Index of Notation

Physically Based Rendering

Physically Based Rendering

FROM THEORY TO IMPLEMENTATION

FOURTH EDITION

MATT PHARR

WENZEL JAKOB

GREG HUMPHREYS

The MIT Press

Cambridge, Massachusetts

London, England

The MIT Press would like to thank the anonymous peer reviewers who provided comments on drafts of this book. The generous work of academic experts is essential for establishing the authority and quality of our publications. We acknowledge with gratitude the contributions of these otherwise uncredited readers.

This book was set in Minion, East Bloc ICG Open, and Univers by Windfall Software. Printed and bound in the United States of America.

Library of Congress Cataloging-in-Publication Data

Names: Pharr, Matt, author. | Jakob, Wenzel, author. | Humphreys, Greg, author.
Title: Physically based rendering : from theory to implementation / Matt Pharr, Wenzel Jakob, Greg Humphreys.
Description: Fourth edition. | Cambridge : The MIT Press, [2023] | Includes bibliographical references and index.
Identifiers: LCCN 2022014718 (print) | LCCN 2022014719 (ebook) |
ISBN 9780262048026 | ISBN 9780262374033 (epub) | ISBN 9780262374040 (pdf)
Subjects: LCSH: Computer graphics. | Three-dimensional display systems. |
Image processing–Digital techniques.
Classification: LCC T385 .P486 2022 (print) | LCC T385 (ebook) |
DDC 006.6–dc23/eng/20220919
LC record available at *https://lccn.loc.gov/2022014718*
LC ebook record available at *https://lccn.loc.gov/2022014719*

10 9 8 7 6 5 4 3 2 1

To **Deirdre**, who even let me bring the manuscript on our honeymoon.

M. P.

To **Olesya**, who thought it was cute that my favorite book is a computer program.

W. J.

To **Isabel and Quinn**, the two most extraordinary people I've ever met. May your pixels never be little squares.

G. H.

ABOUT THE AUTHORS

Matt Pharr is a Distinguished Research Scientist at NVIDIA. He has previously worked at Google, co-founded Neoptica, which was acquired by Intel, and co-founded Exluna, which was acquired by NVIDIA. He has a B.S. degree from Yale and a Ph.D. from the Stanford Graphics Lab, where he worked under the supervision of Pat Hanrahan.

Wenzel Jakob is an assistant professor in the School of Computer and Communication Sciences at École Polytechnique Fédérale de Lausanne (EPFL). His research revolves around inverse and differentiable graphics, material appearance modeling, and physically based rendering. Wenzel obtained his Ph.D. at Cornell University under the supervision of Steve Marschner, after which he joined ETH Zürich for postdoctoral studies under the supervision of Olga Sorkine Hornung. Wenzel is also the lead developer of the *Mitsuba* renderer, a research-oriented rendering system.

Greg Humphreys is currently an engineer at a stealth startup. He has also been part of the Chrome graphics team at Google and the OptiX GPU ray-tracing team at NVIDIA. In a former life, he was a professor of Computer Science at the University of Virginia, where he conducted research in both high-performance and physically based computer graphics, as well as computer architecture and visualization. Greg has a B.S.E. degree from Princeton and a Ph.D. in Computer Science from Stanford under the supervision of Pat Hanrahan. When he's not tracing rays, Greg can usually be found playing tournament bridge.

Contents

---

* An asterisk denotes a section with advanced content that can be skipped on a first reading.

Preface

[Just as] other information should be available to those who want to learn and understand, program source code is the only means for programmers to learn the art from their predecessors. It would be unthinkable for playwrights not to allow other playwrights to read their plays [or to allow them] at theater performances where they would be barred even from taking notes. Likewise, any good author is well read, as every child who learns to write will read hundreds of times more than it writes. Programmers, however, are expected to invent the alphabet and learn to write long novels all on their own. Programming cannot grow and learn unless the next generation of programmers has access to the knowledge and information gathered by other programmers before them. —Erik Naggum

Rendering is a fundamental component of computer graphics. At the highest level of abstraction, rendering is the process of converting a description of a three-dimensional scene into an image. Algorithms for animation, geometric modeling, texturing, and other areas of computer graphics all must pass their results through some sort of rendering process so that they can be made visible in an image. Rendering has become ubiquitous; from movies to games and beyond, it has opened new frontiers for creative expression, entertainment, and visualization.

In the early years of the field, research in rendering focused on solving fundamental problems such as determining which objects are visible from a given viewpoint. As effective solutions to these problems have been found and as richer and more realistic scene descriptions have become available thanks to continued progress in other areas of graphics, modern rendering has grown to include ideas from a broad range of disciplines, including physics and astrophysics, astronomy, biology, psychology and the study of perception, and pure and applied mathematics. The interdisciplinary nature of rendering is one of the reasons that it is such a fascinating area of study.

This book presents a selection of modern rendering algorithms through the documented source code for a complete rendering system. Nearly all of the images in this book, including the one on the front cover, were rendered by this software. All of the algorithms that came together to generate these images are described in these pages. The system, pbrt, is written using a programming methodology called *literate programming* that mixes prose describing the system with the source code that implements it. We believe that the literate programming approach is a valuable way to introduce ideas in computer graphics and computer science in general. Often, some of the subtleties of an algorithm can be unclear or hidden until it is implemented, so seeing an actual implementation is a good way to acquire a solid understanding of that algorithm's details. Indeed, we believe that deep understanding of a number of carefully selected algorithms in this manner provides a better foundation for further study of computer graphics than does superficial understanding of many.

In addition to clarifying how an algorithm is implemented in practice, presenting these algorithms in the context of a complete and nontrivial software system also allows us to address issues in the design and implementation of medium-sized rendering systems. The design of a rendering system's basic abstractions and interfaces has substantial implications for both the elegance of the implementation and the ability to extend it later, yet the trade-offs in this design space are rarely discussed.

pbrt and the contents of this book focus exclusively on *photorealistic rendering*, which can be defined variously as the task of generating images that are indistinguishable from those that a camera would capture in a photograph or as the task of generating images that evoke the same response from a human observer as looking at the actual scene. There are many reasons to focus on photorealism. Photorealistic images are crucial for special effects in movies because computer-generated imagery must often be mixed seamlessly with footage of the real world. In applications like computer games where all of the imagery is synthetic, photorealism is an effective tool for making the observer forget that he or she is looking at an environment that does not actually exist. Finally, photorealism gives a reasonably well-defined metric for evaluating the quality of the rendering system's output.

AUDIENCE

There are three main audiences that this book is intended for. The first is students in graduate or upper-level undergraduate computer graphics classes. This book assumes existing knowledge of computer graphics at the level of an introductory college-level course, although certain key concepts such as basic vector geometry and transformations will be reviewed here. For students who do not have experience with programs that have tens of thousands of lines of source code, the literate programming style gives a gentle introduction to this complexity. We pay special attention to explaining the reasoning behind some of the key interfaces and abstractions in the system in order to give these readers a sense of why the system is structured in the way that it is.

The second audience is advanced graduate students and researchers in computer graphics. For those doing research in rendering, the book provides a broad introduction to the area, and the pbrt source code provides a foundation that can be useful to build upon (or at least to use bits of source code from). For those working in other areas of computer graphics, we believe that having a thorough understanding of rendering can be helpful context to carry along.

Our final audience is software developers in industry. Although many of the basic ideas in this book will be familiar to this audience, seeing explanations of the algorithms presented in the literate style may lead to new perspectives. pbrt also includes carefully crafted and debugged implementations of many algorithms that can be challenging to implement correctly; these should be of particular interest to experienced practitioners in rendering. We hope that delving into one particular organization of a complete and nontrivial rendering system will also be thought provoking to this audience.

OVERVIEW AND GOALS

pbrt is based on the *ray-tracing* algorithm. Ray tracing is an elegant technique that has its origins in lens making; Carl Friedrich Gauß traced rays through lenses by hand in the 19th century. Ray-tracing algorithms on computers follow the path of infinitesimal rays of light through the scene until they intersect a surface. This approach gives a simple method for finding the first visible object as seen from any particular position and direction and is the basis for many rendering algorithms.

pbrt was designed and implemented with three main goals in mind: it should be *complete*, it should be *illustrative*, and it should be *physically based*.

Completeness implies that the system should not lack key features found in high-quality commercial rendering systems. In particular, it means that important practical issues, such as antialiasing, robustness, numerical precision, and the ability to efficiently render complex scenes should all be addressed thoroughly. It is important to consider these issues from the start of the system's design, since these features can have subtle implications for all components of the system and can be quite difficult to retrofit into the system at a later stage of implementation.

Our second goal means that we tried to choose algorithms, data structures, and rendering techniques with care and with an eye toward readability and clarity. Since their implementations will be examined by more readers than is the case for other rendering systems, we tried to select the most elegant algorithms that we were aware of and implement them as well as possible. This goal also required that the system be small enough for a single person to understand completely. We have implemented pbrt using an extensible architecture, with the core of the system implemented in terms of a set of carefully designed interface classes, and as much of the specific functionality as possible in implementations of these interfaces. The result is that one does not need to understand all of the specific implementations in order to understand the basic structure of the system. This makes it easier to delve deeply into parts of interest and skip others, without losing sight of how the overall system fits together.

There is a tension between the two goals of being complete and being illustrative. Implementing and describing every possible useful technique would not only make this book unacceptably long, but would also make the system prohibitively complex for most readers. In cases where pbrt lacks a particularly useful feature, we have attempted to design the architecture so that the feature could be added without altering the overall system design.

The basic foundations for physically based rendering are the laws of physics and their mathematical expression. pbrt was designed to use the correct physical units and concepts for the quantities it computes and the algorithms it implements. pbrt strives to compute images that are *physically correct*; they accurately reflect the lighting as it would be in a real-world version of the scene.[1] One advantage of the decision to use a physical basis is that it gives a concrete standard of program correctness: for simple scenes, where the expected result can be computed in closed form, if pbrt does not compute the same result, we know there must be a bug in the implementation. Similarly, if different physically based lighting algorithms in pbrt give different results for the same scene, or if pbrt does not give the same results as another physically based renderer, there is certainly an error in one of them. Finally, we believe that this physically based approach to rendering is valuable because it is rigorous. When it is not clear how a particular computation should be performed, physics gives an answer that guarantees a consistent result.

Efficiency was given lower priority than these three goals. Since rendering systems often run for many minutes or hours in the course of generating an image, efficiency is clearly important. However, we have mostly confined ourselves to *algorithmic* efficiency rather than low-level code optimization. In some cases, obvious micro-optimizations take a backseat to clear, well-organized code, although we did make some effort to optimize the parts of the system where most of the computation occurs.

---

1   Of course, any computer simulation of physics requires carefully choosing approximations that trade off requirements for fidelity with computational efficiency. See Section 1.2 for further discussion of the choices made in pbrt.

In the course of presenting pbrt and discussing its implementation, we hope to convey some hard-learned lessons from years of rendering research and development. There is more to writing a good renderer than stringing together a set of fast algorithms; making the system both flexible and robust is a difficult task. The system's performance must degrade gracefully as more geometry or light sources are added to it or as any other axis of complexity is stressed.

The rewards for developing a system that addresses all these issues are enormous—it is a great pleasure to write a new renderer or add a new feature to an existing renderer and use it to create an image that could not be generated before. Our most fundamental goal in writing this book was to bring this opportunity to a wider audience. Readers are encouraged to use the system to render the example scenes in the pbrt software distribution as they progress through the book. Exercises at the end of each chapter suggest modifications to the system that will help clarify its inner workings and more complex projects to extend the system by adding new features.

The website for this book is located at *pbrt.org*. This site includes links to the pbrt source code, scenes that can be downloaded to render with pbrt, and a bug tracker, as well as errata. Any errors in this text that are not listed in the errata can be reported to the email address *authors@pbrt.org*. We greatly value your feedback!

CHANGES BETWEEN THE FIRST AND SECOND EDITIONS

Six years passed between the publication of the first edition of this book in 2004 and the second edition in 2010. In that time, thousands of copies of the book were sold, and the pbrt software was downloaded thousands of times from the book's website. The pbrt user base gave us a significant amount of feedback and encouragement, and our experience with the system guided many of the decisions we made in making changes between the version of pbrt presented in the first edition and the version in the second edition. In addition to a number of bug fixes, we also made several significant design changes and enhancements:

- *Removal of the plugin architecture:* The first version of pbrt used a runtime plugin architecture to dynamically load code for implementations of objects like shapes, lights, integrators, cameras, and other objects that were used in the scene currently being rendered. This approach allowed users to extend pbrt with new object types (e.g., new shape primitives) without recompiling the entire rendering system. This approach initially seemed elegant, but it complicated the task of supporting pbrt on multiple platforms and it made debugging more difficult. The only new usage scenario that it truly enabled (binary-only distributions of pbrt or binary plugins) was actually contrary to our pedagogical and open-source goals. Therefore, the plugin architecture was dropped in this edition.
- *Removal of the image-processing pipeline:* The first version of pbrt provided a tone-mapping interface that converted high-dynamic-range (HDR) floating-point output images directly into low-dynamic-range TIFFs for display. This functionality made sense in 2004, as support for HDR images was still sparse. In 2010, however, advances in digital photography had made HDR images commonplace. Although the theory and practice of tone mapping are elegant and worth learning, we decided to focus the new book exclusively on the process of image formation and skip the topic of image display. Interested readers should consult the book written by Reinhard et al. (2010) for a thorough and modern treatment of the HDR image display process.

- *Task parallelism:* Multicore architectures became ubiquitous, and we felt that pbrt would not remain relevant without the ability to scale to the number of locally available cores. We also hoped that the parallel programming implementation details documented in this book would help graphics programmers understand some of the subtleties and complexities in writing scalable parallel code.
- *Appropriateness for "production" rendering:* The first version of pbrt was intended exclusively as a pedagogical tool and a stepping-stone for rendering research. Indeed, we made a number of decisions in preparing the first edition that were contrary to use in a production environment, such as limited support for image-based lighting, no support for motion blur, and a photon mapping implementation that was not robust in the presence of complex lighting. With much improved support for these features as well as support for subsurface scattering and Metropolis light transport, we feel that with the second edition, pbrt became much more suitable for rendering very high-quality images of complex environments.

CHANGES BETWEEN THE SECOND AND THIRD EDITIONS

With the passage of another six years, it was time to update and extend the book and the pbrt system. We continued to learn from readers' and users' experiences to better understand which topics were most useful to cover. Further, rendering research continued apace; many parts of the book were due for an update to reflect current best practices. We made significant improvements on a number of fronts:

- *Bidirectional light transport:* The third version of pbrt added a bidirectional path tracer, including full support for volumetric light transport and multiple importance sampling to weight paths. An all-new Metropolis light transport integrator used components of the bidirectional path tracer, allowing for a particularly succinct implementation of that algorithm.
- *Subsurface scattering:* The appearance of many objects—notably, skin and translucent objects—is a result of subsurface light transport. Our implementation of subsurface scattering in the second edition reflected the state of the art in the early 2000s; we thoroughly updated both BSSRDF models and our subsurface light transport algorithms to reflect the progress made in ten subsequent years of research.
- *Numerically robust intersections:* The effects of floating-point round-off error in geometric ray intersection calculations have been a long-standing challenge in ray tracing: they can cause small errors to be present throughout the image. We focused on this issue and derived conservative (but tight) bounds of this error, which made our implementation more robust to this issue than previous rendering systems.
- *Participating media representation:* We significantly improved the way that scattering media are described and represented in the system; this allows for more accurate results with nested scattering media. A new sampling technique enabled unbiased rendering of heterogeneous media in a way that cleanly integrated with all of the other parts of the system.
- *Measured materials:* This edition added a new technique to represent and evaluate measured materials using a sparse frequency-space basis. This approach is convenient because it allows for exact importance sampling, which was not possible with the representation used in the previous edition.
- *Photon mapping:* A significant step forward for photon mapping algorithms has been the development of variants that do not require storing all of the photons in memory. We

replaced pbrt's photon mapping algorithm with an implementation based on stochastic progressive photon mapping, which efficiently renders many difficult light transport effects.

- *Sample generation algorithms:* The distribution of sample values used for numerical integration in rendering algorithms can have a surprisingly large effect on the quality of the final results. We thoroughly updated our treatment of this topic, covering new approaches and efficient implementation techniques in more depth than before.

Many other parts of the system were improved and updated to reflect progress in the field: microfacet reflection models were treated in more depth, with much better sampling techniques; a new "curve" shape was added for modeling hair and other fine geometry; and a new camera model that simulates realistic lens systems was made available. Throughout the book, we made numerous smaller changes to more clearly explain and illustrate the key concepts in physically based rendering systems like pbrt.

CHANGES BETWEEN THE THIRD AND FOURTH EDITIONS

Innovation in rendering algorithms has shown no sign of slowing down, and so in 2019 we began focused work on a fourth edition of the text. Not only does almost every chapter include substantial additions, but we have updated the order of chapters and ideas introduced, bringing Monte Carlo integration and the basic ideas of path tracing to the fore rather than saving them for the end.

Capabilities of the system that have seen especially significant improvements include:

- *Volumetric scattering:* We have updated the algorithms that model scattering from participating media to the state of the art, adding support for emissive volumes, efficient sampling of volumes with varying densities, and robust support for chromatic media, where the scattering properties vary by wavelength.
- *Spectral rendering:* We have excised all use of RGB color for lighting calculations; pbrt now performs lighting calculations exclusively in terms of samples of wavelength-dependent spectral distributions. Not only is this approach more physically accurate than using RGB, but it also allows pbrt to accurately model effects like dispersion.
- *Reflection models:* Our coverage of the foundations of BSDFs and reflection models has been extensively revised, and we have expanded the range of BSDFs covered to include one that accurately models reflection from hair and another that models scattering from layered materials. The measured BRDF follows a new approach that can represent a wide set of materials' reflection spectra.
- *Light sampling:* Not only have we improved the algorithms for sampling points on individual light sources to better reflect the state of the art, but this edition also includes support for *many-light sampling*, which makes it possible to efficiently render scenes with thousands or millions of light sources by carefully sampling just a few of them.
- *GPU rendering:* This version of pbrt adds support for rendering on GPUs, which can provide 10–100 times higher ray tracing performance than CPUs. We have implemented this capability in a way so that almost all of the code presented in the book runs on both CPUs and GPUs, which has made it possible to localize discussion of GPU-related issues to Chapter 15.

The system has seen numerous other improvements and additions, including a new bilinear patch shape, many updates to the sample-generation algorithms that are at the heart of Monte Carlo integration, support for outputting auxiliary information at each pixel about the visible surface geometry and reflection properties, and many more small improvements to the system.

ACKNOWLEDGMENTS

Pat Hanrahan has contributed to this book in more ways than we could hope to acknowledge; we owe a profound debt to him. He tirelessly argued for clean interfaces and finding the right abstractions to use throughout the system, and his understanding of and approach to rendering deeply influenced its design. His willingness to use pbrt and this manuscript in his rendering course at Stanford was enormously helpful, particularly in the early years of its life when it was still in very rough form; his feedback throughout this process has been crucial for bringing the text to its current state. Finally, the group of people that Pat helped assemble at the Stanford Graphics Lab, and the open environment that he fostered, made for an exciting, stimulating, and fertile environment. Matt and Greg both feel extremely privileged to have been there.

We owe a debt of gratitude to the many students who used early drafts of this book in courses at Stanford and the University of Virginia between 1999 and 2004. These students provided an enormous amount of feedback about the book and pbrt. The teaching assistants for these courses deserve special mention: Tim Purcell, Mike Cammarano, Ian Buck, and Ren Ng at Stanford, and Nolan Goodnight at Virginia. A number of students in those classes gave particularly valuable feedback and sent bug reports and bug fixes; we would especially like to thank Evan Parker and Phil Beatty. A draft of the manuscript of this book was used in classes taught by Bill Mark and Don Fussell at the University of Texas, Austin, and Raghu Machiraju at Ohio State University; their feedback was invaluable, and we are grateful for their adventurousness in incorporating this system into their courses, even while it was still being edited and revised.

Matt Pharr would like to acknowledge colleagues and co-workers in rendering-related endeavors who have been a great source of education and who have substantially influenced his approach to writing renderers and his understanding of the field. Particular thanks go to Craig Kolb, who provided a cornerstone of Matt's early computer graphics education through the freely available source code to the rayshade ray-tracing system, and Eric Veach, who has also been generous with his time and expertise. Thanks also to Doug Shult and Stan Eisenstat for formative lessons in mathematics and computer science during high school and college, respectively, and most important to Matt's parents, for the education they have provided and continued encouragement along the way. Finally, thanks to NVIDIA for supporting the preparation of both the first and this latest edition of the book; at NVIDIA, thanks to Nick Triantos and Jayant Kolhe for their support through the final stages of the preparation of the first edition and thanks to Aaron Lefohn, David Luebke, and Bill Dally for their support of work on the fourth edition.

Greg Humphreys is very grateful to all the professors and TAs who tolerated him when he was an undergraduate at Princeton. Many people encouraged his interest in graphics, specifically Michael Cohen, David Dobkin, Adam Finkelstein, Michael Cox, Gordon Stoll, Patrick Min, and Dan Wallach. Doug Clark, Steve Lyon, and Andy Wolfe also supervised various independent research boondoggles without even laughing once. Once, in a group meeting about a year-long robotics project, Steve Lyon became exasperated and yelled, "Stop telling me why it can't be done, and figure out how to do it!"—an impromptu lesson that will never be forgotten. Eric Ristad fired Greg as a summer research assistant after his freshman year (before the summer even began), pawning him off on an unsuspecting Pat Hanrahan and beginning an advising relationship that would span 10 years and both coasts. Finally,

Dave Hanson taught Greg that literate programming was a great way to work and that computer programming can be a beautiful and subtle art form.

Wenzel Jakob was excited when the first edition of pbrt arrived in his mail during his undergraduate studies in 2004. Needless to say, this had a lasting effect on his career—thus Wenzel would like to begin by thanking his co-authors for inviting him to become a part of the third and fourth editions of this book. Wenzel is extremely indebted to Steve Marschner, who was his Ph.D. advisor during a fulfilling five years at Cornell University. Steve brought him into the world of research and remains a continuous source of inspiration. Wenzel is also thankful for the guidance and stimulating research environment created by the other members of the graphics group, including Kavita Bala, Doug James, and Bruce Walter. Wenzel spent a wonderful postdoc with Olga Sorkine Hornung, who introduced him to geometry processing. Olga's support for Wenzel's involvement in the third edition of this book is deeply appreciated.

We would especially like to thank the reviewers who read drafts in their entirety; all had insightful and constructive feedback about the manuscript at various stages of its progress. For providing feedback on both the first and second editions of the book, thanks to Ian Ashdown, Per Christensen, Doug Epps, Dan Goldman, Eric Haines, Erik Reinhard, Pete Shirley, Peter-Pike Sloan, Greg Ward, and a host of anonymous reviewers. For the second edition, thanks to Janne Kontkanen, Bill Mark, Nelson Max, and Eric Tabellion. For the fourth edition, we are grateful to Thomas Müller and Per Christensen, who both offered extensive feedback that has measurably improved the final version.

Many experts have kindly explained subtleties in their work to us and guided us to best practices. For the first and second editions, we are also grateful to Don Mitchell, for his help with understanding some of the details of sampling and reconstruction; Thomas Kollig and Alexander Keller, for explaining the finer points of low-discrepancy sampling; Christer Ericson, who had a number of suggestions for improving our kd-tree implementation; and Christophe Hery and Eugene d'Eon for helping us with the nuances of subsurface scattering.

For the third edition, we would especially like to thank Leo Grünschloß for reviewing our sampling chapter; Alexander Keller for suggestions about topics for that chapter; Eric Heitz for extensive help with details of microfacets and reviewing our text on that topic; Thiago Ize for thoroughly reviewing the text on floating-point error; Tom van Bussel for reporting a number of errors in our BSSRDF code; Ralf Habel for reviewing our BSSRDF text; and Toshiya Hachisuka and Anton Kaplanyan for extensive review and comments about our light transport chapters.

For the fourth edition, thanks to Alejandro Conty Estevez for reviewing our treatment of many-light sampling; Eugene d'Eon, Bailey Miller, and Jan Novák for comments on the volumetric scattering chapters; Eric Haines, Simon Kallweit, Martin Stich, and Carsten Wächter for reviewing the chapter on GPU rendering; Karl Li for feedback on a number of chapters; Tzu-Mao Li for his review of our discussion of inverse and differentiable rendering; Fabrice Rousselle for feedback on machine learning and rendering; and Gurprit Singh for comments on our discussion of Fourier analysis of Monte Carlo integration. We also appreciate extensive comments and suggestions from Jeppe Revall Frisvad on pbrt's treatment of reflection models in previous editions.

For improvements to pbrt's implementation in this edition, thanks to Pierre Moreau for his efforts in debugging pbrt's GPU support on Windows and to Jim Price, who not only found and fixed numerous bugs in the early release of pbrt's source code, but who also contributed a better representation of chromatic volumetric media than our original implementation. We are also very appreciative of Anders Langlands and Luca Fascione of Weta Digital for providing an implementation of their *PhysLight* system, which has been incorporated into pbrt's PixelSensor class and light source implementations.

Many people have reported errors in the text of previous editions or bugs in pbrt. We'd especially like to thank Solomon Boulos, Stephen Chenney, Per Christensen, John Danks, Mike Day, Kevin Egan, Volodymyr Kachurovskyi, Kostya Smolenskiy, Ke Xu, and Arek Zimny, who have been especially prolific.

For their suggestions and bug reports, we would also like to thank Rachit Agrawal, Frederick Akalin, Thomas de Bodt, Mark Bolstad, Brian Budge, Jonathon Cai, Bryan Catanzaro, Tzu-Chieh Chang, Mark Colbert, Yunjian Ding, Tao Du, Marcos Fajardo, Shaohua Fan, Luca Fascione, Etienne Ferrier, Nigel Fisher, Jeppe Revall Frisvad, Robert G. Graf, Asbjørn Heid, Steve Hill, Wei-Feng Huang, John "Spike" Hughes, Keith Jeffery, Greg Johnson, Aaron Karp, Andrew Kensler, Alan King, Donald Knuth, Martin Kraus, Chris Kulla, Murat Kurt, Larry Lai, Morgan McGuire, Craig McNaughton, Don Mitchell, Swaminathan Narayanan, Anders Nilsson, Jens Olsson, Vincent Pegoraro, Srinath Ravichandiran, Andy Selle, Sébastien Speierer, Nils Thuerey, Eric Veach, Ingo Wald, Zejian Wang, Xiong Wei, Wei-Wei Xu, Tizian Zeltner, and Matthias Zwicker. Finally, we would like to thank the *LuxRender* developers and the *LuxRender* community, particularly Terrence Vergauwen, Jean-Philippe Grimaldi, and Asbjørn Heid; it has been a delight to see the rendering system they have built from pbrt's foundation, and we have learned from reading their source code and implementations of new rendering algorithms.

Special thanks to Martin Preston and Steph Bruning from Framestore for their help with our being able to use a frame from *Gravity* (image courtesy of Warner Bros. and Framestore), and to Weta Digital for their help with the frame from *Alita: Battle Angel* (© 2018 Twentieth Century Fox Film Corporation, All Rights Reserved).

PRODUCTION

For the production of the first edition, we would also like to thank our editor Tim Cox for his willingness to take on this slightly unorthodox project and for both his direction and patience throughout the process. We are very grateful to Elisabeth Beller (project manager), who went well beyond the call of duty for the book; her ability to keep this complex project in control and on schedule was remarkable, and we particularly thank her for the measurable impact she had on the quality of the final result. Thanks also to Rick Camp (editorial assistant) for his many contributions along the way. Paul Anagnostopoulos and Jacqui Scarlott at Windfall Software did the book's composition; their ability to take the authors' homebrew literate programming file format and turn it into high-quality final output while also juggling the multiple unusual types of indexing we asked for is greatly appreciated. Thanks also to Ken DellaPenta (copyeditor) and Jennifer McClain (proofreader), as well as to Max Spector at Chen Design (text and cover designer) and Steve Rath (indexer).

For the second edition, we would like to thank Greg Chalson, who talked us into expanding and updating the book; Greg also ensured that Paul Anagnostopoulos at Windfall Software would again do the book's composition. We would like to thank Paul again for his efforts in working with this book's production complexity. Finally, we would also like to thank Todd Green, Paul Gottehrer, and Heather Scherer at Elsevier.

For the third edition, we would like to thank Todd Green, who oversaw that go-round, and Amy Invernizzi, who kept the train on the rails throughout that process. We were delighted to have Paul Anagnostopoulos at Windfall Software part of this process for a third time; his efforts have been critical to the book's high production value, which is so important to us.

The fourth edition saw us moving to MIT Press; many thanks to Elizabeth Swayze for her enthusiasm for bringing us on board, guidance through the production process, and ensuring that Paul Anagnostopoulos would again handle composition. Our deepest thanks to Paul for coming back for one more edition with us, and many thanks as well to MaryEllen Oliver for her superb work on copyediting and proofreading.

SCENES, MODELS, AND DATA

Many people and organizations have generously provided scenes and models for use in this book and the pbrt distribution. Their generosity has been invaluable in helping us create interesting example images throughout the text.

We are most grateful to Guillermo M. Leal Llaguno of Evolución Visual, *www.evvisual.com*, who modeled and rendered the iconic *San Miguel* scene that was featured on the cover of the second edition and is still used in numerous figures in the book. We would also especially like to thank Marko Dabrovic (*www.3lhd.com*) and Mihovil Odak at RNA Studios (*www.rna.hr*), who supplied a bounty of models and scenes used in earlier editions of the book, including the Sponza atrium, the Sibenik cathedral, and the Audi TT car model that can be seen in Figure 16.1 of this edition.

We sincerely thank Jan-Walter Schliep, Burak Kahraman, and Timm Dapper of Laubwerk (*www.laubwerk.com*) for creating the *Countryside* landscape scene that was on the cover of the previous edition of the book and is used in numerous figures in this edition.

Many thanks to Angelo Ferretti of Lucydreams (*www.lucydreams.it*) for licensing the *Watercolor* and *Kroken* scenes, which have provided a wonderful cover image for this edition, material for numerous figures, and a pair of complex scenes that exercise pbrt's capabilities.

Jim Price kindly provided a number of scenes featuring interesting volumetric media; those have measurably improved the figures for that topic. Thanks also to Beeple for making the *Zero Day* and *Transparent Machines* scenes available under a permissive license and to Martin Lubich for the Austrian Imperial Crown model. Finally, our deepest thanks to Walt Disney Animation Studios for making the production-complexity *Moana Island* scene available as well as providing the detailed volumetric cloud model.

The bunny, Buddha, and dragon models are courtesy of the Stanford Computer Graphics Laboratory's scanning repository. The "killeroo" model is included with permission of Phil Dench and Martin Rezard (3D scan and digital representations by headus, design and clay sculpt by Rezard). The dragon model scan used in Chapter 9 is courtesy of Christian Schüller, and our thanks to Yasutoshi Mori for the material orb and the sports car model. The head model used to illustrate subsurface scattering was made available by Infinite Realities, Inc. under a Creative Commons Attribution 3.0 license. Thanks also to "tyrant monkey" for the BMW M6 car model and "Wig42" for the breakfast table scene; both were posted to *blendswap.com*, also under a Creative Commons Attribution 3.0 license.

We have made use of numerous environment maps from the *PolyHaven* website (*polyhaven .com*) for HDR lighting in various scenes; all are available under a Creative Commons CC0 license. Thanks to Sergej Majboroda and Greg Zaal, whose environment maps we have used.

Marc Ellens provided spectral data for a variety of light sources, and the spectral RGB measurement data for a variety of displays is courtesy of Tom Lianza at X-Rite. Our thanks as well to Danny Pascale (*www.babelcolor.com*) for allowing us to include his measurements of the spectral reflectance of a color chart. Thanks to Mikhail Polyanskiy for index of refraction data via *refractiveindex.info* and to Anders Langlands, Luca Fascione, and Weta Digital for camera sensor response data that is included in pbrt.

ABOUT THE COVER

The *Watercolor* scene on the cover was created by Angelo Ferretti of Lucydreams (*www .lucydreams.it*). It requires a total of 2 GiB of on-disk storage for geometry and 836 MiB for texture maps. Come rendering, the scene description requires 15 GiB of memory to store over 33 million unique triangles, 412 texture maps, and associated data structures.

ADDITIONAL READING

Donald Knuth's article *Literate Programming* (Knuth 1984) describes the main ideas behind literate programming as well as his web programming environment. The seminal TEX typesetting system was written with web and has been published as a series of books (Knuth 1986; Knuth 1993a). Knuth and Levy presented the implementation of the cweb literate programming system as a literate program (Knuth and Levy 1994). Knuth has also published both a collection of graph algorithms in *The Stanford GraphBase* (Knuth 1993b) and a simulator for the *MMIX* instruction set (Knuth 1999) in literate format. These programs are enjoyable to read and are excellent presentations of their respective algorithms. The website *www.literateprogramming.com* has pointers to many articles about literate programming, literate programs to download, and a variety of literate programming systems; many refinements have been made since Knuth's original development of the idea.

Other literate programs we know of that have been published as books include one on the implementation of the lcc compiler, which was written by Christopher Fraser and David Hanson and published as *A Retargetable C Compiler: Design and Implementation* (Fraser and Hanson 1995). See also Hanson's book on program interface design (Hanson 1996), Mehlhorn and Näher's presentation on the implementation of the LEDA library (Mehlhorn and Näher 1999), Valiente's collection of graph algorithms (Valiente 2002), and Ruckert's description of the *mp3* audio format (Ruckert 2005).

CHAPTER ONE

01 INTRODUCTION

Rendering is the process of producing an image from the description of a 3D scene. Obviously, this is a broad task, and there are many ways to approach it. *Physically based* techniques attempt to simulate reality; that is, they use principles of physics to model the interaction of light and matter. While a physically based approach may seem to be the most obvious way to approach rendering, it has only been widely adopted in practice over the past 15 or so years.

This book describes pbrt, a physically based rendering system based on the ray-tracing algorithm. It is capable of rendering realistic images of complex scenes such as the one shown in Figure 1.1. (Other than a few exceptions in this chapter that are noted with their appearance, all the images in this book are rendered with pbrt.)

Most computer graphics books present algorithms and theory, sometimes combined with snippets of code. In contrast, this book couples the theory with a complete implementation of a fully functional rendering system. Furthermore, the full source code of the system is available under an open-source license, and the full text of this book is freely available online at *pbr-book.org/4ed*, as of November 1, 2023. Further information, including example scenes and additional information about pbrt, can be found on the website, *pbrt.org*.

1.1 LITERATE PROGRAMMING

While creating the TEX typesetting system, Donald Knuth developed a new programming methodology based on a simple but revolutionary idea. To quote Knuth, "let us change our traditional attitude to the construction of programs: Instead of imagining that our main task is to instruct a computer what to do, let us concentrate rather on explaining to human beings what we want a computer to do." He named this methodology *literate programming*. This book (including the chapter you are reading now) is a long literate program. This means that in the course of reading this book, you will read the full implementation of the pbrt rendering system, not just a high-level description of it.

Literate programs are written in a metalanguage that mixes a document formatting language (e.g., TEX or HTML) and a programming language (e.g., C++). Two separate systems process the program: a "weaver" that transforms the literate program into a document suitable for typesetting and a "tangler" that produces source code suitable for compilation. Our literate

Figure 1.1: A Scene Rendered by pbrt. The *Kroken* scene features complex geometry, materials, and light transport. Handling all of these effects well in a rendering system makes it possible to render photorealistic images like this one. This scene and many others can be downloaded from the pbrt website. *(Scene courtesy of Angelo Ferretti.)*

programming system is homegrown, but it was heavily influenced by Norman Ramsey's noweb system.

The literate programming metalanguage provides two important features. The first is the ability to mix prose with source code. This feature puts the description of the program on equal footing with its actual source code, encouraging careful design and documentation. Second, the language provides mechanisms for presenting the program code to the reader in an order that is entirely different from the compiler input. Thus, the program can be described in a logical manner. Each named block of code is called a *fragment*, and each fragment can refer to other fragments by name.

As a simple example, consider a function InitGlobals() that is responsible for initializing all of a program's global variables:[1]

1　The example code in this section is merely illustrative and is not part of pbrt itself.

```
void InitGlobals() {
    nMarbles = 25.7;
    shoeSize = 13;
    dielectric = true;
}
```

Despite its brevity, this function is hard to understand without any context. Why, for example, can the variable nMarbles take on floating-point values? Just looking at the code, one would need to search through the entire program to see where each variable is declared and how it is used in order to understand its purpose and the meanings of its legal values. Although this structuring of the system is fine for a compiler, a human reader would much rather see the initialization code for each variable presented separately, near the code that declares and uses the variable.

In a literate program, one can instead write InitGlobals() like this:

⟨*Function Definitions*⟩ ≡
```
    void InitGlobals() {
        ⟨Initialize Global Variables 3⟩
    }
```

This defines a fragment, called ⟨*Function Definitions*⟩, that contains the definition of the InitGlobals() function. The InitGlobals() function itself refers to another fragment, ⟨*Initialize Global Variables*⟩. Because the initialization fragment has not yet been defined, we do not know anything about this function except that it will presumably contain assignments to global variables.

Just having the fragment name is just the right level of abstraction for now, since no variables have been declared yet. When we introduce the global variable shoeSize somewhere later in the program, we can then write

⟨*Initialize Global Variables*⟩ ≡   3
```
    shoeSize = 13;
```

Here we have started to define the contents of ⟨*Initialize Global Variables*⟩. When the literate program is tangled into source code for compilation, the literate programming system will substitute the code shoeSize = 13; inside the definition of the InitGlobals() function.

Later in the text, we may define another global variable, dielectric, and we can append its initialization to the fragment:

⟨*Initialize Global Variables*⟩ +≡   3
```
    dielectric = true;
```

The +≡ symbol after the fragment name shows that we have added to a previously defined fragment.

When tangled, these three fragments turn into the code

```
    void InitGlobals() {
        // Initialize Global Variables
        shoeSize = 13;
        dielectric = true;
    }
```

In this way, we can decompose complex functions into logically distinct parts, making them much easier to understand. For example, we can write a complicated function as a series of fragments:

⟨*Function Definitions*⟩ +≡
```
    void complexFunc(int x, int y, double *values) {
        ⟨Check validity of arguments⟩
        if (x < y) {
            ⟨Swap x and y⟩
        }
        ⟨Do precomputation before loop⟩
        ⟨Loop through and update values array⟩
    }
```

Again, the contents of each fragment are expanded inline in complexFunc() for compilation. In the document, we can introduce each fragment and its implementation in turn. This decomposition lets us present code a few lines at a time, making it easier to understand. Another advantage of this style of programming is that by separating the function into logical fragments, each with a single and well-delineated purpose, each one can then be written, verified, or read independently. In general, we will try to make each fragment less than 10 lines long.

In some sense, the literate programming system is just an enhanced macro substitution package tuned to the task of rearranging program source code. This may seem like a trivial change, but in fact literate programming is quite different from other ways of structuring software systems.

1.1.1 INDEXING AND CROSS-REFERENCING

The following features are designed to make the text easier to navigate. Indices in the page margins give page numbers where the functions, variables, and methods used on that page are defined. Indices at the end of the book collect all of these identifiers so that it's possible to find definitions by name. The index of fragments, starting on page 1183, lists the pages where each fragment is defined and where it is used. An index of class names and their members follows, starting on page 1201, and an index of miscellaneous identifiers can be found on page 1213. Within the text, a defined fragment name is followed by a list of page numbers on which that fragment is used. For example, a hypothetical fragment definition such as

⟨*A fascinating fragment*⟩ ≡   **184, 690**
```
    nMarbles += .001;
```

indicates that this fragment is used on pages 184 and 690. Occasionally we elide fragments from the printed book that are either boilerplate code or substantially the same as other fragments; when these fragments are used, no page numbers will be listed.

When a fragment is used inside another fragment, the page number on which it is first defined appears after the fragment name. For example,

⟨*Do something interesting*⟩+≡   **500**
```
    InitializeSomethingInteresting();
    ⟨Do something else interesting 486⟩
    CleanUp();
```

indicates that the ⟨*Do something else interesting*⟩ fragment is defined on page 486.

1.2 PHOTOREALISTIC RENDERING AND THE RAY-TRACING ALGORITHM

The goal of photorealistic rendering is to create an image of a 3D scene that is indistinguishable from a photograph of the same scene. Before we describe the rendering process, it is important to understand that in this context the word *indistinguishable* is imprecise because it involves a human observer, and different observers may perceive the same image differently. Although we will cover a few perceptual issues in this book, accounting for the precise characteristics of a given observer is a difficult and not fully solved problem. For the most part, we will be satisfied with an accurate simulation of the physics of light and its interaction with matter, relying on our understanding of display technology to present the best possible image to the viewer.

Given this single-minded focus on realistic simulation of light, it seems prudent to ask: *what is light?* Perception through light is central to our very existence, and this simple question has thus occupied the minds of famous philosophers and physicists since the beginning of recorded time. The ancient Indian philosophical school of Vaisheshika (5th–6th century BC) viewed light as a collection of small particles traveling along rays at high velocity. In the fifth century BC, the Greek philosopher Empedocles postulated that a divine fire emerged from human eyes and combined with light rays from the sun to produce vision. Between the 18th and 19th century, polymaths such as Isaac Newton, Thomas Young, and Augustin-Jean Fresnel endorsed conflicting theories modeling light as the consequence of either wave or particle propagation. During the same time period, André-Marie Ampère, Joseph-Louis Lagrange, Carl Friedrich Gauß, and Michael Faraday investigated the relations between electricity and magnetism that culminated in a sudden and dramatic unification by James Clerk Maxwell into a combined theory that is now known as *electromagnetism*.

Light is a wave-like manifestation in this framework: the motion of electrically charged particles such as electrons in a light bulb's filament produces a disturbance of a surrounding *electric field* that propagates away from the source. The electric oscillation also causes a secondary oscillation of the *magnetic field*, which in turn reinforces an oscillation of the electric field, and so on. The interplay of these two fields leads to a self-propagating wave that can travel extremely large distances: millions of light years, in the case of distant stars visible in a clear night sky. In the early 20th century, work by Max Planck, Max Born, Erwin Schrödinger, and Werner Heisenberg led to another substantial shift of our understanding: at a microscopic level, elementary properties like energy and momentum are quantized, which means that they can only exist as an integer multiple of a base amount that is known as a *quantum*. In the case of electromagnetic oscillations, this quantum is referred to as a *photon*. In this sense, our physical understanding has come full circle: once we turn to very small scales, light again betrays a particle-like behavior that coexists with its overall wave-like nature.

How does our goal of simulating light to produce realistic images fit into all of this? Faced with this tower of increasingly advanced explanations, a fundamental question arises: how far must we climb this tower to attain photorealism? To our great fortune, the answer turns out to be "not far at all." Waves comprising visible light are extremely small, measuring only a few hundred nanometers from crest to trough. The complex wave-like behavior of light appears at these small scales, but it is of little consequence when simulating objects at the scale of, say, centimeters or meters. This is excellent news, because detailed wave-level simulations of anything larger than a few micrometers are impractical: computer graphics would not exist in its current form if this level of detail was necessary to render images. Instead, we will mostly work with equations developed between the 16th and early 19th century that model light as particles that travel along rays. This leads to a more efficient computational approach based on a key operation known as *ray tracing*.

Ray tracing is conceptually a simple algorithm; it is based on following the path of a ray of light through a scene as it interacts with and bounces off objects in an environment. Although there are many ways to write a ray tracer, all such systems simulate at least the following objects and phenomena:

- *Cameras:* A camera model determines how and from where the scene is being viewed, including how an image of the scene is recorded on a sensor. Many rendering systems generate viewing rays starting at the camera that are then traced into the scene to determine which objects are visible at each pixel.
- *Ray–object intersections:* We must be able to tell precisely where a given ray intersects a given geometric object. In addition, we need to determine certain properties of the object at the intersection point, such as a surface normal or its material. Most ray tracers also have some facility for testing the intersection of a ray with multiple objects, typically returning the closest intersection along the ray.
- *Light sources:* Without lighting, there would be little point in rendering a scene. A ray tracer must model the distribution of light throughout the scene, including not only the locations of the lights themselves but also the way in which they distribute their energy throughout space.
- *Visibility:* In order to know whether a given light deposits energy at a point on a surface, we must know whether there is an uninterrupted path from the point to the light source. Fortunately, this question is easy to answer in a ray tracer, since we can just construct the ray from the surface to the light, find the closest ray–object intersection, and compare the intersection distance to the light distance.
- *Light scattering at surfaces:* Each object must provide a description of its appearance, including information about how light interacts with the object's surface, as well as the nature of the reradiated (or *scattered*) light. Models for surface scattering are typically parameterized so that they can simulate a variety of appearances.
- *Indirect light transport:* Because light can arrive at a surface after bouncing off or passing through other surfaces, it is usually necessary to trace additional rays to capture this effect.
- *Ray propagation:* We need to know what happens to the light traveling along a ray as it passes through space. If we are rendering a scene in a vacuum, light energy remains constant along a ray. Although true vacuums are unusual on Earth, they are a reasonable approximation for many environments. More sophisticated models are available for tracing rays through fog, smoke, the Earth's atmosphere, and so on.

We will briefly discuss each of these simulation tasks in this section. In the next section, we will show pbrt's high-level interface to the underlying simulation components and will present a simple rendering algorithm that randomly samples light paths through a scene in order to generate images.

1.2.1 CAMERAS AND FILM

Nearly everyone has used a camera and is familiar with its basic functionality: you indicate your desire to record an image of the world (usually by pressing a button or tapping a screen), and the image is recorded onto a piece of film or by an electronic sensor.[2] One of the simplest

---

2   Although digital sensors are now more common than physical film, we will use "film" to encompass both in cases where either could be used.

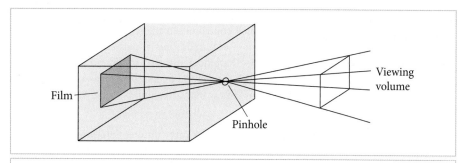

Figure 1.2: A Pinhole Camera. The viewing volume is determined by the projection of the film through the pinhole.

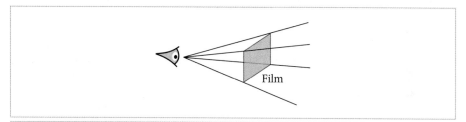

Figure 1.3: When we simulate a pinhole camera, we place the film in front of the hole at the imaging plane, and the hole is renamed the *eye*.

devices for taking photographs is called the *pinhole camera*. Pinhole cameras consist of a light-tight box with a tiny hole at one end (Figure 1.2). When the hole is uncovered, light enters and falls on a piece of photographic paper that is affixed to the other end of the box. Despite its simplicity, this kind of camera is still used today, mostly for artistic purposes. Long exposure times are necessary to get enough light on the film to form an image.

Although most cameras are substantially more complex than the pinhole camera, it is a convenient starting point for simulation. The most important function of the camera is to define the portion of the scene that will be recorded onto the film. In Figure 1.2, we can see how connecting the pinhole to the edges of the film creates a double pyramid that extends into the scene. Objects that are not inside this pyramid cannot be imaged onto the film. Because actual cameras image a more complex shape than a pyramid, we will refer to the region of space that can potentially be imaged onto the film as the *viewing volume*.

Another way to think about the pinhole camera is to place the film plane in front of the pinhole but at the same distance (Figure 1.3). Note that connecting the hole to the film defines exactly the same viewing volume as before. Of course, this is not a practical way to build a real camera, but for simulation purposes it is a convenient abstraction. When the film (or image) plane is in front of the pinhole, the pinhole is frequently referred to as the *eye*.

Now we come to the crucial issue in rendering: at each point in the image, what color does the camera record? The answer to this question is partially determined by what part of the scene is visible at that point. If we recall the original pinhole camera, it is clear that only light rays that travel along the vector between the pinhole and a point on the film can contribute to that film location. In our simulated camera with the film plane in front of the eye, we are interested in the amount of light traveling from the image point to the eye.

Therefore, an important task of the camera simulator is to take a point on the image and generate *rays* along which incident light will contribute to that image location. Because a ray consists of an origin point and a direction vector, this task is particularly simple for the pinhole camera model of Figure 1.3: it uses the pinhole for the origin and the vector from the pinhole to the imaging plane as the ray's direction. For more complex camera models involving multiple lenses, the calculation of the ray that corresponds to a given point on the image may be more involved.

Light arriving at the camera along a ray will generally carry different amounts of energy at different wavelengths. The human visual system interprets this wavelength variation as color. Most camera sensors record separate measurements for three wavelength distributions that correspond to red, green, and blue colors, which is sufficient to reconstruct a scene's visual appearance to a human observer. (Section 4.6 discusses color in more detail.) Therefore, cameras in pbrt also include a film abstraction that both stores the image and models the film sensor's response to incident light.

pbrt's camera and film abstraction is described in detail in Chapter 5. With the process of converting image locations to rays encapsulated in the camera module and with the film abstraction responsible for determining the sensor's response to light, the rest of the rendering system can focus on evaluating the lighting along those rays.

1.2.2 RAY–OBJECT INTERSECTIONS

Each time the camera generates a ray, the first task of the renderer is to determine which object, if any, that ray intersects first and where the intersection occurs. This intersection point is the visible point along the ray, and we will want to simulate the interaction of light with the object at this point. To find the intersection, we must test the ray for intersection against all objects in the scene and select the one that the ray intersects first. Given a ray r, we first start by writing it in *parametric form*:

$$r(t) = o + t\mathbf{d},$$

where o is the ray's origin, $\mathbf{d}$ is its direction vector, and t is a parameter whose legal range is $[0, \infty)$. We can obtain a point along the ray by specifying its parametric t value and evaluating the above equation.

It is often easy to find the intersection between the ray r and a surface defined by an implicit function $F(x, y, z) = 0$. We first substitute the ray equation into the implicit equation, producing a new function whose only parameter is t. We then solve this function for t and substitute the smallest positive root into the ray equation to find the desired point. For example, the implicit equation of a sphere centered at the origin with radius r is

$$x^2 + y^2 + z^2 - r^2 = 0.$$

Substituting the ray equation, we have

$$\left(o_x + t\mathbf{d}_x\right)^2 + \left(o_y + t\mathbf{d}_y\right)^2 + \left(o_z + t\mathbf{d}_z\right)^2 - r^2 = 0,$$

where subscripts denote the corresponding component of a point or vector. For a given ray and a given sphere, all the values besides t are known, giving us an easily solved quadratic equation in t. If there are no real roots, the ray misses the sphere; if there are roots, the smallest positive one gives the intersection point.

The intersection point alone is not enough information for the rest of the ray tracer; it needs to know certain properties of the surface at the point. First, a representation of the material at the point must be determined and passed along to later stages of the ray-tracing algorithm.

Figure 1.4: *Moana Island* Scene, Rendered by pbrt. This model from a feature film exhibits the extreme complexity of scenes rendered for movies (Walt Disney Animation Studios 2018). It features over 146 million unique triangles, though the true geometric complexity of the scene is well into the tens of billions of triangles due to extensive use of object instancing. *(Scene courtesy of Walt Disney Animation Studios.)*

Second, additional geometric information about the intersection point will also be required in order to shade the point. For example, the surface normal **n** is always required. Although many ray tracers operate with only **n**, more sophisticated rendering systems like pbrt require even more information, such as various partial derivatives of position and surface normal with respect to the local parameterization of the surface.

Of course, most scenes are made up of multiple objects. The brute-force approach would be to test the ray against each object in turn, choosing the minimum positive t value of all intersections to find the closest intersection. This approach, while correct, is very slow, even for scenes of modest complexity. A better approach is to incorporate an *acceleration structure* that quickly rejects whole groups of objects during the ray intersection process. This ability to quickly cull irrelevant geometry means that ray tracing frequently runs in $O(m \log n)$ time, where m is the number of pixels in the image and n is the number of objects in the scene.[3] (Building the acceleration structure itself is necessarily at least $O(n)$ time, however.) Thanks to the effectiveness of acceleration structures, it is possible to render highly complex scenes like the one shown in Figure 1.4 in reasonable amounts of time.

pbrt's geometric interface and implementations of it for a variety of shapes are described in Chapter 6, and the acceleration interface and implementations are shown in Chapter 7.

1.2.3 LIGHT DISTRIBUTION

The ray–object intersection stage gives us a point to be shaded and some information about the local geometry at that point. Recall that our eventual goal is to find the amount of light leaving this point in the direction of the camera. To do this, we need to know how much light is *arriving* at this point. This involves both the *geometric* and *radiometric* distribution of light in the scene. For very simple light sources (e.g., point lights), the geometric distribution

---

3   Although ray tracing's logarithmic complexity is often heralded as one of its key strengths, this complexity is typically only true on average. A number of ray-tracing algorithms that have guaranteed logarithmic running time have been published in the computational geometry literature, but these algorithms only work for certain types of scenes and have very expensive preprocessing and storage requirements. Szirmay-Kalos and Márton provide pointers to the relevant literature (Szirmay-Kalos and Márton 1998). In practice, the ray intersection algorithms presented in this book are sublinear, but without expensive preprocessing and huge memory usage it is always possible to construct worst-case scenes where ray tracing runs in $O(mn)$ time. One consolation is that scenes representing realistic environments generally do not exhibit this worst-case behavior.

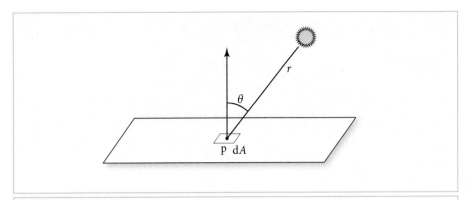

Figure 1.5: Geometric construction for determining the power per area arriving at a point p due to a point light source. The distance from the point to the light source is denoted by r.

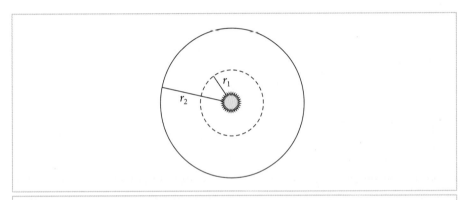

Figure 1.6: Since the point light radiates light equally in all directions, the same total power is deposited on all spheres centered at the light.

of lighting is a simple matter of knowing the position of the lights. However, point lights do not exist in the real world, and so physically based lighting is often based on *area* light sources. This means that the light source is associated with a geometric object that emits illumination from its surface. However, we will use point lights in this section to illustrate the components of light distribution; a more rigorous discussion of light measurement and distribution is the topic of Chapters 4 and 12.

We frequently would like to know the amount of light power being deposited on the differential area surrounding the intersection point p (Figure 1.5). We will assume that the point light source has some power Φ associated with it and that it radiates light equally in all directions. This means that the power per area on a unit sphere surrounding the light is $\Phi/(4\pi)$. (These measurements will be explained and formalized in Section 4.1.)

If we consider two such spheres (Figure 1.6), it is clear that the power per area at a point on the larger sphere must be less than the power at a point on the smaller sphere because the same total power is distributed over a larger area. Specifically, the power per area arriving at a point on a sphere of radius r is proportional to $1/r^2$.

Furthermore, it can be shown that if the tiny surface patch dA is tilted by an angle θ away from the vector from the surface point to the light, the amount of power deposited on dA

Figure 1.7: Scene with Thousands of Light Sources. This scene has far too many lights to consider all of them at each point where the reflected light is computed. Nevertheless, it can be rendered efficiently using stochastic sampling of light sources. *(Scene courtesy of Beeple.)*

is proportional to $\cos\theta$. Putting this all together, the differential power per area $\mathrm{d}E$ (the *differential irradiance*) is

$$\mathrm{d}E = \frac{\Phi\cos\theta}{4\pi r^2}.$$

Readers already familiar with basic lighting in computer graphics will notice two familiar laws encoded in this equation: the cosine falloff of light for tilted surfaces mentioned above, and the one-over-r-squared falloff of light with distance.

Scenes with multiple lights are easily handled because illumination is *linear*: the contribution of each light can be computed separately and summed to obtain the overall contribution. An implication of the linearity of light is that sophisticated algorithms can be applied to randomly sample lighting from only some of the light sources at each shaded point in the scene; this is the topic of Section 12.6. Figure 1.7 shows a scene with thousands of light sources rendered in this way.

1.2.4 VISIBILITY

The lighting distribution described in the previous section ignores one very important component: *shadows*. Each light contributes illumination to the point being shaded only if the path from the point to the light's position is unobstructed (Figure 1.8).

Fortunately, in a ray tracer it is easy to determine if the light is visible from the point being shaded. We simply construct a new ray whose origin is at the surface point and whose direction points toward the light. These special rays are called *shadow rays*. If we trace this ray through the environment, we can check to see whether any intersections are found between the ray's origin and the light source by comparing the parametric t value of any intersections found to the parametric t value along the ray of the light source position. If there is no blocking object between the light and the surface, the light's contribution is included.

1.2.5 LIGHT SCATTERING AT SURFACES

We are now able to compute two pieces of information that are vital for proper shading of a point: its location and the incident lighting. Now we need to determine how the incident lighting is *scattered* at the surface. Specifically, we are interested in the amount of light energy

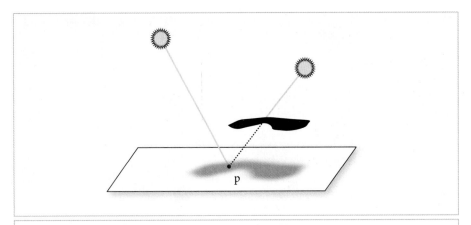

Figure 1.8: A light source only deposits energy on a surface if the source is not obscured as seen from the receiving point. The light source on the left illuminates the point p, but the light source on the right does not.

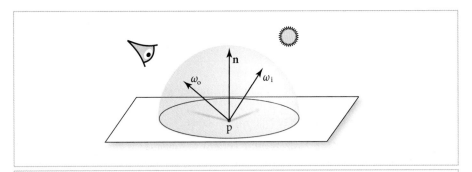

Figure 1.9: The Geometry of Surface Scattering. Incident light arriving along direction ω_i interacts with the surface at point p and is scattered back toward the camera along direction ω_o. The amount of light scattered toward the camera is given by the product of the incident light energy and the BRDF.

scattered back along the ray that we originally traced to find the intersection point, since that ray leads to the camera (Figure 1.9).

Each object in the scene provides a *material*, which is a description of its appearance properties at each point on the surface. This description is given by the *bidirectional reflectance distribution function* (BRDF). This function tells us how much energy is reflected from an incoming direction ω_i to an outgoing direction ω_o. We will write the BRDF at p as $f_r(p, \omega_o, \omega_i)$. (By convention, directions ω are unit vectors.)

It is easy to generalize the notion of a BRDF to transmitted light (obtaining a BTDF) or to general scattering of light arriving from either side of the surface. A function that describes general scattering is called a *bidirectional scattering distribution function* (BSDF). pbrt supports a variety of BSDF models; they are described in Chapter 9. More complex yet is the *bidirectional scattering surface reflectance distribution function* (BSSRDF), which models light that exits a surface at a different point than it enters. This is necessary to reproduce translucent materials such as milk, marble, or skin. The BSSRDF is described in Section 4.3.2. Figure 1.10 shows an image rendered by pbrt based on a model of a human head where scattering from the skin is modeled using a BSSRDF.

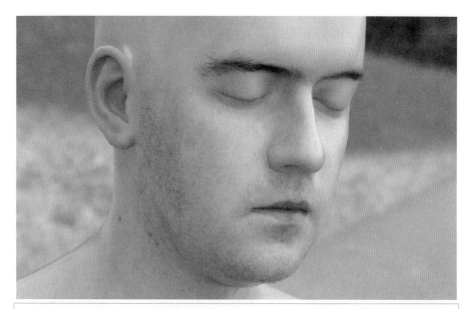

Figure 1.10: Head with Scattering Modeled Using a BSSRDF. Accurately modeling subsurface light transport rather than assuming that light exits the surface at the same point it entered greatly improves the realism of the rendered image. *(Model courtesy of Infinite Realities, Inc.)*

1.2.6 INDIRECT LIGHT TRANSPORT

Turner Whitted's original paper on ray tracing (1980) emphasized its *recursive* nature, which was the key that made it possible to include indirect specular reflection and transmission in rendered images. For example, if a ray from the camera hits a shiny object like a mirror, we can reflect the ray about the surface normal at the intersection point and recursively invoke the ray-tracing routine to find the light arriving at the point on the mirror, adding its contribution to the original camera ray. This same technique can be used to trace transmitted rays that intersect transparent objects. Many early ray-tracing examples showcased mirrors and glass balls (Figure 1.11) because these types of effects were difficult to capture with other rendering techniques.

In general, the amount of light that reaches the camera from a point on an object is given by the sum of light emitted by the object (if it is itself a light source) and the amount of reflected light. This idea is formalized by the *light transport equation* (also often known as the *rendering equation*), which measures light with respect to *radiance*, a radiometric unit that will be defined in Section 4.1. It says that the outgoing radiance $L_o(p, \omega_o)$ from a point p in direction ω_o is the emitted radiance at that point in that direction, $L_e(p, \omega_o)$, plus the incident radiance from all directions on the sphere $\mathbb{S}^2$ around p scaled by the BSDF $f(p, \omega_o, \omega_i)$ and a cosine term:

$$L_o(p, \omega_o) = L_e(p, \omega_o) + \int_{\mathbb{S}^2} f(p, \omega_o, \omega_i)\, L_i(p, \omega_i)\, |\cos \theta_i|\, d\omega_i. \qquad [1.1]$$

We will show a more complete derivation of this equation in Sections 4.3.1 and 13.1.1. Solving this integral analytically is not possible except for the simplest of scenes, so we must either make simplifying assumptions or use numerical integration techniques.

(a)

(b)

Figure 1.11: A Prototypical Early Ray Tracing Scene. Note the use of mirrored and glass objects, which emphasizes the algorithm's ability to handle these kinds of surfaces. (a) Rendered using Whitted's original ray-tracing algorithm from 1980, and (b) rendered using *stochastic progressive photon mapping* (SPPM), a modern advanced light transport algorithm. SPPM is able to accurately simulate the focusing of light that passes through the spheres.

Whitted's ray-tracing algorithm simplifies this integral by ignoring incoming light from most directions and only evaluating $L_i(p, \omega_i)$ for directions to light sources and for the directions of perfect reflection and refraction. In other words, it turns the integral into a sum over a small number of directions. In Section 1.3.6, we will see that simple random sampling of Equation (1.1) can create realistic images that include both complex lighting and complex surface scattering effects. Throughout the remainder of the book, we will show how using more sophisticated random sampling algorithms greatly improves the efficiency of this general approach.

1.2.7 RAY PROPAGATION

The discussion so far has assumed that rays are traveling through a vacuum. For example, when describing the distribution of light from a point source, we assumed that the light's power was distributed equally on the surface of a sphere centered at the light without decreasing along the way. The presence of *participating media* such as smoke, fog, or dust can invalidate this assumption. These effects are important to simulate: a wide class of interesting phenomena can be described using participating media. Figure 1.12 shows an explosion rendered by pbrt. Less dramatically, almost all outdoor scenes are affected substantially by participating media. For example, Earth's atmosphere causes objects that are farther away to appear less saturated.

Figure 1.12: Explosion Modeled Using Participating Media. Because pbrt is capable of simulating light emission, scattering, and absorption in detailed models of participating media, it is capable of rendering images like this one. *(Scene courtesy of Jim Price.)*

There are two ways in which a participating medium can affect the light propagating along a ray. First, the medium can *extinguish* (or *attenuate*) light, either by absorbing it or by scattering it in a different direction. We can capture this effect by computing the *transmittance* T_r between the ray origin and the intersection point. The transmittance tells us how much of the light scattered at the intersection point makes it back to the ray origin.

A participating medium can also add to the light along a ray. This can happen either if the medium emits light (as with a flame) or if the medium scatters light from other directions back along the ray. We can find this quantity by numerically evaluating the *volume light transport equation*, in the same way we evaluated the light transport equation to find the amount of light reflected from a surface. We will leave the description of participating media and volume rendering until Chapters 11 and 14.

1.3 pbrt: SYSTEM OVERVIEW

pbrt is structured using standard object-oriented techniques: for each of a number of fundamental types, the system specifies an interface that implementations of that type must fulfill. For example, pbrt requires the implementation of a particular shape that represents geometry in a scene to provide a set of methods including one that returns the shape's bounding box, and another that tests for intersection with a given ray. In turn, the majority of the system can be implemented purely in terms of those interfaces; for example, the code that checks for occluding objects between a light source and a point being shaded calls the shape intersection methods without needing to consider which particular types of shapes are present in the scene.

There are a total of 14 of these key base types, summarized in Table 1.1. Adding a new implementation of one of these types to the system is straightforward; the implementation must provide the required methods, it must be compiled and linked into the executable, and the scene object creation routines must be modified to create instances of the object as

Table 1.1: **Main Interface Types.** Most of pbrt is implemented in terms of 14 key base types, listed here. Implementations of each of these can easily be added to the system to extend its functionality.

Base type	Source Files	Section
Spectrum	base/spectrum.h, util/spectrum.{h,cpp}	4.5
Camera	base/camera.h, cameras.{h,cpp}	5.1
Shape	base/shape.h, shapes.{h,cpp}	6.1
Primitive	cpu/{primitive,accelerators}.{h,cpp}	7.1
Sampler	base/sampler.h, samplers.{h,cpp}	8.3
Filter	base/filter.h, filters.{h,cpp}	8.8.1
BxDF	base/bxdf.h, bxdfs.{h,cpp}	9.1.2
Material	base/material.h, materials.{h,cpp}	10.5
FloatTexture		
SpectrumTexture	base/texture.h, textures.{h,cpp}	10.3
Medium	base/medium.h, media.{h,cpp}	11.4
Light	base/light.h, lights.{h,cpp}	12.1
LightSampler	base/lightsampler.h, lightsamplers.{h,cpp}	12.6
Integrator	cpu/integrators.{h,cpp}	1.3.3

BxDF 538
Camera 206
Filter 515
FloatTexture 656
Integrator 22
Light 740
LightSampler 781
Material 674
Medium 714
Primitive 398
Sampler 469
Shape 261
Spectrum 165
SpectrumTexture 656

needed as the scene description file is parsed. Section C.4 discusses extending the system in more detail.

Conventional practice in C++ would be to specify the interfaces for each of these types using abstract base classes that define pure virtual functions and to have implementations inherit from those base classes and implement the required virtual functions. In turn, the compiler would take care of generating the code that calls the appropriate method, given a pointer to any object of the base class type. That approach was used in the three previous versions of pbrt, but the addition of support for rendering on graphics processing units (GPUs) in this version motivated a more portable approach based on *tag-based dispatch*, where each specific type implementation is assigned a unique integer that determines its type at runtime. (See Section 1.5.7 for more information about this topic.) The polymorphic types that are implemented in this way in pbrt are all defined in header files in the base/ directory.

This version of pbrt is capable of running on GPUs that support C++17 and provide APIs for ray intersection tests.[4] We have carefully designed the system so that almost all of pbrt's implementation runs on both CPUs and GPUs, just as it is presented in Chapters 2 through 12. We will therefore generally say little about the CPU versus the GPU in most of the following.

The main differences between the CPU and GPU rendering paths in pbrt are in their data flow and how they are parallelized—effectively, how the pieces are connected together. Both the basic rendering algorithm described later in this chapter and the light transport algorithms described in Chapters 13 and 14 are only available on the CPU. The GPU rendering pipeline is discussed in Chapter 15, though it, too, is also capable of running on the CPU (not as efficiently as the CPU-targeted light transport algorithms, however).

While pbrt can render many scenes well with its current implementation, it has frequently been extended by students, researchers, and developers. Throughout this section are a number of notable images from those efforts. Figures 1.13, 1.14, and 1.15 were each created by students in a rendering course where the final class project was to extend pbrt with new functionality in order to render an image that it could not have rendered before. These images are among the best from that course.

1.3.1 PHASES OF EXECUTION

pbrt can be conceptually divided into three phases of execution. First, it parses the scene description file provided by the user. The scene description is a text file that specifies the geometric shapes that make up the scene, their material properties, the lights that illuminate them, where the virtual camera is positioned in the scene, and parameters to all the individual algorithms used throughout the system. The scene file format is documented on the pbrt website, *pbrt.org*.

The result of the parsing phase is an instance of the BasicScene class, which stores the scene specification, but not in a form yet suitable for rendering. In the second phase of execution, pbrt creates specific objects corresponding to the scene; for example, if a perspective projection has been specified, it is in this phase that a PerspectiveCamera object corresponding to the specified viewing parameters is created. Previous versions of pbrt intermixed these first two phases, but for this version we have separated them because the CPU and GPU rendering paths differ in some of the ways that they represent the scene in memory.

BasicScene 1134

PerspectiveCamera 220

---

4   At the time of writing, these capabilities are only available on NVIDIA hardware, but it would not be too difficult to port pbrt to other architectures that provide them in the future.

Figure 1.13: Guillaume Poncin and Pramod Sharma extended pbrt in numerous ways, implementing a number of complex rendering algorithms, to make this prize-winning image for Stanford's CS348b rendering competition. The trees are modeled procedurally with L-systems, a glow image processing filter increases the apparent realism of the lights on the tree, snow was modeled procedurally with metaballs, and a subsurface scattering algorithm gave the snow its realistic appearance by accounting for the effect of light that travels beneath the snow for some distance before leaving it.

In the third phase, the main rendering loop executes. This phase is where pbrt usually spends the majority of its running time, and most of this book is devoted to code that executes during this phase. To orchestrate the rendering, pbrt implements an *integrator*, so-named because its main task is to evaluate the integral in Equation (1.1).

1.3.2 pbrt'S main() FUNCTION

The main() function for the pbrt executable is defined in the file cmd/pbrt.cpp in the directory that holds the pbrt source code, src/pbrt in the pbrt distribution. It is only a hundred and fifty or so lines of code, much of it devoted to processing command-line arguments and related bookkeeping.

⟨*main program*⟩ ≡
```
int main(int argc, char *argv[]) {
    ⟨Convert command-line arguments to vector of strings  19⟩
    ⟨Declare variables for parsed command line  19⟩
    ⟨Process command-line arguments⟩
    ⟨Initialize pbrt  20⟩
    ⟨Parse provided scene description files  20⟩
    ⟨Render the scene  21⟩
    ⟨Clean up after rendering the scene  21⟩
}
```

Rather than operate on the argv values provided to the main() function directly, pbrt converts the provided arguments to a vector of std::strings. It does so not only for the greater

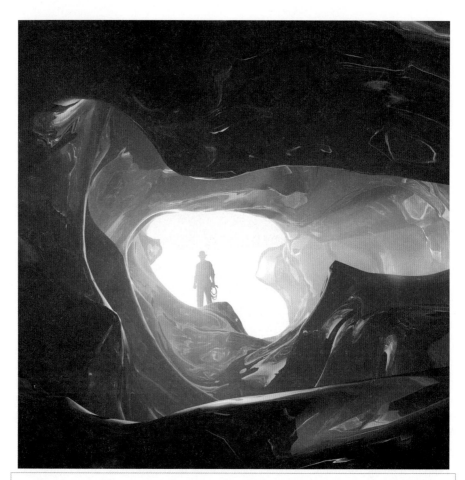

Figure 1.14: Abe Davis, David Jacobs, and Jongmin Baek rendered this amazing image of an ice cave to take the grand prize in the 2009 Stanford CS348b rendering competition. They first implemented a simulation of the physical process of glaciation, the process where snow falls, melts, and refreezes over the course of many years, forming stratified layers of ice. They then simulated erosion of the ice due to melted water runoff before generating a geometric model of the ice. Scattering of light inside the volume was simulated with volumetric photon mapping; the blue color of the ice is entirely due to modeling the wavelength-dependent absorption of light in the ice volume.

convenience of the string class, but also to support non-ASCII character sets. Section B.3.2 has more information about character encodings and how they are handled in pbrt.

⟨*Convert command-line arguments to vector of strings*⟩ ≡   18
```
std::vector<std::string> args = GetCommandLineArguments(argv);
```

We will only include the definitions of some of the main function's fragments in the book text here. Some, such as the one that handles parsing command-line arguments provided by the user, are both simple enough and long enough that they are not worth the few pages that they would add to the book's length. However, we will include the fragment that declares the variables in which the option values are stored.

GetCommandLineArguments()
    1063

PBRTOptions 1032

⟨*Declare variables for parsed command line*⟩ ≡   18
```
PBRTOptions options;
std::vector<std::string> filenames;
```

Figure 1.15: Chenlin Meng, Hubert Teo, and Jiren Zhu rendered this tasty-looking image of cotton candy in a teacup to win the grand prize in the 2018 Stanford CS348b rendering competition. They modeled the cotton candy with multiple layers of curves and then filled the center with a participating medium to efficiently model scattering in its interior.

The GetCommandLineArguments() function and PBRTOptions type appear in a *mini-index* in the page margin, along with the number of the page where they are defined. The mini-indices have pointers to the definitions of almost all the functions, classes, methods, and member variables used or referred to on each page. (In the interests of brevity, we will omit very widely used classes such as Ray from the mini-indices, as well as types or methods that were just introduced in the preceding few pages.)

The PBRTOptions class stores various rendering options that are generally more suited to be specified on the command line rather than in scene description files—for example, how chatty pbrt should be about its progress during rendering. It is passed to the InitPBRT() function, which aggregates the various system-wide initialization tasks that must be performed before any other work is done. For example, it initializes the logging system and launches a group of threads that are used for the parallelization of pbrt.

⟨*Initialize pbrt*⟩ ≡   **18**
    InitPBRT(options);

After the arguments have been parsed and validated, the ParseFiles() function takes over to handle the first of the three phases of execution described earlier. With the assistance of two classes, BasicSceneBuilder and BasicScene, which are respectively described in Sections C.2 and C.3, it loops over the provided filenames, parsing each file in turn. If pbrt is run with no filenames provided, it looks for the scene description from standard input. The mechanics of tokenizing and parsing scene description files will not be described in this book, but the parser implementation can be found in the files parser.h and parser.cpp in the src/pbrt directory.

⟨*Parse provided scene description files*⟩ ≡   **18**
    BasicScene scene;
    BasicSceneBuilder builder(&scene);
    ParseFiles(&builder, filenames);

After the scene description has been parsed, one of two functions is called to render the scene. RenderWavefront() supports both the CPU and GPU rendering paths, processing a million or so image samples in parallel. It is the topic of Chapter 15. RenderCPU() renders the scene using

Figure 1.16: Martin Lubich modeled this scene of the Austrian Imperial Crown using *Blender*; it was originally rendered using *LuxRender,* which started out as a fork of the `pbrt-v1` codebase. The crown consists of approximately 3.5 million triangles that are illuminated by six area light sources with emission spectra based on measured data from a real-world light source. It was originally rendered with 1280 samples per pixel in 73 hours of computation on a quad-core CPU. On a modern GPU, `pbrt` renders this scene at the same sampling rate in 184 seconds.

an `Integrator` implementation and is only available when running on the CPU. It uses much less parallelism than `RenderWavefront()`, rendering only as many image samples as there are CPU threads in parallel.

Both of these functions start by converting the `BasicScene` into a form suitable for efficient rendering and then pass control to a processor-specific integrator. (More information about this process is available in Section C.3.) We will for now gloss past the details of this transformation in order to focus on the main rendering loop in `RenderCPU()`, which is much more interesting. For that, we will take the efficient scene representation as a given.

⟨*Render the scene*⟩ ≡   **18**
```
if (Options->useGPU || Options->wavefront)
    RenderWavefront(scene);
else
    RenderCPU(scene);
```

After the image has been rendered, `CleanupPBRT()` takes care of shutting the system down gracefully, including, for example, terminating the threads launched by `InitPBRT()`.

⟨*Clean up after rendering the scene*⟩ ≡   **18**
```
CleanupPBRT();
```

1.3.3 INTEGRATOR INTERFACE

In the RenderCPU() rendering path, an instance of a class that implements the Integrator interface is responsible for rendering. Because Integrator implementations only run on the CPU, we will define Integrator as a standard base class with pure virtual methods. Integrator and the various implementations are each defined in the files cpu/integrator.h and cpu/integrator.cpp.

```
⟨Integrator Definition⟩ ≡
    class Integrator {
      public:
        ⟨Integrator Public Methods 23⟩
        ⟨Integrator Public Members 22⟩
      protected:
        ⟨Integrator Protected Methods 22⟩
    };
```

The base Integrator constructor takes a single Primitive that represents all the geometric objects in the scene as well as an array that holds all the lights in the scene.

```
⟨Integrator Protected Methods⟩ ≡                                          22
    Integrator(Primitive aggregate, std::vector<Light> lights)
        : aggregate(aggregate), lights(lights) {
        ⟨Integrator constructor implementation 23⟩
    }
```

Each geometric object in the scene is represented by a Primitive, which is primarily responsible for combining a Shape that specifies its geometry and a Material that describes its appearance (e.g., the object's color, or whether it has a dull or glossy finish). In turn, all the geometric primitives in a scene are collected into a single aggregate primitive that is stored in the Integrator::aggregate member variable. This aggregate is a special kind of primitive that itself holds references to many other primitives. The aggregate implementation stores all the scene's primitives in an acceleration data structure that reduces the number of unnecessary ray intersection tests with primitives that are far away from a given ray. Because it implements the Primitive interface, it appears no different from a single primitive to the rest of the system.

```
⟨Integrator Public Members⟩ ≡                                            22
    Primitive aggregate;
    std::vector<Light> lights;
```

Each light source in the scene is represented by an object that implements the Light interface, which allows the light to specify its shape and the distribution of energy that it emits. Some lights need to know the bounding box of the entire scene, which is unavailable when they are first created. Therefore, the Integrator constructor calls their Preprocess() methods, providing those bounds. At this point any "infinite" lights are also stored in a separate array. This sort of light, which will be introduced in Section 12.5, models infinitely far away sources of light, which is a reasonable model for skylight as received on Earth's surface, for example. Sometimes it will be necessary to loop over just those lights, and for scenes with thousands of light sources it would be inefficient to loop over all of them just to find those.

⟨*Integrator constructor implementation*⟩ ≡   22
```
Bounds3f sceneBounds = aggregate ? aggregate.Bounds() : Bounds3f();
for (auto &light : lights) {
    light.Preprocess(sceneBounds);
    if (light.Type() == LightType::Infinite)
        infiniteLights.push_back(light);
}
```

⟨*Integrator Public Members*⟩ +≡   22
```
std::vector<Light> infiniteLights;
```

Integrators must provide an implementation of the Render() method, which takes no further arguments. This method is called by the RenderCPU() function once the scene representation has been initialized. The task of integrators is to render the scene as specified by the aggregate and the lights. Beyond that, it is up to the specific integrator to define what it means to render the scene, using whichever other classes that it needs to do so (e.g., a camera model). This interface is intentionally very general to permit a wide range of implementations—for example, one could implement an Integrator that measures light only at a sparse set of points distributed through the scene rather than generating a regular 2D image.

⟨*Integrator Public Methods*⟩ ≡   22
```
virtual void Render() = 0;
```

The Integrator class provides two methods related to ray–primitive intersection for use of its subclasses. Intersect() takes a ray and a maximum parametric distance tMax, traces the given ray into the scene, and returns a ShapeIntersection object corresponding to the closest primitive that the ray hit, if there is an intersection along the ray before tMax. (The ShapeIntersection structure is defined in Section 6.1.3.) One thing to note is that this method uses the type pstd::optional for the return value rather than std::optional from the C++ standard library; we have reimplemented parts of the standard library in the pstd namespace for reasons that are discussed in Section 1.5.5.

⟨*Integrator Method Definitions*⟩ ≡
```
pstd::optional<ShapeIntersection>
Integrator::Intersect(const Ray &ray, Float tMax) const {
    if (aggregate) return aggregate.Intersect(ray, tMax);
    else           return {};
}
```

Also note the capitalized floating-point type Float in Intersect()'s signature: almost all floating-point values in pbrt are declared as Floats. (The only exceptions are a few cases where a 32-bit float or a 64-bit double is specifically needed (e.g., when saving binary values to files).) Depending on the compilation flags of pbrt, Float is an alias for either float or double, though single precision float is almost always sufficient in practice. The definition of Float is in the pbrt.h header file, which is included by all other source files in pbrt.

⟨*Float Type Definitions*⟩ ≡
```
#ifdef PBRT_FLOAT_AS_DOUBLE
    using Float = double;
#else
    using Float = float;
#endif
```

Integrator::IntersectP() is closely related to the Intersect() method. It checks for the existence of intersections along the ray but only returns a Boolean indicating whether an intersection was found. (The "P" in its name indicates that it is a function that evaluates a predicate, using a common naming convention from the Lisp programming language.) Because it does not need to search for the closest intersection or return additional geometric information about intersections, `IntersectP()` is generally more efficient than `Integrator::Intersect()`. This routine is used for shadow rays.

⟨*Integrator Method Definitions*⟩ +≡
```
bool Integrator::IntersectP(const Ray &ray, Float tMax) const {
    if (aggregate) return aggregate.IntersectP(ray, tMax);
    else           return false;
}
```

1.3.4 ImageTileIntegrator AND THE MAIN RENDERING LOOP

Before implementing a basic integrator that simulates light transport to render an image, we will define two `Integrator` subclasses that provide additional common functionality used by that integrator as well as many of the integrator implementations to come. We start with `ImageTileIntegrator`, which inherits from `Integrator`. The next section defines `RayIntegrator`, which inherits from `ImageTileIntegrator`.

All of pbrt's CPU-based integrators render images using a camera model to define the viewing parameters, and all parallelize rendering by splitting the image into tiles and having different processors work on different tiles. Therefore, pbrt includes an `ImageTileIntegrator` that provides common functionality for those tasks.

⟨*ImageTileIntegrator Definition*⟩ ≡
```
class ImageTileIntegrator : public Integrator {
  public:
    ⟨ImageTileIntegrator Public Methods  24⟩
  protected:
    ⟨ImageTileIntegrator Protected Members  25⟩
};
```

In addition to the aggregate and the lights, the `ImageTileIntegrator` constructor takes a `Camera` that specifies the viewing and lens parameters such as position, orientation, focus, and field of view. `Film` stored by the camera handles image storage. The `Camera` classes are the subject of most of Chapter 5, and `Film` is described in Section 5.4. The `Film` is responsible for writing the final image to a file.

The constructor also takes a `Sampler`; its role is more subtle, but its implementation can substantially affect the quality of the images that the system generates. First, the sampler is responsible for choosing the points on the image plane that determine which rays are initially traced into the scene. Second, it is responsible for supplying random sample values that are used by integrators for estimating the value of the light transport integral, Equation (1.1). For example, some integrators need to choose random points on light sources to compute illumination from area lights. Generating a good distribution of these samples is an important part of the rendering process that can substantially affect overall efficiency; this topic is the main focus of Chapter 8.

⟨*ImageTileIntegrator Public Methods*⟩ ≡   **24**
```
ImageTileIntegrator(Camera camera, Sampler sampler,
        Primitive aggregate, std::vector<Light> lights)
    : Integrator(aggregate, lights), camera(camera),
      samplerPrototype(sampler) {}
```

⟨*ImageTileIntegrator Protected Members*⟩ ≡   **24**
    Camera camera;
    Sampler samplerPrototype;

For all of pbrt's integrators, the final color computed at each pixel is based on random sampling algorithms. If each pixel's final value is computed as the average of multiple samples, then the quality of the image improves. At low numbers of samples, sampling error manifests itself as grainy high-frequency noise in images, though error goes down at a predictable rate as the number of samples increases. (This topic is discussed in more depth in Section 2.1.4.) ImageTileIntegrator::Render() therefore renders the image in *waves* of a few samples per pixel. For the first two waves, only a single sample is taken in each pixel. In the next wave, two samples are taken, with the number of samples doubling after each wave up to a limit. While it makes no difference to the final image if the image was rendered in waves or with all the samples being taken in a pixel before moving on to the next one, this organization of the computation means that it is possible to see previews of the final image during rendering where all pixels have some samples, rather than a few pixels having many samples and the rest having none.

Because pbrt is parallelized to run using multiple threads, there is a balance to be struck with this approach. There is a cost for threads to acquire work for a new image tile, and some threads end up idle at the end of each wave once there is no more work for them to do but other threads are still working on the tiles they have been assigned. These considerations motivated the capped doubling approach.

⟨*ImageTileIntegrator Method Definitions*⟩ ≡
    void ImageTileIntegrator::Render() {
        ⟨*Declare common variables for rendering image in tiles* **25**⟩
        ⟨*Render image in waves* **26**⟩
    }

Before rendering begins, a few additional variables are required. First, the integrator implementations will need to allocate small amounts of temporary memory to store surface scattering properties in the course of computing each ray's contribution. The large number of resulting allocations could easily overwhelm the system's regular memory allocation routines (e.g., new), which must coordinate multi-threaded maintenance of elaborate data structures to track free memory. A naive implementation could potentially spend a fairly large fraction of its computation time in the memory allocator.

To address this issue, pbrt provides a ScratchBuffer class that manages a small preallocated buffer of memory. ScratchBuffer allocations are very efficient, just requiring the increment of an offset. The ScratchBuffer does not allow independently freeing allocations; instead, all must be freed at once, but doing so only requires resetting that offset.

Because ScratchBuffers are not safe for use by multiple threads at the same time, an individual one is created for each thread using the ThreadLocal template class. Its constructor takes a lambda function that returns a fresh instance of the object of the type it manages; here, calling the default ScratchBuffer constructor is sufficient. ThreadLocal then handles the details of maintaining distinct copies of the object for each thread, allocating them on demand.

⟨*Declare common variables for rendering image in tiles*⟩ ≡   **25**
    ThreadLocal<ScratchBuffer> scratchBuffers(
        []() { return ScratchBuffer(); });

Most Sampler implementations find it useful to maintain some state, such as the coordinates of the current pixel. This means that multiple threads cannot use a single Sampler concurrently and ThreadLocal is also used for Sampler management. Samplers provide a Clone() method that creates a new instance of their sampler type. The Sampler first provided to the ImageTileIntegrator constructor, samplerPrototype, provides those copies here.

⟨*Declare common variables for rendering image in tiles*⟩ +≡   **25**
```
ThreadLocal<Sampler> samplers(
    [this]() { return samplerPrototype.Clone(); });
```

It is helpful to provide the user with an indication of how much of the rendering work is done and an estimate of how much longer it will take. This task is handled by the ProgressReporter class, which takes as its first parameter the total number of items of work. Here, the total amount of work is the number of samples taken in each pixel times the total number of pixels. It is important to use 64-bit precision to compute this value, since a 32-bit int may be insufficient for high-resolution images with many samples per pixel.

⟨*Declare common variables for rendering image in tiles*⟩ +≡   **25**
```
Bounds2i pixelBounds = camera.GetFilm().PixelBounds();
int spp = samplerPrototype.SamplesPerPixel();
ProgressReporter progress(int64_t(spp) * pixelBounds.Area(), "Rendering",
                          Options->quiet);
```

In the following, the range of samples to be taken in the current wave is given by waveStart and waveEnd; nextWaveSize gives the number of samples to be taken in the next wave.

⟨*Declare common variables for rendering image in tiles*⟩ +≡   **25**
```
int waveStart = 0, waveEnd = 1, nextWaveSize = 1;
```

With these variables in hand, rendering proceeds until the required number of samples have been taken in all pixels.

⟨*Render image in waves*⟩ ≡   **25**
```
while (waveStart < spp) {
    ⟨Render current wave's image tiles in parallel 27⟩
    ⟨Update start and end wave 28⟩
    ⟨Optionally write current image to disk⟩
}
```

The ParallelFor2D() function loops over image tiles, running multiple loop iterations concurrently; it is part of the parallelism-related utility functions that are introduced in Section B.6. A C++ lambda expression provides the loop body. ParallelFor2D() automatically chooses a tile size to balance two concerns: on one hand, we would like to have significantly more tiles than there are processors in the system. It is likely that some of the tiles will take less processing time than others, so if there was for example a 1:1 mapping between processors and tiles, then some processors will be idle after finishing their work while others continue to work on their region of the image. (Figure 1.17 graphs the distribution of time taken to render tiles of an example image, illustrating this concern.) On the other hand, having too many tiles also hurts efficiency. There is a small fixed overhead for a thread to acquire more work in the parallel for loop and the more tiles there are, the more times this overhead must be paid. ParallelFor2D() therefore chooses a tile size that accounts for both the extent of the region to be processed and the number of processors in the system.

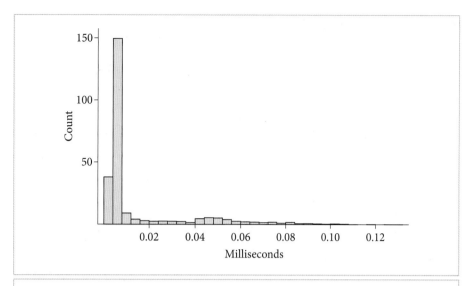

Figure 1.17: Histogram of Time Spent Rendering Each Tile for the Scene in Figure 1.11. The horizontal axis measures time in seconds. Note the wide variation in execution time, illustrating that different parts of the image required substantially different amounts of computation.

⟨*Render current wave's image tiles in parallel*⟩ ≡   **26**
```
ParallelFor2D(pixelBounds, [&](Bounds2i tileBounds) {
    ⟨Render image tile given by tileBounds 27⟩
});
```

Given a tile to render, the implementation starts by acquiring the `ScratchBuffer` and `Sampler` for the currently executing thread. As described earlier, the `ThreadLocal::Get()` method takes care of the details of allocating and returning individual ones of them for each thread.

With those in hand, the implementation loops over all the pixels in the tile using a range-based `for` loop that uses iterators provided by the `Bounds2` class before informing the `ProgressReporter` about how much work has been completed.

⟨*Render image tile given by* tileBounds⟩ ≡   **27**
```
ScratchBuffer &scratchBuffer = scratchBuffers.Get();
Sampler &sampler = samplers.Get();
for (Point2i pPixel : tileBounds) {
    ⟨Render samples in pixel pPixel 28⟩
}
progress.Update((waveEnd - waveStart) * tileBounds.Area());
```

Given a pixel to take one or more samples in, the thread's `Sampler` is notified that it should start generating samples for the current pixel via `StartPixelSample()`, which allows it to set up any internal state that depends on which pixel is currently being processed. The integrator's `EvaluatePixelSample()` method is then responsible for determining the specified sample's value, after which any temporary memory it may have allocated in the `ScratchBuffer` is freed with a call to `ScratchBuffer::Reset()`.

⟨*Render samples in pixel* pPixel⟩ ≡   27
```
    for (int sampleIndex = waveStart; sampleIndex < waveEnd; ++sampleIndex) {
        sampler.StartPixelSample(pPixel, sampleIndex);
        EvaluatePixelSample(pPixel, sampleIndex, sampler, scratchBuffer);
        scratchBuffer.Reset();
    }
```

Having provided an implementation of the pure virtual Integrator::Render() method, ImageTileIntegrator now imposes the requirement on its subclasses that they implement the following EvaluatePixelSample() method.

⟨*ImageTileIntegrator Public Methods*⟩ +≡   24
```
    virtual void EvaluatePixelSample(Point2i pPixel, int sampleIndex,
        Sampler sampler, ScratchBuffer &scratchBuffer) = 0;
```

After the parallel for loop for the current wave completes, the range of sample indices to be processed in the next wave is computed.

⟨*Update start and end wave*⟩ ≡   26
```
    waveStart = waveEnd;
    waveEnd = std::min(spp, waveEnd + nextWaveSize);
    nextWaveSize = std::min(2 * nextWaveSize, 64);
```

If the user has provided the --write-partial-images command-line option, the in-progress image is written to disk before the next wave of samples is processed. We will not include here the fragment that takes care of this, ⟨*Optionally write current image to disk*⟩.

1.3.5 RayIntegrator IMPLEMENTATION

Just as the ImageTileIntegrator centralizes functionality related to integrators that decompose the image into tiles, RayIntegrator provides commonly used functionality to integrators that trace ray paths starting from the camera. All of the integrators implemented in Chapters 13 and 14 inherit from RayIntegrator.

⟨*RayIntegrator Definition*⟩ ≡
```
    class RayIntegrator : public ImageTileIntegrator {
      public:
        ⟨RayIntegrator Public Methods 28⟩
    };
```

Its constructor does nothing more than pass along the provided objects to the ImageTile Integrator constructor.

⟨*RayIntegrator Public Methods*⟩ ≡   28
```
    RayIntegrator(Camera camera, Sampler sampler, Primitive aggregate,
                  std::vector<Light> lights)
        : ImageTileIntegrator(camera, sampler, aggregate, lights) {}
```

RayIntegrator implements the pure virtual EvaluatePixelSample() method from ImageTile Integrator. At the given pixel, it uses its Camera and Sampler to generate a ray into the scene and then calls the Li() method, which is provided by the subclass, to determine the amount of light arriving at the image plane along that ray. As we will see in following chapters, the units of the value returned by this method are related to the incident spectral radiance at the ray origin, which is generally denoted by the symbol L_i in equations—thus, the method name. This value is passed to the Film, which records the ray's contribution to the image.

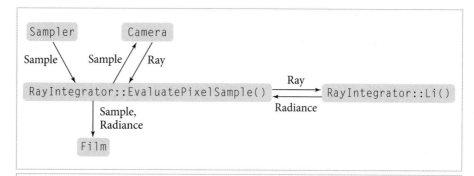

Figure 1.18: Class Relationships for `RayIntegrator::EvaluatePixelSample()`'s computation. The `Sampler` provides sample values for each image sample to be taken. The `Camera` turns a sample into a corresponding ray from the film plane, and the `Li()` method computes the radiance along that ray arriving at the film. The sample and its radiance are passed to the `Film`, which stores their contribution in an image.

Figure 1.18 summarizes the main classes used in this method and the flow of data among them.

⟨*RayIntegrator Method Definitions*⟩ ≡
```
void RayIntegrator::EvaluatePixelSample(Point2i pPixel, int sampleIndex,
        Sampler sampler, ScratchBuffer &scratchBuffer) {
    ⟨Sample wavelengths for the ray 29⟩
    ⟨Initialize CameraSample for current sample 30⟩
    ⟨Generate camera ray for current sample 30⟩
    ⟨Trace cameraRay if valid 30⟩
    ⟨Add camera ray's contribution to image 31⟩
}
```

Each ray carries radiance at a number of discrete wavelengths λ (four, by default). When computing the color at each pixel, pbrt chooses different wavelengths at different pixel samples so that the final result better reflects the correct result over all wavelengths. To choose these wavelengths, a sample value `lu` is first provided by the `Sampler`. This value will be uniformly distributed and in the range [0, 1). The `Film::SampleWavelengths()` method then maps this sample to a set of specific wavelengths, taking into account its model of film sensor response as a function of wavelength. Most `Sampler` implementations ensure that if multiple samples are taken in a pixel, those samples are in the aggregate well distributed over [0, 1). In turn, they ensure that the sampled wavelengths are also well distributed across the range of valid wavelengths, improving image quality.

⟨*Sample wavelengths for the ray*⟩ ≡   29
```
Float lu = sampler.Get1D();
SampledWavelengths lambda = camera.GetFilm().SampleWavelengths(lu);
```

The `CameraSample` structure records the position on the film for which the camera should generate a ray. This position is affected by both a sample position provided by the sampler and the reconstruction filter that is used to filter multiple sample values into a single value for the pixel. `GetCameraSample()` handles those calculations. `CameraSample` also stores a time that is associated with the ray as well as a lens position sample, which are used when rendering scenes with moving objects and for camera models that simulate non-pinhole apertures, respectively.

⟨*Initialize* CameraSample *for current sample*⟩ ≡   29
```
    Filter filter = camera.GetFilm().GetFilter();
    CameraSample cameraSample = GetCameraSample(sampler, pPixel, filter);
```

The Camera interface provides two methods to generate rays: GenerateRay(), which returns the ray for a given image sample position, and GenerateRayDifferential(), which returns a *ray differential*, which incorporates information about the rays that the camera would generate for samples that are one pixel away on the image plane in both the *x* and *y* directions. Ray differentials are used to get better results from some of the texture functions defined in Chapter 10, by making it possible to compute how quickly a texture varies with respect to the pixel spacing, which is a key component of texture antialiasing.

Some CameraSample values may not correspond to valid rays for a given camera. Therefore, pstd::optional is used for the CameraRayDifferential returned by the camera.

⟨*Generate camera ray for current sample*⟩ ≡   29
```
    pstd::optional<CameraRayDifferential> cameraRay =
        camera.GenerateRayDifferential(cameraSample, lambda);
```

If the camera ray is valid, it is passed along to the RayIntegrator subclass's Li() method implementation after some additional preparation. In addition to returning the radiance along the ray L, the subclass is also responsible for initializing an instance of the VisibleSurface class, which records geometric information about the surface the ray intersects (if any) at each pixel for the use of Film implementations like the GBufferFilm that store more information than just color at each pixel.

⟨*Trace* cameraRay *if valid*⟩ ≡   29
```
    SampledSpectrum L(0.);
    VisibleSurface visibleSurface;
    if (cameraRay) {
        ⟨Scale camera ray differentials based on image sampling rate 30⟩
        ⟨Evaluate radiance along camera ray 31⟩
        ⟨Issue warning if unexpected radiance value is returned⟩
    }
```

Before the ray is passed to the Li() method, the ScaleDifferentials() method scales the differential rays to account for the actual spacing between samples on the film plane when multiple samples are taken per pixel.

⟨*Scale camera ray differentials based on image sampling rate*⟩ ≡   30
```
    Float rayDiffScale =
        std::max<Float>(.125f, 1 / std::sqrt((Float)sampler.SamplesPerPixel()));
    cameraRay->ray.ScaleDifferentials(rayDiffScale);
```

For Film implementations that do not store geometric information at each pixel, it is worth saving the work of populating the VisibleSurface class. Therefore, a pointer to this class is only passed in the call to the Li() method if it is necessary, and a null pointer is passed otherwise. Integrator implementations then should only initialize the VisibleSurface if it is non-null.

CameraRayDifferential also carries a weight associated with the ray that is used to scale the returned radiance value. For simple camera models, each ray is weighted equally, but camera models that more accurately simulate the process of image formation by lens systems may generate some rays that contribute more than others. Such a camera model might simulate the effect of less light arriving at the edges of the film plane than at the center, an effect called *vignetting*.

⟨*Evaluate radiance along camera ray*⟩ ≡   30
```
    bool initializeVisibleSurface = camera.GetFilm().UsesVisibleSurface();
    L = cameraRay->weight *
        Li(cameraRay->ray, lambda, sampler, scratchBuffer,
            initializeVisibleSurface ? &visibleSurface : nullptr);
```

Li() is a pure virtual method that RayIntegrator subclasses must implement. It returns the incident radiance at the origin of a given ray, sampled at the specified wavelengths.

⟨*RayIntegrator Public Methods*⟩ +≡   28
```
    virtual SampledSpectrum Li(
        RayDifferential ray, SampledWavelengths &lambda, Sampler sampler,
        ScratchBuffer &scratchBuffer, VisibleSurface *visibleSurface) const = 0;
```

A common side effect of bugs in the rendering process is that impossible radiance values are computed. For example, division by zero results in radiance values equal to either the IEEE floating-point infinity or a "not a number" value. The renderer looks for these possibilities and prints an error message when it encounters them. Here we will not include the fragment that does this, ⟨*Issue warning if unexpected radiance value is returned*⟩. See the implementation in cpu/integrator.cpp if you are interested in its details.

After the radiance arriving at the ray's origin is known, a call to Film::AddSample() updates the corresponding pixel in the image, given the weighted radiance for the sample. The details of how sample values are recorded in the film are explained in Sections 5.4 and 8.8.

⟨*Add camera ray's contribution to image*⟩ ≡   29
```
    camera.GetFilm().AddSample(pPixel, L, lambda, &visibleSurface,
                               cameraSample.filterWeight);
```

1.3.6 RANDOM WALK INTEGRATOR

Although it has taken a few pages to go through the implementation of the integrator infrastructure that culminated in RayIntegrator, we can now turn to implementing light transport integration algorithms in a simpler context than having to start implementing a complete Integrator::Render() method. The RandomWalkIntegrator that we will describe in this section inherits from RayIntegrator and thus all the details of multi-threading, generating the initial ray from the camera and then adding the radiance along that ray to the image, are all taken care of. The integrator operates in a simpler context: a ray has been provided and its task is to compute the radiance arriving at its origin.

Recall that in Section 1.2.7 we mentioned that in the absence of participating media, the light carried by a ray is unchanged as it passes through free space. We will ignore the possibility of participating media in the implementation of this integrator, which allows us to take a first step: given the first intersection of a ray with the geometry in the scene, the radiance arriving at the ray's origin is equal to the radiance leaving the intersection point toward the ray's origin. That outgoing radiance is given by the light transport equation (1.1), though it is hopeless to evaluate it in closed form. Numerical approaches are required, and the ones used in pbrt are based on Monte Carlo integration, which makes it possible to estimate the values of integrals based on pointwise evaluation of their integrands. Chapter 2 provides an introduction to Monte Carlo integration, and additional Monte Carlo techniques will be introduced as they are used throughout the book.

Figure 1.19: A View of the *Watercolor* Scene, Rendered with the RandomWalkIntegrator. Because the RandomWalkIntegrator does not handle perfectly specular surfaces, the two glasses on the table are black. Furthermore, even with the 8,192 samples per pixel used to render this image, the result is still peppered with high-frequency noise. (Note, for example, the far wall and the base of the chair.) *(Scene courtesy of Angelo Ferretti.)*

In order to compute the outgoing radiance, the RandomWalkIntegrator implements a simple Monte Carlo approach that is based on incrementally constructing a *random walk*, where a series of points on scene surfaces are randomly chosen in succession to construct light-carrying paths starting from the camera. This approach effectively models image formation in the real world in reverse, starting from the camera rather than from the light sources. Going backward in this respect is still physically valid because the physical models of light that pbrt is based on are time-reversible.

Although the implementation of the random walk sampling algorithm is in total just over twenty lines of code, it is capable of simulating complex lighting and shading effects; Figure 1.19 shows an image rendered using it. (That image required many hours of computation to achieve that level of quality, however.) For the remainder of this section, we will gloss over a few of the mathematical details of the integrator's implementation and focus on an intuitive understanding of the approach, though subsequent chapters will fill in the gaps and explain this and more sophisticated techniques more rigorously.

⟨*RandomWalkIntegrator Definition*⟩ ≡
```
class RandomWalkIntegrator : public RayIntegrator {
  public:
    ⟨RandomWalkIntegrator Public Methods 33⟩
  private:
    ⟨RandomWalkIntegrator Private Methods 33⟩
    ⟨RandomWalkIntegrator Private Members 34⟩
};
```

This integrator recursively evaluates the random walk. Therefore, its `Li()` method implementation does little more than start the recursion, via a call to the `LiRandomWalk()` method. Most of the parameters to `Li()` are just passed along, though the `VisibleSurface` is ignored for this simple integrator and an additional parameter is added to track the depth of recursion.

⟨*RandomWalkIntegrator Public Methods*⟩ ≡   33
```
SampledSpectrum Li(RayDifferential ray, SampledWavelengths &lambda,
        Sampler sampler, ScratchBuffer &scratchBuffer,
        VisibleSurface *visibleSurface) const {
    return LiRandomWalk(ray, lambda, sampler, scratchBuffer, 0);
}
```

⟨*RandomWalkIntegrator Private Methods*⟩ ≡   33
```
SampledSpectrum LiRandomWalk(RayDifferential ray,
        SampledWavelengths &lambda, Sampler sampler,
        ScratchBuffer &scratchBuffer, int depth) const {
    ⟨Intersect ray with scene and return if no intersection 33⟩
    ⟨Get emitted radiance at surface intersection 34⟩
    ⟨Terminate random walk if maximum depth has been reached 35⟩
    ⟨Compute BSDF at random walk intersection point 35⟩
    ⟨Randomly sample direction leaving surface for random walk 35⟩
    ⟨Evaluate BSDF at surface for sampled direction 35⟩
    ⟨Recursively trace ray to estimate incident radiance at surface 35⟩
}
```

The first step is to find the closest intersection of the ray with the shapes in the scene. If no intersection is found, the ray has left the scene. Otherwise, a `SurfaceInteraction` that is returned as part of the `ShapeIntersection` structure provides information about the local geometric properties of the intersection point.

⟨*Intersect ray with scene and return if no intersection*⟩ ≡   33
```
pstd::optional<ShapeIntersection> si = Intersect(ray);
if (!si) {
    ⟨Return emitted light from infinite light sources 34⟩
}
SurfaceInteraction &isect = si->intr;
```

If no intersection was found, radiance still may be carried along the ray due to light sources such as the `ImageInfiniteLight` that do not have geometry associated with them. The `Light::Le()` method allows such lights to return their radiance for a given ray.

⟨*Return emitted light from infinite light sources*⟩ ≡   33
```
SampledSpectrum Le(0.f);
for (Light light : infiniteLights)
    Le += light.Le(ray, lambda);
return Le;
```

If a valid intersection has been found, we must evaluate the light transport equation at the intersection point. The first term, $L_e(p, \omega_o)$, which is the emitted radiance, is easy: emission is part of the scene specification and the emitted radiance is available by calling the `SurfaceInteraction::Le()` method, which takes the outgoing direction of interest. Here, we are interested in radiance emitted back along the ray's direction. If the object is not emissive, that method returns a zero-valued spectral distribution.

⟨*Get emitted radiance at surface intersection*⟩ ≡   33
```
Vector3f wo = -ray.d;
SampledSpectrum Le = isect.Le(wo, lambda);
```

Evaluating the second term of the light transport equation requires computing an integral over the sphere of directions around the intersection point p. Application of the principles of Monte Carlo integration can be used to show that if directions ω' are chosen with equal probability over all possible directions, then an estimate of the integral can be computed as a weighted product of the BSDF f, which describes the light scattering properties of the material at p, the incident lighting, L_i, and a cosine factor:

$$\int_{\mathcal{S}^2} f(p, \omega_o, \omega_i) \, L_i(p, \omega_i) \, |\cos \theta_i| \, d\omega_i \approx \frac{f(p, \omega_o, \omega') \, L_i(p, \omega') \, |\cos \theta'|}{1/4\pi}. \qquad [1.2]$$

In other words, given a random direction ω', estimating the value of the integral requires evaluating the terms in the integrand for that direction and then scaling by a factor of 4π. (This factor, which is derived in Section A.5.2, relates to the surface area of a unit sphere.) Since only a single direction is considered, there is almost always error in the Monte Carlo estimate compared to the true value of the integral. However, it can be shown that estimates like this one are correct *in expectation*: informally, that they give the correct result on average. Averaging multiple independent estimates generally reduces this error—hence, the practice of taking multiple samples per pixel.

The BSDF and the cosine factor of the estimate are easily evaluated, leaving us with L_i, the incident radiance, unknown. However, note that we have found ourselves right back where we started with the initial call to `LiRandomWalk()`: we have a ray for which we would like to find the incident radiance at the origin—that, a recursive call to `LiRandomWalk()` will provide.

Before computing the estimate of the integral, we must consider terminating the recursion. The `RandomWalkIntegrator` stops at a predetermined maximum depth, maxDepth. Without this termination criterion, the algorithm might never terminate (imagine, e.g., a hall-of-mirrors scene). This member variable is initialized in the constructor based on a parameter that can be set in the scene description file.

⟨*RandomWalkIntegrator Private Members*⟩ ≡   33
```
int maxDepth;
```

⟨*Terminate random walk if maximum depth has been reached*⟩ ≡   33
```
if (depth == maxDepth)
    return Le;
```

If the random walk is not terminated, the SurfaceInteraction::GetBSDF() method is called to find the BSDF at the intersection point. It evaluates texture functions to determine surface properties and then initializes a representation of the BSDF. It generally needs to allocate memory for the objects that constitute the BSDF's representation; because this memory only needs to be active when processing the current ray, the ScratchBuffer is provided to it to use for its allocations.

⟨*Compute BSDF at random walk intersection point*⟩ ≡   33
```
BSDF bsdf = isect.GetBSDF(ray, lambda, camera, scratchBuffer, sampler);
```

Next, we need to sample a random direction ω' to compute the estimate in Equation (1.2). The SampleUniformSphere() function returns a uniformly distributed direction on the unit sphere, given two uniform values in [0, 1) that are provided here by the sampler.

⟨*Randomly sample direction leaving surface for random walk*⟩ ≡   33
```
Point2f u = sampler.Get2D();
Vector3f wp = SampleUniformSphere(u);
```

All the factors of the Monte Carlo estimate other than the incident radiance can now be readily evaluated. The BSDF class provides an f() method that evaluates the BSDF for a pair of specified directions, and the cosine of the angle with the surface normal can be computed using the AbsDot() function, which returns the absolute value of the dot product between two vectors. If the vectors are normalized, as both are here, this value is equal to the absolute value of the cosine of the angle between them (Section 3.3.2).

It is possible that the BSDF will be zero-valued for the provided directions and thus that fcos will be as well—for example, the BSDF is zero if the surface is not transmissive but the two directions are on opposite sides of it.[5] In that case, there is no reason to continue the random walk, since subsequent points will make no contribution to the result.

⟨*Evaluate BSDF at surface for sampled direction*⟩ ≡   33
```
SampledSpectrum fcos = bsdf.f(wo, wp) * AbsDot(wp, isect.shading.n);
if (!fcos)
    return Le;
```

The remaining task is to compute the new ray leaving the surface in the sampled direction ω'. This task is handled by the SpawnRay() method, which returns a ray leaving an intersection in the provided direction, ensuring that the ray is sufficiently offset from the surface that it does not incorrectly reintersect it due to round-off error. Given the ray, the recursive call to LiRandomWalk() can be made to estimate the incident radiance, which completes the estimate of Equation (1.2).

⟨*Recursively trace ray to estimate incident radiance at surface*⟩ ≡   33
```
ray = isect.SpawnRay(wp);
return Le  + fcos * LiRandomWalk(ray, lambda, sampler, scratchBuffer,
                                depth + 1) / (1 / (4 * Pi));
```

---

5   It would be easy enough to check if the BSDF was only reflective and to only sample directions on the same side of the surface as the ray, but for this simple integrator we will not bother.

(a)   (b)

Figure 1.20: *Watercolor* Scene Rendered Using 32 Samples per Pixel. (a) Rendered using the RandomWalkIntegrator. (b) Rendered using the PathIntegrator, which follows the same general approach but uses more sophisticated Monte Carlo techniques. The PathIntegrator gives a substantially better image for roughly the same amount of work, with 54.5× reduction in mean squared error.

This simple approach has many shortcomings. For example, if the emissive surfaces are small, most ray paths will not find any light and many rays will need to be traced to form an accurate image. In the limit case of a point light source, the image will be black, since there is zero probability of intersecting such a light source. Similar issues apply with BSDF models that scatter light in a concentrated set of directions. In the limiting case of a perfect mirror that scatters incident light along a single direction, the RandomWalkIntegrator will never be able to randomly sample that direction.

Those issues and more can be addressed through more sophisticated application of Monte Carlo integration techniques. In subsequent chapters, we will introduce a succession of improvements that lead to much more accurate results. The integrators that are defined in Chapters 13 through 15 are the culmination of those developments. All still build on the same basic ideas used in the RandomWalkIntegrator, but are much more efficient and robust than it is. Figure 1.20 compares the RandomWalkIntegrator to one of the improved integrators and gives a sense of how much improvement is possible.

1.4 HOW TO PROCEED THROUGH THIS BOOK

We have written this book assuming it will be read in roughly front-to-back order. We have tried to minimize the number of forward references to ideas and interfaces that have not yet been introduced, but we do assume that the reader is acquainted with the previous content at any particular point in the text. Some sections go into depth about advanced topics that some readers may wish to skip over, particularly on first reading; each advanced section is identified by an asterisk in its title.

Because of the modular nature of the system, the main requirements are that the reader be familiar with the low-level classes like `Point3f`, `Ray`, and `SampledSpectrum`; the interfaces defined by the abstract base classes listed in Table 1.1; and the rendering loop that culminates in calls to integrators' `RayIntegrator::Li()` methods. Given that knowledge, for example, the reader who does not care about precisely how a camera model based on a perspective projection matrix maps `CameraSamples` to rays can skip over the implementation of that camera and can just remember that the `Camera::GenerateRayDifferential()` method somehow turns a `CameraSample` into a `RayDifferential`.

The remainder of this book is divided into four main parts of a few chapters each. First, Chapters 2 through 4 introduce the foundations of the system. A brief introduction to the key ideas underlying Monte Carlo integration is provided in Chapter 2, and Chapter 3 then describes widely used geometric classes like `Point3f`, `Ray`, and `Bounds3f`. Chapter 4 introduces the physical units used to measure light and the `SampledSpectrum` class that pbrt uses to represent spectral distributions. It also discusses color, the human perception of spectra, which affects how input is provided to the renderer and how it generates output.

The second part of the book covers image formation and how the scene geometry is represented. Chapter 5 defines the `Camera` interface and a few different camera implementations before discussing the overall process of turning spectral radiance arriving at the film into images. Chapter 6 then introduces the `Shape` interface and gives implementations of a number of shapes, including showing how to perform ray intersection tests with them. Chapter 7 describes the implementations of the acceleration structures that make ray tracing more efficient by skipping tests with primitives that a ray can be shown to definitely not intersect. Finally, Chapter 8's topic is the `Sampler` classes that place samples on the image plane and provide random samples for Monte Carlo integration.

The third part of the book is about light and how it scatters from surfaces and participating media. Chapter 9 includes a collection of classes that define a variety of types of reflection from surfaces. Materials, described in Chapter 10, use these reflection functions to implement a number of different surface types, such as plastic, glass, and metal. Spatial variation in material properties (color, roughness, etc.) is modeled by textures, which are also described in Chapter 10. Chapter 11 introduces the abstractions that describe how light is scattered and absorbed in participating media, and Chapter 12 then describes the interface for light sources and a variety of light source implementations.

The last part brings all the ideas from the rest of the book together to implement a number of interesting light transport algorithms. The integrators in Chapters 13 and 14 represent a variety of different applications of Monte Carlo integration to compute more accurate approximations of the light transport equation than the `RandomWalkIntegrator`. Chapter 15 then describes the implementation of a high-performance integrator that runs on the GPU, based on all the same classes that are used in the implementations of the CPU-based integrators.

Chapter 16, the last chapter of the book, provides a brief retrospective and discussion of system design decisions along with a number of suggestions for more far-reaching projects than those in the exercises. Appendices contain more Monte Carlo sampling algorithms, describe utility functions, and explain details of how the scene description is created as the input file is parsed.

1.4.1 THE EXERCISES

At the end of each chapter you will find exercises related to the material covered in that chapter. Each exercise is marked as one of three levels of difficulty:

- ➊ An exercise that should take only an hour or two
- ➋ A reading and/or implementation task that would be suitable for a course assignment and should take between 10 and 20 hours of work
- ➌ A suggested final project for a course that will likely take 40 hours or more to complete

1.4.2 VIEWING THE IMAGES

Figures throughout the book compare the results of rendering the same scene using different algorithms. As with previous editions of the book, we have done our best to ensure that these differences are evident on the printed page, though even high quality printing cannot match modern display technology, especially now with the widespread availability of high dynamic range displays.

We have therefore made all of the rendered images that are used in figures available online. For example, the first image shown in this chapter as Figure 1.1 is available at the URL *pbr-book.org/4ed/fig/1.1*. All of the others follow the same naming scheme.

1.4.3 THE ONLINE EDITION

Starting on November 1, 2023, the full contents of this book will be freely available online at *pbr-book.org/4ed*. (The previous edition of the book is already available at that website.)

The online edition includes additional content that could not be included in the printed book due to page constraints. All of that material is supplementary to the contents of this book. For example, it includes the implementation of an additional camera model, a kd-tree acceleration structure, and a full chapter on bidirectional light transport algorithms. (Almost all of the additional material appeared in the previous edition of the book.)

1.5 USING AND UNDERSTANDING THE CODE

The pbrt source code distribution is available from *pbrt.org*. The website also includes additional documentation, images rendered with pbrt, example scenes, errata, and links to a bug reporting system. We encourage you to visit the website and subscribe to the pbrt mailing list.

pbrt is written in C++, but we have tried to make it accessible to non-C++ experts by limiting the use of esoteric features of the language. Staying close to the core language features also helps with the system's portability. We make use of C++'s extensive standard library whenever it is applicable but will not discuss the semantics of calls to standard library functions in the text. Our expectation is that the reader will consult documentation of the standard library as necessary.

We will occasionally omit short sections of pbrt's source code from the book. For example, when there are a number of cases to be handled, all with nearly identical code, we will present one case and note that the code for the remaining cases has been omitted from the text. Default class constructors are generally not shown, and the text also does not include details like the various #include directives at the start of each source file. All the omitted code can be found in the pbrt source code distribution.

1.5.1 SOURCE CODE ORGANIZATION

The source code used for building pbrt is under the src directory in the pbrt distribution. In that directory are src/ext, which has the source code for various third-party libraries that are used by pbrt, and src/pbrt, which contains pbrt's source code. We will not discuss the third-party libraries' implementations in the book.

The source files in the src/pbrt directory mostly consist of implementations of the various interface types. For example, shapes.h and shapes.cpp have implementations of the Shape interface, materials.h and materials.cpp have materials, and so forth. That directory also holds the source code for parsing pbrt's scene description files.

The pbrt.h header file in src/pbrt is the first file that is included by all other source files in the system. It contains a few macros and widely useful forward declarations, though we have tried to keep it short and to minimize the number of other headers that it includes in the interests of compile time efficiency.

The src/pbrt directory also contains a number of subdirectories. They have the following roles:

- base: Header files defining the interfaces for 12 of the common interface types listed in Table 1.1 (Primitive and Integrator are CPU-only and so are defined in files in the cpu directory).
- cmd: Source files containing the main() functions for the executables that are built for pbrt. (Others besides the pbrt executable include imgtool, which performs various image processing operations, and pbrt_test, which contains unit tests.)
- cpu: CPU-specific code, including Integrator implementations.
- gpu: GPU-specific source code, including functions for allocating memory and launching work on the GPU.
- util: Lower-level utility code, most of it not specific to rendering.
- wavefront: Implementation of the WavefrontPathIntegrator, which is introduced in Chapter 15. This integrator runs on both CPUs and GPUs.

1.5.2 NAMING CONVENTIONS

Functions and classes are generally named using Camel case, with the first letter of each word capitalized and no delineation for spaces. One exception is some methods of container classes, which follow the naming convention of the C++ standard library when they have matching functionality (e.g., size() and begin() and end() for iterators). Variables also use Camel case, though with the first letter lowercase, except for a few global variables.

We also try to match mathematical notation in naming: for example, we use variables like p for points p and w for directions ω. We will occasionally add a p to the end of a variable to denote a primed symbol: wp for ω'. Underscores are used to indicate subscripts in equations: theta_o for θ_o, for example.

Our use of underscores is not perfectly consistent, however. Short variable names often omit the underscore—we use wi for ω_i and we have already seen the use of Li for L_i. We also occasionally use an underscore to separate a word from a lowercase mathematical symbol. For example, we use Sample_f for a method that samples a function f rather than Samplef, which would be more difficult to read, or SampleF, which would obscure the connection to the function f ("where was the function F defined?").

1.5.3 POINTER OR REFERENCE?

C++ provides two different mechanisms for passing an object to a function or method by reference: pointers and references. If a function argument is not intended as an output variable, either can be used to save the expense of passing the entire structure on the stack. The convention in `pbrt` is to use a pointer when the argument will be completely changed by the function or method, a reference when some of its internal state will be changed but it will not be fully reinitialized, and `const` references when it will not be changed at all. One important exception to this rule is that we will always use a pointer when we want to be able to pass `nullptr` to indicate that a parameter is not available or should not be used.

1.5.4 ABSTRACTION VERSUS EFFICIENCY

One of the primary tensions when designing interfaces for software systems is making a reasonable trade-off between abstraction and efficiency. For example, many programmers religiously make all data in all classes `private` and provide methods to obtain or modify the values of the data items. For simple classes (e.g., `Vector3f`), we believe that approach needlessly hides a basic property of the implementation—that the class holds three floating-point coordinates—that we can reasonably expect to never change. Of course, using no information hiding and exposing all details of all classes' internals leads to a code maintenance nightmare, but we believe that there is nothing wrong with judiciously exposing basic design decisions throughout the system. For example, the fact that a `Ray` is represented with a point, a vector, a time, and the medium it is in is a decision that does not need to be hidden behind a layer of abstraction. Code elsewhere is shorter and easier to understand when details like these are exposed.

An important thing to keep in mind when writing a software system and making these sorts of trade-offs is the expected final size of the system. `pbrt` is roughly 70,000 lines of code and it is never going to grow to be a million lines of code; this fact should be reflected in the amount of information hiding used in the system. It would be a waste of programmer time (and likely a source of runtime inefficiency) to design the interfaces to accommodate a system of a much higher level of complexity.

1.5.5 pstd

We have reimplemented a subset of the C++ standard library in the `pstd` namespace; this was necessary in order to use those parts of it interchangeably on the CPU and on the GPU. For the purposes of reading `pbrt`'s source code, anything in `pstd` provides the same functionality with the same type and methods as the corresponding entity in `std`. We will therefore not document usage of `pstd` in the text here.

1.5.6 ALLOCATORS

Almost all dynamic memory allocation for the objects that represent the scene in `pbrt` is performed using an instance of an `Allocator` that is provided to the object creation methods. In `pbrt`, `Allocator` is shorthand for the C++ standard library's `pmr::polymorphic_allocator` type. Its definition is in `pbrt.h` so that it is available to all other source files.

⟨*Define* `Allocator`⟩ ≡
```
using Allocator = pstd::pmr::polymorphic_allocator<std::byte>;
```

`std::pmr::polymorphic_allocator` implementations provide a few methods for allocating and freeing objects. These three are used widely in `pbrt`:[6]

```
void *allocate_bytes(size_t nbytes, size_t alignment);
```

---

6   Because `pmr::polymorphic_allocator` is a recent addition to C++ that is not yet widely used, yet is widely used in `pbrt`, we break our regular habit of not documenting standard library functionality in the text here.

```
template <class T> T *allocate_object(size_t n = 1);
template <class T, class... Args> T *new_object(Args &&... args);
```

The first, allocate_bytes(), allocates the specified number of bytes of memory. Next, allocate_object() allocates an array of n objects of the specified type T, initializing each one with its default constructor. The final method, new_object(), allocates a single object of type T and calls its constructor with the provided arguments. There are corresponding methods for freeing each type of allocation: deallocate_bytes(), deallocate_object(), and delete_object().

A tricky detail related to the use of allocators with data structures from the C++ standard library is that a container's allocator is fixed once its constructor has run. Thus, if one container is assigned to another, the target container's allocator is unchanged even though all the values it stores are updated. (This is the case even with C++'s move semantics.) Therefore, it is common to see objects' constructors in pbrt passing along an allocator in member initializer lists for containers that they store even if they are not yet ready to set the values stored in them.

Using an explicit memory allocator rather than direct calls to new and delete has a few advantages. Not only does it make it easy to do things like track the total amount of memory that has been allocated, but it also makes it easy to substitute allocators that are optimized for many small allocations, as is useful when building acceleration structures in Chapter 7. Using allocators in this way also makes it easy to store the scene objects in memory that is visible to the GPU when GPU rendering is being used.

1.5.7 DYNAMIC DISPATCH

As mentioned in Section 1.3, virtual functions are generally not used for dynamic dispatch with polymorphic types in pbrt (the main exception being the Integrators). Instead, the TaggedPointer class is used to represent a pointer to one of a specified set of types; it includes machinery for runtime type identification and thence dynamic dispatch. (Its implementation can be found in Appendix B.4.4.) Two considerations motivate its use.

First, in C++, an instance of an object that inherits from an abstract base class includes a hidden virtual function table pointer that is used to resolve virtual function calls. On most modern systems, this pointer uses eight bytes of memory. While eight bytes may not seem like much, we have found that when rendering complex scenes with previous versions of pbrt, a substantial amount of memory would be used just for virtual function pointers for shapes and primitives. With the TaggedPointer class, there is no incremental storage cost for type information.

The other problem with virtual function tables is that they store function pointers that point to executable code. Of course, that's what they are supposed to do, but this characteristic means that a virtual function table can be valid for method calls from either the CPU or from the GPU, but not from both simultaneously, since the executable code for the different processors is stored at different memory locations. When using the GPU for rendering, it is useful to be able to call methods from both processors, however.

Spectrum 165

TaggedPointer 1073

For all the code that just calls methods of polymorphic objects, the use of pbrt's Tagged Pointer in place of virtual functions makes no difference other than the fact that method calls are made using the . operator, just as would be used for a C++ reference. Section 4.5.1, which introduces Spectrum, the first class based on TaggedPointer that occurs in the book, has more details about how pbrt's dynamic dispatch scheme is implemented.

1.5.8 CODE OPTIMIZATION

We have tried to make pbrt efficient through the use of well-chosen algorithms rather than through local micro-optimizations, so that the system can be more easily understood. However, efficiency is an integral part of rendering, and so we discuss performance issues throughout the book.

For both CPUs and GPUs, processing performance continues to grow more quickly than the speed at which data can be loaded from main memory into the processor. This means that waiting for values to be fetched from memory can be a major performance limitation. The most important optimizations that we discuss relate to minimizing unnecessary memory access and organizing algorithms and data structures in ways that lead to coherent access patterns; paying attention to these issues can speed up program execution much more than reducing the total number of instructions executed.

1.5.9 DEBUGGING AND LOGGING

Debugging a renderer can be challenging, especially in cases where the result is correct most of the time but not always. pbrt includes a number of facilities to ease debugging.

One of the most important is a suite of unit tests. We have found unit testing to be invaluable in the development of pbrt for the reassurance it gives that the tested functionality is very likely to be correct. Having this assurance relieves the concern behind questions during debugging such as "am I sure that the hash table that is being used here is not itself the source of my bug?" Alternatively, a failing unit test is almost always easier to debug than an incorrect image generated by the renderer; many of the tests have been added along the way as we have debugged pbrt. Unit tests for a file code.cpp are found in code_tests.cpp. All the unit tests are executed by an invocation of the pbrt_test executable and specific ones can be selected via command-line options.

There are many assertions throughout the pbrt codebase, most of them not included in the book text. These check conditions that should never be true and issue an error and exit immediately if they are found to be true at runtime. (See Section B.3.6 for the definitions of the assertion macros used in pbrt.) A failed assertion gives a first hint about the source of an error; like a unit test, an assertion helps focus debugging, at least with a starting point. Some of the more computationally expensive assertions in pbrt are only enabled for debug builds; if the renderer is crashing or otherwise producing incorrect output, it is worthwhile to try running a debug build to see if one of those additional assertions fails and yields a clue.

We have also endeavored to make the execution of pbrt at a given pixel sample deterministic. One challenge with debugging a renderer is a crash that only happens after minutes or hours of rendering computation. With deterministic execution, rendering can be restarted at a single pixel sample in order to more quickly return to the point of a crash. Furthermore, upon a crash pbrt will print a message such as "Rendering failed at pixel (16, 27) sample 821. Debug with --debugstart 16,27,821". The values printed after "debugstart" depend on the integrator being used, but are sufficient to restart its computation close to the point of a crash.

Finally, it is often useful to print out the values stored in a data structure during the course of debugging. We have implemented ToString() methods for nearly all of pbrt's classes. They return a std::string representation of them so that it is easy to print their full object state during program execution. Furthermore, pbrt's custom Printf() and StringPrintf() functions (Section B.3.3) automatically use the string returned by ToString() for an object when a %s specifier is found in the formatting string.

Printf() 1064
StringPrintf() 1064

1.5.10 PARALLELISM AND THREAD SAFETY

In pbrt (as is the case for most ray tracers), the vast majority of data at rendering time is read only (e.g., the scene description and texture images). Much of the parsing of the scene file and creation of the scene representation in memory is done with a single thread of execution, so there are few synchronization issues during that phase of execution.[7] During rendering, concurrent read access to all the read-only data by multiple threads works with no problems on both the CPU and the GPU; we only need to be concerned with situations where data in memory is being modified.

As a general rule, the low-level classes and structures in the system are not thread-safe. For example, the Point3f class, which stores three float values to represent a point in 3D space, is not safe for multiple threads to call methods that modify it at the same time. (Multiple threads can use Point3fs as read-only data simultaneously, of course.) The runtime overhead to make Point3f thread-safe would have a substantial effect on performance with little benefit in return.

The same is true for classes like Vector3f, Normal3f, SampledSpectrum, Transform, Quaternion, and SurfaceInteraction. These classes are usually either created at scene construction time and then used as read-only data or allocated on the stack during rendering and used only by a single thread.

The utility classes ScratchBuffer (used for high-performance temporary memory allocation) and RNG (pseudo-random number generation) are also not safe for use by multiple threads; these classes store state that is modified when their methods are called, and the overhead from protecting modification to their state with mutual exclusion would be excessive relative to the amount of computation they perform. Consequently, in code like the ImageTileIntegrator::Render() method earlier, pbrt allocates per-thread instances of these classes on the stack.

With two exceptions, implementations of the base types listed in Table 1.1 are safe for multiple threads to use simultaneously. With a little care, it is usually straightforward to implement new instances of these base classes so they do not modify any shared state in their methods.

The first exceptions are the Light Preprocess() method implementations. These are called by the system during scene construction, and implementations of them generally modify shared state in their objects. Therefore, it is helpful to allow the implementer to assume that only a single thread will call into these methods. (This is a separate issue from the consideration that implementations of these methods that are computationally intensive may use ParallelFor() to parallelize their computation.)

The second exception is Sampler class implementations; their methods are also not expected to be thread-safe. This is another instance where this requirement would impose an excessive performance and scalability impact; many threads simultaneously trying to get samples from a single Sampler would limit the system's overall performance. Therefore, as described in Section 1.3.4, a unique Sampler is created for each rendering thread using Sampler::Clone().

All stand-alone functions in pbrt are thread-safe (as long as multiple threads do not pass pointers to the same data to them).

---

7 Exceptions include the fact that we try to load image maps and binary geometry files in parallel, some image resampling performed on texture images, and construction of one variant of the BVHAggregate, though all of these are highly localized.

1.5.11 EXTENDING THE SYSTEM

One of our goals in writing this book and building the pbrt system was to make it easier for developers and researchers to experiment with new (or old!) ideas in rendering. One of the great joys in computer graphics is writing new software that makes a new image; even small changes to the system can be fun to experiment with. The exercises throughout the book suggest many changes to make to the system, ranging from small tweaks to major open-ended research projects. Section C.4 in Appendix C has more information about the mechanics of adding new implementations of the interfaces listed in Table 1.1.

1.5.12 BUGS

Although we made every effort to make pbrt as correct as possible through extensive testing, it is inevitable that some bugs are still present.

If you believe you have found a bug in the system, please do the following:

1. Reproduce the bug with an unmodified copy of the latest version of pbrt.
2. Check the online discussion forum and the bug-tracking system at *pbrt.org*. Your issue may be a known bug, or it may be a commonly misunderstood feature.
3. Try to find the simplest possible test case that demonstrates the bug. Many bugs can be demonstrated by scene description files that are just a few lines long, and debugging is much easier with a simple scene than a complex one.
4. Submit a detailed bug report using our online bug-tracking system. Make sure that you include the scene file that demonstrates the bug and a detailed description of why you think pbrt is not behaving correctly with the scene. If you can provide a patch that fixes the bug, all the better!

We will periodically update the pbrt source code repository with bug fixes and minor enhancements. (Be aware that we often let bug reports accumulate for a few months before going through them; do not take this as an indication that we do not value them!) However, we will not make major changes to the pbrt source code so that it does not diverge from the system described here in the book.

1.6 A BRIEF HISTORY OF PHYSICALLY BASED RENDERING

Through the early years of computer graphics in the 1970s, the most important problems to solve were fundamental issues like visibility algorithms and geometric representations. When a megabyte of RAM was a rare and expensive luxury and when a computer capable of a million floating-point operations per second cost hundreds of thousands of dollars, the complexity of what was possible in computer graphics was correspondingly limited, and any attempt to accurately simulate physics for rendering was infeasible.

As computers have become more capable and less expensive, it has become possible to consider more computationally demanding approaches to rendering, which in turn has made physically based approaches viable. This progression is neatly explained by *Blinn's law*: "as technology advances, rendering time remains constant."

Jim Blinn's simple statement captures an important constraint: given a certain number of images that must be rendered (be it a handful for a research paper or over a hundred thousand for a feature film), it is only possible to take so much processing time for each one. One has a certain amount of computation available and one has some amount of time available before rendering must be finished, so the maximum computation per image is necessarily limited.

Blinn's law also expresses the observation that there remains a gap between the images people would like to be able to render and the images that they can render: as computers have become faster, content creators have continued to use increased computational capability to render more complex scenes with more sophisticated rendering algorithms, rather than rendering the same scenes as before, just more quickly. Rendering continues to consume all computational capabilities made available to it.

1.6.1 RESEARCH

Physically based approaches to rendering started to be seriously considered by graphics researchers in the 1980s. Whitted's paper (1980) introduced the idea of using ray tracing for global lighting effects, opening the door to accurately simulating the distribution of light in scenes. The rendered images his approach produced were markedly different from any that had been seen before, which spurred excitement about this approach.

Another notable early advancement in physically based rendering was Cook and Torrance's reflection model (1981, 1982), which introduced microfacet reflection models to graphics. Among other contributions, they showed that accurately modeling microfacet reflection made it possible to render metal surfaces accurately; metal was not well rendered by earlier approaches.

Shortly afterward, Goral et al. (1984) made connections between the thermal transfer literature and rendering, showing how to incorporate global diffuse lighting effects using a physically based approximation of light transport. This method was based on finite-element techniques, where areas of surfaces in the scene exchanged energy with each other. This approach came to be referred to as "radiosity," after a related physical unit. Following work by Cohen and Greenberg (1985) and Nishita and Nakamae (1985) introduced important improvements. Once again, a physically based approach led to images with lighting effects that had not previously been seen in rendered images, which led to many researchers pursuing improvements in this area.

While the radiosity approach was based on physical units and conservation of energy, in time it became clear that it would not lead to practical rendering algorithms: the asymptotic computational complexity was a difficult-to-manage $O(n^2)$, and it was necessary to retessellate geometric models along shadow boundaries for good results; researchers had difficulty developing robust and efficient tessellation algorithms for this purpose. Radiosity's adoption in practice was limited.

During the radiosity years, a small group of researchers pursued physically based approaches to rendering that were based on ray tracing and Monte Carlo integration. At the time, many looked at their work with skepticism; objectionable noise in images due to Monte Carlo integration error seemed unavoidable, while radiosity-based methods quickly gave visually pleasing results, at least on relatively simple scenes.

In 1984, Cook, Porter, and Carpenter introduced distributed ray tracing, which generalized Whitted's algorithm to compute motion blur and defocus blur from cameras, blurry reflection from glossy surfaces, and illumination from area light sources (Cook et al. 1984), showing that ray tracing was capable of generating a host of important soft lighting effects.

Shortly afterward, Kajiya (1986) introduced path tracing; he set out a rigorous formulation of the rendering problem (the light transport integral equation) and showed how to apply Monte Carlo integration to solve it. This work required immense amounts of computation: to render a 256 × 256 pixel image of two spheres with path tracing required 7 hours of computation on an IBM 4341 computer, which cost roughly $280,000 when it was first released (Farmer 1981). With von Herzen, Kajiya also introduced the volume-rendering equation to graphics (Kajiya and von Herzen 1984); this equation describes the scattering of light in participating media.

Both Cook et al.'s and Kajiya's work once again led to images unlike any that had been seen before, demonstrating the value of physically based methods. In subsequent years, important work on Monte Carlo for realistic image synthesis was described in papers by Arvo and Kirk (1990) and Kirk and Arvo (1991). Shirley's Ph.D. dissertation (1990) and follow-on work by Shirley et al. (1996) were important contributions to Monte Carlo–based efforts. Hall's book, *Illumination and Color in Computer Generated Imagery* (1989), was one of the first books to present rendering in a physically based framework, and Andrew Glassner's *Principles of Digital Image Synthesis* laid out foundations of the field (1995). Ward's *Radiance* rendering system was an early open source physically based rendering system, focused on lighting design (Ward 1994), and Slusallek's *Vision* renderer was designed to bridge the gap between physically based approaches and the then widely used *RenderMan* interface, which was not physically based (Slusallek 1996).

Following Torrance and Cook's work, much of the research in the Program of Computer Graphics at Cornell University investigated physically based approaches. The motivations for this work were summarized by Greenberg et al. (1997), who made a strong argument for a physically accurate rendering based on measurements of the material properties of real-world objects and on deep understanding of the human visual system.

A crucial step forward for physically based rendering was Veach's work, described in detail in his dissertation (Veach 1997). Veach advanced key theoretical foundations of Monte Carlo rendering while also developing new algorithms like multiple importance sampling, bidirectional path tracing, and Metropolis light transport that greatly improved its efficiency. Using Blinn's law as a guide, we believe that these significant improvements in efficiency were critical to practical adoption of these approaches.

Around this time, as computers became faster and more parallel, a number of researchers started pursuing real-time ray tracing; Wald, Slusallek, and Benthin wrote an influential paper that described a highly optimized ray tracer that was much more efficient than previous ray tracers (Wald et al. 2001b). Many subsequent papers introduced increasingly more efficient ray-tracing algorithms. Though most of this work was not physically based, the results led to great progress in ray-tracing acceleration structures and performance of the geometric components of ray tracing. Because physically based rendering generally makes substantial use of ray tracing, this work has in turn had the same helpful effect as faster computers have, making it possible to render more complex scenes with physical approaches.

We end our summary of the key steps in the research progress of physically based rendering at this point, though much more has been done. The "Further Reading" sections in all the subsequent chapters of this book cover this work in detail.

1.6.2 PRODUCTION

With more capable computers in the 1980s, computer graphics could start to be used for animation and film production. Early examples include Jim Blinn's rendering of the *Voyager 2* flyby of Saturn in 1981 and visual effects in the movies *Star Trek II: The Wrath of Khan* (1982), *Tron* (1982), and *The Last Starfighter* (1984).

In early production use of computer-generated imagery, rasterization-based rendering (notably, the Reyes algorithm (Cook et al. 1987)) was the only viable option. One reason was that not enough computation was available for complex reflection models or for the global lighting effects that physically based ray tracing could provide. More significantly, rasterization had the important advantage that it did not require that the entire scene representation fit into main memory.

When RAM was much less plentiful, almost any interesting scene was too large to fit into main memory. Rasterization-based algorithms made it possible to render scenes while having only a small subset of the full scene representation in memory at any time. Global lighting effects are difficult to achieve if the whole scene cannot fit into main memory; for many years, with limited computer systems, content creators effectively decided that geometric and texture complexity was more important to visual realism than lighting complexity (and in turn physical accuracy).

Many practitioners at this time also believed that physically based approaches were undesirable for production: one of the great things about computer graphics is that one can cheat reality with impunity to achieve a desired artistic effect. For example, lighting designers on regular movies often struggle to place light sources so that they are not visible to the camera or spend considerable effort placing a light to illuminate an actor without shining too much light on the background. Computer graphics offers the opportunity to, for example, implement a light source model that shines twice as much light on a character as on a background object. For many years, this capability seemed much more useful than physical accuracy.

Visual effects practitioners who had the specific need to match rendered imagery to filmed real-world environments pioneered capturing real-world lighting and shading effects and were early adopters of physically based approaches in the late 1990s and early 2000s. (See Snow (2010) for a history of ILM's early work in this area, for example.)

During this time, Blue Sky Studios adopted a physically based pipeline (Ohmer 1997). The photorealism of an advertisement they made for a Braun shaver in 1992 caught the attention of many, and their short film, *Bunny*, shown in 1998, was an early example of Monte Carlo global illumination used in production. Its visual look was substantially different from those of films and shorts rendered with Reyes and was widely noted. Subsequent feature films from Blue Sky also followed this approach. Unfortunately, Blue Sky never published significant technical details of their approach, limiting their wider influence.

During the early 2000s, the *mental ray* ray-tracing system was used by a number of studios, mostly for visual effects. It was an efficient ray tracer with sophisticated global illumination algorithm implementations. The main focus of its developers was computer-aided design and product design applications, so it lacked features like the ability to handle extremely complex scenes and the enormous numbers of texture maps that film production demanded.

After *Bunny*, another watershed moment came in 2001, when Marcos Fajardo came to the SIGGRAPH conference with an early version of his *Arnold* renderer. He showed images in the Monte Carlo image synthesis course that not only had complex geometry, textures, and global illumination but also were rendered in tens of minutes. While these scenes were not of the complexity of those used in film production at the time, his results showed many the creative opportunities from the combination of global illumination and complex scenes.

Fajardo brought *Arnold* to Sony Pictures Imageworks, where work started to transform it to a production-capable physically based rendering system. Many issues had to be addressed, including efficient motion blur, programmable shading, support for massively complex scenes, and deferred loading of scene geometry and textures. *Arnold* was first used on the movie *Monster House* and is now available as a commercial product.

In the early 2000s, Pixar's *RenderMan* renderer started to support hybrid rasterization and ray-tracing algorithms and included a number of innovative algorithms for computing global

Figure 1.21: *Gravity* (2013) featured spectacular computer-generated imagery of a realistic space environment with volumetric scattering and large numbers of anisotropic metal surfaces. The image was generated using *Arnold,* a physically based rendering system that accounts for global illumination. Image courtesy of Warner Bros. and Framestore.

illumination solutions in complex scenes. *RenderMan* was recently rewritten to be a physically based ray tracer, following the general system architecture of pbrt (Christensen 2015).

One of the main reasons that physically based Monte Carlo approaches to rendering have been successful in production is that they end up improving the productivity of artists. These have been some of the important factors:

- The algorithms involved have essentially just a single quality knob: how many samples to take per pixel; this is extremely helpful for artists. Ray-tracing algorithms are also suited to both progressive refinement and quickly computing rough previews by taking just a few samples per pixel; rasterization-based renderers do not have equivalent capabilities.
- Adopting physically based reflection models has made it easier to design surface materials. Earlier, when reflection models that did not necessarily conserve energy were used, an object might be placed in a single lighting environment while its surface reflection parameters were adjusted. The object might look great in that environment, but it would often appear completely wrong when moved to another lighting environment because surfaces were reflecting too little or too much energy: surface properties had been set to unreasonable values.
- The quality of shadows computed with ray tracing is much better than it is with rasterization. Eliminating the need to tweak shadow map resolutions, biases, and other parameters has eliminated an unpleasant task of lighting artists. Further, physically based methods bring with them bounce lighting and other soft-lighting effects from the method itself, rather than as an artistically tuned manual process.

As of this writing, physically based rendering is used widely for producing computer-generated imagery for movies; Figures 1.21 and 1.22 show images from two recent movies that used physically based approaches.

FURTHER READING

In a seminal early paper, Arthur Appel (1968) first described the basic idea of ray tracing to solve the hidden surface problem and to compute shadows in polygonal scenes. Goldstein and Nagel (1971) later showed how ray tracing could be used to render scenes with quadric

Figure 1.22: This image from *Alita: Battle Angel* (2019) was also rendered using a physically based rendering system. Image by Weta Digital, © 2018 Twentieth Century Fox Film Corporation. All Rights Reserved.

surfaces. Kay and Greenberg (1979) described a ray-tracing approach to rendering transparency, and Whitted's seminal *CACM* article described a general recursive ray-tracing algorithm that accurately simulates reflection and refraction from specular surfaces and shadows from point light sources (Whitted 1980). Whitted has recently written an article describing developments over the early years of ray tracing (Whitted 2020).

In addition to the ones discussed in Section 1.6, notable early books on physically based rendering and image synthesis include Cohen and Wallace's *Radiosity and Realistic Image Synthesis* (1993), Sillion and Puech's *Radiosity and Global Illumination* (1994), and Ashdown's *Radiosity: A Programmer's Perspective* (1994), all of which primarily describe the finite-element radiosity method. The course notes from the Monte Carlo ray-tracing course at SIGGRAPH have a wealth of practical information (Jensen et al. 2001a, 2003), much of it still relevant, now nearly twenty years later.

In a paper on ray-tracing system design, Kirk and Arvo (1988) suggested many principles that have now become classic in renderer design. Their renderer was implemented as a core kernel that encapsulated the basic rendering algorithms and interacted with primitives and shading routines via a carefully constructed object-oriented interface. This approach made it easy to extend the system with new primitives and acceleration methods. pbrt's design is based on these ideas.

To this day, a good reference on basic ray-tracer design is *Introduction to Ray Tracing* (Glassner 1989a), which describes the state of the art in ray tracing at that time and has a chapter by Heckbert that sketches the design of a basic ray tracer. More recently, Shirley and Morley's *Realistic Ray Tracing* (2003) offers an easy-to-understand introduction to ray tracing and includes the complete source code to a basic ray tracer. Suffern's book (2007) also provides a gentle introduction to ray tracing. Shirley's *Ray Tracing in One Weekend* series (2020) is an accessible introduction to the joy of writing a ray tracer.

Researchers at Cornell University have developed a rendering testbed over many years; its design and overall structure were described by Trumbore, Lytle, and Greenberg (1993). Its predecessor was described by Hall and Greenberg (1983). This system is a loosely coupled set of modules and libraries, each designed to handle a single task (ray–object intersection acceleration, image storage, etc.) and written in a way that makes it easy to combine appropriate modules to investigate and develop new rendering algorithms. This testbed has been quite successful, serving as the foundation for much of the rendering research done at Cornell through the 1990s.

Radiance was the first widely available open source renderer based fundamentally on physical quantities. It was designed to perform accurate lighting simulation for architectural design. Ward described its design and history in a paper and a book (Ward 1994; Larson and Shakespeare 1998). *Radiance* is designed in the UNIX style, as a set of interacting programs, each handling a different part of the rendering process. This general type of rendering architecture was first described by Duff (1985).

Glassner's (1993) *Spectrum* rendering architecture also focuses on physically based rendering, approached through a signal-processing-based formulation of the problem. It is an extensible system built with a plug-in architecture; pbrt's approach of using parameter/value lists for initializing implementations of the main abstract interfaces is similar to *Spectrum*'s. One notable feature of *Spectrum* is that all parameters that describe the scene can be functions of time.

Slusallek and Seidel (1995, 1996; Slusallek 1996) described the *Vision* rendering system, which is also physically based and designed to support a wide variety of light transport algorithms. In particular, it had the ambitious goal of supporting both Monte Carlo and finite-element-based light transport algorithms.

Many papers have been written that describe the design and implementation of other rendering systems, including renderers for entertainment and artistic applications. The Reyes architecture, which forms the basis for Pixar's *RenderMan* renderer, was first described by Cook et al. (1987), and a number of improvements to the original algorithm have been summarized by Apodaca and Gritz (2000). Gritz and Hahn (1996) described the *BMRT* ray tracer. The renderer in the *Maya* modeling and animation system was described by Sung et al. (1998), and some of the internal structure of the *mental ray* renderer is described in Driemeyer and Herken's book on its API (Driemeyer and Herken 2002). The design of the high-performance *Manta* interactive ray tracer was described by Bigler et al. (2006).

OptiX introduced a particularly interesting design approach for high-performance ray tracing: it is based on doing JIT compilation at runtime to generate a specialized version of the ray tracer, intermingling user-provided code (such as for material evaluation and sampling) and renderer-provided code (such as high-performance ray–object intersection). It was described by Parker et al. (2010).

More recently, Eisenacher et al. discussed the ray sorting architecture of Disney's *Hyperion* renderer (Eisenacher et al. 2013), and Lee et al. have written about the implementation of the *MoonRay* rendering system at DreamWorks (Lee et al. 2017). The implementation of the *Iray* ray tracer was described by Keller et al. (2017).

In 2018, a special issue of *ACM Transactions on Graphics* included papers describing the implementations of five rendering systems that are used for feature film production. These papers are full of details about the various renderers; reading them is time well spent. They include Burley et al.'s description of Disney's *Hyperion* renderer (2018), Christensen et al. on Pixar's modern *RenderMan* (2018), Fascione et al. describing Weta Digital's *Manuka* (2018), Georgiev et al. on Solid Angle's version of *Arnold* (2018) and Kulla et al. on the version of *Arnold* used at Sony Pictures Imageworks (2018).

Whereas standard rendering algorithms generate images from a 3D scene description, the *Mitsuba 2* system is engineered around the corresponding inverse problem. It computes derivatives with respect to scene parameters using JIT-compiled kernels that efficiently run on GPUs and CPUs. These kernels are then used in the inner loop of an optimization algorithm to reconstruct 3D scenes that are consistent with user-provided input images. This topic is further discussed in Section 16.3.1. The system's design and implementation was described by Nimier-David et al. (2019).

EXERCISE

1.1 A good way to gain an understanding of pbrt is to follow the process of computing the radiance value for a single ray in a debugger. Build a version of pbrt with debugging symbols and set up your debugger to run pbrt with a not-too-complex scene. Set breakpoints in the ImageTileIntegrator::Render() method and trace through the process of how a ray is generated, how its radiance value is computed, and how its contribution is added to the image. The first time you do this, you may want to specify that only a single thread of execution should be used by providing --nthreads 1 as command-line arguments to pbrt; doing so ensures that all computation is done in the main processing thread, which may make it easier to understand what is going on, depending on how easy your debugger makes it to step through the program when it is running multiple threads.

As you gain more understanding about the details of the system later in the book, repeat this process and trace through particular parts of the system more carefully.

CHAPTER TWO

02 MONTE CARLO INTEGRATION

Rendering is full of integration problems. In addition to the light transport equation (1.1), in the following chapters we will see that integral equations also describe a variety of additional quantities related to light, including the sensor response in a camera, the attenuation and scattering of light in participating media, and scattering from materials like skin. These integral equations generally do not have analytic solutions, so we must turn to numerical methods. Although standard numerical integration techniques like trapezoidal integration or Gaussian quadrature are effective at solving low-dimensional smooth integrals, their rate of convergence is poor for the higher dimensional and discontinuous integrals that are common in rendering. Monte Carlo integration techniques provide one solution to this problem. They use random sampling to evaluate integrals with a convergence rate that is independent of the dimensionality of the integrand.

Monte Carlo integration[1] has the useful property that it only requires the ability to evaluate an integrand $f(x)$ at arbitrary points in the domain in order to estimate the value of its integral $\int f(x)\,dx$. This property not only makes Monte Carlo easy to implement but also makes the technique applicable to a broad variety of integrands. It has a natural extension to multidimensional functions; in Chapter 13, we will see that the light transport algorithm implemented in the RandomWalkIntegrator can be shown to be estimating the value of an infinite-dimensional integral.

Judicious use of randomness has revolutionized the field of algorithm design. Randomized algorithms fall broadly into two classes: *Las Vegas* and *Monte Carlo*. Las Vegas algorithms are those that use randomness but always give the same result in the end (e.g., choosing a random array entry as the pivot element in Quicksort). Monte Carlo algorithms, on the other hand, give different results depending on the particular random numbers used along the way but give the right answer *on average*. So, by averaging the results of several runs of a Monte Carlo algorithm (on the same input), it is possible to find a result that is statistically very likely to be close to the true answer.

1   For brevity, we will refer to Monte Carlo integration simply as "Monte Carlo."

The following sections discuss the basic principles of Monte Carlo integration, focusing on those that are widely used in pbrt. See also Appendix A, which has the implementations of additional Monte Carlo sampling functions that are more rarely used in the system.

2.1 MONTE CARLO: BASICS

Because Monte Carlo integration is based on randomization, we will start this chapter with a brief review of ideas from probability and statistics that provide the foundations of the approach. Doing so will allow us to introduce the basic Monte Carlo algorithm as well as mathematical tools for evaluating its error.

2.1.1 BACKGROUND AND PROBABILITY REVIEW

We will start by defining some terms and reviewing basic ideas from probability. We assume that the reader is already familiar with basic probability concepts; readers needing a more complete introduction to this topic should consult a textbook such as Sheldon Ross's *Introduction to Probability Models* (2002).

A *random variable* X is a value chosen by some random process. We will generally use capital letters to denote random variables, with exceptions made for a few Greek symbols that represent special random variables. Random variables are always drawn from some domain, which can be either discrete (e.g., a fixed, finite set of possibilities) or continuous (e.g., the real numbers $\mathbb{R}$). Applying a function f to a random variable X results in a new random variable $Y = f(X)$.

For example, the result of a roll of a die is a discrete random variable sampled from the set of events $X_i \in \{1, 2, 3, 4, 5, 6\}$. Each event has a probability $p_i = \frac{1}{6}$, and the sum of probabilities $\sum p_i$ is necessarily one. A random variable like this one that has the same probability for all potential values of it is said to be *uniform*. A function $p(X)$ that gives a discrete random variable's probability is termed a *probability mass function* (PMF), and so we could equivalently write $p(X) = \frac{1}{6}$ in this case.

Two random variables are *independent* if the probability of one does not affect the probability of the other. In this case, the *joint probability* $p(X, Y)$ of two random variables is given by the product of their probabilities:

$$p(X, Y) = p(X)\, p(Y).$$

For example, two random variables representing random samples of the six sides of a die are independent.

For *dependent* random variables, one's probability affects the other's. Consider a bag filled with some number of black balls and some number of white balls. If we randomly choose two balls from the bag, the probability of the second ball being white is affected by the color of the first ball since its choice changes the number of balls of one type left in the bag. We will say that the second ball's probability is *conditioned* on the choice of the first one. In this case, the joint probability for choosing two balls X and Y is given by

$$p(X, Y) = p(X)\, p(Y|X), \qquad\qquad [2.1]$$

where $p(Y|X)$ is the *conditional probability* of Y given a value of X.

In the following, it will often be the case that a random variable's probability is conditioned on many values; for example, when choosing a light source from which to sample illumination, the BVHLightSampler in Section 12.6.3 considers the 3D position of the receiving point

BVHLightSampler 796

and its surface normal, and so the choice of light is conditioned on them. However, we will often omit the variables that a random variable is conditioned on in cases where there are many of them and where enumerating them would obscure notation.

A particularly important random variable is the *canonical uniform random variable*, which we will write as ξ. This variable takes on all values in its domain $[0, 1)$ independently and with uniform probability. This particular variable is important for two reasons. First, it is easy to generate a variable with this distribution in software—most runtime libraries have a pseudo-random number generator that does just that.[2] Second, we can take the canonical uniform random variable ξ and map it to a discrete random variable, choosing X_i if

$$\sum_{j=1}^{i-1} p_j \leq \xi < \sum_{j=1}^{i} p_j. \tag{2.2}$$

For lighting applications, we might want to define the probability of sampling illumination from each light in the scene based on its power Φ_i relative to the total power from all sources:

$$p_i = \frac{\Phi_i}{\sum_j \Phi_j}.$$

Notice that these p_i values also sum to 1. Given such per-light probabilities, ξ could be used to select a light source from which to sample illumination.

The *cumulative distribution function* (CDF) $P(x)$ of a random variable is the probability that a value from the variable's distribution is less than or equal to some value x:

$$P(x) = \Pr\{X \leq x\}. \tag{2.3}$$

For the die example, $P(2) = \frac{1}{3}$, since two of the six possibilities are less than or equal to 2.

Continuous random variables take on values over ranges of continuous domains (e.g., the real numbers, directions on the unit sphere, or the surfaces of shapes in the scene). Beyond ξ, another example of a continuous random variable is the random variable that ranges over the real numbers between 0 and 2, where the probability of its taking on any particular value x is proportional to the value $2 - x$: it is twice as likely for this random variable to take on a value around 0 as it is to take one around 1, and so forth.

The *probability density function* (PDF) formalizes this idea: it describes the relative probability of a random variable taking on a particular value and is the continuous analog of the PMF. The PDF $p(x)$ is the derivative of the random variable's CDF,

$$p(x) = \frac{dP(x)}{dx}.$$

For uniform random variables, $p(x)$ is a constant; this is a direct consequence of uniformity. For ξ we have

$$p(x) = \begin{cases} 1 & x \in [0, 1) \\ 0 & \text{otherwise.} \end{cases}$$

PDFs are necessarily nonnegative and always integrate to 1 over their domains. Note that their value at a point x is *not* necessarily less than 1, however.

---

2   Although the theory of Monte Carlo is based on using truly random numbers, in practice a well-written pseudo-random number generator (PRNG) is sufficient. pbrt uses a particularly high-quality PRNG that returns a sequence of pseudo-random values that is effectively as "random" as true random numbers. True random numbers, found by measuring random phenomena like atomic decay or atmospheric noise, are available from sources like *www.random.org* for those for whom PRNGs are not acceptable.

Given an interval $[a, b]$ in the domain, integrating the PDF gives the probability that a random variable lies inside the interval:

$$\Pr\{x \in [a, b]\} = \int_a^b p(x)\, dx = P(b) - P(a).$$

This follows directly from the first fundamental theorem of calculus and the definition of the PDF.

2.1.2 EXPECTED VALUES

The *expected value* $E_p[f(x)]$ of a function f is defined as the average value of the function over some distribution of values $p(x)$ over its domain D. It is defined as

$$E_p[f(x)] = \int_D f(x)\, p(x)\, dx. \tag{2.4}$$

As an example, consider finding the expected value of the cosine function between 0 and π, where p is uniform. Because the PDF $p(x)$ must integrate to 1 over the domain, $p(x) = 1/\pi$, so[3]

$$E[\cos x] = \int_0^\pi \frac{\cos x}{\pi}\, dx = \frac{1}{\pi}(\sin \pi - \sin 0) = 0,$$

which is precisely the expected result. (Consider the graph of $\cos x$ over $[0, \pi]$ to see why this is so.)

The expected value has a few useful properties that follow from its definition:

$$E[af(x)] = a E[f(x)]$$

$$E\left[\sum_{i=1}^n f(X_i)\right] = \sum_{i=1}^n E[f(X_i)]. \tag{2.5}$$

We will repeatedly use these properties in derivations in the following sections.

2.1.3 THE MONTE CARLO ESTIMATOR

We can now define the Monte Carlo estimator, which approximates the value of an arbitrary integral $\int_a^b f(x)\, dx$. Suppose that we want to evaluate a 1D integral $\int_a^b f(x)\, dx$. Given a supply of independent uniform random variables $X_i \in [a, b]$, the Monte Carlo estimator says that the expected value of the estimator

$$F_n = \frac{b - a}{n} \sum_{i=1}^n f(X_i), \tag{2.6}$$

$E[F_n]$, is equal to the integral. This fact can be demonstrated with just a few steps. First, note that the PDF $p(x)$ corresponding to the random variable X_i must be equal to $1/(b - a)$, since p must not only be a constant but also integrate to 1 over the domain $[a, b]$. Algebraic manipulation using the properties from Equations (2.4) and (2.5) then shows that

---

3   When computing expected values with a uniform distribution, we will drop the subscript p from E_p.

$$E[F_n] = E\left[\frac{b-a}{n}\sum_{i=1}^{n}f(X_i)\right]$$

$$= \frac{b-a}{n}\sum_{i=1}^{n}E\left[f(X_i)\right]$$

$$= \frac{b-a}{n}\sum_{i=1}^{n}\int_{a}^{b}f(x)\,p(x)\,dx$$

$$= \frac{1}{n}\sum_{i=1}^{n}\int_{a}^{b}f(x)\,dx$$

$$= \int_{a}^{b}f(x)\,dx.$$

Extending this estimator to multiple dimensions or complex integration domains is straight-forward: n independent samples X_i are taken from a uniform multidimensional PDF, and the estimator is applied in the same way. For example, consider the 3D integral

$$\int_{z_0}^{z_1}\int_{y_0}^{y_1}\int_{x_0}^{x_1}f(x,\,y,\,z)\,dx\,dy\,dz.$$

If samples $X_i = (x_i,\,y_i,\,z_i)$ are chosen uniformly from the cube from $[x_0,\,x_1] \times [y_0,\,y_1] \times [z_0,\,z_1]$, then the PDF $p(X)$ is the constant value

$$\frac{1}{(x_1 - x_0)}\frac{1}{(y_1 - y_0)}\frac{1}{(z_1 - z_0)},$$

and the estimator is

$$\frac{(x_1 - x_0)(y_1 - y_0)(z_1 - z_0)}{n}\sum_{i=1}^{n}f(X_i).$$

The restriction to uniform random variables can be relaxed with a small generalization. This is an important step, since carefully choosing the PDF from which samples are drawn leads to a key technique for reducing error in Monte Carlo that will be introduced in Section 2.2.2. If the random variables X_i are drawn from a PDF $p(x)$, then the estimator

$$F_n = \frac{1}{n}\sum_{i=1}^{n}\frac{f(X_i)}{p(X_i)} \tag{2.7}$$

can be used to estimate the integral instead. The only limitation on $p(x)$ is that it must be nonzero for all x where $|f(x)| > 0$.

It is similarly not too hard to see that the expected value of this estimator is the desired integral of f:

$$E[F_n] = E\left[\frac{1}{n}\sum_{i=1}^{n}\frac{f(X_i)}{p(X_i)}\right]$$

$$= \frac{1}{n}\sum_{i=1}^{n}\int_a^b \frac{f(x)}{p(x)}p(x)\,\mathrm{d}x$$

$$= \frac{1}{n}\sum_{i=1}^{n}\int_a^b f(x)\,\mathrm{d}x$$

$$= \int_a^b f(x)\,\mathrm{d}x.$$

We can now understand the factor of $1/(4\pi)$ in the implementation of the RandomWalk Integrator: directions are uniformly sampled over the unit sphere, which has area 4π. Because the PDF is normalized over the sampling domain, it must have the constant value $1/(4\pi)$. When the estimator of Equation (2.7) is applied, that value appears in the divisor.

With Monte Carlo, the number of samples n can be chosen arbitrarily, regardless of the dimensionality of the integrand. This is another important advantage of Monte Carlo over traditional deterministic quadrature techniques, which typically require a number of samples that is exponential in the dimension.

2.1.4 ERROR IN MONTE CARLO ESTIMATORS

Showing that the Monte Carlo estimator converges to the right answer is not enough to justify its use; its rate of convergence is important too. *Variance*, the expected squared deviation of a function from its expected value, is a useful way to characterize Monte Carlo estimators' convergence. The variance of an estimator F is defined as

$$V[F] = E\left[\left(F - E[F]\right)^2\right], \tag{2.8}$$

from which it follows that

$$V[aF] = a^2 V[F].$$

This property and Equation (2.5) yield an alternative expression for the variance:

$$V[F] = E\left[F^2\right] - E[F]^2. \tag{2.9}$$

Thus, the variance is the expected value of the square minus the square of the expected value.

If the estimator is a sum of independent random variables (like the Monte Carlo estimator F_n), then the variance of the sum is the sum of the individual random variables' variances:

$$V\left[\sum_{i=1}^{n}X_i\right] = \sum_{i=1}^{n}V[X_i]. \tag{2.10}$$

From Equation (2.10) it is easy to show that variance decreases linearly with the number of samples n. Because variance is squared error, the error in a Monte Carlo estimate therefore only goes down at a rate of $O(n^{-1/2})$ in the number of samples. Although standard quadrature techniques converge at a faster rate in one dimension, their performance becomes exponentially worse as the dimensionality of the integrand increases, while Monte Carlo's convergence rate is independent of the dimension, making Monte Carlo the only practical numerical integration algorithm for high-dimensional integrals.

The $O(n^{-1/2})$ characteristic of Monte Carlo's rate of error reduction is apparent when watching a progressive rendering of a scene where additional samples are incrementally taken in all pixels. The image improves rapidly for the first few samples when doubling the number of samples is relatively little additional work. Later on, once tens or hundreds of samples have been taken, each additional sample doubling takes much longer and remaining error in the image takes a long time to disappear.

The linear decrease in variance with increasing numbers of samples makes it easy to compare different Monte Carlo estimators. Consider two estimators, where the second has half the variance of the first but takes three times as long to compute an estimate; which of the two is better? In that case, the first is preferable: it could take three times as many samples in the time consumed by the second, in which case it would achieve a 3× variance reduction. This concept can be encapsulated in the *efficiency* of an estimator F, which is defined as

$$\epsilon[F] = \frac{1}{V[F]\, T[F]},$$

where $V[F]$ is its variance and $T[F]$ is the running time to compute its value.

Not all estimators of integrals have expected values that are equal to the value of the integral. Such estimators are said to be *biased*, where the difference

$$\beta = E[F] - \int f(x)\, dx$$

is the amount of bias. Biased estimators may still be desirable if they are able to get close to the correct result more quickly than unbiased estimators. Kalos and Whitlock (1986, pp. 36–37) gave the following example: consider the problem of computing an estimate of the mean value of a uniform distribution $X_i \sim p$ over the interval from 0 to 1. One could use the estimator

$$\frac{1}{n} \sum_{i=1}^{n} X_i,$$

or one could use the biased estimator

$$\frac{1}{2} \max(X_1, X_2, \ldots, X_n).$$

The first estimator is unbiased but has variance with order $O(n^{-1})$. The second estimator's expected value is

$$0.5 \frac{n}{n+1} \neq 0.5,$$

so it is biased, although its variance is $O(n^{-2})$, which is much better. This estimator has the useful property that its error goes to 0 in the limit as the number of samples n goes to infinity; such estimators are *consistent*.[4] Most of the Monte Carlo estimators used in pbrt are unbiased, with the notable exception of the SPPMIntegrator, which implements a photon mapping algorithm.

Closely related to the variance is the *mean squared error* (MSE), which is defined as the expectation of the squared difference of an estimator and the true value,

$$MSE[F] = E\left[\left(F - \int f(x)\, dx\right)^2\right].$$

---

4   As a technical note, it is possible for an estimator with infinite variance to be unbiased but not consistent. Such estimators do not generally come up in rendering, however.

For an unbiased estimator, MSE is equal to the variance; otherwise it is the sum of variance and the squared bias of the estimator.

It is possible to work out the variance and MSE of some simple estimators in closed form, but for most of the ones of interest in rendering, this is not possible. Yet it is still useful to be able to quantify these values. For this purpose, the *sample variance* can be computed using a set of independent random variables X_i. Equation (2.8) points at one way to compute the sample variance for a set of n random variables X_i. If the *sample mean* is computed as their average, $\bar{X} = (1/n) \sum X_i$, then the sample variance is

$$\frac{1}{n-1} \sum_{i=1}^{n} (X_i - \bar{X})^2. \tag{2.11}$$

The division by $n-1$ rather than n is *Bessel's correction*, and ensures that the sample variance is an unbiased estimate of the variance. (See also Section B.2.11, where a numerically stable approach for computing the sample variance is introduced.)

The sample variance is itself an estimate of the variance, so it has variance itself. Consider, for example, a random variable that has a value of 1 99.99% of the time, and a value of one million 0.01% of the time. If we took ten random samples of it that all had the value 1, the sample variance would suggest that the random variable had zero variance even though its variance is actually much higher.

If an accurate estimate of the integral $\tilde{F} \approx \int f(x)\, dx$ can be computed (for example, using a large number of samples), then the mean squared error can be estimated by

$$MSE[F] \approx \frac{1}{n} \sum_{i=1}^{n} \left(f(X_i) - \tilde{F} \right)^2.$$

The `imgtool` utility program that is provided in `pbrt`'s distribution can compute an image's MSE with respect to a reference image via its `diff` option.

2.2 IMPROVING EFFICIENCY

Given an unbiased Monte Carlo estimator, we are in the fortunate position of having a reliable relationship between the number of samples taken and variance (and thus, error). If we have an unacceptably noisy rendered image, increasing the number of samples will reduce error in a predictable way, and—given enough computation—an image of sufficient quality can be generated.

However, computation takes time, and often there is not enough of it. The deadline for a movie may be at hand, or the sixtieth-of-a-second time slice in a real-time renderer may be coming to an end. Given the consequentially limited number of samples, the only option for variance reduction is to find ways to make more of the samples that can be taken. Fortunately, a variety of techniques have been developed to improve the basic Monte Carlo estimator by making the most of the samples that are taken; here we will discuss the most important ones that are used in `pbrt`.

2.2.1 STRATIFIED SAMPLING

A classic and effective family of techniques for variance reduction is based on the careful placement of samples in order to better capture the features of the integrand (or, more accurately, to be less likely to miss important features). These techniques are used extensively in pbrt. Stratified sampling decomposes the integration domain into regions and places samples in each one; here we will analyze that approach in terms of its variance reduction properties. Later, in Section 8.2.1, we will return with machinery based on Fourier analysis that provides further insights about it.

Stratified sampling subdivides the integration domain Λ into n nonoverlapping regions $\Lambda_1, \Lambda_2, \ldots, \Lambda_n$. Each region is called a *stratum*, and they must completely cover the original domain:

$$\bigcup_{i=1}^{n} \Lambda_i = \Lambda.$$

To draw samples from Λ, we will draw n_i samples from each Λ_i, according to densities p_i inside each stratum. A simple example is supersampling a pixel. With stratified sampling, the area around a pixel is divided into a $k \times k$ grid, and a sample is drawn uniformly within each grid cell. This is better than taking k^2 random samples, since the sample locations are less likely to clump together. Here we will show why this technique reduces variance.

Within a single stratum Λ_i, the Monte Carlo estimate is

$$F_i = \frac{1}{n_i} \sum_{j=1}^{n_i} \frac{f(X_{i,j})}{p_i(X_{i,j})},$$

where $X_{i,j}$ is the jth sample drawn from density p_i. The overall estimate is $F = \sum_i v_i F_i$, where v_i is the fractional volume of stratum i ($v_i \in (0, 1]$).

The true value of the integrand in stratum i is

$$\mu_i = E\left[f\left(X_{i,j}\right)\right] = \frac{1}{v_i} \int_{\Lambda_i} f(x) \, dx,$$

and the variance in this stratum is

$$\sigma_i^2 = \frac{1}{v_i} \int_{\Lambda_i} \left(f(x) - \mu_i\right)^2 dx.$$

Thus, with n_i samples in the stratum, the variance of the per-stratum estimator is σ_i^2 / n_i. This shows that the variance of the overall estimator is

$$\begin{aligned} V[F] &= V\left[\sum v_i F_i\right] \\ &= \sum V\left[v_i F_i\right] \\ &= \sum v_i^2 V\left[F_i\right] \\ &= \sum \frac{v_i^2 \sigma_i^2}{n_i}. \end{aligned}$$

If we make the reasonable assumption that the number of samples n_i is proportional to the volume v_i, then we have $n_i = v_i n$, and the variance of the overall estimator is

$$V\left[F_n\right] = \frac{1}{n} \sum v_i \sigma_i^2.$$

To compare this result to the variance without stratification, we note that choosing an unstratified sample is equivalent to choosing a random stratum I according to the discrete probability distribution defined by the volumes v_i and then choosing a random sample X

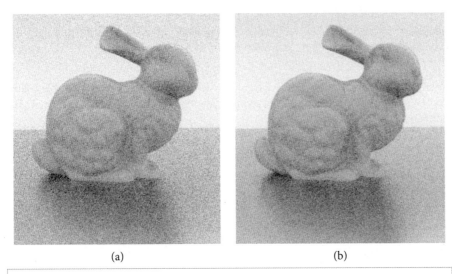

(a)   (b)

Figure 2.1: Variance is higher and the image noisier (a) when independent random sampling is used than (b) when a stratified distribution of sample directions is used instead. *(Bunny model courtesy of the Stanford Computer Graphics Laboratory.)*

in Λ_I. In this sense, X is chosen *conditionally* on I, so it can be shown using conditional probability that

$$V[F] = \frac{1}{n} \left[\sum v_i \sigma_i^2 + \sum v_i \left(\mu_i - Q \right)^2 \right],$$ [2.12]

where Q is the mean of f over the whole domain Λ.[5]

There are two things to notice about Equation (2.12). First, we know that the right-hand sum must be nonnegative, since variance is always nonnegative. Second, it demonstrates that stratified sampling can never increase variance. Stratification always reduces variance unless the right-hand sum is exactly 0. It can only be 0 when the function f has the same mean over each stratum Λ_i. For stratified sampling to work best, we would like to maximize the right-hand sum, so it is best to make the strata have means that are as unequal as possible. This explains why *compact* strata are desirable if one does not know anything about the function f. If the strata are wide, they will contain more variation and will have μ_i closer to the true mean Q.

Figure 2.1 shows the effect of using stratified sampling versus an independent random distribution for sampling when rendering an image that includes glossy reflection. There is a reasonable reduction in variance at essentially no cost in running time.

The main downside of stratified sampling is that it suffers from the same "curse of dimensionality" as standard numerical quadrature. Full stratification in D dimensions with S strata per dimension requires S^D samples, which quickly becomes prohibitive. Fortunately, it is often possible to stratify some of the dimensions independently and then randomly associate samples from different dimensions; this approach will be used in Section 8.5. Choosing which dimensions are stratified should be done in a way that stratifies dimensions that tend to be most highly correlated in their effect on the value of the integrand (Owen 1998).

---

5   See Veach (1997) for a derivation of this result.

2.2.2 IMPORTANCE SAMPLING

Importance sampling is a powerful variance reduction technique that exploits the fact that the Monte Carlo estimator

$$F_n = \frac{1}{n} \sum_{i=1}^{n} \frac{f(X_i)}{p(X_i)}$$

converges more quickly if the samples are taken from a distribution $p(x)$ that is similar to the function $f(x)$ in the integrand. In this case, samples are more likely to be taken when the magnitude of the integrand is relatively large. Importance sampling is one of the most frequently used variance reduction techniques in rendering, since it is easy to apply and is very effective when good sampling distributions are used.

To see why such sampling distributions reduce error, first consider the effect of using a distribution $p(x) \propto f(x)$, or $p(x) = cf(x)$.[6] It is trivial to show that normalization of the PDF requires that

$$c = \frac{1}{\int f(x) \, dx}.$$

Finding such a PDF requires that we know the value of the integral, which is what we were trying to estimate in the first place. Nonetheless, if we *could* sample from this distribution, each term of the sum in the estimator would have the value

$$\frac{f(X_i)}{p(X_i)} = \frac{1}{c} = \int f(x) \, dx.$$

The variance of the estimator is zero! Of course, this is ludicrous since we would not bother using Monte Carlo if we could integrate f directly. However, if a density $p(x)$ can be found that is similar in shape to $f(x)$, variance is reduced.

As a more realistic example, consider the Gaussian function $f(x) = e^{-1000(x-1/4)^2}$, which is plotted in Figure 2.2(a) over [0, 1]. Its value is close to zero over most of the domain. Samples X with $X < 0.2$ or $X > 0.3$ are of little help in estimating the value of the integral since they give no information about the magnitude of the bump in the function's value around 1/4. With uniform sampling and the basic Monte Carlo estimator, variance is approximately 0.0365.

If samples are instead drawn from the piecewise-constant distribution

$$p(x) = \begin{cases} 0.1 & x \in [0, 0.15) \\ 4.6 & x \in [0.15, 0.35) \\ 0.1 & x \in [0.35, 1), \end{cases}$$

which is plotted in Figure 2.2(b), and the estimator from Equation (2.7) is used instead, then variance is reduced by a factor of approximately $6.7\times$. A representative set of 6 points from this distribution is shown in Figure 2.2(c); we can see that most of the evaluations of $f(x)$ are in the interesting region where it is not nearly zero.

---

6   We will generally assume that $f(x) \geq 0$; if it is negative, we might set $p(x) \propto |f(x)|$. See the "Further Reading" section for more discussion of this topic.

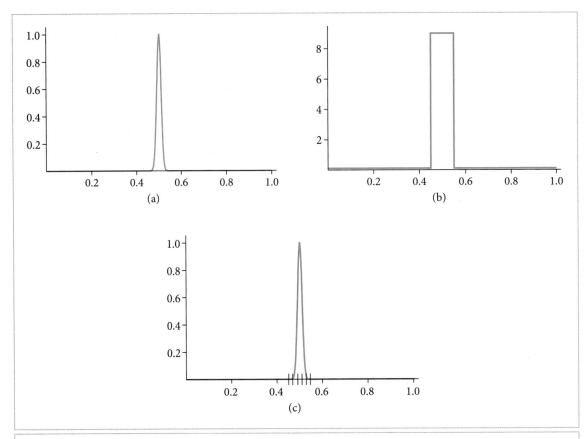

Figure 2.2: (a) A narrow Gaussian function that is close to zero over most of the range [0, 1]. The basic Monte Carlo estimator of Equation (2.6) has relatively high variance if it is used to integrate this function, since most samples have values that are close to zero. (b) A PDF that roughly approximates the function's distribution. If this PDF is used to generate samples, variance is reduced substantially. (c) A representative distribution of samples generated according to (b).

Importance sampling can increase variance if a poorly chosen distribution is used, however. Consider instead using the distribution

$$p(x) = \begin{cases} 1.2 & x \in [0, 0.15) \\ 0.2 & x \in [0.15, 0.35) \\ 1.2 & x \in [0.35, 1), \end{cases}$$

for estimating the integral of the Gaussian function. This PDF increases the probability of sampling the function where its value is close to zero and decreases the probability of sampling it where its magnitude is larger.

Not only does this PDF generate fewer samples where the integrand is large, but when it does, the magnitude of $f(x)/p(x)$ in the Monte Carlo estimator will be especially high since $p(x) = 0.2$ in that region. The result is approximately $5.4\times$ higher variance than uniform sampling, and nearly $36\times$ higher variance than the better PDF above. In the context of Monte Carlo integration for rendering where evaluating the integrand generally involves the expense of tracing a ray, it is desirable to minimize the number of samples taken; using an inferior sampling distribution and making up for it by evaluating more samples is an unappealing option.

2.2.3 MULTIPLE IMPORTANCE SAMPLING

We are frequently faced with integrals that are the product of two or more functions: $\int f_a(x) f_b(x) \, dx$. It is often possible to derive separate importance sampling strategies for individual factors individually, though not one that is similar to their product. This situation is especially common in the integrals involved with light transport, such as in the product of BSDF, incident radiance, and a cosine factor in the light transport equation (1.1).

To understand the challenges involved with applying Monte Carlo to such products, assume for now the good fortune of having two sampling distributions p_a and p_b that match the distributions of f_a and f_b exactly. (In practice, this will not normally be the case.) With the Monte Carlo estimator of Equation (2.7), we have two options: we might draw samples using p_a, which gives the estimator

$$\frac{f(X)}{p_a(X)} = \frac{f_a(X) f_b(X)}{p_a(X)} = c f_b(X),$$

where c is a constant equal to the integral of f_a, since $p_a(x) \propto f_a(x)$. The variance of this estimator is proportional to the variance of f_b, which may itself be high.[7] Conversely, we might sample from p_b, though doing so gives us an estimator with variance proportional to the variance of f_a, which may similarly be high. In the more common case where the sampling distributions only approximately match one of the factors, the situation is usually even worse.

Unfortunately, the obvious solution of taking some samples from each distribution and averaging the two estimators is not much better. Because variance is additive, once variance has crept into an estimator, we cannot eliminate it by adding it to another low-variance estimator.

Multiple importance sampling (MIS) addresses exactly this issue, with an easy-to-implement variance reduction technique. The basic idea is that, when estimating an integral, we should draw samples from multiple sampling distributions, chosen in the hope that at least one of them will match the shape of the integrand reasonably well, even if we do not know which one this will be. MIS then provides a method to weight the samples from each technique that can eliminate large variance spikes due to mismatches between the integrand's value and the sampling density. Specialized sampling routines that only account for unusual special cases are even encouraged, as they reduce variance when those cases occur, with relatively little cost in general.

With two sampling distributions p_a and p_b and a single sample taken from each one, $X \sim p_a$ and $Y \sim p_b$, the MIS Monte Carlo estimator is

$$w_a(X) \frac{f(X)}{p_a(X)} + w_b(Y) \frac{f(Y)}{p_b(Y)}, \qquad\qquad\text{[2.13]}$$

where w_a and w_b are weighting functions chosen such that the expected value of this estimator is the value of the integral of $f(x)$.

More generally, given n sampling distributions p_i with n_i samples $X_{i,j}$ taken from the ith distribution, the MIS Monte Carlo estimator is

$$F_n = \sum_{i=1}^{n} \frac{1}{n_i} \sum_{j=1}^{n_i} w_i(X_{i,j}) \frac{f(X_{i,j})}{p_i(X_{i,j})}.$$

---

7   Note that the definition of variance in Equation (2.8) does not preclude computing the variance of a function itself.

(The full set of conditions on the weighting functions for the estimator to be unbiased are that they sum to 1 when $f(x) \neq 0$, $\sum_{i=1}^{n} w_i(x) = 1$, and that $w_i(x) = 0$ if $p_i(x) = 0$.)

Setting $x_i(X) = 1/n$ corresponds to the case of summing the various estimators, which we have already seen is an ineffective way to reduce variance. It would be better if the weighting functions were relatively large when the corresponding sampling technique was a good match to the integrand and relatively small when it was not, thus reducing the contribution of high-variance samples.

In practice, a good choice for the weighting functions is given by the *balance heuristic*, which attempts to fulfill this goal by taking into account all the different ways that a sample could have been generated, rather than just the particular one that was used to do so. The balance heuristic's weighting function for the ith sampling technique is

$$w_i(x) = \frac{n_i \, p_i(x)}{\sum_j n_j \, p_j(x)}.$$ [2.14]

With the balance heuristic and our example of taking a single sample from each of two sampling techniques, the estimator of Equation (2.13) works out to be

$$\frac{f(X)}{p_a(X) + p_b(X)} + \frac{f(Y)}{p_a(Y) + p_b(Y)}.$$

Each evaluation of f is divided by the sum of all PDFs for the corresponding sample rather than just the one that generated the sample. Thus, if p_a generates a sample with low probability at a point where the p_b has a higher probability, then dividing by $p_a(X) + p_b(X)$ reduces the sample's contribution. Effectively, such samples are downweighted when sampled from p_a, recognizing that the sampling technique associated with p_b is more effective at the corresponding point in the integration domain. As long as just one of the sampling techniques has a reasonable probability of sampling a point where the function's value is large, the MIS weights can lead to a significant reduction in variance.

BalanceHeuristic() computes Equation (2.14) for the specific case of two distributions p_a and p_b. We will not need a more general multidistribution case in pbrt.

⟨*Sampling Inline Functions*⟩ ≡
```
Float BalanceHeuristic(int nf, Float fPdf, int ng, Float gPdf) {
    return (nf * fPdf) / (nf * fPdf + ng * gPdf);
}
```

In practice, the *power heuristic* often reduces variance even further. For an exponent β, the power heuristic is

$$w_i(x) = \frac{(n_i \, p_i(x))^{\beta}}{\sum_j (n_j \, p_j(x))^{\beta}}.$$ [2.15]

Note that the power heuristic has a similar form to the balance heuristic, though it further reduces the contribution of relatively low probabilities. Our implementation has $\beta = 2$ hardcoded in its implementation; that parameter value usually works well in practice.

⟨*Sampling Inline Functions*⟩ +≡
```
Float PowerHeuristic(int nf, Float fPdf, int ng, Float gPdf) {
    Float f = nf * fPdf, g = ng * gPdf;
    return Sqr(f) / (Sqr(f) + Sqr(g));
}
```

Float 23
Sqr() 1034

Multiple importance sampling can be applied even without sampling from all the distributions. This approach is known as the *single sample model*. We will not include the derivation here, but it can be shown that given an integrand $f(x)$, if a sampling technique p_i is chosen from a set of techniques with probability q_i and a sample X is drawn from p_i, then the *single sample estimator*

$$\frac{w_i(X)}{q_i} \frac{f(X)}{p_i(X)} \qquad\qquad [2.16]$$

gives an unbiased estimate of the integral. For the single sample model, the balance heuristic is provably optimal.

One shortcoming of multiple importance sampling is that if one of the sampling techniques is a very good match to the integrand, MIS can slightly increase variance. For rendering applications, MIS is almost always worthwhile for the variance reduction it provides in cases that can otherwise have high variance.

MIS Compensation

Multiple importance sampling is generally applied using probability distributions that are all individually valid for importance sampling the integrand, with nonzero probability of generating a sample anywhere that the integrand is nonzero. However, when MIS is being used, it is not a requirement that all PDFs are nonzero where the function's value is nonzero; only one of them must be.

This observation led to the development of a technique called *MIS compensation*, which can further reduce variance. It is motivated by the fact that if all the sampling distributions allocate some probability to sampling regions where the integrand's value is small, it is often the case that that region of the integrand ends up being oversampled, leaving the region where the integrand is high undersampled.

MIS compensation is based on the idea of sharpening one or more (but not all) the probability distributions—for example, by adjusting them to have zero probability in areas where they earlier had low probability. A new sampling distribution p' can, for example, be defined by

$$p'(x) = \frac{\max(0, \, p(x) - \delta)}{\int \max(0, \, p(x) - \delta) \, dx},$$

for some fixed value δ.

This technique is especially easy to apply in the case of tabularized sampling distributions. In Section 12.5, it is used to good effect for sampling environment map light sources.

2.2.4 RUSSIAN ROULETTE

Russian roulette is a technique that can improve the efficiency of Monte Carlo estimates by skipping the evaluation of samples that would make a small contribution to the final result. In rendering, we often have estimators of the form

$$\frac{f(X) \, v(X)}{p(X)},$$

where the integrand consists of some factors $f(X)$ that are easily evaluated (e.g., those that relate to how the surface scatters light) and others that are more expensive to evaluate, such as a binary visibility factor $v(X)$ that requires tracing a ray. In these cases, most of the computational expense of evaluating the estimator lies in v.

If $f(X)$ is zero, it is obviously worth skipping the work of evaluating $v(X)$, since its value will not affect the value of the estimator. However, if we also skipped evaluating estimators where

$f(X)$ was small but nonzero, then we would introduce bias into the estimator and would systemically underestimate the value of the integrand. Russian roulette solves this problem, making it possible to also skip tracing rays when $f(X)$'s value is small but not necessarily 0, while still computing the correct value on average.

To apply Russian roulette, we select some termination probability q. This value can be chosen in almost any manner; for example, it could be based on an estimate of the value of the integrand for the particular sample chosen, increasing as the integrand's value becomes smaller. With probability q, the estimator is not evaluated for the particular sample, and some constant value c is used in its place ($c = 0$ is often used). With probability $1 - q$, the estimator is still evaluated but is weighted by the factor $1/(1-q)$, which effectively compensates for the samples that were skipped.

We have the new estimator

$$F' = \begin{cases} \frac{F - qc}{1-q} & \xi > q \\ c & \text{otherwise.} \end{cases}$$

It is easy to see that its expected value is the same as the expected value of the original estimator:

$$E[F'] = (1 - q)\left(\frac{E[F] - qc}{1-q}\right) + qc = E[F].$$

Russian roulette never reduces variance. In fact, unless somehow $c = F$, it will always increase variance. However, it does improve Monte Carlo efficiency if the probabilities are chosen so that samples that are likely to make a small contribution to the final result are skipped.

2.2.5 SPLITTING

While Russian roulette reduces the number of samples, splitting increases the number of samples in some dimensions of multidimensional integrals in order to improve efficiency. As an example, consider an integral of the general form

$$\int_A \int_B f(x, y) \, dx \, dy. \tag{2.17}$$

With the standard importance sampling estimator, we might draw n samples from independent distributions, $X_i \sim p_x$ and $Y_i \sim p_y$, and compute

$$\frac{1}{n} \sum_{i=1}^{n} \frac{f(X_i, Y_i)}{p_x(X_i) \, p_y(Y_i)}. \tag{2.18}$$

Splitting allows us to formalize the idea of taking more than one sample for the integral over B for each sample taken in A. With splitting, we might take m samples $Y_{i,j}$ for each sample X_i, giving the estimator

$$\frac{1}{n} \sum_{i=1}^{n} \frac{1}{m} \sum_{j=1}^{m} \frac{f(X_i, Y_{i,j})}{p_x(X_i) \, p_y(Y_{i,j})}.$$

If it is possible to partially evaluate $f(X_i, \cdot)$ for each X_i, then we can compute a total of nm samples more efficiently than we had taken nm independent X_i values using Equation (2.18).

For an example from rendering, an integral of the form of Equation (2.17) is evaluated to compute the color of pixels in an image: an integral is taken over the area of the pixel A where at each point in the pixel x, a ray is traced into the scene and the reflected radiance at the intersection point is computed using an integral over the hemisphere (denoted here by

B) for which one or more rays are traced. With splitting, we can take multiple samples for each lighting integral, improving efficiency by amortizing the cost of tracing the initial ray from the camera over them.

2.3 SAMPLING USING THE INVERSION METHOD

To evaluate the Monte Carlo estimator in Equation (2.7), it is necessary to be able to draw random samples from a chosen probability distribution. There are a variety of techniques for doing so, but one of the most important for rendering is the *inversion method*, which maps uniform samples from [0, 1) to a given 1D probability distribution by inverting the distribution's CDF. (In Section 2.4.2 we will see how this approach can be applied to higher-dimensional functions by considering a sequence of 1D distributions.) When used with well-distributed samples such as those generated by the samplers that are defined in Chapter 8, the inversion method can be particularly effective. Throughout the remainder of the book, we will see the application of the inversion method to generate samples from the distributions defined by BSDFs, light sources, cameras, and scattering media.

2.3.1 DISCRETE CASE

Equation (2.2) leads to an algorithm for sampling from a set of discrete probabilities using a uniform random variable. Suppose we have a process with four possible outcomes where the probabilities of each of the four outcomes are given by p_1, p_2, p_3, and p_4, with $\sum_i p_i = 1$. The corresponding PMF is shown in Figure 2.3.

There is a direct connection between the sums in Equation (2.2) and the definition of the CDF. The discrete CDF is given by

$$P_i = \sum_{j=1}^{i} p_j,$$

which can be interpreted graphically by stacking the bars of the PMF on top of each other, starting at the left. This idea is shown in Figure 2.4.

The sampling operation of Equation (2.2) can be expressed as finding *i* such that

$$P_{i-1} \le \xi < P_i, \tag{2.19}$$

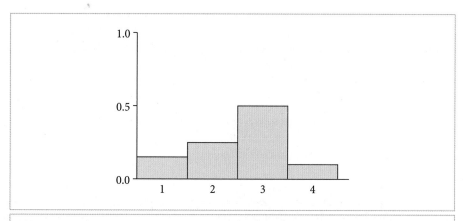

Figure 2.3: A PMF for Four Events, Each with a Probability p_i. The sum of their probabilities $\sum_i p_i$ is necessarily 1.

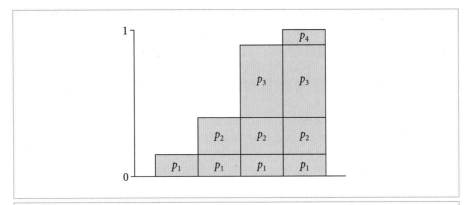

Figure 2.4: A Discrete CDF, Corresponding to the PMF in Figure 2.3. Each column's height is given by the PMF for the event that it represents plus the sum of the PMFs for the previous events, $P_i = \sum_{j=1}^{i} p_j$.

which can be interpreted as inverting the CDF P, and thus, the name of the technique. Continuing the graphical interpretation, this sampling operation can be considered in terms of projecting the events' probabilities onto the vertical axis where they cover the range $[0, 1]$ and using a random variable ξ to select among them (see Figure 2.5). It should be clear that this draws from the correct distribution—the probability of the uniform sample hitting any particular bar is exactly equal to the height of that bar.

The `SampleDiscrete()` function implements this algorithm. It takes a not-necessarily normalized set of nonnegative weights, a uniform random sample u, and returns the index of one of the weights with probability proportional to its weight. The sampling operation it performs corresponds to finding i such that

$$\sum_{j=1}^{i-1} w_j \leq \xi \sum w_i < \sum_{j=1}^{i} w_j, \tag{2.20}$$

which corresponds to multiplying Equation (2.19) by $\sum w_i$. (Not requiring a normalized PMF is a convenience for calling code and not much more work in the function's implementation.) Two optional parameters are provided to return the value of the PMF for the sample as well as a new uniform random sample that is derived from u.

This function is designed for the case where only a single sample needs to be generated from the weights' distribution; if multiple samples are required, the `AliasTable`, which will be introduced in Section A.1, should generally be used instead: it generates samples in $O(1)$ time after an $O(n)$ preprocessing step, whereas `SampleDiscrete()` requires $O(n)$ time for each sample generated.

⟨*Sampling Inline Functions*⟩ +≡
```
int SampleDiscrete(pstd::span<const Float> weights, Float u, Float *pmf,
                Float *uRemapped) {
    ⟨Handle empty weights for discrete sampling 71⟩
    ⟨Compute sum of weights 71⟩
    ⟨Compute rescaled u′ sample 71⟩
    ⟨Find offset in weights corresponding to u′ 71⟩
    ⟨Compute PMF and remapped u value, if necessary 71⟩
    return offset;
}
```

The case of weights being empty is handled first so that subsequent code can assume that there is at least one weight.

⟨*Handle empty* weights *for discrete sampling*⟩ ≡   70
```
if (weights.empty()) {
    if (pmf)
        *pmf = 0;
    return -1;
}
```

The discrete probability of sampling the ith element is given by weights[i] divided by the sum of all weight values. Therefore, the function computes that sum next.

⟨*Compute sum of* weights⟩ ≡   70
```
Float sumWeights = 0;
for (Float w : weights)
    sumWeights += w;
```

Following Equation (2.20), the uniform sample u is scaled by the sum of the weights to get a value u' that will be used to sample from them. Even though the provided u value should be in the range [0, 1), it is possible that u * sumWeights will be equal to sumWeights due to floating-point round-off. In that rare case, up is bumped down to the next lower floating-point value so that subsequent code can assume that up < sumWeights.

⟨*Compute rescaled u' sample*⟩ ≡   70
```
Float up = u * sumWeights;
if (up == sumWeights)
    up = NextFloatDown(up);
```

We would now like to find the last offset in the weights array i where the random sample up is greater than the sum of weights up to i. Sampling is performed using a linear search from the start of the array, accumulating a sum of weights until the sum would be greater than u'.

⟨*Find offset in* weights *corresponding to u'*⟩ ≡   70
```
int offset = 0;
Float sum = 0;
while (sum + weights[offset] <= up)
    sum += weights[offset++];
```

After the while loop terminates, the randomness in the provided sample u has only been used to select an element of the array—a discrete choice. The offset of a sample between the CDF values that bracket it is itself a uniform random value that can easily be remapped to [0, 1). This value is returned to the caller in uRemapped, if requested.

One might ask: why bother? It is not too difficult to generate uniform random variables, so the benefit of providing this option may seem marginal. However, for some of the high-quality sample generation algorithms in Chapter 8, it can be beneficial to reuse samples in this way rather than generating new ones—thus, this option is provided.

⟨*Compute PMF and remapped* u *value, if necessary*⟩ ≡   70
```
if (pmf)
    *pmf = weights[offset] / sumWeights;
if (uRemapped)
    *uRemapped = std::min((up - sum) / weights[offset], OneMinusEpsilon);
```

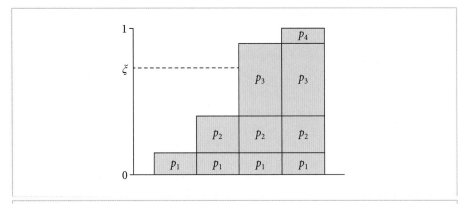

Figure 2.5: To use the inversion method to draw a sample from the distribution described by the PMF in Figure 2.3, a canonical uniform random variable is plotted on the vertical axis. By construction, the horizontal extension of ξ will intersect the box representing the ith outcome with probability p_i. If the corresponding event is chosen for a set of random variables ξ, then the resulting distribution of events will be distributed according to the PMF.

2.3.2 CONTINUOUS CASE

In order to generalize this technique to continuous distributions, consider what happens as the number of discrete possibilities approaches infinity. The PMF from Figure 2.3 becomes a PDF, and the CDF from Figure 2.4 becomes its integral. The projection process is still the same, but it has a convenient mathematical interpretation—it represents inverting the CDF and evaluating the inverse at ξ.

More precisely, we can draw a sample X_i from a PDF $p(x)$ with the following steps:

1. Integrate the PDF to find the CDF[8] $P(x) = \int_0^x p(x')\,dx'$.
2. Obtain a uniformly distributed random number ξ.
3. Generate a sample by solving $\xi = P(X)$ for X; in other words, find $X = P^{-1}(\xi)$.

We will illustrate this algorithm with a simple example; see Section A.4 for its application to a number of additional functions.

Sampling a Linear Function

The function $f(x) = (1 - x)a + xb$ defined over $[0, 1]$ linearly interpolates between a at $x = 0$ and b at $x = 1$. Here we will assume that $a, b \geq 0$; an exercise at the end of the chapter discusses the more general case.

⟨*Math Inline Functions*⟩ ≡
```
Float Lerp(Float x, Float a, Float b) {
    return (1 - x) * a + x * b;
}
```

The function's integral is $\int_0^1 f(x)\,dx = (a + b)/2$, which gives the normalization constant $2/(a + b)$ to define its PDF,

$$p(x) = \frac{2 f(x)}{a + b}.$$

Float 23

---

8   In general, the lower limit of integration should be $-\infty$, although if $p(x) = 0$ for $x < 0$, this equation is equivalent.

⟨*Sampling Inline Functions*⟩ +≡

```
Float LinearPDF(Float x, Float a, Float b) {
    if (x < 0 || x > 1)
        return 0;
    return 2 * Lerp(x, a, b) / (a + b);
}
```

Integrating the PDF gives the CDF, which is the quadratic function

$$P(x) = \frac{x(a(2-x) + bx)}{a+b}.$$

Inverting $\xi = P(X)$ gives a sampling recipe

$$X = \frac{a - \sqrt{(1 - \xi)a^2 + \xi b^2}}{a - b},$$

though note that in this form, the case $a = b$ gives an indeterminate result. The more stable formulation

$$X = \frac{\xi(a+b)}{a + \sqrt{(1 - \xi)a^2 + \xi b^2}}$$

computes the same result and is implemented here.

⟨*Sampling Inline Functions*⟩ +≡

```
Float SampleLinear(Float u, Float a, Float b) {
    if (u == 0 && a == 0) return 0;
    Float x = u * (a + b) / (a + std::sqrt(Lerp(u, Sqr(a), Sqr(b))));
    return std::min(x, OneMinusEpsilon);
}
```

One detail to note is the `std::min` call in the return statement, which ensures that the returned value is within the range [0, 1). Although the sampling algorithm generates values in that range given $\xi \in [0, 1)$, round-off error may cause the result to be equal to 1. Because some of the code that calls the sampling routines depends on the returned values being in the specified range, the sampling routines must ensure this is so.

In addition to providing functions that sample from a distribution and compute the PDF of a sample, pbrt usually also provides functions that invert sampling operations, returning the random sample ξ that corresponds to a value x. In the 1D case, this is equivalent to evaluating the CDF.

⟨*Sampling Inline Functions*⟩ +≡

```
Float InvertLinearSample(Float x, Float a, Float b) {
    return x * (a * (2 - x) + b * x) / (a + b);
}
```

2.4 TRANSFORMING BETWEEN DISTRIBUTIONS

Float 23
Lerp() 72
OneMinusEpsilon 470
Sqr() 1034

In describing the inversion method, we introduced a technique that generates samples according to some distribution by transforming canonical uniform random variables in a particular manner. Here, we will investigate the more general question of which distribution results when we transform samples from an arbitrary distribution to some other distribution with a function f. Understanding the effect of such transformations is useful for a few reasons, though here we will focus on how they allow us to derive multidimensional sampling algorithms.

Suppose we are given a random variable X drawn from some PDF $p(x)$ with CDF $P(x)$. Given a function $f(x)$ with $y = f(x)$, if we compute $Y = f(X)$, we would like to find the distribution of the new random variable Y. In this case, the function $f(x)$ must be a one-to-one transformation; if multiple values of x mapped to the same y value, then it would be impossible to unambiguously describe the probability density of a particular y value. A direct consequence of f being one-to-one is that its derivative must either be strictly greater than 0 or strictly less than 0, which implies that for a given x,

$$\Pr\{Y \le f(x)\} = \Pr\{X \le x\}.$$

From the definition of the CDF, Equation (2.3), we can see that

$$P_f(y) = P_f(f(x)) = P(x).$$

This relationship between CDFs leads directly to the relationship between their PDFs. If we assume that f's derivative is greater than 0, differentiating gives

$$p_f(y)\frac{\mathrm{d}f}{\mathrm{d}x} = p(x),$$

and so

$$p_f(y) = \left(\frac{\mathrm{d}f}{\mathrm{d}x}\right)^{-1} p(x).$$

In general, f's derivative is either strictly positive or strictly negative, and the relationship between the densities is

$$p_f(y) = \left|\frac{\mathrm{d}f}{\mathrm{d}x}\right|^{-1} p(x).$$

How can we use this formula? Suppose that $p(x) = 2x$ over the domain $[0, 1]$, and let $f(x) = \sin x$. What is the PDF of the random variable $Y = f(X)$? Because we know that $\mathrm{d}f/\mathrm{d}x = \cos x$,

$$p_f(y) = \frac{p(x)}{|\cos x|} = \frac{2x}{\cos x} = \frac{2 \arcsin y}{\sqrt{1 - y^2}}.$$

This procedure may seem backward—usually we have some PDF that we want to sample from, not a given transformation. For example, we might have X drawn from some $p(x)$ and would like to compute Y from some distribution $p_f(y)$. What transformation should we use? All we need is for the CDFs to be equal, or $P_f(y) = P(x)$, which immediately gives the transformation

$$f(x) = P_f^{-1}(P(x)).$$

This is a generalization of the inversion method, since if X were uniformly distributed over $[0, 1)$ then $P(x) = x$, and we have the same procedure as was introduced previously.

2.4.1 TRANSFORMATION IN MULTIPLE DIMENSIONS

In the general d-dimensional case, a similar derivation gives the analogous relationship between different densities. We will not show the derivation here; it follows the same form as the 1D case. Suppose we have a d-dimensional random variable X with density function $p(x)$. Now let $Y = T(X)$, where T is a bijection. In this case, the densities are related by

$$p_T(y) = p_T(T(x)) = \frac{p(x)}{|J_T(x)|},$$ (2.21)

where $|J_T|$ is the absolute value of the determinant of T's Jacobian matrix, which is

$$\begin{pmatrix} \partial T_1/\partial x_1 & \cdots & \partial T_1/\partial x_d \\ \vdots & \ddots & \vdots \\ \partial T_d/\partial x_1 & \cdots & \partial T_d/\partial x_d \end{pmatrix},$$

where subscripts index dimensions of $T(x)$ and x.

For a 2D example of the use of Equation (2.21), the polar transformation relates Cartesian (x, y) coordinates to a polar radius and angle,

$$x = r \cos \theta$$
$$y = r \sin \theta.$$

Suppose we draw samples from some density $p(r, \theta)$. What is the corresponding density $p(x, y)$? The Jacobian of this transformation is

$$J_T = \begin{pmatrix} \frac{\partial x}{\partial r} & \frac{\partial x}{\partial \theta} \\ \frac{\partial y}{\partial r} & \frac{\partial y}{\partial \theta} \end{pmatrix} = \begin{pmatrix} \cos \theta & -r \sin \theta \\ \sin \theta & r \cos \theta \end{pmatrix},$$

and the determinant is $r \left(\cos^2 \theta + \sin^2 \theta\right) = r$. So, $p(x, y) = p(r, \theta)/r$. Of course, this is backward from what we usually want—typically we start with a sampling strategy in Cartesian coordinates and want to transform it to one in polar coordinates. In that case, we would have

$$p(r, \theta) = r \, p(x, y).$$ (2.22)

In 3D, given the spherical coordinate representation of directions, Equation (3.7), the Jacobian of this transformation has determinant $|J_T| = r^2 \sin \theta$, so the corresponding density function is

$$p(r, \theta, \phi) = r^2 \sin \theta \, p(x, y, z).$$ (2.23)

This transformation is important since it helps us represent directions as points (x, y, z) on the unit sphere.

2.4.2 SAMPLING WITH MULTIDIMENSIONAL TRANSFORMATIONS

Suppose we have a 2D joint density function $p(x, y)$ that we wish to draw samples (X, Y) from. If the densities are independent, they can be expressed as the product of 1D densities

$$p(x, y) = p_x(x) \, p_y(y),$$

and random variables (X, Y) can be found by independently sampling X from p_x and Y from p_y. Many useful densities are not separable, however, so we will introduce the theory of how to sample from multidimensional distributions in the general case.

Given a 2D density function, the *marginal density function* $p(x)$ is obtained by "integrating out" one of the dimensions:

$$p(x) = \int p(x, y) \, \mathrm{d}y.$$ (2.24)

This can be thought of as the density function for X alone. More precisely, it is the average density for a particular x over *all* possible y values.

If we can draw a sample $X \sim p(x)$, then—using Equation (2.1)—we can see that in order to sample Y, we need to sample from the conditional probability density, $Y \sim p(y|x)$, which is given by:

$$p(y|x) = \frac{p(x, y)}{\int p(x, y) \, dy}.$$

Sampling from higher-dimensional distributions can be performed in a similar fashion, integrating out all but one of the dimensions, sampling that one, and then applying the same technique to the remaining conditional distribution, which has one fewer dimension.

Sampling the Bilinear Function

The bilinear function

$$f(x, y) = (1 - x)(1 - y)w_0 + x(1 - y)w_1 + y(1 - x)w_2 + xyw_3 \qquad \text{(2.25)}$$

interpolates between four values w_i at the four corners of $[0, 1]^2$. (w_0 is at $(0, 0)$, w_1 is at $(1, 0)$, w_2 at $(0, 1)$, and w_3 at $(1, 1)$.) After integration and normalization, we can find that its PDF is

$$p(x, y) = \frac{4f(x, y)}{w_0 + w_1 + w_2 + w_3}.$$

⟨*Sampling Inline Functions*⟩ +≡
```
Float BilinearPDF(Point2f p, pstd::span<const Float> w) {
    if (p.x < 0 || p.x > 1 || p.y < 0 || p.y > 1)
        return 0;
    if (w[0] + w[1] + w[2] + w[3] == 0)
        return 1;
    return 4 * ((1 - p[0]) * (1 - p[1]) * w[0] + p[0] * (1 - p[1]) * w[1] +
                (1 - p[0]) * p[1] * w[2] + p[0] * p[1] * w[3]) /
           (w[0] + w[1] + w[2] + w[3]);
}
```

The two dimensions of this function are not independent, so the sampling method samples a marginal distribution before sampling the resulting conditional distribution.

⟨*Sampling Inline Functions*⟩ +≡
```
Point2f SampleBilinear(Point2f u, pstd::span<const Float> w) {
    Point2f p;
    ⟨Sample y for bilinear marginal distribution 77⟩
    ⟨Sample x for bilinear conditional distribution 77⟩
    return p;
}
```

We can choose either x or y to be the marginal distribution. If we choose y and integrate out x, we find that

$$p(y) = \int_0^1 p(x, y) \, dx = 2\frac{(1 - y)(w_0 + w_1) + y(w_2 + w_3)}{w_0 + w_1 + w_2 + w_3}$$

$$\propto (1 - y)(w_0 + w_1) + y(w_2 + w_3).$$

$p(y)$ performs linear interpolation between two constant values, and so we can use `SampleLinear()` to sample from the simplified proportional function since it normalizes the associated PDF.

⟨*Sample y for bilinear marginal distribution*⟩ ≡   76
```
p.y = SampleLinear(u[1], w[0] + w[1], w[2] + w[3]);
```

Applying Equation (2.1) and again canceling out common factors, we have

$$p(x|y) = \frac{p(x, y)}{p(y)} \propto (1 - x)\left[(1 - y)w_0 + yw_2\right] + x\left[(1 - y)w_1 + yw_3\right],$$

which can also be sampled in x using `SampleLinear()`.

⟨*Sample x for bilinear conditional distribution*⟩ ≡   76
```
p.x = SampleLinear(u[0], Lerp(p.y, w[0], w[2]), Lerp(p.y, w[1], w[3]));
```

Because the bilinear sampling routine is based on the composition of two 1D linear sampling operations, it can be inverted by applying the inverses of those two operations in reverse order.

⟨*Sampling Inline Functions*⟩ +≡
```
Point2f InvertBilinearSample(Point2f p, pstd::span<const Float> w) {
    return {InvertLinearSample(p.x, Lerp(p.y, w[0], w[2]),
                                Lerp(p.y, w[1], w[3])),
            InvertLinearSample(p.y, w[0] + w[1], w[2] + w[3])};
}
```

See Section A.5 for further examples of multidimensional sampling algorithms, including techniques for sampling directions on the unit sphere and hemisphere, sampling unit disks, and other useful distributions for rendering.

FURTHER READING

The Monte Carlo method was introduced soon after the development of the digital computer by Stanislaw Ulam and John von Neumann (Ulam et al. 1947), though it also seems to have been independently invented by Enrico Fermi (Metropolis 1987). An early paper on Monte Carlo was written by Metropolis and Ulam (1949).

Many books have been written on Monte Carlo integration. Hammersley and Handscomb (1964), Spanier and Gelbard (1969), and Kalos and Whitlock (1986) are classic references. More recent books on the topic include those by Sobol' (1994), Fishman (1996), and Liu (2001). We have also found Owen's in-progress book (2019) to be an invaluable resource. Motwani and Raghavan (1995) have written an excellent introduction to the broader topic of randomized algorithms.

Most of the functions of interest in rendering are nonnegative; applying importance sampling to negative functions requires special care. A straightforward option is to define a sampling distribution that is proportional to the absolute value of the function. See also Owen and Zhou (2000) for a more effective sampling approach for such functions.

Float 23
InvertLinearSample() 73
Lerp() 72
Point2f 92
SampleLinear() 73

Multiple importance sampling was developed by Veach and Guibas (Veach and Guibas 1995; Veach 1997). Normally, a predetermined number of samples are taken using each sampling technique; see Pajot et al. (2011) and Lu et al. (2013) for approaches to adaptively distributing the samples over strategies in an effort to reduce variance by choosing those that are the best match to the integrand. Grittmann et al. (2019) tracked the variance of each sampling technique and then dynamically adjusted the MIS weights accordingly. The MIS compensation approach was developed by Karlík et al. (2019).

Sbert and collaborators (2016, 2017, 2018) have performed further variance analysis on MIS estimators and have developed improved methods based on allocating samples according to the variance and cost of each technique. Kondapaneni et al. (2019) considered the generalization of MIS to include negative weights and derived optimal estimators in that setting. West et al. (2020) considered the case where a continuum of sampling techniques are available and derived an optimal MIS estimator for that case, and Grittmann et al. (2021) have developed improved MIS estimators when correlation is present among samples (as is the case, for example, with bidirectional light transport algorithms).

Heitz (2020) described an inversion-based sampling method that can be applied when CDF inversion of a 1D function is not possible. It is based on sampling from a second function that approximates the first and then using a second random variable to adjust the sample to match the original function's distribution. An interesting alternative to manually deriving sampling techniques was described by Anderson et al. (2017), who developed a domain-specific language for sampling where probabilities are automatically computed, given the implementation of a sampling algorithm. They showed the effectiveness of their approach with succinct implementations of a number of tricky sampling techniques.

The numerically stable sampling technique used in `SampleLinear()` is an application of Muller's method (1956) due to Heitz (2020).

In applications of Monte Carlo in graphics, the integrand is often a product of factors, where no sampling distribution is available that fits the full product. While multiple importance sampling can give reasonable results in this case, at least minimizing variance from ineffective sampling techniques, sampling the full product is still preferable. Talbot et al. (2005) applied *importance resampling* to this problem, taking multiple samples from some distribution and then choosing among them with probability proportional to the full integrand. More recently, Hart et al. (2020) presented a simple technique based on warping uniform samples that can be used to approximate product sampling. For more information on this topic, see also the "Further Reading" sections of Chapters 13 and 14, which discuss product sampling approaches in the context of specific light transport algorithms.

Debugging Monte Carlo algorithms can be challenging, since it is their behavior in expectation that determines their correctness: it may be difficult to tell if the program execution for a particular sample is correct. Statistical tests can be an effective approach for checking their correctness. See the papers by Subr and Arvo (2007a) and by Jung et al. (2020) for applicable techniques.

See also the "Further Reading" section in Appendix A, which has information about the sampling algorithms implemented there as well as related approaches.

EXERCISES

● 2.1   Write a program that compares Monte Carlo and one or more alternative numerical integration techniques. Structure this program so that it is easy to replace the particular function being integrated. Verify that the different techniques compute the same result (given a sufficient number of samples for each of them). Modify your program so that it draws samples from distributions other than the uniform distribution for the Monte Carlo estimate, and verify that it still computes the correct result when the correct estimator, Equation (2.7), is used. (Make sure that any alternative distributions you use have nonzero probability of choosing any value of x where $f(x) > 0$.)

SampleLinear() 73

❶ 2.2   Write a program that computes unbiased Monte Carlo estimates of the integral of a given function. Compute an estimate of the variance of the estimates by performing a series of trials with successively more samples and computing the mean squared error for each one. Demonstrate numerically that variance decreases at a rate of $O(n)$.

❷ 2.3   The algorithm for sampling the linear interpolation function in Section 2.3.2 implicitly assumes that $a, b \geq 0$ and that thus $f(x) \geq 0$. If f is negative, then the importance sampling PDF should be proportional to $|f(x)|$. Generalize Sample Linear() and the associated PDF and inversion functions to handle the case where f is always negative as well as the case where it crosses zero due to a and b having different signs.

SampleLinear() 73

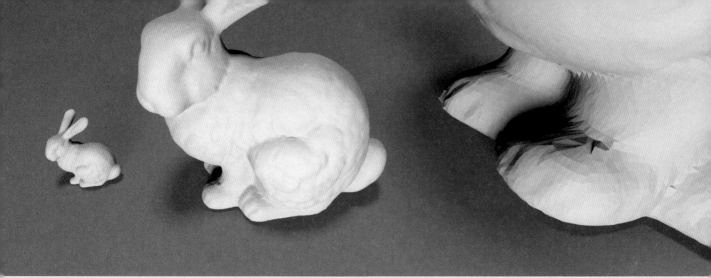

CHAPTER THREE

03 GEOMETRY AND TRANSFORMATIONS

Almost all nontrivial graphics programs are built on a foundation of geometric classes that represent mathematical constructs like points, vectors, and rays. Because these classes are ubiquitous throughout the system, good abstractions and efficient implementations are critical. This chapter presents the interface to and implementation of pbrt's geometric foundation. Note that these are not the classes that represent the actual scene geometry (triangles, spheres, etc.); those classes are the topic of Chapter 6.

3.1 COORDINATE SYSTEMS

As is typical in computer graphics, pbrt represents three-dimensional points, vectors, and normal vectors with three coordinate values: x, y, and z. These values are meaningless without a *coordinate system* that defines the origin of the space and gives three linearly independent vectors that define the x, y, and z axes of the space. Together, the origin and three vectors are called the *frame* that defines the coordinate system. Given an arbitrary point or direction in 3D, its (x, y, z) coordinate values depend on its relationship to the frame. Figure 3.1 shows an example that illustrates this idea in 2D.

In the general n-dimensional case, a frame's origin p_o and its n linearly independent basis vectors define an n-dimensional *affine space*. All vectors $\mathbf{v}$ in the space can be expressed as a linear combination of the basis vectors. Given a vector $\mathbf{v}$ and the basis vectors $\mathbf{v}_i$, there is a unique set of scalar values s_i such that

$$\mathbf{v} = s_1\mathbf{v}_1 + \cdots + s_n\mathbf{v}_n.$$

The scalars s_i are the *representation* of $\mathbf{v}$ with respect to the basis $\{\mathbf{v}_1, \mathbf{v}_2, \ldots, \mathbf{v}_n\}$ and are the coordinate values that we store with the vector. Similarly, for all points p, there are unique scalars s_i such that the point can be expressed in terms of the origin p_o and the basis vectors

$$p = p_o + s_1\mathbf{v}_1 + \cdots + s_n\mathbf{v}_n.$$

Thus, although points and vectors are both represented by x, y, and z coordinates in 3D, they are distinct mathematical entities and are not freely interchangeable.

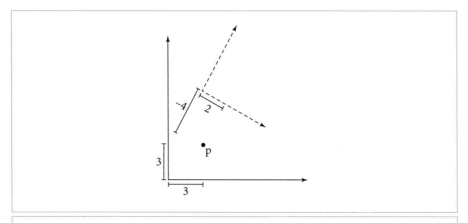

Figure 3.1: In 2D, the (x, y) coordinates of a point p are defined by the relationship of the point to a particular 2D coordinate system. Here, two coordinate systems are shown; the point might have coordinates (3, 3) with respect to the coordinate system with its coordinate axes drawn in solid lines but have coordinates (2, −4) with respect to the coordinate system with dashed axes. In either case, the 2D point p is at the same absolute position in space.

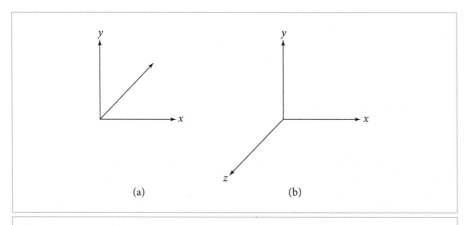

Figure 3.2: (a) In a left-handed coordinate system, the z axis points into the page when the x and y axes are oriented with x pointing to the right and y pointing up. (b) In a right-handed system, the z axis points out of the page.

This definition of points and vectors in terms of coordinate systems reveals a paradox: to define a frame we need a point and a set of vectors, but we can only meaningfully talk about points and vectors with respect to a particular frame. Therefore, in three dimensions we need a *standard frame* with origin (0, 0, 0) and basis vectors (1, 0, 0), (0, 1, 0), and (0, 0, 1). All other frames will be defined with respect to this canonical coordinate system, which we call *world space*.

3.1.1 COORDINATE SYSTEM HANDEDNESS

There are two different ways that the three coordinate axes can be arranged, as shown in Figure 3.2. Given perpendicular x and y coordinate axes, the z axis can point in one of two directions. These two choices are called *left-handed* and *right-handed*. The choice between the two is arbitrary but has a number of implications for how some of the geometric operations throughout the system are implemented. pbrt uses a left-handed coordinate system.

3.2 n-TUPLE BASE CLASSES

pbrt's classes that represent two- and three-dimensional points, vectors, and surface normals are all based on general *n*-tuple classes, whose definitions we will start with. The definitions of these classes as well as the types that inherit from them are defined in the files util/vecmath.h and util/vecmath.cpp under the main pbrt source directory.

Although this and the following few sections define classes that have simple logic in most of their method implementations, they make more use of advanced C++ programming techniques than we generally use in pbrt. Doing so reduces the amount of redundant code needed to implement the point, vector, and normal classes and makes them extensible in ways that will be useful later. If you are not a C++ expert, it is fine to gloss over these details and to focus on understanding the functionality that these classes provide. Alternatively, you could use this as an opportunity to learn more corners of the language.

Both Tuple2 and Tuple3 are template classes. They are templated not just on a type used for storing each coordinate's value but also on the type of the class that inherits from it to define a specific two- or three-dimensional type. If one has not seen it before, this is a strange construction: normally, inheritance is sufficient, and the base class has no need to know the type of the subclass.[1] In this case, having the base class know the child class's type makes it possible to write generic methods that operate on and return values of the child type, as we will see shortly.

⟨*Tuple2 Definition*⟩ ≡
```
template <template <typename> class Child, typename T>
class Tuple2 {
  public:
    ⟨Tuple2 Public Methods⟩
    ⟨Tuple2 Public Members 83⟩
};
```

The two-dimensional tuple stores its values as x and y and makes them available as public member variables. The pair of curly braces after each one ensures that the member variables are *default initialized*; for numeric types, this initializes them to 0.

⟨*Tuple2 Public Members*⟩ ≡   83
```
T x{}, y{};
```

We will focus on the Tuple3 implementation for the remainder of this section. Tuple2 is almost entirely the same but with one fewer coordinate.

⟨*Tuple3 Definition*⟩ ≡
```
template <template <typename> class Child, typename T>
class Tuple3 {
  public:
    ⟨Tuple3 Public Methods 84⟩
    ⟨Tuple3 Public Members 84⟩
};
```

By default, the (x, y, z) values are set to zero, although the user of the class can optionally supply values for each of the components. If the user does supply values, the constructor checks that none of them has the floating-point "not a number" (NaN) value using the

Tuple3 83

---

1   This form of inheritance is often referred to as the *curiously recurring template pattern* (CRTP) in C++.

DCHECK() macro. When compiled in optimized mode, this macro disappears from the compiled code, saving the expense of verifying this case. NaNs almost certainly indicate a bug in the system; if a NaN is generated by some computation, we would like to catch it as soon as possible in order to make isolating its source easier. (See Section 6.8.1 for more discussion of NaN values.)

⟨*Tuple3 Public Methods*⟩ ≡   83
```
Tuple3(T x, T y, T z) : x(x), y(y), z(z) { DCHECK(!HasNaN()); }
```

Readers who have been exposed to object-oriented design may question our decision to make the tuple component values publicly accessible. Typically, member variables are only accessible inside their class, and external code that wishes to access or modify the contents of a class must do so through a well-defined API that may include selector and mutator functions. Although we are sympathetic to the principle of encapsulation, it is not appropriate here. The purpose of selector and mutator functions is to hide the class's internal implementation details. In the case of three-dimensional tuples, hiding this basic part of their design gains nothing and adds bulk to code that uses them.

⟨*Tuple3 Public Members*⟩ ≡   83
```
T x{}, y{}, z{};
```

The HasNaN() test checks each component individually.

⟨*Tuple3 Public Methods*⟩ +≡   83
```
bool HasNaN() const { return IsNaN(x) || IsNaN(y) || IsNaN(z); }
```

An alternate implementation of these two tuple classes would be to have a single template class that is also parameterized with an integer number of dimensions and to represent the coordinates with an array of that many T values. While this approach would reduce the total amount of code by eliminating the need for separate two- and three-dimensional tuple types, individual components of the vector could not be accessed as v.x and so forth. We believe that, in this case, a bit more code in the vector implementations is worthwhile in return for more transparent access to components. However, some routines do find it useful to be able to easily loop over the components of vectors; the tuple classes also provide a C++ operator to index into the components so that, given an instance v, v[0] == v.x and so forth.

⟨*Tuple3 Public Methods*⟩ +≡   83
```
T operator[](int i) const {
    if (i == 0) return x;
    if (i == 1) return y;
    return z;
}
```

If the tuple type is non-const, then indexing returns a reference, allowing components of the tuple to be set.

⟨*Tuple3 Public Methods*⟩ +≡   83
```
T &operator[](int i) {
    if (i == 0) return x;
    if (i == 1) return y;
    return z;
}
```

We can now turn to the implementation of arithmetic operations that operate on the values stored in a tuple. Their code is fairly dense. For example, here is the method that adds together two three-tuples of some type (for example, Child might be Vector3, the forthcoming three-dimensional vector type).

⟨*Tuple3 Public Methods*⟩ +≡   83
```
template <typename U>
auto operator+(Child<U> c) const -> Child<decltype(T{} + U{})> {
    return {x + c.x, y + c.y, z + c.z};
}
```

There are a few things to note in the implementation of operator+. By virtue of being a template method based on another type U, it supports adding two elements of the same Child template type, though they may use different types for storing their components (T and U in the code here). However, because the base type of the method's parameter is Child, it is only possible to add two values of the same child type using this method. If this method instead took a Tuple3 for the parameter, then it would silently allow addition with any type that inherited from Tuple3, which might not be intended.

There are two interesting things in the declaration of the return type, to the right of the -> operator after the method's parameter list. First, the base return type is Child; thus, if one adds two Vector3 values, the returned value will be of Vector3 type. This, too, eliminates a class of potential errors: if a Tuple3 was returned, then it would for example be possible to add two Vector3s and assign the result to a Point3, which is nonsensical. Finally, the component type of the returned type is determined based on the type of an expression adding values of types T and U. Thus, this method follows C++'s standard type promotion rules: if a Vector3 that stored integer values is added to one that stores Floats, the result is a Vector3 storing Floats.

In the interests of space, we will not include the other Tuple3 arithmetic operators here, nor will we include the various other utility functions that perform component-wise operations on them. The full list of capabilities provided by Tuple2 and Tuple3 is:

- The basic arithmetic operators of per-component addition, subtraction, and negation, including the "in place" (e.g., operator+=) forms of them.
- Component-wise multiplication and division by a scalar value, including "in place" variants.
- Abs(a), which returns a value where the absolute value of each component of the tuple type has been taken.
- Ceil(a) and Floor(a), which return a value where the components have been rounded up or down to the nearest integer value, respectively.
- Lerp(t, a, b), which returns the result of the linear interpolation (1-t)*a + t*b.
- FMA(a, b, c), which takes three tuples and returns the result of a component-wise fused multiply-add a*b + c.
- Min(a, b) and Max(a, b), which respectively return the component-wise minimum and maximum of the two given tuples.
- MinComponentValue(a) and MaxComponentValue(a), which respectively return the minimum and maximum value of the tuple's components.
- MinComponentIndex(a) and MaxComponentIndex(a), which respectively return the zero-based index of the tuple element with minimum or maximum value.
- Permute(a, perm), which returns the permutation of the tuple according to an array of indices.
- HProd(a), which returns the horizontal product—the component values multiplied together.

Tuple2 83
Tuple3 83

3.3 VECTORS

pbrt provides both 2D and 3D vector classes that are based on the corresponding two- and three-dimensional tuple classes. Both vector types are themselves parameterized by the type of the underlying vector element, thus making it easy to instantiate vectors of both integer and floating-point types.

⟨*Vector2 Definition*⟩ ≡
```
template <typename T>
class Vector2 : public Tuple2<Vector2, T> {
  public:
      ⟨Vector2 Public Methods⟩
};
```

Two-dimensional vectors of Floats and integers are widely used, so we will define aliases for those two types.

⟨*Vector2* Definitions*⟩ ≡
```
using Vector2f = Vector2<Float>;
using Vector2i = Vector2<int>;
```

As with Tuple2, we will not include any further details of Vector2 since it is very similar to Vector3, which we will discuss in more detail.

A Vector3's tuple of component values gives its representation in terms of the x, y, and z (in 3D) axes of the space it is defined in. The individual components of a 3D vector $\mathbf{v}$ will be written $\mathbf{v}_x$, $\mathbf{v}_y$, and $\mathbf{v}_z$.

⟨*Vector3 Definition*⟩ ≡
```
template <typename T>
class Vector3 : public Tuple3<Vector3, T> {
  public:
      ⟨Vector3 Public Methods 86⟩
};
```

We also define type aliases for two commonly used three-dimensional vector types.

⟨*Vector3* Definitions*⟩ ≡
```
using Vector3f = Vector3<Float>;
using Vector3i = Vector3<int>;
```

Vector3 provides a few constructors, including a default constructor (not shown here) and one that allows specifying each component value directly.

⟨*Vector3 Public Methods*⟩ ≡   **86**
```
Vector3(T x, T y, T z) : Tuple3<pbrt::Vector3, T>(x, y, z) {}
```

There is also a constructor that takes a Vector3 with a different element type. It is qualified with explicit so that it is not unintentionally used in automatic type conversions; a cast must be used to signify the intent of the type conversion.

⟨*Vector3 Public Methods*⟩ +≡   **86**
```
template <typename U>
explicit Vector3(Vector3<U> v)
    : Tuple3<pbrt::Vector3, T>(T(v.x), T(v.y), T(v.z)) {}
```

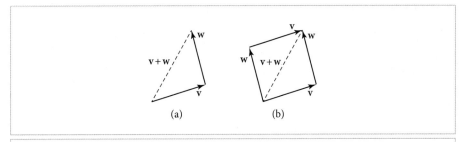

Figure 3.3: (a) Vector addition: $\mathbf{v} + \mathbf{w}$. (b) Notice that the sum $\mathbf{v} + \mathbf{w}$ forms the diagonal of the parallelogram formed by $\mathbf{v}$ and $\mathbf{w}$, which shows the commutativity of vector addition: $\mathbf{v} + \mathbf{w} = \mathbf{w} + \mathbf{v}$.

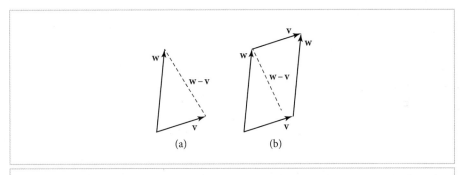

Figure 3.4: (a) Vector subtraction. (b) If we consider the parallelogram formed by two vectors, the diagonals are given by $\mathbf{w} - \mathbf{v}$ (dashed line) and $-\mathbf{v} - \mathbf{w}$ (not shown).

Finally, constructors are provided to convert from the forthcoming `Point3` and `Normal3` types. Their straightforward implementations are not included here. These, too, are `explicit` to help ensure that they are only used in situations where the conversion is meaningful.

⟨*Vector3 Public Methods*⟩ +≡   86
```
template <typename U>
explicit Vector3(Point3<U> p);
template <typename U>
explicit Vector3(Normal3<U> n);
```

Addition and subtraction of vectors is performed component-wise, via methods from `Tuple3`. The usual geometric interpretation of vector addition and subtraction is shown in Figures 3.3 and 3.4. A vector's length can be changed via component-wise multiplication or division by a scalar. These capabilities, too, are provided by `Tuple3` and so do not require any additional implementation in the `Vector3` class.

3.3.1 NORMALIZATION AND VECTOR LENGTH

It is often necessary to *normalize* a vector—that is, to compute a new vector pointing in the same direction but with unit length. A normalized vector is often called a *unit vector*. The notation used in this book for normalized vectors is that $\hat{\mathbf{v}}$ is the normalized version of $\mathbf{v}$. Before getting to normalization, we will start with computing vectors' lengths.

The squared length of a vector is given by the sum of the squares of its component values.

⟨*Vector3 Inline Functions*⟩ ≡
```
template <typename T>
T LengthSquared(Vector3<T> v) { return Sqr(v.x) + Sqr(v.y) + Sqr(v.z); }
```

Moving on to computing the length of a vector leads us to a quandary: what type should the Length() function return? For example, if the Vector3 stores an integer type, that type is probably not an appropriate return type since the vector's length will not necessarily be integer-valued. In that case, Float would be a better choice, though we should not standardize on Float for everything, because given a Vector3 of double-precision values, we should return the length as a double as well. Continuing our journey through advanced C++, we turn to a technique known as *type traits* to solve this dilemma.

First, we define a general TupleLength template class that holds a type definition, type. The default is set here to be Float.

⟨*TupleLength Definition*⟩ ≡
```
template <typename T>
struct TupleLength { using type = Float; };
```

For Vector3s of doubles, we also provide a template specialization that defines double as the type for length given double for the element type.

⟨*TupleLength Definition*⟩ +≡
```
template <>
struct TupleLength<double> { using type = double; };
```

Now we can implement Length(), using TupleLength to determine which type to return. Note that the return type cannot be specified before the function declaration is complete since the type T is not known until the function parameters have been parsed. Therefore, the function is declared as auto with the return type specified after its parameter list.

⟨*Vector3 Inline Functions*⟩ +≡
```
template <typename T>
auto Length(Vector3<T> v) -> typename TupleLength<T>::type {
    using std::sqrt;
    return sqrt(LengthSquared(v));
}
```

There is one more C++ subtlety in these few lines of code: the reader may wonder, why have a using std::sqrt declaration in the implementation of Length() and then call sqrt(), rather than just calling std::sqrt() directly? That construction is used because we would like to be able to use component types T that do not have overloaded versions of std::sqrt() available to them. For example, we will later make use of Vector3s that store intervals of values for each component using a forthcoming Interval class. With the way the code is written here, if std::sqrt() supports the type T, the std variant of the function is called. If not, then so long as we have defined a function named sqrt() that takes our custom type, that version will be used.

With all of this in hand, the implementation of Normalize() is thankfully now trivial. The use of auto for the return type ensures that if for example Normalize() is called with a vector with integer components, then the returned vector type has Float components according to type conversion from the division operator.

⟨*Vector3 Inline Functions*⟩ +≡
```
template <typename T>
auto Normalize(Vector3<T> v) { return v / Length(v); }
```

3.3.2 DOT AND CROSS PRODUCT

Two useful operations on vectors are the dot product (also known as the scalar or inner product) and the cross product. For two 3D vectors **v** and **w**, their *dot product* (**v** · **w**) is defined as

$$\mathbf{v}_x\mathbf{w}_x + \mathbf{v}_y\mathbf{w}_y + \mathbf{v}_z\mathbf{w}_z,$$

and the implementation follows directly.

⟨*Vector3 Inline Functions*⟩ +≡
```
template <typename T>
T Dot(Vector3<T> v, Vector3<T> w) {
    return v.x * w.x + v.y * w.y + v.z * w.z;
}
```

A few basic properties directly follow from the definition of the dot product. For example, if **u**, **v**, and **w** are vectors and *s* is a scalar value, then:

$$(\mathbf{u} \cdot \mathbf{v}) = (\mathbf{v} \cdot \mathbf{u})$$
$$(s\mathbf{u} \cdot \mathbf{v}) = s(\mathbf{u} \cdot \mathbf{v})$$
$$(\mathbf{u} \cdot (\mathbf{v} + \mathbf{w})) = (\mathbf{u} \cdot \mathbf{v}) + (\mathbf{u} \cdot \mathbf{w}).$$

The dot product has a simple relationship to the angle between the two vectors:

$$(\mathbf{v} \cdot \mathbf{w}) = \|\mathbf{v}\|\,\|\mathbf{w}\|\cos\theta, \tag{3.1}$$

where θ is the angle between **v** and **w**, and $\|\mathbf{v}\|$ denotes the length of the vector **v**. It follows from this that (**v** · **w**) is zero if and only if **v** and **w** are perpendicular, provided that neither **v** nor **w** is *degenerate*—equal to (0, 0, 0). A set of two or more mutually perpendicular vectors is said to be *orthogonal*. An orthogonal set of unit vectors is called *orthonormal*.

It follows from Equation (3.1) that if **v** and **w** are unit vectors, their dot product is the cosine of the angle between them. As the cosine of the angle between two vectors often needs to be computed for rendering, we will frequently make use of this property.

If we would like to find the angle between two normalized vectors, we could use the standard library's inverse cosine function, passing it the value of the dot product between the two vectors. However, that approach can suffer from a loss of accuracy when the two vectors are nearly parallel or facing in nearly opposite directions. The following reformulation does more of its computation with values close to the origin where there is more floating-point precision, giving a more accurate result.

⟨*Vector3 Inline Functions*⟩ +≡
```
template <typename T>
Float AngleBetween(Vector3<T> v1, Vector3<T> v2) {
    if (Dot(v1, v2) < 0)
        return Pi - 2 * SafeASin(Length(v1 + v2) / 2);
    else
        return 2 * SafeASin(Length(v2 - v1) / 2);
}
```

We will frequently need to compute the absolute value of the dot product as well. The AbsDot() function does this for us so that a separate call to std::abs() is not necessary in that case.

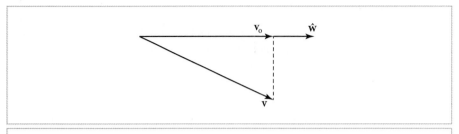

Figure 3.5: The orthogonal projection of a vector $\mathbf{v}$ onto a normalized vector $\hat{\mathbf{w}}$ gives a vector $\mathbf{v}_o$ that is parallel to $\hat{\mathbf{w}}$. The difference vector, $\mathbf{v} - \mathbf{v}_o$, shown here as a dashed line, is perpendicular to $\hat{\mathbf{w}}$.

⟨*Vector3 Inline Functions*⟩ +≡
```
template <typename T>
T AbsDot(Vector3<T> v1, Vector3<T> v2) { return std::abs(Dot(v1, v2)); }
```

A useful operation on vectors that is based on the dot product is the *Gram–Schmidt* process, which transforms a set of non-orthogonal vectors that form a basis into orthogonal vectors that span the same basis. It is based on successive application of the *orthogonal projection* of a vector $\mathbf{v}$ onto a normalized vector $\hat{\mathbf{w}}$, which is given by $(\mathbf{v} \cdot \hat{\mathbf{w}})\hat{\mathbf{w}}$ (see Figure 3.5). The orthogonal projection can be used to compute a new vector

$$\mathbf{v}_\perp = \mathbf{v} - (\mathbf{v} \cdot \hat{\mathbf{w}})\hat{\mathbf{w}} \qquad [3.2]$$

that is orthogonal to $\mathbf{w}$. An advantage of computing $\mathbf{v}_\perp$ in this way is that $\mathbf{v}_\perp$ and $\mathbf{w}$ span the same subspace as $\mathbf{v}$ and $\mathbf{w}$ did.

The GramSchmidt() function implements Equation (3.2); it expects the vector w to already be normalized.

⟨*Vector3 Inline Functions*⟩ +≡
```
template <typename T>
Vector3<T> GramSchmidt(Vector3<T> v, Vector3<T> w) {
    return v - Dot(v, w) * w;
}
```

The *cross product* is another useful operation for 3D vectors. Given two vectors in 3D, the cross product $\mathbf{v} \times \mathbf{w}$ is a vector that is perpendicular to both of them. Given orthogonal vectors $\mathbf{v}$ and $\mathbf{w}$, then $\mathbf{v} \times \mathbf{w}$ is defined to be a vector such that $(\mathbf{v}, \mathbf{w}, \mathbf{v} \times \mathbf{w})$ form an orthogonal coordinate system.

The cross product is defined as:

$$(\mathbf{v} \times \mathbf{w})_x = \mathbf{v}_y \mathbf{w}_z - \mathbf{v}_z \mathbf{w}_y$$
$$(\mathbf{v} \times \mathbf{w})_y = \mathbf{v}_z \mathbf{w}_x - \mathbf{v}_x \mathbf{w}_z$$
$$(\mathbf{v} \times \mathbf{w})_z = \mathbf{v}_x \mathbf{w}_y - \mathbf{v}_y \mathbf{w}_x.$$

A way to remember this is to compute the determinant of the matrix:

$$\mathbf{v} \times \mathbf{w} = \begin{vmatrix} i & j & k \\ \mathbf{v}_x & \mathbf{v}_y & \mathbf{v}_z \\ \mathbf{w}_x & \mathbf{w}_y & \mathbf{w}_z \end{vmatrix},$$

where i, j, and k represent the axes $(1, 0, 0)$, $(0, 1, 0)$, and $(0, 0, 1)$, respectively. Note that this equation is merely a memory aid and not a rigorous mathematical construction, since the matrix entries are a mix of scalars and vectors.

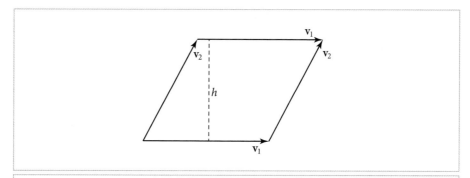

Figure 3.6: The area of a parallelogram with edges given by vectors $\mathbf{v}_1$ and $\mathbf{v}_2$ is equal to $\|\mathbf{v}_1\|h$. From Equation (3.3), the length of the cross product of $\mathbf{v}_1$ and $\mathbf{v}_2$ is equal to the product of the two vector lengths times the sine of the angle between them—the parallelogram area.

The cross product implementation here uses the `DifferenceOfProducts()` function that is introduced in Section B.2.9. Given values a, b, c, and d, it computes a*b-c*d in a way that maintains more floating-point accuracy than a direct implementation of that expression would. This concern is not a theoretical one: previous versions of pbrt have resorted to using double precision for the implementation of `Cross()` so that numerical error would not lead to artifacts in rendered images. Using `DifferenceOfProducts()` is a better solution since it can operate entirely in single precision while still computing a result with low error.

⟨*Vector3 Inline Functions*⟩ +≡

```
template <typename T>
Vector3<T> Cross(Vector3<T> v, Vector3<T> w) {
    return {DifferenceOfProducts(v.y, w.z, v.z, w.y),
            DifferenceOfProducts(v.z, w.x, v.x, w.z),
            DifferenceOfProducts(v.x, w.y, v.y, w.x)};
}
```

From the definition of the cross product, we can derive

$$\|\mathbf{v}\times\mathbf{w}\| = \|\mathbf{v}\|\,\|\mathbf{w}\|\,|\sin\theta|, \tag{3.3}$$

where θ is the angle between $\mathbf{v}$ and $\mathbf{w}$. An important implication of this is that the cross product of two perpendicular unit vectors is itself a unit vector. Note also that the result of the cross product is a degenerate vector if $\mathbf{v}$ and $\mathbf{w}$ are parallel.

This definition also shows a convenient way to compute the area of a parallelogram (Figure 3.6). If the two edges of the parallelogram are given by vectors $\mathbf{v}_1$ and $\mathbf{v}_2$, and it has height h, the area is given by $\|\mathbf{v}_1\|h$. Since $h = \sin\theta\|\mathbf{v}_2\|$, we can use Equation (3.3) to see that the area is $\|\mathbf{v}_1\times\mathbf{v}_2\|$.

3.3.3 COORDINATE SYSTEM FROM A VECTOR

We will sometimes find it useful to construct a local coordinate system given only a single normalized 3D vector. To do so, we must find two additional normalized vectors such that all three vectors are mutually perpendicular.

Given a vector $\mathbf{v}$, it can be shown that the two vectors

$$\left(\frac{1 - \mathbf{v}_x^2}{1 + \mathbf{v}_z}, -\frac{\mathbf{v}_x\mathbf{v}_y}{1 + \mathbf{v}_z}, -\mathbf{v}_x\right) \text{ and } \left(-\frac{\mathbf{v}_x\mathbf{v}_y}{1 + \mathbf{v}_z}, \frac{1 - \mathbf{v}_y^2}{1 + \mathbf{v}_z}, -\mathbf{v}_y\right)$$

fulfill these conditions. However, computing those properties directly has high error when $v_z \approx -1$ due to a loss of accuracy when $1/(1 + v_z)$ is calculated. A reformulation of that computation, used in the following implementation, addresses that issue.

⟨*Vector3 Inline Functions*⟩ +≡
```
template <typename T>
void CoordinateSystem(Vector3<T> v1, Vector3<T> *v2, Vector3<T> *v3) {
    Float sign = pstd::copysign(Float(1), v1.z);
    Float a = -1 / (sign + v1.z);
    Float b = v1.x * v1.y * a;
    *v2 = Vector3<T>(1 + sign * Sqr(v1.x) * a, sign * b, -sign * v1.x);
    *v3 = Vector3<T>(b, sign + Sqr(v1.y) * a, -v1.y);
}
```

3.4 POINTS

A point is a zero-dimensional location in 2D or 3D space. The Point2 and Point3 classes in pbrt represent points in the obvious way: using x, y, z (in 3D) coordinates with respect to a coordinate system. Although the same representation is used for vectors, the fact that a point represents a position whereas a vector represents a direction leads to a number of important differences in how they are treated. Points are denoted in text by p.

In this section, we will continue the approach of only including implementations of the 3D point methods for the Point3 class here.

⟨*Point3 Definition*⟩ ≡
```
template <typename T>
class Point3 : public Tuple3<Point3, T> {
  public:
    ⟨Point3 Public Methods 92⟩
};
```

As with vectors, it is helpful to have shorter type names for commonly used point types.

⟨*Point3* Definitions*⟩ ≡
```
using Point3f = Point3<Float>;
using Point3i = Point3<int>;
```

It is also useful to be able to convert a point with one element type (e.g., a Point3f) to a point of another one (e.g., Point3i) as well as to be able to convert a point to a vector with a different underlying element type. The following constructor and conversion operator provide these conversions. Both also require an explicit cast, to make it clear in source code when they are being used.

⟨*Point3 Public Methods*⟩ ≡   92
```
template <typename U>
explicit Point3(Point3<U> p)
    : Tuple3<pbrt::Point3, T>(T(p.x), T(p.y), T(p.z)) {}
template <typename U>
explicit Point3(Vector3<U> v)
    : Tuple3<pbrt::Point3, T>(T(v.x), T(v.y), T(v.z)) {}
```

Float 23
Point3 92
Sqr() 1034
Tuple3 83
Vector3 86

There are certain Point3 methods that either return or take a Vector3. For instance, one can add a vector to a point, offsetting it in the given direction to obtain a new point. Analogous methods, not included in the text, also allow subtracting a vector from a point.

Figure 3.7: Obtaining the Vector between Two Points. The vector $\mathbf{v} = \mathrm{p}' - \mathrm{p}$ is given by the component-wise subtraction of the points p' and p.

⟨*Point3 Public Methods*⟩ +≡   92
```
template <typename U>
auto operator+(Vector3<U> v) const -> Point3<decltype(T{} + U{})> {
    return {x + v.x, y + v.y, z + v.z};
}
template <typename U>
Point3<T> &operator+=(Vector3<U> v) {
    x += v.x;    y += v.y;    z += v.z;
    return *this;
}
```

Alternately, one can subtract one point from another, obtaining the vector between them, as shown in Figure 3.7.

⟨*Point3 Public Methods*⟩ +≡   92
```
template <typename U>
auto operator-(Point3<U> p) const -> Vector3<decltype(T{} - U{})> {
    return {x - p.x, y - p.y, z - p.z};
}
```

The distance between two points can be computed by subtracting them to compute the vector between them and then finding the length of that vector. Note that we can just use auto for the return type and let it be set according to the return type of Length(); there is no need to use the TupleLength type trait to find that type.

⟨*Point3 Inline Functions*⟩ ≡
```
template <typename T>
auto Distance(Point3<T> p1, Point3<T> p2) { return Length(p1 - p2); }
```

The squared distance between two points can be similarly computed using LengthSquared().

⟨*Point3 Inline Functions*⟩ +≡
```
template <typename T>
auto DistanceSquared(Point3<T> p1, Point3<T> p2) {
    return LengthSquared(p1 - p2);
}
```

3.5 NORMALS

A *surface normal* (or just *normal*) is a vector that is perpendicular to a surface at a particular position. It can be defined as the cross product of any two nonparallel vectors that are tangent to the surface at a point. Although normals are superficially similar to vectors, it is important to distinguish between the two of them: because normals are defined in terms of their relationship to a particular surface, they behave differently than vectors in some situations, particularly when applying transformations. (That difference is discussed in Section 3.10.)

⟨*Normal3 Definition*⟩ ≡
```
template <typename T>
class Normal3 : public Tuple3<Normal3, T> {
  public:
    ⟨Normal3 Public Methods 94⟩
};
```

⟨*Normal3 Definition*⟩ +≡
```
using Normal3f = Normal3<Float>;
```

The implementations of Normal3s and Vector3s are very similar. Like vectors, normals are represented by three components x, y, and z; they can be added and subtracted to compute new normals; and they can be scaled and normalized. However, a normal cannot be added to a point, and one cannot take the cross product of two normals. Note that, in an unfortunate turn of terminology, normals are *not* necessarily normalized.

In addition to the usual constructors (not included here), Normal3 allows conversion from Vector3 values given an explicit typecast, similarly to the other Tuple2- and Tuple3-based classes.

⟨*Normal3 Public Methods*⟩ ≡   94
```
template <typename U>
explicit Normal3<T>(Vector3<U> v)
    : Tuple3<pbrt::Normal3, T>(T(v.x), T(v.y), T(v.z)) {}
```

The Dot() and AbsDot() functions are also overloaded to compute dot products between the various possible combinations of normals and vectors. This code will not be included in the text here. We also will not include implementations of all the various other Normal3 methods here, since they are similar to those for vectors.

One new operation to implement comes from the fact that it is often necessary to flip a surface normal so it lies in the same hemisphere as a given vector—for example, the surface normal that lies in the same hemisphere as a ray leaving a surface is frequently needed. The FaceForward() utility function encapsulates this small computation. (pbrt also provides variants of this function for the other three combinations of Vector3s and Normal3s as parameters.) Be careful when using the other instances, though: when using the version that takes two Vector3s, for example, ensure that the first parameter is the one that should be returned (possibly flipped) and the second is the one to test against. Reversing the two parameters will give unexpected results.

⟨*Normal3 Inline Functions*⟩ ≡
```
template <typename T>
Normal3<T> FaceForward(Normal3<T> n, Vector3<T> v) {
    return (Dot(n, v) < 0.f) ? -n : n;
}
```

3.6 RAYS

A *ray* r is a semi-infinite line specified by its origin o and direction d; see Figure 3.8. pbrt represents Rays using a Point3f for the origin and a Vector3f for the direction; there is no need for non-Float-based rays in pbrt. See the files ray.h and ray.cpp in the pbrt source code distribution for the implementation of the Ray class implementation.

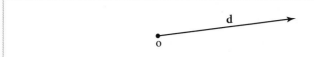

Figure 3.8: A ray is a semi-infinite line defined by its origin o and its direction vector **d**.

⟨*Ray Definition*⟩ ≡
```
class Ray {
  public:
    ⟨Ray Public Methods 95⟩
    ⟨Ray Public Members 95⟩
};
```

Because we will be referring to these variables often throughout the code, the origin and direction members of a Ray are succinctly named o and d. Note that we again make the data publicly available for convenience.

⟨*Ray Public Members*⟩ ≡   95
```
Point3f o;
Vector3f d;
```

The *parametric form* of a ray expresses it as a function of a scalar value t, giving the set of points that the ray passes through:

$$\mathrm{r}(t) = \mathrm{o} + t\mathbf{d} \quad 0 \le t < \infty. \tag{3.4}$$

The Ray class overloads the function application operator for rays in order to match the $\mathrm{r}(t)$ notation in Equation (3.4).

⟨*Ray Public Methods*⟩ ≡   95
```
Point3f operator()(Float t) const { return o + d * t; }
```

Given this method, when we need to find the point at a particular position along a ray, we can write code like:

```
Ray r(Point3f(0, 0, 0), Vector3f(1, 2, 3));
Point3f p = r(1.7);
```

Each ray also has a time value associated with it. In scenes with animated objects, the rendering system constructs a representation of the scene at the appropriate time for each ray.

⟨*Ray Public Members*⟩ +≡   95
```
Float time = 0;
```

Each ray also records the medium at its origin. The Medium class, which will be introduced in Section 11.4, encapsulates the (potentially spatially varying) properties of participating media such as a foggy atmosphere, smoke, or scattering liquids like milk. Associating this information with rays makes it possible for other parts of the system to account correctly for the effect of rays passing from one medium to another.

⟨*Ray Public Members*⟩ +≡   95
```
Medium medium = nullptr;
```

Constructing Rays is straightforward. The default constructor relies on the Point3f and Vector3f constructors to set the origin and direction to (0, 0, 0). Alternately, a particular point and direction can be provided. If an origin and direction are provided, the constructor allows values to be given for the ray's time and medium.

⟨*Ray Public Methods*⟩ +≡   95
```
    Ray(Point3f o, Vector3f d, Float time = 0.f, Medium medium = nullptr)
        : o(o), d(d), time(time), medium(medium) {}
```

3.6.1 RAY DIFFERENTIALS

To be able to perform better antialiasing with the texture functions defined in Chapter 10, pbrt makes use of the RayDifferential class, which is a subclass of Ray that contains additional information about two auxiliary rays. These extra rays represent camera rays offset by one sample in the *x* and *y* direction from the main ray on the film plane. By determining the area that these three rays project to on an object being shaded, a Texture can estimate an area to average over for proper antialiasing (Section 10.1).

Because RayDifferential inherits from Ray, geometric interfaces in the system can be written to take const Ray & parameters, so that either a Ray or RayDifferential can be passed to them. Only the routines that need to account for antialiasing and texturing require RayDifferential parameters.

⟨*RayDifferential Definition*⟩ ≡
```
    class RayDifferential : public Ray {
      public:
        ⟨RayDifferential Public Methods 96⟩
        ⟨RayDifferential Public Members 96⟩
    };
```

The RayDifferential constructor mirrors the Ray's.

⟨*RayDifferential Public Methods*⟩ ≡   96
```
    RayDifferential(Point3f o, Vector3f d, Float time = 0.f,
                    Medium medium = nullptr)
        : Ray(o, d, time, medium) {}
```

In some cases, differential rays may not be available. Routines that take RayDifferential parameters should check the hasDifferentials member variable before accessing the differential rays' origins or directions.

⟨*RayDifferential Public Members*⟩ ≡   96
```
    bool hasDifferentials = false;
    Point3f rxOrigin, ryOrigin;
    Vector3f rxDirection, ryDirection;
```

There is also a constructor to create a RayDifferential from a Ray. As with the previous constructor, the default false value of the hasDifferentials member variable is left as is.

⟨*RayDifferential Public Methods*⟩ +≡   96
```
    explicit RayDifferential(const Ray &ray) : Ray(ray) {}
```

Camera implementations in pbrt compute differentials for rays leaving the camera under the assumption that camera rays are spaced one pixel apart. Integrators usually generate multiple camera rays per pixel, in which case the actual distance between samples is lower and the differentials should be updated accordingly; if this factor is not accounted for, then textures in images will generally be too blurry. The ScaleDifferentials() method below takes care of this, given an estimated sample spacing of s. It is called, for example, by the fragment ⟨*Generate camera ray for current sample*⟩ in Chapter 1.

⟨*RayDifferential Public Methods*⟩ +≡   **96**
```
    void ScaleDifferentials(Float s) {
        rxOrigin = o + (rxOrigin - o) * s;
        ryOrigin = o + (ryOrigin - o) * s;
        rxDirection = d + (rxDirection - d) * s;
        ryDirection = d + (ryDirection - d) * s;
    }
```

3.7 BOUNDING BOXES

Many parts of the system operate on axis-aligned regions of space. For example, multi-threading in pbrt is implemented by subdividing the image into 2D rectangular tiles that can be processed independently, and the bounding volume hierarchy in Section 7.3 uses 3D boxes to bound geometric primitives in the scene. The Bounds2 and Bounds3 template classes are used to represent the extent of these sorts of regions. Both are parameterized by a type T that is used to represent the coordinates of their extents. As with the earlier vector math types, we will focus here on the 3D variant, Bounds3, since Bounds2 is effectively a subset of it.

⟨*Bounds2 Definition*⟩ ≡
```
    template <typename T>
    class Bounds2 {
      public:
        ⟨Bounds2 Public Methods⟩
        ⟨Bounds2 Public Members⟩
    };
```

⟨*Bounds3 Definition*⟩ ≡
```
    template <typename T>
    class Bounds3 {
      public:
        ⟨Bounds3 Public Methods 98⟩
        ⟨Bounds3 Public Members 98⟩
    };
```

We use the same shorthand as before to define names for commonly used bounding types.

⟨*Bounds[23][fi] Definitions*⟩ ≡
```
    using Bounds2f = Bounds2<Float>;
    using Bounds2i = Bounds2<int>;
    using Bounds3f = Bounds3<Float>;
    using Bounds3i = Bounds3<int>;
```

There are a few possible representations for these sorts of bounding boxes; pbrt uses *axis-aligned bounding boxes* (AABBs), where the box edges are mutually perpendicular and aligned with the coordinate system axes. Another possible choice is *oriented bounding boxes* (OBBs), where the box edges on different sides are still perpendicular to each other but not necessarily coordinate-system aligned. A 3D AABB can be described by one of its vertices and three lengths, each representing the distance spanned along the x, y, and z coordinate axes. Alternatively, two opposite vertices of the box can describe it. We chose the two-point

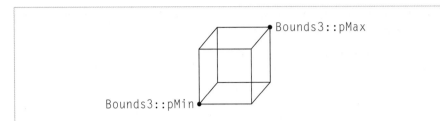

Figure 3.9: An Axis-Aligned Bounding Box. The Bounds2 and Bounds3 classes store only the coordinates of the minimum and maximum points of the box; the other box corners are implicit in this representation.

representation for pbrt's Bounds2 and Bounds3 classes; they store the positions of the vertex with minimum coordinate values and of the one with maximum coordinate values. A 2D illustration of a bounding box and its representation is shown in Figure 3.9.

⟨*Bounds3 Public Members*⟩ ≡   97
```
Point3<T> pMin, pMax;
```

The default constructors create an empty box by setting the extent to an invalid configuration, which violates the invariant that pMin.x <= pMax.x (and similarly for the other dimensions). By initializing two corner points with the largest and smallest representable number, any operations involving an empty box (e.g., Union()) will yield the correct result.

⟨*Bounds3 Public Methods*⟩ ≡   97
```
Bounds3() {
    T minNum = std::numeric_limits<T>::lowest();
    T maxNum = std::numeric_limits<T>::max();
    pMin = Point3<T>(maxNum, maxNum, maxNum);
    pMax = Point3<T>(minNum, minNum, minNum);
}
```

It is also useful to be able to initialize bounds that enclose just a single point:

⟨*Bounds3 Public Methods*⟩ +≡   97
```
explicit Bounds3(Point3<T> p) : pMin(p), pMax(p) {}
```

If the caller passes two corner points (p1 and p2) to define the box, the constructor needs to find their component-wise minimum and maximum values since it is not necessarily the case that p1.x <= p2.x, and so on.

⟨*Bounds3 Public Methods*⟩ +≡   97
```
Bounds3(Point3<T> p1, Point3<T> p2)
    : pMin(Min(p1, p2)), pMax(Max(p1, p2)) {}
```

It can be useful to use array indexing to select between the two points at the corners of the box. Assertions in the debug build, not shown here, check that the provided index is either 0 or 1.

⟨*Bounds3 Public Methods*⟩ +≡   97
```
Point3<T> operator[](int i) const { return (i == 0) ? pMin : pMax; }
Point3<T> &operator[](int i) { return (i == 0) ? pMin : pMax; }
```

The Corner() method returns the coordinates of one of the eight corners of the bounding box. Its logic calls the operator[] method with a zero or one value for each dimension that is based on one of the low three bits of corner and then extracts the corresponding component.

It is worthwhile to verify that this method returns the positions of all eight corners when passed values from 0 to 7 if that is not immediately evident.

⟨*Bounds3 Public Methods*⟩ +≡   97

```
Point3<T> Corner(int corner) const {
    return Point3<T>((*this)[(corner & 1)].x,
                     (*this)[(corner & 2) ? 1 : 0].y,
                     (*this)[(corner & 4) ? 1 : 0].z);
}
```

Given a bounding box and a point, the Union() function returns a new bounding box that encompasses that point as well as the original bounds.

⟨*Bounds3 Inline Functions*⟩ ≡

```
template <typename T>
Bounds3<T> Union(const Bounds3<T> &b, Point3<T> p) {
    Bounds3<T> ret;
    ret.pMin = Min(b.pMin, p);
    ret.pMax = Max(b.pMax, p);
    return ret;
}
```

One subtlety that applies to this and some of the following functions is that it is important that the pMin and pMax members of ret be set directly here, rather than passing the values returned by Min() and Max() to the Bounds3 constructor. The detail stems from the fact that if the provided bounds are both degenerate, the returned bounds should be degenerate as well. If a degenerate extent is passed to the constructor, then it will sort the coordinate values, which in turn leads to what is essentially an infinite bound.

It is similarly possible to construct a new box that bounds the space encompassed by two other bounding boxes. The definition of this function is similar to the earlier Union() method that takes a Point3f; the difference is that the pMin and pMax of the second box are used for the Min() and Max() tests, respectively.

⟨*Bounds3 Inline Functions*⟩ +≡

```
template <typename T>
Bounds3<T> Union(const Bounds3<T> &b1, const Bounds3<T> &b2) {
    Bounds3<T> ret;
    ret.pMin = Min(b1.pMin, b2.pMin);
    ret.pMax = Max(b1.pMax, b2.pMax);
    return ret;
}
```

The intersection of two bounding boxes can be found by computing the maximum of their two respective minimum coordinates and the minimum of their maximum coordinates. (See Figure 3.10.)

⟨*Bounds3 Inline Functions*⟩ +≡

```
template <typename T>
Bounds3<T> Intersect(const Bounds3<T> &b1, const Bounds3<T> &b2) {
    Bounds3<T> b;
    b.pMin = Max(b1.pMin, b2.pMin);
    b.pMax = Min(b1.pMax, b2.pMax);
    return b;
}
```

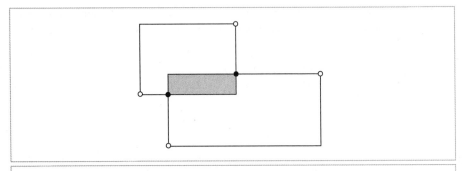

Figure 3.10: Intersection of Two Bounding Boxes. Given two bounding boxes with pMin and pMax points denoted by open circles, the bounding box of their area of intersection (shaded region) has a minimum point (lower left filled circle) with coordinates given by the maximum of the coordinates of the minimum points of the two boxes in each dimension. Similarly, its maximum point (upper right filled circle) is given by the minimums of the boxes' maximum coordinates.

We can also determine if two bounding boxes overlap by seeing if their extents overlap in all of x, y, and z:

⟨*Bounds3 Inline Functions*⟩ +≡
```
template <typename T>
bool Overlaps(const Bounds3<T> &b1, const Bounds3<T> &b2) {
    bool x = (b1.pMax.x >= b2.pMin.x) && (b1.pMin.x <= b2.pMax.x);
    bool y = (b1.pMax.y >= b2.pMin.y) && (b1.pMin.y <= b2.pMax.y);
    bool z = (b1.pMax.z >= b2.pMin.z) && (b1.pMin.z <= b2.pMax.z);
    return (x && y && z);
}
```

Three 1D containment tests determine if a given point is inside a bounding box.

⟨*Bounds3 Inline Functions*⟩ +≡
```
template <typename T>
bool Inside(Point3<T> p, const Bounds3<T> &b) {
    return (p.x >= b.pMin.x && p.x <= b.pMax.x &&
            p.y >= b.pMin.y && p.y <= b.pMax.y &&
            p.z >= b.pMin.z && p.z <= b.pMax.z);
}
```

The InsideExclusive() variant of Inside() does not consider points on the upper boundary to be inside the bounds. It is mostly useful with integer-typed bounds.

⟨*Bounds3 Inline Functions*⟩ +≡
```
template <typename T>
bool InsideExclusive(Point3<T> p, const Bounds3<T> &b) {
    return (p.x >= b.pMin.x && p.x < b.pMax.x &&
            p.y >= b.pMin.y && p.y < b.pMax.y &&
            p.z >= b.pMin.z && p.z < b.pMax.z);
}
```

DistanceSquared() returns the squared distance from a point to a bounding box or zero if the point is inside it. The geometric setting of the computation is shown in Figure 3.11. After the distance from the point to the box is computed in each dimension, the squared distance is found by summing the squares of each of the 1D distances.

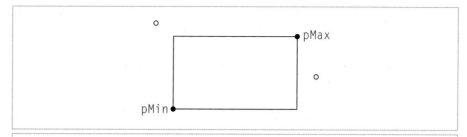

Figure 3.11: Computing the Squared Distance from a Point to an Axis-Aligned Bounding Box. We first find the distance from the point to the box in each dimension. Here, the point represented by an empty circle on the upper left is above to the left of the box, so its x and y distances are respectively pMin.x - p.x and pMin.y - p.y. The other point represented by an empty circle is to the right of the box but overlaps its extent in the y dimension, giving it respective distances of p.x - pMax.x and zero. The logic in Bounds3::DistanceSquared() computes these distances by finding the maximum of zero and the distances to the minimum and maximum points in each dimension.

⟨*Bounds3 Inline Functions*⟩ +≡

```
template <typename T, typename U>
auto DistanceSquared(Point3<T> p, const Bounds3<U> &b) {
    using TDist = decltype(T{} - U{});
    TDist dx = std::max<TDist>({0, b.pMin.x - p.x, p.x - b.pMax.x});
    TDist dy = std::max<TDist>({0, b.pMin.y - p.y, p.y - b.pMax.y});
    TDist dz = std::max<TDist>({0, b.pMin.z - p.z, p.z - b.pMax.z});
    return Sqr(dx) + Sqr(dy) + Sqr(dz);
}
```

It is easy to compute the distance from a point to a bounding box, though some indirection is needed to be able to determine the correct return type using TupleLength.

⟨*Bounds3 Inline Functions*⟩ +≡

```
template <typename T, typename U>
auto Distance(Point3<T> p, const Bounds3<U> &b) {
    auto dist2 = DistanceSquared(p, b);
    using TDist = typename TupleLength<decltype(dist2)>::type;
    return std::sqrt(TDist(dist2));
}
```

The Expand() function pads the bounding box by a constant factor in all dimensions.

⟨*Bounds3 Inline Functions*⟩ +≡

```
template <typename T, typename U>
Bounds3<T> Expand(const Bounds3<T> &b, U delta) {
    Bounds3<T> ret;
    ret.pMin = b.pMin - Vector3<T>(delta, delta, delta);
    ret.pMax = b.pMax + Vector3<T>(delta, delta, delta);
    return ret;
}
```

Diagonal() returns the vector along the box diagonal from the minimum point to the maximum point.

⟨*Bounds3 Public Methods*⟩ +≡   **97**

```
Vector3<T> Diagonal() const { return pMax - pMin; }
```

Methods for computing the surface area of the six faces of the box and the volume inside of it are also useful. (This is a place where Bounds2 and Bounds3 diverge: these methods are not available in Bounds2, though it does have an Area() method.)

⟨*Bounds3 Public Methods*⟩ +≡   97
```
T SurfaceArea() const {
    Vector3<T> d = Diagonal();
    return 2 * (d.x * d.y + d.x * d.z + d.y * d.z);
}
```

⟨*Bounds3 Public Methods*⟩ +≡   97
```
T Volume() const {
    Vector3<T> d = Diagonal();
    return d.x * d.y * d.z;
}
```

The Bounds3::MaxDimension() method returns the index of which of the three axes is longest. This is useful, for example, when deciding which axis to subdivide when building some of the ray-intersection acceleration structures.

⟨*Bounds3 Public Methods*⟩ +≡   97
```
int MaxDimension() const {
    Vector3<T> d = Diagonal();
    if (d.x > d.y && d.x > d.z) return 0;
    else if (d.y > d.z)         return 1;
    else                        return 2;
}
```

Lerp() linearly interpolates between the corners of the box by the given amount in each dimension.

⟨*Bounds3 Public Methods*⟩ +≡   97
```
Point3f Lerp(Point3f t) const {
    return Point3f(pbrt::Lerp(t.x, pMin.x, pMax.x),
                   pbrt::Lerp(t.y, pMin.y, pMax.y),
                   pbrt::Lerp(t.z, pMin.z, pMax.z));
}
```

Offset() is effectively the inverse of Lerp(). It returns the continuous position of a point relative to the corners of the box, where a point at the minimum corner has offset $(0, 0, 0)$, a point at the maximum corner has offset $(1, 1, 1)$, and so forth.

⟨*Bounds3 Public Methods*⟩ +≡   97
```
Vector3f Offset(Point3f p) const {
    Vector3f o = p - pMin;
    if (pMax.x > pMin.x) o.x /= pMax.x - pMin.x;
    if (pMax.y > pMin.y) o.y /= pMax.y - pMin.y;
    if (pMax.z > pMin.z) o.z /= pMax.z - pMin.z;
    return o;
}
```

Bounds3 also provides a method that returns the center and radius of a sphere that bounds the bounding box. In general, this may give a far looser fit than a sphere that bounded the original contents of the Bounds3 directly, although for some geometric operations it is easier to work with a sphere than a box, in which case the worse fit may be an acceptable trade-off.

⟨*Bounds3 Public Methods*⟩ +≡   97
```
    void BoundingSphere(Point3<T> *center, Float *radius) const {
        *center = (pMin + pMax) / 2;
        *radius = Inside(*center, *this) ? Distance(*center, pMax) : 0;
    }
```

Straightforward methods test for empty and degenerate bounding boxes. Note that "empty" means that a bounding box has zero volume but does not necessarily imply that it has zero surface area.

⟨*Bounds3 Public Methods*⟩ +≡   97
```
    bool IsEmpty() const {
        return pMin.x >= pMax.x || pMin.y >= pMax.y || pMin.z >= pMax.z;
    }
    bool IsDegenerate() const {
        return pMin.x > pMax.x || pMin.y > pMax.y || pMin.z > pMax.z;
    }
```

Finally, for integer bounds, there is an iterator class that fulfills the requirements of a C++ forward iterator (i.e., it can only be advanced). The details are slightly tedious and not particularly interesting, so the code is not included in the book. Having this definition makes it possible to write code using range-based for loops to iterate over integer coordinates in a bounding box:

```
        Bounds2i b = ...;
        for (Point2i p : b) {
            .
            .
            .
        }
```

As implemented, the iteration goes up to but does not visit points equal to the maximum extent in each dimension.

3.8 SPHERICAL GEOMETRY

Geometry on the unit sphere is also frequently useful in rendering. 3D unit direction vectors can equivalently be represented as points on the unit sphere, and sets of directions can be represented as areas on the unit sphere. Useful operations such as bounding a set of directions can often be cleanly expressed as bounds on the unit sphere. We will therefore introduce some useful principles of spherical geometry and related classes and functions in this section.

3.8.1 SOLID ANGLES

In 2D, the *planar angle* is the total angle subtended by some object with respect to some position (Figure 3.12). Consider the unit circle around the point p; if we project the shaded object onto that circle, some length of the circle s will be covered by its projection. The arc length of s (which is the same as the angle θ) is the angle subtended by the object. Planar angles are measured in *radians* and the entire unit circle covers 2π radians.

The solid angle extends the 2D unit circle to a 3D unit sphere (Figure 3.13). The total area s is the solid angle subtended by the object. Solid angles are measured in *steradians* (sr). The entire sphere subtends a solid angle of 4π sr, and a hemisphere subtends 2π sr.

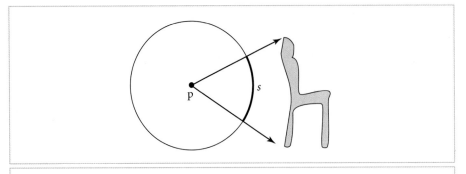

Figure 3.12: Planar Angle. The planar angle of an object as seen from a point p is equal to the angle it subtends as seen from p or, equivalently, as the length of the arc *s* on the unit sphere.

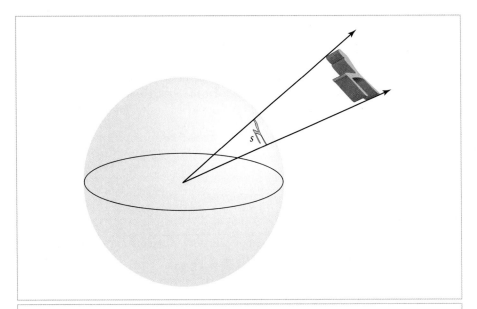

Figure 3.13: Solid Angle. The solid angle *s* subtended by a 3D object is computed by projecting the object onto the unit sphere and measuring the area of its projection.

By providing a way to measure area on the unit sphere (and thus over the unit directions), the solid angle also provides the foundation for a measure for integrating spherical functions; the *differential solid angle* dω corresponds to the differential area measure on the unit sphere.

3.8.2 SPHERICAL POLYGONS

We will sometimes find it useful to consider the set of directions from a point to the surface of a polygon. (Doing so can be useful, for example, when computing the illumination arriving at a point from an emissive polygon.) If a regular planar polygon is projected onto the unit sphere, it forms a *spherical polygon*.

A vertex of a spherical polygon can be found by normalizing the vector from the center of the sphere to the corresponding vertex of the original polygon. Each edge of a spherical polygon is given by the intersection of the unit sphere with the plane that goes through the sphere's center and the corresponding two vertices of the polygon. The result is a *great circle* on the

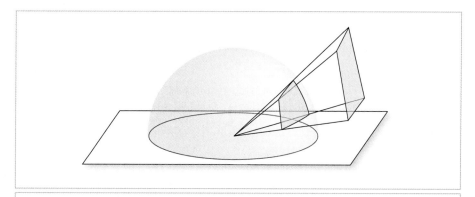

Figure 3.14: A spherical polygon corresponds to the projection of a polygon onto the unit sphere. Its vertices correspond to the unit vectors to the original polygon's vertices and its edges are defined by the intersection of the sphere and the planes that go through the sphere's center and two vertices of the polygon.

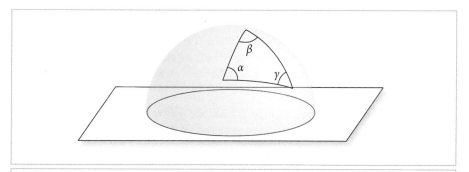

Figure 3.15: A Spherical Triangle. Each vertex's angle is labeled with the Greek letter corresponding to the letter used for its vertex.

sphere that is the shortest distance between the two vertices on the surface of the sphere (Figure 3.14).

The angle at each vertex is given by the angle between the planes corresponding to the two edges that meet at the vertex (Figure 3.15). (The angle between two planes is termed their *dihedral angle*.) We will label the angle at each vertex with the Greek letter that corresponds to its label (α for the vertex **a** and so forth). Unlike planar triangles, the three angles of a spherical triangle do not sum to π radians; rather, their sum is $\pi + A$, where A is the spherical triangle's area. Given the angles α, β, and γ, it follows that the area of a spherical triangle can be computed using *Girard's theorem*, which says that a triangle's surface area A on the unit sphere is given by the "excess angle"

$$A = \alpha + \beta + \gamma - \pi. \qquad (3.5)$$

Direct implementation of Equation (3.5) requires multiple calls to expensive inverse trigonometric functions, and its computation can be prone to error due to floating-point cancellation. A more efficient and accurate approach is to apply the relationship

$$\tan\left(\frac{1}{2}A\right) = \frac{\mathbf{A} \cdot (\mathbf{b} \times \mathbf{b})}{1 + (\mathbf{a} \cdot \mathbf{b}) + (\mathbf{a} \cdot \mathbf{c}) + (\mathbf{b} \cdot \mathbf{c})}, \qquad (3.6)$$

which can be derived from Equation (3.5) using spherical trigonometric identities. That approach is used in SphericalTriangleArea(), which takes three vectors on the unit sphere corresponding to the spherical triangle's vertices.

⟨*Spherical Geometry Inline Functions*⟩ ≡
```
    Float SphericalTriangleArea(Vector3f a, Vector3f b, Vector3f c) {
        return std::abs(2 * std::atan2(Dot(a, Cross(b, c)),
                                 1 + Dot(a, b) + Dot(a, c) + Dot(b, c)));
    }
```

The area of a quadrilateral projected onto the unit sphere is given by $\alpha + \beta + \gamma + \delta - 2\pi$, where α, β, γ, and δ are its interior angles. This value is computed by SphericalQuadArea(), which takes the vertex positions on the unit sphere. Its implementation is very similar to SphericalTriangleArea(), so it is not included here.

⟨*Spherical Geometry Inline Functions*⟩ +≡
```
    Float SphericalQuadArea(Vector3f a, Vector3f b, Vector3f c, Vector3f d);
```

3.8.3 SPHERICAL PARAMETERIZATIONS

The 3D Cartesian coordinates of a point on the unit sphere are not always the most convenient representation of a direction. For example, if we are tabulating a function over the unit sphere, a 2D parameterization that takes advantage of the fact that the sphere's surface is two-dimensional is preferable.

There are a variety of mappings between 2D and the sphere. Developing such mappings that fulfill various goals has been an important part of map making since its beginnings. It can be shown that any mapping from the plane to the sphere introduces some form of distortion; the task then is to choose a mapping that best fulfills the requirements for a particular application. pbrt thus uses three different spherical parameterizations, each with different advantages and disadvantages.

Spherical Coordinates

Spherical coordinates (θ, ϕ) are a well-known parameterization of the sphere. For a general sphere of radius r, they are related to Cartesian coordinates by

$$
\begin{aligned}
x &= r \sin \theta \cos \phi \\
y &= r \sin \theta \sin \phi \\
z &= r \cos \theta.
\end{aligned}
\tag{3.7}
$$

(See Figure 3.16.)

For convenience, we will define a SphericalDirection() function that converts a θ and ϕ pair into a unit (x, y, z) vector, applying these equations directly. Notice that the function is given the sine and cosine of θ, rather than θ itself. This is because the sine and cosine of θ are often already available to the caller. This is not normally the case for ϕ, however, so ϕ is passed in as is.

⟨*Spherical Geometry Inline Functions*⟩ +≡
```
    Vector3f SphericalDirection(Float sinTheta, Float cosTheta, Float phi) {
        return Vector3f(Clamp(sinTheta, -1, 1) * std::cos(phi),
                   Clamp(sinTheta, -1, 1) * std::sin(phi),
                   Clamp(cosTheta, -1, 1));
    }
```

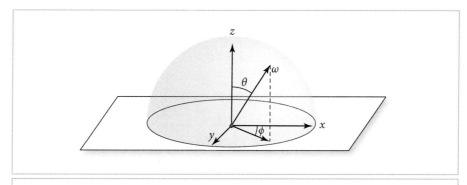

Figure 3.16: A direction vector can be written in terms of spherical coordinates (θ, ϕ) if the x, y, and z basis vectors are given as well. The spherical angle formulae make it easy to convert between the two representations.

The conversion of a direction (x, y, z) to spherical coordinates can be found by

$$\theta = \arccos z$$
$$\phi = \arctan \frac{y}{x}. \qquad \text{[3.8]}$$

The corresponding functions follow. Note that `SphericalTheta()` assumes that the vector v has been normalized before being passed in; using `SafeACos()` in place of `std::acos()` avoids errors if |v.z| is slightly greater than 1 due to floating-point round-off error.

⟨*Spherical Geometry Inline Functions*⟩ +≡
```
Float SphericalTheta(Vector3f v) { return SafeACos(v.z); }
```

`SphericalPhi()` returns an angle in $[0, 2\pi]$, which sometimes requires an adjustment to the value returned by `std::atan2()`.

⟨*Spherical Geometry Inline Functions*⟩ +≡
```
Float SphericalPhi(Vector3f v) {
    Float p = std::atan2(v.y, v.x);
    return (p < 0) ? (p + 2 * Pi) : p;
}
```

Given a direction vector ω, it is easy to compute quantities like the cosine of the angle θ:

$$\cos \theta = ((0, 0, 1) \cdot \omega) = \omega_z.$$

This is a much more efficient computation than it would have been to compute ω's θ value using first an expensive inverse trigonometric function to compute θ and then another expensive function to compute its cosine. The following functions compute this cosine and a few useful variations.

⟨*Spherical Geometry Inline Functions*⟩ +≡
```
Float CosTheta(Vector3f w) { return w.z; }
Float Cos2Theta(Vector3f w) { return Sqr(w.z); }
Float AbsCosTheta(Vector3f w) { return std::abs(w.z); }
```

The value of $\sin^2 \theta$ can be efficiently computed using the trigonometric identity $\sin^2 \theta + \cos^2 \theta = 1$, though we need to be careful to avoid returning a negative value in the rare case that 1 - Cos2Theta(w) is less than zero due to floating-point round-off error.

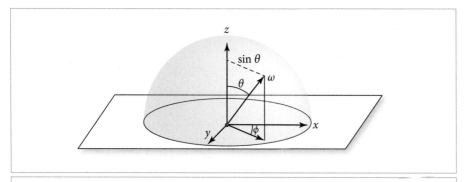

Figure 3.17: The values of $\sin\phi$ and $\cos\phi$ can be computed using the circular coordinate equations $x = r\cos\phi$ and $y = r\sin\phi$, where r, the length of the dashed line, is equal to $\sin\theta$.

⟨*Spherical Geometry Inline Functions*⟩ +≡
```
Float Sin2Theta(Vector3f w) { return std::max<Float>(0, 1 - Cos2Theta(w)); }
Float SinTheta(Vector3f w) { return std::sqrt(Sin2Theta(w)); }
```

The tangent of the angle θ can be computed via the identity $\tan\theta = \sin\theta/\cos\theta$.

⟨*Spherical Geometry Inline Functions*⟩ +≡
```
Float TanTheta(Vector3f w) { return SinTheta(w) / CosTheta(w); }
Float Tan2Theta(Vector3f w) { return Sin2Theta(w) / Cos2Theta(w); }
```

The sine and cosine of the ϕ angle can also be easily found from (x, y, z) coordinates without using inverse trigonometric functions (Figure 3.17). In the $z = 0$ plane, the vector ω has coordinates (x, y), which are given by $r\cos\phi$ and $r\sin\phi$, respectively. The radius r is $\sin\theta$, so

$$\cos\phi = \frac{x}{r} = \frac{x}{\sin\theta}$$
$$\sin\phi = \frac{y}{r} = \frac{y}{\sin\theta}.$$

⟨*Spherical Geometry Inline Functions*⟩ +≡
```
Float CosPhi(Vector3f w) {
    Float sinTheta = SinTheta(w);
    return (sinTheta == 0) ? 1 : Clamp(w.x / sinTheta, -1, 1);
}
Float SinPhi(Vector3f w) {
    Float sinTheta = SinTheta(w);
    return (sinTheta == 0) ? 0 : Clamp(w.y / sinTheta, -1, 1);
}
```

Finally, the cosine of the angle $\Delta\phi$ between two vectors' ϕ values can be found by zeroing their z coordinates to get 2D vectors in the $z = 0$ plane and then normalizing them. The dot product of these two vectors gives the cosine of the angle between them. The implementation below rearranges the terms a bit for efficiency so that only a single square root operation needs to be performed.

⟨*Spherical Geometry Inline Functions*⟩ +≡
```
Float CosDPhi(Vector3f wa, Vector3f wb) {
    Float waxy = Sqr(wa.x) + Sqr(wa.y), wbxy = Sqr(wb.x) + Sqr(wb.y);
    if (waxy == 0 || wbxy == 0) return 1;
    return Clamp((wa.x * wb.x + wa.y * wb.y) / std::sqrt(waxy * wbxy),
                 -1, 1);
}
```

Parameterizing the sphere with spherical coordinates corresponds to the *equirectangular* mapping of the sphere. It is not a particularly good parameterization for representing regularly sampled data on the sphere due to substantial distortion at the sphere's poles.

Octahedral Encoding

While Vector3f is a convenient representation for computation using unit vectors, it does not use storage efficiently: not only does it use 12 bytes of memory (assuming 4-byte Floats), but it is capable of representing 3D direction vectors of arbitrary length. Normalized vectors are a small subset of all the possible Vector3fs, however, which means that the storage represented by those 12 bytes is not well allocated for them. When many normalized vectors need to be stored in memory, a more space-efficient representation can be worthwhile.

Spherical coordinates could be used for this task. Doing so would reduce the storage required to two Floats, though with the disadvantage that relatively expensive trigonometric and inverse trigonometric functions would be required to convert to and from Vector3s. Further, spherical coordinates provide more precision near the poles and less near the equator; a more equal distribution of precision across all unit vectors is preferable. (Due to the way that floating-point numbers are represented, Vector3f suffers from providing different precision in different parts of the unit sphere as well.)

OctahedralVector provides a compact representation for unit vectors with an even distribution of precision and efficient encoding and decoding routines. Our implementation uses just 4 bytes of memory for each unit vector; all the possible values of those 4 bytes correspond to a valid unit vector. Its representation is not suitable for computation, but it is easy to convert between it and Vector3f, which makes it an appealing option for in-memory storage of normalized vectors.

⟨*OctahedralVector Definition*⟩ ≡
```
class OctahedralVector {
  public:
    ⟨OctahedralVector Public Methods 110⟩
  private:
    ⟨OctahedralVector Private Methods 110⟩
    ⟨OctahedralVector Private Members 110⟩
};
```

As indicated by its name, this unit vector is based on an octahedral mapping of the unit sphere that is illustrated in Figure 3.18.

The algorithm to convert a unit vector to this representation is surprisingly simple. The first step is to project the vector onto the faces of the 3D octahedron; this can be done by dividing the vector components by the vector's L1 norm, $|v_x| + |v_y| + |v_z|$. For points in the upper hemisphere (i.e., with $v_z \geq 0$), projection down to the $z = 0$ plane then just requires taking the x and y components directly.

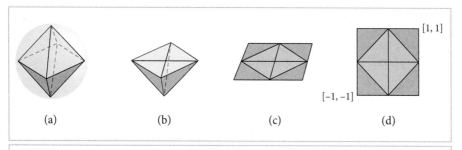

Figure 3.18: The `OctahedralVector`'s parameterization of the unit sphere can be understood by first considering (a) an octahedron inscribed in the sphere. Its 2D parameterization is then defined by (b) flattening the top pyramid into the $z = 0$ plane and (c) unwrapping the bottom half and projecting its triangles onto the same plane. (d) The result allows a simple $[-1, 1]^2$ parameterization. (Figure after Figure 2 in Meyer et al. (2010).)

⟨*OctahedralVector Public Methods*⟩ ≡   **109**
```
OctahedralVector(Vector3f v) {
    v /= std::abs(v.x) + std::abs(v.y) + std::abs(v.z);
    if (v.z >= 0) {
        x = Encode(v.x);
        y = Encode(v.y);
    } else {
        ⟨Encode octahedral vector with z < 0 110⟩
    }
}
```

For directions in the lower hemisphere, the reprojection to the appropriate point in $[-1, 1]^2$ is slightly more complex, though it can be expressed without any conditional control flow with a bit of care. (Here is another concise fragment of code that is worth understanding; consider in comparison code based on `if` statements that handled unwrapping the four triangles independently.)

⟨*Encode octahedral vector with z < 0*⟩ ≡   **110**
```
x = Encode((1 - std::abs(v.y)) * Sign(v.x));
y = Encode((1 - std::abs(v.x)) * Sign(v.y));
```

The helper function `OctahedralVector::Sign()` uses the standard math library function `std::copysign()` to return ±1 according to the sign of v (positive/negative zero are treated like ordinary numbers).

⟨*OctahedralVector Private Methods*⟩ ≡   **109**
```
static Float Sign(Float v) { return std::copysign(1.f, v); }
```

The 2D parameterization in Figure 3.18(d) is then represented using a 16-bit value for each coordinate that quantizes the range $[-1, 1]$ with 2^{16} steps.

⟨*OctahedralVector Private Members*⟩ ≡   **109**
```
uint16_t x, y;
```

`Encode()` performs the encoding from a value in $[-1, 1]$ to the integer encoding.

⟨*OctahedralVector Private Methods*⟩ +≡   **109**
```
static uint16_t Encode(Float f) {
    return pstd::round(Clamp((f + 1) / 2, 0, 1) * 65535.f);
}
```

The mapping back to a `Vector3f` follows the same steps in reverse. For directions in the upper hemisphere, the z value on the octahedron face is easily found. Normalizing that vector then gives the corresponding unit vector.

⟨*OctahedralVector Public Methods*⟩ +≡   109
```
explicit operator Vector3f() const {
    Vector3f v;
    v.x = -1 + 2 * (x / 65535.f);
    v.y = -1 + 2 * (y / 65535.f);
    v.z = 1 - (std::abs(v.x) + std::abs(v.y));
    ⟨Reparameterize directions in the z < 0 portion of the octahedron 111⟩
    return Normalize(v);
}
```

For directions in the lower hemisphere, the inverse of the mapping implemented in the ⟨*Encode octahedral vector with z < 0*⟩ fragment must be performed before the direction is normalized.

⟨*Reparameterize directions in the z < 0 portion of the octahedron*⟩ ≡   111
```
if (v.z < 0) {
    Float xo = v.x;
    v.x = (1 - std::abs(v.y)) * Sign(xo);
    v.y = (1 - std::abs(xo)) * Sign(v.y);
}
```

Equal-Area Mapping

The third spherical parameterization used in pbrt is carefully designed to preserve area: any area on the surface of the sphere maps to a proportional area in the parametric domain. This representation is a good choice for tabulating functions on the sphere, as it is continuous, has reasonably low distortion, and all values stored represent the same solid angle. It combines the octahedral mapping used in the OctahedralVector class with a variant of the square-to-disk mapping from Section A.5.1, which maps the unit square to the hemisphere in a way that preserves area. The mapping splits the unit square into four sectors, each of which is mapped to a sector of the hemisphere (see Figure 3.19).

Given $(u, v) \in [-1, 1]^2$; then in the first sector where $u \geq 0$ and $u - |v| \geq 0$, defining the polar coordinates of a point on the unit disk by

$$r = u$$
$$\phi = \frac{\pi}{4}\frac{u}{v}$$

gives an area-preserving mapping with $\phi \in [-\pi/4, \pi/4]$. Similar mappings can be found for the other three sectors.

Given (r, ϕ), the corresponding point on the positive hemisphere is then given by

$$x = (\cos \phi)r\sqrt{2 - r^2}$$
$$y = (\sin \phi)r\sqrt{2 - r^2} \qquad\qquad [3.9]$$
$$z = 1 - r^2.$$

This mapping is also area-preserving.

This mapping can be extended to the entire sphere using the same octahedral mapping that was used for the OctahedralVector. There are then three steps:

1. First, the octahedral mapping is applied to the direction, giving a point $(u, v) \in [-1, 1]^2$.

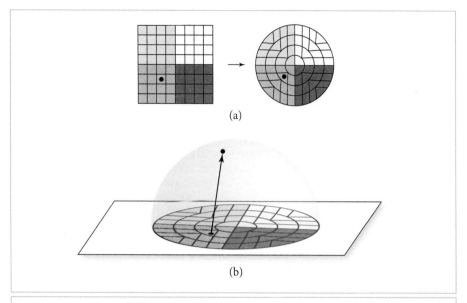

(a)

(b)

Figure 3.19: The uniform hemispherical mapping (a) first transforms the unit square to the unit disk so that the four shaded sectors of the square are mapped to the corresponding shaded sectors of the disk. (b) Points on the disk are then mapped to the hemisphere in a manner that preserves relative area.

2. For directions in the upper hemisphere, the concentric hemisphere mapping, Equation (3.9), is applied to the inner square of the octahedral mapping. Doing so requires accounting for the fact that it is rotated by $45°$ from the square expected by the hemispherical mapping.

3. Directions in the lower hemisphere are mirrored over across their quadrant's diagonal before the hemispherical mapping is applied. The resulting direction vector's z component is then negated.

The following implementation of this approach goes through some care to be *branch free*: no matter what the input value, there is a single path of control flow through the function. When possible, this characteristic is often helpful for performance, especially on the GPU, though we note that this function usually represents a small fraction of pbrt's execution time, so this characteristic does not affect the system's overall performance.

⟨*Square–Sphere Mapping Function Definitions*⟩ ≡
```
Vector3f EqualAreaSquareToSphere(Point2f p) {
    ⟨Transform p to [−1, 1]² and compute absolute values 113⟩
    ⟨Compute radius r as signed distance from diagonal 113⟩
    ⟨Compute angle φ for square to sphere mapping 113⟩
    ⟨Find z coordinate for spherical direction 113⟩
    ⟨Compute cos φ and sin φ for original quadrant and return vector 113⟩
}
```

After transforming the original point p in $[0, 1]^2$ to $(u, v) \in [−1, 1]^2$, the implementation also computes the absolute value of these coordinates $u' = |u|$ and $v' = |v|$. Doing so remaps the three quadrants with one or two negative coordinate values to the positive quadrant, flipping each quadrant so that its upper hemisphere is mapped to $u' + v' < 1$, which corresponds to the upper hemisphere in the original positive quadrant. (Each lower hemisphere is also mapped to the $u' + v' > 1$ region, corresponding to the original negative quadrant.)

Point2f 92

Vector3f 86

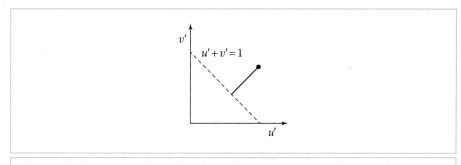

Figure 3.20: Computation of the Radius r for the Square-to-Disk Mapping. The signed distance to the $u' + v' = 1$ line is computed. One minus its absolute value gives a radius between 0 and 1.

⟨*Transform* p *to* $[-1, 1]^2$ *and compute absolute values*⟩ ≡   112
```
Float u = 2 * p.x - 1, v = 2 * p.y - 1;
Float up = std::abs(u), vp = std::abs(v);
```

Most of this function's implementation operates using (u', v') in the positive quadrant. Its next step is to compute the radius r for the mapping to the disk by computing the signed distance to the $u + v = 1$ diagonal that splits the upper and lower hemispheres where the lower hemisphere's signed distance is negative (Figure 3.20).

⟨*Compute radius* r *as signed distance from diagonal*⟩ ≡   112
```
Float signedDistance = 1 - (up + vp);
Float d = std::abs(signedDistance);
Float r = 1 - d;
```

The ϕ computation accounts for the 45° rotation with an added $\pi/4$ term.

⟨*Compute angle* ϕ *for square to sphere mapping*⟩ ≡   112
```
Float phi = (r == 0 ? 1 : (vp - up) / r + 1) * Pi / 4;
```

The sign of the signed distance computed earlier indicates whether the (u', v') point is in the lower hemisphere; the returned z coordinate takes its sign.

⟨*Find z coordinate for spherical direction*⟩ ≡   112
```
Float z = pstd::copysign(1 - Sqr(r), signedDistance);
```

After computing $\cos \phi$ and $\sin \phi$ in the positive quadrant, it is necessary to remap those values to the correct ones for the actual quadrant of the original point (u, v). Associating the sign of u with the computed $\cos \phi$ value and the sign of v with $\sin \phi$ suffices to do so and this operation can be done with another use of copysign().

⟨*Compute* $\cos \phi$ *and* $\sin \phi$ *for original quadrant and return vector*⟩ ≡   112
```
Float cosPhi = pstd::copysign(std::cos(phi), u);
Float sinPhi = pstd::copysign(std::sin(phi), v);
return Vector3f(cosPhi * r * SafeSqrt(2 - Sqr(r)),
                sinPhi * r * SafeSqrt(2 - Sqr(r)), z);
```

The inverse mapping is performed by the EqualAreaSphereToSquare() function, which effectively performs the same operations in reverse and is therefore not included here. Also useful and also not included, WrapEqualAreaSquare() handles the boundary cases of points p that are just outside of $[0, 1]^2$ (as may happen during bilinear interpolation with image texture lookups) and wraps them around to the appropriate valid coordinates that can be passed to EqualAreaSquareToSphere().

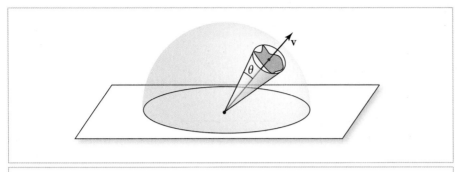

Figure 3.21: Bounding a Set of Directions with a Cone. A set of directions, shown here as a shaded region on the sphere, can be bounded using a cone described by a central direction vector **v** and a spread angle θ set such that all the directions in the set are inside the cone.

3.8.4 BOUNDING DIRECTIONS

In addition to bounding regions of space, it is also sometimes useful to bound a set of directions. For example, if a light source emits illumination in some directions but not others, that information can be used to cull that light source from being included in lighting calculations for points it certainly does not illuminate. pbrt provides the DirectionCone class for such uses; it represents a cone that is parameterized by a central direction and an angular spread (see Figure 3.21).

⟨*DirectionCone Definition*⟩ ≡
```
class DirectionCone {
  public:
    ⟨DirectionCone Public Methods 114⟩
    ⟨DirectionCone Public Members 114⟩
};
```

The DirectionCone provides a variety of constructors, including one that takes the central axis of the cone and the cosine of its spread angle and one that bounds a single direction. For both the constructor parameters and the cone representation stored in the class, the cosine of the spread angle is used rather than the angle itself. Doing so makes it possible to perform some of the following operations with DirectionCones using efficient dot products in place of more expensive trigonometric functions.

⟨*DirectionCone Public Methods*⟩ ≡   **114**
```
DirectionCone() = default;
DirectionCone(Vector3f w, Float cosTheta)
   : w(Normalize(w)), cosTheta(cosTheta) {}
explicit DirectionCone(Vector3f w) : DirectionCone(w, 1) {}
```

The default DirectionCone is empty; an invalid value of infinity for cosTheta encodes that case.

⟨*DirectionCone Public Members*⟩ ≡   **114**
```
Vector3f w;
Float cosTheta = Infinity;
```

A convenience method reports whether the cone is empty.

⟨*DirectionCone Public Methods*⟩ +≡   **114**
```
bool IsEmpty() const { return cosTheta == Infinity; }
```

Another convenience method provides the bound for all directions.

⟨*DirectionCone Public Methods*⟩ +≡   **114**
```
static DirectionCone EntireSphere() {
    return DirectionCone(Vector3f(0, 0, 1), -1);
}
```

Given a `DirectionCone`, it is easy to check if a given direction vector is inside its bounds: the cosine of the angle between the direction and the cone's central direction must be greater than the cosine of the cone's spread angle. (Note that for the angle to be smaller, the cosine must be larger.)

⟨*DirectionCone Inline Functions*⟩ ≡
```
bool Inside(const DirectionCone &d, Vector3f w) {
    return !d.IsEmpty() && Dot(d.w, Normalize(w)) >= d.cosTheta;
}
```

`BoundSubtendedDirections()` returns a `DirectionCone` that bounds the directions subtended by a given bounding box with respect to a point p.

⟨*DirectionCone Inline Functions*⟩ +≡
```
DirectionCone BoundSubtendedDirections(const Bounds3f &b, Point3f p) {
    ⟨Compute bounding sphere for b and check if p is inside 115⟩
    ⟨Compute and return DirectionCone for bounding sphere 115⟩
}
```

First, a bounding sphere is found for the bounds b. If the given point p is inside the sphere, then a direction bound of all directions is returned. Note that the point p may be inside the sphere but outside b, in which case the returned bounds will be overly conservative. This issue is discussed further in an exercise at the end of the chapter.

⟨*Compute bounding sphere for b and check if p is inside*⟩ ≡   **115**
```
Float radius;
Point3f pCenter;
b.BoundingSphere(&pCenter, &radius);
if (DistanceSquared(p, pCenter) < Sqr(radius))
    return DirectionCone::EntireSphere();
```

Otherwise the central axis of the bounds is given by the vector from p to the center of the sphere and the cosine of the spread angle is easily found using basic trigonometry (see Figure 3.22).

⟨*Compute and return DirectionCone for bounding sphere*⟩ ≡   **115**
```
Vector3f w = Normalize(pCenter - p);
Float sin2ThetaMax = Sqr(radius) / DistanceSquared(pCenter, p);
Float cosThetaMax = SafeSqrt(1 - sin2ThetaMax);
return DirectionCone(w, cosThetaMax);
```

Finally, we will find it useful to be able to take the union of two `DirectionCones`, finding a `DirectionCone` that bounds both of them.

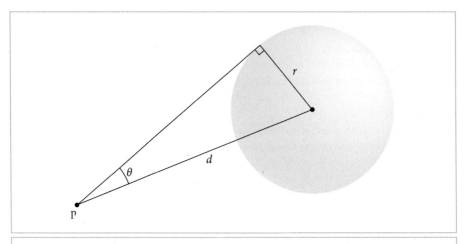

Figure 3.22: Finding the Angle That a Bounding Sphere Subtends from a Point p. Given a bounding sphere and a reference point p outside of the sphere, the cosine of the angle θ can be found by first computing $\sin\theta$ by dividing the sphere's radius r by the distance d between p and the sphere's center and then using the identity $\sin^2\theta + \cos^2\theta = 1$.

⟨*DirectionCone Function Definitions*⟩ ≡
```
DirectionCone Union(const DirectionCone &a, const DirectionCone &b) {
    ⟨Handle the cases where one or both cones are empty 116⟩
    ⟨Handle the cases where one cone is inside the other 116⟩
    ⟨Compute the spread angle of the merged cone, θ_o 117⟩
    ⟨Find the merged cone's axis and return cone union 118⟩
}
```

If one of the cones is empty, we can immediately return the other one.

⟨*Handle the cases where one or both cones are empty*⟩ ≡   **116**
```
if (a.IsEmpty()) return b;
if (b.IsEmpty()) return a;
```

Otherwise the implementation computes a few angles that will be helpful, including the actual spread angle of each cone as well as the angle between their two central direction vectors. These values give enough information to determine if one cone is entirely bounded by the other (see Figure 3.23).

⟨*Handle the cases where one cone is inside the other*⟩ ≡   **116**
```
Float theta_a = SafeACos(a.cosTheta), theta_b = SafeACos(b.cosTheta);
Float theta_d = AngleBetween(a.w, b.w);
if (std::min(theta_d + theta_b, Pi) <= theta_a)
    return a;
if (std::min(theta_d + theta_a, Pi) <= theta_b)
    return b;
```

Otherwise it is necessary to compute a new cone that bounds both of them. As illustrated in Figure 3.24, the sum of θ_a, θ_d, and θ_b gives the full angle that the new cone must cover; half of that is its spread angle.

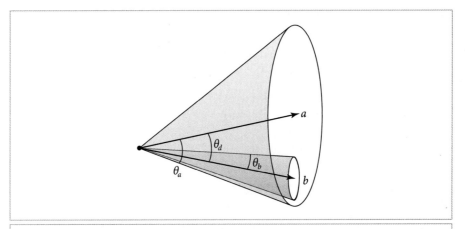

Figure 3.23: Determining If One Cone of Directions Is Entirely inside Another. Given two direction cones a and b, their spread angles θ_a and θ_b, and the angle between their two central direction vectors θ_d, we can determine if one cone is entirely inside the other. Here, $\theta_a > \theta_d + \theta_b$, and so b is inside a.

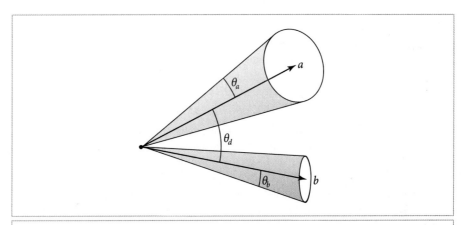

Figure 3.24: Computing the Spread Angle of the Direction Cone That Bounds Two Others. If θ_d is the angle between two cones' central axes and the two cones have spread angles θ_a and θ_b, then the total angle that the cone bounds is $\theta_a + \theta_d + \theta_b$ and so its spread angle is half of that.

⟨*Compute the spread angle of the merged cone, θ_o*⟩ ≡   **116**
```
    Float theta_o = (theta_a + theta_d + theta_b) / 2;
    if (theta_o >= Pi)
        return DirectionCone::EntireSphere();
```

The direction vector for the new cone should *not* be set with the average of the two cones' direction vectors; that vector and a spread angle of θ_o does not necessarily bound the two given cones. Using that vector would require a spread angle of $\theta_d/2 + \max(2\theta_a, 2\theta_b)$, which is never less than θ_o. (It is worthwhile to sketch out a few cases on paper to convince yourself of this.)

Instead, we find the vector perpendicular to the cones' direction vectors using the cross product and rotate a.w by the angle around that axis that causes it to bound both cones' angles. (The Rotate() function used for this will be introduced shortly, in Section 3.9.7.) In the case that LengthSquared(wr) == 0, the vectors face in opposite directions and a bound of the entire sphere is returned.[2]

⟨*Find the merged cone's axis and return cone union*⟩ ≡   **116**
```
Float theta_r = theta_o - theta_a;
Vector3f wr = Cross(a.w, b.w);
if (LengthSquared(wr) == 0)
    return DirectionCone::EntireSphere();
Vector3f w = Rotate(Degrees(theta_r), wr)(a.w);
return DirectionCone(w, std::cos(theta_o));
```

3.9 TRANSFORMATIONS

In general, a *transformation* T is a mapping from points to points and from vectors to vectors:

$$\mathrm{p}' = \mathrm{T}(\mathrm{p}) \qquad \mathrm{v}' = \mathrm{T}(\mathrm{v}).$$

The transformation T may be an arbitrary procedure. However, we will consider a subset of all possible transformations in this chapter. In particular, they will be

- *Linear:* If T is an arbitrary linear transformation and s is an arbitrary scalar, then $\mathrm{T}(s\mathrm{v}) = s\mathrm{T}(\mathrm{v})$ and $\mathrm{T}(\mathrm{v}_1 + \mathrm{v}_2) = \mathrm{T}(\mathrm{v}_1) + \mathrm{T}(\mathrm{v}_2)$. These two properties can greatly simplify reasoning about transformations.
- *Continuous:* Roughly speaking, T maps the neighborhoods around p and v to neighborhoods around p′ and v′.
- *One-to-one and invertible:* For each p, T maps p to a single unique p′. Furthermore, there exists an inverse transform T^{-1} that maps p′ back to p.

We will often want to take a point, vector, or normal defined with respect to one coordinate frame and find its coordinate values with respect to another frame. Using basic properties of linear algebra, a 4 × 4 matrix can be shown to express the linear transformation of a point or vector from one frame to another. Furthermore, such a 4 × 4 matrix suffices to express all linear transformations of points and vectors within a fixed frame, such as translation in space or rotation around a point. Therefore, there are two different (and incompatible!) ways that a matrix can be interpreted:

- *Transformation within the frame:* Given a point, the matrix could express how to compute a *new* point in the same frame that represents the transformation of the original point (e.g., by translating it in some direction).
- *Transformation from one frame to another:* A matrix can express the coordinates of a point or vector in a new frame in terms of the coordinates in the original frame.

Most uses of transformations in pbrt are for transforming points from one frame to another.

In general, transformations make it possible to work in the most convenient coordinate space. For example, we can write routines that define a virtual camera, assuming that the camera is located at the origin, looks down the z axis, and has the y axis pointing up and the x axis pointing right. These assumptions greatly simplify the camera implementation. To place the camera at any point in the scene looking in any direction, we construct a transformation that maps points in the scene's coordinate system to the camera's coordinate system. (See Section 5.1.1 for more information about camera coordinate spaces in pbrt.)

---

2   A tighter bound is possible in this case, but it occurs very rarely and so we have not bothered with handling it more effectively.

3.9.1 HOMOGENEOUS COORDINATES

Given a frame defined by $(p_o, \mathbf{v}_1, \mathbf{v}_2, \mathbf{v}_3)$, there is ambiguity between the representation of a point (p_x, p_y, p_z) and a vector (v_x, v_y, v_z) with the same (x, y, z) coordinates. Using the representations of points and vectors introduced at the start of the chapter, we can write the point as the inner product $[s_1\, s_2\, s_3\, 1][\mathbf{v}_1\, \mathbf{v}_2\, \mathbf{v}_3\, p_o]^T$ and the vector as the inner product $[s_1'\, s_2'\, s_3'\, 0][\mathbf{v}_1\, \mathbf{v}_2\, \mathbf{v}_3\, p_o]^T$. These four-vectors of three s_i values and a zero or one are called the *homogeneous* representations of the point and the vector. The fourth coordinate of the homogeneous representation is sometimes called the *weight*. For a point, its value can be any scalar other than zero: the homogeneous points $[1, 3, -2, 1]$ and $[-2, -6, 4, -2]$ describe the same Cartesian point $(1, 3, -2)$. Converting homogeneous points into ordinary points entails dividing the first three components by the weight:

$$(x, y, z, w) \rightarrow \left(\frac{x}{w}, \frac{y}{w}, \frac{z}{w} \right).$$

We will use these facts to see how a transformation matrix can describe how points and vectors in one frame can be mapped to another frame. Consider a matrix $\mathbf{M}$ that describes the transformation from one coordinate system to another:

$$\mathbf{M} = \begin{pmatrix} m_{0,0} & m_{0,1} & m_{0,2} & m_{0,3} \\ m_{1,0} & m_{1,1} & m_{1,2} & m_{1,3} \\ m_{2,0} & m_{2,1} & m_{2,2} & m_{2,3} \\ m_{3,0} & m_{3,1} & m_{3,2} & m_{3,3} \end{pmatrix}.$$

(In this book, we define matrix element indices starting from zero, so that equations and source code correspond more directly.) Then if the transformation represented by $\mathbf{M}$ is applied to the x axis vector $(1, 0, 0)$, we have

$$\mathbf{Mx} = \mathbf{M}[1\, 0\, 0\, 0]^T = [m_{0,0}\, m_{1,0}\, m_{2,0}\, m_{3,0}]^T.$$

Thus, directly reading the columns of the matrix shows how the basis vectors and the origin of the current coordinate system are transformed by the matrix:

$$\mathbf{My} = [m_{0,1}\, m_{1,1}\, m_{2,1}\, m_{3,1}]^T$$

$$\mathbf{Mz} = [m_{0,2}\, m_{1,2}\, m_{2,2}\, m_{3,2}]^T$$

$$\mathbf{Mp} = [m_{0,3}\, m_{1,3}\, m_{2,3}\, m_{3,3}]^T.$$

In general, by characterizing how the basis is transformed, we know how any point or vector specified in terms of that basis is transformed. Because points and vectors in a coordinate system are expressed in terms of the coordinate system's frame, applying the transformation to them directly is equivalent to applying the transformation to the coordinate system's basis and finding their coordinates in terms of the transformed basis.

We will not use homogeneous coordinates explicitly in our code; there is no Homogeneous Point class in pbrt. However, the various transformation routines in the next section will implicitly convert points, vectors, and normals to homogeneous form, transform the homogeneous points, and then convert them back before returning the result. This isolates the details of homogeneous coordinates in one place (namely, the implementation of transformations).

3.9.2 Transform CLASS DEFINITION

The Transform class represents a 4×4 transformation. Its implementation is in the files util/transform.h and util/transform.cpp.

⟨*Transform Definition*⟩ ≡
```
class Transform {
  public:
    ⟨Transform Public Methods 120⟩
  private:
    ⟨Transform Private Members 120⟩
};
```

The transformation matrix is represented by the elements of the matrix m, which is represented by a SquareMatrix<4> object. (The SquareMatrix class is defined in Section B.2.12.) The matrix m is stored in *row-major* form, so element m[i][j] corresponds to $m_{i,j}$, where i is the row number and j is the column number. For convenience, the Transform also stores the inverse of m in its Transform::mInv member variable; for pbrt's needs, it is better to have the inverse easily available than to repeatedly compute it as needed.

⟨*Transform Private Members*⟩ ≡   **120**
```
    SquareMatrix<4> m, mInv;
```

This representation of transformations is relatively memory hungry: assuming 4 bytes of storage for a Float value, a Transform requires 128 bytes of storage. Used naïvely, this approach can be wasteful; if a scene has millions of shapes but only a few thousand unique transformations, there is no reason to redundantly store the same matrices many times. Therefore, Shapes in pbrt store a pointer to a Transform and the scene specification code defined in Section C.2.3 uses an InternCache of Transforms to ensure that all shapes that share the same transformation point to a single instance of that transformation in memory.

3.9.3 BASIC OPERATIONS

When a new Transform is created, it defaults to the *identity transformation*—the transformation that maps each point and each vector to itself. This transformation is represented by the *identity matrix*:

$$I = \begin{pmatrix} 1 & 0 & 0 & 0 \\ 0 & 1 & 0 & 0 \\ 0 & 0 & 1 & 0 \\ 0 & 0 & 0 & 1 \end{pmatrix}.$$

The implementation here relies on the default SquareMatrix constructor to fill in the identity matrix for m and mInv.

⟨*Transform Public Methods*⟩ ≡   **120**
```
    Transform() = default;
```

A Transform can also be created from a given matrix. In this case, the matrix must be explicitly inverted.

⟨*Transform Public Methods*⟩ +≡   **120**
```
    Transform(const SquareMatrix<4> &m) : m(m) {
        pstd::optional<SquareMatrix<4>> inv = Inverse(m);
        if (inv)
            mInv = *inv;
        else {
            ⟨Initialize mInv with not-a-number values 121⟩
        }
    }
```

If the matrix provided by the caller is degenerate and cannot be inverted, mInv is initialized with floating-point not-a-number values, which poison computations that involve them: arithmetic performed using a not-a-number value always gives a not-a-number value. In this way, a caller who provides a degenerate matrix m can still use the Transform as long as no methods that access mInv are called.

⟨*Initialize* mInv *with not-a-number values*⟩ ≡   120
```
Float NaN = std::numeric_limits<Float>::has_signaling_NaN
                         ? std::numeric_limits<Float>::signaling_NaN()
                         : std::numeric_limits<Float>::quiet_NaN();
for (int i = 0; i < 4; ++i)
    for (int j = 0; j < 4; ++j)
        mInv[i][j] = NaN;
```

Another constructor allows specifying the elements of the matrix using a regular 2D array.

⟨*Transform Public Methods*⟩ +≡   120
```
Transform(const Float mat[4][4]) : Transform(SquareMatrix<4>(mat)) {}
```

The most commonly used constructor takes a reference to the transformation matrix along with an explicitly provided inverse. This is a superior approach to computing the inverse in the constructor because many geometric transformations have simple inverses and we can avoid the expense and potential loss of numeric accuracy from computing a general 4×4 matrix inverse. Of course, this places the burden on the caller to make sure that the supplied inverse is correct.

⟨*Transform Public Methods*⟩ +≡   120
```
Transform(const SquareMatrix<4> &m, const SquareMatrix<4> &mInv)
    : m(m), mInv(mInv) {}
```

Both the matrix and its inverse are made available for callers that need to access them directly.

⟨*Transform Public Methods*⟩ +≡   120
```
const SquareMatrix<4> &GetMatrix() const { return m; }
const SquareMatrix<4> &GetInverseMatrix() const { return mInv; }
```

The Transform representing the inverse of a Transform can be returned by just swapping the roles of mInv and m.

⟨*Transform Inline Functions*⟩ ≡
```
Transform Inverse(const Transform &t) {
    return Transform(t.GetInverseMatrix(), t.GetMatrix());
}
```

Transposing the two matrices in the transform to compute a new transform can also be useful.

⟨*Transform Inline Functions*⟩ +≡
```
Transform Transpose(const Transform &t) {
    return Transform(Transpose(t.GetMatrix()),
                     Transpose(t.GetInverseMatrix()));
}
```

The Transform class also provides equality and inequality testing methods as well as an IsIdentity() method that checks to see if the transformation is the identity.

⟨*Transform Public Methods*⟩ +≡   **120**

```
bool operator==(const Transform &t) const { return t.m == m; }
bool operator!=(const Transform &t) const { return t.m != m; }
bool IsIdentity() const { return m.IsIdentity(); }
```

3.9.4 TRANSLATIONS

One of the simplest transformations is the *translation transformation*, $T(\Delta x, \Delta y, \Delta z)$. When applied to a point p, it translates p's coordinates by Δx, Δy, and Δz, as shown in Figure 3.25. As an example, $T(2, 2, 1)(x, y, z) = (x + 2, y + 2, z + 1)$.

Translation has some basic properties:

$$T(0, 0, 0) = I$$
$$T(x_1, y_1, z_1)T(x_2, y_2, z_2) = T(x_1 + x_2, y_1 + y_2, z_1 + z_2)$$
$$T(x_1, y_1, z_1)T(x_2, y_2, z_2) = T(x_2, y_2, z_2)T(x_1, y_1, z_1)$$
$$T^{-1}(x, y, z) = T(-x, -y, -z).$$

Translation only affects points, leaving vectors unchanged. In matrix form, the translation transformation is

$$T(\Delta x, \Delta y, \Delta z) = \begin{pmatrix} 1 & 0 & 0 & \Delta x \\ 0 & 1 & 0 & \Delta y \\ 0 & 0 & 1 & \Delta z \\ 0 & 0 & 0 & 1 \end{pmatrix}.$$

When we consider the operation of a translation matrix on a point, we see the value of homogeneous coordinates. Consider the product of the matrix for $T(\Delta x, \Delta y, \Delta z)$ with a point p in homogeneous coordinates $[x\ y\ z\ 1]^T$:

$$\begin{pmatrix} 1 & 0 & 0 & \Delta x \\ 0 & 1 & 0 & \Delta y \\ 0 & 0 & 1 & \Delta z \\ 0 & 0 & 0 & 1 \end{pmatrix} \begin{pmatrix} x \\ y \\ z \\ 1 \end{pmatrix} = \begin{pmatrix} x + \Delta x \\ y + \Delta y \\ z + \Delta z \\ 1 \end{pmatrix}.$$

As expected, we have computed a new point with its coordinates offset by $(\Delta x, \Delta y, \Delta z)$. However, if we apply T to a vector v, we have

$$\begin{pmatrix} 1 & 0 & 0 & \Delta x \\ 0 & 1 & 0 & \Delta y \\ 0 & 0 & 1 & \Delta z \\ 0 & 0 & 0 & 1 \end{pmatrix} \begin{pmatrix} x \\ y \\ z \\ 0 \end{pmatrix} = \begin{pmatrix} x \\ y \\ z \\ 0 \end{pmatrix}.$$

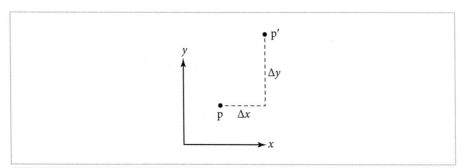

SquareMatrix::IsIdentity()
    1050

Transform 120

Transform::m 120

Figure 3.25: Translation in 2D. Adding offsets Δx and Δy to a point's coordinates correspondingly changes its position in space.

The result is the same vector **v**. This makes sense because vectors represent directions, so translation leaves them unchanged.

The Translate() function returns a Transform that represents a given translation—it is a straightforward application of the translation matrix equation. The inverse of the translation is easily computed, so it is provided to the Transform constructor as well.

⟨*Transform Function Definitions*⟩ ≡
```
Transform Translate(Vector3f delta) {
    SquareMatrix<4> m(1, 0, 0, delta.x,
                      0, 1, 0, delta.y,
                      0, 0, 1, delta.z,
                      0, 0, 0, 1);
    SquareMatrix<4> minv(1, 0, 0, -delta.x,
                         0, 1, 0, -delta.y,
                         0, 0, 1, -delta.z,
                         0, 0, 0, 1);
    return Transform(m, minv);
}
```

3.9.5 SCALING

Another basic transformation is the *scale transformation*, $S(s_x, s_y, s_z)$. It has the effect of taking a point or vector and multiplying its components by scale factors in x, y, and z: $S(2, 2, 1)(x, y, z) = (2x, 2y, z)$. It has the following basic properties:

$$S(1, 1, 1) = I$$
$$S(x_1, y_1, z_1)S(x_2, y_2, z_2) = S(x_1x_2, y_1y_2, z_1z_2)$$
$$S(x_1, y_1, z_1)S(x_2, y_2, z_2) = S(x_2, y_2, z_2)S(x_1, y_1, z_1)$$
$$S^{-1}(x, y, z) = S\left(\frac{1}{x}, \frac{1}{y}, \frac{1}{z}\right).$$

We can differentiate between *uniform scaling*, where all three scale factors have the same value, and *nonuniform scaling*, where they may have different values. The general scale matrix is

$$S(x, y, z) = \begin{pmatrix} x & 0 & 0 & 0 \\ 0 & y & 0 & 0 \\ 0 & 0 & z & 0 \\ 0 & 0 & 0 & 1 \end{pmatrix}.$$

⟨*Transform Function Definitions*⟩ +≡
```
Transform Scale(Float x, Float y, Float z) {
    SquareMatrix<4> m(x, 0, 0, 0,
                      0, y, 0, 0,
                      0, 0, z, 0,
                      0, 0, 0, 1);
    SquareMatrix<4> minv(1 / x,     0,     0, 0,
                             0, 1 / y,     0, 0,
                             0,     0, 1 / z, 0,
                             0,     0,     0, 1);
    return Transform(m, minv);
}
```

It is useful to be able to test if a transformation has a scaling term in it; an easy way to do this is to transform the three coordinate axes and see if any of their lengths are appreciably different from one.

⟨*Transform Public Methods*⟩ +≡   120

```
bool HasScale(Float tolerance = 1e-3f) const {
    Float la2 = LengthSquared((*this)(Vector3f(1, 0, 0)));
    Float lb2 = LengthSquared((*this)(Vector3f(0, 1, 0)));
    Float lc2 = LengthSquared((*this)(Vector3f(0, 0, 1)));
    return (std::abs(la2 - 1) > tolerance ||
            std::abs(lb2 - 1) > tolerance ||
            std::abs(lc2 - 1) > tolerance);
}
```

3.9.6 x, y, AND z AXIS ROTATIONS

Another useful type of transformation is the *rotation transformation*, **R**. In general, we can define an arbitrary axis from the origin in any direction and then rotate around that axis by a given angle. The most common rotations of this type are around the x, y, and z coordinate axes. We will write these rotations as $\mathbf{R}_x(\theta)$, $\mathbf{R}_y(\theta)$, and so on. The rotation around an arbitrary axis (x, y, z) is denoted by $\mathbf{R}_{(x,y,z)}(\theta)$.

Rotations also have some basic properties:

$$\mathbf{R}_a(0) = \mathbf{I}$$
$$\mathbf{R}_a(\theta_1)\mathbf{R}_a(\theta_2) = \mathbf{R}_a(\theta_1 + \theta_2)$$
$$\mathbf{R}_a(\theta_1)\mathbf{R}_a(\theta_2) = \mathbf{R}_a(\theta_2)\mathbf{R}_a(\theta_1)$$
$$\mathbf{R}_a^{-1}(\theta) = \mathbf{R}_a(-\theta) = \mathbf{R}_a^T(\theta),$$

where $\mathbf{R}^T$ is the matrix transpose of $\mathbf{R}$. This last property, that the inverse of $\mathbf{R}$ is equal to its transpose, stems from the fact that $\mathbf{R}$ is an *orthogonal matrix*; its first three columns (or rows) are all normalized and orthogonal to each other. Fortunately, the transpose is much easier to compute than a full matrix inverse.

For a left-handed coordinate system, the matrix for clockwise rotation around the x axis is

$$\mathbf{R}_x(\theta) = \begin{pmatrix} 1 & 0 & 0 & 0 \\ 0 & \cos\theta & -\sin\theta & 0 \\ 0 & \sin\theta & \cos\theta & 0 \\ 0 & 0 & 0 & 1 \end{pmatrix}.$$

Figure 3.26 gives an intuition for how this matrix works.

It is easy to see that the matrix leaves the x axis unchanged:

$$\mathbf{R}_x(\theta)[1\,0\,0\,0]^T = [1\,0\,0\,0]^T.$$

It maps the y axis $(0, 1, 0)$ to $(0, \cos\theta, \sin\theta)$ and the z axis to $(0, -\sin\theta, \cos\theta)$. The y and z axes remain in the same plane, perpendicular to the x axis, but are rotated by the given angle. An arbitrary point in space is similarly rotated about the x axis by this transformation while staying in the same yz plane as it was originally.

The implementation of the RotateX() function is straightforward.

Float 23

LengthSquared() 87

RotateX() 125

Vector3f 86

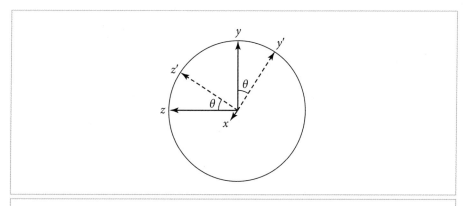

Figure 3.26: Clockwise rotation by an angle θ about the x axis leaves the x coordinate unchanged. The y and z axes are mapped to the vectors given by the dashed lines; y and z coordinates move accordingly.

⟨*Transform Function Definitions*⟩ +≡

```
Transform RotateX(Float theta) {
    Float sinTheta = std::sin(Radians(theta));
    Float cosTheta = std::cos(Radians(theta));
    SquareMatrix<4> m(1,       0,         0, 0,
                      0, cosTheta, -sinTheta, 0,
                      0, sinTheta,  cosTheta, 0,
                      0,       0,         0, 1);
    return Transform(m, Transpose(m));
}
```

Similarly, for clockwise rotation around y and z, we have

$$\mathbf{R}_y(\theta) = \begin{pmatrix} \cos\theta & 0 & \sin\theta & 0 \\ 0 & 1 & 0 & 0 \\ -\sin\theta & 0 & \cos\theta & 0 \\ 0 & 0 & 0 & 1 \end{pmatrix} \qquad \mathbf{R}_z(\theta) = \begin{pmatrix} \cos\theta & -\sin\theta & 0 & 0 \\ \sin\theta & \cos\theta & 0 & 0 \\ 0 & 0 & 1 & 0 \\ 0 & 0 & 0 & 1 \end{pmatrix}.$$

The implementations of RotateY() and RotateZ() follow directly and are not included here.

3.9.7 ROTATION AROUND AN ARBITRARY AXIS

We also provide a routine to compute the transformation that represents rotation around an arbitrary axis. A common derivation of this matrix is based on computing rotations that map the given axis to a fixed axis (e.g., z), performing the rotation there, and then rotating the fixed axis back to the original axis. A more elegant derivation can be constructed with vector algebra.

Consider a normalized direction vector $\mathbf{a}$ that gives the axis to rotate around by angle θ, and a vector $\mathbf{v}$ to be rotated (Figure 3.27).

First, we can compute the vector $\mathbf{v}_c$ along the axis $\mathbf{a}$ that is in the plane through the end point of $\mathbf{v}$ and is parallel to $\mathbf{a}$. Assuming $\mathbf{v}$ and $\mathbf{a}$ form an angle α, we have

$$\mathbf{v}_c = \mathbf{a}\,\|\mathbf{v}\|\cos\alpha = \mathbf{a}(\mathbf{v}\cdot\mathbf{a}).$$

We now compute a pair of basis vectors $\mathbf{v}_1$ and $\mathbf{v}_2$ in this plane. Trivially, one of them is

$$\mathbf{v}_1 = \mathbf{v} - \mathbf{v}_c,$$

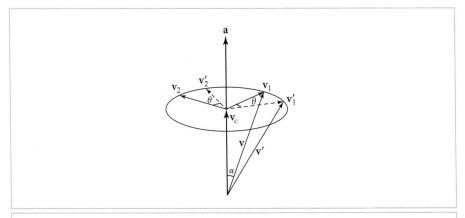

Figure 3.27: A vector **v** can be rotated around an arbitrary axis **a** by constructing a coordinate system $(p, \mathbf{v}_1, \mathbf{v}_2)$ in the plane perpendicular to the axis that passes through **v**'s end point and rotating the vectors $\mathbf{v}_1$ and $\mathbf{v}_2$ about p. Applying this rotation to the axes of the coordinate system $(1, 0, 0)$, $(0, 1, 0)$, and $(0, 0, 1)$ gives the general rotation matrix for this rotation.

and the other can be computed with a cross product

$$\mathbf{v}_2 = (\mathbf{v}_1 \times \mathbf{a}).$$

Because **a** is normalized, $\mathbf{v}_1$ and $\mathbf{v}_2$ have the same length, equal to the length of the vector between **v** and $\mathbf{v}_c$. To now compute the rotation by an angle θ about $\mathbf{v}_c$ in the plane of rotation, the rotation formulae earlier give us

$$\mathbf{v}' = \mathbf{v}_c + \mathbf{v}_1 \cos \theta + \mathbf{v}_2 \sin \theta.$$

To convert this to a rotation matrix, we apply this formula to the basis vectors $(1, 0, 0)$, $(0, 1, 0)$, and $(0, 0, 1)$ to get the values of the rows of the matrix. The result of all this is encapsulated in the following function. As with the other rotation matrices, the inverse is equal to the transpose.

Because some callers of the `Rotate()` function already have $\sin \theta$ and $\cos \theta$ at hand, pbrt provides a variant of the function that takes those values directly.

⟨*Transform Inline Functions*⟩ $+\equiv$
```
Transform Rotate(Float sinTheta, Float cosTheta, Vector3f axis) {
    Vector3f a = Normalize(axis);
    SquareMatrix<4> m;
    ⟨Compute rotation of first basis vector 126⟩
    ⟨Compute rotations of second and third basis vectors⟩
    return Transform(m, Transpose(m));
}
```

⟨*Compute rotation of first basis vector*⟩ $\equiv$ **126**
```
m[0][0] = a.x * a.x + (1 - a.x * a.x) * cosTheta;
m[0][1] = a.x * a.y * (1 - cosTheta) - a.z * sinTheta;
m[0][2] = a.x * a.z * (1 - cosTheta) + a.y * sinTheta;
m[0][3] = 0;
```

The code for the other two basis vectors follows similarly and is not included here.

A second variant of `Rotate()` takes the angle θ in degrees, computes its sine and cosine, and calls the first.

Float 23
Normalize() 88
SquareMatrix 1049
SquareMatrix::Transpose() 1051
Transform 120
Vector3f 86

⟨*Transform Inline Functions*⟩ +≡

```
Transform Rotate(Float theta, Vector3f axis) {
    Float sinTheta = std::sin(Radians(theta).);
    Float cosTheta = std::cos(Radians(theta));
    return Rotate(sinTheta, cosTheta, axis);
}
```

3.9.8 ROTATING ONE VECTOR TO ANOTHER

It is sometimes useful to find the transformation that performs a rotation that aligns one unit vector $\mathbf{f}$ with another $\mathbf{t}$ (where $\mathbf{f}$ denotes "from" and $\mathbf{t}$ denotes "to"). One way to do so is to define a rotation axis by the cross product of the two vectors, compute the rotation angle as the arccosine of their dot product, and then use the Rotate() function. However, this approach not only becomes unstable when the two vectors are nearly parallel but also requires a number of expensive trigonometric function calls.

A different approach to deriving this rotation matrix is based on finding a pair of reflection transformations that reflect $\mathbf{f}$ to an intermediate vector $\mathbf{r}$ and then reflect $\mathbf{r}$ to $\mathbf{t}$. The product of such a pair of reflections gives the desired rotation. The *Householder matrix* $\mathbf{H}(\mathbf{v})$ provides a way to find these reflections: it reflects the given vector $\mathbf{v}$ to its negation $-\mathbf{v}$ while leaving all vectors orthogonal to $\mathbf{v}$ unchanged and is defined as

$$\mathbf{H}(\mathbf{v}) = \mathbf{I} - \frac{2}{\mathbf{v} \cdot \mathbf{v}} \mathbf{v}\mathbf{v}^T,$$

where $\mathbf{I}$ is the identity matrix.

With the product of the two reflections

$$\mathbf{R} = \mathbf{H}(\mathbf{r} - \mathbf{t})\mathbf{H}(\mathbf{r} - \mathbf{f}), \qquad\qquad (3.10)$$

the second matrix reflects $\mathbf{f}$ to $\mathbf{r}$ and the first then reflects $\mathbf{r}$ to $\mathbf{t}$, which together give the desired rotation.

⟨*Transform Inline Functions*⟩ +≡

```
Transform RotateFromTo(Vector3f from, Vector3f to) {
    ⟨Compute intermediate vector for vector reflection 127⟩
    ⟨Initialize matrix r for rotation 128⟩
    return Transform(r, Transpose(r));
}
```

The intermediate reflection direction refl is determined by choosing a basis vector that is not too closely aligned to either of the from and to vectors. In the computation here, because 0.72 is just slightly greater than $\sqrt{2}/2$, the absolute value of at least one pair of matching coordinates must then both be less than 0.72, assuming the vectors are normalized. In this way, a loss of accuracy is avoided when the reflection direction is nearly parallel to either from or to.

⟨*Compute intermediate vector for vector reflection*⟩ ≡   127

```
Vector3f refl;
if (std::abs(from.x) < 0.72f && std::abs(to.x) < 0.72f)
    refl = Vector3f(1, 0, 0);
else if (std::abs(from.y) < 0.72f && std::abs(to.y) < 0.72f)
    refl = Vector3f(0, 1, 0);
else
    refl = Vector3f(0, 0, 1);
```

Given the reflection axis, the matrix elements can be initialized directly.

Float 23
Radians() 1033
Rotate() 126
SquareMatrix::Transpose() 1051
Transform 120
Vector3f 86

⟨*Initialize matrix* r *for rotation*⟩ ≡   **127**
```
   Vector3f u = refl - from, v = refl - to;
   SquareMatrix<4> r;
   for (int i = 0; i < 3; ++i)
       for (int j = 0; j < 3; ++j)
           ⟨Initialize matrix element r[i][j] 128⟩
```

Expanding the product of the Householder matrices in Equation (3.10), we can find that the matrix element $r_{i,j}$ is given by

$$\delta_{i,j} - \frac{2}{\mathbf{u} \cdot \mathbf{u}} \mathbf{u}_i \mathbf{u}_j - \frac{2}{\mathbf{v} \cdot \mathbf{v}} \mathbf{v}_i \mathbf{v}_j + \frac{4(\mathbf{u} \cdot \mathbf{v})}{(\mathbf{u} \cdot \mathbf{u})(\mathbf{v} \cdot \mathbf{v})} \mathbf{v}_i \mathbf{u}_j,$$

where $\delta_{i,j}$ is the Kronecker delta function that is 1 if i and j are equal and 0 otherwise. The implementation follows directly.

⟨*Initialize matrix element* r[i][j]⟩ ≡   **128**
```
   r[i][j] = ((i == j) ? 1 : 0) -
             2 / Dot(u, u) * u[i] * u[j] -
             2 / Dot(v, v) * v[i] * v[j] +
             4 * Dot(u, v) / (Dot(u, u) * Dot(v, v)) * v[i] * u[j];
```

3.9.9 THE LOOK-AT TRANSFORMATION

The *look-at transformation* is particularly useful for placing a camera in the scene. The caller specifies the desired position of the camera, a point the camera is looking at, and an "up" vector that orients the camera along the viewing direction implied by the first two parameters. All of these values are typically given in world-space coordinates; this gives a transformation from world space to camera space (Figure 3.28). We will assume that use in the discussion below, though note that this way of specifying transformations can also be useful for placing light sources in the scene.

In order to find the entries of the look-at transformation matrix, we use principles described earlier in this section: the columns of a transformation matrix give the effect of the transformation on the basis of a coordinate system.

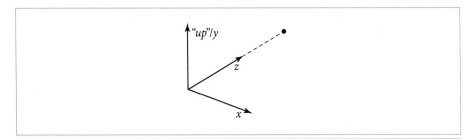

Figure 3.28: Given a camera position, the position being looked at from the camera, and an "up" direction, the look-at transformation describes a transformation from a left-handed viewing coordinate system where the camera is at the origin looking down the $+z$ axis, and the $+y$ axis is along the up direction.

Dot() 89

SquareMatrix 1049

Vector3f 86

⟨*Transform Function Definitions*⟩ +≡

```
Transform LookAt(Point3f pos, Point3f look, Vector3f up) {
    SquareMatrix<4> worldFromCamera;
    ⟨Initialize fourth column of viewing matrix 129⟩
    ⟨Initialize first three columns of viewing matrix 129⟩
    SquareMatrix<4> cameraFromWorld = InvertOrExit(worldFromCamera);
    return Transform(cameraFromWorld, worldFromCamera);
}
```

The easiest column is the fourth one, which gives the point that the camera-space origin, $[0\ 0\ 0\ 1]^T$, maps to in world space. This is clearly just the camera position, supplied by the user.

⟨*Initialize fourth column of viewing matrix*⟩ ≡   **129**

```
worldFromCamera[0][3] = pos.x;
worldFromCamera[1][3] = pos.y;
worldFromCamera[2][3] = pos.z;
worldFromCamera[3][3] = 1;
```

The other three columns are not much more difficult. First, LookAt() computes the normalized direction vector from the camera location to the look-at point; this gives the vector coordinates that the z axis should map to and, thus, the third column of the matrix. (In a left-handed coordinate system, camera space is defined with the viewing direction down the $+z$ axis.) The first column, giving the world-space direction that the $+x$ axis in camera space maps to, is found by taking the cross product of the user-supplied "up" vector with the recently computed viewing direction vector. Finally, the "up" vector is recomputed by taking the cross product of the viewing direction vector with the transformed x axis vector, thus ensuring that the y and z axes are perpendicular and we have an orthonormal viewing coordinate system.

⟨*Initialize first three columns of viewing matrix*⟩ ≡   **129**

```
Vector3f dir = Normalize(look - pos);
Vector3f right = Normalize(Cross(Normalize(up), dir));
Vector3f newUp = Cross(dir, right);
worldFromCamera[0][0] = right.x;
worldFromCamera[1][0] = right.y;
worldFromCamera[2][0] = right.z;
worldFromCamera[3][0] = 0.;
worldFromCamera[0][1] = newUp.x;
worldFromCamera[1][1] = newUp.y;
worldFromCamera[2][1] = newUp.z;
worldFromCamera[3][1] = 0.;
worldFromCamera[0][2] = dir.x;
worldFromCamera[1][2] = dir.y;
worldFromCamera[2][2] = dir.z;
worldFromCamera[3][2] = 0.;
```

3.10 APPLYING TRANSFORMATIONS

We can now define routines that perform the appropriate matrix multiplications to transform points and vectors. We will overload the function application operator to describe these transformations; this lets us write code like:

```
Point3f p = ...;
Transform T = ...;
Point3f pNew = T(p);
```

3.10.1 POINTS

The point transformation routine takes a point (x, y, z) and implicitly represents it as the homogeneous column vector $[x\ y\ z\ 1]^T$. It then transforms the point by premultiplying this vector with the transformation matrix. Finally, it divides by w to convert back to a non-homogeneous point representation. For efficiency, this method skips the division by the homogeneous weight, w, when $w = 1$, which is common for most of the transformations that will be used in pbrt—only the projective transformations defined in Chapter 5 will require this division.

⟨*Transform Inline Methods*⟩ ≡
```
template <typename T>
Point3<T> Transform::operator()(Point3<T> p) const {
    T xp = m[0][0] * p.x + m[0][1] * p.y + m[0][2] * p.z + m[0][3];
    T yp = m[1][0] * p.x + m[1][1] * p.y + m[1][2] * p.z + m[1][3];
    T zp = m[2][0] * p.x + m[2][1] * p.y + m[2][2] * p.z + m[2][3];
    T wp = m[3][0] * p.x + m[3][1] * p.y + m[3][2] * p.z + m[3][3];
    if (wp == 1)
        return Point3<T>(xp, yp, zp);
    else
        return Point3<T>(xp, yp, zp) / wp;
}
```

The Transform class also provides a corresponding ApplyInverse() method for each type it transforms. The one for Point3 applies its inverse transformation to the given point. Calling this method is more succinct and generally more efficient than calling Transform::Inverse() and then calling its operator().

⟨*Transform Public Methods*⟩ +≡   **120**
```
template <typename T>
Point3<T> ApplyInverse(Point3<T> p) const;
```

All subsequent types that can be transformed also have an ApplyInverse() method, though we will not include them in the book text.

3.10.2 VECTORS

The transformations of vectors can be computed in a similar fashion. However, the multiplication of the matrix and the column vector is simplified since the implicit homogeneous w coordinate is zero.

⟨*Transform Inline Methods*⟩ +≡
```
template <typename T>
Vector3<T> Transform::operator()(Vector3<T> v) const {
    return Vector3<T>(m[0][0] * v.x + m[0][1] * v.y + m[0][2] * v.z,
                      m[1][0] * v.x + m[1][1] * v.y + m[1][2] * v.z,
                      m[2][0] * v.x + m[2][1] * v.y + m[2][2] * v.z);
}
```

Point3 92
Transform 120
Transform::Inverse() 121
Transform::m 120
Vector3 86

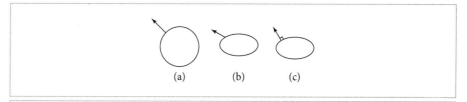

Figure 3.29: Transforming Surface Normals. (a) Original circle, with the normal at a point indicated by an arrow. (b) When scaling the circle to be half as tall in the y direction, simply treating the normal as a direction and scaling it in the same manner gives a normal that is no longer perpendicular to the surface. (c) A properly transformed normal.

3.10.3 NORMALS

Normals do not transform in the same way that vectors do, as shown in Figure 3.29. Although tangent vectors at a surface transform in the straightforward way, normals require special treatment. Because the normal vector $\mathbf{n}$ and any tangent vector $\mathbf{t}$ on the surface are orthogonal by construction, we know that

$$\mathbf{n} \cdot \mathbf{t} = \mathbf{n}^T \mathbf{t} = 0.$$

When we transform a point on the surface by some matrix $\mathbf{M}$, the new tangent vector $\mathbf{t}'$ at the transformed point is $\mathbf{Mt}$. The transformed normal $\mathbf{n}'$ should be equal to $\mathbf{Sn}$ for some 4×4 matrix $\mathbf{S}$. To maintain the orthogonality requirement, we must have

$$0 = (\mathbf{n}')^T \mathbf{t}'$$
$$= (\mathbf{Sn})^T \mathbf{Mt}$$
$$= (\mathbf{n})^T \mathbf{S}^T \mathbf{Mt}.$$

This condition holds if $\mathbf{S}^T \mathbf{M} = \mathbf{I}$, the identity matrix. Therefore, $\mathbf{S}^T = \mathbf{M}^{-1}$, and so $\mathbf{S} = (\mathbf{M}^{-1})^T$, and we see that normals must be transformed by the inverse transpose of the transformation matrix. This detail is one of the reasons why Transforms maintain their inverses.

Note that this method does not explicitly compute the transpose of the inverse when transforming normals. It just indexes into the inverse matrix in a different order (compare to the code for transforming Vector3fs).

⟨*Transform Inline Methods*⟩ $+\equiv$
```
template <typename T>
Normal3<T> Transform::operator()(Normal3<T> n) const {
    T x = n.x, y = n.y, z = n.z;
    return Normal3<T>(mInv[0][0] * x + mInv[1][0] * y + mInv[2][0] * z,
                      mInv[0][1] * x + mInv[1][1] * y + mInv[2][1] * z,
                      mInv[0][2] * x + mInv[1][2] * y + mInv[2][2] * z);
}
```

3.10.4 RAYS

Transforming rays is conceptually straightforward: it is a matter of transforming the constituent origin and direction and copying the other data members. (pbrt also provides a similar method for transforming RayDifferentials.)

The approach used in pbrt to manage floating-point round-off error introduces some subtleties that require a small adjustment to the transformed ray origin. The ⟨*Offset ray origin to edge of error bounds and compute* tMax⟩ fragment handles these details; it is defined in Section 6.8.6, where round-off error and pbrt's mechanisms for dealing with it are discussed.

⟨*Transform Inline Methods*⟩ +≡
```
Ray Transform::operator()(const Ray &r, Float *tMax) const {
    Point3fi o = (*this)(Point3fi(r.o));
    Vector3f d = (*this)(r.d);
    ⟨Offset ray origin to edge of error bounds and compute tMax 383⟩
    return Ray(Point3f(o), d, r.time, r.medium);
}
```

3.10.5 BOUNDING BOXES

The easiest way to transform an axis-aligned bounding box is to transform all eight of its corner vertices and then compute a new bounding box that encompasses those points. The implementation of this approach is shown below; one of the exercises for this chapter is to implement a technique to do this computation more efficiently.

⟨*Transform Method Definitions*⟩ ≡
```
Bounds3f Transform::operator()(const Bounds3f &b) const {
    Bounds3f bt;
    for (int i = 0; i < 8; ++i)
        bt = Union(bt, (*this)(b.Corner(i)));
    return bt;
}
```

3.10.6 COMPOSITION OF TRANSFORMATIONS

Having defined how the matrices representing individual types of transformations are constructed, we can now consider an aggregate transformation resulting from a series of individual transformations. We will finally see the real value of representing transformations with matrices.

Consider a series of transformations **ABC**. We would like to compute a new transformation **T** such that applying **T** gives the same result as applying each of **A**, **B**, and **C** in reverse order; that is, $A(B(C(p))) = T(p)$. Such a transformation **T** can be computed by multiplying the matrices of the transformations **A**, **B**, and **C** together. In pbrt, we can write:

```
Transform T = A * B * C;
```

Then we can apply T to Point3fs p as usual, Point3f pp = T(p), instead of applying each transformation in turn: Point3f pp = A(B(C(p))).

We overload the C++ * operator in the Transform class to compute the new transformation that results from postmultiplying a transformation with another transformation t2. In matrix multiplication, the (i, j)th element of the resulting matrix is the inner product of the ith row of the first matrix with the jth column of the second.

The inverse of the resulting transformation is equal to the product of t2.mInv * mInv. This is a result of the matrix identity

$$(AB)^{-1} = B^{-1}A^{-1}.$$

⟨*Transform Method Definitions*⟩ +≡
```
Transform Transform::operator*(const Transform &t2) const {
    return Transform(m * t2.m, t2.mInv * mInv);
}
```

3.10.7 TRANSFORMATIONS AND COORDINATE SYSTEM HANDEDNESS

Certain types of transformations change a left-handed coordinate system into a right-handed one, or vice versa. Some routines will need to know if the handedness of the source coordinate system is different from that of the destination. In particular, routines that want to ensure that a surface normal always points "outside" of a surface might need to flip the normal's direction after transformation if the handedness changes.

Fortunately, it is easy to tell if handedness is changed by a transformation: it happens only when the determinant of the transformation's upper-left 3×3 submatrix is negative.

⟨*Transform Method Definitions*⟩ +≡
```
bool Transform::SwapsHandedness() const {
    SquareMatrix<3> s(m[0][0], m[0][1], m[0][2],
                      m[1][0], m[1][1], m[1][2],
                      m[2][0], m[2][1], m[2][2]);
    return Determinant(s) < 0;
}
```

3.10.8 VECTOR FRAMES

It is sometimes useful to define a rotation that aligns three orthonormal vectors in a coordinate system with the x, y, and z axes. Applying such a transformation to direction vectors in that coordinate system can simplify subsequent computations. For example, in pbrt, BSDF evaluation is performed in a coordinate system where the surface normal is aligned with the z axis. Among other things, this makes it possible to efficiently evaluate trigonometric functions using functions like the CosTheta() function that was introduced in Section 3.8.3.

The Frame class efficiently represents and performs such transformations, avoiding the full generality (and hence, complexity) of the Transform class. It only needs to store a 3×3 matrix, and storing the inverse is unnecessary since it is just the matrix's transpose, given orthonormal basis vectors.

⟨*Frame Definition*⟩ ≡
```
class Frame {
  public:
    ⟨Frame Public Methods 133⟩
    ⟨Frame Public Members 133⟩
};
```

Given three orthonormal vectors x, y, and z, the matrix F that transforms vectors into their space is

$$\mathbf{F} = \begin{pmatrix} \mathbf{x}_x & \mathbf{x}_y & \mathbf{x}_z \\ \mathbf{y}_x & \mathbf{y}_y & \mathbf{y}_z \\ \mathbf{z}_x & \mathbf{z}_y & \mathbf{z}_z \end{pmatrix} = \begin{pmatrix} \mathbf{x} \\ \mathbf{y} \\ \mathbf{z} \end{pmatrix}.$$

The Frame stores this matrix using three Vector3fs.

⟨*Frame Public Members*⟩ ≡   133
```
Vector3f x, y, z;
```

The three basis vectors can be specified explicitly; in debug builds, DCHECK()s in the constructor ensure that the provided vectors are orthonormal.

⟨*Frame Public Methods*⟩ ≡   133
```
Frame() : x(1, 0, 0), y(0, 1, 0), z(0, 0, 1) {}
Frame(Vector3f x, Vector3f y, Vector3f z);
```

Frame also provides convenience methods that construct a frame from just two of the basis vectors, using the cross product to compute the third.

⟨*Frame Public Methods*⟩ +≡   133
```
static Frame FromXZ(Vector3f x, Vector3f z) {
    return Frame(x, Cross(z, x), z);
}
static Frame FromXY(Vector3f x, Vector3f y) {
    return Frame(x, y, Cross(x, y));
}
```

Only the *z* axis vector can be provided as well, in which case the others are set arbitrarily.

⟨*Frame Public Methods*⟩ +≡   133
```
static Frame FromZ(Vector3f z) {
    Vector3f x, y;
    CoordinateSystem(z, &x, &y);
    return Frame(x, y, z);
}
```

A variety of other functions, not included here, allow specifying a frame using a normal vector and specifying it via just the *x* or *y* basis vector.

Transforming a vector into the frame's coordinate space is done using the F matrix. Because Vector3fs were used to store its rows, the matrix-vector product can be expressed as three dot products.

⟨*Frame Public Methods*⟩ +≡   133
```
Vector3f ToLocal(Vector3f v) const {
    return Vector3f(Dot(v, x), Dot(v, y), Dot(v, z));
}
```

A ToLocal() method is also provided for normal vectors. In this case, we do not need to compute the inverse transpose of F for the transformation normals (recall the discussion of transforming normals in Section 3.10.3). Because F is an orthonormal matrix (its rows and columns are mutually orthogonal and unit length), its inverse is equal to its transpose, so it is its own inverse transpose already.

⟨*Frame Public Methods*⟩ +≡   133
```
Normal3f ToLocal(Normal3f n) const {
    return Normal3f(Dot(n, x), Dot(n, y), Dot(n, z));
}
```

The method that transforms vectors out of the frame's local space transposes F to find its inverse before multiplying by the vector. In this case, the resulting computation can be expressed as the sum of three scaled versions of the matrix columns. As before, surface normals transform as regular vectors. (That method is not included here.)

⟨*Frame Public Methods*⟩ +≡   133
```
Vector3f FromLocal(Vector3f v) const {
    return v.x * x + v.y * y + v.z * z;
}
```

For convenience, there is a Transform constructor that takes a Frame. Its simple implementation is not included here.

⟨*Transform Public Methods*⟩ +≡   120
```
explicit Transform(const Frame &frame);
```

Figure 3.30: Spinning Spheres. Three spheres, reflected in a mirror, spinning at different rates using pbrt's transformation animation code. Note that the reflections of the spheres are blurry as well as the spheres themselves.

3.10.9 ANIMATING TRANSFORMATIONS

pbrt supports time-varying transformation matrices for cameras and geometric primitives in the scene. Rather than just supplying a single transformation to place an object in the scene, the user may supply a number of *keyframe* transformations, each one associated with a particular time. This makes it possible for the camera to move and for objects in the scene to be in motion during the time the simulated camera's shutter is open. Figure 3.30 shows three spheres animated using keyframe matrix animation in pbrt.

Directly interpolating the matrix elements of transformation matrices at different times usually does not work well, especially if a rotation is included in the associated change of transformation. pbrt therefore implements algorithms that decompose transformations into translations, rotations, and scales, each of which can be independently interpolated before they are reassembled to form an interpolated transformation. The AnimatedTransform class that implements those algorithms is not included here in the printed book, though the online edition of the book (recall Section 1.4.3) includes thorough documentation of its implementation. Here we will summarize its interface so that its use in forthcoming text can be understood.

Its constructor takes two transformations and associated times. Due to the computational cost of decomposing and recomposing transformations as well as the storage requirements of AnimatedTransform, which total roughly 400 bytes, it is worthwhile to avoid using AnimatedTransform if the two matrices are equal.

```
AnimatedTransform(Transform startTransform, Float startTime,
                  Transform endTransform, Float endTime);
```

The Interpolate() method returns the interpolated transformation for the given time. If the time is outside of the range specified to the constructor, whichever of startTransform or endTransform is closest in time is returned.

```
Transform Interpolate(Float time) const;
```

Point3f 92

Methods are also available to apply transformations and inverse transformations to pbrt's basic geometric classes. For example, the following two methods transform points. (Because Point3f does not store an associated time, the time must be provided separately. However, classes like Ray and Interaction that do store a time are passed to their transformation methods unaccompanied.)

```
Point3f operator()(Point3f p, Float time) const;
Point3f ApplyInverse(Point3f p, Float time) const;
```

It is usually more efficient to transform a geometric object using those methods than to retrieve the interpolated Transform using the Interpolate() method and then use its transformation methods since the specialized transformation methods can apply optimizations like not computing unneeded inverse transformations.

The other key method provided by AnimatedTransform is MotionBounds(), which computes a bounding box that bounds the motion of a bounding box over the AnimatedTransform's time range. Taking the union of the bounds of the transformed bounding box at startTime and endTime is not sufficient to bound the box's motion over intermediate times; this method therefore takes care of the tricky details of accurately bounding the motion.

```
Bounds3f MotionBounds(const Bounds3f &b) const;
```

3.11 INTERACTIONS

The last abstractions in this chapter, SurfaceInteraction and MediumInteraction, respectively represent local information at points on surfaces and in participating media. For example, the ray–shape intersection routines in Chapter 6 return information about the local differential geometry at intersection points in a SurfaceInteraction. Later, the texturing code in Chapter 10 computes material properties using values from the SurfaceInteraction. The closely related MediumInteraction class is used to represent points where light interacts with participating media like smoke or clouds. The implementations of all of these classes are in the files interaction.h and interaction.cpp.

Both SurfaceInteraction and MediumInteraction inherit from a generic Interaction class that provides common member variables and methods, which allows parts of the system for which the differences between surface and medium interactions do not matter to be implemented purely in terms of Interactions.

⟨Interaction Definition⟩ ≡
```
    class Interaction {
      public:
        ⟨Interaction Public Methods 136⟩
        ⟨Interaction Public Members 137⟩
    };
```

A variety of Interaction constructors are available; depending on what sort of interaction is being constructed and what sort of information about it is relevant, corresponding sets of parameters are accepted. This one is the most general of them.

⟨Interaction Public Methods⟩ ≡   136
```
    Interaction(Point3fi pi, Normal3f n, Point2f uv, Vector3f wo, Float time)
        : pi(pi), n(n), uv(uv), wo(Normalize(wo)), time(time) {}
```

All interactions have a point p associated with them. This point is stored using the Point3fi class, which uses an Interval to represent each coordinate value. Storing a small interval of floating-point values rather than a single Float makes it possible to represent bounds on the numeric error in the intersection point, as occurs when the point p was computed by a ray intersection calculation. This information will be useful for avoiding incorrect self-intersections for rays leaving surfaces, as will be discussed in Section 6.8.6.

⟨*Interaction Public Members*⟩ ≡   **136**
    Point3fi pi;

Interaction provides a convenience method that returns a regular Point3f for the interaction point for the parts of the system that do not need to account for any error in it (e.g., the texture evaluation routines).

⟨*Interaction Public Methods*⟩ +≡   **136**
    Point3f p() const { return Point3f(pi); }

All interactions also have a time associated with them. Among other uses, this value is necessary for setting the time of a spawned ray leaving the interaction.

⟨*Interaction Public Members*⟩ +≡   **136**
    Float time = 0;

For interactions that lie along a ray (either from a ray–shape intersection or from a ray passing through participating media), the negative ray direction is stored in the wo member variable, which corresponds to ω_o, the notation we use for the outgoing direction when computing lighting at points. For other types of interaction points where the notion of an outgoing direction does not apply (e.g., those found by randomly sampling points on the surface of shapes), wo has the value $(0, 0, 0)$.

⟨*Interaction Public Members*⟩ +≡   **136**
    Vector3f wo;

For interactions on surfaces, n stores the surface normal at the point and uv stores its (u, v) parametric coordinates. It is fair to ask, why are these values stored in the base Interaction class rather than in SurfaceInteraction? The reason is that there are some parts of the system that *mostly* do not care about the distinction between surface and medium interactions—for example, some of the routines that sample points on light sources given a point to be illuminated. Those make use of these values if they are available and ignore them if they are set to zero. By accepting the small dissonance of having them in the wrong place here, the implementations of those methods and the code that calls them is made that much simpler.

⟨*Interaction Public Members*⟩ +≡   **136**
    Normal3f n;
    Point2f uv;

It is possible to check if a pointer or reference to an Interaction is one of the two subclasses. A nonzero surface normal is used as a distinguisher for a surface.

⟨*Interaction Public Methods*⟩ +≡   **136**
    bool IsSurfaceInteraction() const { return n != Normal3f(0, 0, 0); }
    bool IsMediumInteraction() const { return !IsSurfaceInteraction(); }

Methods are provided to cast to the subclass types as well. This is a good place for a run-time check to ensure that the requested conversion is valid. The non-const variant of this method as well as corresponding AsMedium() methods follow similarly and are not included in the text.

⟨*Interaction Public Methods*⟩ +≡   **136**
```
    const SurfaceInteraction &AsSurface() const {
        CHECK(IsSurfaceInteraction());
        return (const SurfaceInteraction &)*this;
    }
```

Interactions can also represent either an interface between two types of participating media using an instance of the MediumInterface class, which is defined in Section 11.4, or the properties of the scattering medium at their point using a Medium. Here as well, the Interaction abstraction leaks: surfaces can represent interfaces between media, and at a point inside a medium, there is no interface but there is the current medium. Both of these values are stored in Interaction for the same reasons of expediency that n and uv were.

⟨*Interaction Public Members*⟩ +≡   **136**
```
    const MediumInterface *mediumInterface = nullptr;
    Medium medium = nullptr;
```

3.11.1 SURFACE INTERACTION

As described earlier, the geometry of a particular point on a surface (often a position found by intersecting a ray against the surface) is represented by a SurfaceInteraction. Having this abstraction lets most of the system work with points on surfaces without needing to consider the particular type of geometric shape the points lie on.

⟨*SurfaceInteraction Definition*⟩ ≡
```
    class SurfaceInteraction : public Interaction {
      public:
        ⟨SurfaceInteraction Public Methods 139⟩
        ⟨SurfaceInteraction Public Members 138⟩
    };
```

In addition to the point p, the surface normal n, and (u, v) coordinates from the parameterization of the surface from the Interaction base class, the SurfaceInteraction also stores the parametric partial derivatives of the point $\partial p/\partial u$ and $\partial p/\partial v$ and the partial derivatives of the surface normal $\partial n/\partial u$ and $\partial n/\partial v$. See Figure 3.31 for a depiction of these values.

⟨*SurfaceInteraction Public Members*⟩ ≡   **138**
```
    Vector3f dpdu, dpdv;
    Normal3f dndu, dndv;
```

This representation implicitly assumes that shapes have a parametric description—that for some range of (u, v) values, points on the surface are given by some function f such that $p = f(u, v)$. Although this is not true for all shapes, all of the shapes that pbrt supports do have at least a local parametric description, so we will stick with the parametric representation since this assumption is helpful elsewhere (e.g., for antialiasing of textures in Chapter 10).

The SurfaceInteraction constructor takes parameters that set all of these values. It computes the normal as the cross product of the partial derivatives.

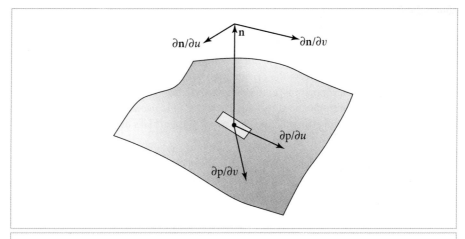

Figure 3.31: The Local Differential Geometry around a Point p. The parametric partial derivatives of the surface, $\partial p/\partial u$ and $\partial p/\partial v$, lie in the tangent plane but are not necessarily orthogonal. The surface normal **n** is given by the cross product of $\partial p/\partial u$ and $\partial p/\partial v$. The vectors $\partial n/\partial u$ and $\partial n/\partial v$ record the differential change in surface normal as we move u and v along the surface.

⟨*SurfaceInteraction Public Methods*⟩ ≡   **138**
```
SurfaceInteraction(Point3fi pi, Point2f uv, Vector3f wo, Vector3f dpdu,
        Vector3f dpdv, Normal3f dndu, Normal3f dndv, Float time,
        bool flipNormal)
    : Interaction(pi, Normal3f(Normalize(Cross(dpdu, dpdv))), uv, wo, time),
      dpdu(dpdu), dpdv(dpdv), dndu(dndu), dndv(dndv) {
    ⟨Initialize shading geometry from true geometry 139⟩
    ⟨Adjust normal based on orientation and handedness 140⟩
}
```

SurfaceInteraction stores a second instance of a surface normal and the various partial derivatives to represent possibly perturbed values of these quantities—as can be generated by bump mapping or interpolated per-vertex normals with meshes. Some parts of the system use this shading geometry, while others need to work with the original quantities.

⟨*SurfaceInteraction Public Members*⟩ +≡   **138**
```
struct {
    Normal3f n;
    Vector3f dpdu, dpdv;
    Normal3f dndu, dndv;
} shading;
```

The shading geometry values are initialized in the constructor to match the original surface geometry. If shading geometry is present, it generally is not computed until some time after the SurfaceInteraction constructor runs. The SetShadingGeometry() method, to be defined shortly, updates the shading geometry.

⟨*Initialize shading geometry from true geometry*⟩ ≡   **139**
```
shading.n = n;
shading.dpdu = dpdu;
shading.dpdv = dpdv;
shading.dndu = dndu;
shading.dndv = dndv;
```

The surface normal has special meaning to pbrt, which assumes that, for closed shapes, the normal is oriented such that it points to the outside of the shape. For geometry used as an area light source, light is by default emitted from only the side of the surface that the normal points toward; the other side is black. Because normals have this special meaning, pbrt provides a mechanism for the user to reverse the orientation of the normal, flipping it to point in the opposite direction. A ReverseOrientation directive in a pbrt input file flips the normal to point in the opposite, non-default direction. Therefore, it is necessary to check if the given Shape has the corresponding flag set and, if so, switch the normal's direction here.

However, one other factor plays into the orientation of the normal and must be accounted for here as well. If a shape's transformation matrix has switched the handedness of the object coordinate system from pbrt's default left-handed coordinate system to a right-handed one, we need to switch the orientation of the normal as well. To see why this is so, consider a scale matrix $S(1, 1, -1)$. We would naturally expect this scale to switch the direction of the normal, although because we have computed the normal by $\mathbf{n} = \partial \mathrm{p}/\partial u \times \partial \mathrm{p}/\partial v$,

$$S(1, 1, -1)\frac{\partial \mathrm{p}}{\partial u} \times S(1, 1, -1)\frac{\partial \mathrm{p}}{\partial v} = S(-1, -1, 1)\left(\frac{\partial \mathrm{p}}{\partial u} \times \frac{\partial \mathrm{p}}{\partial v}\right)$$

$$= S(-1, -1, 1)\mathbf{n}$$

$$\neq S(1, 1, -1)\mathbf{n}.$$

Therefore, it is also necessary to flip the normal's direction if the transformation switches the handedness of the coordinate system, since the flip will not be accounted for by the computation of the normal's direction using the cross product. A flag passed by the caller indicates whether this flip is necessary.

⟨*Adjust normal based on orientation and handedness*⟩ ≡   **139**
```
if (flipNormal) {
    n *= -1;
    shading.n *= -1;
}
```

pbrt also provides the capability to associate an integer index with each face of a polygon mesh. This information is used for certain texture mapping operations. A separate SurfaceInteraction constructor allows its specification.

⟨*SurfaceInteraction Public Members*⟩ +≡   **138**
```
int faceIndex = 0;
```

When a shading coordinate frame is computed, the SurfaceInteraction is updated via its SetShadingGeometry() method.

⟨*SurfaceInteraction Public Methods*⟩ +≡   **138**
```
void SetShadingGeometry(Normal3f ns, Vector3f dpdus, Vector3f dpdvs,
        Normal3f dndus, Normal3f dndvs, bool orientationIsAuthoritative) {
```
   ⟨*Compute* shading.n *for* SurfaceInteraction **141**⟩
   ⟨*Initialize* shading *partial derivative values* **141**⟩
```
}
```

After performing the same cross product (and possibly flipping the orientation of the normal) as before to compute an initial shading normal, the implementation then flips either the shading normal or the true geometric normal if needed so that the two normals lie in the same hemisphere. Since the shading normal generally represents a relatively small perturbation of the geometric normal, the two of them should always be in the same hemisphere.

Depending on the context, either the geometric normal or the shading normal may more authoritatively point toward the correct "outside" of the surface, so the caller passes a Boolean value that determines which should be flipped if needed.

⟨*Compute* shading.n *for* SurfaceInteraction⟩ ≡ **140**
```
    shading.n = ns;
    if (orientationIsAuthoritative)
        n = FaceForward(n, shading.n);
    else
        shading.n = FaceForward(shading.n, n);
```

With the normal set, the various partial derivatives can be copied.

⟨*Initialize* shading *partial derivative values*⟩ ≡ **140**
```
    shading.dpdu = dpdus;
    shading.dpdv = dpdvs;
    shading.dndu = dndus;
    shading.dndv = dndvs;
```

3.11.2 MEDIUM INTERACTION

As described earlier, the MediumInteraction class is used to represent an interaction at a point in a scattering medium like smoke or clouds.

⟨*MediumInteraction Definition*⟩ ≡
```
    class MediumInteraction : public Interaction {
      public:
        ⟨MediumInteraction Public Methods 141⟩
        ⟨MediumInteraction Public Members 141⟩
    };
```

In contrast to SurfaceInteraction, it adds little to the base Interaction class. The only addition is a PhaseFunction, which describes how the particles in the medium scatter light. Phase functions and the PhaseFunction class are introduced in Section 11.3.

⟨*MediumInteraction Public Methods*⟩ ≡ **141**
```
    MediumInteraction(Point3f p, Vector3f wo, Float time, Medium medium,
                      PhaseFunction phase)
        : Interaction(p, wo, time, medium), phase(phase) {}
```

⟨*MediumInteraction Public Members*⟩ ≡ **141**
```
    PhaseFunction phase;
```

FURTHER READING

DeRose, Goldman, and their collaborators have argued for an elegant "coordinate-free" approach to describing vector geometry for graphics, where the fact that positions and directions happen to be represented by (x, y, z) coordinates with respect to a particular coordinate system is deemphasized and where points and vectors themselves record which coordinate system they are expressed in terms of (Goldman 1985; DeRose 1989; Mann, Litke, and DeRose 1997). This makes it possible for a software layer to ensure that common errors like adding a vector in one coordinate system to a point in another coordinate system are transparently handled by transforming them to a common coordinate system first. A related approach was described by Geisler et al. (2020), who encoded coordinate systems using the programming language's type system. We have not followed either of these approaches in pbrt, although the principles behind them are well worth understanding and keeping in mind when working with coordinate systems in computer graphics.

Schneider and Eberly's *Geometric Tools for Computer Graphics* is influenced by the coordinate-free approach and covers the topics of this chapter in much greater depth (Schneider and Eberly 2003). It is also full of useful geometric algorithms for graphics. A classic and more traditional introduction to the topics of this chapter is *Mathematical Elements for Computer Graphics* by Rogers and Adams (1990). Note that their book uses a row-vector representation of points and vectors, however, which means that our matrices would be transposed when expressed in their framework, and that they multiply points and vectors by matrices to transform them (pM), rather than multiplying matrices by points as we do (Mp). Homogeneous coordinates were only briefly mentioned in this chapter, although they are the basis of projective geometry, where they are the foundation of many elegant algorithms. Stolfi's book is an excellent introduction to this topic (Stolfi 1991).

There are many good books on linear algebra and vector geometry. We have found Lang (1986) and Buck (1978) to be good references on these respective topics. See also Akenine-Möller et al.'s *Real-Time Rendering* book (2018) for a solid graphics-based introduction to linear algebra. Ström et al. have written an excellent online linear algebra book, *immersivemath.com*, that features interactive figures that illustrate the key concepts (2020).

Donnay's book (1945) gives a concise but complete introduction to spherical trigonometry. The expression for the solid angle of a triangle in Equation (3.6) is due to Van Oosterom and Strackee (1983).

An alternative approach for designing a vector math library is exemplified by the widely used *eigen* system by Guennebaud, Jacob, and others (2010). In addition to including support for CPU SIMD vector instruction sets, it makes extensive use of *expression templates*, a C++ programming technique that makes it possible to simplify and optimize the evaluation of vector and matrix expressions at compile time.

The subtleties of how normal vectors are transformed were first widely understood in the graphics community after articles by Wallis (1990) and Turkowski (1990b).

Cigolle et al. (2014) compared a wide range of approaches for compactly encoding unit vectors. The approach implemented in OctahedralVector is due to Meyer et al. (2010), who also showed that if 52 bits are used with this representation, the precision is equal to that of normalized Vector3fs. (Our implementation also includes an improvement suggested by Cigolle et al. (2014).) The octahedral encoding it is based on was introduced by Praun and Hoppe (2003).

The equal-area sphere mapping algorithm in Section 3.8.3 is due to Clarberg (2008); our implementation of the mapping functions is derived from the high-performance CPU SIMD implementation that accompanies that paper. The square-to-hemisphere mapping that it is based on was developed by Shirley and Chiu (1997).

The algorithm used in CoordinateSystem() is based on an approach first derived by Frisvad (2012). The reformulation to improve numerical accuracy that we have used in our implementation was derived concurrently by Duff et al. (2017) and by Max (2017). The algorithm implemented in RotateFromTo() was introduced by Möller and Hughes (1999), with an adjustment to the computation of the reflection vector due to Hughes (2021).

The numerically robust AngleBetween() function defined in this chapter is due to Hatch (2003).

An algorithm to compute a tight bounding cone for multiple direction vectors was given by Barequet and Elber (2005).

The algorithms used in the `AnimatedTransform` implementation are based on the polar matrix decomposition approach that was described by Shoemake and Duff (1992); see the online edition of this book for further references to methods for animating transformations.

EXERCISES

3.1 Find a more efficient way to transform axis-aligned bounding boxes by taking advantage of the symmetries of the problem: because the eight corner points are linear combinations of three axis-aligned basis vectors and a single corner point, their transformed bounding box can be found more efficiently than by the method we have presented (Arvo 1990).

3.2 Instead of boxes, tighter bounds around objects could be computed by using the intersections of many nonorthogonal slabs. Extend the bounding box representation in `pbrt` to allow the user to specify a bound comprised of arbitrary slabs.

3.3 The `DirectionCone::BoundSubtendedDirections()` method bounds the directions that a `Bounds3f` subtends from a given reference point by first finding a sphere that bounds the `Bounds3f` and then bounding the directions it subtends. While this gives a valid bound, it is not necessarily the smallest one possible. Derive an improved algorithm that acts directly on the bounding box, update the implementation of `BoundSubtendedDirections()`, and render scenes where that method is used (e.g., those that use a `BVHLightSampler` to sample light sources). How are running time and image quality affected? Can you find a scene where this change gives a significant benefit?

3.4 Change `pbrt` so that it transforms `Normal3f`s just like `Vector3f`s, and create a scene that gives a clearly incorrect image due to this bug. (Do not forget to revert this change from your copy of the source code when you are done!)

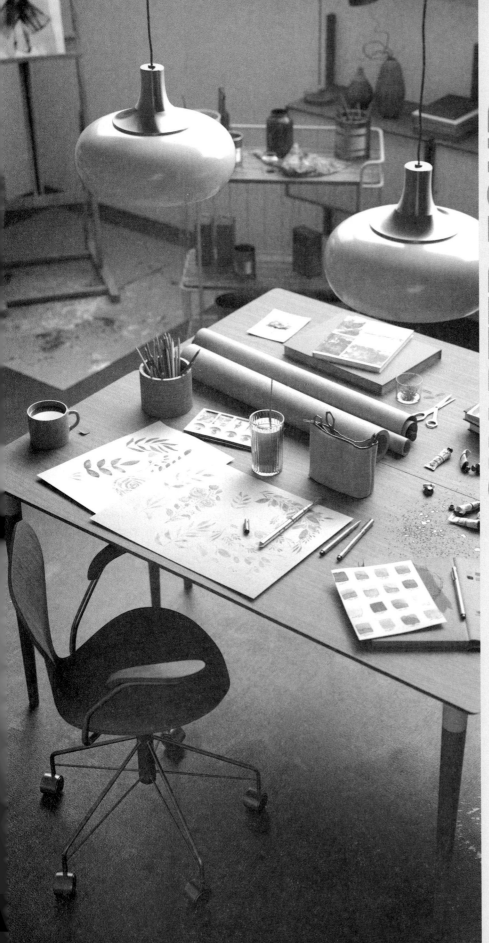

CHAPTER FOUR

04 RADIOMETRY, SPECTRA, AND COLOR

To precisely describe how light is represented and sampled to compute images, we must first establish some background in *radiometry*—the study of the propagation of electromagnetic radiation in an environment. In this chapter, we will first introduce four key quantities that describe electromagnetic radiation: flux, intensity, irradiance, and radiance.

These radiometric quantities generally vary as a function of wavelength. The variation of each is described by its *spectral distribution*—a distribution function that gives the amount of light at each wavelength. (We will interchangeably use *spectrum* to describe spectral distributions, and *spectra* for a plurality of them.) Of particular interest in rendering are the wavelengths (λ) of electromagnetic radiation between approximately 380 nm and 780 nm, which account for light visible to humans.[1] A variety of classes that are used to represent spectral distributions in pbrt are defined in Section 4.5.

While spectral distributions are a purely physical concept, color is related to how humans perceive spectra. The lower wavelengths of light ($\lambda \approx 400$ nm) are said to be bluish colors, the middle wavelengths ($\lambda \approx 550$ nm) greens, and the upper wavelengths ($\lambda \approx 650$ nm) reds. It is important to have accurate models of color for two reasons: first, display devices like monitors expect colors rather than spectra to describe pixel values, so accurately converting spectra to appropriate colors is important for displaying rendered images. Second, emission and reflection properties of objects in scenes are often specified using colors; these colors must be converted into spectra for use in rendering. Section 4.6, at the end of this chapter, describes the properties of color in more detail and includes implementations of pbrt's color-related functionality.

---

1   The full range of perceptible wavelengths slightly extends beyond this interval, though the eye's sensitivity at these wavelengths is lower by many orders of magnitude. The range 360–830 nm is often used as a conservative bound when tabulating spectral curves.

4.1 RADIOMETRY

Radiometry provides a set of ideas and mathematical tools to describe light propagation and reflection. It forms the basis of the derivation of the rendering algorithms that will be used throughout the rest of this book. Interestingly enough, radiometry was not originally derived from first principles using the physics of light but was built on an abstraction of light based on particles flowing through space. As such, effects like polarization of light do not naturally fit into this framework, although connections have since been made between radiometry and Maxwell's equations, giving radiometry a solid basis in physics.

Radiative transfer is the phenomenological study of the transfer of radiant energy. It is based on radiometric principles and operates at the *geometric optics* level, where macroscopic properties of light suffice to describe how light interacts with objects much larger than the light's wavelength. It is not uncommon to incorporate phenomena from wave optics models of light, but these results need to be expressed in the language of radiative transfer's basic abstractions.

In this manner, it is possible to describe interactions of light with objects of approximately the same size as the wavelength of the light, and thereby model effects like dispersion and interference. At an even finer level of detail, quantum mechanics is needed to describe light's interaction with atoms. Fortunately, direct simulation of quantum mechanical principles is unnecessary for solving rendering problems in computer graphics, so the intractability of such an approach is avoided.

In pbrt, we will assume that geometric optics is an adequate model for the description of light and light scattering. This leads to a few basic assumptions about the behavior of light that will be used implicitly throughout the system:

- *Linearity:* The combined effect of two inputs to an optical system is always equal to the sum of the effects of each of the inputs individually. Nonlinear scattering behavior is only observed in physical experiments involving extremely high energies, so this is generally a reasonable assumption.
- *Energy conservation:* When light scatters from a surface or from participating media, the scattering events can never produce more energy than they started with.
- *No polarization:* Electromagnetic radiation including visible light is *polarized*. A good mental analogy of polarization is a vibration propagating along a taut string. Shaking one end of the string will produce perpendicular waves that travel toward the other end. However, besides a simple linear motion, the taut string can also conduct other kinds of oscillations: the motion could, for example, be clockwise or counter-clockwise and in a circular or elliptical shape. All of these possibilities exist analogously in the case of light. Curiously, this additional polarization state of light is essentially imperceptible to humans without additional aids like specialized cameras or polarizing sunglasses. In pbrt, we will therefore make the common assumption that light is unpolarized—that is, a superposition of waves with many different polarizations so that only their average behavior is perceived. Therefore, the only relevant property of light is its distribution by wavelength (or, equivalently, frequency).
- *No fluorescence or phosphorescence:* The behavior of light at one wavelength is completely independent of light's behavior at other wavelengths or times. As with polarization, it is not too difficult to include these effects if they are required.
- *Steady state:* Light in the environment is assumed to have reached equilibrium, so its radiance distribution is not changing over time. This happens nearly instantaneously with light in realistic scenes, so it is not a limitation in practice. Note that phosphorescence also violates the steady-state assumption.

The most significant loss from adopting a geometric optics model is the incompatibility with diffraction and interference effects. Even though this incompatibility can be circumvented— for example, by replacing radiance with the concept of a *Wigner distribution function* (Oh et al. 2010, Cuypers et al. 2012)—such extensions are beyond the scope of this book.

4.1.1 BASIC QUANTITIES

There are four radiometric quantities that are central to rendering: flux, irradiance/radiant exitance, intensity, and radiance. They can each be derived from energy by successively taking limits over time, area, and directions. All of these radiometric quantities are in general wavelength dependent, though we will defer that topic until Section 4.1.3.

Energy

Our starting point is energy, which is measured in joules (J). Sources of illumination emit photons, each of which is at a particular wavelength and carries a particular amount of energy. All the basic radiometric quantities are effectively different ways of measuring photons. A photon at wavelength λ carries energy

$$Q = \frac{hc}{\lambda},$$

where c is the speed of light, $299{,}472{,}458$ m/s, and h is Planck's constant, $h \approx 6.626 \times 10^{-34}$ m^2 kg/s.

Flux

Energy measures work over some period of time, though under the steady-state assumption generally used in rendering, we are mostly interested in measuring light at an instant. *Radiant flux*, also known as *power*, is the total amount of energy passing through a surface or region of space per unit time. Radiant flux can be found by taking the limit of differential energy per differential time:

$$\Phi = \lim_{\Delta t \to 0} \frac{\Delta Q}{\Delta t} = \frac{dQ}{dt}.$$

Its units are joules/second (J/s), or more commonly, watts (W).

For example, given a light that emitted $Q = 200{,}000$ J over the course of an hour, if the same amount of energy was emitted at all times over the hour, we can find that the light source's flux was

$$\Phi = 200{,}000 \text{ J}/3600 \text{ s} \approx 55.6 \text{ W}.$$

Conversely, given flux as a function of time, we can integrate over a range of times to compute the total energy:

$$Q = \int_{t_0}^{t_1} \Phi(t) \, dt.$$

Note that our notation here is slightly informal: among other issues, because photons are discrete quanta, it is not meaningful to take limits that go to zero for differential time. For the purposes of rendering, where the number of photons is enormous with respect to the measurements we are interested in, this detail is not problematic.

Total emission from light sources is generally described in terms of flux. Figure 4.1 shows flux from a point light source measured by the total amount of energy passing through imaginary spheres around the light. Note that the total amount of flux measured on either of the two spheres in Figure 4.1 is the same—although less energy is passing through any local part of

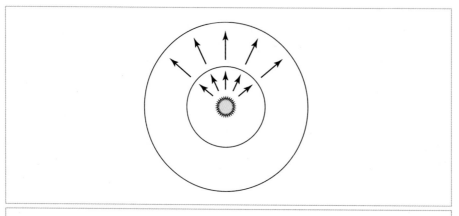

Figure 4.1: Radiant flux, Φ, measures energy passing through a surface or region of space. Here, flux from a point light source is measured at spheres that surround the light.

the large sphere than the small sphere, the greater area of the large sphere means that the total flux is the same.

Irradiance and Radiant Exitance

Any measurement of flux requires an area over which photons per time is being measured. Given a finite area A, we can define the average density of power over the area by $E = \Phi/A$. This quantity is either *irradiance* (E), the area density of flux arriving at a surface, or *radiant exitance* (M), the area density of flux leaving a surface. These measurements have units of W/m^2. (The term *irradiance* is sometimes also used to refer to flux leaving a surface, but for clarity we will use different terms for the two cases.)

For the point light source example in Figure 4.1, irradiance at a point on the outer sphere is less than the irradiance at a point on the inner sphere, since the surface area of the outer sphere is larger. In particular, if the point source is emitting the same amount of illumination in all directions, then for a sphere in this configuration that has radius r,

$$E = \frac{\Phi}{4\pi r^2}.$$

This fact explains why the amount of energy received from a light at a point falls off with the squared distance from the light.

More generally, we can define irradiance and radiant exitance by taking the limit of differential power per differential area at a point p:

$$E(\mathrm{p}) = \lim_{\Delta A \to 0} \frac{\Delta \Psi(\mathrm{p})}{\Delta A} = \frac{\mathrm{d}\Phi(\mathrm{p})}{\mathrm{d}A}.$$

We can also integrate irradiance over an area to find power:

$$\Phi = \int_A E(\mathrm{p})\,\mathrm{d}A. \tag{4.1}$$

The irradiance equation can also help us understand the origin of *Lambert's law*, which says that the amount of light energy arriving at a surface is proportional to the cosine of the angle between the light direction and the surface normal (Figure 4.2). Consider a light source with area A and flux Φ that is illuminating a surface. If the light is shining directly down on the surface (as on the left side of the figure), then the area on the surface receiving light A_1 is

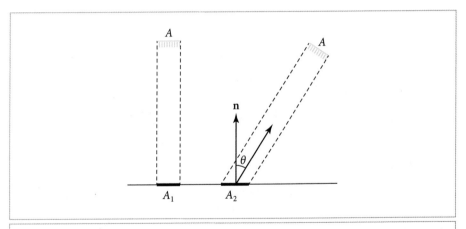

Figure 4.2: Lambert's Law. Irradiance arriving at a surface varies according to the cosine of the angle of incidence of illumination, since illumination is over a larger area at larger incident angles.

equal to A. Irradiance at any point inside A_1 is then

$$E_1 = \frac{\Phi}{A}.$$

However, if the light is at an angle to the surface, the area on the surface receiving light is larger. If A is small, then the area receiving flux, A_2, is roughly $A / \cos \theta$. For points inside A_2, the irradiance is therefore

$$E_2 = \frac{\Phi \cos \theta}{A}.$$

Intensity

Consider now an infinitesimal light source emitting photons. If we center this light source within the unit sphere, we can compute the angular density of emitted power. *Intensity*, denoted by I, is this quantity; it has units W/sr. Over the entire sphere of directions, we have

$$I = \frac{\Phi}{4\pi},$$

but more generally we are interested in taking the limit of a differential cone of directions:

$$I = \lim_{\Delta\omega \to 0} \frac{\Delta\Phi}{\Delta\omega} = \frac{d\Phi}{d\omega}.$$

As usual, we can go back to power by integrating intensity: given intensity as a function of direction $I(\omega)$, we can integrate over a finite set of directions Ω to recover the power:

$$\Phi = \int_{\Omega} I(\omega) \, d\omega. \tag{4.2}$$

Intensity describes the directional distribution of light, but it is only meaningful for point light sources.

Radiance

The final, and most important, radiometric quantity is *radiance*, L. Irradiance and radiant exitance give us differential power per differential area at a point p, but they do not distinguish the directional distribution of power. Radiance takes this last step and measures

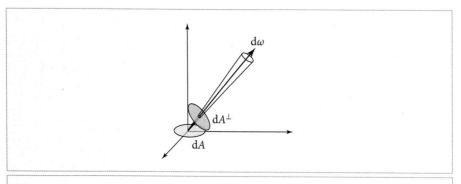

Figure 4.3: Radiance L is defined as flux per unit solid angle $d\omega$ per unit projected area $dA^{\perp}$.

irradiance or radiant exitance with respect to solid angles. It is defined by

$$L(\mathrm{p}, \omega) = \lim_{\Delta\omega \to 0} \frac{\Delta E_{\omega}(\mathrm{p})}{\Delta\omega} = \frac{dE_{\omega}(\mathrm{p})}{d\omega},$$

where we have used E_{ω} to denote irradiance at the surface that is perpendicular to the direction ω. In other words, radiance is not measured with respect to the irradiance incident at the surface p lies on. In effect, this change of measurement area serves to eliminate the $\cos\theta$ factor from Lambert's law in the definition of radiance.

Radiance is the flux density per unit area, per unit solid angle. In terms of flux, it is defined by

$$L = \frac{d^2\Phi}{d\omega \, dA^{\perp}}, \qquad\qquad [4.3]$$

where $dA^{\perp}$ is the projected area of dA on a hypothetical surface perpendicular to ω (Figure 4.3). Thus, it is the limit of the measurement of incident light at the surface as a cone of incident directions of interest $d\omega$ becomes very small and as the local area of interest on the surface dA also becomes very small.

Of all of these radiometric quantities, radiance will be the one used most frequently throughout the rest of the book. An intuitive reason for this is that in some sense it is the most fundamental of all the radiometric quantities; if radiance is given, then all the other values can be computed in terms of integrals of radiance over areas and directions. Another nice property of radiance is that it remains constant along rays through empty space. It is thus a natural quantity to compute with ray tracing.

4.1.2 INCIDENT AND EXITANT RADIANCE FUNCTIONS

When light interacts with surfaces in the scene, the radiance function L is generally not continuous across the surface boundaries. In the most extreme case of a fully opaque surface (e.g., a mirror), the radiance function slightly above and slightly below a surface could be completely unrelated.

It therefore makes sense to take one-sided limits at the discontinuity to distinguish between the radiance function just above and below

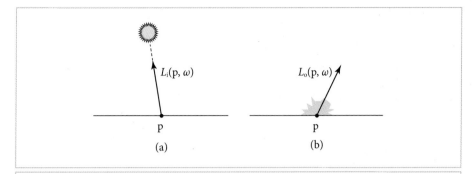

Figure 4.4: (a) The incident radiance function $L_i(p, \omega)$ describes the distribution of radiance arriving at a point as a function of position and direction. (b) The exitant radiance function $L_o(p, \omega)$ gives the distribution of radiance leaving the point. Note that for both functions, ω is oriented to point away from the surface, and thus, for example, $L_i(p, -\omega)$ gives the radiance arriving on the other side of the surface than the one where ω lies.

$$L^+(p, \omega) = \lim_{t \to 0^+} L(p + t\mathbf{n}_p, \omega),$$

$$L^-(p, \omega) = \lim_{t \to 0^-} L(p + t\mathbf{n}_p, \omega),$$

$$[4.4]$$

where $\mathbf{n}_p$ is the surface normal at p. However, keeping track of one-sided limits throughout the text is unnecessarily cumbersome.

We prefer to solve this ambiguity by making a distinction between radiance arriving at the point (e.g., due to illumination from a light source) and radiance leaving that point (e.g., due to reflection from a surface).

Consider a point p on the surface of an object. There is some distribution of radiance arriving at the point that can be described mathematically by a function of position and direction. This function is denoted by $L_i(p, \omega)$ (Figure 4.4). The function that describes the outgoing reflected radiance from the surface at that point is denoted by $L_o(p, \omega)$. Note that in both cases the direction vector ω is oriented to point away from p, but be aware that some authors use a notation where ω is reversed for L_i terms so that it points toward p.

There is a simple relation between these more intuitive incident and exitant radiance functions and the one-sided limits from Equation (4.4):

$$L_i(p, \omega) = \begin{cases} L^+(p, -\omega), & \omega \cdot \mathbf{n}_p > 0 \\ L^-(p, -\omega), & \omega \cdot \mathbf{n}_p < 0 \end{cases}$$

$$L_o(p, \omega) = \begin{cases} L^+(p, \omega), & \omega \cdot \mathbf{n}_p > 0 \\ L^-(p, \omega), & \omega \cdot \mathbf{n}_p < 0. \end{cases}$$

Throughout the book, we will use the idea of incident and exitant radiance functions to resolve ambiguity in the radiance function at boundaries.

Another property to keep in mind is that at a point in space where there is no surface (i.e., in free space), L is continuous, so $L^+ = L^-$, which means

$$L_o(p, \omega) = L_i(p, -\omega) = L(p, \omega).$$

In other words, L_i and L_o only differ by a direction reversal.

4.1.3 RADIOMETRIC SPECTRAL DISTRIBUTIONS

Thus far, all the radiometric quantities have been defined without considering variation in their distribution over wavelengths. They have therefore effectively been the integrals of wavelength-dependent quantities over an (unspecified) range of wavelengths of interest. Just as we were able to define the various radiometric quantities in terms of limits of other quantities, we can also define their spectral variants by taking their limits over small wavelength ranges.

For example, we can define *spectral radiance* L_λ as the limit of radiance over an infinitesimal interval of wavelengths $\Delta\lambda$,

$$L_\lambda = \lim_{\Delta\lambda \to 0} \frac{\Delta L}{\Delta\lambda} = \frac{dL}{d\lambda}.$$

In turn, radiance can be found by integrating spectral radiance over a range of wavelengths:

$$L = \int_{\lambda_0}^{\lambda_1} L_\lambda(\lambda)\, d\lambda. \qquad\qquad [4.5]$$

Definitions for the other radiometric quantities follow similarly. All of these spectral variants have an additional factor of $1/m$ in their units.

4.1.4 LUMINANCE AND PHOTOMETRY

All the radiometric measurements like flux, radiance, and so forth have corresponding photometric measurements. *Photometry* is the study of visible electromagnetic radiation in terms of its perception by the human visual system. Each spectral radiometric quantity can be converted to its corresponding photometric quantity by integrating against the spectral response curve $V(\lambda)$, which describes the relative sensitivity of the human eye to various wavelengths.[2]

Luminance measures how bright a spectral power distribution appears to a human observer. For example, luminance accounts for the fact that a spectral distribution with a particular amount of energy in the green wavelengths will appear brighter to a human than a spectral distribution with the same amount of energy in blue.

We will denote luminance by Y; it is related to spectral radiance by

$$Y = \int_\lambda L_\lambda(\lambda)\, V(\lambda)\, d\lambda. \qquad\qquad [4.6]$$

Luminance and the spectral response curve $V(\lambda)$ are closely related to the XYZ representation of color, which will be introduced in Section 4.6.1.

The units of luminance are candelas per meter squared (cd/m^2), where the candela is the photometric equivalent of radiant intensity. Some representative luminance values are given in Table 4.1.

All the other radiometric quantities that we have introduced in this chapter have photometric equivalents; they are summarized in Table 4.2.[3]

---

2   The spectral response curve model is based on experiments done in a normally illuminated indoor environment. Because sensitivity to color decreases in dark environments, it does not model the human visual system's response well under all lighting situations. Nonetheless, it forms the basis for the definition of luminance and other related photometric properties.

3   The various photometric quantities have fairly unusual names; the somewhat confusing state of affairs was nicely summarized by Jim Kajiya: "Thus one nit is one lux per steradian is one candela per square meter is one lumen per square meter per steradian. Got it?"

Table 4.1: Representative Luminance Values for a Number of Lighting Conditions.	
Condition	Luminance (cd/m^2, or nits)
Sun at horizon	600,000
60-watt lightbulb	120,000
Clear sky	8,000
Typical office	100–1,000
Typical computer display	1–100
Street lighting	1–10
Cloudy moonlight	0.25

Table 4.2: Radiometric Measurements and Their Photometric Analogs.			
Radiometric	Unit	Photometric	Unit
Radiant energy	joule (J)	Luminous energy	talbot (T)
Radiant flux	watt (W)	Luminous flux	lumen (lm)
Intensity	W/sr	Luminous intensity	lm/sr = candela (cd)
Irradiance	W/m^2	Illuminance	lm/m^2 = lux (lx)
Radiance	W/(m^{2}sr)	Luminance	lm/(m^{2}sr) = cd/m^2 = nit

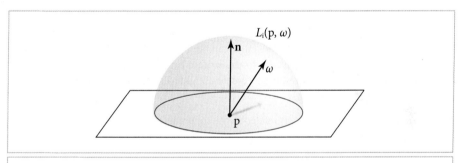

Figure 4.5: Irradiance at a point p is given by the integral of radiance times the cosine of the incident direction over the entire upper hemisphere above the point.

4.2 WORKING WITH RADIOMETRIC INTEGRALS

A frequent task in rendering is the evaluation of integrals of radiometric quantities. In this section, we will present some tricks that can make it easier to do this. To illustrate the use of these techniques, we will take the computation of irradiance at a point as an example. Irradiance at a point p with surface normal **n** due to radiance over a set of directions Ω is

$$E(\mathrm{p}, \mathbf{n}) = \int_{\Omega} L_{\mathrm{i}}(\mathrm{p}, \omega) \, |\cos \theta| \, \mathrm{d}\omega, \qquad \text{[4.7]}$$

where $L_{\mathrm{i}}(\mathrm{p}, \omega)$ is the incident radiance function (Figure 4.5) and the $\cos \theta$ factor in the integrand is due to the $\mathrm{d}A^{\perp}$ factor in the definition of radiance. θ is measured as the angle between ω and the surface normal **n**. Irradiance is usually computed over the hemisphere $\mathcal{H}^2(\mathbf{n})$ of directions about a given surface normal **n**.

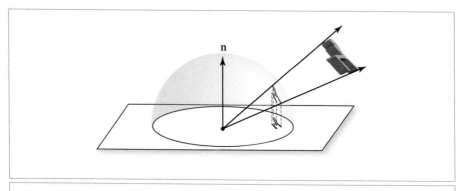

Figure 4.6: The projected solid angle subtended by an object is the cosine-weighted solid angle that it subtends. It can be computed by finding the object's solid angle, projecting it down to the plane perpendicular to the surface normal, and measuring its area there. Thus, the projected solid angle depends on the surface normal where it is being measured, since the normal orients the plane of projection.

The integral in Equation (4.7) is with respect to solid angle on the hemisphere and the measure $d\omega$ corresponds to surface area on the unit hemisphere. (Recall the definition of solid angle in Section 3.8.1.)

4.2.1 INTEGRALS OVER PROJECTED SOLID ANGLE

The various cosine factors in the integrals for radiometric quantities can often distract from what is being expressed in the integral. This problem can be avoided using *projected solid angle* rather than solid angle to measure areas subtended by objects being integrated over. The projected solid angle subtended by an object is determined by projecting the object onto the unit sphere, as was done for the solid angle, but then projecting the resulting shape down onto the unit disk that is perpendicular to the surface normal (Figure 4.6). Integrals over hemispheres of directions with respect to cosine-weighted solid angle can be rewritten as integrals over projected solid angle.

The projected solid angle measure is related to the solid angle measure by

$$d\omega^\perp = |\cos\theta|\, d\omega,$$

so the irradiance-from-radiance integral over the hemisphere can be written more simply as

$$E(\mathrm{p}, \mathbf{n}) = \int_{\mathcal{H}^2(\mathbf{n})} L_i(\mathrm{p}, \omega)\, d\omega^\perp.$$

For the rest of this book, we will write integrals over directions in terms of solid angle, rather than projected solid angle. In other sources, however, projected solid angle may be used, so it is always important to be aware of the integrand's actual measure.

4.2.2 INTEGRALS OVER SPHERICAL COORDINATES

It is often convenient to transform integrals over solid angle into integrals over spherical coordinates (θ, ϕ) using Equation (3.7). In order to convert an integral over a solid angle to an integral over (θ, ϕ), we need to be able to express the relationship between the differential area of a set of directions $d\omega$ and the differential area of a (θ, ϕ) pair (Figure 4.7). The differential area on the unit sphere $d\omega$ is the product of the differential lengths of its sides, $\sin\theta\, d\phi$ and $d\theta$. Therefore,

$$d\omega = \sin\theta\, d\theta\, d\phi. \tag{4.8}$$

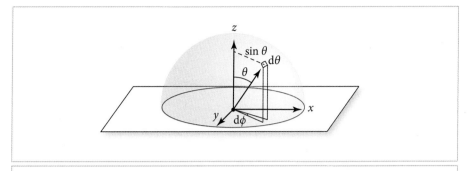

Figure 4.7: The differential area $d\omega$ subtended by a differential solid angle is the product of the differential lengths of the two edges $\sin\theta d\phi$ and $d\theta$. The resulting relationship, $d\omega = \sin\theta d\theta d\phi$, is the key to converting between integrals over solid angles and integrals over spherical angles.

(This result can also be derived using the multidimensional transformation approach from Section 2.4.1.)

We can thus see that the irradiance integral over the hemisphere, Equation (4.7) with $\Omega = \mathcal{H}^2(\mathbf{n})$, can equivalently be written as

$$E(\mathrm{p}, \mathbf{n}) = \int_0^{2\pi} \int_0^{\pi/2} L_\mathrm{i}(\mathrm{p}, \theta, \phi) \cos\theta \, \sin\theta \, d\theta \, d\phi.$$

If the radiance is the same from all directions, the equation simplifies to $E = \pi L_\mathrm{i}$.

4.2.3 INTEGRALS OVER AREA

One last useful transformation is to turn integrals over directions into integrals over area. Consider the irradiance integral in Equation (4.7) again, and imagine there is a quadrilateral with constant outgoing radiance and that we could like to compute the resulting irradiance at a point p. Computing this value as an integral over directions ω or spherical coordinates (θ, ϕ) is in general not straightforward, since given a particular direction it is nontrivial to determine if the quadrilateral is visible in that direction or (θ, ϕ). It is much easier to compute the irradiance as an integral over the area of the quadrilateral.

Differential area dA on a surface is related to differential solid angle as viewed from a point p by

$$d\omega = \frac{dA \cos\theta}{r^2}, \tag{4.9}$$

where θ is the angle between the surface normal of dA and the vector to p, and r is the distance from p to dA (Figure 4.8). We will not derive this result here, but it can be understood intuitively: if dA is at distance 1 from p and is aligned exactly so that it is perpendicular to $d\omega$, then $d\omega = dA$, $\theta = 0$, and Equation (4.9) holds. As dA moves farther away from p, or as it rotates so that it is not aligned with the direction of $d\omega$, the r^2 and $\cos\theta$ factors compensate accordingly to reduce $d\omega$.

Therefore, we can write the irradiance integral for the quadrilateral source as

$$E(\mathrm{p}, \mathbf{n}) = \int_A L \cos\theta_\mathrm{i} \, \frac{\cos\theta_\mathrm{o} \, dA}{r^2},$$

where L is the emitted radiance from the surface of the quadrilateral, θ_i is the angle between the surface normal at p and the direction from p to the point p$'$ on the light, and θ_o is the angle between the surface normal at p$'$ on the light and the direction from p$'$ to p (Figure 4.9).

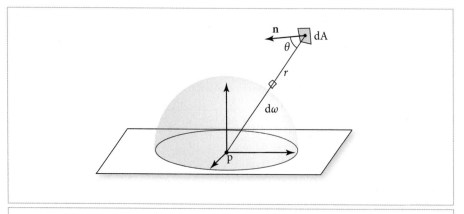

Figure 4.8: The differential solid angle $d\omega$ subtended by a differential area dA is equal to $dA \cos\theta / r^2$, where θ is the angle between dA's surface normal and the vector to the point p and r is the distance from p to dA.

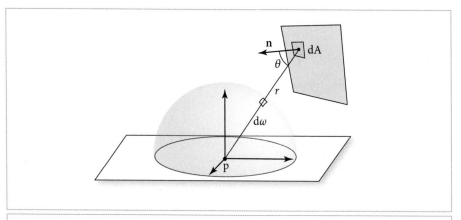

Figure 4.9: To compute irradiance at a point p from a quadrilateral source, it is easier to integrate over the surface area of the source than to integrate over the irregular set of directions that it subtends. The relationship between solid angles and areas given by Equation (4.9) lets us go back and forth between the two approaches.

4.3 SURFACE REFLECTION

When light is incident on a surface, the surface scatters the light, reflecting some of it back into the environment. There are two main effects that need to be described to model this reflection: the spectral distribution of the reflected light and its directional distribution. For example, the skin of a lemon mostly absorbs light in the blue wavelengths but reflects most of the light in the red and green wavelengths. Therefore, when it is illuminated with white light, its color is yellow. It has much the same color no matter what direction it is being observed from, although for some directions a highlight—a brighter area that is more white than yellow—is visible. In contrast, the light reflected from a point in a mirror depends almost entirely on the viewing direction. At a fixed point on the mirror, as the viewing angle changes, the object that is reflected in the mirror changes accordingly.

Reflection from translucent surfaces is more complex; a variety of materials ranging from skin and leaves to wax and liquids exhibit *subsurface light transport*, where light that enters the surface at one point exits it some distance away. (Consider, for example, how shining a flashlight in one's mouth makes one's cheeks light up, as light that enters the inside of the cheeks passes through the skin and exits the face.)

There are two abstractions for describing these mechanisms for light reflection: the BRDF and the BSSRDF, described in Sections 4.3.1 and 4.3.2, respectively. The BRDF describes surface reflection at a point neglecting the effect of subsurface light transport. For materials where this transport mechanism does not have a significant effect, this simplification introduces little error and makes the implementation of rendering algorithms much more efficient. The BSSRDF generalizes the BRDF and describes the more general setting of light reflection from translucent materials.

4.3.1 THE BRDF AND THE BTDF

The *bidirectional reflectance distribution function* (BRDF) gives a formalism for describing reflection from a surface. Consider the setting in Figure 4.10: we would like to know how much radiance is leaving the surface in the direction ω_o toward the viewer, $L_o(p, \omega_o)$, as a result of incident radiance along the direction ω_i, $L_i(p, \omega_i)$. (When considering light scattering at a surface location, pbrt uses the convention that ω_i refers to the direction from which the quantity of interest (radiance in this case) arrives, rather than the direction from which the Integrator reached the surface.)

If the direction ω_i is considered as a differential cone of directions, the differential irradiance at p is

$$dE(p, \omega_i) = L_i(p, \omega_i) \, \cos \theta_i \, d\omega_i. \tag{4.10}$$

A differential amount of radiance will be reflected in the direction ω_o due to this irradiance. Because of the linearity assumption from geometric optics, the reflected differential radiance is proportional to the irradiance

$$dL_o(p, \omega_o) \propto dE(p, \omega_i).$$

The constant of proportionality defines the surface's BRDF f_r for the particular pair of directions ω_i and ω_o:

$$f_r(p, \omega_o, \omega_i) = \frac{dL_o(p, \omega_o)}{dE(p, \omega_i)} = \frac{dL_o(p, \omega_o)}{L_i(p, \omega_i) \cos \theta_i \, d\omega_i}. \tag{4.11}$$

The spectral BRDF is defined by using spectral radiance in place of radiance.

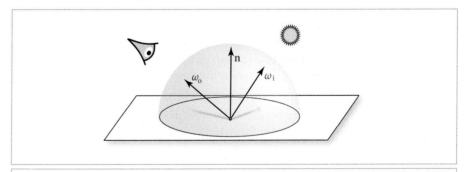

Figure 4.10: The BRDF. The bidirectional reflectance distribution function is a 4D function over pairs of directions ω_i and ω_o that describes how much incident light along ω_i is scattered from the surface in the direction ω_o.

Physically based BRDFs have two important qualities:

1. *Reciprocity:* For all pairs of directions ω_i and ω_o, $f_r(p, \omega_i, \omega_o) = f_r(p, \omega_o, \omega_i)$.
2. *Energy conservation:* The total energy of light reflected is less than or equal to the energy of incident light. For all directions ω_o,

$$\int_{\mathcal{H}^2(n)} f_r(p, \omega_o, \omega') \, \cos \theta' \, d\omega' \le 1.$$

Note that the value of the BRDF for a pair of directions ω_i and ω_o is *not* necessarily less than 1; it is only its integral that has this normalization constraint.

Two quantities that are based on the BRDF will occasionally be useful. First, the *hemispherical-directional reflectance* is a 2D function that gives the total reflection in a given direction due to constant illumination over the hemisphere, or, equivalently, the total reflection over the hemisphere due to light from a given direction.[4] It is defined as

$$\rho_{hd}(\omega_o) = \int_{\mathcal{H}^2(n)} f_r(p, \omega_o, \omega_i) \, |\cos \theta_i| \, d\omega_i. \qquad [4.12]$$

The *hemispherical-hemispherical reflectance* of a BRDF, denoted by ρ_{hh}, gives the fraction of incident light reflected by a surface when the incident light is the same from all directions. It is

$$\rho_{hh} = \frac{1}{\pi} \int_{\mathcal{H}^2(n)} \int_{\mathcal{H}^2(n)} f_r(p, \omega_o, \omega_i) \, |\cos \theta_o \cos \theta_i| \, d\omega_o \, d\omega_i. \qquad [4.13]$$

A surface's *bidirectional transmittance distribution function* (BTDF), which describes the distribution of transmitted light, can be defined in a manner similar to that for the BRDF. The BTDF is generally denoted by $f_t(p, \omega_o, \omega_i)$, where ω_i and ω_o are in opposite hemispheres around p. Remarkably, the BTDF does not obey reciprocity as defined above; we will discuss this issue in detail in Section 9.5.2.

For convenience in equations, we will denote the BRDF and BTDF when considered together as $f(p, \omega_o, \omega_i)$; we will call this the *bidirectional scattering distribution function* (BSDF). Chapter 9 is entirely devoted to describing a variety of BSDFs that are useful for rendering.

Using the definition of the BSDF, we have

$$dL_o(p, \omega_o) = f(p, \omega_o, \omega_i) \, L_i(p, \omega_i) \, |\cos \theta_i| \, d\omega_i.$$

Here an absolute value has been added to the $\cos \theta_i$ factor. This is done because surface normals in pbrt are not reoriented to lie on the same side of the surface as ω_i (many other rendering systems do this, although we find it more useful to leave them in their natural orientation as given by the Shape). Doing so makes it easier to consistently apply conventions like "the surface normal is assumed to point outside the surface" elsewhere in the system. Thus, applying the absolute value to $\cos \theta$ factors like these ensures that the desired quantity is calculated.

We can integrate this equation over the sphere of incident directions around p to compute the outgoing radiance in direction ω_o due to the incident illumination at p from all directions:

$$L_o(p, \omega_o) = \int_{\mathcal{S}^2} f(p, \omega_o, \omega_i) \, L_i(p, \omega_i) \, |\cos \theta_i| \, d\omega_i. \qquad [4.14]$$

Shape 261

4　The fact that these two quantities are equal is due to the reciprocity of reflection functions.

This is a fundamental equation in rendering; it describes how an incident distribution of light at a point is transformed into an outgoing distribution, based on the scattering properties of the surface. It is often called the *scattering equation* when the sphere S^2 is the domain (as it is here), or the *reflection equation* when just the upper hemisphere $\mathcal{H}^2(\mathbf{n})$ is being integrated over. One of the key tasks of the integration routines in Chapters 13 through 15 is to evaluate this integral at points on surfaces in the scene.

4.3.2 THE BSSRDF

The *bidirectional scattering surface reflectance distribution function* (BSSRDF) is the formalism that describes scattering from materials that exhibit subsurface light transport. It is a distribution function $S(p_o, \omega_o, p_i, \omega_i)$ that describes the ratio of exitant differential radiance at point p_o in direction ω_o to the incident differential flux at p_i from direction ω_i (Figure 4.11):

$$S(p_o, \omega_o, p_i, \omega_i) = \frac{dL_o(p_o, \omega_o)}{d\Phi(p_i, \omega_i)}. \qquad [4.15]$$

The generalization of the scattering equation for the BSSRDF requires integration over surface area *and* incoming direction, turning the 2D scattering Equation (4.14) into a 4D integral.

$$L_o(p_o, \omega_o) = \int_A \int_{\mathcal{H}^2(\mathbf{n})} S(p_o, \omega_o, p_i, \omega_i)\, L_i(p_i, \omega_i)\, |\cos \theta_i|\, d\omega_i\, dA. \qquad [4.16]$$

With two more dimensions to integrate over, it is more complex to account for in rendering algorithms than Equation (4.14) is. However, as the distance between points p_i and p_o increases, the value of S generally diminishes. This fact can be a substantial help in implementations of subsurface scattering algorithms.

Light transport beneath a surface is described by the same principles as volume light transport in participating media and is described by the equation of transfer, which is introduced in Section 14.1. Subsurface scattering is thus based on the same effects as light scattering in clouds and smoke—just at a smaller scale.

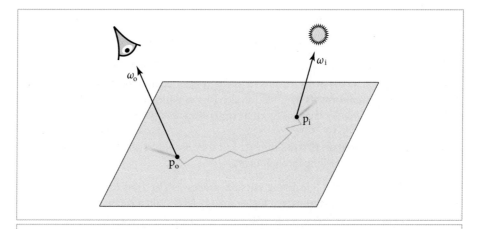

Figure 4.11: The bidirectional scattering surface reflectance distribution function generalizes the BSDF to account for light that exits the surface at a point other than where it enters. It is often more difficult to evaluate than the BSDF, although subsurface light transport makes a substantial contribution to the appearance of many real-world objects.

4.4 LIGHT EMISSION

The atoms of an object with temperature above absolute zero are moving. In turn, as described by Maxwell's equations, the motion of atomic particles that hold electrical charges causes objects to emit electromagnetic radiation over a range of wavelengths. As we will see shortly, at room temperature most of the emission is at infrared frequencies; objects need to be much warmer to emit meaningful amounts of electromagnetic radiation at visible frequencies.

Many different types of light sources have been invented to convert energy into emitted electromagnetic radiation. An object that emits light is called a *lamp* or an *illuminant*, though we avoid the latter terminology since we generally use "illuminant" to refer to a spectral distribution of emission (Section 4.4.2). A lamp is housed in a *luminaire*, which consists of all the objects that hold and protect the light as well as any objects like reflectors or diffusers that shape the distribution of light.

Understanding some of the physical processes involved in emission is helpful for accurately modeling light sources for rendering. A number of corresponding types of lamps are in wide use today:

* Incandescent (tungsten) lamps have a small tungsten filament. The flow of electricity through the filament heats it, which in turn causes it to emit electromagnetic radiation with a distribution of wavelengths that depends on the filament's temperature. A frosted glass enclosure is often present to diffuse the emission over a larger area than just the filament and to absorb some of the wavelengths generated in order to achieve a desired distribution of emission by wavelength. With an incandescent light, much of the emitted power is in the infrared bands, which in turn means that much of the energy consumed by the light is turned into heat rather than light.
* Halogen lamps also have a tungsten filament, but the enclosure around them is filled with halogen gas. Over time, part of the filament in an incandescent light evaporates when it is heated; the halogen gas causes this evaporated tungsten to return to the filament, which lengthens the life of the light. Because it returns to the filament, the evaporated tungsten does not adhere to the bulb surface (as it does with regular incandescent bulbs), which also prevents the bulb from darkening.
* Gas-discharge lamps pass electrical current through hydrogen, neon, argon, or vaporized metal gas, which causes light to be emitted at specific wavelengths that depend on the particular atom in the gas. (Atoms that emit relatively little of their electromagnetic radiation in the not-useful infrared frequencies are selected for the gas.) Because a broader spectrum of wavelengths is generally more visually desirable than wavelengths that the chosen atoms generate directly, a fluorescent coating on the bulb's interior is often used to transform the emitted wavelengths to a broader range. (The fluorescent coating also improves efficiency by converting ultraviolet wavelengths to visible wavelengths.)
* LED lights are based on electroluminescence: they use materials that emit photons due to electrical current passing through them.

For all of these sources, the underlying physical process is electrons colliding with atoms, which pushes their outer electrons to a higher energy level. When such an electron returns to a lower energy level, a photon is emitted. There are many other interesting processes that create light, including chemoluminescence (as seen in light sticks) and bioluminescence—a form of chemoluminescence seen in fireflies. Though interesting in their own right, we will not consider their mechanisms further here.

Luminous efficacy measures how effectively a light source converts power to visible illumination, accounting for the fact that for human observers, emission in non-visible wavelengths is of little value. Interestingly enough, it is the ratio of a photometric quantity (the emitted luminous flux) to a radiometric quantity (either the total power it uses or the total power that it emits over all wavelengths, measured in flux):

$$\frac{\int \Phi_e(\lambda)\, V(\lambda)\, d\lambda}{\int \Phi_i(\lambda)\, d\lambda},$$

where $V(\lambda)$ is the spectral response curve that was introduced in Section 4.1.4.

Luminous efficacy has units of lumens per watt. If Φ_i is the power consumed by the light source (rather than the emitted power), then luminous efficacy also incorporates a measure of how effectively the light source converts power to electromagnetic radiation. Luminous efficacy can also be defined as a ratio of luminous exitance (the photometric equivalent of radiant exitance) to irradiance at a point on a surface, or as the ratio of exitant luminance to radiance at a point on a surface in a particular direction.

A typical value of luminous efficacy for an incandescent tungsten lightbulb is around 15 lm/W. The highest value it can possibly have is 683, for a perfectly efficient light source that emits all of its light at $\lambda = 555$ nm, the peak of the $V(\lambda)$ function. (While such a light would have high efficacy, it would not necessarily be a pleasant one as far as human observers are concerned.)

4.4.1 BLACKBODY EMITTERS

A *blackbody* is a perfect emitter: it converts power to electromagnetic radiation as efficiently as physically possible. While true blackbodies are not physically realizable, some emitters exhibit near-blackbody behavior. Blackbodies also have a useful closed-form expression for their emission by wavelength as a function of temperature that is useful for modeling non-blackbody emitters.

Blackbodies are so-named because they absorb absolutely all incident power, reflecting none of it. Intuitively, the reasons that perfect absorbers are also perfect emitters stem from the fact that absorption is the reverse operation of emission. Thus, if time was reversed, all the perfectly absorbed power would be perfectly efficiently re-emitted.

Planck's law gives the radiance emitted by a blackbody as a function of wavelength λ and temperature T measured in kelvins:

$$L_e(\lambda, T) = \frac{2hc^2}{\lambda^5 \left(e^{hc/\lambda k_b T} - 1\right)}, \qquad \text{[4.17]}$$

where c is the speed of light in the medium (299,792,458 m/s in a vacuum), h is Planck's constant, $6.62606957 \times 10^{-34}$ J s, and k_b is the Boltzmann constant, $1.3806488 \times 10^{-23}$ J/K, where kelvin (K) is the unit of temperature. Blackbody emitters are perfectly diffuse; they emit radiance equally in all directions.

Figure 4.12 plots the emitted radiance distributions of a blackbody for a number of temperatures.

The `Blackbody()` function computes emitted radiance at the given temperature T in Kelvin for the given wavelength `lambda`.

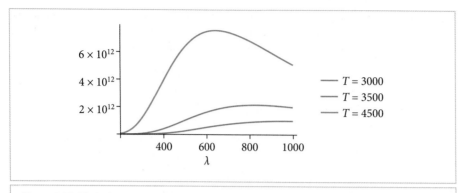

Figure 4.12: Plots of emitted radiance as a function of wavelength for blackbody emitters at a few temperatures, as given by Equation (4.17). Note that as temperature increases, more of the emitted light is in the visible frequencies (roughly 380 nm–780 nm) and that the spectral distribution shifts from reddish colors to bluish colors. The total amount of emitted energy grows quickly as temperature increases, as described by the Stefan–Boltzmann law in Equation (4.19).

⟨*Spectrum Function Declarations*⟩ ≡
```
Float Blackbody(Float lambda, Float T) {
    if (T <= 0) return 0;
    const Float c = 299792458.f;
    const Float h = 6.62606957e-34f;
    const Float kb = 1.3806488e-23f;
    ⟨Return emitted radiance for blackbody at wavelength lambda 162⟩
}
```

The wavelength passed to Blackbody() is in nm, but the constants for Equation (4.17) are in terms of meters. Therefore, it is necessary to first convert the wavelength to meters by scaling it by 10^{-9}.

⟨*Return emitted radiance for blackbody at wavelength* lambda⟩ ≡   162
```
Float l = lambda * 1e-9f;
Float Le = (2 * h * c * c) /
    (Pow<5>(l) * (FastExp((h * c) / (l * kb * T)) - 1));
return Le;
```

The emission of non-blackbodies is described by *Kirchhoff's law*, which says that the emitted radiance distribution at any frequency is equal to the emission of a perfect blackbody at that frequency times the fraction of incident radiance at that frequency that is absorbed by the object. (This relationship follows from the object being assumed to be in thermal equilibrium.) The fraction of radiance absorbed is equal to 1 minus the amount reflected, and so the emitted radiance is

$$L'_e(T, \omega, \lambda) = L_e(T, \lambda)(1 - \rho_{hd}(\omega)), \qquad\qquad [4.18]$$

where $L_e(T, \lambda)$ is the emitted radiance given by Planck's law, Equation (4.17), and $\rho_{hd}(\omega)$ is the hemispherical-directional reflectance from Equation (4.12).

The *Stefan–Boltzmann law* gives the radiant exitance (recall that this is the outgoing irradiance) at a point p for a blackbody emitter:

$$M(\text{p}) = \sigma T^4, \qquad\qquad [4.19]$$

FastExp() 1036
Float 23
Pow() 1034

where σ is the Stefan–Boltzmann constant, 5.67032×10^{-8} W m^{-2} K^{-4}. Note that the total emission over all frequencies grows very rapidly—at the rate T^4. Thus, doubling the temperature of a blackbody emitter increases the total energy emitted by a factor of 16.

The blackbody emission distribution provides a useful metric for describing the emission characteristics of non-blackbody emitters through the notion of *color temperature*. If the shape of the emitted spectral distribution of an emitter is similar to the blackbody distribution at some temperature, then we can say that the emitter has the corresponding color temperature. One approach to find color temperature is to take the wavelength where the light's emission is highest and find the corresponding temperature using *Wien's displacement law*, which gives the wavelength where emission of a blackbody is maximum given its temperature:

$$\lambda_{\text{max}} = \frac{b}{T}, \tag{4.20}$$

where b is Wien's displacement constant, 2.8977721×10^{-3} m K.

Incandescent tungsten lamps are generally around 2700 K color temperature, and tungsten halogen lamps are around 3000 K. Fluorescent lights may range all the way from 2700 K to 6500 K. Generally speaking, color temperatures over 5000 K are described as "cool," while 2700–3000 K is described as "warm."

4.4.2 STANDARD ILLUMINANTS

Another useful way of categorizing light emission distributions is a number of "standard illuminants" that have been defined by Commission Internationale de l'Éclairage (CIE).

The Standard Illuminant A was introduced in 1931 and was intended to represent average incandescent light. It corresponds to a blackbody radiator of about 2856 K. (It was originally defined as a blackbody at 2850 K, but the accuracy of the constants used in Planck's law subsequently improved. Therefore, the specification was updated to be in terms of the 1931 constants, so that the illuminant was unchanged.) Figure 4.13 shows a plot of the spectral distribution of the A illuminant.

(The B and C illuminants were intended to model daylight at two times of day and were generated with an A illuminant in combination with specific filters. They are no longer used.

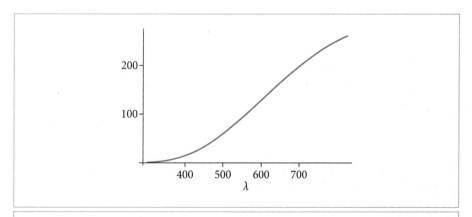

Figure 4.13: Plot of the CIE Standard Illuminant A's Spectral Power Distribution as a Function of Wavelength in nm. This illuminant represents incandescent illumination and is close to a blackbody at 2856 K.

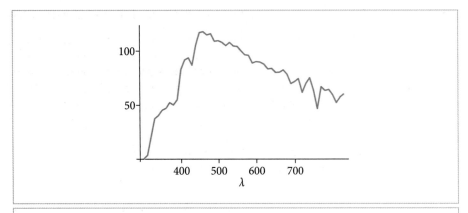

Figure 4.14: Plot of the CIE Standard D65 Illuminant Spectral Distribution as a Function of Wavelength in nm. This illuminant represents noontime daylight at European latitudes and is commonly used to define the whitepoint of color spaces (Section 4.6.3).

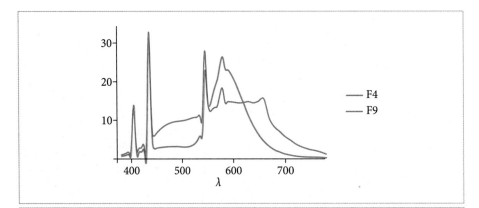

Figure 4.15: Plots of the F4 and F9 Standard Illuminants as a Function of Wavelength in nm. These represent two fluorescent lights. Note that the distributions are quite different. Spikes in the two distributions correspond to the wavelengths directly emitted by atoms in the gas, while the other wavelengths are generated by the bulb's fluorescent coating. The F9 illuminant is a "broadband" emitter that uses multiple phosphors to achieve a more uniform spectral distribution.

The E illuminant is defined as having a constant spectral distribution and is used only for comparisons to other illuminants.)

The D illuminant describes various phases of daylight. It was defined based on characteristic vector analysis of a variety of daylight spectra, which made it possible to express daylight in terms of a linear combination of three terms (one fixed and two weighted), with one weight essentially corresponding to yellow-blue color change due to cloudiness and the other corresponding to pink-green due to water in the atmosphere (from haze, etc.). D65 is roughly 6504 K color temperature (not 6500 K—again due to changes in the values used for the constants in Planck's law) and is intended to correspond to mid-day sunlight in Europe. (See Figure 4.14.) The CIE recommends that this illuminant be used for daylight unless there is a specific reason not to.

Finally, the F series of illuminants describes fluorescents; it is based on measurements of a number of actual fluorescent lights. Figure 4.15 shows the spectral distributions of two of them.

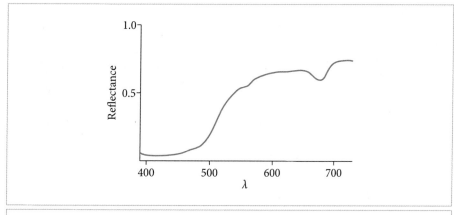

Figure 4.16: Spectral Distribution of Reflection from Lemon Skin.

4.5 REPRESENTING SPECTRAL DISTRIBUTIONS

Spectral distributions in the real world can be complex; we have already seen a variety of complex emission spectra and Figure 4.16 shows a graph of the spectral distribution of the reflectance of lemon skin. In order to render images of scenes that include a variety of complex spectra, a renderer must have efficient and accurate representations of spectral distributions. This section will introduce pbrt's abstractions for representing and performing computation with them; the corresponding code can be found in the files util/spectrum.h and util/spectrum.cpp.

We will start by defining constants that give the range of visible wavelengths. Both here and for the remainder of the spectral code in pbrt, wavelengths are specified in nanometers, which are of a magnitude that gives easily human-readable values for the visible wavelengths.

⟨*Spectrum Constants*⟩ ≡
```
constexpr Float Lambda_min = 360, Lambda_max = 830;
```

4.5.1 SPECTRUM INTERFACE

We will find a variety of spectral representations useful in pbrt, ranging from spectral sample values tabularized by wavelength to functional descriptions such as the blackbody function. This brings us to our first interface class, Spectrum. A Spectrum corresponds to a pointer to a class that implements one such spectral representation.

Spectrum inherits from TaggedPointer, which handles the details of runtime polymorphism. TaggedPointer requires that all the types of Spectrum implementations be provided as template parameters, which allows it to associate a unique integer identifier with each type. (See Section B.4.4 for details of its implementation.)

⟨*Spectrum Definition*⟩ ≡
```
class Spectrum
    : public TaggedPointer<ConstantSpectrum, DenselySampledSpectrum,
                           PiecewiseLinearSpectrum, RGBAlbedoSpectrum,
                           RGBUnboundedSpectrum, RGBIlluminantSpectrum,
                           BlackbodySpectrum> {
  public:
    ⟨Spectrum Interface 166⟩
};
```

As with other classes that are based on TaggedPointer, Spectrum defines an interface that must be implemented by all the spectral representations. Typical practice in C++ would be for such an interface to be specified by pure virtual methods in Spectrum and for Spectrum implementations to inherit from Spectrum and implement those methods. With the TaggedPointer approach, the interface is specified implicitly: for each method in the interface, there is a method in Spectrum that dispatches calls to the appropriate type's implementation. We will discuss the details of how this works for a single method here but will omit them for other Spectrum methods and for other interface classes since they all follow the same boilerplate.

The most important method that Spectrum defines is operator(), which takes a single wavelength λ and returns the value of the spectral distribution for that wavelength.

⟨*Spectrum Interface*⟩ ≡   **165**
```
Float operator()(Float lambda) const;
```

The corresponding method implementation is brief, though dense. A call to TaggedPointer::Dispatch() begins the process of dispatching the method call. The TaggedPointer class stores an integer tag along with the object's pointer that encodes its type; in turn, Dispatch() is able to determine the specific type of the pointer at runtime. It then calls the callback function provided to it with a pointer to the object, cast to be a pointer to its actual type.

The lambda function that is called here, op, takes a pointer with the auto type specifier for its parameter. In C++17, such a lambda function acts as a templated function; a call to it with a concrete type acts as an instantiation of a lambda that takes that type. Thus, the call (*ptr)(lambda) in the lambda body ends up as a direct call to the appropriate method.

⟨*Spectrum Inline Method Definitions*⟩ ≡
```
inline Float Spectrum::operator()(Float lambda) const {
    auto op = [&](auto ptr) { return (*ptr)(lambda); };
    return Dispatch(op);
}
```

Spectrum implementations must also provide a MaxValue() method that returns a bound on the maximum value of the spectral distribution over its wavelength range. This method's main use in pbrt is for computing bounds on the power emitted by light sources so that lights can be sampled according to their expected contribution to illumination in the scene.

⟨*Spectrum Interface*⟩ +≡   **165**
```
Float MaxValue() const;
```

4.5.2 GENERAL SPECTRAL DISTRIBUTIONS

With the Spectrum interface specified, we will start by defining a few Spectrum class implementations that explicitly tabularize values of the spectral distribution function. Constant Spectrum is the simplest: it represents a constant spectral distribution over all wavelengths. The most common use of the ConstantSpectrum class in pbrt is to define a zero-valued spectral distribution in cases where a particular form of scattering is not present.

The ConstantSpectrum implementation is straightforward and we omit its trivial MaxValue() method here. Note that it does not inherit from Spectrum. This is another difference from using traditional C++ abstract base classes with virtual functions—as far as the C++ type system is concerned, there is no explicit connection between ConstantSpectrum and Spectrum.

⟨*Spectrum Definitions*⟩ ≡
```
class ConstantSpectrum {
  public:
    ConstantSpectrum(Float c) : c(c) {}
    Float operator()(Float lambda) const { return c; }
  private:
    Float c;
};
```

More expressive is `DenselySampledSpectrum`, which stores a spectral distribution sampled at 1 nm intervals over a given range of integer wavelengths $[\lambda_{min}, \lambda_{max}]$.

⟨*Spectrum Definitions*⟩ +≡
```
class DenselySampledSpectrum {
  public:
    ⟨DenselySampledSpectrum Public Methods 167⟩
  private:
    ⟨DenselySampledSpectrum Private Members 167⟩
};
```

Its constructor takes another `Spectrum` and evaluates that spectral distribution at each wavelength in the range. `DenselySampledSpectrum` can be useful if the provided spectral distribution is computationally expensive to evaluate, as it allows subsequent evaluations to be performed by reading a single value from memory.

⟨*DenselySampledSpectrum Public Methods*⟩ ≡   **167**
```
DenselySampledSpectrum(Spectrum spec, int lambda_min = Lambda_min,
                       int lambda_max = Lambda_max, Allocator alloc = {})
  : lambda_min(lambda_min), lambda_max(lambda_max),
    values(lambda_max - lambda_min + 1, alloc) {
    if (spec)
        for (int lambda = lambda_min; lambda <= lambda_max; ++lambda)
            values[lambda - lambda_min] = spec(lambda);
}
```

⟨*DenselySampledSpectrum Private Members*⟩ ≡   **167**
```
int lambda_min, lambda_max;
pstd::vector<Float> values;
```

Finding the spectrum's value for a given wavelength `lambda` is a matter of returning zero for wavelengths outside of the valid range and indexing into the stored values otherwise.

⟨*DenselySampledSpectrum Public Methods*⟩ +≡   **167**
```
Float operator()(Float lambda) const {
    int offset = std::lround(lambda) - lambda_min;
    if (offset < 0 || offset >= values.size()) return 0;
    return values[offset];
}
```

While sampling a spectral distribution at 1 nm wavelengths gives sufficient accuracy for most uses in rendering, doing so requires nearly 2 kB of memory to store a distribution that covers the visible wavelengths. `PiecewiseLinearSpectrum` offers another representation that is often more compact; its distribution is specified by a set of pairs of values (λ_i, v_i) where the spectral

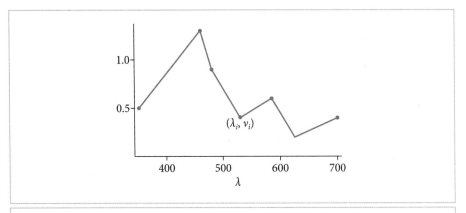

Figure 4.17: PiecewiseLinearSpectrum defines a spectral distribution using a set of sample values (λ_i, v_i). A continuous distribution is then defined by linearly interpolating between them.

distribution is defined by linearly interpolating between them; see Figure 4.17. For spectra that are smooth in some regions and change rapidly in others, this representation makes it possible to specify the distribution at a higher rate in regions where its variation is greatest.

⟨*Spectrum Definitions*⟩ +≡
```
class PiecewiseLinearSpectrum {
  public:
    ⟨PiecewiseLinearSpectrum Public Methods 168⟩
  private:
    ⟨PiecewiseLinearSpectrum Private Members 168⟩
};
```

The PiecewiseLinearSpectrum constructor, not included here, checks that the provided lambda values are sorted and then stores them and the associated spectrum values in corresponding member variables.

⟨*PiecewiseLinearSpectrum Public Methods*⟩ ≡   168
```
PiecewiseLinearSpectrum(pstd::span<const Float> lambdas,
    pstd::span<const Float> values, Allocator alloc = {});
```

⟨*PiecewiseLinearSpectrum Private Members*⟩ ≡   168
```
pstd::vector<Float> lambdas, values;
```

Finding the value for a given wavelength requires first finding the pair of values in the lambdas array that bracket it and then linearly interpolating between them.

⟨*Spectrum Method Definitions*⟩ ≡
```
Float PiecewiseLinearSpectrum::operator()(Float lambda) const {
    ⟨Handle PiecewiseLinearSpectrum corner cases 168⟩
    ⟨Find offset to largest lambdas below lambda and interpolate 169⟩
}
```

As with DenselySampledSpectrum, wavelengths outside of the specified range are given a value of zero.

⟨*Handle* PiecewiseLinearSpectrum *corner cases*⟩ ≡   168
```
if (lambdas.empty() || lambda < lambdas.front() || lambda > lambdas.back())
    return 0;
```

If lambda is in range, then FindInterval() gives the offset to the largest value of lambdas that is less than or equal to lambda. In turn, lambda's offset between that wavelength and the next gives the linear interpolation parameter to use with the stored values.

⟨*Find offset to largest* lambdas *below* lambda *and interpolate*⟩ ≡   **168**
```
int o = FindInterval(lambdas.size(),
                     [&](int i) { return lambdas[i] <= lambda; });
Float t = (lambda - lambdas[o]) / (lambdas[o + 1] - lambdas[o]);
return Lerp(t, values[o], values[o + 1]);
```

The maximum value of the distribution is easily found using std::max_element(), which performs a linear search. This function is not currently called in any performance-sensitive parts of pbrt; if it was, it would likely be worth caching this value to avoid recomputing it.

⟨*Spectrum Method Definitions*⟩ +≡
```
Float PiecewiseLinearSpectrum::MaxValue() const {
    if (values.empty()) return 0;
    return *std::max_element(values.begin(), values.end());
}
```

Another useful Spectrum implementation, BlackbodySpectrum, gives the spectral distribution of a blackbody emitter at a specified temperature.

⟨*Spectrum Definitions*⟩ +≡
```
class BlackbodySpectrum {
  public:
    ⟨BlackbodySpectrum Public Methods 169⟩
  private:
    ⟨BlackbodySpectrum Private Members 169⟩
};
```

The temperature of the blackbody in Kelvin is the constructor's only parameter.

⟨*BlackbodySpectrum Public Methods*⟩ ≡   **169**
```
BlackbodySpectrum(Float T) : T(T) {
    ⟨Compute blackbody normalization constant for given temperature 169⟩
}
```

⟨*BlackbodySpectrum Private Members*⟩ ≡   **169**
```
Float T;
```

Because the power emitted by a blackbody grows so quickly with temperature (recall the Stefan–Boltzmann law, Equation (4.19)), the BlackbodySpectrum represents a normalized blackbody spectral distribution where the maximum value at any wavelength is 1. Wien's displacement law, Equation (4.20), gives the wavelength in meters where emitted radiance is at its maximum; we must convert this value to nm before calling Blackbody() to find the corresponding radiance value.

⟨*Compute blackbody normalization constant for given temperature*⟩ ≡   **169**
```
Float lambdaMax = 2.8977721e-3f / T;
normalizationFactor = 1 / Blackbody(lambdaMax * 1e9f, T);
```

⟨*BlackbodySpectrum Private Members*⟩ +≡   **169**
```
Float normalizationFactor;
```

The method that returns the value of the distribution at a wavelength then returns the product of the value returned by Blackbody() and the normalization factor.

⟨*BlackbodySpectrum Public Methods*⟩ +≡   **169**
```
Float operator()(Float lambda) const {
    return Blackbody(lambda, T) * normalizationFactor;
}
```

4.5.3 EMBEDDED SPECTRAL DATA

pbrt's scene description format provides multiple ways to specify spectral data, ranging from blackbody temperatures to arrays of λ-value pairs to specify a piecewise-linear spectrum. For convenience, a variety of useful spectral distributions are also embedded directly in the pbrt binary, including ones that describe the emission profiles of various types of light source, the scattering properties of various conductors, and the wavelength-dependent indices of refraction of various types of glass. See the online pbrt file format documentation for a list of all of them.

The GetNamedSpectrum() function searches through these spectra and returns a Spectrum corresponding to a given named spectrum if it is available.

⟨*Spectral Function Declarations*⟩ ≡
```
Spectrum GetNamedSpectrum(std::string name);
```

A number of important spectra are made available directly through corresponding functions, all of which are in a Spectra namespace. Among them are Spectra::X(), Spectra::Y(), and Spectra::Z(), which return the color matching curves that are described in Section 4.6.1, and Spectra::D(), which returns a DenselySampledSpectrum representing the D illuminant at the given temperature.

⟨*Spectrum Function Declarations*⟩ +≡
```
DenselySampledSpectrum D(Float T, Allocator alloc);
```

4.5.4 SAMPLED SPECTRAL DISTRIBUTIONS

The attentive reader may have noticed that although Spectrum makes it possible to evaluate spectral distribution functions, it does not provide the ability to do very much computation with them other than sampling their value at a specified wavelength. Yet, for example, evaluating the integrand of the reflection equation, (4.14), requires taking the product of two spectral distributions, one for the BSDF and one for the incident radiance function.

Providing this functionality with the abstractions that have been introduced so far would quickly become unwieldy. For example, while the product of two DenselySampledSpectrums could be faithfully represented by another DenselySampledSpectrum, consider taking the product of two PiecewiseLinearSpectrums: the resulting function would be piecewise-quadratic and subsequent products would only increase its degree. Further, operations between Spectrum implementations of different types would not only require a custom implementation for each pair, but would require choosing a suitable Spectrum representation for each result.

pbrt avoids this complexity by performing spectral calculations at a set of discrete wavelengths as part of the Monte Carlo integration that is already being performed for image synthesis. To understand how this works, consider computing the (non-spectral) irradiance at some point p with surface normal **n** over some range of wavelengths of interest, $[\lambda_0, \lambda_1]$. Using Equation (4.7), which expresses irradiance in terms of incident radiance, and Equation (4.5), which expresses radiance in terms of spectral radiance, we have

$$E = \int_{\Omega} \int_{\lambda_0}^{\lambda_1} L_i(p, \omega, \lambda) \, |\cos\theta| \, d\omega \, d\lambda,$$

where $L_i(p, \omega, \lambda)$ is the incident spectral radiance at wavelength λ.

Applying the standard Monte Carlo estimator and taking advantage of the fact that ω and λ are independent, we can see that estimates of E can be computed by sampling directions ω_i from some distribution p_ω, wavelengths λ_i from some distribution p_λ, and then evaluating:

$$E \approx \frac{1}{n} \sum_{i=1}^{n} \frac{L_i(\mathrm{p}, \omega_i, \lambda_i) \, |\cos \theta_i|}{p_\omega(\omega_i) \, p_\lambda(\lambda_i)}. \qquad [4.21]$$

Thus, we only need to be able to evaluate the integrand at the specified discrete wavelengths to estimate the irradiance. More generally, we will see that it is possible to express all the spectral quantities that pbrt outputs as integrals over wavelength. For example, Section 4.6 shows that when rendering an image represented using RGB colors, each pixel's color can be computed by integrating the spectral radiance arriving at a pixel with functions that model red, green, and blue color response. pbrt therefore uses only discrete spectral samples for spectral computation.

So that we can proceed to the implementation of the classes related to sampling spectra and performing computations with spectral samples, we will define the constant that sets the number of spectral samples here. (Section 4.6.5 will discuss in more detail the trade-offs involved in choosing this value.) pbrt uses 4 wavelength samples by default; this value can easily be changed, though doing so requires recompiling the system.

⟨*Spectrum Constants*⟩ +≡
```
static constexpr int NSpectrumSamples = 4;
```

SampledSpectrum

The SampledSpectrum class stores an array of NSpectrumSamples values that represent values of the spectral distribution at discrete wavelengths. It provides methods that allow a variety of mathematical operations to be performed with them.

⟨*SampledSpectrum Definition*⟩ ≡
```
class SampledSpectrum {
  public:
    ⟨SampledSpectrum Public Methods 171⟩
  private:
    pstd::array<Float, NSpectrumSamples> values;
};
```

Its constructors include one that allows providing a single value for all wavelengths and one that takes an appropriately sized pstd::span of per-wavelength values.

⟨*SampledSpectrum Public Methods*⟩ ≡   171
```
explicit SampledSpectrum(Float c) { values.fill(c); }
SampledSpectrum(pstd::span<const Float> v) {
    for (int i = 0; i < NSpectrumSamples; ++i)
        values[i] = v[i];
}
```

The usual indexing operations are also provided for accessing and setting each wavelength's value.

⟨*SampledSpectrum Public Methods*⟩ +≡   171
```
Float operator[](int i) const { return values[i]; }
Float &operator[](int i) { return values[i]; }
```

It is often useful to know if all the values in a SampledSpectrum are zero. For example, if a surface has zero reflectance, then the light transport routines can avoid the computational cost of casting reflection rays that have contributions that would eventually be multiplied by zeros. This capability is provided through a type conversion operator to bool.[5]

⟨*SampledSpectrum Public Methods*⟩ +≡   **171**
```
explicit operator bool() const {
    for (int i = 0; i < NSpectrumSamples; ++i)
        if (values[i] != 0) return true;
    return false;
}
```

All the standard arithmetic operations on SampledSpectrum objects are provided; each operates component-wise on the stored values. The implementation of operator+= is below. The others are analogous and are therefore not included in the text.

⟨*SampledSpectrum Public Methods*⟩ +≡   **171**
```
SampledSpectrum &operator+=(const SampledSpectrum &s) {
    for (int i = 0; i < NSpectrumSamples; ++i)
        values[i] += s.values[i];
    return *this;
}
```

SafeDiv() divides two sampled spectra, but generates zero for any sample where the divisor is zero.

⟨*SampledSpectrum Inline Functions*⟩ ≡
```
SampledSpectrum SafeDiv(SampledSpectrum a, SampledSpectrum b) {
    SampledSpectrum r;
    for (int i = 0; i < NSpectrumSamples; ++i)
        r[i] = (b[i] != 0) ? a[i] / b[i] : 0.;
    return r;
}
```

In addition to the basic arithmetic operations, SampledSpectrum also provides Lerp(), Sqrt(), Clamp(), ClampZero(), Pow(), Exp(), and FastExp() functions that operate (again, component-wise) on SampledSpectrum objects; some of these operations are necessary for evaluating some of the reflection models in Chapter 9 and for evaluating volume scattering models in Chapter 14. Finally, MinComponentValue() and MaxComponentValue() return the minimum and maximum of all the values, and Average() returns their average. These methods are all straightforward and are therefore not included in the text.

SampledWavelengths

A separate class, SampledWavelengths, stores the wavelengths for which a SampledSpectrum stores samples. Thus, it is important not only to keep careful track of the SampledWavelengths that are represented by an individual SampledSpectrum but also to not perform any operations that combine SampledSpectrums that have samples at different wavelengths.

---

5   C++ arcana: the explicit qualifier ensures that a SampledSpectrum is not unintentionally passed as a bool argument to a function without an explicit cast. However, if a SampledSpectrum is used as the condition in an "if" test, it is still automatically converted to a Boolean value without a cast.

⟨*SampledWavelengths Definitions*⟩ ≡
```
class SampledWavelengths {
  public:
    ⟨SampledWavelengths Public Methods 173⟩
  private:
    ⟨SampledWavelengths Private Members 173⟩
};
```

To be used in the context of Monte Carlo integration, the wavelengths stored in `Sampled Wavelengths` must be sampled from some probability distribution. Therefore, the class stores the wavelengths themselves as well as each one's probability density.

⟨*SampledWavelengths Private Members*⟩ ≡   173
```
pstd::array<Float, NSpectrumSamples> lambda, pdf;
```

The easiest way to sample wavelengths is uniformly over a given range. This approach is implemented in the `SampleUniform()` method, which takes a single uniform sample u and a range of wavelengths.

⟨*SampledWavelengths Public Methods*⟩ ≡   173
```
static SampledWavelengths SampleUniform(Float u,
        Float lambda_min = Lambda_min, Float lambda_max = Lambda_max) {
    SampledWavelengths swl;
    ⟨Sample first wavelength using u 173⟩
    ⟨Initialize lambda for remaining wavelengths 173⟩
    ⟨Compute PDF for sampled wavelengths 173⟩
    return swl;
}
```

It chooses the first wavelength uniformly within the range.

⟨*Sample first wavelength using* u⟩ ≡   173
```
swl.lambda[0] = Lerp(u, lambda_min, lambda_max);
```

The remaining wavelengths are chosen by taking uniform steps `delta` starting from the first wavelength and wrapping around if `lambda_max` is passed. The result is a set of stratified wavelength samples that are generated using a single random number. One advantage of sampling wavelengths in this way rather than using a separate uniform sample for each one is that the value of `NSpectrumSamples` can be changed without requiring the modification of code that calls `SampleUniform()` to adjust the number of sample values that are passed to this method.

⟨*Initialize* lambda *for remaining wavelengths*⟩ ≡   173
```
Float delta = (lambda_max - lambda_min) / NSpectrumSamples;
for (int i = 1; i < NSpectrumSamples; ++i) {
    swl.lambda[i] = swl.lambda[i - 1] + delta;
    if (swl.lambda[i] > lambda_max)
        swl.lambda[i] = lambda_min + (swl.lambda[i] - lambda_max);
}
```

The probability density for each sample is easily computed, since the sampling distribution is uniform.

⟨*Compute PDF for sampled wavelengths*⟩ ≡   173
```
for (int i = 0; i < NSpectrumSamples; ++i)
    swl.pdf[i] = 1 / (lambda_max - lambda_min);
```

Additional methods provide access to the individual wavelengths and to all of their PDFs. PDF values are returned in the form of a SampledSpectrum, which makes it easy to compute the value of associated Monte Carlo estimators.

⟨*SampledWavelengths Public Methods*⟩ +≡   **173**
```
    Float operator[](int i) const { return lambda[i]; }
    Float &operator[](int i) { return lambda[i]; }
    SampledSpectrum PDF() const { return SampledSpectrum(pdf); }
```

In some cases, different wavelengths of light may follow different paths after a scattering event. The most common example is when light undergoes dispersion and different wavelengths of light refract to different directions. When this happens, it is no longer possible to track multiple wavelengths of light with a single ray. For this case, SampledWavelengths provides the capability of terminating all but one of the wavelengths; subsequent computations can then consider the single surviving wavelength exclusively.

⟨*SampledWavelengths Public Methods*⟩ +≡   **173**
```
    void TerminateSecondary() {
        if (SecondaryTerminated()) return;
        ⟨Update wavelength probabilities for termination 174⟩
    }
```

The wavelength stored in lambda[0] is always the survivor: there is no need to randomly select the surviving wavelength so long as each lambda value was randomly sampled from the same distribution as is the case with SampleUniform(), for example. Note that this means that it would be incorrect for SampledWavelengths::SampleUniform() to always place lambda[0] in a first wavelength stratum between lambda_min and lambda_min+delta, lambda[1] in the second, and so forth.[6]

Terminated wavelengths have their PDF values set to zero; code that computes Monte Carlo estimates using SampledWavelengths must therefore detect this case and ignore terminated wavelengths accordingly. The surviving wavelength's PDF is updated to account for the termination event by multiplying it by the probability of a wavelength surviving termination, 1 / NSpectrumSamples. (This is similar to how applying Russian roulette affects the Monte Carlo estimator—see Section 2.2.4.)

⟨*Update wavelength probabilities for termination*⟩ ≡   **174**
```
    for (int i = 1; i < NSpectrumSamples; ++i)
        pdf[i] = 0;
    pdf[0] /= NSpectrumSamples;
```

SecondaryTerminated() indicates whether TerminateSecondary() has already been called. Because path termination is the only thing that causes zero-valued PDFs after the first wavelength, checking the PDF values suffices for this test.

⟨*SampledWavelengths Public Methods*⟩ +≡   **173**
```
    bool SecondaryTerminated() const {
        for (int i = 1; i < NSpectrumSamples; ++i)
            if (pdf[i] != 0)
                return false;
        return true;
    }
```

---

6   This mistake is one of the bugs that the authors encountered during the initial development of this functionality in pbrt.

We will often have a Spectrum and a set of wavelengths for which we would like to evaluate it. Therefore, we will add a method to the Spectrum interface that provides a Sample() method that takes a set of wavelengths, evaluates its spectral distribution function at each one, and returns a SampledSpectrum. This convenience method eliminates the need for an explicit loop over wavelengths with individual calls to Spectrum::operator() in this common case. The implementations of this method are straightforward and not included here.

⟨*Spectrum Interface*⟩ +≡   **165**
```
    SampledSpectrum Sample(const SampledWavelengths &lambda) const;
```

Discussion

Now that SampledWavelengths and SampledSpectrum have been introduced, it is reasonable to ask the question: why are they separate classes, rather than a single class that stores both wavelengths and their sample values? Indeed, an advantage of such a design would be that it would be possible to detect at runtime if an operation was performed with two SampledSpectrum instances that stored values for different wavelengths—such an operation is nonsensical and would signify a bug in the system.

However, in practice many SampledSpectrum objects are created during rendering, many as temporary values in the course of evaluating expressions involving spectral computation. It is therefore worthwhile to minimize the object's size, if only to avoid initialization and copying of additional data. While the pbrt's CPU-based integrators do not store many SampledSpectrum values in memory at the same time, the GPU rendering path stores a few million of them, giving further motivation to minimize their size.

Our experience has been that bugs from mixing computations at different wavelengths have been rare. With the way that computation is structured in pbrt, wavelengths are generally sampled at the start of following a ray's path through the scene, and then the same wavelengths are used throughout for all spectral calculations along the path. There ends up being little opportunity for inadvertent mingling of sampled wavelengths in SampledSpectrum instances. Indeed, in an earlier version of the system, SampledSpectrum did carry along a SampledWavelengths member variable in debug builds in order to be able to check for that case. It was eliminated in the interests of simplicity after a few months' existence without finding a bug.

4.6 COLOR

"Spectral distribution" and "color" might seem like two names for the same thing, but they are distinct. A spectral distribution is a purely physical concept, while color describes the human perception of a spectrum. Color is thus closely connected to the physiology of the human visual system and the brain's processing of visual stimulus.

Although the majority of rendering computation in pbrt is based on spectral distributions, color still must be treated carefully. For example, the spectral distribution at each pixel in a rendered image must be converted to RGB color to be displayed on a monitor. Performing this conversion accurately requires using information about the monitor's color characteristics. The renderer also finds color in scene descriptions that use it to describe reflectance and light emission. Although it is convenient for humans to use colors to describe the appearance of modeled scenes, these colors must be converted to spectra if a renderer uses spectral distributions in its light transport simulation. Unfortunately, doing so is an underspecified problem. A variety of approaches have been developed for it; the one implemented in pbrt is described in Section 4.6.6.

The *tristimulus theory* of color perception says that all visible spectral distributions can be accurately represented for human observers using three scalar values. Its basis is that there are three types of photoreceptive cone cells in the eye, each sensitive to different wavelengths of light. This theory, which has been tested in numerous experiments since its introduction in the 1800s, has led to the development of *spectral matching functions*, which are functions of wavelength that can be used to compute a tristimulus representation of a spectral distribution.

Integrating the product of a spectral distribution $S(\lambda)$ with three tristimulus matching functions $m_{\{1,2,3\}}(\lambda)$ gives three *tristimulus values* v_i:

$$v_i = \int S(\lambda)\, m_i(\lambda)\, d\lambda.$$

The matching functions thus define a *color space*, which is a 3D vector space of the tristimulus values: the tristimulus values for the sum of two spectra are given by the sum of their tristimulus values and the tristimulus values associated with a spectrum that has been scaled by a constant can be found by scaling the tristimulus values by the same factor. Note that from these definitions, the tristimulus values for the product of two spectral distributions are *not* given by the product of their tristimulus values. This nit is why using tristimulus color like RGB for rendering may not give accurate results; we will say more about this topic in Section 4.6.6.

The files util/color.h and util/color.cpp in the pbrt distribution contain the implementation of the functionality related to color that is introduced in this section.

4.6.1 XYZ COLOR

An important set of color matching functions were determined by the Commission Internationale de l'Éclairage (CIE) standards body after a series of experiments with human test subjects. They define the *XYZ color space* and are graphed in Figure 4.18. XYZ is a *device-independent* color space, which means that it does not describe the characteristics of a particular display or color measurement device.

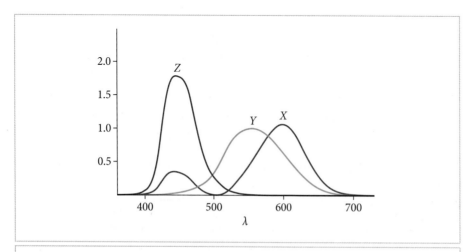

Figure 4.18: The XYZ Color Matching Curves. A given spectral distribution can be converted to XYZ by multiplying it by each of the three matching curves and integrating the result to compute the values x_λ, y_λ, and z_λ, using Equation (4.22).

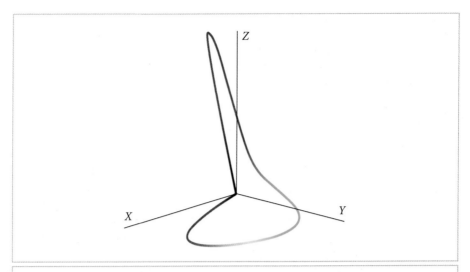

Figure 4.19: Plot of XYZ color coefficients for the wavelengths of light in the visible range. The curve is shaded with the RGB color associated with each wavelength.

Given a spectral distribution $S(\lambda)$, its XYZ color space coordinates x_λ, y_λ, and z_λ are computed by integrating its product with the $X(\lambda)$, $Y(\lambda)$, and $Z(\lambda)$ spectral matching curves:[7]

$$x_\lambda = \frac{1}{\int_\lambda Y(\lambda)\,d\lambda} \int_\lambda S(\lambda)\,X(\lambda)\,d\lambda$$

$$y_\lambda = \frac{1}{\int_\lambda Y(\lambda)\,d\lambda} \int_\lambda S(\lambda)\,Y(\lambda)\,d\lambda \qquad\qquad [4.22]$$

$$z_\lambda = \frac{1}{\int_\lambda Y(\lambda)\,d\lambda} \int_\lambda S(\lambda)\,Z(\lambda)\,d\lambda.$$

The CIE $Y(\lambda)$ tristimulus curve was chosen to be proportional to the $V(\lambda)$ spectral response curve used to define photometric quantities such as luminance in Equation (4.6). Their relationship is: $V(\lambda) = 683\,Y(\lambda)$.

Remarkably, spectra with substantially different distributions may have very similar x_λ, y_λ, and z_λ values. To the human observer, such spectra appear the same. Pairs of such spectra are called *metamers*.

Figure 4.19 shows a 3D plot of the curve in the XYZ space corresponding to the XYZ coefficients for single wavelengths of light over the visible range. The coefficients for more complex spectral distributions therefore correspond to linear combinations of points along this curve. Although all spectral distributions can be represented with XYZ coefficients, not all values of XYZ coefficients correspond to realizable spectra; such sets of coefficients are termed *imaginary colors*.

Three functions in the Spectra namespace provide the CIE XYZ matching curves sampled at 1-nm increments from 360 nm to 830 nm.

---

7   A variety of conventions are used to define these integrals, sometimes with other or no normalization factors. For use in pbrt, the normalization by one over the integral of the Y matching curve is convenient, as it causes a spectral distribution with a constant value of 1 to have $y_\lambda = 1$.

⟨*Spectral Function Declarations*⟩ +≡
```
namespace Spectra {
    const DenselySampledSpectrum &X();
    const DenselySampledSpectrum &Y();
    const DenselySampledSpectrum &Z();
}
```

The integral of $Y(\lambda)$ is precomputed and available in a constant.

⟨*Spectrum Constants*⟩ +≡
```
static constexpr Float CIE_Y_integral = 106.856895;
```

There is also an XYZ class that represents XYZ colors.

⟨*XYZ Definition*⟩ ≡
```
class XYZ {
  public:
    ⟨XYZ Public Methods 178⟩
    ⟨XYZ Public Members 178⟩
};
```

Its implementation is the obvious one, using three Float values to represent the three color components. All the regular arithmetic operations are provided for XYZ in methods that are not included in the text here.

⟨*XYZ Public Methods*⟩ ≡   **178**
```
XYZ(Float X, Float Y, Float Z) : X(X), Y(Y), Z(Z) {}
```

⟨*XYZ Public Members*⟩ ≡   **178**
```
Float X = 0, Y = 0, Z = 0;
```

The SpectrumToXYZ() function computes the XYZ coefficients of a spectral distribution following Equation (4.22) using the following InnerProduct() utility function to handle each component.

⟨*Spectrum Function Definitions*⟩ ≡
```
XYZ SpectrumToXYZ(Spectrum s) {
    return XYZ(InnerProduct(&Spectra::X(), s),
               InnerProduct(&Spectra::Y(), s),
               InnerProduct(&Spectra::Z(), s)) / CIE_Y_integral;
}
```

Monte Carlo is not necessary for a simple 1D integral of two spectra, so InnerProduct() computes a Riemann sum over integer wavelengths instead:

$$\int_{\lambda_{\min}}^{\lambda_{\max}} f(\lambda)\, g(\lambda)\, \mathrm{d}\lambda \approx \sum_{\lambda=\lambda_{\min}}^{\lambda_{\max}} f(\lambda)\, g(\lambda).$$

⟨*Spectrum Inline Functions*⟩ ≡
```
Float InnerProduct(Spectrum f, Spectrum g) {
    Float integral = 0;
    for (Float lambda = Lambda_min; lambda <= Lambda_max; ++lambda)
        integral += f(lambda) * g(lambda);
    return integral;
}
```

It is also useful to be able to compute XYZ coefficients for a `SampledSpectrum`. Because `SampledSpectrum` only has point samples of the spectral distribution at predetermined wavelengths, they are found via a Monte Carlo estimate of Equation (4.22) using the sampled spectral values s_i at wavelengths λ_i and their associated PDFs:

$$x_\lambda \approx \frac{1}{\int_\lambda Y(\lambda)\,d\lambda}\left(\frac{1}{n}\sum_{i=1}^{n}\frac{s_i\,X(\lambda_i)}{p(\lambda_i)}\right), \qquad\qquad [4.23]$$

and so forth, where n is the number of wavelength samples.

`SampledSpectrum::ToXYZ()` computes the value of this estimator.

⟨*Spectrum Method Definitions*⟩ +≡
```
XYZ SampledSpectrum::ToXYZ(const SampledWavelengths &lambda) const {
    ⟨Sample the X, Y, and Z matching curves at lambda 179⟩
    ⟨Evaluate estimator to compute (x, y, z) coefficients 179⟩
}
```

The first step is to sample the matching curves at the specified wavelengths.

⟨*Sample the X, Y, and Z matching curves at* lambda⟩ ≡   **179**
```
SampledSpectrum X = Spectra::X().Sample(lambda);
SampledSpectrum Y = Spectra::Y().Sample(lambda);
SampledSpectrum Z = Spectra::Z().Sample(lambda);
```

The summand in Equation (4.23) is easily computed with values at hand. Here, we evaluate all terms of each sum with a single expression. Using `SampledSpectrum::SafeDiv()` to divide by the PDF values handles the case of the PDF being equal to zero for some wavelengths, as can happen if `SampledWavelengths::TerminateSecondary()` was called. Finally, `SampledSpectrum::Average()` conveniently takes care of summing the individual terms and dividing by n to compute the estimator's value for each coefficient.

⟨*Evaluate estimator to compute* (x, y, z) *coefficients*⟩ ≡   **179**
```
SampledSpectrum pdf = lambda.PDF();
return XYZ(SafeDiv(X * *this, pdf).Average(),
          SafeDiv(Y * *this, pdf).Average(),
          SafeDiv(Z * *this, pdf).Average()) / CIE_Y_integral;
```

To avoid the expense of computing the X and Z coefficients when only luminance is needed, there is a `y()` method that only returns Y. Its implementation is the obvious subset of `XYZ()` and so is not included here.

Chromaticity and xyY Color

Color can be separated into *lightness*, which describes how bright it is relative to something white, and *chroma*, which describes its relative colorfulness with respect to white. One approach to quantifying chroma is the *xyz chromaticity coordinates*, which are defined in terms of XYZ color space coordinates by

$$x = \frac{x_\lambda}{x_\lambda + y_\lambda + z_\lambda}$$

$$y = \frac{y_\lambda}{x_\lambda + y_\lambda + z_\lambda}$$

$$z = \frac{z_\lambda}{x_\lambda + y_\lambda + z_\lambda} = 1 - x - y.$$

Note that any two of them are sufficient to specify chromaticity.

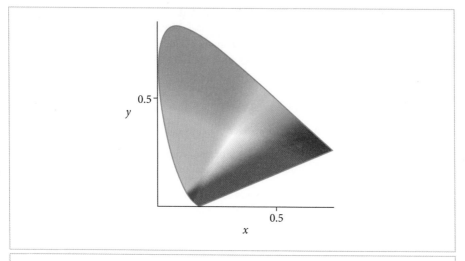

Figure 4.20: xy **Chromaticity Diagram.** All valid colors lie inside the shaded region.

Considering just x and y, we can plot a *chromaticity diagram* to visualize their values; see Figure 4.20. Spectra with light at just a single wavelength—the pure spectral colors—lie along the curved part of the chromaticity diagram. This part corresponds to the xy projection of the 3D XYZ curve that was shown in Figure 4.19. All the valid colors lie inside the upside-down horseshoe shape; points outside that region correspond to imaginary colors.

The xyY color space separates a color's chromaticity from its lightness. It uses the x and y chromaticity coordinates and y_λ from XYZ, since the $Y(\lambda)$ matching curve was defined to be proportional to luminance. pbrt makes limited use of xyY colors and therefore does not provide a class to represent them, but the XYZ class does provide a method that returns its xy chromaticity coordinates as a Point2f.

⟨*XYZ Public Methods*⟩ +≡   **178**
```
Point2f xy() const {
    return Point2f(X / (X + Y + Z), Y / (X + Y + Z));
}
```

A corresponding method converts from xyY to XYZ, given xy and optionally y_λ coordinates.

⟨*XYZ Public Methods*⟩ +≡   **178**
```
static XYZ FromxyY(Point2f xy, Float Y = 1) {
    if (xy.y == 0)
        return XYZ(0, 0, 0);
    return XYZ(xy.x * Y / xy.y, Y, (1 - xy.x - xy.y) * Y / xy.y);
}
```

4.6.2 RGB COLOR

RGB color is used more commonly than XYZ in rendering applications. In RGB color spaces, colors are represented by a triplet of values corresponding to red, green, and blue colors, often referred to as *RGB*. However, an RGB triplet on its own is meaningless; it must be defined with respect to a specific RGB color space.

To understand why, consider what happens when an RGB color is shown on a display: the spectrum that is displayed is given by the weighted sum of three spectral emission curves, one

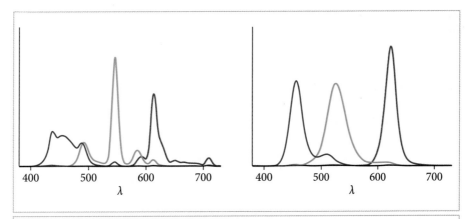

Figure 4.21: Red, Green, and Blue Emission Curves for an LCD Display and an LED Display. The first plot shows the curves for an LCD display, and the second shows them for an LED. These two displays have quite different emission profiles. *(Data courtesy of X-Rite, Inc.)*

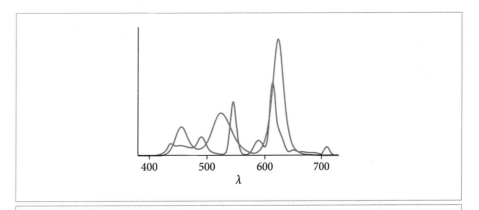

Figure 4.22: Spectral Distributions from Displaying the RGB Color (0.6, 0.3, 0.2) **on LED (red) and LCD (blue) Displays.** The resulting emitted distributions are remarkably different, even given the same RGB values, due to the different emission curves illustrated in Figure 4.21.

for each of red, green, and blue, as emitted by the display elements, be they phosphors, LED or LCD elements, or plasma cells.[8] Figure 4.21 plots the red, green, and blue distributions emitted by an LCD display and an LED display; note that they are remarkably different. Figure 4.22 in turn shows the spectral distributions that result from displaying the RGB color (0.6, 0.3, 0.2) on those displays. Not surprisingly, the resulting spectra are quite different as well.

If a display's $R(\lambda)$, $G(\lambda)$, and $B(\lambda)$ curves are known, the RGB coefficients for displaying a spectral distribution $S(\lambda)$ on that display can be found by integrating $S(\lambda)$ with each curve:

$$r = \int R(\lambda)\, S(\lambda)\, d\lambda,$$

---

8   This model is admittedly a simplification in that it neglects any additional processing the display does; in particular, many displays perform nonlinear remappings of the displayed values; this topic will be discussed in Section B.5.6.

and so forth. The same approaches that were used to compute XYZ values for spectra in the previous section can be used to compute the values of these integrals.

Alternatively, if we already have the $(x_\lambda, y_\lambda, z_\lambda)$ representation of $S(\lambda)$, it is possible to convert the XYZ coefficients directly to corresponding RGB coefficients. Consider, for example, computing the value of the red component for a spectral distribution $S(\lambda)$:

$$
\begin{aligned}
r &= \int R(\lambda)\, S(\lambda)\, d\lambda \\
&\approx \int R(\lambda)(x_\lambda X(\lambda) + y_\lambda Y(\lambda) + z_\lambda Z(\lambda))\, d\lambda \\
&= x_\lambda \int R(\lambda)\, X(\lambda)\, d\lambda + y_\lambda \int R(\lambda)\, Y(\lambda)\, d\lambda + z_\lambda \int R(\lambda)\, Z(\lambda)\, d\lambda,
\end{aligned}
$$

[4.24]

where the second step takes advantage of the tristimulus theory of color perception.

The integrals of the products of an RGB response function and XYZ matching function can be precomputed for given response curves, making it possible to express the full conversion as a matrix:

$$
\begin{bmatrix} r \\ g \\ b \end{bmatrix} = \begin{pmatrix} \int R(\lambda) X(\lambda)\, d\lambda & \int R(\lambda) Y(\lambda)\, d\lambda & \int R(\lambda) Z(\lambda)\, d\lambda \\ \int G(\lambda) X(\lambda)\, d\lambda & \int G(\lambda) Y(\lambda)\, d\lambda & \int G(\lambda) Z(\lambda)\, d\lambda \\ \int B(\lambda) X(\lambda)\, d\lambda & \int B(\lambda) Y(\lambda)\, d\lambda & \int B(\lambda) Z(\lambda)\, d\lambda \end{pmatrix} \begin{bmatrix} x_\lambda \\ y_\lambda \\ z_\lambda \end{bmatrix}.
$$

pbrt frequently uses this approach in order to efficiently convert colors from one color space to another.

An RGB class that has the obvious representation and provides a variety of useful arithmetic operations (not included in the text) is also provided by pbrt.

⟨RGB Definition⟩ ≡
```
class RGB {
  public:
    ⟨RGB Public Methods 182⟩
    ⟨RGB Public Members 182⟩
};
```

⟨RGB Public Methods⟩ ≡   182
```
RGB(Float r, Float g, Float b) : r(r), g(g), b(b) {}
```

⟨RGB Public Members⟩ ≡   182
```
Float r = 0, g = 0, b = 0;
```

4.6.3 RGB COLOR SPACES

Full spectral response curves are not necessary to define color spaces. For example, a color space can be defined using xy chromaticity coordinates to specify three *color primaries*. From them, it is possible to derive matrices that convert XYZ colors to and from that color space. In cases where we do not otherwise need explicit spectral response curves, this is a convenient way to specify a color space.

The RGBColorSpace class, which is defined in the files util/colorspace.h and util/color space.cpp, uses this approach to encapsulate a representation of an RGB color space as well as a variety of useful operations like converting XYZ colors to and from its color space.

Float 23
RGB 182

⟨*RGBColorSpace Definition*⟩ ≡
```
class RGBColorSpace {
  public:
    ⟨RGBColorSpace Public Methods 184⟩
  private:
    ⟨RGBColorSpace Private Members 184⟩
};
```

An RGB color space is defined using the chromaticities of red, green, and blue color primaries. The primaries define the *gamut* of the color space, which is the set of colors it can represent with RGB values between 0 and 1. For three primaries, the gamut forms a triangle on the chromaticity diagram where each primary's chromaticity defines one of the vertices.[9]

In addition to the primaries, it is necessary to specify the color space's *whitepoint*, which is the color that is displayed when all three primaries are activated to their maximum emission. It may be surprising that this is necessary—after all, should not white correspond to a spectral distribution with the same value at every wavelength? White is, however, a color, and as a color it is what humans *perceive* as being uniform and label "white." The spectra for white colors tend to have more power in the lower wavelengths that correspond to blues and greens than they do at higher wavelengths that correspond to oranges and reds. The D65 illuminant, which was described in Section 4.4.2 and plotted in Figure 4.14, is a common choice for specifying color spaces' whitepoints.

While the chromaticities of the whitepoint are sufficient to define a color space, the RGBColorSpace constructor takes its full spectral distribution, which is useful for forthcoming code that converts from color to spectral distributions. Storing the illuminant spectrum allows users of the renderer to specify emission from light sources using RGB color; the provided illuminant then gives the spectral distribution for RGB white, (1, 1, 1).

⟨*RGBColorSpace Method Definitions*⟩ ≡
```
RGBColorSpace::RGBColorSpace(Point2f r, Point2f g, Point2f b,
        Spectrum illuminant, const RGBToSpectrumTable *rgbToSpec,
        Allocator alloc)
    : r(r), g(g), b(b), illuminant(illuminant, alloc),
      rgbToSpectrumTable(rgbToSpec) {
    ⟨Compute whitepoint primaries and XYZ coordinates 184⟩
    ⟨Initialize XYZ color space conversion matrices 184⟩
}
```

RGBColorSpace represents the illuminant as a DenselySampledSpectrum for efficient lookups by wavelength.

⟨*RGBColorSpace Public Members*⟩ ≡
```
Point2f r, g, b, w;
DenselySampledSpectrum illuminant;
```

RGBColorSpaces also store a pointer to an RGBToSpectrumTable class that stores information related to converting RGB values in the color space to full spectral distributions; it will be introduced shortly, in Section 4.6.6.

---

9 Some displays use more than three primaries to increase the size of the gamut, though we will assume conventional RGB here.

⟨*RGBColorSpace Private Members*⟩ ≡   **183**
```
const RGBToSpectrumTable *rgbToSpectrumTable;
```

To find RGB values in the color space, it is useful to be able to convert to and from XYZ. This can be done using 3×3 matrices. To compute them, we will require the XYZ coordinates of the chromaticities and the whitepoint.

⟨*Compute whitepoint primaries and XYZ coordinates*⟩ ≡   **183**
```
XYZ W = SpectrumToXYZ(illuminant);
w = W.xy();
XYZ R = XYZ::FromxyY(r), G = XYZ::FromxyY(g), B = XYZ::FromxyY(b);
```

We will first derive the matrix M that transforms from RGB coefficients in the color space to XYZ:

$$\begin{bmatrix} x_\lambda \\ y_\lambda \\ z_\lambda \end{bmatrix} = M \begin{bmatrix} r \\ g \\ b \end{bmatrix}.$$

This matrix can be found by considering the relationship between the RGB triplet $(1, 1, 1)$ and the whitepoint in XYZ coordinates, which is available in W. In this case, we know that w_{x_λ} must be proportional to the sum of the x_λ coordinates of the red, green, and blue primaries, since we are considering the case of a $(1, 1, 1)$ RGB. The same follows for y_λ and z_λ. This relationship can be expressed as

$$\begin{bmatrix} w_{x_\lambda} \\ w_{y_\lambda} \\ w_{z_\lambda} \end{bmatrix} = \begin{pmatrix} r_{x_\lambda} & g_{x_\lambda} & b_{x_\lambda} \\ r_{y_\lambda} & g_{y_\lambda} & b_{y_\lambda} \\ r_{z_\lambda} & g_{z_\lambda} & b_{z_\lambda} \end{pmatrix} \begin{pmatrix} c_r & 0 & 0 \\ 0 & c_g & 0 \\ 0 & 0 & c_b \end{pmatrix} \begin{bmatrix} 1 \\ 1 \\ 1 \end{bmatrix} = \begin{pmatrix} r_{x_\lambda} & g_{x_\lambda} & b_{x_\lambda} \\ r_{y_\lambda} & g_{y_\lambda} & b_{y_\lambda} \\ r_{z_\lambda} & g_{z_\lambda} & b_{z_\lambda} \end{pmatrix} \begin{bmatrix} c_r \\ c_g \\ c_b \end{bmatrix},$$

which only has unknowns c_r, c_g, and c_b. These can be found by multiplying the whitepoint XYZ coordinates by the inverse of the remaining matrix. Inverting this matrix then gives the matrix that goes to RGB from XYZ.

⟨*Initialize XYZ color space conversion matrices*⟩ ≡   **183**
```
SquareMatrix<3> rgb(R.X, G.X, B.X,
                    R.Y, G.Y, B.Y,
                    R.Z, G.Z, B.Z);
XYZ C = InvertOrExit(rgb) * W;
XYZFromRGB = rgb * SquareMatrix<3>::Diag(C[0], C[1], C[2]);
RGBFromXYZ = InvertOrExit(XYZFromRGB);
```

⟨*RGBColorSpace Public Members*⟩ +≡
```
SquareMatrix<3> XYZFromRGB, RGBFromXYZ;
```

Given a color space's XYZ/RGB conversion matrices, a matrix-vector multiplication is sufficient to convert any XYZ triplet into the color space and to convert any RGB in the color space to XYZ.

⟨*RGBColorSpace Public Methods*⟩ ≡   **183**
```
RGB ToRGB(XYZ xyz) const { return Mul<RGB>(RGBFromXYZ, xyz); }
XYZ ToXYZ(RGB rgb) const { return Mul<XYZ>(XYZFromRGB, rgb); }
```

Furthermore, it is easy to compute a matrix that converts from one color space to another by using these matrices and converting by way of XYZ colors.

⟨*RGBColorSpace Method Definitions*⟩ +≡
```
SquareMatrix<3> ConvertRGBColorSpace(const RGBColorSpace &from,
                                     const RGBColorSpace &to) {
    if (from == to) return {};
    return to.RGBFromXYZ * from.XYZFromRGB;
}
```

SampledSpectrum provides a convenience method that converts to RGB in a given color space, again via XYZ.

⟨*Spectrum Method Definitions*⟩ +≡
```
RGB SampledSpectrum::ToRGB(const SampledWavelengths &lambda,
                           const RGBColorSpace &cs) const {
    XYZ xyz = ToXYZ(lambda);
    return cs.ToRGB(xyz);
}
```

Standard Color Spaces

There are a number of widely used standard color spaces for which pbrt includes built-in support. A few examples include:

- sRGB, which was developed in the 1990s and was widely used for monitors for many years. One of the original motivations for its development was to standardize color on the web.
- DCI-P3, which was developed for digital film projection and covers a wider gamut than sRGB. At the time of writing, it is increasingly being adopted for computer displays and mobile phones.
- Rec2020, which covers an even wider gamut, and is used in the UHDTV television standard.
- ACES2065-1, which has primaries that are outside of the representable colors and are placed so that all colors can be represented by it. One reason for this choice was for it to be suitable as a format for long-term archival storage.

The gamuts of each are shown in Figure 4.23.

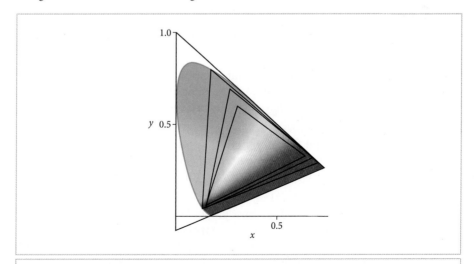

Figure 4.23: The gamuts of the sRGB, DCI-P3, Rec2020, and ACES2065-1 color spaces, visualized using the chromaticity diagram. sRGB covers the smallest gamut, DCI-P3 the next largest, Rec2020 an even larger one. ACES2065-1, which corresponds to the large triangle, is distinguished by using primaries that correspond to imaginary colors. In doing so, it is able to represent all valid colors, unlike the others.

The `RGBColorSpace` class provides pre-initialized instances of the `RGBColorSpaces` for each of these.

⟨*RGBColorSpace Public Members*⟩ +≡
```
static const RGBColorSpace *sRGB, *DCI_P3, *Rec2020, *ACES2065_1;
```

It is also possible to look color spaces up by name or by specifying the chromaticity of primaries and a whitepoint.

⟨*RGBColorSpace Public Methods*⟩ +≡   183
```
static const RGBColorSpace *GetNamed(std::string name);
static const RGBColorSpace *Lookup(Point2f r, Point2f g, Point2f b,
                                   Point2f w);
```

4.6.4 WHY SPECTRAL RENDERING?

Thus far, we have been proceeding with the description of pbrt's implementation with the understanding that it uses point-sampled spectra to represent spectral quantities. While that may seem natural given pbrt's physical basis and general adoption of Monte Carlo integration, it does not fit with the current widespread practice of using RGB color for spectral computations in rendering. We hinted at a significant problem with that practice at the start of this section; having introduced RGB color spaces, we can now go farther.

As discussed earlier, because color spaces are vector spaces, addition of two colors in the same color space gives the same color as adding the underlying spectra and then finding the resulting spectrum's color. That is not so for multiplication. To understand the problem, suppose that we are rendering a uniformly colored object (e.g., green) that is uniformly illuminated by light of the same color. For simplicity, assume that both illumination and the object's reflectance value are represented by the RGB color (0, 1, 0). The scattered light is then given by a product of reflectance and incident illumination:

$$\begin{pmatrix} 0 \\ 1 \\ 0 \end{pmatrix} \odot \begin{pmatrix} 0 \\ 1 \\ 0 \end{pmatrix} = \begin{pmatrix} 0 \\ 1 \\ 0 \end{pmatrix},$$

where componentwise multiplication of RGB colors is indicated by the "⊙" operator.

In the sRGB color space, the green color (0, 1, 0) maps to the upper vertex of the gamut of representable colors (Figure 4.24), and this RGB color value furthermore remains unchanged by the multiplication.

Now suppose that we change to the wide-gamut color space ACES2065-1. The sRGB color (0, 1, 0) can be found to be (0.38, 0.82, 0.12) in this color space—it thus maps to a location that lies in the interior of the set of representable colors. Performing the same component-wise multiplication gives the result:

$$\begin{pmatrix} 0.38 \\ 0.82 \\ 0.12 \end{pmatrix} \odot \begin{pmatrix} 0.38 \\ 0.82 \\ 0.12 \end{pmatrix} \approx \begin{pmatrix} 0.14 \\ 0.67 \\ 0.01 \end{pmatrix}$$

This time, the resulting color has lower intensity than it started with and has also become more saturated due to an increase in the relative proportion of green light. That leads to the somewhat bizarre situation shown in Figure 4.24: component-wise multiplication in this new color space not only produces a different color—it also increases saturation so severely that the color is pushed outside of the CIE horseshoe shape of physically realizable colors!

The ability to multiply spectral values is crucial for evaluating the interaction of materials and light sources in the context of rendering. At the same time, this example demonstrates

Point2f 92

RGBColorSpace 183

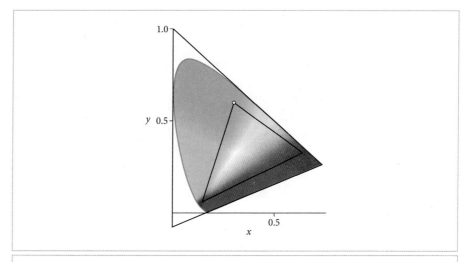

Figure 4.24: The same color can have very different RGB values when expressed in RGB color spaces with differently shaped gamuts. The green primary (0, 1, 0) in the sRGB color gamut (inner triangle) has chromaticity coordinates (0.3, 0.6) (white dot). In the wide-gamut ACES2065-1 color space (outer triangle), the same color has the RGB value (0.38, 0.82, 0.12).

the problem when RGB values are used for this purpose: the multiplication operation is in some sense arbitrary, because its behavior heavily depends on the chosen color space. Thus, rendering using a spectral model is preferable even in situations where RGB output is ultimately desired, as is the case with pbrt.

Additional benefits come from using spectral representations for rendering: they allow dispersion to easily be modeled and advanced reflectance models often have a natural dependence on wavelength to account for iridescence in thin layers or diffraction from surface microstructure.

4.6.5 CHOOSING THE NUMBER OF WAVELENGTH SAMPLES

Even though it uses a spectral model for light transport simulation, pbrt's output is generally an image in a tristimulus color representation like RGB. Having described how those colors are computed—Monte Carlo estimates of the products of spectra and matching functions of the form of Equation (4.23)—we will briefly return to the question of how many spectral samples are used for the SampledSpectrum class. The associated Monte Carlo estimators are easy to evaluate, but error in them leads to *color noise* in images. Figure 4.25 shows an example of this phenomenon.

Figure 4.25(a) shows a scene illuminated by a point light source where only direct illumination from the light is included. In this simple setting, the Monte Carlo estimator for the scattered light has zero variance at all wavelengths, so the only source of Monte Carlo error is the integrals of the color matching functions. With a single ray path per pixel and each one tracking a single wavelength, the image is quite noisy, as shown in Figure 4.25(b). Intuitively, the challenge in this case can be understood from the fact that the renderer is trying to estimate three values at each pixel—red, green, and blue—all from the spectral value at a single wavelength.

SampledSpectrum 171

Increasing the number of pixel samples can reduce this error (as long as they sample different wavelengths), though it is more effective to associate multiple wavelength samples with each ray. The path that a ray takes through the scene is usually independent of wavelength and the

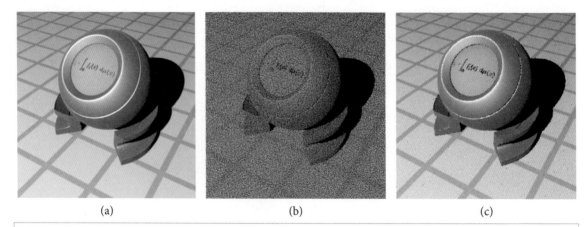

$$(a) \qquad\qquad (b) \qquad\qquad (c)$$

Figure 4.25: (a) Reference image of the example scene. (b) If the scene is rendered using only a single image sample per pixel, each sampling only a single wavelength, there is a substantial amount of variance from error in the Monte Carlo estimates of the pixels' RGB colors. (c) With four wavelength samples (pbrt's default), this variance is substantially reduced, though color noise is still evident. In practice, four wavelength samples is usually sufficient since multiple image samples are generally taken at each pixel. *(Model courtesy of Yasutoshi Mori.)*

incremental cost to compute lighting at multiple wavelengths is generally small compared to the cost of finding ray intersections and computing other wavelength-independent quantities. (Considering multiple wavelengths for each ray can be seen as an application of the Monte Carlo splitting technique that is described in Section 2.2.5.) Figure 4.25(c) shows the improvement from associating four wavelengths with each ray; color noise is substantially reduced.

However, computing scattering from too many wavelengths with each ray can harm efficiency due to the increased computation required to compute spectral quantities. To investigate this trade-off, we rendered the scene from Figure 4.25 with a variety of numbers of wavelength samples, both with wavelengths sampled independently and with stratified sampling of wavelengths. (For both, wavelengths were sampled uniformly over the range 360–830 nm.[10]) Figure 4.26 shows the results.

Figure 4.26(a) shows that for this scene, rendering with 32 wavelength samples requires nearly 1.6× more time than rendering with a single wavelength sample. (Rendering performance with both independent and stratified sampling is effectively the same.) However, as shown in Figure 4.26(b), the benefit of more wavelength samples is substantial. On the log–log plot there, we can see that with independent samples, mean squared error decreases at a rate $O(1/n)$, in line with the rate at which variance decreases with more samples. Stratified sampling does remarkably well, not only delivering orders of magnitude lower error, but at a faster asymptotic convergence rate as well.

Figure 4.26(c) plots Monte Carlo efficiency for both approaches (note, with a logarithmic scale for the y axis). The result seems clear; 32 stratified wavelength samples is over a million times more efficient than one sample and there the curve has not yet leveled off. Why stop

---

10 In Section 5.4.2, we will see that nonuniform sampling of wavelengths is beneficial but will stick to uniform sampling here for simplicity.

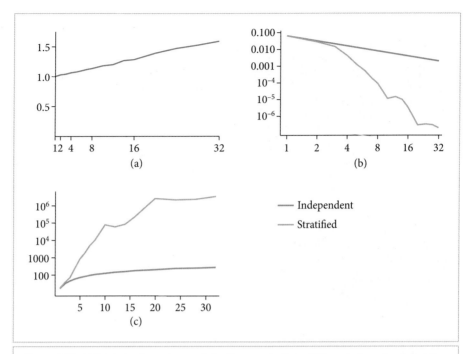

Figure 4.26: (a) Rendering time when rendering the scene in Figure 4.25 graphed as a function of the number of wavelength samples, normalized to rendering time with one wavelength sample. (b) Mean squared error as a function of number of wavelength samples for both independent and stratified samples. (c) Monte Carlo efficiency as a function of number of stratified wavelength samples. These results suggest that at least 32 wavelength samples are optimal.

measuring at 32, and why is pbrt stuck with a default of four wavelength samples for its NSpectrumSamples parameter?

There are three main reasons for the current setting. First, although Figure 4.26(a) shows nearly a 500× reduction in error from 8 to 32 wavelength samples, the two images are nearly indistinguishable—the difference in error is irrelevant due to limitations in display technology and the human visual system. Second, scenes are usually rendered following multiple ray paths in each pixel in order to reduce error from other Monte Carlo estimators. As more pixel samples are taken with fewer wavelengths, the total number of wavelengths that contribute to each pixel's value increases.

Finally, and most importantly, those other sources of Monte Carlo error often make larger contributions to the overall error than wavelength sampling. Figure 4.27(a) shows a much more complex scene with challenging lighting that is sampled using Monte Carlo. A graph of mean squared error as a function of the number of wavelength samples is shown in Figure 4.27(b) and Monte Carlo efficiency is shown in Figure 4.27(c). It is evident that after eight wavelength samples, the incremental cost of more of them is not beneficial.

4.6.6 FROM RGB TO SPECTRA

Although converting spectra to RGB for image output is a well-specified operation, the same is not true for converting RGB colors to spectral distributions. That is an important task, since much of the input to a renderer is often in the form of RGB colors. Scenes authored in current 3D modeling tools normally specify objects' reflection properties and lights' emission

NSpectrumSamples 171

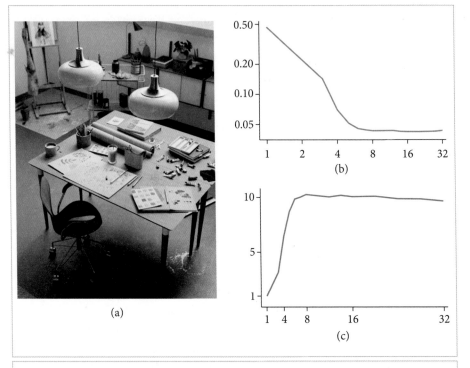

Figure 4.27: (a) A more complex scene, where variance in the Monte Carlo estimator is present from a variety of sources beyond wavelength sampling. (b) Graph of mean squared error versus the number of stratified wavelength samples. The benefits of additional wavelength samples are limited after six of them. (c) Monte Carlo efficiency versus number of stratified wavelength samples, normalized to efficiency with one wavelength sample. For this scene, eight samples is optimal.

using RGB parameters and textures. In a spectral renderer, these RGB values must somehow be converted into equivalent color spectra, but unfortunately any such conversion is inherently ambiguous due to the existence of metamers. How we can expect to find a reasonable solution if the problem is so poorly defined? On the flip side, this ambiguity can also be seen positively: it leaves a large space of possible answers containing techniques that are simple and efficient.

Further complicating this task, we must account for three fundamentally different types of spectral distributions:

- *Illuminant spectra*, which specify the spectral dependence of a light source's emission profile. These are nonnegative and unbounded; their shapes range from smooth (incandescent light sources, LEDs) to extremely spiky (stimulated emission in lasers or gas discharge in xenon arc and fluorescent lamps).
- *Reflectance spectra*, which describe reflection from absorbing surfaces. Reflectance spectra conserve the amount of energy at each wavelength, meaning that values cannot be outside of the [0, 1] range. They are typically smooth functions in the visible wavelength range.[11] (Figure 4.28 shows a few examples of reflectance spectra from a color checker.)

---

11 Note that this observation does not always hold: in the ultraviolet and infrared wavelength range, absorption bands cause sharp spikes in reflectance spectra. Furthermore, wave-optical effects such as iridescence produce oscillatory spectral variation. These behaviors could likely be handled using specialized conversion techniques, which are beyond the scope of the simple approach discussed here.

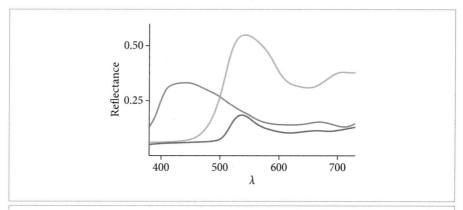

Figure 4.28: Spectral reflectances of several color checker patches. Each curve is shaded with the associated RGB color.

- *Unbounded spectra*, which are nonnegative and unbounded but do not describe emission. Common examples include spectrally varying indices of refraction and coefficients used to describe medium scattering properties.

This section first presents an approach for converting an RGB color value with components between 0 and 1 into a corresponding reflectance spectrum, followed by a generalization to unbounded and illuminant spectra. The conversion exploits the ambiguity of the problem to achieve the following goals:

- *Identity*: If an RGB value is converted to a spectrum, converting that spectrum back to RGB should give the same RGB coefficients.
- *Smoothness*: Motivated by the earlier observation about real-world reflectance spectra, the output spectrum should be as smooth as possible. Another kind of smoothness is also important: slight perturbations of the input RGB color should lead to a corresponding small change of the output spectrum. Discontinuities are undesirable, since they would cause visible seams on textured objects if observed under different illuminants.
- *Energy conservation*: Given RGB values in [0, 1], the associated spectral distribution should also be within [0, 1].

Although real-world reflectance spectra exist in a wide variety of shapes, they are often well-approximated by constant (white, black), approximately linear, or peaked curves with one (green, yellow) or two modes (bluish-purple).

The approach chosen here attempts to represent such spectra using a function family that is designed to be simple, smooth, and efficient to evaluate at runtime, while exposing a sufficient number of degrees of freedom to precisely reproduce arbitrary RGB color values.

Polynomials are typically a standard building block in such constructions; indeed, a quadratic polynomial could represent constant and linear curves, as well as ones that peak in the middle or toward the endpoints of the wavelength range. However, their lack of energy conservation poses a problem that we address using a sigmoid function:

$$s(x) = \frac{1}{2} + \frac{x}{2\sqrt{1 + x^2}}. \tag{4.25}$$

This function, plotted in Figure 4.29, is strictly monotonic and smoothly approaches the endpoints 0 and 1 as $x \to \mp\infty$.

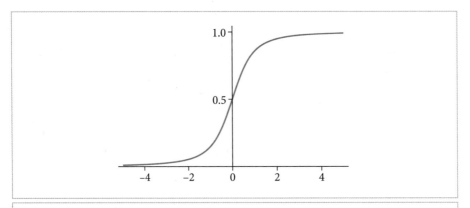

Figure 4.29: Sigmoid curve. The term *sigmoid* refers to smooth S-shaped curves that map all inputs to a bounded output interval. The particular type of sigmoid used here is defined in terms of algebraic functions, enabling highly efficient evaluation at runtime.

We apply this sigmoid to a quadratic polynomial defined by three coefficients c_i, squashing its domain to the interval $[0, 1]$ to ensure energy conservation.

$$S(\lambda) = s(c_0\lambda^2 + c_1\lambda + c_2). \qquad\qquad [4.26]$$

Representing ideally absorptive and reflective spectra (i.e., $S(\lambda) = \pm 1$) is somewhat awkward using this representation, since the polynomial must evaluate to positive or negative infinity to reach these two limits. This in turn leads to a fraction of the form $\pm\infty/\infty$ in Equation (4.25), which evaluates to a not-a-number value in IEEE-754 arithmetic. We will need to separately handle this limit case.

We begin with the definition of a class that encapsulates the coefficients c_i and evaluates Equation (4.26).

⟨*RGBSigmoidPolynomial Definition*⟩ ≡
```
class RGBSigmoidPolynomial {
  public:
    ⟨RGBSigmoidPolynomial Public Methods 192⟩
  private:
    ⟨RGBSigmoidPolynomial Private Methods 193⟩
    ⟨RGBSigmoidPolynomial Private Members 192⟩
};
```

It has the expected constructor and member variables.

⟨*RGBSigmoidPolynomial Public Methods*⟩ ≡   192
```
RGBSigmoidPolynomial(Float c0, Float c1, Float c2)
    : c0(c0), c1(c1), c2(c2) {}
```

⟨*RGBSigmoidPolynomial Private Members*⟩ ≡   192
```
Float c0, c1, c2;
```

Given coefficient values, it is easy to evaluate the spectral function at a specified wavelength.

⟨*RGBSigmoidPolynomial Public Methods*⟩ +≡   192
```
Float operator()(Float lambda) const {
    return s(EvaluatePolynomial(lambda, c2, c1, c0));
}
```

The sigmoid function follows the earlier definition and adds a special case to handle positive and negative infinity.

⟨*RGBSigmoidPolynomial Private Methods*⟩ ≡   192

```
static Float s(Float x) {
    if (IsInf(x)) return x > 0 ? 1 : 0;
    return .5f + x / (2 * std::sqrt(1 + Sqr(x)));
};
```

The `MaxValue()` method returns the maximum value of the spectral distribution over the visible wavelength range 360–830 nm. Because the sigmoid function is monotonically increasing, this problem reduces to locating the maximum of the quadratic polynomial from Equation (4.25) and evaluating the model there.

We conservatively check the endpoints of the interval along with the extremum found by setting the polynomial's derivative to zero and solving for the wavelength `lambda`. The value will be ignored if it happens to be a local minimum.

⟨*RGBSigmoidPolynomial Public Methods*⟩ +≡   192

```
Float MaxValue() const {
    Float result = std::max((*this)(360), (*this)(830));
    Float lambda = -c1 / (2 * c0);
    if (lambda >= 360 && lambda <= 830)
        result = std::max(result, (*this)(lambda));
    return result;
}
```

We now turn to the second half of `RGBSigmoidPolynomial`, which is the computation that determines suitable coefficients c_0, c_1, c_2 for a given RGB color. This step depends on the spectral emission curves of the color primaries and generally does not have an explicit solution. We instead formulate it as an optimization problem that minimizes the round-trip error (i.e., the *identity* goal mentioned above) by computing the difference between input and output RGB values following forward and reverse conversion. The precise optimization goal is

$$(c_0^*, c_1^*, c_2^*) = \operatorname*{argmin}_{c_0, c_1, c_2} \left\| \begin{bmatrix} r \\ g \\ b \end{bmatrix} - \int \begin{bmatrix} R(\lambda) \\ G(\lambda) \\ B(\lambda) \end{bmatrix} S(\lambda, c_0, c_1, c_2) \, W(\lambda) \, \mathrm{d}\lambda \right\|,$$

where $R(\lambda)$, $G(\lambda)$, $B(\lambda)$ describe emission curves of the color primaries and $W(\lambda)$ represents the whitepoint (e.g., D65 shown in Figure 4.14 in the case of the sRGB color space). Including the whitepoint in this optimization problem ensures that monochromatic RGB values map to uniform reflectance spectra.

In spaces with a relatively compact gamut like sRGB, this optimization can achieve zero error regardless of the method used to quantify color distances. In larger color spaces, particularly those including imaginary colors like ACES2065-1, zero round-trip error is clearly not achievable, and the choice of norm $\| \cdot \|$ becomes relevant. In principle, we could simply use the 2-norm—however, a problem with such a basic choice is that it is not *perceptually uniform*: whether a given amount of error is actually visible depends on its position within the RGB cube. We instead use CIE76 ΔE, which first transforms both colors into a color space known as CIELAB before evaluating the L_2-distance.

We then solve this optimization problem using the Gauss–Newton algorithm, an approximate form of Newton's method. This optimization takes on the order of a few microseconds,

Float 23
IsInf() 363
RGBSigmoidPolynomial::c0 192
RGBSigmoidPolynomial::c1 192
Sqr() 1034

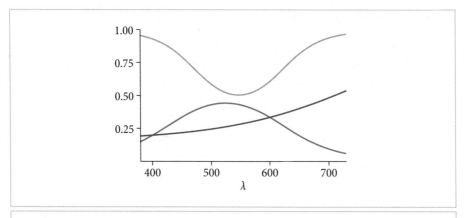

Figure 4.30: Spectra Computed from RGB Values. Plots of reflectance spectra represented by the RGBSigmoidPolynomial for the RGB colors (0.7, 0.5, 0.8) (purple line), (0.25, 0.44, 0.33) (green line), and (0.36, 0.275, 0.21) (brown line). Each line is colored with its corresponding RGB color.

which would lead to inefficiencies if performed every time an RGB value must be converted to a spectrum (e.g., once for every pixel of a high-resolution texture).

To avoid this inefficiency, we precompute coefficient tables spanning the $[0, 1]^3$ RGB color cube when pbrt is first compiled. It is worth noting that the tabulation could in principle also be performed over a lower-dimensional 2D space of chromaticities: for example, a computed spectrum representing the maximally saturated color red (1, 0, 0) could simply be scaled to reproduce less saturated RGB colors $(c, 0, 0)$, where $c \in (0, 1)$. However, spectra for highly saturated colors must necessarily peak within a small wavelength range to achieve this saturation, while less saturated colors can be represented by smoother spectra. This is generally preferable whenever possible due to the inherent smoothness of reflectance spectra encountered in physical reality.

We therefore precompute a full 3D tabulation for each RGB color space that pbrt supports (currently, sRGB, DCI-P3, Rec2020, and ACES2065-1). The implementation of this optimization step is contained in the file cmd/rgb2spec_opt.cpp, though we will not discuss it in detail here; see the "Further Reading" section for additional information. Figure 4.30 shows plots of spectra corresponding to a few RGB values.

The resulting tables are stored in the pbrt binary. At system startup time, an RGBToSpectrum Table for each of the RGB color spaces is created.

⟨*RGBToSpectrumTable Definition*⟩ ≡
```
class RGBToSpectrumTable {
  public:
    ⟨RGBToSpectrumTable Public Constants 195⟩
    ⟨RGBToSpectrumTable Public Methods⟩
  private:
    ⟨RGBToSpectrumTable Private Members 196⟩
};
```

RGBSigmoidPolynomial 192

The principal method of RGBToSpectrumTable returns the RGBSigmoidPolynomial corresponding to the given RGB color.

⟨*RGBToSpectrumTable Method Definitions*⟩ ≡
```
RGBSigmoidPolynomial RGBToSpectrumTable::operator()(RGB rgb) const {
    ⟨Handle uniform rgb values 195⟩
    ⟨Find maximum component and compute remapped component values 195⟩
    ⟨Compute integer indices and offsets for coefficient interpolation 196⟩
    ⟨Trilinearly interpolate sigmoid polynomial coefficients c 197⟩
    return RGBSigmoidPolynomial(c[0], c[1], c[2]);
}
```

If the three RGB values are equal, it is useful to ensure that the returned spectrum is exactly constant. (In some cases, a slight color shift may otherwise be evident if interpolated values from the coefficient tables are used.) A constant spectrum results if $c_0 = c_1 = 0$ in Equation (4.26) and the appropriate value of c_2 can be found by inverting the sigmoid function.

⟨*Handle uniform rgb values*⟩ ≡   195
```
if (rgb[0] == rgb[1] && rgb[1] == rgb[2])
    return RGBSigmoidPolynomial(
        0, 0, (rgb[0] - .5f) / std::sqrt(rgb[0] * (1 - rgb[0])));
```

The coefficients c_i from the optimization are generally smoothly varying; small changes in RGB generally lead to small changes in their values. (This property also ends up being helpful for the *smoothness* goal.) However, there are a few regions of the RGB space where they change rapidly, which makes direct 3D tabularization of them prone to error in those regions—see Figure 4.31(a), (b), and (c). A better approach is to tabularize them independently based on which of the red, green, or blue RGB coefficients has the largest magnitude. This partitioning matches the coefficient discontinuities well, as is shown in Figure 4.31(d).

A 3D tabularization problem remains within each of the three partitions. We will use the partition where the red component r has the greatest magnitude to explain how the table is indexed. For a given (r, g, b), the first step is to compute a renormalized coordinate

$$(x, y, z) = \left(\frac{g}{r}, \frac{b}{r}, r \right).$$

(By convention, the largest component is always mapped to z.) A similar remapping is applied if g or b is the maximum. With this mapping, all three coordinates span the range $[0, 1]$, which makes it possible to make better use of samples in a fixed grid.

⟨*Find maximum component and compute remapped component values*⟩ ≡   195
```
int maxc = (rgb[0] > rgb[1]) ? ((rgb[0] > rgb[2]) ? 0 : 2) :
                               ((rgb[1] > rgb[2]) ? 1 : 2);
float z = rgb[maxc];
float x = rgb[(maxc + 1) % 3] * (res - 1) / z;
float y = rgb[(maxc + 2) % 3] * (res - 1) / z;
```

The resolution of the tabularization, res, is the same in all three dimensions. Because it is set to be a compile time constant here, changing the size of the tables would require recompiling pbrt.

⟨*RGBToSpectrumTable Public Constants*⟩ ≡   194
```
static constexpr int res = 64;
```

An equally spaced discretization is used for the x and y coordinates in the coefficient tables, though z is remapped through a nonlinear function that allocates more samples near both 0 and 1. The c_i coefficients vary most rapidly in that region, so this remapping allocates samples more effectively.

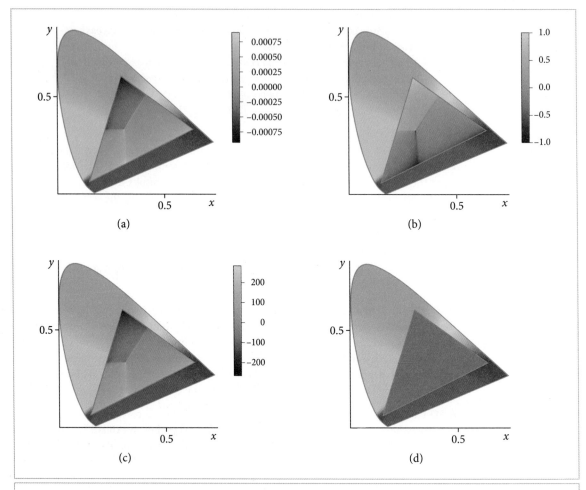

Figure 4.31: Plots of Spectrum Polynomial Coefficients c_i. These plots show the polynomial coefficients for the corresponding xy chromaticities in the sRGB color space. Each of (a) c_0, (b) c_1, and (c) c_2 mostly vary smoothly, though they exhibit sharp transitions. (d) Partitioning the gamut according to which of red, green, or blue has the largest magnitude closely corresponds to these transitions; coefficients are therefore independently tabularized in those three regions.

The zNodes array (which is of res elements) stores the result of the remapping where if f is the remapping function then the ith element of zNodes stores $f(i/\text{res})$.

⟨*RGBToSpectrumTable Private Members*⟩ ≡   **194**
```
const float *zNodes;
```

Finding integer coordinates in the table is simple for x and y given the equally spaced discretization. For z, a binary search through zNodes is required. Given these coordinates, floating-point offsets from them are then found for use in interpolation.

⟨*Compute integer indices and offsets for coefficient interpolation*⟩ ≡   **195**
```
int xi = std::min((int)x, res - 2), yi = std::min((int)y, res - 2),
    zi = FindInterval(res, [&](int i) { return zNodes[i] < z; });
Float dx = x - xi, dy = y - yi,
    dz = (z - zNodes[zi]) / (zNodes[zi + 1] - zNodes[zi]);
```

FindInterval() 1039

Float 23

RGBToSpectrumTable::zNodes 196

We can now implement the fragment that trilinearly interpolates between the eight coefficients around the (x, y, z) lookup point. The details of indexing into the coefficient tables are handled by the co lambda function, which we will define shortly, after describing the layout of the tables in memory. Note that although the z coordinate has a nonlinear mapping applied to it, we still linearly interpolate between coefficient samples in z. In practice, the error from doing so is minimal.

⟨*Trilinearly interpolate sigmoid polynomial coefficients* c⟩ ≡   **195**
```
pstd::array<Float, 3> c;
for (int i = 0; i < 3; ++i) {
    ⟨Define co lambda for looking up sigmoid polynomial coefficients 197⟩
    c[i] = Lerp(dz, Lerp(dy, Lerp(dx, co(0, 0, 0), co(1, 0, 0)),
                             Lerp(dx, co(0, 1, 0), co(1, 1, 0))),
                    Lerp(dy, Lerp(dx, co(0, 0, 1), co(1, 0, 1)),
                             Lerp(dx, co(0, 1, 1), co(1, 1, 1))));
}
```

The coefficients are stored in a five-dimensional array. The first dimension corresponds to whether r, g, or b had the largest magnitude and the next three correspond to z, y, and x, respectively. The last dimension is over the three coefficients c_i.

⟨*RGBToSpectrumTable Public Constants*⟩ +≡   **194**
```
using CoefficientArray = float[3][res][res][res][3];
```

⟨*RGBToSpectrumTable Private Members*⟩ +≡   **194**
```
const CoefficientArray *coeffs;
```

The coefficient lookup lambda function is now just a matter of using the correct values for each dimension of the array. The provided integer deltas are applied in x, y, and z when doing so.

⟨*Define* co *lambda for looking up sigmoid polynomial coefficients*⟩ ≡   **197**
```
auto co = [&](int dx, int dy, int dz) {
    return (*coeffs)[maxc][zi + dz][yi + dy][xi + dx][i];
};
```

With RGBSigmoidPolynomial's implementation complete, we can now add a method to RGBColorSpace to transform an RGB in its color space to an RGBSigmoidPolynomial.

⟨*RGBColorSpace Method Definitions*⟩ +≡
```
RGBSigmoidPolynomial RGBColorSpace::ToRGBCoeffs(RGB rgb) const {
    return (*rgbToSpectrumTable)(ClampZero(rgb));
}
```

With these capabilities, we can now define the RGBAlbedoSpectrum class, which implements the Spectrum interface to return spectral samples according to the sigmoid-polynomial model.

⟨*Spectrum Definitions*⟩ +≡
```
class RGBAlbedoSpectrum {
  public:
    ⟨RGBAlbedoSpectrum Public Methods 198⟩
  private:
    ⟨RGBAlbedoSpectrum Private Members 198⟩
};
```

Runtime assertions in the constructor, not shown here, verify that the provided RGB value is between 0 and 1.

⟨*Spectrum Method Definitions*⟩ +≡
```
RGBAlbedoSpectrum::RGBAlbedoSpectrum(const RGBColorSpace &cs, RGB rgb) {
    rsp = cs.ToRGBCoeffs(rgb);
}
```

The only member variable necessary is one to store the polynomial coefficients.

⟨*RGBAlbedoSpectrum Private Members*⟩ ≡   **197**
```
RGBSigmoidPolynomial rsp;
```

Implementation of the required Spectrum methods is a matter of forwarding the requests on to the appropriate RGBSigmoidPolynomial methods. As with most Spectrum implementations, we will not include the Sample() method here since it just loops over the wavelengths and evaluates Equation (4.26) at each one.

⟨*RGBAlbedoSpectrum Public Methods*⟩ ≡   **197**
```
Float operator()(Float lambda) const { return rsp(lambda); }
Float MaxValue() const { return rsp.MaxValue(); }
```

Unbounded RGB

For unbounded (positive-valued) RGB values, the RGBSigmoidPolynomial foundation can still be used—just with the addition of a scale factor that remaps its range to the necessary range for the given RGB. That approach is implemented in the RGBUnboundedSpectrum class.

⟨*Spectrum Definitions*⟩ +≡
```
class RGBUnboundedSpectrum {
  public:
    ⟨RGBUnboundedSpectrum Public Methods 199⟩
  private:
    ⟨RGBUnboundedSpectrum Private Members 198⟩
};
```

A natural choice for a scale factor would be one over the maximum of the red, green, and blue color components. We would then use that to normalize the RGB value before finding polynomial coefficients and then rescale values returned by RGBSigmoidPolynomial accordingly. However, it is possible to get better results by instead normalizing RGB to have a maximum value of 1/2 rather than 1. The reason is illustrated in Figure 4.32: because reflectance spectra must not exceed one, when highly saturated colors are provided, the resulting spectra may have unusual features, including large magnitudes in the unsaturated region of the spectrum. Rescaling to 1/2 gives the fit more room to work with, since the normalization constraint does not immediately affect it.

⟨*Spectrum Method Definitions*⟩ +≡
```
RGBUnboundedSpectrum::RGBUnboundedSpectrum(const RGBColorSpace &cs,
                                           RGB rgb) {
    Float m = std::max({rgb.r, rgb.g, rgb.b});
    scale = 2 * m;
    rsp = cs.ToRGBCoeffs(scale ? rgb / scale : RGB(0, 0, 0));
}
```

⟨*RGBUnboundedSpectrum Private Members*⟩ ≡   **198**
```
Float scale = 1;
RGBSigmoidPolynomial rsp;
```

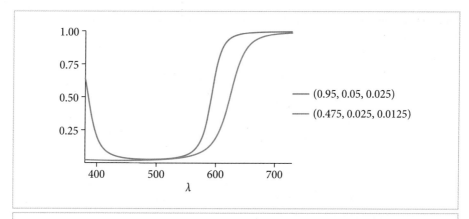

Figure 4.32: With the sigmoid polynomial representation, highly saturated colors may end up with unexpected features in their spectra. Here we have plotted the spectrum returned by `RGBAlbedoSpectrum` for the RGB color (0.95, 0.05, 0.025) as well as that color with all components divided by two. With the original color, we see a wide range of the higher wavelengths are near 1 and that the lower wavelengths have more energy than expected. If that color is divided by two, the resulting spectrum is better behaved, though note that its magnitude exceeds the original red value of 0.475 in the higher wavelengths.

In comparison to the `RGBAlbedoSpectrum` implementation, the wavelength evaluation and `MaxValue()` methods here are just augmented with a multiplication by the scale factor. The `Sample()` method has been updated similarly, but is not included here.

⟨*RGBUnboundedSpectrum Public Methods*⟩ ≡   **198**
```
Float operator()(Float lambda) const { return scale * rsp(lambda); }
Float MaxValue() const { return scale * rsp.MaxValue(); }
```

RGB Illuminants

As illustrated in the plots of illuminant spectra in Section 4.4.2, real-world illuminants often have complex spectral distributions. Given a light source specified using RGB color, we do not attempt to infer a complex spectral distribution but will stick with a smooth spectrum, scaled appropriately. The details are handled by the `RGBIlluminantSpectrum` class.

⟨*Spectrum Definitions*⟩ +≡
```
class RGBIlluminantSpectrum {
  public:
    ⟨RGBIlluminantSpectrum Public Methods 200⟩
  private:
    ⟨RGBIlluminantSpectrum Private Members 200⟩
};
```

Beyond a scale factor that is equivalent to the one used in `RGBUnboundedSpectrum` to allow an arbitrary maximum RGB value, the `RGBIlluminantSpectrum` also multiplies the value returned at the given wavelength by the value of the color space's standard illuminant at that wavelength. A non-intuitive aspect of spectral modeling of illuminants is that uniform spectra generally do not map to neutral white colors following conversion to RGB. Color spaces always assume that the viewer is adapted to some type of environmental illumination that influences color perception and the notion of a neutral color. For example, the commonly used D65 whitepoint averages typical daylight illumination conditions. To reproduce illuminants with a desired color, we therefore use a crude but effective solution, which is to multiply the whitepoint with a suitable reflectance spectra. Conceptually, this resembles viewing a white reference light source through a colored film. It also ensures that white objects lit by white lights lead to white pixel values in the rendered image.

⟨*Spectrum Method Definitions*⟩ +≡

```
RGBIlluminantSpectrum::RGBIlluminantSpectrum(const RGBColorSpace &cs,
                                             RGB rgb)
    : illuminant(&cs.illuminant) {
    Float m = std::max({rgb.r, rgb.g, rgb.b});
    scale = 2 * m;
    rsp = cs.ToRGBCoeffs(scale ? rgb / scale : RGB(0, 0, 0));
}
```

Thus, a pointer to the illuminant is held in a member variable.

⟨*RGBIlluminantSpectrum Private Members*⟩ ≡   **199**

```
Float scale;
RGBSigmoidPolynomial rsp;
const DenselySampledSpectrum *illuminant;
```

Implementations of the various `Spectrum` interface methods follow; here is the one that evaluates the spectral distribution at a single wavelength. One detail is that it must handle the case of a `nullptr` illuminant, as will happen if an `RGBIlluminantSpectrum` is default-initialized. In that case, a zero-valued spectrum should be the result.

⟨*RGBIlluminantSpectrum Public Methods*⟩ ≡   **199**

```
Float operator()(Float lambda) const {
    if (!illuminant) return 0;
    return scale * rsp(lambda) * (*illuminant)(lambda);
}
```

We will not include the implementations of the `Sample()` or `MaxValue()` methods here, as their implementations are as would be expected.

FURTHER READING

McCluney's book on radiometry is an excellent introduction to the topic (McCluney 1994). Preisendorfer (1965) also covered radiometry in an accessible manner and delved into the relationship between radiometry and the physics of light. Nicodemus et al. (1977) carefully defined the BRDF, BSSRDF, and various quantities that can be derived from them.

Books by Moon and Spencer (1936, 1948) and Gershun (1939) are classic early introductions to radiometry. Lambert's seminal early writings about photometry from the mid-18th century have been translated into English by DiLaura (Lambert 1760).

Preisendorfer (1965) has connected radiative transfer theory to Maxwell's classical equations describing electromagnetic fields, and further work was done in this area by Fante (1981). Going well beyond earlier work that represented radiance with Wigner distribution functions to model wave effects (Oh et al. 2010, Cuypers et al. 2012), Steinberg and Yan (2021) have recently introduced a comprehensive model of light transport based on a wave model, including a generalization of the light transport equation.

Correctly implementing radiometric computations can be tricky: one missed cosine factor and one is computing a completely different quantity than expected. Debugging these sorts of issues can be quite time-consuming. Ou and Pellacini (2010) showed how to use C++'s type system to associate units with each term of these sorts of computations so that, for example, trying to add a radiance value to another value that represents irradiance would trigger a compile time error.

The books by McCluney (1994) and Malacara (2002) discuss blackbody emitters and the standard illuminants in detail. The Standard Illuminants are defined in a CIE Technical Report (2004); Judd et al. (1964) developed the approach that was used to define the D Standard Illuminant.

Wilkie and Weidlich (2011) noted that common practice in rendering has been to use the blackbody distribution of Equation (4.17) to model light emission for rendering, while Kirchhoff's law, Equation (4.18), would be more accurate. They also pointed out that as objects become hot, their BRDFs often change, which makes Kirchhoff's law more difficult to adopt, especially in that models that account for the effect of temperature variation on BRDFs generally are not available.

Spectral Representations

Meyer was one of the first researchers to closely investigate spectral representations in graphics (Meyer and Greenberg 1980; Meyer et al. 1986). Hall (1989) summarized the state of the art in spectral representations through 1989, and Glassner's *Principles of Digital Image Synthesis* (1995) covers the topic through the mid-1990s. Survey articles by Hall (1999), Johnson and Fairchild (1999), and Devlin et al. (2002) are good resources on early work on this topic.

Borges (1991) analyzed the error introduced from the tristimulus representation when used for spectral computation. A variety of approaches based on representing spectra using basis functions have been developed, including Peercy (1993), who developed a technique based on choosing basis functions in a scene-dependent manner by considering the spectral distributions of the lights and reflecting objects in the scene. Rougeron and Péroche (1997) projected all spectra in the scene onto a hierarchical basis (the Haar wavelets), and showed that this adaptive representation can be used to stay within a desired error bound. Ward and Eydelberg-Vileshin (2002) developed a method for improving the spectral fidelity of regular RGB-only rendering systems by carefully adjusting the color values provided to the system before rendering.

Another approach to spectral representation was investigated by Sun et al. (2001), who partitioned spectral distributions into a smooth base distribution and a set of spikes. Each part was represented differently, using basis functions that worked well for each of these parts of the distribution. Drew and Finlayson (2003) applied a "sharp" basis, which is adaptive but has the property that computing the product of two functions in the basis does not require a full matrix multiplication as many other basis representations do.

Both Walter et al. (1997) and Morley et al. (2006) described light transport algorithms based on associating a single wavelength with each light path. Evans and McCool (1999) generalized these techniques with *stratified wavelength clusters*, which are effectively the approach implemented in `SampledSpectrum` and `SampledWavelengths`.

Radziszewski et al. (2009) noted that it is not necessary to terminate all secondary spectral wavelengths when effects like dispersion happen at non-specular interfaces; they showed that it is possible to compute all wavelengths' contributions for a single path, weighting the results using multiple importance sampling. Wilkie et al. (2014) used equally spaced point samples in the wavelength domain and showed how this approach can also be used for photon mapping and rendering of participating media.

SampledSpectrum 171

SampledWavelengths 173

Color

For background information on properties of the human visual system, Wandell's book on vision is an excellent starting point (Wandell 1995). Ferwerda (2001) presented an overview of the human visual system for applications in graphics, and Malacara (2002) gave a concise overview of color theory and basic properties of how the human visual system processes color. Ciechanowski (2019) presented an excellent interactive introduction to color spaces; his treatment has influenced our presentation of the XYZ color space and chromaticity.

A number of different approaches have been developed for mapping out-of-gamut colors to ones that can be displayed on a device with particular display primaries. This problem can manifest itself in a few ways: a color's chromaticity may be outside of the displayed range, its chromaticity may be valid but it may be too bright for display, or both may be out of range.

For the issue of how to handle colors with undisplayable chromaticities, see Rougeron and Péroche's survey article, which includes references to many approaches (Rougeron and Péroche 1998). This topic was also covered by Hall (1989). Morovič's book (2008) covers this topic, and a more recent survey has been written by Faridul et al. (2016).

While high dynamic range displays that can display a wide range of intensities are now starting to become available, most of them are still not able to reproduce the full range of brightness in rendered images. This problem can be addressed with *tone reproduction* algorithms that use models of human visual response to make the most of displays' available dynamic ranges. This topic became an active area of research starting with the work of Tumblin and Rushmeier (1993). The survey article of Devlin et al. (2002) summarizes most of the work in this area through 2002, giving pointers to the original papers. See Reinhard et al.'s book (2010) on high dynamic range imaging, which includes comprehensive coverage of this topic through 2010. More recently, Reinhard et al. (2012) have developed tone reproduction algorithms that consider both accurate brightness and color reproduction together, also accounting for the display and viewing environment, and Eilertsen et al. (2017) surveyed algorithms for tone mapping of video.

From RGB to Spectra

Glassner (1989b) did early work on converting RGB values to spectral distributions. Smits (1999) optimized discrete reflectance spectra to reproduce primaries (red, green, blue) and combinations of primaries (yellow, cyan, magenta, white) based on the observation that linear interpolation in such an extended space tends to produce smoother reflectance spectra. Mallett and Yuksel (2019) presented a surprising result showing that linear interpolation of three carefully chosen spectra can fully cover the sRGB gamut, albeit at some cost in terms of smoothness. Meng et al. (2015) optimized a highly smooth spectral interpolant based on a dense sampling of the xy space of chromaticities, enabling usage independent of any specific RGB gamut.

The method described in Section 4.6.6 was developed by Jakob and Hanika (2019). Several properties motivated its choice in pbrt: the spectral representation is based on a smooth function family with 3 parameters (i.e., the same dimension as an RGB). Conversion can then occur in two steps: a preprocessing step (e.g., per texel) replaces RGB values with polynomial coefficients, while the performance-critical evaluation at render time only requires a few floating-point instructions. Jung et al. (2019) extended this approach, using fluorescence to permit conversion of highly saturated RGB values that cannot be recreated using reflection alone.

Peters et al. (2019) proposed a powerful parameterization of smooth reflectance spectra in terms of Fourier coefficients. Instead of using them in a truncated Fourier series, which would suffer from ringing, they built on the theory of moments to reconstruct smooth and energy-conserving spectra.

The previous methods all incorporated smoothness as a central design constraint. While natural spectra indeed often tend to be smooth, maximally smooth spectra are not necessarily the most natural, especially when more information about the underlying type of material is available. Otsu et al. (2018) processed a large database of measured spectra, using principal component analysis to create a data-driven interpolant. Tódová et al. (2021) built on the moment-based method by Peters et al. (2019) to precompute an efficient spectral interpolant that is designed to reproduce user-specified spectra for certain RGB inputs.

EXERCISES

4.1 How many photons would a 50-W lightbulb that emits light at the single wavelength $\lambda = 600$ nm emit in 1 second?

4.2 Compute the irradiance at a point due to a unit-radius disk h units directly above its normal with constant outgoing radiance of 10 W/m^2 sr. Do the computation twice, once as an integral over solid angle and once as an integral over area. (Hint: If the results do not match at first, see Section A.5.1.)

4.3 Similarly, compute the irradiance at a point due to a square quadrilateral with outgoing radiance of 10 W/m^2 sr that has sides of length 1 and is 1 unit directly above the point in the direction of its surface normal.

4.4 Modify the SampledSpectrum class to also store the wavelengths associated with the samples and their PDFs. Using pbrt's assertion macros, add checks to ensure that no computations are performed using SampledSpectrum values associated with different wavelengths. Measure the performance of pbrt with and without your changes. How much runtime overhead is there? Did you find any bugs in pbrt?

CHAPTER FIVE

05 CAMERAS AND FILM

In Chapter 1, we described the pinhole camera model that is commonly used in computer graphics. This model is easy to describe and simulate, but it neglects important effects that physical lenses have on light passing through them. For example, everything rendered with a pinhole camera is in sharp focus—a state of affairs not possible with real lens systems. Such images often look computer generated for their perfection. More generally, the distribution of radiance leaving a lens system is quite different from the distribution entering it; modeling this effect of lenses is important for accurately simulating the radiometry of image formation.

Camera lens systems introduce various aberrations that affect the images that they form; for example, *vignetting* causes a darkening toward the edges of images due to less light making it through to the edges of the film or sensor than to the center. Lenses can also cause *pincushion* or *barrel* distortion, which causes straight lines to be imaged as curves. Although lens designers work to minimize aberrations in their designs, they can still have a meaningful effect on images.

This chapter starts with a description of the Camera interface, after which we present a few implementations, starting with ideal pinhole models. We then generalize those models to account for the effect of finite aperture using a simple approximation of a single lens. (The online edition of this book includes a more sophisticated camera implementation that simulates light passing through a collection of glass lens elements to form an image, similar to real-world cameras.)

After light has been captured by a camera, it is measured by a sensor. While traditional film uses a chemical process to measure light, most modern cameras use solid-state sensors that are divided into pixels, each of which counts the number of photons that arrive over a period of time for some range of wavelengths. Accurately modeling the radiometry of how sensors measure light is an important part of simulating the process of image formation.

Film 244
PixelSensor 234

To that end, all of pbrt's camera models use an instance of the Film class, which defines the basic interface for the classes that represent images captured by cameras. We describe two film implementations in this chapter, both of which use the PixelSensor class to model the spectral response of a particular image sensor, be it film or digital. The film and sensor classes are described in the final section of this chapter.

5.1 CAMERA INTERFACE

The Camera class uses the usual TaggedPointer-based approach to dynamically dispatch interface method calls to the correct implementation based on the actual type of the camera. (As usual, we will not include the implementations of those methods in the book here.) Camera is defined in the file base/camera.h.

⟨*Camera Definition*⟩ ≡
```
class Camera : public TaggedPointer<PerspectiveCamera, OrthographicCamera,
                                SphericalCamera, RealisticCamera> {
  public:
    ⟨Camera Interface 206⟩
};
```

The implementation of the first three Cameras follows in this chapter. RealisticCamera is described only in the online edition.

The first method that cameras must implement is GenerateRay(), which computes the ray corresponding to a given image sample. It is important that the direction component of the returned ray be normalized—many other parts of the system will depend on this behavior. If for some reason there is no valid ray for the given CameraSample, then the pstd::optional return value should be unset. The SampledWavelengths for the ray are passed as a non-const reference so that cameras can model dispersion in their lenses, in which case only a single wavelength of light is tracked by the ray and the GenerateRay() method will call SampledWavelengths::TerminateSecondary().

⟨*Camera Interface*⟩ ≡   **206**
```
pstd::optional<CameraRay> GenerateRay(CameraSample sample,
                                SampledWavelengths &lambda) const;
```

The CameraSample structure that is passed to GenerateRay() holds all the sample values needed to specify a camera ray. Its pFilm member gives the point on the film to which the generated ray should carry radiance. The point on the lens the ray passes through is in pLens (for cameras that include the notion of lenses), and time gives the time at which the ray should sample the scene. If the camera itself is in motion, the time value determines what camera position to use when generating the ray.

Finally, the filterWeight member variable is an additional scale factor that is applied when the ray's radiance is added to the image stored by the film; it accounts for the reconstruction filter used to filter image samples at each pixel. This topic is discussed in Sections 5.4.3 and 8.8.

⟨*CameraSample Definition*⟩ ≡
```
struct CameraSample {
    Point2f pFilm;
    Point2f pLens;
    Float time = 0;
    Float filterWeight = 1;
};
```

The CameraRay structure that is returned by GenerateRay() includes both a ray and a spectral weight associated with it. Simple camera models leave the weight at the default value of one, while more sophisticated ones like RealisticCamera return a weight that is used in modeling the radiometry of image formation. (Section 5.4.1 contains more information about how exactly this weight is computed and used in the latter case.)

⟨*CameraRay Definition*⟩ ≡
```
struct CameraRay {
    Ray ray;
    SampledSpectrum weight = SampledSpectrum(1);
};
```

Cameras must also provide an implementation of `GenerateRayDifferential()`, which computes a main ray like `GenerateRay()` but also computes the corresponding rays for pixels shifted one pixel in the *x* and *y* directions on the film plane. This information about how camera rays change as a function of position on the film helps give other parts of the system a notion of how much of the film area a particular camera ray's sample represents, which is useful for antialiasing texture lookups.

⟨*Camera Interface*⟩ +≡   206
```
pstd::optional<CameraRayDifferential> GenerateRayDifferential(
    CameraSample sample, SampledWavelengths &lambda) const;
```

`GenerateRayDifferential()` returns an instance of the `CameraRayDifferential` structure, which is equivalent to `CameraRay`, except it stores a `RayDifferential`.

⟨*CameraRayDifferential Definition*⟩ ≡
```
struct CameraRayDifferential {
    RayDifferential ray;
    SampledSpectrum weight = SampledSpectrum(1);
};
```

Camera implementations must provide access to their `Film`, which allows other parts of the system to determine things such as the resolution of the output image.

⟨*Camera Interface*⟩ +≡   206
```
Film GetFilm() const;
```

Just like real-world cameras, pbrt's camera models include the notion of a shutter that opens for a short period of time to expose the film to light. One result of this nonzero exposure time is *motion blur*: objects that are in motion relative to the camera during the exposure are blurred. Time is yet another thing that is amenable to point sampling and Monte Carlo integration: given an appropriate distribution of ray times between the shutter open time and the shutter close time, it is possible to compute images that exhibit motion blur.

The `SampleTime()` interface method should therefore map a uniform random sample u in the range [0, 1) to a time when the camera's shutter is open. Normally, it is just used to linearly interpolate between the shutter open and close times.

⟨*Camera Interface*⟩ +≡   206
```
Float SampleTime(Float u) const;
```

The last interface method allows camera implementations to set fields in the `ImageMetadata` class to specify transformation matrices related to the camera. If the output image format has support for storing this sort of auxiliary information, it will be included in the final image that is written to disk.

⟨*Camera Interface*⟩ +≡   206
```
void InitMetadata(ImageMetadata *metadata) const;
```

5.1.1 CAMERA COORDINATE SPACES

Before we start to describe the implementation of pbrt's camera models, we will define some of the coordinate spaces that they use. In addition to world space, which was introduced in Section 3.1, we will now introduce four additional coordinate spaces, *object space, camera space, camera-world space*, and *rendering space*.[1] In sum, we have:

- *Object space:* This is the coordinate system in which geometric primitives are defined. For example, spheres in pbrt are defined to be centered at the origin of their object space.
- *World space:* While each primitive may have its own object space, all objects in the scene are placed in relation to a single world space. A world-from-object transformation determines where each object is located in world space. World space is the standard frame that all other spaces are defined in terms of.
- *Camera space:* A camera is placed in the scene at some world space point with a particular viewing direction and orientation. This camera defines a new coordinate system with its origin at the camera's location. The z axis of this coordinate system is mapped to the viewing direction, and the y axis is mapped to the up direction.
- *Camera-world space:* Like camera space, the origin of this coordinate system is the camera's position, but it maintains the orientation of world space (i.e., unlike camera space, the camera is not necessarily looking down the z axis).
- *Rendering space:* This is the coordinate system into which the scene is transformed for the purposes of rendering. In pbrt, it may be world space, camera space, or camera-world space.

Renderers based on rasterization traditionally do most of their computations in camera space: triangle vertices are transformed all the way from object space to camera space before being projected onto the screen and rasterized. In that context, camera space is a handy space for reasoning about which objects are potentially visible to the camera. For example, if an object's camera space bounding box is entirely behind the $z = 0$ plane (and the camera does not have a field of view wider than 180 degrees), the object will not be visible.

Conversely, many ray tracers (including all versions of pbrt prior to this one) render in world space. Camera implementations may start out in camera space when generating rays, but they transform those rays to world space where all subsequent ray intersection and shading calculations are performed. A problem with that approach stems from the fact that floating-point numbers have more precision close to the origin than far away from it. If the camera is placed far from the origin, there may be insufficient precision to accurately represent the part of the scene that it is looking at.

Figure 5.1 illustrates the precision problem with rendering in world space. In Figure 5.1(a), the scene is rendered with the camera and objects as they were provided in the original scene specification, which happened to be in the range of ± 10 in each coordinate in world space. In Figure 5.1(b), both the camera and the scene have been translated 1,000,000 units in each dimension. In principle, both images should be the same, but much less precision is available for the second viewpoint, to the extent that the discretization of floating-point numbers is visible in the geometric model.

Rendering in camera space naturally provides the most floating-point precision for the objects closest to the camera. If the scene in Figure 5.1 is rendered in camera space, translating both the camera and the scene geometry by 1,000,000 units has no effect—the translations

---

1   "Camera-world space" and "rendering space" are non-standard names, though we are unaware of generally accepted names for those coordinate spaces.

(a)

(b)

(c)

Figure 5.1: Effect of the Loss of Floating-Point Precision Far from the Origin. (a) As originally specified, this scene is within 10 units of the origin. Rendering the scene in world space produces the expected image. (b) If both the scene and the camera are translated 1,000,000 units from the origin and the scene is rendered in world space, there is significantly less floating-point precision to represent the scene, giving this poor result. (c) If the translated scene is rendered in camera-world space, much more precision is available and the geometric detail is preserved. However, the viewpoint has shifted slightly due to a loss of accuracy in the representation of the camera position. *(Model courtesy of Yasutoshi Mori.)*

cancel. However, there is a problem with using camera space with ray tracing. Scenes are often modeled with major features aligned to the coordinate axes (e.g., consider an architectural model, where the floor and ceiling might be aligned with y planes). Axis-aligned bounding boxes of such features are degenerate in one dimension, which reduces their surface area. Acceleration structures like the BVH that will be introduced in Chapter 7 are particularly effective with such bounding boxes. In turn, if the camera is rotated with respect to the scene, axis-aligned bounding boxes are less effective at bounding such features and rendering performance is affected: for the scene in Figure 5.1, rendering time increases by 27%.

Rendering using camera-world space gives the best of both worlds: the camera is at the origin and the scene is translated accordingly. However, the rotation is not applied to the scene geometry, thus preserving good bounding boxes for the acceleration structures. With camera-world space, there is no increase in rendering time and higher precision is maintained, as is shown in Figure 5.1(c).

The CameraTransform class abstracts the choice of which particular coordinate system is used for rendering by handling the details of transforming among the various spaces.

⟨*CameraTransform Definition*⟩ ≡
```
class CameraTransform {
  public:
    ⟨CameraTransform Public Methods⟩
  private:
    ⟨CameraTransform Private Members 210⟩
};
```

Camera implementations must make their CameraTransform available to other parts of the system, so we will add one more method to the Camera interface.

⟨*Camera Interface*⟩ +≡   206
```
const CameraTransform &GetCameraTransform() const;
```

CameraTransform maintains two transformations: one from camera space to the rendering space, and one from the rendering space to world space. In pbrt, the latter transformation cannot be animated; any animation in the camera transformation is kept in the first transformation. This ensures that a moving camera does not cause static geometry in the scene to become animated, which in turn would harm performance.[2]

⟨*CameraTransform Private Members*⟩ ≡   210
```
AnimatedTransform renderFromCamera;
Transform worldFromRender;
```

The CameraTransform constructor takes the world-from-camera transformation as specified in the scene description and decomposes it into the two transformations described earlier. The default rendering space is camera-world, though this choice can be overridden using a command-line option.

⟨*CameraTransform Method Definitions*⟩ ≡
```
CameraTransform::CameraTransform(const AnimatedTransform &worldFromCamera) {
    switch (Options->renderingSpace) {
    case RenderingCoordinateSystem::Camera: {
        ⟨Compute worldFromRender for camera-space rendering 211⟩
```

---

2   A moving camera generally does not affect ray tracing performance, as rendering with one just causes different camera rays to be traced. Moving geometry requires larger bounding boxes to bound the motion of objects, which in turn reduces the effectiveness of acceleration structures. Thus, it is undesirable to make objects move that do not need to be in motion.

```
    } case RenderingCoordinateSystem::CameraWorld: {
        ⟨Compute worldFromRender for camera-world space rendering 211⟩
    } case RenderingCoordinateSystem::World: {
        ⟨Compute worldFromRender for world-space rendering 211⟩
    }
    }
    ⟨Compute renderFromCamera transformation 211⟩
}
```

For camera-space rendering, the world-from-camera transformation should be used for worldFromRender and an identity transformation for the render-from-camera transformation, since those two coordinate systems are equivalent. However, because worldFromRender cannot be animated, the implementation takes the world-from-camera transformation at the midpoint of the frame and then folds the effect of any animation in the camera transformation into renderFromCamera.

⟨*Compute* worldFromRender *for camera-space rendering*⟩ ≡   **210**
```
    Float tMid = (worldFromCamera.startTime + worldFromCamera.endTime) / 2;
    worldFromRender = worldFromCamera.Interpolate(tMid);
    break;
```

For the default case of rendering in camera-world space, the world-from-render transformation is given by translating to the camera's position at the midpoint of the frame.

⟨*Compute* worldFromRender *for camera-world space rendering*⟩ ≡   **210**
```
    Float tMid = (worldFromCamera.startTime + worldFromCamera.endTime) / 2;
    Point3f pCamera = worldFromCamera(Point3f(0, 0, 0), tMid);
    worldFromRender = Translate(Vector3f(pCamera));
    break;
```

For world-space rendering, worldFromRender is the identity transformation.

⟨*Compute* worldFromRender *for world-space rendering*⟩ ≡   **210**
```
    worldFromRender = Transform();
    break;
```

Once worldFromRender has been set, whatever transformation remains in worldFromCamera is extracted and stored in renderFromCamera.

⟨*Compute* renderFromCamera *transformation*⟩ ≡   **210**
```
    Transform renderFromWorld = Inverse(worldFromRender);
    Transform rfc[2] = { renderFromWorld * worldFromCamera.startTransform,
                         renderFromWorld * worldFromCamera.endTransform };
    renderFromCamera = AnimatedTransform(rfc[0], worldFromCamera.startTime,
                                         rfc[1], worldFromCamera.endTime);
```

The CameraTransform class provides a variety of overloaded methods named RenderFromCamera(), CameraFromRender(), and RenderFromWorld() that transform points, vectors, normals, and rays among the coordinate systems it manages. Other methods return the corresponding transformations directly. Their straightforward implementations are not included here.

5.1.2 THE CameraBase CLASS

All of the camera implementations in this chapter share some common functionality that we have factored into a single class, CameraBase, from which all of them inherit.[3] CameraBase, as well as all the camera implementations, is defined in the files cameras.h and cameras.cpp.

⟨*CameraBase Definition*⟩ ≡
```
class CameraBase {
  public:
    ⟨CameraBase Public Methods 213⟩
  protected:
    ⟨CameraBase Protected Members 212⟩
    ⟨CameraBase Protected Methods 212⟩
};
```

The CameraBase constructor takes a variety of parameters that are applicable to all of pbrt's cameras:

- One of the most important is the transformation that places the camera in the scene, which is represented by a CameraTransform and is stored in the cameraTransform member variable.
- Next is a pair of floating-point values that give the times at which the camera's shutter opens and closes.
- A Film instance stores the final image and models the film sensor.
- Last is a Medium instance that represents the scattering medium that the camera lies in, if any (Medium is described in Section 11.4).

A small structure bundles them together and helps shorten the length of the parameter lists for Camera constructors.

⟨*CameraBaseParameters Definition*⟩ ≡
```
struct CameraBaseParameters {
    CameraTransform cameraTransform;
    Float shutterOpen = 0, shutterClose = 1;
    Film film;
    Medium medium;
};
```

We will only include the constructor's prototype here because its implementation does no more than assign the parameters to the corresponding member variables.

⟨*CameraBase Protected Methods*⟩ ≡   212
```
    CameraBase(CameraBaseParameters p);
```

⟨*CameraBase Protected Members*⟩ ≡   212
```
    CameraTransform cameraTransform;
    Float shutterOpen, shutterClose;
    Film film;
    Medium medium;
```

CameraBase 212
CameraBaseParameters 212
CameraTransform 210
Film 244
Float 23
Medium 714

---

3   One inconvenience with pbrt's custom dynamic dispatch approach is that the interface class cannot provide such functionality via default method implementations. It is not too much work to do so with an explicitly shared base class as is done here, however.

CameraBase can implement a number of the methods required by the Camera interface directly, thus saving the trouble of needing to redundantly implement them in the camera implementations that inherit from it.

For example, accessor methods make the Film and CameraTransform available.

⟨*CameraBase Public Methods*⟩ ≡   212
```
    Film GetFilm() const { return film; }
    const CameraTransform &GetCameraTransform() const {
        return cameraTransform;
    }
```

The SampleTime() method is implemented by linearly interpolating between the shutter open and close times using the sample u.

⟨*CameraBase Public Methods*⟩ +≡   212
```
    Float SampleTime(Float u) const {
        return Lerp(u, shutterOpen, shutterClose);
    }
```

CameraBase provides a GenerateRayDifferential() method that computes a ray differential via multiple calls to a camera's GenerateRay() method. One subtlety is that camera implementations that use this method still must implement a Camera GenerateRayDifferential() method themselves, but then call this method from theirs. (Note that this method's signature is different than that one.) Cameras pass their this pointer as a Camera parameter, which allows it to call the camera's GenerateRay() method. This additional complexity stems from our not using virtual functions for the camera interface, which means that the CameraBase class does not on its own have the ability to call that method unless a Camera is provided to it.

⟨*CameraBase Method Definitions*⟩ ≡
```
    pstd::optional<CameraRayDifferential>
    CameraBase::GenerateRayDifferential(Camera camera,
            CameraSample sample, SampledWavelengths &lambda) {
```
      ⟨*Generate regular camera ray cr for ray differential* 213⟩
      ⟨*Find camera ray after shifting one pixel in the x direction* 214⟩
      ⟨*Find camera ray after shifting one pixel in the y direction*⟩
      ⟨*Return approximate ray differential and weight* 214⟩
```
    }
```

The primary ray is found via a first call to GenerateRay(). If there is no valid ray for the given sample, then there can be no ray differential either.

⟨*Generate regular camera ray cr for ray differential*⟩ ≡   213
```
    pstd::optional<CameraRay> cr = camera.GenerateRay(sample, lambda);
    if (!cr) return {};
    RayDifferential rd(cr->ray);
```

Two attempts are made to find the *x* ray differential: one using forward differencing and one using backward differencing by a fraction of a pixel. It is important to try both of these due to vignetting at the edges of images formed by realistic camera models—sometimes the main ray is valid but shifting in one direction moves past the image formed by the lens system. In that case, trying the other direction may successfully generate a ray.

⟨*Find camera ray after shifting one pixel in the x direction*⟩ ≡   213
```
    pstd::optional<CameraRay> rx;
    for (Float eps : {.05f, -.05f}) {
        CameraSample sshift = sample;
        sshift.pFilm.x += eps;
        ⟨Try to generate ray with sshift and compute x differential 214⟩
    }
```

If it was possible to generate the auxiliary *x* ray, then the corresponding pixel-wide differential is initialized via differencing.

⟨*Try to generate ray with* sshift *and compute x differential*⟩ ≡   214
```
    if (rx = camera.GenerateRay(sshift, lambda); rx) {
        rd.rxOrigin = rd.o + (rx->ray.o - rd.o) / eps;
        rd.rxDirection = rd.d + (rx->ray.d - rd.d) / eps;
        break;
    }
```

The implementation of the fragment ⟨*Find camera ray after shifting one pixel in the y direction*⟩ follows similarly and is not included here.

If a valid ray was found for both *x* and *y*, we can go ahead and set the hasDifferentials member variable to true. Otherwise, the main ray can still be traced, just without differentials available.

⟨*Return approximate ray differential and weight*⟩ ≡   213
```
    rd.hasDifferentials = rx && ry;
    return CameraRayDifferential{rd, cr->weight};
```

Finally, for the convenience of its subclasses, CameraBase provides various transformation methods that use the CameraTransform. We will only include the Ray method here; the others are analogous.

⟨*CameraBase Protected Methods*⟩ +≡   212
```
    Ray RenderFromCamera(const Ray &r) const {
        return cameraTransform.RenderFromCamera(r);
    }
```

5.2 PROJECTIVE CAMERA MODELS

One of the fundamental issues in 3D computer graphics is the *3D viewing problem:* how to project a 3D scene onto a 2D image for display. Most of the classic approaches can be expressed by a 4 × 4 projective transformation matrix. Therefore, we will introduce a projection matrix camera class, ProjectiveCamera, and then define two camera models based on it. The first implements an orthographic projection, and the other implements a perspective projection—two classic and widely used projections.

⟨*ProjectiveCamera Definition*⟩ ≡
```
    class ProjectiveCamera : public CameraBase {
      public:
        ⟨ProjectiveCamera Public Methods 216⟩
      protected:
        ⟨ProjectiveCamera Protected Members 216⟩
    };
```

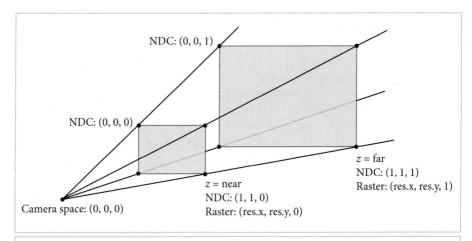

NDC: (0, 0, 1)

NDC: (0, 0, 0)

$z = \text{far}$
NDC: (1, 1, 1)
Raster: (res.x, res.y, 1)

$z = \text{near}$
NDC: (1, 1, 0)
Raster: (res.x, res.y, 0)

Camera space: (0, 0, 0)

Figure 5.2: Several camera-related coordinate spaces are commonly used to simplify the implementation of `Cameras`. The camera class holds transformations between them. Scene objects in rendering space are viewed by the camera, which sits at the origin of camera space and points along the $+z$ axis. Objects between the near and far planes are projected onto the film plane at $z = \text{near}$ in camera space. The film plane is at $z = 0$ in raster space, where x and y range from $(0, 0)$ to the image resolution in pixels. Normalized device coordinate (NDC) space normalizes raster space so that x and y range from $(0, 0)$ to $(1, 1)$.

The orthographic and perspective projections both require the specification of two planes perpendicular to the viewing direction: the *near* and *far* planes. When rasterization is used for rendering, objects that are not between those two planes are culled and not included in the final image. (Culling objects in front of the near plane is particularly important in order to avoid a singularity at the depth 0 and because otherwise the projection matrices map points behind the camera to appear to be in front of it.) In a ray tracer, the projection matrices are used purely to determine rays leaving the camera and these concerns do not apply; there is therefore less need to worry about setting those planes' depths carefully in this context.

Three more coordinate systems (summarized in Figure 5.2) are useful for defining and discussing projective cameras:

- *Screen space:* Screen space is defined on the film plane. The camera projects objects in camera space onto the film plane; the parts inside the *screen window* are visible in the image that is generated. Points at the near plane are mapped to a depth z value of 0 and points at the far plane are mapped to 1. Note that, although this is called "screen" space, it is still a 3D coordinate system, since z values are meaningful.
- *Normalized device coordinate (NDC) space:* This is the coordinate system for the actual image being rendered. In x and y, this space ranges from $(0, 0)$ to $(1, 1)$, with $(0, 0)$ being the upper-left corner of the image. Depth values are the same as in screen space, and a linear transformation converts from screen to NDC space.
- *Raster space:* This is almost the same as NDC space, except the x and y coordinates range from $(0, 0)$ to the resolution of the image in x and y pixels.

Projective cameras use 4×4 matrices to transform among all of these spaces.

In addition to the parameters required by the `CameraBase` class, the `ProjectiveCamera` takes the projective transformation matrix, the screen space extent of the image, and additional parameters related to the distance at which the camera is focused and the size of its lens aperture. If the lens aperture is not an infinitesimal pinhole, then parts of the image may be

ProjectiveCamera 214

blurred, as happens for out-of-focus objects with real lens systems. Simulation of this effect will be discussed later in this section.

⟨*ProjectiveCamera Public Methods*⟩ ≡   214
```
    ProjectiveCamera(CameraBaseParameters baseParameters,
            const Transform &screenFromCamera, Bounds2f screenWindow,
            Float lensRadius, Float focalDistance)
        : CameraBase(baseParameters), screenFromCamera(screenFromCamera),
          lensRadius(lensRadius), focalDistance(focalDistance) {
        ⟨Compute projective camera transformations 216⟩
    }
```

ProjectiveCamera implementations pass the projective transformation up to the base class constructor shown here. This transformation gives the screen-from-camera projection; from that, the constructor can easily compute the other transformations that go all the way from raster space to camera space.

⟨*Compute projective camera transformations*⟩ ≡   216
```
    ⟨Compute projective camera screen transformations 216⟩
    cameraFromRaster = Inverse(screenFromCamera) * screenFromRaster;
```

⟨*ProjectiveCamera Protected Members*⟩ ≡   214
```
    Transform screenFromCamera, cameraFromRaster;
```

The only nontrivial transformation to compute in the constructor is the raster-from-screen projection. It is computed in two steps, via composition of the raster-from-NDC and NDC-from-screen transformations. An important detail here is that the y coordinate is inverted by the final transformation; this is necessary because increasing y values move up the image in screen coordinates but down in raster coordinates.

⟨*Compute projective camera screen transformations*⟩ ≡   216
```
    Transform NDCFromScreen =
        Scale(1 / (screenWindow.pMax.x - screenWindow.pMin.x),
              1 / (screenWindow.pMax.y - screenWindow.pMin.y), 1) *
        Translate(Vector3f(-screenWindow.pMin.x, -screenWindow.pMax.y, 0));
    Transform rasterFromNDC =
        Scale(film.FullResolution().x, -film.FullResolution().y, 1);
    rasterFromScreen = rasterFromNDC * NDCFromScreen;
    screenFromRaster = Inverse(rasterFromScreen);
```

⟨*ProjectiveCamera Protected Members*⟩ +≡   214
```
    Transform rasterFromScreen, screenFromRaster;
```

5.2.1 ORTHOGRAPHIC CAMERA

The orthographic camera is based on the orthographic projection transformation. The orthographic transformation takes a rectangular region of the scene and projects it onto the front face of the box that defines the region. It does not give the effect of *foreshortening*— objects becoming smaller on the image plane as they get farther away—but it does leave parallel lines parallel, and it preserves relative distance between objects. Figure 5.3 shows how this rectangular volume defines the visible region of the scene.

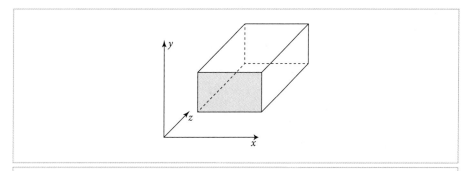

Figure 5.3: The orthographic view volume is an axis-aligned box in camera space, defined such that objects inside the region are projected onto the $z = $ near face of the box.

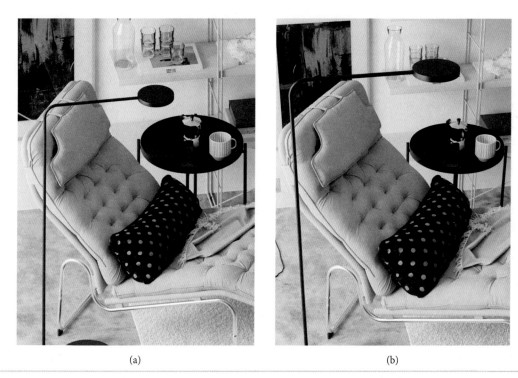

(a)   (b)

Figure 5.4: *Kroken* **Scene Rendered with Different Camera Models.** Images are rendered from the same viewpoint with (a) orthographic and (b) perspective cameras. The lack of foreshortening makes the orthographic view feel like it has less depth, although it does preserve parallel lines, which can be a useful property. *(Scene courtesy of Angelo Ferretti.)*

⟨*OrthographicCamera Definition*⟩ ≡
```
class OrthographicCamera : public ProjectiveCamera {
  public:
    ⟨OrthographicCamera Public Methods 218⟩
  private:
    ⟨OrthographicCamera Private Members 218⟩
};
```

ProjectiveCamera 214

Figure 5.4 compares the result of using the orthographic projection for rendering to that of the perspective projection defined in the next section.

The orthographic camera constructor generates the orthographic transformation matrix with the `Orthographic()` function, which will be defined shortly.

⟨*OrthographicCamera Public Methods*⟩ ≡   **217**
```
    OrthographicCamera(CameraBaseParameters baseParameters,
                    Bounds2f screenWindow, Float lensRadius, Float focalDist)
        : ProjectiveCamera(baseParameters, Orthographic(0, 1), screenWindow,
                        lensRadius, focalDist) {
        ⟨Compute differential changes in origin for orthographic camera rays 218⟩
        ⟨Compute minimum differentials for orthographic camera 640⟩
    }
```

The orthographic viewing transformation leaves x and y coordinates unchanged but maps z values at the near plane to 0 and z values at the far plane to 1. To do this, the scene is first translated along the z axis so that the near plane is aligned with $z = 0$. Then, the scene is scaled in z so that the far plane maps to $z = 1$. The composition of these two transformations gives the overall transformation. For a ray tracer like pbrt, we would like the near plane to be at 0 so that rays start at the plane that goes through the camera's position; the far plane's position does not particularly matter.

⟨*Transform Function Definitions*⟩ +≡
```
    Transform Orthographic(Float zNear, Float zFar) {
        return Scale(1, 1, 1 / (zFar - zNear)) *
                Translate(Vector3f(0, 0, -zNear));
    }
```

Thanks to the simplicity of the orthographic projection, it is easy to directly compute the differential rays in the x and y directions in the `GenerateRayDifferential()` method. The directions of the differential rays will be the same as the main ray (as they are for all rays generated by an orthographic camera), and the difference in origins will be the same for all rays. Therefore, the constructor here precomputes how much the ray origins shift in camera space coordinates due to a single pixel shift in the x and y directions on the film plane.

⟨*Compute differential changes in origin for orthographic camera rays*⟩ ≡   **218**
```
    dxCamera = cameraFromRaster(Vector3f(1, 0, 0));
    dyCamera = cameraFromRaster(Vector3f(0, 1, 0));
```

⟨*OrthographicCamera Private Members*⟩ ≡   **217**
```
    Vector3f dxCamera, dyCamera;
```

We can now go through the code that takes a sample point in raster space and turns it into a camera ray. The process is summarized in Figure 5.5. First, the raster space sample position is transformed into a point in camera space, giving a point located on the near plane, which is the origin of the camera ray. Because the camera space viewing direction points down the z axis, the camera space ray direction is $(0, 0, 1)$.

If the lens aperture is not a pinhole, the ray's origin and direction are modified so that defocus blur is simulated. Finally, the ray is transformed into rendering space before being returned.

⟨*OrthographicCamera Method Definitions*⟩ ≡
```
    pstd::optional<CameraRay> OrthographicCamera::GenerateRay(
            CameraSample sample, SampledWavelengths &lambda) const {
        ⟨Compute raster and camera sample positions 219⟩
        Ray ray(pCamera, Vector3f(0, 0, 1), SampleTime(sample.time), medium);
        ⟨Modify ray for depth of field 226⟩
        return CameraRay{RenderFromCamera(ray)};
    }
```

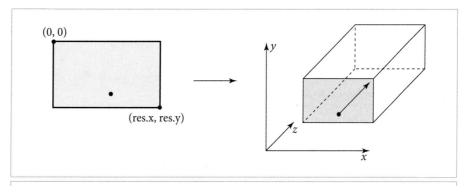

Figure 5.5: To create a ray with the orthographic camera, a raster space position on the film plane is transformed to camera space, giving the ray's origin on the near plane. The ray's direction in camera space is (0, 0, 1), down the *z* axis.

Once all the transformation matrices have been set up, it is easy to transform the raster space sample point to camera space.

⟨*Compute raster and camera sample positions*⟩ ≡   **218, 222**
```
Point3f pFilm = Point3f(sample.pFilm.x, sample.pFilm.y, 0);
Point3f pCamera = cameraFromRaster(pFilm);
```

The implementation of GenerateRayDifferential() performs the same computation to generate the main camera ray. The differential ray origins are found using the offsets computed in the OrthographicCamera constructor, and then the full ray differential is transformed to rendering space.

⟨*OrthographicCamera Method Definitions*⟩ +≡
```
pstd::optional<CameraRayDifferential>
OrthographicCamera::GenerateRayDifferential(CameraSample sample,
        SampledWavelengths &lambda) const {
    ⟨Compute main orthographic viewing ray⟩
    ⟨Compute ray differentials for OrthographicCamera 219⟩
    ray.hasDifferentials = true;
    return CameraRayDifferential{RenderFromCamera(ray)};
}
```

⟨*Compute ray differentials for* OrthographicCamera⟩ ≡   **219**
```
if (lensRadius > 0) {
    ⟨Compute OrthographicCamera ray differentials accounting for lens⟩
} else {
    ray.rxOrigin = ray.o + dxCamera;
    ray.ryOrigin = ray.o + dyCamera;
    ray.rxDirection = ray.ryDirection = ray.d;
}
```

5.2.2 PERSPECTIVE CAMERA

The perspective projection is similar to the orthographic projection in that it projects a volume of space onto a 2D film plane. However, it includes the effect of foreshortening: objects that are far away are projected to be smaller than objects of the same size that are closer. Unlike the orthographic projection, the perspective projection does not preserve distances or angles, and parallel lines no longer remain parallel. The perspective projection is a reasonably close match to how an eye or camera lens generates images of the 3D world.

⟨*PerspectiveCamera Definition*⟩ ≡
```
class PerspectiveCamera : public ProjectiveCamera {
  public:
    ⟨PerspectiveCamera Public Methods 220⟩
  private:
    ⟨PerspectiveCamera Private Members 221⟩
};
```

⟨*PerspectiveCamera Public Methods*⟩ ≡   **220**
```
PerspectiveCamera(CameraBaseParameters baseParameters, Float fov,
                  Bounds2f screenWindow, Float lensRadius, Float focalDist)
    : ProjectiveCamera(baseParameters, Perspective(fov, 1e-2f, 1000.f),
                       screenWindow, lensRadius, focalDist) {
    ⟨Compute differential changes in origin for perspective camera rays 221⟩
    ⟨Compute cosTotalWidth for perspective camera 222⟩
    ⟨Compute image plane area at z = 1 for PerspectiveCamera⟩
    ⟨Compute minimum differentials for PerspectiveCamera 640⟩
}
```

The perspective projection describes perspective viewing of the scene. Points in the scene are projected onto a viewing plane perpendicular to the z axis. The Perspective() function computes this transformation; it takes a field-of-view angle in fov and the distances to a near z plane and a far z plane (Figure 5.6).

⟨*Transform Function Definitions*⟩ +≡
```
Transform Perspective(Float fov, Float n, Float f) {
    ⟨Perform projective divide for perspective projection 221⟩
    ⟨Scale canonical perspective view to specified field of view 221⟩
}
```

The transformation is most easily understood in two steps:

1. Points p in camera space are projected onto the viewing plane. A bit of algebra shows that the projected x' and y' coordinates on the viewing plane can be computed by dividing x and y by the point's z coordinate value. The projected z depth is remapped so

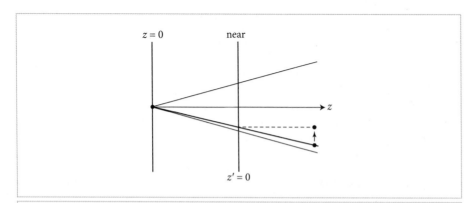

Figure 5.6: The perspective transformation matrix projects points in camera space onto the near plane. The x' and y' coordinates of the projected points are equal to the unprojected x and y coordinates divided by the z coordinate. That operation is depicted here, where the effect of the projection is indicated by an arrow. The projected z' coordinate is then computed so that points on the near plane map to $z' = 0$ and points on the far plane map to $z' = 1$.

that z values at the near plane are 0 and z values at the far plane are 1. The computation we would like to do is

$$x' = x/z$$
$$y' = y/z$$
$$z' = \frac{f(z - n)}{z(f - n)}.$$

All of this computation can be encoded in a 4×4 matrix that can then be applied to homogeneous coordinates:

$$
\begin{bmatrix}
1 & 0 & 0 & 0 \\
0 & 1 & 0 & 0 \\
0 & 0 & \frac{f}{f-n} & -\frac{fn}{f-n} \\
0 & 0 & 1 & 0
\end{bmatrix}
$$

⟨*Perform projective divide for perspective projection*⟩ ≡   **220**
```
SquareMatrix<4> persp(1, 0,            0,              0,
                      0, 1,            0,              0,
                      0, 0, f / (f - n), -f*n / (f - n),
                      0, 0,            1,              0);
```

2. The angular field of view (fov) specified by the user is accounted for by scaling the (x, y) values on the projection plane so that points inside the field of view project to coordinates between $[-1, 1]$ on the view plane. For square images, both x and y lie between $[-1, 1]$ in screen space. Otherwise, the direction in which the image is narrower maps to $[-1, 1]$, and the wider direction maps to a proportionally larger range of screen space values. Recall that the tangent is equal to the ratio of the opposite side of a right triangle to the adjacent side. Here the adjacent side has length 1, so the opposite side has the length $\tan(fov/2)$. Scaling by the reciprocal of this length maps the field of view to the range $[-1, 1]$.

⟨*Scale canonical perspective view to specified field of view*⟩ ≡   **220**
```
Float invTanAng = 1 / std::tan(Radians(fov) / 2);
return Scale(invTanAng, invTanAng, 1) * Transform(persp);
```

As with the OrthographicCamera, the PerspectiveCamera's constructor computes information about how the rays it generates change with shifts in pixels. In this case, the ray origins are unchanged and the ray differentials are only different in their directions. Here, we compute the change in position on the near perspective plane in camera space with respect to shifts in pixel location.

⟨*Compute differential changes in origin for perspective camera rays*⟩ ≡   **220**
```
dxCamera = cameraFromRaster(Point3f(1, 0, 0)) -
           cameraFromRaster(Point3f(0, 0, 0));
dyCamera = cameraFromRaster(Point3f(0, 1, 0)) -
           cameraFromRaster(Point3f(0, 0, 0));
```

⟨*PerspectiveCamera Private Members*⟩ ≡   **220**
```
Vector3f dxCamera, dyCamera;
```

The cosine of the maximum angle of the perspective camera's field of view will occasionally be useful. In particular, points outside the field of view can be quickly culled via a dot product with the viewing direction and comparison to this value. This cosine can be found by computing the angle between the camera's viewing vector and a vector to one of the corners

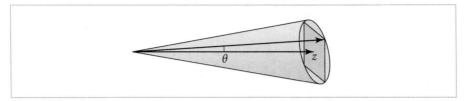

Figure 5.7: Computing the Cosine of the Perspective Camera's Maximum View Angle. A cone that bounds the viewing directions of a `PerspectiveCamera` can be found by using the camera's viewing direction as the center axis and by computing the cosine of the angle θ between that axis and a vector to one of the corners of the image. In camera space, that simplifies to be the z component of that vector, normalized.

of the image (see Figure 5.7). This corner needs a small adjustment here to account for the width of the filter function centered at each pixel that is used to weight image samples according to their location (this topic is discussed in Section 8.8).

⟨*Compute* `cosTotalWidth` *for perspective camera*⟩ ≡   **220**
```
Point2f radius = Point2f(film.GetFilter().Radius());
Point3f pCorner(-radius.x, -radius.y, 0.f);
Vector3f wCornerCamera = Normalize(Vector3f(cameraFromRaster(pCorner)));
cosTotalWidth = wCornerCamera.z;
```

⟨*PerspectiveCamera Private Members*⟩ +≡   **220**
```
Float cosTotalWidth;
```

With the perspective projection, camera space rays all originate from the origin, (0, 0, 0). A ray's direction is given by the vector from the origin to the point on the near plane, pCamera, that corresponds to the provided CameraSample's pFilm location. In other words, the ray's vector direction is component-wise equal to this point's position, so rather than doing a useless subtraction to compute the direction, we just initialize the direction directly from the point pCamera.

⟨*PerspectiveCamera Method Definitions*⟩ ≡
```
pstd::optional<CameraRay> PerspectiveCamera::GenerateRay(
        CameraSample sample, SampledWavelengths &lambda) const {
    ⟨Compute raster and camera sample positions 219⟩
    Ray ray(Point3f(0, 0, 0), Normalize(Vector3f(pCamera)),
            SampleTime(sample.time), medium);
    ⟨Modify ray for depth of field 226⟩
    return CameraRay{RenderFromCamera(ray)};
}
```

The `GenerateRayDifferential()` method follows the implementation of `GenerateRay()`, except for this additional fragment that computes the differential rays.

⟨*Compute offset rays for* PerspectiveCamera *ray differentials*⟩ ≡
```
if (lensRadius > 0) {
    ⟨Compute PerspectiveCamera ray differentials accounting for lens⟩
} else {
    ray.rxOrigin = ray.ryOrigin = ray.o;
    ray.rxDirection = Normalize(Vector3f(pCamera) + dxCamera);
    ray.ryDirection = Normalize(Vector3f(pCamera) + dyCamera);
}
```

5.2.3 THE THIN LENS MODEL AND DEPTH OF FIELD

An ideal pinhole camera that only allows rays passing through a single point to reach the film is not physically realizable; while it is possible to make cameras with extremely small apertures that approach this behavior, small apertures allow relatively little light to reach the film sensor. With a small aperture, long exposure times are required to capture enough photons to accurately capture the image, which in turn can lead to blur from objects in the scene moving while the camera shutter is open.

Real cameras have lens systems that focus light through a finite-sized aperture onto the film plane. Camera designers (and photographers using cameras with adjustable apertures) face a trade-off: the larger the aperture, the more light reaches the film and the shorter the exposures that are needed. However, lenses can only focus on a single plane (the *focal plane*), and the farther objects in the scene are from this plane, the blurrier they are. The larger the aperture, the more pronounced this effect is.

The `RealisticCamera` (included only in the online edition of the book) implements a fairly accurate simulation of lens systems in real-world cameras. For the simple camera models introduced so far, we can apply a classic approximation from optics, the *thin lens approximation*, to model the effect of finite apertures with traditional computer graphics projection models. The thin lens approximation models an optical system as a single lens with spherical profiles, where the thickness of the lens is small relative to the radius of curvature of the lens.

Under the thin lens approximation, incident rays that are parallel to the optical axis and pass through the lens focus at a point behind the lens called the *focal point*. The distance the focal point is behind the lens, f, is the lens's *focal length*. If the film plane is placed at a distance equal to the focal length behind the lens, then objects infinitely far away will be in focus, as they image to a single point on the film.

Figure 5.8 illustrates the basic setting. Here we have followed the typical lens coordinate system convention of placing the lens perpendicular to the z axis, with the lens at $z = 0$ and the scene along $-z$. (Note that this is a different coordinate system from the one we used for camera space, where the viewing direction is $+z$.) Distances on the scene side of the lens are denoted with unprimed variables z, and distances on the film side of the lens (positive z) are primed, z'.

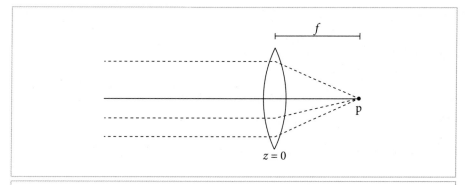

Figure 5.8: A thin lens, located along the z axis at $z = 0$. Incident rays that are parallel to the optical axis and pass through a thin lens (dashed lines) all pass through a point p, the focal point. The distance between the lens and the focal point, f, is the lens's focal length.

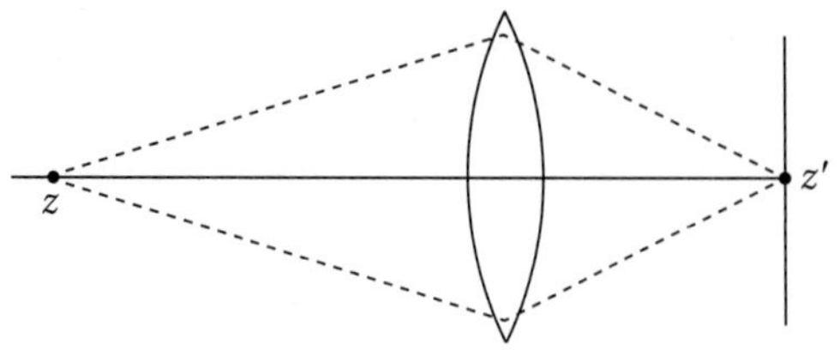

Figure 5.9: To focus a thin lens at a depth z in the scene, Equation (5.2) can be used to compute the distance z' on the film side of the lens that points at z focus to. Focusing is performed by adjusting the distance between the lens and the film plane.

For points in the scene at a depth z from a thin lens with focal length f, the *Gaussian lens equation* relates the distances from the object to the lens and from the lens to the image of the point:

$$\frac{1}{z'} - \frac{1}{z} = \frac{1}{f}. \tag{5.1}$$

Note that for $z = -\infty$, we have $z' = f$, as expected.

We can use the Gaussian lens equation to solve for the distance between the lens and the film that sets the plane of focus at some z, the *focal distance* (Figure 5.9):

$$z' = \frac{fz}{f + z}. \tag{5.2}$$

A point that does not lie on the plane of focus is imaged to a disk on the film plane, rather than to a single point. The boundary of this disk is called the *circle of confusion*. The size of the circle of confusion is affected by the diameter of the aperture that light rays pass through, the focal distance, and the distance between the object and the lens. Although the circle of confusion only has zero radius for a single depth, a range of nearby depths have small enough circles of confusion that they still appear to be in focus. (As long as its circle of confusion is smaller than the spacing between pixels, a point will effectively appear to be in focus.) The range of depths that appear in focus are termed the *depth of field*.

Figure 5.10 shows this effect, in the *Watercolor* scene. As the size of the lens aperture increases, blurriness increases the farther a point is from the plane of focus. Note that the pencil cup in the center remains in focus throughout all the images, as the plane of focus has been placed at its depth. Figure 5.11 shows depth of field used to render the landscape scene. Note how the effect draws the viewer's eye to the in-focus grass in the center of the image.

The Gaussian lens equation also lets us compute the size of the circle of confusion; given a lens with focal length f that is focused at a distance z_f, the film plane is at z_f'. Given another point at depth z, the Gaussian lens equation gives the distance z' that the lens focuses the point to. This point is either in front of or behind the film plane; Figure 5.12(a) shows the case where it is behind.

The diameter of the circle of confusion is given by the intersection of the cone between z' and the lens with the film plane. If we know the diameter of the lens d_l, then we can use similar triangles to solve for the diameter of the circle of confusion d_c (Figure 5.12(b)):

$$\frac{d_l}{z'} = \frac{d_c}{|z' - z_f'|}.$$

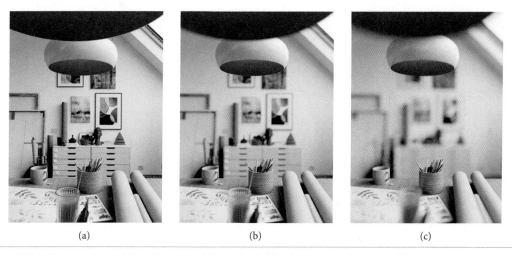

(a)   (b)   (c)

Figure 5.10: (a) Scene rendered with no defocus blur, (b) extensive depth of field due to a relatively small lens aperture, which gives only a small amount of blurriness in the out-of-focus regions, and (c) a very large aperture, giving a larger circle of confusion in the out-of-focus areas, resulting in a greater amount of blur on the film plane. *(Scene courtesy of Angelo Ferretti.)*

Figure 5.11: Depth of field gives a greater sense of depth and scale to this part of the landscape scene. *(Scene courtesy of Laubwerk.)*

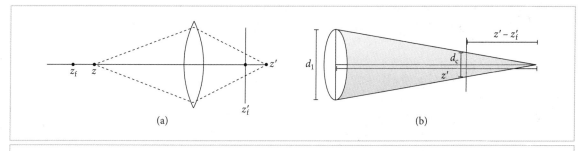

(a)   (b)

Figure 5.12: (a) If a thin lens with focal length f is focused at some depth z_f, then the distance from the lens to the focus plane is z'_f, given by the Gaussian lens equation. A point in the scene at depth $z \neq z_f$ will be imaged as a circle on the film plane; here z focuses at z', which is behind the film plane. (b) To compute the diameter of the circle of confusion, we can apply similar triangles: the ratio of d_l, the diameter of the lens, to z' must be the same as the ratio of d_c, the diameter of the circle of confusion, to $z' - z'_f$.

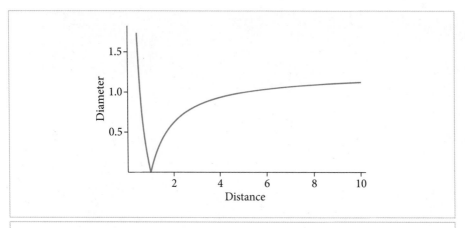

Figure 5.13: The diameter of the circle of confusion as a function of depth for a 50-mm focal length lens with 25-mm aperture, focused at 1 meter.

Solving for d_c, we have

$$d_c = \left| \frac{d_l\,(z' - z'_f)}{z'} \right|.$$

Applying the Gaussian lens equation to express the result in terms of scene depths, we can find that

$$d_c = \left| \frac{d_l\,f\,(z - z_f)}{z(f + z_f)} \right|.$$

Note that the diameter of the circle of confusion is proportional to the diameter of the lens. The lens diameter is often expressed as the lens's *f-number n*, which expresses diameter as a fraction of focal length, $d_l = f/n$.

Figure 5.13 shows a graph of this function for a 50-mm focal length lens with a 25-mm aperture, focused at $z_f = 1$ m. Note that the blur is asymmetric with depth around the focal plane and grows much more quickly for objects in front of the plane of focus than for objects behind it.

Modeling a thin lens in a ray tracer is remarkably straightforward: all that is necessary is to choose a point on the lens and find the appropriate ray that starts on the lens at that point such that objects in the plane of focus are in focus on the film (Figure 5.14). Therefore, projective cameras take two extra parameters for depth of field: one sets the size of the lens aperture, and the other sets the focal distance.

⟨*ProjectiveCamera Protected Members*⟩ +≡   214
    Float lensRadius, focalDistance;

It is generally necessary to trace many rays for each image pixel in order to adequately sample the lens for smooth defocus blur. Figure 5.15 shows the landscape scene from Figure 5.11 with only four samples per pixel (Figure 5.11 had 2048 samples per pixel).

⟨*Modify ray for depth of field*⟩ ≡   218, 222
    if (lensRadius > 0) {
        ⟨*Sample point on lens* 228⟩
        ⟨*Compute point on plane of focus* 228⟩
        ⟨*Update ray for effect of lens* 228⟩
    }

Float 23

ProjectiveCamera::lensRadius
226

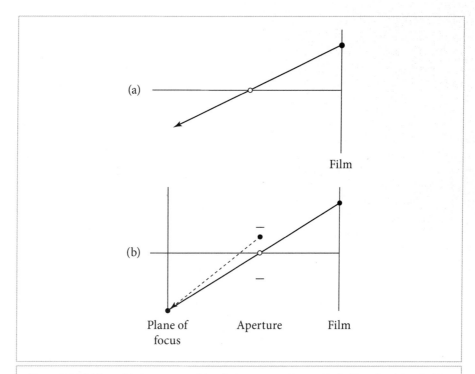

(a)

Film

(b)

Plane of
focus

Aperture

Film

Figure 5.14: (a) For a pinhole camera model, a single camera ray is associated with each point on the film plane (filled circle), given by the ray that passes through the single point of the pinhole lens (empty circle). (b) For a camera model with a finite aperture, we sample a point (filled circle) on the disk-shaped lens for each ray. We then compute the ray that passes through the center of the lens (corresponding to the pinhole model) and the point where it intersects the plane of focus (solid line). We know that all objects in the plane of focus must be in focus, regardless of the lens sample position. Therefore, the ray corresponding to the lens position sample (dashed line) is given by the ray starting on the lens sample point and passing through the computed intersection point on the plane of focus.

Figure 5.15: Landscape scene with depth of field and only four samples per pixel: the depth of field is undersampled and the image is grainy. *(Scene courtesy of Laubwerk.)*

The SampleUniformDiskConcentric() function, which is defined in Section A.5.1, takes a (u, v) sample position in $[0, 1)^2$ and maps it to a 2D unit disk centered at the origin $(0, 0)$. To turn this into a point on the lens, these coordinates are scaled by the lens radius. The CameraSample class provides the (u, v) lens-sampling parameters in the pLens member variable.

⟨*Sample point on lens*⟩ ≡   226
```
Point2f pLens = lensRadius * SampleUniformDiskConcentric(sample.pLens);
```

The ray's origin is this point on the lens. Now it is necessary to determine the proper direction for the new ray. We know that *all* rays from the given image sample through the lens must converge at the same point on the plane of focus. Furthermore, we know that rays pass through the center of the lens without a change in direction, so finding the appropriate point of convergence is a matter of intersecting the unperturbed ray from the pinhole model with the plane of focus and then setting the new ray's direction to be the vector from the point on the lens to the intersection point.

For this simple model, the plane of focus is perpendicular to the z axis and the ray starts at the origin, so intersecting the ray through the lens center with the plane of focus is straightforward. The t value of the intersection is given by

$$t = \frac{focalDistance}{\mathrm{d}_z}.$$

⟨*Compute point on plane of focus*⟩ ≡   226
```
Float ft = focalDistance / ray.d.z;
Point3f pFocus = ray(ft);
```

Now the ray can be initialized. The origin is set to the sampled point on the lens, and the direction is set so that the ray passes through the point on the plane of focus, pFocus.

⟨*Update ray for effect of lens*⟩ ≡   226
```
ray.o = Point3f(pLens.x, pLens.y, 0);
ray.d = Normalize(pFocus - ray.o);
```

To compute ray differentials with the thin lens, the approach used in the fragment ⟨*Update ray for effect of lens*⟩ is applied to rays offset one pixel in the x and y directions on the film plane. The fragments that implement this, ⟨*Compute* OrthographicCamera *ray differentials accounting for lens*⟩ and ⟨*Compute* PerspectiveCamera *ray differentials accounting for lens*⟩, are not included here.

5.3 SPHERICAL CAMERA

One advantage of ray tracing compared to scan line or rasterization-based rendering methods is that it is easy to employ unusual image projections. We have great freedom in how the image sample positions are mapped into ray directions, since the rendering algorithm does not depend on properties such as straight lines in the scene always projecting to straight lines in the image.

In this section, we will describe a camera model that traces rays in all directions around a point in the scene, giving a view of everything that is visible from that point. The Spherical Camera supports two spherical parameterizations from Section 3.8 to map points in the image to associated directions. Figure 5.16 shows this camera in action with the *San Miguel* model.

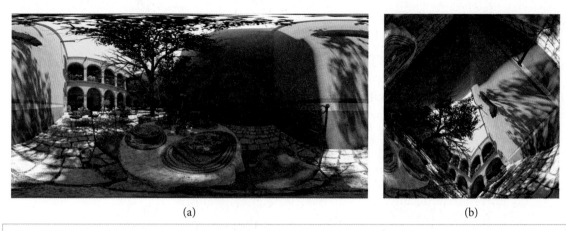

(a)

(b)

Figure 5.16: The *San Miguel* scene rendered with the `SphericalCamera`, which traces rays in all directions from the camera position. (a) Rendered using an equirectangular mapping. (b) Rendered with an equal-area mapping. *(Scene courtesy of Guillermo M. Leal Llaguno.)*

⟨*SphericalCamera Definition*⟩ ≡
```
class SphericalCamera : public CameraBase {
  public:
    ⟨SphericalCamera::Mapping Definition 230⟩
    ⟨SphericalCamera Public Methods 229⟩
  private:
    ⟨SphericalCamera Private Members 230⟩
};
```

`SphericalCamera` does not derive from `ProjectiveCamera` since the projections that it uses are nonlinear and cannot be captured by a single 4×4 matrix.

⟨*SphericalCamera Public Methods*⟩ ≡   229
```
SphericalCamera(CameraBaseParameters baseParameters, Mapping mapping)
    : CameraBase(baseParameters), mapping(mapping) {
    ⟨Compute minimum differentials for SphericalCamera⟩
}
```

The first mapping that `SphericalCamera` supports is the equirectangular mapping that was defined in Section 3.8.3. In the implementation here, θ values range from 0 at the top of the image to π at the bottom of the image, and ϕ values range from 0 to 2π, moving from left to right across the image.

The equirectangular mapping is easy to evaluate and has the advantage that lines of constant latitude and longitude on the sphere remain straight. However, it preserves neither area nor angles between curves on the sphere (i.e., it is not *conformal*). These issues are especially evident at the top and bottom of the image in Figure 5.16(a).

Therefore, the `SphericalCamera` also supports the equal-area mapping from Section 3.8.3. With this mapping, any finite solid angle of directions on the sphere maps to the same area in the image, regardless of where it is on the sphere. (This mapping is also used by the `ImageInfiniteLight`, which is described in Section 12.5.2, and so images rendered using this camera can be used as light sources.) The equal-area mapping's use with the `SphericalCamera` is shown in Figure 5.16(b).

An enumeration reflects which mapping should be used.

⟨*SphericalCamera::Mapping Definition*⟩ ≡   **229**
    enum Mapping { EquiRectangular, EqualArea };

⟨*SphericalCamera Private Members*⟩ ≡   **229**
    Mapping mapping;

The main task of the GenerateRay() method is to apply the requested mapping. The rest of it
follows the earlier GenerateRay() methods.

⟨*SphericalCamera Method Definitions*⟩ ≡
    pstd::optional<CameraRay> SphericalCamera::GenerateRay(
            CameraSample sample, SampledWavelengths &lambda) const {
        ⟨*Compute spherical camera ray direction* **230**⟩
        Ray ray(Point3f(0, 0, 0), dir, SampleTime(sample.time), medium);
        return CameraRay{RenderFromCamera(ray)};
    }

For the use of both mappings, (u, v) coordinates in NDC space are found by dividing the
raster space sample location by the image's overall resolution. Then, after the mapping is
applied, the y and z coordinates are swapped to account for the fact that both mappings are
defined with z as the "up" direction, while y is "up" in camera space.

⟨*Compute spherical camera ray direction*⟩ ≡   **230**
    Point2f uv(sample.pfilm.x / film.FullResolution().x,
                sample.pfilm.y / film.FullResolution().y);
    Vector3f dir;
    if (mapping == EquiRectangular) {
        ⟨*Compute ray direction using equirectangular mapping* **230**⟩
    } else {
        ⟨*Compute ray direction using equal-area mapping* **230**⟩
    }
    pstd::swap(dir.y, dir.z);

For the equirectangular mapping, the (u, v) coordinates are scaled to cover the (θ, ϕ) range
and the spherical coordinate formula is used to compute the ray direction.

⟨*Compute ray direction using equirectangular mapping*⟩ ≡   **230**
    Float theta = Pi * uv[1], phi = 2 * Pi * uv[0];
    dir = SphericalDirection(std::sin(theta), std::cos(theta), phi);

The (u, v) values for the CameraSample may be slightly outside of the range $[0, 1]^2$, due to
the pixel sample filter function. A call to WrapEqualAreaSquare() takes care of handling the
boundary conditions before EqualAreaSquareToSphere() performs the actual mapping.

⟨*Compute ray direction using equal-area mapping*⟩ ≡   **230**
    uv = WrapEqualAreaSquare(uv);
    dir = EqualAreaSquareToSphere(uv);

5.4 FILM AND IMAGING

After the camera's projection or lens system forms an image of the scene on the film, it is
necessary to model how the film measures light to create the final image generated by the
renderer. This section starts with an overview of the radiometry of how light is measured on
the film and then continues with the topic of how spectral energy is converted to tristimulus
colors (typically, RGB). This leads to the PixelSensor class, which models that process as

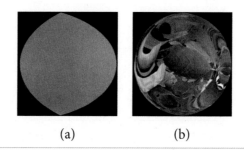

(a)   (b)

Figure 5.17: The Image of the Scene on the Lens, as Seen from Two Points on the Film Plane. Both are from a rendering of the *San Miguel* scene. (a) As seen from a point where the scene is in sharp focus; the incident radiance is effectively constant over its area. (b) As seen from a pixel in an out-of-focus area, a small image of part of the scene is visible, with potentially rapidly varying radiance.

well as further processing that is generally performed by cameras. After next considering how image samples on the film are accumulated into the pixels of the final image, we introduce the Film interface and then two implementations of it that put this model into practice.

5.4.1 THE CAMERA MEASUREMENT EQUATION

Given a simulation of the process of real image formation, it is also worthwhile to more carefully define the radiometry of the measurement made by a film or a camera sensor. Rays from the rear of the lens to the film carry radiance from the scene. As considered from a point on the film plane, there is thus a set of directions from which radiance is incident. The distribution of radiance leaving the lens is affected by the amount of defocus blur seen by the point on the film—Figure 5.17 shows two images of the radiance from the lens as seen from two points on the film.

Given the incident radiance function, we can define the irradiance at a point on the film plane. If we start with the definition of irradiance in terms of radiance, Equation (4.7), we can then convert from an integral over solid angle to an integral over area (in this case, an area A_e of the plane tangent to the rear lens element) using Equation (4.9). This gives us the irradiance for a point p on the film plane:

$$E(\mathrm{p}) = \int_{A_e} L_i(\mathrm{p}, \mathrm{p}') \, \frac{|\cos\theta \cos\theta'|}{||\mathrm{p}' - \mathrm{p}||^2} \, dA_e.$$

Figure 5.18 shows the geometry of the situation.

Because the film plane is perpendicular to the lens's plane, $\theta = \theta'$. We can further take advantage of the fact that the distance between p and p' is equal to the axial distance from the film plane to the lens (which we will denote here by z) divided by $\cos\theta$. Putting this all together, we have

$$E(\mathrm{p}) = \frac{1}{z^2} \int_{A_e} L_i(\mathrm{p}, \mathrm{p}') \, |\cos^4\theta| \, dA_e. \tag{5.3}$$

For cameras where the extent of the film is relatively large with respect to the distance z, the $\cos^4\theta$ term can meaningfully reduce the incident irradiance—this factor also contributes to vignetting. Most modern digital cameras correct for this effect with preset correction factors that increase pixel values toward the edges of the sensor.

Film 244

Integrating irradiance at a point on the film over the time that the shutter is open gives *radiant exposure*, which is the radiometric unit for energy per area, J/m^2.

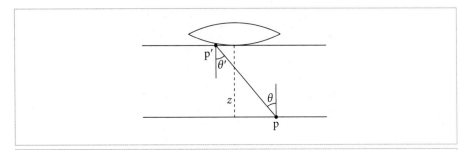

Figure 5.18: Geometric setting for the irradiance measurement equation, (5.3). Radiance can be measured as it passes through points p′ on the plane tangent to the rear lens element to a point on the film plane p. z is the axial distance from the film plane to the rear element tangent plane, and θ is the angle between the vector from p′ to p and the optical axis.

$$H(\mathrm{p}) = \frac{1}{z^2} \int_{t_0}^{t_1} \int_{A_\mathrm{e}} L_\mathrm{i}(\mathrm{p}, \mathrm{p}', t') \, |\cos^4 \theta| \, dA_\mathrm{e} \, dt'. \qquad (5.4)$$

(Radiant exposure is also known as *fluence*.) Measuring radiant exposure at a point captures the effect that the amount of energy received on the film plane is partially related to the length of time the camera shutter is open.

Photographic film (or CCD or CMOS sensors in digital cameras) measures radiant energy over a small area.[4] Taking Equation (5.4) and also integrating over sensor pixel area, A_p, we have

$$J = \frac{1}{z^2} \int_{A_\mathrm{p}} \int_{t_0}^{t_1} \int_{A_\mathrm{e}} L_\mathrm{i}(\mathrm{p}, \mathrm{p}', t') \, |\cos^4 \theta| \, dA_\mathrm{e} \, dt' \, dA_\mathrm{p}, \qquad (5.5)$$

the Joules arriving at a pixel; this is called the *camera measurement equation*.

Although these factors apply to all of the camera models introduced in this chapter, they are only included in the implementation of the `RealisticCamera`. The reason is purely pragmatic: most renderers do not model this effect, so omitting it from the simpler camera models makes it easier to compare images rendered by pbrt with those rendered by other systems.

5.4.2 MODELING SENSOR RESPONSE

Traditional film is based on a chemical process where silver halide crystals produce silver bromide when they are exposed to light. Silver halide is mostly sensitive to blue light, but color images can be captured using multiple layers of crystals with color filters between them and dyes that make silver halide more responsive to other wavelengths.

Modern digital cameras use CCD or CMOS sensors where each pixel effectively counts the number of photons it is exposed to by transforming photons into electrical charge. A variety of approaches to capturing color images have been developed, but the most common of them is to have a color filter over each pixel so that each measures red, green, or blue by counting only the photons that make it through the filter. Each pixel is often supplemented with a *microlens* that increases the amount of light that reaches the sensor.

For both film and digital sensors, color measurements at pixels can be modeled using spectral response curves that characterize the color filter or film's chemical response to light as a

---

4   A typical size for pixels in digital cameras in 2022-era mobile phones is 1.8 microns per side.

function of wavelength. These functions are defined such that, for example, given an incident spectral distribution $s(\lambda)$, a pixel's red component is given by

$$r = \int s(\lambda)\, \bar{r}(\lambda)\, \mathrm{d}\lambda. \tag{5.6}$$

Digital sensor pixels are typically arranged in a *mosaic*, with twice as many green pixels as red and blue, due to the human visual system's greater sensitivity to green. One implication of pixel mosaics is that a *demosaicing* algorithm must be used to convert these sensor pixels to image pixels where the red, green, and blue color components are colocated. The naive approach of taking quads of mosaiced pixels and using their color values as is does not work well, since the constituent sensor pixels are at slightly different locations.

There are many challenges in designing digital sensors, most of them stemming from the small size of pixels, which is a result of demand for high-resolution images. The smaller a pixel is, the fewer photons it is exposed to given a lens and exposure time, and in turn, the harder it is to accurately measure the light. Pixel arrays suffer from a variety of types of noise, of which *shot noise* is generally the most significant. It is due to the discrete nature of photons: there is random fluctuation in the number of photons that are counted, which matters more the fewer of them that are captured. Shot noise can be modeled using a Poisson distribution.

Each pixel must receive a sufficient amount of light either to cause the necessary chemical reactions or to count enough photons to capture an accurate image. In Equation (5.5), we saw that the energy captured at a pixel depends on the incident radiance, the pixel area, the exit pupil area, and the exposure time. With pixel area fixed for a given camera design, both increasing the lens aperture area and increasing the exposure time may introduce undesired side-effects in return for the additional light provided. A larger aperture reduces depth of field, which may lead to undesired defocus blur. Longer exposures can also cause blur due to moving objects in the scene or due to camera motion while the shutter is open. Sensors and film therefore provide an additional control in the form of an *ISO setting*.

For physical film, ISO encodes its responsiveness to light (higher ISO values require less light to record an image). In digital cameras, ISO controls the *gain*—a scaling factor that is applied to pixel values as they are read from the sensor. With physical cameras, increasing gain exacerbates noise, as noise in the initial pixel measurements is amplified. Because pbrt does not model the noise present in readings from physical sensors, the ISO value can be set arbitrarily to achieve a desired exposure.

In pbrt's sensor model, we model neither mosaicing nor noise, nor other effects like blooming, where a pixel that is exposed to enough light will "spill over" and start increasing the measured value at adjacent pixels. We also do not simulate the process of image readout from the sensor: many cameras use a *rolling shutter* where scanlines are read in succession. For scenes with rapidly moving objects, this can give surprising results. Exercises at the end of the chapter suggest modifying pbrt in various ways to explore these effects.

The PixelSensor class implements pbrt's semi-idealized model of pixel color measurement. It is defined in the files film.h and film.cpp.[5]

---

5   Its original implementation is due to Anders Langlands and Luca Fascione and is based on the sensor model in Weta Digital's *PhysLight* system, which is used in Weta's *Manuka* renderer.

⟨*PixelSensor Definition*⟩ ≡

```
    class PixelSensor {
      public:
          ⟨PixelSensor Public Methods 234⟩
          ⟨PixelSensor Public Members 237⟩
      private:
          ⟨PixelSensor Private Methods 236⟩
          ⟨PixelSensor Private Members 234⟩
    };
```

PixelSensor models three components of sensor pixels' operation:

1. *Exposure controls:* These are the user-settable parameters that control how bright or dark the image is.
2. *RGB response:* PixelSensor uses spectral response curves that are based on measurements of physical camera sensors to model the conversion of spectral radiance to tristimulus colors.
3. *White balance:* Cameras generally process the images they capture, including adjusting initial RGB values according to the color of illumination to model chromatic adaptation in the human visual system. Thus, captured images appear visually similar to what a human observer would remember having seen when taking a picture.

pbrt includes a realistic camera model as well as idealized models based on projection matrices. Because pinhole cameras have apertures with infinitesimal area, we make some pragmatic trade-offs in the implementation of the PixelSensor so that images rendered with pinhole models are not completely black. We leave it the Camera's responsibility to model the effect of the aperture size. The idealized models do not account for it at all, while the RealisticCamera does so in the ⟨*Compute weighting for* RealisticCamera *ray*⟩ fragment. The PixelSensor then only accounts for the shutter time and the ISO setting. These two factors are collected into a single quantity called the *imaging ratio*.

The PixelSensor constructor takes the sensor's RGB matching functions—$\bar{r}$, $\bar{g}$, and $\bar{b}$—and the imaging ratio as parameters. It also takes the color space requested by the user for the final output RGB values as well as the spectrum of an illuminant that specifies what color to consider to be white in the scene; together, these will make it possible to convert spectral energy to RGB as measured by the sensor and then to RGB in the output color space.

Figure 5.19 shows the effect of modeling camera response, comparing rendering a scene using the XYZ matching functions to compute initial pixel colors with rendering with the matching functions for an actual camera sensor.

⟨*PixelSensor Public Methods*⟩ ≡   **234**

```
    PixelSensor(Spectrum r, Spectrum g, Spectrum b,
          const RGBColorSpace *outputColorSpace, Spectrum sensorIllum,
          Float imagingRatio, Allocator alloc)
        : r_bar(r, alloc), g_bar(g, alloc), b_bar(b, alloc),
          imagingRatio(imagingRatio) {
        ⟨Compute XYZ from camera RGB matrix 236⟩
    }
```

⟨*PixelSensor Private Members*⟩ ≡   **234**

```
    DenselySampledSpectrum r_bar, g_bar, b_bar;
    Float imagingRatio;
```

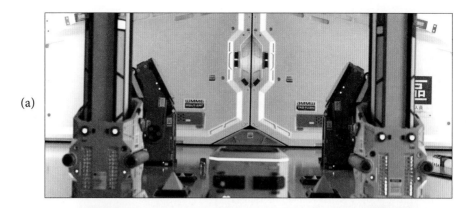

(a)

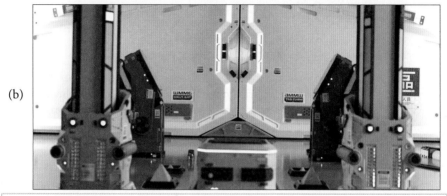

(b)

Figure 5.19: The Effect of Accurately Modeling Camera Sensor Response. (a) Scene rendered using the XYZ matching functions for the `PixelSensor`. (b) Scene rendered using measured sensor response curves for a Canon EOS 5D camera. Note that the color tones are slightly cooler—they have less orange and more blue to them. *(Scene courtesy of Beeple.)*

The RGB color space in which a sensor pixel records light is generally not the same as the RGB color space that the user has specified for the final image. The former is generally specific to a camera and is determined by the physical properties of its pixel color filters, and the latter is generally a device-independent color space like sRGB or one of the other color spaces described in Section 4.6.3. Therefore, the `PixelSensor` constructor computes a 3×3 matrix that converts from its RGB space to XYZ. From there, it is easy to convert to a particular output color space.

This matrix is found by solving an optimization problem. It starts with over twenty spectral distributions, representing the reflectance of patches with a variety of colors from a standardized color chart. The constructor computes the RGB colors of those patches under the camera's illuminant in the camera's color space as well as their XYZ colors under the illuminant of the output color space. If these colors are respectively denoted by column vectors, then we can consider the problem of finding a 3×3 matrix $\mathbf{M}$:

$$\mathbf{M} \begin{bmatrix} r_1 & r_2 & & r_n \\ g_1 & g_2 & \cdots & g_n \\ b_1 & b_2 & & b_n \end{bmatrix} \approx \begin{bmatrix} x_1 & x_2 & & x_n \\ y_1 & y_2 & \cdots & y_n \\ z_1 & z_2 & & z_n \end{bmatrix}. \tag{5.7}$$

As long as there are more than three reflectances, this is an over-constrained problem that can be solved using linear least squares.

⟨*Compute XYZ from camera RGB matrix*⟩ ≡   **234**
    ⟨*Compute* rgbCamera *values for training swatches* **236**⟩
    ⟨*Compute* xyzOutput *values for training swatches*⟩
    ⟨*Initialize* XYZFromSensorRGB *using linear least squares* **237**⟩

Given the sensor's illuminant, the work of computing the RGB coefficients for each reflectance is handled by the ProjectReflectance() method.

⟨*Compute* rgbCamera *values for training swatches*⟩ ≡   **236**
```
Float rgbCamera[nSwatchReflectances][3];
for (int i = 0; i < nSwatchReflectances; ++i) {
    RGB rgb = ProjectReflectance<RGB>(swatchReflectances[i], sensorIllum,
                            &r_bar, &g_bar, &b_bar);
    for (int c = 0; c < 3; ++c)
        rgbCamera[i][c] = rgb[c];
}
```

For good results, the spectra used for this optimization problem should present a good variety of representative real-world spectra. The ones used in pbrt are based on measurements of a standard color chart.[6]

⟨*PixelSensor Private Members*⟩ +≡   **234**
```
static constexpr int nSwatchReflectances = 24;
static Spectrum swatchReflectances[nSwatchReflectances];
```

The ProjectReflectance() utility method takes spectral distributions for a reflectance and an illuminant as well as three spectral matching functions $\bar{b}_i$ for a tristimulus color space. It returns a triplet of color coefficients c_i given by

$$c_i = \int r(\lambda)\, L(\lambda)\, \bar{b}_i(\lambda)\, d\lambda,$$

where r is the spectral reflectance function, L is the illuminant's spectral distribution, and $\bar{b}_i$ is a spectral matching function. Under the assumption that the second matching function $\bar{b}_2$ generally corresponds to luminance or at least something green, the color that causes the greatest response by the human visual system, the returned color triplet is normalized by $\int L(\lambda)\, \bar{b}_2(\lambda)\, d\lambda$. In this way, the linear least squares fit at least roughly weights each RGB/XYZ pair according to visual importance.

The ProjectReflectance() utility function takes the color space triplet type as a template parameter and is therefore able to return both RGB and XYZ values as appropriate. Its implementation follows the same general form as Spectrum::InnerProduct(), computing a Riemann sum over 1 nm spaced wavelengths, so it is not included here.

⟨*PixelSensor Private Methods*⟩ ≡   **234**
```
template <typename Triplet>
static Triplet ProjectReflectance(Spectrum r, Spectrum illum,
                        Spectrum b1, Spectrum b2, Spectrum b3);
```

The fragment that computes XYZ coefficients in the output color space, ⟨*Compute* xyzOutput *values for training swatches*⟩, is generally similar to the one for RGB, with the differences that

---

6   These reflectance measurements are courtesy of Danny Pascale and are used with permission.

it uses the output illuminant and the XYZ spectral matching functions and initializes the xyzOutput array. It is therefore also not included here.

Given the two matrices of color coefficients, a call to the LinearLeastSquares() function solves the optimization problem of Equation (5.7).

⟨*Initialize* XYZFromSensorRGB *using linear least squares*⟩ ≡   **236**
```
pstd::optional<SquareMatrix<3>> m =
    LinearLeastSquares(rgbCamera, xyzOutput, nSwatchReflectances);
if (!m) ErrorExit("Sensor XYZ from RGB matrix could not be solved.");
XYZFromSensorRGB = *m;
```

Because the RGB and XYZ colors are computed using the color spaces' respective illuminants, the matrix **M** also performs white balancing.

⟨*PixelSensor Public Members*⟩ ≡   **234**
```
SquareMatrix<3> XYZFromSensorRGB;
```

A second PixelSensor constructor uses XYZ matching functions for the pixel sensor's spectral response curves. If a specific camera sensor is not specified in the scene description file, this is the default. Note that with this usage, the member variables r_bar, g_bar, and b_bar are misnamed in that they are actually X, Y, and Z.

⟨*PixelSensor Public Methods*⟩ +≡   **234**
```
PixelSensor(const RGBColorSpace *outputColorSpace, Spectrum sensorIllum,
        Float imagingRatio, Allocator alloc)
    : r_bar(&Spectra::X(), alloc), g_bar(&Spectra::Y(), alloc),
      b_bar(&Spectra::Z(), alloc), imagingRatio(imagingRatio) {
    ⟨Compute white balancing matrix for XYZ PixelSensor 237⟩
}
```

By default, no white balancing is performed when PixelSensor converts to XYZ coefficients; that task is left for post-processing. However, if the user does specify a color temperature, white balancing is handled by the XYZFromSensorRGB matrix. (It is otherwise the identity matrix.) The WhiteBalance() function that computes this matrix will be described shortly; it takes the chromaticities of the white points of two color spaces and returns a matrix that maps the first to the second.

⟨*Compute white balancing matrix for XYZ PixelSensor*⟩ ≡   **237**
```
if (sensorIllum) {
    Point2f sourceWhite = SpectrumToXYZ(sensorIllum).xy();
    Point2f targetWhite = outputColorSpace->w;
    XYZFromSensorRGB = WhiteBalance(sourceWhite, targetWhite);
}
```

The main functionality provided by the PixelSensor is the ToSensorRGB() method, which converts a point-sampled spectral distribution $L(\lambda_i)$ in a SampledSpectrum to RGB coefficients in the sensor's color space. It does so via Monte Carlo evaluation of the sensor response integral, Equation (5.6), giving estimators of the form

$$r \approx \frac{1}{n} \sum_{i}^{n} \frac{L(\lambda_i)\,\bar{r}(\lambda_i)}{p(\lambda_i)}, \tag{5.8}$$

where n is equal to NSpectrumSamples. The associated PDF values are available from the SampledWavelengths and the sum over wavelengths and division by n is handled using

`SampledSpectrum::Average()`. These coefficients are scaled by the imaging ratio, which completes the conversion.

⟨*PixelSensor Public Methods*⟩ +≡   **234**
```
RGB ToSensorRGB(SampledSpectrum L,
                const SampledWavelengths &lambda) const {
    L = SafeDiv(L, lambda.PDF());
    return imagingRatio *
        RGB((r_bar.Sample(lambda) * L).Average(),
            (g_bar.Sample(lambda) * L).Average(),
            (b_bar.Sample(lambda) * L).Average());
}
```

Chromatic Adaptation and White Balance

One of the remarkable properties of the human visual system is that the color of objects is generally seen as the same, even under different lighting conditions; this effect is called *chromatic adaptation*. Cameras perform a similar function so that photographs capture the colors that the person taking the picture remembers seeing; in that context, this process is called *white balancing*.

pbrt provides a `WhiteBalance()` function that implements a white balancing algorithm called the *von Kries transform*. It takes two chromaticities: one is the chromaticity of the illumination and the other the chromaticity of the color white. (Recall the discussion in Section 4.6.3 of why white is not usually a constant spectrum but is instead defined as the color that humans perceive as white.) It returns a 3 × 3 matrix that applies the corresponding white balancing operation to XYZ colors.

⟨*White Balance Definitions*⟩ ≡
```
SquareMatrix<3> WhiteBalance(Point2f srcWhite, Point2f targetWhite) {
    ⟨Find LMS coefficients for source and target white 238⟩
    ⟨Return white balancing matrix for source and target white 239⟩
}
```

White balance with the von Kries transform is performed in the *LMS* color space, which is a color space where the responsivity of the three matching functions is specified to match the three types of cone in the human eye. By performing white balancing in the LMS space, we can model the effect of modulating the contribution of each type of cone in the eye, which is believed to be how chromatic adaptation is implemented in humans. After computing normalized XYZ colors corresponding to the provided chromaticities, the `LMSFromXYZ` matrix can be used to transform to LMS from XYZ.

⟨*Find LMS coefficients for source and target white*⟩ ≡   **238**
```
XYZ srcXYZ = XYZ::FromxyY(srcWhite), dstXYZ = XYZ::FromxyY(targetWhite);
auto srcLMS = LMSFromXYZ * srcXYZ, dstLMS = LMSFromXYZ * dstXYZ;
```

3 × 3 matrices that convert between LMS and XYZ are available as constants.

⟨*Color Space Constants*⟩ ≡
```
extern const SquareMatrix<3> LMSFromXYZ, XYZFromLMS;
```

Given a color in LMS space, white balancing is performed by dividing out the color of the scene's illuminant and then multiplying by the color of the desired illuminant, which can be represented by a diagonal matrix. The complete white balance matrix that operates on XYZ colors follows directly.

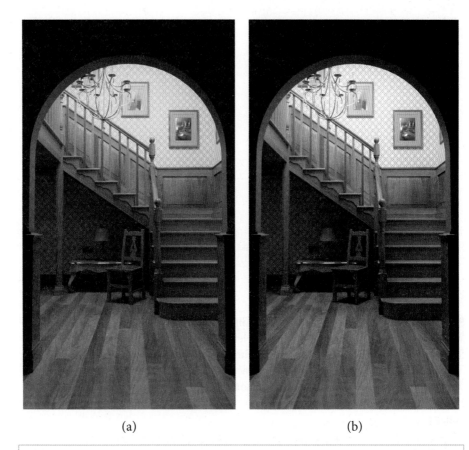

(a)   (b)

Figure 5.20: The Effect of White Balance. (a) Image of a scene with a yellow illuminant that has a similar spectral distribution to an incandescent light bulb. (b) White balanced image, using a color temperature of 3000 K. Due to chromatic adaptation, this image is much closer than (a) to what a human observer would perceive viewing this scene. *(Scene courtesy of Wig42 from Blend Swap, via Benedikt Bitterli.)*

⟨*Return white balancing matrix for source and target white*⟩ ≡   **238**
```
SquareMatrix<3> LMScorrect = SquareMatrix<3>::Diag(
    dstLMS[0] / srcLMS[0], dstLMS[1] / srcLMS[1], dstLMS[2] / srcLMS[2]);
return XYZFromLMS * LMScorrect * LMSFromXYZ;
```

Figure 5.20 shows an image rendered with a yellowish illuminant and the image after white balancing with the illuminant's chromaticity.

Sampling Sensor Response

Because the sensor response functions used by a PixelSensor describe the sensor's wavelength-dependent response to radiance, it is worth at least approximately accounting for their variation when sampling the wavelengths of light that a ray is to carry. At minimum, a wavelength where all of them are zero should never be chosen, as that wavelength will make no contribution to the final image. More generally, applying importance sampling according to the sensor response functions is desirable as it offers the possibility of reducing error in the estimates of Equation (5.8).

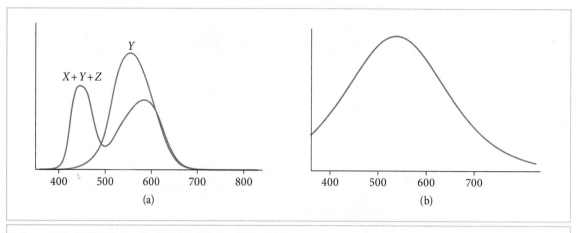

Figure 5.21: (a) Plot of normalized PDFs corresponding to the CIE Y matching function and the sum of the X, Y, and Z matching functions. (b) Plot of the parametric distribution $p_v(\lambda)$ from Equation (5.9).

However, choosing a distribution to use for sampling is challenging since the goal is minimizing error perceived by humans rather than strictly minimizing numeric error. Figure 5.21(a) shows the plots of both the CIE Y matching function and the sum of X, Y, and Z matching functions, both of which could be used. In practice, sampling according to Y alone gives excessive chromatic noise, but sampling by the sum of all three matching functions devotes too many samples to wavelengths between 400 nm and 500 nm, which are relatively unimportant visually.

A parametric probability distribution function that balances these concerns and works well for sampling the visible wavelengths is

$$p_v(\lambda) = \left(\int_{\lambda_{\min}}^{\lambda_{\max}} f(\lambda)\, d\lambda \right)^{-1} f(\lambda), \tag{5.9}$$

with

$$f(\lambda) = \frac{1}{\cosh^2(A(\lambda - B))},$$

$A = 0.0072 \text{ nm}^{-1}$, and $B = 538$ nm. Figure 5.21(b) shows a plot of $p_v(\lambda)$.

Our implementation samples over the wavelength range from 360 nm to 830 nm. The normalization constant that converts f into a PDF is precomputed.

⟨*Sampling Inline Functions*⟩ +≡
```
Float VisibleWavelengthsPDF(Float lambda) {
    if (lambda < 360 || lambda > 830)
        return 0;
    return 0.0039398042f / Sqr(std::cosh(0.0072f * (lambda - 538)));
}
```

Float 23

Sqr() 1034

The PDF can be sampled using the inversion method; the result is implemented in Sample VisibleWavelengths().

⟨*Sampling Inline Functions*⟩ +≡
```
Float SampleVisibleWavelengths(Float u) {
    return 538 - 138.888889f * std::atanh(0.85691062f - 1.82750197f * u);
}
```

We can now implement another sampling method in the `SampledWavelengths` class, `Sample Visible()`, which uses this technique.

⟨*SampledWavelengths Public Methods*⟩ +≡   173
```
static SampledWavelengths SampleVisible(Float u) {
    SampledWavelengths swl;
    for (int i = 0; i < NSpectrumSamples; ++i) {
        ⟨Compute up for i th wavelength sample 241⟩
        swl.lambda[i] = SampleVisibleWavelengths(up);
        swl.pdf[i] = VisibleWavelengthsPDF(swl.lambda[i]);
    }
    return swl;
}
```

Like `SampledWavelengths::SampleUniform()`, `SampleVisible()` uses a single random sample to generate all wavelength samples. It uses a slightly different approach, taking uniform steps across the [0, 1) sample space before sampling each wavelength.

⟨*Compute* up *for i th wavelength sample*⟩ ≡   241
```
Float up = u + Float(i) / NSpectrumSamples;
if (up > 1)
    up -= 1;
```

Using this distribution for sampling in place of a uniform distribution is worthwhile. Figure 5.22 shows two images of a scene, one rendered using uniform wavelength samples and the other rendered using `SampleVisible()`. Color noise is greatly reduced, with only a 1% increase in runtime.

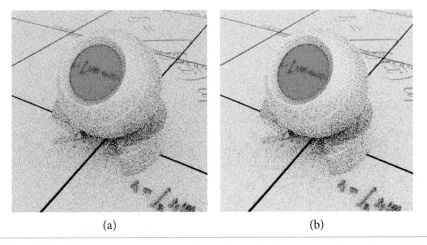

(a)   (b)

Figure 5.22: (a) Scene rendered with 4 samples per pixel, each with 4 wavelength samples, sampled uniformly over the visible range. (b) Rendered at the same sampling rates but instead sampling wavelengths using `SampledWavelengths::SampleVisible()`. This image has substantially less color noise, at a negligible cost in additional computation. *(Model courtesy of Yasutoshi Mori.)*

5.4.3 FILTERING IMAGE SAMPLES

The main responsibility of Film implementations is to aggregate multiple spectral samples at each pixel in order to compute a final value for it. In a physical camera, each pixel integrates light over a small area. Its response may have some spatial variation over that area that depends on the physical design of the sensor. In Chapter 8 we will consider this operation from the perspective of signal processing and will see that the details of where the image function is sampled and how those samples are weighted can significantly affect the final image quality.

Pending those details, for now we will assume that some filter function f is used to define the spatial variation in sensor response around each image pixel. These filter functions quickly go to zero, encoding the fact that pixels only respond to light close to them on the film. They also encode any further spatial variation in the pixel's response. With this approach, if we have an image function $r(x, y)$ that gives the red color at an arbitrary position on the film (e.g., as measured using a sensor response function $\bar{r}(\lambda)$ with Equation (5.6)), then the filtered red value r_f at a position (x, y) is given by

$$r_f(x, y) = \int f(x - x', y - y')\, r(x', y')\, dx'\, dy', \qquad \text{(5.10)}$$

where the filter function f is assumed to integrate to 1.

As usual, we will estimate this integral using point samples of the image function. The estimator is

$$r_f(x, y) \approx \frac{1}{n} \sum_i^n \frac{f(x - x_i, y - y_i)\, r(x_i, y_i)}{p(x_i, y_i)}. \qquad \text{(5.11)}$$

Two approaches have been used in graphics to sample the integrand. The first, which was used in all three previous versions of pbrt, is to sample the image uniformly. Each image sample may then contribute to multiple pixels' final values, depending on the extent of the filter function being used. This approach gives the estimator

$$r_f(x, y) \approx \frac{A}{n} \sum_i^n f(x - x_i, y - y_i)\, r(x_i, y_i), \qquad \text{(5.12)}$$

where A is the film area. Figure 5.23 illustrates the approach; it shows a pixel at location (x, y) that has a pixel filter with extent radius.x in the x direction and radius.y in the y direction. All the samples at positions (x_i, y_i) inside the box given by the filter extent may contribute to the pixel's value, depending on the filter function's value for $f(x - x_i, y - y_i)$.

While Equation (5.12) gives an unbiased estimate of the pixel value, variation in the filter function leads to variance in the estimates. Consider the case of a constant image function r: in that case, we would expect the resulting image pixels to all be exactly equal to r. However, the sum of filter values $f(x - x_i, y - y_i)$ will not generally be equal to 1: it only equals 1 in expectation. Thus, the image will include noise, even in this simple setting. If the alternative estimator

$$r_f(x, y) \approx \frac{\sum_i f(x - x_i, y - y_i)\, r(x_i, y_i)}{\sum_i f(x - x_i, y - y_i)}$$

is used instead, that variance is eliminated at the cost of a small amount of bias. (This is the *weighted importance sampling* Monte Carlo estimator.) In practice, this trade-off is worthwhile.

Film 244

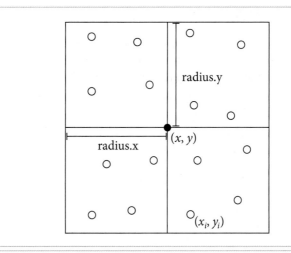

Figure 5.23: 2D Image Filtering. To compute a filtered pixel value for the pixel marked with a filled circle located at (x, y), all the image samples inside the box around (x, y) with extent `radius.x` and `radius.y` need to be considered. Each of the image samples (x_i, y_i), denoted by open circles, is weighted by a 2D filter function, $f(x - x_i, y - y_i)$. The weighted average of all samples is the final pixel value.

Equation (5.10) can also be estimated independently at each pixel. This is the approach used in this version of pbrt. In this case, it is worthwhile to sample points on the film using a distribution based on the filter function. This approach is known as *filter importance sampling*. With it, the spatial variation of the filter is accounted for purely via the distribution of sample locations for a pixel rather than scaling each sample's contribution according to the filter's value.

If $p \propto f$, then those two factors cancel in Equation (5.11) and we are left with an average of the $r(x_i, y_i)$ sample values scaled by the constant of proportionality. However, here we must handle the rare (for rendering) case of estimating an integral that may be negative: as we will see in Chapter 8, filter functions that are partially negative can give better results than those that are nonnegative. In that case, we have $p \propto |f|$, which gives

$$r_{\mathrm{f}}(x, y) \approx \left(\int |f(x', y')| \, dx' \, dy' \right) \left(\frac{1}{n} \sum_i^n \operatorname{sign}(f(x - x_i, y - y_i)) \, r(x_i, y_i) \right),$$

where $\operatorname{sign}(x)$ is 1 if $x > 0$, 0 if it is 0, and -1 otherwise. However, this estimator has the same problem as Equation (5.12): even with a constant function r, the estimates will have variance depending on how many of the sign function evaluations give 1 and how many give -1.

Therefore, this version of pbrt continues to use the weighted importance sampling estimator, computing pixel values as

$$r_{\mathrm{f}}(x, y) \approx \frac{\sum_i w(x - x_i, y - y_i) \, r(x_i, y_i)}{\sum_i w(x - x_i, y - y_i)} \tag{5.13}$$

with $w(x, y) = f(x, y)/p(x, y)$.

The first of these two approaches has the advantage that each image sample can contribute to multiple pixels' final filtered values. This can be beneficial for rendering efficiency, as all the computation involved in computing the radiance for an image sample can be used to improve the accuracy of multiple pixels. However, using samples generated for other pixels is not always helpful: some of the sample generation algorithms implemented in Chapter 8 carefully position samples in ways that ensure good coverage of the sampling domain in a pixel. If samples from other pixels are mixed in with those, the full set of samples for a pixel may no longer have that same structure, which in turn can increase error. By not sharing samples across pixels, filter importance sampling does not have this problem.

Filter importance sampling has further advantages. It makes parallel rendering easier: if the renderer is parallelized in a way that has different threads working on different pixels, there is never a chance that multiple threads will need to concurrently modify the same pixel's value. A final advantage is that if there are any samples that are much brighter than the others due to a variance spike from a poorly sampled integrand, then those samples only contribute to a single pixel, rather than being smeared over multiple pixels. It is easier to fix up the resulting single-pixel artifacts than a neighborhood of them that have been affected by such a sample.

5.4.4 THE FILM INTERFACE

With the foundations of sensor response and pixel sample filtering established, we can introduce the Film interface. It is defined in the file base/film.h.

⟨*Film Definition*⟩ ≡
```
class Film : public TaggedPointer<RGBFilm, GBufferFilm, SpectralFilm> {
  public:
    ⟨Film Interface 244⟩
};
```

SpectralFilm, which is not described here, records spectral images over a specified wavelength range that is discretized into non-overlapping ranges. See the documentation of pbrt's file format for more information about the SpectralFilm's use.

Samples can be provided to the film in two ways. The first is from the Sampler selecting points on the film at which the Integrator estimates the radiance. These samples are provided to the Film via the AddSample() method, which takes the following parameters:

- The sample's pixel coordinates, pFilm.
- The spectral radiance of the sample, L.
- The sample's wavelengths, lambda.
- An optional VisibleSurface that describes the geometry at the first visible point along the sample's camera ray.
- A weight for the sample to use in computing Equation (5.13) that is returned by Filter::Sample().

Film implementations can assume that multiple threads will not call AddSample() concurrently with the same pFilm location (though they should assume that threads will call it concurrently with different ones). Therefore, it is not necessary to worry about mutual exclusion in this method's implementation unless some data that is not unique to a pixel is modified.

⟨*Film Interface*⟩ ≡   244
```
void AddSample(Point2i pFilm, SampledSpectrum L,
    const SampledWavelengths &lambda,
    const VisibleSurface *visibleSurface, Float weight);
```

The Film interface also includes a method that returns a bounding box of all the samples that may be generated. Note that this is different than the bounding box of the image pixels in the common case that the pixel filter extents are wider than a pixel.

⟨*Film Interface*⟩ +≡   **244**
   Bounds2f SampleBounds() const;

VisibleSurface holds an assortment of information about a point on a surface.

⟨*VisibleSurface Definition*⟩ ≡
   class VisibleSurface {
   public:
      ⟨*VisibleSurface Public Methods* **245**⟩
      ⟨*VisibleSurface Public Members* **245**⟩
   };

In addition to the point, normal, shading normal, and time, VisibleSurface stores the partial derivatives of depth at each pixel, $\partial z/\partial x$ and $\partial z/\partial y$, where x and y are in raster space and z in camera space. These values are useful in image denoising algorithms, since they make it possible to test whether the surfaces in adjacent pixels are coplanar. The surface's albedo is its spectral distribution of reflected light under uniform illumination; this quantity can be useful for separating texture from illumination before denoising.

⟨*VisibleSurface Public Members*⟩ ≡   **245**
   Point3f p;
   Normal3f n, ns;
   Point2f uv;
   Float time = 0;
   Vector3f dpdx, dpdy;
   SampledSpectrum albedo;

We will not include the VisibleSurface constructor here, as its main function is to copy appropriate values from the SurfaceInteraction into its member variables.

⟨*VisibleSurface Public Methods*⟩ ≡   **245**
   VisibleSurface(const SurfaceInteraction &si, SampledSpectrum albedo,
           const SampledWavelengths &lambda);

The set member variable indicates whether a VisibleSurface has been initialized.

⟨*VisibleSurface Public Members*⟩ +≡   **245**
   bool set = false;

⟨*VisibleSurface Public Methods*⟩ +≡   **245**
   operator bool() const { return set; }

Film implementations can indicate whether they use the VisibleSurface * passed to their AddSample() method via UsesVisibleSurface(). Providing this information allows integrators to skip the expense of initializing a VisibleSurface if it will not be used.

⟨*Film Interface*⟩ +≡   **244**
   bool UsesVisibleSurface() const;

Light transport algorithms that sample paths starting from the light sources (such as bidirectional path tracing) require the ability to "splat" contributions to arbitrary pixels. Rather than computing the final pixel value as a weighted average of contributing splats, splats are simply summed. Generally, the more splats that are around a given pixel, the brighter the pixel will be. AddSplat() splats the provided value at the given location in the image.

In contrast to AddSample(), this method may be called concurrently by multiple threads that end up updating the same pixel. Therefore, Film implementations must either implement some form of mutual exclusion or use atomic operations in their implementations of this method.

⟨*Film Interface*⟩ +≡   244
```
    void AddSplat(Point2f p, SampledSpectrum v,
                  const SampledWavelengths &lambda);
```

Film implementations must also provide a SampleWavelengths() method that samples from the range of wavelengths that the film's sensor responds to (e.g., using SampledWavelengths::SampleVisible()).

⟨*Film Interface*⟩ +≡   244
```
    SampledWavelengths SampleWavelengths(Float u) const;
```

In addition, they must provide a handful of methods that give the extent of the image and the diagonal length of its sensor, measured in meters.

⟨*Film Interface*⟩ +≡   244
```
    Point2i FullResolution() const;
    Bounds2i PixelBounds() const;
    Float Diagonal() const;
```

A call to the Film::WriteImage() method directs the film to do the processing necessary to generate the final image and store it in a file. In addition to the camera transform, this method takes a scale factor that is applied to the samples provided to the AddSplat() method.

⟨*Film Interface*⟩ +≡   244
```
    void WriteImage(ImageMetadata metadata, Float splatScale = 1);
```

The ToOutputRGB() method allows callers to find the output RGB value that results for given spectral radiance samples from applying the PixelSensor's model, performing white balancing, and then converting to the output color space. (This method is used by the SPPMIntegrator included in the online edition, which has requirements that cause it to maintain the final image itself rather than using a Film implementation.)

⟨*Film Interface*⟩ +≡   244
```
    RGB ToOutputRGB(SampledSpectrum L, const SampledWavelengths &lambda) const;
```

A caller can also request the entire image to be returned, as well as the RGB value for a single pixel. The latter method is used for displaying in-progress images during rendering.

⟨*Film Interface*⟩ +≡   244
```
    Image GetImage(ImageMetadata *metadata, Float splatScale = 1);
    RGB GetPixelRGB(Point2i p, Float splatScale = 1) const;
```

Finally, Film implementations must provide access to a few additional values for use in other parts of the system.

⟨*Film Interface*⟩ +≡   244
```
    Filter GetFilter() const;
    const PixelSensor *GetPixelSensor() const;
    std::string GetFilename() const;
```

5.4.5 COMMON FILM FUNCTIONALITY

As we did with `CameraBase` for `Camera` implementations, we have written a `FilmBase` class that `Film` implementations can inherit from. It collects commonly used member variables and is able to provide a few of the methods required by the `Film` interface.

⟨*FilmBase Definition*⟩ ≡
```
class FilmBase {
  public:
    ⟨FilmBase Public Methods 247⟩
  protected:
    ⟨FilmBase Protected Members 247⟩
};
```

The `FilmBase` constructor takes a number of values: the overall resolution of the image in pixels; a bounding box that may specify a subset of the full image; a filter function; a `PixelSensor`; the length of the diagonal of the film's physical area; and the filename for the output image. These are all bundled up into a small structure in order to shorten the parameter lists of forthcoming constructors.

⟨*FilmBaseParameters Definition*⟩ ≡
```
struct FilmBaseParameters {
    Point2i fullResolution;
    Bounds2i pixelBounds;
    Filter filter;
    Float diagonal;
    const PixelSensor *sensor;
    std::string filename;
};
```

The `FilmBase` constructor then just copies the various values from the parameter structure, converting the film diagonal length from millimeters (as specified in scene description files) to meters, the unit used for measuring distance in pbrt.

⟨*FilmBase Public Methods*⟩ ≡   247
```
FilmBase(FilmBaseParameters p)
    : fullResolution(p.fullResolution), pixelBounds(p.pixelBounds),
      filter(p.filter), diagonal(p.diagonal * .001f), sensor(p.sensor),
      filename(p.filename) {
}
```

⟨*FilmBase Protected Members*⟩ ≡   247
```
Point2i fullResolution;
Bounds2i pixelBounds;
Filter filter;
Float diagonal;
const PixelSensor *sensor;
std::string filename;
```

Having these values makes it possible to immediately implement a number of the methods required by the `Film` interface.

⟨*FilmBase Public Methods*⟩ +≡   **247**

```
Point2i FullResolution() const { return fullResolution; }
Bounds2i PixelBounds() const { return pixelBounds; }
Float Diagonal() const { return diagonal; }
Filter GetFilter() const { return filter; }
const PixelSensor *GetPixelSensor() const { return sensor; }
std::string GetFilename() const { return filename; }
```

An implementation of SampleWavelengths() samples according to the distribution in Equation (5.9).

⟨*FilmBase Public Methods*⟩ +≡   **247**

```
SampledWavelengths SampleWavelengths(Float u) const {
    return SampledWavelengths::SampleVisible(u);
}
```

The Film::SampleBounds() method can also be easily implemented, given the Filter. Computing the sample bounds involves both expanding by the filter radius and accounting for half-pixel offsets that come from the conventions used in pbrt for pixel coordinates; these are explained in more detail in Section 8.1.4.

⟨*FilmBase Method Definitions*⟩ ≡

```
Bounds2f FilmBase::SampleBounds() const {
    Vector2f radius = filter.Radius();
    return Bounds2f(pixelBounds.pMin - radius + Vector2f(0.5f, 0.5f),
                    pixelBounds.pMax + radius - Vector2f(0.5f, 0.5f));
}
```

5.4.6 RGBFilm

RGBFilm records an image represented by RGB color.

⟨*RGBFilm Definition*⟩ ≡

```
class RGBFilm : public FilmBase {
  public:
    ⟨RGBFilm Public Methods 249⟩
  private:
    ⟨RGBFilm::Pixel Definition 249⟩
    ⟨RGBFilm Private Members 249⟩
};
```

In addition to the parameters that are passed along to FilmBase, RGBFilm takes a color space to use for the output image, a parameter that allows specifying the maximum value of an RGB color component, and a parameter that controls the floating-point precision in the output image.

⟨*RGBFilm Method Definitions*⟩ ≡

```
RGBFilm::RGBFilm(FilmBaseParameters p, const RGBColorSpace *colorSpace,
                 Float maxComponentValue, bool writeFP16, Allocator alloc)
    : FilmBase(p), pixels(p.pixelBounds, alloc), colorSpace(colorSpace),
      maxComponentValue(maxComponentValue), writeFP16(writeFP16) {
    filterIntegral = filter.Integral();
    ⟨Compute outputRGBFromSensorRGB matrix 249⟩
}
```

The integral of the filter function will be useful to normalize the filter values used for samples provided via AddSplat(), so it is cached in a member variable.

⟨*RGBFilm Private Members*⟩ ≡   248
```
const RGBColorSpace *colorSpace;
Float maxComponentValue;
bool writeFP16;
Float filterIntegral;
```

The color space for the final image is given by a user-specified RGBColorSpace that is unlikely to be the same as the sensor's RGB color space. The constructor therefore computes a 3 × 3 matrix that transforms sensor RGB values to the output color space.

⟨*Compute* outputRGBFromSensorRGB *matrix*⟩ ≡   248
```
outputRGBFromSensorRGB = colorSpace->RGBFromXYZ *
    sensor->XYZFromSensorRGB;
```

⟨*RGBFilm Private Members*⟩ +≡   248
```
SquareMatrix<3> outputRGBFromSensorRGB;
```

Given the pixel resolution of the (possibly cropped) image, the constructor allocates a 2D array of Pixel structures, with one for each pixel. The running weighted sums of pixel contributions are represented using RGB colors in the rgbSum member variable. weightSum holds the sum of filter weight values for the sample contributions to the pixel. These respectively correspond to the numerator and denominator in Equation (5.13). Finally, rgbSplat holds an (unweighted) sum of sample splats.

Double-precision floating point is used for all of these quantities. Single-precision floats are almost always sufficient, but when used for reference images rendered with high sample counts they may have insufficient precision to accurately store their associated sums. Although it is rare for this error to be visually evident, it can cause problems with reference images that are used to evaluate the error of Monte Carlo sampling algorithms.

Figure 5.24 shows an example of this problem. We rendered a reference image of a test scene using 4 million samples in each pixel, using both 32-bit and 64-bit floating-point values for the RGBFilm pixel values. We then plotted mean squared error (MSE) as a function of sample count. For an unbiased Monte Carlo estimator, MSE is $O(1/n)$ in the number of samples taken n; on a log–log plot, it should be a straight line with slope -1. However, we can see that for $n > 1000$ with a 32-bit float reference image, the reduction in MSE seems to flatten out—more samples do not seem to reduce error. With 64-bit floats, the curve maintains its expected path.

⟨*RGBFilm::Pixel Definition*⟩ ≡   248
```
struct Pixel {
    double rgbSum[3] = {0., 0., 0.};
    double weightSum = 0.;
    AtomicDouble rgbSplat[3];
};
```

⟨*RGBFilm Private Members*⟩ +≡   248
```
Array2D<Pixel> pixels;
```

The RGBFilm does not use the VisibleSurface * passed to AddSample().

⟨*RGBFilm Public Methods*⟩ ≡   248
```
bool UsesVisibleSurface() const { return false; }
```

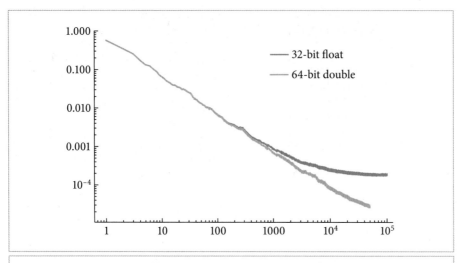

Figure 5.24: Mean Squared Error as a Function of Sample Count. When rendering a scene using an unbiased Monte Carlo estimator, we expect MSE to be related to the number of samples n by $O(1/n)$. With a log–log plot, this rate corresponds to a straight line with slope -1. For the test scene considered here, we can see that using 32-bit `float`s for the reference image causes reported error to inaccurately stop decreasing after 1,000 or so samples.

`AddSample()` converts spectral radiance to sensor RGB before updating the `Pixel` corresponding to the point `pFilm`.

⟨*RGBFilm Public Methods*⟩ +≡   **248**
```
void AddSample(Point2i pFilm, SampledSpectrum L,
        const SampledWavelengths &lambda,
        const VisibleSurface *, Float weight) {
    ⟨Convert sample radiance to PixelSensor RGB 250⟩
    ⟨Optionally clamp sensor RGB value 251⟩
    ⟨Update pixel values with filtered sample contribution 251⟩
}
```

The radiance value is first converted to RGB by the sensor.

⟨*Convert sample radiance to* `PixelSensor` *RGB*⟩ ≡   **250, 252**
```
RGB rgb = sensor->ToSensorRGB(L, lambda);
```

Images rendered with Monte Carlo integration can exhibit bright spikes of noise in pixels where the sampling distributions that were used do not match the integrand well such that when $f(x)/p(x)$ is computed in the Monte Carlo estimator, $f(x)$ is very large and $p(x)$ is very small. (Such pixels are colloquially called "fireflies.") Many additional samples may be required to get an accurate estimate for that pixel.

A widely used technique to reduce the effect of fireflies is to clamp all sample contributions to some maximum amount. Doing so introduces error: energy is lost, and the image is no longer an unbiased estimate of the true image. However, when the aesthetics of rendered images are more important than their mathematics, this can be a useful remedy. Figure 5.25 shows an example of its use.

The `RGBFilm`'s `maxComponentValue` parameter can be set to a threshold that is used for clamping. It is infinite by default, and no clamping is performed.

(a)

(b)

Figure 5.25: Image with High Variance in Some Pixels. This scene suffers from variance spikes in pixels due to difficult-to-sample light paths that occasionally intersect the sun. (a) Image rendered normally. (b) Image rendered with clamping, where pixel sample RGB values are clamped to have values no larger than 10. The image looks much better with clamping, though at a cost of some loss of energy. *(Model courtesy of Yasutoshi Mori.)*

⟨*Optionally clamp sensor RGB value*⟩ ≡   **250, 252**
```
Float m = std::max({rgb.r, rgb.g, rgb.b});
if (m > maxComponentValue)
    rgb *= maxComponentValue / m;
```

Float 23

RGBFilm::maxComponentValue 249

RGBFilm::Pixel::rgbSum 249

RGBFilm::Pixel::weightSum 249

RGBFilm::pixels 249

Given the possibly clamped RGB value, the pixel it lies in can be updated by adding its contributions to the running sums of the numerator and denominator of Equation (5.13).

⟨*Update pixel values with filtered sample contribution*⟩ ≡   **250**
```
Pixel &pixel = pixels[pFilm];
for (int c = 0; c < 3; ++c)
    pixel.rgbSum[c] += weight * rgb[c];
pixel.weightSum += weight;
```

The AddSplat() method first reuses the first two fragments from AddSample() to compute the RGB value of the provided radiance L.

⟨*RGBFilm Method Definitions*⟩ +≡
```
    void RGBFilm::AddSplat(Point2f p, SampledSpectrum L,
                           const SampledWavelengths &lambda) {
        ⟨Convert sample radiance to PixelSensor RGB 250⟩
        ⟨Optionally clamp sensor RGB value 251⟩
        ⟨Compute bounds of affected pixels for splat, splatBounds 252⟩
        for (Point2i pi : splatBounds) {
            ⟨Evaluate filter at pi and add splat contribution 252⟩
        }
    }
```

Because splatted contributions are not a result of pixel samples but are points in the scene that are projected onto the film plane, it is necessary to consider their contribution to multiple pixels, since each pixel's reconstruction filter generally extends out to include contributions from nearby pixels.

First, a bounding box of potentially affected pixels is found using the filter's radius. See Section 8.1.4, which explains the conventions for indexing into pixels in pbrt and, in particular, the addition of (0.5, 0.5) to the pixel coordinate here.

⟨*Compute bounds of affected pixels for splat*, splatBounds⟩ ≡   252
```
    Point2f pDiscrete = p + Vector2f(0.5, 0.5);
    Vector2f radius = filter.Radius();
    Bounds2i splatBounds(Point2i(Floor(pDiscrete - radius)),
                         Point2i(Floor(pDiscrete + radius)) + Vector2i(1, 1));
    splatBounds = Intersect(splatBounds, pixelBounds);
```

If the filter weight is nonzero, the splat's weighted contribution is added. Unlike with AddSample(), no sum of filter weights is maintained; normalization is handled later using the filter's integral, as per Equation (5.10).

⟨*Evaluate filter at* pi *and add splat contribution*⟩ ≡   252
```
    Float wt = filter.Evaluate(Point2f(p - pi - Vector2f(0.5, 0.5)));
    if (wt != 0) {
        Pixel &pixel = pixels[pi];
        for (int i = 0; i < 3; ++i)
            pixel.rgbSplat[i].Add(wt * rgb[i]);
    }
```

GetPixelRGB() returns the final RGB value for a given pixel in the RGBFilm's output color space.

⟨*RGBFilm Public Methods*⟩ +≡   248
```
    RGB GetPixelRGB(Point2i p, Float splatScale = 1) const {
        const Pixel &pixel = pixels[p];
        RGB rgb(pixel.rgbSum[0], pixel.rgbSum[1], pixel.rgbSum[2]);
        ⟨Normalize rgb with weight sum 253⟩
        ⟨Add splat value at pixel 253⟩
        ⟨Convert rgb to output RGB color space 253⟩
        return rgb;
    }
```

First, the final pixel contribution from the values provided by AddSample() is computed via Equation (5.13).

⟨*Normalize* rgb *with weight sum*⟩ ≡   **252**
```
Float weightSum = pixel.weightSum;
if (weightSum != 0)
    rgb /= weightSum;
```

Then Equation (5.10) can be applied to incorporate any splatted values.

⟨*Add splat value at pixel*⟩ ≡   **252**
```
for (int c = 0; c < 3; ++c)
    rgb[c] += splatScale * pixel.rgbSplat[c] / filterIntegral;
```

Finally, the color conversion matrix brings the RGB value into the output color space.

⟨*Convert* rgb *to output RGB color space*⟩ ≡   **252**
```
rgb = outputRGBFromSensorRGB * rgb;
```

ToOutputRGB()'s implementation first uses the sensor to compute a sensor RGB and then converts to the output color space.

⟨*RGBFilm Public Methods*⟩ +≡   **248**
```
RGB ToOutputRGB(SampledSpectrum L, const SampledWavelengths &lambda) const {
    RGB sensorRGB = sensor->ToSensorRGB(L, lambda);
    return outputRGBFromSensorRGB * sensorRGB;
}
```

We will not include the straightforward RGBFilm WriteImage() or GetImage() method implementations in the book. The former calls GetImage() before calling Image::Write(), and the latter fills in an image using GetPixelRGB() to get each pixel's value.

5.4.7 GBufferFilm

The GBufferFilm stores not only RGB at each pixel, but also additional information about the geometry at the first visible intersection point. This additional information is useful for a variety of applications, ranging from image denoising algorithms to providing training data for machine learning applications.

⟨*GBufferFilm Definition*⟩ ≡
```
class GBufferFilm : public FilmBase {
  public:
    ⟨GBufferFilm Public Methods⟩
  private:
    ⟨GBufferFilm::Pixel Definition 254⟩
    ⟨GBufferFilm Private Members⟩
};
```

We will not include any of the GBufferFilm implementation other than its Pixel structure, which augments the one used in RGBFilm with additional fields that store geometric information. It also stores estimates of the variance of the red, green, and blue color values at each pixel using the VarianceEstimator class, which is defined in Section B.2.11. The rest of the implementation is a straightforward generalization of RGBFilm that also updates these additional values.

⟨*GBufferFilm::Pixel Definition*⟩ ≡   **253**
```
struct Pixel {
    double rgbSum[3] = {0., 0., 0.};
    double weightSum = 0., gBufferWeightSum = 0.;
    AtomicDouble rgbSplat[3];
    Point3f pSum;
    Float dzdxSum = 0, dzdySum = 0;
    Normal3f nSum, nsSum;
    Point2f uvSum;
    double rgbAlbedoSum[3] = {0., 0., 0.};
    VarianceEstimator<Float> rgbVariance[3];
};
```

FURTHER READING

In his seminal *Sketchpad* system, Sutherland (1963) was the first to use projection matrices for computer graphics. Akenine-Möller et al. (2018) have provided a particularly well-written derivation of the orthographic and perspective projection matrices. Other good references for projections are Rogers and Adams's *Mathematical Elements for Computer Graphics* (1990) and Eberly's book (2001) on game engine design. See Adams and Levoy (2007) for a broad analysis of the types of radiance measurements that can be taken with cameras that have non-pinhole apertures.

An unusual projection method was used by Greene and Heckbert (1986) for generating images for OMNIMAX® theaters.

Potmesil and Chakravarty (1981, 1982, 1983) did early work on depth of field and motion blur in computer graphics. Cook and collaborators developed a more accurate model for these effects based on the thin lens model; this is the approach used for the depth of field calculations in Section 5.2.3 (Cook et al. 1984; Cook 1986). An alternative approach to motion blur was described by Gribel and Akenine-Möller (2017), who analytically computed the time ranges of ray–triangle intersections to eliminate stochastic sampling in time.

Kolb, Mitchell, and Hanrahan (1995) showed how to simulate complex camera lens systems with ray tracing in order to model the imaging effects of real cameras; the RealisticCamera is based on their approach. Steinert et al. (2011) improved a number of details of this simulation, incorporating wavelength-dependent effects and accounting for both diffraction and glare. Joo et al. (2016) extended this approach to handle aspheric lenses and modeled diffraction at the aperture stop, which causes some brightening at the edges of the circle of confusion in practice. See the books by Hecht (2002) and Smith (2007) for excellent introductions to optics and lens systems.

Hullin et al. (2012) used polynomials to model the effect of lenses on rays passing through them; they were able to construct polynomials that approximate entire lens systems from polynomial approximations of individual lenses. This approach saves the computational expense of tracing rays through lenses, though for complex scenes, this cost is generally negligible in relation to the rest of the rendering computations. Hanika and Dachsbacher (2014) improved the accuracy of this approach and showed how to combine it with bidirectional path tracing. Schrade et al. (2016) showed good results with approximation of wide-angle lenses using sparse higher-degree polynomials.

AtomicDouble 1100
Float 23
Normal3f 94
Point2f 92
Point3f 92
RGBFilm 248
VarianceEstimator 1048

Film and Imaging

The film sensor model presented in Section 5.4.2 and the `PixelSensor` class implementation are from the *PhysLight* system described by Langlands and Fascione (2020). See also Chen et al. (2009), who described the implementation of a fairly complete simulation of a digital camera, including the analog-to-digital conversion and noise in the measured pixel values inherent in this process.

Filter importance sampling, as described in Section 8.8, was described in a paper by Ernst et al. (2006). This technique is also proposed in Shirley's Ph.D. thesis (1990).

The idea of storing additional information about the properties of the visible surface in a pixel was introduced by Perlin (1985a) and Saito and Takahashi (1990), who also coined the term *G-Buffer*. Shade et al. (1998) introduced the generalization of storing information about all the surfaces along each camera ray and applied this representation to view interpolation, using the originally hidden surfaces to handle disocclusion.

Celarek et al. (2019) developed techniques for evaluating sampling schemes based on computing both the expectation and variance of MSE and described approaches for evaluating error in rendered images across both pixels and frequencies.

The sampling technique that approximates the XYZ matching curves is due to Radziszewski et al. (2009).

The `SpectralFilm` uses a representation for spectral images in the OpenEXR format that was introduced by Fichet et al. (2021).

As discussed in Section 5.4.2, the human visual system generally factors out the illumination color to perceive surfaces' colors independently of it. A number of methods have been developed to process photographs to perform white balancing to eliminate the tinge of light source colors; see Gijsenij et al. (2011) for a survey. White balancing photographs can be challenging, since the only information available to white balancing algorithms is the final pixel values. In a renderer, the problem is easier, as information about the light sources is directly available; Wilkie and Weidlich (2009) developed an efficient method to perform accurate white balancing in a renderer.

Denoising

A wide range of approaches have been developed for removing Monte Carlo noise from rendered images. Here we will discuss those that are based on the statistical characteristics of the sample values themselves. In the "Further Reading" section of Chapter 8, we will discuss ones that derive filters that account for the underlying light transport equations used to form the image. Zwicker et al.'s report (2015) has thorough coverage of both approaches to denoising through 2015. We will therefore focus here on some of the foundational work as well as more recent developments.

Lee and Redner (1990) suggested using an alpha-trimmed mean filter for this task; it discards some number of samples at the low and high range of the sample values. The median filter, where all but a single sample are discarded, is a special case of it. Jensen and Christensen (1995) observed that it can be effective to separate out the contributions to pixel values based on the type of illumination they represent; low-frequency indirect illumination can be filtered differently from high-frequency direct illumination, thus reducing noise in the final image. They developed an effective filtering technique based on this observation.

PixelSensor 234

SpectralFilm 244

McCool (1999) used the depth, surface normal, and color at each pixel to determine how to blend pixel values with their neighbors in order to better preserve edges in the filtered image. Keller and collaborators introduced the *discontinuity buffer* (Keller 1998; Wald et al. 2002).

In addition to filtering slowly varying quantities like indirect illumination separately from more quickly varying quantities like surface reflectance, the discontinuity buffer also uses geometric quantities like the surface normal to determine filter extents.

Dammertz et al. (2010) introduced a denoising algorithm based on edge-aware image filtering, applied hierarchically so that very wide kernels can be used with good performance. This approach was improved by Schied et al. (2017), who used estimates of variance at each pixel to set filter widths and incorporated temporal reuse, using filtered results from the previous frame in a real-time ray tracer. Bitterli et al. (2016) analyzed a variety of previous denoising techniques in a unified framework and derived a new approach based on a first-order regression of pixel values. Boughida and Boubekeur (2017) described a Bayesian approach based on statistics of all the samples in a pixel, and Vicini et al. (2019) considered the problem of denoising "deep" images, where each pixel may contain multiple color values, each at a different depth.

Some filtering techniques focus solely on the outlier pixels that result when the sampling probability in the Monte Carlo estimator is a poor match to the integrand and is far too small for a sample. (As mentioned previously, the resulting pixels are sometimes called "fireflies," in a nod to their bright transience.) Rushmeier and Ward (1994) developed an early technique to address this issue based on detecting outlier pixels and spreading their energy to nearby pixels in order to maintain an unbiased estimate of the true image. DeCoro et al. (2010) suggested storing all pixel sample values and then rejecting outliers before filtering them to compute final pixel values. Zirr et al. (2018) proposed an improved approach that uses the distribution of sample values at each pixel to detect and reweight outlier samples. Notably, their approach does not need to store all the individual samples, but can be implemented by partitioning samples into one of a small number of image buffers based on their magnitude. More recently, Buisine et al. (2021) proposed using a median of means filter, which is effective at removing outliers but has slower convergence than the mean. They therefore dynamically select between the mean and median of means depending on the characteristics of the sample values.

As with many other areas of image processing and understanding, techniques based on machine learning have recently been applied to denoising rendered images. This work started with Kalantari et al. (2015), who used relatively small neural networks to determine parameters for conventional denoising filters. Approaches based on deep learning and convolutional neural networks soon followed with Bako et al. (2017), Chaitanya et al. (2017), and Vogels et al. (2018) developing autoencoders based on the u-net architecture (Ronneberger et al. 2015). Xu et al. (2019) applied adversarial networks to improve the training of such denoisers. Gharbi et al. (2019) showed that filtering the individual samples with a neural network can give much better results than sampling the pixels with the samples already averaged. Munkberg and Hasselgren (2020) described an architecture that reduces the memory and computation required for this approach.

EXERCISES

⊘ 5.1   Some types of cameras expose the film by sliding a rectangular slit across the film. This leads to interesting effects when objects are moving in a different direction from the exposure slit (Glassner 1999; Stephenson 2007). Furthermore, most digital cameras read out pixel values from scanlines in succession over a period of a few milliseconds; this leads to *rolling shutter* artifacts, which have similar visual characteristics. Modify the way that time samples are generated in one or more of the camera implementations in this chapter to model such effects. Render images with moving objects that clearly show the effect of accounting for this issue.

● 5.2   Write an application that loads images rendered by the SphericalCamera and uses texture mapping to apply them to a sphere centered at the eyepoint such that they can be viewed interactively. The user should be able to freely change the viewing direction. If the correct texture-mapping function is used for generating texture coordinates on the sphere, the image generated by the application will appear as if the viewer was at the camera's location in the scene when it was rendered, thus giving the user the ability to interactively look around the scene.

● 5.3   *Focal stack rendering:* A focal stack is a series of images of a fixed scene where the camera is focused at a different distance for each image. Hasinoff and Kutulakos (2011) and Jacobs et al. (2012) introduced a number of applications of focal stacks, including freeform depth of field, where the user can specify arbitrary depths that are in focus, achieving effects not possible with traditional optics. Render focal stacks with pbrt and write an interactive tool to control focus effects with them.

● 5.4   *Light field camera:* Ng et al. (2005) discussed the physical design and applications of a camera that captures small images of the exit pupil across the film, rather than averaging the radiance over the entire exit pupil at each pixel, as conventional cameras do. Such a camera captures a representation of the *light field*—the spatially and directionally varying distribution of radiance arriving at the camera sensor. By capturing the light field, a number of interesting operations are possible, including refocusing photographs after they have been taken. Read Ng et al.'s paper and implement a Camera in pbrt that captures the light field of a scene. Write a tool to allow users to interactively refocus these light fields.

● 5.5   The Cameras in this chapter place the film at the center of and perpendicular to the optical axis. While this is the most common configuration of actual cameras, interesting effects can be achieved by adjusting the film's placement with respect to the lens system.

For example, the plane of focus in the current implementation is always perpendicular to the optical axis; if the film plane (or the lens system) is tilted so that the film is not perpendicular to the optical axis, then the plane of focus is no longer perpendicular to the optical axis. (This can be useful for landscape photography, for example, where aligning the plane of focus with the ground plane allows greater depth of field even with larger apertures.) Alternatively, the film plane can be shifted so that it is not centered on the optical axis; this shift can be used to keep the plane of focus aligned with a very tall object, for example.

Modify the PerspectiveCamera to allow one or both of these adjustments and render images showing the result. (You may find Kensler's (2021) chapter useful.)

● 5.6   The clamping approach used to suppress outlier sample values in the RGBFilm and GBufferFilm is a heavy-handed solution that can cause a significant amount of energy loss in the image. (Consider, for example, pixels where the sun is directly visible—the radiance along rays in those pixels may be extremely high, though it is not a cause of spiky pixels and should not be clamped.) Implement a more principled solution to this problem such as the technique of Zirr et al. (2018). Render images with your implementation and pbrt's current approach and compare the results.

⊘ 5.7   Investigate the sources of noise in camera sensors and mathematical models to simulate them. Then, modify the `PixelSensor` class to model the effect of noise. In addition to shot noise, which depends on the number of photons reaching each pixel, you may also want to model factors like read noise and dark noise, which are independent of the number of photons. Render images that exhibit noise and show the effect of different types of it as exposure time varies.

⊘ 5.8   Because they are based on floating-point addition, which is not associative, the `AddSplat()` methods implemented in this chapter do not live up to pbrt's goal of producing deterministic output: if different threads add splats to the same pixel in a different order over multiple runs of pbrt, the final image may differ. An alternative implementation might allocate a separate buffer for each thread's splats and then sum the buffers at the end of rendering, which would be deterministic but would incur a memory cost proportional to the number of threads. Either implement that approach or come up with another one to address this issue and implement it in pbrt. Measure the memory and performance overhead of your approach as well as how often the current implementation is non-deterministic. Is the current implementation defensible?

➌ 5.9   Image-based rendering is the general name for a set of techniques that use one or more images of a scene to synthesize new images from viewpoints different from the original ones. One such approach is light field rendering, where a set of images from a densely spaced set of positions is used—as described by Levoy and Hanrahan (1996) and Gortler et al. (1996). Read these two papers on light fields, and modify pbrt to directly generate light fields of scenes, without requiring that the renderer be run multiple times, once for each camera position. It will probably be necessary to write a specialized `Camera`, `Sampler`, and `Film` to do this. Also, write an interactive light field viewer that loads light fields generated by your implementation and that generates new views of the scene.

CHAPTER SIX

06 SHAPES

In this chapter, we will present pbrt's abstraction for geometric primitives such as spheres and triangles. Careful abstraction of geometric shapes in a ray tracer is a key component of a clean system design, and shapes are the ideal candidate for an object-oriented approach. All geometric primitives implement a common interface, and the rest of the renderer can use this interface without needing any details about the underlying shape. This makes it possible to separate the geometric and shading subsystems of pbrt.

pbrt hides details about primitives behind a two-level abstraction. The Shape interface provides access to the basic geometric properties of the primitive, such as its surface area and bounding box, and provides a ray intersection routine. Then, the Primitive interface encapsulates additional non-geometric information about the primitive, such as its material properties. The rest of the renderer then deals only with the abstract Primitive interface. This chapter will focus on the geometry-only Shape class; the Primitive interface is a key topic of Chapter 7.

6.1 BASIC SHAPE INTERFACE

The interface for Shapes is defined in the file base/shape.h, and the shape implementations can be found in shapes.h and shapes.cpp. The Shape class defines the general shape interface.

⟨*Shape Definition*⟩ ≡
```
class Shape : public TaggedPointer<Sphere, Cylinder, Disk, Triangle,
                                   BilinearPatch, Curve> {
  public:
    ⟨Shape Interface 262⟩
};
```

6.1.1 BOUNDING

The scenes that pbrt renders often contain objects that are computationally expensive to process. For many operations, it is useful to have a 3D *bounding volume* that encloses an object. For example, if a ray does not pass through a particular bounding volume, pbrt can avoid processing all the objects inside of it for that ray.

Axis-aligned bounding boxes are a convenient bounding volume, as they require only six floating-point values to store. They fit many shapes well and it is fairly inexpensive to test for the intersection of a ray with an axis-aligned bounding box. Each Shape implementation must therefore be capable of bounding itself with an axis-aligned bounding box represented by a Bounds3f. The returned bounding box should be in the rendering coordinate system (recall the discussion of coordinate systems in Section 5.1.1).

⟨Shape Interface⟩ ≡   261
```
Bounds3f Bounds() const;
```

In addition to bounding their spatial extent, shapes must also be able to bound their range of surface normals. The NormalBounds() method should return such a bound using a DirectionCone, which was defined in Section 3.8.4. Normal bounds are specifically useful in lighting calculations: when a shape is emissive, they sometimes make it possible to efficiently determine that the shape does not illuminate a particular point in the scene.

⟨Shape Interface⟩ +≡   261
```
DirectionCone NormalBounds() const;
```

6.1.2 RAY–BOUNDS INTERSECTIONS

Given the use of Bounds3f instances to bound shapes, we will add a Bounds3 method, Bounds3::IntersectP(), that checks for a ray–box intersection and returns the two parametric t values of the intersection, if any.

One way to think of bounding boxes is as the intersection of three slabs, where a slab is the region of space between two parallel planes. To intersect a ray with a box, we intersect the ray with each of the box's three slabs in turn. Because the slabs are aligned with the three coordinate axes, a number of optimizations can be made in the ray–slab tests.

The basic ray–bounding box intersection algorithm works as follows: we start with a parametric interval that covers that range of positions t along the ray where we are interested in finding intersections; typically, this is $(0, \infty)$. We will then successively compute the two parametric t positions where the ray intersects each axis-aligned slab. We compute the set intersection of the per-slab intersection interval with the current intersection interval, returning failure if we find that the resulting interval is degenerate. If, after checking all three slabs, the interval is nondegenerate, we have the parametric range of the ray that is inside the box. Figure 6.1 illustrates this process, and Figure 6.2 shows the basic geometry of a ray intersecting a slab.

If the Bounds3::IntersectP() method returns true, the intersection's parametric range is returned in the optional arguments hitt0 and hitt1. Intersections outside of the (0, tMax) range of the ray are ignored. If the ray's origin is inside the box, 0 is returned for hitt0.

⟨Bounds3 Inline Functions⟩ +≡
```
template <typename T>
bool Bounds3<T>::IntersectP(Point3f o, Vector3f d, Float tMax,
                            Float *hitt0, Float *hitt1) const {
    Float t0 = 0, t1 = tMax;
    for (int i = 0; i < 3; ++i) {
        ⟨Update interval for ith bounding box slab 264⟩
    }
    if (hitt0) *hitt0 = t0;
    if (hitt1) *hitt1 = t1;
    return true;
}
```

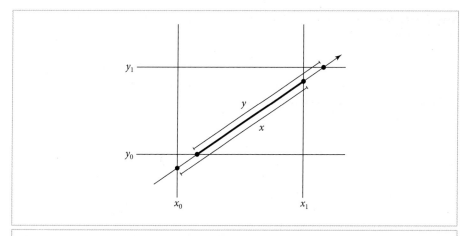

Figure 6.1: Intersecting a Ray with an Axis-Aligned Bounding Box. We compute intersection points with each slab in turn, progressively narrowing the parametric interval. Here, in 2D, the intersection of the x and y extents along the ray (thick segment) gives the extent where the ray is inside the box.

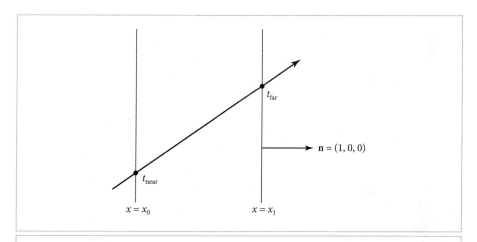

Figure 6.2: Intersecting a Ray with an Axis-Aligned Slab. The two planes shown here are described by $x = c$ for constant values c. The normal of each plane is $(1, 0, 0)$. Unless the ray is parallel to the planes, it will intersect the slab twice, at parametric positions t_near and t_far.

For each pair of planes, this routine needs to compute two ray–plane intersections. For example, the slab described by two planes perpendicular to the x axis can be described by planes through points $(x_0, 0, 0)$ and $(x_1, 0, 0)$, each with normal $(1, 0, 0)$. Consider the first t value for a plane intersection, t_0. The parametric t value for the intersection between a ray with origin o and direction $\mathbf{d}$ and a plane $ax + by + cz + d = 0$ can be found by substituting the ray equation into the plane equation:

$$0 = a(\mathrm{o}_x + t\mathbf{d}_x) + b(\mathrm{o}_y + t\mathbf{d}_y) + c(\mathrm{o}_z + t\mathbf{d}_z) + d$$
$$= (a, b, c) \cdot \mathrm{o} + t(a, b, c) \cdot \mathbf{d} + d.$$

Solving for t gives

$$t = \frac{-d - ((a, b, c) \cdot \mathrm{o})}{((a, b, c) \cdot \mathbf{d})}.$$

Because the y and z components of the plane's normal are zero, b and c are zero, and a is one. The plane's d coefficient is $-x_0$. We can use this information and the definition of the dot product to simplify the calculation substantially:

$$t_0 = \frac{x_0 - o_x}{\mathrm{d}_x}.$$

The code to compute the t values of the slab intersections starts by computing the reciprocal of the corresponding component of the ray direction so that it can multiply by this factor instead of performing multiple divisions. Note that, although it divides by this component, it is not necessary to verify that it is nonzero. If it is zero, then invRayDir will hold an infinite value, either $-\infty$ or ∞, and the rest of the algorithm still works correctly.[1]

⟨*Update interval for* i*th bounding box slab*⟩ ≡   262
```
Float invRayDir = 1 / d[i];
Float tNear = (pMin[i] - o[i]) * invRayDir;
Float tFar  = (pMax[i] - o[i]) * invRayDir;
```
⟨*Update parametric interval from slab intersection t values* **264**⟩

The two distances are reordered so that tNear holds the closer intersection and tFar the farther one. This gives a parametric range [tNear, tFar], which is used to compute the set intersection with the current range [t0, t1] to compute a new range. If this new range is empty (i.e., t0 > t1), then the code can immediately return failure.

There is another floating-point-related subtlety here: in the case where the ray origin is in the plane of one of the bounding box slabs and the ray lies in the plane of the slab, it is possible that tNear or tFar will be computed by an expression of the form 0/0, which results in a floating-point "not a number" (NaN) value. Like infinity values, NaNs have well-specified semantics: for example, any logical comparison involving a NaN always evaluates to false. Therefore, the code that updates the values of t0 and t1 is carefully written so that if tNear or tFar is NaN, then t0 or t1 will not ever take on a NaN value but will always remain unchanged.

⟨*Update parametric interval from slab intersection t values*⟩ ≡   264
```
if (tNear > tFar) pstd::swap(tNear, tFar);
```
⟨*Update* tFar *to ensure robust ray–bounds intersection* **370**⟩
```
t0 = tNear > t0 ? tNear : t0;
t1 = tFar  < t1 ? tFar  : t1;
if (t0 > t1) return false;
```

Bounds3 also provides a specialized IntersectP() method that takes the reciprocal of the ray's direction as an additional parameter, so that the three reciprocals do not need to be computed each time IntersectP() is called.

This version of the method also takes precomputed values that indicate whether each direction component is negative, which makes it possible to eliminate the comparisons of the computed tNear and tFar values in the original routine and to directly compute the respective near and far values. Because the comparisons that order these values from low to high in the original code are dependent on computed values, they can be inefficient for processors to execute, since the computation of their values must be finished before the comparison can

---

Bounds3::pMax 98
Bounds3::pMin 98
Float 23

1   This assumes that the architecture being used supports IEEE floating-point arithmetic, which is universal on modern systems. The relevant properties of IEEE floating-point arithmetic are that for all $v > 0$, $v/0 = \infty$ and for all $w < 0$, $w/0 = -\infty$, where ∞ is a special value such that any positive number multiplied by ∞ gives ∞ and any negative number multiplied by ∞ gives $-\infty$, and so on. See Section 6.8.1 for more information about floating-point arithmetic.

be made. Because many ray–bounds intersection tests may be performed during rendering, this small optimization is worth using.

This routine returns true if the ray segment is entirely inside the bounding box, even if the intersections are not within the ray's (0, tMax) range.

⟨*Bounds3 Inline Functions*⟩ +≡
```
template <typename T>
bool Bounds3<T>::IntersectP(Point3f o, Vector3f d, Float raytMax,
                           Vector3f invDir, const int dirIsNeg[3]) const {
    const Bounds3f &bounds = *this;
    ⟨Check for ray intersection against x and y slabs 265⟩
    ⟨Check for ray intersection against z slab⟩
    return (tMin < raytMax) && (tMax > 0);
}
```

If the ray direction vector is negative, the "near" parametric intersection will be found with the slab with the larger of the two bounding values, and the far intersection will be found with the slab with the smaller of them. The implementation can use this observation to compute the near and far parametric values in each direction directly.

⟨*Check for ray intersection against x and y slabs*⟩ ≡   265
```
Float tMin  = (bounds[  dirIsNeg[0]].x - o.x) * invDir.x;
Float tMax  = (bounds[1-dirIsNeg[0]].x - o.x) * invDir.x;
Float tyMin = (bounds[  dirIsNeg[1]].y - o.y) * invDir.y;
Float tyMax = (bounds[1-dirIsNeg[1]].y - o.y) * invDir.y;
⟨Update tMax and tyMax to ensure robust bounds intersection⟩
if (tMin > tyMax || tyMin > tMax)
    return false;
if (tyMin > tMin) tMin = tyMin;
if (tyMax < tMax) tMax = tyMax;
```

The fragment ⟨*Check for ray intersection against z slab*⟩ is analogous and is not included here.

This intersection test is at the heart of traversing the BVHAggregate acceleration structure, which is introduced in Section 7.3. Because so many ray–bounding box intersection tests are performed while traversing the BVH tree, we found that this optimized method provided approximately a 15% performance improvement in overall rendering time compared to using the Bounds3::IntersectP() variant that did not take the precomputed direction reciprocals and signs.

6.1.3 INTERSECTION TESTS

Shape implementations must provide an implementation of two methods that test for ray intersections with their shape. The first, Intersect(), returns geometric information about a single ray–shape intersection corresponding to the first intersection, if any, in the (0, tMax) parametric range along the given ray.

⟨*Shape Interface*⟩ +≡   261
```
pstd::optional<ShapeIntersection> Intersect(const Ray &ray,
                                            Float tMax = Infinity) const;
```

In the event that an intersection is found, a SurfaceInteraction corresponding to the intersection point and the parametric *t* distance along the ray where the intersection occurred are returned via a ShapeIntersection instance.

⟨*ShapeIntersection Definition*⟩ ≡
```
struct ShapeIntersection {
    SurfaceInteraction intr;
    Float tHit;
};
```

There are a few important things to keep in mind when reading (and writing) intersection routines:

- The provided `tMax` value defines the endpoint of the ray. Intersection routines must ignore any intersections that occur after this point.
- If there are multiple intersections with a shape along the ray, the closest one should be reported.
- The rays passed into intersection routines are in rendering space, so shapes are responsible for transforming them to object space if needed for intersection tests. The intersection information returned should be in rendering space.

The second intersection test method, `Shape::IntersectP()`, is a predicate function that determines whether or not an intersection occurs without returning any details about the intersection itself. That test is often more efficient than a full intersection test. This method is used in particular for shadow rays that are testing the visibility of a light source from a point in the scene.

⟨*Shape Interface*⟩ +≡   **261**
```
bool IntersectP(const Ray &ray, Float tMax = Infinity) const;
```

6.1.4 INTERSECTION COORDINATE SPACES

For some shapes, intersection routines are most naturally expressed in their object space. For example, the following `Sphere` shape computes the intersection with a sphere of a given radius positioned at the origin. The sphere being at the origin allows various simplifications to the intersection algorithm. Other shapes, like the `Triangle`, transform their representation to rendering space and perform intersection tests there.

Shapes like `Sphere` that operate in object space must transform the specified ray to object space and then transform any intersection results back to rendering space. Most of this is handled easily using associated methods in the `Transform` class that were introduced in Section 3.10, though a natural question to ask is, "What effect does the object-from-rendering-space transformation have on the correct parametric distance to return?" The intersection method has found a parametric t distance to the intersection for the object-space ray, which may have been translated, rotated, scaled, or worse when it was transformed from rendering space.

Using the properties of transformations, it is possible to show that the t distance to the intersection is unaffected by the transformation. Consider a rendering-space ray r_r with associated origin o_r and direction $\mathbf{d}_r$. Given an object-from-rendering-space transformation matrix $\mathbf{M}$, we can then find the object-space ray r_o with origin $\mathbf{M}o_o$ and direction $\mathbf{M}\mathbf{d}_o$.

If the ray–shape intersection algorithm finds an object-space intersection at a distance t along the ray, then the object-space intersection point is

$$p_o = o_o + t\mathbf{d}_o.$$

Now consider the rendering-space intersection point p_r that is found by applying $\mathbf{M}$'s inverse to both sides of that equation:

$$M^{-1}p_o = M^{-1}\left(o_o + t d_o\right)$$
$$M^{-1}p_o = M^{-1}o_o + M^{-1}\left(t d_o\right)$$
$$M^{-1}p_o = M^{-1}o_o + t M^{-1}\left(d_o\right)$$
$$p_r = o_r + t d_r.$$

Therefore, the t value that was computed in object space is the correct t value for the intersection point in rendering space as well. Note that if the object-space ray's direction had been normalized after the transformation, then this would no longer be the case and a correction factor related to the unnormalized ray's length would be needed. This is one reason that pbrt does not normalize object-space rays' directions after transformation.

6.1.5 SIDEDNESS

Many rendering systems, particularly those based on scanline or z-buffer algorithms, support the concept of shapes being "one-sided"—the shape is visible if seen from the front but disappears when viewed from behind. In particular, if a geometric object is closed and always viewed from the outside, then the backfacing parts of it can be discarded without changing the resulting image. This optimization can substantially improve the speed of these types of hidden surface removal algorithms. The potential for improved performance is reduced when using this technique with ray tracing, however, since it is often necessary to perform the ray–object intersection before determining the surface normal to do the backfacing test. Furthermore, this feature can lead to a physically inconsistent scene description if one-sided objects are not in fact closed. For example, a surface might block light when a shadow ray is traced from a light source to a point on another surface, but not if the shadow ray is traced in the other direction. For all of these reasons, pbrt does not support this feature.

6.1.6 AREA

In pbrt, area lights are defined by attaching an emission profile to a Shape. To use Shapes as area lights, it is necessary that shapes be able to return their surface area of a shape in rendering space.

⟨Shape Interface⟩ +≡   **261**
```
Float Area() const;
```

6.1.7 SAMPLING

A few methods are necessary to sample points on the surface of shapes in order to use them as emitters. Additional Shape methods make this possible.

There are two shape sampling methods, both named Sample(). The first chooses points on the surface of the shape using a sampling distribution with respect to surface area and returns the local geometric information about the sampled point in a ShapeSample. The provided sample value u, a uniform sample in $[0, 1)^2$, should be used to determine the point on the shape.

⟨Shape Interface⟩ +≡   **261**
```
pstd::optional<ShapeSample> Sample(Point2f u) const;
```

Float 23
Interaction 136
Point2f 92
ShapeSample 268

The ShapeSample structure that is returned stores an Interaction corresponding to a sampled point on the surface as well as the probability density with respect to surface area on the shape for sampling that point.

⟨*ShapeSample Definition*⟩ ≡
```
struct ShapeSample {
    Interaction intr;
    Float pdf;
};
```

Shapes must also provide an associated PDF() method that returns probability density for sampling the specified point on the shape that corresponds to the given Interaction. This method should only be called with interactions that are on the shape's surface. Although Sample() already returns the probability density for the point it samples, this method is useful when using multiple importance sampling, in which case it is necessary to compute the probability density for samples generated using other sampling techniques. An important detail is that implementations are allowed to assume that the provided point is on their surface; callers are responsible for ensuring that this is the case.

⟨*Shape Interface*⟩ +≡   261
```
Float PDF(const Interaction &) const;
```

The second shape sampling method takes a reference point from which the shape is being viewed. This method is particularly useful for lighting, since the caller can pass in the point to be lit and allow shape implementations to ensure that they only sample the portion of the shape that is potentially visible from that point.

Unlike the first Shape sampling method, which generates points on the shape according to a probability density with respect to surface area on the shape, the second one uses a density with respect to solid angle from the reference point. This difference stems from the fact that the area light sampling routines evaluate the direct lighting integral as an integral over directions from the reference point—expressing these sampling densities with respect to solid angle at the point is more convenient.

⟨*Shape Interface*⟩ +≡   261
```
pstd::optional<ShapeSample> Sample(const ShapeSampleContext &ctx,
                                   Point2f u) const;
```

Information about the reference point and its geometric and shading normals is provided by the ShapeSampleContext structure. The reference point position is specified using the Point3fi class, which can represent the numerical uncertainty in a ray intersection point computed using floating-point arithmetic. Discussion of related topics is in Section 6.8. For points in participating media that are not associated with a surface, the normal and shading normal are left with their default values of (0, 0, 0).

⟨*ShapeSampleContext Definition*⟩ ≡
```
struct ShapeSampleContext {
    ⟨ShapeSampleContext Public Methods 269⟩
    Point3fi pi;
    Normal3f n, ns;
    Float time;
};
```

ShapeSampleContext provides a variety of convenience constructors that allow specifying the member variable values directly or from various types of Interaction.

⟨*ShapeSampleContext Public Methods*⟩ ≡   **268**
```
ShapeSampleContext(Point3fi pi, Normal3f n, Normal3f ns, Float time)
  : pi(pi), n(n), ns(ns), time(time) {}
ShapeSampleContext(const SurfaceInteraction &si)
  : pi(si.pi), n(si.n), ns(si.shading.n), time(si.time) {}
ShapeSampleContext(const MediumInteraction &mi)
  : pi(mi.pi), time(mi.time) {}
```

For code that does not need to be aware of numeric error in the intersection point, a method provides it as a regular Point3.

⟨*ShapeSampleContext Public Methods*⟩ +≡   **268**
```
Point3f p() const { return Point3f(pi); }
```

A second PDF() method comes along with this sampling approach. It returns the shape's probability of sampling a point on the light such that the incident direction ω_i at the reference point is wi. As with the corresponding sampling method, this density should be with respect to solid angle at the reference point. As with the other Shape PDF() method, this should only be called for a direction that is known to intersect the shape from the reference point; as such, implementations are not responsible for checking that case.

⟨*Shape Interface*⟩ +≡   **261**
```
Float PDF(const ShapeSampleContext &ctx, Vector3f wi) const;
```

Some of the PDF() method implementations will need to trace a ray from the reference point in the direction ω_i to see if it intersects the shape. The following ShapeSampleContext methods should be used to find the origin or the ray itself rather than using the point returned by ShapeSampleContext::p(). This, too, stems from a subtlety related to handling numeric error in intersection points. The implementation of these methods and discussion of the underlying issues can be found in Section 6.8.6.

⟨*ShapeSampleContext Public Methods*⟩ +≡   **268**
```
Point3f OffsetRayOrigin(Vector3f w) const;
Point3f OffsetRayOrigin(Point3f pt) const;
Ray SpawnRay(Vector3f w) const;
```

6.2 SPHERES

Spheres are a special case of a general type of surface called *quadrics*—surfaces described by quadratic polynomials in x, y, and z. They offer a good starting point for introducing ray intersection algorithms. In conjunction with a transformation matrix, pbrt's Sphere shape can also take the form of an ellipsoid. pbrt supports two other basic types of quadrics: cylinders and disks. Other quadrics such as the cone, hyperboloid, and paraboloid are less useful for most rendering applications, and so are not included in the system.

Many surfaces can be described in one of two main ways: in *implicit form* and in *parametric form*. An implicit function describes a 3D surface as

$$f(x, y, z) = 0.$$

The set of all points (x, y, z) that fulfill this condition defines the surface. For a unit sphere at the origin, the familiar implicit equation is $x^2 + y^2 + z^2 - 1 = 0$. Only the set of points one unit from the origin satisfies this constraint, giving the unit sphere's surface.

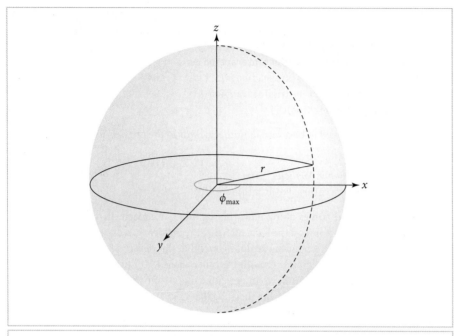

Figure 6.3: Basic Setting for the Sphere Shape. It has a radius of r and is centered at the object space origin. A partial sphere may be described by specifying a maximum ϕ value.

Many surfaces can also be described parametrically using a function to map 2D points to 3D points on the surface. For example, a sphere of radius r can be described as a function of 2D spherical coordinates (θ, ϕ), where θ ranges from 0 to π and ϕ ranges from 0 to 2π (Figure 6.3):

$$\begin{aligned} x &= r\ \sin\theta\ \cos\phi \\ y &= r\ \sin\theta\ \sin\phi \\ z &= r\ \cos\theta. \end{aligned} \quad\quad [6.1]$$

We can transform this function $f(\theta, \phi)$ into a function $f(u, v)$ over $[0, 1]^2$ and generalize it slightly to allow partial spheres that only sweep out $\theta \in [\theta_{\min}, \theta_{\max}]$ and $\phi \in [0, \phi_{\max}]$ with the substitution

$$\begin{aligned} \phi &= u\ \phi_{\max} \\ \theta &= \theta_{\min} + v(\theta_{\max} - \theta_{\min}). \end{aligned} \quad\quad [6.2]$$

This form is particularly useful for texture mapping, where it can be directly used to map a texture defined over $[0, 1]^2$ to the sphere. Figure 6.4 shows an image of two spheres; a grid image map has been used to show the (u, v) parameterization.

As we describe the implementation of the sphere shape, we will make use of both the implicit and parametric descriptions of the shape, depending on which is a more natural way to approach the particular problem we are facing.

The Sphere class represents a sphere that is centered at the origin. As with all the other shapes, its implementation is in the files shapes.h and shapes.cpp.

Sphere 271

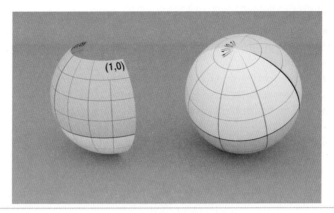

Figure 6.4: Two Spheres. On the left is a partial sphere (with $z_{max} < r$ and $\phi_{max} < 2\pi$) and on the right is a complete sphere. Note that the texture image used shows the (u, v) parameterization of the shape; the singularity at one of the poles is visible in the complete sphere.

⟨*Sphere Definition*⟩ ≡
```
class Sphere {
  public:
    ⟨Sphere Public Methods 272⟩
  private:
    ⟨Sphere Private Members 272⟩
};
```

As mentioned earlier, spheres in pbrt are defined in a coordinate system where the center of the sphere is at the origin. The sphere constructor is provided transformations that map between the sphere's object space and rendering space.

Although pbrt supports animated transformation matrices, the transformations here are not AnimatedTransforms. (Such is also the case for all the shapes defined in this chapter.) Animated shape transformations are instead handled by using a TransformedPrimitive to represent the shape in the scene. Doing so allows us to centralize some of the tricky details related to animated transformations in a single place, rather than requiring all Shapes to handle this case.

The radius of the sphere can have an arbitrary positive value, and the sphere's extent can be truncated in two different ways. First, minimum and maximum z values may be set; the parts of the sphere below and above these planes, respectively, are cut off. Second, considering the parameterization of the sphere in spherical coordinates, a maximum ϕ value can be set. The sphere sweeps out ϕ values from 0 to the given ϕ_{max} such that the section of the sphere with spherical ϕ values above ϕ_{max} is also removed.

Finally, the Sphere constructor also takes a Boolean parameter, reverseOrientation, that indicates whether their surface normal directions should be reversed from the default (which is pointing outside the sphere). This capability is useful because the orientation of the surface normal is used to determine which side of a shape is "outside." For example, shapes that emit illumination are by default emissive only on the side the surface normal lies on. The value of this parameter is managed via the ReverseOrientation statement in pbrt scene description files.

AnimatedTransform 135
Shape 261
TransformedPrimitive 403

⟨*Sphere Public Methods*⟩ ≡   271
```
Sphere(const Transform *renderFromObject, const Transform *objectFromRender,
        bool reverseOrientation, Float radius, Float zMin, Float zMax,
        Float phiMax)
    : renderFromObject(renderFromObject), objectFromRender(objectFromRender),
      reverseOrientation(reverseOrientation),
      transformSwapsHandedness(renderFromObject->SwapsHandedness()),
      radius(radius),
      zMin(Clamp(std::min(zMin, zMax), -radius, radius)),
      zMax(Clamp(std::max(zMin, zMax), -radius, radius)),
      thetaZMin(std::acos(Clamp(std::min(zMin, zMax) / radius, -1, 1))),
      thetaZMax(std::acos(Clamp(std::max(zMin, zMax) / radius, -1, 1))),
      phiMax(Radians(Clamp(phiMax, 0, 360))) {}
```

⟨*Sphere Private Members*⟩ ≡   271
```
Float radius;
Float zMin, zMax;
Float thetaZMin, thetaZMax, phiMax;
const Transform *renderFromObject, *objectFromRender;
bool reverseOrientation, transformSwapsHandedness;
```

6.2.1 BOUNDING

Computing an object-space bounding box for a sphere is straightforward. The implementation here uses the values of $z_{\min}$ and $z_{\max}$ provided by the user to tighten up the bound when less than an entire sphere is being rendered. However, it does not do the extra work to compute a tighter bounding box when $\phi_{\max}$ is less than $3\pi/2$. This improvement is left as an exercise. This object-space bounding box is transformed to rendering space before being returned.

⟨*Sphere Method Definitions*⟩ ≡
```
Bounds3f Sphere::Bounds() const {
    return (*renderFromObject)(
        Bounds3f(Point3f(-radius, -radius, zMin),
                 Point3f( radius,  radius, zMax)));
}
```

The Sphere's NormalBounds() method does not consider any form of partial spheres but always returns the bounds for an entire sphere, which is all possible directions.

⟨*Sphere Public Methods*⟩ +≡   271
```
DirectionCone NormalBounds() const { return DirectionCone::EntireSphere(); }
```

6.2.2 INTERSECTION TESTS

The ray intersection test is broken into two stages. First, BasicIntersect() does the basic ray–sphere intersection test and returns a small structure, QuadricIntersection, if an intersection is found. A subsequent call to the InteractionFromIntersection() method transforms the QuadricIntersection into a full-blown SurfaceInteraction, which can be returned from the Intersection() method.

There are two motivations for separating the intersection test into two stages like this. One is that doing so allows the IntersectP() method to be implemented as a trivial wrapper around BasicIntersect(). The second is that pbrt's GPU rendering path is organized such that the closest intersection among all shapes is found before the full SurfaceInteraction is constructed; this decomposition fits that directly.

⟨*Sphere Public Methods*⟩ +≡   **271**
```
pstd::optional<ShapeIntersection> Intersect(const Ray &ray,
                                            Float tMax = Infinity) const {
    pstd::optional<QuadricIntersection> isect = BasicIntersect(ray, tMax);
    if (!isect) return {};
    SurfaceInteraction intr =
        InteractionFromIntersection(*isect, -ray.d, ray.time);
    return ShapeIntersection{intr, isect->tHit};
}
```

QuadricIntersection stores the parametric t along the ray where the intersection occurred, the object-space intersection point, and the sphere's ϕ value there. As its name suggests, this structure will be used by the other quadrics in the same way it is here.

⟨*QuadricIntersection Definition*⟩ ≡
```
struct QuadricIntersection {
    Float tHit;
    Point3f pObj;
    Float phi;
};
```

The basic intersection test transforms the provided rendering-space ray to object space and intersects it with the complete sphere. If a partial sphere has been specified, some additional tests reject intersections with portions of the sphere that have been removed.

⟨*Sphere Public Methods*⟩ +≡   **271**
```
pstd::optional<QuadricIntersection> BasicIntersect(const Ray &r,
                                                   Float tMax) const {
    Float phi;
    Point3f pHit;
    ⟨Transform Ray origin and direction to object space 273⟩
    ⟨Solve quadratic equation to compute sphere t0 and t1 274⟩
    ⟨Check quadric shape t0 and t1 for nearest intersection 275⟩
    ⟨Compute sphere hit position and φ 275⟩
    ⟨Test sphere intersection against clipping parameters 276⟩
    ⟨Return QuadricIntersection for sphere intersection 276⟩
}
```

The transformed ray origin and direction are respectively stored using Point3fi and Vector3fi classes rather than the usual Point3f and Vector3f. These classes represent those quantities as small intervals in each dimension that bound the floating-point round-off error that was introduced by applying the transformation. Later, we will see that these error bounds will be useful for improving the geometric accuracy of the intersection computation. For the most part, these classes can respectively be used just like Point3f and Vector3f.

⟨*Transform Ray origin and direction to object space*⟩ ≡   **273, 288, 293**
```
Point3fi oi = (*objectFromRender)(Point3fi(r.o));
Vector3fi di = (*objectFromRender)(Vector3fi(r.d));
```

If a sphere is centered at the origin with radius r, its implicit representation is

$$x^2 + y^2 + z^2 - r^2 = 0.$$

By substituting the parametric representation of the ray from Equation (3.4) into the implicit sphere equation, we have

$$\left(o_x + t\mathbf{d}_x\right)^2 + \left(o_y + t\mathbf{d}_y\right)^2 + \left(o_z + t\mathbf{d}_z\right)^2 = r^2.$$

Note that all elements of this equation besides t are known values. The t values where the equation holds give the parametric positions along the ray where the implicit sphere equation is satisfied and thus the points along the ray where it intersects the sphere. We can expand this equation and gather the coefficients for a general quadratic equation in t,

$$at^2 + bt + c = 0,$$

where[2]

$$
\begin{aligned}
a &= \mathbf{d}_x^2 + \mathbf{d}_y^2 + \mathbf{d}_z^2 \\
b &= 2(\mathbf{d}_x o_x + \mathbf{d}_y o_y + \mathbf{d}_z o_z) \\
c &= o_x^2 + o_y^2 + o_z^2 - r^2.
\end{aligned}
\qquad [6.3]
$$

The Interval class stores a small range of floating-point values to maintain bounds on floating-point rounding error. It is defined in Section B.2.15 and is analogous to Float in the way that Point3fi is to Point3f, for example.

⟨*Solve quadratic equation to compute sphere* t0 *and* t1⟩ ≡   **273**
```
Interval t0, t1;
```
    ⟨*Compute sphere quadratic coefficients* **274**⟩
    ⟨*Compute sphere quadratic discriminant* discrim **372**⟩
    ⟨*Compute quadratic t values* **275**⟩

Given Interval, Equation (6.3) directly translates to the following fragment of source code.

⟨*Compute sphere quadratic coefficients*⟩ ≡   **274**
```
Interval a = Sqr(di.x) + Sqr(di.y) + Sqr(di.z);
Interval b = 2 * (di.x * oi.x + di.y * oi.y + di.z * oi.z);
Interval c = Sqr(oi.x) + Sqr(oi.y) + Sqr(oi.z) - Sqr(Interval(radius));
```

The fragment ⟨*Compute sphere quadratic discriminant* discrim⟩ computes the discriminant $b^2 - 4ac$ in a way that maintains numerical accuracy in tricky cases. It is defined later, in Section 6.8.3, after related topics about floating-point arithmetic have been introduced. Proceeding here with its value in discrim, the quadratic equation can be applied. Here we use a variant of the traditional $-b \pm \sqrt{b^2 - 4ac}/(2a)$ approach that gives more accuracy; it is described in Section B.2.10.

Float 23
Interval 1057
Interval::Sqr() 1060
Point3f 92
Point3fi 1061
Sphere::radius 272
Sqr() 1034

---

2   Some ray tracers require that the direction vector of a ray be normalized, meaning $a = 1$. This can lead to subtle errors, however, if the caller forgets to normalize the ray direction. Of course, these errors can be avoided by normalizing the direction in the ray constructor, but this wastes effort when the provided direction is *already* normalized. To avoid this needless complexity, pbrt never insists on vector normalization in intersection routines. This is particularly helpful since it reduces the amount of computation needed to transform rays to object space, because no normalization is necessary there.

⟨*Compute quadratic t values*⟩ ≡   274, 288
```
Interval rootDiscrim = Sqrt(discrim);
Interval q;
if ((Float)b < 0) q = -.5f * (b - rootDiscrim);
else              q = -.5f * (b + rootDiscrim);
t0 = q / a;
t1 = c / q;
```
⟨*Swap quadratic t values so that* t0 *is the lesser* 275⟩

Because t0 and t1 represent intervals of floating-point values, it may be ambiguous which of them is less than the other. We use their lower bound for this test, so that in ambiguous cases, at least we do not risk returning a hit that is potentially farther away than an actual closer hit.

⟨*Swap quadratic t values so that* t0 *is the lesser*⟩ ≡   275
```
if (t0.LowerBound() > t1.LowerBound())
    pstd::swap(t0, t1);
```

A similar ambiguity must be accounted for when testing the *t* values against the acceptable range. In ambiguous cases, we err on the side of returning no intersection rather than an invalid one. The closest valid *t* is then stored in tShapeHit.

⟨*Check quadric shape* t0 *and* t1 *for nearest intersection*⟩ ≡   273, 288
```
if (t0.UpperBound() > tMax || t1.LowerBound() <= 0)
    return {};
Interval tShapeHit = t0;
if (tShapeHit.LowerBound() <= 0) {
    tShapeHit = t1;
    if (tShapeHit.UpperBound() > tMax)
        return {};
}
```

Given the parametric distance along the ray to the intersection with a full sphere, the intersection point pHit can be computed as that offset along the ray. In its initializer, all the respective interval types are cast back to their non-interval equivalents, which gives their midpoint. (The remainder of the intersection test no longer needs the information provided by the intervals.) Due to floating-point precision limitations, this computed intersection point pHit may lie a bit to one side of the actual sphere surface; the ⟨*Refine sphere intersection point*⟩ fragment, which is defined in Section 6.8.5, improves the accuracy of this value.

It is next necessary to handle partial spheres with clipped *z* or *ϕ* ranges—intersections that are in clipped areas must be ignored. The implementation starts by computing the *ϕ* value for the hit point. Using the parametric representation of the sphere,

$$\frac{y}{x} = \frac{r\ \sin\theta\ \sin\phi}{r\ \sin\theta\ \cos\phi} = \tan\phi,$$

so $\phi = \arctan y/x$. It is necessary to remap the result of the standard library's std::atan() function to a value between 0 and 2π, to match the sphere's original definition.

⟨*Compute sphere hit position and* ϕ⟩ ≡   273, 276
```
pHit = Point3f(oi) + (Float)tShapeHit * Vector3f(di);
```
⟨*Refine sphere intersection point* 375⟩
```
if (pHit.x == 0 && pHit.y == 0) pHit.x = 1e-5f * radius;
phi = std::atan2(pHit.y, pHit.x);
if (phi < 0) phi += 2 * Pi;
```

The hit point can now be tested against the specified minima and maxima for z and ϕ. One subtlety is that it is important to skip the z tests if the z range includes the entire sphere; the computed pHit.z value may be slightly out of the z range due to floating-point round-off, so we should only perform this test when the user expects the sphere to be partially incomplete. If the t_0 intersection is not valid, the routine tries again with t_1.

⟨*Test sphere intersection against clipping parameters*⟩ ≡   273
```
    if ((zMin > -radius && pHit.z < zMin) ||
        (zMax < radius && pHit.z > zMax) || phi > phiMax) {
        if (tShapeHit == t1) return {};
        if (t1.UpperBound() > tMax) return {};
        tShapeHit = t1;
        ⟨Compute sphere hit position and φ 275⟩
        if ((zMin > -radius && pHit.z < zMin) ||
            (zMax < radius && pHit.z > zMax) || phi > phiMax)
            return {};
    }
```

At this point in the routine, it is certain that the ray hits the sphere. A QuadricIntersection is returned that encapsulates sufficient information about it to determine the rest of the geometric information at the intersection point. Recall from Section 6.1.4 that even though tShapeHit was computed in object space, it is also the correct t value in rendering space. Therefore, it can be returned directly.

⟨*Return* QuadricIntersection *for sphere intersection*⟩ ≡   273
```
    return QuadricIntersection{Float(tShapeHit), pHit, phi};
```

With BasicIntersect() implemented, Sphere::IntersectP() is easily taken care of.

⟨*Sphere Public Methods*⟩ +≡   271
```
    bool IntersectP(const Ray &r, Float tMax = Infinity) const {
        return BasicIntersect(r, tMax).has_value();
    }
```

A QuadricIntersection can be upgraded to a SurfaceInteraction with a call to Interaction FromIntersection().

⟨*Sphere Public Methods*⟩ +≡   271
```
    SurfaceInteraction InteractionFromIntersection(
            const QuadricIntersection &isect, Vector3f wo, Float time) const {
        Point3f pHit = isect.pObj;
        Float phi = isect.phi;
        ⟨Find parametric representation of sphere hit 277⟩
        ⟨Compute error bounds for sphere intersection 375⟩
        ⟨Return SurfaceInteraction for quadric intersection 279⟩
    }
```

The method first computes u and v values by scaling the previously computed ϕ value for the hit to lie between 0 and 1 and by computing a θ value between 0 and 1 for the hit point based on the range of θ values for the given sphere. Then it finds the parametric partial derivatives of position $\partial p/\partial u$ and $\partial p/\partial v$ and surface normal $\partial n/\partial u$ and $\partial n/\partial v$.

⟨*Find parametric representation of sphere hit*⟩ ≡   **276**
```
Float u = phi / phiMax;
Float cosTheta = pHit.z / radius;
Float theta = SafeACos(cosTheta);
Float v = (theta - thetaZMin) / (thetaZMax - thetaZMin);
```
⟨*Compute sphere ∂p/∂u and ∂p/∂v* **277**⟩
⟨*Compute sphere ∂n/∂u and ∂n/∂v* **278**⟩

Computing the partial derivatives of a point on the sphere is a short exercise in algebra. Here we will show how the x component of $\partial p/\partial u$, $\partial p_x/\partial u$, is calculated; the other components are found similarly. Using the parametric definition of the sphere, we have

$$x = r \sin\theta \cos\phi$$

$$\frac{\partial p_x}{\partial u} = \frac{\partial}{\partial u}(r \sin\theta \cos\phi)$$

$$= r \sin\theta \frac{\partial}{\partial u}(\cos\phi)$$

$$= r \sin\theta(-\phi_{max} \sin\phi).$$

Using a substitution based on the parametric definition of the sphere's y coordinate, this simplifies to

$$\frac{\partial p_x}{\partial u} = -\phi_{max} y.$$

Similarly,

$$\frac{\partial p_y}{\partial u} = \phi_{max} x,$$

and

$$\frac{\partial p_z}{\partial u} = 0.$$

A similar process gives $\partial p/\partial v$. The complete result is

$$\frac{\partial p}{\partial u} = (-\phi_{max} y, \phi_{max} x, 0)$$

$$\frac{\partial p}{\partial v} = (\theta_{max} - \theta_{min})(z \cos\phi, z \sin\phi, -r \sin\theta),$$

and the implementation follows directly.

⟨*Compute sphere ∂p/∂u and ∂p/∂v*⟩ ≡   **277**
```
Float zRadius = std::sqrt(Sqr(pHit.x) + Sqr(pHit.y));
Float cosPhi = pHit.x / zRadius, sinPhi = pHit.y / zRadius;
Vector3f dpdu(-phiMax * pHit.y, phiMax * pHit.x, 0);
Float sinTheta = SafeSqrt(1 - Sqr(cosTheta));
Vector3f dpdv = (thetaZMax - thetaZMin) *
    Vector3f(pHit.z * cosPhi, pHit.z * sinPhi, -radius * sinTheta);
```

It is also useful to determine how the normal changes as we move along the surface in the u and v directions. (For example, the antialiasing techniques in Chapter 10 use this information to antialias textures on objects that are seen reflected in curved surfaces.) The differential changes in normal $\partial\mathbf{n}/\partial u$ and $\partial\mathbf{n}/\partial v$ are given by the *Weingarten equations* from differential geometry:

$$\frac{\partial\mathbf{n}}{\partial u} = \frac{fF - eG}{EG - F^2}\frac{\partial\mathbf{p}}{\partial u} + \frac{eF - fE}{EG - F^2}\frac{\partial\mathbf{p}}{\partial v}$$

$$\frac{\partial\mathbf{n}}{\partial v} = \frac{gF - fG}{EG - F^2}\frac{\partial\mathbf{p}}{\partial u} + \frac{fF - gE}{EG - F^2}\frac{\partial\mathbf{p}}{\partial v},$$

where E, F, and G are coefficients of the *first fundamental form* and are given by

$$E = \left|\frac{\partial\mathbf{p}}{\partial u}\right|^2$$

$$F = \left(\frac{\partial\mathbf{p}}{\partial u}\cdot\frac{\partial\mathbf{p}}{\partial v}\right)$$

$$G = \left|\frac{\partial\mathbf{p}}{\partial v}\right|^2.$$

These are easily computed with the $\partial\mathbf{p}/\partial u$ and $\partial\mathbf{p}/\partial v$ values found earlier. The e, f, and g are coefficients of the *second fundamental form*,

$$e = \left(\mathbf{n}\cdot\frac{\partial^2\mathbf{p}}{\partial u^2}\right)$$

$$f = \left(\mathbf{n}\cdot\frac{\partial^2\mathbf{p}}{\partial u\partial v}\right)$$

$$g = \left(\mathbf{n}\cdot\frac{\partial^2\mathbf{p}}{\partial v^2}\right).$$

The two fundamental forms capture elementary metric properties of a surface, including notions of distance, angle, and curvature; see a differential geometry textbook such as Gray (1993) for details. To find e, f, and g, it is necessary to compute the second-order partial derivatives $\partial^2\mathbf{p}/\partial u^2$ and so on.

For spheres, a little more algebra gives the second derivatives:

$$\frac{\partial^2\mathbf{p}}{\partial u^2} = -\phi_{max}^2(x, y, 0)$$

$$\frac{\partial^2\mathbf{p}}{\partial u\partial v} = (\theta_{max} - \theta_{min})\, z\, \phi_{max}(-\sin\phi, \cos\phi, 0)$$

$$\frac{\partial^2\mathbf{p}}{\partial v^2} = -(\theta_{max} - \theta_{min})^2(x, y, z).$$

The translation into code is straightforward.

⟨*Compute sphere* $\partial\mathbf{n}/\partial u$ *and* $\partial\mathbf{n}/\partial v$⟩ ≡   277

```
Vector3f d2Pduu = -phiMax * phiMax * Vector3f(pHit.x, pHit.y, 0);
Vector3f d2Pduv = (thetaZMax - thetaZMin) * pHit.z * phiMax *
    Vector3f(-sinPhi, cosPhi, 0.);
Vector3f d2Pdvv = -Sqr(thetaZMax - thetaZMin) * Vector3f(pHit.x,pHit.y,pHit.z);
⟨Compute coefficients for fundamental forms 279⟩
⟨Compute ∂n/∂u and ∂n/∂v from fundamental form coefficients 279⟩
```

Given all the partial derivatives, it is also easy to compute the coefficients of the fundamental forms.

⟨*Compute coefficients for fundamental forms*⟩ ≡   278, 290, 337
```
Float E = Dot(dpdu, dpdu), F = Dot(dpdu, dpdv), G = Dot(dpdv, dpdv);
Vector3f n = Normalize(Cross(dpdu, dpdv));
Float e = Dot(n, d2Pduu), f = Dot(n, d2Pduv), g = Dot(n, d2Pdvv);
```

We now have all the values necessary to apply the Weingarten equations. For this computation, we have found it worthwhile to use `DifferenceOfProducts()` to compute $EG - F^2$ for the greater numerical accuracy it provides than the direct expression of that computation. Note also that we must be careful to avoid dividing by 0 if that expression is zero-valued so that dndu and dndv do not take on not-a-number values in that case.

⟨*Compute* $\partial\mathbf{n}/\partial u$ *and* $\partial\mathbf{n}/\partial v$ *from fundamental form coefficients*⟩ ≡   278, 290, 337
```
Float EGF2 = DifferenceOfProducts(E, G, F, F);
Float invEGF2 = (EGF2 == 0) ? Float(0) : 1 / EGF2;
Normal3f dndu = Normal3f((f * F - e * G) * invEGF2 * dpdu +
                         (e * F - f * E) * invEGF2 * dpdv);
Normal3f dndv = Normal3f((g * F - f * G) * invEGF2 * dpdu +
                         (f * F - g * E) * invEGF2 * dpdv);
```

Having computed the surface parameterization and all the relevant partial derivatives, a `SurfaceInteraction` structure that contains all the necessary geometric information for this intersection can be returned. There are three things to note in the parameter values passed to the `SurfaceInteraction` constructor.

1. The intersection point is provided as a `Point3i` that takes the pHit point computed earlier and an error bound pError that is initialized in the fragment ⟨*Compute error bounds for sphere intersection*⟩, which is defined later, in Section 6.8.5.
2. The `SurfaceInteraction` is initialized with object-space geometric quantities (pHit, dpdu, etc.) and is then transformed to rendering space when it is returned. However, one of the parameters is the outgoing direction, ω_0. This is passed in to `Interaction FromIntersection()`, but must be transformed to object space before being passed to the constructor so that the returned `Interaction::wo` value is in rendering space again.
3. The `flipNormal` parameter indicates whether the surface normal should be flipped after it is initially computed with the cross product of dpdu and dpdv. This should be done either if the `ReverseOrientation` directive has been enabled or if the object-to-rendering-space transform swaps coordinate system handedness (but not if both of these are the case). (The need for the latter condition was discussed in Section 3.11.1.)

Cross() 91
DifferenceOfProducts() 1044
Dot() 89
Float 23
Normal3f 94
Normalize() 88
Point2f 92
Point3fi 1061
Point3i 92
Sphere::objectFromRender 272
Sphere::reverseOrientation 272
Sphere:: transformSwapsHandedness 272
SurfaceInteraction 138
Vector3f 86

⟨*Return* SurfaceInteraction *for quadric intersection*⟩ ≡   276, 290, 295
```
bool flipNormal = reverseOrientation ^ transformSwapsHandedness;
Vector3f woObject = (*objectFromRender)(wo);
return (*renderFromObject)(
    SurfaceInteraction(Point3fi(pHit, pError), Point2f(u, v), woObject,
                       dpdu, dpdv, dndu, dndv, time, flipNormal));
```

6.2.3 SURFACE AREA

To compute the surface area of quadrics, we use a standard formula from integral calculus. If a curve $y = f(x)$ from $x = a$ to $x = b$ is revolved around the x axis, the surface area of the resulting swept surface is

$$2\pi \int_a^b f(x)\sqrt{1 + \left(f'(x)\right)^2}\, dx,$$

where $f'(x)$ denotes the derivative $d f/dx$. Since most of our surfaces of revolution are only partially swept around the axis, we will instead use the formula

$$\phi_{max} \int_a^b f(x)\sqrt{1 + \left(f'(x)\right)^2}\, dx.$$

The sphere is a surface of revolution of a circular arc. The function that defines the profile curve along the z axis of the sphere is

$$f(z) = \sqrt{r^2 - z^2},$$

and its derivative is

$$f'(z) = -\frac{z}{\sqrt{r^2 - z^2}}.$$

Recall that the sphere is clipped at z_{min} and z_{max}. The surface area is therefore

$$\begin{aligned}
A &= \phi_{max} \int_{z_{min}}^{z_{max}} \sqrt{r^2 - z^2}\sqrt{1 + \frac{z^2}{r^2 - z^2}}\, dz \\
&= \phi_{max} \int_{z_{min}}^{z_{max}} \sqrt{r^2 - z^2 + z^2}\, dz \\
&= \phi_{max} \int_{z_{min}}^{z_{max}} r\, dz \\
&= \phi_{max}\, r\, (z_{max} - z_{min}).
\end{aligned}$$

For the full sphere $\phi_{max} = 2\pi$, $z_{min} = -r$, and $z_{max} = r$, so we have the standard formula $A = 4\pi r^2$, confirming that the formula makes sense.

⟨*Sphere Public Methods*⟩ +≡   **271**
```
Float Area() const { return phiMax * radius * (zMax - zMin); }
```

6.2.4 SAMPLING

Uniformly sampling a point on the sphere's area is easy: `Sphere::Sample()` generates a point on the unit sphere using `SampleUniformSphere()` and then scales the point by the sphere's radius. A bound on the numeric error in this value is found in a fragment that will be defined later.

⟨*Sphere Method Definitions*⟩ +≡
```
pstd::optional<ShapeSample> Sphere::Sample(Point2f u) const {
    Point3f pObj = Point3f(0, 0, 0) + radius * SampleUniformSphere(u);
    ⟨Reproject pObj to sphere surface and compute pObjError 376⟩
    ⟨Compute surface normal for sphere sample and return ShapeSample 281⟩
}
```

Float 23
Point2f 92
Point3f 92
Point3fi 1061
SampleUniformSphere() 1016
ShapeSample 268
Sphere::phiMax 272
Sphere::radius 272
Sphere::zMax 272
Sphere::zMin 272

Because the object-space sphere is at the origin, the object-space surface normal is easily found by converting the object-space point to a normal vector and then normalizing it. A `Point3fi` for the sample point can be initialized from `pObj` and its error bounds. The final sample is returned in rendering space with a PDF equal to one over the surface area, since this `Sample()` method samples uniformly by surface area.

⟨*Compute surface normal for sphere sample and return* ShapeSample⟩ ≡   **280**
```
Normal3f nObj(pObj.x, pObj.y, pObj.z);
Normal3f n = Normalize((*renderFromObject)(nObj));
if (reverseOrientation)
    n *= -1;
```
⟨*Compute* (*u*, *v*) *coordinates for sphere sample* **281**⟩
```
Point3fi pi = (*renderFromObject)(Point3fi(pObj, pObjError));
return ShapeSample{Interaction(pi, n, uv), 1 / Area()};
```

The (*u*, *v*) parametric coordinates for the point are given by inverting Equations (6.1) and (6.2).

⟨*Compute* (*u*, *v*) *coordinates for sphere sample*⟩ ≡   **281**
```
Float theta = SafeACos(pObj.z / radius);
Float phi = std::atan2(pObj.y, pObj.x);
if (phi < 0) phi += 2 * Pi;
Point2f uv(phi / phiMax, (theta - thetaZMin) / (thetaZMax - thetaZMin));
```

The associated PDF() method returns the same PDF.

⟨*Sphere Public Methods*⟩ +≡   **271**
```
Float PDF(const Interaction &) const { return 1 / Area(); }
```

For the sphere sampling method that is given a point being illuminated, we can do much better than sampling over the sphere's entire area. While uniform sampling over its surface would be perfectly correct, a better approach is not to sample points on the sphere that are definitely not visible (such as those on the back side of the sphere as seen from the point). The sampling routine here instead uniformly samples directions over the solid angle subtended by the sphere from the reference point and then computes the point on the sphere corresponding to the sampled direction.

⟨*Sphere Public Methods*⟩ +≡   **271**
```
pstd::optional<ShapeSample> Sample(const ShapeSampleContext &ctx,
                                   Point2f u) const {
    ⟨Sample uniformly on sphere if p is inside it 281⟩
    ⟨Sample sphere uniformly inside subtended cone 282⟩
    ⟨Return ShapeSample for sampled point on sphere 284⟩
}
```

For points that lie inside the sphere, the entire sphere should be sampled, since the whole sphere is visible from inside it. Note that the reference point used in this determination, pOrigin, is computed using the OffsetRayOrigin() function. Doing so ensures that if the reference point came from a ray intersecting the sphere, the point tested does not lie on the wrong side of the sphere due to rounding error.

⟨*Sample uniformly on sphere if* p *is inside it*⟩ ≡   **281**
```
Point3f pCenter = (*renderFromObject)(Point3f(0, 0, 0));
Point3f pOrigin = ctx.OffsetRayOrigin(pCenter);
if (DistanceSquared(pOrigin, pCenter) <= Sqr(radius)) {
    ⟨Sample shape by area and compute incident direction wi 282⟩
    ⟨Convert area sampling PDF in ss to solid angle measure 282⟩
    return ss;
}
```

A call to the first Sample() method gives an initial ShapeSample for a point on the sphere. The direction vector from the reference point to the sampled point wi is computed and then normalized, so long as it is non-degenerate.

⟨*Sample shape by area and compute incident direction* wi⟩ ≡   **281, 291, 317, 343**
```
pstd::optional<ShapeSample> ss = Sample(u);
ss->intr.time = ctx.time;
Vector3f wi = ss->intr.p() - ctx.p();
if (LengthSquared(wi) == 0) return {};
wi = Normalize(wi);
```

To compute the value of the PDF, the method converts the value of the PDF with respect to surface area from the call to Sample() to a PDF with respect to solid angle from the reference point. Doing so requires division by the factor

$$\frac{d\omega_i}{dA} = \frac{\cos\theta_o}{r^2},$$

where θ_o is the angle between the direction of the ray from the point on the light to the reference point and the light's surface normal, and r^2 is the distance between the point on the light and the point being shaded (recall the discussion about transforming between area and directional integration domains in Section 4.2.3).

In the rare case that the surface normal and wi are perpendicular, this results in an infinite value, in which case no valid sample is returned.

⟨*Convert area sampling PDF in* ss *to solid angle measure*⟩ ≡   **281, 291, 317, 343**
```
ss->pdf /= AbsDot(ss->intr.n, -wi) /
        DistanceSquared(ctx.p(), ss->intr.p());
if (IsInf(ss->pdf))
    return {};
```

For the more common case of a point outside the sphere, sampling within the cone proceeds.

⟨*Sample sphere uniformly inside subtended cone*⟩ ≡   **281**
    ⟨*Compute quantities related to the* θ_{max} *for cone* **283**⟩
    ⟨*Compute* θ *and* ϕ *values for sample in cone* **283**⟩
    ⟨*Compute angle* α *from center of sphere to sampled point on surface* **284**⟩
    ⟨*Compute surface normal and sampled point on sphere* **284**⟩

If the reference point is outside the sphere, then as seen from the reference point p the sphere subtends an angle

$$\theta_{max} = \arcsin\left(\frac{r}{|p - p_c|}\right) = \arccos\sqrt{1 - \left(\frac{r}{|p - p_c|}\right)^2}, \qquad [6.4]$$

where r is the radius of the sphere and p_c is its center (Figure 6.5). The sampling method here computes the cosine of the subtended angle θ_{max} using Equation (6.4) and then uniformly samples directions inside this cone of directions using an approach that is derived for the SampleUniformCone() function in Section A.5.4, sampling an offset θ from the center vector ω_c and then uniformly sampling a rotation angle ϕ around the vector. That function is not used here, however, as we will need some of the intermediate values in the following fragments.

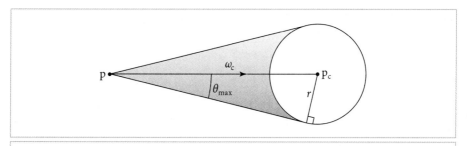

Figure 6.5: To sample points on a spherical light source, we can uniformly sample within the cone of directions around a central vector ω_c with an angular spread of up to θ_{max}. Trigonometry can be used to derive the value of $\sin\theta_{max}$, $r/|p_c - p|$.

⟨*Compute quantities related to the θ_{max} for cone*⟩ ≡   282
```
Float sinThetaMax = radius / Distance(ctx.p(), pCenter);
Float sin2ThetaMax = Sqr(sinThetaMax);
Float cosThetaMax = SafeSqrt(1 - sin2ThetaMax);
Float oneMinusCosThetaMax = 1 - cosThetaMax;
```

As shown in Section A.5.4, uniform sampling of $\cos\theta$ between $\cos\theta_{max}$ and 1 gives the cosine of a uniformly sampled direction in the cone.

⟨*Compute θ and ϕ values for sample in cone*⟩ ≡   282
```
Float cosTheta = (cosThetaMax - 1) * u[0] + 1;
Float sin2Theta = 1 - Sqr(cosTheta);
if (sin2ThetaMax < 0.00068523f /* sin^2(1.5 deg) */) {
    ⟨Compute cone sample via Taylor series expansion for small angles 283⟩
}
```

For very small θ_{max} angles, $\cos^2\theta_{max}$ is close to one. Computing $\sin^2\theta$ by subtracting this value from 1 gives a value close to 0, but with very little accuracy, since there is much less floating-point precision close to 1 than there is by 0. Therefore, in this case, we use single-term Taylor expansions near 0 to compute $\sin^2\theta$ and related terms, which gives much better accuracy.

⟨*Compute cone sample via Taylor series expansion for small angles*⟩ ≡   283
```
sin2Theta = sin2ThetaMax * u[0];
cosTheta = std::sqrt(1 - sin2Theta);
oneMinusCosThetaMax = sin2ThetaMax / 2;
```

Given a sample angle (θ, ϕ) with respect to the sampling coordinate system computed earlier, we can directly compute the corresponding point on the sphere. The first step is to find the angle γ between the vector from the reference point p_r to the sampled point on the sphere p_s and the vector from the center of the sphere p_c to p_s. The basic setting is shown in Figure 6.6.

We denote the distance from the reference point to the center of the sphere by d_c. Applying the law of sines, we can find that

$$\sin\gamma = \frac{d_c}{r}\sin\theta.$$

Because γ is an obtuse angle, $\gamma = \pi - \arcsin(d_c/r\sin\theta)$. Given two of the three angles of the triangle, it follows that

$$\alpha = \pi - \gamma - \theta = \arcsin\left(\frac{d_c}{r}\sin\theta\right) - \theta.$$

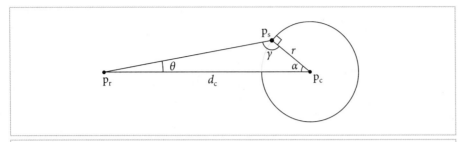

Figure 6.6: Geometric Setting for Computing the Sampled Point on the Sphere Corresponding to a Sampled Angle θ. Consider the triangle shown here. The lengths of two sides are known: one is the radius of the sphere r and the other is d_c, the distance from the reference point to the center of the sphere. We also know one angle, θ. Given these, we first solve for the angle γ before finding $\cos \alpha$.

We can avoid expensive inverse trigonometric functions by taking advantage of the fact that we only need the sine and cosine of α. If we take the cosine of both sides of this equation, apply the cosine angle addition formula, and then use the two relationships $\sin \theta_{\max} = r/d_c$ and $\cos(\arcsin x) = \sqrt{1 - x^2}$, we can find

$$\cos \alpha = \frac{\sin^2 \theta}{\sin \theta_{\max}} + \cos \theta \sqrt{1 - \frac{\sin^2 \theta}{\sin^2 \theta_{\max}}}.$$

The value of $\sin \alpha$ follows from the identity $\sin \alpha = \sqrt{1 - \cos^2 \alpha}$.

⟨*Compute angle α from center of sphere to sampled point on surface*⟩ ≡   282
```
Float cosAlpha = sin2Theta / sinThetaMax +
                 cosTheta * SafeSqrt(1 - sin2Theta / Sqr(sinThetaMax));
Float sinAlpha = SafeSqrt(1 - Sqr(cosAlpha));
```

The α angle and ϕ give the spherical coordinates for the sampled direction with respect to a coordinate system with z axis centered around the vector from the sphere center to the reference point. We can use an instance of the Frame class to transform the direction from that coordinate system to rendering space. The surface normal on the sphere can then be computed as the negation of that vector and the point on the sphere can be found by scaling by the radius and translating by the sphere's center point.

⟨*Compute surface normal and sampled point on sphere*⟩ ≡   282
```
Float phi = u[1] * 2 * Pi;
Vector3f w = SphericalDirection(sinAlpha, cosAlpha, phi);
Frame samplingFrame = Frame::FromZ(Normalize(pCenter - ctx.p()));
Normal3f n(samplingFrame.FromLocal(-w));
Point3f p = pCenter + radius * Point3f(n.x, n.y, n.z);
if (reverseOrientation)
    n *= -1;
```

The ⟨*Compute (u, v) coordinates for sampled point on sphere*⟩ fragment applies the same mapping using the object space sampled point as is done in the Intersect() method, and so it is elided. The PDF for uniform sampling in a cone is $1/(2\pi(1 - \cos \theta_{\max}))$. (A derivation is in Section A.5.4.)

⟨*Return ShapeSample for sampled point on sphere*⟩ ≡   281
```
⟨Compute pError for sampled point on sphere⟩
⟨Compute (u, v) coordinates for sampled point on sphere⟩
return ShapeSample{Interaction(Point3fi(p, pError), n, ctx.time, uv),
        1 / (2 * Pi * oneMinusCosThetaMax)};
```

The method that computes the PDF for sampling a direction toward a sphere from a reference point also differs depending on which of the two sampling strategies would be used for the point.

⟨*Sphere Public Methods*⟩ +≡   271
```
Float PDF(const ShapeSampleContext &ctx, Vector3f wi) const {
    Point3f pCenter = (*renderFromObject)(Point3f(0, 0, 0));
    Point3f pOrigin = ctx.OffsetRayOrigin(pCenter);
    if (DistanceSquared(pOrigin, pCenter) <= Sqr(radius)) {
        ⟨Return solid angle PDF for point inside sphere 285⟩
    }
    ⟨Compute general solid angle sphere PDF 285⟩
}
```

If the reference point is inside the sphere, a uniform area sampling strategy would have been used.

⟨*Return solid angle PDF for point inside sphere*⟩ ≡   285
```
    ⟨Intersect sample ray with shape geometry 285⟩
    ⟨Compute PDF in solid angle measure from shape intersection point 285⟩
    return pdf;
```

First, the corresponding point on the sphere is found by intersecting a ray leaving the reference point in direction wi with the sphere. Note that this is a fairly efficient computation since it is only intersecting the ray with a single sphere and not the entire scene.

⟨*Intersect sample ray with shape geometry*⟩ ≡   285, 291, 324, 345
```
    Ray ray = ctx.SpawnRay(wi);
    pstd::optional<ShapeIntersection> isect = Intersect(ray);
    if (!isect) return 0;
```

In turn, the uniform area density of one over the surface area is converted to a solid angle density following the same approach as was used in the previous Sample() method.

⟨*Compute PDF in solid angle measure from shape intersection point*⟩ ≡   285, 291, 324
```
    Float pdf = (1 / Area()) / (AbsDot(isect->intr.n, -wi) /
                                DistanceSquared(ctx.p(), isect->intr.p()));
    if (IsInf(pdf)) pdf = 0;
```

The value of the PDF is easily computed using the same trigonometric identities as were used in the sampling routine.

⟨*Compute general solid angle sphere PDF*⟩ ≡   285
```
    Float sin2ThetaMax = radius * radius / DistanceSquared(ctx.p(), pCenter);
    Float cosThetaMax = SafeSqrt(1 - sin2ThetaMax);
    Float oneMinusCosThetaMax = 1 - cosThetaMax;
    ⟨Compute more accurate oneMinusCosThetaMax for small solid angle 285⟩
    return 1 / (2 * Pi * oneMinusCosThetaMax);
```

Here it is also worth considering numerical accuracy when the sphere subtends a small solid angle from the reference point. In that case, cosThetaMax will be close to 1 and the value of oneMinusCosThetaMax will be relatively inaccurate; we then switch to the one-term Taylor approximation of $1 - \cos\theta \approx 1/2 \sin^2\theta$, which is more accurate near zero.

⟨*Compute more accurate oneMinusCosThetaMax for small solid angle*⟩ ≡   285
```
    if (sin2ThetaMax < 0.00068523f /* sin^2(1.5 deg) */)
        oneMinusCosThetaMax = sin2ThetaMax / 2;
```

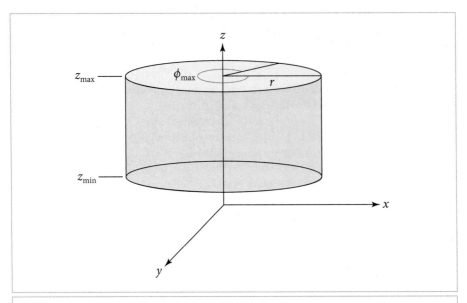

Figure 6.7: Basic Setting for the Cylinder Shape. The cylinder has a radius of r and covers a range along the z axis. A partial cylinder may be swept by specifying a maximum ϕ value.

6.3 CYLINDERS

Another useful quadric is the cylinder; pbrt provides a cylinder Shape that is centered around the z axis. The user can supply a minimum and maximum z value for the cylinder, as well as a radius and maximum ϕ sweep value (Figure 6.7).

⟨*Cylinder Definition*⟩ ≡
```
  class Cylinder {
    public:
      ⟨Cylinder Public Methods 287⟩
    private:
      ⟨Cylinder Private Members 287⟩
  };
```

In parametric form, a cylinder is described by the following equations:

$$\phi = u\,\phi_{\max}$$
$$x = r\cos\phi$$
$$y = r\sin\phi$$
$$z = z_{\min} + v(z_{\max} - z_{\min}).$$

Figure 6.8 shows a rendered image of two cylinders. Like the sphere image, the right cylinder is a complete cylinder, while the left one is a partial cylinder because it has a $\phi_{\max}$ value less than 2π.

Similar to the Sphere constructor, the Cylinder constructor takes transformations that define its object space and the parameters that define the cylinder itself. Its constructor just initializes the corresponding member variables, so we will not include it here.

Cylinder 286
Shape 261
Sphere 271

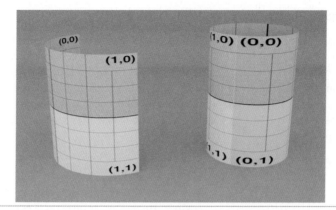

Figure 6.8: Two Cylinders. A partial cylinder is on the left, and a complete cylinder is on the right.

⟨*Cylinder Public Methods*⟩ ≡   286
```
Cylinder(const Transform *renderFromObj, const Transform *objFromRender,
    bool reverseOrientation, Float radius, Float zMin, Float zMax,
    Float phiMax);
```

⟨*Cylinder Private Members*⟩ ≡   286
```
const Transform *renderFromObject, *objectFromRender;
bool reverseOrientation, transformSwapsHandedness;
Float radius, zMin, zMax, phiMax;
```

6.3.1 AREA AND BOUNDING

A cylinder is a rolled-up rectangle. If you unroll the rectangle, its height is $z_{max} - z_{min}$, and its width is $r\phi_{max}$:

⟨*Cylinder Public Methods*⟩ +≡   286
```
Float Area() const { return (zMax - zMin) * radius * phiMax; }
```

As was done with the sphere, the cylinder's spatial bounding method computes a conservative bounding box using the z range but does not take into account the maximum ϕ.

⟨*Cylinder Method Definitions*⟩ ≡
```
Bounds3f Cylinder::Bounds() const {
    return (*renderFromObject)(Bounds3f({-radius, -radius, zMin},
                                        { radius,  radius, zMax}));
}
```

Its surface normal bounding function is conservative in two ways: not only does it not account for $\phi_{max} < 2\pi$, but the actual set of normals of a cylinder can be described by a circle on the sphere of all directions. However, DirectionCone's representation is not able to bound such a distribution more tightly than with the entire sphere of directions, and so that is the bound that is returned.

⟨*Cylinder Public Methods*⟩ +≡   286
```
DirectionCone NormalBounds() const { return DirectionCone::EntireSphere(); }
```

6.3.2 INTERSECTION TESTS

Also similar to the sphere (and for similar reasons), Cylinder provides a BasicIntersect() method that returns a QuadricIntersection as well as an InteractionFromIntersection() method that converts that to a full SurfaceInteraction. Given these, the Intersect() method is again a simple composition of them. (If pbrt used virtual functions, a design alternative would be to have a QuadricShape class that provided a default Intersect() method and left BasicIntersect() and InteractionFromIntersection() as pure virtual functions for subclasses to implement.)

⟨*Cylinder Public Methods*⟩ +≡   286
```
    pstd::optional<ShapeIntersection> Intersect(const Ray &ray,
                                      Float tMax = Infinity) const {
        pstd::optional<QuadricIntersection> isect = BasicIntersect(ray, tMax);
        if (!isect) return {};
        SurfaceInteraction intr =
            InteractionFromIntersection(*isect, -ray.d, ray.time);
        return ShapeIntersection{intr, isect->tHit};
    }
```

The form of the BasicIntersect() method also parallels the sphere's, computing appropriate quadratic coefficients, solving the quadratic equation, and then handling the various cases for partial cylinders. A number of fragments can be reused from the Sphere's implementation.

⟨*Cylinder Public Methods*⟩ +≡   286
```
    pstd::optional<QuadricIntersection> BasicIntersect(const Ray &r,
                                          Float tMax) const {
        Float phi;
        Point3f pHit;
        ⟨Transform Ray origin and direction to object space 273⟩
        ⟨Solve quadratic equation to find cylinder t0 and t1 values 288⟩
        ⟨Check quadric shape t0 and t1 for nearest intersection 275⟩
        ⟨Compute cylinder hit point and φ 289⟩
        ⟨Test cylinder intersection against clipping parameters 289⟩
        ⟨Return QuadricIntersection for cylinder intersection 289⟩
    }
```

As before, the fragment that computes the quadratic discriminant, ⟨*Compute cylinder quadratic discriminant* discrim⟩, is defined in Section 6.8.3 after topics related to floating-point accuracy have been discussed.

⟨*Solve quadratic equation to find cylinder t0 and t1 values*⟩ ≡   288
```
    Interval t0, t1;
    ⟨Compute cylinder quadratic coefficients 289⟩
    ⟨Compute cylinder quadratic discriminant discrim 372⟩
    ⟨Compute quadratic t values 275⟩
```

As with spheres, the ray–cylinder intersection formula can be found by substituting the ray equation into the cylinder's implicit equation. The implicit equation for an infinitely long cylinder centered on the z axis with radius r is

$$x^2 + y^2 - r^2 = 0.$$

Substituting the ray equation, Equation (3.4), we have

$$\left(o_x + t\mathbf{d}_x\right)^2 + \left(o_y + t\mathbf{d}_y\right)^2 = r^2.$$

When we expand this equation and find the coefficients of the quadratic equation $at^2 + bt + c = 0$, we have

$$a = \mathbf{d}_x^2 + \mathbf{d}_y^2$$
$$b = 2(\mathbf{d}_x o_x + \mathbf{d}_y o_y)$$
$$c = o_x^2 + o_y^2 - r^2.$$

⟨*Compute cylinder quadratic coefficients*⟩ ≡   288
```
Interval a = Sqr(di.x) + Sqr(di.y);
Interval b = 2 * (di.x * oi.x + di.y * oi.y);
Interval c = Sqr(oi.x) + Sqr(oi.y) - Sqr(Interval(radius));
```

As with spheres, the implementation refines the computed intersection point to reduce the rounding error in the point computed by evaluating the ray equation; see Section 6.8.5. Afterward, we invert the parametric description of the cylinder to compute ϕ from x and y; it turns out that the result is the same as for the sphere.

⟨*Compute cylinder hit point and* ϕ⟩ ≡   288, 289
```
pHit = Point3f(oi) + (Float)tShapeHit * Vector3f(di);
```
⟨*Refine cylinder intersection point* **375**⟩
```
phi = std::atan2(pHit.y, pHit.x);
if (phi < 0) phi += 2 * Pi;
```

The next step in the intersection method makes sure that the hit is in the specified z range and that the angle ϕ is acceptable. If not, it rejects the hit and checks t_1 if it has not already been considered—these tests resemble the conditional logic in Sphere::Intersect().

⟨*Test cylinder intersection against clipping parameters*⟩ ≡   288
```
if (pHit.z < zMin || pHit.z > zMax || phi > phiMax) {
    if (tShapeHit == t1)
        return {};
    tShapeHit = t1;
    if (t1.UpperBound() > tMax)
        return {};
    ⟨Compute cylinder hit point and ϕ 289⟩
    if (pHit.z < zMin || pHit.z > zMax || phi > phiMax)
        return {};
}
```

For a successful intersection, the same three values suffice to provide enough information to later compute the corresponding SurfaceInteraction.

⟨*Return* QuadricIntersection *for cylinder intersection*⟩ ≡   288
```
return QuadricIntersection{Float(tShapeHit), pHit, phi};
```

As with the sphere, IntersectP()'s implementation is a simple wrapper around Basic Intersect().

⟨*Cylinder Public Methods*⟩ +≡   286
```
bool IntersectP(const Ray &r, Float tMax = Infinity) const {
    return BasicIntersect(r, tMax).has_value();
}
```

InteractionFromIntersection() computes all the quantities needed to initialize a Surface Interaction from a cylinder's QuadricIntersection.

⟨*Cylinder Public Methods*⟩ +≡   **286**
```
    SurfaceInteraction InteractionFromIntersection(
            const QuadricIntersection &isect, Vector3f wo, Float time) const {
        Point3f pHit = isect.pObj;
        Float phi = isect.phi;
        ⟨Find parametric representation of cylinder hit 290⟩
        ⟨Compute error bounds for cylinder intersection 375⟩
        ⟨Return SurfaceInteraction for quadric intersection 279⟩
    }
```

Again the parametric *u* value is computed by scaling ϕ to lie between 0 and 1. Inversion of the parametric equation for the cylinder's *z* value gives the *v* parametric coordinate.

⟨*Find parametric representation of cylinder hit*⟩ ≡   **290**
```
    Float u = phi / phiMax;
    Float v = (pHit.z - zMin) / (zMax - zMin);
    ⟨Compute cylinder ∂p/∂u and ∂p/∂v 290⟩
    ⟨Compute cylinder ∂n/∂u and ∂n/∂v 290⟩
```

The partial derivatives for a cylinder are easy to derive:

$$\frac{\partial \mathbf{p}}{\partial u} = (-\phi_{\max} y, \ \phi_{\max} x, \ 0)$$

$$\frac{\partial \mathbf{p}}{\partial v} = (0, \ 0, \ z_{\max} - z_{\min}).$$

⟨*Compute cylinder ∂p/∂u and ∂p/∂v*⟩ ≡   **290**
```
    Vector3f dpdu(-phiMax * pHit.y, phiMax * pHit.x, 0);
    Vector3f dpdv(0, 0, zMax - zMin);
```

We again use the Weingarten equations to compute the parametric partial derivatives of the cylinder normal. The relevant partial derivatives are

$$\frac{\partial^2 \mathbf{p}}{\partial u^2} = -\phi_{\max}^2 (x, \ y, \ 0)$$

$$\frac{\partial^2 \mathbf{p}}{\partial u \partial v} = (0, 0, 0)$$

$$\frac{\partial^2 \mathbf{p}}{\partial v^2} = (0, 0, 0).$$

⟨*Compute cylinder ∂n/∂u and ∂n/∂v*⟩ ≡   **290**
```
    Vector3f d2Pduu = -phiMax * phiMax * Vector3f(pHit.x, pHit.y, 0);
    Vector3f d2Pduv(0, 0, 0), d2Pdvv(0, 0, 0);
    ⟨Compute coefficients for fundamental forms 279⟩
    ⟨Compute ∂n/∂u and ∂n/∂v from fundamental form coefficients 279⟩
```

6.3.3 SAMPLING

Uniformly sampling the surface area of a cylinder is straightforward: uniform sampling of the height and ϕ give uniform area sampling. Intuitively, it can be understood that this approach works because a cylinder is just a rolled-up rectangle.

⟨*Cylinder Public Methods*⟩ +≡   286
```
    pstd::optional<ShapeSample> Sample(Point2f u) const {
        Float z = Lerp(u[0], zMin, zMax);
        Float phi = u[1] * phiMax;
        ⟨Compute cylinder sample position pi and normal n from z and φ 291⟩
        Point2f uv(phi / phiMax, (pObj.z - zMin) / (zMax - zMin));
        return ShapeSample{Interaction(pi, n, uv), 1 / Area()};
    }
```

Given z and ϕ, the corresponding object-space position and normal are easily found.

⟨*Compute cylinder sample position* pi *and normal* n *from z and φ*⟩ ≡   291
```
    Point3f pObj = Point3f(radius * std::cos(phi), radius * std::sin(phi), z);
    ⟨Reproject pObj to cylinder surface and compute pObjError 376⟩
    Point3fi pi = (*renderFromObject)(Point3fi(pObj, pObjError));
    Normal3f n = Normalize((*renderFromObject)(Normal3f(pObj.x, pObj.y, 0)));
    if (reverseOrientation)
        n *= -1;
```

⟨*Cylinder Public Methods*⟩ +≡   286
```
    Float PDF(const Interaction &) const { return 1 / Area(); }
```

Unlike the Sphere, pbrt's Cylinder does not have a specialized solid angle sampling method. Instead, it samples a point on the cylinder uniformly by area without making use of the reference point before converting the area density for that point to a solid angle density before returning it. Both the Sample() and PDF() methods can be implemented using the same fragments that were used for solid angle sampling of reference points inside spheres.

⟨*Cylinder Public Methods*⟩ +≡   286
```
    pstd::optional<ShapeSample> Sample(const ShapeSampleContext &ctx,
                                       Point2f u) const {
        ⟨Sample shape by area and compute incident direction wi 282⟩
        ⟨Convert area sampling PDF in ss to solid angle measure 282⟩
        return ss;
    }
```

⟨*Cylinder Public Methods*⟩ +≡   286
```
    Float PDF(const ShapeSampleContext &ctx, Vector3f wi) const {
        ⟨Intersect sample ray with shape geometry 285⟩
        ⟨Compute PDF in solid angle measure from shape intersection point 285⟩
        return pdf;
    }
```

6.4 DISKS

The disk is an interesting quadric since it has a particularly straightforward intersection routine that avoids solving the quadratic equation. In pbrt, a Disk is a circular disk of radius r at height h along the z axis.

To describe partial disks, the user may specify a maximum ϕ value beyond which the disk is cut off (Figure 6.9). The disk can also be generalized to an annulus by specifying an inner radius, r_i. In parametric form, it is described by

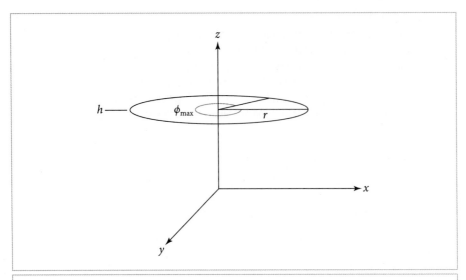

Figure 6.9: Basic Setting for the Disk Shape. The disk has radius r and is located at height h along the z axis. A partial disk may be swept by specifying a maximum ϕ value and an inner radius r_i.

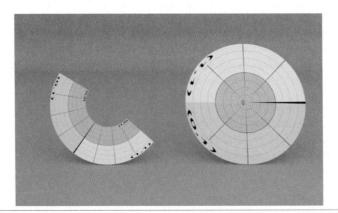

Figure 6.10: Two Disks. A partial disk is on the left, and a complete disk is on the right.

$$\phi = u\,\phi_{max}$$
$$x = ((1-v)r + vr_i)\cos\phi$$
$$y = ((1-v)r + vr_i)\sin\phi$$
$$z = h.$$

Figure 6.10 is a rendered image of two disks.

⟨*Disk Definition*⟩ ≡
```
class Disk {
  public:
    ⟨Disk Public Methods 293⟩
  private:
    ⟨Disk Private Members 293⟩
};
```

The Disk constructor directly initializes its various member variables from the values passed to it. We have omitted it here because it is trivial.

⟨*Disk Private Members*⟩ ≡   **292**
```
const Transform *renderFromObject, *objectFromRender;
bool reverseOrientation, transformSwapsHandedness;
Float height, radius, innerRadius, phiMax;
```

6.4.1 AREA AND BOUNDING

Disks have easily computed surface area, since they are just portions of an annulus:

$$A = \frac{\phi_{\max}}{2}(r^2 - r_i^2).$$

⟨*Disk Public Methods*⟩ ≡   **292**
```
Float Area() const {
    return phiMax * 0.5f * (Sqr(radius) - Sqr(innerRadius));
}
```

The bounding method is also quite straightforward; it computes a bounding box centered at the height of the disk along z, with extent of radius in both the x and y directions.

⟨*Disk Method Definitions*⟩ ≡
```
Bounds3f Disk::Bounds() const {
    return (*renderFromObject)(
        Bounds3f(Point3f(-radius, -radius, height),
                 Point3f( radius,  radius, height)));
}
```

A disk has a single surface normal.

⟨*Disk Method Definitions*⟩ +≡
```
DirectionCone Disk::NormalBounds() const {
    Normal3f n = (*renderFromObject)(Normal3f(0, 0, 1));
    if (reverseOrientation) n = -n;
    return DirectionCone(Vector3f(n));
}
```

6.4.2 INTERSECTION TESTS

The Disk intersection test methods follow the same form as the earlier quadrics. We omit Intersect(), as it is exactly the same as Sphere::Intersect() and Cylinder::Intersect(), with calls to BasicIntersect() and then InteractionFromIntersection().

The basic intersection test for a ray with a disk is easy. The intersection of the ray with the $z = h$ plane that the disk lies in is found and then the intersection point is checked to see if it lies inside the disk.

⟨*Disk Public Methods*⟩ +≡   **292**
```
pstd::optional<QuadricIntersection> BasicIntersect(const Ray &r,
                                                   Float tMax) const {
    ⟨Transform Ray origin and direction to object space 273⟩
    ⟨Compute plane intersection for disk 294⟩
    ⟨See if hit point is inside disk radii and φmax 294⟩
    ⟨Return QuadricIntersection for disk intersection 295⟩
}
```

The first step is to compute the parametric t value where the ray intersects the plane that the disk lies in. We want to find t such that the z component of the ray's position is equal to the height of the disk. Thus,

$$h = o_z + t\mathbf{d}_z$$

and so

$$t = \frac{h - o_z}{\mathbf{d}_z}.$$

The intersection method computes a t value and checks to see if it is inside the range of values $(0, \text{tMax})$. If not, the routine can report that there is no intersection.

⟨*Compute plane intersection for disk*⟩ ≡   293
    ⟨*Reject disk intersections for rays parallel to the disk's plane* 294⟩
    ```
Float tShapeHit = (height - Float(oi.z)) / Float(di.z);
if (tShapeHit <= 0 || tShapeHit >= tMax)
    return {};
```

If the ray is parallel to the disk's plane (i.e., the z component of its direction is zero), no intersection is reported. The case where a ray is both parallel to the disk's plane and lies within the plane is somewhat ambiguous, but it is most reasonable to define intersecting a disk edge-on as "no intersection." This case must be handled explicitly so that not-a-number floating-point values are not generated by the following code.

⟨*Reject disk intersections for rays parallel to the disk's plane*⟩ ≡   294
```
if (Float(di.z) == 0)
    return {};
```

Now the intersection method can compute the point pHit where the ray intersects the plane. Once the plane intersection is known, an invalid intersection is returned if the distance from the hit to the center of the disk is more than Disk::radius or less than Disk::innerRadius. This check can be optimized by computing the squared distance to the center, taking advantage of the fact that the x and y coordinates of the center point (0, 0, height) are zero, and the z coordinate of pHit is equal to height.

⟨*See if hit point is inside disk radii and* $\phi_{\max}$⟩ ≡   293
```
Point3f pHit = Point3f(oi) + (Float)tShapeHit * Vector3f(di);
Float dist2 = Sqr(pHit.x) + Sqr(pHit.y);
if (dist2 > Sqr(radius) || dist2 < Sqr(innerRadius))
    return {};
```
    ⟨*Test disk* ϕ *value against* $\phi_{\max}$ 294⟩

If the distance check passes, a final test makes sure that the ϕ value of the hit point is between zero and $\phi_{\max}$, specified by the caller. Inverting the disk's parameterization gives the same expression for ϕ as the other quadric shapes. Because a ray can only intersect a disk once, there is no need to consider a second intersection if this test fails, as was the case with the two earlier quadrics.

⟨*Test disk* ϕ *value against* $\phi_{\max}$⟩ ≡   294
```
Float phi = std::atan2(pHit.y, pHit.x);
if (phi < 0) phi += 2 * Pi;
if (phi > phiMax)
    return {};
```

⟨*Return* QuadricIntersection *for disk intersection*⟩ ≡   **293**
```
    return QuadricIntersection{tShapeHit, pHit, phi};
```

Finding the SurfaceInteraction corresponding to a disk intersection follows the same process of inverting the parametric representation we have seen before.

⟨*Disk Public Methods*⟩ +≡   **292**
```
    SurfaceInteraction InteractionFromIntersection(
            const QuadricIntersection &isect, Vector3f wo, Float time) const {
        Point3f pHit = isect.pObj;
        Float phi = isect.phi;
```
        ⟨*Find parametric representation of disk hit* **295**⟩
        ⟨*Refine disk intersection point* **375**⟩
        ⟨*Compute error bounds for disk intersection* **376**⟩
        ⟨*Return* SurfaceInteraction *for quadric intersection* **279**⟩
```
    }
```

The parameter u is first scaled to reflect the partial disk specified by ϕ_{max}, and v is computed by inverting the parametric equation. The equations for the partial derivatives at the hit point can be derived with a process similar to that used for the previous quadrics. Because the normal of a disk is the same everywhere, the partial derivatives $\partial \mathbf{n}/\partial u$ and $\partial \mathbf{n}/\partial v$ are both trivially $(0, 0, 0)$.

⟨*Find parametric representation of disk hit*⟩ ≡   **295**
```
    Float u = phi / phiMax;
    Float rHit = std::sqrt(Sqr(pHit.x) + Sqr(pHit.y));
    Float v = (radius - rHit) / (radius - innerRadius);
    Vector3f dpdu(-phiMax * pHit.y, phiMax * pHit.x, 0);
    Vector3f dpdv = Vector3f(pHit.x, pHit.y, 0) * (innerRadius - radius) / rHit;
    Normal3f dndu(0, 0, 0), dndv(0, 0, 0);
```

As usual, the implementation of IntersectP() is straightforward.

⟨*Disk Public Methods*⟩ +≡   **292**
```
    bool IntersectP(const Ray &r, Float tMax = Infinity) const {
        return BasicIntersect(r, tMax).has_value();
    }
```

6.4.3 SAMPLING

The Disk area sampling method uses a utility routine, SampleUniformDiskConcentric(), that uniformly samples a unit disk. (It is defined in Section A.5.1.) The point that it returns is then scaled by the radius and offset in z so that it lies on the disk of a given radius and height. Note that our implementation here does not account for partial disks due to Disk::innerRadius being nonzero or Disk::phiMax being less than 2π. Fixing this bug is left for an exercise at the end of the chapter.

⟨*Disk Public Methods*⟩ +≡   **292**
```
    pstd::optional<ShapeSample> Sample(Point2f u) const {
        Point2f pd = SampleUniformDiskConcentric(u);
        Point3f pObj(pd.x * radius, pd.y * radius, height);
        Point3fi pi = (*renderFromObject)(Point3fi(pObj));
        Normal3f n = Normalize((*renderFromObject)(Normal3f(0, 0, 1)));
```

```
        if (reverseOrientation)
            n *= -1;
      ⟨Compute (u, v) for sampled point on disk 296⟩
      return ShapeSample{Interaction(pi, n, uv), 1 / Area()};
  }
```

The same computation as in the `Intersect()` method gives the parametric (u, v) for the sampled point.

⟨*Compute (u, v) for sampled point on disk*⟩ ≡   295
```
      Float phi = std::atan2(pd.y, pd.x);
      if (phi < 0) phi += 2 * Pi;
      Float radiusSample = std::sqrt(Sqr(pObj.x) + Sqr(pObj.y));
      Point2f uv(phi / phiMax, (radius - radiusSample) / (radius - innerRadius));
```

⟨*Disk Public Methods*⟩ +≡   292
```
      Float PDF(const Interaction &) const { return 1 / Area(); }
```

We do not provide a specialized solid angle sampling method for disks, but follow the same approach that we did for cylinders, sampling uniformly by area and then computing the probability density to be with respect to solid angle. The implementations of those methods are not included here, as they are the same as they were for cylinders.

6.5 TRIANGLE MESHES

The triangle is one of the most commonly used shapes in computer graphics; complex scenes may be modeled using millions of triangles to achieve great detail. (Figure 6.11 shows an image of a complex triangle mesh of over four million triangles.)

While a natural representation would be to have a `Triangle` shape implementation where each triangle stored the positions of its three vertices, a more memory-efficient representation is to separately store entire triangle meshes with an array of vertex positions where each individual triangle just stores three offsets into this array for its three vertices. To see why this is the case, consider the celebrated Euler–Poincaré formula, which relates the number of vertices V, edges E, and faces F on closed discrete meshes as

$$V - E + F = 2(1 - g),$$

where $g \in \mathbb{N}$ is the *genus* of the mesh. The genus is usually a small number and can be interpreted as the number of "handles" in the mesh (analogous to a handle of a teacup). On a triangle mesh, the number of edges and vertices is furthermore related by the identity

$$E = \frac{3}{2}F.$$

This can be seen by dividing each edge into two parts associated with the two adjacent triangles. There are $3F$ such half-edges, and all colocated pairs constitute the E mesh edges. For large closed triangle meshes, the overall effect of the genus usually becomes negligible and we can combine the previous two equations (with $g = 0$) to obtain

$$F \approx 2V.$$

In other words, there are approximately twice as many faces as vertices. Since each face references three vertices, every vertex is (on average) referenced a total of six times. Thus, when vertices are shared, the total amortized storage required per triangle will be 12 bytes of

Figure 6.11: Ganesha Model. This triangle mesh contains over four million individual triangles. It was created from a real statue using a 3D scanner that uses structured light to determine shapes of objects.

memory for the offsets (at 4 bytes for three 32-bit integer offsets) plus half of the storage for one vertex—6 bytes, assuming three 4-byte floats are used to store the vertex position—for a total of 18 bytes per triangle. This is much better than the 36 bytes per triangle that storing the three positions directly would require. The relative storage savings are even better when there are per-vertex surface normals or texture coordinates in a mesh.

6.5.1 MESH REPRESENTATION AND STORAGE

pbrt uses the TriangleMesh class to store the shared information about a triangle mesh. It is defined in the files util/mesh.h and util/mesh.cpp.

⟨*TriangleMesh Definition*⟩ ≡
    class TriangleMesh {
      public:
        ⟨*TriangleMesh Public Methods*⟩
        ⟨*TriangleMesh Public Members* **298**⟩
    };

TriangleMesh 297

In addition to the mesh vertex positions and vertex indices, per-vertex normals n, tangent vectors s, and texture coordinates uv may be provided. The corresponding vectors should be empty if there are no such values or should be the same size as p otherwise.

⟨*TriangleMesh Method Definitions*⟩ ≡
```
    TriangleMesh::TriangleMesh(
            const Transform &renderFromObject, bool reverseOrientation,
            std::vector<int> indices, std::vector<Point3f> p,
            std::vector<Vector3f> s, std::vector<Normal3f> n,
            std::vector<Point2f> uv, std::vector<int> faceIndices, Allocator alloc)
        : nTriangles(indices.size() / 3), nVertices(p.size()) {
        ⟨Initialize mesh vertexIndices 298⟩
        ⟨Transform mesh vertices to rendering space and initialize mesh p 301⟩
        ⟨Remainder of TriangleMesh constructor⟩
    }
```

The mesh data is made available via public member variables; as with things like coordinates of points or rays' directions, there would be little benefit and some bother from information hiding in this case.

⟨*TriangleMesh Public Members*⟩ ≡   297
```
    int nTriangles, nVertices;
    const int *vertexIndices = nullptr;
    const Point3f *p = nullptr;
```

Although its constructor takes `std::vector` parameters, `TriangleMesh` stores plain pointers to its data arrays. The `vertexIndices` pointer points to 3 * `nTriangles` values, and the per-vertex pointers, if not `nullptr`, point to `nVertices` values.

We chose this design so that different `TriangleMeshes` could potentially point to the same arrays in memory in the case that they were both given the same values for some or all of their parameters. Although pbrt offers capabilities for object instancing, where multiple copies of the same geometry can be placed in the scene with different transformation matrices (e.g., via the `TransformedPrimitive` that is described in Section 7.1.2), the scenes provided to it do not always make full use of this capability. For example, with the landscape scene in Figures 5.11 and 7.2, over 400 MB is saved from detecting such redundant arrays.

The `BufferCache` class handles the details of storing a single unique copy of each buffer provided to it. Its `LookupOrAdd()` method, to be defined shortly, takes a `std::vector` of the type it manages and returns a pointer to memory that stores the same values.

⟨*Initialize mesh* vertexIndices⟩ ≡   298
```
    vertexIndices = intBufferCache->LookupOrAdd(indices, alloc);
```

The `BufferCaches` are made available through global variables in the pbrt namespace. Additional ones, not included here, handle normals, tangent vectors, and texture coordinates.

⟨*BufferCache Global Declarations*⟩ ≡
```
    extern BufferCache<int> *intBufferCache;
    extern BufferCache<Point3f> *point3BufferCache;
```

The `BufferCache` class is templated based on the array element type that it stores.

⟨*BufferCache Definition*⟩ ≡
```
template <typename T> class BufferCache {
  public:
    ⟨BufferCache Public Methods 300⟩
  private:
    ⟨BufferCache::Buffer Definition 299⟩
    ⟨BufferCache::BufferHasher Definition 300⟩
    ⟨BufferCache Private Members 299⟩
};
```

BufferCache allows concurrent use by multiple threads so that multiple meshes can be added to the scene in parallel; the scene construction code in Appendix C takes advantage of this capability. While a single mutex could be used to manage access to it, contention over that mutex by multiple threads can inhibit concurrency, reducing the benefits of multi-threading. Therefore, the cache is broken into 64 independent *shards*, each holding a subset of the entries. Each shard has its own mutex, allowing different threads to concurrently access different shards.

⟨*BufferCache Private Members*⟩ ≡   **299**
```
static constexpr int logShards = 6;
static constexpr int nShards = 1 << logShards;
std::shared_mutex mutex[nShards];
std::unordered_set<Buffer, BufferHasher> cache[nShards];
```

Buffer is a small helper class that wraps an allocation managed by the BufferCache.

⟨*BufferCache::Buffer Definition*⟩ ≡   **299**
```
struct Buffer {
    ⟨BufferCache::Buffer Public Methods 299⟩
    const T *ptr = nullptr;
    size_t size = 0, hash;
};
```

The Buffer constructor computes the buffer's hash, which is stored in a member variable.

⟨*BufferCache::Buffer Public Methods*⟩ ≡   **299**
```
Buffer(const T *ptr, size_t size) : ptr(ptr), size(size) {
    hash = HashBuffer(ptr, size);
}
```

An equality operator, which is required by the std::unordered_set, only returns true if both buffers are the same size and store the same values.

⟨*BufferCache::Buffer Public Methods*⟩ +≡   **299**
```
bool operator==(const Buffer &b) const {
    return size == b.size && hash == b.hash &&
           std::memcmp(ptr, b.ptr, size * sizeof(T)) == 0;
}
```

BufferHasher is another helper class, used by std::unordered_set. It returns the buffer's already-computed hash.

⟨*BufferCache::BufferHasher Definition*⟩ ≡   **299**
```
    struct BufferHasher {
        size_t operator()(const Buffer &b) const {
            return b.hash;
        }
    };
```

The `BufferCache` `LookUpOrAdd()` method checks to see if the values stored by the provided buffer are already in the cache and returns a pointer to them if so. Otherwise, it allocates memory to store them and returns a pointer to it.

⟨*BufferCache Public Methods*⟩ ≡   **299**
```
    const T *LookupOrAdd(pstd::span<const T> buf, Allocator alloc) {
```
⟨*Return pointer to data if* buf *contents are already in the cache* **300**⟩
⟨*Add* buf *contents to cache and return pointer to cached copy* **300**⟩
```
    }
```

The `pstd::span`'s contents need to be wrapped in a `Buffer` instance to be able to search for a matching buffer in the cache. The buffer's pointer is returned if it is already present. Because the cache is only read here and is not being modified, the `lock_shared()` capability of `std::shared_mutex` is used here, allowing multiple threads to read the hash table concurrently.

⟨*Return pointer to data if* buf *contents are already in the cache*⟩ ≡   **300**
```
    Buffer lookupBuffer(buf.data(), buf.size());
    int shardIndex = uint32_t(lookupBuffer.hash) >> (32 - logShards);
    mutex[shardIndex].lock_shared();
    if (auto iter = cache[shardIndex].find(lookupBuffer);
        iter != cache[shardIndex].end()) {
        const T *ptr = iter->ptr;
        mutex[shardIndex].unlock_shared();
        return ptr;
    }
```

Otherwise, memory is allocated using the allocator to store the buffer, and the values are copied from the provided span before the `Buffer` is added to the cache. An exclusive lock to the mutex must be held in order to modify the cache; one is acquired by giving up the shared lock and then calling the regular `lock()` method.

⟨*Add* buf *contents to cache and return pointer to cached copy*⟩ ≡   **300**
```
    mutex[shardIndex].unlock_shared();
    T *ptr = alloc.allocate_object<T>(buf.size());
    std::copy(buf.begin(), buf.end(), ptr);
    mutex[shardIndex].lock();
```
⟨*Handle the case of another thread adding the buffer first* **301**⟩
```
    cache[shardIndex].insert(Buffer(ptr, buf.size()));
    mutex[shardIndex].unlock();
    return ptr;
```

Allocator 40

BufferCache::Buffer::hash
  299

BufferCache::cache 299

BufferCache::mutex 299

std::pmr::
  polymorphic_allocator::
  allocate_object()
  41

It is possible that another thread may have added the buffer to the cache before the current thread is able to; if the same buffer is being added by multiple threads concurrently, then one will end up acquiring the exclusive lock before the other. In that rare case, a pointer to the already-added buffer is returned and the memory allocated by this thread is released.

⟨*Handle the case of another thread adding the buffer first*⟩ ≡   **300**
```
if (auto iter = cache[shardIndex].find(lookupBuffer);
    iter != cache[shardIndex].end()) {
    const T *cachePtr = iter->ptr;
    mutex[shardIndex].unlock();
    alloc.deallocate_object(ptr, buf.size());
    return cachePtr;
}
```

Returning now to the TriangleMesh constructor, the vertex positions are processed next. Unlike the other shapes that leave the shape description in object space and then transform incoming rays from rendering space to object space, triangle meshes transform the shape into rendering space and thus save the work of transforming incoming rays into object space and the work of transforming the intersection's geometric representation out to rendering space. This is a good idea because this operation can be performed once at startup, avoiding transforming rays many times during rendering. Using this approach with quadrics is more complicated, although possible—see Exercise 6.1 at the end of the chapter.

The resulting points are also provided to the buffer cache, though after the rendering from object transformation has been applied. Because the positions were transformed to rendering space, this cache lookup is rarely successful. The hit rate would likely be higher if positions were left in object space, though doing so would require additional computation to transform vertex positions when they were accessed. Vertex indices and uv texture coordinates fare better with the buffer cache, however.

⟨*Transform mesh vertices to rendering space and initialize mesh* p⟩ ≡   **298**
```
for (Point3f &pt : p)
    pt = renderFromObject(pt);
this->p = point3BufferCache->LookupOrAdd(p, alloc);
```

We will omit the remainder of the TriangleMesh constructor, as handling the other per-vertex buffer types is similar to how the positions are processed. The remainder of its member variables are below. In addition to the remainder of the mesh vertex and face data, the TriangleMesh records whether the normals should be flipped by way of the values of reverseOrientation and transformSwapsHandedness. Because these two have the same value for all triangles in a mesh, memory can be saved by storing them once with the mesh itself rather than redundantly with each of the triangles.

⟨*TriangleMesh Public Members*⟩ +≡   **297**
```
const Normal3f *n = nullptr;
const Vector3f *s = nullptr;
const Point2f *uv = nullptr;
bool reverseOrientation, transformSwapsHandedness;
```

6.5.2 Triangle CLASS

The Triangle class actually implements the Shape interface. It represents a single triangle.

⟨*Triangle Definition*⟩ ≡
```
class Triangle {
  public:
    ⟨Triangle Public Methods 302⟩
  private:
    ⟨Triangle Private Methods 302⟩
    ⟨Triangle Private Members 302⟩
};
```

Because complex scenes may have billions of triangles, it is important to minimize the amount of memory that each triangle uses. pbrt stores pointers to all the TriangleMeshes for the scene in a vector, which allows each triangle to be represented using just two integers: one to record which mesh it is a part of and another to record which triangle in the mesh it represents. With 4-byte ints, each Triangle uses just 8 bytes of memory.

Given this compact representation of triangles, recall the discussion in Section 1.5.7 about the memory cost of classes with virtual functions: if Triangle inherited from an abstract Shape base class that defined pure virtual functions, the virtual function pointer with each Triangle alone would double its size, assuming a 64-bit architecture with 8-byte pointers.

⟨*Triangle Public Methods*⟩ ≡   **301**
```
Triangle(int meshIndex, int triIndex)
    : meshIndex(meshIndex), triIndex(triIndex) {}
```

⟨*Triangle Private Members*⟩ ≡   **301**
```
int meshIndex = -1, triIndex = -1;
static pstd::vector<const TriangleMesh *> *allMeshes;
```

The bounding box of a triangle is easily found by computing a bounding box that encompasses its three vertices. Because the vertices have already been transformed to rendering space, no transformation of the bounds is necessary.

⟨*Triangle Method Definitions*⟩ ≡
```
Bounds3f Triangle::Bounds() const {
    ⟨Get triangle vertices in p0, p1, and p2 302⟩
    return Union(Bounds3f(p0, p1), p2);
}
```

Finding the positions of the three triangle vertices requires some indirection: first the mesh pointer must be found; then the indices of the three triangle vertices can be found given the triangle's index in the mesh; finally, the positions can be read from the mesh's p array. We will reuse this fragment repeatedly in the following, as the vertex positions are needed in many of the Triangle methods.

⟨*Get triangle vertices in p0, p1, and p2*⟩ ≡   302, 303, 309, 313, 317, 325
```
const TriangleMesh *mesh = GetMesh();
const int *v = &mesh->vertexIndices[3 * triIndex];
Point3f p0 = mesh->p[v[0]], p1 = mesh->p[v[1]], p2 = mesh->p[v[2]];
```

The GetMesh() method encapsulates the indexing operation to get the mesh's pointer.

⟨*Triangle Private Methods*⟩ ≡   **301**
```
const TriangleMesh *GetMesh() const {
    return (*allMeshes)[meshIndex];
}
```

Using the fact that the area of a parallelogram is given by the length of the cross product of the two vectors along its sides, the Area() method computes the triangle area as half the area of the parallelogram formed by two of its edge vectors (see Figure 6.13).

⟨*Triangle Public Methods*⟩ +≡   **301**
```
Float Area() const {
    ⟨Get triangle vertices in p0, p1, and p2 302⟩
    return 0.5f * Length(Cross(p1 - p0, p2 - p0));
}
```

Bounding the triangle's normal should be trivial: a cross product of appropriate edges gives its single normal vector direction. However, two subtleties that affect the orientation of the normal must be handled before the bounds are returned.

⟨*Triangle Method Definitions*⟩ +≡
```
DirectionCone Triangle::NormalBounds() const {
    ⟨Get triangle vertices in p0, p1, and p2 302⟩
    Normal3f n = Normalize(Normal3f(Cross(p1 - p0, p2 - p0)));
    ⟨Ensure correct orientation of geometric normal for normal bounds 303⟩
    return DirectionCone(Vector3f(n));
}
```

The first issue with the returned normal comes from the presence of per-vertex normals, even though it is a bound on geometric normals that NormalBounds() is supposed to return. pbrt requires that both the geometric normal and the interpolated per-vertex normal lie on the same side of the surface. If the two of them are on different sides, then pbrt follows the convention that the geometric normal is the one that should be flipped.

Furthermore, if there are not per-vertex normals, then—as with earlier shapes—the normal is flipped if either ReverseOrientation was specified in the scene description or the rendering to object transformation swaps the coordinate system handedness, but not both. Both of these considerations must be accounted for in the normal returned for the normal bounds.

⟨*Ensure correct orientation of geometric normal for normal bounds*⟩ ≡   303
```
if (mesh->n) {
    Normal3f ns(mesh->n[v[0]] + mesh->n[v[1]] + mesh->n[v[2]]);
    n = FaceForward(n, ns);
} else if (mesh->reverseOrientation ^ mesh->transformSwapsHandedness)
    n *= -1;
```

Although it is not required by the Shape interface, we will find it useful to be able to compute the solid angle that a triangle subtends from a reference point. The previously defined SphericalTriangleArea() function takes care of this directly.

⟨*Triangle Public Methods*⟩ +≡   301
```
Float SolidAngle(Point3f p) const {
    ⟨Get triangle vertices in p0, p1, and p2 302⟩
    return SphericalTriangleArea(Normalize(p0 - p), Normalize(p1 - p),
                                 Normalize(p2 - p));
}
```

6.5.3 RAY–TRIANGLE INTERSECTION

Unlike the other shapes so far, pbrt provides a stand-alone triangle intersection function that takes a ray and the three triangle vertices directly. Having this functionality available without needing to instantiate both a Triangle and a TriangleMesh in order to do a ray–triangle intersection test is helpful in a few other parts of the system. The Triangle class intersection methods, described next, use this function in their implementations.

⟨*Triangle Functions*⟩ ≡
```
pstd::optional<TriangleIntersection>
IntersectTriangle(const Ray &ray, Float tMax, Point3f p0, Point3f p1,
                  Point3f p2) {
    ⟨Return no intersection if triangle is degenerate 304⟩
    ⟨Transform triangle vertices to ray coordinate space 304⟩
```

⟨*Compute edge function coefficients* e0, e1, *and* e2 **307**⟩
⟨*Fall back to double-precision test at triangle edges*⟩
⟨*Perform triangle edge and determinant tests* **308**⟩
⟨*Compute scaled hit distance to triangle and test against ray t range* **308**⟩
⟨*Compute barycentric coordinates and t value for triangle intersection* **309**⟩
⟨*Ensure that computed triangle t is conservatively greater than zero* **384**⟩
⟨*Return* TriangleIntersection *for intersection* **309**⟩
}

pbrt's ray–triangle intersection test is based on first computing an affine transformation that transforms the ray such that its origin is at $(0, 0, 0)$ in the transformed coordinate system and such that its direction is along the $+z$ axis. Triangle vertices are also transformed into this coordinate system before the intersection test is performed. In the following, we will see that applying this coordinate system transformation simplifies the intersection test logic since, for example, the x and y coordinates of any intersection point must be zero. Later, in Section 6.8.4, we will see that this transformation makes it possible to have a *watertight* ray–triangle intersection algorithm, such that intersections with tricky rays like those that hit the triangle right on the edge are never incorrectly reported as misses.

One side effect of the transformation that we will apply to the vertices is that, due to floating-point round-off error, a degenerate triangle may be transformed into a non-degenerate triangle. If an intersection is reported with a degenerate triangle, then later code that tries to compute the geometric properties of the intersection will be unable to compute valid results. Therefore, this function starts with testing for a degenerate triangle and returning immediately if one was provided.

⟨*Return no intersection if triangle is degenerate*⟩ ≡   303
    if (LengthSquared(Cross(p2 - p0, p1 - p0)) == 0)
        return {};

There are three steps to computing the transformation from rendering space to the ray–triangle intersection coordinate space: a translation **T**, a coordinate permutation **P**, and a shear **S**. Rather than computing explicit transformation matrices for each of these and then computing an aggregate transformation matrix $\mathbf{M} = \mathbf{SPT}$ to transform vertices to the coordinate space, the following implementation applies each step of the transformation directly, which ends up being a more efficient approach.

⟨*Transform triangle vertices to ray coordinate space*⟩ ≡   303
    ⟨*Translate vertices based on ray origin* **305**⟩
    ⟨*Permute components of triangle vertices and ray direction* **305**⟩
    ⟨*Apply shear transformation to translated vertex positions* **305**⟩

The translation that places the ray origin at the origin of the coordinate system is:

$$\mathbf{T} = \begin{pmatrix} 1 & 0 & 0 & -o_x \\ 0 & 1 & 0 & -o_y \\ 0 & 0 & 1 & -o_z \\ 0 & 0 & 0 & 1 \end{pmatrix}.$$

Cross() 91
LengthSquared() 87

This transformation does not need to be explicitly applied to the ray origin, but we will apply it to the three triangle vertices.

⟨*Translate vertices based on ray origin*⟩ ≡   304
```
Point3f p0t = p0 - Vector3f(ray.o);
Point3f p1t = p1 - Vector3f(ray.o);
Point3f p2t = p2 - Vector3f(ray.o);
```

Next, the three dimensions of the space are permuted so that the z dimension is the one where the absolute value of the ray's direction is largest. The x and y dimensions are arbitrarily assigned to the other two dimensions. This step ensures that if, for example, the original ray's z direction is zero, then a dimension with nonzero magnitude is mapped to $+z$.

For example, if the ray's direction had the largest magnitude in x, the permutation would be:

$$\mathbf{P} = \begin{pmatrix} 0 & 1 & 0 & 0 \\ 0 & 0 & 1 & 0 \\ 1 & 0 & 0 & 0 \\ 0 & 0 & 0 & 1 \end{pmatrix}.$$

As before, it is easiest to permute the dimensions of the ray direction and the translated triangle vertices directly.

⟨*Permute components of triangle vertices and ray direction*⟩ ≡   304
```
int kz = MaxComponentIndex(Abs(ray.d));
int kx = kz + 1; if (kx == 3) kx = 0;
int ky = kx + 1; if (ky == 3) ky = 0;
Vector3f d = Permute(ray.d, {kx, ky, kz});
p0t = Permute(p0t, {kx, ky, kz});
p1t = Permute(p1t, {kx, ky, kz});
p2t = Permute(p2t, {kx, ky, kz});
```

Finally, a shear transformation aligns the ray direction with the $+z$ axis:

$$\mathbf{S} = \begin{pmatrix} 1 & 0 & -\mathbf{d}_x/\mathbf{d}_z & 0 \\ 0 & 1 & -\mathbf{d}_y/\mathbf{d}_z & 0 \\ 0 & 0 & 1/\mathbf{d}_z & 0 \\ 0 & 0 & 0 & 1 \end{pmatrix}.$$

To see how this transformation works, consider its operation on the ray direction vector $[\mathbf{d}_x \ \mathbf{d}_y \ \mathbf{d}_z \ 0]^T$.

For now, only the x and y dimensions are sheared; we can wait and shear the z dimension only if the ray intersects the triangle.

⟨*Apply shear transformation to translated vertex positions*⟩ ≡   304
```
Float Sx = -d.x / d.z;
Float Sy = -d.y / d.z;
Float Sz = 1 / d.z;
p0t.x += Sx * p0t.z;
p0t.y += Sy * p0t.z;
p1t.x += Sx * p1t.z;
p1t.y += Sy * p1t.z;
p2t.x += Sx * p2t.z;
p2t.y += Sy * p2t.z;
```

Note that the calculations for the coordinate permutation and the shear coefficients only depend on the given ray; they are independent of the triangle. In a high-performance ray tracer, it may be worthwhile to compute these values once and store them in the Ray class, rather than recomputing them for each triangle the ray is intersected with.

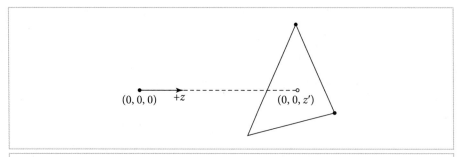

Figure 6.12: In the ray–triangle intersection coordinate system, the ray starts at the origin and goes along the $+z$ axis. The intersection test can be performed by considering only the xy projection of the ray and the triangle vertices, which in turn reduces to determining if the 2D point $(0, 0)$ is within the triangle.

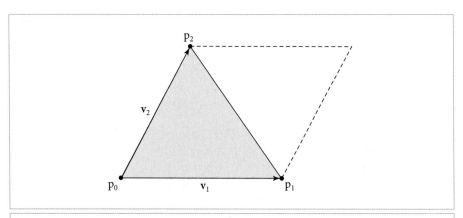

Figure 6.13: The area of a triangle with two edges given by vectors $\mathbf{v}_1$ and $\mathbf{v}_2$ is one-half of the area of the parallelogram shown here. The parallelogram area is given by the length of the cross product of $\mathbf{v}_1$ and $\mathbf{v}_2$.

With the triangle vertices transformed to this coordinate system, our task now is to find whether the ray starting from the origin and traveling along the $+z$ axis intersects the transformed triangle. Because of the way the coordinate system was constructed, this problem is equivalent to the 2D problem of determining if the x, y coordinates $(0, 0)$ are inside the xy projection of the triangle (Figure 6.12).

To understand how the intersection algorithm works, first recall from Figure 3.6 that the length of the cross product of two vectors gives the area of the parallelogram that they define. In 2D, with vectors $\mathbf{a}$ and $\mathbf{b}$, the area is

$$\mathbf{a}_x\mathbf{b}_y - \mathbf{b}_x\mathbf{a}_y.$$

Half of this area is the area of the triangle that they define. Thus, we can see that in 2D, the area of a triangle with vertices $\mathbf{p}_0$, $\mathbf{p}_1$, and $\mathbf{p}_2$ is

$$\frac{1}{2}\left((\mathbf{p}_{1x} - \mathbf{p}_{0x})(\mathbf{p}_{2y} - \mathbf{p}_{0y}) - (\mathbf{p}_{2x} - \mathbf{p}_{0x})(\mathbf{p}_{1y} - \mathbf{p}_{0y})\right).$$

Figure 6.13 visualizes this idea geometrically.

We will use this expression of triangle area to define a signed *edge function*: given two triangle vertices $\mathbf{p}_0$ and $\mathbf{p}_1$, we can define the directed edge function e as the function that gives twice the area of the triangle given by $\mathbf{p}_0$, $\mathbf{p}_1$, and a given third point $\mathbf{p}$:

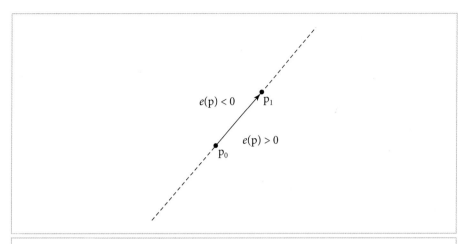

Figure 6.14: The edge function $e(p)$ characterizes points with respect to an oriented line between two points p_0 and p_1. The value of the edge function is positive for points p to the right of the line, zero for points on the line, and negative for points to the left of the line. The ray–triangle intersection algorithm uses an edge function that is twice the signed area of the triangle formed by the three points.

$$e(p) = (p_{1x} - p_{0x})(p_y - p_{0y}) - (p_x - p_{0x})(p_{1y} - p_{0y}). \qquad [6.5]$$

(See Figure 6.14.)

The edge function gives a positive value for points to the left of the line, and a negative value for points to the right. Thus, if a point has edge function values of the same sign for all three edges of a triangle, it must be on the same side of all three edges and thus must be inside the triangle.

Thanks to the coordinate system transformation, the point p that we are testing has coordinates $(0, 0)$. This simplifies the edge function expressions. For example, for the edge e_0 from p_1 to p_2, we have:

$$
\begin{aligned}
e_0(p) &= (p_{2x} - p_{1x})(p_y - p_{1y}) - (p_x - p_{1x})(p_{2y} - p_{1y}) \\
&= (p_{2x} - p_{1x})(-p_{1y}) - (-p_{1x})(p_{2y} - p_{1y}) \\
&= p_{1x}\,p_{2y} - p_{2x}\,p_{1y}.
\end{aligned}
\qquad [6.6]
$$

In the following, we will use the indexing scheme that the edge function e_i corresponds to the directed edge from vertex $p_{(i+1) \bmod 3}$ to $p_{(i+2) \bmod 3}$.

⟨*Compute edge function coefficients* e0, e1, *and* e2⟩ ≡   303
```
Float e0 = DifferenceOfProducts(p1t.x, p2t.y, p1t.y, p2t.x);
Float e1 = DifferenceOfProducts(p2t.x, p0t.y, p2t.y, p0t.x);
Float e2 = DifferenceOfProducts(p0t.x, p1t.y, p0t.y, p1t.x);
```

In the rare case that any of the edge function values is exactly zero, it is not possible to be sure if the ray hits the triangle or not, and the edge equations are reevaluated using double-precision floating-point arithmetic. (Section 6.8.4 discusses the need for this step in more detail.) The fragment that implements this computation, ⟨*Fall back to double-precision test at triangle edges*⟩, is just a reimplementation of ⟨*Compute edge function coefficients* e0, e1, *and* e2⟩ using doubles and so is not included here.

DifferenceOfProducts() 1044

Float 23

Given the values of the three edge functions, we have our first two opportunities to determine that there is no intersection. First, if the signs of the edge function values differ, then the point $(0, 0)$ is not on the same side of all three edges and therefore is outside the triangle. Second, if the sum of the three edge function values is zero, then the ray is approaching the triangle edge-on, and we report no intersection. (For a closed triangle mesh, the ray will hit a neighboring triangle instead.)

⟨*Perform triangle edge and determinant tests*⟩ ≡   303
```
    if ((e0 < 0 || e1 < 0 || e2 < 0) && (e0 > 0 || e1 > 0 || e2 > 0))
        return {};
    Float det = e0 + e1 + e2;
    if (det == 0)
        return {};
```

Because the ray starts at the origin, has unit length, and is along the $+z$ axis, the z coordinate value of the intersection point is equal to the intersection's parametric t value. To compute this z value, we first need to go ahead and apply the shear transformation to the z coordinates of the triangle vertices. Given these z values, the *barycentric coordinates* of the intersection point in the triangle can be used to interpolate them across the triangle. They are given by dividing each edge function value by the sum of edge function values:

$$b_i = \frac{e_i}{e_0 + e_1 + e_2}.$$

Thus, the b_i sum to one.

The interpolated z value is given by

$$z = b_0 z_0 + b_1 z_1 + b_2 z_2,$$

where z_i are the coordinates of the three vertices in the ray–triangle intersection coordinate system.

To save the cost of the floating-point division to compute b_i in cases where the final t value is out of the range of valid t values, the implementation here first computes t by interpolating z_i with e_i (in other words, not yet performing the division by $d = e_0 + e_1 + e_2$). If the sign of d and the sign of the interpolated t value are different, then the final t value will certainly be negative and thus not a valid intersection.

Along similar lines, the check $t < t_{max}$ can be equivalently performed in two ways:

$$\sum_i e_i z_i < t_{max}(e_0 + e_1 + e_2) \qquad \text{if } e_0 + e_1 + e_2 > 0$$

$$\sum_i e_i z_i > t_{max}(e_0 + e_1 + e_2) \qquad \text{otherwise.}$$

⟨*Compute scaled hit distance to triangle and test against ray t range*⟩ ≡   303
```
    p0t.z *= Sz;
    p1t.z *= Sz;
    p2t.z *= Sz;
    Float tScaled = e0 * p0t.z + e1 * p1t.z + e2 * p2t.z;
    if (det < 0 && (tScaled >= 0 || tScaled < tMax * det))
        return {};
    else if (det > 0 && (tScaled <= 0 || tScaled > tMax * det))
        return {};
```

Float 23

Given a valid intersection, the actual barycentric coordinates and t value for the intersection are found.

⟨*Compute barycentric coordinates and t value for triangle intersection*⟩ ≡   303
```
Float invDet = 1 / det;
Float b0 = e0 * invDet, b1 = e1 * invDet, b2 = e2 * invDet;
Float t = tScaled * invDet;
```

After a final test on the *t* value that will be discussed in Section 6.8.7, a TriangleIntersection object that represents the intersection can be returned.

⟨*Return* TriangleIntersection *for intersection*⟩ ≡   303
```
return TriangleIntersection{b0, b1, b2, t};
```

TriangleIntersection just records the barycentric coordinates and the *t* value along the ray where the intersection occurred.

⟨*TriangleIntersection Definition*⟩ ≡
```
struct TriangleIntersection {
    Float b0, b1, b2;
    Float t;
};
```

The structure of the Triangle::Intersect() method follows the form of earlier intersection test methods.

⟨*Triangle Method Definitions*⟩ +≡
```
pstd::optional<ShapeIntersection> Triangle::Intersect(const Ray &ray,
                                                      Float tMax) const {
```
    ⟨*Get triangle vertices in* p0, p1, *and* p2 **302**⟩
```
    pstd::optional<TriangleIntersection> triIsect =
        IntersectTriangle(ray, tMax, p0, p1, p2);
    if (!triIsect) return {};
    SurfaceInteraction intr = InteractionFromIntersection(
        mesh, triIndex, *triIsect, ray.time, -ray.d);
    return ShapeIntersection{intr, triIsect->t};
}
```

We will not include the Triangle::IntersectP() method here, as it is just based on calling IntersectTriangle().

The InteractionFromIntersection() method is different than the corresponding methods in the quadrics in that it is a stand-alone function rather than a regular member function. Because a call to it is thus not associated with a specific Triangle instance, it takes a TriangleMesh and the index of a triangle in the mesh as parameters. In the context of its usage in the Intersect() method, this may seem gratuitous—why pass that information as parameters rather than access it directly in a non-static method?

We have designed the interface in this way so that we are able to use this method in pbrt's GPU rendering path, where the Triangle class is not used. There, the representation of triangles in the scene is abstracted by a ray intersection API and the geometric ray–triangle intersection test is performed using specialized hardware. Given an intersection, it provides the triangle index, a pointer to the mesh that the triangle is a part of, and the barycentric coordinates of the intersection. That information is sufficient to call this method, which then allows us to find the SurfaceInteraction for such intersections using the same code as executes on the CPU.

⟨*Triangle Public Methods*⟩ +≡   **301**
```
    static SurfaceInteraction InteractionFromIntersection(
            const TriangleMesh *mesh, int triIndex,
            TriangleIntersection ti, Float time, Vector3f wo) {
        const int *v = &mesh->vertexIndices[3 * triIndex];
        Point3f p0 = mesh->p[v[0]], p1 = mesh->p[v[1]], p2 = mesh->p[v[2]];
```
        ⟨*Compute triangle partial derivatives* 311⟩
        ⟨*Interpolate* (*u, v*) *parametric coordinates and hit point* 311⟩
        ⟨*Return* SurfaceInteraction *for triangle hit* 312⟩
```
    }
```

To generate consistent tangent vectors over triangle meshes, it is necessary to compute the partial derivatives $\partial p/\partial u$ and $\partial p/\partial v$ using the parametric (u, v) values at the triangle vertices, if provided. Although the partial derivatives are the same at all points on the triangle, the implementation here recomputes them each time an intersection is found. Although this results in redundant computation, the storage savings for large triangle meshes can be significant.

A triangle can be described by the set of points

$$p_o + u\frac{\partial p}{\partial u} + v\frac{\partial p}{\partial v},$$

for some p_o, where u and v range over the parametric coordinates of the triangle. We also know the three vertex positions p_i, $i = 0, 1, 2$, and the texture coordinates (u_i, v_i) at each vertex. From this it follows that the partial derivatives of p must satisfy

$$p_i = p_o + u_i\frac{\partial p}{\partial u} + v_i\frac{\partial p}{\partial v}.$$

In other words, there is a unique affine mapping from the 2D (u, v) space to points on the triangle. (Such a mapping exists even though the triangle is specified in 3D because the triangle is planar.) To compute expressions for $\partial p/\partial u$ and $\partial p/\partial v$, we start by computing the differences $p_0 - p_2$ and $p_1 - p_2$, giving the matrix equation

$$\begin{pmatrix} u_0 - u_2 & v_0 - v_2 \\ u_1 - u_2 & v_1 - v_2 \end{pmatrix} \begin{pmatrix} \partial p/\partial u \\ \partial p/\partial v \end{pmatrix} = \begin{pmatrix} p_0 - p_2 \\ p_1 - p_2 \end{pmatrix}.$$

Thus,

$$\begin{pmatrix} \partial p/\partial u \\ \partial p/\partial v \end{pmatrix} = \begin{pmatrix} u_0 - u_2 & v_0 - v_2 \\ u_1 - u_2 & v_1 - v_2 \end{pmatrix}^{-1} \begin{pmatrix} p_0 - p_2 \\ p_1 - p_2 \end{pmatrix}.$$

Inverting a 2×2 matrix is straightforward. The inverse of the (u, v) differences matrix is

$$\frac{1}{(u_0 - u_2)(v_1 - v_2) - (v_0 - v_2)(u_1 - u_2)} \begin{pmatrix} v_1 - v_2 & -(v_0 - v_2) \\ -(u_1 - u_2) & u_0 - u_2 \end{pmatrix}. \qquad \text{[6.7]}$$

This computation is performed by the ⟨*Compute triangle partial derivatives*⟩ fragment, with handling for various additional corner cases.

⟨*Compute triangle partial derivatives*⟩ ≡   310
  ⟨*Compute deltas and matrix determinant for triangle partial derivatives* 311⟩
  `Vector3f dpdu, dpdv;`
  `bool degenerateUV = std::abs(determinant) < 1e-9f;`
  `if (!degenerateUV) {`
    ⟨*Compute triangle* ∂p/∂u *and* ∂p/∂v *via matrix inversion* 311⟩
  `}`
  ⟨*Handle degenerate triangle* (u, v) *parameterization or partial derivatives* 311⟩

The triangle's uv coordinates are found by indexing into the `TriangleMesh::uv` array, if present. Otherwise, a default parameterization is used. We will not include the fragment that initializes uv here.

⟨*Compute deltas and matrix determinant for triangle partial derivatives*⟩ ≡   311
  ⟨*Get triangle texture coordinates in* uv *array*⟩
  `Vector2f duv02 = uv[0] - uv[2], duv12 = uv[1] - uv[2];`
  `Vector3f dp02 = p0 - p2, dp12 = p1 - p2;`
  `Float determinant =`
    `DifferenceOfProducts(duv02[0], duv12[1], duv02[1], duv12[0]);`

In the usual case, the 2×2 matrix is non-degenerate, and the partial derivatives are computed using Equation (6.7).

⟨*Compute triangle* ∂p/∂u *and* ∂p/∂v *via matrix inversion*⟩ ≡   311
  `Float invdet = 1 / determinant;`
  `dpdu = DifferenceOfProducts(duv12[1], dp02, duv02[1], dp12) * invdet;`
  `dpdv = DifferenceOfProducts(duv02[0], dp12, duv12[0], dp02) * invdet;`

However, there are a number of rare additional cases that must be handled. For example, the user may have provided (u, v) coordinates that specify a degenerate parameterization, such as the same (u, v) at all three vertices. Alternatively, the computed dpdu and dpdv values may have a degenerate cross product due to rounding error. In such cases we fall back to computing dpdu and dpdv that at least give the correct normal vector.

⟨*Handle degenerate triangle* (u, v) *parameterization or partial derivatives*⟩ ≡   311
  `if (degenerateUV || LengthSquared(Cross(dpdu, dpdv)) == 0) {`
    `Vector3f ng = Cross(p2 - p0, p1 - p0);`
    `if (LengthSquared(ng) == 0)`
      `ng = Vector3f(Cross(Vector3<double>(p2 - p0),`
             `Vector3<double>(p1 - p0)));`
    `CoordinateSystem(Normalize(ng), &dpdu, &dpdv);`
  `}`

To compute the intersection point and the (u, v) parametric coordinates at the hit point, the barycentric interpolation formula is applied to the vertex positions and the (u, v) coordinates at the vertices. As we will see in Section 6.8.5, this gives a more accurate result for the intersection point than evaluating the parametric ray equation using t.

⟨*Interpolate* (u, v) *parametric coordinates and hit point*⟩ ≡   310
  `Point3f pHit = ti.b0 * p0 + ti.b1 * p1 + ti.b2 * p2;`
  `Point2f uvHit = ti.b0 * uv[0] + ti.b1 * uv[1] + ti.b2 * uv[2];`

Unlike with the shapes we have seen so far, it is not necessary to transform the Surface Interaction here to rendering space, since the geometric per-vertex values are already in rendering space. Like the disk, the partial derivatives of the triangle's normal are also both (0, 0, 0), since it is flat.

⟨*Return* SurfaceInteraction *for triangle hit*⟩ ≡   310
    bool flipNormal = mesh->reverseOrientation ^ mesh->transformSwapsHandedness;
    ⟨*Compute error bounds* pError *for triangle intersection* 377⟩
    SurfaceInteraction isect(Point3fi(pHit, pError), uvHit, wo, dpdu, dpdv,
                             Normal3f(), Normal3f(), time, flipNormal);
    ⟨*Set final surface normal and shading geometry for triangle* 312⟩
    return isect;

Before the SurfaceInteraction is returned, some final details related to its surface normal and shading geometry must be taken care of.

⟨*Set final surface normal and shading geometry for triangle*⟩ ≡   312
    ⟨*Override surface normal in* isect *for triangle* 312⟩
    if (mesh->n || mesh->s) {
        ⟨*Initialize* Triangle *shading geometry* 312⟩
    }

The SurfaceInteraction constructor initializes the geometric normal n as the normalized cross product of dpdu and dpdv. This works well for most shapes, but in the case of triangle meshes it is preferable to rely on an initialization that does not depend on the underlying texture coordinates: it is fairly common to encounter meshes with bad parameterizations that do not preserve the orientation of the mesh, in which case the geometric normal would have an incorrect orientation.

We therefore initialize the geometric normal using the normalized cross product of the edge vectors dp02 and dp12, which results in the same normal up to a potential sign difference that depends on the exact order of triangle vertices (also known as the triangle's *winding order*).[3] 3D modeling packages generally try to ensure that triangles in a mesh have consistent winding orders, which makes this approach more robust.

⟨*Override surface normal in* isect *for triangle*⟩ ≡   312
    isect.n = isect.shading.n = Normal3f(Normalize(Cross(dp02, dp12)));
    if (mesh->reverseOrientation ^ mesh->transformSwapsHandedness)
        isect.n = isect.shading.n = -isect.n;

With Triangles, the user can provide normal vectors and tangent vectors at the vertices of the mesh that are interpolated to give normals and tangents at points on the faces of triangles. Shading geometry with interpolated normals can make otherwise faceted triangle meshes appear to be smoother than they geometrically are. If either shading normals or shading tangents have been provided, they are used to initialize the shading geometry in the SurfaceInteraction.

⟨*Initialize* Triangle *shading geometry*⟩ ≡   312
    ⟨*Compute shading normal* ns *for triangle* 313⟩
    ⟨*Compute shading tangent* ss *for triangle* 313⟩
    ⟨*Compute shading bitangent* ts *for triangle and adjust* ss 313⟩
    ⟨*Compute* ∂n/∂u *and* ∂n/∂v *for triangle shading geometry*⟩
    isect.SetShadingGeometry(ns, ss, ts, dndu, dndv, true);

Given the barycentric coordinates of the intersection point, it is easy to compute the shading normal by interpolating among the appropriate vertex normals, if present.

---

3   This computation implicitly assumes a counterclockwise vertex ordering.

⟨*Compute shading normal* ns *for triangle*⟩ ≡   312
```
Normal3f ns;
if (mesh->n) {
    ns = ti.b0 * mesh->n[v[0]] + ti.b1 * mesh->n[v[1]] + ti.b2 * mesh->n[v[2]];
    ns = LengthSquared(ns) > 0 ? Normalize(ns) : isect.n;
} else
    ns = isect.n;
```

The shading tangent is computed similarly.

⟨*Compute shading tangent* ss *for triangle*⟩ ≡   312
```
Vector3f ss;
if (mesh->s) {
    ss = ti.b0 * mesh->s[v[0]] + ti.b1 * mesh->s[v[1]] + ti.b2 * mesh->s[v[2]];
    if (LengthSquared(ss) == 0)
        ss = isect.dpdu;
} else
    ss = isect.dpdu;
```

The bitangent vector ts is found using the cross product of ns and ss, giving a vector orthogonal to the two of them. Next, ss is overwritten with the cross product of ts and ns; this ensures that the cross product of ss and ts gives ns. Thus, if per-vertex **n** and **s** values are provided and if the interpolated **n** and **s** values are not perfectly orthogonal, **n** will be preserved and **s** will be modified so that the coordinate system is orthogonal.

⟨*Compute shading bitangent* ts *for triangle and adjust* ss⟩ ≡   312
```
Vector3f ts = Cross(ns, ss);
if (LengthSquared(ts) > 0)
    ss = Cross(ts, ns);
else
    CoordinateSystem(ns, &ss, &ts);
```

The code to compute the partial derivatives $\partial \mathbf{n}/\partial u$ and $\partial \mathbf{n}/\partial v$ of the shading normal is almost identical to the code to compute the partial derivatives $\partial \mathbf{p}/\partial u$ and $\partial \mathbf{p}/\partial v$. Therefore, it has been elided from the text here.

★ 6.5.4 SAMPLING

The uniform area triangle sampling method is based on mapping the provided random sample u to barycentric coordinates that are uniformly distributed over the triangle.

⟨*Triangle Public Methods*⟩ +≡   301
```
pstd::optional<ShapeSample> Sample(Point2f u) const {
    ⟨Get triangle vertices in p0, p1, and p2 302⟩
    ⟨Sample point on triangle uniformly by area 314⟩
    ⟨Compute surface normal for sampled point on triangle 314⟩
    ⟨Compute (u, v) for sampled point on triangle 314⟩
    ⟨Compute error bounds pError for sampled point on triangle 377⟩
    return ShapeSample{Interaction(Point3fi(p, pError), n, uvSample),
                       1 / Area()};
}
```

★   This section covers advanced topics and may be skipped on a first reading.

Uniform barycentric sampling is provided via a stand-alone utility function (to be described shortly), which makes it easier to reuse this functionality elsewhere.

⟨*Sample point on triangle uniformly by area*⟩ ≡   313
```
pstd::array<Float, 3> b = SampleUniformTriangle(u);
Point3f p = b[0] * p0 + b[1] * p1 + b[2] * p2;
```

As with `Triangle::NormalBounds()`, the surface normal of the sampled point is affected by the orientation of the shading normal, if present.

⟨*Compute surface normal for sampled point on triangle*⟩ ≡   313, 318
```
Normal3f n = Normalize(Normal3f(Cross(p1 - p0, p2 - p0)));
if (mesh->n) {
    Normal3f ns(b[0] * mesh->n[v[0]] + b[1] * mesh->n[v[1]] +
                (1 - b[0] - b[1]) * mesh->n[v[2]]);
    n = FaceForward(n, ns);
} else if (mesh->reverseOrientation ^ mesh->transformSwapsHandedness)
    n *= -1;
```

The (u, v) coordinates for the sampled point are also found with barycentric interpolation.

⟨*Compute (u, v) for sampled point on triangle*⟩ ≡   313, 318
```
⟨Get triangle texture coordinates in uv array⟩
Point2f uvSample = b[0] * uv[0] + b[1] * uv[1] + b[2] * uv[2];
```

Because barycentric interpolation is linear, it can be shown that if we can find barycentric coordinates that uniformly sample a specific triangle, then those barycentrics can be used to uniformly sample any triangle. To derive the sampling algorithm, we will therefore consider the case of uniformly sampling a unit right triangle. Given a uniform sample in $[0, 1)^2$ that we would like to map to the triangle, the task can also be considered as finding an area-preserving mapping from the unit square to the unit triangle.

A straightforward approach is suggested by Figure 6.15: the unit square could be folded over onto itself, such that samples that are on the side of the diagonal that places them outside the triangle are reflected across the diagonal to be inside it. While this would provide a valid sampling technique, it is undesirable since it causes samples that were originally far away in $[0, 1)^2$ to be close together on the triangle. (For example, (0.01, 0.01) and (0.99, 0.99) in the unit square would both map to the same point in the triangle.) The effect would be that sampling techniques that generate well-distributed uniform samples such as those discussed in Chapter 8 were less effective at reducing error.

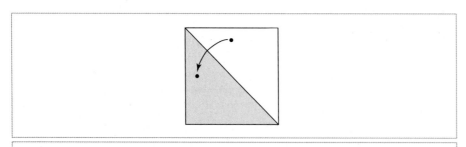

Figure 6.15: Samples from the unit square can be mapped to the unit right triangle by reflecting across the $x + y = 1$ diagonal, though doing so causes far away samples on the square to map to nearby points on the triangle.

A better mapping translates points along the diagonal by a varying amount that brings the two opposite sides of the unit square to the triangle's diagonal.

$$f(\xi_1, \xi_2) = (\xi_1 - \delta, \xi_2 - \delta), \text{ where } \delta = \begin{cases} \xi_1/2 & \xi_1 < \xi_2 \\ \xi_2/2 & \text{otherwise.} \end{cases}$$

The determinant of the Jacobian matrix for this mapping is a constant and therefore this mapping is area preserving and uniformly distributed samples in the unit square are uniform in the triangle. (Recall Section 2.4.1, which presented the mathematics of transforming samples from one domain to the other; there it was shown that if the Jacobian of the transformation is constant, the mapping is area-preserving.)

⟨*Sampling Inline Functions*⟩ +≡
```
pstd::array<Float, 3> SampleUniformTriangle(Point2f u) {
    Float b0, b1;
    if (u[0] < u[1]) {
        b0 = u[0] / 2;
        b1 = u[1] - b0;
    } else {
        b1 = u[1] / 2;
        b0 = u[0] - b1;
    }
    return {b0, b1, 1 - b0 - b1};
}
```

The usual normalization constraint gives the PDF in terms of the triangle's surface area.

⟨*Triangle Public Methods*⟩ +≡   301
```
Float PDF(const Interaction &) const { return 1 / Area(); }
```

In order to sample points on spheres with respect to solid angle from a reference point, we derived a specialized sampling method that only sampled from the potentially visible region of the sphere. For the cylinder and disk, we just sampled uniformly by area and rescaled the PDF to account for the change of measure from area to solid angle. It is tempting to do the same for triangles (and, indeed, all three previous editions of this book did so), but going through the work to apply a solid angle sampling approach can lead to much better results.

To see why, consider a simplified form of the reflection integral from the scattering equation, (4.14):

$$\int_{S^2} \rho \, L_i(p, \omega_i) \, |\cos \theta_i| \, d\omega_i,$$

where the BRDF f has been replaced with a constant ρ, which corresponds to a diffuse surface. If we consider the case of incident radiance only coming from a triangular light source that emits uniform diffuse radiance L_e, then we can rewrite this integral as

$$\rho L_e \int_{S^2} V(p, \omega_i) \, |\cos \theta_i| \, d\omega_i,$$

Float 23
Interaction 136
Point2f 92
Triangle::Area() 302

where V is a visibility function that is 1 if the ray from p in direction ω_i hits the light source and 0 if it misses or is occluded by another object. If we sample the triangle uniformly within the solid angle that it subtends from the reference point, we end up with the estimator

$$\frac{\rho L_e}{1/A_{\text{solid}}} \left(V(p, \omega_i) \, |\cos \theta'| \right)$$

where A_{solid} is the subtended solid angle. The constant values have been pulled out, leaving just the two factors in parentheses that vary based on p'. They are the only source of variance in estimates of the integral.

As an alternative, consider a Monte Carlo estimate of this function where a point p' has been uniformly sampled on the surface of the triangle. If the triangle's area is A, then the PDF is $p(p') = 1/A$. Applying the standard Monte Carlo estimator and defining a new visibility function V that is between two points, we end up with

$$\frac{\rho L_e}{1/A} \left(V(p, p') \, |\cos \theta'| \frac{|\cos \theta_1|}{\|p' - p\|^2} \right),$$

where the last factor accounts for the change of variables and where $\cos \theta_1$ is the angle between the light source's surface normal and the vector between the two points. The values of the four factors inside the parentheses in this estimator all depend on the choice of p'.

With area sampling, the $|\cos \theta_1|$ factor adds some additional variance, though not too much, since it is between 0 and 1. However, $1/\|p' - p\|^2$ can have unbounded variation over the surface of the triangle, which can lead to high variance in the estimator since the method used to sample p' does not account for it at all. This variance increases the larger the triangle is and the closer the reference point is to it. Figure 6.16 shows a scene where solid angle sampling significantly reduces error.

The `Triangle::Sample()` method that takes a reference point therefore samples a point according to solid angle.

Figure 6.16: A Scene Where Solid Angle Triangle Sampling Is Beneficial. When points on triangles are sampled using uniform area sampling, error is high at points on the ground close to the emitter. If points are sampled on the triangle by uniformly sampling the solid angle the triangle subtends, then the remaining non-constant factors in the estimator are both between 0 and 1, which results in much lower error. For this scene, mean squared error (MSE) is reduced by a factor of 3.86. *(Dragon model courtesy of the Stanford Computer Graphics Laboratory.)*

⟨*Triangle Public Methods*⟩ +≡   **301**
```
pstd::optional<ShapeSample> Sample(const ShapeSampleContext &ctx,
                                   Point2f u) const {
```
   ⟨*Get triangle vertices in* p0, p1, *and* p2 **302**⟩
   ⟨*Use uniform area sampling for numerically unstable cases* **317**⟩
   ⟨*Sample spherical triangle from reference point* **317**⟩
   ⟨*Compute error bounds* pError *for sampled point on triangle* **377**⟩
   ⟨*Return* ShapeSample *for solid angle sampled point on triangle* **318**⟩
```
}
```

Triangles that subtend a very small solid angle as well as ones that cover nearly the whole hemisphere can encounter problems with floating-point accuracy in the following solid angle sampling approach. The sampling method falls back to uniform area sampling in those cases, which does not hurt results in practice: for very small triangles, the various additional factors tend not to vary as much over the triangle's area. pbrt also samples the BSDF as part of the direct lighting calculation, which is an effective strategy for large triangles, so uniform area sampling is fine in that case as well.

⟨*Use uniform area sampling for numerically unstable cases*⟩ ≡   **317**
```
Float solidAngle = SolidAngle(ctx.p());
if (solidAngle < MinSphericalSampleArea ||
    solidAngle > MaxSphericalSampleArea) {
```
    ⟨*Sample shape by area and compute incident direction* wi **282**⟩
    ⟨*Convert area sampling PDF in* ss *to solid angle measure* **282**⟩
```
    return ss;
}
```

⟨*Triangle Private Members*⟩ +≡   **301**
```
static constexpr Float MinSphericalSampleArea = 3e-4;
static constexpr Float MaxSphericalSampleArea = 6.22;
```

pbrt also includes an approximation to the effect of the $|\cos\theta'|$ factor in its triangle sampling algorithm, which leaves visibility and error in that approximation as the only sources of variance. We will defer discussion of the fragment that handles that, ⟨*Apply warp product sampling for cosine factor at reference point*⟩, until after we have discussed the uniform solid angle sampling algorithm. For now we will note that it affects the final sampling PDF, which turns out to be the product of the PDF for uniform solid angle sampling of the triangle and a correction factor.

Uniform sampling of the solid angle that a triangle subtends is equivalent to uniformly sampling the spherical triangle that results from its projection on the unit sphere (recall Section 3.8.2). Spherical triangle sampling is implemented in a separate function described shortly, SampleSphericalTriangle(), that returns the barycentric coordinates for the sampled point.

⟨*Sample spherical triangle from reference point*⟩ ≡   **317**
   ⟨*Apply warp product sampling for cosine factor at reference point* **324**⟩
```
Float triPDF;
pstd::array<Float, 3> b =
    SampleSphericalTriangle({p0, p1, p2}, ctx.p(), u, &triPDF);
if (triPDF == 0) return {};
pdf *= triPDF;
```

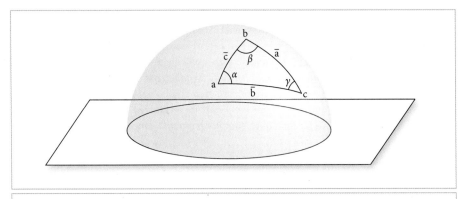

Figure 6.17: Geometric Setting for Spherical Triangles. Given vertices a, b, and c, the respective opposite edges are labeled $\bar{a}$, $\bar{b}$, and $\bar{c}$ and the interior angles are labeled with Greek letters α, β, and γ.

Given the barycentric coordinates, it is simple to compute the sampled point. With that as well as the surface normal, computed by reusing a fragment from the other triangle sampling method, we have everything necessary to return a ShapeSample.

⟨*Return* ShapeSample *for solid angle sampled point on triangle*⟩ ≡   **317**
```
Point3f p = b[0] * p0 + b[1] * p1 + b[2] * p2;
⟨Compute surface normal for sampled point on triangle 314⟩
⟨Compute (u, v) for sampled point on triangle 314⟩
return ShapeSample{Interaction(Point3fi(p, pError), n, ctx.time, uvSample),
                   pdf};
```

The spherical triangle sampling function takes three triangle vertices v, a reference point p, and a uniform sample u. The value of the PDF for the sampled point is optionally returned via pdf, if it is not nullptr. Figure 6.17 shows the geometric setting.

⟨*Sampling Function Definitions*⟩ ≡
```
pstd::array<Float, 3> SampleSphericalTriangle(
      const pstd::array<Point3f, 3> &v, Point3f p, Point2f u, Float *pdf) {
    ⟨Compute vectors a, b, and c to spherical triangle vertices 318⟩
    ⟨Compute normalized cross products of all direction pairs 319⟩
    ⟨Find angles α, β, and γ at spherical triangle vertices 319⟩
    ⟨Uniformly sample triangle area A to compute A′ 320⟩
    ⟨Find cos β′ for point along b for sampled area 321⟩
    ⟨Sample c′ along the arc between b′ and a 321⟩
    ⟨Compute sampled spherical triangle direction and return barycentrics 322⟩
}
```

Given the reference point, it is easy to project the vertices on the unit sphere to find the spherical triangle vertices a, b, and c.

Float 23
Interaction 136
Normalize() 88
Point2f 92
Point3f 92
Point3fi 1061
ShapeSample 268
ShapeSampleContext::time 268
Vector3f 86

⟨*Compute vectors* a, b, *and* c *to spherical triangle vertices*⟩ ≡   **318, 325**
```
Vector3f a(v[0] - p), b(v[1] - p), c(v[2] - p);
a = Normalize(a);
b = Normalize(b);
c = Normalize(c);
```

Because the plane containing an edge also passes through the origin, we can compute the plane normal for an edge from a to b as

It can be simplified in a similar manner to find the equation

$$0 = (\cos \phi + \cos \alpha) \cos \beta' + (\sin \phi - \sin \alpha \cos \bar{c}) \sin \beta'.$$

The terms in parentheses are all known. We will denote them by $k_1 = \cos \phi + \cos \alpha$ and $k_2 = \sin \phi - \sin \alpha \cos \bar{c}$. It is then easy to see that solutions to the equation

$$0 = k_1 \cos \beta' + k_2 \sin \beta'$$

are given by

$$\cos \beta' = \frac{\pm k_2}{\sqrt{k_1^2 + k_2^2}} \quad \text{and} \quad \sin \beta' = \frac{\mp k_1}{\sqrt{k_1^2 + k_2^2}}.$$

Substituting these into Equation (6.9), taking the solution with a positive cosine, and simplifying gives

$$\cos \bar{b}' = \frac{k_2 + (k_2 \cos \phi - k_1 \sin \phi) \cos \alpha}{(k_2 \sin \phi + k_1 \cos \phi) \sin \alpha},$$

which finally has only known values on the right hand side.

The code to compute this cosine follows directly from this solution. In it, we have also applied trigonometric identities to compute $\sin \phi$ and $\cos \phi$ in terms of other sines and cosines.

⟨*Find* cos β′ *for point along* b *for sampled area*⟩ ≡   318
```
Float cosAlpha = std::cos(alpha), sinAlpha = std::sin(alpha);
Float sinPhi = std::sin(Ap_pi) * cosAlpha - std::cos(Ap_pi) * sinAlpha;
Float cosPhi = std::cos(Ap_pi) * cosAlpha + std::sin(Ap_pi) * sinAlpha;
Float k1 = cosPhi + cosAlpha;
Float k2 = sinPhi - sinAlpha * Dot(a, b) /* cos c */;
Float cosBp =
    (k2 + (DifferenceOfProducts(k2, cosPhi, k1, sinPhi)) * cosAlpha) /
    ((SumOfProducts(k2, sinPhi, k1, cosPhi)) * sinAlpha);
cosBp = Clamp(cosBp, -1, 1);
```

The arc of the great circle between the two points a and c can be parameterized by $\cos \theta \mathbf{a} + \sin \theta \mathbf{c}_\perp$, where $\mathbf{c}_\perp$ is the normalized perpendicular component of c with respect to a. This vector is given by the GramSchmidt() function introduced earlier, which makes the computation of $\mathbf{c}'$ straightforward. In this case, $\sin \bar{b}'$ can then be found using $\cos \bar{b}'$ with the Pythagorean identity, since we know that it must be nonnegative.

⟨*Sample* c′ *along the arc between* b′ *and* a⟩ ≡   318
```
Float sinBp = SafeSqrt(1 - Sqr(cosBp));
Vector3f cp = cosBp * a + sinBp * Normalize(GramSchmidt(c, a));
```

For the sample points to be uniformly distributed in the spherical triangle, it can be shown that if the edge from b to c′ is parameterized using θ in the same way as was used for the edge from a to c, then $\cos \theta$ should be sampled as

$$\cos \theta = 1 - \xi_1(1 - (\mathbf{c}' \cdot \mathbf{b})). \tag{6.10}$$

(The "Further Reading" section has pointers to the details.)

With that, we can compute the final sampled direction ω. The remaining step is to compute the barycentric coordinates for the sampled direction.

Clamp() 1033

DifferenceOfProducts() 1044

Dot() 89

Float 23

GramSchmidt() 90

Normalize() 88

SafeSqrt() 1034

Sqr() 1034

SumOfProducts() 1044

Vector3f 86

⟨*Compute sampled spherical triangle direction and return barycentrics*⟩ ≡   318
```
Float cosTheta = 1 - u[1] * (1 - Dot(cp, b));
Float sinTheta = SafeSqrt(1 - Sqr(cosTheta));
Vector3f w = cosTheta * b + sinTheta * Normalize(GramSchmidt(cp, b));
⟨Find barycentric coordinates for sampled direction w 322⟩
⟨Return clamped barycentrics for sampled direction 322⟩
```

The barycentric coordinates of the corresponding point in the planar triangle can be found using part of a ray–triangle intersection algorithm that finds the barycentrics along the way (Möller and Trumbore 1997). It starts with equating the parametric form of the ray with the barycentric interpolation of the triangle's vertices v_i,

$$o + t\mathbf{d} = (1 - b_0 - b_1)v_0 + b_1v_1 + b_2v_2,$$

expressing this as a matrix equation, and solving the resulting linear system for the barycentrics. The solution is implemented in the following fragment, which includes the result of factoring out various common subexpressions.

⟨*Find barycentric coordinates for sampled direction* w⟩ ≡   322
```
Vector3f e1 = v[1] - v[0], e2 = v[2] - v[0];
Vector3f s1 = Cross(w, e2);
Float divisor = Dot(s1, e1);
Float invDivisor = 1 / divisor;
Vector3f s = p - v[0];
Float b1 = Dot(s, s1) * invDivisor;
Float b2 = Dot(w, Cross(s, e1)) * invDivisor;
```

The computed barycentrics may be invalid for very small and very large triangles. This happens rarely, but to protect against it, they are clamped to be within the triangle before they are returned.

⟨*Return clamped barycentrics for sampled direction*⟩ ≡   322
```
b1 = Clamp(b1, 0, 1);
b2 = Clamp(b2, 0, 1);
if (b1 + b2 > 1) {
    b1 /= b1 + b2;
    b2 /= b1 + b2;
}
return {Float(1 - b1 - b2), Float(b1), Float(b2)};
```

As noted earlier, uniform solid angle sampling does not account for the incident cosine factor at the reference point. Indeed, there is no known analytic method to do so. However, it is possible to apply a warping function to the uniform samples u that approximately accounts for this factor.

To understand the idea, first note that $\cos\theta$ varies smoothly over the spherical triangle. Because the spherical triangle sampling algorithm that we have just defined maintains a continuous relationship between sample values and points in the triangle, then if we consider the image of the $\cos\theta$ function back in the $[0, 1]^2$ sampling domain, as would be found by mapping it through the inverse of the spherical triangle sampling algorithm, the $\cos\theta$ function is smoothly varying there as well. (See Figure 6.19.)

It can be shown through simple application of the chain rule that a suitable transformation of uniform $[0, 1]^2$ sample points can account for the $\cos\theta$ factor. Specifically, if transformed points are distributed according to the distribution of $\cos\theta$ in $[0, 1]^2$ and then used with the

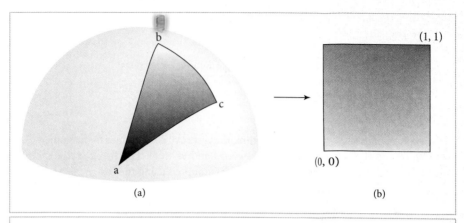

(a)   (b)

Figure 6.19: (a) The $\cos\theta$ factor varies smoothly over the area of a spherical triangle. (b) If it is mapped back to the $[0, 1]^2$ sampling domain, it also varies smoothly there, thanks to the sampling algorithm not introducing any discontinuities or excessive distortion.

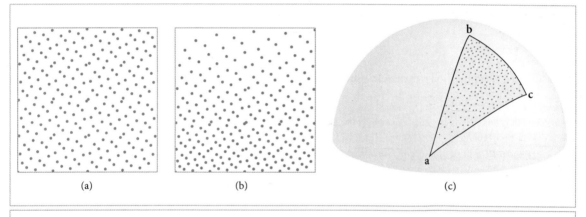

(a)   (b)   (c)

Figure 6.20: If (a) uniform sample points are warped to (b) approximate the distribution of the incident cosine factor in $[0, 1]^2$ before being used with the spherical triangle sampling algorithm, then (c) the resulting points in the triangle are approximately cosine-distributed.

spherical triangle sampling algorithm, then the distribution of directions on the sphere will include the $\cos\theta$ factor.

The true function has no convenient analytic form, but because it is smoothly varying, here we will approximate it with a bilinear function. Each corner of the $[0, 1]^2$ sampling domain maps to one of the three vertices of the spherical triangle, and so we set the bilinear function's value at each corner according to the $\cos\theta$ factor computed at the associated triangle vertex.

Sampling a point in the triangle then proceeds by using the initial uniform sample to sample the bilinear distribution and to use the resulting nonuniform point in $[0, 1]^2$ with the triangle sampling algorithm. (See Figure 6.20.)

Applying the principles of transforming between distributions that were introduced in Section 2.4.1, we can find that the overall PDF of such a sample is given by the product of the PDF for the bilinear sample and the PDF of the spherical triangle sample.

ShapeSampleContext::ns 268

This technique is only applied for reference points on surfaces. For points in scattering media, the surface normal ShapeSampleContext::ns is degenerate and no sample warping is applied.

⟨Apply warp product sampling for cosine factor at reference point⟩ ≡   317
```
Float pdf = 1;
if (ctx.ns != Normal3f(0, 0, 0)) {
    ⟨Compute cos θ-based weights w at sample domain corners 324⟩
    u = SampleBilinear(u, w);
    pdf = BilinearPDF(u, w);
}
```

For the spherical triangle sampling algorithm, the vertex v0 corresponds to the sample (0, 1), v1 to (0, 0) and (1, 0) (and the line in between), and v2 to (1, 1). Therefore, the sampling weights at the corners of the $[0, 1]^2$ domain are computed using the cosine of the direction to the corresponding vertex.

⟨Compute cos θ-based weights w at sample domain corners⟩ ≡   324, 325
```
Point3f rp = ctx.p();
Vector3f wi[3] = {Normalize(p0 - rp), Normalize(p1 - rp),
                  Normalize(p2 - rp)};
pstd::array<Float, 4> w =
    pstd::array<Float, 4>{std::max<Float>(0.01, AbsDot(ctx.ns, wi[1])),
                          std::max<Float>(0.01, AbsDot(ctx.ns, wi[1])),
                          std::max<Float>(0.01, AbsDot(ctx.ns, wi[0])),
                          std::max<Float>(0.01, AbsDot(ctx.ns, wi[2]))};
```

The associated PDF() method is thankfully much simpler than the sampling routine.

⟨Triangle Public Methods⟩ +≡   301
```
Float PDF(const ShapeSampleContext &ctx, Vector3f wi) const {
    Float solidAngle = SolidAngle(ctx.p());
    ⟨Return PDF based on uniform area sampling for challenging triangles 324⟩
    Float pdf = 1 / solidAngle;
    ⟨Adjust PDF for warp product sampling of triangle cos θ factor 325⟩
    return pdf;
}
```

It is important that the PDF() method makes exactly the same decisions about which technique is used to sample the triangle as the Sample() method does. This method therefore starts with the same check for very small and very large triangles to determine whether it should fall back to returning the PDF based on uniform area sampling.

⟨Return PDF based on uniform area sampling for challenging triangles⟩ ≡   324
```
if (solidAngle < MinSphericalSampleArea ||
    solidAngle > MaxSphericalSampleArea) {
    ⟨Intersect sample ray with shape geometry 285⟩
    ⟨Compute PDF in solid angle measure from shape intersection point 285⟩
    return pdf;
}
```

If Sample() would have warped the initial uniform random sample to account for the incident cos θ factor, it is necessary to incorporate the corresponding change of variables factor in the returned PDF here. To do so, we need to be able to invert the spherical triangle sampling algorithm in order to determine the sample value u that samples a point on the triangle that gives the incident direction wi at the reference point. The InvertSphericalTriangleSample() function performs this computation.

⟨*Adjust PDF for warp product sampling of triangle cos θ factor*⟩ ≡   **324**
```
if (ctx.ns != Normal3f(0, 0, 0)) {
    ⟨Get triangle vertices in p0, p1, and p2 302⟩
    Point2f u = InvertSphericalTriangleSample({p0, p1, p2}, ctx.p(), wi);
    ⟨Compute cos θ-based weights w at sample domain corners 324⟩
    pdf *= BilinearPDF(u, w);
}
```

The pair of sample values that give a sampled direction ω can be found by inverting each of the sampling operations individually. The function that performs this computation starts out with a few reused fragments to compute the angles at the three vertices of the spherical triangle.

⟨*Sampling Function Definitions*⟩ +≡
```
Point2f InvertSphericalTriangleSample(const pstd::array<Point3f, 3> &v,
                                       Point3f p, Vector3f w) {
    ⟨Compute vectors a, b, and c to spherical triangle vertices 318⟩
    ⟨Compute normalized cross products of all direction pairs 319⟩
    ⟨Find angles α, β, and γ at spherical triangle vertices 319⟩
    ⟨Find vertex c′ along ac arc for ω 326⟩
    ⟨Invert uniform area sampling to find u0 326⟩
    ⟨Invert arc sampling to find u1 and return result 326⟩
}
```

Next, it finds the vertex c' along the arc between **a** and **c** that defines the subtriangle that would have been sampled when sampling ω. This vertex can be found by computing the intersection of the great circle defined by **b** and ω and the great circle defined by **a** and **c**; see Figure 6.21.

Recall from Section 3.8.2 that the great circle passing through two points on the sphere is given by the intersection of the sphere with a plane passing through the origin and those two points. Therefore, we can find the intersection between the two corresponding planes, which is a line. In 3D, the cross product of the plane normals gives this line's direction. This line intersects the sphere at two points and so it is necessary to choose the one of them that is between **a** and **c**.

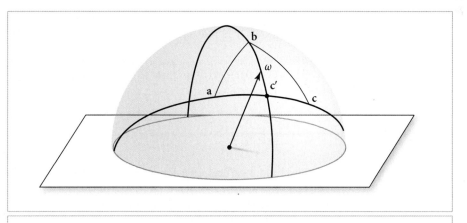

Figure 6.21: Given a spherical triangle **abc** and a direction ω that is inside it, the vertex c' along the edge from **a** to **c** can be found from the intersection of the great circle that passes through **b** and ω and the great circle that passes through **a** and **c**.

⟨*Find vertex* **c**′ *along* **ac** *arc for* ω⟩ ≡   325
```
    Vector3f cp = Normalize(Cross(Cross(b, w), Cross(c, a)));
    if (Dot(cp, a + c) < 0)
        cp = -cp;
```

Given **c**′, it is easy to compute the area of the triangle **abc**′; the ratio of that area to the original area gives the first sample value u0. However, it is necessary to be aware of the case where **a** and **c**′ are nearly coincident; in that case, computation of the angle γ′ may have high error, sometimes to the point that the subtriangle **abc**′ seems to have larger area than the original triangle **abc**. That case is caught with a dot product test.

⟨*Invert uniform area sampling to find* u0⟩ ≡   325
```
    Float u0;
    if (Dot(a, cp) > 0.99999847691f /* 0.1 degrees */)
        u0 = 0;
    else {
        ⟨Compute area A′ of subtriangle 326⟩
        ⟨Compute sample u0 that gives the area A′ 326⟩
    }
```

Otherwise, the area of the subtriangle A' is computed using Girard's theorem.

⟨*Compute area* A' *of subtriangle*⟩ ≡   326
```
    Vector3f n_cpb = Cross(cp, b), n_acp = Cross(a, cp);
    if (LengthSquared(n_cpb) == 0 || LengthSquared(n_acp) == 0)
        return Point2f(0.5, 0.5);
    n_cpb = Normalize(n_cpb);
    n_acp = Normalize(n_acp);
    Float Ap =
        alpha + AngleBetween(n_ab, n_cpb) + AngleBetween(n_acp, -n_cpb) - Pi;
```

The first sample value is then easily found given these two areas.

⟨*Compute sample* u0 *that gives the area* A'⟩ ≡   326
```
    Float A = alpha + beta + gamma - Pi;
    u0 = Ap / A;
```

The sampling method for choosing ω along the arc through **b** and **c**′, Equation (6.10), is also easily inverted.

⟨*Invert arc sampling to find* u1 *and return result*⟩ ≡   325
```
    Float u1 = (1 - Dot(w, b)) / (1 - Dot(cp, b));
    return Point2f(Clamp(u0, 0, 1), Clamp(u1, 0, 1));
```

6.6 BILINEAR PATCHES

It is useful to have a shape defined by four vertices. One option would be a planar quadrilateral, though not requiring all four vertices to be coplanar is preferable, as it is less restrictive. Such a shape is the bilinear patch, which is a parametric surface defined by four vertices $p_{0,0}$, $p_{1,0}$, $p_{0,1}$, and $p_{1,1}$. Each vertex gives the position associated with a corner of the parametric (u, v) domain $[0, 1]^2$ and points on the surface are defined via bilinear interpolation:

$$f(u, v) = (1 - u)(1 - v)p_{0,0} + u(1 - v)p_{1,0} + (1 - u)vp_{0,1} + uvp_{1,1}.$$ [6.11]

AngleBetween() 89
Clamp() 1033
Cross() 91
Dot() 89
Float 23
LengthSquared() 87
Normalize() 88
Pi 1033
Point2f 92
Vector3f 86

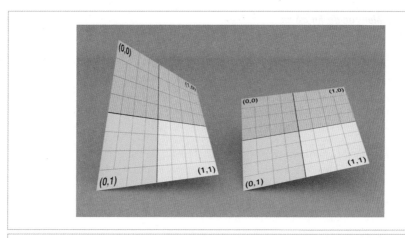

Figure 6.22: Two Bilinear Patches. The bilinear patch is defined by four vertices that are not necessarily planar. It is able to represent a variety of simple curved surfaces.

The bilinear patch is a *doubly ruled surface*: there are two straight lines through every point on it. (This can be seen by considering a parametric point on the surface (u, v) and then fixing either of u and v and considering the function that results: it is linear.)

Not only can bilinear patches be used to represent planar quadrilaterals, but they can also represent simple curved surfaces. They are a useful target for converting higher-order parametric surfaces to simpler shapes that are amenable to direct ray intersection. Figure 6.22 shows two bilinear patches.

pbrt allows the specification of bilinear patch meshes for the same reasons that triangle meshes can be specified: to allow per-vertex attributes like position and surface normal to be shared by multiple patches and to allow mesh-wide properties to be stored just once. To this end, BilinearPatchMesh plays the equivalent role to the TriangleMesh.

⟨*BilinearPatchMesh Definition*⟩ ≡
```
class BilinearPatchMesh {
  public:
    ⟨BilinearPatchMesh Public Methods⟩
    ⟨BilinearPatchMesh Public Members 327⟩
};
```

We will skip past the BilinearPatchMesh constructor, as it mirrors the TriangleMesh's, transforming the positions and normals to rendering space and using the BufferCache to avoid storing redundant buffers in memory.

⟨*BilinearPatchMesh Public Members*⟩ ≡   327
```
bool reverseOrientation, transformSwapsHandedness;
int nPatches, nVertices;
const int *vertexIndices = nullptr;
const Point3f *p = nullptr;
const Normal3f *n = nullptr;
const Point2f *uv = nullptr;
```

The BilinearPatch class implements the Shape interface and represents a single patch in a bilinear patch mesh.

⟨*BilinearPatch Definition*⟩ ≡
```
class BilinearPatch {
  public:
    ⟨BilinearPatch Public Methods 330⟩
  private:
    ⟨BilinearPatch Private Methods 328⟩
    ⟨BilinearPatch Private Members 328⟩
};
```

⟨*BilinearPatch Method Definitions*⟩ ≡
```
BilinearPatch::BilinearPatch(const BilinearPatchMesh *mesh, int meshIndex,
                             int blpIndex)
    : meshIndex(meshIndex), blpIndex(blpIndex) {
    ⟨Store area of bilinear patch in area 329⟩
}
```

Also similar to triangles, each `BilinearPatch` stores the index of the mesh that it is a part of as well as its own index in the mesh's patches.

⟨*BilinearPatch Private Members*⟩ ≡   328
```
int meshIndex, blpIndex;
```

The `GetMesh()` method makes it easy for a `BilinearPatch` to get the pointer to its associated mesh.

⟨*BilinearPatch Private Methods*⟩ ≡   328
```
const BilinearPatchMesh *GetMesh() const {
    return (*allMeshes)[meshIndex];
}
```

There is a subtlety that comes with the use of a vector to store the meshes. pbrt's scene initialization code in Appendix C does its best to parallelize its work, which includes the parallelization of reading binary files that encode meshes from disk. A mutex is used to protect adding meshes to this vector, though as this vector grows, it is periodically reallocated to make more space. A consequence is that the `BilinearPatch` constructor must not call the `GetMesh()` method to get its `BilinearPatchMesh *`, since `GetMesh()` accesses `allMeshes` without mutual exclusion. Thus, the mesh is passed to the constructor as a parameter above.

⟨*BilinearPatch Private Members*⟩ +≡   328
```
static pstd::vector<const BilinearPatchMesh *> *allMeshes;
```

The area of a parametric surface defined over $[0, 1]^2$ is given by the integral

$$\int_0^1 \int_0^1 \left\| \frac{\partial \mathrm{p}}{\partial u} \times \frac{\partial \mathrm{p}}{\partial v} \right\| \, du \, dv. \qquad [6.12]$$

The partial derivatives of a bilinear patch are easily derived. They are:

$$\frac{\partial \mathrm{p}}{\partial u} = (1 - v)(\mathrm{p}_{1,0} - \mathrm{p}_{0,0}) + v(\mathrm{p}_{1,1} - \mathrm{p}_{0,1})$$

$$\frac{\partial \mathrm{p}}{\partial v} = (1 - u)(\mathrm{p}_{0,1} - \mathrm{p}_{0,0}) + u(\mathrm{p}_{1,1} - \mathrm{p}_{1,0}). \qquad [6.13]$$

However, it is not generally possible to evaluate the area integral from Equation (6.12) in closed form with these partial derivatives. Therefore, the `BilinearPatch` constructor caches the patch's surface area in a member variable, using numerical integration to compute its value if necessary.

Because bilinear patches are often used to represent rectangles, the constructor checks for that case and takes the product of the lengths of the sides of the rectangle to compute the area when appropriate. In the general case, the fragment ⟨*Compute approximate area of bilinear patch*⟩ uses a Riemann sum evaluated at 3×3 points to approximate Equation (6.12). We do not include that code fragment here.

⟨*Store area of bilinear patch in* area⟩ ≡   **328**
```
⟨Get bilinear patch vertices in p00, p01, p10, and p11 329⟩
if (IsRectangle(mesh))
    area = Distance(p00, p01) * Distance(p00, p10);
else {
    ⟨Compute approximate area of bilinear patch⟩
}
```

⟨*BilinearPatch Private Members*⟩ +≡   **328**
```
Float area;
```

This fragment, which loads the four vertices of a patch into local variables, will be reused in many of the following methods.

⟨*Get bilinear patch vertices in* p00, p01, p10, *and* p11⟩ ≡   **329, 330, 335, 338, 342, 343, 344**
```
const int *v = &mesh->vertexIndices[4 * blpIndex];
Point3f p00 = mesh->p[v[0]], p10 = mesh->p[v[1]];
Point3f p01 = mesh->p[v[2]], p11 = mesh->p[v[3]];
```

In addition to the surface area computation, there will be a number of additional cases where we will find it useful to use specialized algorithms if a BilinearPatch is a rectangle. Therefore, this check is encapsulated in the IsRectangle() method.

It first tests to see if any two neighboring vertices are coincident, in which case the patch is certainly not a rectangle. This check is important to perform first, since the following ones would otherwise end up trying to perform invalid operations like normalizing degenerate vectors in that case.

⟨*BilinearPatch Private Methods*⟩ +≡   **328**
```
bool IsRectangle(const BilinearPatchMesh *mesh) const {
    ⟨Get bilinear patch vertices in p00, p01, p10, and p11 329⟩
    if (p00 == p01 || p01 == p11 || p11 == p10 || p10 == p00)
        return false;
    ⟨Check if bilinear patch vertices are coplanar 329⟩
    ⟨Check if planar vertices form a rectangle 330⟩
}
```

If the four vertices are not coplanar, then they do not form a rectangle. We can check this case by computing the surface normal of the plane formed by three of the vertices and then testing if the vector from one of those three to the fourth vertex is not (nearly) perpendicular to the plane normal.

⟨*Check if bilinear patch vertices are coplanar*⟩ ≡   **329**
```
Normal3f n(Normalize(Cross(p10 - p00, p01 - p00)));
if (AbsDot(Normalize(p11 - p00), n) > 1e-5f)
    return false;
```

Four coplanar vertices form a rectangle if they all have the same distance from the average of their positions. The implementation here computes the squared distance to save the square root operations and then tests the relative error with respect to the first squared distance.

Because the test is based on relative error, it is not sensitive to the absolute size of the patch; scaling all the vertex positions does not affect it.

⟨*Check if planar vertices form a rectangle*⟩ ≡   **329**

```
Point3f pCenter = (p00 + p01 + p10 + p11) / 4;
Float d2[4] = {
    DistanceSquared(p00, pCenter), DistanceSquared(p01, pCenter),
    DistanceSquared(p10, pCenter), DistanceSquared(p11, pCenter) };
for (int i = 1; i < 4; ++i)
    if (std::abs(d2[i] - d2[0]) / d2[0] > 1e-4f)
        return false;
return true;
```

With the area cached, implementation of the Area() method is trivial.

⟨*BilinearPatch Public Methods*⟩ ≡   **328**

```
Float Area() const { return area; }
```

The bounds of a bilinear patch are given by the bounding box that bounds its four corner vertices. As with Triangles, the mesh vertices are already in rendering space, so no further transformation is necessary here.

⟨*BilinearPatch Method Definitions*⟩ +≡

```
Bounds3f BilinearPatch::Bounds() const {
    const BilinearPatchMesh *mesh = GetMesh();
    ⟨Get bilinear patch vertices in p00, p01, p10, and p11 329⟩
    return Union(Bounds3f(p00, p01), Bounds3f(p10, p11));
}
```

Although a planar patch has a single surface normal, the surface normal of a nonplanar patch varies across its surface.

⟨*BilinearPatch Method Definitions*⟩ +≡

```
DirectionCone BilinearPatch::NormalBounds() const {
    const BilinearPatchMesh *mesh = GetMesh();
    ⟨Get bilinear patch vertices in p00, p01, p10, and p11 329⟩
    ⟨If patch is a triangle, return bounds for single surface normal⟩
    ⟨Compute bilinear patch normal n00 at (0, 0) 331⟩
    ⟨Compute bilinear patch normals n10, n01, and n11⟩
    ⟨Compute average normal and return normal bounds for patch 331⟩
}
```

If the bilinear patch is actually a triangle, the ⟨*If patch is a triangle, return bounds for single surface normal*⟩ fragment evaluates its surface normal and returns the corresponding DirectionCone. We have not included that straightforward fragment here.

Otherwise, the normals are computed at the four corners of the patch. The following fragment computes the normal at the (0, 0) parametric position. It is particularly easy to evaluate the partial derivatives at the corners; they work out to be the differences with the adjacent vertices in u and v. Some care is necessary with the orientation of the normals, however. As with triangle meshes, if per-vertex shading normals were specified, they determine which side of the surface the geometric normal lies on. Otherwise, the normal may need to be flipped, depending on the user-specified orientation and the handedness of the rendering-to-object-space transformation.

⟨*Compute bilinear patch normal* n00 *at* (0, 0)⟩ ≡   330

```
    Vector3f n00 = Normalize(Cross(p10 - p00, p01 - p00));
    if (mesh->n)
        n00 = FaceForward(n00, mesh->n[v[0]]);
    else if (mesh->reverseOrientation ^ mesh->transformSwapsHandedness)
        n00 = -n00;
```

Normals at the other three vertices are computed in an equivalent manner, so the fragment that handles the rest is not included here.

A bounding cone for the normals is found by taking their average and then finding the cosine of the maximum angle that any of them makes with their average. Although this does not necessarily give an optimal bound, it usually works well in practice. (See the "Further Reading" section in Chapter 3 for more information on this topic.)

⟨*Compute average normal and return normal bounds for patch*⟩ ≡   330

```
    Vector3f n = Normalize(n00 + n10 + n01 + n11);
    Float cosTheta = std::min({Dot(n, n00), Dot(n, n01),
                               Dot(n, n10), Dot(n, n11)});
    return DirectionCone(n, Clamp(cosTheta, -1, 1));
```

6.6.1 INTERSECTION TESTS

Unlike triangles (but like spheres and cylinders), a ray may intersect a bilinear patch twice, in which case the closest of the two intersections is returned. An example is shown in Figure 6.23.

As with triangles, it is useful to have a stand-alone ray–bilinear patch intersection test function rather than only providing this functionality through an instance of a `BilinearPatch` object. Rather than being based on computing t values along the ray and then finding the (u, v) coordinates for any found intersections, the algorithm here first determines the parametric u coordinates of any intersections. Only if any are found within $[0, 1]$ are the corresponding v and t values computed to find the full intersection information.

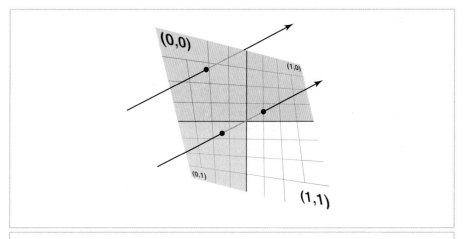

Figure 6.23: Ray–Bilinear Patch Intersections. Rays may intersect a bilinear patch either once or two times.

⟨*Bilinear Patch Inline Functions*⟩ ≡
```
    pstd::optional<BilinearIntersection>
    IntersectBilinearPatch(const Ray &ray, Float tMax, Point3f p00, Point3f p10,
                           Point3f p01, Point3f p11) {
        ⟨Find quadratic coefficients for distance from ray to u iso-lines 333⟩
        ⟨Solve quadratic for bilinear patch u intersection 333⟩
        ⟨Find epsilon eps to ensure that candidate t is greater than zero 386⟩
        ⟨Compute v and t for the first u intersection 334⟩
        ⟨Compute v and t for the second u intersection⟩
        ⟨Check intersection t against tMax and possibly return intersection 335⟩
    }
```

Going back to the definition of the bilinear surface, Equation (6.11), we can see that if we fix one of u or v, then we are left with an equation that defines a line. For example, with u fixed, we have

$$f_u(v) = (1 - v)\mathrm{p}_{u,0} + v\mathrm{p}_{u,1},$$

with

$$\mathrm{p}_{u,0} = (1 - u)\mathrm{p}_{0,0} + u\mathrm{p}_{1,0}$$
$$\mathrm{p}_{u,1} = (1 - u)\mathrm{p}_{0,1} + u\mathrm{p}_{1,1}.$$

[6.14]

(See Figure 6.24.)

The first step of the intersection test considers the set of all such lines defined by the patch's vertices. For any intersection, the minimum distance from a point along the ray to a point along one of these lines will be zero. Therefore, we start with the task of trying to find u values that give lines with zero distance to a point on the ray.

Given two infinite and non-parallel lines, one defined by the two points p_a and p_b and the other defined by p_c and p_d, the minimum distance between them can be found by determining the pair of parallel planes that each contain one of the lines and then finding the distance between them. (See Figure 6.25.)

To find the coefficients of those plane equations, we start by taking the cross product $(\mathrm{p}_b - \mathrm{p}_a) \times (\mathrm{p}_d - \mathrm{p}_c)$. This gives a vector that is perpendicular to both lines and provides the first

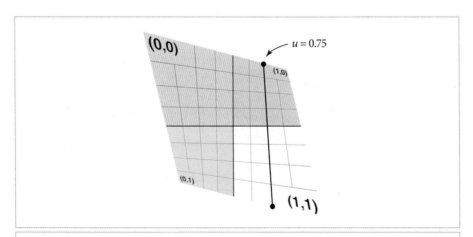

Figure 6.24: Fixing the u parameter of a bilinear patch gives a linear function between two opposite edges of the patch.

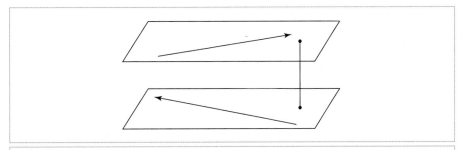

Figure 6.25: The minimum distance between two lines can be computed by finding two parallel planes that contain each line and then computing the distance between them.

three coefficients of the plane equation $ax + by + cz + d = 0$. In turn, the d_{ab} and d_{cd} coefficients can be found for each line's plane by substituting a point along the respective line into the plane equation and solving for d. Because the planes are parallel, the distance between them is then

$$\frac{|d_{ab} - d_{cd}|}{\sqrt{a^2 + b^2 + c^2}}. \tag{6.15}$$

In the case of ray–bilinear patch intersection, one line corresponds to the ray and the other to a line from the family of lines given by f_u.

Given a ray and the bilinear patch vertices, we have $p_a = o$, the ray's origin, and p_b can be set as the point along the ray $p_b = o + \mathbf{d}$. Then, p_c and p_d can be set as $p_c = p_{u,0}$ and $p_d = p_{u,1}$ from Equation (6.14). After taking the cross product to find the plane coefficients, finding each d value, and simplifying, we can find that $d_{ray} - d_u$ is a quadratic equation in u. (That it is quadratic is reassuring, since a ray can intersect a bilinear patch up to two times.)

Because we only care about finding zeros of the distance function, we can neglect the denominator of Equation (6.15). After equating the difference $d_{ray} - d_u$ to 0, collecting terms and simplifying, we end up with the following code to compute the quadratic coefficients.[4]

⟨*Find quadratic coefficients for distance from ray to u iso-lines*⟩ ≡   332
```
Float a = Dot(Cross(p10 - p00, p01 - p11), ray.d);
Float c = Dot(Cross(p00 - ray.o, ray.d), p01 - p00);
Float b = Dot(Cross(p10 - ray.o, ray.d), p11 - p10) - (a + c);
```

The u values where the ray intersects the patch are given by the solution to the corresponding quadratic equation. If there are no real solutions, then there is no intersection and the function returns.

⟨*Solve quadratic for bilinear patch u intersection*⟩ ≡   332
```
Float u1, u2;
if (!Quadratic(a, b, c, &u1, &u2))
    return {};
```

The two u values are handled in turn. The first step is to check whether each is between 0 and 1. If not, it does not represent a valid intersection in the patch's parametric domain. Otherwise, the v and t values for the intersection point are computed.

Cross() 91
Dot() 89
Float 23
Quadratic() 1045
Ray::d 95

---

4   Note that these are coefficients to the equation $au^2 + bu + c = 0$ and not a, b, and c plane coefficients.

⟨*Compute v and t for the first u intersection*⟩ ≡   332
```
    Float t = tMax, u, v;
    if (0 <= u1 && u1 <= 1) {
        ⟨Precompute common terms for v and t computation 334⟩
        ⟨Compute matrix determinants for v and t numerators 334⟩
        ⟨Set u, v, and t if intersection is valid 335⟩
    }
```

One way to compute the v and t values is to find the parametric values along the ray and the line f_u where the distance between them is minimized. Although this distance should be zero since we have determined that there is an intersection between the ray and f_u, there may be some round-off error in the computed u value. Thus, formulating this computation in terms of minimizing that distance is a reasonable way to make the most of the values at hand.

With o the ray's origin and **d** its direction, the parameter values where the distances are minimized are given by

$$t = \frac{\det(f_u(0) - \text{o}, \ f_u(1) - f_u(0), \ \mathbf{d} \times (f_u(1) - f_u(0)))}{\|\mathbf{d} \times (f_u(1) - f_u(0))\|^2}$$

and

$$v = \frac{\det(f_u(0) - \text{o}, \ \mathbf{d}, \ \mathbf{d} \times (f_u(1) - f_u(0)))}{\|\mathbf{d} \times (f_u(1) - f_u(0))\|^2}$$

where det is shorthand for the determinant of the 3×3 matrix formed from the three column vectors. We will not derive these equations here. The "Further Reading" section has more details.

We start by computing a handful of common values that are used in computing the matrix determinants and final parametric values.

⟨*Precompute common terms for v and t computation*⟩ ≡   334
```
    Point3f uo = Lerp(u1, p00, p10);
    Vector3f ud = Lerp(u1, p01, p11) - uo;
    Vector3f deltao = uo - ray.o;
    Vector3f perp = Cross(ray.d, ud);
    Float p2 = LengthSquared(perp);
```

The matrix determinants in the numerators can easily be computed using the `SquareMatrix` class. Note that there are some common subexpressions among the two of them, though we leave it to the compiler to handle them. In a more optimized implementation, writing out the determinant computations explicitly in order to do so manually could be worthwhile.

⟨*Compute matrix determinants for v and t numerators*⟩ ≡   334
```
    Float v1 = Determinant(SquareMatrix<3>(deltao.x, ray.d.x, perp.x,
                                           deltao.y, ray.d.y, perp.y,
                                           deltao.z, ray.d.z, perp.z));
    Float t1 = Determinant(SquareMatrix<3>(deltao.x, ud.x, perp.x,
                                           deltao.y, ud.y, perp.y,
                                           deltao.z, ud.z, perp.z));
```

Float 23
Point3f 92
SquareMatrix 1049
SquareMatrix::Determinant()
  1051
Vector3f 86

Due to round-off error, it is possible that the computed t distance is positive and seemingly represents a valid intersection even though the true value of t is negative and corresponds to a point behind the ray's origin. Testing t against an epsilon value (which is discussed further in Section 6.8.7) helps avoid reporting incorrect intersections in such cases. Because we defer the division to compute the final *t* value, it is necessary to test t1 against p2 * eps here.

⟨*Set* u, v, *and* t *if intersection is valid*⟩ ≡   334
```
if (t1 > p2 * eps && 0 <= v1 && v1 <= p2) {
    u = u1;
    v = v1 / p2;
    t = t1 / p2;
}
```

The second *u* root is handled with equivalent code, though with added logic to keep the closer of the intersections if there are two of them. That fragment is not included here.

If the final closest *t* value is less than the given tMax, then an intersection is returned.

⟨*Check intersection* t *against* tMax *and possibly return intersection*⟩ ≡   332
```
if (t >= tMax)
    return {};
return BilinearIntersection{{u, v}, t};
```

The (*u*, *v*) coordinates and ray parametric *t* value are sufficient to encapsulate the intersection so that the rest of its geometric properties can be computed later.

⟨*BilinearIntersection Definition*⟩ ≡
```
struct BilinearIntersection {
    Point2f uv;
    Float t;
};
```

The InteractionFromIntersection() method computes all the geometric information necessary to return the SurfaceInteraction corresponding to a specified (*u*, *v*) point on a bilinear path, as is found by the intersection routine.

⟨*BilinearPatch Public Methods*⟩ +≡   328
```
static SurfaceInteraction InteractionFromIntersection(
        const BilinearPatchMesh *mesh, int blpIndex, Point2f uv,
        Float time, Vector3f wo) {
    ⟨Compute bilinear patch point p, ∂p/∂u, and ∂p/∂v for (u, v) 335⟩
    ⟨Compute (s, t) texture coordinates at bilinear patch (u, v) 336⟩
    ⟨Find partial derivatives ∂n/∂u and ∂n/∂v for bilinear patch 337⟩
    ⟨Initialize bilinear patch intersection point error pError 377⟩
    ⟨Initialize SurfaceInteraction for bilinear patch intersection 337⟩
    ⟨Compute bilinear patch shading normal if necessary 337⟩
    return isect;
}
```

Given the parametric (*u*, *v*) coordinates of an intersection point, it is easy to compute the corresponding point on the bilinear patch using Equation (6.11) and its partial derivatives with Equation (6.13).

⟨*Compute bilinear patch point* p, ∂p/∂u, *and* ∂p/∂v *for* (u, v)⟩ ≡   335
```
⟨Get bilinear patch vertices in p00, p01, p10, and p11 329⟩
Point3f p = Lerp(uv[0], Lerp(uv[1], p00, p01), Lerp(uv[1], p10, p11));
Vector3f dpdu = Lerp(uv[1], p10, p11) - Lerp(uv[1], p00, p01);
Vector3f dpdv = Lerp(uv[0], p01, p11) - Lerp(uv[0], p00, p10);
```

If per-vertex texture coordinates have been specified, then they, too, are interpolated at the intersection point. Otherwise, the parametric (u, v) coordinates are used for texture mapping. For the remainder of this method, we will denote the texture coordinates as (s, t) to distinguish them from the patch's (u, v) parameterization. (Because this method does not use the parametric t distance along the ray, this notation is unambiguous.)

Variables are also defined here to store the partial derivatives between the two sets of coordinates: $\partial u/\partial s$, $\partial u/\partial t$, $\partial v/\partial s$, and $\partial v/\partial t$. These are initialized for now to the appropriate values for when $(s, t) = (u, v)$.

⟨*Compute (s, t) texture coordinates at bilinear patch (u, v)*⟩ ≡   335
```
Point2f st = uv;
Float duds = 1, dudt = 0, dvds = 0, dvdt = 1;
if (mesh->uv) {
    ⟨Compute texture coordinates for bilinear patch intersection point 336⟩
    ⟨Update bilinear patch ∂p/∂u and ∂p/∂v accounting for (s, t) 336⟩
}
```

If per-vertex texture coordinates have been specified, they are bilinearly interpolated in the usual manner.

⟨*Compute texture coordinates for bilinear patch intersection point*⟩ ≡   336, 341, 344
```
Point2f uv00 = mesh->uv[v[0]], uv10 = mesh->uv[v[1]];
Point2f uv01 = mesh->uv[v[2]], uv11 = mesh->uv[v[3]];
st = Lerp(uv[0], Lerp(uv[1], uv00, uv01), Lerp(uv[1], uv10, uv11));
```

Because the partial derivatives $\partial p/\partial u$ and $\partial p/\partial v$ in the SurfaceInteraction are in terms of the (u, v) parameterization used for texturing, these values must be updated if texture coordinates have been specified.

⟨*Update bilinear patch $\partial p/\partial u$ and $\partial p/\partial v$ accounting for (s, t)*⟩ ≡   336
```
⟨Compute partial derivatives of (u, v) with respect to (s, t) 336⟩
⟨Compute partial derivatives of p with respect to (s, t) 337⟩
⟨Set dpdu and dpdv to updated partial derivatives 337⟩
```

The first step is to compute the updated partial derivatives $\partial u/\partial s$ and so forth. These can be found by first taking the corresponding partial derivatives of the bilinear interpolation used to compute (s, t) to find $\partial(s, t)/\partial u$ and $\partial(s, t)/\partial v$. (Note the similar form to how the partial derivatives of p were computed earlier.) The desired partial derivatives can be found by taking reciprocals.

⟨*Compute partial derivatives of (u, v) with respect to (s, t)*⟩ ≡   336
```
Vector2f dstdu = Lerp(uv[1], uv10, uv11) - Lerp(uv[1], uv00, uv01);
Vector2f dstdv = Lerp(uv[0], uv01, uv11) - Lerp(uv[0], uv00, uv10);
duds = std::abs(dstdu[0]) < 1e-8f ? 0 : 1 / dstdu[0];
dvds = std::abs(dstdv[0]) < 1e-8f ? 0 : 1 / dstdv[0];
dudt = std::abs(dstdu[1]) < 1e-8f ? 0 : 1 / dstdu[1];
dvdt = std::abs(dstdv[1]) < 1e-8f ? 0 : 1 / dstdv[1];
```

Given the partial derivatives, the chain rule can be applied to compute the updated partial derivatives of position. For example,

$$\frac{\partial \mathrm{p}}{\partial s} = \frac{\partial \mathrm{p}}{\partial u}\frac{\partial u}{\partial s} + \frac{\partial \mathrm{p}}{\partial v}\frac{\partial v}{\partial s},$$

and similarly for $\partial \mathrm{p}/\partial t$.

⟨*Compute partial derivatives of* p *with respect to* (s, t)⟩ ≡   336
```
Vector3f dpds = dpdu * duds + dpdv * dvds;
Vector3f dpdt = dpdu * dudt + dpdv * dvdt;
```

If the provided texture coordinates specify a degenerate mapping, $\partial p/\partial s$ or $\partial p/\partial t$ may be zero. In that case, dpdu and dpdv are left unchanged, as at least their cross product provides a correct normal vector. A dot product checks that the normal given by $\partial p/\partial s \times \partial p/\partial t$ lies in the same hemisphere as the normal given by the cross product of the original partial derivatives of p, flipping $\partial p/\partial t$ if necessary. Finally, dpdu and dpdv can be updated.

⟨*Set* dpdu *and* dpdv *to updated partial derivatives*⟩ ≡   336
```
if (Cross(dpds, dpdt) != Vector3f(0, 0, 0)) {
    if (Dot(Cross(dpdu, dpdv), Cross(dpds, dpdt)) < 0)
        dpdt = -dpdt;
    dpdu = dpds;
    dpdv = dpdt;
}
```

The second partial derivatives of p are easily found to compute the partial derivatives of the surface normal; all but $\partial^2 p/\partial u \partial v$ are zero vectors. Thence, the partial derivatives of the normal can be computed using the regular approach. These are then adjusted to account for the (s, t) parameterization in the same way that $\partial p/\partial u$ and $\partial p/\partial v$ were. The corresponding fragment follows the same form as ⟨*Compute partial derivatives of* p *with respect to* (s, t)⟩ and is therefore not included here.

⟨*Find partial derivatives* $\partial \mathbf{n}/\partial u$ *and* $\partial \mathbf{n}/\partial v$ *for bilinear patch*⟩ ≡   335
```
Vector3f d2Pduu(0, 0, 0), d2Pdvv(0, 0, 0);
Vector3f d2Pduv = (p00 - p01) + (p11 - p10);
```
⟨*Compute coefficients for fundamental forms* **279**⟩
⟨*Compute* $\partial \mathbf{n}/\partial u$ *and* $\partial \mathbf{n}/\partial v$ *from fundamental form coefficients* **279**⟩
⟨*Update* $\partial \mathbf{n}/\partial u$ *and* $\partial \mathbf{n}/\partial v$ *to account for* (s, t) *parameterization*⟩

All the necessary information for initializing the SurfaceInteraction is now at hand.

⟨*Initialize* SurfaceInteraction *for bilinear patch intersection*⟩ ≡   335
```
bool flipNormal = mesh->reverseOrientation ^ mesh->transformSwapsHandedness;
SurfaceInteraction isect(Point3fi(p, pError), st, wo, dpdu, dpdv,
                         dndu, dndv, time, flipNormal);
```

Shading geometry is set in the SurfaceInteraction after it is created. Therefore, per-vertex shading normals are handled next.

⟨*Compute bilinear patch shading normal if necessary*⟩ ≡   335
```
if (mesh->n) {
    ⟨Compute shading normals for bilinear patch intersection point 338⟩
}
```

The usual bilinear interpolation is performed and if the resulting normal is non-degenerate, the shading geometry is provided to the SurfaceInteraction.

⟨*Compute shading normals for bilinear patch intersection point*⟩ ≡   337
```
Normal3f n00 = mesh->n[v[0]], n10 = mesh->n[v[1]];
Normal3f n01 = mesh->n[v[2]], n11 = mesh->n[v[3]];
Normal3f ns = Lerp(uv[0], Lerp(uv[1], n00, n01), Lerp(uv[1], n10, n11));
if (LengthSquared(ns) > 0) {
    ns = Normalize(ns);
    ⟨Set shading geometry for bilinear patch intersection 338⟩
}
```

The partial derivatives of the shading normal are computed in the same manner as the partial derivatives of p were found, including the adjustment for the parameterization given by per-vertex texture coordinates, if provided. Because shading geometry is specified via shading $\partial p/\partial u$ and $\partial p/\partial v$ vectors, here we find the rotation matrix that takes the geometric normal to the shading normal and apply it to dpdu and dpdv. The cross product of the resulting vectors then gives the shading normal.

⟨*Set shading geometry for bilinear patch intersection*⟩ ≡   338
```
Normal3f dndu = Lerp(uv[1], n10, n11) - Lerp(uv[1], n00, n01);
Normal3f dndv = Lerp(uv[0], n01, n11) - Lerp(uv[0], n00, n10);
⟨Update ∂n/∂u and ∂n/∂v to account for (s, t) parameterization⟩
Transform r = RotateFromTo(Vector3f(Normalize(isect.n)), Vector3f(ns));
isect.SetShadingGeometry(ns, r(dpdu), r(dpdv), dndu, dndv, true);
```

Given the intersection and InteractionFromIntersection() methods, both of the Bilinear Patch::Intersect() and IntersectP() methods are easy to implement. Since they both follow what should be by now a familiar form, we have not included them here.

6.6.2 SAMPLING

The sampling routines for bilinear patches select between sampling algorithms depending on the characteristics of the patch. For area sampling, both rectangular patches and patches that have an emission distribution defined by an image map are given special treatment. When sampling by solid angle from a reference point, rectangular patches are projected on to the sphere and sampled as spherical rectangles. For both cases, general-purpose sampling routines are used otherwise.

The area sampling method first samples parametric (u, v) coordinates, from which the rest of the necessary geometric values are derived.

⟨*BilinearPatch Method Definitions*⟩ +≡
```
pstd::optional<ShapeSample> BilinearPatch::Sample(Point2f u) const {
    const BilinearPatchMesh *mesh = GetMesh();
    ⟨Get bilinear patch vertices in p00, p01, p10, and p11 329⟩
    ⟨Sample bilinear patch parametric (u, v) coordinates 339⟩
    ⟨Compute bilinear patch geometric quantities at sampled (u, v) 341⟩
    ⟨Return ShapeSample for sampled bilinear patch point 341⟩
}
```

While all the Shape implementations we have implemented so far can be used as area light sources, none of their sampling routines have accounted for the fact that pbrt's DiffuseArea Light allows specifying an image that is used to represent spatially varying emission over the shape's (u, v) surface. Because such emission profiles are most frequently used with rectangular light sources, the BilinearPatch has the capability of sampling in (u, v) according to the emission function. Figure 6.26 demonstrates the value of doing so.

(a)

(b)

Figure 6.26: Area Sampling Accounting for Image-Based Emission. For a scene with an emissive bilinear patch where the amount of emission varies across the patch based on an image, (a) uniformly sampling in the patch's (u, v) parametric space leads to high variance since some samples have much higher contributions than others. (b) Sampling according to the image's distribution of brightness gives a significantly better result for the same number of rays. Here, MSE is improved by a factor of 2.28×. *(Bunny model courtesy of the Stanford Computer Graphics Laboratory.)*

Otherwise, if the patch is not a rectangle, an approximation to uniform area sampling is used. If it is a rectangle, then uniform area sampling is trivial and the provided sample value is used directly for (u, v). In all of these cases, the pdf value is with respect to the (u, v) parametric domain over $[0, 1)^2$.

⟨*Sample bilinear patch parametric (u, v) coordinates*⟩ ≡   **338**

```
Float pdf = 1;
Point2f uv;
if (mesh->imageDistribution)
    uv = mesh->imageDistribution->Sample(u, &pdf);
else if (!IsRectangle(mesh)) {
    ⟨Sample patch (u, v) with approximate uniform area sampling 340⟩
} else
    uv = u;
```

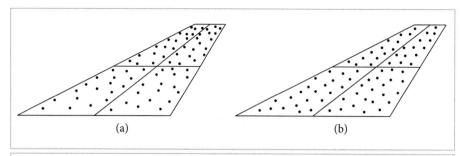

Figure 6.27: Nonuniform Sample Distribution from Uniform Parametric Sampling. (a) When a bilinear patch is sampled uniformly in (u, v), the sample points are denser close to pairs of nearby vertices. (b) When using an approximate equal-area distribution, the points are more uniformly distributed over the patch.

⟨*BilinearPatchMesh Public Members*⟩ +≡   327
```
PiecewiseConstant2D *imageDistribution;
```

For patches without an emissive image to sample from, we would like to uniformly sample over their surface area, as we have done with all the shapes so far. Unfortunately, an exact equal-area sampling algorithm cannot be derived for bilinear patches. This is a consequence of the fact that it is not possible to integrate the expression that gives the area of a bilinear patch, Equation (6.12). It is easy to uniformly sample in parametric (u, v) space, but doing so can give a poor distribution of samples, especially for bilinear patches where two vertices are close together and the others are far apart. Figure 6.27 shows such a patch as well as the distribution of points that results from uniform parametric sampling. While the nonuniform distribution of points can be accounted for in the PDF such that Monte Carlo estimates using such samples still converge to the correct result, the resulting estimators will generally have higher error than if a more uniform distribution is used.

An exact equal-area sampling algorithm would sample points p with probability proportional to its differential surface area $\|\partial p/\partial u \times \partial p/\partial v\|$. Lacking the ability to sample directly from this distribution, we will approximate it with a bilinear function where the value of the function at each corner is given by the patch's differential surface area there. Sampling a (u, v) location from that distribution generally works well to approximate exact equal-area sampling; see Figure 6.28.

⟨*Sample patch (u, v) with approximate uniform area sampling*⟩ ≡   339
```
    ⟨Initialize w array with differential area at bilinear patch corners 340⟩
    uv = SampleBilinear(u, w);
    pdf = BilinearPDF(uv, w);
```

It is especially easy to compute the partial derivatives at the patch corners; they are just differences with the adjacent vertices.

⟨*Initialize w array with differential area at bilinear patch corners*⟩ ≡   340, 342
```
    pstd::array<Float, 4> w = {
        Length(Cross(p10 - p00, p01 - p00)),
        Length(Cross(p10 - p00, p11 - p10)),
        Length(Cross(p01 - p00, p11 - p01)),
        Length(Cross(p11 - p10, p11 - p01)) };
```

BilinearPDF() 76
Cross() 91
Float 23
Length() 88
PiecewiseConstant2D 1019
SampleBilinear() 76

Given a (u, v) position on the patch, the corresponding position, partial derivatives, and surface normal can all be computed, following the same approach as was implemented in InteractionFromIntersection(). The fragment ⟨*Compute* p, $\partial p/\partial u$, *and* $\partial p/\partial v$ *for sampled*

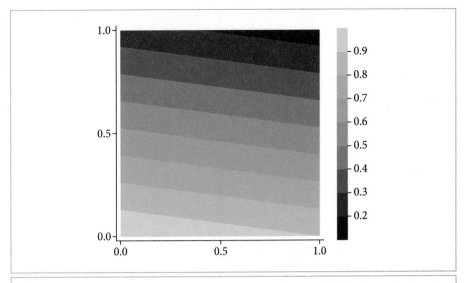

Figure 6.28: Plot of differential area $\|\partial p/\partial u \times \partial p/\partial v\|$ in parametric space for the bilinear patch shown in Figure 6.27. Although the differential area is not a bilinear function, a bilinear fit to it has low error and is easy to draw samples from.

$(u, v)\rangle$ is therefore not included here, and (s, t) texture coordinates for the sampled point are computed using a fragment defined earlier.

⟨*Compute bilinear patch geometric quantities at sampled* (u, v)⟩ ≡   **338**
    ⟨*Compute* p, $\partial p/\partial u$, *and* $\partial p/\partial v$ *for sampled* (u, v)⟩
    Point2f st = uv;
    if (mesh->uv) {
        ⟨*Compute texture coordinates for bilinear patch intersection point* **336**⟩
    }
    ⟨*Compute surface normal for sampled bilinear patch* (u, v) **341**⟩
    ⟨*Compute* pError *for sampled bilinear patch* (u, v) **377**⟩

Only the geometric normal is needed for sampled points. It is easily found via the cross product of partial derivatives of the position. The ⟨*Flip normal at sampled* (u, v) *if necessary*⟩ fragment negates the normal if necessary, depending on the mesh properties and shading normals, if present. It follows the same form as earlier fragments that orient the geometric normal based on the shading normal, if present, and otherwise the reverseOrientation and transformSwapsHandedness properties of the mesh.

⟨*Compute surface normal for sampled bilinear patch* (u, v)⟩ ≡   **341**
    Normal3f n = Normal3f(Normalize(Cross(dpdu, dpdv)));
    ⟨*Flip normal at sampled* (u, v) *if necessary*⟩

The PDF value stored in pdf gives the probability of sampling the position uv in parametric space. In order to return a PDF defined with respect to the patch's surface area, it is necessary to account for the corresponding change of variables, which results in an additional factor of $1/\|\partial p/\partial u \times \partial p/\partial v\|$.

⟨*Return* ShapeSample *for sampled bilinear patch point*⟩ ≡   **338**
    return ShapeSample{Interaction(Point3fi(p, pError), n, st),
                       pdf / Length(Cross(dpdu, dpdv))};

The PDF for sampling a given point on a bilinear patch is found by first computing the probability density for sampling its (u, v) position in parametric space and then transforming that density to be with respect to the patch's surface area.

⟨*BilinearPatch Method Definitions*⟩ +≡
```
Float BilinearPatch::PDF(const Interaction &intr) const {
    const BilinearPatchMesh *mesh = GetMesh();
    ⟨Get bilinear patch vertices in p00, p01, p10, and p11 329⟩
    ⟨Compute parametric (u, v) of point on bilinear patch 342⟩
    ⟨Compute PDF for sampling the (u, v) coordinates given by intr.uv 342⟩
    ⟨Find ∂p/∂u and ∂p/∂v at bilinear patch (u, v)⟩
    ⟨Return final bilinear patch area sampling PDF 342⟩
}
```

If (u, v) coordinates have been specified at the vertices of a bilinear patch, then the member variable `Interaction::uv` stores interpolated texture coordinates. In the following, we will need the parametric (u, v) coordinates over the patch's $[0, 1]^2$ domain, which can be found via a call to `InvertBilinear()`.

⟨*Compute parametric (u, v) of point on bilinear patch*⟩ ≡   342
```
Point2f uv = intr.uv;
if (mesh->uv) {
    Point2f uv00 = mesh->uv[v[0]], uv10 = mesh->uv[v[1]];
    Point2f uv01 = mesh->uv[v[2]], uv11 = mesh->uv[v[3]];
    uv = InvertBilinear(uv, {uv00, uv10, uv01, uv11});
}
```

Regardless of which (u, v) sampling technique is used for a bilinear patch, finding the PDF for a (u, v) sample is straightforward.

⟨*Compute PDF for sampling the (u, v) coordinates given by* `intr.uv`⟩ ≡   342
```
Float pdf;
if (mesh->imageDistribution)
    pdf = mesh->imageDistribution->PDF(uv);
else if (!IsRectangle(mesh)) {
    ⟨Initialize w array with differential area at bilinear patch corners 340⟩
    pdf = BilinearPDF(uv, w);
} else
    pdf = 1;
```

The partial derivatives are computed from (u, v) as they have been before and so we omit the corresponding fragment. Given `dpdu` and `dpdv`, the same scaling factor as was used in `Sample()` is used to transform the PDF.

⟨*Return final bilinear patch area sampling PDF*⟩ ≡   342
```
return pdf / Length(Cross(dpdu, dpdv));
```

The solid angle sampling method handles general bilinear patches with the same approach that was used for `Cylinder`s and `Disk`s: a sample is taken with respect to surface area on the surface using the first sampling method and is returned with a probability density expressed in terms of solid angle. Rectangular patches are handled using a specialized sampling technique that gives better results.

⟨*BilinearPatch Method Definitions*⟩ +≡
```
pstd::optional<ShapeSample>
BilinearPatch::Sample(const ShapeSampleContext &ctx, Point2f u) const {
    const BilinearPatchMesh *mesh = GetMesh();
    ⟨Get bilinear patch vertices in p00, p01, p10, and p11 329⟩
    ⟨Sample bilinear patch with respect to solid angle from reference point 343⟩
}
```

If the patch is not a rectangle, is very small, or has a sampling distribution associated with it to match textured emission, then the regular area sampling method is used and the PDF with respect to area is converted to be with respect to solid angle. Otherwise, a specialized solid angle sampling technique is used.

⟨*Sample bilinear patch with respect to solid angle from reference point*⟩ ≡   343
```
Vector3f v00 = Normalize(p00 - ctx.p()), v10 = Normalize(p10 - ctx.p());
Vector3f v01 = Normalize(p01 - ctx.p()), v11 = Normalize(p11 - ctx.p());
if (!IsRectangle(mesh) || mesh->imageDistribution ||
    SphericalQuadArea(v00, v10, v11, v01) <= MinSphericalSampleArea) {
    ⟨Sample shape by area and compute incident direction wi 282⟩
    ⟨Convert area sampling PDF in ss to solid angle measure 282⟩
    return ss;
}
⟨Sample direction to rectangular bilinear patch 343⟩
```

⟨*BilinearPatch Private Members*⟩ +≡   328
```
static constexpr Float MinSphericalSampleArea = 1e-4;
```

Rectangular patches are projected on the sphere to form a spherical rectangle that can then be sampled directly. Doing so gives similar benefits to sampling spherical triangles, as was implemented in Section 6.5.4.

⟨*Sample direction to rectangular bilinear patch*⟩ ≡   343
```
Float pdf = 1;
⟨Warp uniform sample u to account for incident cos θ factor 343⟩
⟨Sample spherical rectangle at reference point 344⟩
⟨Compute (u, v) and surface normal for sampled point on rectangle 344⟩
⟨Compute (s, t) texture coordinates for sampled (u, v) 344⟩
return ShapeSample{Interaction(p, n, ctx.time, st), pdf};
```

Also as with triangles, we incorporate an approximation to the $\cos\theta$ factor at the reference point by warping the uniform sample u using a bilinear approximation to the $\cos\theta$ function in the $[0, 1]^2$ sampling space.

⟨*Warp uniform sample u to account for incident cos θ factor*⟩ ≡   343
```
if (ctx.ns != Normal3f(0, 0, 0)) {
    ⟨Compute cos θ weights for rectangle seen from reference point 344⟩
    u = SampleBilinear(u, w);
    pdf *= BilinearPDF(u, w);
}
```

The spherical rectangle sampling algorithm maintains the relationship between each corner of the $[0, 1]^2$ sampling space and the corresponding corner of the patch in its parametric space. Therefore, each bilinear sampling weight is set using the $\cos\theta$ factor to the corresponding vertex of the patch.

⟨*Compute* cos θ *weights for rectangle seen from reference point*⟩ ≡   343, 345
```
pstd::array<Float, 4> w = pstd::array<Float, 4>{
    std::max<Float>(0.01, AbsDot(v00, ctx.ns)),
    std::max<Float>(0.01, AbsDot(v10, ctx.ns)),
    std::max<Float>(0.01, AbsDot(v01, ctx.ns)),
    std::max<Float>(0.01, AbsDot(v11, ctx.ns))};
```

In addition to the sample u, `SampleSphericalRectangle()` takes a reference point, the $(0, 0)$ corner of the rectangle, and two vectors that define its edges. It returns a point on the patch and the sampling PDF, which is one over the solid angle that it subtends.

⟨*Sample spherical rectangle at reference point*⟩ ≡   343
```
Vector3f eu = p10 - p00, ev = p01 - p00;
Float quadPDF;
Point3f p = SampleSphericalRectangle(ctx.p(), p00, eu, ev, u, &quadPDF);
pdf *= quadPDF;
```

The implementation of the `SampleSphericalRectangle()` function is another interesting exercise in spherical trigonometry, like `SampleSphericalTriangle()` was. However, in the interests of space, we will not include discussion of its implementation here; the "Further Reading" section has a pointer to the paper that introduced the approach and describes its derivation.

⟨*Sampling Function Declarations*⟩ ≡
```
Point3f SampleSphericalRectangle(Point3f p, Point3f v00, Vector3f eu,
                                 Vector3f ev, Point2f u,
                                 Float *pdf = nullptr);
```

A rectangle has the same surface normal across its entire surface, which can be found by taking the cross product of the two edge vectors. The parametric (u, v) coordinates for the point p are then found by computing the normalized projection of p onto each of the edges.

⟨*Compute* (u, v) *and surface normal for sampled point on rectangle*⟩ ≡   343
```
Point2f uv(Dot(p - p00, eu) / DistanceSquared(p10, p00),
           Dot(p - p00, ev) / DistanceSquared(p01, p00));
Normal3f n = Normal3f(Normalize(Cross(eu, ev)));
```
⟨*Flip normal at sampled* (u, v) *if necessary*⟩

If the bilinear patch has per-vertex texture coordinates associated with it, the interpolated texture coordinates at the sampled point are easily computed.

⟨*Compute* (s, t) *texture coordinates for sampled* (u, v)⟩ ≡   343
```
Point2f st = uv;
if (mesh->uv) {
    ⟨Compute texture coordinates for bilinear patch intersection point 336⟩
}
```

The associated `PDF()` method follows the usual form, determining which sampling method would be used for the patch and then computing its solid angle PDF.

⟨*BilinearPatch Method Definitions*⟩ +≡
```
Float BilinearPatch::PDF(const ShapeSampleContext &ctx, Vector3f wi) const {
    const BilinearPatchMesh *mesh = GetMesh();
    ⟨Get bilinear patch vertices in p00, p01, p10, and p11 329⟩
    ⟨Compute solid angle PDF for sampling bilinear patch from ctx 345⟩
}
```

In all cases, the `SurfaceInteraction` corresponding to the intersection of the ray from `ctx` in the direction `wi` will be needed, so the method starts by performing a ray–patch intersection test.

⟨*Compute solid angle PDF for sampling bilinear patch from* `ctx`⟩ ≡   **344**
    ⟨*Intersect sample ray with shape geometry* **285**⟩
```
Vector3f v00 = Normalize(p00 - ctx.p()), v10 = Normalize(p10 - ctx.p());
Vector3f v01 = Normalize(p01 - ctx.p()), v11 = Normalize(p11 - ctx.p());
if (!IsRectangle(mesh) || mesh->imageDistribution ||
    SphericalQuadArea(v00, v10, v11, v01) <= MinSphericalSampleArea) {
```
        ⟨*Return solid angle PDF for area-sampled bilinear patch* **345**⟩
```
} else {
```
        ⟨*Return PDF for sample in spherical rectangle* **345**⟩
```
}
```

If one of the area sampling approaches was used, then a call to the other `PDF()` method provides the PDF with respect to surface area, which is converted to be with respect to solid angle before it is returned.

⟨*Return solid angle PDF for area-sampled bilinear patch*⟩ ≡   **345**
```
Float pdf = PDF(isect->intr) * (DistanceSquared(ctx.p(), isect->intr.p()) /
                                AbsDot(isect->intr.n, -wi));
return IsInf(pdf) ? 0 : pdf;
```

Otherwise, the spherical rectangle sampling technique was used. The uniform solid angle PDF is 1 over the solid angle that the rectangle subtends. If the reference point is on a surface and the approximation to the $\cos\theta$ factor would be applied in the `Sample()` method, then the PDF for sampling u must be included as well.

⟨*Return PDF for sample in spherical rectangle*⟩ ≡   **345**
```
Float pdf = 1 / SphericalQuadArea(v00, v10, v11, v01);
if (ctx.ns != Normal3f(0, 0, 0)) {
```
    ⟨*Compute* $\cos\theta$ *weights for rectangle seen from reference point* **344**⟩
```
    Point2f u = InvertSphericalRectangleSample(ctx.p(), p00, p10 - p00,
                                               p01 - p00, isect->intr.p());
    return BilinearPDF(u, w) * pdf;
} else
    return pdf;
```

The `InvertSphericalRectangleSample()` function, not included here, returns the sample value u that maps to the given point pRect on the rectangle when the `SampleSphericalRectangle()` is called with the given reference point pRef.

⟨*Sampling Function Declarations*⟩ +≡
```
Point2f InvertSphericalRectangleSample(
    Point3f pRef, Point3f v00, Vector3f eu, Vector3f ev, Point3f pRect);
```

*6.7 CURVES

While triangles or bilinear patches can be used to represent thin shapes for modeling fine geometry like hair, fur, or fields of grass, it is worthwhile to have a specialized Shape in order to more efficiently render these sorts of objects, since many individual instances of them are often present. The Curve shape, introduced in this section, represents thin geometry modeled with cubic Bézier curves, which are defined by four control points, p_0, p_1, p_2, and p_3. The

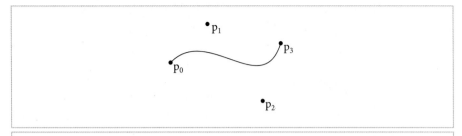

Figure 6.29: A cubic Bézier curve is defined by four control points, p_i. The curve $p(u)$, defined in Equation (6.16), passes through the first and last control points at $u = 0$ and $u = 1$, respectively.

Figure 6.30: Basic Geometry of the Curve Shape. A 1D Bézier curve is offset by half of the specified width in both the directions orthogonal to the curve at each point along it. The resulting area represents the curve's surface.

Bézier spline passes through the first and last control points. Points along it are given by the polynomial

$$p(u) = (1 - u)^3 p_0 + 3(1 - u)^2 u p_1 + 3(1 - u)u^2 p_2 + u^3 p_3. \qquad \text{(6.16)}$$

(See Figure 6.29.) Curves specified using another basis (e.g., Hermite splines or b-splines) must therefore be converted to the Bézier basis to be used with this Shape.

The Curve shape is defined by a 1D Bézier curve along with a width that is linearly interpolated from starting and ending widths along its extent. Together, these define a flat 2D surface (Figure 6.30).[5] It is possible to directly intersect rays with this representation without tessellating it, which in turn makes it possible to efficiently render smooth curves without using too much storage.

Figure 6.31 shows a bunny model with fur modeled with over one million Curves.

⟨*Curve Definition*⟩ ≡
```
class Curve {
  public:
    ⟨Curve Public Methods 348⟩
  private:
    ⟨Curve Private Methods⟩
    ⟨Curve Private Members 348⟩
};
```

There are three types of curves that the Curve shape can represent, shown in Figure 6.32.

- *Flat:* Curves with this representation are always oriented to face the ray being intersected with them; they are useful for modeling fine swept cylindrical shapes like hair or fur.

---

5   Note the abuse of terminology: while a curve is a 1D mathematical entity, a Curve shape represents a 2D surface. In the following, we will generally refer to the Shape as a curve. The 1D entity will be distinguished by the name "Bézier curve" when the distinction would not otherwise be clear.

Figure 6.31: Furry Bunny. Bunny model with over one million Curve shapes used to model fur. Here, we have used unrealistically long curves to better show off the Curve's capabilities, giving an unrealistically shaggy bunny. *(Underlying bunny mesh courtesy of the Stanford Computer Graphics Laboratory.)*

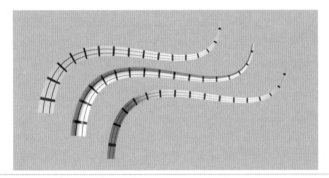

Figure 6.32: The Three Types of Curves That the Curve Shape Can Represent. On the top is a flat curve that is always oriented to be perpendicular to a ray approaching it. The middle is a variant of this curve where the shading normal is set so that the curve appears to be cylindrical. On the bottom is a ribbon, which has a fixed orientation at its starting and ending points; intermediate orientations are smoothly interpolated between them.

- *Cylinder:* For curves that span a few pixels on the screen (like spaghetti seen from not too far away), the Curve shape can compute a shading normal that makes the curve appear to actually be a cylinder.
- *Ribbon:* This variant is useful for modeling shapes that do not actually have a cylindrical cross section (such as a blade of grass).

The CurveType enumerator records which of them a given Curve instance models.

The flat and cylinder curve variants are intended to be used as convenient approximations of deformed cylinders. It should be noted that intersections found with respect to them do not correspond to a physically realizable 3D shape, which can potentially lead to minor inconsistencies when taking a scene with true cylinders as a reference.

Curve 346

⟨*CurveType Definition*⟩ ≡
```
enum class CurveType { Flat, Cylinder, Ribbon };
```

Given a curve specified in a pbrt scene description file, it can be worthwhile to split it into a few segments, each covering part of the *u* parametric range of the curve. (One reason for doing so is that axis-aligned bounding boxes do not tightly bound wiggly curves, but subdividing Bézier curves makes them less wiggly—the *variation diminishing property* of polynomials.) Therefore, the Curve constructor takes a parametric range of *u* values, $[u_{min}, u_{max}]$, as well as a pointer to a CurveCommon structure, which stores the control points and other information about the curve that is shared across curve segments. In this way, the memory footprint for individual curve segments is reduced, which makes it easier to keep many of them in memory.

⟨*Curve Public Methods*⟩ ≡   346
```
Curve(const CurveCommon *common, Float uMin, Float uMax)
    : common(common), uMin(uMin), uMax(uMax) {}
```

⟨*Curve Private Members*⟩ ≡   346
```
const CurveCommon *common;
Float uMin, uMax;
```

The CurveCommon constructor initializes member variables with values passed into it for the control points, the curve width, etc. The control points provided to it should be in the curve's object space.

For Ribbon curves, CurveCommon stores a surface normal to orient the curve at each endpoint. The constructor precomputes the angle between the two normal vectors and one over the sine of this angle; these values will be useful when computing the orientation of the curve at arbitrary points along its extent.

⟨*CurveCommon Definition*⟩ ≡
```
struct CurveCommon {
    ⟨CurveCommon Public Methods⟩
    ⟨CurveCommon Public Members 348⟩
};
```

⟨*CurveCommon Public Members*⟩ ≡   348
```
CurveType type;
Point3f cpObj[4];
Float width[2];
Normal3f n[2];
Float normalAngle, invSinNormalAngle;
const Transform *renderFromObject, *objectFromRender;
bool reverseOrientation, transformSwapsHandedness;
```

6.7.1 BOUNDING CURVES

The object-space bound of a curve can be found by first bounding the spline along the center of the curve and then expanding that bound by half the maximum width the curve takes on over its extent. The Bounds() method then transforms that bound to rendering space before returning it.

⟨*Curve Method Definitions*⟩ ≡
```
Bounds3f Curve::Bounds() const {
    pstd::span<const Point3f> cpSpan(common->cpObj);
    Bounds3f objBounds = BoundCubicBezier(cpSpan, uMin, uMax);
    ⟨Expand objBounds by maximum curve width over u range 349⟩
    return (*common->renderFromObject)(objBounds);
}
```

⟨*Expand* objBounds *by maximum curve width over u range*⟩ ≡   **348**
```
Float width[2] = {Lerp(uMin, common->width[0], common->width[1]),
                  Lerp(uMax, common->width[0], common->width[1])};
objBounds = Expand(objBounds, std::max(width[0], width[1]) * 0.5f);
```

The Curve shape cannot be used as an area light, as it does not provide implementations of the required sampling methods. It does provide a NormalBounds() method that returns a conservative bound.

⟨*Curve Public Methods*⟩ +≡   **346**
```
DirectionCone NormalBounds() const { return DirectionCone::EntireSphere(); }
```

6.7.2 INTERSECTION TESTS

Both of the intersection methods required by the Shape interface are implemented via another Curve method, IntersectRay(). Rather than returning an optional ShapeIntersection, it takes a pointer to one.

⟨*Curve Method Definitions*⟩ +≡
```
pstd::optional<ShapeIntersection>
Curve::Intersect(const Ray &ray, Float tMax) const {
    pstd::optional<ShapeIntersection> si;
    IntersectRay(ray, tMax, &si);
    return si;
}
```

IntersectP() passes nullptr to IntersectRay(), which indicates that it can return immediately if an intersection is found.

⟨*Curve Method Definitions*⟩ +≡
```
bool Curve::IntersectP(const Ray &ray, Float tMax) const {
    return IntersectRay(ray, tMax, nullptr);
}
```

The Curve intersection algorithm is based on discarding curve segments as soon as it can be determined that the ray definitely does not intersect them and otherwise recursively splitting the curve in half to create two smaller segments that are then tested. Eventually, the curve is linearly approximated for an efficient intersection test. That process starts after some initial preparation and early culling tests in IntersectRay().

⟨*Curve Method Definitions*⟩ +≡
```
bool Curve::IntersectRay(const Ray &r, Float tMax,
                         pstd::optional<ShapeIntersection> *si) const {
    ⟨Transform Ray to curve's object space 349⟩
    ⟨Get object-space control points for curve segment, cpObj 350⟩
    ⟨Project curve control points to plane perpendicular to ray 350⟩
    ⟨Test ray against bound of projected control points 351⟩
    ⟨Compute refinement depth for curve, maxDepth⟩
    ⟨Recursively test for ray–curve intersection 351⟩
}
```

⟨*Transform* Ray *to curve's object space*⟩ ≡   **349**
```
Ray ray = (*common->objectFromRender)(r);
```

The CurveCommon class stores the control points for the full curve, but a Curve instance generally needs the four control points that represent the Bézier curve for its *u* extent. The CubicBezierControlPoints() utility function performs this computation.

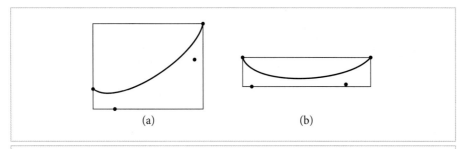

Figure 6.33: 2D Bounding Boxes of a Bézier Curve. (a) Bounding box computed using the curve's control points as given. (b) The effect of rotating the curve so that the vector from its first to last control point is aligned with the x axis before computing bounds. The resulting bounding box is a much tighter fit.

⟨*Get object-space control points for curve segment*, cpObj⟩ ≡   **349**
```
pstd::array<Point3f, 4> cpObj =
    CubicBezierControlPoints(pstd::span<const Point3f>(common->cpObj),
                             uMin, uMax);
```

Like the ray–triangle intersection algorithm from Section 6.5.3, the ray–curve intersection test is based on transforming the curve to a coordinate system with the ray's origin at the origin of the coordinate system and the ray's direction aligned to be along the $+z$ axis. Performing this transformation at the start greatly reduces the number of operations that must be performed for intersection tests.

For the Curve shape, we will need an explicit representation of the transformation, so the LookAt() function is used to generate it here. The origin is the ray's origin and the "look at" point is a point offset from the origin along the ray's direction. The "up" direction is set to be perpendicular to both the ray's direction and the vector from the first to the last control point. Doing so helps orient the curve to be roughly parallel to the x axis in the ray coordinate system, which in turn leads to tighter bounds in y (see Figure 6.33). This improvement in the fit of the bounds often makes it possible to terminate the recursive intersection tests earlier than would be possible otherwise.

If the ray and the vector between the first and last control points are parallel, dx will be degenerate. In that case we find an arbitrary "up" vector direction so that intersection tests can proceed in this unusual case.

⟨*Project curve control points to plane perpendicular to ray*⟩ ≡   **349**
```
Vector3f dx = Cross(ray.d, cpObj[3] - cpObj[0]);
if (LengthSquared(dx) == 0) {
    Vector3f dy;
    CoordinateSystem(ray.d, &dx, &dy);
}
Transform rayFromObject = LookAt(ray.o, ray.o + ray.d, dx);
pstd::array<Point3f, 4> cp = {
    rayFromObject(cpObj[0]), rayFromObject(cpObj[1]),
    rayFromObject(cpObj[2]), rayFromObject(cpObj[3]) };
```

Along the lines of the implementation in Curve::Bounds(), a conservative bounding box for a curve segment can be found by taking the bounds of the curve's control points and expanding by half of the maximum width of the curve over the u range being considered.

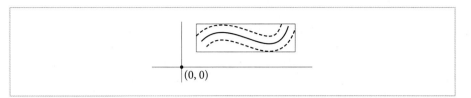

(0, 0)

Figure 6.34: Ray–Curve Bounds Test. In the ray coordinate system, the ray's origin is at (0, 0, 0) and its direction is aligned with the +z axis. Therefore, if the 2D point $(x, y) = (0, 0)$ is outside the xy bounding box of the curve segment, then it is impossible that the ray intersects the curve.

Because the ray's origin is at (0, 0, 0) and its direction is aligned with the +z axis in the intersection space, its bounding box only includes the origin in x and y (Figure 6.34); its z extent is given by the z range that its parametric extent covers. Before proceeding with the recursive intersection testing algorithm, the ray's bounding box is tested for intersection with the curve's bounding box. The method can return immediately if they do not intersect.

⟨*Test ray against bound of projected control points*⟩ ≡   **349**
```
Float maxWidth = std::max(Lerp(uMin, common->width[0], common->width[1]),
                          Lerp(uMax, common->width[0], common->width[1]));
Bounds3f curveBounds = Union(Bounds3f(cp[0], cp[1]), Bounds3f(cp[2], cp[3]));
curveBounds = Expand(curveBounds, 0.5f * maxWidth);
Bounds3f rayBounds(Point3f(0, 0, 0), Point3f(0, 0, Length(ray.d) * tMax));
if (!Overlaps(rayBounds, curveBounds))
    return false;
```

The maximum number of times to subdivide the curve is computed so that the maximum distance from the eventual linearized curve at the finest refinement level is bounded to be less than a small fixed distance. We will not go into the details of this computation, which is implemented in the fragment ⟨*Compute refinement depth for curve,* maxDepth⟩. With the culling tests passed and that value in hand, the recursive intersection tests begin.

⟨*Recursively test for ray–curve intersection*⟩ ≡   **349**
```
pstd::span<const Point3f> cpSpan(cp);
return RecursiveIntersect(ray, tMax, cpSpan, Inverse(rayFromObject),
                          uMin, uMax, maxDepth, si);
```

The RecursiveIntersect() method then tests whether the given ray intersects the given curve segment over the given parametric range [u0, u1]. It assumes that the ray has already been tested against the curve's bounding box and found to intersect it.

⟨*Curve Method Definitions*⟩ +≡
```
bool Curve::RecursiveIntersect(
        const Ray &ray, Float tMax, pstd::span<const Point3f> cp,
        const Transform &objectFromRay, Float u0, Float u1,
        int depth, pstd::optional<ShapeIntersection> *si) const {
    Float rayLength = Length(ray.d);
    if (depth > 0) {
        ⟨Split curve segment into subsegments and test for intersection 352⟩
    } else {
        ⟨Intersect ray with curve segment 352⟩
    }
}
```

If the maximum depth has not been reached, a call to `SubdivideCubicBezier()` gives the control points for the two Bézier curves that result in splitting the Bézier curve given by `cp` in half. The last control point of the first curve is the same as the first control point of the second, so 7 values are returned for the total of 8 control points. The `u` array is then initialized so that it holds the parametric range of the two curves before each one is processed in turn.

⟨*Split curve segment into subsegments and test for intersection*⟩ ≡   351
```
pstd::array<Point3f, 7> cpSplit = SubdivideCubicBezier(cp);
Float u[3] = {u0, (u0 + u1) / 2, u1};
for (int seg = 0; seg < 2; ++seg) {
    ⟨Check ray against curve segment's bounding box⟩
    ⟨Recursively test ray-segment intersection 352⟩
}
return si ? si->has_value() : false;
```

The bounding box test in the ⟨*Check ray against curve segment's bounding box*⟩ fragment is essentially the same as the one in ⟨*Test ray against bound of projected control points*⟩ except that it takes *u* values from the `u` array when computing the curve's maximum width over the *u* range and it uses control points from `cpSplit`. Therefore, it is not included here.

If the ray does intersect the bounding box, the corresponding segment is given to a recursive call of `RecursiveIntersect()`. If an intersection is found and the ray is a shadow ray, `si` will be `nullptr` and an intersection can immediately be reported. For non-shadow rays, even if an intersection has been found, it may not be the closest intersection, so the other segment still must be considered.

⟨*Recursively test ray-segment intersection*⟩ ≡   352
```
bool hit = RecursiveIntersect(ray, tMax, cps, objectFromRay, u[seg],
                              u[seg + 1], depth - 1, si);
if (hit && !si)
    return true;
```

The intersection test is made more efficient by using a linear approximation of the curve; the variation diminishing property allows us to make this approximation without introducing too much error.

⟨*Intersect ray with curve segment*⟩ ≡   351
```
⟨Test ray against segment endpoint boundaries 352⟩
⟨Find line w that gives minimum distance to sample point 355⟩
⟨Compute u coordinate of curve intersection point and hitWidth 355⟩
⟨Test intersection point against curve width 355⟩
if (si) {
    ⟨Initialize ShapeIntersection for curve intersection 356⟩
}
return true;
```

It is important that the intersection test only accepts intersections that are on the Curve's surface for the *u* segment currently under consideration. Therefore, the first step of the intersection test is to compute edge functions for lines perpendicular to the curve starting point and ending point and to classify the potential intersection point against them (Figure 6.35).

⟨*Test ray against segment endpoint boundaries*⟩ ≡   352
```
⟨Test sample point against tangent perpendicular at curve start 353⟩
⟨Test sample point against tangent perpendicular at curve end⟩
```

⟨*Find line w that gives minimum distance to sample point*⟩ ≡   352
```
Vector2f segmentDir = Point2f(cp[3].x, cp[3].y) - Point2f(cp[0].x, cp[0].y);
Float denom = LengthSquared(segmentDir);
if (denom == 0)
    return false;
Float w = Dot(-Vector2f(cp[0].x, cp[0].y), segmentDir) / denom;
```

The parametric u coordinate of the (presumed) closest point on the Bézier curve to the candidate intersection point is computed by linearly interpolating along the u range of the segment. Given this u value, the width of the curve at that point can be computed.

⟨*Compute u coordinate of curve intersection point and* hitWidth⟩ ≡   352
```
Float u = Clamp(Lerp(w, u0, u1), u0, u1);
Float hitWidth = Lerp(u, common->width[0], common->width[1]);
Normal3f nHit;
if (common->type == CurveType::Ribbon) {
    ⟨Scale hitWidth based on ribbon orientation 355⟩
}
```

For Ribbon curves, the curve is not always oriented to face the ray. Rather, its orientation is interpolated between two surface normals given at each endpoint. Here, spherical linear interpolation is used to interpolate the normal at u. The curve's width is then scaled by the cosine of the angle between the normalized ray direction and the ribbon's orientation so that it corresponds to the visible width of the curve from the given direction.

⟨*Scale* hitWidth *based on ribbon orientation*⟩ ≡   355
```
if (common->normalAngle == 0)
    nHit = common->n[0];
else {
    Float sin0 = std::sin((1 - u) * common->normalAngle) *
        common->invSinNormalAngle;
    Float sin1 = std::sin(u * common->normalAngle) *
        common->invSinNormalAngle;
    nHit = sin0 * common->n[0] + sin1 * common->n[1];
}
hitWidth *= AbsDot(nHit, ray.d) / rayLength;
```

To finally classify the potential intersection as a hit or miss, the Bézier curve must still be evaluated at u. (Because the control points cp represent the curve segment currently under consideration, it is important to use w rather than u in the function call, however, since w is in the range $[0, 1]$.) The derivative of the curve at this point will be useful shortly, so it is recorded now.

We would like to test whether the distance from p to this point on the curve pc is less than half the curve's width. Because $p = (0, 0)$, we can equivalently test whether the distance from pc to the origin is less than half the width or whether the squared distance is less than one quarter the width squared. If this test passes, the last thing to check is if the intersection point is in the ray's parametric t range.

⟨*Test intersection point against curve width*⟩ ≡   352
```
Vector3f dpcdw;
Point3f pc = EvaluateCubicBezier(pstd::span<const Point3f>(cp),
                                 Clamp(w, 0, 1), &dpcdw);
Float ptCurveDist2 = Sqr(pc.x) + Sqr(pc.y);
```

```
    if (ptCurveDist2 > Sqr(hitWidth) * 0.25f)
        return false;
    if (pc.z < 0 || pc.z > rayLength * tMax)
        return false;
```

For non-shadow rays, the ShapeIntersection for the intersection can finally be initialized. Doing so requires computing the ray *t* value for the intersection as well as its Surface Interaction.

⟨*Initialize* ShapeIntersection *for curve intersection*⟩ ≡   352
  ⟨*Compute* tHit *for curve intersection* 356⟩
  ⟨*Initialize* SurfaceInteraction intr *for curve intersection* 356⟩
  *si = ShapeIntersection{intr, tHit};

After the tHit value has been computed, it is compared against the tHit of a previously found ray–curve intersection, if there is one. This check ensures that the closest intersection is returned.

⟨*Compute* tHit *for curve intersection*⟩ ≡   356
```
    Float tHit = pc.z / rayLength;
    if (si->has_value() && tHit > si->value().tHit)
        return false;
```

A variety of additional quantities need to be computed in order to be able to initialize the intersection's SurfaceInteraction.

⟨*Initialize* SurfaceInteraction intr *for curve intersection*⟩ ≡   356
  ⟨*Compute v coordinate of curve intersection point* 356⟩
  ⟨*Compute* ∂p/∂u *and* ∂p/∂v *for curve intersection* 357⟩
  ⟨*Compute error bounds for curve intersection* 378⟩
```
    bool flipNormal = common->reverseOrientation ^
                        common->transformSwapsHandedness;
    Point3fi pi(ray(tHit), pError);
    SurfaceInteraction intr(pi, {u, v}, -ray.d, dpdu, dpdv, Normal3f(),
                        Normal3f(), ray.time, flipNormal);
    intr = (*common->renderFromObject)(intr);
```

We have gotten this far without computing the v coordinate of the intersection point, which is now needed. The curve's v coordinate ranges from 0 to 1, taking on the value 0.5 at the center of the curve; here, we classify the intersection point, (0, 0), with respect to an edge function going through the point on the curve pc and a point along its derivative to determine which side of the center the intersection point is on and in turn how to compute v.

⟨*Compute v coordinate of curve intersection point*⟩ ≡   356
```
    Float ptCurveDist = std::sqrt(ptCurveDist2);
    Float edgeFunc = dpcdw.x * -pc.y + pc.x * dpcdw.y;
    Float v = (edgeFunc > 0) ? 0.5f + ptCurveDist / hitWidth :
                                0.5f - ptCurveDist / hitWidth;
```

The partial derivative ∂p/∂u comes directly from the derivative of the underlying Bézier curve. The second partial derivative, ∂p/∂v, is computed in different ways based on the type of the curve. For ribbons, we have ∂p/∂u and the surface normal, and so ∂p/∂v must be the vector such that ∂p/∂u × ∂p/∂v = **n** and has length equal to the curve's width.

⟨*Compute ∂p/∂u and ∂p/∂v for curve intersection*⟩ ≡   356
```
Vector3f dpdu, dpdv;
EvaluateCubicBezier(pstd::MakeConstSpan(common->cpObj), u, &dpdu);
if (common->type == CurveType::Ribbon)
    dpdv = Normalize(Cross(nHit, dpdu)) * hitWidth;
else {
    ⟨Compute curve ∂p/∂v for flat and cylinder curves 357⟩
}
```

For flat and cylinder curves, we transform $\partial p/\partial u$ to the intersection coordinate system. For flat curves, we know that $\partial p/\partial v$ lies in the xy plane, is perpendicular to $\partial p/\partial u$, and has length equal to hitWidth. We can find the 2D perpendicular vector using the same approach as was used earlier for the perpendicular curve segment boundary edges.

⟨*Compute curve ∂p/∂v for flat and cylinder curves*⟩ ≡   357
```
Vector3f dpduPlane = objectFromRay.ApplyInverse(dpdu);
Vector3f dpdvPlane = Normalize(Vector3f(-dpduPlane.y, dpduPlane.x, 0)) *
                     hitWidth;
if (common->type == CurveType::Cylinder) {
    ⟨Rotate dpdvPlane to give cylindrical appearance 357⟩
}
dpdv = objectFromRay(dpdvPlane);
```

The $\partial p/\partial v$ vector for cylinder curves is rotated around the dpduPlane axis so that its appearance resembles a cylindrical cross-section.

⟨*Rotate dpdvPlane to give cylindrical appearance*⟩ ≡   357
```
Float theta = Lerp(v, -90, 90);
Transform rot = Rotate(-theta, dpduPlane);
dpdvPlane = rot(dpdvPlane);
```

*6.8 MANAGING ROUNDING ERROR

Thus far, we have been discussing ray–shape intersection algorithms with respect to idealized arithmetic operations based on the real numbers. This approach has gotten us far, although the fact that computers can only represent finite quantities and therefore cannot actually represent all the real numbers is important. In place of real numbers, computers use floating-point numbers, which have fixed storage requirements. However, error may be introduced each time a floating-point operation is performed, since the result may not be representable in the designated amount of memory.

The accumulation of this error has several implications for the accuracy of intersection tests. First, it is possible that it will cause valid intersections to be missed completely—for example, if a computed intersection's t value is negative even though the precise value is positive. Furthermore, computed ray–shape intersection points may be above or below the actual surface of the shape. This leads to a problem: when new rays are traced starting from computed intersection points for shadow rays and reflection rays, if the ray origin is below the actual surface, we may find an incorrect reintersection with the surface. Conversely, if the origin is too far above the surface, shadows and reflections may appear detached. (See Figure 6.38.)

Typical practice to address this issue in ray tracing is to offset spawned rays by a fixed "ray epsilon" value, ignoring any intersections along the ray $p + t\mathbf{d}$ closer than some t_{min} value.

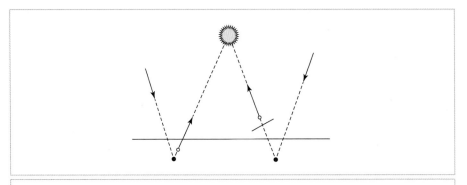

Figure 6.38: Geometric Settings for Rounding-Error Issues That Can Cause Visible Errors in Images. The incident ray on the left intersects the surface. On the left, the computed intersection point (black circle) is slightly below the surface and a too-low "epsilon" offsetting the origin of the shadow ray leads to an incorrect self-intersection, as the shadow ray origin (white circle) is still below the surface; thus the light is incorrectly determined to be occluded. On the right, a too-high "epsilon" causes a valid intersection to be missed as the ray's origin is past the occluding surface.

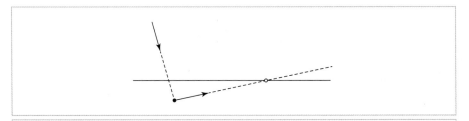

Figure 6.39: If the computed intersection point (filled circle) is below the surface and the spawned ray is oblique, incorrect reintersections may occur some distance from the ray origin (open circle). If a minimum t value along the ray is used to discard nearby intersections, a relatively large t_{min} is needed to handle oblique rays well.

Figure 6.39 shows why this approach requires fairly high t_{min} values to work effectively: if the spawned ray is oblique to the surface, incorrect ray intersections may occur quite some distance from the ray origin. Unfortunately, large t_{min} values cause ray origins to be relatively far from the original intersection points, which in turn can cause valid nearby intersections to be missed, leading to loss of fine detail in shadows and reflections.

In this section, we will introduce the ideas underlying floating-point arithmetic and describe techniques for analyzing the error in floating-point computations. We will then apply these methods to the ray–shape algorithms introduced earlier in this chapter and show how to compute ray intersection points with bounded error. This will allow us to conservatively position ray origins so that incorrect self-intersections are never found, while keeping ray origins extremely close to the actual intersection point so that incorrect misses are minimized. In turn, no additional "ray epsilon" values are needed.

6.8.1 FLOATING-POINT ARITHMETIC

Computation must be performed on a finite representation of numbers that fits in a finite amount of memory; the infinite set of real numbers cannot be represented on a computer. One such finite representation is fixed point, where given a 16-bit integer, for example, one might map it to positive real numbers by dividing by 256. This would allow us to represent the range $[0, 65535/256] = [0, 255 + 255/256]$ with equal spacing of $1/256$ between values.

Fixed-point numbers can be implemented efficiently using integer arithmetic operations (a property that made them popular on early PCs that did not support floating-point computation), but they suffer from a number of shortcomings; among them, the maximum number they can represent is limited, and they are not able to accurately represent very small numbers near zero.

An alternative representation for real numbers on computers is floating-point numbers. These are based on representing numbers with a sign, a significand,[6] and an exponent: essentially, the same representation as scientific notation but with a fixed number of digits devoted to significand and exponent. (In the following, we will assume base-2 digits exclusively.) This representation makes it possible to represent and perform computations on numbers with a wide range of magnitudes while using a fixed amount of storage.

Programmers using floating-point arithmetic are generally aware that floating-point values may be inaccurate; this understanding sometimes leads to a belief that floating-point arithmetic is unpredictable. In this section we will see that floating-point arithmetic has a carefully designed foundation that in turn makes it possible to compute conservative bounds on the error introduced in a particular computation. For ray-tracing calculations, this error is often surprisingly small.

Modern CPUs and GPUs nearly ubiquitously implement a model of floating-point arithmetic based on a standard promulgated by the Institute of Electrical and Electronics Engineers (1985, 2008). (Henceforth when we refer to floats, we will specifically be referring to 32-bit floating-point numbers as specified by IEEE 754.) The IEEE 754 technical standard specifies the format of floating-point numbers in memory as well as specific rules for precision and rounding of floating-point computations; it is these rules that make it possible to reason rigorously about the error present in a computed floating-point value.

Floating-Point Representation

The IEEE standard specifies that 32-bit floats are represented with a sign bit, 8 bits for the exponent, and 23 bits for the significand. The exponent stored in a float ranges from 0 to 255. We will denote it by e_b, with the subscript indicating that it is biased; the actual exponent used in computation, e, is computed as

$$e = e_b - 127. \tag{6.17}$$

The significand actually has 24 bits of precision when a *normalized* floating-point value is stored. When a number expressed with significand and exponent is normalized, there are no leading 0s in the significand. In binary, this means that the leading digit of the significand must be one; in turn, there is no need to store this value explicitly. Thus, the implicit leading 1 digit with the 23 digits encoding the fractional part of the significand gives a total of 24 bits of precision.

Given a sign $s = \pm1$, significand m, and biased exponent e_b, the corresponding floating-point value is

$$s \times 1.m \times 2^{e_b - 127}.$$

For example, with a normalized significand, the floating-point number 6.5 is written as $1.101_2 \times 2^2$, where the 2 subscript denotes a base-2 value. (If non-whole binary numbers are not immediately intuitive, note that the first number to the right of the radix point

---

6   The word *mantissa* is often used in place of *significand,* though floating-point purists note that *mantissa* has a different meaning in the context of logarithms and thus prefer *significand*. We follow this usage here.

contributes $2^{-1} = 1/2$, and so forth.) Thus, we have

$$(1 \times 2^0 + 1 \times 2^{-1} + 0 \times 2^{-2} + 1 \times 2^{-3}) \times 2^2 = 1.625 \times 2^2 = 6.5.$$

$e = 2$, so $e_b = 129 = 10000001_2$ and $m = 10100000000000000000000_2$.

Floats are laid out in memory with the sign bit at the most significant bit of the 32-bit value (with negative signs encoded with a 1 bit), then the exponent, and the significand. Thus, for the value 6.5 the binary in-memory representation of the value is

$$0\ \ 10000001\ \ 10100000000000000000000 = 40d00000_{16}.$$

Similarly, the floating-point value 1.0 has $m = 0 \ldots 0_2$ and $e = 0$, so $e_b = 127 = 01111111_2$ and its binary representation is:

$$0\ \ 01111111\ \ 00000000000000000000000 = 3f800000_{16}.$$

This hexadecimal number is a value worth remembering, as it often comes up in memory dumps when debugging graphics programs.

An implication of this representation is that the spacing between representable floats between two adjacent powers of two is uniform throughout the range. (It corresponds to increments of the significand bits by one.) In a range $[2^e, 2^{e+1})$, the spacing is

$$2^{e-23}. \hspace{2cm} \text{[6.18]}$$

Thus, for floating-point numbers between 1 and 2, $e = 0$, and the spacing between floating-point values is $2^{-23} \approx 1.19209 \ldots \times 10^{-7}$. This spacing is also referred to as the magnitude of a *unit in last place* ("ulp"); note that the magnitude of an ulp is determined by the floating-point value that it is with respect to—ulps are relatively larger at numbers with larger magnitudes than they are at numbers with smaller magnitudes.

As we have described the representation so far, it is impossible to exactly represent zero as a floating-point number. This is obviously an unacceptable state of affairs, so the minimum exponent $e_b = 0$, or $e = -127$, is set aside for special treatment. With this exponent, the floating-point value is interpreted as not having the implicit leading 1 bit in the significand, which means that a significand of all 0 bits results in

$$s \times 0.0 \cdots 0_2 \times 2^{-127} = 0.$$

Eliminating the leading 1 significand bit also makes it possible to represent *denormalized* numbers:[7] if the leading 1 was always present, then the smallest 32-bit float would be

$$1.0 \cdots 0_2 \times 2^{-127} \approx 5.8774718 \times 10^{-39}.$$

Without the leading 1 bit, the minimum value is

$$0.00 \cdots 1_2 \times 2^{-126} = 2^{-23} \times 2^{-126} \approx 1.4012985 \times 10^{-45}.$$

(The -126 exponent is used because denormalized numbers are encoded with $e_b = 0$ but are interpreted as if $e_b = 1$ so that there is no excess gap between them and the adjacent smallest regular floating-point number.) Providing some capability to represent these small values can make it possible to avoid needing to round very small values to zero.

Note that there is both a "positive" and "negative" zero value with this representation. This detail is mostly transparent to the programmer. For example, the standard guarantees that the comparison -0.0 == 0.0 evaluates to true, even though the in-memory representations

---

7 Denormalized numbers are also known as *subnormal numbers*.

of these two values are different. Conveniently, a floating-point zero value with an unset sign bit is represented by the value 0 in memory.

The maximum exponent, $e_b = 255$, is also reserved for special treatment. Therefore, the largest regular floating-point value that can be represented has $e_b = 254$ (or $e = 127$) and is approximately

$$3.402823\ldots \times 10^{38}.$$

With $e_b = 255$, if the significand bits are all 0, the value corresponds to positive or negative infinity, according to the sign bit. Infinite values result when performing computations like $1/0$ in floating point, for example. Arithmetic operations with infinity and a noninfinite value usually result in infinity, though dividing a finite value by infinity gives 0. For comparisons, positive infinity is larger than any noninfinite value and similarly for negative infinity.

The Infinity constant is initialized to be the "infinity" floating-point value. We make it available in a separate constant so that code that uses its value does not need to use the wordy C++ standard library call.

⟨*Floating-point Constants*⟩ ≡
```
static constexpr Float Infinity = std::numeric_limits<Float>::infinity();
```

With $e_b = 255$, nonzero significand bits correspond to special "not a number" (NaN) values (defined on page 83), which result from invalid operations like taking the square root of a negative number or trying to compute $0/0$. NaNs propagate through computations: any arithmetic operation where one of the operands is a NaN itself always returns NaN. Thus, if a NaN emerges from a long chain of computations, we know that something went awry somewhere along the way. In debug builds, pbrt has many assertion statements that check for NaN values, as we almost never expect them to come up in the regular course of events. Any comparison with a NaN value returns false; thus, checking for !(x == x) serves to check if a value is not a number.[8]

By default, the majority of floating-point computation in pbrt uses 32-bit floats. However, as discussed in Section 1.3.3, it is possible to configure it to use 64-bit double-precision values instead. In addition to the sign bit, doubles allocate 11 bits to the exponent and 52 to the significand. pbrt also supports 16-bit floats (which are known as halfs) as an in-memory representation for floating-point values stored at pixels in images. Halfs use 5 bits for the exponent and 10 for the significand. (A convenience Half class, not discussed further in the text, provides capabilities for working with halfs and converting to and from 32-bit floats.)

Arithmetic Operations

IEEE 754 provides important guarantees about the properties of floating-point arithmetic: specifically, it guarantees that addition, subtraction, multiplication, division, and square root give the same results given the same inputs and that these results are the floating-point number that is closest to the result of the underlying computation if it had been performed in infinite-precision arithmetic.[9] It is remarkable that this is possible on finite-precision digital computers at all; one of the achievements in IEEE 754 was the demonstration that this level of accuracy is possible and can be implemented fairly efficiently in hardware.

Float 23

8   This is one of a few places where compilers must not perform seemingly obvious and safe algebraic simplifi-
    cations with expressions that include floating-point values—this particular comparison must not be simplified
    to false. Enabling compiler "fast math" or "perform unsafe math optimizations" flags may allow these opti-
    mizations to be performed. In turn, buggy behavior may be introduced in pbrt.
9   IEEE float allows the user to select one of a number of rounding modes, but we will assume the default—round
    to nearest even—here.

Figure 6.40: The IEEE standard specifies that floating-point calculations must be implemented as if the calculation was performed with infinite-precision real numbers and then rounded to the nearest representable float. Here, an infinite-precision result in the real numbers is denoted by a filled dot, with the representable floats around it denoted by ticks on a number line. We can see that the error introduced by rounding to the nearest float, δ, can be no more than half the spacing between floats.

Using circled operators to denote floating-point arithmetic operations and sqrt for floating-point square root, these accuracy guarantees can be written as:

$$a \oplus b = \text{round}(a + b)$$
$$a \ominus b = \text{round}(a - b)$$
$$a \otimes b = \text{round}(a * b)$$
$$a \oslash b = \text{round}(a/b) \tag{6.19}$$
$$\text{sqrt(a)} = \text{round}(\sqrt{a})$$
$$\text{FMA(a, b, c)} = \text{round}(a * b + c)$$

where round(x) indicates the result of rounding a real number to the closest floating-point value and where FMA denotes the *fused multiply add* operation, which only rounds once. It thus gives better accuracy than computing $(a \otimes b) \oplus c$.

This bound on the rounding error can also be represented with an interval of real numbers: for example, for addition, we can say that the rounded result is within an interval

$$a \oplus b = \text{round}(a + b) \in (a + b)(1 \pm \epsilon)$$
$$= [(a + b)(1 - \epsilon), (a + b)(1 + \epsilon)] \tag{6.20}$$

for some ϵ. The amount of error introduced from this rounding can be no more than half the floating-point spacing at $a + b$—if it was more than half the floating-point spacing, then it would be possible to round to a different floating-point number with less error (Figure 6.40).

For 32-bit floats, we can bound the floating-point spacing at $a + b$ from above using Equation (6.18) (i.e., an ulp at that value) by $(a + b)2^{-23}$, so half the spacing is bounded from above by $(a + b)2^{-24}$ and so $|\epsilon| \le 2^{-24}$. This bound is the *machine epsilon*.[10] For 32-bit floats, $\epsilon_m = 2^{-24} \approx 5.960464 \ldots \times 10^{-8}$.

⟨*Floating-point Constants*⟩ +≡
```
static constexpr Float MachineEpsilon =
    std::numeric_limits<Float>::epsilon() * 0.5;
```

Thus, we have

$$a \oplus b = \text{round}(a + b) \in (a + b)(1 \pm \epsilon_m)$$
$$= [(a + b)(1 - \epsilon_m), (a + b)(1 + \epsilon_m)].$$

Analogous relations hold for the other arithmetic operators and the square root operator.[11]

---

10 The C and C++ standards define the machine epsilon as the magnitude of one ulp above the number 1. For a 32-bit float, this value is 2^{-23}, which is twice as large as the machine epsilon as the term is generally used in numerical analysis.

11 This bound assumes that there is no overflow or underflow in the computation; these possibilities can be easily handled (Higham 2002, p. 56) but are not generally important for our application here.

Float 23

A number of useful properties follow directly from Equation (6.19). For a floating-point number x,

- $1 \otimes x = x$.
- $x \oslash x = 1$.
- $x \oplus 0 = x$.
- $x \ominus x = 0$.
- $2 \otimes x$ and $x \oslash 2$ are exact; no rounding is performed to compute the final result. More generally, any multiplication by or division by a power of two gives an exact result (assuming there is no overflow or underflow).
- $x \oslash 2^i = x \otimes 2^{-i}$ for all integer i, assuming 2^i does not overflow.

All of these properties follow from the principle that the result must be the nearest floating-point value to the actual result; when the result can be represented exactly, the exact result must be computed.

Utility Routines

A few basic utility routines will be useful in the following. First, we define our own IsNaN() function to check for NaN values. It comes with the baggage of a use of C++'s enable_if construct to declare its return type in a way that requires that this function only be called with floating-point types.

⟨*Floating-point Inline Functions*⟩ ≡
```
template <typename T> inline
typename std::enable_if_t<std::is_floating_point_v<T>, bool>
IsNaN(T v) {
    return std::isnan(v);
}
```

We also define IsNaN() for integer-based types; it trivially returns false, since NaN is not representable in those types. One might wonder why we have bothered with enable_if and this second definition that tells us something that we already know. One motivation is the templated Tuple2 and Tuple3 classes from Section 3.2, which are used with both Float and int for their element types. Given these two functions, they can freely have assertions that their elements do not store NaN values without worrying about which particular type their elements are.

⟨*Floating-point Inline Functions*⟩ +≡
```
template <typename T> inline
typename std::enable_if_t<std::is_integral_v<T>, bool>
IsNaN(T v) { return false; }
```

For similar motivations, we define a pair of IsInf() functions that test for infinity.

⟨*Floating-point Inline Functions*⟩ +≡
```
template <typename T> inline
typename std::enable_if_t<std::is_floating_point_v<T>, bool>
IsInf(T v) {
    return std::isinf(v);
}
```

Float 23
Tuple2 83
Tuple3 83

Once again, because infinity is not representable with integer types, the integer variant of this function returns false.

⟨*Floating-point Inline Functions*⟩ +≡

```
template <typename T> inline
typename std::enable_if_t<std::is_integral_v<T>, bool>
IsInf(T v) { return false; }
```

A pair of IsFinite() functions check whether a number is neither infinite or NaN.

⟨*Floating-point Inline Functions*⟩ +≡

```
template <typename T> inline
typename std::enable_if_t<std::is_floating_point_v<T>, bool>
IsFinite(T v) {
    return std::isfinite(v);
}
template <typename T> inline
typename std::enable_if_t<std::is_integral_v<T>, bool>
IsFinite(T v) { return true; }
```

Although fused multiply add is available through the standard library, we also provide our own FMA() function.

⟨*Floating-point Inline Functions*⟩ +≡

```
float FMA(float a, float b, float c) { return std::fma(a, b, c); }
```

A separate version for integer types allows calling FMA() from code regardless of the numeric type being used.

⟨*Math Inline Functions*⟩ +≡

```
template <typename T> inline
typename std::enable_if_t<std::is_integral_v<T>, T>
FMA(T a, T b, T c) { return a * b + c; }
```

For certain low-level operations, it can be useful to be able to interpret a floating-point value in terms of its constituent bits and to convert the bits representing a floating-point value to an actual float or double. A natural approach to this would be to take a pointer to a value to be converted and cast it to a pointer to the other type:

```
float f = ...;
uint32_t bits = *((uint32_t *)&f);
```

However, modern versions of C++ specify that it is illegal to cast a pointer of one type, float, to a different type, uint32_t. (This restriction allows the compiler to optimize more aggressively in its analysis of whether two pointers may point to the same memory location, which can inhibit storing values in registers.) Another popular alternative, using a union with elements of both types, assigning to one type and reading from the other, is also illegal: the C++ standard says that reading an element of a union different from the last one assigned to is undefined behavior.

Fortunately, as of C++20, the standard library provides a std::bit_cast function that performs such conversions. Because this version of pbrt only requires C++17, we provide an implementation in the pstd library that is used by the following conversion functions.

⟨*Floating-point Inline Functions*⟩ +≡

```
inline uint32_t FloatToBits(float f) {
    return pstd::bit_cast<uint32_t>(f);
}
```

⟨*Floating-point Inline Functions*⟩ +≡
```
inline float BitsToFloat(uint32_t ui) {
    return pstd::bit_cast<float>(ui);
}
```

(Versions of these functions that convert between `double` and `uint64_t` are also available but are similar and are therefore not included here.)

The corresponding integer type with a sufficient number of bits to store pbrt's `Float` type is available through `FloatBits`.

⟨*Float Type Definitions*⟩ +≡
```
#ifdef PBRT_FLOAT_AS_DOUBLE
using FloatBits = uint64_t;
#else
using FloatBits = uint32_t;
#endif // PBRT_FLOAT_AS_DOUBLE
```

Given the ability to extract the bits of a floating-point value and given the description of their layout in Section 6.8.1, it is easy to extract various useful quantities from a float.

⟨*Floating-point Inline Functions*⟩ +≡
```
inline int Exponent(float v) { return (FloatToBits(v) >> 23) - 127; }
```

⟨*Floating-point Inline Functions*⟩ +≡
```
inline int Significand(float v) { return FloatToBits(v) & ((1 << 23) - 1); }
```

⟨*Floating-point Inline Functions*⟩ +≡
```
inline uint32_t SignBit(float v) { return FloatToBits(v) & 0x80000000; }
```

These conversions can be used to implement functions that bump a floating-point value up or down to the next greater or next smaller representable floating-point value.[12] They are useful for some conservative rounding operations that we will need in code to follow. Thanks to the specifics of the in-memory representation of floats, these operations are quite efficient.

⟨*Floating-point Inline Functions*⟩ +≡
```
inline float NextFloatUp(float v) {
    ⟨Handle infinity and negative zero for NextFloatUp() 365⟩
    ⟨Advance v to next higher float 366⟩
}
```

There are two important special cases: first, if v is positive infinity, then this function just returns v unchanged. Second, negative zero is skipped forward to positive zero before continuing on to the code that advances the significand. This step must be handled explicitly, since the bit patterns for −0.0 and 0.0 are not adjacent.

⟨*Handle infinity and negative zero for* NextFloatUp()⟩ ≡   365
```
if (IsInf(v) && v > 0.f)
    return v;
if (v == -0.f)
    v = 0.f;
```

Conceptually, given a floating-point value, we would like to increase the significand by one, where if the result overflows, the significand is reset to zero and the exponent is increased by

---

12 These functions are equivalent to `std::nextafter(v, Infinity)` and `std::nextafter(v, -Infinity)`, but are more efficient since they do not try to handle NaN values or deal with signaling floating-point exceptions.

one. Fortuitously, adding one to the in-memory integer representation of a float achieves this: because the exponent lies at the high bits above the significand, adding one to the low bit of the significand will cause a one to be carried all the way up into the exponent if the significand is all ones and otherwise will advance to the next higher significand for the current exponent. (This is yet another example of the careful thought that was applied to the development of the IEEE floating-point specification.) Note also that when the highest representable finite floating-point value's bit representation is incremented, the bit pattern for positive floating-point infinity is the result.

For negative values, subtracting one from the bit representation similarly advances to the next higher value.

⟨*Advance v to next higher float*⟩ ≡   365
```
    uint32_t ui = FloatToBits(v);
    if (v >= 0) ++ui;
    else          --ui;
    return BitsToFloat(ui);
```

The NextFloatDown() function, not included here, follows the same logic but effectively in reverse. pbrt also provides versions of these functions for doubles.

Error Propagation

Using the guarantees of IEEE floating-point arithmetic, it is possible to develop methods to analyze and bound the error in a given floating-point computation. For more details on this topic, see the excellent book by Higham (2002), as well as Wilkinson's earlier classic (1994).

Two measurements of error are useful in this effort: absolute and relative. If we perform some floating-point computation and get a rounded result $\tilde{a}$, we say that the magnitude of the difference between $\tilde{a}$ and the result of doing that computation in the real numbers is the *absolute error*, δ_a:

$$\delta_a = |\tilde{a} - a|.$$

Relative error, δ_r, is the ratio of the absolute error to the precise result:

$$\delta_r = \left| \frac{\tilde{a} - a}{a} \right| = \left| \frac{\delta_a}{a} \right|, \qquad\qquad [6.21]$$

as long as $a \neq 0$. Using the definition of relative error, we can thus write the computed value $\tilde{a}$ as a perturbation of the exact result a:

$$\tilde{a} \in a \pm \delta_a = a(1 \pm \delta_r).$$

As a first application of these ideas, consider computing the sum of four numbers, a, b, c, and d, represented as floats. If we compute this sum as r = (((a + b) + c) + d), Equation (6.20) gives us

$$(((a \oplus b) \oplus c) \oplus d) \in ((((a + b)(1 \pm \epsilon_m)) + c)(1 \pm \epsilon_m) + d)(1 \pm \epsilon_m)$$

$$= (a + b)(1 \pm \epsilon_m)^3 + c(1 \pm \epsilon_m)^2 + d(1 \pm \epsilon_m).$$

Because ϵ_m is small, higher-order powers of ϵ_m can be bounded by an additional ϵ_m term, and so we can bound the $(1 \pm \epsilon_m)^n$ terms with

$$(1 \pm \epsilon_m)^n \leq (1 \pm (n + 1)\epsilon_m).$$

BitsToFloat() 365
FloatToBits() 364

(As a practical matter, $(1 \pm n\epsilon_m)$ almost bounds these terms, since higher powers of ϵ_m get very small very quickly, but the above is a fully conservative bound.)

This bound lets us simplify the result of the addition to:

$$(a + b)(1 \pm 4\epsilon_m) + c(1 \pm 3\epsilon_m) + d(1 \pm 2\epsilon_m) =$$
$$a + b + c + d + [\pm 4\epsilon_m(a + b) \pm 3\epsilon_m c \pm 2\epsilon_m d].$$

The term in square brackets gives the absolute error: its magnitude is bounded by

$$4\epsilon_m|a + b| + 3\epsilon_m|c| + 2\epsilon_m|d|. \qquad [6.22]$$

Thus, if we add four floating-point numbers together with the above parenthesization, we can be certain that the difference between the final rounded result and the result we would get if we added them with infinite-precision real numbers is bounded by Equation (6.22); this error bound is easily computed given specific values of a, b, c, and d.

This is a fairly interesting result; we see that the magnitude of $a + b$ makes a relatively large contribution to the error bound, especially compared to d. (This result gives a sense for why, if adding a large number of floating-point numbers together, sorting them from small to large magnitudes generally gives a result with a lower final error than an arbitrary ordering.)

Our analysis here has implicitly assumed that the compiler would generate instructions according to the expression used to define the sum. Compilers are required to follow the form of the given floating-point expressions in order to not break carefully crafted computations that may have been designed to minimize round-off error. Here again is a case where certain transformations that would be valid on expressions with integers cannot be safely applied when floats are involved.

What happens if we change the expression to the algebraically equivalent float r = (a + b) + (c + d)? This corresponds to the floating-point computation

$$((a \oplus b) \oplus (c \oplus d)).$$

If we use the same process of applying Equation (6.20), expanding out terms, converting higher-order $(1 \pm \epsilon_m)^n$ terms to $(1 \pm (n + 1)\epsilon_m)$, we get absolute error bounds of

$$3\epsilon_m|a + b| + 3\epsilon_m|c + d|,$$

which are lower than the first formulation if $|a + b|$ is relatively large, but possibly higher if $|c + d|$ is relatively large.

This approach to computing error is known as *forward error analysis*; given inputs to a computation, we can apply a fairly mechanical process that provides conservative bounds on the error in the result. The derived bounds in the result may overstate the actual error—in practice, the signs of the error terms are often mixed, so that there is cancellation when they are added.[13] An alternative approach is *backward error analysis*, which treats the computed result as exact and finds bounds on perturbations on the inputs that give the same result. This approach can be more useful when analyzing the stability of a numerical algorithm but is less applicable to deriving conservative error bounds on the geometric computations we are interested in here.

The conservative bounding of $(1 \pm \epsilon_m)^n$ by $(1 \pm (n + 1)\epsilon_m)$ is somewhat unsatisfying since it adds a whole ϵ_m term purely to conservatively bound the sum of various higher powers of ϵ_m. Higham (2002, Section 3.1) gives an approach to more tightly bound products of $(1 \pm \epsilon_m)$ error terms. If we have $(1 \pm \epsilon_m)^n$, it can be shown that this value is bounded by $1 + \theta_n$, where

$$|\theta_n| \le \frac{n\,\epsilon_m}{1 - n\,\epsilon_m}, \qquad [6.23]$$

---

13 Some numerical analysts use a rule of thumb that the number of ulps of error in practice is often close to the square root of the bound's number of ulps, thanks to the cancellation of error in intermediate results.

as long as $n \, \epsilon_m < 1$ (which will certainly be the case for the calculations we consider). Note that the denominator of this expression will be just less than one for reasonable n values, so it just barely increases $n\epsilon_m$ to achieve a conservative bound.

We will denote this bound by γ_n:

$$\gamma_n = \frac{n \, \epsilon_m}{1 - n \, \epsilon_m}.$$

The function that computes its value is declared as `constexpr` so that any invocations with compile-time constants will be replaced with the corresponding floating-point return value.

⟨*Floating-point Inline Functions*⟩ +≡
```
inline constexpr Float gamma(int n) {
    return (n * MachineEpsilon) / (1 - n * MachineEpsilon);
}
```

Using the γ notation, our bound on the error of the first sum of four values is

$$|a + b|\gamma_3 + |c|\gamma_2 + |d|\gamma_1.$$

An advantage of this approach is that quotients of $(1 \pm \epsilon_m)^n$ terms can also be bounded with the γ function. Given

$$\frac{(1 \pm \epsilon_m)^m}{(1 \pm \epsilon_m)^n},$$

the interval is bounded by $(1 \pm \gamma_{m+n})$. Thus, γ can be used to collect ϵ_m terms from both sides of an equality over to one side by dividing them through; this will be useful in some of the following derivations. (Note that because $(1 \pm \epsilon_m)$ terms represent intervals, canceling them would be incorrect:

$$\frac{(1 \pm \epsilon_m)^m}{(1 \pm \epsilon_m)^n} \neq (1 \pm \epsilon_m)^{m-n};$$

the γ_{m+n} bounds must be used instead.)

Given inputs to some computation that themselves carry some amount of error, it is instructive to see how this error is carried through various elementary arithmetic operations. Given two values, $a(1 \pm \gamma_i)$ and $b(1 \pm \gamma_j)$, that each carry accumulated error from earlier operations, consider their product. Using the definition of $\otimes$, the result is in the interval:

$$a(1 \pm \gamma_i) \otimes b(1 \pm \gamma_j) \in ab(1 \pm \gamma_{i+j+1}),$$

where we have used the relationship $(1 \pm \gamma_i)(1 \pm \gamma_j) \in (1 \pm \gamma_{i+j})$, which follows directly from Equation (6.23).

The relative error in this result is bounded by

$$\left| \frac{ab \, \gamma_{i+j+1}}{ab} \right| = \gamma_{i+j+1},$$

and so the final error is no more than roughly $(i + j + 1)/2$ ulps at the value of the product—about as good as we might hope for, given the error going into the multiplication. (The situation for division is similarly good.)

Unfortunately, with addition and subtraction, it is possible for the relative error to increase substantially. Using the same definitions of the values being operated on, consider

$$a(1 \pm \gamma_i) \oplus b(1 \pm \gamma_j),$$

Float 23

MachineEpsilon 362

which is in the interval $a(1 \pm \gamma_{i+1}) + b(1 \pm \gamma_{j+1})$, and so the absolute error is bounded by $|a|\gamma_{i+1} + |b|\gamma_{j+1}$.

If the signs of a and b are the same, then the absolute error is bounded by $|a + b|\gamma_{i+j+1}$ and the relative error is approximately $(i + j + 1)/2$ ulps around the computed value.

However, if the signs of a and b differ (or, equivalently, they are the same but subtraction is performed), then the relative error can be quite high. Consider the case where $a \approx -b$: the relative error is

$$\frac{|a|\gamma_{i+1} + |b|\gamma_{j+1}}{a + b} \approx \frac{2|a|\gamma_{i+j+1}}{a + b}.$$

The numerator's magnitude is proportional to the original value $|a|$ yet is divided by a very small number, and thus the relative error is quite high. This substantial increase in relative error is called *catastrophic cancellation*. Equivalently, we can have a sense of the issue from the fact that the absolute error is in terms of the magnitude of $|a|$, though it is in relation to a value much smaller than a.

Running Error Analysis

In addition to working out error bounds algebraically, we can also have the computer do this work for us as some computation is being performed. This approach is known as *running error analysis*. The idea behind it is simple: each time a floating-point operation is performed, we compute intervals based on Equation (6.20) that bound its true value.

The Interval class, which is defined in Section B.2.15, provides this functionality. The Interval class also tracks rounding errors in floating-point arithmetic and is useful even if none of the initial values are intervals. While computing error bounds in this way has higher runtime overhead than using derived expressions that give an error bound directly, it can be convenient when derivations become unwieldy.

6.8.2 CONSERVATIVE RAY–BOUNDS INTERSECTIONS

Floating-point round-off error can cause the ray–bounding box intersection test to miss cases where a ray actually does intersect the box. While it is acceptable to have occasional false positives from ray–box intersection tests, we would like to never miss an intersection—getting this right is important for the correctness of the BVHAggregate acceleration data structure in Section 7.3 so that valid ray–shape intersections are not missed.

The ray–bounding box test introduced in Section 6.1.2 is based on computing a series of ray–slab intersections to find the parametric $t_{\min}$ along the ray where the ray enters the bounding box and the $t_{\max}$ where it exits. If $t_{\min} < t_{\max}$, the ray passes through the box; otherwise, it misses it. With floating-point arithmetic, there may be error in the computed t values—if the computed $t_{\min}$ value is greater than $t_{\max}$ purely due to round-off error, the intersection test will incorrectly return a false result.

Recall that the computation to find the t value for a ray intersection with a plane perpendicular to the x axis at a point x is $t = (x - o_x)/d_x$. Expressed as a floating-point computation and applying Equation (6.19), we have

$$t = (x \ominus o_x) \otimes (1 \oslash \mathbf{d}_x) \in \frac{x - o_x}{\mathbf{d}_x}(1 \pm \epsilon)^3,$$

BVHAggregate 407
Interval 1057

and so

$$\frac{x - o_x}{\mathbf{d}_x} \in t(1 \pm \gamma_3).$$

The difference between the computed result t and the precise result is bounded by $\gamma_3|t|$.

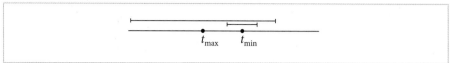

Figure 6.41: If the error bounds of the computed t_{min} and t_{max} values overlap, the comparison $t_{min} < t_{max}$ may not indicate if a ray hit a bounding box. It is better to conservatively return true in this case than to miss an intersection. Extending t_{max} by twice its error bound ensures that the comparison is conservative.

If we consider the intervals around the computed t values that bound the true value of t, then the case we are concerned with is when the intervals overlap; if they do not, then the comparison of computed values will give the correct result (Figure 6.41). If the intervals do overlap, it is impossible to know the true ordering of the t values. In this case, increasing t_{max} by twice the error bound, $2\gamma_3 t_{max}$, before performing the comparison ensures that we conservatively return true in this case.

We can now define the fragment for the ray–bounding box test in Section 6.1.2 that makes this adjustment.

⟨*Update* tFar *to ensure robust ray–bounds intersection*⟩ ≡   264
    tFar *= 1 + 2 * gamma(3);

The fragments for the Bounds3::IntersectP() method, ⟨*Update* tMax *and* tyMax *to ensure robust bounds intersection*⟩ and ⟨*Update* tzMax *to ensure robust bounds intersection*⟩, are similar and therefore not included here.

6.8.3 ACCURATE QUADRATIC DISCRIMINANTS

Recall from Sections 6.2.2 and 6.3.2 that intersecting a ray with a sphere or cylinder involves finding the zeros of a quadratic equation, which requires calculating its discriminant, $b^2 - 4ac$. If the discriminant is computed as written, then when the sphere is far from the ray origin, $b^2 \approx 4ac$ and catastrophic cancellation occurs. This issue is made worse since the magnitudes of the two terms of the discriminant are related to the *squared* distance between the sphere and the ray origin. Even for rays that are far from ever hitting the sphere, a discriminant may be computed that is exactly equal to zero, leading to the intersection code reporting an invalid intersection. See Figure 6.42, which shows that this error can be meaningful in practice.

Algebraically rewriting the discriminant computation makes it possible to compute it with more accuracy. First, if we rewrite the quadratic discriminant as

$$b^2 - 4ac = 4a\left(\frac{b^2}{4a} - c\right)$$

and then substitute in the values of a, b, and c from Equation (6.3) to the terms inside the parentheses, we have

$$4a\left(\frac{4(\mathbf{o} \cdot \mathbf{d})^2}{4(\mathbf{d} \cdot \mathbf{d})} - ((\mathbf{o} \cdot \mathbf{o}) - r^2)\right)$$

$$= 4a\left([(\mathbf{o} \cdot \hat{\mathbf{d}})^2 - (\mathbf{o} \cdot \mathbf{o})] + r^2\right),$$ [6.24]

gamma() 368

where we have denoted the vector from $(0, 0, 0)$ to the ray's origin as $\mathbf{o}$ and $\hat{\mathbf{d}}$ is the ray's normalized direction.

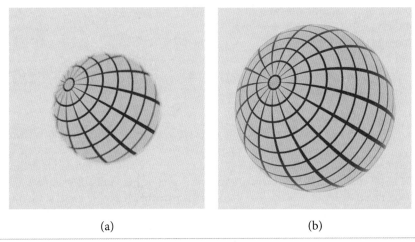

(a)   (b)

Figure 6.42: The Effect of Reducing the Error in the Computation of the Discriminant for Ray–Sphere Intersection. Unit sphere, viewed using an orthographic projection with a camera 400 units away. (a) If the quadratic discriminant is computed in the usual fashion, numeric error causes intersections at the edges to be missed. In the found intersections, the inaccuracy is evident in the wobble of the textured lines. (b) With the more precise formulation described in this section, the sphere is rendered correctly. (With the improved discriminant, such a sphere can be translated as far as 7,500 or so units from an orthographic camera and still be rendered accurately.)

Now consider the decomposition of $\mathbf{o}$ into the sum of two vectors, $\mathbf{d}_\perp$ and $\mathbf{d}_\parallel$, where $\mathbf{d}_\parallel$ is parallel to $\hat{\mathbf{d}}$ and $\mathbf{d}_\perp$ is perpendicular to it. Those vectors are given by

$$\mathbf{d}_\parallel = (\mathbf{o} \cdot \hat{\mathbf{d}})\hat{\mathbf{d}}$$
$$\mathbf{d}_\perp = \mathbf{o} - \mathbf{d}_\parallel = \mathbf{o} - (\mathbf{o} \cdot \hat{\mathbf{d}})\hat{\mathbf{d}}.$$

(6.25)

These three vectors form a right triangle, and therefore $\|\mathbf{o}\|^2 = \|\mathbf{d}_\perp\|^2 + \|\mathbf{d}_\parallel\|^2$. Applying Equation (6.25),

$$(\mathbf{o} \cdot \mathbf{o}) = \|\mathbf{o} - (\mathbf{o} \cdot \hat{\mathbf{d}})\hat{\mathbf{d}}\|^2 + (\mathbf{o} \cdot \hat{\mathbf{d}})^2\|\hat{\mathbf{d}}\|^2$$
$$= \|\mathbf{o} - (\mathbf{o} \cdot \hat{\mathbf{d}})\hat{\mathbf{d}}\|^2 + (\mathbf{o} \cdot \hat{\mathbf{d}})^2.$$

Rearranging terms gives

$$(\mathbf{o} \cdot \hat{\mathbf{d}})^2 - (\mathbf{o} \cdot \mathbf{o}) = -\|\mathbf{o} - (\mathbf{o} \cdot \hat{\mathbf{d}})\hat{\mathbf{d}}\|^2.$$

Expressing the right hand side in terms of the sphere quadratic coefficients from Equation (6.3) gives

$$(\mathbf{o} \cdot \hat{\mathbf{d}})^2 - (\mathbf{o} \cdot \mathbf{o}) = -\left\|\mathbf{o} - \frac{b}{2a}\mathbf{d}\right\|^2.$$

Note that the left hand side is equal to the term in square brackets in Equation (6.24).

Computing that term in this way eliminates c from the discriminant, which is of great benefit since its magnitude is proportional to the squared distance to the origin, with accordingly limited accuracy. In the implementation below, we take advantage of the fact that the discriminant is now the difference of squared values and make use of the identity $x^2 - y^2 = (x + y)(x - y)$ to reduce the magnitudes of the intermediate values, which further reduces error.

⟨*Compute sphere quadratic discriminant* discrim⟩ ≡   **274**
```
    Vector3fi v(oi - b / (2 * a) * di);
    Interval length = Length(v);
    Interval discrim = 4 * a * (Interval(radius) + length) *
                                (Interval(radius) - length);
    if (discrim.LowerBound() < 0)
        return {};
```

One might ask, why go through this trouble when we could use the DifferenceOfProducts() function to compute the discriminant, presumably with low error? The reason that is not an equivalent alternative is that the values a, b, and c already suffer from rounding error. In turn, a result computed by DifferenceOfProducts() will be inaccurate if its inputs already are inaccurate themselves. $c = o_x^2 + o_y^2 + o_z^2 - r^2$ is particularly problematic, since it is the difference of two positive values, so is susceptible to catastrophic cancellation.

A similar derivation gives a more accurate discriminant for the cylinder.

⟨*Compute cylinder quadratic discriminant* discrim⟩ ≡   **288**
```
    Interval f = b / (2 * a);
    Interval vx = oi.x - f * di.x, vy = oi.y - f * di.y;
    Interval length = Sqrt(Sqr(vx) + Sqr(vy));
    Interval discrim = 4 * a * (Interval(radius) + length) *
                                (Interval(radius) - length);
    if (discrim.LowerBound() < 0)
        return {};
```

6.8.4 ROBUST TRIANGLE INTERSECTIONS

The details of the ray–triangle intersection algorithm described in Section 6.5.3 were carefully designed to avoid cases where rays could incorrectly pass through an edge or vertex shared by two adjacent triangles without generating an intersection. Fittingly, an intersection algorithm with this guarantee is referred to as being *watertight*.

Recall that the algorithm is based on transforming triangle vertices into a coordinate system with the ray's origin at its origin and the ray's direction aligned along the $+z$ axis. Although round-off error may be introduced by transforming the vertex positions to this coordinate system, this error does not affect the watertightness of the intersection test, since the same transformation is applied to all triangles. (Further, this error is quite small, so it does not significantly impact the accuracy of the computed intersection points.)

Given vertices in this coordinate system, the three edge functions defined in Equation (6.5) are evaluated at the point $(0, 0)$; the corresponding expressions, Equation (6.6), are quite straightforward. The key to the robustness of the algorithm is that with floating-point arithmetic, the edge function evaluations are guaranteed to have the correct sign. In general, we have

$$(a \otimes b) \ominus (c \otimes d). \tag{6.26}$$

First, note that if $ab = cd$, then Equation (6.26) evaluates to exactly zero, even in floating point. We therefore just need to show that if $ab > cd$, then $(a \otimes b) \ominus (c \otimes d)$ is never negative. If $ab > cd$, then $(a \otimes b)$ must be greater than or equal to $(c \otimes d)$. In turn, their difference must be greater than or equal to zero. (These properties both follow from the fact that floating-point arithmetic operations are all rounded to the nearest representable floating-point value.)

If the value of the edge function is zero, then it is impossible to tell whether it is exactly zero or whether a small positive or negative value has rounded to zero. In this case, the fragment ⟨*Fall back to double-precision test at triangle edges*⟩ reevaluates the edge function with double precision; it can be shown that doubling the precision suffices to accurately distinguish these cases, given 32-bit floats as input.

The overhead caused by this additional precaution is minimal: in a benchmark with 88 million ray intersection tests, the double-precision fallback had to be used in less than 0.0000023% of the cases.

6.8.5 BOUNDING INTERSECTION POINT ERROR

We can apply the machinery introduced in this section for analyzing rounding error to derive conservative bounds on the absolute error in computed ray–shape intersection points, which allows us to construct bounding boxes that are guaranteed to include an intersection point on the actual surface (Figure 6.43). These bounding boxes provide the basis of the algorithm for generating spawned ray origins that will be introduced in Section 6.8.6.

It is illuminating to start by looking at the sources of error in conventional approaches to computing intersection points. It is common practice in ray tracing to compute 3D intersection points by first solving the parametric ray equation $o + t\mathbf{d}$ for a value t_{hit} where a ray intersects a surface and then computing the hit point p with $p = o + t_{\text{hit}}\mathbf{d}$. If t_{hit} carries some error δ_t, then we can bound the error in the computed intersection point. Considering the x coordinate, for example, we have

$$
\begin{aligned}
x &= o_x \oplus (t_{\text{hit}} \pm \delta_t) \otimes \mathbf{d}_x \\
&\in o_x \oplus (t_{\text{hit}} \pm \delta_t)\mathbf{d}_x(1 \pm \gamma_1) \\
&\subset o_x(1 \pm \gamma_1) + (t_{\text{hit}} \pm \delta_t)\mathbf{d}_x(1 \pm \gamma_2) \\
&= o_x + t_{\text{hit}}\mathbf{d}_x + [\pm o_x\gamma_1 \pm \delta_t\mathbf{d}_x \pm t_{\text{hit}}\mathbf{d}_x\gamma_2 \pm \delta_t\mathbf{d}_x\gamma_2].
\end{aligned}
$$

The error term (in square brackets) is bounded by

$$
\gamma_1|o_x| + \delta_t(1 + \gamma_2)|\mathbf{d}_x| + \gamma_2|t_{\text{hit}}\mathbf{d}_x|. \tag{6.27}
$$

There are two things to see from Equation (6.27): first, the magnitudes of the terms that contribute to the error in the computed intersection point (o_x, $\mathbf{d}_x$, and $t_{\text{hit}}\mathbf{d}_x$) may be quite different from the magnitude of the intersection point. Thus, there is a danger of catastrophic cancellation in the intersection point's computed value. Second, ray intersection algorithms generally perform tens of floating-point operations to compute t values, which in turn means

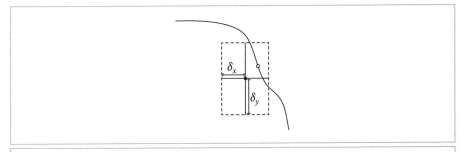

Figure 6.43: Shape intersection algorithms in `pbrt` compute an intersection point, shown here in the 2D setting with a filled circle. The absolute error in this point is bounded by δ_x and δ_y, giving a small box around the point. Because these bounds are conservative, we know that the actual intersection point on the surface (open circle) must lie somewhere within the box.

that we can expect δ_t to be at least of magnitude $\gamma_n t$, with n in the tens (and possibly much more, due to catastrophic cancellation).

Each of these terms may introduce a significant amount of error in the computed point x. We introduce better approaches in the following.

Reprojection: Quadrics

We would like to reliably compute surface intersection points with just a few ulps of error rather than the orders of magnitude greater error that intersection points computed with the parametric ray equation may have. Previously, Woo et al. (1996) suggested using the first intersection point computed as a starting point for a second ray–plane intersection, for ray–polygon intersections. From the bounds in Equation (6.27), we can see why the second intersection point will often be much closer to the surface than the first: the t_{hit} value along the second ray will be quite close to zero, so that the magnitude of the absolute error in t_{hit} will be quite small, and thus using this value in the parametric ray equation will give a point quite close to the surface (Figure 6.44). Further, the ray origin will have similar magnitude to the intersection point, so the $\gamma_1 |o_x|$ term will not introduce much additional error.

Although the second intersection point computed with this approach is much closer to the plane of the surface, it still suffers from error by being offset due to error in the first computed intersection. The farther away the ray origin is from the intersection point (and thus, the larger the absolute error is in t_{hit}), the larger this error will be. In spite of this error, the approach has merit: we are generally better off with a computed intersection point that is quite close to the actual surface, even if offset from the most accurate possible intersection point, than we are with a point that is some distance above or below the surface (and likely also far from the most accurate intersection point).

Rather than doing a full reintersection computation, which may not only be computationally costly but also will still have error in the computed t value, an effective alternative is to refine computed intersection points by reprojecting them to the surface. The error bounds for these reprojected points are often remarkably small. (It should be noted that these reprojection error bounds do not capture tangential errors that were present in the original intersection p—the main focus here is to detect errors that might cause the reprojected point p' to fall below the surface.)

Consider a ray–sphere intersection: given a computed intersection point (e.g., from the ray equation) p with a sphere at the origin with radius r, we can reproject the point onto the surface of the sphere by scaling it with the ratio of the sphere's radius to the computed point's

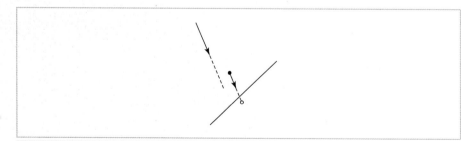

Figure 6.44: Reintersection to Improve the Accuracy of the Computed Intersection Point. Given a ray and a surface, an initial intersection point has been computed with the ray equation (filled circle). This point may be fairly inaccurate due to rounding error but can be used as the origin for a second ray–shape intersection. The intersection point computed from this second intersection (open circle) is much closer to the surface, though it may be shifted from the true intersection point due to error in the first computed intersection.

distance to the origin, computing a new point $p' = (x', y', z')$ with

$$x' = x \frac{r}{\sqrt{x^2 + y^2 + z^2}},$$

and so forth. The floating-point computation is

$$x' = x \otimes r \oslash \mathsf{sqrt}((x \otimes x) \oplus (y \otimes y) \oplus (z \otimes z))$$

$$\in \frac{xr(1 \pm \epsilon_m)^2}{\sqrt{x^2(1 \pm \epsilon_m)^3 + y^2(1 \pm \epsilon_m)^3 + z^2(1 \pm \epsilon_m)^2(1 \pm \epsilon_m)}}$$

$$\subset \frac{xr(1 \pm \gamma_2)}{\sqrt{x^2(1 \pm \gamma_3) + y^2(1 \pm \gamma_3) + z^2(1 \pm \gamma_2)(1 \pm \gamma_1)}}.$$

Because x^2, y^2, and z^2 are all positive, the terms in the square root can share the same γ term, and we have

$$x' \in \frac{xr(1 \pm \gamma_2)}{\sqrt{(x^2 + y^2 + z^2)(1 \pm \gamma_4)}(1 \pm \gamma_1)}$$

$$= \frac{xr(1 \pm \gamma_2)}{\sqrt{(x^2 + y^2 + z^2)}\sqrt{(1 \pm \gamma_4)}(1 \pm \gamma_1)} \qquad [6.28]$$

$$\subset \frac{xr}{\sqrt{(x^2 + y^2 + z^2)}}(1 \pm \gamma_5)$$

$$= x'(1 \pm \gamma_5).$$

Thus, the absolute error of the reprojected x coordinate is bounded by $\gamma_5|x'|$ (and similarly for y' and z') and is thus no more than 2.5 ulps in each dimension from a point on the surface of the sphere.

Here is the fragment that reprojects the intersection point for the Sphere shape.

⟨*Refine sphere intersection point*⟩ ≡   275
```
pHit *= radius / Distance(pHit, Point3f(0, 0, 0));
```

The error bounds follow from Equation (6.28).

⟨*Compute error bounds for sphere intersection*⟩ ≡   276
```
Vector3f pError = gamma(5) * Abs((Vector3f)pHit);
```

Reprojection algorithms and error bounds for other quadrics can be defined similarly: for example, for a cylinder along the z axis, only the x and y coordinates need to be reprojected, and the error bounds in x and y turn out to be only γ_3 times their magnitudes.

⟨*Refine cylinder intersection point*⟩ ≡   289
```
Float hitRad = std::sqrt(Sqr(pHit.x) + Sqr(pHit.y));
pHit.x *= radius / hitRad;
pHit.y *= radius / hitRad;
```

⟨*Compute error bounds for cylinder intersection*⟩ ≡   290
```
Vector3f pError = gamma(3) * Abs(Vector3f(pHit.x, pHit.y, 0));
```

The disk shape is particularly easy; we just need to set the z coordinate of the point to lie on the plane of the disk.

⟨*Refine disk intersection point*⟩ ≡   295
```
pHit.z = height;
```

In turn, we have a point with zero error; it lies exactly on the surface on the disk.

⟨*Compute error bounds for disk intersection*⟩ ≡   295
```
Vector3f pError(0, 0, 0);
```

The quadrics' `Sample()` methods also use reprojection. For example, the Sphere's area sampling method is based on `SampleUniformSphere()`, which uses `std::sin()` and `std::cos()`. Therefore, the error bounds on the computed pObj value depend on the accuracy of those functions. By reprojecting the sampled point to the sphere's surface, the error bounds derived earlier in Equation (6.28) can be used without needing to worry about those functions' accuracy.

⟨*Reproject* pObj *to sphere surface and compute* pObjError⟩ ≡   280
```
pObj *= radius / Distance(pObj, Point3f(0, 0, 0));
Vector3f pObjError = gamma(5) * Abs((Vector3f)pObj);
```

The same issue and solution apply to sampling cylinders.

⟨*Reproject* pObj *to cylinder surface and compute* pObjError⟩ ≡   291
```
Float hitRad = std::sqrt(Sqr(pObj.x) + Sqr(pObj.y));
pObj.x *= radius / hitRad;
pObj.y *= radius / hitRad;
Vector3f pObjError = gamma(3) * Abs(Vector3f(pObj.x, pObj.y, 0));
```

Parametric Evaluation: Triangles

Another effective approach to computing accurate intersection points near the surface of a shape uses the shape's parametric representation. For example, the triangle intersection algorithm in Section 6.5.3 computes three edge function values e_0, e_1, and e_2 and reports an intersection if all three have the same sign. Their values can be used to find the barycentric coordinates

$$b_i = \frac{e_i}{e_0 + e_1 + e_2}.$$

Attributes v_i at the triangle vertices (including the vertex positions) can be interpolated across the face of the triangle by

$$v' = b_0 v_0 + b_1 v_1 + b_2 v_2.$$

We can show that interpolating the positions of the vertices in this manner gives a point very close to the surface of the triangle. First consider precomputing the reciprocal of the sum of e_i:

$$d = 1 \oslash (e_0 \oplus e_1 \oplus e_2)$$
$$\in \frac{1}{(e_0 + e_1)(1 \pm \epsilon_m)^2 + e_2(1 \pm \epsilon_m)}(1 \pm \epsilon_m).$$

Because all e_i have the same sign if there is an intersection, we can collect the e_i terms and conservatively bound d:

$$d \in \frac{1}{(e_0 + e_1 + e_2)(1 \pm \epsilon_m)^2}(1 \pm \epsilon_m)$$
$$\subset \frac{1}{e_0 + e_1 + e_2}(1 \pm \gamma_3).$$

If we now consider interpolation of the x coordinate of the position in the triangle corresponding to the edge function values, we have

$$x' = ((e_0 \otimes x_0) \oplus (e_1 \otimes x_1) \oplus (e_2 \otimes x_2)) \otimes d$$

$$\in (e_0 x_0 (1 \pm \epsilon_m)^3 + e_1 x_1 (1 \pm \epsilon_m)^3 + e_2 x_2 (1 \pm \epsilon_m)^2) d (1 \pm \epsilon_m)$$

$$\subset (e_0 x_0 (1 \pm \gamma_4) + e_1 x_1 (1 \pm \gamma_4) + e_2 x_2 (1 \pm \gamma_3)) d.$$

Using the bounds on d,

$$x \in \frac{e_0 x_0 (1 \pm \gamma_7) + e_1 x_1 (1 \pm \gamma_7) + e_2 x_2 (1 \pm \gamma_6)}{e_0 + e_1 + e_2}$$

$$= b_0 x_0 (1 \pm \gamma_7) + b_1 x_1 (1 \pm \gamma_7) + b_2 x_2 (1 \pm \gamma_6).$$

Thus, we can finally see that the absolute error in the computed x' value is in the interval

$$\pm b_0 x_0 \gamma_7 \pm b_1 x_1 \gamma_7 \pm b_2 x_2 \gamma_7,$$

which is bounded by

$$\gamma_7 (|b_0 x_0| + |b_1 x_1| + |b_2 x_2|). \hspace{2cm} \text{(6.29)}$$

(Note that the $b_2 x_2$ term could have a γ_6 factor instead of γ_7, but the difference between the two is very small, so we choose a slightly simpler final expression.) Equivalent bounds hold for y' and z'.

Equation (6.29) lets us bound the error in the interpolated point computed in `Triangle::Intersect()`.

⟨*Compute error bounds* pError *for triangle intersection*⟩ ≡   312
```
Point3f pAbsSum = Abs(ti.b0 * p0) + Abs(ti.b1 * p1) + Abs(ti.b2 * p2);
Vector3f pError = gamma(7) * Vector3f(pAbsSum);
```

The bounds for a sampled point on a triangle can be found in a similar manner.

⟨*Compute error bounds* pError *for sampled point on triangle*⟩ ≡   313, 317
```
Point3f pAbsSum = Abs(b[0] * p0) + Abs(b[1] * p1) +
                  Abs((1 - b[0] - b[1]) * p2);
Vector3f pError = Vector3f(gamma(6) * pAbsSum);
```

Parametric Evaluation: Bilinear Patches

Bilinear patch intersection points are found by evaluating the bilinear function from Equation (6.11). The computation performed is

$$\left[(1 \ominus u) \otimes ((1 \ominus v) \otimes p_{0,0} \oplus v \otimes p_{0,1}) \right] \oplus \left[u \otimes ((1 \ominus v) \otimes p_{1,0} \oplus v \otimes p_{1,1}) \right].$$

Considering just the x coordinate, we can find that its error is bounded by

$$\gamma_6 |(1-u)(1-v) x_{0,0}| + \gamma_5 |(1-u) v x_{0,1}| + \gamma_5 |u (1-v) x_{1,0}| + \gamma_4 |uv x_{1,1}|.$$

Because u and v are between 0 and 1, here we will use the looser but more computationally efficient bounds of the form

$$\gamma_6 \left(|x_{0,0}| + |x_{0,1}| + |x_{1,0}| + |x_{1,1}| \right).$$

⟨*Initialize bilinear patch intersection point error* pError⟩ ≡   335
```
Point3f pAbsSum = Abs(p00) + Abs(p01) + Abs(p10) + Abs(p11);
Vector3f pError = gamma(6) * Vector3f(pAbsSum);
```

The same bounds apply for points sampled in the `BilinearPatch::Sample()` method.

⟨*Compute* pError *for sampled bilinear patch* (u, v)⟩ ≡   341
```
Point3f pAbsSum = Abs(p00) + Abs(p01) + Abs(p10) + Abs(p11);
Vector3f pError = gamma(6) * Vector3f(pAbsSum);
```

Parametric Evaluation: Curves

Because the Curve shape orients itself to face incident rays, rays leaving it must be offset by the curve's width in order to not incorrectly reintersect it when it is reoriented to face them. For wide curves, this bound is significant and may lead to visible errors in images. In that case, the Curve shape should probably be replaced with one or more bilinear patches.

⟨*Compute error bounds for curve intersection*⟩ ≡   **356**
```
    Vector3f pError(hitWidth, hitWidth, hitWidth);
```

Effect of Transformations

The last detail to attend to in order to bound the error in computed intersection points is the effect of transformations, which introduce additional rounding error when they are applied.

The quadric Shapes in pbrt transform rendering-space rays into object space before performing ray–shape intersections, and then transform computed intersection points back to rendering space. Both of these transformation steps introduce rounding error that needs to be accounted for in order to maintain robust rendering-space bounds around intersection points.

If possible, it is best to try to avoid coordinate-system transformations of rays and intersection points. For example, it is better to transform triangle vertices to rendering space and intersect rendering-space rays with them than to transform rays to object space and then transform intersection points to rendering space.[14] Transformations are still useful—for example, for the quadrics and for object instancing—so we will show how to bound the error that they introduce.

We will discuss these topics in the context of the Transform operator() method that takes a Point3fi, which is the Point3 variant that uses an Interval for each of the coordinates.

⟨*Transform Public Methods*⟩ +≡   **120**
```
    Point3fi operator()(const Point3fi &p) const {
        Float x = Float(p.x), y = Float(p.y), z = Float(p.z);
        ⟨Compute transformed coordinates from point (x, y, z)⟩
        ⟨Compute absolute error for transformed point, pError 379⟩
        if (wp == 1)
            return Point3fi(Point3f(xp, yp, zp), pError);
        else
            return Point3fi(Point3f(xp, yp, zp), pError) / wp;
    }
```

This method starts by computing the transformed position of the point (x, y, z) where each coordinate is at the midpoint of its respective interval in p. The fragment that implements that computation, ⟨*Compute transformed coordinates from point* (x, y, z)⟩, is not included here; it implements the same matrix/point multiplication as in Section 3.10.

Next, error bounds are computed, accounting both for rounding error when applying the transformation as well as the effect of non-empty intervals, if p is not exact.

---

14 Although rounding error is introduced when transforming triangle vertices to rendering space (for example), this error does not add error that needs to be handled in computing intersection points. In other words, the transformed vertices may represent a perturbed representation of the scene, but they are the most accurate representation available given the transformation.

⟨*Compute absolute error for transformed point*, pError⟩ ≡   378

```
Vector3f pError;
if (p.IsExact()) {
    ⟨Compute error for transformed exact p 379⟩
} else {
    ⟨Compute error for transformed approximate p⟩
}
```

If (x, y, z) has no accumulated error, then given a 4×4 non-projective transformation matrix with elements denoted by $m_{i,j}$, the transformed coordinate x' is

$$x' = ((m_{0,0} \otimes x) \oplus (m_{0,1} \otimes y)) \oplus ((m_{0,2} \otimes z) \oplus m_{0,3})$$

$$\in m_{0,0}x(1 \pm \epsilon_m)^3 + m_{0,1}y(1 \pm \epsilon_m)^3 + m_{0,2}z(1 \pm \epsilon_m)^3 + m_{0,3}(1 \pm \epsilon_m)^2$$

$$\subset (m_{0,0}x + m_{0,1}y + m_{0,2}z + m_{0,3}) + \gamma_3(\pm m_{0,0}x \pm m_{0,1}y \pm m_{0,2}z \pm m_{0,3})$$

$$\subset (m_{0,0}x + m_{0,1}y + m_{0,2}z + m_{0,3}) \pm \gamma_3(|m_{0,0}x| + |m_{0,1}y| + |m_{0,2}z| + |m_{0,3}|).$$

Thus, the absolute error in the result is bounded by

$$\gamma_3(|m_{0,0}x| + |m_{0,1}y| + |m_{0,2}z| + |m_{0,3}|). \tag{6.30}$$

Similar bounds follow for the transformed y' and z' coordinates, and the implementation follows directly.

⟨*Compute error for transformed exact* p⟩ ≡   379

```
pError.x = gamma(3) * (std::abs(m[0][0] * x) + std::abs(m[0][1] * y) +
                       std::abs(m[0][2] * z) + std::abs(m[0][3]));
pError.y = gamma(3) * (std::abs(m[1][0] * x) + std::abs(m[1][1] * y) +
                       std::abs(m[1][2] * z) + std::abs(m[1][3]));
pError.z = gamma(3) * (std::abs(m[2][0] * x) + std::abs(m[2][1] * y) +
                       std::abs(m[2][2] * z) + std::abs(m[2][3]));
```

Now consider the case of the point p having error that is bounded by δ_x, δ_y, and δ_z in each dimension. The transformed x coordinate is given by:

$$x' = (m_{0,0} \otimes (x \pm \delta_x) \oplus m_{0,1} \otimes (y \pm \delta_y)) \oplus (m_{0,2} \otimes (z \pm \delta_z) \oplus m_{0,3}).$$

Applying the definitions of floating-point addition and multiplication and their error bounds, we have

$$x' = m_{0,0}(x \pm \delta_x)(1 \pm \epsilon_m)^3 + m_{0,1}(y \pm \delta_y)(1 \pm \epsilon_m)^3$$
$$+ m_{0,2}(z \pm \delta_z)(1 \pm \epsilon_m)^3 + m_{0,3}(1 \pm \epsilon_m)^2.$$

Transforming to use γ, we can find the absolute error term to be bounded by

$$(\gamma_3 + 1)(|m_{0,0}|\delta_x + |m_{0,1}|\delta_y + |m_{0,2}|\delta_z)$$
$$+ \gamma_3(|m_{0,0}x| + |m_{0,1}y| + |m_{0,2}z| + |m_{0,3}|). \tag{6.31}$$

We have not included the fragment ⟨*Compute error for transformed approximate* p⟩ that implements this computation, as it is nearly 20 lines of code for the direct translation of Equation (6.31).

It would have been much easier to implement this method using the Interval class to automatically compute error bounds. We found that that approach gives bounds that are generally 3–6× wider and cause the method to be six times slower than the implementation presented

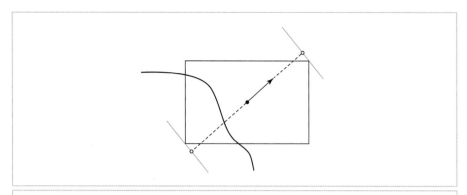

Figure 6.45: Given a computed intersection point (filled circle) with surface normal (arrow) and error bounds (rectangle), we compute two planes offset along the normal that are offset just far enough so that they do not intersect the error bounds. The points on these planes along the normal from the computed intersection point give us the origins for spawned rays (open circles); one of the two is selected based on the ray direction so that the spawned ray will not pass through the error bounding box. By construction, such rays cannot incorrectly reintersect the actual surface (thick line).

here. Given that transformations are frequently applied during rendering, deriving and then using tighter bounds is worthwhile.

Note that the code that computes error bounds is buggy if the matrix is projective and the homogeneous w coordinate of the projected point is not one; this nit is not currently a problem for pbrt's usage of this method.

The Transform class also provides methods to transform vectors and rays, returning the resulting error. The vector error bound derivations (and thence, implementations) are very similar to those for points, and so also are not included here.

6.8.6 ROBUST SPAWNED RAY ORIGINS

Computed intersection points and their error bounds give us a small 3D box that bounds a region of space. We know that the precise intersection point must be somewhere inside this box and that thus the surface must pass through the box (at least enough to present the point where the intersection is). (Recall Figure 6.43.) Having these boxes makes it possible to position the origins of rays leaving the surface so that they are always on the right side of the surface and do not incorrectly reintersect it. When tracing spawned rays leaving the intersection point p, we offset their origins enough to ensure that they are past the boundary of the error box and thus will not incorrectly reintersect the surface.

In order to ensure that the spawned ray origin is definitely on the right side of the surface, we move far enough along the normal so that the plane perpendicular to the normal is outside the error bounding box. To see how to do this, consider a computed intersection point at the origin, where the equation for the plane going through the intersection point is

$$f(x, y, z) = \mathbf{n}_x x + \mathbf{n}_y y + \mathbf{n}_z z.$$

The plane is implicitly defined by $f(x, y, z) = 0$, and the normal is $(\mathbf{n}_x, \mathbf{n}_y, \mathbf{n}_z)$.

For a point not on the plane, the value of the plane equation $f(x, y, z)$ gives the offset along the normal that gives a plane that goes through the point. We would like to find the maximum value of $f(x, y, z)$ for the eight corners of the error bounding box; if we offset the plane plus and minus this offset, we have two planes that do not intersect the error box that should be (locally) on opposite sides of the surface, at least at the computed intersection point offset along the normal (Figure 6.45).

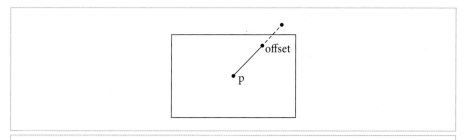

Figure 6.46: The rounded value of the offset point p+offset computed in OffsetRayOrigin() may end up in the interior of the error box rather than on its boundary, which in turn introduces the risk of incorrect self-intersections if the rounded point is on the wrong side of the surface. Advancing each coordinate of the computed point one floating-point value away from p ensures that it is outside of the error box.

If the eight corners of the error bounding box are given by $(\pm\delta_x, \pm\delta_y, \pm\delta_z)$, then the maximum value of $f(x, y, z)$ is easily computed:

$$d = |\mathbf{n}_x|\delta_x + |\mathbf{n}_y|\delta_y + |\mathbf{n}_z|\delta_z.$$

Computing spawned ray origins by offsetting along the surface normal in this way has a few advantages: assuming that the surface is locally planar (a reasonable assumption, especially at the very small scale of the intersection point error bounds), moving along the normal allows us to get from one side of the surface to the other while moving the shortest distance. In general, minimizing the distance that ray origins are offset is desirable for maintaining shadow and reflection detail.

OffsetRayOrigin() is a short function that implements this computation.

⟨*Ray Inline Functions*⟩ ≡
```
Point3f OffsetRayOrigin(Point3fi pi, Normal3f n, Vector3f w) {
    ⟨Find vector offset to corner of error bounds and compute initial po 381⟩
    ⟨Round offset point po away from p 382⟩
    return po;
}
```

⟨*Find vector* offset *to corner of error bounds and compute initial po*⟩ ≡   **381**
```
Float d = Dot(Abs(n), pi.Error());
Vector3f offset = d * Vector3f(n);
if (Dot(w, n) < 0)
    offset = -offset;
Point3f po = Point3f(pi) + offset;
```

We also must handle round-off error when computing the offset point: when offset is added to p, the result will in general need to be rounded to the nearest floating-point value. In turn, it may be rounded down toward p such that the resulting point is in the interior of the error box rather than on its boundary (Figure 6.46). Therefore, the offset point is rounded away from p here to ensure that it is not inside the box.[15]

Alternatively, the floating-point rounding mode could have been set to round toward plus or minus infinity (based on the sign of the value). Changing the rounding mode is fairly

---

15 The observant reader may now wonder about the effect of rounding error when computing the error bounds that are passed into this function. Indeed, these bounds should also be computed with rounding toward positive infinity. We ignore that issue under the expectation that the additional offset of one ulp here will be enough to cover that error.

expensive on many processors, so we just shift the floating-point value by one ulp here. This will sometimes cause a value already outside of the error box to go slightly farther outside it, but because the floating-point spacing is so small, this is not a problem in practice.

⟨*Round offset point* po *away from* p⟩ ≡   **381**
```
for (int i = 0; i < 3; ++i) {
    if (offset[i] > 0)      po[i] = NextFloatUp(po[i]);
    else if (offset[i] < 0) po[i] = NextFloatDown(po[i]);
}
```

For convenience, Interaction provides two variants of this functionality via methods that perform the ray offset computation using its stored position and surface normal. The first takes a ray direction, like the stand-alone OffsetRayOrigin() function.

⟨*Interaction Public Methods*⟩ +≡   **136**
```
Point3f OffsetRayOrigin(Vector3f w) const {
    return pbrt::OffsetRayOrigin(pi, n, w);
}
```

The second takes a position for the ray's destination that is used to compute a direction w to pass to the first method.

⟨*Interaction Public Methods*⟩ +≡   **136**
```
Point3f OffsetRayOrigin(Point3f pt) const {
    return OffsetRayOrigin(pt - p());
}
```

There are also some helper functions for the Ray class that generate rays leaving intersection points that account for these offsets.

⟨*Ray Inline Functions*⟩ +≡
```
Ray SpawnRay(Point3fi pi, Normal3f n, Float time, Vector3f d) {
    return Ray(OffsetRayOrigin(pi, n, d), d, time);
}
```

⟨*Ray Inline Functions*⟩ +≡
```
Ray SpawnRayTo(Point3fi pFrom, Normal3f n, Float time, Point3f pTo) {
    Vector3f d = pTo - Point3f(pFrom);
    return SpawnRay(pFrom, n, time, d);
}
```

To generate a ray between two points requires offsets at both endpoints before the vector between them is computed.

⟨*Ray Inline Functions*⟩ +≡
```
Ray SpawnRayTo(Point3fi pFrom, Normal3f nFrom, Float time, Point3fi pTo,
               Normal3f nTo) {
    Point3f pf = OffsetRayOrigin(pFrom, nFrom,
                                 Point3f(pTo) - Point3f(pFrom));
    Point3f pt = OffsetRayOrigin(pTo, nTo, pf - Point3f(pTo));
    return Ray(pf, pt - pf, time);
}
```

We can also implement Interaction methods that generate rays leaving intersection points.

⟨*Interaction Public Methods*⟩ +≡   136
```
RayDifferential SpawnRay(Vector3f d) const {
    return RayDifferential(OffsetRayOrigin(d), d, time, GetMedium(d));
}
```

⟨*Interaction Public Methods*⟩ +≡   136
```
Ray SpawnRayTo(Point3f p2) const {
    Ray r = pbrt::SpawnRayTo(pi, n, time, p2);
    r.medium = GetMedium(r.d);
    return r;
}
```

A variant of Interaction::SpawnRayTo() that takes an Interaction is similar and not included here.

The ShapeSampleContext class also provides OffsetRayOrigin() and SpawnRay() helper methods that correspond to the ones we have added to Interaction here. Their implementations are essentially the same, so they are not included here.

The approach we have developed so far addresses the effect of floating-point error at the origins of rays leaving surfaces; there is a related issue for shadow rays to area light sources: we would like to find any intersections with shapes that are close to the light source and actually occlude it, while avoiding reporting incorrect intersections with the surface of the light source. Unfortunately, our implementation does not address this issue, so we set the tMax value of shadow rays to be just under one so that they stop before the surface of light sources.

⟨*Mathematical Constants*⟩ ≡
```
constexpr Float ShadowEpsilon = 0.0001f;
```

One last issue must be dealt with in order to maintain robust spawned ray origins: error introduced when performing transformations. Given a ray in one coordinate system where its origin was carefully computed to be on the appropriate side of some surface, transforming that ray to another coordinate system may introduce error in the transformed origin such that the origin is no longer on the correct side of the surface it was spawned from.

Therefore, whenever a ray is transformed by the Ray variant of Transform::operator() (which was implemented in Section 3.10.4), its origin is advanced to the edge of the bounds on the error that was introduced by the transformation. This ensures that the origin conservatively remains on the correct side of the surface it was spawned from, if any.

⟨*Offset ray origin to edge of error bounds and compute* tMax⟩ ≡   132
```
if (Float lengthSquared = LengthSquared(d); lengthSquared > 0) {
    Float dt = Dot(Abs(d), o.Error()) / lengthSquared;
    o += d * dt;
    if (tMax)
        *tMax -= dt;
}
```

6.8.7 AVOIDING INTERSECTIONS BEHIND RAY ORIGINS

Bounding the error in computed intersection points allows us to compute ray origins that are guaranteed to be on the right side of the surface so that a ray with infinite precision would not incorrectly intersect the surface it is leaving. However, a second source of rounding error must also be addressed: the error in parametric *t* values computed for ray–shape intersections. Rounding error can lead to an intersection algorithm computing a value $t > 0$ for the intersection point even though the t value for the actual intersection is negative (and thus should be ignored).

It is possible to show that some intersection test algorithms always return a t value with the correct sign; this is the best case, as no further computation is needed to bound the actual error in the computed t value. For example, consider the ray–axis-aligned slab computation: $t = (x \ominus o_x) \oslash \mathbf{d}_x$. The IEEE floating-point standard guarantees that if $a > b$, then $a \ominus b \geq 0$ (and if $a < b$, then $a \ominus b \leq 0$). To see why this is so, note that if $a > b$, then the real number $a - b$ must be greater than zero. When rounded to a floating-point number, the result must be either zero or a positive float; there is no a way a negative floating-point number could be the closest floating-point number. Second, floating-point division returns the correct sign; these together guarantee that the sign of the computed t value is correct. (Or that $t = 0$, but this case is fine, since our test for an intersection is carefully chosen to be $t > 0$.)

For shape intersection routines that are based on the Interval class, the computed t value in the end has an error bound associated with it, and no further computation is necessary to perform this test. See the definition of the fragment ⟨*Check quadric shape* t0 *and* t1 *for nearest intersection*⟩ in Section 6.2.2.

Triangles

Interval introduces computational overhead that we would prefer to avoid for more commonly used shapes where efficient intersection code is more important. For these shapes, we can derive efficient-to-evaluate conservative bounds on the error in computed t values. The ray–triangle intersection algorithm in Section 6.5.3 computes a final t value by computing three edge function values e_i and using them to compute a barycentric-weighted sum of transformed vertex z coordinates, z_i:

$$t = \frac{e_0 z_0 + e_1 z_1 + e_2 z_2}{e_0 + e_1 + e_2}. \tag{6.32}$$

By successively bounding the error in these terms and then in the final t value, we can conservatively check that it is positive.

⟨*Ensure that computed triangle* t *is conservatively greater than zero*⟩ ≡   303
    ⟨*Compute* δ_z *term for triangle* t *error bounds* 384⟩
    ⟨*Compute* δ_x *and* δ_y *terms for triangle* t *error bounds* 385⟩
    ⟨*Compute* δ_e *term for triangle* t *error bounds* 385⟩
    ⟨*Compute* δ_t *term for triangle* t *error bounds and check* t 385⟩

Given a ray r with origin o, direction $\mathbf{d}$, and a triangle vertex p, the projected z coordinate is

$$z = (1 \oslash \mathbf{d}_z) \otimes (\mathbf{p}_z \ominus o_z).$$

Applying the usual approach, we can find that the maximum error in z_i for each of three vertices of the triangle $\mathbf{p}_i$ is bounded by $\gamma_3 |z_i|$, and we can thus find a conservative upper bound for the error in *any* of the z positions by taking the maximum of these errors:

$$\delta_z = \gamma_3 \max_i |z_i|.$$

⟨*Compute* δ_z *term for triangle* t *error bounds*⟩ ≡   384
    Float maxZt = MaxComponentValue(Abs(Vector3f(p0t.z, p1t.z, p2t.z)));
    Float deltaZ = gamma(3) * maxZt;

The edge function values are computed as the difference of two products of transformed x and y vertex positions:

$$e_0 = (x_1 \otimes y_2) \ominus (y_1 \otimes x_2)$$
$$e_1 = (x_2 \otimes y_0) \ominus (y_2 \otimes x_0)$$
$$e_2 = (x_0 \otimes y_1) \ominus (y_0 \otimes x_1).$$

Bounds for the error in the transformed positions x_i and y_i are

$$\delta_x = \gamma_5(\max_i |x_i| + \max_i |z_i|)$$
$$\delta_y = \gamma_5(\max_i |y_i| + \max_i |z_i|).$$

⟨*Compute δ_x and δ_y terms for triangle t error bounds*⟩ ≡   384
```
Float maxXt = MaxComponentValue(Abs(Vector3f(p0t.x, p1t.x, p2t.x)));
Float maxYt = MaxComponentValue(Abs(Vector3f(p0t.y, p1t.y, p2t.y)));
Float deltaX = gamma(5) * (maxXt + maxZt);
Float deltaY = gamma(5) * (maxYt + maxZt);
```

Taking the maximum error over all three of the vertices, the $x_i \otimes y_j$ products in the edge functions are bounded by

$$(\max_i |x_i| + \delta_x)(\max_i |y_i| + \delta_y)(1 \pm \epsilon_m),$$

which have an absolute error bound of

$$\delta_{xy} = \gamma_1 \max_i |x_i| \max_i |y_i| + \delta_y \max_i |x_i| + \delta_x \max_i |y_i| + \cdots.$$

Dropping the (negligible) higher-order terms of products of γ and δ terms, the error bound on the difference of two x and y terms for the edge function is

$$\delta_e = 2(\gamma_2 \max_i |x_i| \max_i |y_i| + \delta_y \max_i |x_i| + \delta_x \max_i |y_i|).$$

⟨*Compute δ_e term for triangle t error bounds*⟩ ≡   384
```
Float deltaE = 2 * (gamma(2) * maxXt * maxYt + deltaY * maxXt +
                    deltaX * maxYt);
```

Again bounding error by taking the maximum of error over all the e_i terms, the error bound for the computed value of the numerator of t in Equation (6.32) is

$$\delta_t = 3(\gamma_3 \max_i |e_i| \max_i |z_i| + \delta_e \max_i |z_i| + \delta_z \max_i |e_i|).$$

A computed t value (before normalization by the sum of e_i) must be greater than this value for it to be accepted as a valid intersection that definitely has a positive t value.

⟨*Compute δ_t term for triangle t error bounds and check* t⟩ ≡   384
```
Float maxE = MaxComponentValue(Abs(Vector3f(e0, e1, e2)));
Float deltaT = 3 * (gamma(3) * maxE * maxZt + deltaE * maxZt +
                    deltaZ * maxE) * std::abs(invDet);
if (t <= deltaT)
    return {};
```

Float 23
gamma() 368
Tuple3::Abs() 85
Tuple3::MaxComponentValue()
  85
Vector3f 86

Although it may seem that we have made a number of choices to compute looser bounds than we might have, in practice the bounds on error in t are extremely small. For a regular scene that fills a bounding box roughly ± 10 in each dimension, our t error bounds near ray origins are generally around 10^{-7}.

Bilinear Patches

Recall from Section 6.6.1 that the t value for a bilinear patch intersection is found by taking the determinant of a 3×3 matrix. Each matrix element includes round-off error from the series of floating-point computations used to compute its value. While it is possible to derive bounds on the error in the computed t using a similar approach as was used for triangle intersections, the algebra becomes unwieldy because the computation involves many more operations.

Therefore, here we compute an epsilon value that is based on the magnitudes of all of the inputs of the computation of t.

⟨*Find epsilon* eps *to ensure that candidate t is greater than zero*⟩ ≡   **332**
```
    Float eps = gamma(10) *
        (MaxComponentValue(Abs(ray.o)) + MaxComponentValue(Abs(ray.d)) +
         MaxComponentValue(Abs(p00))   + MaxComponentValue(Abs(p10))   +
         MaxComponentValue(Abs(p01))   + MaxComponentValue(Abs(p11)));
```

6.8.8 DISCUSSION

Minimizing and bounding numerical error in other geometric computations (e.g., partial derivatives of surface positions, interpolated texture coordinates, etc.) are much less important than they are for the positions of ray intersections. In a similar vein, the computations involving color and light in physically based rendering generally do not present trouble with respect to round-off error; they involve sums of products of positive numbers (usually with reasonably close magnitudes); hence catastrophic cancellation is not a commonly encountered issue. Furthermore, these sums are of few enough terms that accumulated error is small: the variance that is inherent in the Monte Carlo algorithms used for them dwarfs any floating-point error in computing them.

Interestingly enough, we saw an increase of roughly 20% in overall ray-tracing execution time after replacing the previous version of pbrt's old *ad hoc* method to avoid incorrect self-intersections with the method described in this section. (In comparison, rendering with double-precision floating point causes an increase in rendering time of roughly 30%.) Profiling showed that very little of the additional time was due to the additional computation to find error bounds; this is not surprising, as the incremental computation our approach requires is limited—most of the error bounds are just scaled sums of absolute values of terms that have already been computed.

The majority of this slowdown is due to an increase in ray–object intersection tests. The reason for this increase in intersection tests was first identified by Wächter (2008, p. 30); when ray origins are very close to shape surfaces, more nodes of intersection acceleration hierarchies must be visited when tracing spawned rays than if overly loose offsets are used. Thus, more intersection tests are performed near the ray origin. While this reduction in performance is unfortunate, it is a direct result of the greater accuracy of the method; it is the price to be paid for more accurate resolution of valid nearby intersections.

FURTHER READING

An Introduction to Ray Tracing has an extensive survey of algorithms for ray–shape intersection (Glassner 1989a). Goldstein and Nagel (1971) discussed ray–quadric intersections, and Heckbert (1984) discussed the mathematics of quadrics for graphics applications in detail, with many citations to literature in mathematics and other fields. Hanrahan (1983) described a system that automates the process of deriving a ray intersection routine for surfaces defined by implicit polynomials; his system emits C source code to perform the intersection test and normal computation for a surface described by a given equation. Mitchell (1990) showed

Float 23
gamma() 368
Tuple3::Abs() 85
Tuple3::MaxComponentValue()
     85

that interval arithmetic could be applied to develop algorithms for robustly computing intersections with implicit surfaces that cannot be described by polynomials and are thus more difficult to accurately compute intersections for (more recent work in this area was done by Knoll et al. (2009)).

Other notable early papers related to ray–shape intersection include Kajiya's (1983) work on computing intersections with surfaces of revolution and procedurally generated fractal terrains. Fournier et al.'s (1982) paper on rendering procedural stochastic models and Hart et al.'s (1989) paper on finding intersections with fractals illustrate the broad range of shape representations that can be used with ray-tracing algorithms.

The ray–triangle intersection test in Section 6.5 was developed by Woop et al. (2013). See Möller and Trumbore (1997) for another widely used ray–triangle intersection algorithm. A ray–quadrilateral intersection routine was developed by Lagae and Dutré (2005). An interesting approach for developing a fast ray–triangle intersection routine was introduced by Kensler and Shirley (2006): they implemented a program that performed a search across the space of mathematically equivalent ray–triangle tests, automatically generating software implementations of variations and then benchmarking them. In the end, they found a more efficient ray–triangle routine than had been in use previously.

Kajiya (1982) developed the first algorithm for computing intersections with parametric patches. Subsequent work on more efficient techniques for direct ray intersection with patches includes papers by Stürzlinger (1998), Martin et al. (2000), Roth et al. (2001), and Benthin et al. (2006), who also included additional references to previous work. Related to this, Ogaki and Tokuyoshi (2011) introduced a technique for directly intersecting smooth surfaces generated from triangle meshes with per-vertex normals.

Ramsey et al. (2004) described an algorithm for computing intersections with bilinear patches, though double-precision computation was required for robust results. Reshetov (2019) derived a more efficient algorithm that operates in single precision; that algorithm is used in pbrt's `BilinearPatch` implementation. See Akenine-Möller et al. (2018) for explanations of the algorithms used in its implementation that are related to the distance between lines.

Phong and Crow (1975) introduced the idea of interpolating per-vertex shading normals to give the appearance of smooth surfaces from polygonal meshes. The use of shading normals may cause rays reflected from a surface to be on the wrong side of the true surface; Reshetov et al. (2010) described a normal interpolation technique that avoids this problem.

The layout of triangle meshes in memory can have a measurable impact on performance. In general, if triangles that are close together in 3D space are close together in memory, cache hit rates will be higher, and overall system performance will benefit. See Yoon et al. (2005) and Yoon and Lindstrom (2006) for algorithms for creating cache-friendly mesh layouts in memory. Relatedly, reducing the storage required for meshes can improve performance, in addition to making it possible to render more complex scenes; see for example Lauterbach et al. (2008).

Subdivision surfaces are a widely used representation of smooth surfaces; they were invented by Doo and Sabin (1978) and Catmull and Clark (1978). Warren's book provides a good introduction to them (Warren 2002). Müller et al. (2003) described an approach that refines a subdivision surface on demand for the rays to be tested for intersection with it, and Benthin et al. (2007, 2015) described a related approach. A more memory-efficient approach was described by Tejima et al. (2015), who converted subdivision surfaces to Bézier patches and

BilinearPatch   328

intersected rays with those. Previous editions of this book included a section in this chapter on the implementation of subdivision surfaces, which may also be of interest.

The curve intersection algorithm in Section 6.7 is based on the approach developed by Nakamaru and Ohno (2002). Earlier methods for computing ray intersections with generalized cylinders are also applicable to rendering curves, though they are much less efficient (Bronsvoort and Klok 1985; de Voogt et al. 2000). Binder and Keller (2018) improved the recursive culling of curve intersections using cylinders to bound the curve in place of axis-aligned bounding boxes. Their approach is better suited for GPUs than the current implementation in the Curve shape, as it uses a compact bit field to record work to be done, in place of recursive evaluation.

More efficient intersection algorithms for curves have recently been developed by Reshetov (2017) and Reshetov and Luebke (2018). Related is a tube primitive described by a poly-line with a specified radius at each vertex that Han et al. (2019) provided an efficient intersection routine for.

One challenge with rendering thin geometry like hair and fur is that thin geometry may require many pixel samples to be accurately resolved, which in turn increases rendering time. One approach to this problem was described by Qin et al. (2014), who used cone tracing for rendering fur, where narrow cones are traced instead of rays. In turn, all the curves that intersect a cone can be considered in computing the cone's contribution, allowing high-quality rendering with a small number of cones per pixel.

An excellent introduction to differential geometry was written by Gray (1993); Section 14.3 of his book presents the Weingarten equations.

Intersection Accuracy

Higham's (2002) book on floating-point computation is excellent; it also develops the γ_n notation that we have used in Section 6.8. Other good references to this topic are Wilkinson (1994) and Goldberg (1991). While we have derived floating-point error bounds manually, see the *Gappa* system by Daumas and Melquiond (2010) for a tool that automatically derives forward error bounds of floating-point computations. The *Herbgrind* (Sanchez-Stern et al. 2018) system implements an interesting approach, automatically finding floating-point computations that suffer from excessive error during the course of a program's execution.

The incorrect self-intersection problem has been a known problem for ray-tracing practitioners for quite some time (Haines 1989; Amanatides and Mitchell 1990). In addition to offsetting rays by an "epsilon" at their origin, approaches that have been suggested include ignoring intersections with the object that was previously intersected; "root polishing" (Haines 1989; Woo et al. 1996), where the computed intersection point is refined to become more numerically accurate; and using higher-precision floating-point representations (e.g., double instead of float).

Kalra and Barr (1989) and Dammertz and Keller (2006) developed algorithms for numerically robust intersections based on recursively subdividing object bounding boxes, discarding boxes that do not encompass the object's surface, and discarding boxes missed by the ray. Both of these approaches are much less efficient than traditional ray–object intersection algorithms as well as the techniques introduced in Section 6.8.

Ize showed how to perform numerically robust ray–bounding box intersections (Ize 2013); his approach is implemented in Section 6.8.2. (With a more careful derivation, he showed that a scale factor of $2\gamma_2$ can be used to increase tMax, rather than the $2\gamma_3$ we derived.) Wächter (2008) discussed self-intersection issues in his thesis; he suggested recomputing the intersection point starting from the initial intersection (root polishing) and offsetting

Curve 346

spawned rays along the normal by a fixed small fraction of the intersection point's magnitude. The approach implemented in this chapter uses his approach of offsetting ray origins along the normal but uses conservative bounds on the offsets based on the numerical error present in computed intersection points. (As it turns out, our bounds are generally tighter than Wächter's offsets while also being provably conservative.)

The method used for computing accurate discriminants for ray–quadratic intersections in Section 6.8.3 is due to Hearn and Baker (2004), via Haines et al. (2019).

Geometric accuracy has seen much more attention in computational geometry than in rendering. Examples include Salesin et al. (1989), who introduced techniques to derive robust primitive operations for computational geometry that accounted for floating-point round-off error, and Shewchuk (1997), who applied adaptive-precision floating-point arithmetic to geometric predicates, using just enough precision to compute a correct result for given input values.

The precision requirements of ray tracing have implications beyond practical implementation, which has been our focus. Reif et al. (1994) showed how to construct Turing machines based entirely on ray tracing and the geometric optics, which implies that ray tracing is *undecidable* in the sense of complexity theory. Yet in practice, optical computing systems can be constructed, though they are not able to solve undecidable problems. Blakey (2012) showed that this can be explained by careful consideration of such optical Turing machines' precision requirements, which can grow exponentially.

Sampling Shapes

Turk (1990) described two approaches for uniformly sampling the surface area of triangles. The approach implemented in SampleUniformTriangle(), which is more efficient and better preserves sample stratification than the algorithms given by Turk, is due to Talbot (2011) and Heitz (2019). Shirley et al. (1996) derived methods for sampling a number of other shapes, and Arvo and Novins (2007) showed how to sample convex quadrilaterals.

The aforementioned approaches are all based on warping samples from the unit square to the surface of the shape; an interesting alternative was given by Basu and Owen (2015, 2017), who showed how to recursively decompose triangles and disks to directly generate low-discrepancy points on their surfaces. Marques et al. (2013) showed how to generate low-discrepancy samples directly on the unit sphere; see also Christensen's report (2018), which shows an error reduction from imposing structure on the distribution of multiple sample points on disk light sources.

Uniformly sampling the visible area of a shape from a reference point is an improvement to uniform area sampling for direct lighting calculations. Gardner et al. (1987) and Zimmerman (1995) derived methods to do so for cylinders, and Wang et al. (2006) found an algorithm to sample the visible area of cones. (For planar shapes like triangles, the visible area is trivially the entire area.)

Uniform solid angle sampling of shapes has also seen attention by a number of researchers. Wang (1992) introduced an approach for solid angle sampling of spheres. Arvo showed how to sample the projection of a triangle on the sphere of directions with respect to a reference point (Arvo 1995b); his approach is implemented in SampleSphericalTriangle(). (A more efficient approach to solid angle sampling of triangles was recently developed by Peters (2021b, Section 5).) Ureña et al. (2013) and Pekelis and Hery (2014) developed analogous techniques for sampling quadrilateral light sources; Ureña et al.'s method is used in SampleSphericalRectangle(). (To better understand these techniques for sampling projected polygons, Donnay's book on spherical trigonometry provides helpful background (Donnay

1945).) The approach implemented in Section 6.2.4 to convert an angle (θ, ϕ) in a cone to a point on a sphere was derived by Akalin (2015).

The algorithm for inverting the spherical triangle sampling algorithm that is implemented in `InvertSphericalTriangleSample()` is due to Arvo (2001b).

Gamito (2016) presented an approach for uniform solid angle sampling of disk and cylindrical lights based on bounding the solid angle they subtend in order to fit a quadrilateral, which is then sampled using Ureña et al.'s method (2013). Samples that do not correspond to points on the light source are rejected. A related approach was developed by Tsai et al. (2006), who approximate shapes with collections of triangles that are then sampled by solid angle. Guillén et al. (2017) subsequently developed an algorithm for directly sampling disks by solid angle that avoids rejection sampling.

Spheres are the only shapes for which we are aware of algorithms for direct sampling of their projected solid angle. An algorithm to do so was presented by Ureña and Georgiev (2018). Peters and Dachsbacher developed a more efficient approach (2019) and Peters (2019) described how to use this method to compute the PDF associated with a direction so that it can be used with multiple importance sampling.

A variety of additional techniques for projected solid angle sampling have been developed. Arvo (2001a) described a general framework for deriving sampling algorithms and showed its application to projected solid angle sampling of triangles, though numeric inversion of the associated CDF is required. Ureña (2000) approximated projected solid angle sampling of triangles by progressively decomposing them into smaller triangles until solid angle sampling is effectively equivalent. The approach based on warping uniform samples to approximate projected solid angle sampling that we implemented for triangles and quadrilateral bilinear patches was described by Hart et al. (2020). Peters (2021b) has recently shown how to efficiently and accurately perform projected solid angle sampling of polygons.

EXERCISES

⊘ **6.1** One nice property of mesh-based shapes like triangle meshes and subdivision surfaces is that the shape's vertices can be transformed into rendering space, so that it is not necessary to transform rays into object space before performing ray intersection tests. Interestingly enough, it is possible to do the same thing for ray–quadric intersections.

The implicit forms of the quadrics in this chapter were all of the form

$$ax^2 + bxy + cxz + dy^2 + eyz + fz^2 + g = 0,$$

where some of the constants $a \ldots g$ were zero. More generally, we can define quadric surfaces by the equation

$$ax^2 + by^2 + cz^2 + 2dxy + 2eyz + 2fxz + 2gx + 2hy + 2iz + j = 0,$$

where most of the parameters $a \ldots j$ do not directly correspond to the earlier $a \ldots g$. In this form, the quadric can be represented by a 4×4 symmetric matrix $\mathbf{Q}$:

$$
\begin{bmatrix} x & y & z & 1 \end{bmatrix}
\begin{pmatrix} a & d & f & g \\ d & b & e & h \\ f & e & c & i \\ g & h & i & j \end{pmatrix}
\begin{bmatrix} x \\ y \\ z \\ 1 \end{bmatrix}
= \mathbf{p}^T \mathbf{Q} \mathbf{p} = 0.
$$

InvertSphericalTriangleSample()
325

Given this representation, first show that the matrix $\mathbf{Q}'$ representing a quadric transformed by the matrix $\mathbf{M}$ is

$$\mathbf{Q}' = (\mathbf{M}^T)^{-1}\mathbf{Q}\mathbf{M}^{-1}.$$

To do so, show that for any point p where $p^T \mathbf{Q} p = 0$, if we apply a transformation $\mathbf{M}$ to p and compute $p' = \mathbf{M}p$, we would like to find $\mathbf{Q}'$ so that $(p')^T \mathbf{Q}' p' = 0$.

Next, substitute the ray equation into the earlier, more general quadric equation to compute coefficients for the quadratic equation in terms of entries of the matrix $\mathbf{Q}$ to pass to the `Quadratic()` function.

Now implement this approach in pbrt and use it instead of the original quadric intersection routines. Note that you will still need to transform the resulting rendering space hit points into object space to test against θ_{max}, if it is not 2π, and so on. How does performance compare to the original scheme?

● 6.2 Transforming the object-space bounding box of a quadric to rendering space does not necessarily give an optimal bounding box. However, the matrix form of a quadric described in Exercise 6.1 can also be applied to computing optimal bounds. Read the article by Barnes (2014) on this topic and implement the approach he described in pbrt. How much are bounding boxes improved with this approach? Measure the effect of your changes on rendering performance for a scene with many transformed quadrics.

● 6.3 Improve the object-space bounding box routines for the quadrics to properly account for $\phi_{max} < 3\pi/2$, and compute tighter bounding boxes when possible. How much does this improve performance when rendering scenes with partial quadric shapes?

● 6.4 There is room to optimize the implementations of the various quadric primitives in pbrt in a number of ways. For example, for complete spheres some of the tests in the intersection routine related to partial spheres are unnecessary. Furthermore, some of the quadrics have calls to trigonometric functions that could be turned into simpler expressions using insight about the geometry of the particular primitives. Investigate ways to speed up these methods. How much does doing so improve the overall run time of pbrt when rendering scenes with quadrics?

● 6.5 Fix the buggy `Sphere::Sample()` and `Disk::Sample()` methods, which currently do not properly account for partial spheres and disks when they sample points on the surface. Create a scene that demonstrates the error from the current implementations and for which your solution is clearly an improvement.

● 6.6 It is possible to derive a sampling method for cylinder area light sources that only chooses points over the visible area as seen from the receiving point, similar to the improved sphere sampling method in this chapter (Gardner et al. 1987; Zimmerman 1995). Write a new implementation of `Cylinder::Sample()` that implements such an algorithm. Verify that pbrt still generates correct images with your method, and measure how much the improved version reduces variance for a fixed number of samples taken. How much does it improve efficiency? How do you explain any discrepancy between the amount of reduction in variance and the amount of improvement in efficiency?

● 6.7 Implement one of the approaches for sampling the spheres according to the projected solid angle in their visible region (Ureña and Georgiev 2018; Peters and

Dachsbacher 2019). Measure the change in pbrt's execution time when the alternative algorithm is used and discuss your results.

Then, measure the MSE of pbrt's current approach as well as your approach for a few scenes with spherical light sources, using an image rendered with thousands of samples per pixel as a reference. How do the results differ if the light is always unoccluded versus if it is sometimes partially occluded? How does the BSDF of scene surfaces affect the results?

● **6.8** Currently pbrt recomputes the partial derivatives $\partial p/\partial u$ and $\partial p/\partial v$ for triangles every time they are needed, even though they are constant for each triangle. Precompute these vectors and analyze the speed/storage trade-off, especially for large triangle meshes. How do the depth complexity of the scene and the size of triangles in the image affect this trade-off?

● **6.9** Implement a general polygon primitive that supports an arbitrary number of vertices and convex or concave polygons as a new Shape in pbrt. You can assume that a valid polygon has been provided and that all the vertices of the polygon lie on the same plane, although you might want to issue a warning when this is not the case.

An efficient technique for computing ray–polygon intersections is to find the plane equation for the polygon from its normal and a point on the plane. Then compute the intersection of the ray with that plane and project the intersection point and the polygon vertices to 2D. You can then apply a 2D point-in-polygon test to determine if the point is inside the polygon. An easy way to do this is to effectively do a 2D ray-tracing computation: intersect the ray with each of the edge segments, and count how many it goes through. If it goes through an odd number of them, the point is inside the polygon and there is an intersection. See Figure 6.47 for an illustration of this idea.

You may find it helpful to read the article by Haines (1994) that surveys a number of approaches for efficient point-in-polygon tests. Some of the techniques described there may be helpful for optimizing this test. Furthermore, Section 13.3.3 of Schneider and Eberly (2003) discusses strategies for getting all the corner cases right: for example, when the 2D ray is aligned precisely with an edge or passes through a vertex of the polygon.

● **6.10** Constructive solid geometry (CSG) is a solid modeling technique where complex shapes are built up by considering the union, intersection, and differences of more primitive shapes. For example, a sphere could be used to create pits in a cylinder if

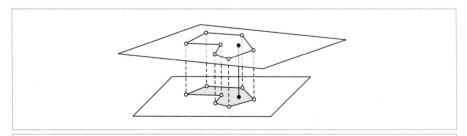

Figure 6.47: A ray–polygon intersection test can be performed by finding the point where the ray intersects the polygon's plane, projecting the hit point and polygon vertices onto an axis-aligned plane, and doing a 2D point-in-polygon test there.

Shape 261

a shape was modeled as the difference of a cylinder and set of spheres that partially overlapped it. See Hoffmann (1989) for further information about CSG.

Add support for CSG to pbrt and render images that demonstrate interesting shapes that can be rendered using CSG. You may want to read Roth (1982), which first described how ray tracing could be used to render models described by CSG, as well as Amanatides and Mitchell (1990), which discusses accuracy-related issues for CSG ray tracing.

❷ **6.11** *Procedurally described parametric surfaces*: Write a Shape that takes a general mathematical expression of the form $f(u, v) \rightarrow (x, y, z)$ that describes a parametric surface as a function of (u, v). Evaluate the given function at a grid of (u, v) positions, and create a bilinear patch mesh that approximates the given surface. Render images of interesting shapes using your new Shape.

❷ **6.12** *Adaptive curve refinement*: Adjust the number of levels of recursive refinement used for intersection with Curve shapes based on the on-screen area that they cover. One approach is to take advantage of the RayDifferential class, which represents the image space area that a given ray represents. (However, currently, only Rays— not RayDifferentials—are passed to the Shape::Intersect() method implementation, so you would need to modify other parts of the system to make ray differentials available.) Alternatively, you could modify the Camera to provide information about the projected length of vectors between points in rendering space on the image plane and make the camera available during Curve intersection.

Render images that show the benefit of adaptive refinement when the camera is close to curves. Measure performance, varying the camera-to-curves distance. Does performance improve when the camera is far away? How does it change when the camera is close?

❷ **6.13** Implement one of the more efficient ray–curve intersection algorithms described by Reshetov (2017) or by Reshetov and Luebke (2018). Measure the performance of pbrt's current Curve implementation as well as your new one and discuss the results. Do rendered images match with both approaches? Can you find differences in the intersections returned that lead to changes in images, especially when the camera is close to a curve? Explain your findings.

❸ **6.14** *Ray-tracing point-sampled geometry*: Extending methods for rendering complex models represented as a collection of point samples (Levoy and Whitted 1985; Pfister et al. 2000; Rusinkiewicz and Levoy 2000), Schaufler and Jensen (2000) have described a method for intersecting rays with collections of oriented point samples in space. Their algorithm probabilistically determined that an intersection has occurred when a ray approaches a sufficient local density of point samples and computes a surface normal with a weighted average of the nearby samples. Read their paper and extend pbrt to support a point-sampled geometry shape. Do any of pbrt's basic interfaces need to be extended or generalized to support a shape like this?

❸ **6.15** *Deformation motion blur*: The TransformedPrimitive in Section 7.1.2 of Chapter 7 supports animated shapes via transformations of primitives that vary over time. However, this type of animation is not general enough to represent a triangle mesh where each vertex has a position given at the start time and another one at the end time. (For example, this type of animation description can be used to describe a running character model where different parts of the body are moving in different ways.) Implement a more general `Triangle` or `BilinearPatch` shape that supports specifying vertex positions at the start and end of frame and interpolates between them based on the ray time passed to the intersection methods. Be sure to update the bounding routines appropriately.

Meshes with very large amounts of motion may exhibit poor performance due to individual triangles or patches sweeping out large bounding boxes and thus many intersection tests being performed that do not hit the shape. Can you come up with approaches that could be used to reduce the impact of this problem?

● 6.16   *Implicit functions*: Just as implicit definitions of the quadric shapes are a useful starting point for deriving ray-intersection algorithms, more complex implicit functions can also be used to define interesting shapes. In particular, difficult-to-model organic shapes, water drops, and so on can be well represented by implicit surfaces. Blinn (1982a) introduced the idea of directly rendering implicit surfaces, and Wyvill and Wyvill (1989) gave a basis function for implicit surfaces with a number of advantages compared to Blinn's.

Implement a method for finding ray intersections with implicit surfaces and add it to pbrt. You may wish to read papers by Kalra and Barr (1989), Hart (1996), and Sabbadin and Droske (2021) for methods for ray tracing them. Mitchell's algorithm for robust ray intersections with implicit surfaces using interval arithmetic gives another effective method for finding these intersections (Mitchell 1990), and more recently Knoll et al. (2009) described refinements to this idea. You may find an approach along these lines easier to implement than the others. See Moore's book on interval arithmetic as needed for reference (Moore 1966).

● 6.17   *L-systems*: A very successful technique for procedurally modeling plants was introduced to graphics by Alvy Ray Smith (1984), who applied *Lindenmayer systems* (L-systems) to model branching plant structures. Prusinkiewicz and collaborators have generalized this approach to encompass a much wider variety of types of plants and effects that determine their appearance (Prusinkiewicz 1986; Prusinkiewicz, James, and Mech 1994; Deussen et al. 1998; Prusinkiewicz et al. 2001). L-systems describe the branching structure of these types of shapes via a grammar. The grammar can be evaluated to form expressions that describe a topological representation of a plant, which can then be translated into a geometric representation. Add an L-system primitive to pbrt that takes a grammar as input and evaluates it to create the shape it describes.

● 6.18   Given an arbitrary point (x, y, z), what bound on the error from applying a scale transformation of $(2, 1, 4)$ is given by Equation (6.30)? How much error is actually introduced?

● 6.19   The quadric shapes all use the `Interval` class for their intersection tests in order to be able to bound the error in the computed t value so that intersections behind the ray origin are not incorrectly reported as intersections. First, measure the performance difference when using regular `Float`s for one or more quadrics when rendering a scene that includes those shapes. Next, manually derive conservative error bounds for t values computed by those shapes as was done for triangles in Section 6.8.7. Implement your method. You may find it useful to use the `Interval`

Interval 1057

class to empirically test your derivation's correctness. Measure the performance difference with your implementation.

⊘ **6.20** One detail thwarts the watertightness of the current `Triangle` shape implementation: the translation and shearing of triangle vertices introduces round-off error, which must be accounted for in the extent of triangles' bounding boxes; see Section 3.3 of Woop et al. (2013) for discussion (and a solution). Modify pbrt to incorporate a solution to this shortcoming. Can you find scenes where small image errors are eliminated thanks to your fix?

CHAPTER SEVEN

07 PRIMITIVES AND INTERSECTION ACCELERATION

The classes described in the last chapter focus exclusively on representing geometric properties of 3D objects. Although the Shape interface provides a convenient abstraction for geometric operations such as intersection and bounding, it is not sufficiently expressive to fully describe an object in a scene. For example, it is necessary to bind material properties to each shape in order to specify its appearance.

pbrt's CPU and GPU rendering paths diverge in how they address this issue. The classes in this chapter implement the approach used on the CPU. On the GPU, some of the details of how properties such as materials are associated with shapes are handled by the GPU's ray-tracing APIs and so a different representation is used there; the equivalents for the GPU are discussed in Section 15.3.6.

For the CPU, this chapter introduces the Primitive interface and provides a number of implementations that allow various properties of primitives to be specified. It then presents an additional Primitive implementation that acts as an aggregate—a container that can hold many primitives. This allows us to implement an *acceleration structure*—a data structure that helps reduce the otherwise $O(n)$ complexity of testing a ray for intersection with all n objects in a scene.

BVHAggregate 407
KdTreeAggregate 406
Shape 261

The acceleration structure, BVHAggregate, is based on building a hierarchy of bounding boxes around objects in the scene. The online edition of this book also includes the implementation of a second acceleration structure, KdTreeAggregate, which is based on adaptive recursive spatial subdivision. While many other acceleration structures have been proposed, almost all ray tracers today use one of these two. The "Further Reading" section at the end of this chapter has extensive references to other possibilities. Because construction and use of intersection acceleration structures is an integral part of GPU ray-tracing APIs, the acceleration structures in this chapter are only used on the CPU.

7.1 PRIMITIVE INTERFACE AND GEOMETRIC PRIMITIVES

The Primitive class defines the Primitive interface. It and the Primitive implementations that are described in this section are defined in the files cpu/primitive.h and cpu/primitive.cpp.

⟨*Primitive Definition*⟩ ≡
```
class Primitive
    : public TaggedPointer<SimplePrimitive, GeometricPrimitive,
                           TransformedPrimitive, AnimatedPrimitive,
                           BVHAggregate, KdTreeAggregate> {
  public:
    ⟨Primitive Interface 398⟩
};
```

The Primitive interface is composed of only three methods, each of which corresponds to a Shape method. The first, Bounds(), returns a bounding box that encloses the primitive's geometry in rendering space. There are many uses for such a bound; one of the most important is to place the Primitive in the acceleration data structures.

⟨*Primitive Interface*⟩ ≡   398
```
    Bounds3f Bounds() const;
```

The other two methods provide the two types of ray intersection tests.

⟨*Primitive Interface*⟩ +≡   398
```
    pstd::optional<ShapeIntersection> Intersect(const Ray &r,
                                                Float tMax = Infinity) const;
    bool IntersectP(const Ray &r, Float tMax = Infinity) const;
```

Upon finding an intersection, a Primitive's Intersect() method is also responsible for initializing a few member variables in the SurfaceInteraction in the ShapeIntersection that it returns. The first two are representations of the shape's material and its emissive properties, if it is itself an emitter. For convenience, SurfaceInteraction provides a method to set these, which reduces the risk of inadvertently not setting all of them. The second two are related to medium scattering properties and the fragment that initializes them will be described later, in Section 11.4.

⟨*SurfaceInteraction Public Methods*⟩ +≡   138
```
    void SetIntersectionProperties(Material mtl, Light area,
            const MediumInterface *primMediumInterface, Medium rayMedium) {
        material = mtl;
        areaLight = area;
        ⟨Set medium properties at surface intersection 716⟩
    }
```

⟨*SurfaceInteraction Public Members*⟩ +≡   138
```
    Material material;
    Light areaLight;
```

7.1.1 GEOMETRIC PRIMITIVES

The GeometricPrimitive class provides a basic implementation of the Primitive interface that stores a variety of properties that may be associated with a shape.

⟨*GeometricPrimitive Definition*⟩ ≡
```
class GeometricPrimitive {
  public:
    ⟨GeometricPrimitive Public Methods⟩
  private:
    ⟨GeometricPrimitive Private Members 399⟩
};
```

Each `GeometricPrimitive` holds a `Shape` with a description of its appearance properties, including its material, its emissive properties if it is a light source, the participating media on each side of its surface, and an optional *alpha texture*, which can be used to make some parts of a shape's surface disappear.

⟨*GeometricPrimitive Private Members*⟩ ≡   399
```
Shape shape;
Material material;
Light areaLight;
MediumInterface mediumInterface;
FloatTexture alpha;
```

The `GeometricPrimitive` constructor initializes these variables from the parameters passed to it. It is straightforward, so we do not include it here.

Most of the methods of the `Primitive` interface start out with a call to the corresponding `Shape` method. For example, its `Bounds()` method directly returns the bounds from the `Shape`.

⟨*GeometricPrimitive Method Definitions*⟩ ≡
```
Bounds3f GeometricPrimitive::Bounds() const {
    return shape.Bounds();
}
```

`GeometricPrimitive::Intersect()` calls the `Intersect()` method of its `Shape` to do the actual intersection test and to initialize a `ShapeIntersection` to describe the intersection, if any. If an intersection is found, then additional processing specific to the `GeometricPrimitive` is performed.

⟨*GeometricPrimitive Method Definitions*⟩ +≡
```
pstd::optional<ShapeIntersection>
GeometricPrimitive::Intersect(const Ray &r, Float tMax) const {
    pstd::optional<ShapeIntersection> si = shape.Intersect(r, tMax);
    if (!si) return {};
    ⟨Test intersection against alpha texture, if present 400⟩
    ⟨Initialize SurfaceInteraction after Shape intersection 401⟩
    return si;
}
```

If an alpha texture is associated with the shape, then the intersection point is tested against the alpha texture before a successful intersection is reported. (The definition of the texture interface and a number of implementations are in Chapter 10.) The alpha texture can be thought of as a scalar function over the shape's surface that indicates whether the surface is actually present at each point. An alpha value of 0 indicates that it is not, and 1 that it is. Alpha textures are useful for representing objects like leaves: a leaf might be modeled as a single triangle or bilinear patch, with an alpha texture cutting out the edges so that a detailed outline of a leaf remains.

⟨*Test intersection against alpha texture, if present*⟩ ≡   399
```
if (alpha) {
    if (Float a = alpha.Evaluate(si->intr); a < 1) {
        ⟨Possibly ignore intersection based on stochastic alpha test 400⟩
    }
}
```

If the alpha texture has a value of 0 or 1 at the intersection point, then it is easy to decide whether or not the intersection reported by the shape is valid. For intermediate alpha values, the correct answer is less clear.

One possibility would be to use a fixed threshold—for example, accepting all intersections with an alpha of 1 and ignoring them otherwise. However, this approach leads to hard transitions at the resulting boundary. Another option would be to return the alpha from the intersection method and leave calling code to handle it, effectively treating the surface as partially transparent at such points. However, that approach would not only make the Primitive intersection interfaces more complex, but it would place a new burden on integrators, requiring them to compute the shading at such intersection points as well as to trace an additional ray to find what was visible behind them.

A *stochastic alpha test* addresses these issues. With it, intersections with the shape are randomly reported with probability proportional to the value of the alpha texture. This approach is easy to implement, gives the expected results for an alpha of 0 or 1, and with a sufficient number of samples gives a better result than using a fixed threshold. Figure 7.1 compares the approaches.

One challenge in performing the stochastic alpha test is generating a uniform random number to apply it. For a given ray and shape, we would like this number to be the same across multiple runs of the system; doing so is a part of making the set of computations performed by pbrt be deterministic, which is a great help for debugging. If a different random number was used on different runs of the system, then we might hit a runtime error on some runs but not others. However, it is important that different random numbers be used for different rays; otherwise, the approach could devolve into the same as using a fixed threshold.

The HashFloat() utility function provides a solution to this problem. Here it is used to compute a random floating-point value between 0 and 1 for the alpha test; this value is determined by the ray's origin and direction.

⟨*Possibly ignore intersection based on stochastic alpha test*⟩ ≡   400
```
Float u = (a <= 0) ? 1.f : HashFloat(r.o, r.d);
if (u > a) {
    ⟨Ignore this intersection and trace a new ray 401⟩
}
```

Float 23

FloatTexture::Evaluate() 656

GeometricPrimitive::alpha
    399

HashFloat() 1042

Ray::d 95

Ray::o 95

ShapeIntersection::intr 266

If the alpha test indicates that the intersection should be ignored, then another intersection test is performed with the current GeometricPrimitive, with a recursive call to Intersect(). This additional test is important for shapes like spheres, where we may reject the closest intersection but then intersect the shape again further along the ray. This recursive call requires adjustment of the tMax value passed to it to account for the distance along the ray to the initial alpha tested intersection point. Then, if it reports an intersection, the reported tHit value should account for that segment as well.

(a)

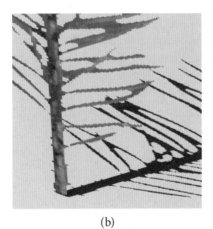

(b)   (c)

Figure 7.1: **Comparison of Stochastic Alpha Testing to Using a Fixed Threshold.** (a) Example scene: the two fir branches are modeled using a single quadrilateral with an alpha texture. (b) If a fixed threshold is used for the alpha test, the shape is not faithfully reproduced. Here a threshold of 1 was used, leading to shrinkage and jagged edges. (c) If a stochastic alpha test is used, the result is a smoother and more realistic transition.

⟨*Ignore this intersection and trace a new ray*⟩ ≡   **400**
```
Ray rNext = si->intr.SpawnRay(r.d);
pstd::optional<ShapeIntersection> siNext = Intersect(rNext, tMax - si->tHit);
if (siNext)
    siNext->tHit += si->tHit;
return siNext;
```

Given a valid intersection, the GeometricPrimitive can go ahead and finalize the Surface Interaction's representation of the intersection.

⟨*Initialize* SurfaceInteraction *after* Shape *intersection*⟩ ≡   **399**
```
si->intr.SetIntersectionProperties(material, areaLight, &mediumInterface,
                                   r.medium);
```

The `IntersectP()` method must also handle the case of the `GeometricPrimitive` having an alpha texture associated with it. In that case, it may be necessary to consider all the intersections of the ray with the shape in order to determine if there is a valid intersection. Because `IntersectP()` implementations in shapes return early when they find any intersection and because they do not return the geometric information associated with an intersection, a full intersection test is performed in this case. In the more common case of no alpha texture, `Shape::IntersectP()` can be called directly.

⟨*GeometricPrimitive Method Definitions*⟩ +≡
```
bool GeometricPrimitive::IntersectP(const Ray &r, Float tMax) const {
    if (alpha)
        return Intersect(r, tMax).has_value();
    else
        return shape.IntersectP(r, tMax);
}
```

Most objects in a scene are neither emissive nor have alpha textures. Further, only a few of them typically represent the boundary between two different types of participating media. It is wasteful to store `nullptr` values for the corresponding member variables of `GeometricPrimitive` in that common case. Therefore, pbrt also provides `SimplePrimitive`, which also implements the `Primitive` interface but does not store those values. The code that converts the parsed scene representation into the scene for rendering uses a `SimplePrimitive` in place of a `GeometricPrimitive` when it is possible to do so.

⟨*SimplePrimitive Definition*⟩ ≡
```
class SimplePrimitive {
  public:
    ⟨SimplePrimitive Public Methods⟩
  private:
    ⟨SimplePrimitive Private Members 402⟩
};
```

Because `SimplePrimitive` only stores a shape and a material, it saves 32 bytes of memory. For scenes with millions of primitives, the overall savings can be meaningful.

⟨*SimplePrimitive Private Members*⟩ ≡   402
```
Shape shape;
Material material;
```

We will not include the remainder of the `SimplePrimitive` implementation here; it is effectively a simplified subset of `GeometricPrimitive`'s.

7.1.2 OBJECT INSTANCING AND PRIMITIVES IN MOTION

Object instancing is a classic technique in rendering that reuses transformed copies of a single collection of geometry at multiple positions in a scene. For example, in a model of a concert hall with thousands of identical seats, the scene description can be compressed substantially if all the seats refer to a shared geometric representation of a single seat. The ecosystem scene in Figure 7.2 has 23,241 individual plants of various types, although only 31 unique plant models. Because each plant model is instanced multiple times with a different transformation for each instance, the complete scene has a total of 3.1 billion triangles. However, only 24 million triangles are stored in memory thanks to primitive reuse through object instancing. pbrt uses just over 4 GB of memory when rendering this scene with object instancing (1.7 GB

Figure 7.2: This outdoor scene makes heavy use of instancing as a mechanism for compressing the scene's description. There are only 24 million unique triangles in the scene, although, thanks to object reuse through instancing, the total geometric complexity is 3.1 billion triangles. *(Scene courtesy of Laubwerk.)*

for BVHs, 707 MB for `Primitives`, 877 MB for triangle meshes, and 846 MB for texture images), but would need upward of 516 GB to render it without instancing.[1]

The `TransformedPrimitive` implementation of the `Primitive` interface makes object instancing possible in pbrt. Rather than holding a shape, it stores a single `Primitive` as well as a `Transform` that is injected in between the underlying primitive and its representation in the scene. This extra transformation enables object instancing.

Recall that the `Shapes` of Chapter 6 themselves had rendering from object space transformations applied to them to place them in the scene. If a shape is held by a `TransformedPrimitive`, then the shape's notion of rendering space is not the actual scene rendering space—only after the `TransformedPrimitive`'s transformation is also applied is the shape actually in rendering space. For this application here, it makes sense for the shape to not be at all aware of the additional transformation being applied. For instanced primitives, letting `Shapes` know all the instance transforms is of limited utility: we would not want the `TriangleMesh` to make a copy of its vertex positions for each instance transformation and transform them all the way to rendering space, since this would negate the memory savings of object instancing.

⟨*TransformedPrimitive Definition*⟩ ≡
```
class TransformedPrimitive {
  public:
    ⟨TransformedPrimitive Public Methods 404⟩
  private:
    ⟨TransformedPrimitive Private Members 404⟩
};
```

---

1   The previous version of pbrt used 7 GB of memory when rendering this scene, with most of that difference due to less memory-efficient `Primitive` representations, virtual function pointers stored with each `Shape` and each `Primitive`, and the use of 32-bit floats for image texture pixels even for textures that were originally stored with 8-bit values.

The `TransformedPrimitive` constructor takes a `Primitive` that represents the model and the transformation that places it in the scene. If the instanced geometry is described by multiple `Primitive`s, the calling code is responsible for placing them in an aggregate so that only a single `Primitive` needs to be stored here.

⟨*TransformedPrimitive Public Methods*⟩ ≡   **403**
```
TransformedPrimitive(Primitive primitive,
                     const Transform *renderFromPrimitive)
    : primitive(primitive), renderFromPrimitive(renderFromPrimitive) { }
```

⟨*TransformedPrimitive Private Members*⟩ ≡   **403**
```
Primitive primitive;
const Transform *renderFromPrimitive;
```

The key task of `TransformedPrimitive` is to bridge between the `Primitive` interface that it implements and the `Primitive` that it holds, accounting for the effects of the rendering from primitive space transformation. If the `primitive` member has its own transformation, that should be interpreted as the transformation from object space to the `TransformedPrimitive`'s coordinate system. The complete transformation to rendering space requires both of these transformations together.

⟨*TransformedPrimitive Public Methods*⟩ +≡   **403**
```
Bounds3f Bounds() const {
    return (*renderFromPrimitive)(primitive.Bounds());
}
```

The `Intersect()` method also must account for the transformation, both for the ray passed to the held primitive and for any intersection information it returns.

⟨*TransformedPrimitive Method Definitions*⟩ ≡
```
pstd::optional<ShapeIntersection>
TransformedPrimitive::Intersect(const Ray &r, Float tMax) const {
    ⟨Transform ray to primitive-space and intersect with primitive 404⟩
    ⟨Return transformed instance's intersection information 404⟩
}
```

The method first transforms the given ray to the primitive's coordinate system and passes the transformed ray to its `Intersect()` routine.

⟨*Transform ray to primitive-space and intersect with primitive*⟩ ≡   **404**
```
Ray ray = renderFromPrimitive->ApplyInverse(r, &tMax);
pstd::optional<ShapeIntersection> si = primitive.Intersect(ray, tMax);
if (!si) return {};
```

Given an intersection, the `SurfaceInteraction` needs to be transformed to rendering space; the `primitive`'s intersection method will already have transformed the `SurfaceInteraction` to its notion of rendering space, so here we only need to apply the effect of the additional transformation held by `TransformedPrimitive`.

Note that any returned `ShapeIntersection::tHit` value from the primitive can be returned to the caller as is; recall the discussion of intersection coordinate spaces and ray *t* values in Section 6.1.4.

⟨*Return transformed instance's intersection information*⟩ ≡   **404**
```
si->intr = (*renderFromPrimitive)(si->intr);
return si;
```

The IntersectP() method is similar and is therefore elided.

The AnimatedPrimitive class uses an AnimatedTransform in place of the Transform stored by TransformedPrimitives. It thus enables rigid-body animation of primitives in the scene. See Figure 3.30 for an image that exhibits motion blur due to animated transformations.

⟨*AnimatedPrimitive Definition*⟩ ≡
```
class AnimatedPrimitive {
  public:
    ⟨AnimatedPrimitive Public Methods 405⟩
  private:
    ⟨AnimatedPrimitive Private Members 405⟩
};
```

The AnimatedTransform class uses substantially more memory than Transform. On the system used to develop pbrt, the former uses 696 bytes of memory, while the latter uses 128. Thus, just as was the case with GeometricPrimitive and SimplePrimitive, it is worthwhile to only use AnimatedPrimitive for shapes that actually are animated. Making this distinction is the task of the code that constructs the scene specification used for rendering.

⟨*AnimatedPrimitive Private Members*⟩ ≡   405
```
    Primitive primitive;
    AnimatedTransform renderFromPrimitive;
```

A bounding box of the primitive over the frame's time range is found via the Animated Transform::MotionBounds() method.

⟨*AnimatedPrimitive Public Methods*⟩ ≡   405
```
    Bounds3f Bounds() const {
        return renderFromPrimitive.MotionBounds(primitive.Bounds());
    }
```

We will also skip past the rest of the implementations of the AnimatedPrimitive intersection methods; they parallel those of TransformedPrimitive, just using an AnimatedTransform.

7.2 AGGREGATES

Ray intersection acceleration structures are one of the components at the heart of any ray tracer. Without algorithms to reduce the number of unnecessary ray intersection tests, tracing a single ray through a scene would take time linear in the number of primitives in the scene, since the ray would need to be tested against each primitive to find the closest intersection. However, doing so is extremely wasteful in most scenes, since the ray passes nowhere near the vast majority of primitives. The goals of acceleration structures are to allow the quick, simultaneous rejection of groups of primitives and to order the search process so that nearby intersections are likely to be found first and farther away ones can potentially be ignored.

Because ray–object intersections can account for the bulk of execution time in ray tracers, there has been a substantial amount of research into algorithms for ray intersection acceleration. We will not try to explore all of this work here but refer the interested reader to references in the "Further Reading" section at the end of this chapter.

Broadly speaking, there are two main approaches to this problem: spatial subdivision and object subdivision. Spatial subdivision algorithms decompose 3D space into regions (e.g., by superimposing a grid of axis-aligned boxes on the scene) and record which primitives overlap which regions. In some algorithms, the regions may also be adaptively subdivided based on the number of primitives that overlap them. When a ray intersection needs to be found, the sequence of these regions that the ray passes through is computed and only the primitives in the overlapping regions are tested for intersection.

In contrast, object subdivision is based on progressively breaking the objects in the scene down into smaller groups of nearby objects. For example, a model of a room might be broken down into four walls, a ceiling, and a chair. If a ray does not intersect the room's bounding volume, then all of its primitives can be culled. Otherwise, the ray is tested against each of them. If it hits the chair's bounding volume, for example, then it might be tested against each of its legs, the seat, and the back. Otherwise, the chair is culled.

Both of these approaches have been quite successful at solving the general problem of ray intersection computational requirements; there is no fundamental reason to prefer one over the other. The BVHAggregate is based on object subdivision and the KdTreeAggregate (which is described in the online edition of this book) is based on spatial subdivision. Both are defined in the files cpu/aggregates.h and cpu/aggregates.cpp.

As with the TransformedPrimitive and AnimatedPrimitive classes, the intersection methods for aggregates are not responsible for setting the material, area light, and medium information at the intersection point: those are all set by the actually intersected primitive and should be left unchanged by the aggregate.

7.3 BOUNDING VOLUME HIERARCHIES

Bounding volume hierarchies (BVHs) are an approach for ray intersection acceleration based on primitive subdivision, where the primitives are partitioned into a hierarchy of disjoint sets. (In contrast, spatial subdivision generally partitions space into a hierarchy of disjoint sets.) Figure 7.3 shows a bounding volume hierarchy for a simple scene. Primitives are stored in the leaves, and each node stores a bounding box of the primitives in the nodes beneath it. Thus, as a ray traverses through the tree, any time it does not intersect a node's bounds, the subtree beneath that node can be skipped.

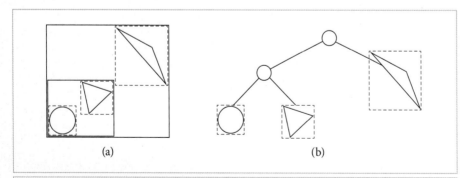

Figure 7.3: Bounding Volume Hierarchy for a Simple Scene. (a) A small collection of primitives, with bounding boxes shown by dashed lines. The primitives are aggregated based on proximity; here, the sphere and the equilateral triangle are bounded by another bounding box before being bounded by a bounding box that encompasses the entire scene (both shown in solid lines). (b) The corresponding bounding volume hierarchy. The root node holds the bounds of the entire scene. Here, it has two children, one storing a bounding box that encompasses the sphere and equilateral triangle (that in turn has those primitives as its children) and the other storing the bounding box that holds the skinny triangle.

One property of primitive subdivision is that each primitive appears in the hierarchy only once. In contrast, a primitive may overlap multiple spatial regions with spatial subdivision and thus may be tested for intersection multiple times as the ray passes through them.[2] Another implication of this property is that the amount of memory needed to represent the primitive subdivision hierarchy is bounded. For a binary BVH that stores a single primitive in each leaf, the total number of nodes is $2n - 1$, where n is the number of primitives. (There are n leaf nodes and $n - 1$ interior nodes.) If leaves store multiple primitives, fewer nodes are needed.

BVHs are more efficient to build than kd-trees, and are generally more numerically robust and less prone to missed intersections due to round-off errors than kd-trees are. The BVH aggregate, BVHAggregate, is therefore the default acceleration structure in pbrt.

⟨*BVHAggregate Definition*⟩ ≡
```
class BVHAggregate {
  public:
    ⟨BVHAggregate Public Types 407⟩
    ⟨BVHAggregate Public Methods⟩
  private:
    ⟨BVHAggregate Private Methods⟩
    ⟨BVHAggregate Private Members 407⟩
};
```

Its constructor takes an enumerator value that describes which of four algorithms to use when partitioning primitives to build the tree. The default, SAH, indicates that an algorithm based on the "surface area heuristic," discussed in Section 7.3.2, should be used. An alternative, HLBVH, which is discussed in Section 7.3.3, can be constructed more efficiently (and more easily parallelized), but it does not build trees that are as effective as SAH. The remaining two approaches use even less computation but create fairly low-quality trees. They are mostly useful for illuminating the superiority of the first two approaches.

⟨*BVHAggregate Public Types*⟩ ≡   **407**
```
enum class SplitMethod { SAH, HLBVH, Middle, EqualCounts };
```

In addition to the enumerator, the constructor takes the primitives themselves and the maximum number of primitives that can be in any leaf node.

⟨*BVHAggregate Method Definitions*⟩ ≡
```
BVHAggregate::BVHAggregate(std::vector<Primitive> prims,
        int maxPrimsInNode, SplitMethod splitMethod)
    : maxPrimsInNode(std::min(255, maxPrimsInNode)),
      primitives(std::move(prims)), splitMethod(splitMethod) {
    ⟨Build BVH from primitives 408⟩
}
```

⟨*BVHAggregate Private Members*⟩ ≡   **407**
```
int maxPrimsInNode;
std::vector<Primitive> primitives;
SplitMethod splitMethod;
```

---

2   The *mailboxing* technique can be used to avoid these multiple intersections for accelerators that use spatial subdivision, though its implementation can be tricky in the presence of multi-threading. More information on mailboxing is available in the "Further Reading" section.

7.3.1 BVH CONSTRUCTION

There are three stages to BVH construction in the implementation here. First, bounding information about each primitive is computed and stored in an array that will be used during tree construction. Next, the tree is built using the algorithm choice encoded in splitMethod. The result is a binary tree where each interior node holds pointers to its children and each leaf node holds references to one or more primitives. Finally, this tree is converted to a more compact (and thus more efficient) pointerless representation for use during rendering. (The implementation is easier with this approach, versus computing the pointerless representation directly during tree construction, which is also possible.)

⟨*Build BVH from* primitives⟩ ≡   **407**
   ⟨*Initialize* bvhPrimitives *array for primitives* **408**⟩
   ⟨*Build BVH for primitives using* bvhPrimitives **408**⟩
   ⟨*Convert BVH into compact representation in* nodes *array* **429**⟩

For each primitive to be stored in the BVH, an instance of the BVHPrimitive structure stores its complete bounding box and its index in the primitives array.

⟨*Initialize* bvhPrimitives *array for primitives*⟩ ≡   **408**
```
std::vector<BVHPrimitive> bvhPrimitives(primitives.size());
for (size_t i = 0; i < primitives.size(); ++i)
    bvhPrimitives[i] = BVHPrimitive(i, primitives[i].Bounds());
```

⟨*BVHPrimitive Definition*⟩ ≡
```
struct BVHPrimitive {
    BVHPrimitive(size_t primitiveIndex, const Bounds3f &bounds)
        : primitiveIndex(primitiveIndex), bounds(bounds) {}
    size_t primitiveIndex;
    Bounds3f bounds;
    ⟨BVHPrimitive Public Methods 408⟩
};
```

A simple method makes the centroid of the bounding box available.

⟨*BVHPrimitive Public Methods*⟩ ≡   **408**
```
Point3f Centroid() const { return .5f * bounds.pMin + .5f * bounds.pMax; }
```

Hierarchy construction can now begin. In addition to initializing the pointer to the root note of the BVH, root, an important side effect of the tree construction process is that a new array of Primitives is stored in orderedPrims; this array stores the primitives ordered so that the primitives in each leaf node occupy a contiguous range in the array. It is swapped with the original primitives array after tree construction.

⟨*Build BVH for primitives using* bvhPrimitives⟩ ≡   **408**
   ⟨*Declare* Allocators *used for BVH construction* **409**⟩
```
std::vector<Primitive> orderedPrims(primitives.size());
BVHBuildNode *root;
```
   ⟨*Build BVH according to selected* splitMethod **409**⟩

Memory for the initial BVH is allocated using the following Allocators. Note that all are based on the C++ standard library's pmr::monotonic_buffer_resource, which efficiently allocates memory from larger buffers. This approach is not only more computationally efficient than using a general-purpose allocator, but also uses less memory in total due to keeping less bookkeeping information with each allocation. We have found that using the default memory allocation algorithms in the place of these uses approximately 10% more memory and takes approximately 10% longer for complex scenes.

Because the pmr::monotonic_buffer_resource class cannot be used concurrently by multiple threads without mutual exclusion, in the parts of BVH construction that execute in parallel each thread uses per-thread allocation of them with help from the ThreadLocal class. Non-parallel code can use alloc directly.

⟨*Declare* Allocators *used for BVH construction*⟩ ≡   **408**
```
    pstd::pmr::monotonic_buffer_resource resource;
    Allocator alloc(&resource);
    using Resource = pstd::pmr::monotonic_buffer_resource;
    std::vector<std::unique_ptr<Resource>> threadBufferResources;
    ThreadLocal<Allocator> threadAllocators([&threadBufferResources]() {
        threadBufferResources.push_back(std::make_unique<Resource>());
        auto ptr = threadBufferResources.back().get();
        return Allocator(ptr);
    });
```

If the HLBVH construction algorithm has been selected, buildHLBVH() is called to build the tree. The other three construction algorithms are all handled by buildRecursive(). The initial calls to these functions are passed all the primitives to be stored. Each returns a pointer to the root of a BVH for the primitives they are given, which is represented with the BVHBuildNode structure and the total number of nodes created, which is stored in totalNodes. This value is represented by a std::atomic variable so that it can be modified correctly by multiple threads executing in parallel.

⟨*Build BVH according to selected* splitMethod⟩ ≡   **408**
```
    std::atomic<int> totalNodes{0};
    if (splitMethod == SplitMethod::HLBVH) {
        root = buildHLBVH(alloc, bvhPrimitives, &totalNodes, orderedPrims);
    } else {
        std::atomic<int> orderedPrimsOffset{0};
        root = buildRecursive(threadAllocators,
                            pstd::span<BVHPrimitive>(bvhPrimitives),
                            &totalNodes, &orderedPrimsOffset, orderedPrims);
    }
    primitives.swap(orderedPrims);
```

Each BVHBuildNode represents a node of the BVH. All nodes store a Bounds3f that represents the bounds of all the children beneath the node. Each interior node stores pointers to its two children in children. Interior nodes also record the coordinate axis along which primitives were partitioned for distribution to their two children; this information is used to improve the performance of the traversal algorithm. Leaf nodes record which primitive or primitives are stored in them; the elements of the BVHAggregate::primitives array from the offset firstPrimOffset up to but not including firstPrimOffset + nPrimitives are the primitives in the leaf. (This is why the primitives array needs to be reordered—so that this representation can be used, rather than, for example, storing a variable-sized array of primitive indices at each leaf node.)

⟨*BVHBuildNode Definition*⟩ ≡
```
    struct BVHBuildNode {
        ⟨BVHBuildNode Public Methods 410⟩
        Bounds3f bounds;
        BVHBuildNode *children[2];
        int splitAxis, firstPrimOffset, nPrimitives;
    };
```

We will distinguish between leaf and interior nodes by whether their child pointers have the value `nullptr` or not, respectively.

⟨*BVHBuildNode Public Methods*⟩ ≡   409
```
void InitLeaf(int first, int n, const Bounds3f &b) {
    firstPrimOffset = first;
    nPrimitives = n;
    bounds = b;
    children[0] = children[1] = nullptr;
}
```

The `InitInterior()` method requires that the two child nodes already have been created, so that their pointers can be passed in. This requirement makes it easy to compute the bounds of the interior node, since the children bounds are immediately available.

⟨*BVHBuildNode Public Methods*⟩ +≡   409
```
void InitInterior(int axis, BVHBuildNode *c0, BVHBuildNode *c1) {
    children[0] = c0;
    children[1] = c1;
    bounds = Union(c0->bounds, c1->bounds);
    splitAxis = axis;
    nPrimitives = 0;
}
```

In addition to the allocators used for BVH nodes and the array of `BVHPrimitive` structures, `buildRecursive()` takes a pointer `totalNodes` that is used to track the total number of BVH nodes that have been created; this value makes it possible to allocate exactly the right number of the more compact `LinearBVHNodes` later.

The `orderedPrims` array is used to store primitive references as primitives are stored in leaf nodes of the tree. It is initially allocated with enough entries to store all the primitives, though all entries are `nullptr`. When a leaf node is created, `buildRecursive()` claims enough entries in the array for its primitives; `orderedPrimsOffset` starts at 0 and keeps track of where the next free entry is. It, too, is an atomic variable so that multiple threads can allocate space from the array concurrently. Recall that when tree construction is finished, `BVHAggregate::primitives` is replaced with the ordered primitives array created here.

⟨*BVHAggregate Method Definitions*⟩ +≡
```
BVHBuildNode *BVHAggregate::buildRecursive(
        ThreadLocal<Allocator> &threadAllocators,
        pstd::span<BVHPrimitive> bvhPrimitives,
        std::atomic<int> *totalNodes, std::atomic<int> *orderedPrimsOffset,
        std::vector<Primitive> &orderedPrims) {
    Allocator alloc = threadAllocators.Get();
    BVHBuildNode *node = alloc.new_object<BVHBuildNode>();
    ⟨Initialize BVHBuildNode for primitive range 411⟩
    return node;
}
```

If `bvhPrimitives` has only a single primitive, then the recursion has bottomed out and a leaf node is created. Otherwise, this method partitions its elements using one of the partitioning algorithms and reorders the array elements so that they represent the partitioned subsets. If the partitioning is successful, these two primitive sets are in turn passed to recursive calls that will themselves return pointers to nodes for the two children of the current node.

⟨*Initialize* BVHBuildNode *for primitive range*⟩ ≡   **410**
    `++*totalNodes;`
    ⟨*Compute bounds of all primitives in BVH node* **411**⟩
    `if (bounds.SurfaceArea() == 0 || bvhPrimitives.size() == 1) {`
        ⟨*Create leaf* BVHBuildNode **411**⟩
    `} else {`
        ⟨*Compute bound of primitive centroids and choose split dimension* dim **412**⟩
        ⟨*Partition primitives into two sets and build children* **412**⟩
    `}`

The primitive bounds will be needed regardless of whether an interior or leaf node is created, so they are computed before that determination is made.

⟨*Compute bounds of all primitives in BVH node*⟩ ≡   **411**
    `Bounds3f bounds;`
    `for (const auto &prim : bvhPrimitives)`
        `bounds = Union(bounds, prim.bounds);`

At leaf nodes, the primitives overlapping the leaf are appended to the orderedPrims array and a leaf node object is initialized. Because orderedPrimsOffset is a std::atomic variable and fetch_add() is an atomic operation, multiple threads can safely perform this operation concurrently without further synchronization: each one is able to allocate its own span of the orderedPrimitives array that it can then safely write to.

⟨*Create leaf* BVHBuildNode⟩ ≡   **411, 412, 419**
    `int firstPrimOffset = orderedPrimsOffset->fetch_add(bvhPrimitives.size());`
    `for (size_t i = 0; i < bvhPrimitives.size(); ++i) {`
        `int index = bvhPrimitives[i].primitiveIndex;`
        `orderedPrims[firstPrimOffset + i] = primitives[index];`
    `}`
    `node->InitLeaf(firstPrimOffset, bvhPrimitives.size(), bounds);`
    `return node;`

For interior nodes, the collection of primitives must be partitioned between the two children's subtrees. Given n primitives, there are in general $2^{n-1} - 2$ possible ways to partition them into two non-empty groups. In practice when building BVHs, one generally considers partitions along a coordinate axis, meaning that there are about $3n$ candidate partitions. (Along each axis, each primitive may be put into the first partition or the second partition.)

Here, we choose just one of the three coordinate axes to use in partitioning the primitives. We select the axis with the largest extent of bounding box centroids for the primitives in bvhPrimitives. (An alternative would be to try partitioning the primitives along all three axes and select the one that gave the best result, but in practice this approach works well.) This approach gives good partitions in many scenes; Figure 7.4 illustrates the strategy.

The general goal is to select a partition of primitives that does not have too much overlap of the bounding boxes of the two resulting primitive sets—if there is substantial overlap, then it will more frequently be necessary to traverse both children's subtrees when traversing the tree, requiring more computation than if it had been possible to more effectively prune away collections of primitives. This idea of finding effective primitive partitions will be made more rigorous shortly, in the discussion of the surface area heuristic.

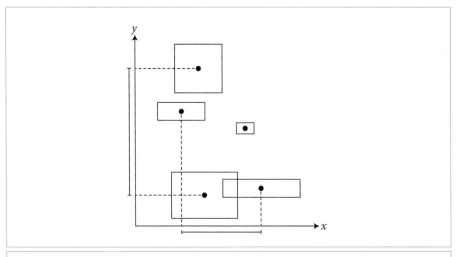

Figure 7.4: Choosing the Axis along which to Partition Primitives. The BVHAggregate chooses an axis along which to partition the primitives based on which axis has the largest range of the centroids of the primitives' bounding boxes. Here, in two dimensions, their extent is largest along the y axis (filled points on the axes), so the primitives will be partitioned in y.

⟨*Compute bound of primitive centroids and choose split dimension* dim⟩ ≡   **411**
```
    Bounds3f centroidBounds;
    for (const auto &prim : bvhPrimitives)
        centroidBounds = Union(centroidBounds, prim.Centroid());
    int dim = centroidBounds.MaxDimension();
```

If all the centroid points are at the same position (i.e., the centroid bounds have zero volume), then recursion stops and a leaf node is created with the primitives; none of the splitting methods here is effective in that (unusual) case. The primitives are otherwise partitioned using the chosen method and passed to two recursive calls to buildRecursive().

⟨*Partition primitives into two sets and build children*⟩ ≡   **411**
```
    if (centroidBounds.pMax[dim] == centroidBounds.pMin[dim]) {
        ⟨Create leaf BVHBuildNode 411⟩
    } else {
        int mid = bvhPrimitives.size() / 2;
        ⟨Partition primitives based on splitMethod⟩
        BVHBuildNode *children[2];
        ⟨Recursively build BVHs for children 412⟩
        node->InitInterior(dim, children[0], children[1]);
    }
```

The two recursive calls access independent data, other than when they allocate space in the orderedPrims array by incrementing orderedPrimsOffset, which we already have seen is thread safe. Therefore, when there are a reasonably large number of active primitives, those calls can be performed in parallel, which improves the performance of BVH construction.

⟨*Recursively build BVHs for* children⟩ ≡   **412**
```
    if (bvhPrimitives.size() > 128 * 1024) {
        ⟨Recursively build child BVHs in parallel 413⟩
    } else {
        ⟨Recursively build child BVHs sequentially⟩
    }
```

A parallel for loop over two items is sufficient to expose the available parallelism. With pbrt's implementation of ParallelFor(), the current thread will end up handling the first recursive call, while another thread, if available, can take the second. ParallelFor() does not return until all the loop iterations have completed, so we can safely proceed, knowing that both children are fully initialized when it does.

⟨*Recursively build child BVHs in parallel*⟩ ≡   412
```
ParallelFor(0, 2, [&](int i) {
    if (i == 0)
        children[0] =
            buildRecursive(threadAllocators, bvhPrimitives.subspan(0, mid),
                           totalNodes, orderedPrimsOffset, orderedPrims);
    else
        children[1] =
            buildRecursive(threadAllocators, bvhPrimitives.subspan(mid),
                           totalNodes, orderedPrimsOffset, orderedPrims);
});
```

The code for the non-parallel case, ⟨*Recursively build child BVHs sequentially*⟩, is equivalent, just without the parallel for loop. We have therefore not included it here.

We also will not include the code fragment ⟨*Partition primitives based on* splitMethod⟩ here; it just uses the value of BVHAggregate::splitMethod to determine which primitive partitioning scheme to use. These three schemes will be described in the following few pages.

A simple splitMethod is Middle, which first computes the midpoint of the primitives' centroids along the splitting axis. This method is implemented in the fragment ⟨*Partition primitives through node's midpoint*⟩. The primitives are classified into the two sets, depending on whether their centroids are above or below the midpoint. This partitioning is easily done with the std::partition() C++ standard library function, which takes a range of elements in an array and a comparison function and orders the elements in the array so that all the elements that return true for the given predicate function appear in the range before those that return false for it. std::partition() returns a pointer to the first element that had a false value for the predicate. Figure 7.5 illustrates this approach, including cases where it does and does not work well.

If the primitives all have large overlapping bounding boxes, this splitting method may fail to separate the primitives into two groups. In that case, execution falls through to the SplitMethod::EqualCounts approach to try again.

⟨*Partition primitives through node's midpoint*⟩ ≡
```
Float pmid = (centroidBounds.pMin[dim] + centroidBounds.pMax[dim]) / 2;
auto midIter =
    std::partition(bvhPrimitives.begin(), bvhPrimitives.end(),
        [dim, pmid](const BVHPrimitive &pi) {
            return pi.Centroid()[dim] < pmid;
        });
mid = midIter - bvhPrimitives.begin();
if (midIter != bvhPrimitives.begin() && midIter != bvhPrimitives.end())
    break;
```

When splitMethod is SplitMethod::EqualCounts, the ⟨*Partition primitives into equally sized subsets*⟩ fragment runs. It partitions the primitives into two equal-sized subsets such that the first half of the *n* of them are the *n*/2 with smallest centroid coordinate values along the chosen axis, and the second half are the ones with the largest centroid coordinate values.

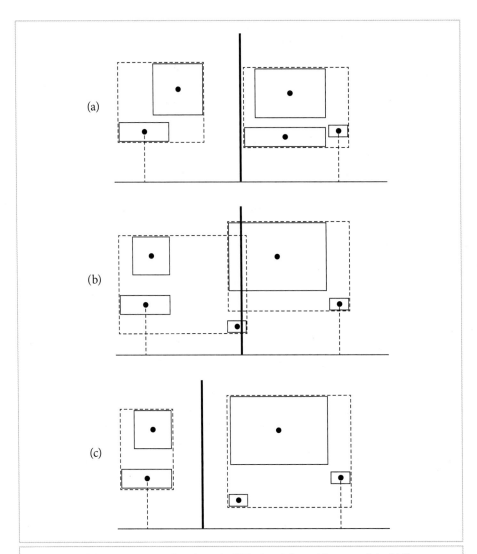

Figure 7.5: Splitting Primitives Based on the Midpoint of Centroids on an Axis. (a) For some distributions of primitives, such as the one shown here, splitting based on the midpoint of the centroids along the chosen axis (thick vertical line) works well. (The bounding boxes of the two resulting primitive groups are shown with dashed lines.) (b) For distributions like this one, the midpoint is a suboptimal choice; the two resulting bounding boxes overlap substantially. (c) If the same group of primitives from (b) is instead split along the line shown here, the resulting bounding boxes are smaller and do not overlap at all, leading to better performance when rendering.

While this approach can sometimes work well, the case in Figure 7.5(b) is one where this method also fares poorly.

This scheme is also easily implemented with a standard library call, std::nth_element(). It takes a start, middle, and ending iterator as well as a comparison function. It orders the array so that the element at the middle iterator is the one that would be there if the array was fully sorted, and such that all the elements before the middle one compare to less than the middle element and all the elements after it compare to greater than it. This ordering can be done in $O(n)$ time, with n the number of elements, which is more efficient than the $O(n \log n)$ cost of completely sorting the array.

⟨*Partition primitives into equally sized subsets*⟩ ≡   416
```
    mid = bvhPrimitives.size() / 2;
    std::nth_element(bvhPrimitives.begin(), bvhPrimitives.begin() + mid,
                     bvhPrimitives.end(),
        [dim](const BVHPrimitive &a, const BVHPrimitive &b) {
            return a.Centroid()[dim] < b.Centroid()[dim];
        });
```

7.3.2 THE SURFACE AREA HEURISTIC

The two primitive partitioning approaches described so far can work well for some distributions of primitives, but they often choose partitions that perform poorly in practice, leading to more nodes of the tree being visited by rays and hence unnecessarily inefficient ray–primitive intersection computations at rendering time. Most of the best current algorithms for building acceleration structures for ray tracing are based on the "surface area heuristic" (SAH), which provides a well-grounded cost model for answering questions like "which of a number of partitions of primitives will lead to a better BVH for ray–primitive intersection tests?" or "which of a number of possible positions to split space in a spatial subdivision scheme will lead to a better acceleration structure?"

The SAH model estimates the computational expense of performing ray intersection tests, including the time spent traversing nodes of the tree and the time spent on ray–primitive intersection tests for a particular partitioning of primitives. Algorithms for building acceleration structures can then follow the goal of minimizing total cost. Typically, a greedy algorithm is used that minimizes the cost for each single node of the hierarchy being built individually.

The ideas behind the SAH cost model are straightforward: at any point in building an adaptive acceleration structure (primitive subdivision or spatial subdivision), we could just create a leaf node for the current region and geometry. In that case, any ray that passes through this region will be tested against all the overlapping primitives and will incur a cost of

$$\sum_{i=1}^{n} t_{\text{isect}}(i),$$

where n is the number of primitives and $t_{\text{isect}}(i)$ is the time to compute a ray–object intersection with the ith primitive.

The other option is to split the region. In that case, rays will incur the cost

$$c(A, B) = t_{\text{trav}} + p_A \sum_{i=1}^{n_A} t_{\text{isect}}(a_i) + p_B \sum_{i=1}^{n_B} t_{\text{isect}}(b_i), \qquad [7.1]$$

where t_{trav} is the time it takes to traverse the interior node and determine which of the children the ray passes through, p_A and p_B are the probabilities that the ray passes through each of the child nodes (assuming binary subdivision), a_i and b_i are the indices of primitives in the two child nodes, and n_A and n_B are the number of primitives that overlap the regions of the two child nodes, respectively. The choice of how primitives are partitioned affects the values of the two probabilities as well as the set of primitives on each side of the split.

In pbrt, we will make the simplifying assumption that $t_{\text{isect}}(i)$ is the same for all the primitives; this assumption is probably not too far from reality, and any error that it introduces does not seem to affect the performance of accelerators very much. Another possibility would be to add a method to Primitive that returned an estimate of the number of processing cycles that its intersection test requires.

BVHPrimitive 408
BVHPrimitive::Centroid() 408
Primitive 398

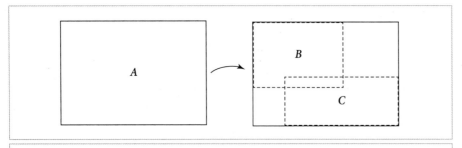

Figure 7.6: If a node of the bounding hierarchy with surface area s_A is split into two children with surface areas s_B and s_C, the probabilities that a ray passing through A also passes through B and C are given by s_B/s_A and s_C/s_A, respectively.

The probabilities p_A and p_B can be computed using ideas from geometric probability. It can be shown that for a convex volume A contained in another convex volume B, the conditional probability that a uniformly distributed random ray passing through B will also pass through A is the ratio of their surface areas, s_A and s_B:

$$p(A|B) = \frac{s_A}{s_B}.$$

Because we are interested in the cost for rays passing through the node, we can use this result directly. Thus, if we are considering refining a region of space A such that there are two new subregions with bounds B and C (Figure 7.6), the probability that a ray passing through A will also pass through either of the subregions is easily computed.

When `splitMethod` has the value `SplitMethod::SAH`, the SAH is used for building the BVH; a partition of the primitives along the chosen axis that gives a minimal SAH cost estimate is found by considering a number of candidate partitions. (This is the default `SplitMethod`, and it creates the most efficient hierarchies of the partitioning options.) However, once it has refined down to two primitives, the implementation switches over to directly partitioning them in half. The incremental computational cost for applying the SAH at that point is not beneficial.

⟨*Partition primitives using approximate SAH*⟩ ≡
```
    if (bvhPrimitives.size() <= 2) {
        ⟨Partition primitives into equally sized subsets 415⟩
    } else {
        ⟨Allocate BVHSplitBucket for SAH partition buckets 417⟩
        ⟨Initialize BVHSplitBucket for SAH partition buckets 417⟩
        ⟨Compute costs for splitting after each bucket 418⟩
        ⟨Find bucket to split at that minimizes SAH metric 419⟩
        ⟨Either create leaf or split primitives at selected SAH bucket 419⟩
    }
```

Rather than exhaustively considering all $2n$ possible partitions along the axis, computing the SAH for each to select the best, the implementation here instead divides the range along the axis into a small number of buckets of equal extent. It then only considers partitions at bucket boundaries. This approach is more efficient than considering all partitions while usually still producing partitions that are nearly as effective. This idea is illustrated in Figure 7.7.

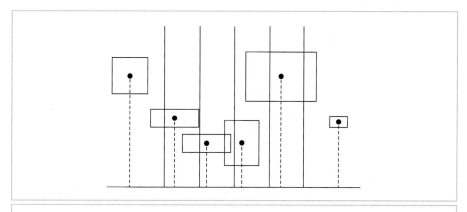

Figure 7.7: Choosing a Splitting Plane with the Surface Area Heuristic for BVHs. The projected extent of primitive bounds centroids is projected onto the chosen split axis. Each primitive is placed in a bucket along the axis based on the centroid of its bounds. The implementation then estimates the cost for splitting the primitives using the planes at each of the bucket boundaries (solid vertical lines); whichever one gives the minimum cost per the surface area heuristic is selected.

⟨*BVHSplitBucket Definition*⟩ ≡
```
struct BVHSplitBucket {
    int count = 0;
    Bounds3f bounds;
};
```

We have found that 12 buckets usually work well in practice. An improvement may be to increase this value when there are many primitives and to decrease it when there are few.

⟨*Allocate* BVHSplitBucket *for SAH partition buckets*⟩ ≡   416
```
constexpr int nBuckets = 12;
BVHSplitBucket buckets[nBuckets];
```

For each primitive, the following fragment determines the bucket that its centroid lies in and updates the bucket's bounds to include the primitive's bounds.

⟨*Initialize* BVHSplitBucket *for SAH partition buckets*⟩ ≡   416
```
for (const auto &prim : bvhPrimitives) {
    int b = nBuckets * centroidBounds.Offset(prim.Centroid())[dim];
    if (b == nBuckets) b = nBuckets - 1;
    buckets[b].count++;
    buckets[b].bounds = Union(buckets[b].bounds, prim.bounds);
}
```

For each bucket, we now have a count of the number of primitives and the bounds of all of their respective bounding boxes. We want to use the SAH to estimate the cost of splitting at each of the bucket boundaries. The fragment below loops over all the buckets and initializes the cost[i] array to store the estimated SAH cost for splitting after the ith bucket. (It does not consider a split after the last bucket, which by definition would not split the primitives.)

We arbitrarily set the estimated intersection cost to 1, and then set the estimated traversal cost to 1/2. (One of the two of them can always be set to 1 since it is the relative, rather than absolute, magnitudes of the estimated traversal and intersection costs that determine their effect.) However, not only is the absolute amount of computation necessary for node traversal—a ray–bounding box intersection—much less than the amount of computation needed to intersect a ray with a shape, the full cost of a shape intersection test is even higher. It includes the overhead of at least two instances of dynamic dispatch (one or more via Primitives and one via a Shape), the cost of computing all the geometric information needed to initialize a SurfaceInteraction if an intersection is found, and any resulting costs from possibly applying additional transformations and interpolating animated transformations.

We have intentionally underestimated the performance ratio between these two costs because the raw amount of computation each performs does not measure their full expense. With a lower traversal cost, the resulting BVHs would be deeper and require more nodes. For complex scenes, this additional memory use may be undesirable. Even for simpler scenes, visiting more nodes when a ray is traced will generally incur the cost of cache misses, which not only may reduce performance for that ray, but may harm future performance from displacing other useful data from the cache. We have found the 2 : 1 ratio that we have used here to make a reasonable trade-off between all of these issues.

In order to be able to choose a split in linear time, the implementation first performs a forward scan over the buckets and then a backward scan over the buckets that incrementally compute each bucket's cost.[3] There is one fewer candidate split than the number of buckets, since all splits are between pairs of buckets.

⟨*Compute costs for splitting after each bucket*⟩ ≡   **416**
```
constexpr int nSplits = nBuckets - 1;
Float costs[nSplits] = {};
```
  ⟨*Partially initialize* costs *using a forward scan over splits* **418**⟩
  ⟨*Finish initializing* costs *using a backward scan over splits* **418**⟩

The loop invariant is that countBelow stores the number of primitives that are below the corresponding candidate split, and boundsBelow stores their bounds. With these values in hand, the value of the first sum in Equation (7.1) can be evaluated for each split.

⟨*Partially initialize* costs *using a forward scan over splits*⟩ ≡   **418**
```
int countBelow = 0;
Bounds3f boundBelow;
for (int i = 0; i < nSplits; ++i) {
    boundBelow = Union(boundBelow, buckets[i].bounds);
    countBelow += buckets[i].count;
    costs[i] += countBelow * boundBelow.SurfaceArea();
}
```

A similar backward scan over the buckets finishes initializing the costs array.

⟨*Finish initializing* costs *using a backward scan over splits*⟩ ≡   **418**
```
int countAbove = 0;
Bounds3f boundAbove;
for (int i = nSplits; i >= 1; --i) {
    boundAbove = Union(boundAbove, buckets[i].bounds);
    countAbove += buckets[i].count;
    costs[i - 1] += countAbove * boundAbove.SurfaceArea();
}
```

---

3   Previous versions of pbrt instead computed these values from scratch for each candidate split, which resulted in $O(n^2)$ performance. Even with the small n here, we have found that this implementation speeds up BVH construction by approximately 2×.

Given all the costs, a linear search over the potential splits finds the partition with minimum cost.

⟨*Find bucket to split at that minimizes SAH metric*⟩ ≡   **416**
```
int minCostSplitBucket = -1;
Float minCost = Infinity;
for (int i = 0; i < nSplits; ++i) {
    ⟨Compute cost for candidate split and update minimum if necessary 419⟩
}
⟨Compute leaf cost and SAH split cost for chosen split 419⟩
```

To find the best split, we evaluate a simplified version of Equation (7.1), neglecting the traversal cost and the division by the surface area of the bounding box of all the primitives to compute the probabilities p_A and p_B; these have no effect on the choice of the best split. That cost is precisely what is stored in costs, so the split with minimum cost is easily found.

⟨*Compute cost for candidate split and update minimum if necessary*⟩ ≡   **419**
```
if (costs[i] < minCost) {
    minCost = costs[i];
    minCostSplitBucket = i;
}
```

To compute the final SAH cost for a split, we need to divide by the surface area of the overall bounding box to compute the probabilities p_A and p_B before adding the estimated traversal cost, $1/2$. Because we set the estimated intersection cost to 1 previously, the estimated cost for just creating a leaf node is equal to the number of primitives.

⟨*Compute leaf cost and SAH split cost for chosen split*⟩ ≡   **419**
```
Float leafCost = bvhPrimitives.size();
minCost = 1.f / 2.f + minCost / bounds.SurfaceArea();
```

If the chosen bucket boundary for partitioning has a lower estimated cost than building a node with the existing primitives or if more than the maximum number of primitives allowed in a node is present, the std::partition() function is used to do the work of reordering nodes in the bvhPrimitives array. Recall from its use earlier that it ensures that all elements of the array that return true from the given predicate appear before those that return false and that it returns a pointer to the first element where the predicate returns false.

⟨*Either create leaf or split primitives at selected SAH bucket*⟩ ≡   **416**
```
if (bvhPrimitives.size() > maxPrimsInNode || minCost < leafCost) {
    auto midIter = std::partition(bvhPrimitives.begin(),
        bvhPrimitives.end(),
        [=](const BVHPrimitive &bp) {
            int b = nBuckets * centroidBounds.Offset(bp.Centroid())[dim];
            if (b == nBuckets) b = nBuckets - 1;
            return b <= minCostSplitBucket;
        });
    mid = midIter - bvhPrimitives.begin();
} else {
    ⟨Create leaf BVHBuildNode 411⟩
}
```

7.3.3 LINEAR BOUNDING VOLUME HIERARCHIES

While building bounding volume hierarchies using the surface area heuristic gives very good results, that approach does have two disadvantages: first, many passes are taken over the scene primitives to compute the SAH costs at all the levels of the tree. Second, top-down BVH construction is difficult to parallelize well: the approach used in buildRecursive()—performing parallel construction of independent subtrees—suffers from limited independent work until the top few levels of the tree have been built, which in turn inhibits parallel scalability. (This second issue is particularly an issue on GPUs, which perform poorly if massive parallelism is not available.)

Linear bounding volume hierarchies (LBVHs) were developed to address these issues. With LBVHs, the tree is built with a small number of lightweight passes over the primitives; tree construction time is linear in the number of primitives. Further, the algorithm quickly partitions the primitives into clusters that can be processed independently. This processing can be fairly easily parallelized and is well suited to GPU implementation.

The key idea behind LBVHs is to turn BVH construction into a sorting problem. Because there is no single ordering function for sorting multidimensional data, LBVHs are based on *Morton codes*, which map nearby points in n dimensions to nearby points along the 1D line, where there is an obvious ordering function. After the primitives have been sorted, spatially nearby clusters of primitives are in contiguous segments of the sorted array.

Morton codes are based on a simple transformation: given n-dimensional integer coordinate values, their Morton-coded representation is found by interleaving the bits of the coordinates in base 2. For example, consider a 2D coordinate (x, y) where the bits of x and y are denoted by x_i and y_i. The corresponding Morton-coded value is

$$\cdots y_3 \, x_3 \, y_2 \, x_2 \, y_1 \, x_1 \, y_0 \, x_0.$$

Figure 7.8 shows a plot of the 2D points in Morton order—note that they are visited along a path that follows a reversed "z" shape. (The Morton path is sometimes called "z-order" for this reason.) We can see that points with coordinates that are close together in 2D are generally close together along the Morton curve.[4]

A Morton-encoded value also encodes useful information about the position of the point that it represents. Consider the case of 4-bit coordinate values in 2D: the x and y coordinates are integers in $[0, 15]$ and the Morton code has 8 bits: $y_3 \, x_3 \, y_2 \, x_2 \, y_1 \, x_1 \, y_0 \, x_0$. Many interesting properties follow from the encoding; a few examples include:

- For a Morton-encoded 8-bit value where the high bit y_3 is set, we then know that the high bit of its underlying y coordinate is set and thus $y \geq 8$ (Figure 7.9(a)).
- The next bit value, x_3, splits the x axis in the middle (Figure 7.9(b)). If y_3 is set and x_3 is off, for example, then the corresponding point must lie in the shaded area of Figure 7.9(c). In general, points with a number of matching high bits lie in a power-of-two sized and axis-aligned region of space determined by the matching bit values.
- The value of y_2 splits the y axis into four regions (Figure 7.9(d)).

Another way to interpret these bit-based properties is in terms of Morton-coded values. For example, Figure 7.9(a) corresponds to the index being in the range $[8, 15]$, and Figure 7.9(c) corresponds to $[8, 11]$. Thus, given a set of sorted Morton indices, we could find the range of

---

4 Many GPUs store texture images in memory using a Morton layout. One advantage of doing so is that when performing bilinear interpolation between four texel values, the values are much more likely to be close together in memory than if the texture is laid out in scanline order. In turn, texture cache performance benefits.

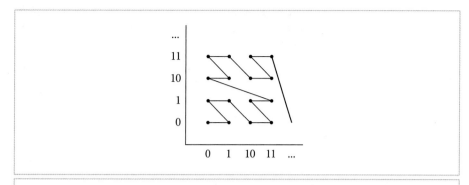

Figure 7.8: The Order That Points Are Visited along the Morton Curve. Coordinate values along the x and y axes are shown in binary. If we connect the integer coordinate points in the order of their Morton indices, we see that the Morton curve visits the points along a hierarchical "z"-shaped path.

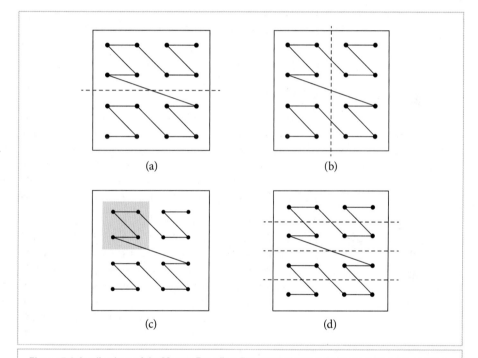

Figure 7.9: Implications of the Morton Encoding. The values of various bits in the Morton value indicate the region of space that the corresponding coordinate lies in. (a) In 2D, the high bit of the Morton-coded value of a point's coordinates defines a splitting plane along the middle of the y axis. If the high bit is set, the point is above the plane. (b) Similarly, the second-highest bit of the Morton value splits the x axis in the middle. (c) If the high y bit is 1 and the high x bit is 0, then the point must lie in the shaded region. (d) The second-from-highest y bit splits the y axis into four regions.

points corresponding to an area like Figure 7.9(c) by performing a binary search to find each endpoint in the array.

LBVHs are BVHs built by partitioning primitives using splitting planes that are at the midpoint of each region of space (i.e., equivalent to the `SplitMethod::Middle` path defined earlier). Partitioning is extremely efficient, as it takes advantage of properties of the Morton encoding described above.

Just reimplementing Middle in a different manner is not particularly interesting, so in the implementation here, we will build a *hierarchical linear bounding volume hierarchy* (HLBVH). With this approach, Morton-curve-based clustering is used to first build trees for the lower levels of the hierarchy (referred to as "treelets" in the following), and the top levels of the tree are then created using the surface area heuristic. The buildHLBVH() method implements this approach and returns the root node of the resulting tree.

⟨*BVHAggregate Method Definitions*⟩ +≡
```
    BVHBuildNode *BVHAggregate::buildHLBVH(
            Allocator alloc, const std::vector<BVHPrimitive> &bvhPrimitives,
            std::atomic<int> *totalNodes,
            std::vector<Primitive> &orderedPrims) {
        ⟨Compute bounding box of all primitive centroids 422⟩
        ⟨Compute Morton indices of primitives 422⟩
        ⟨Radix sort primitive Morton indices 423⟩
        ⟨Create LBVH treelets at bottom of BVH 424⟩
        ⟨Create and return SAH BVH from LBVH treelets 428⟩
    }
```

The BVH is built using only the centroids of primitive bounding boxes to sort them—it does not account for the actual spatial extent of each primitive. This simplification is critical to the performance that HLBVHs offer, but it also means that for scenes with primitives that span a wide range of sizes, the tree that is built will not account for this variation as an SAH-based tree would.

Because the Morton encoding operates on integer coordinates, we first need to bound the centroids of all the primitives so that we can quantize centroid positions with respect to the overall bounds.

⟨*Compute bounding box of all primitive centroids*⟩ ≡   422
```
    Bounds3f bounds;
    for (const BVHPrimitive &prim : bvhPrimitives)
        bounds = Union(bounds, prim.Centroid());
```

Given the overall bounds, we can now compute the Morton code for each primitive. This is a fairly lightweight calculation, but given that there may be millions of primitives, it is worth parallelizing.

⟨*Compute Morton indices of primitives*⟩ ≡   422
```
    std::vector<MortonPrimitive> mortonPrims(bvhPrimitives.size());
    ParallelFor(0, bvhPrimitives.size(), [&](int64_t i) {
        ⟨Initialize mortonPrims[i] for ith primitive 423⟩
    });
```

A MortonPrimitive instance is created for each primitive; it stores the index of the primitive, as well as its Morton code, in the bvhPrimitives array.

⟨*MortonPrimitive Definition*⟩ ≡
```
    struct MortonPrimitive {
        int primitiveIndex;
        uint32_t mortonCode;
    };
```

We use 10 bits for each of the x, y, and z dimensions, giving a total of 30 bits for the Morton code. This granularity allows the values to fit into a single 32-bit variable. Floating-point centroid offsets inside the bounding box are in [0, 1], so we scale them by 2^{10} to get integer coordinates that fit in 10 bits. The EncodeMorton3() function, which is defined with other bitwise utility functions in Section B.2.7, returns the 3D Morton code for the given integer values.

⟨*Initialize* mortonPrims[i] *for ith primitive*⟩ ≡   **422**
```
constexpr int mortonBits = 10;
constexpr int mortonScale = 1 << mortonBits;
mortonPrims[i].primitiveIndex = bvhPrimitives[i].primitiveIndex;
Vector3f centroidOffset = bounds.Offset(bvhPrimitives[i].Centroid());
Vector3f offset = centroidOffset * mortonScale;
mortonPrims[i].mortonCode = EncodeMorton3(offset.x, offset.y, offset.z);
```

Once the Morton indices have been computed, we will sort the mortonPrims by Morton index value using a radix sort. We have found that for BVH construction, our radix sort implementation is noticeably faster than using std::sort() from our system's standard library (which is a mixture of a quicksort and an insertion sort).

⟨*Radix sort primitive Morton indices*⟩ ≡   **422**
```
RadixSort(&mortonPrims);
```

Recall that a radix sort differs from most sorting algorithms in that it is not based on comparing pairs of values but rather is based on bucketing items based on some key. Radix sort can be used to sort integer values by sorting them one digit at a time, going from the rightmost digit to the leftmost. Especially with binary values, it is worth sorting multiple digits at a time; doing so reduces the total number of passes taken over the data. In the implementation here, bitsPerPass sets the number of bits processed per pass; with the value 6, we have 5 passes to sort the 30 bits.

⟨*BVHAggregate Utility Functions*⟩ ≡   **422**
```
static void RadixSort(std::vector<MortonPrimitive> *v) {
    std::vector<MortonPrimitive> tempVector(v->size());
    constexpr int bitsPerPass = 6;
    constexpr int nBits = 30;
    constexpr int nPasses = nBits / bitsPerPass;
    for (int pass = 0; pass < nPasses; ++pass) {
        ⟨Perform one pass of radix sort, sorting bitsPerPass bits 423⟩
    }
    ⟨Copy final result from tempVector, if needed 424⟩
}
```

Each pass sorts bitsPerPass bits, starting at lowBit.

⟨*Perform one pass of radix sort, sorting* bitsPerPass *bits*⟩ ≡   **423**
```
int lowBit = pass * bitsPerPass;
⟨Set in and out vector references for radix sort pass 424⟩
⟨Count number of zero bits in array for current radix sort bit 424⟩
⟨Compute starting index in output array for each bucket 424⟩
⟨Store sorted values in output array 424⟩
```

The in and out references correspond to the vector to be sorted and the vector to store the sorted values in, respectively. Each pass through the loop alternates between the input vector *v and the temporary vector for each of them.

⟨*Set in and out vector references for radix sort pass*⟩ ≡   423
```
std::vector<MortonPrimitive> &in = (pass & 1) ? tempVector : *v;
std::vector<MortonPrimitive> &out = (pass & 1) ? *v : tempVector;
```

If we are sorting n bits per pass, then there are 2^n buckets that each value may land in. We first count how many values will land in each bucket; this will let us determine where to store sorted values in the output array. To compute the bucket index for the current value, the implementation shifts the index so that the bit at index `lowBit` is at bit 0 and then masks off the low `bitsPerPass` bits.

⟨*Count number of zero bits in array for current radix sort bit*⟩ ≡   423
```
constexpr int nBuckets = 1 << bitsPerPass;
int bucketCount[nBuckets] = { 0 };
constexpr int bitMask = (1 << bitsPerPass) - 1;
for (const MortonPrimitive &mp : in) {
    int bucket = (mp.mortonCode >> lowBit) & bitMask;
    ++bucketCount[bucket];
}
```

Given the count of how many values land in each bucket, we can compute the offset in the output array where each bucket's values start; this is just the sum of how many values land in the preceding buckets.

⟨*Compute starting index in output array for each bucket*⟩ ≡   423
```
int outIndex[nBuckets];
outIndex[0] = 0;
for (int i = 1; i < nBuckets; ++i)
    outIndex[i] = outIndex[i - 1] + bucketCount[i - 1];
```

Now that we know where to start storing values for each bucket, we can take another pass over the primitives to recompute the bucket that each one lands in and to store their `MortonPrimitive`s in the output array. This completes the sorting pass for the current group of bits.

⟨*Store sorted values in output array*⟩ ≡   423
```
for (const MortonPrimitive &mp : in) {
    int bucket = (mp.mortonCode >> lowBit) & bitMask;
    out[outIndex[bucket]++] = mp;
}
```

When sorting is done, if an odd number of radix sort passes were performed, then the final sorted values need to be copied from the temporary vector to the output vector that was originally passed to `RadixSort()`.

⟨*Copy final result from* `tempVector`, *if needed*⟩ ≡   423
```
if (nPasses & 1)
    std::swap(*v, tempVector);
```

Given the sorted array of primitives, we can now find clusters of primitives with nearby centroids and then create an LBVH over the primitives in each cluster. This step is a good one to parallelize as there are generally many clusters and each cluster can be processed independently.

MortonPrimitive 422

MortonPrimitive::mortonCode 422

⟨*Create LBVH treelets at bottom of BVH*⟩ ≡   422
    ⟨*Find intervals of primitives for each treelet* **425**⟩
    ⟨*Create LBVHs for treelets in parallel* **426**⟩

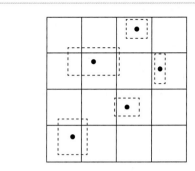

Figure 7.10: Primitive Clusters for LBVH Treelets. Primitive centroids are clustered in a uniform grid over their bounds. An LBVH is created for each cluster of primitives within a cell that are in contiguous sections of the sorted Morton index values.

Each primitive cluster is represented by an `LBVHTreelet`. It encodes the index in the `morton Prims` array of the first primitive in the cluster as well as the number of following primitives. (See Figure 7.10.)

⟨*LBVHTreelet Definition*⟩ ≡
```
struct LBVHTreelet {
    size_t startIndex, nPrimitives;
    BVHBuildNode *buildNodes;
};
```

Recall from Figure 7.9 that a set of points with Morton codes that match in their high bit values lie in a power-of-two aligned and sized subset of the original volume. Because we have already sorted the `mortonPrims` array by Morton-coded value, primitives with matching high bit values are already together in contiguous sections of the array.

Here we will find sets of primitives that have the same values for the high 12 bits of their 30-bit Morton codes. Clusters are found by taking a linear pass through the `mortonPrims` array and finding the offsets where any of the high 12 bits changes. This corresponds to clustering primitives in a regular grid of $2^{12} = 4096$ total grid cells with $2^4 = 16$ cells in each dimension. In practice, many of the grid cells will be empty, though we will still expect to find many independent clusters here.

⟨*Find intervals of primitives for each treelet*⟩ ≡   **424**
```
std::vector<LBVHTreelet> treeletsToBuild;
for (size_t start = 0, end = 1; end <= mortonPrims.size(); ++end) {
    uint32_t mask = 0b00111111111111000000000000000000;
    if (end == (int)mortonPrims.size() ||
        ((mortonPrims[start].mortonCode & mask) !=
         (mortonPrims[end].mortonCode & mask))) {
        ⟨Add entry to treeletsToBuild for this treelet 426⟩
        start = end;
    }
}
```

When a cluster of primitives has been found for a treelet, `BVHBuildNodes` are immediately allocated for it. (Recall that the number of nodes in a BVH is bounded by twice the number of leaf nodes, which in turn is bounded by the number of primitives.) It is simpler to preallocate this memory now in a serial phase of execution than during parallel construction of LBVHs.

⟨*Add entry to* `treeletsToBuild` *for this treelet*⟩ ≡   **425**
```
    size_t nPrimitives = end - start;
    int maxBVHNodes = 2 * nPrimitives - 1;
    BVHBuildNode *nodes = alloc.allocate_object<BVHBuildNode>(maxBVHNodes);
    treeletsToBuild.push_back({start, nPrimitives, nodes});
```

Once the primitives for each treelet have been identified, we can create LBVHs for them in parallel. When construction is finished, the `buildNodes` pointer for each `LBVHTreelet` will point to the root of the corresponding LBVH.

There are two places where the worker threads building LBVHs must coordinate with each other. First, the total number of nodes in all the LBVHs needs to be computed and returned via the `totalNodes` pointer passed to `buildHLBVH()`. Second, when leaf nodes are created for the LBVHs, a contiguous segment of the `orderedPrims` array is needed to record the indices of the primitives in the leaf node. Our implementation uses atomic variables for both.

⟨*Create LBVHs for treelets in parallel*⟩ ≡   **424**
```
    std::atomic<int> orderedPrimsOffset(0);
    ParallelFor(0, treeletsToBuild.size(), [&](int i) {
        ⟨Generate ith LBVH treelet 426⟩
    });
```

The work of building the treelet is performed by `emitLBVH()`, which takes primitives with centroids in some region of space and successively partitions them with splitting planes that divide the current region of space into two halves along the center of the region along one of the three axes.

Note that instead of taking a pointer to the atomic variable `totalNodes` to count the number of nodes created, `emitLBVH()` updates a non-atomic local variable. The fragment here then only updates `totalNodes` once per treelet when each treelet is done. This approach gives measurably better performance than the alternative—having the worker threads frequently modify `totalNodes` over the course of their execution. (To understand why this is so, see the discussion of the overhead of multi-core memory coherence models in Appendix B.6.3.)

⟨*Generate ith LBVH treelet*⟩ ≡   **426**
```
    int nodesCreated = 0;
    const int firstBitIndex = 29 - 12;
    LBVHTreelet &tr = treeletsToBuild[i];
    tr.buildNodes =
        emitLBVH(tr.buildNodes, bvhPrimitives, &mortonPrims[tr.startIndex],
                 tr.nPrimitives, &nodesCreated, orderedPrims,
                 &orderedPrimsOffset, firstBitIndex);
    *totalNodes += nodesCreated;
```

Thanks to the Morton encoding, the current region of space does not need to be explicitly represented in `emitLBVH()`: the sorted `MortonPrims` passed in have some number of matching high bits, which in turn corresponds to a spatial bound. For each of the remaining bits in the Morton codes, this function tries to split the primitives along the plane corresponding to the `bitIndex` bit (recall Figure 7.9(d)) and then calls itself recursively. The index of the next bit to try splitting with is passed as the last argument to the function: initially it is $29 - 12$, since 29 is the index of the 30th bit with zero-based indexing, and we previously used the high 12 bits of the Morton-coded value to cluster the primitives; thus, we know that those bits must all match for the cluster.

⟨*BVHAggregate Method Definitions*⟩ +≡
```
    BVHBuildNode *BVHAggregate::emitLBVH(BVHBuildNode *&buildNodes,
            const std::vector<BVHPrimitive> &bvhPrimitives,
            MortonPrimitive *mortonPrims, int nPrimitives, int *totalNodes,
            std::vector<Primitive> &orderedPrims,
            std::atomic<int> *orderedPrimsOffset, int bitIndex) {
        if (bitIndex == -1 || nPrimitives < maxPrimsInNode) {
            ⟨Create and return leaf node of LBVH treelet 427⟩
        } else {
            int mask = 1 << bitIndex;
            ⟨Advance to next subtree level if there is no LBVH split for this bit 427⟩
            ⟨Find LBVH split point for this dimension 428⟩
            ⟨Create and return interior LBVH node 428⟩
        }
    }
```

After `emitLBVH()` has partitioned the primitives with the final low bit, no more splitting is possible and a leaf node is created. Alternatively, it also stops and makes a leaf node if it is down to a small number of primitives.

Recall that `orderedPrimsOffset` is the offset to the next available element in the ordered Prims array. Here, the call to `fetch_add()` atomically adds the value of `nPrimitives` to `orderedPrimsOffset` and returns its old value before the addition. Given space in the array, leaf construction is similar to the approach implemented earlier in ⟨*Create leaf* BVHBuildNode⟩.

⟨*Create and return leaf node of LBVH treelet*⟩ ≡   427
```
    ++*totalNodes;
    BVHBuildNode *node = buildNodes++;
    Bounds3f bounds;
    int firstPrimOffset = orderedPrimsOffset->fetch_add(nPrimitives);
    for (int i = 0; i < nPrimitives; ++i) {
        int primitiveIndex = mortonPrims[i].primitiveIndex;
        orderedPrims[firstPrimOffset + i] = primitives[primitiveIndex];
        bounds = Union(bounds, bvhPrimitives[primitiveIndex].bounds);
    }
    node->InitLeaf(firstPrimOffset, nPrimitives, bounds);
    return node;
```

It may be the case that all the primitives lie on the same side of the splitting plane; since the primitives are sorted by their Morton index, this case can be efficiently checked by seeing if the first and last primitive in the range both have the same bit value for this plane. In this case, `emitLBVH()` proceeds to the next bit without unnecessarily creating a node.

⟨*Advance to next subtree level if there is no LBVH split for this bit*⟩ ≡   427
```
    if ((mortonPrims[0].mortonCode & mask) ==
        (mortonPrims[nPrimitives - 1].mortonCode & mask))
        return emitLBVH(buildNodes, bvhPrimitives, mortonPrims, nPrimitives,
                        totalNodes, orderedPrims, orderedPrimsOffset,
                        bitIndex - 1);
```

If there are primitives on both sides of the splitting plane, then a binary search efficiently finds the dividing point where the bitIndexth bit goes from 0 to 1 in the current set of primitives.

⟨*Find LBVH split point for this dimension*⟩ ≡   427
```
int splitOffset = FindInterval(nPrimitives, [&](int index) {
    return ((mortonPrims[0].mortonCode & mask) ==
            (mortonPrims[index].mortonCode & mask));
});
++splitOffset;
```

Given the split offset, the method can now claim a node to use as an interior node and recursively build LBVHs for both partitioned sets of primitives. Note a further efficiency benefit from Morton encoding: entries in the mortonPrims array do not need to be copied or reordered for the partition: because they are all sorted by their Morton code value and because it is processing bits from high to low, the two spans of primitives are already on the correct sides of the partition plane.

⟨*Create and return interior LBVH node*⟩ ≡   427
```
(*totalNodes)++;
BVHBuildNode *node = buildNodes++;
BVHBuildNode *lbvh[2] = {
    emitLBVH(buildNodes, bvhPrimitives, mortonPrims, splitOffset,
            totalNodes, orderedPrims, orderedPrimsOffset, bitIndex - 1),
    emitLBVH(buildNodes, bvhPrimitives, &mortonPrims[splitOffset],
            nPrimitives - splitOffset, totalNodes, orderedPrims,
            orderedPrimsOffset, bitIndex - 1)
};
int axis = bitIndex % 3;
node->InitInterior(axis, lbvh[0], lbvh[1]);
return node;
```

Once all the LBVH treelets have been created, buildUpperSAH() creates a BVH of all the treelets. Since there are generally tens or hundreds of them (and in any case, no more than 4096), this step takes very little time.

⟨*Create and return SAH BVH from LBVH treelets*⟩ ≡   422
```
std::vector<BVHBuildNode *> finishedTreelets;
for (LBVHTreelet &treelet : treeletsToBuild)
    finishedTreelets.push_back(treelet.buildNodes);
return buildUpperSAH(alloc, finishedTreelets, 0,
                    finishedTreelets.size(), totalNodes);
```

The implementation of buildUpperSAH() is not included here, as it follows the same approach as fully SAH-based BVH construction, just over treelet root nodes rather than scene primitives.

7.3.4 COMPACT BVH FOR TRAVERSAL

Once the BVH is built, the last step is to convert it into a compact representation—doing so improves cache, memory, and thus overall system performance. The final BVH is stored in a linear array in memory. The nodes of the original tree are laid out in depth-first order, which means that the first child of each interior node is immediately after the node in memory. In this case, only the offset to the second child of each interior node must be stored explicitly.

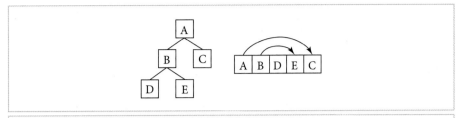

Figure 7.11: Linear Layout of a BVH in Memory. The nodes of the BVH (left) are stored in memory in depth-first order (right). Therefore, for any interior node of the tree (A and B in this example), the first child is found immediately after the parent node in memory. The second child is found via an offset pointer, represented here by lines with arrows. Leaf nodes of the tree (D, E, and C) have no children.

See Figure 7.11 for an illustration of the relationship between tree topology and node order in memory.

The LinearBVHNode structure stores the information needed to traverse the BVH. In addition to the bounding box for each node, for leaf nodes it stores the offset and primitive count for the primitives in the node. For interior nodes, it stores the offset to the second child as well as which of the coordinate axes the primitives were partitioned along when the hierarchy was built; this information is used in the traversal routine below to try to visit nodes in front-to-back order along the ray.

The structure is declared to require 32-byte alignment in memory. It could otherwise be allocated at an alignment that was sufficient to satisfy the first member variable, which would be 4 bytes for the Float-valued Bounds3f::pMin::x member variable. Because modern processor caches are organized into cache lines of a size that is a multiple of 32, a more stringent alignment constraint ensures that no LinearBVHNode straddles two cache lines. In turn, no more than a single cache miss will be incurred when one is accessed, which improves performance.

⟨*LinearBVHNode Definition*⟩ ≡
```
struct alignas(32) LinearBVHNode {
    Bounds3f bounds;
    union {
        int primitivesOffset;    // leaf
        int secondChildOffset;   // interior
    };
    uint16_t nPrimitives;  // 0 -> interior node
    uint8_t axis;          // interior node: xyz
};
```

The built tree is transformed to the LinearBVHNode representation by the flattenBVH() method, which performs a depth-first traversal and stores the nodes in memory in linear order. It is helpful to release the memory in the bvhPrimitives array before doing so, since that may be a significant amount of storage for complex scenes and is no longer needed at this point. This is handled by the resize(0) call.

Bounds3f 97
BVHAggregate::flattenBVH() 430
LinearBVHNode 429

⟨*Convert BVH into compact representation in* nodes *array*⟩ ≡   **408**
```
bvhPrimitives.resize(0);
nodes = new LinearBVHNode[totalNodes];
int offset = 0;
flattenBVH(root, &offset);
```

The pointer to the array of LinearBVHNodes is stored as a BVHAggregate member variable.

⟨*BVHAggregate Private Members*⟩ +≡   **407**
```
LinearBVHNode *nodes = nullptr;
```

Flattening the tree to the linear representation is straightforward; the *offset parameter tracks the current offset into the BVHAggregate::nodes array. Note that the current node is added to the array before any recursive calls to process its children.

⟨*BVHAggregate Method Definitions*⟩ +≡
```
int BVHAggregate::flattenBVH(BVHBuildNode *node, int *offset) {
    LinearBVHNode *linearNode = &nodes[*offset];
    linearNode->bounds = node->bounds;
    int nodeOffset = (*offset)++;
    if (node->nPrimitives > 0) {
        linearNode->primitivesOffset = node->firstPrimOffset;
        linearNode->nPrimitives = node->nPrimitives;
    } else {
        ⟨Create interior flattened BVH node 430⟩
    }
    return nodeOffset;
}
```

At interior nodes, recursive calls are made to flatten the two subtrees. The first one ends up immediately after the current node in the array, as desired, and the offset of the second one, returned by its recursive flattenBVH() call, is stored in this node's secondChildOffset member.

⟨*Create interior flattened BVH node*⟩ ≡   **430**
```
linearNode->axis = node->splitAxis;
linearNode->nPrimitives = 0;
flattenBVH(node->children[0], offset);
linearNode->secondChildOffset = flattenBVH(node->children[1], offset);
```

7.3.5 BOUNDING AND INTERSECTION TESTS

Given a built BVH, the implementation of the Bounds() method is easy: by definition, the root node's bounds are the bounds of all the primitives in the tree, so those can be returned directly.

⟨*BVHAggregate Method Definitions*⟩ +≡
```
Bounds3f BVHAggregate::Bounds() const {
    return nodes[0].bounds;
}
```

The BVH traversal code is quite simple—there are no recursive function calls and a small amount of data to maintain about the current state of the traversal. The Intersect() method starts by precomputing a few values related to the ray that will be used repeatedly.

⟨*BVHAggregate Method Definitions*⟩ +≡
```
pstd::optional<ShapeIntersection>
BVHAggregate::Intersect(const Ray &ray, Float tMax) const {
    pstd::optional<ShapeIntersection> si;
    Vector3f invDir(1 / ray.d.x, 1 / ray.d.y, 1 / ray.d.z);
    int dirIsNeg[3] = {int(invDir.x < 0), int(invDir.y < 0),
                       int(invDir.z < 0)};
    ⟨Follow ray through BVH nodes to find primitive intersections 431⟩
    return si;
}
```

Each time the following `while` loop starts an iteration, `currentNodeIndex` holds the offset into the nodes array of the node to be visited. It starts with a value of 0, representing the root of the tree. The nodes that still need to be visited are stored in the `nodesToVisit[]` array, which acts as a stack; `toVisitOffset` holds the offset to the next free element in the stack. With the following traversal algorithm, the number of nodes in the stack is never more than the maximum tree depth. A statically allocated stack of 64 entries is sufficient in practice.

⟨*Follow ray through BVH nodes to find primitive intersections*⟩ ≡   431
```
int toVisitOffset = 0, currentNodeIndex = 0;
int nodesToVisit[64];
while (true) {
    const LinearBVHNode *node = &nodes[currentNodeIndex];
    ⟨Check ray against BVH node 431⟩
}
```

At each node, the first step is to check if the ray intersects the node's bounding box (or starts inside of it). The node is visited if so, with its primitives tested for intersection if it is a leaf node or its children are visited if it is an interior node. If no intersection is found, then the offset of the next node to be visited is retrieved from `nodesToVisit[]` (or traversal is complete if the stack is empty). See Figures 7.12 and 7.13 for visualizations of how many nodes are visited and how many intersection tests are performed at each pixel for two complex scenes.

⟨*Check ray against BVH node*⟩ ≡   431
```
if (node->bounds.IntersectP(ray.o, ray.d, tMax, invDir, dirIsNeg)) {
    if (node->nPrimitives > 0) {
        ⟨Intersect ray with primitives in leaf BVH node 433⟩
    } else {
        ⟨Put far BVH node on nodesToVisit stack, advance to near node 434⟩
    }
} else {
    if (toVisitOffset == 0) break;
    currentNodeIndex = nodesToVisit[--toVisitOffset];
}
```

If the current node is a leaf, then the ray must be tested for intersection with the primitives inside it. The next node to visit is then found from the `nodesToVisit` stack; even if an intersection is found in the current node, the remaining nodes must be visited in case one of them yields a closer intersection.

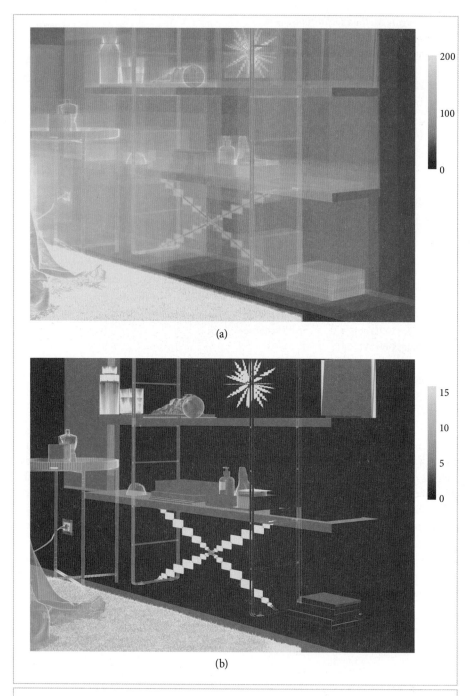

(a)

(b)

Figure 7.12: Visualization of BVH Performance with the *Kroken* Scene. (a) Number of BVH nodes visited when tracing the camera ray at each pixel for the scene shown in Figure 1.1. Not only are more nodes visited in geometrically complex regions of the scene such as the rug, but objects that are not accurately bounded by axis-aligned bounding boxes such as the support under the bottom shelf lead to many nodes being visited. (b) Number of ray–triangle intersection tests performed for the camera ray at each pixel. The BVH is effective at limiting the number of intersection tests even in highly complex regions of the scene like the rug. However, objects that are poorly fit by axis-aligned bounding boxes lead to many intersection tests for rays in their vicinity. *(Kroken scene courtesy of Angelo Ferretti.)*

(a)

(b)

Figure 7.13: Visualization of BVH Performance with the *Moana Island* Scene. (a) Number of BVH nodes visited when tracing the camera ray at each pixel for the scene shown in Figure 1.4. As with the *Kroken* scene, silhouette edges and regions where the ray passes by many objects before finding an intersection see the most nodes visited. (b) Number of ray–triangle intersection tests performed for the camera ray at each pixel. The most geometrically complex trees and the detailed ground cover on the beach require the most intersection tests. *(Scene courtesy of Walt Disney Animation Studios.)*

⟨*Intersect ray with primitives in leaf BVH node*⟩ ≡   **431**
```
    for (int i = 0; i < node->nPrimitives; ++i) {
        ⟨Check for intersection with primitive in BVH node 434⟩
    }
    if (toVisitOffset == 0) break;
    currentNodeIndex = nodesToVisit[--toVisitOffset];
```

LinearBVHNode::nPrimitives
429

If an intersection is found, the tMax value can be updated to the intersection's parametric distance along the ray; this makes it possible to efficiently discard any remaining nodes that are farther away than the intersection.

⟨*Check for intersection with primitive in BVH node*⟩ ≡   433
```
    pstd::optional<ShapeIntersection> primSi =
        primitives[node->primitivesOffset + i].Intersect(ray, tMax);
    if (primSi) {
        si = primSi;
        tMax = si->tHit;
    }
```

For an interior node that the ray hits, it is necessary to visit both of its children. As described above, it is desirable to visit the first child that the ray passes through before visiting the second one in case the ray intersects a primitive in the first one. If so, the ray's tMax value can be updated, thus reducing the ray's extent and thus the number of node bounding boxes it intersects.

An efficient way to perform a front-to-back traversal without incurring the expense of intersecting the ray with both child nodes and comparing the distances is to use the sign of the ray's direction vector for the coordinate axis along which primitives were partitioned for the current node: if the sign is negative, we should visit the second child before the first child, since the primitives that went into the second child's subtree were on the upper side of the partition point. (And conversely for a positive-signed direction.) Doing this is straightforward: the offset for the node to be visited first is copied to currentNodeIndex, and the offset for the other node is added to the nodesToVisit stack. (Recall that the first child is immediately after the current node due to the depth-first layout of nodes in memory.)

⟨*Put far BVH node on* nodesToVisit *stack, advance to near node*⟩ ≡   431
```
    if (dirIsNeg[node->axis]) {
        nodesToVisit[toVisitOffset++] = currentNodeIndex + 1;
        currentNodeIndex = node->secondChildOffset;
    } else {
        nodesToVisit[toVisitOffset++] = node->secondChildOffset;
        currentNodeIndex = currentNodeIndex + 1;
    }
```

The BVHAggregate::IntersectP() method is essentially the same as the regular intersection method, with the two differences that Primitive's IntersectP() methods are called rather than Intersect(), and traversal stops immediately when any intersection is found. It is thus not included here.

FURTHER READING

The stochastic alpha test implemented in Section 7.1.1 builds on ideas introduced in Enderton et al.'s stochastic approach for transparency (2010) and Wyman and McGuire's hashed alpha testing algorithm (2017), both of which were focused on rasterization-based rendering.

After the introduction of the ray-tracing algorithm, an enormous amount of research was done to try to find effective ways to speed it up, primarily by developing improved raytracing acceleration structures. Arvo and Kirk's chapter in *An Introduction to Ray Tracing* (Glassner 1989a) summarizes the state of the art as of 1989 and still provides an excellent taxonomy for categorizing different approaches to ray intersection acceleration.

Kirk and Arvo (1988) introduced the unifying principle of *meta-hierarchies*. They showed that by implementing acceleration data structures to conform to the same interface as is used for primitives in the scene, it is easy to mix and match different intersection acceleration schemes. pbrt follows this model.

Grids

Fujimoto, Tanaka, and Iwata (1986) introduced uniform grids, a spatial subdivision approach where the scene bounds are decomposed into equally sized grid cells. More efficient grid-traversal methods were described by Amanatides and Woo (1987) and Cleary and Wyvill (1988). Snyder and Barr (1987) described a number of key improvements to this approach and showed the use of grids for rendering extremely complex scenes. Hierarchical grids, where grid cells with many primitives in them are themselves refined into grids, were introduced by Jevans and Wyvill (1989). More sophisticated techniques for hierarchical grids were developed by Cazals, Drettakis, and Puech (1995) and Klimaszewski and Sederberg (1997).

Ize et al. (2006) developed an efficient algorithm for parallel construction of grids. One of their interesting findings was that grid construction performance quickly became limited by memory bandwidth as the number of cores used increased.

Choosing an optimal grid resolution is important for getting good performance from grids. A good paper on this topic is by Ize et al. (2007), who provided a solid foundation for automatically selecting the resolution and for deciding when to refine into subgrids when using hierarchical grids. They derived theoretical results using a number of simplifying assumptions and then showed the applicability of the results to rendering real-world scenes. Their paper also includes a good selection of pointers to previous work in this area.

Lagae and Dutré (2008a) described an innovative representation for uniform grids based on hashing that has the desirable properties that not only does each primitive have a single index into a grid cell, but also each cell has only a single primitive index. They showed that this representation has very low memory usage and is still quite efficient.

Hunt and Mark (2008a) showed that building grids in perspective space, where the center of projection is the camera or a light source, can make tracing rays from the camera or light substantially more efficient. Although this approach requires multiple acceleration structures, the performance benefits from multiple specialized structures for different classes of rays can be substantial. Their approach is also notable in that it is in some ways a middle ground between rasterization and ray tracing.

Bounding Volume Hierarchies

Clark (1976) first suggested using bounding volumes to cull collections of objects for standard visible-surface determination algorithms. Building on this work, Rubin and Whitted (1980) developed the first hierarchical data structures for scene representation for fast ray tracing, although their method depended on the user to define the hierarchy. Kay and Kajiya (1986) implemented one of the first practical object subdivision approaches based on bounding objects with collections of slabs.

Goldsmith and Salmon (1987) described the first algorithm for automatically computing bounding volume hierarchies. Although their algorithm was based on estimating the probability of a ray intersecting a bounding volume using the volume's surface area, it was much less effective than modern SAH BVH approaches. The first use of the SAH for BVH construction was described by Müller and Fellner (1999); another early application is due to Massó and López (2003).

The BVHAggregate implementation in this chapter is based on the construction algorithm described by Wald (2007) and Günther et al. (2007). The bounding box test is the one introduced by Williams et al. (2005). An even more efficient bounding box test that does additional precomputation in exchange for higher performance when the same ray is tested for intersection against many bounding boxes was developed by Eisemann et al. (2007); we leave implementing their method for an exercise. Ize's robust ray–bounding box intersection algorithm ensures that the BVH is *watertight* and that valid intersections are not missed due to numeric error (Ize 2013).

The BVH traversal algorithm used in pbrt was concurrently developed by a number of researchers; see the notes by Boulos and Haines (2006) for more details and background. Another option for tree traversal is that of Kay and Kajiya (1986); they maintained a heap of nodes ordered by ray distance. On GPUs, which have relatively limited amounts of on-chip memory, maintaining a stack of to-be-visited nodes for each ray may have a prohibitive memory cost. Foley and Sugerman (2005) introduced a "stackless" kd-tree traversal algorithm that periodically backtracks and searches starting from the tree root to find the next node to visit, rather than storing all nodes to visit explicitly. Laine (2010) made a number of improvements to this approach, reducing the frequency of re-traversals from the tree root and applying the approach to BVHs. See also Binder and Keller (2016), who applied perfect hashing to finding subsequent nodes to visit with the stackless approach.

An innovative approach to BVH traversal is described by Hendrich et al. (2019), who created a spatio-directional 5D data structure that records a set of BVH nodes that are used to seed the traversal stack for sets of rays. Given a particular ray, traversal starts immediately with an appropriate stack, which in turn improves performance by entirely skipping processing of BVH nodes that are either certain to be intersected or certain not to be intersected for rays in a particular set.

A number of researchers have developed techniques for improving the quality of BVHs after construction. Yoon et al. (2007) and Kensler (2008) presented algorithms that make local adjustments to the BVH. See also Bittner et al. (2013, 2014), Karras and Aila (2013), and Meister and Bittner (2018a) for further work in this area. An interesting approach was described by Gu et al. (2015), who constructed a BVH, traced a relatively small number of representative rays, and gathered statistics about how frequently each bounding box was intersected, and then tuned the BVH to be more efficient for rays with similar statistics.

Most current methods for building BVHs are based on top-down construction of the tree, first creating the root node and then partitioning the primitives into children and continuing recursively. An alternative approach was demonstrated by Walter et al. (2008), who showed that bottom-up construction, where the leaves are created first and then agglomerated into parent nodes, is a viable option. Gu et al. (2013b) developed a much more efficient implementation of this approach and showed its suitability for parallel implementation, and Meister and Bittner (2018b) described a bottom-up approach that is suitable for GPU implementation.

One shortcoming of BVHs is that even a small number of relatively large primitives that have overlapping bounding boxes can substantially reduce the efficiency of the BVH: many of the nodes of the tree will be overlapping, solely due to the overlapping bounding boxes of geometry down at the leaves. Ernst and Greiner (2007) proposed "split clipping" as a solution; the restriction that each primitive only appears once in the tree is lifted, and the bounding boxes of large input primitives are subdivided into a set of tighter subbounds that are then used for tree construction.

BVHAggregate 407

Dammertz and Keller (2008a) observed that the problematic primitives are the ones with a large amount of empty space in their bounding box relative to their surface area, so they subdivided the most egregious triangles and reported substantial performance improvements. Stich et al. (2009) developed an approach that splits primitives during BVH construction, making it possible to only split primitives when an SAH cost reduction was found. See also Popov et al.'s paper (2009) on a theoretically optimal BVH partitioning algorithm and its relationship to previous approaches, and Karras and Aila (2013) for improved criteria for deciding when to split triangles. Woop et al. (2014) developed an approach to building BVHs for long, thin geometry like hair and fur; because this sort of geometry is quite thin with respect to the volume of its bounding boxes, it normally has poor performance with most acceleration structures. Ganestam and Doggett (2016) have proposed a splitting approach that has benefits to both BVH construction and traversal efficiency.

The memory requirements for BVHs can be significant. In our implementation, each node is 32 bytes. With up to 2 BVH nodes needed per primitive in the scene, the total overhead may be as high as 64 bytes per primitive. Cline et al. (2006) suggested a more compact representation for BVH nodes, at some expense of efficiency. First, they quantized the bounding box stored in each node using 8 or 16 bytes to encode its position with respect to the node's parent's bounding box. Second, they used *implicit indexing*, where the node i's children are at positions $2i$ and $2i + 1$ in the node array (assuming a $2\times$ branching factor). They showed substantial memory savings, with moderate performance impact. Bauszat et al. (2010) developed another space-efficient BVH representation. See also Segovia and Ernst (2010), who developed compact representations of both BVH nodes and triangle meshes. A BVH specialized for space-efficient storage of parametric surfaces was described by Selgrad et al. (2017) and an adoption of this approach for displaced subdivision surfaces was presented by Lier et al. (2018a).

Other work in the area of space-efficient BVHs includes that of Vaidyanathan et al. (2016), who introduced a reduced-precision representation of the BVH that still guarantees conservative intersection tests with respect to the original BVH. Liktor and Vaidyanathan (2016) introduced a BVH node representation based on clustering nodes that improves cache performance and reduces storage requirements for child node pointers. Ylitie et al. (2017) showed how to optimally convert binary BVHs into wider BVHs with more children at each node, from which they derived a compressed BVH representation that shows a substantial bandwidth reduction with incoherent rays. Vaidyanathan et al. (2019) developed an algorithm for efficiently traversing such wide BVHs using a small stack. Benthin et al. (2018) focused on compressing sets of adjacent leaf nodes of BVHs under the principle that most of the memory is used at the leaves, and Lin et al. (2019) described an approach that saves both computation and storage by taking advantage of shared planes among the bounds of the children of a BVH node.

Yoon and Manocha (2006) described algorithms for cache-efficient layout of BVHs and kd-trees and demonstrated performance improvements from using them. See also Ericson's book (2004) for extensive discussion of this topic.

The linear BVH was introduced by Lauterbach et al. (2009); Morton codes were first described in a report by Morton (1966). Pantaleoni and Luebke (2010) developed the HLBVH generalization, using the SAH at the upper levels of the tree. They also noted that the upper bits of the Morton-coded values can be used to efficiently find clusters of primitives—both of these ideas are used in our HLBVH implementation. Garanzha et al. (2011) introduced further improvements to the HLBVH, most of them targeting GPU implementations.

Vinkler et al. (2017) described improved techniques for mapping values to the Morton index coordinates that lead to higher-quality BVHs, especially for scenes with a range of primitive sizes.

Wald (2012) described an approach for high-performance parallel BVH construction on CPUs that uses the SAH throughout. More recently, Benthin et al. (2017) have described a two-level BVH construction technique based on building high-quality second-level BVHs for collections of objects in a scene, collecting them into a single BVH, and then iteratively refining the overall tree, including moving subtrees from one of the initial BVHs to another. Hendrich et al. (2017) described a related technique, quickly building an initial LBVH and then progressively building a higher-quality BVH based on it.

A comprehensive survey of work in bounding volume hierarchies, spanning construction, representation, traversal, and hardware acceleration, was recently published by Meister et al. (2021).

kd-trees

Glassner (1984) introduced the use of octrees for ray intersection acceleration. Use of the kd-tree for ray tracing was first described by Kaplan (1985). Kaplan's tree construction algorithm always split nodes down their middle; MacDonald and Booth (1990) introduced the SAH approach, estimating ray–node traversal probabilities using relative surface areas. Naylor (1993) has also written on general issues of constructing good kd-trees. Havran and Bittner (2002) revisited many of these issues and introduced useful improvements. Adding a bonus factor to the SAH for tree nodes that are completely empty was suggested by Hurley et al. (2002). See Havran's Ph.D. thesis (2000) for an excellent overview of high-performance kd-construction and traversal algorithms.

Jansen (1986) first developed the efficient ray-traversal algorithm for kd-trees. Arvo (1988) also investigated this problem and discussed it in a note in *Ray Tracing News*. Sung and Shirley (1992) described a ray-traversal algorithm's implementation for a BSP-tree accelerator; our `KdTreeAggregate` traversal code (included in the online edition) is loosely based on theirs.

The asymptotic complexity of the kd-tree construction algorithm in pbrt is $O(n \log^2 n)$. Wald and Havran (2006) showed that it is possible to build kd-trees in $O(n \log n)$ time with some additional implementation complexity; they reported a 2 to 3× speedup in construction time for typical scenes.

The best kd-trees for ray tracing are built using "perfect splits," where the primitive being inserted into the tree is clipped to the bounds of the current node at each step. This eliminates the issue that, for example, an object's bounding box may intersect a node's bounding box and thus be stored in it, even though the object itself does not intersect the node's bounding box. This approach was introduced by Havran and Bittner (2002) and discussed further by Hurley et al. (2002), Wald and Havran (2006), and Soupikov et al. (2008). Even with perfect splits, large primitives may still be stored in many kd-tree leaves; Choi et al. (2013) suggested storing some primitives in interior nodes to address this issue.

kd-tree construction tends to be much slower than BVH construction (especially if "perfect splits" are used), so parallel construction algorithms are of particular interest. Work in this area includes that of Shevtsov et al. (2007b) and Choi et al. (2010), who presented efficient parallel kd-tree construction algorithms with good scalability to multiple processors.

The Surface Area Heuristic

A number of researchers have investigated improvements to the SAH since its introduction to ray tracing by MacDonald and Booth (1990). Fabianowski et al. (2009) derived a

KdTreeAggregate 406

version that replaces the assumption that rays are uniformly distributed throughout space with the assumption that ray origins are uniformly distributed inside the scene's bounding box. Hunt and Mark (2008b) introduced a modified SAH that accounts for the fact that rays generally are not uniformly distributed but rather that many of them originate from a single point or a set of nearby points (cameras and light sources, respectively). Hunt (2008) showed how the SAH should be modified when the "mailboxing" optimization is being used, and Vinkler et al. (2012) used assumptions about the visibility of primitives to adjust their SAH cost. Ize and Hansen (2011) derived a "ray termination surface area heuristic" (RTSAH), which they used to adjust BVH traversal order for shadow rays in order to more quickly find intersections with occluders. See also Moulin et al. (2015), who adapted the SAH to account for shadow rays being occluded during kd-tree traversal.

While the SAH has led to very effective kd-trees and BVHs, a number of researchers have noted that it is not unusual to encounter cases where a kd-tree or BVH with a higher SAH-estimated cost gives better performance than one with lower estimated cost. Aila et al. (2013) surveyed some of these results and proposed two additional heuristics that help address them; one accounts for the fact that most rays start on surfaces—ray origins are not actually randomly distributed throughout the scene—and another accounts for SIMD divergence when multiple rays traverse the hierarchy together. While these new heuristics are effective at explaining why a given tree delivers the performance that it does, it is not yet clear how to incorporate them into tree construction algorithms.

Evaluating the SAH can be costly, particularly when many different splits or primitive partitions are being considered. One solution to this problem is to only compute it at a subset of the candidate points—for example, along the lines of the bucketing approach used in the BVHAggregate in pbrt. Hurley et al. (2002) suggested this approach for building kd-trees, and Popov et al. (2006) discussed it in detail. Shevtsov et al. (2007b) introduced the improvement of binning the full extents of triangles, not just their centroids.

Wodniok and Goesele constructed BVHs where the SAH cost estimate is not based on primitive counts and primitive bounds but is instead found by actually building BVHs for various partitions and computing their SAH cost (Wodniok and Goesele 2016). They showed a meaningful improvement in ray intersection performance, though at a cost of impractically long BVH construction times.

Hunt et al. (2006) noted that if you only have to evaluate the SAH at one point, for example, you do not need to sort the primitives but only need to do a linear scan over them to compute primitive counts and bounding boxes at the point. pbrt's implementation follows that approach. They also showed that approximating the SAH with a piecewise quadratic based on evaluating it at a number of individual positions, and using that to choose a good split, leads to effective trees. A similar approximation was used by Popov et al. (2006).

Other Topics in Acceleration Structures

Weghorst, Hooper, and Greenberg (1984) discussed the trade-offs of using various shapes for bounding volumes and suggested projecting objects to the screen and using a z-buffer rendering to accelerate finding intersections for camera rays.

A number of researchers have investigated the applicability of general BSP trees, where the splitting planes are not necessarily axis aligned, as they are with kd-trees. Kammaje and Mora (2007) built BSP trees using a preselected set of candidate splitting planes. Budge et al. (2008) developed a number of improvements to their approach, though their results only approached kd-tree performance in practice due to a slower construction stage and slower

BVHAggregate 407

traversal than kd-trees. Ize et al. (2008) showed a BSP implementation that renders scenes faster than kd-trees but at the cost of extremely long construction times.

There are many techniques for traversing a collection of rays through the acceleration structure together, rather than just one at a time. This approach ("packet tracing") is an important component of many high-performance ray tracing approaches; it is discussed in more detail in Section 16.2.3.

Animated primitives present two challenges to ray tracers: first, renderers that try to reuse acceleration structures over multiple frames of an animation must update the acceleration structures if objects are moving. Lauterbach et al. (2006) and Wald et al. (2007a) showed how to incrementally update BVHs in this case, and Kopta et al. (2012) reused BVHs over multiple frames of an animation, maintaining their quality by updating the parts that bound moving objects. Garanzha (2009) suggested creating clusters of nearby primitives and then building BVHs of those clusters (thus lightening the load on the BVH construction algorithm).

A second challenge from animated primitives is that for primitives that are moving quickly, the bounding boxes of their full motion over the frame time may be quite large, leading to many unnecessary ray–primitive intersection tests. Notable work on this issue includes Glassner (1988), who generalized ray tracing (and an octree for acceleration) to four dimensions, adding time. More recently, Grünschloß et al. (2011) developed improvements to BVHs for moving primitives. See also Wald et al.'s (2007b) survey paper on ray tracing animated scenes. Woop et al. (2017) described a generalization of BVHs that also allows nodes to split in time, with child nodes of such a split accounting for different time ranges.

An innovative approach to acceleration structures was suggested by Arvo and Kirk (1987), who introduced a 5D data structure that subdivided based on both 3D spatial and 2D ray directions. Another interesting approach for scenes described with triangle meshes was developed by Lagae and Dutré (2008b): they computed a constrained tetrahedralization, where all triangle faces of the model are represented in the tetrahedralization. Rays are then stepped through tetrahedra until they intersect a triangle from the scene description. This approach is still a few times slower than the state of the art in kd-trees and BVHs but is an interesting new way to think about the problem.

There is a middle ground between kd-trees and BVHs, where the tree node holds a splitting plane for each child rather than just a single splitting plane. This refinement makes it possible to do object subdivision in a kd-tree-like acceleration structure, putting each primitive in just one subtree and allowing the subtrees to overlap, while still preserving many of the benefits of efficient kd-tree traversal. Ooi et al. (1987) first introduced this refinement to kd-trees for storing spatial data, naming it the "spatial kd-tree" (skd-tree). Skd-trees have been applied to ray tracing by a number of researchers, including Zachmann (2002), Woop et al. (2006), Wächter and Keller (2006), Havran et al. (2006), and Zuniga and Uhlmann (2006).

When spatial subdivision approaches like grids or kd-trees are used, primitives may overlap multiple nodes of the structure and a ray may be tested for intersection with the same primitive multiple times as it passes through the structure. Arnaldi, Priol, and Bouatouch (1987) and Amanatides and Woo (1987) developed the "mailboxing" technique to address this issue: each ray is given a unique integer identifier, and each primitive records the id of the last ray that was tested against it. If the ids match, then the intersection test is unnecessary and can be skipped.

While effective, mailboxing does not work well with a multi-threaded ray tracer. To address this issue, Benthin (2006) suggested storing a small per-ray hash table to record ids of recently intersected primitives. Shevtsov et al. (2007a) maintained a small array of the last n intersected primitive ids and searched it linearly before performing intersection tests. Although some primitives may still be checked multiple times with both of these approaches, they usually eliminate most redundant tests.

EXERCISES

◐ 7.1   What kinds of scenes are worst-case scenarios for the two acceleration structures in pbrt? (Consider specific geometric configurations that the approaches will respectively be unable to handle well.) Construct scenes with these characteristics, and measure the performance of pbrt as you add more primitives. How does the worst case for one behave when rendered with the other?

◐ 7.2   Implement a hierarchical grid accelerator where cells that have an excessive number of primitives overlapping them are refined to instead hold a finer subgrid to store its geometry. (See, for example, Jevans and Wyvill (1989) for one approach to this problem and Ize et al. (2007) for effective methods for deciding when refinement is worthwhile.) Compare both accelerator construction performance and rendering performance to a non-hierarchical grid as well as to pbrt's built-in accelerators.

◐ 7.3   Implement "split clipping" in pbrt's BVH implementation. Read one or more papers on this topic, including ones by Ernst and Greiner (2007), Dammertz and Keller (2008a), Stich et al. (2009), Karras and Aila (2013), and Ganestam and Doggett (2016), and implement one of their approaches to subdivide primitives with large bounding boxes relative to their surface area into multiple subprimitives for tree construction. (Doing so will probably require modification to the Shape interface; you will probably want to design a new interface that allows some shapes to indicate that they are unable to subdivide themselves, so that you only need to implement this method for triangles, for example.)

             Measure the improvement for rendering actual scenes; a compelling way to gather this data is to do the experiment that Dammertz and Keller did, where a scene is rotated around an axis over progressive frames of an animation. Typically, many triangles that are originally axis aligned will have very loose bounding boxes as they rotate more, leading to a substantial performance degradation if split clipping is not used.

◐ 7.4   The 30-bit Morton codes used for the HLBVH construction algorithm in the BVHAggregate may be insufficient for scenes with large spatial extents because they can only represent $2^{10} = 1024$ steps in each dimension. Modify the BVHAggregate to use 64-bit integers with 63-bit Morton codes for HLBVHs. Compare the performance of your approach to the original one with a variety of scenes. Are there scenes where performance is substantially improved? Are there any where there is a loss of performance?

◐ 7.5   Investigate alternative SAH cost functions for building BVHs or kd-trees. How much can a poor cost function hurt its performance? How much improvement can be had compared to the current one? (See the discussion in the "Further Reading" section for ideas about how the SAH may be improved.)

7.6   The idea of using spatial data structures for ray intersection acceleration can be generalized to include spatial data structures that themselves hold other spatial data structures rather than just primitives. Not only could we have a grid that has subgrids inside the grid cells that have many primitives in them, but we could also have the scene organized into a hierarchical bounding volume where the leaf nodes are grids that hold smaller collections of spatially nearby primitives. Such hybrid techniques can bring the best of a variety of spatial data structure–based ray intersection acceleration methods. In pbrt, because both geometric primitives and intersection accelerators implement the Primitive interface and thus provide the same interface, it is easy to mix and match in this way.

Modify pbrt to build hybrid acceleration structures—for example, using a BVH to coarsely partition the scene geometry and then uniform grids at the leaves of the tree to manage dense, spatially local collections of geometry. Measure the running time and memory use for rendering scenes with this method compared to the current aggregates.

7.7   Eisemann et al. (2007) described an even more efficient ray–box intersection test than is used in the BVHAggregate. It does more computation at the start for each ray but makes up for this work with fewer computations to do tests for individual bounding boxes. Implement their method in pbrt, and measure the change in rendering time for a variety of scenes. Are there simple scenes where the additional upfront work does not pay off? How does the improvement for highly complex scenes compare to the improvement for simpler scenes?

7.8   Although the intersection algorithm implemented in the IntersectTriangle() function is watertight, a source of inaccuracy in ray–triangle intersections computed in pbrt remains: because the triangle intersection algorithm shears the vertices of the triangle, it may no longer lie in its original bounding box. In turn, the BVH traversal algorithm must be modified to account for this error so that valid intersections are not missed. Read the discussion of this issue in Woop et al.'s paper (2013) and modify pbrt to fix this issue. What is the performance impact of your fix? Can you find any scenes where the image changes as a result of it?

7.9   Read the paper by Segovia and Ernst (2010) on memory-efficient BVHs, and implement their approach in pbrt. How does memory usage with their approach compare to that for the BVHAggregate? Compare rendering performance with your approach to pbrt's current performance. Discuss how your results compare to the results reported in their paper.

7.10   Consider a scene with an animated camera that is tracking a moving object such that there is no relative motion between the two. For such a scene, it may be more efficient to represent it with the camera and object being static and with a corresponding relative animated transformation applied to the rest of the scene. In this way, ray intersections with the tracked object will be more efficient since its bounding box is not expanded by its motion.

Construct such a scene and then measure the performance of rendering it with both ways of representing the motion by making corresponding changes to the scene description file. How is performance affected by the size of the tracked object in the image? Next, modify pbrt to automatically perform this optimization when this situation occurs. Can you find a way to have these benefits when the motion of the camera and some objects in the scene are close but not exactly the same?

BVHAggregate 407
IntersectTriangle() 303
Primitive 398

● **7.11** It is often possible to introduce some approximation into the computation of shadows from very complex geometry (consider, e.g., the branches and leaves of a tree casting a shadow). Lacewell et al. (2008) suggested augmenting the acceleration structure with a prefiltered directionally varying representation of occlusion for regions of space. As shadow rays pass through these regions, an approximate visibility probability can be returned rather than a binary result, and the cost of tree traversal and object intersection tests is reduced. Implement such an approach in pbrt, and compare its performance to the current implementation. Do you see any changes in rendered images?

CHAPTER EIGHT

08 SAMPLING AND RECONSTRUCTION

Although the final output of a renderer is generally a 2D grid of colored pixels, incident radiance is actually a continuous function defined over the film plane. The manner in which the discrete pixel values are computed from this continuous function can noticeably affect the quality of the final image generated by the renderer; if this process is not performed carefully, artifacts will be present. Conversely, if it is performed well, a relatively small amount of additional computation to this end can substantially improve the quality of the rendered images. We have thus far approached this topic from the perspective of Monte Carlo integration, though other viewpoints can also give useful insight.

This chapter starts by introducing *sampling theory*—the theory of taking discrete sample values from functions defined over continuous domains and then using those samples to reconstruct new functions that are similar to the original. In pbrt, integration is more often the goal than reconstruction is, though we will see that Fourier analysis—the foundation of sampling theory—also provides insight about error in Monte Carlo integration. We discuss those connections as well as other approaches for evaluating the quality of sampling algorithms in the second section of this chapter.

With these ideas in hand, the implementations of six Samplers make up the bulk of this chapter. They span a wide variety of approaches to the sampling problem. The chapter concludes with the Filter class, which determines how multiple samples near each pixel are blended together to compute the final pixel value. Both of pbrt's Film implementations use these filters to accumulate image sample contributions into pixels of images.

8.1 SAMPLING THEORY

Filter 515

A digital image is represented as a set of pixel values, typically aligned on a rectangular grid. When a digital image is displayed on a physical device, these values are used to determine the spectral power emitted by pixels on the display. When thinking about digital images, it is important to differentiate between image pixels, which represent the value of a function at a particular sample location, and display pixels, which are physical objects that emit light with some spatial and directional distribution. (For example, in an LCD display, the color and brightness may change substantially when the display is viewed at oblique angles.) Displays use the image pixel values to construct a new image function over the display surface. This function is defined at all points on the display, not just the infinitesimal points of the digital image's pixels. This process of taking a collection of sample values and converting them back to a continuous function is called *reconstruction*.

In order to compute the discrete pixel values in the digital image, it is necessary to sample the original continuously defined image function. In pbrt, like most other ray-tracing renderers, the only way to get information about the image function is to sample it by tracing rays. For example, there is no general method that can compute bounds on the variation of the image function between two points on the film plane. While an image could be generated by just sampling the function precisely at the pixel positions, a better result can be obtained by taking more samples at different positions and incorporating this additional information about the image function into the final pixel values. Indeed, for the best quality result, the pixel values should be computed such that the reconstructed image on the display device is as close as possible to the original image of the scene on the virtual camera's film plane. Note that this is a subtly different goal from expecting the display's pixels to take on the image function's actual value at their positions. Handling this difference is the main goal of the algorithms implemented in this chapter.[1]

Because the sampling and reconstruction process involves approximation, it introduces error known as *aliasing,* which can manifest itself in many ways, including jagged edges or flickering in animations. These errors occur because the sampling process is not able to capture all the information from the continuously defined image function.

As an example of these ideas, consider a 1D function (which we will interchangeably refer to as a signal), given by $f(x)$, where we can evaluate $f(x')$ at any desired location x' in the function's domain. Each such x' is called a *sample position*, and the value of $f(x')$ is the *sample value*. Figure 8.1 shows a set of samples of a smooth 1D function, along with a reconstructed signal $\tilde{f}$ that approximates the original function f. In this example, $\tilde{f}$ is a piecewise linear function that approximates f by linearly interpolating neighboring sample values (readers already familiar with sampling theory will recognize this as reconstruction with a hat function). Because the only information available about f comes from the sample values at the positions x', $\tilde{f}$ is unlikely to match f perfectly since there is no information about f's behavior between the samples.

Fourier analysis can be used to evaluate the quality of the match between the reconstructed function and the original. This section will introduce the main ideas of Fourier analysis with enough detail to work through some parts of the sampling and reconstruction processes but will omit proofs of many properties and skip details that are not directly relevant to the sampling algorithms used in pbrt. The "Further Reading" section of this chapter has pointers to more detailed information about these topics.

8.1.1 THE FREQUENCY DOMAIN AND THE FOURIER TRANSFORM

One of the foundations of Fourier analysis is the Fourier transform, which represents a function in the *frequency domain*. (We will say that functions are normally expressed in

---

1   In this book, we will ignore issues related to the characteristics of physical display pixels and will work under the assumption that the display performs the ideal reconstruction process described later in this section. This assumption is patently at odds with how actual displays work, but it avoids unnecessary complication of the analysis here. Chapter 3 of Glassner (1995) has a good treatment of nonidealized display devices and their impact on the image sampling and reconstruction process.

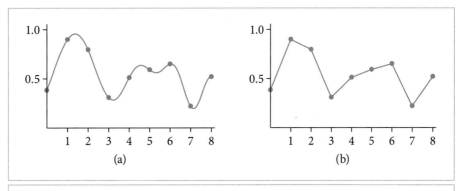

Figure 8.1: (a) By taking a set of *point samples* of $f(x)$ (indicated by dots), we determine the value of the function at those positions. (b) The sample values can be used to *reconstruct* a function $\tilde{f}(x)$ that is an approximation to $f(x)$. The sampling theorem, introduced in Section 8.1.3, makes a precise statement about the conditions on $f(x)$, the number of samples taken, and the reconstruction technique used under which $\tilde{f}(x)$ is exactly the same as $f(x)$. The fact that the original function can sometimes be reconstructed exactly from point samples alone is remarkable.

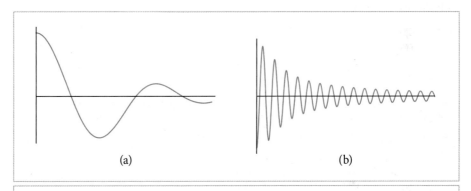

Figure 8.2: (a) Low-frequency function and (b) high-frequency function. Roughly speaking, the higher frequency a function is, the more quickly it varies over a given region.

the *spatial domain*.) Consider the two functions graphed in Figure 8.2. The function in Figure 8.2(a) varies relatively slowly as a function of x, while the function in Figure 8.2(b) varies much more rapidly. The more slowly varying function is said to have lower-frequency content.

Figure 8.3 shows the frequency space representations of these two functions; the lower-frequency function's representation goes to 0 more quickly than does the higher-frequency function.

Most functions can be decomposed into a weighted sum of shifted sinusoids. This remarkable fact was first described by Joseph Fourier, and the Fourier transform converts a function into this representation. This frequency space representation of a function gives insight into some of its characteristics—the distribution of frequencies in the sine functions corresponds to the distribution of frequencies in the original function. Using this form, it is possible to use Fourier analysis to gain insight into the error that is introduced by the sampling and reconstruction process and how to reduce the perceptual impact of this error.

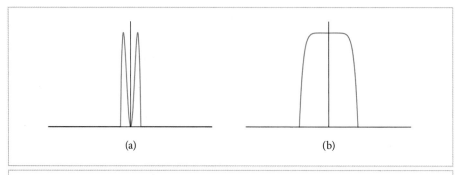

(a)   (b)

Figure 8.3: Frequency Space Representations of the Functions in Figure 8.2. The graphs show the contribution of each frequency ω to each of the functions in the spatial domain.

The Fourier transform of a 1D function $f(x)$ is[2]

$$F(\omega) = \int_{-\infty}^{\infty} f(x)\,e^{-i2\pi\omega x}\,dx. \qquad [8.1]$$

(Recall that $e^{ix} = \cos x + i \sin x$, where $i = \sqrt{-1}$.) For simplicity, here we will consider only *even* functions where $f(-x) = f(x)$, in which case the Fourier transform of f has no imaginary terms. The new function F is a function of *frequency*, ω.[3] We will denote the Fourier transform operator by $\mathcal{F}$, such that $\mathcal{F}\{f(x)\} = F(\omega)$. $\mathcal{F}$ is clearly a linear operator—that is, $\mathcal{F}\{af(x)\} = a\mathcal{F}\{f(x)\}$ for any scalar a, and $\mathcal{F}\{f(x) + g(x)\} = \mathcal{F}\{f(x)\} + \mathcal{F}\{g(x)\}$. The Fourier transform has a straightforward generalization to multidimensional functions where ω is a corresponding multidimensional value, though we will generally stick to the 1D case for notational simplicity.

Equation (8.1) is called the *Fourier analysis* equation, or sometimes just the *Fourier transform*. We can also transform from the frequency domain back to the spatial domain using the *Fourier synthesis* equation, or the *inverse Fourier transform*:

$$f(x) = \int_{-\infty}^{\infty} F(\omega)\,e^{i2\pi\omega x}\,d\omega. \qquad [8.2]$$

Table 8.1 shows a number of important functions and their frequency space representations. A number of these functions are based on the Dirac delta distribution, which is defined such that $\int \delta(x)\,dx = 1$, and for all $x \neq 0$, $\delta(x) = 0$. An important consequence of these properties is that

$$\int f(x)\,\delta(x)\,dx = f(0).$$

The delta distribution cannot be expressed as a standard mathematical function, but instead is generally thought of as the limit of a unit area box function centered at the origin with width approaching 0.

---

2   The reader should be warned that the constants in front of these integrals are not always the same in different fields. For example, some authors (including many in the physics community) prefer to multiply both integrals by $1/\sqrt{2\pi}$.

3   In this chapter, we will use the ω symbol to denote frequency. Throughout the rest of the book, ω denotes normalized direction vectors. This overloading of notation should never be confusing, given the contexts where these symbols are used. Similarly, when we refer to a function's "spectrum" in this chapter, we are referring to its distribution of frequencies in its frequency space representation.

Table 8.1: Fourier Pairs. Functions in the spatial domain and their frequency space representations. Because of the symmetry properties of the Fourier transform, if the left column is instead considered to be frequency space, then the right column is the spatial equivalent of those functions as well.

Spatial Domain	Frequency Space Representation
Box: $f(x) = 1$ if $\|x\| < 1/2$, 0 otherwise	Sinc: $f(\omega) = \mathrm{sinc}(\omega) = \sin(\pi\omega)/(\pi\omega)$
Gaussian: $f(x) = e^{-\pi x^2}$	Gaussian: $f(\omega) = e^{-\pi\omega^2}$
Constant: $f(x) = 1$	Delta: $f(\omega) = \delta(\omega)$
Sinusoid: $f(x) = \cos x$	Translated delta: $f(\omega) = \pi(\delta(1 - 2\pi\omega) + \delta(1 + 2\pi\omega))$
Shah: $f(x) = \text{Ш}_T(x) = T \sum_i \delta(x - Ti)$	Shah: $f(\omega) = \text{Ш}_{1/T}(\omega) = (1/T) \sum_i \delta(\omega - i/T)$

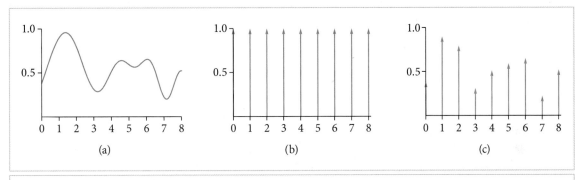

Figure 8.4: Formalizing the Sampling Process. (a) The function $f(x)$ is multiplied by (b) the shah function $\text{Ш}_T(x)$, giving (c) an infinite sequence of scaled delta functions that represent its value at each sample point.

8.1.2 IDEAL SAMPLING AND RECONSTRUCTION

Using frequency space analysis, we can now formally investigate the properties of sampling. Recall that the sampling process requires us to choose a set of equally spaced sample positions and compute the function's value at those positions. Formally, this corresponds to multiplying the function by a "shah," or "impulse train," function, an infinite sum of equally spaced delta functions. The shah $\text{Ш}_T(x)$ is defined as

$$\text{Ш}_T(x) = T \sum_{i=-\infty}^{\infty} \delta(x - iT),$$

where T defines the period, or *sampling rate*. This formal definition of sampling is illustrated in Figure 8.4. The multiplication yields an infinite sequence of values of the function at equally spaced points:

$$\text{Ш}_T(x) f(x) = T \sum_i \delta(x - iT) f(iT).$$

These sample values can be used to define a reconstructed function $\tilde{f}$ by choosing a reconstruction filter function $r(x)$ and computing the *convolution*

$$\big(\text{Ш}_T(x) f(x)\big) \otimes r(x),$$

where the convolution operation $\otimes$ is defined as

$$f(x) \otimes g(x) = \int_{-\infty}^{\infty} f(x')\, g(x - x')\, dx'.$$

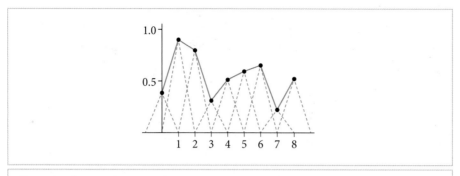

Figure 8.5: The sum of instances of the triangle reconstruction filter, shown with dashed lines, gives the reconstructed approximation to the original function, shown with a solid line.

For reconstruction, convolution gives a weighted sum of scaled instances of the reconstruction filter centered at the sample points:

$$\tilde{f}(x) = T \sum_{i=-\infty}^{\infty} f(iT)\, r(x - iT).$$

For example, in Figure 8.1, the triangle reconstruction filter, $r(x) = \max(0, 1 - |x|)$, was used. Figure 8.5 shows the scaled triangle functions used for that example.

We have gone through a process that may seem gratuitously complex in order to end up at an intuitive result: the reconstructed function $\tilde{f}(x)$ can be obtained by interpolating among the samples in some manner. By setting up this background carefully, however, we can now apply Fourier analysis to the process more easily.

We can gain a deeper understanding of the sampling process by analyzing the sampled function in the frequency domain. In particular, we will be able to determine the conditions under which the original function can be exactly recovered from its values at the sample locations—a very powerful result. For the discussion here, we will assume for now that the function $f(x)$ is *band limited*—there exists some frequency ω_0 such that $f(x)$ contains no frequencies greater than ω_0. By definition, band-limited functions have frequency space representations with compact support, such that $F(\omega) = 0$ for all $|\omega| > \omega_0$. Both of the spectra in Figure 8.3 are band limited.

An important idea used in Fourier analysis is the fact that the Fourier transform of the product of two functions $\mathcal{F}\{f(x)g(x)\}$ can be shown to be the convolution of their individual Fourier transforms $F(\omega)$ and $G(\omega)$:

$$\mathcal{F}\{f(x)g(x)\} = F(\omega) \otimes G(\omega). \tag{8.3}$$

It is similarly the case that convolution in the spatial domain is equivalent to multiplication in the frequency domain:

$$\mathcal{F}\{f(x) \otimes g(x)\} = F(\omega)G(\omega). \tag{8.4}$$

These properties are derived in the standard references on Fourier analysis. Using these ideas, the original sampling step in the spatial domain, where the product of the shah function and the original function $f(x)$ is found, can be equivalently described by the convolution of $F(\omega)$ with another shah function in frequency space.

We also know the spectrum of the shah function $\text{Ш}_T(x)$ from Table 8.1; the Fourier transform of a shah function with period T is another shah function with period $1/T$. This

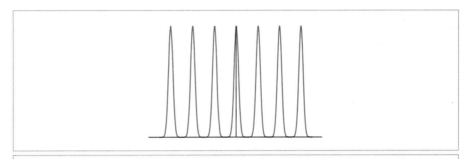

Figure 8.6: The Convolution of $F(\omega)$ **and the Shah Function.** The result is infinitely many copies of F.

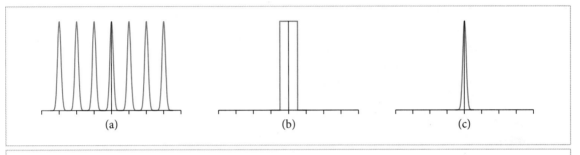

(a)   (b)   (c)

Figure 8.7: Multiplying (a) a series of copies of $F(\omega)$ by (b) the appropriate box function yields (c) the original spectrum.

reciprocal relationship between periods is important to keep in mind: it means that if the samples are farther apart in the spatial domain, they are closer together in the frequency domain.

Thus, the frequency domain representation of the sampled signal is given by the convolution of $F(\omega)$ and this new shah function. Convolving a function with a delta function just yields a copy of the function, so convolving with a shah function yields an infinite sequence of copies of the original function, with spacing equal to the period of the shah (Figure 8.6). This is the frequency space representation of the series of samples.

Now that we have this infinite set of copies of the function's spectrum, how do we reconstruct the original function? Looking at Figure 8.6, the answer is obvious: just discard all of the spectrum copies except the one centered at the origin, giving the original $F(\omega)$.

In order to throw away all but the center copy of the spectrum, we multiply by a box function of the appropriate width (Figure 8.7). The box function $\Pi_T(x)$ of width T is defined as

$$\Pi_T(x) = \begin{cases} 1/T & |x| < T/2 \\ 0 & \text{otherwise.} \end{cases}$$

This multiplication step corresponds to convolution with the reconstruction filter in the spatial domain. This is the ideal sampling and reconstruction process. To summarize:

$$\tilde{F} = \left(F(\omega) \otimes \text{Ш}_{1/T}(\omega)\right) \Pi_{1/T}(\omega).$$

This is a remarkable result: we have been able to determine the exact frequency space representation of $f(x)$, purely by sampling it at a set of regularly spaced points. Other than knowing that the function was band limited, no additional information about the composition of the function was used.

Applying the equivalent process in the spatial domain will likewise recover $f(x)$ exactly. Because the inverse Fourier transform of the box function is the sinc function, ideal reconstruction in the spatial domain is

$$\tilde{f} = \big(f(x)\text{Ш}_T(x)\big) \otimes \text{sinc}_T(x),$$

where $\text{sinc}_T(x) = \text{sinc}(Tx)$, and thus

$$\tilde{f}(x) = \sum_{i=-\infty}^{\infty} \text{sinc}(x - Ti)f(Ti). \qquad [8.5]$$

Unfortunately, because the sinc function has infinite extent, it is necessary to use all the sample values $f(Ti)$ to compute any particular value of $\tilde{f}(x)$ in the spatial domain. Filters with finite spatial extent are preferable for practical implementations even though they do not reconstruct the original function perfectly.

A commonly used alternative in graphics is to use the box function for reconstruction, effectively averaging all the sample values within some region around x. This is a poor choice, as can be seen by considering the box filter's behavior in the frequency domain: This technique attempts to isolate the central copy of the function's spectrum by *multiplying by a sinc*, which not only does a bad job of selecting the central copy of the function's spectrum but includes high-frequency contributions from the infinite series of other copies of it as well.

8.1.3 ALIASING

Beyond the issue of the sinc function's infinite extent, one of the most serious practical problems with the ideal sampling and reconstruction approach is the assumption that the signal is band limited. For signals that are not band limited, or signals that are not sampled at a sufficiently high sampling rate for their frequency content, the process described earlier will reconstruct a function that is different from the original signal. Both the underlying problem and mitigation strategies for it can be understood using Fourier analysis.

The key to successful reconstruction is the ability to exactly recover the original spectrum $F(\omega)$ by multiplying the sampled spectrum with a box function of the appropriate width. Notice that in Figure 8.6, the copies of the signal's spectrum are separated by empty space, so perfect reconstruction is possible. Consider what happens, however, if the original function was sampled with a lower sampling rate. Recall that the Fourier transform of a shah function Ш_T with period T is a new shah function with period $1/T$. This means that if the spacing between samples increases in the spatial domain, the sample spacing decreases in the frequency domain, pushing the copies of the spectrum $F(\omega)$ closer together. If the copies get too close together, they start to overlap.

Because the copies are added together, the resulting spectrum no longer looks like many copies of the original (Figure 8.8). When this new spectrum is multiplied by a box function, the result is a spectrum that is similar but not equal to the original $F(\omega)$: high-frequency details in the original signal leak into lower-frequency regions of the spectrum of the reconstructed signal. These new low-frequency artifacts are called *aliases* (because high frequencies are "masquerading" as low frequencies), and the resulting signal is said to be *aliased*. It is sometimes useful to distinguish between artifacts due to sampling and those due to reconstruction; when we wish to be precise we will call sampling artifacts *prealiasing* and reconstruction artifacts *postaliasing*. Any attempt to fix these errors is broadly classified as *antialiasing*.

Figure 8.9 shows the effects of aliasing from undersampling and then reconstructing the 1D function $f(x) = 1 + \cos(4\pi x^2)$.

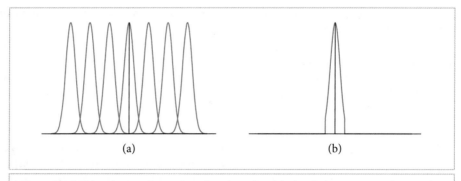

Figure 8.8: (a) When the sampling rate is too low, the copies of the function's spectrum overlap, resulting in (b) aliasing when reconstruction is performed.

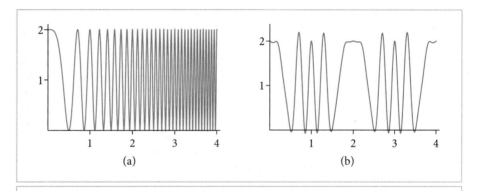

Figure 8.9: Aliasing from Point Sampling the Function $1 + \cos(4\pi x^2)$. (a) The function. (b) The reconstructed function from sampling it with samples spaced 0.125 units apart and performing perfect reconstruction with the sinc filter. Aliasing causes the high-frequency information in the original function to be lost and to reappear as lower-frequency error.

A possible solution to the problem of overlapping spectra is to simply increase the sampling rate until the copies of the spectrum are sufficiently far apart not to overlap, thereby eliminating aliasing completely. The *sampling theorem* tells us exactly what rate is required. This theorem says that as long as the frequency of uniformly spaced sample points ω_s is greater than twice the maximum frequency present in the signal ω_0, it is possible to reconstruct the original signal perfectly from the samples. This minimum sampling frequency is called the *Nyquist frequency*.

However, increasing the sampling rate is expensive in a ray tracer: the time to render an image is directly proportional to the number of samples taken. Furthermore, for signals that are not band limited ($\omega_0 = \infty$), it is impossible to sample at a high enough rate to perform perfect reconstruction. Non-band-limited signals have spectra with infinite support, so no matter how far apart the copies of their spectra are (i.e., how high a sampling rate we use), there will always be overlap.

Unfortunately, few of the interesting functions in computer graphics are band limited. In particular, any function containing a discontinuity cannot be band limited, and therefore we cannot perfectly sample and reconstruct it. This makes sense because the function's discontinuity will always fall between two samples and the samples provide no information about the location of the discontinuity. Thus, it is necessary to apply different methods besides just increasing the sampling rate in order to counteract the error that aliasing can introduce to the renderer's results.

8.1.4 UNDERSTANDING PIXELS

With this understanding of sampling and reconstruction in mind, it is worthwhile to establish some terminology and conventions related to pixels.

The word "pixel" is used to refer to two different things: physical elements that either emit or measure light (as used in displays and digital cameras) and regular samples of an image function (as used for image textures, for example). Although the pixels in an image may be measured by the pixels in a camera's sensor, and although the pixels in an image may be used to set the emission from pixels in a display, it is important to be attentive to the differences between them.

The pixels that constitute an image are defined to be point samples of an image function at discrete points on the image plane; there is no "area" associated with an image pixel. As Alvy Ray Smith (1995) has emphatically pointed out, thinking of the pixels in an image as small squares with finite area is an incorrect mental model that leads to a series of errors. We may filter the continuously defined image function over an area to compute an image pixel value, though we will maintain the distinction in that case that a pixel represents a point sample of a filtered function.

A related issue is that the pixels in an image are naturally defined at discrete integer (x, y) coordinates on a pixel grid, but it will often be useful to consider an image as a continuous function of (x, y) positions. The natural way to map between these two domains is to round continuous coordinates to the nearest discrete coordinate; doing so is appealing since it maps continuous coordinates that happen to have the same value as discrete coordinates to that discrete coordinate. However, the result is that given a set of discrete coordinates spanning a range $[x_0, x_1]$, the set of continuous coordinates that covers that range is $[x_0 - 1/2, x_1 + 1/2)$. Thus, any code that generates continuous sample positions for a given discrete pixel range is littered with 1/2 offsets. It is easy to forget some of these, leading to subtle errors.

A better convention is to truncate continuous coordinates c to discrete coordinates d by

$$d = \lfloor c \rfloor,$$

and convert from discrete to continuous by

$$c = d + 1/2.$$

In this case, the range of continuous coordinates for the discrete range $[x_0, x_1]$ is naturally $[x_0, x_1 + 1)$, and the resulting code is much simpler (Heckbert 1990a). This convention, which we have adopted in pbrt, is shown graphically in Figure 8.10.

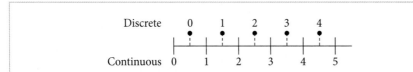

Figure 8.10: Pixels in an image can be addressed with either *discrete* or *continuous* coordinates. A discrete image five pixels wide covers the continuous pixel range [0, 5). A particular discrete pixel d's coordinate in the continuous representation is $d + 1/2$.

8.1.5 SAMPLING AND ALIASING IN RENDERING

The application of the principles of sampling theory to the 2D case of sampling and reconstructing images of rendered scenes is straightforward: we have an image, which we can think of as a function of 2D (x, y) image locations to radiance values L:

$$f(x, y) \rightarrow L.$$

It is useful to generalize the definition of the scene function to a higher-dimensional function that also depends on the time t and (u, v) lens position at which it is sampled. Because the rays from the camera are based on these five quantities, varying any of them gives a different ray and thus a potentially different value of f. For a particular image position, the radiance at that point will generally vary across both time (if there are moving objects in the scene) and position on the lens (if the camera has a finite-aperture lens).

Even more generally, because the integrators defined in Chapters 13 through 15 use Monte Carlo integration to estimate the radiance along a given ray, they may return a different radiance value when repeatedly given the same ray. If we further extend the scene radiance function to include sample values used by the integrator (e.g., values used to choose points on area light sources for illumination computations), we have an even higher-dimensional image function

$$f(x, y, t, u, v, i_1, i_2, \ldots) \rightarrow L.$$

Sampling all of these dimensions well is an important part of generating high-quality imagery efficiently. For example, if we ensure that nearby (x, y) positions on the image tend to have dissimilar (u, v) positions on the lens, the resulting rendered images will have less error because each sample is more likely to account for information about the scene that its neighboring samples do not. The Sampler class implementations later in this chapter will address the issue of sampling all of these dimensions effectively.

Sources of Aliasing

Geometry is one of the most common causes of aliasing in rendered images. When projected onto the image plane, an object's boundary introduces a step function—the image function's value instantaneously jumps from one value to another. Not only do step functions have infinite frequency content as mentioned earlier, but, even worse, the perfect reconstruction filter causes artifacts when applied to aliased samples: ringing artifacts appear in the reconstructed function, an effect known as the *Gibbs phenomenon*. Figure 8.11 shows an example of this

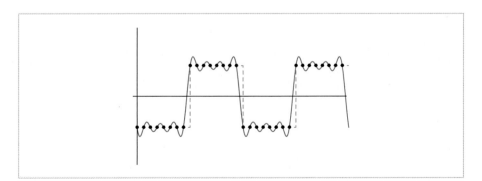

Sampler 469

Figure 8.11: Illustration of the Gibbs Phenomenon. When a function has not been sampled at the Nyquist rate and the set of aliased samples is reconstructed with the sinc filter, the reconstructed function will have "ringing" artifacts, where it oscillates around the true function. Here a 1D step function (dashed line) has been sampled with a sample spacing of 0.125. When reconstructed with the sinc, the ringing appears (solid line).

effect for a 1D function. Choosing an effective reconstruction filter in the face of aliasing requires a mix of science, artistry, and personal taste, as we will see later in this chapter.

Very small objects in the scene can also cause geometric aliasing. If the geometry is small enough that it falls between samples on the image plane, it can unpredictably disappear and reappear over multiple frames of an animation.

Another source of aliasing can come from the texture and materials on an object. *Shading aliasing* can be caused by textures that have not been filtered correctly (addressing this problem is the topic of much of Chapter 10) or from small highlights on shiny surfaces. If the sampling rate is not high enough to sample these features adequately, aliasing will result. Furthermore, a sharp shadow cast by an object introduces another step function in the final image. While it is possible to identify the position of step functions from geometric edges on the image plane, detecting step functions from shadow boundaries is more difficult.

The inescapable conclusion about aliasing in rendered images is that we can never remove all of its sources, so we must develop techniques to mitigate its impact on the quality of the final image.

Adaptive Sampling

One approach that has been applied to combat aliasing is *adaptive supersampling*: if we can identify the regions of the signal with frequencies higher than the Nyquist limit, we can take additional samples in those regions without needing to incur the computational expense of increasing the sampling frequency everywhere. It can be difficult to get this approach to work well in practice, because finding all the places where supersampling is needed is difficult. Most techniques for doing so are based on examining adjacent sample values and finding places where there is a significant change in value between the two; the assumption is that the signal has high frequencies in that region.

In general, adjacent sample values cannot tell us with certainty what is really happening between them: even if the values are the same, the functions may have huge variation between them. Alternatively, adjacent samples may have substantially different values without any aliasing actually being present. For example, the texture-filtering algorithms in Chapter 10 work hard to eliminate aliasing due to image maps and procedural textures on surfaces in the scene; we would not want an adaptive sampling routine to needlessly take extra samples in an area where texture values are changing quickly but no excessively high frequencies are actually present.

Prefiltering

Another approach to eliminating aliasing that sampling theory offers is to filter (i.e., blur) the original function so that no high frequencies remain that cannot be captured accurately at the sampling rate being used. This approach is applied in the texture functions of Chapter 10. While this technique changes the character of the function being sampled by removing information from it, blurring is generally less objectionable than aliasing.

Recall that we would like to multiply the original function's spectrum with a box filter with width chosen so that frequencies above the Nyquist limit are removed. In the spatial domain, this corresponds to convolving the original function with a sinc filter,

$$f(x) \otimes \mathrm{sinc}(2\omega_s x).$$

In practice, we can use a filter with finite extent that works well. The frequency space representation of this filter can help clarify how well it approximates the behavior of the ideal sinc filter.

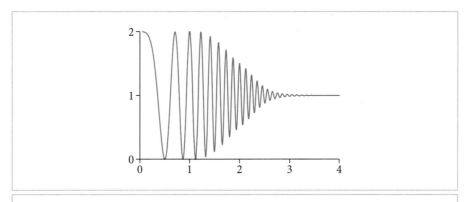

Figure 8.12: Graph of the function $1 + \cos(4\pi x^2)$ convolved with a filter that removes frequencies beyond the Nyquist limit for a sampling rate of $T = 0.125$. High-frequency detail has been removed from the function, so that the new function can at least be sampled and reconstructed without aliasing.

Figure 8.12 shows the function $1 + \cos(4\pi x^2)$ convolved with a variant of the sinc with finite extent that will be introduced in Section 8.8. Note that the high-frequency details have been eliminated; this function can be sampled and reconstructed at the sampling rate used in Figure 8.9 without aliasing.

8.1.6 SPECTRAL ANALYSIS OF SAMPLING PATTERNS

Given a fixed sampling rate, the remaining option to improve image quality is to consider how the distribution of sample positions affects the result. We can understand the behavior of deterministic sampling patterns like the shah function in frequency space by considering the convolution of its frequency space representation with a function's frequency space representation. However, we will find it worthwhile to consider *stochastic sampling* methods where the sample positions are specified by one or more random variables. In that case, we will distinguish between the statistical properties of all the sets of samples that the algorithm may generate and a single set of points generated by it (which we will call a *sample pattern*); the former gives much more insight about an algorithm's behavior.

A concept known as the *power spectral density* (PSD) is helpful for this task. For a function $f(x)$ that is represented by $F(\omega)$ in the Fourier basis, the PSD is defined as:

$$\mathcal{P}_f(\omega) = F(\omega)\overline{F(\omega)},$$

where $\overline{F(\omega)}$ is the complex conjugate of $F(\omega)$. (Under the assumption of an even function $f(x)$, $\mathcal{P}_f(\omega) = F(\omega)^2$.) Because the PSD discards information about the phase of the signal, the original Fourier coefficients cannot be recovered from it.

A useful property of the PSD is that the PSD of the product of two functions f and g in the spatial domain is given by the convolution of their PSDs in the Fourier domain:

$$\mathcal{P}_{fg}(\omega) = \mathcal{P}_f(\omega) \otimes \mathcal{P}_g(\omega).$$

This property follows directly from Equation (8.3). Therefore, if we have a point-sampling technique represented by a function $s(x)$ that is defined as a sum of Dirac delta distributions (as the shah function was), then the frequency content from sampling a function f is given by the convolution of $\mathcal{P}_f$ and $\mathcal{P}_s$.

In some cases, the PSD of a sampling pattern can be derived analytically: doing so is easy for uniform random sampling, for example. For stochastic sampling patterns without an

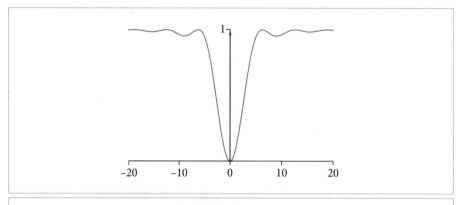

Figure 8.13: Graph of the PSD of jittered samples with $T = 1$, as given by Equation (8.7).

analytic PSD, the PSD can be computed numerically by averaging over random instances of the sample points. Because each sample point is represented as a Dirac delta distribution, their Fourier transform, Equation (8.1), ends up as a sum over the sample points.[4]

The ideal sampling pattern's PSD would have a single delta distribution spike at the origin and be zero everywhere else: in that case, sampling would exactly replicate $\mathcal{P}_f$. Unfortunately, such a sampling pattern would require an infinite sampling density. (This can be understood by considering the inverse Fourier transform of $S(\omega) = \delta(\omega)$, which is a constant function.)

The PSD makes it possible to analyze the effects of stochastic sampling. One way to do so is through *jittering*, which adds uniform random offsets to regularly spaced sample points. With a uniform random number ξ between 0 and 1, a random set of samples based on the impulse train is

$$s_T(x) = \sum_{i=-\infty}^{\infty} \delta\left(x - \left(i + \frac{1}{2} - \xi\right)T\right).$$

[8.6]

It is possible to derive the expectation of the analytic PSD of this sampling strategy,[5]

$$\mathcal{P}_s(\omega) = 1 - \operatorname{sinc}^2\left(\frac{T\omega}{2}\right) + \delta(\omega).$$

[8.7]

This function is graphed in Figure 8.13. Note that there is a spike at the origin, that its value is otherwise close to 0 in the low frequencies, and that it settles in to an increasingly narrow range around 1 at the higher frequencies.

We can use the PSD to compare the effect of undersampling a function in two different ways: using regularly spaced samples and using jittered samples. Figure 8.14(a) shows the frequency space representation of a function with energy in frequencies $|\omega| > 1/2$, which is the maximum frequency content that can be perfectly reconstructed with regular sampling with $T = 1$. Figure 8.14(b) then shows the result of convolving the function's PSD with regular samples and Figure 8.14(c) shows the result with jittered samples.

---

4   The pspec program, found in the file cmd/pspec.cpp in the pbrt distribution, efficiently computes high-quality visualizations of various sampling patterns' power spectra, using the GPU when one is available.

5   In the following, when we speak of the PSD of a stochastic sampling method, we mean the expectation of its PSD, but we will often omit that qualifier.

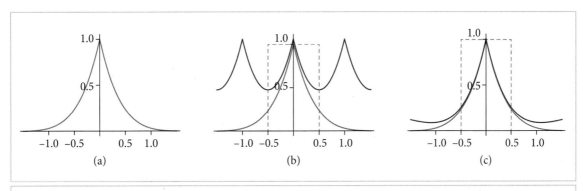

Figure 8.14: The Effect of Jittered Sampling on Aliasing. (a) The power spectral density of a function that cannot be perfectly reconstructed with regularly spaced samples at a rate $T = 1$. (b) The PSD from sampling the function with a shah function with $T = 1$ (red), which is given by the convolution of their PSDs. The original function is shown in blue and the extent of the ideal reconstruction filter is shown with dashed lines. (c) The PSD from jittered sampling (red), which is given by convolving $\mathcal{P}_f$ with Equation (8.7). (The original function is again in blue and the perfect reconstruction filter is indicated by the dashed box.)

In general, aliasing is reduced most effectively if there is minimal energy in the PSD of the sampling function at low frequencies. This characteristic prevents higher frequencies in the function being sampled from appearing as aliases at lower frequencies. (It is implicit in this assumption that the function f's energy is concentrated in the lower frequencies. This is the case for most natural images, though if this is not the case, then the behavior of the sampling function's PSD at the lower frequencies does not matter as much.)

While the shah function is effective by this measure, the uniformity of its sampling rate can lead to structured error, as was shown in Figure 8.14. With jittered sampling, the copies of the sampled signal end up being randomly shifted, so that when reconstruction is performed the result is random error rather than coherent aliasing. Because jittered sampling has roughly the same amount of energy in all the higher frequencies of its PSD, it spreads high-frequency energy in the function being sampled over many frequencies, converting aliasing into high-frequency noise, which is more visually pleasing to human observers than lower-frequency aliasing.

PSDs are sometimes described in terms of their color. For example, a *white noise* distribution has equal power at all frequencies, just as white light has (more or less) equal power at all visible frequencies. *Blue noise* corresponds to a distribution with its power concentrated at the higher frequencies and less power at low frequencies, again corresponding to the relationship between power and frequency exhibited by blue light.

We will occasionally find precomputed 2D tables of values that have blue noise characteristics to be useful; pbrt includes a number of such tables that are made available through the following function. Tables are reused once the provided tableIndex value goes past their number.

⟨*Blue noise lookup functions*⟩ ≡
```
float BlueNoise(int tableIndex, Point2i p);
```

Point2i 92

Figure 8.15 shows one such table along with a white noise image. With a blue noise distribution, the values at nearby pixels differ, corresponding to higher-frequency variation. Because the white noise image does not have this characteristic, there are visible clumps of pixels with similar values.

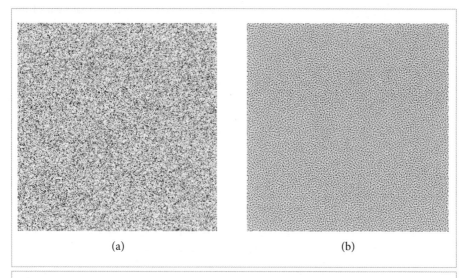

(a)   (b)

Figure 8.15: 256 × 256 pixels with (a) values distributed with white noise characteristics, and (b) with blue noise. *(Blue noise table courtesy of Christoph Peters.)*

8.2 SAMPLING AND INTEGRATION

The lighting integration algorithms used throughout pbrt are based on Monte Carlo integration, yet the focus of Section 8.1 was on sampling and reconstruction. That topic is an important one for understanding aliasing and the use of filters for image reconstruction, but it is a different one than minimizing Monte Carlo integration error. There are a number of connections between Monte Carlo and both Fourier analysis and other approaches to analyzing point-sampling algorithms, however. For example, jittered sampling is a form of stratified sampling, a variance reduction technique that was introduced in Section 2.2.1. Thus, we can see that jittered sampling is advantageous from both perspectives.

Given multiple perspectives on the problem, one might ask, what is the best sampling approach to use for Monte Carlo integration? There is no easy answer to this question, which is reflected by the fact that this chapter presents a total of 6 classes that implement the upcoming Sampler interface to generate sample points, though a number of them offer a few variations of an underlying sampling approach, giving a total of 17 different techniques.

Although some of this variety is for pedagogy, it is largely due to the fact that the question of which sampling technique is best is not easily answered. Not only do the various mathematical approaches to analyzing sampling techniques often disagree, but another difficulty comes from the human visual system: rendered images are generally for human consumption and most mathematical approaches for evaluating sampling patterns do not account for this fact. Later in this chapter, we will see that sampling patterns that lead to errors in the image having blue noise characteristics are visually preferable, yet may not have any lower numeric error than those that do not. Thus, pbrt provides a variety of options, allowing the user to make their own choice among them.

* ### 8.2.1 FOURIER ANALYSIS OF VARIANCE

Sampler 469

Fourier analysis can also be applied to evaluate sampling patterns in the context of Monte Carlo integration, leading to insights about both variance and the convergence rates of various sampling algorithms. We will make three simplifications in our treatment of this topic here. There are more general forms of the theory that do not require these, though they are more complex. (As always, see the "Further Reading" section for more information.) We assume that:

1. The sample points are uniformly distributed and equally weighted (i.e., importance sampling is not being used).
2. The Monte Carlo estimator used is unbiased.
3. The properties of the sample points are homogeneous with respect to toroidal translation over the sampling domain. (If they are not, the analysis is effectively over all possible random translations of the sample points.)

Excluding importance sampling has obvious implications, though we note that the last assumption, homogeneity, is also significant. Many of the sampling approaches later in this chapter are based on decomposing the $[0, 1)^n$ sampling domain into strata and placing a single sample in each one. Homogenizing such algorithms causes some of those regions to wrap around the boundaries of the domain, which harms their effectiveness. Equivalently, homogenization can be seen as toroidally translating the function being integrated, which can introduce discontinuities that were not previously present. Nevertheless, we will see that there is still much useful insight to be had about the behavior of sampling patterns in spite of these simplifications.

Our first step is to introduce the *Fourier series* representation of functions, which we will use as the basis for analysis of sampling patterns for the remainder of this section. The Fourier transform assumes that the function $f(x)$ has infinite extent, while for rendering we are generally operating over the $[0, 1)^n$ domain or on mappings from there to other finite domains such as the unit hemisphere. While it is tempting to apply the Fourier transform as is, defining $f(x)$ to be zero outside the domain of interest, doing so introduces a discontinuity in the function at the boundaries that leads to error due to the Gibbs phenomenon in the Fourier coefficients. Fourier series are defined over a specific finite domain and so do not suffer from this problem.

The Fourier series represents a function using an infinite set of coefficients f_j for all integer-valued $j \geq 0$. (We use j to index coefficients in order to avoid confusion with the use of i for the unit imaginary number.) For the $[0, 1)$ domain, the coefficients are given by[6]

$$f_j = \int_{[0,1)} f(x)\, e^{-i2\pi j x}\, \mathrm{d}x. \tag{8.8}$$

(Domains other than $[0, 1)$ can be handled using a straightforward reparameterization.)

Expressed using the Fourier series coefficients, the original function is

$$f(x) = \sum_{j \in \mathbb{Z}} f_j\, e^{-i2\pi j x}. \tag{8.9}$$

It can be shown that the continuous Fourier transform corresponds to the limit of taking the Fourier series with an infinite extent.

The PSD of a function in the Fourier series basis is given by the product of each coefficient with its complex conjugate,

$$\mathcal{P}_f(j) = f_j \overline{f_j}.$$

---

6   We will continue to stick with 1D for Fourier analysis, though as before, all concepts extend naturally to multiple dimensions.

In order to analyze Monte Carlo integration in frequency space, we will start by defining the sampling function $s(x)$ for a set of sample points x_i as the averaged sum of n samples, each represented by a delta distribution,

$$s(x) = \frac{1}{n} \sum_{i=1}^{n} \delta(x - x_i).$$

Given the sampling function, it is possible to rewrite the Monte Carlo estimator as an integral:

$$\int_{[0,1)} f(x) \, dx \approx \frac{1}{n} \sum_{i=1}^{n} f(x_i)$$

$$= \int_{[0,1)} f(x) \, s(x) \, dx. \tag{8.10}$$

It may seem like we are moving backward: after all, the point of Monte Carlo integration is to transform integrals into sums. However, this transformation is key to being able to apply the Fourier machinery to the problem.

If we substitute the Fourier series expansion of Equation (8.9) into Equation (8.10), we can find that

$$\int_{[0,1)} f(x) \, s(x) \, dx = \sum_{j \in \mathbb{Z}} \overline{f_j} \, s_j.$$

From the definition of the Fourier series coefficients, we know that $f_0 = \overline{f_0} = \int f(x) \, dx$. Furthermore, $s_0 = 1$ from the definition of $s(x)$ and the assumption of uniform and unweighted samples. Therefore, the error in the Monte Carlo estimate is given by

$$\left| \int_{[0,1)} f(x) \, dx - \int_{[0,1)} f(x) \, s(x) \, dx \right| = \left| f_0 - \sum_{j \in \mathbb{Z}} \overline{f_j} \, s_j \right| = \sum_{j \in \mathbb{Z}^*} \overline{f_j} \, s_j, \tag{8.11}$$

where $\mathbb{Z}^*$ denotes the set of all integers except for zero.

Equation (8.11) is the key result that gives us insight about integration error. It is worth taking the time to understand and to consider the implications of it. For example, if f is band limited, then $f_j = 0$ for all j after some value $j_{\max}$. In that case, if s's sampling rate is at least equal to f's highest frequency, then $s_j = 0$ for all $0 < j < j_{\max}$ and a zero variance estimator is the result. Only half the sampling rate is necessary for perfect integration compared to what is needed for perfect reconstruction!

Using Equation (8.11) with the definition of variance, it can be shown that the variance of the estimator is given by the sum of products of $f(x)$'s and $s(x)$'s PSDs:

$$V \left[\frac{1}{n} \sum_{i=1}^{n} f(x_i) \right] = \sum_{j \in \mathbb{Z}^*} \mathcal{P}_f(j) \mathcal{P}_s(j). \tag{8.12}$$

This gives a clear direction about how to reduce variance: it is best if the power spectrum of the sampling pattern is low where the function's power spectrum is high. In rendering, the function is generally not available analytically, let alone in the Fourier series basis, so we follow the usual expectation that the function has most of its frequency content in lower frequencies. This assumption argues for a sampling pattern with its energy concentrated in higher frequencies and minimal energy in the lower frequencies—precisely the same blue noise criterion that we earlier saw was effective for antialiasing.

An insight that directly follows from Equation (8.12) is that with uniform random sampling (i.e., white noise), $\mathcal{P}_s$ is the constant $1/n$, which leads to the variance of

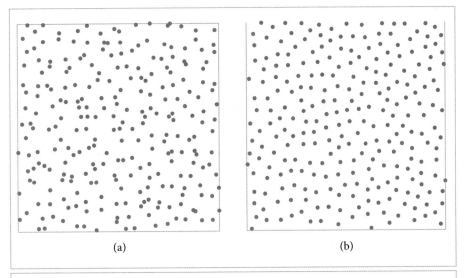

Figure 8.16: 256 sample points distributed using (a) a jittered distribution, and (b) a Poisson disk distribution. Poisson disk point sets combine some randomness in the locations of the points with some structure from no two of them being too close together.

$$\frac{1}{n} \sum_{j \in \mathbb{Z}^*} \mathcal{P}_f(j) = O\left(\frac{1}{n}\right),$$

which is the same variance of the Monte Carlo estimator that was derived earlier using different means in Section 2.1.4. More generally, if the PSD for a sampling technique can be asymptotically bounded, it can be shown that the technique exhibits a higher rate of variance reduction given a suitable function being integrated. One example is that in 2D, a jittered sampling pattern can achieve $O(n^{-2})$ variance, given a smooth integrand.

Fourier analysis has also revealed that *Poisson disk* sampling patterns have unexpectedly bad asymptotic convergence. Poisson disk point sets are constructed such that no two points can be closer than some minimum distance d (see Figure 8.16). For many years, they were believed to be superior to jittered patterns. The Poisson disk criterion is an appealing one, as it prohibits multiple samples from clumping close together, as is possible with adjacent jittered samples.

Part of the appeal of Poisson disk patterns is that initially they seem to have superior blue noise characters to jittered patterns, with a much larger range of frequencies around the origin where the PSD is low. Figure 8.17 shows the PSDs of 2D jittered and Poisson disk sample points. Both feature a spike at the origin, a ring of low energy around it, and then a transition to fairly equal-energy noise at higher frequencies.

Radially averaged plots of the distribution of energy in these PSDs, however, makes their behavior in the low frequencies more clear; see Figure 8.18.[7] We can see that although the Poisson disk pattern has low energy for a larger range of frequencies than the jittered pattern, its PSD retains a small amount of energy all the way until 0, while the jittered pattern does not.

---

7   Some of the sampling patterns that we will see later in the chapter have anisotropic PSDs, in which case a radial average loses some information about their behavior, though these two patterns are both isotropic and thus radially symmetric.

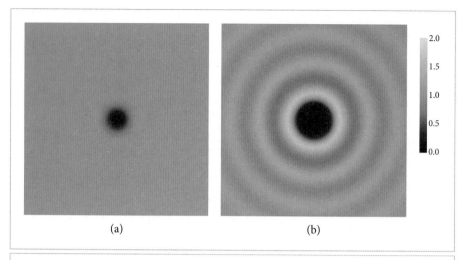

Figure 8.17: PSDs of (a) jittered and (b) Poisson disk–distributed sample points. The origin with the central spike is at the center of each image.

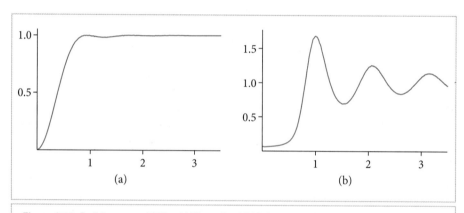

Figure 8.18: Radially averaged PSDs of (a) jittered and (b) Poisson disk–distributed sample points.

Using Fourier analysis of variance, it can be shown that due to this lingering energy, the variance when using Poisson disk sampling is never any better than $O(n^{-1})$—worse than jittered points for some integrands. (Though remember that these are asymptotic bounds, and that for small n, Poisson disk–distributed points may give lower variance.) Nevertheless, the poor asymptotic convergence for what seems like it should be an effective sampling approach was a surprise, and points to the value of this form of analysis.

8.2.2 LOW DISCREPANCY AND QUASI MONTE CARLO

Outside of Fourier analysis, another useful approach for evaluating the quality of sample points is based on a concept called *discrepancy*. Well-distributed sampling patterns have low discrepancy, and thus the sample pattern generation problem can be considered to be one of finding a suitable pattern of points with low discrepancy.

In discussing the discrepancy of sample points, we will draw a distinction between *sample sets*, which are a specific number of points, and *sample sequences*, which are defined by an algorithm that can generate an arbitrary number of points. For a fixed number of samples, it

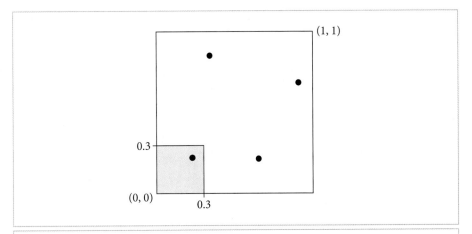

Figure 8.19: The discrepancy of a box (shaded) given a set of 2D sample points in $[0, 1)^2$. One of the four sample points is inside the box, so this set of points would estimate the box's area to be 1/4. The true area of the box is $0.3 \times 0.3 = .09$, so the discrepancy for this particular box is $.25 - .09 = .16$. In general, we are interested in finding the maximum discrepancy of all possible boxes (or some other shape).

is generally possible to distribute points in a sample set slightly better than the same number of points in a sample sequence. However, sequences can be especially useful with adaptive sampling algorithms, thanks to their flexibility in the number of points they generate.

The basic idea of discrepancy is that the quality of a set of points in a d-dimensional space $[0, 1)^d$ can be evaluated by looking at regions of the domain $[0, 1)^d$, counting the number of points inside each region, and comparing the volume of each region to the number of sample points inside. In general, a given fraction of the volume should have roughly the same fraction of the total number of sample points inside of it. While it is not possible for this always to be the case, we can still try to use patterns that minimize the maximum difference between the actual volume and the volume estimated by the points (the *discrepancy*). Figure 8.19 shows an example of the idea in two dimensions.

To compute the discrepancy of a set of points, we first pick a family of shapes B that are subsets of $[0, 1)^d$. For example, boxes with one corner at the origin are often used. This corresponds to

$$B = \{[0, v_1] \times [0, v_2] \times \cdots \times [0, v_d]\},$$

where $0 \le v_i < 1$. Given a set of n sample points $P = \{x_1, \ldots, x_n\}$, the discrepancy of P with respect to B is[8]

$$D_n(B, P) = \sup_{b \in B} \left| \frac{\sharp\{x_i \in b\}}{n} - V(b) \right|, \qquad \text{[8.13]}$$

where $\sharp\{x_i \in b\}$ is the number of points in b and $V(b)$ is the volume of b.

The intuition for why Equation (8.13) is a reasonable measure of quality is that the value $\sharp\{x_i \in b\}/n$ is an approximation of the volume of the box b given by the particular points P. Therefore, the discrepancy is the worst error over all possible boxes from this way of approximating the volume. When the set of shapes B is the set of boxes with a corner at

---

8   The sup operator, also referred to as the *least upper bound*, gives the tightest-possible upper bound of the value of the function over its domain.

the origin, this value is called the *star discrepancy*, $D_n^*(P)$. Another popular option for B is the set of all axis-aligned boxes, where the restriction that one corner be at the origin has been removed.

For some point sets, the discrepancy can be computed analytically. For example, consider the set of points in one dimension

$$x_i = \frac{i}{n}.$$

We can see that the star discrepancy of x_i is

$$D_n^*(x_1, \ldots, x_n) = \frac{1}{n}.$$

For example, take the interval $b = [0, 1/n)$. Then $V(b) = 1/n$, but $\sharp\{x_i \in b\} = 0$. This interval (and the intervals $[0, 2/n)$, etc.) is the interval where the largest differences between volume and fraction of points inside the volume are seen.

The star discrepancy of this point set can be improved by modifying it slightly:

$$x_i = \frac{i - \frac{1}{2}}{n}. \tag{8.14}$$

Then

$$D_n^*(x_i) = \frac{1}{2n}.$$

The bounds for the star discrepancy of a sequence of points in one dimension have been shown to be

$$D_n^*(x_i) = \frac{1}{2n} + \max_{1 \le i \le n} \left| x_i - \frac{2i - 1}{2n} \right|.$$

Thus, the earlier set from Equation (8.14) has the lowest possible discrepancy for a sequence in 1D. In general, it is much easier to analyze and compute bounds for the discrepancy of sequences in 1D than for those in higher dimensions. When it is not possible to derive the discrepancy of a sampling technique analytically, it can be estimated numerically by constructing a large number of shapes b, computing their discrepancy, and reporting the maximum value found.

The astute reader will notice that according to the discrepancy measure, the uniform sequence in 1D is optimal, but Fourier analysis indicated that jittering was superior to uniform sampling. Fortunately, low-discrepancy patterns in higher dimensions are much less uniform than they are in one dimension and thus usually work reasonably well as sample patterns in practice. Nevertheless, their underlying uniformity means that low-discrepancy patterns can be more prone to visually objectionable aliasing than patterns with pseudo-random variation.

A d-dimensional sequence of points is said to have *low discrepancy* if its discrepancy is of the order

$$O\left(\frac{(\log n)^d}{n}\right). \tag{8.15}$$

These bounds are the best that are known for arbitrary d.

Low-discrepancy point sets and sequences are often generated using deterministic algorithms; we will see a number of such algorithms in Sections 8.6 and 8.7. Using such points to sample functions for integration brings us to *quasi–Monte Carlo* (QMC) methods. Many of the techniques used in regular Monte Carlo algorithms can be shown to work equally well with such *quasi-random* sample points.

The *Koksma–Hlawka inequality* relates the discrepancy of a set of points used for integration to the error of an estimate of the integral of a function f. It is:

$$\left| \int f(x)\,dx - \frac{1}{n}\sum_i f(x_i) \right| \le D_n(B, P)\mathcal{V}_f, \qquad \text{[8.16]}$$

where $\mathcal{V}_f$ is the *total variation* of the function f being integrated. It is defined as

$$\mathcal{V}_f = \sup_{0 = y_1 < y_2 < \cdots < y_m = 1} \sum_{i=1}^{m} \left| f(y_i) - f(y_{i+1}) \right|,$$

over all partitions of the $[0, 1)$ domain at points y_i. In essence, the total variation represents how quickly the function's value ever changes between points, and the discrepancy represents how effective the points used for integration are at catching the function's variation.

Given the definition of low discrepancy from Equation (8.15), we can see from the Koksma–Hlawka inequality that as the dimensionality d of the integrand increases, the integration error with low discrepancy approaches $O(n^{-1})$, which is asymptotically much better than the $O(n^{-1/2})$ error from Monte Carlo integration (Section 2.1.4). Note also that these error bounds are asymptotic; in practice, QMC usually has an even better rate of convergence.

However, because QMC integration is deterministic, it is not possible to use variance as a measure of an estimator's quality, though of course one can still compute the mean squared error. Alternatively, the sample points can be randomized using approaches that are carefully designed not to harm their discrepancy. We will see later in the chapter that randomization can even lead to improved rates of convergence. Such approaches are *randomized quasi–Monte Carlo* (RQMC) methods and again allow the use of variance. RQMC is the foundation of most of pbrt's Monte Carlo integration algorithms.

In most of this text, we have glossed over the differences between Monte Carlo, QMC, and RQMC, and have localized the choice among them in the Samplers in this chapter. Doing so introduces the possibility of subtle errors if a Sampler generates quasi-random sample points that an Integrator then improperly uses as part of an implementation of an algorithm that is not suitable for quasi Monte Carlo, though none of the integrators described in the text do so.

8.3 SAMPLING INTERFACE

pbrt's Sampler interface makes it possible to use a variety of sample generation algorithms for rendering. The sample points that they provide are used by pbrt's Integrators in a multitude of ways, ranging from determining points on the image plane from which camera rays originate to selecting which light source to trace a shadow ray to and at which point on it the shadow ray should terminate.

Integrator 22

Sampler 469

As we will see in the following sections, the benefits of carefully crafted sampling patterns are not just theoretical; they can substantially improve the quality of rendered images. The runtime expense for using good sampling algorithms is relatively small; because evaluating

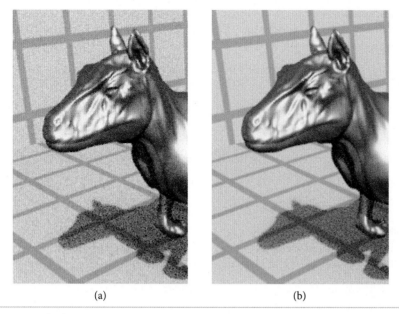

(a)   (b)

Figure 8.20: Scene rendered with (a) a relatively ineffective sampler and (b) a carefully designed sampler, using the same number of samples for each. The improvement in image quality, ranging from the shadow on the floor to the quality of the glossy reflections, is noticeable. Both images are rendered with 8 samples per pixel. *(Killeroo model courtesy of headus/Rezard.)*

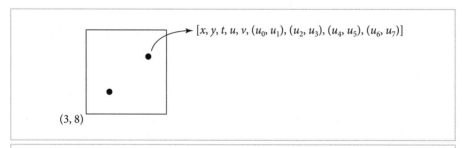

Figure 8.21: Samplers generate a d-dimensional sample point for each of the image samples taken to generate the final image. Here, the pixel $(3, 8)$ is being sampled, and there are two image samples in the pixel area. The first two dimensions of the sample give the (x, y) offset of the sample within the pixel, and the next three dimensions determine the time and lens position of the corresponding camera ray. Subsequent dimensions are used by the Monte Carlo light transport algorithms implemented in pbrt's Integrators.

the radiance for each image sample is much more expensive than computing the sample's component values, doing this work pays dividends (Figure 8.20).

The task of a Sampler is to generate uniform d-dimensional sample points, where each coordinate's value is in the range $[0, 1)$. The total number of dimensions in each point is not set ahead of time; Samplers must generate additional dimensions on demand, depending on the number of dimensions required for the calculations performed by the light transport algorithms. (See Figure 8.21.) While this design makes implementing a Sampler slightly more complex than if its task was to generate all the dimensions of each sample point up front, it is more convenient for integrators, which end up needing a different number of dimensions depending on the particular path they follow through the scene.

⟨*Sampler Definition*⟩ ≡
```
class Sampler : public TaggedPointer<⟨Sampler Types 469⟩> {
  public:
    ⟨Sampler Interface 469⟩
};
```

All the samplers save for `MLTSampler` are defined in this chapter; that one is used solely by the `MLTIntegrator`, which is described in the online version of the book.

⟨*Sampler Types*⟩ ≡   469
```
IndependentSampler, StratifiedSampler, HaltonSampler, PaddedSobolSampler,
SobolSampler, ZSobolSampler, MLTSampler
```

`Sampler` implementations specify the number of samples to be taken in each pixel and return this value via `SamplesPerPixel()`. Most samplers already store this value as a member variable and return it directly in their implementations of this method. We will usually not include the straightforward implementations of this method in the text.

⟨*Sampler Interface*⟩ ≡   469
```
int SamplesPerPixel() const;
```

When an `Integrator` is ready to start work on a given pixel sample, it starts by calling `StartPixelSample()`, providing the coordinates of the pixel in the image and the index of the sample within the pixel. (The index should be greater than or equal to zero and less than the value returned by `SamplesPerPixel()`.) The `Integrator` may also provide a starting dimension at which sample generation should begin.

This method serves two purposes. First, some `Sampler` implementations use the knowledge of which pixel is being sampled to improve the overall distribution of the samples that they generate—for example, by ensuring that adjacent pixels do not take two samples that are close together. Attending to this detail, while it may seem minor, can substantially improve image quality.

Second, this method allows samplers to put themselves in a deterministic state before generating each sample point. Doing so is an important part of making pbrt's operation deterministic, which in turn is crucial for debugging. It is expected that all samplers will be implemented so that they generate precisely the same sample coordinate values for a given pixel and sample index across multiple runs of the renderer. This way, for example, if pbrt crashes in the middle of a lengthy run, debugging can proceed starting at the specific pixel and pixel sample index where the renderer crashed. With a deterministic renderer, the crash will reoccur without taking the time to perform all the preceding rendering work.

⟨*Sampler Interface*⟩ +≡   469
```
void StartPixelSample(Point2i p, int sampleIndex, int dimension = 0);
```

Integrators can request dimensions of the d-dimensional sample point one or two at a time, via the `Get1D()` and `Get2D()` methods. While a 2D sample value could be constructed by using values returned by a pair of calls to `Get1D()`, some samplers can generate better point distributions if they know that two dimensions will be used together. However, the interface does not support requests for 3D or higher-dimensional sample values from samplers because these are generally not needed for the types of rendering algorithms implemented here. In that case, multiple values from lower-dimensional components can be used to construct higher-dimensional sample points.

⟨*Sampler Interface*⟩ +≡   **469**
```
   Float Get1D();
   Point2f Get2D();
```

A separate method, GetPixel2D(), is called to retrieve the 2D sample used to determine the point on the film plane that is sampled. Some of the following Sampler implementations handle those dimensions of the sample differently from the way they handle 2D samples in other dimensions; other Samplers implement this method by calling their Get2D() methods.

⟨*Sampler Interface*⟩ +≡   **469**
```
   Point2f GetPixel2D();
```

Because each sample coordinate must be strictly less than 1, it is useful to define a constant, OneMinusEpsilon, that represents the largest representable floating-point value that is less than 1. Later, the Sampler implementations will sometimes clamp sample values to be no larger than this.

⟨*Floating-point Constants*⟩ +≡
```
   static constexpr double DoubleOneMinusEpsilon = 0x1.fffffffffffffp-1;
   static constexpr float FloatOneMinusEpsilon = 0x1.fffffep-1;
   #ifdef PBRT_FLOAT_AS_DOUBLE
   static constexpr double OneMinusEpsilon = DoubleOneMinusEpsilon;
   #else
   static constexpr float OneMinusEpsilon = FloatOneMinusEpsilon;
   #endif
```

A sharp edge of these interfaces is that code that uses sample values must be carefully written so that it always requests sample dimensions in the same order. Consider the following code:

```
       sampler->StartPixelSample(pPixel, sampleIndex);
       Float v = a(sampler->Get1D());
       if (v > 0)
           v += b(sampler->Get1D());
       v += c(sampler->Get1D());
```

In this case, the first dimension of the sample will always be passed to the function a(); when the code path that calls b() is executed, b() will receive the second dimension. However, if the if test is not always true or false, then c() will sometimes receive a sample value from the second dimension of the sample and otherwise receive a sample value from the third dimension. This will thus thwart efforts by the sampler to provide well-distributed sample points in each dimension being evaluated. Code that uses Samplers should therefore be carefully written so that it consistently consumes sample dimensions, to avoid this issue.

Clone(), the final method required by the interface, returns a copy of the Sampler. Because Sampler implementations store a variety of state about the current sample—which pixel is being sampled, how many dimensions of the sample have been used, and so forth— it is unsafe for a single Sampler to be used concurrently by multiple threads. Therefore, Integrators call Clone() to make copies of an initial Sampler so that each thread has its own. The implementations of the various Clone() methods are not generally interesting, so they will not be included in the text here.

⟨*Sampler Interface*⟩ +≡   **469**
```
   Sampler Clone(Allocator alloc = {});
```

8.4 INDEPENDENT SAMPLER

The IndependentSampler is perhaps the simplest possible (correct) implementation of the Sampler interface. It returns independent uniform sample values for each sample request without making any further effort to ensure the quality of the distribution of samples. The IndependentSampler should never be used for rendering if image quality is a concern, but it is useful for setting a baseline to compare against better samplers.

⟨*IndependentSampler Definition*⟩ ≡
```
class IndependentSampler {
  public:
    ⟨IndependentSampler Public Methods 471⟩
  private:
    ⟨IndependentSampler Private Members 471⟩
};
```

Like many of the following samplers, IndependentSampler takes a seed to use when initializing the pseudo-random number generator with which it produces sample values. Setting different seeds makes it possible to generate independent sets of samples across multiple runs of the renderer, which can be useful when measuring the convergence of various sampling algorithms.

⟨*IndependentSampler Public Methods*⟩ ≡   471
```
IndependentSampler(int samplesPerPixel, int seed = 0)
    : samplesPerPixel(samplesPerPixel), seed(seed) {}
```

An instance of the RNG class is used to generate sample coordinate values.

⟨*IndependentSampler Private Members*⟩ ≡   471
```
int samplesPerPixel, seed;
RNG rng;
```

So that the IndependentSampler always gives the same sample value for a given pixel sample, it is important to reset the RNG to a deterministic state rather than, for example, leaving it in whatever state it was at the end of the last pixel sample it was used for. To do so, we take advantage of the fact that the RNG in pbrt allows not only for specifying one of 2^{64} sequences of pseudo-random values but also for specifying an offset in that sequence. The implementation below chooses a sequence deterministically, based on the pixel coordinates and seed value. Then, an initial offset into the sequence is found based on the index of the sample, so that different samples in a pixel will start far apart in the sequence. If a nonzero starting dimension is specified, it gives an additional offset into the sequence that skips over earlier dimensions.

⟨*IndependentSampler Public Methods*⟩ +≡   471
```
void StartPixelSample(Point2i p, int sampleIndex, int dimension) {
    rng.SetSequence(Hash(p, seed));
    rng.Advance(sampleIndex * 65536ull + dimension);
}
```

Given a seeded RNG, the implementations of the methods that return 1D and 2D samples are trivial. Note that Get2D() uses C++'s uniform initialization syntax, which ensures that the two calls to Uniform() happen in a well-defined order, which in turn gives consistent results across different compilers.

⟨*IndependentSampler Public Methods*⟩ +≡   **471**
```
    Float Get1D() { return rng.Uniform<Float>(); }
    Point2f Get2D() { return {rng.Uniform<Float>(), rng.Uniform<Float>()}; }
    Point2f GetPixel2D() { return Get2D(); }
```

All the methods for analyzing sampling patterns from Section 8.2 are in agreement about the IndependentSampler: it is a terrible sampler. Independent uniform samples contain all frequencies equally (they are the definition of white noise), so they do not push aliasing out to higher frequencies. Further, the discrepancy of uniform random samples is 1—the worst possible. (To see why, consider the case of all sample dimensions either having the value 0 or 1.) This sampler's only saving grace comes in the case of integrating a function with a significant amount of energy in its high frequencies (with respect to the sampling rate). In that case, it does about as well as any of the more sophisticated samplers.

8.5 STRATIFIED SAMPLER

The IndependentSampler's weakness is that it makes no effort to ensure that its sample points have good coverage of the sampling domain. All the subsequent Samplers in this chapter are based on various ways of ensuring that. As we saw in Section 2.2.1, stratification is one such approach. The StratifiedSampler applies this technique, subdividing the $[0, 1)^d$ sampling domain into regions and generating a single sample inside each one. Because a sample is taken in each region, it is less likely that important features in the integrand will be missed, since the samples are guaranteed not to all be close together.

The StratifiedSampler places each sample at a random point inside each stratum by jittering the center point of the stratum by a uniform random amount so that all points inside the stratum are sampled with equal probability. The nonuniformity that results from this jittering helps turn aliasing into noise, as discussed in Section 8.1.6. The sampler also offers an unjittered mode, which gives uniform sampling in the strata; this mode is mostly useful for comparisons between different sampling techniques rather than for rendering high-quality images.

Direct application of stratification to high-dimensional sampling quickly leads to an intractable number of samples. For example, if we divided the 5D image, lens, and time sample space into four strata in each dimension, the total number of samples per pixel would be $4^5 = 1024$. We could reduce this impact by taking fewer samples in some dimensions (or not stratifying some dimensions, effectively using a single stratum), but we would then lose the benefit of having well-stratified samples in those dimensions. This problem with stratification is known as the *curse of dimensionality*.

We can reap most of the benefits of stratification without paying the price in excessive total sampling by computing lower-dimensional stratified patterns for subsets of the domain's dimensions and then randomly associating samples from each set of dimensions. (This process is sometimes called *padding*.) Figure 8.22 shows the basic idea: we might want to take just four samples per pixel but still require the samples to be stratified over all dimensions. We independently generate four 2D stratified image samples, four 1D stratified time samples, and four 2D stratified lens samples. Then we randomly associate a time and lens sample value with each image sample. The result is that each pixel has samples that together have good coverage of the sample space.

Rendering a scene without complex lighting but including defocus blur due to a finite aperture is useful for understanding the behavior of sampling patterns. This is a case where the integral is over four dimensions—more than just the two of the image plane, but not the

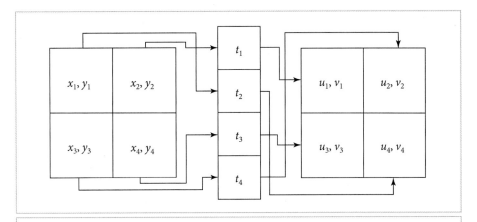

Figure 8.22: We can generate a good sample pattern that reaps the benefits of stratification without requiring all the sampling dimensions to be stratified simultaneously. Here, we have split (x, y) image position, time t, and (u, v) lens position into independent strata with four regions each. Each is sampled independently, and then a time sample and a lens sample are randomly associated with each image sample. We retain the benefits of stratification in each stratification domain without having to exponentially increase the total number of samples.

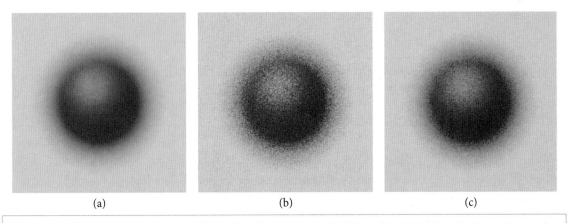

(a)   (b)   (c)

Figure 8.23: Effect of Sampling Patterns in Rendering a Purple Sphere with Defocus Blur. (a) A high-quality reference image of a blurry sphere. (b) An image generated with independent random sampling without stratification. (c) An image generated with the same number of samples, but with the `StratifiedSampler`, which stratified both the image and, more importantly for this image, the lens samples. Stratification gives a substantial improvement and a 3× reduction in mean squared error.

full high-dimensional integral when complex light transport is sampled. Figure 8.23 shows the improvement in image quality from using stratified lens and image samples versus using unstratified independent samples when rendering such a scene.

Figure 8.24 shows a comparison of a few sampling patterns. The first is an independent uniform random pattern generated by the `IndependentSampler`. The result is terrible; some regions have few samples and other areas have clumps of many samples. The second is an unjittered stratified pattern. In the last, the uniform pattern has been jittered, with a random offset added to each sample's location, keeping it inside its cell. This gives a better overall distribution than the purely random pattern while preserving the benefits of stratification, though there are still some clumps of samples and some regions that are undersampled.

IndependentSampler 471
StratifiedSampler 474

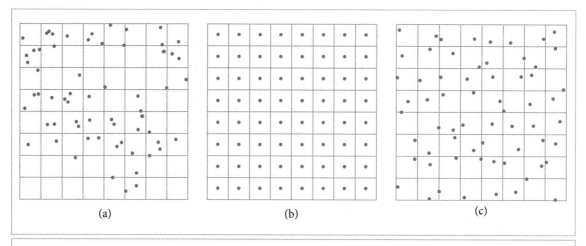

(a)   (b)   (c)

Figure 8.24: Three 2D Sampling Patterns. (a) The independent uniform pattern is an ineffective pattern, with many clumps of samples that leave large sections of the image poorly sampled. (b) An unjittered pattern is better distributed but can exacerbate aliasing artifacts. (c) A stratified jittered pattern turns aliasing from the unjittered pattern into high-frequency noise while generally maintaining the benefits of stratification. (See Figure 8.26 for a danger of jittering, however.)

Figure 8.25 shows images rendered using the StratifiedSampler and shows how jittered sample positions turn aliasing artifacts into less objectionable noise.

⟨*StratifiedSampler Definition*⟩ ≡
```
class StratifiedSampler {
  public:
    ⟨StratifiedSampler Public Methods 474⟩
  private:
    ⟨StratifiedSampler Private Members 474⟩
};
```

The StratifiedSampler constructor takes a specification of how many 2D strata should be used via specification of *x* and *y* sample counts. Parameters that specify whether jittering is enabled and a seed for the random number generator can also be provided to the constructor.

⟨*StratifiedSampler Public Methods*⟩ ≡   474
```
StratifiedSampler(int xPixelSamples, int yPixelSamples, bool jitter,
                  int seed = 0)
    : xPixelSamples(xPixelSamples), yPixelSamples(yPixelSamples),
      seed(seed), jitter(jitter) {}
```

⟨*StratifiedSampler Private Members*⟩ ≡   474
```
int xPixelSamples, yPixelSamples, seed;
bool jitter;
RNG rng;
```

The total number of samples in each pixel is the product of the two dimensions' sample counts.

⟨*StratifiedSampler Public Methods*⟩ +≡   474
```
int SamplesPerPixel() const { return xPixelSamples * yPixelSamples; }
```

This sampler needs to keep track of the current pixel, sample index, and dimension for use in the sample generation methods. After recording them in member variables, the RNG is seeded

RNG 1054
StratifiedSampler 474
StratifiedSampler::jitter 474
StratifiedSampler::seed 474
StratifiedSampler:: xPixelSamples 474
StratifiedSampler:: yPixelSamples 474

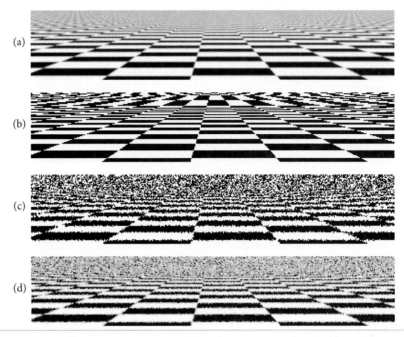

Figure 8.25: Comparison of Image Sampling Methods with a Checkerboard Texture. This is a difficult image to render well, since the checkerboard's frequency with respect to the pixel spacing tends toward infinity as we approach the horizon. (a) A reference image, rendered with 256 samples per pixel, showing something close to an ideal result. (b) An image rendered with one sample per pixel, with no jittering. Note the jaggy artifacts at the edges of checks in the foreground. Notice also the artifacts in the distance where the checker function goes through many cycles between samples; as expected from the signal processing theory presented earlier, that detail reappears incorrectly as lower-frequency aliasing. (c) The result of jittering the image samples, still with just one sample per pixel. The regular aliasing of the second image has been replaced by less objectionable noise artifacts. (d) The result of four jittered samples per pixel is still inferior to the reference image but is substantially better than the previous result.

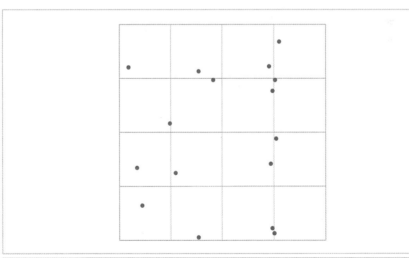

Figure 8.26: A Worst-Case Situation for Stratified Sampling. In an $n \times n$ 2D pattern, up to $2n$ of the points may project to essentially the same point on one of the axes. When "unlucky" patterns like this are generated, the quality of the results computed with them usually suffers. (Here, 8 of the samples have nearly the same x value.)

so that deterministic values are returned for the sample point, following the same approach as was used in IndependentSampler::StartPixelSample().

⟨*StratifiedSampler Public Methods*⟩ +≡   **474**
```
void StartPixelSample(Point2i p, int index, int dim) {
    pixel = p;
    sampleIndex = index;
    dimension = dim;
    rng.SetSequence(Hash(p, seed));
    rng.Advance(sampleIndex * 65536ull + dimension);
}
```

⟨*StratifiedSampler Private Members*⟩ +≡   **474**
```
Point2i pixel;
int sampleIndex = 0, dimension = 0;
```

The StratifiedSampler's implementation is made more complex by the fact that its task is not to generate a full set of sample points for all of the pixel samples at once. If that was the task of the sampler, then the following code suggests how 1D stratified samples for some dimension might be generated: each array element is first initialized with a random point in its corresponding stratum and then the array is randomly shuffled.

This shuffling operation is necessary for padding, so that there is no correlation between the pixel sample index and which stratum its sample comes from. If this shuffling was not done, then the sample dimensions' values would be correlated in a way that would lead to errors in images—for example, the first 2D sample used to choose the film location, as well as the first 2D lens sample, would always each be in the lower left stratum adjacent to the origin.

```
constexpr int n = ...;
std::array<Float, n> samples;
for (int i = 0; i < n; ++i)
    samples[i] = (i + rng.Uniform<Float>()) / n;
std::shuffle(samples.begin(), samples.end(), rng);
```

In the context of pbrt's sampling interface, we would like to perform this random sample shuffling without explicitly representing all the dimension's sample values. The Stratified Sampler therefore uses a random permutation of the sample index to determine which stratum to sample. Given the stratum index, generating a 1D sample is easy.

⟨*StratifiedSampler Public Methods*⟩ +≡   **474**
```
Float Get1D() {
    ⟨Compute stratum index for current pixel and dimension 477⟩
    ++dimension;
    Float delta = jitter ? rng.Uniform<Float>() : 0.5f;
    return (stratum + delta) / SamplesPerPixel();
}
```

It is possible to perform the sample index permutation without representing the permutation explicitly thanks to the PermutationElement() routine, which is defined in Section B.2.8. It takes an index, a total permutation size, and a random seed, and returns the element that the given index is mapped to, doing so in such a way that a valid permutation is returned across all indices up to the permutation size. Thus, we just need to compute a consistent seed value that is the same whenever a particular dimension is sampled at a particular pixel. Hash() takes care of this, though note that sampleIndex must not be included in the hashed values, as doing so would lead to different permutations for different samples in a pixel.

⟨*Compute* stratum *index for current pixel and dimension*⟩ ≡   **476, 477**
```
uint64_t hash = Hash(pixel, dimension, seed);
int stratum = PermutationElement(sampleIndex, SamplesPerPixel(), hash);
```

Generating a 2D sample follows a similar approach, though the stratum index has to be mapped into separate *x* and *y* stratum coordinates. Given these, the remainder of the sampling operation is straightforward.

⟨*StratifiedSampler Public Methods*⟩ +≡   **474**
```
Point2f Get2D() {
    ⟨Compute stratum index for current pixel and dimension 477⟩
    dimension += 2;
    int x = stratum % xPixelSamples, y = stratum / xPixelSamples;
    Float dx = jitter ? rng.Uniform<Float>() : 0.5f;
    Float dy = jitter ? rng.Uniform<Float>() : 0.5f;
    return {(x + dx) / xPixelSamples, (y + dy) / yPixelSamples};
}
```

The pixel sample is not handled differently than other 2D samples with this sampler, so the GetPixel2D() method just calls Get2D().

⟨*StratifiedSampler Public Methods*⟩ +≡   **474**
```
Point2f GetPixel2D() { return Get2D(); }
```

With a *d*-dimensional stratification, the star discrepancy of jittered points has been shown to be

$$O\left(\frac{\sqrt{d \log n}}{n^{1/2+1/(2d)}}\right),$$ [8.17]

which means that stratified samples do not qualify as having low discrepancy.

The PSD of 2D stratified samples was plotted earlier, in Figure 8.17(a). Other than the central spike at the origin (at the center of the image), power is low at low frequencies and settles in to be fairly constant at higher frequencies, which means that this sampling approach is effective at transforming aliasing into high-frequency noise.

⋆ 8.6 HALTON SAMPLER

The underlying goal of the StratifiedSampler is to generate a well-distributed but randomized set of sample points, with no two sample points too close together and no excessively large regions of the sample space that have no samples. As Figure 8.24 showed, a jittered stratified pattern is better at this than an independent uniform random pattern, although its quality can suffer when samples in adjacent strata happen to be close to the shared boundary of their two strata.

This section introduces the HaltonSampler, which is based on algorithms that directly generate low-discrepancy sample points that are simultaneously well distributed over all the dimensions of the sample—not just one or two dimensions at a time, as the StratifiedSampler did.

8.6.1 HAMMERSLEY AND HALTON POINTS

Hammersley and Halton points are two closely related types of low-discrepancy points that are constructed using the *radical inverse*. The radical inverse is based on the fact that a positive integer value a can be expressed in a base b with a sequence of digits $d_m(a) \ldots d_2(a)d_1(a)$ uniquely determined by

$$a = \sum_{i=1}^{m} d_i(a)b^{i-1}, \qquad\qquad \text{[8.18]}$$

where all digits $d_i(a)$ are between 0 and $b - 1$.

The radical inverse function Φ_b in base b converts a nonnegative integer a to a fractional value in $[0, 1)$ by reflecting these digits about the radix point:

$$\Phi_b(a) = 0.d_1(a)d_2(a) \ldots d_m(a) = \sum_{i=1}^{m} d_i(a)b^{-i}. \qquad\qquad \text{[8.19]}$$

One of the simplest low-discrepancy sequences is the *van der Corput sequence*, which is a 1D sequence given by the radical inverse function in base 2:

$$x_a = \Phi_2(a),$$

with $a = 0, 1, \ldots$. Note that van der Corput points are a point sequence because an arbitrary number of them can be generated in succession; the total number need not be specified in advance. (However, if the number of points n is not a power of 2, then the gaps between points will be of different sizes.)

Table 8.2 shows the first few values of the van der Corput sequence. Notice how it recursively splits the intervals of the 1D line in half, generating a sample point at the center of each interval.

The discrepancy of this sequence is

$$D_n^*(P) = O\left(\frac{\log n}{n}\right),$$

which is optimal.

The d-dimensional Halton sequence is defined using the radical inverse base b, with a different base for each dimension. The bases used must all be relatively prime to each other, so a natural choice is to use the first d prime numbers $(p_1, \ldots, p_d)$:

$$x_a = (\Phi_2(a), \Phi_3(a), \Phi_5(a), \ldots, \Phi_{p_d}(a)).$$

Table 8.2: The radical inverse $\Phi_2(a)$ of the first few nonnegative integers, computed in base 2. Notice how successive values of $\Phi_2(a)$ are not close to any of the previous values of $\Phi_2(a)$. As more and more values of the sequence are generated, samples are necessarily closer to previous samples, although with a minimum distance that is guaranteed to be reasonably good.

a	Base 2	$\Phi_2(a)$
0	0	0
1	1	$0.1 = 1/2$
2	10	$0.01 = 1/4$
3	11	$0.11 = 3/4$
4	100	$0.001 = 1/8$
5	101	$0.101 = 5/8$
$\vdots$		

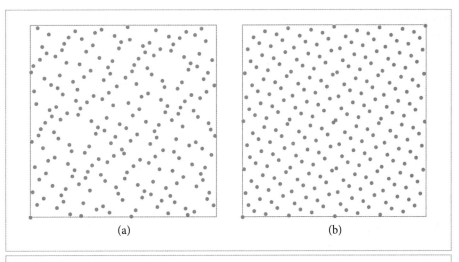

(a)   (b)

Figure 8.27: The First Points of Two Low-Discrepancy Sequences in 2D. (a) Halton (216 points), (b) Hammersley (256 points).

Like the van der Corput sequence, the Halton sequence can be used even if the total number of samples needed is not known in advance; all prefixes of the sequence are well distributed, so as additional samples are added to the sequence, low discrepancy will be maintained. (However, its distribution is best when the total number of samples is the product of powers of the bases $\Pi p_i^{k_i}$ for integer k_i.)

The discrepancy of a d-dimensional Halton sequence is

$$D_n^*(x_a) = O\left(\frac{(\log n)^d}{n}\right),$$

which is asymptotically optimal.

If the number of samples n is fixed, the *Hammersley point set* can be used, giving slightly lower discrepancy. Hammersley point sets are defined by

$$x_a = \left(\frac{a}{n}, \Phi_{b_1}(a), \Phi_{b_2}(a), \ldots, \Phi_{b_{d-1}}(a)\right),$$

again with $a = 0, 1, \ldots$, where n is the total number of samples to be taken, and as before all the bases b_i are relatively prime. Figure 8.27(a) shows a plot of the first 216 points of the 2D Halton sequence and Figure 8.27(b) shows a set of 256 Hammersley points. (216 Halton points were used in this figure, since they are based on the radical inverses in base 2 and 3, and $2^3 3^3 = 216$.)

The RadicalInverse() function computes the radical inverse for a given number a using the baseIndexth prime number as the base. (It and related functions are defined in the files util/lowdiscrepancy.h and util/lowdiscrepancy.cpp.) It does so by computing the digits d_i starting with d_1 and then computing a series v_i where $v_1 = d_1$, $v_2 = bd_1 + d_2$, such that

$$v_n = b^{n-1}d_1 + b^{n-2}d_2 + \cdots + d_n.$$

RadicalInverse() 480

(For example, with base 10, it would convert the value 1234 to 4321.) The value of v_n can be found entirely using integer arithmetic, without accumulating any round-off error.

The final value of the radical inverse is then found by converting to floating-point and multiplying by $1/b^m$, where m is the number of digits in the value, to get the value in Equation (8.19). The factor for this multiplication is built up in invBaseM as the digits are processed.

⟨*Low Discrepancy Inline Functions*⟩ ≡
```
Float RadicalInverse(int baseIndex, uint64_t a) {
    int base = Primes[baseIndex];
    Float invBase = (Float)1 / (Float)base, invBaseM = 1;
    uint64_t reversedDigits = 0;
    while (a) {
        ⟨Extract least significant digit from a and update reversedDigits 480⟩
    }
    return std::min(reversedDigits * invBaseM, OneMinusEpsilon);
}
```

The value of a for the next loop iteration is found by dividing by the base; the remainder is the least significant digit of the current value of a.

⟨*Extract least significant digit from* a *and update* reversedDigits⟩ ≡   480
```
uint64_t next = a / base;
uint64_t digit = a - next * base;
reversedDigits = reversedDigits * base + digit;
invBaseM *= invBase;
a = next;
```

It will also be useful to be able to compute the inverse of the radical inverse function; the InverseRadicalInverse() function takes the reversed integer digits in a given base, corresponding to the final value of reversedDigits in the RadicalInverse() function, and returns the index a that corresponds to them. Note that in order to be able to compute the inverse correctly, the total number of digits in the original value must be provided: for example, both 1234 and 123400 are converted to 4321 after the integer-only part of the radical inverse algorithm; trailing zeros become leading zeros, which are lost.

⟨*Low Discrepancy Inline Functions*⟩ +≡
```
uint64_t InverseRadicalInverse(uint64_t inverse, int base, int nDigits) {
    uint64_t index = 0;
    for (int i = 0; i < nDigits; ++i) {
        uint64_t digit = inverse % base;
        inverse /= base;
        index = index * base + digit;
    }
    return index;
}
```

8.6.2 RANDOMIZATION VIA SCRAMBLING

One disadvantage of the fact that the Hammersley set and Halton sequence are both fully deterministic is that it is not possible to estimate variance by computing multiple independent estimates of an integral with them. Furthermore, they both have the shortcoming that as the base b increases, lower-dimensional projections of sample values can exhibit regular patterns (see Figure 8.28(a)). Because, for example, 2D projections of these points are used for sampling points on light sources, these patterns can lead to visible error in rendered images.

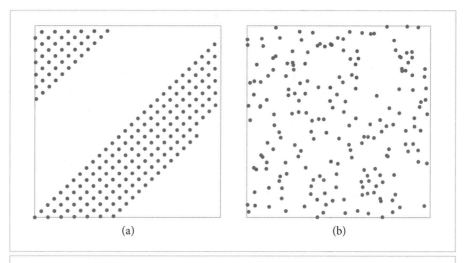

Figure 8.28: Plot of Halton Sample Values with and without Scrambling. (a) In higher dimensions, projections of sample values start to exhibit regular structure. Here, points from the dimensions $(\Phi_{29}(a), \Phi_{31}(a))$ are shown. (b) Scrambled sequences based on Equation (8.20) break up this structure by permuting the digits of sample indices.

These issues can be addressed using techniques that randomize the points that are generated by these algorithms while still maintaining low discrepancy. A family of such techniques are based on randomizing the digits of each sample coordinate with random permutations. Over all permutations, each coordinate value is then uniformly distributed over [0, 1), unlike as with the original point. These techniques are often referred to as *scrambling*.

Scrambling can be performed by defining a set of permutations π_i for each base b, where each digit has a distinct permutation of $\{0, 1, \ldots, b - 1\}$ associated with it. (In the following, we will consider scrambling a single dimension of a d-dimensional sample point and thus drop the base b from our notation, leaving it implicit. In practice, all dimensions are independently scrambled.)

Given such a set of permutations, we can define the scrambled radical inverse where a corresponding permutation is applied to each digit:

$$\Psi_b(a) = 0.\pi_1(d_1)\pi_2(d_2) \ldots \pi_m(d_m).$$

[8.20]

Note that the same permutations π_i must be used for generating all the sample points for a given base.

There are a few subtleties related to the permutations. First, with the regular radical inverse, computation of a sample dimension's value can stop once the remaining digits d_i are 0, as they will have no effect on the final result. With the scrambled radical inverse, the zero digits must continue to be processed. If they are not, then scrambling only corresponds to a permutation of the unscrambled sample values in each dimension, which does not give a uniform distribution over [0, 1). (In practice, it is only necessary to consider enough digits so that any more digits make no difference to the result given the limits of floating-point precision.)

Second, it is important that each digit has its own permutation. One way to see why this is important is to consider the trailing 0 digits: if the same permutation is used for all of them, then all scrambled values will have the same digit value repeating infinitely at their end. Once again, [0, 1) would not be sampled uniformly.

The choice of permutations can affect the quality of the resulting points. In the following implementation, we will use random permutations. That alone is enough to break up the structure of the points, as shown in Figure 8.28(b). However, carefully constructed deterministic permutations have been shown to reduce error for some integration problems. See the "Further Reading" section for more information.

The `DigitPermutation` utility class manages allocation and initialization of a set of digit permutations for a single base b.

⟨*DigitPermutation Definition*⟩ ≡
```
class DigitPermutation {
  public:
    ⟨DigitPermutation Public Methods 482⟩
  private:
    ⟨DigitPermutation Private Members 482⟩
};
```

All the permutations are stored in a single flat array: the first `base` elements of it are the permutation for the first digit, the next `base` elements are the second digit's permutation, and so forth. The `DigitPermutation` constructor's two tasks are to determine how many digits must be handled and then to generate a permutation for each one.

⟨*DigitPermutation Public Methods*⟩ ≡   482
```
DigitPermutation(int base, uint32_t seed, Allocator alloc)
    : base(base) {
    ⟨Compute number of digits needed for base 482⟩
    permutations = alloc.allocate_object<uint16_t>(nDigits * base);
    ⟨Compute random permutations for all digits 483⟩
}
```

To save a bit of storage, unsigned 16-bit integers are used for the digit values. As such, the maximum base allowed is 2^{16}. pbrt only supports up to 1,000 dimensions for Halton points, which corresponds to a maximum base of 7,919, the 1,000th prime number, which is comfortably below that limit.

⟨*DigitPermutation Private Members*⟩ ≡   482
```
int base, nDigits;
uint16_t *permutations;
```

The trailing zero-valued digits must be processed until the digit d_m is reached where b^{-m} is small enough that if the product of b^{-m} with the largest digit is subtracted from 1 using floating-point arithmetic, the result is still 1. At this point, no subsequent digits matter, regardless of the permutation. The `DigitPermutation` constructor performs this check using precisely the same logic as the (soon to be described) `ScrambledRadicalInverse()` function does, to be sure that they are in agreement about how many digits need to be handled.

⟨*Compute number of digits needed for base*⟩ ≡   482
```
nDigits = 0;
Float invBase = (Float)1 / (Float)base, invBaseM = 1;
while (1 - (base - 1) * invBaseM < 1) {
    ++nDigits;
    invBaseM *= invBase;
}
```

The permutations are computed using PermutationElement(), which is provided with a different seed for each digit index so that the permutations are independent.

⟨*Compute random permutations for all digits*⟩ ≡   482
```
for (int digitIndex = 0; digitIndex < nDigits; ++digitIndex) {
    uint64_t dseed = Hash(base, digitIndex, seed);
    for (int digitValue = 0; digitValue < base; ++digitValue) {
        int index = digitIndex * base + digitValue;
        permutations[index] = PermutationElement(digitValue, base, dseed);
    }
}
```

The Permute() method takes care of indexing into the permutations array to return the permuted digit value for a given digit index and the unpermuted value of the digit.

⟨*DigitPermutation Public Methods*⟩ +≡   482
```
int Permute(int digitIndex, int digitValue) const {
    return permutations[digitIndex * base + digitValue];
}
```

Finally, the ComputeRadicalInversePermutations() utility function returns a vector of Digit Permutations, one for each base up to the maximum.

⟨*Low Discrepancy Function Definitions*⟩ ≡
```
pstd::vector<DigitPermutation> *
ComputeRadicalInversePermutations(uint32_t seed, Allocator alloc) {
    pstd::vector<DigitPermutation> *perms =
        alloc.new_object<pstd::vector<DigitPermutation>>(alloc);
    perms->resize(PrimeTableSize);
    for (int i = 0; i < PrimeTableSize; ++i)
        (*perms)[i] = DigitPermutation(Primes[i], seed, alloc);
    return perms;
}
```

With DigitPermutations available, we can implement the ScrambledRadicalInverse() function. Its structure is generally the same as RadicalInverse(), though here we can see that it uses a different termination criterion, as was discussed with the implementation of ⟨*Compute number of digits needed for* base⟩ above.

⟨*Low Discrepancy Inline Functions*⟩ +≡
```
Float ScrambledRadicalInverse(int baseIndex, uint64_t a,
                              const DigitPermutation &perm) {
    int base = Primes[baseIndex];
    Float invBase = (Float)1 / (Float)base, invBaseM = 1;
    uint64_t reversedDigits = 0;
    int digitIndex = 0;
    while (1 - (base - 1) * invBaseM < 1) {
        ⟨Permute least significant digit from a and update reversedDigits 484⟩
    }
    return std::min(invBaseM * reversedDigits, OneMinusEpsilon);
}
```

Each digit is handled the same way as in RadicalInverse(), with the only change being that it is permuted using the provided DigitPermutation.

⟨*Permute least significant digit from* a *and update* reversedDigits⟩ ≡   **483**

```
uint64_t next = a / base;
int digitValue = a - next * base;
reversedDigits =
    reversedDigits * base + perm.Permute(digitIndex, digitValue);
invBaseM *= invBase;
++digitIndex;
a = next;
```

An even more effective scrambling approach defines digit permutations that not only depend on the index of the current digit i, but that also depend on the values of the previous digits $d_1 d_2 \ldots d_{i-1}$. This approach is known as *Owen scrambling*, after its inventor. Remarkably, it can be shown that for a class of smooth functions, the integration error with this scrambling technique decreases at a rate

$$O\left(n^{-\frac{3}{2}}(\log n)^{(d-1)/2}\right),$$

which is a substantial improvement over the $O(n^{-1/2})$ error rate for regular Monte Carlo.

The reason for this benefit can be understood in terms of Owen scrambling being more effective at breaking up structure in the sample values while still maintaining their low discrepancy. Its effect is easiest to see when considering the trailing zero digits that are present in all sample values: if they are all permuted with the same permutation at each digit, they will end up with the same values, which effectively means that there is some structure shared among all the samples. Owen scrambling eliminates this regularity, to the benefit of integration error. (It also benefits the earlier digits in a similar manner, though the connection is less immediately intuitive.)

The challenge with Owen scrambling is that it is infeasible to explicitly store all the permutations, as the number of them that are required grows exponentially with the number of digits. In this case, we can once again take advantage of the PermutationElement() function and its capability of permuting without explicitly representing the full permutation.

⟨*Low Discrepancy Inline Functions*⟩ +≡

```
Float OwenScrambledRadicalInverse(int baseIndex, uint64_t a,
                                  uint32_t hash) {
    int base = Primes[baseIndex];
    Float invBase = (Float)1 / (Float)base, invBaseM = 1;
    uint64_t reversedDigits = 0;
    int digitIndex = 0;
    while (1 - invBaseM < 1) {
        ⟨Compute Owen-scrambled digit for digitIndex 485⟩
    }
    return std::min(invBaseM * reversedDigits, OneMinusEpsilon);
}
```

The computation for each digit is similar to the two previous radical inverse functions; only the third and fourth lines of code in the following fragment are different. At the third line, the values of the previous digits are available in reversedDigits, so hashing them to get a seed for the random permutation suffices to implement Owen scrambling.[9] (Here we have used MixBits() rather than Hash(), as it takes a 64-bit value (which we have at hand) and is more

---

9   Randomly permuting the current digit based on either the previous digits or their permuted values is equivalent in terms of Owen scrambling.

efficient, which is important here since the hashing operation is performed for each digit.) A call to PermutationElement() then gives the corresponding permuted digit value, which is then processed as before.

⟨*Compute Owen-scrambled digit for* digitIndex⟩ ≡   **484**
```
uint64_t next = a / base;
int digitValue = a - next * base;
uint32_t digitHash = MixBits(hash ^ reversedDigits);
digitValue = PermutationElement(digitValue, base, digitHash);
reversedDigits = reversedDigits * base + digitValue;
invBaseM *= invBase;
++digitIndex;
a = next;
```

8.6.3 HALTON SAMPLER IMPLEMENTATION

Given all the capabilities introduced so far in this section, it is not too hard to implement the HaltonSampler, which generates samples using the Halton sequence.

⟨*HaltonSampler Definition*⟩ ≡
```
class HaltonSampler {
  public:
    ⟨HaltonSampler Public Methods 488⟩
  private:
    ⟨HaltonSampler Private Methods 488⟩
    ⟨HaltonSampler Private Members 486⟩
};
```

For the pixel samples, the HaltonSampler scales the domain of the first two dimensions of the Halton sequence from $[0, 1)^2$ so that it covers an integral number of pixels in each dimension.[10] In doing so, it ensures that the pixel samples for adjacent pixels are well distributed with respect to each other. (This is a useful property that the stratified sampler does not guarantee.)

Its constructor takes the full image resolution, even if only a subwindow of it is being rendered. This allows it to always produce the same sample values at each pixel, regardless of whether only some of the pixels are being rendered. This is another place where we have tried to ensure that the renderer's operation is deterministic: rendering a small crop window of an image when debugging does not affect the sample values generated at those pixels if the HaltonSampler is being used.

⟨*HaltonSampler Method Definitions*⟩ ≡
```
HaltonSampler::HaltonSampler(int samplesPerPixel, Point2i fullRes,
        RandomizeStrategy randomize, int seed, Allocator alloc)
    : samplesPerPixel(samplesPerPixel), randomize(randomize) {
    if (randomize == RandomizeStrategy::PermuteDigits)
        digitPermutations = ComputeRadicalInversePermutations(seed, alloc);
    ⟨Find radical inverse base scales and exponents that cover sampling area 487⟩
    ⟨Compute multiplicative inverses for baseScales⟩
}
```

---

10 The following implementation scales by no more than 128, so multiple instances are usually required to cover the full image. Some of the samples may fall outside the image; they are simply not considered.

⟨*HaltonSampler Private Members*⟩ ≡   485
```
int samplesPerPixel;
RandomizeStrategy randomize;
pstd::vector<DigitPermutation> *digitPermutations = nullptr;
```

For this and the following samplers that allow the user to select a randomization strategy, it will be helpful to have an enumeration that encodes them. (Note that the FastOwen option is not supported by the HaltonSampler.)

⟨*RandomizeStrategy Definition*⟩ ≡
```
enum class RandomizeStrategy { None, PermuteDigits, FastOwen, Owen };
```

Some sample generation approaches are naturally pixel-based and fit in easily to the Sampler interface as it has been presented so far. For example, the StratifiedSampler can easily start generating samples in a new pixel after its StartPixelSample() method has been called—it just needs to set RNG state so that it is consistent over all the samples in the pixel.

Others, like the HaltonSampler, naturally generate consecutive samples that are spread across the entire image, visiting completely different pixels if the samples are generated in succession. (Many such samplers are effectively placing each additional sample such that it fills the largest hole in the n-dimensional sample space, which leads to subsequent samples being inside different pixels.) These sampling algorithms are somewhat problematic with the Sampler interface as described so far: the StartPixelSample() method must be able to set the sampler's state so that it is able to generate samples for any requested pixel.

Table 8.3 illustrates the issue for Halton samples. The second column shows 2D Halton sample values in $[0, 1)^2$, which are then multiplied by the image resolution in each dimension to get sample positions in the image plane (here we are considering a 2×3 image for simplicity). Note that here, each pixel is visited by each sixth sample. If we are rendering an image with three samples per pixel, then to generate all the samples for the pixel $(0, 0)$, we need to generate the samples with indices 0, 6, and 12.

Table 8.3: The HaltonSampler generates the coordinates in the middle column for the first two dimensions, which are scaled by 2 in the first dimension and 3 in the second dimension so that they cover a 2×3 pixel image. To fulfill the Sampler interface, it is necessary to be able to work backward from a given pixel and sample number within that pixel to find the corresponding sample index in the full Halton sequence.

Sample index	$[0, 1)^2$ sample coordinates	Pixel sample coordinates
0	(0.000000, 0.000000)	(0.000000, 0.000000)
1	(0.500000, 0.333333)	(1.000000, 1.000000)
2	(0.250000, 0.666667)	(0.500000, 2.000000)
3	(0.750000, 0.111111)	(1.500000, 0.333333)
4	(0.125000, 0.444444)	(0.250000, 1.333333)
5	(0.625000, 0.777778)	(1.250000, 2.333333)
6	(0.375000, 0.222222)	(0.750000, 0.666667)
7	(0.875000, 0.555556)	(1.750000, 1.666667)
8	(0.062500, 0.888889)	(0.125000, 2.666667)
9	(0.562500, 0.037037)	(1.125000, 0.111111)
10	(0.312500, 0.370370)	(0.625000, 1.111111)
11	(0.812500, 0.703704)	(1.625000, 2.111111)
12	(0.187500, 0.148148)	(0.375000, 0.444444)
⋮		

To map the first two dimensions of samples from $[0, 1)^2$ to pixel coordinates, the Halton Sampler finds the smallest scale factor $(2^j, 3^k)$ that is larger than the lower of either the image resolution or MaxHaltonResolution in each dimension. (We will explain shortly how this specific choice of scales makes it easy to see which pixel a sample lands in.) After scaling, any samples outside the image extent will be simply ignored.

For images with resolution greater than MaxHaltonResolution in one or both dimensions, a tile of Halton points is repeated across the image. This resolution limit helps maintain sufficient floating-point precision in the computed sample values.

⟨*Find radical inverse base scales and exponents that cover sampling area*⟩ ≡   485
```
for (int i = 0; i < 2; ++i) {
    int base = (i == 0) ? 2 : 3;
    int scale = 1, exp = 0;
    while (scale < std::min(fullRes[i], MaxHaltonResolution)) {
        scale *= base;
        ++exp;
    }
    baseScales[i] = scale;
    baseExponents[i] = exp;
}
```

For each dimension, baseScales holds the scale factor, 2^j or 3^k, and baseExponents holds the exponents j and k.

⟨*HaltonSampler Private Members*⟩ +≡   485
```
static constexpr int MaxHaltonResolution = 128;
Point2i baseScales, baseExponents;
```

To see why the HaltonSampler uses this scheme to map samples to pixel coordinates, consider the effect of scaling a value computed with the radical inverse base b by a factor b^m. If the digits of a expressed in base b are $d_i(a)$, then recall that the radical inverse is the value $0.d_1(a)d_2(a)\ldots$ in base b. If we multiply this value by b^2, for example, we have $d_1(a)d_2(a).d_3(a)\ldots$; the first two digits have moved to the left of the radix point, and the fractional component of the value starts with $d_3(a)$.

This operation—scaling by b^m—forms the core of being able to determine which sample indices land in which pixels. Considering the first two digits in the above example, we can see that the integer component of the scaled value ranges from 0 to $b^2 - 1$ and that as a increases, its last two digits in base b take on any particular value after each b^2 sample index values.

Given a value x, $0 \le x \le b^2 - 1$, we can find the first value a that gives the value x in the integer components. By definition, the digits of x in base b are $d_2(x)d_1(x)$. Thus, if $d_1(a) = d_2(x)$ and $d_2(a) = d_1(x)$, then the scaled value of a's radical inverse will have an integer component equal to x.

Computing the index of the first sample in a given pixel (x, y) where the samples have been scaled by $(2^j, 3^k)$ involves computing the inverse radical inverse of the last j digits of x in base 2, which we will denote by x_r, and of the last k digits of y in base 3, y_r. This gives us a system of equations

$$x_r \equiv (i \bmod 2^j)$$
$$y_r \equiv (i \bmod 3^k),$$
    (8.21)

where the index i that satisfies these equations is the index of a sample that lies within the given pixel, after scaling.

Given this insight, we can now finally implement the `StartPixelSample()` method. The code that solves Equation (8.21) for i is in the ⟨*Compute Halton sample index for first sample in pixel* p⟩, which is not included here in the book; see Grünschloß et al. (2012) for details of the algorithm.

Given the index into the Halton sequence that corresponds to the first sample for the pixel, we need to find the index for the requested sample, `sampleIndex`. Because the bases $b = 2$ and $b = 3$ used in the `HaltonSampler` for pixel samples are relatively prime, it follows that if the sample values are scaled by some $(2^j, 3^k)$, then any particular pixel in the range $(0, 0) \rightarrow (2^j - 1, 3^k - 1)$ will be visited once every $2^j 3^k$ samples. That product is stored in `sampleStride` and the final Halton index is found by adding the product of that and the current `sampleIndex`.

⟨*HaltonSampler Public Methods*⟩ ≡   485

```
void StartPixelSample(Point2i p, int sampleIndex, int dim) {
    haltonIndex = 0;
    int sampleStride = baseScales[0] * baseScales[1];
    ⟨Compute Halton sample index for first sample in pixel p⟩
    haltonIndex += sampleIndex * sampleStride;
    dimension = std::max(2, dim);
}
```

⟨*HaltonSampler Private Members*⟩ +≡   485

```
int64_t haltonIndex = 0;
int dimension = 0;
```

The methods that generate Halton sample dimensions are straightforward; they just increment the `dimension` member variable based on how many dimensions they have consumed and call the appropriate radical inverse function. In the unlikely case that the maximum supported number of dimensions have been used, the implementation wraps around to the start and then skips over the first two dimensions, which are used solely for pixel samples.

⟨*HaltonSampler Public Methods*⟩ +≡   485

```
Float Get1D() {
    if (dimension >= PrimeTableSize)
        dimension = 2;
    return SampleDimension(dimension++);
}
```

The `SampleDimension()` method takes care of calling the appropriate radical inverse function for the current sample in the current dimension according to the selected randomization strategy.

⟨*HaltonSampler Private Methods*⟩ ≡   485

```
Float SampleDimension(int dimension) const {
    if (randomize == RandomizeStrategy::None)
        return RadicalInverse(dimension, haltonIndex);
    else if (randomize == RandomizeStrategy::PermuteDigits)
        return ScrambledRadicalInverse(dimension, haltonIndex,
                (*digitPermutations)[dimension]);
    else
        return OwenScrambledRadicalInverse(dimension, haltonIndex,
                                MixBits(1 + (dimension << 4)));
}
```

The Get2D() method is easily implemented using SampleDimension().

⟨*HaltonSampler Public Methods*⟩ +≡   **485**
```
    Point2f Get2D() {
        if (dimension + 1 >= PrimeTableSize)
            dimension = 2;
        int dim = dimension;
        dimension += 2;
        return {SampleDimension(dim), SampleDimension(dim + 1)};
    }
```

GetPixel2D() has to account for two important details in the rest of the HaltonSampler implementation. First, because the computation of the sample index, haltonIndex, in StartPixel Sample() does not account for random digit permutations, those must not be included in the samples returned for the first two dimensions: a call to RadicalInverse() is always used here.

Second, because the first baseExponents[i] digits of the first two dimensions' radical inverses are used to select which pixel is sampled, these digits must be discarded before computing the radical inverse for the first two dimensions of the sample, since the GetPixel2D() method is supposed to return the fractional offset in $[0, 1)^2$ within the pixel being sampled. This is most easily done by removing the trailing digits of the sample index before computing the radical inverse. Because the first dimension is base 2, this can efficiently be done using a shift, though a divide is necessary for base 3 in the second dimension.

⟨*HaltonSampler Public Methods*⟩ +≡   **485**
```
    Point2f GetPixel2D() {
        return {RadicalInverse(0, haltonIndex >> baseExponents[0]),
                RadicalInverse(1, haltonIndex / baseScales[1])};
    }
```

8.6.4 EVALUATION

Figure 8.29 shows plots of the power spectra for the HaltonSampler with each of the three randomization strategies. The frequency space perspective is revealing. First, note that all three strategies have low energy along the two axes: this indicates that they all do well with functions that mostly vary in only one dimension. This behavior can be understood from their construction: because each dimension uses an independent radical inverse, 1D projections of the sample points are stratified. (Consider in comparison the jittered sampling pattern's PSD, which had a radially symmetric distribution around the origin. Given n 2D stratified samples, only $\sqrt{n}$ are guaranteed to be stratified along either of the dimensions, whereas with the Halton sampler, all n are.)

However, the non-randomized Halton sampler has wide variation in its PSD at higher frequencies. Ideally, those frequencies would all have roughly unit energy, but in this case, some frequencies have over a hundred times more and others a hundred times less. Results will be poor if the frequencies of the function match the ones with high power in the PSD. This issue can be seen in rendered images; Figure 8.30 compares the visual results from sampling a checkerboard texture using a Halton-based sampler to using the stratified sampler from the previous section. Note the unpleasant pattern along edges in the foreground and toward the horizon.

Returning to the power spectra in Figure 8.29, we can see that random digit permutations give a substantial improvement in the power spectrum, though there is still clear structure, with some frequencies having very low power and others still having high power. The benefit

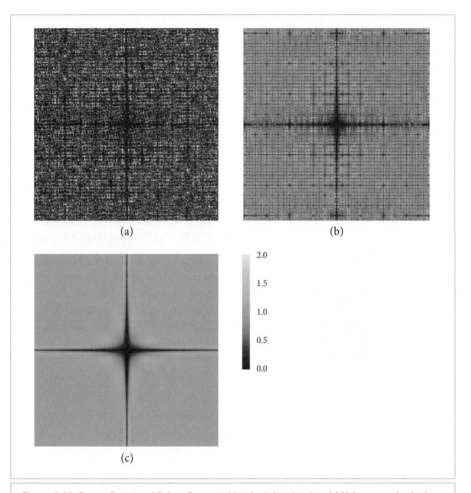

Figure 8.29: Power Spectra of Points Generated by the HaltonSampler. (a) Using no randomization, with substantial variation in power at the higher frequencies. (b) Using random digit scrambling, which improves the regularity of the PSD but still contains some spikes. (c) Using Owen scrambling, which gives near unit power at the higher frequencies, making it especially effective for antialiasing and integration.

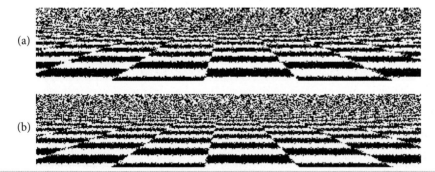

Figure 8.30: Comparison of the Stratified Sampler to a Low-Discrepancy Sampler Based on Halton Points on the Image Plane. (a) The stratified sampler with a single sample per pixel and (b) the Halton sampler with a single sample per pixel and no scrambling. Note that although the Halton pattern is able to reproduce the checker pattern farther toward the horizon than the stratified pattern, there is a regular structure to the error that is visually distracting; it does not turn aliasing into less objectionable noise as well as jittering does.

HaltonSampler 485

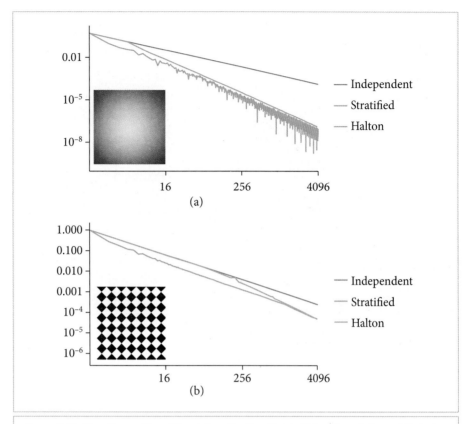

Figure 8.31: Mean Squared Error When Integrating Two Simple 2D Functions. Both are plotted using a log–log scale so that the asymptotic convergence rate can be seen from the slopes of the lines. For the stratified sampler, only square $n \times n$ stratifications are plotted. (a) With the smooth Gaussian function shown, the Halton sampler has a higher asymptotic rate of convergence than both stratified and independent sampling. Its performance is particularly good for sample counts of $2^i 3^i$ for integer i. (b) With the rotated checkerboard, stratified sampling is initially no better than independent sampling since the strata are not aligned with the checks. However, once the strata start to become smaller than the checks (around 256 samples), its asymptotic rate of convergence improves.

of Owen scrambling in this case is striking: it gives a uniform power spectrum at higher frequencies while maintaining low power along the axes.

It can also be illuminating to measure the performance of samplers with simple functions that can be integrated analytically.[11] Figure 8.31 shows plots of mean squared error (MSE) for using the independent, stratified, and Halton samplers for integrating a Gaussian and a checkerboard function (shown in the plots). In this case, using a log–log scale has the effect of causing convergence rates of the form $O(n^c)$ to appear as lines with slope c, which makes it easier to compare asymptotic convergence of various techniques. For both functions, both stratified and Halton sampling have a higher rate of convergence than the $O(1/n)$ of independent sampling, as can be seen by the steeper slopes of their error curves. The Halton sampler does especially well with the Gaussian, achieving nearly two thousand times lower MSE than independent sampling at 4,096 samples.

---

11 The data for these plots was gathered using pbrt's FunctionIntegrator, which is not discussed further in the text. It is a simple Integrator that can evaluate integrals of a handful of simple 2D functions with the specified sampler.

Figure 8.32: Test Scene for Sampler Evaluation. This scene requires integrating a function of tens of dimensions, including defocus blur, a moving camera, and multiply scattered illumination from an environment map light source. *(Dragon model courtesy of the Stanford Computer Graphics Laboratory.)*

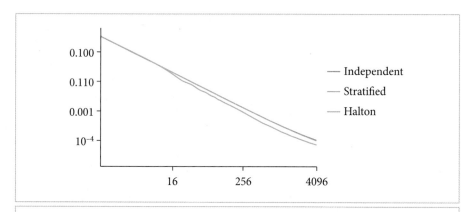

Figure 8.33: Log–Log Plot of MSE versus Number of Samples for the Scene in Figure 8.32. The Halton sampler gives consistently lower error than both the independent and stratified samplers and converges at a slightly higher rate.

Figure 8.32 shows the image of a test scene that we will use for comparing samplers. It features a moving camera, defocus blur, illumination from an environment map light source, and multiply scattered light from sources to give an integral with tens of dimensions. Figure 8.33 is a log–log plot of MSE versus number of samples for these samplers with this scene. With a more complex integrand than the simple ones in Figure 8.31, the Halton sampler does not have the enormous benefit it did there. Nevertheless, it makes a significant improvement to error—for example, MSE is 1.09× lower than independent sampling at 4,096 samples per pixel.

*8.7 SOBOL' SAMPLERS

While the Halton sequence is effective for Monte Carlo integration, each radical inverse computation requires one integer division for each digit. The integer division instruction is one of the slowest ones on most processors, which can affect overall rendering performance, especially in highly optimized renderers. Therefore, in this section we will describe three Samplers that are based on the Sobol' sequence, a low-discrepancy sequence that is defined entirely in base 2, which leads to efficient implementations.

The base-2 radical inverse can be computed more efficiently than the way that the base-agnostic RadicalInverse() function computes it. The key is to take advantage of the fact that numbers are already represented in base 2 on digital computers. If a is a 64-bit value, then from Equation (8.18),

$$a = \sum_{i=1}^{64} d_i(a) 2^{i-1},$$

where $d_i(a)$ are its bits. First, consider reversing its bits, still represented as an integer value, which gives

$$\sum_{i=1}^{64} d_i(a) 2^{64-i}.$$

If we then divide this value by 2^{64}, we have

$$\sum_{i=1}^{64} d_i(a) 2^{-i},$$

which equals $\Phi_2(a)$ (recall Equation (8.19)). Thus, the base-2 radical inverse can equivalently be computed using a bit reverse and a power-of-two division. The division can be replaced with multiplication by the corresponding inverse power-of-two, which gives the same result with IEEE floating point. Some processors provide a native instruction that directly reverses the bits in a register; otherwise it can be done in $O(\log_2 n)$ operations, where n is the number of bits. (See the implementation of ReverseBits32() in Section B.2.7.)

While the implementation of a function that generates Halton points could be optimized by taking advantage of this for the first dimension where $b = 2$, performance would not improve for any of the remaining dimensions, so the overall benefit would be low. The Sobol' sequence uses $b = 2$ for all dimensions, which allows it to benefit in all cases from computers' use of base 2 internally. So that each dimension has a different set of sample values, it uses a different *generator matrix* for each dimension, where the generator matrices are carefully chosen so that the resulting sequence has low discrepancy.

To see how generator matrices are used, consider an n-digit number a in base b, where the ith digit of a is $d_i(a)$ and where we have an $n \times n$ generator matrix C. Then the corresponding sample point $x_a \in [0, 1)$ is defined by

$$x_a = [b^{-1}\ b^{-2}\ \cdots\ b^{-n}] \begin{bmatrix} c_{1,1} & c_{1,2} & \cdots & c_{1,n} \\ c_{2,1} & \ddots & & c_{2,n} \\ \vdots & & \ddots & \vdots \\ c_{n,1} & \cdots & \cdots & c_{n,n} \end{bmatrix} \begin{bmatrix} d_1(a) \\ d_2(a) \\ \vdots \\ d_n(a) \end{bmatrix}, \tag{8.22}$$

where all arithmetic is performed in the ring $\mathbb{Z}_b$ (in other words, when all operations are performed modulo b). This construction gives a total of b^n points as a ranges from 0 to $b^n - 1$. If the generator matrix is the identity matrix, then this definition corresponds to the regular radical inverse, base b. (It is worth pausing to make sure you see this connection between Equations (8.19) and (8.22) before continuing.)

In this section, we will exclusively use $b = 2$ and $n = 32$. While introducing a 32×32 matrix to each dimension of the sample generation algorithm may not seem like a step toward better performance, we will see that in the end the sampling code can be mapped to an implementation that uses a small number of bit operations that perform this computation in an extremely efficient manner.

The first step toward high performance comes from the fact that we are working in base 2; as such, all entries of $\mathbf{C}$ are either 0 or 1 and thus we can represent either each row or each column of the matrix with a single unsigned 32-bit integer. We will choose to represent columns of the matrix as `uint32_ts`; this choice leads to an efficient algorithm for multiplying the d_i column vector by $\mathbf{C}$.

Now consider the task of computing the $\mathbf{C}[d_i(a)]^T$ matrix-vector product; using the definition of matrix-vector multiplication, we have:

$$
\begin{bmatrix}
c_{1,1} & c_{1,2} & \cdots & c_{1,n} \\
c_{2,1} & \ddots & & c_{2,n} \\
\vdots & & \ddots & \vdots \\
c_{n,1} & \cdots & \cdots & c_{n,n}
\end{bmatrix}
\begin{bmatrix}
d_1(a) \\
d_2(a) \\
\vdots \\
d_n(a)
\end{bmatrix}
= d_1
\begin{bmatrix}
c_{1,1} \\
c_{2,1} \\
\vdots \\
c_{n,1}
\end{bmatrix}
+ \cdots + d_n
\begin{bmatrix}
c_{1,n} \\
c_{2,n} \\
\vdots \\
c_{n,n}
\end{bmatrix}.
\tag{8.23}
$$

In other words, for each digit of d_i that has a value of 1, the corresponding column of $\mathbf{C}$ should be summed. This addition can in turn be performed efficiently in $\mathbb{Z}_2$: in that setting, addition corresponds to the bitwise exclusive OR operation. (Consider the combinations of the two possible operand values—0 and 1—and the result of adding them mod 2, and compare to the values computed by exclusive OR with the same operand values.) Thus, the multiplication $\mathbf{C}[d_i(a)]^T$ is just a matter of exclusive ORing together the columns i of $\mathbf{C}$ where $d_i(a)$'s bit is 1. This computation is implemented in the `MultiplyGenerator()` function.

⟨*Low Discrepancy Inline Functions*⟩ +≡
```
uint32_t MultiplyGenerator(pstd::span<const uint32_t> C, uint32_t a) {
    uint32_t v = 0;
    for (int i = 0; a != 0; ++i, a >>= 1)
        if (a & 1)
            v ^= C[i];
    return v;
}
```

Going back to Equation (8.22), if we denote the column vector from the product $v = \mathbf{C}[d_i(a)]^T$, then consider the vector product

$$
x_a = \begin{bmatrix} 2^{-1} & 2^{-2} & \cdots & 2^{-n} \end{bmatrix}
\begin{bmatrix} v_1 \\ v_2 \\ \vdots \\ v_n \end{bmatrix}
= \sum_{i=1}^{32} 2^{-i} v_i.
\tag{8.24}
$$

Applying the same ideas as we did before to derive an efficient base-2 radical inverse algorithm, this value can also be computed by reversing the bits of v and dividing by 2^{32}. To save the small cost of reversing the bits, we can equivalently reverse the bits in all the columns of the generator matrix before passing it to `MultiplyGenerator()`. We will use that convention in what follows.

MultiplyGenerator() 494

We will not discuss how the Sobol' matrices are derived in a way that leads to a low-discrepancy sequence; the "Further Reading" section has pointers to more details. However,

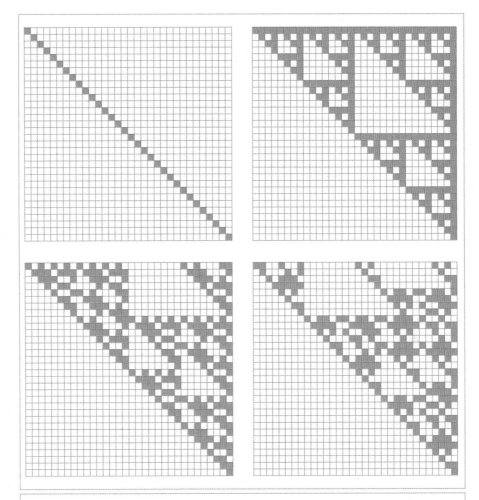

Figure 8.34: Generator matrices for the first four dimensions of the Sobol' sequence. Note their regular structure.

the first few Sobol' generator matrices are shown in Figure 8.34. Note that the first is the identity, corresponding to the van der Corput sequence. Subsequent dimensions have various fractal-like structures to their entries.

8.7.1 STRATIFICATION OVER ELEMENTARY INTERVALS

The first two dimensions of the Sobol' sequence are stratified in a very general way that makes them particularly effective in integration. For example, the first 16 samples satisfy the stratification constraint from stratified sampling in Section 8.5, meaning there is just one sample in each of the boxes of extent $(\frac{1}{4}, \frac{1}{4})$. However, they are also stratified over all the boxes of extent $(\frac{1}{16}, 1)$ and $(1, \frac{1}{16})$. Furthermore, there is only one sample in each of the boxes of extent $(\frac{1}{2}, \frac{1}{8})$ and $(\frac{1}{8}, \frac{1}{2})$. Figure 8.35 shows all the possibilities for dividing the domain into regions where the first 16 Sobol' samples satisfy these stratification properties.

Not only are corresponding stratification constraints obeyed by any power-of-2 set of samples starting from the beginning of the sequence, but subsequent power-of-2-sized sets of

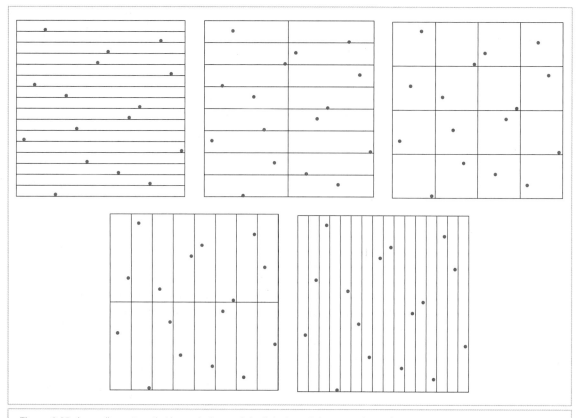

Figure 8.35: A sampling pattern that has a single sample in all the base-2 elementary intervals.

samples fulfill them as well. More formally, any sequence of length $2^{l_1+l_2}$ (where l_i is a non-negative integer) satisfies this general stratification constraint. The set of *elementary intervals* in two dimensions, base 2, is defined as

$$E = \left\{ \left[\frac{a_1}{2^{l_1}}, \frac{a_1 + 1}{2^{l_1}} \right) \times \left[\frac{a_2}{2^{l_2}}, \frac{a_2 + 1}{2^{l_2}} \right) \right\},$$

where the integer $a_i = 0, 1, 2, 3, \ldots, 2^{l_i} - 1$. One sample from each of the first $2^{l_1+l_2}$ values in the sequence will be in each of the elementary intervals. Furthermore, the same property is true for each subsequent set of $2^{l_1+l_2}$ values. Such a sequence is called a $(0, 2)$-*sequence*.

8.7.2 RANDOMIZATION AND SCRAMBLING

For the same reasons as were discussed in Section 8.6.2 in the context of the Halton sequence, it is also useful to be able to scramble the Sobol′ sequence. We will now define a few small classes that scramble a given sample value using various approaches. As with the generation of Sobol′ samples, scrambling algorithms for them can also take advantage of their base-2 representation to improve their efficiency.

All the following randomization classes take an unsigned 32-bit integer that they should interpret as a fixed-point number with 0 digits before and 32 digits after the radix point. Put another way, after randomization, this value will be divided by 2^{32} to yield the final sample value in $[0, 1)$.

The simplest approach is not to randomize the sample at all. In that case, the value is returned unchanged; this is implemented by NoRandomizer.

⟨*NoRandomizer Definition*⟩ ≡
```
struct NoRandomizer {
    uint32_t operator()(uint32_t v) const { return v; }
};
```

Alternatively, random permutations can be applied to the digits, such as was done using the DigitPermutation class with the Halton sampler. In base 2, however, a random permutation of {0, 1} can be represented with a single bit, as there are only two unique permutations. If the permutation {1, 0} is denoted by a bit with value 1 and the permutation {0, 1} is denoted by 0, then the permutation can be applied by computing the exclusive OR of the permutation bit with a digit's bit. Therefore, the permutation for all 32 bits can be represented by a 32-bit integer and all of the permutations can be applied in a single operation by computing the exclusive OR of the provided value with the permutation.

⟨*BinaryPermuteScrambler Definition*⟩ ≡
```
struct BinaryPermuteScrambler {
    BinaryPermuteScrambler(uint32_t perm) : permutation(perm) {}
    uint32_t operator()(uint32_t v) const { return permutation ^ v; }
    uint32_t permutation;
};
```

Owen scrambling is also effective with Sobol' points. pbrt provides two implementations of it, both of which take advantage of their base-2 representation. FastOwenScrambler implements a highly efficient approach, though the spectral properties of the resulting points are not quite as good as a true Owen scramble.

⟨*FastOwenScrambler Definition*⟩ ≡
```
struct FastOwenScrambler {
    FastOwenScrambler(uint32_t seed) : seed(seed) {}
    ⟨FastOwenScrambler Public Methods 498⟩
    uint32_t seed;
};
```

Its implementation builds on the fact that in base 2, if a number is multiplied by an even value, then the value of any particular bit in it only affects the bits above it in the result. Equivalently, for any bit in the result, it is only affected by the bits below it and the even multiplicand. One way to see why this is so is to consider long multiplication (as taught in grade school) applied to binary numbers. Given two n-digit binary numbers a and b where $d_i(b)$ is the ith digit of b, then using Equation (8.18), we have

$$a\,b = \sum_{i=1}^{} a\,d_i(b)\,2^{i-1}. \qquad \text{(8.25)}$$

Thus, for any digit $i > 1$ where $d_i(b)$ is one, the value of a is shifted $i - 1$ bits to the left and added to the final result and so any digit of the result only depends on lower digits of a.

The bits in the value provided to the randomization class must be reversed so that the low bit corresponds to 1/2 in the final sample value. Then, the properties illustrated in Equation (8.25) can be applied: the product of an even value with the sample value v can be interpreted as a bitwise permutation as was done in the BinaryPermuteScrambler, allowing the use of an exclusive OR to permute all the bits. After a few rounds of this and a few operations to mix the seed value in, the bits are reversed again before being returned.

⟨*FastOwenScrambler Public Methods*⟩ ≡   497
```
uint32_t operator()(uint32_t v) const {
    v = ReverseBits32(v);
    v ^= v * 0x3d20adea;
    v += seed;
    v *= (seed >> 16) | 1;
    v ^= v * 0x05526c56;
    v ^= v * 0x53a22864;
    return ReverseBits32(v);
}
```

The OwenScrambler class implements a full Owen scramble, operating on each bit in turn.

⟨*OwenScrambler Definition*⟩ ≡
```
struct OwenScrambler {
    OwenScrambler(uint32_t seed) : seed(seed) {}
    ⟨OwenScrambler Public Methods 498⟩
    uint32_t seed;
};
```

The first bit (corresponding to 1/2 in the final sample value) is handled specially, since there are no bits that precede it to affect its randomization. It is randomly flipped according to the seed value provided to the constructor.

⟨*OwenScrambler Public Methods*⟩ ≡   498
```
uint32_t operator()(uint32_t v) const {
    if (seed & 1)
        v ^= 1u << 31;
    for (int b = 1; b < 32; ++b) {
        ⟨Apply Owen scrambling to binary digit b in v 498⟩
    }
    return v;
}
```

For all the following bits, a bit mask is computed such that the bitwise AND of the mask with the value gives the bits above b—the values of which should determine the permutation that is used for the current bit. Those are run through MixBits() to get a hashed value that is then used to determine whether or not to flip the current bit.

⟨*Apply Owen scrambling to binary digit* b *in* v⟩ ≡   498
```
uint32_t mask = (~0u) << (32 - b);
if ((uint32_t)MixBits((v & mask) ^ seed) & (1u << b))
    v ^= 1u << (31 - b);
```

8.7.3 SOBOL′ SAMPLE GENERATION

We now have the pieces needed to implement functions that generate Sobol′ samples. The SobolSample() function performs this task for a given sample index a and dimension, applying the provided randomizer to the sample before returning it.

Because this function is templated on the type of the randomizer, a specialized instance of it will be compiled using the provided randomizer, leading to the randomization algorithm being expanded inline in the function. For pbrt's purposes, there is no need for a more general mechanism for sample randomization, so the small performance benefit is worth taking in this implementation approach.

⟨*Low Discrepancy Inline Functions*⟩ +≡
```
template <typename R>
Float SobolSample(int64_t a, int dimension, R randomizer) {
    ⟨Compute initial Sobol' sample v using generator matrices 499⟩
    ⟨Randomize Sobol' sample and return floating-point value 499⟩
}
```

Samples are computed using the Sobol' generator matrices, following the approach described by Equation (8.23). All the generator matrices are stored consecutively in the Sobol Matrices32 array. Each one has SobolMatrixSize columns, so scaling the dimension by SobolMatrixSize brings us to the first column of the matrix for the given dimension.

⟨*Compute initial Sobol' sample* v *using generator matrices*⟩ ≡   **499**
```
uint32_t v = 0;
for (int i = dimension * SobolMatrixSize; a != 0; a >>= 1, i++)
    if (a & 1)
        v ^= SobolMatrices32[i];
```

⟨*Sobol Matrix Declarations*⟩ ≡
```
static constexpr int NSobolDimensions = 1024;
static constexpr int SobolMatrixSize = 52;
PBRT_CONST uint32_t SobolMatrices32[NSobolDimensions * SobolMatrixSize];
```

The value is then randomized with the given randomizer before being rescaled to $[0, 1)$. (The constant 0x1p-32 is 2^{-32}, expressed as a hexadecimal floating-point number.)

⟨*Randomize Sobol' sample and return floating-point value*⟩ ≡   **499**
```
v = randomizer(v);
return std::min(v * 0x1p-32f, FloatOneMinusEpsilon);
```

8.7.4 GLOBAL SOBOL' SAMPLER

The SobolSampler generates samples by direct evaluation of the d-dimensional Sobol' sequence. Like the HaltonSampler, it scales the first two dimensions of the sequence to cover a range of image pixels. Thus, in a similar fashion, nearby pixels have well-distributed d-dimensional sample points not just individually but also with respect to nearby pixels.

⟨*SobolSampler Definition*⟩ ≡
```
class SobolSampler {
  public:
    ⟨SobolSampler Public Methods 500⟩
  private:
    ⟨SobolSampler Private Methods 501⟩
    ⟨SobolSampler Private Members 500⟩
};
```

The SobolSampler uniformly scales the first two dimensions by the smallest power of 2 that causes the $[0, 1)^2$ sample domain to cover the image area to be sampled. As with the HaltonSampler, this specific scaling scheme is chosen in order to make it easier to compute the reverse mapping from pixel coordinates to the sample indices that land in each pixel.

⟨*SobolSampler Public Methods*⟩ ≡   **499**
```
    SobolSampler(int samplesPerPixel, Point2i fullResolution,
                 RandomizeStrategy randomize, int seed = 0)
        : samplesPerPixel(samplesPerPixel), seed(seed), randomize(randomize) {
        scale = RoundUpPow2(std::max(fullResolution.x, fullResolution.y));
    }
```

All four of the randomization approaches from Section 8.7.2 are supported by the Sobol
Sampler; randomize encodes which one to apply.

⟨*SobolSampler Private Members*⟩ ≡   **499**
```
    int samplesPerPixel, scale, seed;
    RandomizeStrategy randomize;
```

The sampler needs to record the current pixel for use in its GetPixel2D() method and, like
other samplers, tracks the current dimension in its dimension member variable.

⟨*SobolSampler Public Methods*⟩ +≡   **499**
```
    void StartPixelSample(Point2i p, int sampleIndex, int dim) {
        pixel = p;
        dimension = std::max(2, dim);
        sobolIndex = SobolIntervalToIndex(Log2Int(scale), sampleIndex, pixel);
    }
```

⟨*SobolSampler Private Members*⟩ +≡   **499**
```
    Point2i pixel;
    int dimension;
    int64_t sobolIndex;
```

The SobolIntervalToIndex() function returns the index of the sampleIndexth sample in the
pixel p, if the $[0, 1)^2$ sampling domain has been scaled by $2^{\texttt{log2Scale}}$ to cover the pixel sampling
area.

⟨*Low Discrepancy Declarations*⟩ ≡
```
    uint64_t SobolIntervalToIndex(uint32_t log2Scale, uint64_t sampleIndex,
                                  Point2i p);
```

The general approach used to derive the algorithm it implements is similar to that used by
the Halton sampler in its StartPixelSample() method. Here, scaling by a power of two means
that the base-2 logarithm of the scale gives the number of digits of the $\mathbf{C}[d_i(a)]^T$ product that
form the scaled sample's integer component. To find the values of a that give a particular
integer value after scaling, we can compute the inverse of C: given

$$v = \mathbf{C}[d_i(a)]^T,$$

then equivalently

$$\mathbf{C}^{-1}v = [d_i(a)]^T.$$

We will not include the implementation of this function here.

Sample generation is now straightforward. There is the usual management of the dimension
value, again with the first two dimensions reserved for the pixel sample, and then a call to
SampleDimension() gives the sample for a single Sobol′ dimension.

⟨*SobolSampler Public Methods*⟩ +≡   **499**
```
Float Get1D() {
    if (dimension >= NSobolDimensions)
        dimension = 2;
    return SampleDimension(dimension++);
}
```

The `SampleDimension()` method takes care of calling `SobolSample()` for the current sample index and specified dimension using the appropriate randomizer.

⟨*SobolSampler Private Methods*⟩ ≡   **499**
```
Float SampleDimension(int dimension) const {
    ⟨Return un-randomized Sobol' sample if appropriate⟩
    ⟨Return randomized Sobol' sample using randomize 501⟩
}
```

⟨*Return un-randomized Sobol' sample if appropriate*⟩ ≡
```
if (randomize == RandomizeStrategy::None)
    return SobolSample(sobolIndex, dimension, NoRandomizer());
```

If a randomizer is being used, a seed value must be computed for it. Note that the hash value passed to each randomizer is based solely on the current dimension and user-provided seed, if any. It must *not* be based on the current pixel or the current sample index within the pixel, since the same randomization should be used at all the pixels and all the samples within them.

⟨*Return randomized Sobol' sample using* randomize⟩ ≡   **501**
```
uint32_t hash = Hash(dimension, seed);
if (randomize == RandomizeStrategy::PermuteDigits)
    return SobolSample(sobolIndex, dimension, BinaryPermuteScrambler(hash));
else if (randomize == RandomizeStrategy::FastOwen)
    return SobolSample(sobolIndex, dimension, FastOwenScrambler(hash));
else
    return SobolSample(sobolIndex, dimension, OwenScrambler(hash));
```

2D sample generation is easily implemented using `SampleDimension()`. If all sample dimensions have been consumed, `Get2D()` goes back to the start and skips the first two dimensions, as was done in the `HaltonSampler`.

⟨*SobolSampler Public Methods*⟩ +≡   **499**
```
Point2f Get2D() {
    if (dimension + 1 >= NSobolDimensions)
        dimension = 2;
    Point2f u(SampleDimension(dimension), SampleDimension(dimension + 1));
    dimension += 2;
    return u;
}
```

Pixel samples are generated using the first two dimensions of the Sobol' sample. `Sobol IntervalToIndex()` does not account for randomization, so the `NoRandomizer` is always used for the pixel sample, regardless of the value of `randomize`.

⟨*SobolSampler Public Methods*⟩ +≡   **499**
```
    Point2f GetPixel2D() {
        Point2f u(SobolSample(sobolIndex, 0, NoRandomizer()),
                  SobolSample(sobolIndex, 1, NoRandomizer()));
        ⟨Remap Sobol′ dimensions used for pixel samples 502⟩
        return u;
    }
```

The samples returned for the pixel position need to be adjusted so that they are offsets within the current pixel. Similar to what was done in the `HaltonSampler`, the sample value is scaled so that the pixel coordinates are in the integer component of the result. The remaining fractional component gives the offset within the pixel that the sampler returns.

⟨*Remap Sobol′ dimensions used for pixel samples*⟩ ≡   **502**
```
    for (int dim = 0; dim < 2; ++dim)
        u[dim] = Clamp(u[dim] * scale - pixel[dim], 0, OneMinusEpsilon);
```

8.7.5 PADDED SOBOL′ SAMPLER

The `SobolSampler` generates sample points that have low discrepancy over all of their d dimensions. However, the distribution of samples in two-dimensional slices of the d-dimensional space is not necessarily particularly good. Figure 8.36 shows an example.

For rendering, this state of affairs means that, for example, the samples taken over the surface of a light source at a given pixel may not be well distributed. It is of only slight solace to know that the full set of d-dimensional samples are well distributed in return. Figure 8.37 shows this problem in practice with the `SobolSampler`: 2D projections of the form shown in Figure 8.36 end up generating a characteristic checkerboard pattern in the image at low sampling rates.

Therefore, the `PaddedSobolSampler` generates samples from the Sobol′ sequence in a way that focuses on returning good distributions for the dimensions used by each 1D and 2D sample

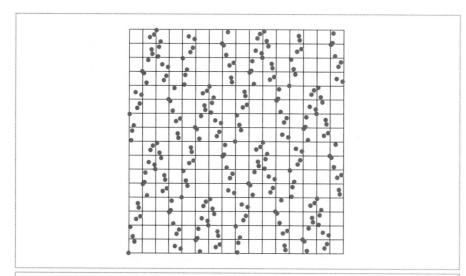

Figure 8.36: Plot of the first 256 points from dimensions 4 and 5 of the Sobol′ sequence. The 2D projection of these two dimensions is not well distributed and is not stratified over elementary intervals.

Figure 8.37: Scene Rendered Using the SobolSampler at a Low Sampling Rate. With that sampler, these sorts of checkerboard patterns can result due to structure in the lower-dimensional projections of the form shown in Figure 8.36. *(Killeroo model courtesy of headus/Rezard.)*

independently. It does so via padding samples, similarly to the StratifiedSampler, but here using Sobol' samples rather than jittered samples.

⟨*PaddedSobolSampler Definition*⟩ ≡
```
class PaddedSobolSampler {
  public:
    ⟨PaddedSobolSampler Public Methods 504⟩
  private:
    ⟨PaddedSobolSampler Private Methods 504⟩
    ⟨PaddedSobolSampler Private Members 503⟩
};
```

The constructor, not included here, initializes the following member variables from provided values. As with the SobolSampler, using a pixel sample count that is not a power of 2 will give suboptimal results; a warning is issued in this case.

⟨*PaddedSobolSampler Private Members*⟩ ≡   **503**
```
int samplesPerPixel, seed;
RandomizeStrategy randomize;
```

`StartPixelSample()`, also not included here, just records the specified pixel, sample index, and dimension.

⟨*PaddedSobolSampler Private Members*⟩ +≡   **503**
```
Point2i pixel;
int sampleIndex, dimension;
```

1D samples are generated by randomly shuffling a randomized van der Corput sequence.

⟨*PaddedSobolSampler Public Methods*⟩ ≡   **503**
```
Float Get1D() {
    ⟨Get permuted index for current pixel sample 504⟩
    int dim = dimension++;
    ⟨Return randomized 1D van der Corput sample for dimension dim 504⟩
}
```

Here, the permutation used for padding is based on the current pixel and dimension. It must not be based on the sample index, as the same permutation should be applied to all sample indices of a given dimension in a given pixel.

⟨*Get permuted index for current pixel sample*⟩ ≡   **504, 505**
```
uint64_t hash = Hash(pixel, dimension, seed);
int index = PermutationElement(sampleIndex, samplesPerPixel, hash);
```

Given the permuted sample index value `index`, a separate method, `SampleDimension()`, takes care of generating the corresponding Sobol′ sample. The high bits of the hash value are reused for the sample's randomization; doing so should be safe, since `PermutationElement()` uses the hash it is passed in an entirely different way than any of the sample randomization schemes do.

⟨*Return randomized 1D van der Corput sample for dimension* dim⟩ ≡   **504**
```
return SampleDimension(0, index, hash >> 32);
```

`SampleDimension()` follows the same approach as the corresponding method in `SobolSampler`, creating the appropriate randomizer before calling `SobolSample()`.

⟨*PaddedSobolSampler Private Methods*⟩ ≡   **503**
```
Float SampleDimension(int dimension, uint32_t a, uint32_t hash) const {
    if (randomize == RandomizeStrategy::None)
        return SobolSample(a, dimension, NoRandomizer());
    else if (randomize == RandomizeStrategy::PermuteDigits)
        return SobolSample(a, dimension, BinaryPermuteScrambler(hash));
    else if (randomize == RandomizeStrategy::FastOwen)
        return SobolSample(a, dimension, FastOwenScrambler(hash));
    else
        return SobolSample(a, dimension, OwenScrambler(hash));
}
```

Padded 2D samples are generated starting with a similar permutation of sample indices.

⟨*PaddedSobolSampler Public Methods*⟩ +≡   **503**
```
    Point2f Get2D() {
        ⟨Get permuted index for current pixel sample 504⟩
        int dim = dimension;
        dimension += 2;
        ⟨Return randomized 2D Sobol' sample 505⟩
    }
```

Randomization also parallels the 1D case; again, bits from hash are used both for the random permutation of sample indices and for sample randomization.

⟨*Return randomized 2D Sobol' sample*⟩ ≡   **505**
```
    return Point2f(SampleDimension(0, index, uint32_t(hash)),
                   SampleDimension(1, index, hash >> 32));
```

For this sampler, pixel samples are generated in the same manner as all other 2D samples, so the sample generation request is forwarded on to Get2D().

⟨*PaddedSobolSampler Public Methods*⟩ +≡   **503**
```
    Point2f GetPixel2D() { return Get2D(); }
```

8.7.6 BLUE NOISE SOBOL' SAMPLER

ZSobolSampler is a third sampler based on the Sobol' sequence. It is also based on padding 1D and 2D Sobol' samples, but uses sample indices in a way that leads to a blue noise distribution of sample values. This tends to push error to higher frequencies, which in turn makes it appear more visually pleasing. Figure 8.38 compares a scene rendered with the PaddedSobolSampler and the ZSobolSampler; both have essentially the same MSE, but the one rendered using ZSobolSampler looks better to most human observers. This Sampler is the default one used by pbrt if no sampler is specified in the scene description.

⟨*ZSobolSampler Definition*⟩ ≡
```
    class ZSobolSampler {
      public:
        ⟨ZSobolSampler Public Methods 508⟩
      private:
        ⟨ZSobolSampler Private Members 508⟩
    };
```

This sampler generates blue noise samples by taking advantage of the properties of (0, 2)-sequences. To understand the idea behind its implementation, first consider rendering a two-pixel image using 16 samples per pixel where a set of 2D samples are used for area light source sampling in each pixel. If the first 16 samples from a (0, 2)-sequence are used for the first pixel and the next 16 for the second, then not only will each pixel individually use well-stratified samples, but the set of all 32 samples will collectively be well stratified thanks to the stratification of (0, 2)-sequences over elementary intervals (Section 8.7.1). Consequently, the samples used in each pixel will generally be in different locations than in the other pixel, which is precisely the sample decorrelation exhibited by blue noise. (See Figure 8.39.)

More generally, if all the pixels in an image take different power-of-2 aligned and sized segments of samples from a single large set of Sobol' samples in a way that nearby pixels generally take adjacent segments, then the distribution of samples across the entire image will be such that pixels generally use different sample values than their neighbors. Allocating segments of samples in scanline order would give good distributions along scanlines, but

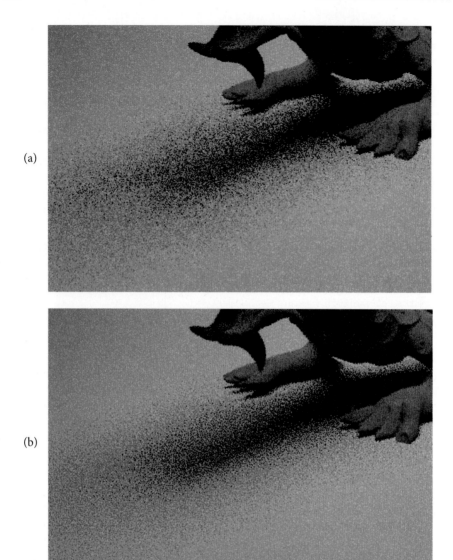

(a)

(b)

Figure 8.38: **The Benefit of Blue Noise with Padded Sobol′ Points.** (a) Rendered using the `PaddedSobol Sampler`. (b) Rendered with the `ZSobolSampler`. Both images are rendered using 1 sample per pixel and have the same overall error, but the second image looks much better thanks to a blue noise distribution of error. *(Dragon model courtesy of the Stanford Computer Graphics Laboratory.)*

it would not do much from scanline to scanline. The Morton curve, which was introduced earlier in Section 7.3.3 in the context of linear bounding volume hierarchies, gives a better mechanism for this task: if we compute the Morton code for each pixel (x, y) and then use that to determine the pixel's starting index into the full set of Sobol′ samples, then nearby pixels—those that are nearby in both x and y—will tend to use nearby segments of the samples. This idea is illustrated in Figure 8.40.

Used directly in this manner, the Morton curve can lead to visible structure in the image; see Figure 8.41, where samples were allocated in that way. This issue can be addressed with a random permutation of the Morton indices interpreted as base-4 numbers, which effectively groups pairs of one bit from x and one bit from y in the Morton index into single base-4

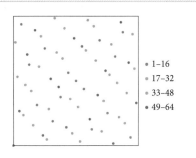

Figure 8.39: The First 64 2D Sobol′ Points, Colored in Sets of 16. If four adjacent pixels each use one of these sets for sampling, then each would not only have well-distributed points individually, but the points collectively would be decorrelated due to being from a (0, 2)-sequence.

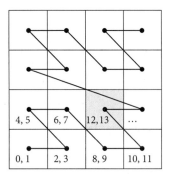

Figure 8.40: Allocating Sobol′ Samples in Morton Curve Order. With a 4 × 4 pixel image rendered using 2 samples per pixel, we can take the full set of 2 × 4 × 4 Sobol′ samples and then allocate segments of samples to pixels according to their Morton indices. For example, pixel (2, 1) has Morton index 6, so it uses samples with indices 12 and 13.

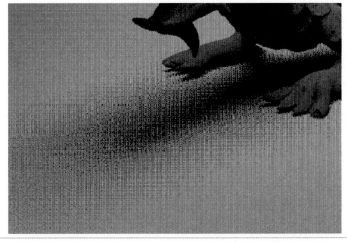

Figure 8.41: If a regular Morton curve without permutations is used to allocate Sobol′ indices in pixels, visible structure will be present in the rendered image. (Compare with Figure 8.38(b) where such a permutation is used.) *(Dragon model courtesy of the Stanford Computer Graphics Laboratory.)*

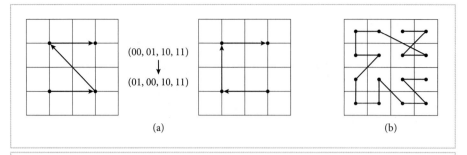

(00, 01, 10, 11)

↓

(01, 00, 10, 11)

(a)   (b)

Figure 8.42: If pixels' Morton indices are interpreted as base-4 numbers and their digits are randomly permuted, the resulting curve is still spatially coherent. (a) Applying the permutation shown to the first base-4 digit for a 4 × 4 pixel image causes the 2 × 2 blocks of pixels to be visited in a different order than the usual Morton curve. (b) If the second base-4 digit is also permuted (here with different permutations for each 2 × 2 block, not shown), then the pixels within each block are also visited in different orders.

digits. Randomly permuting these digits still maintains much of the spatial coherence of the Morton curve; see Figure 8.42 for an illustration of the permutation approach. Figure 8.38(b) shows the resulting improvement in a rendered image.

A second problem with the approach as described so far is that it does not randomize the order of sample indices within a pixel, as is necessary for padding samples across different dimensions. This shortcoming can be addressed by appending the bits of the sample index within a pixel to the pixel's Morton code and then including those in the index randomization as well.

In addition to the usual configuration parameters, the ZSobolSampler constructor also stores the base-2 logarithm of the number of samples per pixel as well as the number of base-4 digits in the full extended Morton index that includes the sample index.

⟨*ZSobolSampler Public Methods*⟩ ≡   505
```
    ZSobolSampler(int samplesPerPixel, Point2i fullResolution,
                  RandomizeStrategy randomize, int seed = 0)
        : randomize(randomize), seed(seed) {
        log2SamplesPerPixel = Log2Int(samplesPerPixel);
        int res = RoundUpPow2(std::max(fullResolution.x, fullResolution.y));
        int log4SamplesPerPixel = (log2SamplesPerPixel + 1) / 2;
        nBase4Digits = Log2Int(res) + log4SamplesPerPixel;
    }
```

⟨*ZSobolSampler Private Members*⟩ ≡   505
```
    RandomizeStrategy randomize;
    int seed, log2SamplesPerPixel, nBase4Digits;
```

The StartPixelSample() method's main task is to construct the initial unpermuted sample index by computing the pixel's Morton code and then appending the sample index, using a left shift to make space for it. This value is stored in mortonIndex.

⟨*ZSobolSampler Public Methods*⟩ +≡   505
```
    void StartPixelSample(Point2i p, int index, int dim) {
        dimension = dim;
        mortonIndex = (EncodeMorton2(p.x, p.y) << log2SamplesPerPixel) | index;
    }
```

⟨*ZSobolSampler Private Members*⟩ +≡   505
```
uint64_t mortonIndex;
int dimension;
```

Sample generation is similar to the PaddedSobolSampler with the exception that the index of the sample is found with a call to the GetSampleIndex() method (shown next), which randomizes mortonIndex. The ⟨*Generate 1D Sobol' sample at* sampleIndex⟩ fragment then calls SobolSample() to generate the sampleIndexth sample using the appropriate randomizer. It is otherwise effectively the same as the PaddedSobolSampler::SampleDimension() method, so its implementation is not included here.

⟨*ZSobolSampler Public Methods*⟩ +≡   505
```
Float Get1D() {
    uint64_t sampleIndex = GetSampleIndex();
    ++dimension;
    ⟨Generate 1D Sobol' sample at sampleIndex⟩
}
```

2D samples are generated in a similar manner, using the first two Sobol' sequence dimensions and a sample index returned by GetSampleIndex(). Here as well, the fragment that dispatches calls to SobolSample() corresponding to the chosen randomization scheme is not included.

⟨*ZSobolSampler Public Methods*⟩ +≡   505
```
Point2f Get2D() {
    uint64_t sampleIndex = GetSampleIndex();
    dimension += 2;
    ⟨Generate 2D Sobol' sample at sampleIndex⟩
}
```

Pixel samples are generated the same way as other 2D sample distributions.

⟨*ZSobolSampler Public Methods*⟩ +≡   505
```
Point2f GetPixel2D() { return Get2D(); }
```

The GetSampleIndex() method is where most of the complexity of this sampler lies. It computes a random permutation of the digits of mortonIndex, including handling the case where the number of samples per pixel is only a power of 2 but not a power of 4; that case needs special treatment since the total number of bits in the index is odd, which means that only one of the two bits needed for the last base-4 digit is available.

⟨*ZSobolSampler Public Methods*⟩ +≡   505
```
uint64_t GetSampleIndex() const {
    ⟨Define the full set of 4-way permutations in permutations 510⟩
    uint64_t sampleIndex = 0;
    ⟨Apply random permutations to full base-4 digits 510⟩
    ⟨Handle power-of-2 (but not 4) sample count 510⟩
    return sampleIndex;
}
```

We will find it useful to have all of the $4! = 24$ permutations of four elements explicitly enumerated; they are stored in the permutations array.

⟨*Define the full set of 4-way permutations in* permutations⟩ ≡   **509**
```
static const uint8_t permutations[24][4] = {
    {0, 1, 2, 3}, {0, 1, 3, 2}, {0, 2, 1, 3}, {0, 2, 3, 1},
    ⟨Define remaining 20 4-way permutations⟩
};
```

The digits are randomized from most significant to least significant. In the case of the number of samples only being a power of 2, the loop terminates before the last bit, which is handled specially since it is not a full base-4 digit.

⟨*Apply random permutations to full base-4 digits*⟩ ≡   **509**
```
bool pow2Samples = log2SamplesPerPixel & 1;
int lastDigit = pow2Samples ? 1 : 0;
for (int i = nBase4Digits - 1; i >= lastDigit; --i) {
    ⟨Randomly permute ith base-4 digit in mortonIndex 510⟩
}
```

After the current digit is extracted from mortonIndex, it is permuted using the selected permutation before being shifted back into place to be added to sampleIndex.

⟨*Randomly permute ith base-4 digit in* mortonIndex⟩ ≡   **510**
```
int digitShift = 2 * i - (pow2Samples ? 1 : 0);
int digit = (mortonIndex >> digitShift) & 3;
⟨Choose permutation p to use for digit 510⟩
digit = permutations[p][digit];
sampleIndex |= uint64_t(digit) << digitShift;
```

Which permutation to use is determined by hashing both the higher-order digits and the current sample dimension. In this way, the index is hashed differently for different dimensions, which randomizes the association of samples in different dimensions for padding. The use of the higher-order digits in this way means that this approach bears some resemblance to Owen scrambling, though here it is applied to sample indices rather than sample values. The result is a top-down hierarchical randomization of the Morton curve.

⟨*Choose permutation* p *to use for* digit⟩ ≡   **510**
```
uint64_t higherDigits = mortonIndex >> (digitShift + 2);
int p = (MixBits(higherDigits ^ (0x55555555u * dimension)) >> 24) % 24;
```

In the case of a power-of-2 sample count, the single remaining bit in mortonIndex is handled specially, though following the same approach as the other digits: the higher-order bits and dimension are hashed to choose a permutation. In this case, there are only two possible permutations, and as with the BinaryPermuteScrambler, an exclusive OR is sufficient to apply whichever of them was selected.

⟨*Handle power-of-2 (but not 4) sample count*⟩ ≡   **509**
```
if (pow2Samples) {
    int digit = mortonIndex & 1;
    sampleIndex |= digit ^
        (MixBits((mortonIndex >> 1) ^ (0x55555555u * dimension)) & 1);
}
```

8.7.7 EVALUATION

In this section we have defined three Samplers, each of which supports four randomization algorithms, giving a total of 12 different ways of generating samples. All are effective

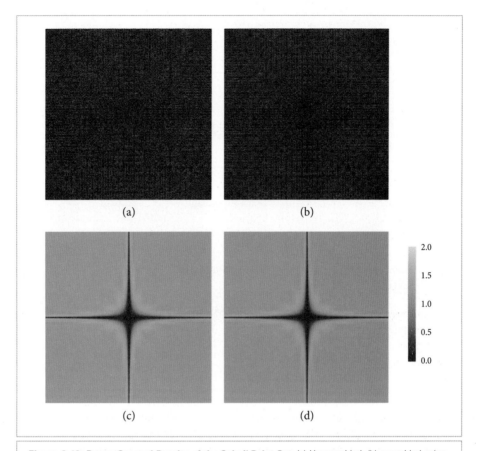

Figure 8.43: Power Spectral Density of the Sobol' Point Set. (a) Unscrambled, (b) scrambled using random digit permutations, (c) scrambled using the `FastOwenScrambler`, (d) scrambled using hashed Owen scrambling. The unscrambled Sobol' points have a remarkably bad power spectral density (PSD) and random digit permutations are of only slight benefit. Owen scrambling greatly improves the PSD.

samplers, though their characteristics vary. In the interest of space, we will not include evaluations of every one of them here but will focus on the most significant differences among them.

Figure 8.43(a) shows the PSD of the unscrambled 2D Sobol' point set; it is an especially bad power spectrum. Like the Halton points, the 2D Sobol' points have low energy along the two axes thanks to well-distributed 1D projections, but there is significant structured variation at higher off-axis frequencies, including regions with very high PSD values. As seen in Figure 8.43(b), randomizing the Sobol' points with random digit permutations only slightly improves the power spectrum. Only with the Owen scrambling algorithms does the power spectrum start to become uniform at higher frequencies, though some structure still remains (Figures 8.43(c) and (d)).

These well-distributed 1D projections are one reason why low-discrepancy sequences are generally more effective than stratified patterns: they are more robust with respect to preserving their good distribution properties after being transformed to other domains. Figure 8.44 shows what happens when a set of 16 sample points are transformed to be points on a skinny quadrilateral by scaling them to cover its surface; samples from the Sobol' sequence remain well distributed, but samples from a stratified pattern fare worse.

FastOwenScrambler 497

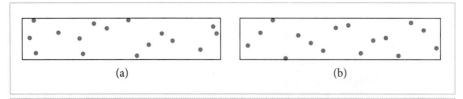

Figure 8.44: (a) Transforming a 4 × 4 stratified sampling pattern to points on a long and thin quadrilateral light source effectively gives fewer than 16 well-distributed samples; stratification in the vertical direction is not helpful. (b) Samples from the Sobol′ sequence remain well distributed even after this transformation.

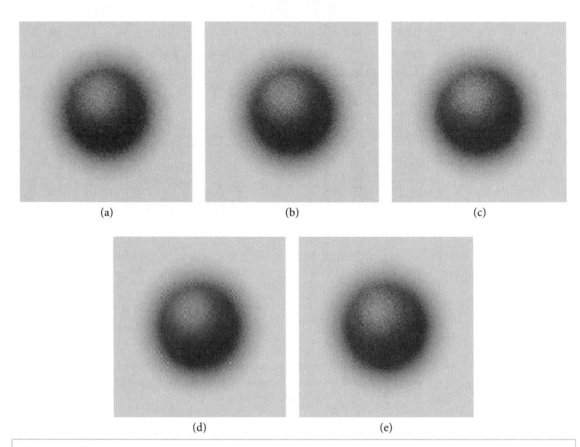

Figure 8.45: Comparisons of the Halton and Various Sobol′ Samplers for Rendering Depth of Field. Mean squared error is reported normalized to that of the stratified sampler. (a) An image rendered using the `StratifiedSampler` (normalized MSE 1), (b) an image rendered using the `HaltonSampler` (normalized MSE 1.44), (c) an image rendered using the `PaddedSobolSampler` (normalized MSE 0.96), (d) an image rendered using the `SobolSampler` (normalized MSE 0.64), and (e) an image rendered using the `ZSobolSampler` (normalized MSE 0.84). All the low-discrepancy samplers use hashed Owen scrambling for randomization and 16 samples per pixel.

Returning to the simple scene with defocus blur that was used in Figure 8.23, Figure 8.45 compares using the Halton sampler to the three Sobol′ samplers for rendering that scene. We can see that the Halton sampler has higher error than the `StratifiedSampler`, which is due to its 2D projections (as are used for sampling the lens) not necessarily being well distributed. The `PaddedSobolSampler` gives little benefit over the stratified sampler, since for sampling a lens, the 4 × 4 stratification is the most important one and both fulfill that. The `SobolSampler` has remarkably low error, even though the rendered image shows the characteristic structure

HaltonSampler 485
PaddedSobolSampler 503
SobolSampler 499
StratifiedSampler 474
ZSobolSampler 505

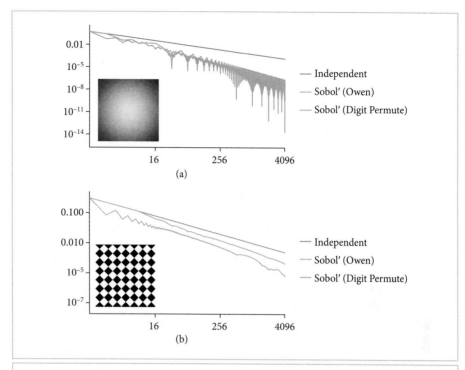

Figure 8.46: Error When Integrating Simple 2D Functions with Sobol' Samples. (a) Sobol' sampling exhibits lower error and a faster asymptotic rate of convergence than independent sampling does. For a smooth function like the Gaussian, Owen scrambling the sample points gives an even better rate of convergence, especially at power-of-two numbers of sample points. (b) Using Sobol' points is also effective for the rotated checkerboard function. Owen scrambling gives a further benefit, though without the substantial improvement in rate of convergence that was seen with the Gaussian.

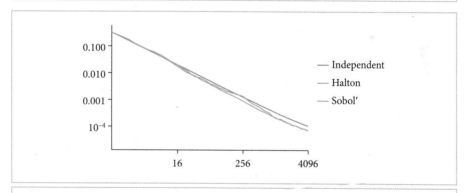

Figure 8.47: Log–Log Plot of MSE When Rendering the Scene in Figure 8.32 with Low-Discrepancy Samplers. For this scene, both the Halton and Sobol' samplers are similarly effective.

of 2D projections of the Sobol' sequence. The ZSobolSampler combines reasonably low error with the visual benefit of distributing its error with blue noise.

Figure 8.46 shows the performance of Sobol' sample points with the two test functions. It does well with both, but especially so with Owen scrambled points and the smooth Gaussian function, where it has an asymptotically faster rate of convergence. Figure 8.47 graphs MSE versus the sample count for the blurry dragon test scene from Figure 8.32. Both the Halton and Sobol' samplers have roughly 10% lower MSE than independent sampling at equivalent sample counts.

ZSobolSampler 505

8.8 IMAGE RECONSTRUCTION

As discussed in Section 5.4.3, each pixel in the Film computes an estimate of the integral of the product of a filter function with samples taken from the image function. In Section 8.1, we saw that sampling theory provides a mathematical foundation for how this filtering operation should be performed in order to achieve an antialiased result. We should, in principle:

1. Reconstruct a continuous image function from the set of image samples.
2. Prefilter that function to remove any frequencies past the Nyquist limit for the pixel spacing.
3. Sample the prefiltered function at the pixel locations to compute the final pixel values.

Because we know that we will be resampling the function at only the pixel locations, it is not necessary to construct an explicit representation of the function. Instead, we can combine the first two steps using a single filter function.

Recall that if the original function had been uniformly sampled at a frequency greater than the Nyquist frequency and reconstructed with the sinc filter, then the reconstructed function in the first step would match the original image function perfectly—quite a feat since we only have point samples. But because the image function almost always will have higher frequencies than could be accounted for by the sampling rate (due to edges, etc.), we chose to sample it nonuniformly, trading off noise for aliasing.

The theory behind ideal reconstruction depends on the samples being uniformly spaced. While a number of attempts have been made to extend the theory to nonuniform sampling, there is not yet an accepted approach to this problem. Furthermore, because the sampling rate is known to be insufficient to capture the function, perfect reconstruction is not possible. Recent research in the field of sampling theory has revisited the issue of reconstruction with the explicit acknowledgment that perfect reconstruction is not generally attainable in practice. This slight shift in perspective has led to powerful new reconstruction techniques. In particular, the goal of research in reconstruction theory has shifted from perfect reconstruction to developing reconstruction techniques that can be shown to minimize error between the reconstructed function and the original function, *regardless of whether the original was band limited*.

The sinc filter is not an appropriate choice here: recall that the ideal sinc filter is prone to ringing when the underlying function has frequencies beyond the Nyquist limit, meaning edges in the image have faint replicated copies of the edge in nearby pixels (the Gibbs phenomenon; see Section 8.1.5). Furthermore, the sinc filter has *infinite support*: it does not fall off to zero at a finite distance from its center, so all the image samples would need to be filtered for each output pixel. In practice, there is no single best filter function. Choosing the best one for a particular scene takes a mixture of quantitative evaluation and qualitative judgment. pbrt therefore provides a variety of choices.

Figure 8.48 shows comparisons of zoomed-in regions of images rendered using a variety of the filters from this section to reconstruct pixel values.

8.8.1 FILTER INTERFACE

Film 244

The Filter class defines the interface for pixel reconstruction filters in pbrt. It is defined in the file base/filter.h.

| (a) | (b) | (c) |

Figure 8.48: The pixel reconstruction filter used to convert the image samples into pixel values can have a noticeable effect on the character of the final image. Here, we see enlargements of a region of the imperial crown model, filtered with (a) the box filter, (b) Gaussian filter, and (c) Mitchell–Netravali filter. Note that the Mitchell filter gives the sharpest image, while the Gaussian blurs it. The box filter is the least desirable, since it allows high-frequency aliasing to leak into the final image. (Note the stair-step pattern along bright gold edges, for example.) *(Crown model courtesy of Martin Lubich.)*

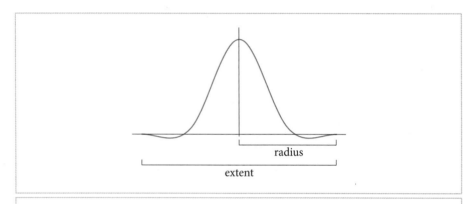

Figure 8.49: The extent of filters in pbrt is specified in terms of each one's radius from the origin to its cutoff point. The support of a filter is its total nonzero extent, here equal to twice its radius.

⟨*Filter Definition*⟩ ≡
```
class Filter :
        public TaggedPointer<BoxFilter, GaussianFilter, MitchellFilter,
                             LanczosSincFilter, TriangleFilter> {
    public:
      ⟨Filter Interface 515⟩
};
```

All filters are 2D functions that are centered at the origin and define a radius beyond which they have a value of 0. The radii are different in the x and y directions but are assumed to be symmetric in each. A filter provides its radius via the Radius() method. The filter's overall extent in each direction (its *support*) is twice the value of its corresponding radius (Figure 8.49).

⟨*Filter Interface*⟩ ≡   **515**
```
    Vector2f Radius() const;
```

Filter implementations must also provide a method that evaluates their filter function. This function may be called with points that are outside of the filter's radius; in this case it is the responsibility of the implementation to detect this case and return the value 0. It is not required for the filter values returned by Evaluate() to integrate to 1 since the estimator used to compute pixel values, Equation (5.13), is self-normalizing.

⟨*Filter Interface*⟩ +≡   **515**
```
    Float Evaluate(Point2f p) const;
```

Filters also must be able to return their integral. Most are able to compute this value in closed form. Thus, if calling code requires a normalized filter function, it is easy enough to find it by dividing values returned by `Evaluate()` by the integral.

⟨*Filter Interface*⟩ +≡   **515**
```
    Float Integral() const;
```

Filters must also provide an importance sampling method, `Sample`, which takes a random sample u in $[0, 1)^2$.

⟨*Filter Interface*⟩ +≡   **515**
```
    FilterSample Sample(Point2f u) const;
```

The returned `FilterSample` structure stores both the sampled position p and a weight, which is the ratio of the value of the filter function at p to the value of the PDF used for sampling there. Because some filters are able to exactly sample from their distribution, returning this ratio directly allows them to save the trouble of evaluating those two values and instead to always return a weight of 1.

⟨*FilterSample Definition*⟩ ≡
```
    struct FilterSample {
        Point2f p;
        Float weight;
    };
```

Given the specification of this interface, we can now implement the `GetCameraSample()` function that most integrators use to compute the `CameraSamples` that they pass to the `Camera::GenerateRay()` methods.

⟨*Sampler Inline Functions*⟩ ≡
```
    template <typename S>
    CameraSample GetCameraSample(S sampler, Point2i pPixel, Filter filter) {
        FilterSample fs = filter.Sample(sampler.GetPixel2D());
        CameraSample cs;
        ⟨Initialize CameraSample member variables 517⟩
        return cs;
    }
```

One subtlety in the definition of this function is that it is templated based on the type of the sampler passed to it. If a value of type `Sampler` is passed to this method, then it proceeds using pbrt's usual dynamic dispatch mechanism to call the corresponding methods of the `Sampler` implementation. However, if a concrete sampler type (e.g., `HaltonSampler`) is passed to it, then the corresponding methods can be called directly (and are generally expanded inline in the function). This capability is used to improve performance in pbrt's GPU rendering path; see Section 15.3.3.

After the filter's `Sample()` method has returned a `FilterSample`, the image sample position can be found by adding the filter's sampled offset to the pixel coordinate before a shift of 0.5 in each dimension accounts for the mapping from discrete to continuous pixel coordinates (recall Section 8.1.4). The filter's weight is passed along in the `CameraSample` so that it is available to the `Film` when its `AddSample()` method is called.

516

⟨*Initialize* CameraSample *member variables*⟩ ≡

```
cs.pFilm = pPixel + fs.p + Vector2f(0.5f, 0.5f);
cs.time = sampler.Get1D();
cs.pLens = sampler.Get2D();
cs.filterWeight = fs.weight;
```

8.8.2 FilterSampler

Not all Filters are able to easily sample from the distributions of their filter functions. Therefore, pbrt provides a FilterSampler class that wraps up the details of sampling based on a tabularized representation of the filter.

⟨*FilterSampler Definition*⟩ ≡

```
class FilterSampler {
  public:
    ⟨FilterSampler Public Methods 518⟩
  private:
    ⟨FilterSampler Private Members 517⟩
};
```

Only the Filter and an allocator are provided to the constructor. We have not found it particularly useful to allow the caller to specify the rate at which the filter function is sampled to construct the table used for sampling, so instead hardcode a sampling rate of 32 times per unit filter extent in each dimension.

⟨*FilterSampler Method Definitions*⟩ ≡

```
FilterSampler::FilterSampler(Filter filter, Allocator alloc)
    : domain(Point2f(-filter.Radius()), Point2f(filter.Radius())),
      f(int(32 * filter.Radius().x), int(32 * filter.Radius().y), alloc),
      distrib(alloc) {
    ⟨Tabularize unnormalized filter function in f 517⟩
    ⟨Compute sampling distribution for filter 518⟩
}
```

domain gives the bounds of the filter and f stores tabularized filter function values.

⟨*FilterSampler Private Members*⟩ ≡   517

```
Bounds2f domain;
Array2D<Float> f;
```

All the filters currently implemented in pbrt are symmetric about the origin, which means that they could be tabularized over a single xy quadrant. Further, they are all separable into the product of two 1D functions. Either of these properties could be exploited to reduce the amount of storage required for the tables used for sampling. However, to allow full flexibility with the definition of additional filter functions, the FilterSampler simply evaluates the filter at equally spaced positions over its entire domain to initialize the f array.

⟨*Tabularize unnormalized filter function in* f⟩ ≡   517

```
for (int y = 0; y < f.YSize(); ++y)
    for (int x = 0; x < f.XSize(); ++x) {
        Point2f p = domain.Lerp(Point2f((x + 0.5f) / f.XSize(),
                                        (y + 0.5f) / f.YSize()));
        f(x, y) = filter.Evaluate(p);
    }
```

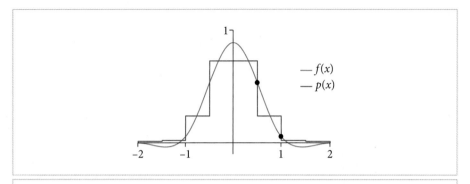

Figure 8.50: Filter function $f(x)$ and a piecewise-constant sampling distribution $p(x)$ found by evaluating it at the center of each cell, as is done by the `FilterSampler`. If filter positions are found by sampling from $p(x)$ and contributions are weighted using the ratio $f(x)/p(x)$, then different samples may have very different contributions. For example, the two points shown have a 10× difference in their $f(x)/p(x)$ values. This variation in filter weights can lead to variance in images and therefore the `FilterSampler` uses the same piecewise-constant approximation of $f(x)$ for evaluation as is used for sampling.

Given a tabularized function, it is easy to initialize the sampling distribution.

⟨*Compute sampling distribution for filter*⟩ ≡   517
    distrib = PiecewiseConstant2D(f, domain, alloc);

⟨*FilterSampler Private Members*⟩ +≡   517
    PiecewiseConstant2D distrib;

There are two important details in the implementation of its `Sample()` method. First, the implementation does not use `Filter::Evaluate()` to evaluate the filter function but instead uses the tabularized version of it in `f`. By using the piecewise constant approximation of the filter function, it ensures that the returned weight $f(\mathrm{p}')/p(\mathrm{p}')$ for a sampled point p' is always $\pm c$ for a constant c. If it did not do this, there would be variation in the returned weight for non-constant filter functions, due to the sampling distribution not being exactly proportional to the filter function—see Figure 8.50, which illustrates the issue.

A second important detail is that the integer coordinates of the sample returned by `Piecewise Constant2D::Sample()` are used to index into `f` for filter function evaluation. If instead the point `p` was scaled up by the size of the `f` array in each dimension and converted to an integer, the result would occasionally differ from the integer coordinates computed during sampling by `PiecewiseConstant2D` due to floating-point round-off error. (Using the notation of Section 6.8.1, the issue is that with floating-point arithmetic, $(a \oslash b) \otimes b \neq (a/b)b = a$.) Again, variance would result, as the ratio $f(x)/p(x)$ might not be $\pm c$.

⟨*FilterSampler Public Methods*⟩ ≡   517
    FilterSample Sample(Point2f u) const {
        Float pdf;
        Point2i pi;
        Point2f p = distrib.Sample(u, &pdf, &pi);
        return FilterSample{p, f[pi] / pdf};
    }

8.8.3 BOX FILTER

One of the most commonly used filters in graphics is the *box filter* (and, in fact, when filtering and reconstruction are not addressed explicitly, the box filter is the *de facto* result). The

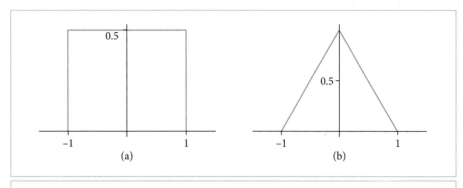

Figure 8.51: Graphs of the (a) box filter and (b) triangle filter. Although neither of these is a particularly good filter, they are both computationally efficient, easy to implement, and good baselines for evaluating other filters.

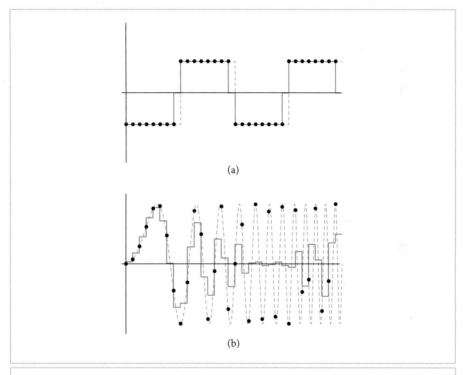

Figure 8.52: The box filter reconstructing (a) a step function and (b) a sinusoidal function with increasing frequency as x increases. This filter does well with the step function, as expected, but does an extremely poor job with the sinusoidal function.

box filter equally weights all samples within a square region of the image. Although computationally efficient, it is just about the worst filter possible. Recall from the discussion in Section 8.1.2 that the box filter allows high-frequency sample data to leak into the reconstructed values. This causes postaliasing—even if the original sample values were at a high enough frequency to avoid aliasing, errors are introduced by poor filtering.

Figure 8.51(a) shows a graph of the box filter, and Figure 8.52 shows the result of using the box filter to reconstruct two 1D functions.

For the step function we used previously to illustrate the Gibbs phenomenon, the box does reasonably well. However, the results are much worse for a sinusoidal function that has increasing frequency along the x axis. Not only does the box filter do a poor job of reconstructing the function when the frequency is low, giving a discontinuous result even though the original function was smooth, but it also does an extremely poor job of reconstruction as the function's frequency approaches and passes the Nyquist limit.

⟨*BoxFilter Definition*⟩ ≡
```
class BoxFilter {
  public:
    ⟨BoxFilter Public Methods 520⟩
  private:
    Vector2f radius;
};
```

For this filter and all the following ones, we will not include the rudimentary constructors and Radius() method implementations.

Evaluating the box filter requires checking that the given point is inside the box.

⟨*BoxFilter Public Methods*⟩ ≡   520
```
Float Evaluate(Point2f p) const {
    return (std::abs(p.x) <= radius.x && std::abs(p.y) <= radius.y) ? 1 : 0;
}
```

Sampling is also easy: the random sample u is used to linearly interpolate within the filter's extent. Since sampling is exact and the filter function is positive, the weight is always 1.

⟨*BoxFilter Public Methods*⟩ +≡   520
```
FilterSample Sample(Point2f u) const {
    Point2f p(Lerp(u[0], -radius.x, radius.x),
              Lerp(u[1], -radius.y, radius.y));
    return {p, Float(1)};
}
```

Finally, the integral is equal to the filter's area.

⟨*BoxFilter Public Methods*⟩ +≡   520
```
Float Integral() const { return 2 * radius.x * 2 * radius.y; }
```

8.8.4 TRIANGLE FILTER

The triangle filter gives slightly better results than the box: the weight falls off linearly from the filter center over the square extent of the filter. See Figure 8.51(b) for a graph of the triangle filter.

⟨*TriangleFilter Definition*⟩ ≡
```
class TriangleFilter {
  public:
    ⟨TriangleFilter Public Methods 521⟩
  private:
    Vector2f radius;
};
```

Evaluating the triangle filter is simple: it is the product of two linear functions that go to 0 after the width of the filter in both the x and y directions. Here we have defined the filter to have a slope of ± 1, though the filter could alternatively have been defined to have a value of 1 at the origin and a slope that depends on the radius.

⟨*TriangleFilter Public Methods*⟩ ≡ 520

```
Float Evaluate(Point2f p) const {
    return std::max<Float>(0, radius.x - std::abs(p.x)) *
           std::max<Float>(0, radius.y - std::abs(p.y));
}
```

Because the filter is separable, its PDF is as well, and so each dimension can be sampled independently. The sampling method uses a separate `SampleTent()` utility function that is defined in Section A.4.1. Once again, the weight returned in the `FilterSample` is always 1 because the filter is positive and sampling is exact.

⟨*TriangleFilter Public Methods*⟩ +≡ 520

```
FilterSample Sample(Point2f u) const {
    return {Point2f(SampleTent(u[0], radius.x),
                    SampleTent(u[1], radius.y)), Float(1)};
}
```

Finally, the triangle filter is easily integrated.

⟨*TriangleFilter Public Methods*⟩ +≡ 520

```
Float Integral() const { return Sqr(radius.x) * Sqr(radius.y); }
```

8.8.5 GAUSSIAN FILTER

Unlike the box and triangle filters, the Gaussian filter gives a reasonably good result in practice. This filter applies a Gaussian bump that is centered at the pixel and radially symmetric around it. Figure 8.53 compares plots of the Gaussian filter and the Mitchell filter (described in Section 8.8.6). The Gaussian does tend to cause slight blurring of the final image compared to some of the other filters, but this blurring can help mask any remaining aliasing. This filter is the default one used in pbrt.

FilterSample 516
Float 23
Point2f 92
SampleTent() 1002
Sqr() 1034
TriangleFilter::radius 520

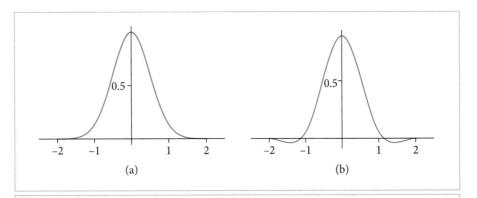

Figure 8.53: Graphs of (a) the Gaussian filter and (b) the Mitchell filter with $B = \frac{1}{3}$ and $C = \frac{1}{3}$, each with a width of 2. The Gaussian gives images that tend to be a bit blurry, while the negative lobes of the Mitchell filter help to accentuate and sharpen edges in final images.

⟨*GaussianFilter Definition*⟩ ≡
```
class GaussianFilter {
  public:
    ⟨GaussianFilter Public Methods 522⟩
  private:
    ⟨GaussianFilter Private Members 522⟩
};
```

The *Gaussian function* is parameterized by the position of the peak μ and the standard deviation σ:

$$g(x, \mu, \sigma) = \frac{1}{\sqrt{2\pi\sigma^2}} e^{-\frac{(x-\mu)^2}{2\sigma^2}}.$$

Larger values of σ cause a slower falloff, which leads to a blurrier image when the Gaussian is used as a filter.

The GaussianFilter is centered at the origin, so $\mu = 0$. Further, the filter function subtracts the value of the Gaussian at the end of its extent r from the filter value in order to make the filter go to 0 at its limit:

$$f(x) = \begin{cases} g(x, 0, \sigma) - g(r, 0, \sigma) & |x| < r \\ 0 & \text{otherwise.} \end{cases} \qquad [8.26]$$

For efficiency, the constructor precomputes the constant term for $g(r, 0, \sigma)$ in each direction.

⟨*GaussianFilter Public Methods*⟩ ≡   522
```
GaussianFilter(Vector2f radius, Float sigma = 0.5f, Allocator alloc = {})
    : radius(radius), sigma(sigma), expX(Gaussian(radius.x, 0, sigma)),
      expY(Gaussian(radius.y, 0, sigma)), sampler(this, alloc) {}
```

⟨*GaussianFilter Private Members*⟩ ≡   522
```
Vector2f radius;
Float sigma, expX, expY;
FilterSampler sampler;
```

The product of the two 1D Gaussian functions gives the overall filter value according to Equation (8.26). The calls to std::max() ensure that the value of 0 is returned for points outside of the filter's extent.

⟨*GaussianFilter Public Methods*⟩ +≡   522
```
Float Evaluate(Point2f p) const {
    return (std::max<Float>(0, Gaussian(p.x, 0, sigma) - expX) *
            std::max<Float>(0, Gaussian(p.y, 0, sigma) - expY));
}
```

The integral of the Gaussian is

$$\int g(x, \mu, \sigma) \, dx = \frac{1}{2}\text{erf}\left(\frac{\mu - x}{\sqrt{2}\sigma}\right),$$

where erf is the error function. GaussianIntegral() evaluates its value over a given range. The filter function's integral can be computed by evaluating the Gaussian's integral over the filter's range and subtracting the integral of the offset that takes the filter to zero at the end of its extent.

⟨*GaussianFilter Public Methods*⟩ +≡   **522**
```
Float Integral() const {
    return ((GaussianIntegral(-radius.x, radius.x, 0, sigma) -
            2 * radius.x * expX) *
            (GaussianIntegral(-radius.y, radius.y, 0, sigma) -
            2 * radius.y * expY));
}
```

It is possible to sample from the Gaussian function using a polynomial approximation to the inverse error function, though that is not sufficient in this case, given the presence of the second term of the filter function in Equation (8.26). pbrt's GaussianFilter implementation therefore uses a FilterSampler for sampling.

⟨*GaussianFilter Public Methods*⟩ +≡   **522**
```
FilterSample Sample(Point2f u) const { return sampler.Sample(u); }
```

8.8.6 MITCHELL FILTER

Filter design is notoriously difficult, mixing mathematical analysis and perceptual experiments. Mitchell and Netravali (1988) developed a family of parameterized filter functions in order to be able to explore this space in a systematic manner. After analyzing test subjects' subjective responses to images filtered with a variety of parameter values, they developed a filter that tends to do a good job of trading off between *ringing* (phantom edges next to actual edges in the image) and *blurring* (excessively blurred results)—two common artifacts from poor reconstruction filters.

Note from the graph in Figure 8.53(b) that this filter function takes on negative values out by its edges; it has *negative lobes*. In practice these negative regions improve the sharpness of edges, giving crisper images (reduced blurring). If they become too large, however, ringing tends to start to enter the image. Furthermore, because the final pixel values can become negative, they will eventually need to be clamped to a legal output range.

Figure 8.54 shows this filter reconstructing the two test functions. It does extremely well with both of them: there is minimal ringing with the step function, and it does a good job with the sinusoidal function, up until the point where the sampling rate is not sufficient to capture the function's detail.

⟨*MitchellFilter Definition*⟩ ≡
```
class MitchellFilter {
  public:
    ⟨MitchellFilter Public Methods 524⟩
  private:
    ⟨MitchellFilter Private Methods⟩
    ⟨MitchellFilter Private Members 523⟩
};
```

The Mitchell filter has two parameters called b and c. Although any values can be used for these parameters, Mitchell and Netravali recommend that they lie along the line $b + 2c = 1$.

⟨*MitchellFilter Private Members*⟩ ≡   **523**
```
Vector2f radius;
Float b, c;
FilterSampler sampler;
```

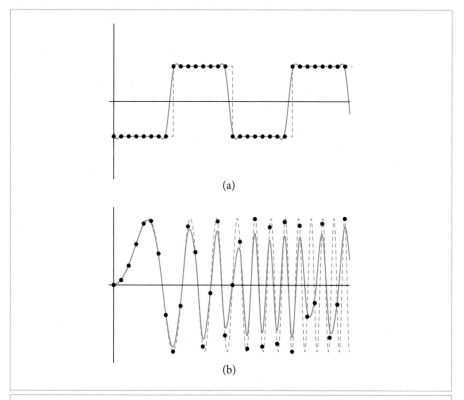

(a)

(b)

Figure 8.54: The Mitchell–Netravali Filter Used to Reconstruct the Example Functions. It does a good job with both of these functions, (a) introducing minimal ringing with the step function and (b) accurately representing the sinusoid until aliasing from undersampling starts to dominate.

The Mitchell–Netravali filter is the product of 1D filter functions in the x and y directions and is therefore separable.

⟨*MitchellFilter Public Methods*⟩ ≡   **523**
```
Float Evaluate(Point2f p) const {
    return Mitchell1D(2 * p.x / radius.x) * Mitchell1D(2 * p.y / radius.y);
}
```

The 1D function used in the Mitchell filter is an even function defined over the range $[-2, 2]$. This function is made by joining a cubic polynomial defined over $[0, 1]$ with another cubic polynomial defined over $[1, 2]$. This combined polynomial is also reflected around the $x = 0$ plane to give the complete function. These polynomials are controlled by the b and c parameters and are chosen carefully to guarantee C^0 and C^1 continuity at $x = 0$, $x = 1$, and $x = 2$. The polynomials are

$$
f(x)
= \frac{1}{6}
\begin{cases}
(12 - 9b - 6c)|x|^3 + (-18 + 12b + 6c)|x|^2 + (6 - 2b) & |x| < 1 \\
(-b - 6c)|x|^3 + (6b + 30c)|x|^2 + (-12b - 48c)|x| \\
\quad + (8b + 24c) & 1 \le |x| < 2 \\
0 & \text{otherwise.}
\end{cases}
$$

Float 23

MitchellFilter::Mitchell1D() 524

MitchellFilter::radius 523

Point2f 92

Mitchell1D() evaluates this function. Its implementation is straightforward and is not included here.

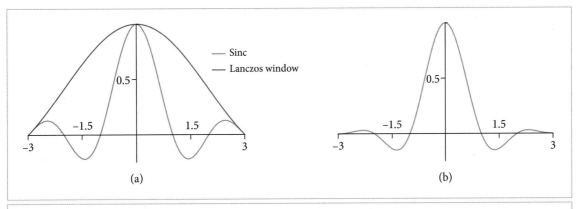

Figure 8.55: Graphs of the Sinc Filter. (a) The sinc function, truncated after three cycles (blue line) and the Lanczos windowing function (red line). (b) The product of these two functions, as implemented in the `LanczosSincFilter`.

As a cubic polynomial, sampling this filter function directly would require inverting a quartic. Therefore, the `MitchellFilter` uses the `FilterSampler` for sampling.

⟨*MitchellFilter Public Methods*⟩ +≡   523
```
FilterSample Sample(Point2f u) const { return sampler.Sample(u); }
```

However, the function is easily integrated. The result is independent of the values of b and c.

⟨*MitchellFilter Public Methods*⟩ +≡   523
```
Float Integral() const { return radius.x * radius.y / 4; }
```

8.8.7 WINDOWED SINC FILTER

Finally, the `LanczosSincFilter` class implements a filter based on the sinc function. In practice, the sinc filter is often multiplied by another function that goes to 0 after some distance. This gives a filter function with finite extent. An additional parameter τ controls how many cycles the sinc function passes through before it is clamped to a value of 0. Figure 8.55 shows a graph of three cycles of the sinc function, along with a graph of the windowing function we use, which was developed by Lanczos. The Lanczos window is just the central lobe of the sinc function, scaled to cover the τ cycles:

$$w(x) = \mathrm{sinc}\left(\frac{x}{\tau}\right) = \frac{\sin(\pi x/\tau)}{\pi x/\tau}. \tag{8.27}$$

Figure 8.55 also shows the filter that we will implement here, which is the product of the sinc function and the windowing function. It is evaluated by the `WindowedSinc()` utility function.

⟨*Math Inline Functions*⟩ +≡
```
Float WindowedSinc(Float x, Float radius, Float tau) {
    if (std::abs(x) > radius)
        return 0;
    return Sinc(x) * Sinc(x / tau);
}
```

Its implementation uses the `Sinc()` function, which in turn is implemented using the numerically robust `SinXOverX()` function.

⟨*Math Inline Functions*⟩ +≡
```
Float Sinc(Float x) { return SinXOverX(Pi * x); }
```

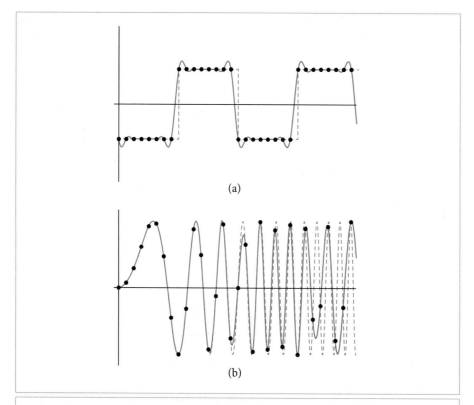

(a)

(b)

Figure 8.56: Results of Using the Windowed Sinc Filter to Reconstruct the Example Functions. Here, $\tau = 3$. (a) Like the infinite sinc, it suffers from ringing with the step function, although there is much less ringing in the windowed version. (b) The filter does quite well with the sinusoid, however.

Figure 8.56 shows the windowed sinc's reconstruction results for uniform 1D samples. Thanks to the windowing, the reconstructed step function exhibits far less ringing than the reconstruction using the infinite-extent sinc function (compare to Figure 8.11). The windowed sinc filter also does extremely well at reconstructing the sinusoidal function until prealiasing begins.

⟨*LanczosSincFilter Definition*⟩ ≡
```
class LanczosSincFilter {
  public:
    ⟨LanczosSincFilter Public Methods 527⟩
  private:
    ⟨LanczosSincFilter Private Members 526⟩
};
```

⟨*LanczosSincFilter Private Members*⟩ ≡   **526**
```
Vector2f radius;
Float tau;
FilterSampler sampler;
```

FilterSampler 517
Float 23
Vector2f 86

The evaluation method is easily implemented in terms of the WindowedSinc() function.

⟨*LanczosSincFilter Public Methods*⟩ ≡ 526
```
Float Evaluate(Point2f p) const {
    return WindowedSinc(p.x, radius.x, tau) *
           WindowedSinc(p.y, radius.y, tau);
}
```

There is no convenient closed-form approach for sampling from the windowed sinc function's distribution, so a FilterSampler is used here as well.

⟨*LanczosSincFilter Public Methods*⟩ +≡ 526
```
FilterSample Sample(Point2f u) const { return sampler.Sample(u); }
```

There is no closed-form expression of the filter's integral, so its Integral() method, not included in the text, approximates it using a Riemann sum.

⟨*LanczosSincFilter Public Methods*⟩ +≡ 526
```
Float Integral() const;
```

FURTHER READING

Heckbert (1990a) wrote an article that explains possible pitfalls when using floating-point coordinates for pixels and develops the conventions that are introduced in Section 8.1.4.

Sampling Theory and Aliasing

One of the best books on signal processing, sampling, reconstruction, and the Fourier transform is Bracewell's *The Fourier Transform and Its Applications* (2000). Glassner's *Principles of Digital Image Synthesis* (1995) has a series of chapters on the theory and application of uniform and nonuniform sampling and reconstruction to computer graphics. For an extensive survey of the history of and techniques for interpolation of sampled data, including the sampling theorem, see Meijering (2002). Unser (2000) also surveyed developments in sampling and reconstruction theory, including the move away from focusing purely on band-limited functions. For more recent work in this area, see Eldar and Michaeli (2009).

Crow (1977) was the first to identify aliasing as a major source of artifacts in computer-generated images. Using nonuniform sampling to turn aliasing into noise was introduced by Cook (1986) and Dippé and Wold (1985); their work was based on experiments by Yellot (1983), who investigated the distribution of photoreceptors in the eyes of monkeys. Dippé and Wold also first introduced the pixel filtering equation to graphics and developed a Poisson sample pattern with a minimum distance between samples.

Mitchell (1987, 1991) extensively investigated sampling patterns for ray tracing. His papers on this topic have many key insights, especially on the importance of blue noise distributions for sampling patterns. See also Ulichney (1988), who demonstrated the effectiveness of blue noise in the context of dithering.

Compressed sensing is an alternative approach to sampling where the required sampling rate depends on the sparsity of the signal, not its frequency content. Sen and Darabi (2011) applied compressed sensing to rendering, allowing them to generate high-quality images at very low sampling rates.

Lessig et al. (2014) proposed a general framework for constructing quadrature rules tailored to specific integration problems such as stochastic ray tracing, spherical harmonics projection, and scattering by surfaces. When targeting band-limited functions, their approach subsumes the frequency space approach presented in this chapter. An excellent tutorial about the underlying theory of *reproducing kernel bases* is provided in the article's supplemental material.

Analysis of Monte Carlo Integration

Starting with Ramamoorthi and Hanrahan's (2004) and Durand et al.'s foundational work (2005), a number of researchers have analyzed light transport and Monte Carlo integration using Fourier analysis. Singh et al.'s survey (2019a) has comprehensive coverage of work in this area.

Durand (2011) was the first to express variance using Fourier analysis, converting the Monte Carlo estimator to the continuous form (our Equation (8.10)) in order to demonstrate that the sampling rate only has to equal the function's highest frequency in order to achieve zero variance. He further derived the variance in terms of the integral of the product of the function's and sampling pattern's power spectra.

Subr and Kautz (2013) subsequently expressed variance in terms of a product of the variance of the sampling pattern and the function being integrated in frequency space. Pilleboue et al. (2015) applied homogenization to sampling patterns in order to express variance in terms of the power spectra in a more general setting than Durand (2011) and extended the analysis to functions on the sphere. They further derived asymptotic convergence rates for various sampling techniques and showed that they matched empirical measurements. These results not only provided a theoretical basis to explain earlier measurements made by Mitchell (1996) but included the surprising result that Poisson disk patterns have asymptotically worse convergence rates than simple jittered patterns.

Öztireli (2016) applied point process statistics to study stochastic sampling patterns for integration, deriving closed-form expressions for bias and variance of a number of approaches and analyzing integrands with discontinuities due to visibility. Singh and Jarosz (2017) analyzed the variance of anisotropic sampling patterns (of which jittered sampling is a notable example), and Singh et al. (2017) investigated the variance of sampling with line segments rather than points. The use of Fourier series to analyze sampling patterns was introduced by Singh et al. (2019b), which allowed the analysis of nonhomogeneous sampling patterns and also made it possible to incorporate the effect of importance sampling.

Öztireli (2020) provided a comprehensive review of work in blue noise sampling for rendering through 2019 and then applied the theory of stochastic point processes to derive the expected error spectrum from sampling a function with a given sampling technique in terms of the associated power spectra. This result makes clear why having minimal power in the low frequencies and as close to uniform unit power as possible at higher frequencies is best for antialiasing.

Sample Generation Algorithms

After the introduction of jittered sampling, Mitchell (1987) introduced an approach to generate sampling patterns with good blue noise characteristics using error diffusion and later developed an algorithm for generating sampling patterns that were also optimized for sampling motion blur and depth of field (Mitchell 1991). A key observation in the second paper was that a d-dimensional Poisson disk distribution is not the ideal one for general integration problems in graphics; while it is useful for the projection of the first two dimensions on the image plane to have the Poisson-disk property, it is important that the other dimensions be more widely distributed than the Poisson-disk quality alone guarantees.

The utility of such approaches was recently understood more widely after work by Georgiev and Fajardo (2016), who also described a method to generate tables of samples where nearby points are decorrelated for such applications. Heitz and Belcour (2019) developed a technique that permutes random seeds across nearby pixels in order to decorrelate the *error* in the image, rather than just the sample values themselves.

The blue noise points provided via the `BlueNoise()` function are thanks to Peters (2016) and were generated using Ulichney's "void and cluster" algorithm (1993).

Chiu, Shirley, and Wang (1994) suggested a *multi-jittered* 2D sampling technique based on randomly shuffling the *x* and *y* coordinates of a canonical jittered pattern that combines the properties of stratified and Latin hypercube sampling patterns. More recently, Kensler (2013) showed that using the same permutation for both dimensions with their method gives much better results than independent permutations; he showed that this approach gives lower discrepancy than the Sobol′ pattern while also maintaining the perceptual advantages of turning aliasing into noise due to using jittered samples. Christensen et al. further improved this approach (2018), generating point sets that were also stratified with respect to the elementary intervals and had good blue noise properties. Pharr (2019) proposed a more efficient algorithm to generate these points, though Grünschloß et al. (2008) had earlier developed an efficient elementary interval test that is similar to the one described there.

Lagae and Dutré (2008c) surveyed the state of the art in generating Poisson disk sample patterns and compared the quality of the point sets that various algorithms generated. Reinert et al. (2015) proposed a construction for *d*-dimensional Poisson disk samples that retain their characteristic sample separation under projection onto lower-dimensional subsets, which ensures good performance if the variation in the function is focused along only some of the dimensions.

Jarosz et al. (2019) applied *orthogonal array sampling* to generating multidimensional sample points that retain good distribution across lower-dimensional projections and showed that this approach gives much better results than randomly padding lower-dimensional samples as pbrt does in the `PaddedSobolSampler`, for example.

The error analysis framework derived in Öztireli's paper (2020) further makes it possible to express the desired properties of a point set in a form that is suitable to solve as an optimization problem. This made it possible to generate point sets with superior antialiasing capabilities to previous approaches. (That paper also includes an extensive review of the state of the art in blue noise and Poisson disk sample point generation.)

Low-Discrepancy Sampling and QMC

Shirley (1991) first introduced the use of discrepancy to evaluate the quality of sample patterns in computer graphics. This work was built upon by Mitchell (1992), Dobkin and Mitchell (1993), and Dobkin, Eppstein, and Mitchell (1996). One important observation in Dobkin et al.'s paper is that the box discrepancy measure used in this chapter and in other work that applies discrepancy to pixel sampling patterns is not particularly appropriate for measuring a sampling pattern's accuracy at randomly oriented edges through a pixel and that a discrepancy measure based on random edges should be used instead.

Mitchell's first paper on discrepancy introduced the idea of using deterministic low-discrepancy sequences for sampling, removing all randomness in the interest of lower discrepancy (Mitchell 1992). The seminal book on quasi-random sampling and algorithms for generating low-discrepancy patterns was written by Niederreiter (1992). For a more recent treatment, see Dick and Pillichshammer's excellent book (2010).

Keller and collaborators have investigated quasi-random sampling patterns for a variety of applications in graphics (Keller 1996, 1997, 2001, Kollig and Keller 2000). Keller's "Quasi-Monte Carlo image synthesis in a nutshell" (2012) is a good introduction to quasi–Monte Carlo for rendering. Friedel and Keller (2002) described an approach for efficient evaluation of the radical inverse based on reusing some values across multiple sample points. Both the sampling approach based on (0, 2)-sequences that is used in the PaddedSobolSampler and the algorithm implemented in the BinaryPermuteScrambler are described in a paper by Kollig and Keller (2002). Basu and Owen (2016) analyzed the effect of the distortion from warping uniform samples in the context of quasi–Monte Carlo.

The discrepancy bounds for jittered sampling in Equation (8.17) are due to Pausinger and Steinerberger (2016).

(0, 2)-sequences are one instance of a general type of low-discrepancy sequence known as (t, s)-sequences and (t, m, s)-nets. These were discussed further by Niederreiter (1992) and Dick and Pillichshammer (2010).

Sobol' (1967) introduced the family of generator matrices used in Section 8.7. Antonov and Saleev (1979) showed that enumerating Sobol' sample points in Gray code order leads to a highly efficient implementation; see also Bratley and Fox (1988) and Wächter's Ph.D. dissertation (2008) for further discussion of high-performance implementation of base-2 generator matrix operations. The Sobol' generator matrices our implementation uses are enhanced versions derived by Joe and Kuo (2008) that improve the 2D projections of sample points. Grünschloß and collaborators found generator matrices for 2D sampling that satisfy the base-2 elementary intervals and are also optimized to improve the sampling pattern's blue noise properties (Grünschloß et al. 2008, Grünschloß and Keller 2009).

Braaten and Weller introduced the idea of using digit permutations to improve Halton sample points (1979); they used a single permutation for all the digits in a given base, but determined permutations incrementally in order to optimize the d-dimensional distribution of points. Better results can be had by using per-digit permutations (as is done in the DigitPermutation class) and by using carefully constructed deterministic permutations (as is not). Faure (1992) described a deterministic approach for computing permutations for scrambled radical inverses; more recently, Faure and Lemieux (2009) surveyed a variety of approaches for doing so and proposed a new approach that ensures that the 1- and 2-dimensional projections of scrambled sample points are well distributed.

The nested uniform digit scrambling that has become known as Owen scrambling was introduced by Owen (1995), though in its original form it had high storage requirements for the permutations. Tan and Boyle (2000) proposed switching to a fixed permutation after some number of digits, and Friedel and Keller (2002) cached lazily generated permutations. Owen (2003) proposed the hash-based permutation approach that is implemented in both OwenScrambledRadicalInverse() and the OwenScrambler class. Laine and Karras (2011) noted that in base 2, nested uniform digit scrambling could be implemented in parallel across all the digits. The specific function used to do so in the FastOwenScrambler is due to Vegdahl (2021). See also Burley (2020) for further discussion of this approach.

The algorithms used for computing sample indices within given pixels in Sections 8.6.3 and 8.7.4 were introduced by Grünschloß et al. (2012).

Rank-1 lattices are a deterministic approach for constructing well-distributed point sets. They were introduced to graphics by Keller (2004) and Dammertz and Keller (2008b). More recently, Liu et al. (2021) extended them to high-dimensional integration problems in rendering.

As the effectiveness of both low-discrepancy sampling and blue noise has become better understood, a number of researchers have developed sampling techniques that target both metrics. Examples include Ahmed et al. (2016), who rearranged low-discrepancy sample points to improve blue noise properties, and Perrier et al. (2018), who found Owen scrambling permutations that led to good blue noise characteristics. Heitz et al. (2019) started with an Owen-scrambled point set and then improved its blue noise characteristics by solving an optimization problem that sets per-pixel seeds for randomization of the points in a way that decorrelates the error in integrating a set of test functions at nearby pixels. The approach implemented in the ZSobolSampler based on permuted Morton indices to achieve blue noise was introduced by Ahmed and Wonka (2020).

An exciting recent development in this area is the recent paper by Ahmed and Wonka (2021) that presents algorithms to directly enumerate all the valid digital $(0, m, 2)$-nets. In turn, it is possible to apply various optimization algorithms to the generated point sets (e.g., to improve their blue noise characteristics). See also recent work by Helmer et al. (2021) for algorithms that incrementally generate sequences of Owen-scrambled Halton, Sobol', and Faure points, allowing both optimization of the distribution of the points and highly efficient point generation.

Filtering and Reconstruction

Cook (1986) first introduced the Gaussian filter to graphics. Mitchell and Netravali (1988) investigated a family of filters using experiments with human observers to find the most effective ones; the MitchellFilter in this chapter is the one they chose as the best. Kajiya and Ullner (1981) investigated image filtering methods that account for the effect of the reconstruction characteristics of Gaussian falloff from pixels in CRTs. Betrisey et al. (2000) described Microsoft's ClearType technology for display of text on LCDs. Alim (2013) applied reconstruction techniques that attempt to minimize the error between the reconstructed image and the original continuous image, even in the presence of discontinuities.

There has been quite a bit of research into reconstruction filters for image resampling applications. Although this application is not the same as reconstructing nonuniform samples for image synthesis, much of this experience is applicable. Turkowski (1990a) reported that the Lanczos windowed sinc filter gives the best results among a number of filters for image resampling. Meijering et al. (1999) tested a variety of filters for image resampling by applying a series of transformations to images such that if perfect resampling had been done, the final image would be the same as the original. They also found that the Lanczos window performed well (as did a few others) and that truncating the sinc without a window gave some of the worst results. Other work in this area includes papers by Möller et al. (1997) and Machiraju and Yagel (1996).

Adaptive Sampling and Reconstruction

pbrt does not include samplers that perform adaptive sampling. Though adaptive sampling has been an active area of research, our own experience with the resulting algorithms has been that while most work well in some cases, few are robust across a wide range of scenes. (Adaptive sampling further introduces a coupling between the Sampler and the Film that we prefer to avoid.)

Early work on adaptive sampling includes that of Lee, Redner, and Uselton (1985), who developed a technique for adaptive sampling based on statistical tests that made it possible to compute images to a given error tolerance; Mitchell (1987), who investigated the use of contrast differences for adaptive sampling; and Purgathofer (1987), who applied statistical tests. Kajiya applied adaptive sampling to the Monte Carlo light transport integral (1986).

Mitchell (1987) observed that standard image reconstruction techniques fail in the presence of adaptive sampling: the contribution of a dense clump of samples in part of the filter's extent may incorrectly have a large effect on the final value purely due to the number of samples taken in that region. He described a multi-stage box filter that addresses this issue. Kirk and Arvo (1991) identified a subtle problem with adaptive sampling algorithms: in short, if a set of samples is not only used to decide if more samples should be taken but is also added to the image, bias is introduced.

Zwicker et al.'s survey article (2015) includes a thorough summary of work in adaptive sampling through 2015. More recently, Ahmed et al. (2017) described an approach for generating adaptive samples that maintains good blue noise properties. Vogels et al. (2018), Kuznetsov et al. (2018), and Hasselgren et al. (2020) have all trained neural nets to determine where additional samples should be taken in a noisy image.

Much recent work on adaptive sampling has been based on the foundation of Durand et al.'s (2005) frequency analysis of light transport. Much of it not only adapts sampling based on frequency space insights but also applies filters that are tailored to the frequency content of the functions being sampled. Shinya (1993) and Egan et al. (2009) developed adaptive sampling and reconstruction methods focused on rendering motion blur. Belcour et al. (2013) computed 5D covariance of image, time, and lens defocus and applied adaptive sampling and high-quality reconstruction. While most earlier work focused on single effects—soft shadows, motion blur, etc.—Wu et al. (2017) showed how to efficiently filter according to multiple such effects at once.

EXERCISES

⊘ 8.1   The third through fifth dimensions of every sample are currently consumed for time and lens samples in pbrt, even though not all scenes need these sample values. For some sample generation algorithms, lower dimensions in the sample are better distributed than higher ones and so this can cause an unnecessary reduction in image quality.

Modify pbrt so that the camera can report its sample requirements and then use this information when samples are requested to initialize CameraSamples. Render images and compare results to the current implementation. Do you see an improvement? How do results differ with different samplers? How do you explain any differences you see across samplers?

⊘ 8.2   Keller (2004) and Dammertz and Keller (2008b) described the application of *rank-1 lattices* to image synthesis. Rank-1 lattices are another way of efficiently generating high-quality low-discrepancy sets of sample points. Read their papers and implement a Sampler based on this approach. Compare results to the other samplers in pbrt.

⊘ 8.3   Implement a Sampler based on orthogonal array sampling, as described by Jarosz et al. (2019). Compare both MSE and Monte Carlo efficiency of this sampler to pbrt's current samplers.

⊚ 8.4   Mitchell and Netravali (1988) noted that there is a family of reconstruction filters that use both the value of a function and its derivative at the point to do substantially better reconstruction than if just the value of the function is known. Furthermore, they report that they have derived closed-form expressions for the

CameraSample 206

Sampler 469

screen space derivatives of Lambertian and Phong reflection models, although they do not include these expressions in their paper. Investigate derivative-based reconstruction, and extend pbrt to support this technique. If you decide to shy away from deriving expressions for the screen space derivatives for general shapes and BSDF models, you may want to investigate approximations based on finite differencing and the ideas behind the ray differentials of Section 10.1.

⊚ 8.5   Read some of the papers on adaptive sampling and reconstruction techniques from the "Further Reading" section and implement one of these techniques in pbrt. Note that you will likely need to both write a new Sampler and add additional Film functionality. Measure the effectiveness of the approach you have implemented using Monte Carlo efficiency in order to account for any increased computational cost. How well does your implementation perform compared to non-adaptive samplers?

Film 244
Sampler 469

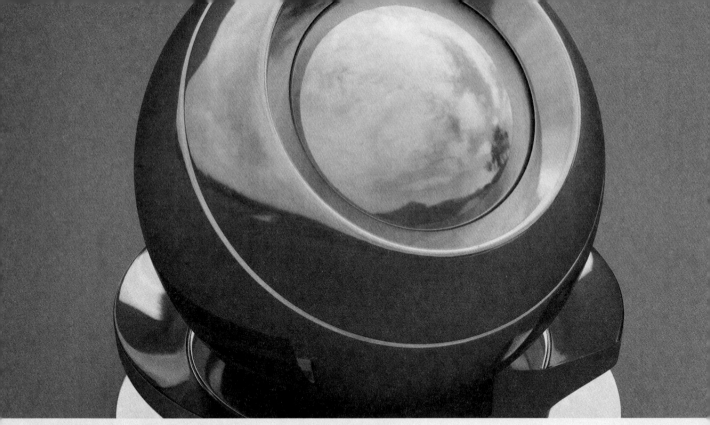

CHAPTER NINE

Given a particular category of reflection, the reflectance distribution function may be *isotropic* or *anisotropic*. With an isotropic material, if you choose a point on the surface and rotate it around its normal axis at that point, the distribution of light reflected at that point does not change. Diffuse materials like paper or wall paint are usually isotropic due to the directionally random arrangement of wood fibers or paint particles.

In contrast, anisotropic materials reflect different amounts of light as you rotate them in this way. Examples of anisotropic materials include hair and many types of cloth. Industrial processes such as milling, rolling, extrusion, and 3D printing also tend to produce highly anisotropic surfaces, an extreme example being brushed metal.

9.1 BSDF REPRESENTATION

There are two components of pbrt's representation of BSDFs: the BxDF interface and its implementations (described in Section 9.1.2) and the BSDF class (described in Section 9.1.5). The former models specific types of scattering at surfaces, while the latter provides a convenient wrapper around a pointer to a specific BxDF implementation. The BSDF class also centralizes general functionality so that BxDF implementations do not individually need to handle it, and it records information about the local geometric properties of the surface.

9.1.1 GEOMETRIC SETTING AND CONVENTIONS

Reflection computations in pbrt are performed in a reflection coordinate system where the two tangent vectors and the normal vector at the point being shaded are aligned with the x, y, and z axes, respectively (Figure 9.2). All direction vectors passed to and returned from the BxDF evaluation and sampling routines will be defined with respect to this coordinate system. It is important to understand this coordinate system in order to understand the BxDF implementations in this chapter.

Section 3.8 introduced a range of utility functions—like SinTheta(), CosPhi(), etc.—that efficiently evaluate trigonometric functions of unit vectors expressed in Cartesian coordinates matching the convention used here. They will be used extensively in this chapter, as quantities like the cosine of the elevation angle play a central role in most reflectance models.

We will frequently find it useful to check whether two direction vectors lie in the same hemisphere with respect to the surface normal in the BSDF coordinate system; the Same Hemisphere() function performs this check.

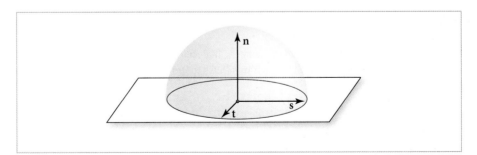

Figure 9.2: The Basic BSDF Coordinate Setting. The shading coordinate system is defined by the orthonormal basis vectors $(\mathbf{s}, \mathbf{t}, \mathbf{n})$. We will orient these vectors such that they lie along the x, y, and z axes in this coordinate system. Direction vectors ω in rendering space are transformed into the shading coordinate system before any of the BRDF or BTDF methods are called.

⟨*Spherical Geometry Inline Functions*⟩ +≡
```
bool SameHemisphere(Vector3f w, Vector3f wp) {
    return w.z * wp.z > 0;
}
```

There are some additional conventions that are important to keep in mind when reading the code in this chapter and when adding BRDFs and BTDFs to pbrt:

- The incident light direction ω_i and the outgoing viewing direction ω_o will both be normalized and *outward facing* after being transformed into the local coordinate system at the surface. In other words, the directions will not model the physical propagation of light, which is helpful in bidirectional rendering algorithms that generate light paths in reverse order.
- In pbrt, the surface normal **n** always points to the "outside" of the object, which makes it easy to determine if light is entering or exiting transmissive objects: if the incident light direction ω_i is in the same hemisphere as **n**, then light is entering; otherwise, it is exiting. Therefore, the normal may be on the opposite side of the surface than one or both of the ω_i and ω_o direction vectors. Unlike many other renderers, pbrt does not flip the normal to lie on the same side as ω_o.
- The local coordinate system used for shading may not be exactly the same as the coordinate system returned by the Shape::Intersect() routines from Chapter 6; it may have been modified between intersection and shading to achieve effects like bump mapping. See Chapter 10 for examples of this kind of modification.

9.1.2 BxDF INTERFACE

The interface for the individual BRDF and BTDF functions is defined by BxDF, which is in the file base/bxdf.h.

⟨*BxDF Definition*⟩ ≡
```
class BxDF
    : public TaggedPointer<
            DiffuseBxDF, CoatedDiffuseBxDF, CoatedConductorBxDF,
            DielectricBxDF, ThinDielectricBxDF, HairBxDF, MeasuredBxDF,
            ConductorBxDF, NormalizedFresnelBxDF> {
  public:
    ⟨BxDF Interface 538⟩
};
```

The BxDF interface provides a method to query the material type following the earlier categorization, which some light transport algorithms in Chapters 13 through 15 use to specialize their behavior.

⟨*BxDF Interface*⟩ ≡   538
```
BxDFFlags Flags() const;
```

The BxDFFlags enumeration lists the previously mentioned categories and also distinguishes reflection from transmission. Note that retroreflection is treated as glossy reflection in this list.

⟨*BxDFFlags Definition*⟩ ≡
```
enum BxDFFlags {
    Unset = 0,
    Reflection = 1 << 0,
    Transmission = 1 << 1,
    Diffuse = 1 << 2,
    Glossy = 1 << 3,
    Specular = 1 << 4,
    ⟨Composite BxDFFlags definitions 539⟩
};
```

These constants can also be combined via a binary OR operation to characterize materials that simultaneously exhibit multiple traits. A number of commonly used combinations are provided with their own names for convenience:

⟨*Composite* BxDFFlags *definitions*⟩ ≡   **539**
```
DiffuseReflection = Diffuse | Reflection,
DiffuseTransmission = Diffuse | Transmission,
GlossyReflection = Glossy | Reflection,
GlossyTransmission = Glossy | Transmission,
SpecularReflection = Specular | Reflection,
SpecularTransmission = Specular | Transmission,
All = Diffuse | Glossy | Specular | Reflection | Transmission
```

A few utility functions encapsulate the logic for testing various flag characteristics.

⟨*BxDFFlags Inline Functions*⟩ ≡
```
bool IsReflective(BxDFFlags f) { return f & BxDFFlags::Reflection; }
bool IsTransmissive(BxDFFlags f) { return f & BxDFFlags::Transmission; }
bool IsDiffuse(BxDFFlags f) { return f & BxDFFlags::Diffuse; }
bool IsGlossy(BxDFFlags f) { return f & BxDFFlags::Glossy; }
bool IsSpecular(BxDFFlags f) { return f & BxDFFlags::Specular; }
bool IsNonSpecular(BxDFFlags f) {
    return f & (BxDFFlags::Diffuse | BxDFFlags::Glossy); }
```

The key method that BxDFs provide is f(), which returns the value of the distribution function for the given pair of directions. The provided directions must be expressed in the local reflection coordinate system introduced in the previous section.

This interface implicitly assumes that light in different wavelengths is decoupled—energy at one wavelength will not be reflected at a different wavelength. In this case, the effect of reflection can be described by a per-wavelength factor returned in the form of a SampledSpectrum. Fluorescent materials that redistribute energy between wavelengths would require that this method return an $n \times n$ matrix to encode the transfer between the n spectral samples of SampledSpectrum.

Neither constructors nor methods of BxDF implementations will generally be informed about the specific wavelengths associated with SampledSpectrum entries, since they do not require this information.

⟨*BxDF Interface*⟩ +≡   **538**
```
SampledSpectrum f(Vector3f wo, Vector3f wi, TransportMode mode) const;
```

The function also takes a `TransportMode` enumerator that indicates whether the outgoing direction is toward the camera or toward a light source (and the corresponding opposite for the incident direction). This is necessary to handle cases where scattering is non-symmetric; this subtle aspect is discussed further in Section 9.5.2.

BxDFs must also provide a method that uses importance sampling to draw a direction from a distribution that approximately matches the scattering function's shape. Not only is this operation crucial for efficient Monte Carlo integration of the light transport equation (1.1), it is the only way to evaluate some BSDFs. For example, perfect specular objects like a mirror, glass, or water only scatter light from a single incident direction into a single outgoing direction. Such BxDFs are best described with *Dirac delta distributions* (covered in more detail in Section 9.1.4) that are zero except for the single direction where light is scattered. Their `f()` and `PDF()` methods always return zero.

Implementations of the `Sample_f()` method should determine the direction of incident light ω_i given an outgoing direction ω_o and return the value of the BxDF for the pair of directions. They take three uniform samples in the range $[0, 1)^2$ via the `uc` and `u` parameters. Implementations can use these however they wish, though it is generally best if they use the 1D sample `uc` to choose between different types of scattering (e.g., reflection or transmission) and the 2D sample to choose a specific direction. Using `uc` and `u[0]` to choose a direction, for example, would likely give inferior results to using `u[0]` and `u[1]`, since `uc` and `u[0]` are not necessarily jointly well distributed. Not all the sample values need be used, and BxDFs that need additional sample values must generate them themselves. (The `LayeredBxDF` described in Section 14.3 is one such example.)

Note the potentially counterintuitive direction convention: the outgoing direction ω_o is given, and the implementation then samples an incident direction ω_i. The Monte Carlo methods in this book construct light paths in *reverse* order—that is, counter to the propagation direction of the transported quantity (radiance or importance)—motivating this choice.

Callers of this method must be prepared for the possibility that sampling fails, in which case an unset `optional` value will be returned.

⟨*BxDF Interface*⟩ +≡   **538**
```
pstd::optional<BSDFSample>
Sample_f(Vector3f wo, Float uc, Point2f u,
         TransportMode mode = TransportMode::Radiance,
         BxDFReflTransFlags sampleFlags = BxDFReflTransFlags::All) const;
```

The sample generation can optionally be restricted to the reflection or transmission component via the `sampleFlags` parameter. A sampling failure will occur in invalid cases—for example, if the caller requests a transmission sample on an opaque surface.

⟨*BxDFReflTransFlags Definition*⟩ ≡
```
enum class BxDFReflTransFlags {
    Unset = 0,
    Reflection = 1 << 0,
    Transmission = 1 << 1,
    All = Reflection | Transmission
};
```

If sampling succeeds, the method returns a `BSDFSample` that includes the value of the BSDF f, the sampled direction wi, its probability density function (PDF) measured with respect to solid angle, and a `BxDFFlags` instance that describes the characteristics of the particular sample. BxDFs should specify the direction wi with respect to the local reflection coordinate system, though BSDF::Sample_f() will transform this direction to rendering space before returning it.

Some BxDF implementations (notably, the LayeredBxDF described in Section 14.3) generate samples via simulation, following a random light path. The distribution of paths that escape is the BxDF's exact (probabilistic) distribution, but the returned f and pdf are only proportional to their true values. (Fortunately, by the same proportion!) This case needs special handling in light transport algorithms, and is indicated by the pdfIsProportional field. For all the BxDFs in this chapter, it can be left set to its default false value.

⟨*BSDFSample Definition*⟩ ≡
```
struct BSDFSample {
    ⟨BSDFSample Public Methods 541⟩
    SampledSpectrum f;
    Vector3f wi;
    Float pdf = 0;
    BxDFFlags flags;
    Float eta = 1;
    bool pdfIsProportional = false;
};
```

⟨*BSDFSample Public Methods*⟩ ≡   541
```
BSDFSample(SampledSpectrum f, Vector3f wi, Float pdf, BxDFFlags flags,
           Float eta = 1, bool pdfIsProportional = false)
  : f(f), wi(wi), pdf(pdf), flags(flags), eta(eta),
    pdfIsProportional(pdfIsProportional) {}
```

Several convenience methods can be used to query characteristics of the sample using previously defined functions like BxDFFlags::IsReflective(), etc.

⟨*BSDFSample Public Methods*⟩ +≡   541
```
bool IsReflection() const { return pbrt::IsReflective(flags); }
bool IsTransmission() const { return pbrt::IsTransmissive(flags); }
bool IsDiffuse() const { return pbrt::IsDiffuse(flags); }
bool IsGlossy() const { return pbrt::IsGlossy(flags); }
bool IsSpecular() const { return pbrt::IsSpecular(flags); }
```

The PDF() method returns the value of the PDF for a given pair of directions, which is useful for techniques like multiple importance sampling that compare probabilities of multiple strategies for obtaining a given sample.

⟨*BxDF Interface*⟩ +≡   538
```
Float PDF(Vector3f wo, Vector3f wi, TransportMode mode,
          BxDFReflTransFlags sampleFlags = BxDFReflTransFlags::All) const;
```

9.1.3 HEMISPHERICAL REFLECTANCE

With the BxDF methods described so far, it is possible to implement methods that compute the reflectance of a BxDF by applying the Monte Carlo estimator to the definitions of reflectance from Equations (4.12) and (4.13).

A first variant of BxDF::rho() computes the reflectance function ρ_{hd}. Its caller is responsible for determining how many samples should be taken and for providing the uniform sample values to be used in computing the estimate. Thus, depending on the context, callers have control over sampling and the quality of the returned estimate.

⟨*BxDF Method Definitions*⟩ ≡
```
SampledSpectrum BxDF::rho(Vector3f wo, pstd::span<const Float> uc,
                          pstd::span<const Point2f> u2) const {
    SampledSpectrum r(0.);
    for (size_t i = 0; i < uc.size(); ++i) {
        ⟨Compute estimate of ρhd 542⟩
    }
    return r / uc.size();
}
```

Each term of the estimator

$$\frac{1}{n} \sum_{j}^{n} \frac{f_{\mathrm{r}}(\omega, \omega_j)\,|\cos\theta_j|}{p(\omega_j)}$$

is easily evaluated.

⟨*Compute estimate of ρ*hd⟩ ≡   542
```
pstd::optional<BSDFSample> bs = Sample_f(wo, uc[i], u2[i]);
if (bs)
    r += bs->f * AbsCosTheta(bs->wi) / bs->pdf;
```

The hemispherical-hemispherical reflectance is found in the second BxDF::rho() method that evaluates Equation (4.13). As with the first rho() method, the caller is responsible for passing in uniform sample values—in this case, five dimensions' worth of them.

⟨*BxDF Method Definitions*⟩ +≡
```
SampledSpectrum BxDF::rho(pstd::span<const Point2f> u1,
        pstd::span<const Float> uc, pstd::span<const Point2f> u2) const {
    SampledSpectrum r(0.f);
    for (size_t i = 0; i < uc.size(); ++i) {
        ⟨Compute estimate of ρhh 542⟩
    }
    return r / (Pi * uc.size());
}
```

Our implementation samples the first direction wo uniformly over the hemisphere. Given this, the second direction can be sampled using BxDF::Sample_f().[1]

⟨*Compute estimate of ρ*hh⟩ ≡   542
```
Vector3f wo = SampleUniformHemisphere(u1[i]);
if (wo.z == 0)
    continue;
Float pdfo = UniformHemispherePDF();
pstd::optional<BSDFSample> bs = Sample_f(wo, uc[i], u2[i]);
if (bs)
    r += bs->f * AbsCosTheta(bs->wi) * AbsCosTheta(wo) / (pdfo * bs->pdf);
```

---

1   It could be argued that a shortcoming of the BxDF sampling interface is that there are not entry points to sample from the 4D distribution of $f(\omega, \omega')$. This is a reasonably esoteric case for the applications envisioned for pbrt, however.

9.1.4 DELTA DISTRIBUTIONS IN BSDFs

Several BSDF models in this chapter make use of Dirac delta distributions to represent interactions with perfect specular materials like smooth metal or glass surfaces. They represent a curious corner case in implementations, and we therefore establish a few important conventions.

Recall from Section 8.1.1 that the Dirac delta distribution is defined such that

$$\delta(x) = 0 \quad \text{for all } x \neq 0$$

and

$$\int_{-\infty}^{\infty} \delta(x) \, dx = 1.$$

According to these equations, δ can be interpreted as a normalized density function that is zero for all $x \neq 0$. Generating a sample from such a distribution is trivial, since there is only one value that it can take. In this sense, the forthcoming implementations of `Sample_f()` involving delta functions naturally fit into the Monte Carlo sampling framework.

However, sampling alone is not enough: two methods (`Sample_f()` and `PDF`) also provide sampling densities, and it is considerably less clear what values should be returned here. Strictly speaking, the delta distribution is not a true function but constitutes the limit of a sequence of functions—for example, one describing a box of unit area whose width approaches 0; see Chapter 5 of Bracewell (2000) for details. In the limit, the value of $\delta(0)$ must then necessarily tend toward infinity. This important theoretical realization does not easily translate into C++ code: certainly, returning an infinite or very large PDF value is not going to lead to correct results from the renderer.

To resolve this conflict, BSDFs may only contain matched pairs of delta functions in their f_r function and PDF. For example, suppose that the PDF factors into a remainder term and a delta function involving a particular direction ω':

$$p(\omega_i) = p^{\text{rem}}(\omega_i) \, \delta(\omega' - \omega_i).$$

If the same holds true for f_r, then a Monte Carlo estimator that divides f_r by the PDF will never require evaluation of the delta function:

$$\frac{f_r(p, \omega_o, \omega_i)}{p(\omega_i)} = \frac{\delta(\omega' - \omega_i) \, f_r^{\text{rem}}(p, \omega_o, \omega_i)}{\delta(\omega' - \omega_i) \, p^{\text{rem}}(\omega_i)} = \frac{f_r^{\text{rem}}(p, \omega_o, \omega_i)}{p^{\text{rem}}(\omega_i)}.$$

Implementations of perfect specular materials will thus return a constant PDF of 1 when `Sample_f()` generates a direction associated with a delta function, with the understanding that the delta function will cancel in the estimator.

In contrast, the respective `PDF()` methods should return 0 for all directions, since there is zero probability that another sampling method will randomly find the direction from a delta distribution.[2]

9.1.5 BSDFs

`BxDF` class implementations perform all computation in a local shading coordinate system that is most appropriate for this task. In contrast, rendering algorithms operate in *rendering*

BxDF 538

---

2   Strictly speaking, this is not always true: for example, the other method might also involve a delta distribution with matching direction ω'. pbrt does not consider this case, which may lead to a small loss of sampling efficiency in this rare corner case.

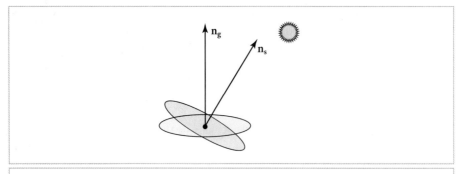

Figure 9.3: The geometric normal, $\mathbf{n_g}$, defined by the surface geometry, and the shading normal, $\mathbf{n_s}$, given by per-vertex normals and/or bump mapping, will generally define different hemispheres for integrating incident illumination to compute surface reflection. It is important to handle this inconsistency carefully since it can otherwise lead to artifacts in images.

space (Section 5.1.1); hence a transformation between these two spaces must be performed somewhere. The BSDF is a small wrapper around a BxDF that handles this transformation.

⟨*BSDF Definition*⟩ ≡
```
class BSDF {
  public:
    ⟨BSDF Public Methods 544⟩
  private:
    ⟨BSDF Private Members 544⟩
};
```

In addition to an encapsulated BxDF, the BSDF holds a shading frame based on the Frame class.

⟨*BSDF Private Members*⟩ ≡   544
```
BxDF bxdf;
Frame shadingFrame;
```

The constructor initializes the latter from the shading normal $\mathbf{n_s}$ and $\partial p/\partial u$ using the shading coordinate system convention (Figure 9.3).

⟨*BSDF Public Methods*⟩ ≡   544
```
BSDF() = default;
BSDF(Normal3f ns, Vector3f dpdus, BxDF bxdf)
    : bxdf(bxdf),
      shadingFrame(Frame::FromXZ(Normalize(dpdus), Vector3f(ns))) {}
```

The default constructor creates a BSDF with a nullptr-valued bxdf, which is useful to represent transitions between different media that do not themselves scatter light. An operator bool() method checks whether the BSDF represents a real material interaction, in which case the Flags() method provides further information about its high-level properties.

⟨*BSDF Public Methods*⟩ +≡   544
```
operator bool() const { return (bool)bxdf; }
BxDFFlags Flags() const { return bxdf.Flags(); }
```

The BSDF provides methods that perform transformations to and from the reflection coordinate system used by BxDFs.

⟨*BSDF Public Methods*⟩ +≡   544
```
    Vector3f RenderToLocal(Vector3f v) const { return shadingFrame.ToLocal(v); }
    Vector3f LocalToRender(Vector3f v) const {
        return shadingFrame.FromLocal(v);
    }
```

The f() function performs the required coordinate frame conversion and then queries the BxDF. The rare case in which the wo direction lies exactly in the surface's tangent plane often leads to not-a-number (NaN) values in BxDF implementations that further propagate and may eventually contaminate the rendered image. The BSDF avoids this case by immediately returning a zero-valued SampledSpectrum.

⟨*BSDF Public Methods*⟩ +≡   544
```
    SampledSpectrum f(Vector3f woRender, Vector3f wiRender,
                      TransportMode mode = TransportMode::Radiance) const {
        Vector3f wi = RenderToLocal(wiRender), wo = RenderToLocal(woRender);
        if (wo.z == 0) return {};
        return bxdf.f(wo, wi, mode);
    }
```

The BSDF also provides a second templated f() method that can be parameterized by the underlying BxDF. If the caller knows the specific type of BSDF::bxdf, it can call this variant directly without involving the dynamic method dispatch used in the method above. This approach is used by pbrt's wavefront rendering path, which groups evaluations based on the underlying BxDF to benefit from vectorized execution on the GPU. The implementation of this specialized version simply casts the BxDF to the provided type before invoking its f() method.

⟨*BSDF Public Methods*⟩ +≡   544
```
    template <typename BxDF>
    SampledSpectrum f(Vector3f woRender, Vector3f wiRender,
                      TransportMode mode = TransportMode::Radiance) const {
        Vector3f wi = RenderToLocal(wiRender), wo = RenderToLocal(woRender);
        if (wo.z == 0) return {};
        const BxDF *specificBxDF = bxdf.CastOrNullptr<BxDF>();
        return specificBxDF->f(wo, wi, mode);
    }
```

The BSDF::Sample_f() method similarly forwards the sampling request on to the BxDF after transforming the ω_o direction to the local coordinate system.

⟨*BSDF Public Methods*⟩ +≡   544
```
    pstd::optional<BSDFSample> Sample_f(
            Vector3f woRender, Float u, Point2f u2,
            TransportMode mode = TransportMode::Radiance,
            BxDFReflTransFlags sampleFlags = BxDFReflTransFlags::All) const {
        Vector3f wo = RenderToLocal(woRender);
        if (wo.z == 0 ||!(bxdf.Flags() & sampleFlags)) return {};
        ⟨Sample bxdf and return BSDFSample 546⟩
    }
```

If the BxDF implementation returns a sample that has a zero-valued BSDF or PDF or an incident direction in the tangent plane, this method nevertheless returns an unset sample value. This allows calling code to proceed without needing to check those cases.

⟨*Sample* bxdf *and return* BSDFSample⟩ ≡   **545**
```
    pstd::optional<BSDFSample> bs = bxdf.Sample_f(wo, u, u2, mode, sampleFlags);
    if (!bs || !bs->f || bs->pdf == 0 || bs->wi.z == 0)
        return {};
    bs->wi = LocalToRender(bs->wi);
    return bs;
```

BSDF::PDF() follows the same pattern.

⟨*BSDF Public Methods*⟩ +≡   **544**
```
    Float PDF(Vector3f woRender, Vector3f wiRender,
              TransportMode mode = TransportMode::Radiance,
              BxDFReflTransFlags sampleFlags = BxDFReflTransFlags::All) const {
        Vector3f wo = RenderToLocal(woRender), wi = RenderToLocal(wiRender);
        if (wo.z == 0) return 0;
        return bxdf.PDF(wo, wi, mode, sampleFlags);
    }
```

We have omitted the definitions of additional templated Sample_f() and PDF() variants that are parameterized by the BxDF type.

Finally, BSDF provides rho() methods to compute the reflectance that forward the call on to its underlying bxdf. They are trivial and therefore not included here.

9.2 DIFFUSE REFLECTION

One of the simplest BRDFs is the Lambertian model, which describes a perfect diffuse surface that scatters incident illumination equally in all directions. It is a reasonable approximation to many real-world surfaces such as paper or matte paint. The Lambertian model captures the behavior of such diffuse materials relatively well, though the approximation tends to perform worse for light arriving at a grazing angle, where specular reflection causes a noticeable deviation from uniformity. (Microfacet models such as those presented in Section 9.6 can account for such effects.)

It is interesting to note that surfaces created from polytetrafluoroethylene (PTFE) powder are known to be particularly good Lambertian reflectors. They are commonly used to calibrate laboratory equipment for this reason.

⟨*DiffuseBxDF Definition*⟩ ≡
```
    class DiffuseBxDF {
      public:
        ⟨DiffuseBxDF Public Methods 546⟩
      private:
        SampledSpectrum R;
    };
```

The constructor takes a reflectance spectrum R with values in the range [0, 1] that specify the fraction of incident light that is scattered.

⟨*DiffuseBxDF Public Methods*⟩ ≡   **546**
```
    DiffuseBxDF(SampledSpectrum R) : R(R) {}
```

The reflection distribution function is just a constant, though it requires a normalization factor equal to $\frac{1}{\pi}$ so that the total integrated reflectance equals R.

$$\int_{\mathcal{H}^2(\mathbf{n})} f_{\mathrm{r}}(\mathrm{p}, \omega_{\mathrm{o}}, \omega') \, \cos \theta' \, \mathrm{d}\omega' = \int_0^{2\pi} \int_0^{\frac{\pi}{2}} \frac{R}{\pi} \cos \theta' \sin \theta' \, \mathrm{d}\theta' \, \mathrm{d}\phi' = R.$$

With this correction, the f() implementation is given by

⟨*DiffuseBxDF Public Methods*⟩ +≡   **546**
```
    SampledSpectrum f(Vector3f wo, Vector3f wi, TransportMode mode) const {
        if (!SameHemisphere(wo, wi))
            return SampledSpectrum(0.f);
        return R * InvPi;
    }
```

The sampling function returns an invalid sample if the caller specified that reflection components of the BSDF should not be sampled. Otherwise, it draws a direction from a suitable distribution and returns all the sample-related information via a BSDFSample instance.

⟨*DiffuseBxDF Public Methods*⟩ +≡   **546**
```
    pstd::optional<BSDFSample> Sample_f(
            Vector3f wo, Float uc, Point2f u, TransportMode mode,
            BxDFReflTransFlags sampleFlags = BxDFReflTransFlags::All) const {
        if (!(sampleFlags & BxDFReflTransFlags::Reflection))
            return {};
```
        ⟨*Sample cosine-weighted hemisphere to compute* wi *and* pdf **547**⟩
```
        return BSDFSample(R * InvPi, wi, pdf, BxDFFlags::DiffuseReflection);
    }
```

Working in a canonical reflection coordinate system greatly simplifies the central sampling step: in particular, a direction generated by SampleCosineHemisphere() can be directly used, and we must only pay attention that wo and wi lie in the same hemisphere, as indicated by wo.z and wi.z.

Although the Lambertian BRDF is uniform over the hemisphere, BSDFs are sampled in the context of the light transport equation, (1.1), where the BSDF is multiplied by the incident radiance and a cosine factor. It is worthwhile for BxDFs to include the cosine factor in their sampling distribution if possible; see Figure 9.4, which compares uniform and cosine-weighted hemisphere sampling for the DiffuseBxDF.

⟨*Sample cosine-weighted hemisphere to compute* wi *and* pdf⟩ ≡   **547**
```
    Vector3f wi = SampleCosineHemisphere(u);
    if (wo.z < 0) wi.z *= -1;
    Float pdf = CosineHemispherePDF(AbsCosTheta(wi));
```

The PDF() method just needs to ensure that the caller has included reflection in the types of scattering that it is interested in and that the two directions both lie in the same hemisphere.

⟨*DiffuseBxDF Public Methods*⟩ +≡   **546**
```
    Float PDF(Vector3f wo, Vector3f wi, TransportMode mode,
            BxDFReflTransFlags sampleFlags = BxDFReflTransFlags::All) const {
        if (!(sampleFlags & BxDFReflTransFlags::Reflection) ||
            !SameHemisphere(wo, wi))
            return 0;
        return CosineHemispherePDF(AbsCosTheta(wi));
    }
```

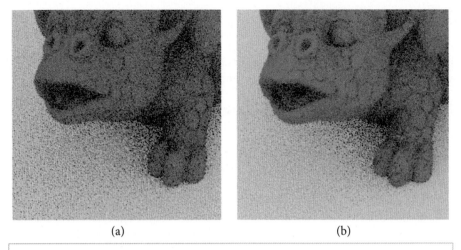

(a)   (b)

> **Figure 9.4: Comparison of Sampling Methods for a Lambertian BSDF.** Both images are rendered using 4 samples per pixel. (a) Uniform hemisphere sampling. (b) Cosine-weighted hemisphere sampling. By incorporating the cosine factor in the light transport equation's integrand, cosine-weighted hemisphere sampling improves mean squared error (MSE) by a factor of 2.34 for this test scene, without additional computational cost.

9.3 SPECULAR REFLECTION AND TRANSMISSION

Following the discussion of diffuse surfaces with their perfectly uniform reflectance, we now turn to the opposite extreme: specular materials that only reflect light into a discrete set of directions. Following a review of the physical principles underlying such materials in this section, we will introduce concrete BxDF implementations in Sections 9.4 and 9.5.

Our initial focus is on perfect specular surfaces. However, many real-world materials are fairly rough at a microscopic scale, and this can have a profound influence on their reflection behavior. Sections 9.6 and 9.7 will generalize our understanding of the perfect specular case to such rough surface microstructures.

9.3.1 PHYSICAL PRINCIPLES

For the most part, this book is concerned with *geometric optics*, which describes the scattering and transport of radiance along rays. This is an approximation of the wave nature of light, albeit an excellent one: visible light waves occur at scales that are negligible ($\sim \frac{1}{2}\mu$m) compared to the size of objects rendered in pbrt ($\sim$ millimeters to meters), and hence wave-like phenomena normally do not manifest in rendered images.

Yet, to understand and model what happens when light strikes a surface, it is helpful to briefly turn toward this deeper understanding of light in terms of waves. Using wave-optical results within an overall geometric simulation is often possible and has become a common design pattern in computer graphics.

The theory of electromagnetism describes light as an oscillation of the *electric and magnetic fields*. What does this mean? These terms refer to *vector fields*, which are convenient mathematical abstractions that assign a 3D vector to every point in space. These vectors describe the force that a small charged particle would feel due to such a light wave passing around it. For our purposes, only the electric field is interesting, and the charged particle that will be influenced by this force is an *electron* surrounding the nucleus of an atom.

When a beam of light arrives at a surface, it stimulates the electrons of the atoms comprising the material, causing them to begin to oscillate rapidly. These moving electric charges induce secondary oscillations in the electric field, whose superposition is then subject to constructive and destructive interference. This constitutes the main mechanism in which atoms reflect light, though the specifics of this process can vary significantly based on the type of atom and the way in which it is bound to other atoms. The electromagnetic theory of light distinguishes the following three major classes of behaviors.

The large class of *dielectrics* includes any substance (whether gaseous, liquid, or solid) that acts as an electric insulator, including glass, water, mineral oil, and air. In such materials, the oscillating electrons are firmly bound to their atoms. Note that a liquid like water can be made electrically conductive by adding ions (e.g., table salt), but that is irrelevant in this classification of purely atomic properties.

The second class of electric *conductors* includes metals and metal alloys, but also semi-metals like graphite. Some of the electrons can freely move within their atomic lattice; hence an oscillation induced by an incident electromagnetic wave can move electrons over larger distances. At the same time, migration through the lattice dissipates some of the incident energy in the form of heat, causing rapid absorption of the light wave as it travels deeper into the material. Total absorption typically occurs within the top 0.1 μm of the material; hence only extremely thin metal films are capable of transmitting appreciable amounts of light. We ignore this effect in pbrt and treat metallic surfaces as opaque.

A third class of *semiconductors*, such as silicon or germanium, exhibits properties of both dielectrics and conductors. For example, silicon appears metallic in the visible spectrum. At the same time, its transparency in the infrared range makes it an excellent material for optical elements in IR cameras. We do not explicitly consider semiconductors in pbrt, though adding a suitable BxDF to handle them would be relatively easy.

9.3.2 THE INDEX OF REFRACTION

When an incident light wave stimulates an electron, the oscillation induces its own electromagnetic oscillation. The oscillation of this re-emitted light incurs a small delay compared to the original wave. The compound effect of many such delays within a solid material causes the light wave to travel at a slower velocity compared to the original speed of light.

The speed reduction is commonly summarized using the *index of refraction* (IOR). For example, a material with an IOR of 2 propagates light at half the speed of light. For common materials, the value is in the range 1.0–2.5 and furthermore varies with the wavelength of light. We will use the Greek letter η, pronounced "eta," to denote this quantity.

Light waves undergo significant reflection when they encounter boundaries with a sudden change in the IOR value. For example, an air–diamond interface with a comparably high IOR difference of 2.42 will appear more reflective than an air–glass surface with a difference around 1.5. In this sense, the IOR provides the main mathematical explanation of why we perceive objects around us: it is because their IOR differs from the surrounding medium (e.g., air). The specific value of η controls the appearance of surfaces; hence a good estimate of this value is important for physically based rendering.

Table 9.1: Indices of refraction for a variety of objects, giving the ratio of the speed of light in a vacuum to the speed of light in the medium. These are generally wavelength-dependent quantities; these values are averages over the visible wavelengths.

Medium	Index of refraction η
Vacuum	1.0
Air at sea level	1.00029
Ice	1.31
Water (20°C)	1.333
Fused quartz	1.46
Glass	1.5–1.6
Sapphire	1.77
Diamond	2.42

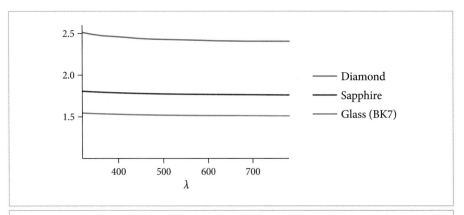

Figure 9.5: Plots of the Wavelength-Dependent Index of Refraction for Various Materials. All have only a few percent variation in index of refraction over the range of visible wavelengths, though even that is sufficient to be visible in rendered images.

Table 9.1 provides IOR values for a number of dielectric materials and Figure 9.5 shows plots of the wavelength-dependent IOR for a few materials. pbrt also includes wavelength-dependent IORs for various materials that can be referred to by name in scene description files; see the file format documentation for more information.

In the following, we assume that the IOR on both sides of the surface in question is known. We first review *in which direction(s)* light travels following an interaction, which is described by the law of specular reflection and Snell's law. Subsequently, we discuss *how much* of the scattered light travels in those directions, which is given by the Fresnel equations.

9.3.3 THE LAW OF SPECULAR REFLECTION

Given incident light from a direction (θ_i, ϕ_i), the single reflected direction (θ_r, ϕ_r) following an interaction with a perfect specular surface is easy to characterize: it makes the same angle with the normal as the incoming direction and is rotated around it by 180°—that is,

$$\theta_r = \theta_i \quad \text{and} \quad \phi_r = \phi_i + \pi.$$

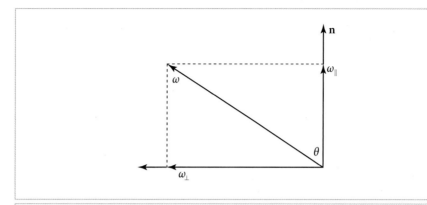

Figure 9.6: The parallel projection of a vector ω on to the normal $\mathbf{n}$ is given by $\omega_\| = (\cos\theta)\mathbf{n} = (\mathbf{n}\cdot\omega)\mathbf{n}$. The perpendicular component is given by $\omega_\perp = (\sin\theta)\mathbf{n}$ but is more easily computed by $\omega_\perp = \omega - \omega_\|$.

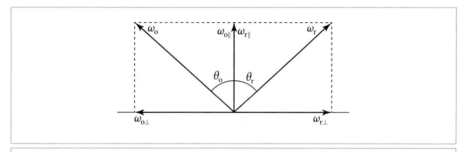

Figure 9.7: Because the angles θ_o and θ_r are equal, the parallel component of the perfect reflection direction $\omega_{r\|}$ is the same as the incident direction's: $\omega_{r\|} = \omega_{o\|}$. Its perpendicular component is just the incident direction's perpendicular component, negated.

This direction can also be computed using vectorial arithmetic instead of angles, which is more convenient in subsequent implementation. For this, note that surface normal, incident, and outgoing directions all lie in the same plane.

We can decompose vectors ω that lie in a plane into a sum of two components: one parallel to $\mathbf{n}$, which we will denote by $\omega_\|$, and one perpendicular to it, denoted $\omega_\perp$. These vectors are easily computed: if $\mathbf{n}$ and ω are normalized, then $\omega_\|$ is $(\cos\theta)\mathbf{n} = (\mathbf{n}\cdot\omega)\mathbf{n}$ (Figure 9.6). Because $\omega_\| + \omega_\perp = \omega$,

$$\omega_\perp = \omega - \omega_\| = \omega - (\mathbf{n}\cdot\omega)\mathbf{n}.$$

Figure 9.7 shows the setting for computing the reflected direction ω_r. We can see that both vectors have the same $\omega_\|$ component, and the value of $\omega_{r\perp}$ is the negation of $\omega_{o\perp}$. Therefore, we have

$$\begin{aligned}
\omega_r = \omega_{r\perp} + \omega_{r\|} &= -\omega_{o\perp} + \omega_{o\|} \\
&= -(\omega_o - (\mathbf{n}\cdot\omega_o)\,\mathbf{n}) + (\mathbf{n}\cdot\omega_o)\,\mathbf{n} \qquad\qquad \text{[9.1]}\\
&= -\omega_o + 2(\mathbf{n}\cdot\omega_o)\,\mathbf{n}.
\end{aligned}$$

The Reflect() function implements this computation.

⟨*Scattering Inline Functions*⟩ ≡
```
Vector3f Reflect(Vector3f wo, Vector3f n) {
    return -wo + 2 * Dot(wo, n) * n;
}
```

9.3.4 SNELL'S LAW

At a specular interface, incident light with direction (θ_i, ϕ_i) about the surface normal *refracts* into a single transmitted direction (θ_t, ϕ_t) located on the opposite side of the interface. The specifics of this process are described by *Snell's law*, which depends on the directions and IOR values η_i and η_t on both sides of the interface.

Snell's law states that

$$\eta_i \ \sin \theta_i = \eta_t \ \sin \theta_t \quad \text{and} \quad \phi_t = \phi_i + \pi. \tag{9.2}$$

If the target medium is optically denser (i.e., $\eta_t > \eta_i$), this means that the refracted light bends toward the surface normal. Snell's law can be derived using Fermat's principle, which is the subject of one of the exercises at the end of this chapter. Figure 9.8 shows the effect of perfect specular reflection and transmission.

The index of refraction normally varies with respect to wavelength; hence light consisting of multiple wavelengths will split into multiple transmitted directions at the boundary between two different media—an effect known as *dispersion*. This effect can be seen when a prism splits incident white light into its spectral components. See Figure 9.9 for a rendered image that includes dispersion.

One useful observation about Snell's law is that it technically does not depend on the precise values of η_i and η_t, but rather on their ratio. In other words, the law can be rewritten as

$$\sin \theta_i = \eta \ \sin \theta_t, \tag{9.3}$$

where the *relative index of refraction* $\eta = \frac{\eta_t}{\eta_i}$ specifies the proportional slowdown incurred when light passes through the interface. We will generally follow the convention that relevant laws and implementations are based on this relative quantity.

As with the law of specular reflection, we shall now derive a more convenient vectorial form of this relationship, illustrated in Figure 9.10.

(a)   (b)

Dot() 89
Vector3f 86

Figure 9.8: Dragon model rendered with (a) perfect specular reflection and (b) perfect specular transmission. Image (b) excludes the effects of external and internal reflection; the resulting energy loss produces conspicuous dark regions. *(Model courtesy of Christian Schüller.)*

(a)

(b)

Figure 9.9: The Effect of Dispersion When Rendering Glass. (a) Rendered using a constant index of refraction, and (b) rendered using a wavelength-dependent index of refraction based on measurements of glass, which causes different wavelengths of light to be scattered in different directions. As a result, white colors are separated, making their individual wavelengths of light distinct. *(Scene courtesy of Beeple.)*

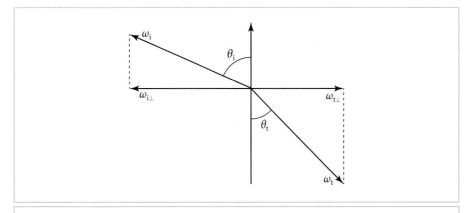

Figure 9.10: The Geometry of Specular Transmission. Given an incident direction ω_i and surface normal **n** with angle θ_i between them, the specularly transmitted direction makes an angle θ_t with the surface normal. This direction, ω_t, can be computed by using Snell's law to find its perpendicular component $\omega_{t\perp}$ and then computing the $\omega_{t\|}$ that gives a normalized result ω_t.

The trigonometric expressions above are closely related to the parallel and perpendicular components of the incident and transmitted directions. For example, the magnitudes of the perpendicular components equal the sines of the corresponding elevation angles. Since these directions all lie in a common reflection plane, Equation (9.3) can be rewritten as

$$\omega_{t\perp} = -\frac{\omega_{i\perp}}{\eta}.$$

Equivalently, because $\omega_\perp = \omega - \omega_\parallel$,

$$\omega_{t\perp} = \frac{-\omega_i + (\omega_i \cdot \mathbf{n})\,\mathbf{n}}{\eta}.$$

The parallel component points into the direction $-\mathbf{n}$, and its magnitude is given by $\cos\theta_t$—that is,

$$\omega_{t\parallel} = -\cos\theta_t\,\mathbf{n}.$$

Putting all the above together, then, the vector ω_t equals

$$\omega_t = \omega_{t\perp} + \omega_{t\parallel} = -\frac{\omega_i}{\eta} + \left[\frac{(\omega_i \cdot \mathbf{n})}{\eta} - \cos\theta_t\right]\mathbf{n}. \tag{9.4}$$

The function `Refract()` computes the refracted direction `wt` via Equation (9.4) given an incident direction `wi`, surface normal `n` in the same hemisphere as `wi`, and the relative index of refraction `eta`. An adjusted relative IOR may be returned via `*etap`—we will discuss this detail shortly. The function returns a Boolean variable to indicate if the refracted direction was computed successfully.

⟨*Scattering Inline Functions*⟩ +≡
```
bool Refract(Vector3f wi, Normal3f n, Float eta, Float *etap,
             Vector3f *wt) {
    Float cosTheta_i = Dot(n, wi);
    ⟨Potentially flip interface orientation for Snell's law 555⟩
    ⟨Compute cos θt using Snell's law 555⟩
    *wt = -wi / eta + (cosTheta_i / eta - cosTheta_t) * Vector3f(n);
    ⟨Provide relative IOR along ray to caller 555⟩
    return true;
}
```

The function's convention for the relative index of refraction `eta` slightly differs from the previous definition: it specifies the IOR ratio of the object interior relative to the outside, as indicated by the surface normal $\mathbf{n}$ that anchors the spherical coordinate system of quantities like θ_i and θ_t.

When the incident ray lies *within* the object, this convention is no longer compatible with our previous use of Snell's law, assuming positive angle cosines and a relative IOR relating the incident and transmitted rays. We detect this case and, if needed, flip the interface by inverting the sign of `n` and `cosTheta_i` and swapping the IOR values, which is equivalent to taking the reciprocal of the relative IOR. Figure 9.11 illustrates this special case. Including this logic directly in `Refract()` facilitates its usage in rendering algorithms.

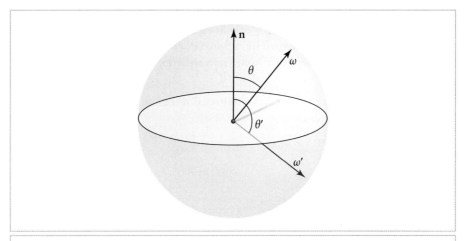

Figure 9.11: The cosine of the angle θ between a direction ω and the geometric surface normal indicates whether the direction is pointing outside the surface (in the same hemisphere as the normal) or inside the surface. In the standard reflection coordinate system, this test just requires checking the z component of the direction vector. Here, ω is in the upper hemisphere, with a positive-valued cosine, while ω' is in the lower hemisphere.

⟨*Potentially flip interface orientation for Snell's law*⟩ ≡   554
```
if (cosTheta_i < 0) {
    eta = 1 / eta;
    cosTheta_i = -cosTheta_i;
    n = -n;
}
```

It is sometimes useful for the caller of Refract() to know the relative IOR along the ray, while handling the case when the ray arrives from the object's interior. To make this accessible, we store the updated eta value into the etap pointer if provided.

⟨*Provide relative IOR along ray to caller*⟩ ≡   554
```
if (etap)
    *etap = eta;
```

We have not yet explained how the cosine of the transmitted angle θ_t should be computed. It can be derived from Equation (9.3) and the identity $\sin^2\theta + \cos^2\theta = 1$, which yields

$$\cos\theta_t = \sqrt{1 - \frac{\sin^2\theta_i}{\eta^2}}. \tag{9.5}$$

The following fragment implements this computation.

⟨*Compute* cos θ_t *using Snell's law*⟩ ≡   554
```
Float sin2Theta_i = std::max<Float>(0, 1 - Sqr(cosTheta_i));
Float sin2Theta_t = sin2Theta_i / Sqr(eta);
```
⟨*Handle total internal reflection case* 556⟩
```
Float cosTheta_t = SafeSqrt(1 - sin2Theta_t);
```

Float 23
SafeSqrt() 1034
Sqr() 1034

We must deal with one potential complication: when light travels into a medium that is *less* optically dense (i.e., $\eta_t < \eta_i$), the interface turns into an ideal reflector at certain angles so that no light is transmitted. This special case denoted *total internal reflection* arises when θ_i is greater than *critical angle* $\theta_c = \sin^{-1}(1/\eta)$, at which point the argument of the square root function in Equation (9.5) turns *negative*. This occurs at roughly 42° in the case of an air–glass interface. Total internal reflection is easy to experience personally inside a swimming pool: observing the air–water interface from below reveals a striking circular pattern that separates a refracted view of the outside from a pure reflection of the pool's interior, and this circle exactly corresponds to a viewing angle of θ_c.

In the case of total internal reflection, the refracted direction *wt is undefined, and the function returns false to indicate this.

⟨*Handle total internal reflection case*⟩ ≡   **555**
```
if (sin2Theta_t >= 1)
    return false;
```

9.3.5 THE FRESNEL EQUATIONS

The previous two subsections focused on *where* light travels following an interaction with a specular material. We now turn to the question of *how much*?

Light is normally both reflected and transmitted at the boundary between two materials with a different index of refraction, though the transmission rapidly decays in the case of conductors. For physically accurate rendering, we must account for the fraction of reflected and transmitted light, which is directionally dependent and therefore cannot be captured by a fixed per-surface scaling constant. The *Fresnel equations*, which are the solution to Maxwell's equations at smooth surfaces, specify the precise proportion of reflected light.

Recall the conscious decision to ignore polarization effects in Section 4.1. In spite of that, we must briefly expand on how polarization is represented to express the Fresnel equations in their natural form that emerges within the framework of electromagnetism.

At surfaces, it is convenient to distinguish between waves, whose polarization is perpendicular ("⊥") or parallel ("∥") to the place of incidence containing the incident direction and surface normal. There is no loss of generality, since the polarization state of any incident wave can be modeled as a superposition of two such orthogonal oscillations.

The Fresnel equations relate the *amplitudes* of the reflected wave (E_r) given an incident wave with a known amplitude (E_i). The ratio of these amplitudes depends on the properties of the specular interface specified in terms of the IOR values η_i and η_t, and the angle θ_i of the incident ray. Furthermore, parallel and perpendicularly polarized waves have different amounts of reflectance, which is the reason there are *two* equations:

$$r_{\parallel} = \frac{E_r^{\parallel}}{E_i^{\parallel}} = \frac{\eta_t \cos\theta_i - \eta_i \cos\theta_t}{\eta_t \cos\theta_i + \eta_i \cos\theta_t},$$

$$r_{\perp} = \frac{E_r^{\perp}}{E_i^{\perp}} = \frac{\eta_i \cos\theta_i - \eta_t \cos\theta_t}{\eta_i \cos\theta_i + \eta_t \cos\theta_t}.$$

(9.6)

(The elevation angle of the transmitted light θ_t is determined by Snell's law.)

As with Snell's law, only the *relative index of refraction* $\eta = \frac{\eta_t}{\eta_i}$ matters, and we therefore prefer the equivalent expressions

$$r_{\parallel} = \frac{\eta \cos\theta_i - \cos\theta_t}{\eta \cos\theta_i + \cos\theta_t}, \quad r_{\perp} = \frac{\cos\theta_i - \eta \cos\theta_t}{\cos\theta_i + \eta \cos\theta_t}.$$

(9.7)

In the wave-optics framework, the quantities of interest are the amplitude and phase of the reflected wave. In contrast, pbrt simulates light geometrically, and we care about the overall *power* carried by the wave, which is given by the square of the amplitude.

Combining this transformation together with the assumption of unpolarized light leads to the *Fresnel reflectance,* expressing an average of the parallel and perpendicular oscillations:

$$F_{\mathrm{r}} = \frac{1}{2}\left(r_{\|}^2 + r_{\perp}^2\right).$$

Dielectrics, conductors, and semiconductors are all governed by the same Fresnel equations. In the common dielectric case, there are additional simplification opportunities; hence it makes sense to first define specialized dielectric evaluation routines. We discuss the more general case in Section 9.3.6.

The function `FrDielectric()` computes the unpolarized Fresnel reflection of a dielectric interface given its relative IOR η and angle cosine $\cos\theta_{\mathrm{i}}$ provided via parameters `cosTheta_i` and `eta`.

⟨*Fresnel Inline Functions*⟩ ≡
```
Float FrDielectric(Float cosTheta_i, Float eta) {
    cosTheta_i = Clamp(cosTheta_i, -1, 1);
    ⟨Potentially flip interface orientation for Fresnel equations 557⟩
    ⟨Compute cos θt for Fresnel equations using Snell's law⟩
    Float r_parl = (eta * cosTheta_i - cosTheta_t) /
                   (eta * cosTheta_i + cosTheta_t);
    Float r_perp = (cosTheta_i - eta * cosTheta_t) /
                   (cosTheta_i + eta * cosTheta_t);
    return (Sqr(r_parl) + Sqr(r_perp)) / 2;
}
```

Recall that our numerical implementation of Snell's law included a fragment ⟨*Potentially flip interface orientation for Snell's law*⟩ to implement the convention that eta always specifies a relative IOR relating the inside to the outside of an object, as determined by the surface normal. We include a similar step in `FrDielectric()` so that these two functions are consistent with each other.

⟨*Potentially flip interface orientation for Fresnel equations*⟩ ≡   557
```
if (cosTheta_i < 0) {
    eta = 1 / eta;
    cosTheta_i = -cosTheta_i;
}
```

The omitted fragment ⟨*Compute* cos θ_t *for Fresnel equations using Snell's law*⟩ matches the previously explained fragment ⟨*Compute* cos θ_t *using Snell's law*⟩ except for one small difference: in the case of total internal reflection, the previous fragment returned a failure to compute a refracted direction. Here, we must instead return a reflectance value of 1 to indicate that all scattering takes place via the reflection component.

9.3.6 THE FRESNEL EQUATIONS FOR CONDUCTORS

Characterizing the reflection behavior of conductors involves an additional twist: the IOR turns into a complex number! Its real component describes the decrease in the speed of light as before. The newly added imaginary component models the decay of light as it travels deeper into the material. This decay occurs so rapidly that it also has a significant effect on the reflection component; hence it is important that we account for it even if the transmitted portion of light is of no interest.

The emergence of complex numbers may appear counterintuitive at this stage. They are best thought of as a convenient mathematical tool employed in derivations based on electromagnetism; they exploit the property that imaginary exponentiation produces complex values with sinusoidal components:

$$e^{ix} = \cos x + i \sin x.$$

Incident and outgoing light is normally modeled using *plane waves* describing an oscillatory electric field that varies with respect to both time and distance z along the wave's direction of travel. For example, the spatial variation in the amplitude of such a wave can be expressed using an exponential function $E(z) = e^{-i\alpha \eta z}$ containing the imaginary unit i in the exponent. The value α denotes the spatial frequency, and η is the index of refraction. Only the real component of this field matters, which equals $\Re[E(z)] = \cos(\alpha \eta z)$. In other words, the plane wave describes a sinusoidal oscillation that propagates unimpeded through the material, which is the expected behavior in a transparent dielectric.

Note, however, what happens when a negative imaginary component is added. By standard convention, the complex index of refraction is defined as $\eta - ik$, where η retains the former meaning and the $k > 0$ term now leads to an exponential decay with increasing depth z inside the medium—that is, $\Re[E(z)] = e^{-\alpha z k} \cos(\alpha \eta z)$. For this reason, k is referred to as the *absorption coefficient*. Although it superficially resembles the volumetric absorption coefficient defined in Section 11.1, those two processes occur at vastly different scales and should not be confused.

Figure 9.12 shows a plot of the index of refraction and absorption coefficient for gold; both of these are wavelength-dependent quantities. Figure 9.13 shows a model rendered with a metal material.

A wondrous aspect of the Fresnel equations is that these two deceptively simple formulae span all major classes of material behavior including dielectrics, conductors, and semiconductors. In the latter two cases, one must simply evaluate these equations using complex arithmetic. The FrComplex() function realizes this change. It takes the angle cosine of the incident direction and a relative index of refraction $\eta = \frac{\eta_t}{\eta_i}$ obtained using complex division.

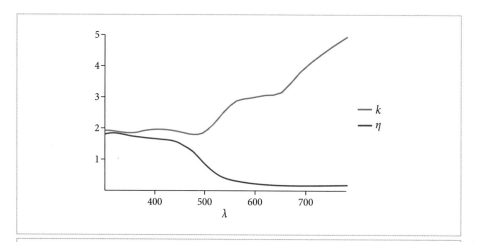

Figure 9.12: Absorption Coefficient and Index of Refraction of Gold. This plot shows the spectrally varying values of the absorption coefficient k and the index of refraction η for gold, where the horizontal axis is wavelength in nm.

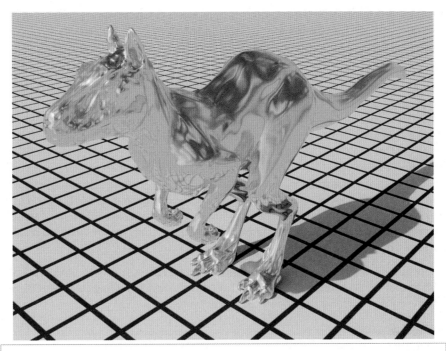

Figure 9.13: Killeroo with a Gold Surface. The killeroo model is rendered here using the `ConductorBxDF`. See Figure 9.12 for a plot of the associated absorption coefficient and index of refraction that lead to its appearance. *(Killeroo model courtesy of headus/Rezard.)*

⟨*Fresnel Inline Functions*⟩ +≡
```
Float FrComplex(Float cosTheta_i, pstd::complex<Float> eta) {
    using Complex = pstd::complex<Float>;
    cosTheta_i = Clamp(cosTheta_i, 0, 1);
    ⟨Compute complex cos θt for Fresnel equations using Snell's law 559⟩
    Complex r_parl = (eta * cosTheta_i - cosTheta_t) /
                     (eta * cosTheta_i + cosTheta_t);
    Complex r_perp = (cosTheta_i - eta * cosTheta_t) /
                     (cosTheta_i + eta * cosTheta_t);
    return (pstd::norm(r_parl) + pstd::norm(r_perp)) / 2;
}
```

Compared to `FrDielectric()`, the main change in the implementation is the type replacement of `Float` by `pstd::complex<Float>`. The function `pstd::norm(x)` computes the squared magnitude—that is, the square of the distance from the origin of the complex plane to the point x.

Computation of $\cos\theta_t$ using Snell's law reveals another curious difference: due to the dependence on η, this value now generally has an imaginary component, losing its original meaning as the cosine of the transmitted angle.

⟨*Compute complex* cos θ_t *for Fresnel equations using Snell's law*⟩ ≡   **559**
```
Float sin2Theta_i = 1 - Sqr(cosTheta_i);
Complex sin2Theta_t = sin2Theta_i / Sqr(eta);
Complex cosTheta_t = pstd::sqrt(1 - sin2Theta_t);
```

This is expected in the case of the Fresnel equations—computation of the actual transmitted angle in absorbing materials is more involved, and we sidestep this case in pbrt (recall that conductors were assumed to be opaque).

Complex numbers play a larger role within the Fresnel equations when polarization is modeled: recall how we detected the total internal reflection when a number under a square root became negative, which is nonsensical in real arithmetic. With complex arithmetic, this imaginary square root can be computed successfully. The angles of the resulting complex numbers $r_\parallel$ and $r_\perp$ relative to the origin of the complex plane encode a delay (also known as the *phase*) that influences the polarization state of the reflected superposition of parallel and perpendicularly polarized waves. It is also worth noting that a number of different sign conventions exist—for example, depending on the definition of a plane wave, the imaginary IOR component k of conductors is either positive or negative. Some sources also flip the sign of the $r_\parallel$ component. Such subtle details are a common source of bugs in renderers that account for polarization, but they are of no concern for pbrt since it only requires the amplitude of the reflected wave.

Before turning to BxDFs using the helper functions defined in the last subsections, we define a convenient wrapper around FrComplex() that takes a spectrally varying complex IOR split into the eta and k, evaluating it NSpectrumSamples times.

⟨*Fresnel Inline Functions*⟩ +≡
```
SampledSpectrum FrComplex(Float cosTheta_i, SampledSpectrum eta,
                          SampledSpectrum k) {
    SampledSpectrum result;
    for (int i = 0; i < NSpectrumSamples; ++i)
        result[i] = FrComplex(cosTheta_i,
                        pstd::complex<Float>(eta[i], k[i]));
    return result;
}
```

9.4 CONDUCTOR BRDF

Having described the relevant physical principles, we now turn to the implementation of a BRDF that models specular reflection from an interface between a dielectric (e.g., air or water) and a conductor (e.g., a polished metal surface). We initially focus on the smooth case, and later generalize the implementation to rough interfaces in Section 9.6.

⟨*ConductorBxDF Definition*⟩ ≡
```
class ConductorBxDF {
  public:
    ⟨ConductorBxDF Public Methods 561⟩
  private:
    ⟨ConductorBxDF Private Members 561⟩
};
```

The internal state of the ConductorBxDF consists of the real (eta) and imaginary (k) component of the index of refraction. Furthermore, the implementation requires a microfacet distribution that statistically describes its roughness. The TrowbridgeReitzDistribution class handles the details here. The constructor, not included here, takes these fields as input and stores them in the ConductorBxDF instance.

⟨*ConductorBxDF Private Members*⟩ ≡   560
```
TrowbridgeReitzDistribution mfDistrib;
SampledSpectrum eta, k;
```

We will sidestep all discussion of microfacets for the time being and only cover the *effectively smooth* case in this section, where the surface is either perfectly smooth or so close to it that it can be modeled as such. The `TrowbridgeReitzDistribution` provides an `EffectivelySmooth()` method that indicates this case, in which the microfacet distribution plays no further role. The `ConductorBxDF::Flags()` method returns `BxDFFlags` accordingly.

⟨*ConductorBxDF Public Methods*⟩ ≡   560
```
BxDFFlags Flags() const {
    return mfDistrib.EffectivelySmooth() ? BxDFFlags::SpecularReflection :
        BxDFFlags::GlossyReflection;
}
```

The conductor BRDF builds on two physical ideas: the law of specular reflection assigns a specific reflected direction to each ray, and the Fresnel equations determine the portion of reflected light. Any remaining light refracts into the conductor, where it is rapidly absorbed and converted into heat.

Let $F_r(\omega)$ denote the unpolarized Fresnel reflectance of a given direction ω (which only depends on the angle θ that this direction makes with the surface normal $\mathbf{n}$). Because the law of specular reflection states that $\theta_r = \theta_o$, we have $F_r(\omega_r) = F_r(\omega_o)$. We thus require a BRDF f_r such that

$$L_o(\omega_o) = \int_{\mathcal{H}^2(\mathbf{n})} f_r(\omega_o, \omega_i)\, L_i(\omega_i)\, |\cos\theta_i|\, d\omega_i = F_r(\omega_r)\, L_i(\omega_r),$$

where $\omega_r = R(\omega_o, \mathbf{n})$ is the specular reflection vector for ω_o reflected about the surface normal $\mathbf{n}$. Such a BRDF can be constructed using the Dirac delta distribution that represents an infinitely peaked signal. Recall from Section 8.1 that the delta distribution has the useful property that

$$\int f(x)\, \delta(x - x_0)\, dx = f(x_0).$$ [9.8]

A first guess might be to use delta functions to restrict the incident direction to the specular reflection direction ω_r. This would yield a BRDF of

$$f_r(\omega_o, \omega_i) = \delta(\omega_i - \omega_r)\, F_r(\omega_i).$$

Although this seems appealing, plugging it into the scattering equation, Equation (4.14), reveals a problem:

$$L_o(\omega_o) = \int_{\mathcal{H}^2(\mathbf{n})} \delta(\omega_i - \omega_r)\, F_r(\omega_i)\, L_i(\omega_i)\, |\cos\theta_i|\, d\omega_i$$
$$= F_r(\omega_r)\, L_i(\omega_r)\, |\cos\theta_r|.$$

This is not correct because it contains an extra factor of $\cos\theta_r$. However, we can divide out this factor to find the correct BRDF for perfect specular reflection:

$$f_r(\mathrm{p}, \omega_o, \omega_i) = F_r(\omega_r)\frac{\delta(\omega_i - \omega_r)}{|\cos\theta_r|}.$$ [9.9]

The `Sample_f()` method of the `ConductorBxDF` method implements Equation (9.9).

⟨*ConductorBxDF Public Methods*⟩ +≡   **560**
```
pstd::optional<BSDFSample>
Sample_f(Vector3f wo, Float uc, Point2f u, TransportMode mode,
        BxDFReflTransFlags sampleFlags = BxDFReflTransFlags::All) const {
    if (!(sampleFlags & BxDFReflTransFlags::Reflection)) return {};
    if (mfDistrib.EffectivelySmooth()) {
        ⟨Sample perfect specular conductor BRDF 562⟩
    }
    ⟨Sample rough conductor BRDF 585⟩
}
```

Note that Dirac delta distributions require special handling compared to standard functions. In particular, the probability of successfully drawing a point on the peak is zero, unless the sampling probability is also a delta distribution. In other words, the distribution must be used to determine the sample location.

Because the surface normal $\mathbf{n}_g$ is (0, 0, 1) in the reflection coordinate system, the equation for the perfect specular reflection direction, (9.1), simplifies substantially; the x and y components only need to be negated to compute this direction and there is no need to call Reflect() (the rough case will require this function, however).

⟨*Sample perfect specular conductor BRDF*⟩ ≡   **562**
```
Vector3f wi(-wo.x, -wo.y, wo.z);
SampledSpectrum f = FrComplex(AbsCosTheta(wi), eta, k) / AbsCosTheta(wi);
return BSDFSample(f, wi, 1, BxDFFlags::SpecularReflection);
```

The PDF value in the returned BSDFSample is set to one, as per the discussion of delta distribution BSDFs in Section 9.1.2. Following the other conventions outlined in that section, BRDF evaluation always returns zero in the smooth case, since the specular peak is considered unreachable by other sampling methods.

⟨*ConductorBxDF Public Methods*⟩ +≡   **560**
```
SampledSpectrum f(Vector3f wo, Vector3f wi, TransportMode mode) const {
    if (!SameHemisphere(wo, wi)) return {};
    if (mfDistrib.EffectivelySmooth()) return {};
    ⟨Evaluate rough conductor BRDF 585⟩
}
```

The same convention also applies to the PDF() method.

⟨*ConductorBxDF Public Methods*⟩ +≡   **560**
```
Float PDF(Vector3f wo, Vector3f wi, TransportMode mode,
          BxDFReflTransFlags sampleFlags) const {
    if (!(sampleFlags & BxDFReflTransFlags::Reflection)) return 0;
    if (!SameHemisphere(wo, wi)) return 0;
    if (mfDistrib.EffectivelySmooth()) return 0;
    ⟨Evaluate sampling PDF of rough conductor BRDF 584⟩
}
```

The missing three fragments—⟨*Sample rough conductor BRDF*⟩, ⟨*Evaluate rough conductor BRDF*⟩, and ⟨*Evaluate sampling PDF of rough conductor BRDF*⟩—will be presented in Section 9.6.

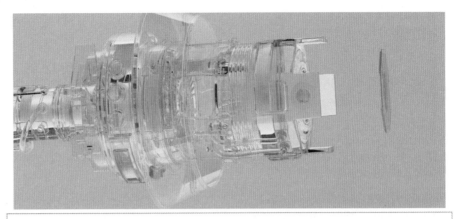

Figure 9.14: When the BRDF for specular reflection and the BTDF for specular transmission are modulated with the Fresnel formula for dielectrics, the realistic angle-dependent variation of the amount of reflection and transmission gives a visually accurate representation of the glass. *(Scene courtesy of Beeple.)*

9.5 DIELECTRIC BSDF

In the dielectric case, the relative index of refraction is real-valued, and specular transmission must be considered in addition to reflection. The `DielectricBxDF` handles this scenario for smooth and rough interfaces.

Figure 9.14 shows an image of an abstract model using this BxDF to model a glass material.

⟨*DielectricBxDF Definition*⟩ ≡
```
class DielectricBxDF {
  public:
    ⟨DielectricBxDF Public Methods 563⟩
  private:
    ⟨DielectricBxDF Private Members 563⟩
};
```

The constructor takes a single `Float`-valued `eta` parameter and a microfacet distribution `mfDistrib`. Spectrally varying IORs that disperse light into different directions are handled by randomly sampling a single wavelength to follow and then instantiating a corresponding `DielectricBxDF`. Section 10.5.1 discusses this topic in more detail.

⟨*DielectricBxDF Public Methods*⟩ ≡   563
```
DielectricBxDF(Float eta, TrowbridgeReitzDistribution mfDistrib)
    : eta(eta), mfDistrib(mfDistrib) {}
```

⟨*DielectricBxDF Private Members*⟩ ≡   563
```
Float eta;
TrowbridgeReitzDistribution mfDistrib;
```

The `Flags()` method handles three different cases. The first is when the dielectric interface is *index-matched*—that is, with an equal IOR on both sides (in which case $\eta = 1$)—and light is only transmitted. Otherwise, in the other two cases, the BSDF has both reflected and transmitted components. In both of these cases, the `TrowbridgeReitzDistribution`'s `EffectivelySmooth()` method differentiates between specular and glossy scattering.

⟨*DielectricBxDF Public Methods*⟩ +≡   **563**
```
BxDFFlags Flags() const {
    BxDFFlags flags = (eta == 1) ? BxDFFlags::Transmission :
                      (BxDFFlags::Reflection | BxDFFlags::Transmission);
    return flags | (mfDistrib.EffectivelySmooth() ? BxDFFlags::Specular
                                                  : BxDFFlags::Glossy);
}
```

The Sample_f() method must choose between sampling perfect specular reflection or transmission. As before, we postpone handling of rough surfaces and only discuss the perfect specular case for now.

⟨*DielectricBxDF Method Definitions*⟩ ≡
```
pstd::optional<BSDFSample>
DielectricBxDF::Sample_f(Vector3f wo, Float uc, Point2f u,
        TransportMode mode, BxDFReflTransFlags sampleFlags) const {
    if (eta == 1 || mfDistrib.EffectivelySmooth()) {
        ⟨Sample perfect specular dielectric BSDF 564⟩
    } else {
        ⟨Sample rough dielectric BSDF 590⟩
    }
}
```

Since dielectrics are characterized by both reflection and transmission, the sampling scheme must randomly choose between these two components, which influences the density function. While any discrete distribution is in principle admissible, an efficient approach from a Monte Carlo variance standpoint is to sample according to the contribution that these two components make—in other words, proportional to the Fresnel reflectance R and the complementary transmittance 1-R. Figure 9.15 shows the benefit of sampling in this way compared to an equal split between reflection and transmission.

⟨*Sample perfect specular dielectric BSDF*⟩ ≡   **564**
```
Float R = FrDielectric(CosTheta(wo), eta), T = 1 - R;
⟨Compute probabilities pr and pt for sampling reflection and transmission 564⟩
if (uc < pr / (pr + pt)) {
    ⟨Sample perfect specular dielectric BRDF 565⟩
} else {
    ⟨Sample perfect specular dielectric BTDF 566⟩
}
```

Because BSDF components can be selectively enabled or disabled via the sampleFlags argument, the component choice is based on adjusted probabilities pr and pt that take this into account.

⟨*Compute probabilities pr and pt for sampling reflection and transmission*⟩ ≡   **564, 568, 587, 590**
```
Float pr = R, pt = T;
if (!(sampleFlags & BxDFReflTransFlags::Reflection)) pr = 0;
if (!(sampleFlags & BxDFReflTransFlags::Transmission)) pt = 0;
if (pr == 0 && pt == 0)
    return {};
```

In the most common case where both reflection and transmission are sampled, the BSDF value and sample probability contain the common factor F or T, which cancels when their

(a)

(b)

Figure 9.15: Glass Object Rendered Using the DielectricBxDF. (a) Choosing between specular reflection and transmission with equal probability at each scattering event. (b) Choosing with probability based on the value of the Fresnel equations, as is implemented in the Sample_f() method. Choosing between scattering modes with probability proportional to their contribution significantly reduces error by following fewer paths with low contributions.

ratio is taken. Thus, all sampled rays end up making the same contribution, and the Fresnel factor manifests in the relative proportion of reflected and transmitted rays.

Putting all of this together, the only change in the following code compared to the analogous fragment ⟨*Sample perfect specular conductor BRDF*⟩ is the incorporation of the discrete probability of the sample.

⟨*Sample perfect specular dielectric BRDF*⟩ ≡   564, 568
```
Vector3f wi(-wo.x, -wo.y, wo.z);
SampledSpectrum fr(R / AbsCosTheta(wi));
return BSDFSample(fr, wi, pr / (pr + pt), BxDFFlags::SpecularReflection);
```

Specular transmission is handled along similar lines, though using the refracted ray direction for wi. The equation for the corresponding BTDF is similar to the case for perfect specular reflection, Equation (9.9), though there is an additional subtle technical detail: depending on the IOR η, refraction either compresses or expands radiance in the angular domain, and the implementation must scale ft to account for this. This correction does not change the amount of radiant power in the scene—rather, it models how the same power is contained in a different solid angle. The details of this step differ depending on the direction of propagation in bidirectional rendering algorithms, and we therefore defer the corresponding fragment ⟨*Account for non-symmetry with transmission to different medium*⟩ to Section 9.5.2.

⟨*Sample perfect specular dielectric BTDF*⟩ ≡   **564**
```
    ⟨Compute ray direction for specular transmission 566⟩
    SampledSpectrum ft(T / AbsCosTheta(wi));
    ⟨Account for non-symmetry with transmission to different medium 571⟩
    return BSDFSample(ft, wi, pt / (pr + pt),
                      BxDFFlags::SpecularTransmission, etap);
```

The function Refract() computes the refracted direction wi via Snell's law, which fails in the case of total internal reflection. In principle, this should never happen: the transmission case is sampled with probability T, which is zero in the case of total internal reflection. However, due to floating-point rounding errors, inconsistencies can occasionally arise here. We handle this corner case by returning an invalid sample.

⟨*Compute ray direction for specular transmission*⟩ ≡   **566**
```
    Vector3f wi;
    Float etap;
    bool valid = Refract(wo, Normal3f(0, 0, 1), eta, &etap, &wi);
    if (!valid) return {};
```

As with the ConductorBxDF, zero is returned from the f() method if the interface is smooth and all scattering is perfect specular.

⟨*DielectricBxDF Method Definitions*⟩ +≡
```
    SampledSpectrum DielectricBxDF::f(Vector3f wo, Vector3f wi,
                                      TransportMode mode) const {
        if (eta == 1 || mfDistrib.EffectivelySmooth())
            return SampledSpectrum(0.f);
        ⟨Evaluate rough dielectric BSDF 589⟩
    }
```

Also, a PDF value of zero is returned if the BSDF is represented using delta distributions.

⟨*DielectricBxDF Method Definitions*⟩ +≡
```
    Float DielectricBxDF::PDF(Vector3f wo, Vector3f wi, TransportMode mode,
            BxDFReflTransFlags sampleFlags) const {
        if (eta == 1 || mfDistrib.EffectivelySmooth())
            return 0;
        ⟨Evaluate sampling PDF of rough dielectric BSDF 587⟩
    }
```

The missing three fragments—⟨*Sample rough dielectric BSDF*⟩, ⟨*Evaluate rough dielectric BSDF*⟩, and ⟨*Evaluate sampling PDF of rough dielectric BSDF*⟩—will be presented in Section 9.7.

9.5.1 THIN DIELECTRIC BSDF

Dielectric interfaces rarely occur in isolation: a particularly common configuration involves two nearby index of refraction changes that are smooth, locally parallel, and mutually reciprocal—that is, with relative IOR η and a corresponding interface with the inverse $1/\eta$. Examples include plate- and acrylic glass in windows or plastic foil used to seal and preserve food.

This important special case is referred to as a *thin dielectric* due to the spatial proximity of the two interfaces compared to the larger lateral dimensions. When incident light splits into a reflected and a transmitted component with two separate interfaces, it is scattered in a recursive process that traps some of the light within the two interfaces (though this amount progressively decays as it undergoes an increasing number of reflections).

While the internal scattering process within a general dielectric may be daunting, simple analytic solutions can fully describe what happens inside such a thin dielectric—that is, an interface pair satisfying the above simplifying conditions. pbrt provides a specialized BSDF named ThinDielectricBxDF that exploits these insights to efficiently represent an infinite number of internal interactions. It further allows such surfaces to be represented with a single interface, saving the ray intersection expense of tracing ray paths between the two surfaces.

⟨*ThinDielectricBxDF Definition*⟩ ≡
```
class ThinDielectricBxDF {
  public:
    ⟨ThinDielectricBxDF Public Methods 567⟩
  private:
    Float eta;
};
```

The only parameter to this BxDF is the relative index of refraction of the interior medium.

⟨*ThinDielectricBxDF Public Methods*⟩ ≡   567
```
ThinDielectricBxDF(Float eta) : eta(eta) {}
```

Since this BxDF models only perfect specular scattering, both its f() and PDF() methods just return zero and are therefore not included here.

The theory of the thin dielectric BSDF goes back to seminal work by Stokes (1860), who investigated light propagation in stacks of glass plates. Figure 9.16 illustrates the most common case involving only a single glass plate: an incident light ray (red) reflects and transmits in proportions R and $T = 1 - R$. When the transmitted ray encounters the bottom interface, reciprocity causes it to reflect and transmit according to the same proportions. This process repeats in perpetuity.

Of course, rays beyond the first interaction are displaced relative to the entrance point. Due to the assumption of a *thin* dielectric, this spatial shift is considered to be negligible; only the total amount of reflected or transmitted light matters. By making this simplification, it is possible to aggregate the effect of the infinite number of scattering events into a simple modification of the reflectance and transmittance factors.

Consider the paths that are reflected out from the top layer. Their aggregate reflectance R' is given by a geometric series that can be converted into an explicit form:

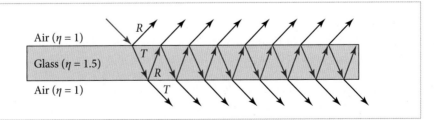

Figure 9.16: Light Paths in a Thin Plane-Parallel Dielectric Medium. An incident light ray (red) gives rise to an infinite internal scattering process that occurs within the glass plate (blue). At each scattering event, some fraction of the light manages to escape, causing a successive decay of the trapped energy.

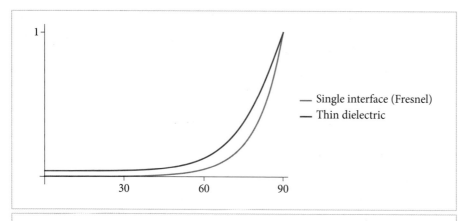

Figure 9.17: Reflectance of a Fresnel Interface and a Thin Dielectric. This plot compares the reflectance of a single dielectric interface with $\eta = 1.5$ as determined by the Fresnel equations (9.6) to that of a matching thin dielectric according to Equation (9.10).

$$R' = R + TRT + TRRRT + \cdots = R + \frac{T^2 R}{1 - R^2}. \tag{9.10}$$

A similar series gives how much light is transmitted, but it can be just as easily computed as $T' = 1 - R'$, due to energy conservation. Figure 9.17 plots R' and R as a function of incident angle θ. The second interface has the effect of increasing the overall amount of reflection compared to a single Fresnel interaction.

The Sample_f() method computes the R' and T' coefficients and then computes probabilities for sampling reflection and transmission, just as the DielectricBxDF did, reusing the corresponding code fragment.

⟨*ThinDielectricBxDF Public Methods*⟩ +≡   **567**
```
pstd::optional<BSDFSample>
Sample_f(Vector3f wo, Float uc, Point2f u, TransportMode mode,
        BxDFReflTransFlags sampleFlags) const {
    Float R = FrDielectric(AbsCosTheta(wo), eta), T = 1 - R;
    ⟨Compute R and T accounting for scattering between interfaces 568⟩
    ⟨Compute probabilities pr and pt for sampling reflection and transmission 564⟩
    if (uc < pr / (pr + pt)) {
        ⟨Sample perfect specular dielectric BRDF 565⟩
    } else {
        ⟨Sample perfect specular transmission at thin dielectric interface 569⟩
    }
}
```

The updated reflection and transmission coefficients are easily computed using Equation (9.10), though care must be taken to avoid a division by zero in the case of $R = 1$.

⟨*Compute R and T accounting for scattering between interfaces*⟩ ≡   **568**
```
if (R < 1) {
    R += Sqr(T) * R / (1 - Sqr(R));
    T = 1 - R;
}
```

The `DielectricBxDF` fragment that samples perfect specular reflection is also reused in this method's implementation, inheriting the computed R value. The transmission case slightly deviates from the `DielectricBxDF`, as the transmitted direction is simply the negation of wo.

⟨*Sample perfect specular transmission at thin dielectric interface*⟩ ≡   568
```
Vector3f wi = -wo;
SampledSpectrum ft(T / AbsCosTheta(wi));
return BSDFSample(ft, wi, pt / (pr + pt), BxDFFlags::SpecularTransmission);
```

∗ 9.5.2 NON-SYMMETRIC SCATTERING AND REFRACTION

All physically based BRDFs are symmetric: the incident and outgoing directions can be interchanged without changing the function's value. However, the same is not generally true for BTDFs. Non-symmetry with BTDFs is due to the fact that when light refracts into a material with a higher index of refraction than the incident medium's index of refraction, energy is compressed into a smaller set of angles (and vice versa, when going in the opposite direction). This effect is easy to see yourself, for instance, by looking at the sky from underwater in a quiet outdoor swimming pool. Because no light can be refracted above the critical angle (∼ 48.6° for water), the incident hemisphere of light is squeezed into a considerably smaller subset of the hemisphere, which covers the remaining set of angles (Figure 9.18). Radiance along rays that do refract therefore must increase so that energy is preserved when light passes through the interface.

More formally, consider incident radiance arriving at the boundary between two media, with indices of refraction η_i and η_o (Figure 9.19). Assuming for now that all the incident light is transmitted, the amount of transmitted differential flux is then

$$d^2\Phi_o = d^2\Phi_i.$$

If we use the definition of radiance, Equation (4.3), we equivalently have

$$L_o \cos\theta_o \, dA \, d\omega_o = L_i \cos\theta_i \, dA \, \omega_i.$$

Figure 9.18: Snell's Window. If one looks upward when underwater in a swimming pool, the sky is only visible through a circular window because no light is refracted beyond the critical angle. Outside of the window, only the reflection of the pool bottom is seen.

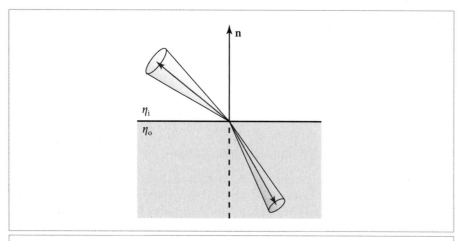

Figure 9.19: The amount of transmitted radiance at the boundary between media with different indices of refraction is scaled by the squared ratio of the two indices of refraction. Intuitively, this can be understood as the result of the radiance's differential solid angle being compressed or expanded as a result of transmission.

Expanding the solid angles to spherical angles gives

$$L_o \cos \theta_o \, dA \sin \theta_o \, d\theta_o \, d\phi_o = L_i \cos \theta_i \, dA \sin \theta_i \, d\theta_i \, d\phi_i. \tag{9.11}$$

Differentiating Snell's law, Equation (9.2), with respect to θ gives the useful relation

$$\eta_o \cos \theta_o \, d\theta_o = \eta_i \cos \theta_i \, d\theta_i,$$

or

$$\frac{\cos \theta_o \, d\theta_o}{\cos \theta_i \, d\theta_i} = \frac{\eta_i}{\eta_o}.$$

Substituting both Snell's law and this relationship into Equation (9.11) and then simplifying, we have

$$L_o \, \eta_i^2 \, d\phi_o = L_i \, \eta_o^2 \, d\phi_i.$$

Finally, $d\phi_i = d\phi_o$, which gives the final relationship between incident and transmitted radiance:

$$L_o = L_i \frac{\eta_o^2}{\eta_i^2}. \tag{9.12}$$

The symmetry relationship satisfied by a BTDF is thus

$$\eta_o^2 f_t(p, \omega_o, \omega_i) = \eta_i^2 f_t(p, \omega_i, \omega_o). \tag{9.13}$$

Non-symmetric scattering can be particularly problematic for bidirectional light transport algorithms that sample light paths starting both from the camera and from the lights. If non-symmetry is not accounted for, then such algorithms may produce incorrect results, since the design of such algorithms is fundamentally based on the principle of symmetry.[3]

We will say that light paths sampled starting from the lights carry *importance* while paths starting from the camera carry radiance. These terms correspond to the quantity that is

---

3   See the online edition of the book for an additional chapter devoted to bidirectional light transport algorithms.

recorded at a path's starting point. With importance transport, the incident and outgoing direction arguments of the BSDFs will be (incorrectly) reversed unless special precautions are taken.

We thus define the *adjoint BSDF* f^*, whose only role is to evaluate the original BSDF with swapped arguments:

$$f^*(\mathrm{p}, \omega_\mathrm{o}, \omega_\mathrm{i}) = f(\mathrm{p}, \omega_\mathrm{i}, \omega_\mathrm{o}).$$

All sampling steps based on importance transport use the adjoint form of the BSDF rather than its original version. Most BSDFs in pbrt are symmetric so that there is no actual difference between f and f^*. However, non-symmetric cases require additional attention.

The `TransportMode` enumeration is used to inform such non-symmetric BSDFs about the transported quantity so that they can correctly switch between the adjoint and non-adjoint forms.

⟨*TransportMode Definition*⟩ ≡
```
enum class TransportMode { Radiance, Importance };
```

The adjoint BTDF is then

$$f_\mathrm{t}^*(\mathrm{p}, \omega_\mathrm{o}, \omega_\mathrm{i}) = f_\mathrm{t}(\mathrm{p}, \omega_\mathrm{i}, \omega_\mathrm{o}) = \frac{\eta_\mathrm{i}^2}{\eta_\mathrm{o}^2} f_\mathrm{t}(\mathrm{p}, \omega_\mathrm{o}, \omega_\mathrm{i}),$$

which effectively cancels out the scale factor in Equation (9.12).

With these equations, we can now define the remaining missing piece in the implementation of the `DielectricBxDF` evaluation and sampling methods. Whenever radiance is transported over a refractive boundary, we apply the scale factor from Equation (9.12). For importance transport, we use the adjoint BTDF, which lacks the scaling factor due to the combination of Equations (9.12) and (9.13).

⟨*Account for non-symmetry with transmission to different medium*⟩ ≡   566, 590, 591
```
if (mode == TransportMode::Radiance)
    ft /= Sqr(etap);
```

9.6 ROUGHNESS USING MICROFACET THEORY

The preceding discussion of the `ConductorBxDF` and `DielectricBxDF` only considered the perfect specular case, where the interface between materials was assumed to be ideally smooth and devoid of any roughness or other surface imperfections. However, many real-world materials are rough at a microscopic scale, which affects the way in which they reflect or transmit light.

We will now turn to a generalization of these BxDFs using *microfacet theory*, which models rough surfaces as a collection of small surface patches denoted as *microfacets*. These microfacets are assumed to be individually very small so that they cannot be resolved by the camera. Yet, despite their small size, they can have a profound impact on the angular distribution of scattered light. Figure 9.20 shows cross sections of a relatively rough surface and a much smoother microfacet surface. We will use the term *macrosurface* to describe the original coarse surface (e.g., as represented by a Shape) and *microsurface* to describe the fine-scale geometry based on microfacets.

It is worth noting that pbrt can in principle already render rough surfaces without resorting to microfacet theory: users could simply create extremely high-resolution triangular meshes

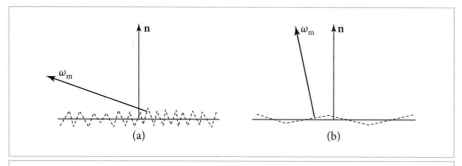

Figure 9.20: Microfacet surface models are often described by a function that gives the distribution of microfacet normals ω_m with respect to the surface normal $\mathbf{n}$. (a) The greater the variation of microfacet normals, the rougher the surface is. (b) Smooth surfaces have relatively little variation of microfacet normals.

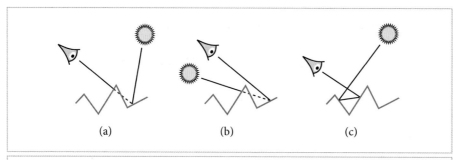

Figure 9.21: Three Important Geometric Effects to Consider with Microfacet Reflection Models. (a) *Masking*: the microfacet of interest is not visible to the viewer due to occlusion by another microfacet. (b) *Shadowing*: analogously, light does not reach the microfacet. (c) *Interreflection*: light bounces among the microfacets before reaching the viewer.

containing such micro-scale surface variations and render them using perfect specular BxDFs. There are two fundamental problems with such an approach:

- *Storage and ray tracing efficiency:* Representing micro-scale roughness using triangular geometry would require staggeringly large triangle budgets. The overheads to store and ray trace such large scenes are prohibitive.
- *Monte Carlo sampling efficiency:* A fundamental issue with perfect specular scattering distributions is that they contain Dirac delta terms, which preclude BSDF evaluation (their f() method returns zero, making BSDF sampling the only supported operation). This aspect disables *light sampling* strategies (Section 12.1), which are crucial for efficiency in Monte Carlo rendering.

A key insight of microfacet theory is that large numbers of microfacets can be efficiently modeled statistically, since it is only their aggregate behavior that determines the observed scattering. (A similar statistical physics approach is used to avoid the costly storage of vast numbers of small particles comprising participating media in Chapter 11.) This approach addresses both of the above issues: BSDF models based on microfacet theory do not require explicit storage of the microgeometry, and they replace the infinitely peaked Dirac delta terms with smooth distributions that enable more efficient Monte Carlo sampling.

Several factors related to the geometry of the microfacets affect how they scatter light (Figure 9.21): for example, a microfacet may be occluded ("masked") or lie in the shadow of a neighboring microfacet, and incident light may interreflect among microfacets. Widely used microfacet BSDFs ignore interreflection and model the remaining masking and shadowing effects using statistical approximations with efficient evaluation procedures.

The two main components of microfacet models are a representation of the statistical distribution of facets and a BSDF that describes how light scatters from an individual microfacet. For the latter part, pbrt supports perfect specular conductors and dielectrics, though other choices are in principle also possible. Given these two ingredients, the aggregate BSDF arising from the microsurface can be determined.

9.6.1 THE MICROFACET DISTRIBUTION

Microgeometry principally affects scattering via variation of the surface normal, which is a consequence of the central role of the surface normal in Snell's law and the law of specular reflection. Under the assumption that the light source and observer are distant with respect to the scale of the microfacets, the precise surface profile has a lesser effect on masking and shadowing that we will study in Section 9.6.2. For now, our focus is on the *microfacet distribution*, which represents roughness in terms of its effect on the surface normal.

Let us denote a small region of a macrosurface as dA. The corresponding microsurface dA_μ is obtained by displacing the macrosurface along its normal $\mathbf{n}$, which means that perpendicular projection of the microsurface exactly covers the macrosurface:

$$\int_{dA_\mu} (\omega_m(p) \cdot \mathbf{n}) \, dp = \int_{dA} dp, \qquad (9.14)$$

where $\omega_m(p)$ specifies the microfacet normal at p. However, tracking the orientation of vast numbers of microfacets would be impractical as previously discussed.

We therefore turn to a statistical approach: the *microfacet distribution function* $D(\omega_m)$ gives the relative differential area of microfacets with the surface normal ω_m. For example, a perfectly smooth surface has a Dirac delta peak in the direction of the original surface normal—that is, $D(\omega_m) = \delta(\omega_m - \mathbf{n})$. The function is generally expressed in the standard reflection coordinate system with $\mathbf{n} = (0, 0, 1)$.

Cast into the directional domain, Equation (9.14) provides a useful normalization condition ensuring that a particular microfacet distribution is physically plausible, as illustrated in Figure 9.22.

$$\int_{\mathcal{H}^2(\mathbf{n})} D(\omega_m) \, (\omega_m \cdot \mathbf{n}) \, d\omega_m = \int_{\mathcal{H}^2(\mathbf{n})} D(\omega_m) \cos \theta_m \, d\omega_m = 1. \qquad (9.15)$$

The most common type of microfacet distribution is *isotropic*, which also leads to an isotropic aggregate BSDF. Recall that the local scattering behavior of an isotropic BSDF does not change when the surface is rotated about the macroscopic surface normal. In the isotropic case, a spherical coordinate parameterization $\omega_m = (\theta_m, \phi_m)$ yields a distribution that only depends on the elevation angle θ_m.

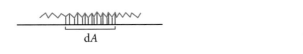

dA

Figure 9.22: Given a differential area on a surface dA, the microfacet normal distribution function $D(\omega_m)$ must be normalized such that the projected surface area of the microfacets above the area is equal to dA.

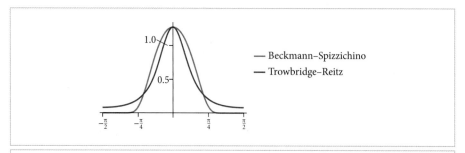

Figure 9.23: Graphs of isotropic Beckmann–Spizzichino and Trowbridge–Reitz microfacet distribution functions as a function of θ for $\alpha = 0.5$. Note that Trowbridge–Reitz has higher tails at larger values of θ.

In contrast, an anisotropic microfacet distribution also depends on the azimuth ϕ_{m} to capture directional variation in the surface roughness. Many real-world materials are anisotropic: for example, rolled or milled steel surfaces feature grooves that are aligned with the direction of extrusion. Rotating a flat sheet of such material about the surface normal results in noticeable variation—for example, in the reflection profile of indirectly observed light sources. Brushed metal is an extreme case: its microfacet distribution varies from almost a single direction to almost uniform over the hemisphere.

Many functional representations of microfacet distributions have been proposed over the years. Geometric analysis of a truncated ellipsoid leads to one of the most widely used distributions proposed by Trowbridge and Reitz (1975), in which the conceptual microsurface is composed of vast numbers of ellipsoidal bumps.[4] Scaled along its different semi-axes, an ellipsoid can take on a variety of configurations including sphere-, pancake-, and cigar-shaped surfaces. It is enough to study the density of surface normals on a single representative ellipsoid, which has an analytic solution:

$$D(\omega_{\mathrm{m}}) = \frac{1}{\pi \, \alpha_x \, \alpha_y \, \cos^4 \theta_{\mathrm{m}} \left(1 + \tan^2 \theta_{\mathrm{m}} \left(\frac{\cos^2 \phi_{\mathrm{m}}}{\alpha_x^2} + \frac{\sin^2 \phi_{\mathrm{m}}}{\alpha_y^2} \right) \right)^2}. \qquad [9.16]$$

This equation assumes that the semi-axes of the ellipsoid are aligned with the shading frame, and the reciprocals of the two variables $1/\alpha_x$, $1/\alpha_y > 0$ encode a scale transformation applied along the two tangential axes. When $\alpha_x, \alpha_y \approx 0$, the ellipsoid has been stretched to such a degree that it essentially collapses into a flat surface, and the aggregate BSDF approximates a perfect specular material. For larger values (e.g., $\alpha_x, \alpha_y \approx 0.3$), the ellipsoidal bumps introduce significant normal variation that blurs the directional distribution of reflected and transmitted light. When $\alpha_x = \alpha_y$, the azimuth dependence drops out, and the model becomes isotropic.

A characteristic feature of the Trowbridge–Reitz model compared to other microfacet distributions is its long tails: the density of microfacets decays comparably slowly as ω_{m} approaches grazing configurations ($\theta_m \to 90°$). This matches the properties of many real-world surfaces well. See Figure 9.23 for a graph of it and another commonly used microfacet distribution function.

The `TrowbridgeReitzDistribution` class encapsulates the state and functionality needed to use this microfacet distribution in a Monte Carlo renderer.

---

4   The same model was also independently derived by Walter et al. (2007), who dubbed it "GGX."

⟨*TrowbridgeReitzDistribution Definition*⟩ ≡
```
class TrowbridgeReitzDistribution {
  public:
    ⟨TrowbridgeReitzDistribution Public Methods 575⟩
  private:
    ⟨TrowbridgeReitzDistribution Private Members 575⟩
};
```

⟨*TrowbridgeReitzDistribution Public Methods*⟩ ≡   **575**
```
TrowbridgeReitzDistribution(Float alpha_x, Float alpha_y)
    : alpha_x(alpha_x), alpha_y(alpha_y) {}
```

⟨*TrowbridgeReitzDistribution Private Members*⟩ ≡   **575**
```
Float alpha_x, alpha_y;
```

The `D()` method is a fairly direct transcription of Equation (9.16) with some additional handling of numerical edge cases.

⟨*TrowbridgeReitzDistribution Public Methods*⟩ +≡   **575**
```
Float D(Vector3f wm) const {
    Float tan2Theta = Tan2Theta(wm);
    if (IsInf(tan2Theta)) return 0;
    Float cos4Theta = Sqr(Cos2Theta(wm));
    Float e = tan2Theta * (Sqr(CosPhi(wm) / alpha_x) +
                           Sqr(SinPhi(wm) / alpha_y));
    return 1 / (Pi * alpha_x * alpha_y * cos4Theta * Sqr(1 + e));
}
```

Even with those precautions, numerical issues involving infinite or not-a-number values tend to arise at very low roughnesses. It is better to treat such surfaces as perfectly smooth and fall back to the previously discussed specialized implementations. The `EffectivelySmooth()` method tests the α values for this case.

⟨*TrowbridgeReitzDistribution Public Methods*⟩ +≡   **575**
```
bool EffectivelySmooth() const {
    return std::max(alpha_x, alpha_y) < 1e-3f;
}
```

9.6.2 THE MASKING FUNCTION

A microfacet distribution alone is not enough to construct a valid energy-conserving BSDF. Observed from a specific direction, only a subset of microfacets is visible, which must be considered to avoid non-physical energy gains. In particular, microfacets may be *masked* because they are backfacing, or due to occlusion by other microfacets. Our approach is once more to capture this effect in a statistically averaged manner instead of tracking the properties of an actual microsurface.

Recall Equation (9.15), which stated that the micro- and macrosurfaces occupy the same area under perpendicular projection along the surface normal **n**. The *masking function* $G_1(\omega, \omega_m)$ enables a generalization of this statement to other projection directions ω. We will shortly discuss how G_1 is derived and simply postulate its existence for now. The function specifies the fraction of microfacets with normal ω_m that are visible from direction ω, and it therefore satisfies $0 \le G_1(\omega, \omega_m) \le 1$ for all arguments.

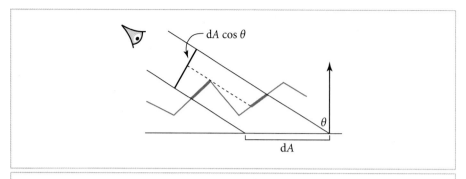

Figure 9.24: As seen from a viewer or a light source, a differential area on the surface has area $dA \cos \theta$, where $\cos \theta$ is the angle of the incident direction with the surface normal. The projected surface area of visible microfacets (thick lines) must be equal to $dA \cos \theta$ as well; the masking function G_1 gives the fraction of the total microfacet area over dA that is visible in the given direction.

Figure 9.24 illustrates the oblique generalization of Equation (9.15), whose left hand side integrates over microfacets and computes the area of their perpendicular projection along ω. A maximum is taken to ignore backfacing microfacets, and G_1 accounts for masking by other facets. The right hand side captures the relative size of the macrosurface, which shrinks by a factor of $\cos \theta$.

$$\int_{\mathcal{H}^2(\mathbf{n})} D(\omega_{\mathrm{m}})\, G_1(\omega, \omega_{\mathrm{m}}) \max(0, \omega \cdot \omega_{\mathrm{m}})\, d\omega_{\mathrm{m}} = \omega \cdot \mathbf{n} = \cos \theta. \qquad [9.17]$$

We expect that physically plausible combinations of microfacet distribution $D(\omega_{\mathrm{m}})$ (the Trowbridge–Reitz distribution in our case) and masking function $G_1(\omega, \omega_{\mathrm{m}})$ should satisfy this equation. Unfortunately, the microfacet distribution alone does not impose enough conditions to imply a specific $G_1(\omega, \omega_{\mathrm{m}})$; an infinite family of functions could fulfill the constraint in Equation (9.17). More information about the specific surface height profile is necessary to narrow down this large set of possibilities.

At this point, an approximation is often taken: if the height and normals of different points on the surface are assumed to be *statistically independent*, the material conceptually turns from a connected surface into an opaque soup of little surface fragments that float in space (hence the name "microfacets"). A consequence of this simplification is that masking becomes independent of the microsurface normal ω_{m}, except for the constraint that backfacing facets are ignored ($\omega \cdot \omega_{\mathrm{m}} > 0$). The masking term can then be moved out of the integral of Equation (9.17):

$$G_1(\omega) \int_{\mathcal{H}^2(\mathbf{n})} D(\omega_{\mathrm{m}}) \max(0, \omega \cdot \omega_{\mathrm{m}})\, d\omega_{\mathrm{m}} = \cos \theta,$$

which can be rearranged to solve for $G_1(\omega)$:

$$G_1(\omega) = \frac{\cos \theta}{\int_{\mathcal{H}^2(\mathbf{n})} D(\omega_{\mathrm{m}}) \max(0, \omega \cdot \omega_{\mathrm{m}})\, d\omega_{\mathrm{m}}}. \qquad [9.18]$$

This is *Smith's approximation*. Despite the rather severe simplification, it has been found to be in good agreement with both brute-force simulation of scattering on randomly generated surface microstructures and real-world measurements.

The integral in Equation (9.18) has analytic solutions for various common choices of micro-facet distributions $D(\omega_{\mathrm{m}})$, including the Trowbridge–Reitz model. In practice, the masking function is often expressed in terms of an auxiliary function $\Lambda(\omega)$ that arises naturally when the derivation of masking is conducted in the slope domain. This has some benefits that we shall see shortly, and we therefore adopt the same approach that relates G_1 and Λ as follows:

$$G_1(\omega) = \frac{1}{1 + \Lambda(\omega)}. \qquad (9.19)$$

The Lambda() method computes this function.

⟨*TrowbridgeReitzDistribution Public Methods*⟩ +≡   575
```
    Float G1(Vector3f w) const { return 1 / (1 + Lambda(w)); }
```

Under the uncorrelated height assumption, $\Lambda(\omega)$ has the following analytic solution for the Trowbridge–Reitz distribution:

$$\Lambda(\omega) = \frac{\sqrt{1 + \alpha^2 \tan^2 \theta} - 1}{2}, \qquad (9.20)$$

where α denotes the isotropic surface roughness. An anisotropic generalization follows from the observation that anisotropy implies tangential scaling of the microsurface based on $1/\alpha_x$ and $1/\alpha_y$. A 1-dimensional ray ω that is not aligned with the *x*- or *y*-axis will observe a different scaling amount that lies between these extremes. The associated interpolated roughness is given by

$$\alpha = \sqrt{\alpha_x^2 \cos^2 \phi + \alpha_y^2 \sin^2 \phi}. \qquad (9.21)$$

Anisotropic masking reuses the isotropic Λ with this definition of α. The "Further Reading" section at the end of this chapter provides more details on these steps. The Lambda() function implements Equation (9.20) in the general case.

⟨*TrowbridgeReitzDistribution Public Methods*⟩ +≡   575
```
    Float Lambda(Vector3f w) const {
        Float tan2Theta = Tan2Theta(w);
        if (IsInf(tan2Theta)) return 0;
        Float alpha2 = Sqr(CosPhi(w) * alpha_x) + Sqr(SinPhi(w) * alpha_y);
        return (std::sqrt(1 + alpha2 * tan2Theta) - 1) / 2;
    }
```

Figure 9.25 compares the appearance of two spheres with an isotropic and an anisotropic microfacet model lit by a light source simulating a distant environment.

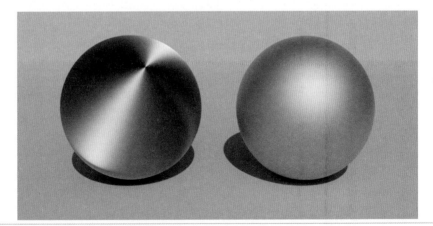

Figure 9.25: Spheres rendered with (left) an anisotropic microfacet distribution and (right) an isotropic distribution. Note the different specular highlight shapes from the anisotropic model. We have used spheres here instead of the dragon, since anisotropic models like these depend on a globally consistent set of tangent vectors over the surface to orient the direction of anisotropy in a reasonable way.

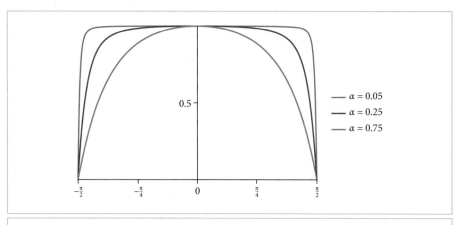

Figure 9.26: The Masking Function $G_1(\omega)$ **for the Trowbridge–Reitz Distribution.** Increasing surface roughness (higher α values) causes the function to fall off to zero more quickly.

Figure 9.26 shows a plot of the Trowbridge–Reitz $G_1(\omega)$ function for a few values of α. Observe how the function is close to one over much of the domain but falls to zero at grazing angles, where masking becomes dominant. Increasing the surface roughness (i.e., higher values of α) causes the function to fall off more quickly.

9.6.3 THE MASKING-SHADOWING FUNCTION

The BSDF is a function of two directional arguments, and each is subject to occlusion effects caused by the surface microstructure. For viewing and lighting directions, these are respectively denoted as *masking* and *shadowing*. To handle both cases, the masking function G_1 must be generalized into a *masking-shadowing function* G that gives the fraction of microfacets in a differential area that are simultaneously visible from both directions ω_o and ω_i.

We know that $G_1(\omega_o)$ gives the fraction of microfacets that are visible from the direction ω_o, and $G_1(\omega_i)$ gives the fraction for ω_i. If we assume that masking and shadowing are statistically independent events, then these probabilities can simply be multiplied together:

$$G(\omega_o, \omega_i) = G_1(\omega_o)\, G_1(\omega_i).$$

However, this independence assumption is a rather severe approximation that tends to overestimate the amount of shadowing and masking. This can produce undesirable dark regions in rendered images.

We instead rely on an approximation that accounts for the property that a microfacet with a higher amount of elevation relative to the macrosurface is more likely to be observed from both ω_i and ω_o. If the heights of microfacets are normally distributed, a less conservative model for G taking height-based correlation into account can be derived:

$$G(\omega_o, \omega_i) = \frac{1}{1 + \Lambda(\omega_o) + \Lambda(\omega_i)}. \qquad \text{(9.22)}$$

The bidirectional form of G implements this equation based on the previously defined `Lambda()` function.

⟨*TrowbridgeReitzDistribution Public Methods*⟩ +≡   575
```
Float G(Vector3f wo, Vector3f wi) const {
    return 1 / (1 + Lambda(wo) + Lambda(wi));
}
```

Float 23

TrowbridgeReitzDistribution::
    Lambda()
        577

Vector3f 86

9.6.4 SAMPLING THE DISTRIBUTION OF VISIBLE NORMALS

Efficient rendering using microfacet theory hinges on our ability to determine the microfacet encountered by a particular incident ray—in essence, this operation must emulate the process of finding an intersection with the surface microstructure. Thanks to its stochastic definition, an actual ray tracing operation is fortunately not needed: the intersected microfacet follows a known statistical distribution that depends on the roughness and the direction of the incident ray.

Recall the normalization criterion from Equation (9.17), which stated that the set of visible microfacets (left hand side) occupy the same area as the underlying macrosurface (right hand side) when observed from given direction ω with elevation angle θ:

$$\int_{\mathcal{H}^2(\mathrm{n})} D(\omega_\mathrm{m}) \, G_1(\omega) \, \max(0, \omega \cdot \omega_\mathrm{m}) \, \mathrm{d}\omega_\mathrm{m} = \cos\theta.$$

The probability of a ray interacting with a particular microfacet is directly proportional to its visible area; hence this equation can be seen to encapsulate the distribution that should be used. Following division of both sides by $\cos\theta$, the integral on the left hand side equals one—in other words, it turns into a normalized density $D_\omega(\omega_\mathrm{m})$ that we shall refer to as the distribution of *visible normals*:

$$D_\omega(\omega_\mathrm{m}) = \frac{G_1(\omega)}{\cos\theta} \, D(\omega_\mathrm{m}) \, \max(0, \omega \cdot \omega_\mathrm{m}). \qquad [9.23]$$

It describes the projected area of forward-facing normals, where the first term involving the masking function specifies an ω-dependent normalization factor. The method D() evaluates this density function.

⟨*TrowbridgeReitzDistribution Public Methods*⟩ +≡   **575**
```
Float D(Vector3f w, Vector3f wm) const {
    return G1(w) / AbsCosTheta(w) * D(wm) * AbsDot(w, wm);
}
```

Two upcoming microfacet BSDFs will rely on the ability to sample microfacet normals ω_m according to this density. At this point, one would ordinarily apply the inversion method (Section 2.3) to Equation (9.23) to build a sampling algorithm, but this leads to a relatively complex and approximate method: part of the problem is that the central inversion step lacks an analytic solution. We instead follow a simple geometric approach that exploits the definition of the microsurface in terms of an arrangement of many identical truncated spheres or ellipsoids.

Before implementing the sampling routine, we will quickly take care of the method that returns the associated PDF, which is simply another name for the D() method.

⟨*TrowbridgeReitzDistribution Public Methods*⟩ +≡   **575**
```
Float PDF(Vector3f w, Vector3f wm) const { return D(w, wm); }
```

Figure 9.27 illustrates the high-level idea: it suffices to focus on a single ellipsoidal or spherical bump and perpendicularly project parallel rays from an incident direction ω onto its surface. The resulting normal directions ω_m will then be distributed according to the density function $D_\omega(\omega_\mathrm{m})$.

An observation illustrated in Figure 9.28 can be used to further simplify this task: by applying the inverse of the ellipsoid's scaling transformation, the problem reduces to the simpler isotropic case. For this, we must transform the incident direction ω to the hemispherical configuration, perform a hemispherical sampling step, and then re-transform the resulting points back to the ellipsoidal state. The Sample_wm() method realizes this sequence of steps.

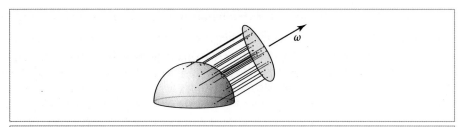

Figure 9.27: Sampling the distribution of visible normals $D_\omega(\omega_m)$ is equivalent to casting rays against the surface microstructure that is composed of many truncated spherical or ellipsoidal bumps. It suffices to consider a single bump in this process.

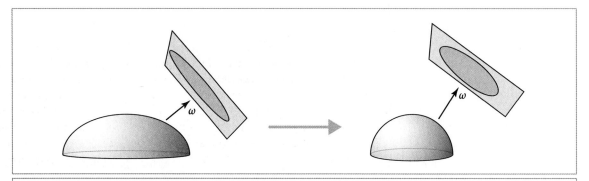

Figure 9.28: Sampling the anisotropic variant of the Trowbridge–Reitz distribution entails perpendicular projection of uniformly distributed points onto a truncated ellipsoid. Applying the inverse of the ellipsoid's scaling transformation to all parts of this problem (ellipsoid and incident ray) reduces this problem to the easier hemispherical/isotropic case.

⟨*TrowbridgeReitzDistribution Public Methods*⟩ +≡   **575**

```
Vector3f Sample_wm(Vector3f w, Point2f u) const {
    ⟨Transform w to hemispherical configuration 580⟩
    ⟨Find orthonormal basis for visible normal sampling 581⟩
    ⟨Generate uniformly distributed points on the unit disk 581⟩
    ⟨Warp hemispherical projection for visible normal sampling 581⟩
    ⟨Reproject to hemisphere and transform normal to ellipsoid configuration 582⟩
}
```

The first transformation to the hemispherical configuration is accomplished by applying the component-wise scaling factors α_x and α_y to the incident direction ω and renormalizing. By convention, microfacet normals point into the upper hemisphere, and we potentially flip the incident direction so that both directions are consistently oriented.

⟨*Transform w to hemispherical configuration*⟩ ≡   **580**

```
Vector3f wh =
    Normalize(Vector3f(alpha_x * w.x, alpha_y * w.y, w.z));
if (wh.z < 0)
    wh = -wh;
```

Next, we complete the unit vector wh to an orthonormal basis (T1, T2, wh). The particular construction below satisfies the additional constraint that T1 is perpendicular to the macroscopic normal (0, 0, 1).

Normalize() 88

Point2f 92

TrowbridgeReitzDistribution::
  alpha_x
  575

TrowbridgeReitzDistribution::
  alpha_y
  575

Vector3f 86

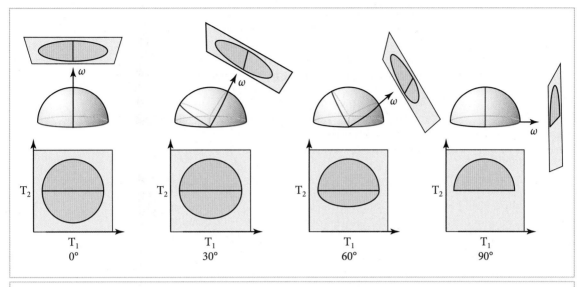

Figure 9.29: The perpendicular projection of a truncated hemisphere can be decomposed into the projection of two half-disks highlighted in red and blue. The size and shape of the projected tangential half-disk (blue) depends on the incident direction ω and vanishes at grazing incidence.

⟨*Find orthonormal basis for visible normal sampling*⟩ ≡   **580**
```
Vector3f T1 = (wh.z < 0.99999f) ? Normalize(Cross(Vector3f(0, 0, 1), wh))
                                : Vector3f(1, 0, 0);
Vector3f T2 = Cross(wh, T1);
```

Figure 9.29 illustrates the geometry of the projection. When ω is perpendicularly incident (first column), the hemisphere projects onto a disk. Non-perpendicular incidence (columns 2–4) reveals more interesting behavior: the bottom half that corresponds to the perpendicular projection of the tangential half-disk (blue) undergoes a scaling given by $\cos\theta = \omega \cdot \mathbf{n}$ along the vertical axis (i.e., the T2 axis). Because the transformation is uniform, we can sample this set using a vertical affine transformation of uniform points on the disk.

⟨*Generate uniformly distributed points on the unit disk*⟩ ≡   **580**
```
Point2f p = SampleUniformDiskPolar(u);
```

Let $p = (x, y)$ denote a point on the unit disk. For a given $x \in [-1, 1]$, the y-component lies on the interval $[-h, h]$, where $h = \sqrt{1 - x^2}$ specifies the maximum height. Due to non-perpendicular projection, this interval must now be reduced to $[-h\cos\theta, h]$, which requires an affine transformation with scale $\frac{1}{2}(1 + \cos\theta)$ and offset $\frac{h}{2}(1 - \cos\theta)$. The following fragment efficiently performs this transformation using the Lerp() function.

⟨*Warp hemispherical projection for visible normal sampling*⟩ ≡   **580**
```
Float h = std::sqrt(1 - Sqr(p.x));
p.y = Lerp((1 + wh.z) / 2, h, p.y);
```

The last step projects the computed position onto the hemisphere and computes its 3D coordinates. Finally, it reapplies the ellipsoidal transformation and returns the result.

⟨*Reproject to hemisphere and transform normal to ellipsoid configuration*⟩ ≡   **580**

```
    Float pz = std::sqrt(std::max<Float>(0, 1 - LengthSquared(Vector2f(p))));
    Vector3f nh = p.x * T1 + p.y * T2 + pz * wh;
    return Normalize(Vector3f(alpha_x * nh.x, alpha_y * nh.y,
                              std::max<Float>(1e-6f, nh.z)));
```

Note that it may seem that we should *divide* instead of multiplying by α_x and α_y to realize the inverse of the transformation from the fragment ⟨*Transform w to hemispherical configuration*⟩. This ostensible blunder is explained by the property that normals transform according to the inverse transpose of linear transformations (Section 3.10.3).

9.6.5 THE TORRANCE–SPARROW MODEL

We can finally explain how the ConductorBxDF handles rough microstructures via a BRDF model due to Torrance and Sparrow (1967). Instead of directly deriving their approach from first principles, we will instead explain how this model is sampled in pbrt, and then reverse-engineer the implied BRDF.

Combined with the visible normal sampling approach, the sampling routine of this model consists of three physically intuitive steps:

1. Given a viewing ray from direction ω_o, a microfacet normal ω_m is sampled from the visible normal distribution $D_{\omega_o}(\omega_m)$. This step encapsulates the process of intersecting the viewing ray with the random microstructure.
2. Reflection from the sampled microfacet is modeled using the law of specular reflection and the Fresnel equations, which yields the incident direction ω_i and a reflection coefficient that attenuates the light carried by the path.
3. The scattered light is finally scaled by $G_1(\omega_i)$ to account for the effect of masking by other microfacets.

Our goal will be to determine the BRDF that represents this sequence of steps. For this, we must first find the probability density of the sampled incident direction ω_i. Although visible normal sampling was involved, it is important to note that ω_i is *not* distributed according to the visible normal distribution—to find its density, we must consider the sequence of steps that were used to obtain ω_i from ω_m.

Taking stock of the available information, we know that the probability density of ω_m is given by $D_{\omega_o}(\omega_m)$, and that ω_i is obtained from ω_m and ω_o using the law of specular reflection—that is,

$$\omega_r = -\omega_o + 2(\omega_m \cdot \omega_o)\,\omega_m. \qquad [9.24]$$

This reflection mapping also has an inverse: the normal responsible for a specific reflection can be determined via

$$\omega_m = \frac{\omega_i + \omega_o}{\|\omega_i + \omega_o\|}, \qquad [9.25]$$

which is known as the *half-angle* or *half-direction* transform, as it gives the unique direction vector that lies halfway between ω_i and ω_o.

The Half-Direction Transform

Transitioning between half- and incident directions is effectively a change of variables, and the Jacobian determinant $d\omega_i/d\omega_m$ of the associated mapping enables the conversion of probability densities between these two spaces. The determinant is simple to find in flatland,

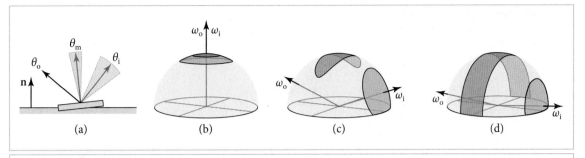

Figure 9.30: Microfacet normals, incident directions, and outgoing directions satisfy an interesting geometric relationship. We hold the outgoing direction ω_o fixed and visualize the set of microfacets (shaded in blue) that will yield a valid reflection from an arc/cone of directions around the incident direction (shaded in green). In the flatland setting shown in (a), the set of admissible microfacets is simply a smaller arc. The 3D case is more complex and involves spherical conic sections. In (b), with the center of the ω_i cone aligned with ω_o, the admissible microfacets form a spherical circle. (c) With a 140° angle between ω_o and the central ω_i direction, the microfacets form a spherical ellipse. (d) A spherical hyperbola is the result with a 170° angle. The Torrance–Sparrow model depends on the ratio of the surface area of these shaded sets, which has a succinct analytic solution in the infinitesimally small case.

as shown in Figure 9.30(a). In the two-dimensional setting, the half-direction mapping simplifies to

$$\theta_m = \frac{\theta_o + \theta_i}{2}. \tag{9.26}$$

A slight perturbation of the incident angle θ_i (shaded green region) while keeping θ_o fixed requires a corresponding change to the microfacet angle θ_m (shaded blue region) to ensure that the law of specular reflection continues to hold. However, this perturbation to θ_m is smaller—half as small, to be precise—which directly follows from Equation (9.26). Indeed, the derivative of Equation (9.26) yields $d\theta_m/d\theta_i = 1/2$ for the 2D case.

The 3D case initially appears challenging due to the varied behavior shown in Figure 9.30(b–d). Fortunately, working with infinitesimal sets leads to a simple analytic expression that can be derived by expressing differential solid angles around ω_m and ω_r using spherical coordinates:

$$\frac{d\omega_m}{d\omega_i} = \frac{\sin\theta_m \, d\theta_m \, d\phi_m}{\sin\theta_i \, d\theta_i \, d\phi_i}.$$

The expression can be simplified by noting that the law of specular reflection implies $\theta_i = 2\theta_m$ and $\phi_i = \phi_m$ in a spherical coordinate system oriented around ω_o:

$$\begin{aligned}
\frac{d\omega_m}{d\omega_i} &= \frac{\sin\theta_m \, d\theta_m \, d\phi_m}{\sin 2\theta_m \, 2 \, d\theta_m \, d\phi_m} \\
&= \frac{\sin\theta_m}{4\cos\theta_m \sin\theta_m} \\
&= \frac{1}{4\cos\theta_m} \\
&= \frac{1}{4(\omega_i \cdot \omega_m)} = \frac{1}{4(\omega_o \cdot \omega_m)}.
\end{aligned} \tag{9.27}$$

The resulting Jacobian determinant can be thus conveniently expressed in terms of the microfacet normal and either ω_i or ω_o.

Torrance–Sparrow PDF

With the relationship of Equation (9.27) at hand, we are now able to evaluate the probability per unit solid angle of the sampled incident directions ω_i obtained through the combination of visible normal sampling and the reflection mapping:

$$p(\omega_i) = D_{\omega_o}(\omega_m) \frac{d\omega_m}{d\omega_i} = \frac{D_{\omega_o}(\omega_m)}{4(\omega_o \cdot \omega_m)}, \tag{9.28}$$

where ω_m depends on ω_i via the half-direction transform in Equation (9.25). The following previously undefined fragment incorporates these observations into `ConductorBxDF::PDF()`.

⟨*Evaluate sampling PDF of rough conductor BRDF*⟩ ≡   562
```
Vector3f wm = wo + wi;
if (LengthSquared(wm) == 0) return 0;
wm = FaceForward(Normalize(wm), Normal3f(0, 0, 1));
return mfDistrib.PDF(wo, wm) / (4 * AbsDot(wo, wm));
```

The sign-related differences between equation and implementation ensure correct operation when the incident ray lies below the surface.

Torrance–Sparrow BRDF

The sampling routine of any BRDF model encodes a local strategy for importance sampling the scattering equation, (4.14). Here, we are dealing with an opaque surface, so the integral is only over the hemisphere. The single-sample Monte Carlo estimator is then

$$\begin{aligned}
L_o(p, \omega_o) &= \int_{\mathcal{H}^2(n)} f_r(p, \omega_o, \omega_i)\, L_i(p, \omega_i)\, |\cos\theta_i|\, d\omega_i \\
&\approx \frac{f_r(p, \omega_o, \omega_i)\, L_i(p, \omega_i)\, |\cos\theta_i|}{p(\omega_i)},
\end{aligned} \tag{9.29}$$

where $p(\omega_i)$ denotes the sample's probability per unit solid angle.

Recall our earlier introduction of the Torrance–Sparrow sampling routine as a composition of physically intuitive steps: intersecting a ray against the random microstructure via visible normal sampling, computation of ω_i via the law of reflection, and attenuation of the incident radiance by the Fresnel and masking factors. The radiance computed in this way should agree with the Monte Carlo estimate from Equation (9.29), which means that f_r must satisfy the identity

$$\frac{f_r(p, \omega_o, \omega_i)\, L_i(p, \omega_i)\, |\cos\theta_i|}{p(\omega_i)} \stackrel{!}{=} F(\omega_o \cdot \omega_m)\, G_1(\omega_i)\, L_i(p, \omega_i). \tag{9.30}$$

We will simply solve this equation to obtain $f_r(p, \omega_o, \omega_i)$. Further substituting the PDF of the Torrance–Sparrow model from Equation (9.28) yields the BRDF

$$f_r(p, \omega_o, \omega_i) = \frac{D_{\omega_o}(\omega_m)\, F(\omega_o \cdot \omega_m)\, G_1(\omega_i)}{4\,(\omega_o \cdot \omega_m)\, |\cos\theta_i|}. \tag{9.31}$$

Inserting the definition of the visible normal distribution from Equation (9.23) and assuming directions in the positive hemisphere results in the common form of the Torrance–Sparrow BRDF:

$$f_r(p, \omega_o, \omega_i) = \frac{D(\omega_m)\, F(\omega_o \cdot \omega_m)\, G_1(\omega_i)\, G_1(\omega_o)}{4\cos\theta_i\,\cos\theta_o}. \tag{9.32}$$

We will, however, make a small adjustment to the above expression: Section 9.6.3 introduced a more accurate bidirectional masking-shadowing factor G that accounts for height correlations on the microstructure. We use it to replace the product of unidirectional G_1 factors:

$$f_r(p, \omega_o, \omega_i) = \frac{D(\omega_m) \; F(\omega_o \cdot \omega_m) \; G(\omega_i, \omega_o)}{4 \cos \theta_i \; \cos \theta_o}. \qquad [9.33]$$

One of the nice things about the Torrance–Sparrow model is that the derivation does not depend on the particular microfacet distribution being used. Furthermore, it does not depend on a particular Fresnel function and can be used for both conductors and dielectrics. However, the relationship between $d\omega_m$ and $d\omega_o$ used in the derivation does depend on the assumption of specular reflection from microfacets, and the refractive variant of this model will require suitable modifications.

Evaluating the terms of the Torrance–Sparrow BRDF is straightforward.

⟨*Evaluate rough conductor BRDF*⟩ ≡   562
    ⟨*Compute cosines and* ω_m *for conductor BRDF* 585⟩
    ⟨*Evaluate Fresnel factor* F *for conductor BRDF* 585⟩
    return mfDistrib.D(wm) * F * mfDistrib.G(wo, wi) /
        (4 * cosTheta_i * cosTheta_o);

Incident and outgoing directions at glancing angles need to be handled explicitly to avoid the generation of NaN values:

⟨*Compute cosines and* ω_m *for conductor BRDF*⟩ ≡   585
    Float cosTheta_o = AbsCosTheta(wo), cosTheta_i = AbsCosTheta(wi);
    if (cosTheta_i == 0 || cosTheta_o == 0) return {};
    Vector3f wm = wi + wo;
    if (LengthSquared(wm) == 0) return {};
    wm = Normalize(wm);

Note that the Fresnel term is based on the angle of incidence relative to the microfacet (i.e., $\omega_o \cdot \omega_m$) rather than the macrosurface.

⟨*Evaluate Fresnel factor* F *for conductor BRDF*⟩ ≡   585
    SampledSpectrum F = FrComplex(AbsDot(wo, wm), eta, k);

Torrance–Sparrow Sampling

The sampling procedure follows the sequence of steps outlined at the beginning of this subsection. It first uses Sample_wm() to find a microfacet orientation and reflects the outgoing direction about the microfacet's normal to find ω_i before evaluating the BRDF and density function.

⟨*Sample rough conductor BRDF*⟩ ≡   562
    ⟨*Sample microfacet normal* ω_m *and reflected direction* ω_i 586⟩
    ⟨*Compute PDF of* wi *for microfacet reflection*⟩
    Float cosTheta_o = AbsCosTheta(wo), cosTheta_i = AbsCosTheta(wi);
    ⟨*Evaluate Fresnel factor* F *for conductor BRDF* 585⟩
    SampledSpectrum f = mfDistrib.D(wm) * F * mfDistrib.G(wo, wi) /
                    (4 * cosTheta_i * cosTheta_o);
    return BSDFSample(f, wi, pdf, BxDFFlags::GlossyReflection);

A curious situation arises when the sampled microfacet normal leads to a computed direction that lies *below* the macroscopic surface. In a real microstructure, this would mean that light travels deeper into a crevice, to be scattered a second or third time. However, the presented ConductorBxDF only simulates a single interaction and thus marks such samples as invalid. This reveals one of the main flaws of the presented model: objects with significant roughness may appear too dark due to this lack of multiple scattering. Addressing issues related to energy loss is an active topic of research; see the "Further Reading" section for more information.

⟨*Sample microfacet normal ω_m and reflected direction ω_i*⟩ ≡   **585**
```
    Vector3f wm = mfDistrib.Sample_wm(wo, u);
    Vector3f wi = Reflect(wo, wm);
    if (!SameHemisphere(wo, wi)) return {};
```

We omit the fragment ⟨*Compute PDF of* wi *for microfacet reflection*⟩ that follows Conductor BxDF::PDF().

Visible normal sampling is still a relatively new development: for several decades, microfacet models relied on sampling ω_m directly proportional to the microfacet distribution, which tends to produce noisier renderings since some terms of the BRDF are not sampled exactly. Figure 9.31 compares this classical approach to what is now implemented in pbrt.

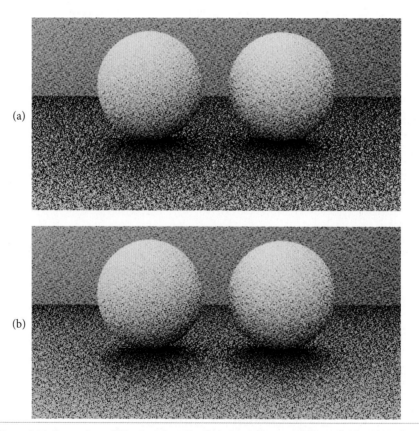

(a)

(b)

Figure 9.31: Comparison of Microfacet Sampling Techniques. The ground plane under the spheres has a metal material modeled using the Torrance–Sparrow BRDF with a roughness of $\alpha = 0.01$. Even with this relatively smooth microsurface, (a) sampling the full microfacet distribution $D(\omega_m)$ gives visibly higher error from unusable samples taken from backfacing microfacets than (b) directly sampling the visible microfacet distribution $D_{\omega_o}(\omega_m)$.

ConductorBxDF::mfDistrib 561

ConductorBxDF::PDF() 562

Reflect() 552

SameHemisphere() 538

TrowbridgeReitzDistribution::
    Sample_wm()
    580

Vector3f 86

(a) (b)

Figure 9.32: Dragon models rendered with the Torrance–Sparrow microfacet model featuring both reflection (a) and transmission (b). *(Model courtesy of Christian Schüller.)*

9.7 ROUGH DIELECTRIC BSDF

We will now extend the microfacet approach from Section 9.6 to the case of rough dielectrics. This involves two notable changes: since dielectrics are characterized by both reflection and transmission, the model must be aware of these two separate components. In the case of transmission, Snell's law will furthermore replace the law of reflection in the computation that determines the incident direction.

Figure 9.32 shows the dragon rendered with the Torrance–Sparrow model and both reflection and transmission.

As before, we will begin by characterizing the probability density of generated samples. The implied BSDF then directly follows from this density and the sequence of events encapsulated by a scattering interaction: visible normal sampling, reflection or refraction, and attenuation by the Fresnel and masking terms.

Rough Dielectric PDF
The density evaluation occurs in the following fragment that we previously omitted during the discussion of the smooth dielectric case.

⟨*Evaluate sampling PDF of rough dielectric BSDF*⟩ ≡   **566**
    ⟨*Compute generalized half vector* wm **588**⟩
    ⟨*Discard backfacing microfacets* **588**⟩
    ⟨*Determine Fresnel reflectance of rough dielectric boundary* **588**⟩
    ⟨*Compute probabilities* pr *and* pt *for sampling reflection and transmission* **564**⟩
    ⟨*Return PDF for rough dielectric* **589**⟩

We now turn to the generalized half-direction vector, whose discussion requires a closer look at Snell's law (Equation (9.2)) relating the elevation and azimuth of the incident and outgoing directions at a refractive interface:

$$\eta_o \sin \theta_o = \eta_i \sin \theta_i \quad \text{and} \quad \phi_o = \phi_i + \pi.$$

Since the refraction takes place at the level of the microgeometry, all of these angles are to be understood within a coordinate frame aligned with the microfacet normal ω_m. Recall also that the sines in the first equation refer to the length of the tangential component of ω_i and ω_o perpendicular to ω_m.

A generalized half-direction vector builds on this observation by scaling and adding these directions to cancel out the tangential components, which yields the surface normal responsible for a particular refraction after normalization. It is defined as

$$\omega_m = \frac{\eta_i\,\omega_i + \eta_o\,\omega_o}{\|\eta_i\,\omega_i + \eta_o\,\omega_o\|} = \frac{\eta\,\omega_i + \omega_o}{\|\eta\,\omega_i + \omega_o\|}, \qquad [9.34]$$

where $\eta = \eta_i/\eta_o$ is the relative index of refraction toward the sampled direction ω_i. The reflective case is trivially subsumed, since $\eta_i = \eta_o$ when no refraction takes place. The next fragment implements this computation, including handling of invalid configurations (e.g., perfectly grazing incidence) where both the BSDF and its sampling density evaluate to zero.

⟨*Compute generalized half vector* wm⟩ ≡   587, 589
```
    Float cosTheta_o = CosTheta(wo), cosTheta_i = CosTheta(wi);
    bool reflect = cosTheta_i * cosTheta_o > 0;
    float etap = 1;
    if (!reflect)
        etap = cosTheta_o > 0 ? eta : (1 / eta);
    Vector3f wm = wi * etap + wo;
    if (cosTheta_i == 0 || cosTheta_o == 0 || LengthSquared(wm) == 0) return {};
    wm = FaceForward(Normalize(wm), Normal3f(0, 0, 1));
```

The last line reflects an important implementation detail: with the previous definition in Equation (9.34), ω_m always points toward the denser medium, whereas pbrt uses the convention that micro- and macro-normal are consistently oriented (i.e., $\omega_m \cdot \mathbf{n} > 0$). In practice, we therefore compute the following modified half-direction vector, where $\mathbf{n} = (0, 0, 1)$ in local coordinates:

$$\omega'_m = \text{sign}(\omega_m \cdot \mathbf{n})\,\omega_m. \qquad [9.35]$$

Next, microfacets that are backfacing with respect to either the incident or outgoing direction do not contribute and must be discarded.

⟨*Discard backfacing microfacets*⟩ ≡   587, 589
```
    if (Dot(wm, wi) * cosTheta_i < 0 || Dot(wm, wo) * cosTheta_o < 0)
        return {};
```

Given ω_m, we can evaluate the Fresnel reflection and transmission terms using the specialized dielectric evaluation of the Fresnel equations.

⟨*Determine Fresnel reflectance of rough dielectric boundary*⟩ ≡   587
```
    Float R = FrDielectric(Dot(wo, wm), eta);
    Float T = 1 - R;
```

We now have the values necessary to compute the PDF for ω_i, which depends on whether it reflects or transmits at the surface.

⟨*Return PDF for rough dielectric*⟩ ≡   587

```
Float pdf;
if (reflect) {
    ⟨Compute PDF of rough dielectric reflection 589⟩
} else {
    ⟨Compute PDF of rough dielectric transmission 589⟩
}
return pdf;
```

As before, the bijective mapping between ω_m and ω_i provides a change of variables whose Jacobian determinant is crucial so that we can correctly deduce the probability density of sampled directions ω_i. The derivation is more involved in the refractive case; see the "Further Reading" section for pointers to its derivation. The final determinant is given by

$$
\begin{aligned}
d\omega_m &= \frac{\eta_i^2 \, |\omega_i \cdot \omega_m|}{(\eta_i (\omega_i \cdot \omega_m) + \eta_o (\omega_o \cdot \omega_m))^2} \, d\omega_i \\
&= \frac{|\omega_o \cdot \omega_m|}{((\omega_i \cdot \omega_m) + (\omega_o \cdot \omega_m)/\eta)^2} \, d\omega_i.
\end{aligned}
\tag{9.36}
$$

Once more, this relationship makes it possible to evaluate the probability per unit solid angle of the sampled incident directions ω_i obtained through the combination of visible normal sampling and scattering:

$$
p(\omega_i) = D_{\omega_o}(\omega_m) \frac{d\omega_m}{d\omega_i} = \frac{D_{\omega_o}(\omega_m) \, |\omega_o \cdot \omega_m|}{((\omega_i \cdot \omega_m) + (\omega_o \cdot \omega_m)/\eta)^2}.
\tag{9.37}
$$

The following fragment implements this computation, while additionally accounting for the discrete probability pt / (pr + pt) of sampling the transmission component.

⟨*Compute PDF of rough dielectric transmission*⟩ ≡   589, 591

```
Float denom = Sqr(Dot(wi, wm) + Dot(wo, wm) / etap);
Float dwm_dwi = AbsDot(wi, wm) / denom;
pdf = mfDistrib.PDF(wo, wm) * dwm_dwi * pt / (pr + pt);
```

Finally, the density of the reflection component agrees with the model used for conductors but for the additional discrete probability pr / (pr + pt) of choosing the reflection component.

⟨*Compute PDF of rough dielectric reflection*⟩ ≡   589, 591

```
pdf = mfDistrib.PDF(wo, wm) / (4 * AbsDot(wo, wm)) * pr / (pr + pt);
```

Rough Dielectric BSDF

BSDF evaluation is similarly split into reflective and transmissive components.

⟨*Evaluate rough dielectric BSDF*⟩ ≡   566

```
⟨Compute generalized half vector wm 588⟩
⟨Discard backfacing microfacets 588⟩
Float F = FrDielectric(Dot(wo, wm), eta);
if (reflect) {
    ⟨Compute reflection at rough dielectric interface 590⟩
} else {
    ⟨Compute transmission at rough dielectric interface 590⟩
}
```

The reflection component follows the approach used for conductors in the fragment ⟨*Evaluate rough conductor BRDF*⟩:

⟨*Compute reflection at rough dielectric interface*⟩ ≡   **589**
```
    return SampledSpectrum(mfDistrib.D(wm) * mfDistrib.G(wo, wi) * F /
                        std::abs(4 * cosTheta_i * cosTheta_o));
```

For the transmission component, we can again derive the effective scattering distribution by equating a single-sample Monte Carlo estimate of the rendering equation with the product of Fresnel transmission, masking, and the incident radiance. This results in the equation

$$\frac{f_t(p, \omega_o, \omega_i) \, L_i(p, \omega_i) \, |\cos \theta_i|}{p(\omega_i)} \stackrel{!}{=} (1 - F(\omega_o \cdot \omega_m)) \, G_1(\omega_i) \, L_i(p, \omega_i). \qquad [9.38]$$

Substituting the PDF from Equation (9.37) and solving for the BTDF $f_t(p, \omega_o, \omega_i)$ results in

$$f_t(p, \omega_o, \omega_i) = \frac{D_{\omega_o}(\omega_m) \, |\omega_o \cdot \omega_m| D_{\omega_o}(\omega_m) \, (1 - F(\omega_o \cdot \omega_m)) \, G_1(\omega_i)}{((\omega_i \cdot \omega_m) + (\omega_o \cdot \omega_m)/\eta)^2 \, |\cos \theta_i|}. \qquad [9.39]$$

Finally, inserting the definition of the visible normal distribution from Equation (9.23) and switching to the more accurate bidirectional masking-shadowing factor G yields

$$f_t(p, \omega_o, \omega_i) = \frac{D(\omega_m) \, (1 - F(\omega_o \cdot \omega_m)) \, G(\omega_i, \omega_o)}{((\omega_i \cdot \omega_m) + (\omega_o \cdot \omega_m)/\eta)^2} \frac{|\omega_i \cdot \omega_m| \, |\omega_o \cdot \omega_m|}{|\cos \theta_i| \, |\cos \theta_o|}. \qquad [9.40]$$

The next fragment implements this expression. It also incorporates the earlier orientation test and handling of non-symmetric scattering that was previously encountered in the perfect specular case (Section 9.5.2).

⟨*Compute transmission at rough dielectric interface*⟩ ≡   **589**
```
    Float denom = Sqr(Dot(wi, wm) + Dot(wo, wm)/etap) * cosTheta_i * cosTheta_o;
    Float ft = mfDistrib.D(wm) * (1 - F) * mfDistrib.G(wo, wi) *
                std::abs(Dot(wi, wm) * Dot(wo, wm) / denom);
    ⟨Account for non-symmetry with transmission to different medium 571⟩
    return SampledSpectrum(ft);
```

Rough Dielectric Sampling
Sampling proceeds by drawing a microfacet normal from the visible normal distribution, computing the Fresnel term, and stochastically selecting between reflection and transmission.

⟨*Sample rough dielectric BSDF*⟩ ≡   **564**
```
    Vector3f wm = mfDistrib.Sample_wm(wo, u);
    Float R = FrDielectric(Dot(wo, wm), eta);
    Float T = 1 - R;
    ⟨Compute probabilities pr and pt for sampling reflection and transmission 564⟩
    Float pdf;
    if (uc < pr / (pr + pt)) {
        ⟨Sample reflection at rough dielectric interface 591⟩
    } else {
        ⟨Sample transmission at rough dielectric interface 591⟩
    }
```

Once again, handling of the reflection component is straightforward and mostly matches the case for conductors except for extra factors that arise due to the discrete choice between reflection and transmission components.

⟨*Sample reflection at rough dielectric interface*⟩ ≡   590
```
    Vector3f wi = Reflect(wo, wm);
    if (!SameHemisphere(wo, wi)) return {};
    ⟨Compute PDF of rough dielectric reflection 589⟩
    SampledSpectrum f(mfDistrib.D(wm) * mfDistrib.G(wo, wi) * R /
                      (4 * CosTheta(wi) * CosTheta(wo)));
    return BSDFSample(f, wi, pdf, BxDFFlags::GlossyReflection);
```

The transmission case invokes Refract() to determine wi. A subsequent test excludes inconsistencies that can rarely arise due to the approximate nature of floating-point arithmetic. For example, Refract() may sometimes indicate a total internal reflection configuration, which is inconsistent as the transmission component should not have been sampled in this case.

⟨*Sample transmission at rough dielectric interface*⟩ ≡   590
```
    Float etap;
    Vector3f wi;
    bool tir = !Refract(wo, (Normal3f)wm, eta, &etap, &wi);
    if (SameHemisphere(wo, wi) || wi.z == 0 || tir)
        return {};
    ⟨Compute PDF of rough dielectric transmission 589⟩
    ⟨Evaluate BRDF and return BSDFSample for rough transmission 591⟩
```

The last step evaluates the BTDF from Equation (9.40) and packs the sample information into a BSDFSample.

⟨*Evaluate BRDF and return* BSDFSample *for rough transmission*⟩ ≡   591
```
    SampledSpectrum ft(T * mfDistrib.D(wm) * mfDistrib.G(wo, wi) *
        std::abs(Dot(wi, wm) * Dot(wo, wm) /
        (CosTheta(wi) * CosTheta(wo) * denom)));
    ⟨Account for non-symmetry with transmission to different medium 571⟩
    return BSDFSample(ft, wi, pdf, BxDFFlags::GlossyTransmission, etap);
```

*9.8 MEASURED BSDFs

The reflection models introduced up to this point represent index of refraction changes at smooth and rough boundaries, which constitute the basic building blocks of surface appearance. More complex materials (e.g., paint on primer, metal under a layer of enamel) can sometimes be approximated using multiple interfaces with participating media between them; the layered material model presented in Section 14.3 is based on that approach.

However, many real-world materials are beyond the scope of even such layered models. Examples include:

- *Materials characterized by wave-optical phenomena that produce striking directionally varying coloration.* Examples include iridescent paints, insect wings, and holographic paper.
- *Materials with rough interfaces.* In pbrt, we have chosen to model such surfaces using microfacet theory and the Trowbridge–Reitz distribution. However, it is important to remember that both of these are models that generally do not match real-world behavior perfectly.
- *Surfaces with non-standard microstructure.* For example, a woven fabric composed of two different yarns looks like a surface from a distance, but its directional intensity and color variation are not well-described by any standard BRDF model due to the distinct reflectance properties of fiber-based microgeometry.

Instead of developing numerous additional specialized BxDFs, we will now pursue another way of reproducing such challenging materials in a renderer: by interpolating measurements of real-world material samples to create a *data-driven* reflectance model. The resulting MeasuredBxDF only models surface reflection, though the approach can in principle generalize to transmission as well.

⟨*MeasuredBxDF Definition*⟩ ≡
```
class MeasuredBxDF {
  public:
    ⟨MeasuredBxDF Public Methods⟩
  private:
    ⟨MeasuredBxDF Private Methods 601⟩
    ⟨MeasuredBxDF Private Members 600⟩
};
```

Measuring reflection in a way that is practical while producing information in a form that is convenient for rendering is a challenging problem. We begin by explaining these challenges for motivation.

Consider the task of measuring the BRDF of a sheet of brushed aluminum: we could illuminate a sample of the material from a set of n incident directions $(\theta_i^{(k)}, \phi_i^{(k)})$ with $k = 1, \ldots, n$ and use some kind of sensor (e.g., a photodiode) to record the reflected light scattered along a set of m outgoing directions $(\theta_o^{(l)}, \phi_o^{(l)})$ with $l = 1, \ldots, m$. These $n \times m$ measurements could be stored on disk and interpolated at runtime to approximate the BRDF at intermediate configurations $(\theta_i, \phi_i, \theta_o, \phi_o)$. However, closer scrutiny of such an approach reveals several problems:

- BSDFs of polished materials are highly directionally peaked. Perturbing the incident or outgoing direction by as little as 1 degree can change the measured reflectance by orders of magnitude. This implies that the set of incident and outgoing directions must be sampled fairly densely.
- Accurate positioning in spherical coordinates is difficult to perform by hand and generally requires mechanical aids. For this reason, such measurements are normally performed using a motorized gantry known as a *goniophotometer* or *gonioreflectometer*. Figure 9.33 shows two examples of such machines. *Light stages* consisting of a rigid assembly of hundreds of LEDs around a sample are sometimes used to accelerate measurement, though at the cost of reduced directional resolution.
- Sampling each direction using a 1 degree spacing in spherical coordinates requires roughly one billion sample points. Storing gigabytes of measurement data is possible but undesirable, yet the time that would be spent for a full measurement is even more problematic: assuming that the goniophotometer can reach a configuration $(\theta_i, \phi_i, \theta_o, \phi_o)$ within 1 second (a reasonable estimate for the devices shown in Figure 9.33), over 34 years of sustained operation would be needed to measure a single material.

In sum, the combination of high-frequency signals, the 4D domain of the BRDF, and the curse of dimensionality conspire to make standard measurement approaches all but impractical.

While there is no general antidote against the curse of dimensionality, the previous example involving a dense discretization of the 4D domain is clearly excessive. For example, peaked BSDFs that concentrate most of their energy into a small set of angles tend to be relatively smooth away from the peak. Figure 9.34 shows how a more specialized sample placement that is informed by the principles of specular reflection can drastically reduce the number of

BxDF 538

MeasuredBxDF 592

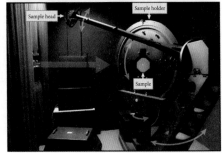

Figure 9.33: Specialized Hardware for BSDF Acquisition. The term *goniophotometer* (or *gonioreflec-tometer*) refers to a typically motorized platform that can simultaneously illuminate and observe a material sample from arbitrary pairs of directions. The device on the left (at Cornell University, built by Cyberware Inc., image courtesy of Steve Marschner) rotates camera (2 degrees of freedom) and light arms (1 degree of freedom) around a centered sample pedestal that can also rotate about its vertical axis. The device on the right (at EPFL, built by pab advanced technologies Ltd) instead uses a static light source and a rotating sensor arm (2 degrees of freedom). The vertical material sample holder then provides 2 rotational degrees of freedom to cover the full 4D domain of the BSDF.

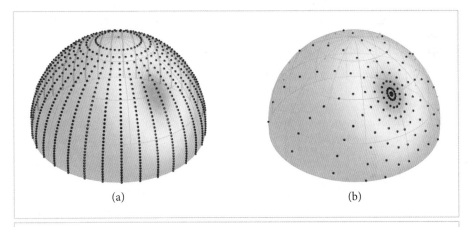

(a)   (b)

Figure 9.34: Adaptive BRDF Sample Placement. (a) Regular sampling of the incident and outgoing directions is a prohibitively expensive way of measuring and storing BRDFs due to the curse of dimensionality (here, only 2 of the 4 dimensions are shown). (b) A smaller number of samples can yield a more accurate interpolant if their placement is informed by the material's reflectance behavior.

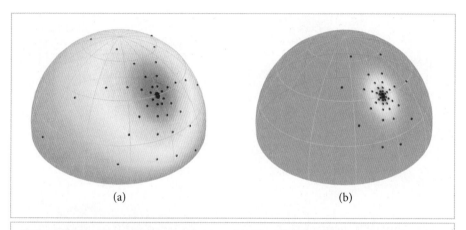

(a)   (b)

Figure 9.35: The Effect of Surface Roughness on Adaptive BRDF Sample Placement. The two plots visualize BRDF values of two materials with different roughnesses for varying directions ω_i and fixed ω_o. Circles indicate adaptively chosen measurement locations, which are used to create the interpolant implemented in the `MeasuredBxDF` class. (a) The measurement locations broadly cover the hemisphere given a relatively rough material. (b) For a more specular material the samples are concentrated in the region around the specular peak. Changing the outgoing direction moves the specular peak; hence the sample locations must depend on ω_o.

sample points that are needed to obtain a desired level of accuracy. Figure 9.35 shows how the roughness of the surface affects the desired distribution of samples—for example, smooth surfaces allow sparse sampling outside of the specular lobe.

The `MeasuredBxDF` therefore builds on microfacet theory and the distribution of visible normals to create a more efficient physically informed sampling pattern. The rationale underlying this choice is that while microfacet theory may not perfectly predict the reflectance of a specific material, it can at least approximately represent how energy is (re-)distributed throughout the 4D domain. Applying it enables the use of a relatively coarse set of measurement locations that suffice to capture the function's behavior.

Concretely, the method works by transforming regular grid points using visible normal sampling (Section 9.6.4) and performing a measurement at each sampled position. If the microfacet sampling routine is given by a function $R : \mathcal{S}^2 \times [0, 1]^2 \to \mathcal{S}^2$ and $u^{(k)}$ with $k = 1, \ldots, n$ denotes input samples arranged on a grid covering the 2D unit square, then we have a sequence of measurements $\mathcal{M}^{(k)}$:

$$\mathcal{M}^{(k)} = f_r(\omega_o, R(\omega_o, u^{(k)})), \qquad\qquad [9.41]$$

where $f_r(\omega_o, \omega_i)$ refers to the real-world BRDF of a material sample, as measured by a goniophotometer (or similar device) in directions ω_o and $\omega_i = R(\omega_o, u^{(k)})$. This process must be repeated for different values of ω_o to also capture variation in the other direction argument. Evaluating the BRDF requires the inverse R^{-1} of the transformation, which yields a position on $[0, 1]^2$ that can be used to interpolate the measurements $\mathcal{M}^{(k)}$. Figure 9.36 illustrates both directions of this mapping.

This procedure raises several questions: first, the non-random use of a method designed for Monte Carlo sampling may be unexpected. To see why this works, remember that the inversion method (Section 2.3) evaluates the inverse of a distribution's cumulative distribution function (CDF). Besides being convenient for sampling, this inverse CDF can also be interpreted as a parameterization of the target domain from the unit square. This param-

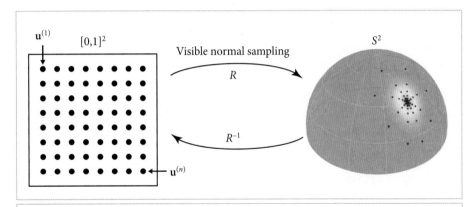

Figure 9.36: Visible Normal Sampling as a Parameterization. The `MeasuredBxDF` leverages visible normal sampling as a parameterization R of the unit sphere. Here, it is used in a deterministic fashion to transform a set of grid points $u^{(k)}$ with $k = 1, \ldots, n$ into spherical directions to be measured. Evaluating the resulting BRDF representation requires the inverse R^{-1} followed by linear interpolation within the regular grid of measurements.

eterization smoothly warps the domain so that regions with a high contribution occupy a correspondingly large amount of the unit square. The `MeasuredBxDF` then simply measures and stores BRDF values in these "improved" coordinates. Note that the material does not have to agree with microfacet theory for this warping to be valid, though the sampling pattern is much less efficient and requires a denser discretization when the material's behavior deviates significantly.

Another challenge is that parameterization guiding the measurement requires a microfacet approximation of the material, but such an approximation would normally be derived from an existing measurement. We will shortly show how to resolve this chicken-and-egg problem and assume for now that a suitable model is available.

Measurement Through a Parameterization

A flaw of the reparameterized measurement sequence in Equation (9.41) is that the values $\mathcal{M}^{(k)}$ may differ by many orders of magnitude, which means that simple linear interpolation between neighboring data points is unlikely to give satisfactory results. We instead use the following representation that transforms measurements prior to storage in an effort to reduce this variation:

$$\mathcal{M}^{(k)} = \frac{f_r(\omega_o, \omega_i^{(k)}) \cos \theta_i^{(k)}}{p(\omega_i^{(k)})}, \tag{9.42}$$

where $\omega_i^{(k)} = R(\omega_o, u^{(k)})$, and $p(\omega_i^{(k)})$ denotes the density of direction $\omega_i^{(k)}$ according to visible normal sampling.

If f_r was an analytic BRDF (e.g., a microfacet model) and $u^{(k)}$ a 2D uniform variate, then Equation (9.42) would simply be the weight of a Monte Carlo importance sampling strategy, typically with a carefully designed mapping R and density p that make this weight near-constant to reduce variance.

In the present context, f_r represents real-world data, while p and R encapsulate a microfacet approximation of the material under consideration. We therefore expect $\mathcal{M}^{(k)}$ to take on near-constant values when the material is well-described by a microfacet model, and more marked deviations otherwise. This can roughly be interpreted as measuring the difference (in

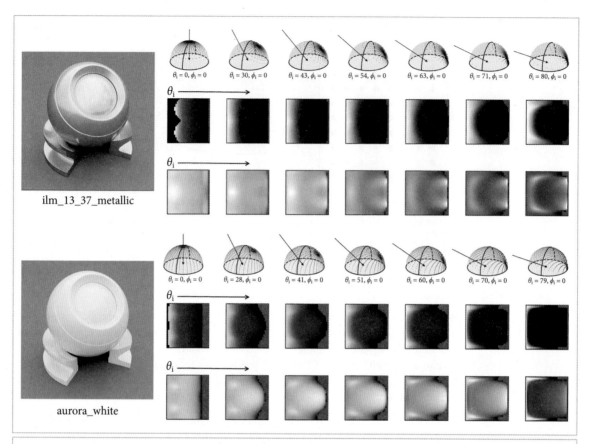

Figure 9.37: Reparameterized BRDF Visualization. This figure illustrates the representation of two material samples: a metallic sample swatch from the L3-37 robot in the film *Solo: A Star Wars Story* (Walt Disney Studios Motion Pictures) and a pearlescent vehicle vinyl wrap (TeckWrap International Inc.). Each column represents a measurement of a separate outgoing direction ω_o. For both materials, the first row visualizes the measured directions $\omega_i^{(k)}$. The subsequent row plots the "raw" reparameterized BRDF of Equation (9.41), where each pixel represents one of the grid points $u^{(k)} \in [0, 1]^2$ identified with $\omega_i^{(k)}$. The final row shows transformed measurements corresponding to Equation (9.42) that are more uniform and easier to interpolate. Note that these samples are both isotropic, which is why a few measurements for different elevation angles suffice. In the anisotropic case, the (θ_o, ϕ_o) domain must be covered more densely.

a multiplicative sense) between the real world and the microfacet simplification. Figure 9.37 visualizes the effect of the transformation in Equation (9.42).

BRDF Evaluation

Evaluating the data-driven BRDF requires the inverse of these steps. Suppose that $\mathcal{M}(\cdot)$ implements an interpolation based on the grid of measurement points $\mathcal{M}^{(k)}$. Furthermore, suppose that we have access to the inverse $R^{-1}(\omega_o, \omega_i)$ that returns the "random numbers" u that would cause visible normal sampling to generate a particular incident direction (i.e., $R(\omega_o, u) = \omega_i$). Accessing $\mathcal{M}(\cdot)$ through R^{-1} then provides a spherical interpolation of the measurement data.

We must additionally multiply by the density $p(\omega_i)$, and divide by the cosine factor[5] to undo corresponding transformations introduced in Equation (9.42), which yields the final form of the data-driven BRDF:

5　Both steps use ω_i instead of $\omega_i^{(k)}$ to improve the smoothness of the interpolation.

$$f_r(\omega_o, \omega_i) = \frac{\mathcal{M}(R^{-1}(\omega_o, \omega_i))\, p(\omega_i)}{\cos\theta_i}. \qquad \text{[9.43]}$$

Generalized Microfacet Model

A major difference between the microfacet model underlying the ConductorBxDF and the approximation used here is that we replace the Trowbridge–Reitz model with an arbitrary data-driven microfacet distribution. This improves the model's ability to approximate the material being measured. At the same time, it implies that previously used simplifications and analytic solutions are no longer available and must be revisited.

We begin with the Torrance–Sparrow sampling density from Equation (9.28),

$$p(\omega_i) = \frac{D_{\omega_o}(\omega_m)}{4(\omega_o \cdot \omega_m)},$$

which references the visible normal sampling density $D_\omega(\omega_m)$ from Equation (9.23). Substituting the definition of the masking function from Equation (9.18) into $D_{\omega_o}(\omega_m)$ and rearranging terms yields

$$D_{\omega_o}(\omega_m) = \frac{1}{\sigma(\omega_o)}\, D(\omega_m)\, \max(0, \omega_o \cdot \omega_m),$$

where

$$\sigma(\omega_o) = \int_{\mathcal{H}^2(\mathbf{n})} D(\omega)\, \max(0, \omega_o \cdot \omega)\, d\omega$$

provides a direction-dependent normalization of the visible normal distribution. For valid reflection directions ($\omega_o \cdot \omega_m > 0$), the PDF of generated samples then simplifies to

$$p(\omega_i) = \frac{D(\omega_m)}{4\,\sigma(\omega_o)}. \qquad \text{[9.44]}$$

Substituting this density into the BRDF from Equation (9.43) produces

$$f_r(\omega_o, \omega_i) = \frac{\mathcal{M}(R^{-1}(\omega_o, \omega_i))\, D(\omega_m)}{4\,\sigma(\omega_o)\cos\theta_i}. \qquad \text{[9.45]}$$

The MeasuredBxDF implements this expression using data-driven representations of $D(\cdot)$ and $\sigma(\cdot)$.

Finding the Initial Microfacet Model

We finally revisit the chicken-and-egg problem from before: practical measurement using the presented approach requires a suitable microfacet model—specifically, a microfacet distribution $D(\omega_m)$. Yet it remains unclear how this distribution could be obtained without access to an already existing BRDF measurement.

The key idea to resolve this conundrum is that the microfacet distribution $D(\omega_m)$ is a 2D quantity, which means that it remains mostly unaffected by the curse of dimensionality. Acquiring this function is therefore substantially cheaper than a measurement of the full 4D BRDF.

Suppose that the material being measured perfectly matches microfacet theory in the sense that it is described by the Torrance–Sparrow BRDF from Equation (9.33). Then we can measure the material's retroreflection (i.e., $\omega_i = \omega_o = \omega$), which is given by

$$f_r(\mathrm{p}, \omega, \omega) = \frac{D(\omega)\, F(\omega \cdot \omega)\, G(\omega, \omega)}{4\cos^2\theta} \propto \frac{D(\omega)\, G_1(\omega)}{\cos^2\theta}.$$

The last step of the above equation removes constant terms including the Fresnel reflectance and introduces the reasonable assumption that shadowing/masking is perfectly correlated given $\omega_i = \omega_o$ and thus occurs only once. Substituting the definition of G_1 from Equation (9.18) and rearranging yields the following relationship of proportionality:

$$D(\omega) \propto f_r(p, \omega, \omega) \cos\theta \int_{\mathcal{H}^2(n)} D(\omega_m) \max(0, \omega \cdot \omega_m) \, d\omega_m. \qquad [9.46]$$

This integral equation can be solved by measuring $f_r(p, \omega_j, \omega_j)$ for n directions ω_j and using those measurements for initial guesses of $D(\omega_j)$. A more accurate estimate of D can then be found using an iterative solution procedure where the estimated values of D are used to estimate the integrals on the right hand side of Equation (9.46) for all of the ω_js. This process quickly converges within a few iterations.

9.8.1 BASIC DATA STRUCTURES

MeasuredBxDFData holds data pertaining to reflectance measurements and the underlying parameterization. Because the data for an isotropic BRDF is typically a few megabytes and the data for an anisotropic BRDF may be over 100, each measured BRDF that is used in the scene is stored in memory only once. As instances of MeasuredBxDF are created at surface intersections during rendering, they can then store just a pointer to the appropriate MeasuredBxDFData. Code not included here adds the ability to initialize instances of this type from binary .bsdf files containing existing measurements.[6]

⟨*MeasuredBxDFData Definition*⟩ ≡
```
struct MeasuredBxDFData {
    ⟨MeasuredBxDFData Public Members 598⟩
};
```

Measured BRDFs are represented by spectral measurements at a set of discrete wavelengths that are stored in wavelengths. The actual measurements are stored in spectra.

⟨*MeasuredBxDFData Public Members*⟩ ≡   598
```
pstd::vector<float> wavelengths;
PiecewiseLinear2D<3> spectra;
```

The template class PiecewiseLinear2D represents a piecewise-linear interpolant on the 2D unit square with samples arranged on a regular grid. The details of its implementation are relatively technical and reminiscent of other interpolants in this book; hence we only provide an overview of its capabilities and do not include its full implementation here.

The class is parameterized by a Dimension template parameter that extends the 2D interpolant to higher dimensions—for example, PiecewiseLinear2D<1> stores a 3D grid of values, and PiecewiseLinear2D<3> used above for spectra is a 5D quantity. The class provides three key methods:

```
template <size_t Dimension> class PiecewiseLinear2D {
public:
    Float Evaluate(Point2f pos, Float... params);
    PLSample Sample(Point2f u, Float... params);
    PLSample Invert(Point2f p, Float... params);
};
```

---

6   A repository of compatible files that cover the 360–1000 nm interval at roughly 4 nm resolution is available at http://rgl.epfl.ch/materials.

PiecewiseLinear2D 598

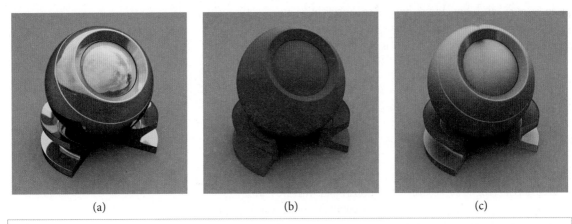

(a)   (b)   (c)

Figure 9.38: Three Measured BRDFs. (a) TeckWrap *Amber Citrine* vinyl wrapping film. (b) Purple acrylic felt. (c) Silk from an Indian sari with two colors of yarn.

where `PLSample` is defined as

```
struct PLSample { Point2f p; Float pdf; };
```

`Evaluate()` takes a position pos $\in [0, 1]^2$ and then additional `Float` parameters to perform a lookup using multidimensional linear interpolation according to the value of `Dimension`.

`Sample()` warps $u \in [0, 1]^2$ via inverse transform sampling (i.e., proportional to the stored linear interpolant), returning both the sampled position on $[0, 1]^2$ and the associated density as a `PLSample`. The additional parameters passed via `params` are used as conditional variables that restrict sampling to a 2D slice of a higher-dimensional function. For example, invoking the method `PiecewiseLinear2D<3>::Sample()` with a uniform 2D variate and parameters 0.1, 0.2, and 0.3 would importance sample the 2D slice $I(0.1, 0.2, 0.3, \cdot, \cdot)$ of a pentalinear interpolant I.

Finally, `Invert()` implements the exact inverse of `Sample()`. Invoking it with the position computed by `Sample()` will recover the input u value up to rounding error.

Additional `PiecewiseLinear1D` instances are used to (redundantly) store the normal distribution $D(\omega_m)$ in ndf, the visible normal distribution $D_{\omega_o}(\omega_m)$ parameterized by $\omega_o = (\theta_o, \phi_o)$ in vndf, and the normalization constant $\sigma(\omega_o)$ in sigma. The data structure also records whether the material is isotropic, in which case the dimensionality of some of the piecewise-linear interpolants can be reduced.

⟨*MeasuredBxDFData Public Members*⟩ +≡   **598**
```
    PiecewiseLinear2D<0> ndf;
    PiecewiseLinear2D<2> vndf;
    PiecewiseLinear2D<0> sigma;
    bool isotropic;
```

9.8.2 EVALUATION

PiecewiseLinear2D 598

Following these preliminaries, we can now turn to evaluating the measured BRDF for a pair of directions. See Figure 9.38 for examples of the variety of types of reflection that the measured representation can reproduce.

The only information that must be stored as `MeasuredBxDF` member variables in order to implement the `BxDF` interface methods is a pointer to the BRDF measurement data and the set of wavelengths at which the BRDF is to be evaluated.

⟨*MeasuredBxDF Private Members*⟩ ≡   592
```
const MeasuredBxDFData *brdf;
SampledWavelengths lambda;
```

BRDF evaluation then follows the approach described in Equation (9.45).

⟨*MeasuredBxDF Method Definitions*⟩ ≡
```
SampledSpectrum MeasuredBxDF::f(Vector3f wo, Vector3f wi,
                               TransportMode mode) const {
    ⟨Check for valid reflection configurations 600⟩
    ⟨Determine half-direction vector ωₘ 600⟩
    ⟨Map ωₒ and ωₘ to the unit square [0, 1]²⟩
    ⟨Evaluate inverse parameterization R⁻¹ 601⟩
    ⟨Evaluate spectral 5D interpolant 601⟩
    ⟨Return measured BRDF value 601⟩
}
```

Zero reflection is returned if the specified directions correspond to transmission through the surface. Otherwise, the directions ω_i and ω_o are mirrored onto the positive hemisphere if necessary.

⟨*Check for valid reflection configurations*⟩ ≡   600
```
if (!SameHemisphere(wo, wi))
    return SampledSpectrum(0);
if (wo.z < 0) {
    wo = -wo;
    wi = -wi;
}
```

The next code fragment determines the associated microfacet normal and handles an edge case that occurs in near-grazing configurations.

⟨*Determine half-direction vector ωₘ*⟩ ≡   600
```
Vector3f wm = wi + wo;
if (LengthSquared(wm) == 0)
    return SampledSpectrum(0);
wm = Normalize(wm);
```

A later step requires that ω_o and ω_m are mapped onto the unit square $[0, 1]^2$, which we do in two steps: first, by converting the directions to spherical coordinates, which are then further transformed by helper methods `theta2u()` and `phi2u()`.

In the isotropic case, the mapping used for ω_m subtracts ϕ_o from ϕ_m, which allows the stored tables to be invariant to rotation about the surface normal. This may cause the second dimension of u_wm to fall out of the [0, 1] interval; a subsequent correction fixes this using the periodicity of the azimuth parameter.

⟨*Map ω_o and ω_m to the unit square* $[0, 1]^2$⟩ ≡

```
Float theta_o = SphericalTheta(wo), phi_o = std::atan2(wo.y, wo.x);
Float theta_m = SphericalTheta(wm), phi_m = std::atan2(wm.y, wm.x);
Point2f u_wo(theta2u(theta_o), phi2u(phi_o));
Point2f u_wm(theta2u(theta_m), phi2u(brdf->isotropic ? (phi_m - phi_o) :
                                                        phi_m));

u_wm[1] = u_wm[1] - pstd::floor(u_wm[1]);
```

The two helper functions encapsulate an implementation detail of the storage representation. The function phi2u() uniformly maps $[-\pi, \pi]$ onto $[0, 1]$, while theta2u() uses a nonlinear transformation that places more resolution near $\theta \approx 0$ to facilitate storing the microfacet distribution of highly specular materials.

⟨*MeasuredBxDF Private Methods*⟩ ≡   592

```
static Float theta2u(Float theta) { return std::sqrt(theta * (2 / Pi)); }
static Float phi2u(Float phi) { return phi * (1 / (2 * Pi)) + .5f; }
```

With this information at hand, we can now evaluate the inverse parameterization to determine the sample values ui.p that would cause visible normal sampling to generate the current incident direction (i.e., $R(\omega_o, u) = \omega_i$).

⟨*Evaluate inverse parameterization* R^{-1}⟩ ≡   600

```
PLSample ui = brdf->vndf.Invert(u_wm, phi_o, theta_o);
```

This position is then used to evaluate a 5D linear interpolant parameterized by the fractional 2D position ui.p $\in [0, 1]^2$ on the reparameterized incident hemisphere, ϕ_o, θ_o, and the wavelength in nanometers. The interpolant must be evaluated once per sample of SampledSpectrum.

⟨*Evaluate spectral 5D interpolant*⟩ ≡   600

```
SampledSpectrum fr;
for (int i = 0; i < NSpectrumSamples; ++i)
    fr[i] = std::max<Float>(0, brdf->spectra.Evaluate(ui.p, phi_o, theta_o,
                                                        lambda[i]));
```

Finally, fr must be scaled to undo the transformations that were applied to the data to improve the quality of the interpolation and to reduce the required measurement density, giving the computation that corresponds to Equation (9.45).

⟨*Return measured BRDF value*⟩ ≡   600

```
return fr * brdf->ndf.Evaluate(u_wm) /
       (4 * brdf->sigma.Evaluate(u_wo) * CosTheta(wi));
```

In principle, implementing the Sample_f() and PDF() methods required by the BxDF interface is straightforward: the Sample_f() method could evaluate the forward mapping R to perform visible normal sampling based on the measured microfacet distribution using PiecewiseLinear2D::Sample(), and PDF() could evaluate the associated sampling density from Equation (9.44). However, a flaw of such a basic sampling scheme is that the transformed BRDF measurements from Equation (9.42) are generally nonuniform on $[0, 1]^2$, which can inject unwanted variance into the rendering process. The implementation therefore uses yet another reparameterization based on a luminance tensor that stores the product integral of the spectral dimension of MeasuredBxDFData::spectra and the CIE Y color matching curve.

⟨*MeasuredBxDFData Public Members*⟩ +≡   **598**
    `PiecewiseLinear2D<2> luminance;`

The actual BRDF sampling routine then consists of two steps. First it converts a uniformly distributed sample on $[0, 1]^2$ into another sample $u \in [0, 1]^2$ that is distributed according to the luminance of the reparameterized BRDF. Following this, visible normal sampling transforms u into a sampled direction ω_i and a sampling weight that will have near-constant luminance. Apart from this step, the implementations of `Sample_f()` and `PDF()` are similar to the evaluation method and therefore not included here.

*9.9 SCATTERING FROM HAIR

Human hair and animal fur can be modeled with a rough dielectric interface surrounding a pigmented translucent core. Reflectance at the interface is generally the same for all wavelengths and it is therefore wavelength-variation in the amount of light that is absorbed inside the hair that determines its color. While these scattering effects could be modeled using a combination of the `DielectricBxDF` and the volumetric scattering models from Chapters 11 and 14, not only would doing so be computationally expensive, requiring ray tracing within the hair geometry, but importance sampling the resulting model would be difficult. Therefore, this section introduces a specialized BSDF for hair and fur that encapsulates these lower-level scattering processes into a model that can be efficiently evaluated and sampled.

See Figure 9.39 for an example of the visual complexity of scattering in hair and a comparison to rendering using a conventional BRDF model with hair geometry.

9.9.1 GEOMETRY

Before discussing the mechanisms of light scattering from hair, we will start by defining a few ways of measuring incident and outgoing directions at ray intersection points on hair. In doing so, we will assume that the hair BSDF is used with the `Curve` shape from Section 6.7, which allows us to make assumptions about the parameterization of the hair

(a)   (b)

Figure 9.39: Comparison of a BSDF that Models Hair to a Coated Diffuse BSDF. (a) Geometric model of hair rendered using a BSDF based on a diffuse base layer with a rough dielectric interface above it (Section 14.3.3). (b) Model rendered using the `HairBxDF` from this section. Because the `HairBxDF` is based on an accurate model of the hair microgeometry and also models light transmission through hair, it gives a much more realistic appearance. *(Hair geometry courtesy of Cem Yuksel.)*

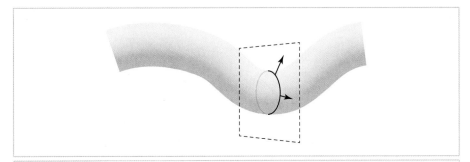

Figure 9.40: At any parametric point along a `Curve` shape, the cross-section of the curve is defined by a circle. All of the circle's surface normals (arrows) lie in a plane (dashed lines), dubbed the "normal plane."

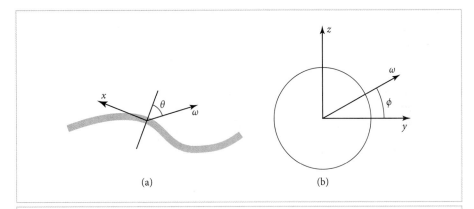

(a)   (b)

Figure 9.41: (a) Given a direction ω at a point on a curve, the longitudinal angle θ is defined by the angle between ω and the normal plane at the point (thick line). The curve's tangent vector at the point is aligned with the x axis in the BSDF coordinate system. (b) For a direction ω, the azimuthal angle ϕ is found by projecting the direction into the normal plane and computing its angle with the y axis, which corresponds to the curve's $\partial p/\partial v$ in the BSDF coordinate system.

geometry. For the geometric discussion in this section, we will assume that the `Curve` variant corresponding to a flat ribbon that is always facing the incident ray is being used. However, in the BSDF model, we will interpret intersection points as if they were on the surface of the corresponding swept cylinder. If there is no interpenetration between hairs and if the hair's width is not much larger than a pixel's width, there is no harm in switching between these interpretations.

Throughout the implementation of this scattering model, we will find it useful to separately consider scattering in the longitudinal plane, effectively using a side view of the curve, and scattering in the azimuthal plane, considering the curve head-on at a particular point along it. To understand these parameterizations, first recall that `Curves` are parameterized such that the u direction is along the length of the curve and v spans its width. At a given u, all the possible surface normals of the curve are given by the surface normals of the circular cross-section at that point. All of these normals lie in a plane that is called the *normal plane* (Figure 9.40).

We will find it useful to represent directions at a ray–curve intersection point with respect to coordinates (θ, ϕ) that are defined with respect to the normal plane at the u position where the ray intersected the curve. The angle θ is the *longitudinal angle*, which is the offset of the ray with respect to the normal plane (Figure 9.41(a)); θ ranges from $-\pi/2$ to $\pi/2$, where

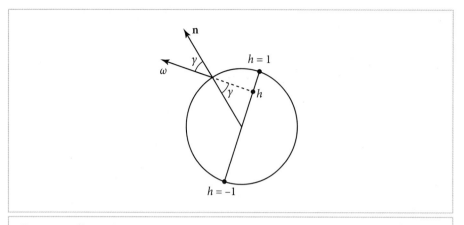

Figure 9.42: Given an incident direction ω of a ray that intersected a `Curve` projected to the normal plane, we can parameterize the curve's width with $h \in [-1, 1]$. Given the h for a ray that has intersected the curve, trigonometry shows how to compute the angle γ between ω and the surface normal on the curve's surface at the intersection point. The two angles γ are equal, and because the circle's radius is 1, $\sin \gamma = h$.

$\pi/2$ corresponds to a direction aligned with $\partial p/\partial u$ and $-\pi/2$ corresponds to $-\partial p/\partial u$. As explained in Section 9.1.1, in pbrt's regular BSDF coordinate system, $\partial p/\partial u$ is aligned with the $+x$ axis, so given a direction in the BSDF coordinate system, we have $\sin \theta = \omega_x$, since the normal plane is perpendicular to $\partial p/\partial u$.

In the BSDF coordinate system, the normal plane is spanned by the y and z coordinate axes. (y corresponds to $\partial p/\partial v$ for curves, which is always perpendicular to the curve's $\partial p/\partial u$, and z is aligned with the ribbon normal.) The *azimuthal angle* ϕ is found by projecting a direction ω into the normal plane and computing its angle with the y axis. It thus ranges from 0 to 2π (Figure 9.41(b)).

One more measurement with respect to the curve will be useful in the following. Consider incident rays with some direction ω: at any given parametric u value, all such rays that intersect the curve can only possibly intersect one half of the circle swept along the curve (Figure 9.42). We will parameterize the circle's diameter with the variable h, where $h = \pm 1$ corresponds to the ray grazing the edge of the circle, and $h = 0$ corresponds to hitting it edge-on. Because pbrt parameterizes curves with $v \in [0, 1]$ across the curve, we can compute $h = -1 + 2v$.

Given the h for a ray intersection, we can compute the angle between the surface normal of the inferred swept cylinder (which is by definition in the normal plane) and the direction ω, which we will denote by γ. (Note: this is unrelated to the γ_n notation used for floating-point error bounds in Section 6.8.) See Figure 9.42, which shows that $\sin \gamma = h$.

9.9.2 SCATTERING FROM HAIR

Geometric setting in hand, we will now turn to discuss the general scattering behaviors that give hair its distinctive appearance and some of the assumptions that we will make in the following.

Hair and fur have three main components:

Curve 346

- *Cuticle:* The outer layer, which forms the boundary with air. The cuticle's surface is a nested series of scales at a slight angle to the hair surface.

- *Cortex:* The next layer inside the cuticle. The cortex generally accounts for around 90% of hair's volume but less for fur. It is typically colored with pigments that mostly absorb light.
- *Medulla:* The center core at the middle of the cortex. It is larger and more significant in thicker hair and fur. The medulla is also pigmented. Scattering from the medulla is much more significant than scattering from the medium in the cortex.

For the following scattering model, we will make a few assumptions. (Approaches for relaxing some of them are discussed in the exercises at the end of this chapter.) First, we assume that the cuticle can be modeled as a rough dielectric cylinder with scales that are all angled at the same angle α (effectively giving a nested series of cones; see Figure 9.43). We also treat the hair interior as a homogeneous medium that only absorbs light—scattering inside the hair is not modeled directly. (Chapters 11 and 14 have detailed discussion of light transport in participating media.)

We will also make the assumption that scattering can be modeled accurately by a BSDF—we model light as entering and exiting the hair at the same place. (A BSSRDF could certainly be used instead; the "Further Reading" section has pointers to work that has investigated that alternative.) Note that this assumption requires that the hair's diameter be fairly small with respect to how quickly illumination changes over the surface; this assumption is generally fine in practice at typical viewing distances.

Incident light arriving at a hair may be scattered one or more times before leaving the hair; Figure 9.44 shows a few of the possible cases. We will use p to denote the number of path segments it follows inside the hair before being scattered back out to air. We will sometimes

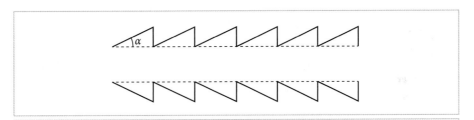

Figure 9.43: The surface of hair is formed by scales that deviate by a small angle α from the ideal cylinder. (α is generally around $2-4°$; the angle shown here is larger for illustrative purposes.)

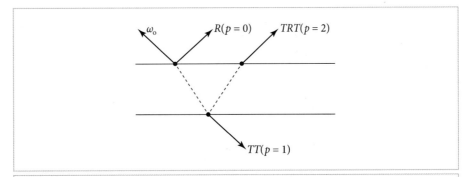

Figure 9.44: Incident light arriving at a hair can be scattered in a variety of ways. $p = 0$ corresponds to light reflected from the surface of the cuticle. Light may also be transmitted through the hair and leave the other side: $p = 1$. It may be transmitted into the hair and reflected back into it again before being transmitted back out: $p = 2$, and so forth.

refer to terms with a shorthand that describes the corresponding scattering events at the boundary: $p = 0$ corresponds to R, for reflection, $p = 1$ is TT, for two transmissions $p = 2$ is TRT, $p = 3$ is $TRRT$, and so forth.

In the following, we will find it useful to consider these scattering modes separately and so will write the hair BSDF as a sum over terms p:

$$f(\omega_o, \omega_i) = \sum_{p=0}^{\infty} f_p(\omega_o, \omega_i). \tag{9.47}$$

To make the scattering model evaluation and sampling easier, many hair scattering models factor f into terms where one depends only on the angles θ and another on ϕ, the difference between ϕ_o and ϕ_i. This *semi-separable* model is given by:

$$f_p(\omega_o, \omega_i) = \frac{M_p(\theta_o, \theta_i) \, A_p(\omega_o) \, N_p(\phi)}{|\cos \theta_i|}, \tag{9.48}$$

where we have a *longitudinal scattering function M_p*, an *attenuation function A_p*, and an *azimuthal scattering function N_p*.[7] The division by $|\cos \theta_i|$ cancels out the corresponding factor in the reflection equation.

In the following implementation, we will evaluate the first few terms of the sum in Equation (9.47) and then represent all higher-order terms with a single one. The pMax constant controls how many are evaluated before the switch-over.

⟨*HairBxDF Constants*⟩ ≡   **606**
```
static constexpr int pMax = 3;
```

The model implemented in the HairBxDF is parameterized by six values:

- h: the $[-1, 1]$ offset along the curve width where the ray intersected the oriented ribbon.
- eta: the index of refraction of the interior of the hair (typically, 1.55).
- sigma_a: the absorption coefficient of the hair interior, where distance is measured with respect to the hair cylinder's diameter. (The absorption coefficient is introduced in Section 11.1.1.)
- beta_m: the longitudinal roughness of the hair, mapped to the range $[0, 1]$.
- beta_n: the azimuthal roughness, also mapped to $[0, 1]$.
- alpha: the angle at which the small scales on the surface of hair are offset from the base cylinder, expressed in degrees (typically, 2).

⟨*HairBxDF Definition*⟩ ≡
```
class HairBxDF {
  public:
    ⟨HairBxDF Public Methods⟩
  private:
    ⟨HairBxDF Constants 606⟩
    ⟨HairBxDF Private Methods 608⟩
    ⟨HairBxDF Private Members 607⟩
};
```

Beyond initializing corresponding member variables, the HairBxDF constructor performs some additional precomputation of values that will be useful for sampling and evaluation

---

7   Other authors generally include A_p in the N_p term, though we find it more clear to keep them separate for the following exposition. Here we also use f for the BSDF, which most hair scattering papers denote by S.

of the scattering model. The corresponding code will be added to the ⟨HairBxDF *constructor implementation*⟩ fragment in the following, closer to where the corresponding values are defined and used. Note that alpha is not stored in a member variable; it is used to compute a few derived quantities that will be, however.

⟨*HairBxDF Private Members*⟩ ≡   **606**
```
Float h, eta;
SampledSpectrum sigma_a;
Float beta_m, beta_n;
```

We will start with the method that evaluates the BSDF.

⟨*HairBxDF Method Definitions*⟩ ≡
```
SampledSpectrum HairBxDF::f(Vector3f wo, Vector3f wi,
                           TransportMode mode) const {
    ⟨Compute hair coordinate system terms related to wo 607⟩
    ⟨Compute hair coordinate system terms related to wi 607⟩
    ⟨Compute cos θₜ for refracted ray 610⟩
    ⟨Compute γₜ for refracted ray 610⟩
    ⟨Compute the transmittance T of a single path through the cylinder 611⟩
    ⟨Evaluate hair BSDF 616⟩
}
```

There are a few quantities related to the directions ω_o and ω_i that are needed for evaluating the hair scattering model—specifically, the sine and cosine of the angle θ that each direction makes with the plane perpendicular to the curve, and the angle ϕ in the azimuthal coordinate system.

As explained in Section 9.9.1, $\sin \theta_o$ is given by the x component of ω_o in the BSDF coordinate system. Given $\sin \theta_o$, because $\theta_o \in [-\pi/2, \pi/2]$, we know that $\cos \theta_o$ must be positive, and so we can compute $\cos \theta_o$ using the identity $\sin^2 \theta + \cos^2 \theta = 1$. The angle ϕ_o in the perpendicular plane can be computed with std::atan.

⟨*Compute hair coordinate system terms related to wo*⟩ ≡   **607, 619**
```
Float sinTheta_o = wo.x;
Float cosTheta_o = SafeSqrt(1 - Sqr(sinTheta_o));
Float phi_o = std::atan2(wo.z, wo.y);
Float gamma_o = SafeASin(h);
```

Equivalent code computes these values for wi.

⟨*Compute hair coordinate system terms related to wi*⟩ ≡   **607**
```
Float sinTheta_i = wi.x;
Float cosTheta_i = SafeSqrt(1 - Sqr(sinTheta_i));
Float phi_i = std::atan2(wi.z, wi.y);
```

With these values available, we will consider in turn the factors of the BSDF model—M_p, A_p, and N_p—before returning to the completion of the f() method.

9.9.3 LONGITUDINAL SCATTERING

M_p defines the component of scattering related to the angles θ—longitudinal scattering. Longitudinal scattering is responsible for the specular lobe along the length of hair and the longitudinal roughness β_m controls the size of this highlight. Figure 9.45 shows hair geometry rendered with three different longitudinal scattering roughnesses.

Float 23
SafeASin() 1035
SafeSqrt() 1034
SampledSpectrum 171
Sqr() 1034
TransportMode 571
Vector3f 86

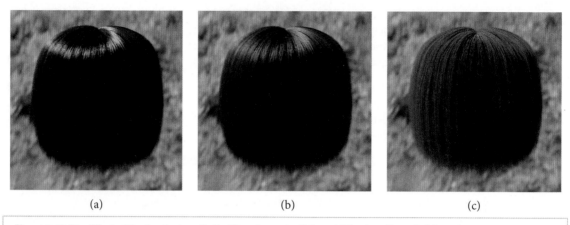

(a)   (b)   (c)

Figure 9.45: The Effect of Varying the Longitudinal Roughness β_m. Hair model illuminated by a skylight environment map rendered with varying longitudinal roughness. (a) With a very low roughness, $\beta_m = 0.1$, the hair appears too shiny—almost metallic. (b) With $\beta_m = 0.25$, the highlight is similar to typical human hair. (c) At high roughness, $\beta_m = 0.7$, the hair is unrealistically flat and diffuse. *(Hair geometry courtesy of Cem Yuksel.)*

The mathematical details of the derivation of the scattering model are complex, so we will not include them here; as always, the "Further Reading" section has references to the details. The design goals of the model implemented here were that it be normalized (ensuring both energy conservation and no energy loss) and that it could be sampled directly. Although this model is not directly based on a physical model of how hair scatters light, it matches measured data well and has parametric control of roughness v.[8]

The model is:

$$M_p(\theta_o, \theta_i) = \frac{1}{2v \sinh(1/v)} e^{-\frac{\sin \theta_i \sin \theta_o}{v}} I_0 \left(\frac{\cos \theta_o \cos \theta_i}{v} \right),$$ [9.49]

where I_0 is the modified Bessel function of the first kind and v is the roughness variance. Figure 9.46 shows plots of M_p.

This model is not numerically stable for low roughness variance values, so our implementation uses a different approach for that case that operates on the logarithm of I_0 before taking an exponent at the end. The v <= .1 test in the implementation below selects between the two formulations.

⟨*HairBxDF Private Methods*⟩ ≡   **606**

```
Float Mp(Float cosTheta_i, Float cosTheta_o, Float sinTheta_i,
         Float sinTheta_o, Float v) {
    Float a = cosTheta_i * cosTheta_o / v, b = sinTheta_i * sinTheta_o / v;
    Float mp = (v <= .1) ?
                (FastExp(LogI0(a) - b - 1 / v + 0.6931f +
                    std::log(1 / (2 * v)))) :
                (FastExp(-b) * I0(a)) / (std::sinh(1 / v) * 2 * v);
    return mp;
}
```

---

8   Note that this is a different usage of v than in earlier chapters when it was used for the parametric coordinate along the width of a curve.

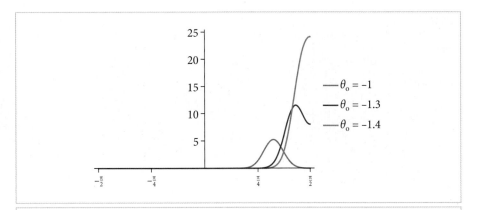

Figure 9.46: Plots of the Longitudinal Scattering Function. The shape of M_p as a function of θ_i for three values of θ_o. In all cases a roughness variance of $v = 0.02$ was used. The peaks are slightly shifted from the perfect specular reflection directions (at $\theta_i = 1$, 1.3, and 1.4, respectively). *(After d'Eon et al. (2011), Figure 4.)*

One challenge with this model is choosing a roughness v to achieve a desired look. Here we have implemented a perceptually uniform mapping from roughness $\beta_m \in [0, 1]$ to v where a roughness of 0 is nearly perfectly smooth and 1 is extremely rough. Different roughness values are used for different values of p. For $p = 1$, roughness is reduced by an empirical factor that models the focusing of light due to refraction through the circular boundary of the hair. It is then increased for $p = 2$ and subsequent terms, which models the effect of light spreading out after multiple reflections at the rough cylinder boundary in the interior of the hair.

⟨HairBxDF *constructor implementation*⟩ ≡
```
v[0] = Sqr(0.726f * beta_m + 0.812f * Sqr(beta_m) + 3.7f * Pow<20>(beta_m));
v[1] = .25 * v[0];
v[2] = 4 * v[0];
for (int p = 3; p <= pMax; ++p)
    v[p] = v[2];
```

⟨*HairBxDF Private Members*⟩ +≡   606
```
Float v[pMax + 1];
```

9.9.4 ABSORPTION IN FIBERS

The A_p factor describes how the incident light is affected by each of the scattering modes p. It incorporates two effects: Fresnel reflection and transmission at the hair–air boundary and absorption of light that passes through the hair (for $p > 0$). Figure 9.47 has rendered images of hair with varying absorption coefficients, showing the effect of absorption. The A_p function that we have implemented models all reflection and transmission at the hair boundary as perfect specular—a very different assumption than M_p and N_p (to come), which model glossy reflection and transmission. This assumption simplifies the implementation and gives reasonable results in practice (presumably in that the specular paths are, in a sense, averages over all the possible glossy paths).

We will start by finding the fraction of incident light that remains after a path of a single transmitted segment through the hair. To do so, we need to find the distance the ray travels until it exits the cylinder; the easiest way to do this is to compute the distances in the longitudinal and azimuthal projections separately.

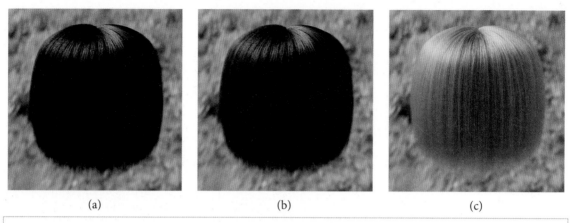

(a)   (b)   (c)

Figure 9.47: Hair Rendered with Various Absorption Coefficients. In all cases, $\beta_m = 0.25$ and $\beta_n = 0.3$. (a) $\sigma_a = (3.35, 5.58, 10.96)$ (RGB coefficients): in black hair, almost all transmitted light is absorbed. The white specular highlight from the $p = 0$ term is the main visual feature. (b) $\sigma_a = (0.84, 1.39, 2.74)$, giving brown hair, where the $p > 1$ terms all introduce color to the hair. (c) With a very low absorption coefficient of $\sigma_a = (0.06, 0.10, 0.20)$, we have blonde hair. *(Hair geometry courtesy of Cem Yuksel.)*

To compute these distances, we need the transmitted angles of the ray ω_o, in the longitudinal and azimuthal planes, which we will denote by θ_t and γ_t, respectively. Application of Snell's law using the hair's index of refraction η allows us to compute $\sin \theta_t$ and $\cos \theta_t$.

⟨*Compute* $\cos \theta_t$ *for refracted ray*⟩ ≡   607, 618
```
Float sinTheta_t = sinTheta_o / eta;
Float cosTheta_t = SafeSqrt(1 - Sqr(sinTheta_t));
```

For γ_t, although we could compute the transmitted direction ω_t from ω_o and then project ω_t into the normal plane, it is possible to compute γ_t directly using a *modified index of refraction* that accounts for the effect of the longitudinal angle on the refracted direction in the normal plane. The modified index of refraction is given by

$$\eta' = \frac{\sqrt{\eta^2 - \sin^2 \theta_o}}{\cos \theta_o}.$$

Given η', we can compute the refracted direction γ_t directly in the normal plane.[9] Since $h = \sin \gamma_o$, we can apply Snell's law to compute γ_t.

⟨*Compute* γ_t *for refracted ray*⟩ ≡   607, 618, 619
```
Float etap = SafeSqrt(Sqr(eta) - Sqr(sinTheta_o)) / cosTheta_o;
Float sinGamma_t = h / etap;
Float cosGamma_t = SafeSqrt(1 - Sqr(sinGamma_t));
Float gamma_t = SafeASin(sinGamma_t);
```

If we consider the azimuthal projection of the transmitted ray in the normal plane, we can see that the segment makes the same angle γ_t with the circle normal at both of its endpoints (Figure 9.48). If we denote the total length of the segment by l_a, then basic trigonometry tells us that $l_a/2 = \cos \gamma_t$, assuming a unit radius circle.

Float 23

HairBxDF::eta 607

HairBxDF::h 607

SafeASin() 1035

SafeSqrt() 1034

Sqr() 1034

---

9   This is due to the *Bravais properties* of cylindrical scattering. See Appendix B of Marschner et al. (2003) for a
    derivation and further explanation.

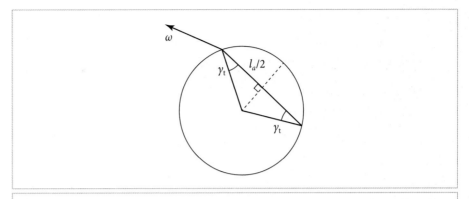

Figure 9.48: Computing the Transmitted Segment's Distance. For a transmitted ray with angle γ_t with respect to the circle's surface normal, half of the total distance l_a is given by $\cos \gamma$, assuming a unit radius. Because γ_t is the same at both halves of the segment, $l_a = 2 \cos \gamma_t$.

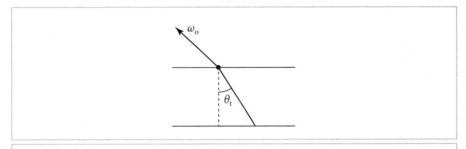

Figure 9.49: The Effect of θ_t on the Transmitted Segment's Length. The length of the transmitted segment through the cylinder is increased by a factor of $1/\cos \theta_t$ versus a direct vertical path.

Now considering the longitudinal projection, we can see that the distance that a transmitted ray travels before exiting is scaled by a factor of $1/\cos \theta_t$ as it passes through the cylinder (Figure 9.49). Putting these together, the total segment length in terms of the hair diameter is

$$l = \frac{2 \cos \gamma_t}{\cos \theta_t}.$$

Given the segment length and the medium's absorption coefficient, the fraction of light transmitted can be computed using Beer's law, which is introduced in Section 11.2. Because the HairBxDF defined σ_a to be measured with respect to the hair diameter (so that adjusting the hair geometry's width does not completely change its color), we do not consider the hair cylinder diameter when we apply Beer's law, and the fraction of light remaining at the end of the segment is given by

$$T_r = e^{-\sigma_a l}. \tag{9.50}$$

⟨*Compute the transmittance* T *of a single path through the cylinder*⟩ ≡   607, 618
```
    SampledSpectrum T = Exp(-sigma_a * (2 * cosGamma_t / cosTheta_t));
```

HairBxDF::sigma_a 607
SampledSpectrum 171
SampledSpectrum::Exp() 172

Given a single segment's transmittance, we can now describe the function that evaluates the full A_p function. Ap() returns an array with the values of A_p up to p_{max} and a final value that is the sum of attenuations for all the higher-order scattering terms.

⟨*HairBxDF Private Methods*⟩ +≡   **606**

```
    pstd::array<SampledSpectrum, pMax + 1>
    Ap(Float cosTheta_o, Float eta, Float h, SampledSpectrum T) {
        pstd::array<SampledSpectrum, pMax + 1> ap;
```
        ⟨*Compute p = 0 attenuation at initial cylinder intersection* **612**⟩
        ⟨*Compute p = 1 attenuation term* **612**⟩
        ⟨*Compute attenuation terms up to p =* pMax **613**⟩
        ⟨*Compute attenuation term accounting for remaining orders of scattering* **613**⟩
```
        return ap;
    }
```

For the A_0 term, corresponding to light that reflects at the cuticle, the Fresnel reflectance at the air–hair boundary gives the fraction of light that is reflected. We can find the cosine of the angle between the surface normal and the direction vector with angles θ_o and γ_o in the hair coordinate system by $\cos\theta_o \cos\gamma_o$.

⟨*Compute p = 0 attenuation at initial cylinder intersection*⟩ ≡   **612**

```
    Float cosGamma_o = SafeSqrt(1 - Sqr(h));
    Float cosTheta = cosTheta_o * cosGamma_o;
    Float f = FrDielectric(cosTheta, eta);
    ap[0] = SampledSpectrum(f);
```

For the TT term, $p = 1$, we have two $1 - f$ factors, accounting for transmission into and out of the cuticle boundary, and a single T factor for one transmission path through the hair.

⟨*Compute p = 1 attenuation term*⟩ ≡   **612**

```
    ap[1] = Sqr(1 - f) * T;
```

The $p = 2$ term has one more reflection event, reflecting light back into the hair, and then a second transmission term. Since we assume perfect specular reflection at the cuticle boundary, both segments inside the hair make the same angle γ_t with the circle's normal (Figure 9.50). From this, we can see that both segments must have the same length (and so forth for subsequent segments). In general, for $p > 0$,

$$A_p = A_{p-1} T f = (1 - f)^2 T^p f^{p-1}.$$

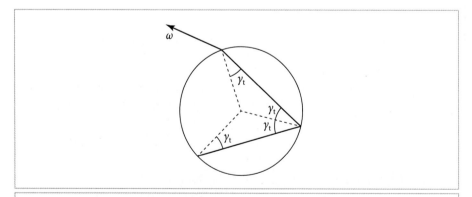

Figure 9.50: When a transmitted ray undergoes specular reflection at the interior of the hair cylinder, it makes the same angle γ_t with the circle's surface normal as the original transmitted ray did. From this, it follows that the lengths of all ray segments for a path inside the cylinder must be equal.

⟨*Compute attenuation terms up to p = pMax*⟩ ≡   612
```
for (int p = 2; p < pMax; ++p)
    ap[p] = ap[p - 1] * T * f;
```

After pMax, a final term accounts for all further orders of scattering. The sum of the infinite series of remaining terms can fortunately be found in closed form, since both $T < 1$ and $f < 1$:

$$\sum_{p=p_{\max}}^{\infty} (1-f)^2 T^p f^{p-1} = \frac{(1-f)^2 T^{p_{\max}} f^{p_{\max}-1}}{1-Tf}.$$

⟨*Compute attenuation term accounting for remaining orders of scattering*⟩ ≡   612
```
if (1 - T * f)
    ap[pMax] = ap[pMax - 1] * f * T / (1 - T * f);
```

9.9.5 AZIMUTHAL SCATTERING

Finally, we will model the component of scattering dependent on the angle ϕ. We will do this work entirely in the normal plane. The azimuthal scattering model is based on first computing a new azimuthal direction assuming perfect specular reflection and transmission and then defining a distribution of directions around this central direction, where increasing roughness gives a wider distribution. Therefore, we will first consider how an incident ray is deflected by specular reflection and transmission in the normal plane; Figure 9.51 illustrates the cases for the first two values of p.

Following the reasoning from Figure 9.51, we can derive the function Φ, which gives the net change in azimuthal direction:

$$\Phi(p, h) = 2p\gamma_t - 2\gamma_o + p\pi.$$

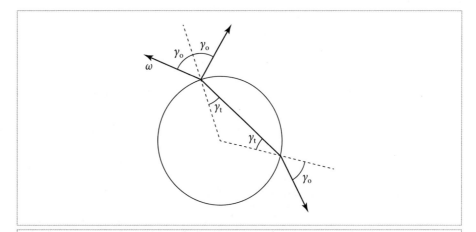

Figure 9.51: For specular reflection, with $p = 0$, the incident and reflected directions make the same angle γ_o with the surface normal. The net change in angle is thus $-2\gamma_o$. For $p = 1$, the ray is deflected from γ_o to γ_t when it enters the cylinder and then correspondingly on the way out. We can also see that when the ray is transmitted again out of the circle, it makes an angle γ_o with the surface normal there. Adding up the angles, the net deflection is $2\gamma_t - 2\gamma_o + \pi$.

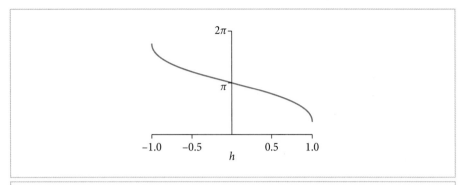

Figure 9.52: Plot of $\Phi(p, h)$ for $p = 1$. As h varies from -1 to 1, we can see that the range of orientations ϕ for the specularly transmitted ray varies rapidly. By examining the range of ϕ values, we can see that the possible transmitted directions cover roughly 2/3 of all possible directions on the circle.

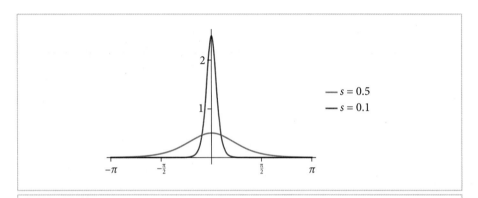

Figure 9.53: Plots of the Trimmed Logistic Function over $\pm\pi$. The curve for $s = 0.5$ (blue line) is broad and flat, while at $s = 0.1$ (red line), the curve is peaked. Because the function is normalized, the peak at 0 generally does not have the value 1, unlike the Gaussian.

(Recall that γ_o and γ_t are derived from h.) Figure 9.52 shows a plot of this function for $p = 1$.

⟨*HairBxDF Private Methods*⟩ +≡   **606**
```
Float Phi(int p, Float gamma_o, Float gamma_t) {
    return 2 * p * gamma_t - 2 * gamma_o + p * Pi;
}
```

Now that we know how to compute new angles in the normal plane after specular transmission and reflection, we need a way to represent surface roughness, so that a range of directions centered around the specular direction can contribute to scattering. The *logistic distribution* provides a good option: it is a generally useful one for rendering, since it has a similar shape to the Gaussian, while also being normalized and integrable in closed form (unlike the Gaussian); see Section B.2.5 for more information.

In the following, we will find it useful to define a normalized logistic function over a range $[a, b]$; we will call this the *trimmed logistic*, l_t.

$$l_t(x, s, [a, b]) = \frac{l(x, s)}{\int_a^b l(x', s) \, dx'}.$$

Float 23
Pi 1033

Figure 9.53 shows plots of the trimmed logistic distribution for a few values of s.

Now we have the pieces to be able to implement the azimuthal scattering distribution. The Np() function computes the N_p term, finding the angular difference between ϕ and $\Phi(p, h)$ and evaluating the azimuthal distribution with that angle.

⟨*HairBxDF Private Methods*⟩ +≡   606
```
Float Np(Float phi, int p, Float s, Float gamma_o, Float gamma_t) {
    Float dphi = phi - Phi(p, gamma_o, gamma_t);
    ⟨Remap dphi to [−π, π] 615⟩
    return TrimmedLogistic(dphi, s, -Pi, Pi);
}
```

The difference between ϕ and $\Phi(p, h)$ may be outside the range we have defined the logistic over, $[-\pi, \pi]$, so we rotate around the circle as needed to get the value to the right range. Because dphi never gets too far out of range for the small p used here, we use the simple approach of adding or subtracting 2π as needed.

⟨*Remap* dphi *to* $[−\pi, \pi]$⟩ ≡   615
```
while (dphi > Pi) dphi -= 2 * Pi;
while (dphi < -Pi) dphi += 2 * Pi;
```

As with the longitudinal roughness, it is helpful to have a roughly perceptually linear mapping from azimuthal roughness $\beta_n \in [0, 1]$ to the logistic scale factor s.

⟨*HairBxDF constructor implementation*⟩ +≡
```
static const Float SqrtPiOver8 = 0.626657069f;
s = SqrtPiOver8 * (0.265f * beta_n + 1.194f * Sqr(beta_n) +
                   5.372f * Pow<22>(beta_n));
```

⟨*HairBxDF Private Members*⟩ +≡   606
```
Float s;
```

Figure 9.54 shows polar plots of azimuthal scattering for the TT term, $p = 1$, with a fairly low roughness. The scattering distributions for the two different points on the curve's width are quite different. Because we expect the hair width to be roughly pixel-sized, many rays per pixel are needed to resolve this variation well.

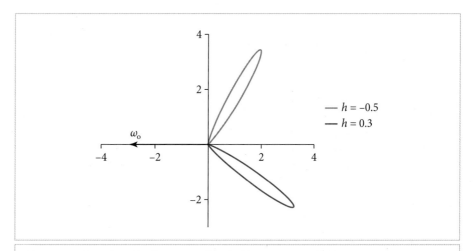

Figure 9.54: Polar plots of N_p for $p = 1$, θ_o aligned with the $-x$ axis, and with a low roughness, $\beta_n = 0.1$, for (blue) $h = -0.5$ and (red) $h = 0.3$. We can see that N_p varies rapidly over the width of the hair.

9.9.6 SCATTERING MODEL EVALUATION

We now have almost all the pieces we need to be able to evaluate the model. The last detail is to account for the effect of scales on the hair surface (recall Figure 9.43). Suitable adjustments to θ_o work well to model this characteristic of hair.

For the R term, adding the angle 2α to θ_o can model the effect of evaluating the hair scattering model with respect to the surface normal of a scale. We can then go ahead and evaluate M_0 with this modification to θ_o. For TT, we have to account for two transmission events through scales. Rotating by α in the opposite direction approximately compensates. (Because the refraction angle is nonlinear with respect to changes in normal orientation, there is some error in this approximation, though the error is low for the typical case of small values of α.) TRT has a reflection term inside the hair; a rotation by -4α compensates for the overall effect.

The effects of these shifts are that the primary reflection lobe R is offset to be above the perfect specular direction and the secondary TRT lobe is shifted below it. Together, these lead to two distinct specular highlights of different colors, since R is not affected by the hair's color, while TRT picks up the hair color due to absorption. This effect can be seen in human hair and is evident in the images in Figure 9.45, for example.

Because we only need the sine and cosine of the angle θ_i to evaluate M_p, we can use the trigonometric identities

$$\sin(\theta_o \pm \alpha) = \sin\theta_o \cos\alpha \pm \cos\theta_o \sin\alpha$$

$$\cos(\theta_o \pm \alpha) = \cos\theta_o \cos\alpha \mp \sin\theta_o \sin\alpha$$

to efficiently compute the rotated angles without needing to evaluate any additional trigonometric functions. The `HairBxDF` constructor therefore precomputes $\sin(2^k\alpha)$ and $\cos(2^k\alpha)$ for $k = 0, 1, 2$. These values can be computed particularly efficiently using trigonometric double angle identities: $\cos 2\theta = \cos^2\theta - \sin^2\theta$ and $\sin 2\theta = 2\cos\theta\sin\theta$.

⟨HairBxDF *constructor implementation*⟩ +≡
```
sin2kAlpha[0] = std::sin(Radians(alpha));
cos2kAlpha[0] = SafeSqrt(1 - Sqr(sin2kAlpha[0]));
for (int i = 1; i < pMax; ++i) {
    sin2kAlpha[i] = 2 * cos2kAlpha[i - 1] * sin2kAlpha[i - 1];
    cos2kAlpha[i] = Sqr(cos2kAlpha[i - 1]) - Sqr(sin2kAlpha[i - 1]);
}
```

⟨*HairBxDF Private Members*⟩ +≡   **606**
```
Float sin2kAlpha[pMax], cos2kAlpha[pMax];
```

Evaluating the model is now mostly just a matter of calling functions that have already been defined and summing the individual terms f_p.

⟨*Evaluate hair BSDF*⟩ ≡   **607**
```
Float phi = phi_i - phi_o;
pstd::array<SampledSpectrum, pMax + 1> ap = Ap(cosTheta_o, eta, h, T);
SampledSpectrum fsum(0.);
```

```
for (int p = 0; p < pMax; ++p) {
    ⟨Compute sin θ₀ and cos θ₀ terms accounting for scales  617⟩
    fsum += Mp(cosTheta_i, cosThetap_o, sinTheta_i, sinThetap_o, v[p]) *
            ap[p] * Np(phi, p, s, gamma_o, gamma_t);
}
⟨Compute contribution of remaining terms after pMax  617⟩
if (AbsCosTheta(wi) > 0)
    fsum /= AbsCosTheta(wi);
return fsum;
```

The rotations that account for the effect of scales are implemented using the trigonometric identities listed above. Here is the code for the $p = 0$ case, where θ_o is rotated by 2α. The remaining cases follow the same structure. (The rotation is by $-\alpha$ for $p = 1$ and by -4α for $p = 2$.)

⟨*Compute* sin θ_o *and* cos θ_o *terms accounting for scales*⟩ ≡   616, 619, 620
```
    Float sinThetap_o, cosThetap_o;
    if (p == 0) {
        sinThetap_o = sinTheta_o * cos2kAlpha[1] - cosTheta_o * sin2kAlpha[1];
        cosThetap_o = cosTheta_o * cos2kAlpha[1] + sinTheta_o * sin2kAlpha[1];
    }
    ⟨Handle remainder of p values for hair scale tilt⟩
    ⟨Handle out-of-range cos θ₀ from scale adjustment  617⟩
```

When ω_i is nearly parallel with the hair, the scale adjustment may give a slightly negative value for cos θ_i—effectively, in this case, it represents a θ_i that is slightly greater than $\pi/2$, the maximum expected value of θ in the hair coordinate system. This angle is equivalent to $\pi - \theta_i$, and $\cos(\pi - \theta_i) = |\cos\theta_i|$, so we can easily handle that here.

⟨*Handle out-of-range* cos θ_o *from scale adjustment*⟩ ≡   617, 620
```
    cosThetap_o = std::abs(cosThetap_o);
```

A final term accounts for all higher-order scattering inside the hair. We just use a uniform distribution $N(\phi) = 1/(2\pi)$ for the azimuthal distribution; this is a reasonable choice, as the direction offsets from $\Phi(p, h)$ for $p \geq p_{\max}$ generally have wide variation and the final A_p term generally represents less than 15% of the overall scattering, so little error is introduced in the final result.

⟨*Compute contribution of remaining terms after* pMax⟩ ≡   616
```
    fsum += Mp(cosTheta_i, cosTheta_o, sinTheta_i, sinTheta_o, v[pMax]) *
            ap[pMax] / (2 * Pi);
```

A Note on Reciprocity

Although we included reciprocity in the properties of physically valid BRDFs in Section 4.3.1, the model we have implemented in this section is, unfortunately, not reciprocal. An immediate issue is that the rotation for hair scales is applied only to θ_i. However, there are more problems: first, all terms $p > 0$ that involve transmission are not reciprocal since the transmission terms use values based on ω_t, which itself only depends on ω_o. Thus, if ω_o and ω_i are interchanged, a completely different ω_t is computed, which in turn leads to different cos θ_t and γ_t values, which in turn give different values from the A_p and N_p functions. In practice, however, we have not observed artifacts in images from these shortcomings.

9.9.7 SAMPLING

Being able to generate sampled directions and compute the PDF for sampling a given direction according to a distribution that is similar to the overall BSDF is critical for efficient rendering, especially at low roughnesses, where the hair BSDF varies rapidly as a function of direction. In the approach implemented here, samples are generated with a two-step process: first we choose a p term to sample according to a probability based on each term's A_p function value, which gives its contribution to the overall scattering function. Then, we find a direction by sampling the corresponding M_p and N_p terms.[10] Fortunately, both the M_p and N_p terms of the hair BSDF can be sampled perfectly, leaving us with a sampling scheme that exactly matches the PDF of the full BSDF.

We will first define the ApPDF() method, which returns a discrete PDF with probabilities for sampling each term A_p according to its contribution relative to all the A_p terms, given θ_o.

⟨*HairBxDF Method Definitions*⟩ +≡
```
    pstd::array<Float, HairBxDF::pMax + 1>
    HairBxDF::ApPDF(Float cosTheta_o) const {
        ⟨Initialize array of A_p values for cosTheta_o 618⟩
        ⟨Compute A_p PDF from individual A_p terms 618⟩
        return apPDF;
    }
```

The method starts by computing the values of A_p for cosTheta_o. We are able to reuse some previously defined fragments to make this task easier.

⟨*Initialize array of A_p values for* cosTheta_o⟩ ≡   618
```
    Float sinTheta_o = SafeSqrt(1 - Sqr(cosTheta_o));
    ⟨Compute cos θ_t for refracted ray 610⟩
    ⟨Compute γ_t for refracted ray 610⟩
    ⟨Compute the transmittance T of a single path through the cylinder 611⟩
    pstd::array<SampledSpectrum, pMax + 1> ap = Ap(cosTheta_o, eta, h, T);
```

Next, the spectral A_p values are converted to scalars using their luminance and these values are normalized to make a proper PDF.

⟨*Compute A_p PDF from individual A_p terms*⟩ ≡   618
```
    pstd::array<Float, pMax + 1> apPDF;
    Float sumY = 0;
    for (const SampledSpectrum &as : ap)
        sumY += as.Average();
    for (int i = 0; i <= pMax; ++i)
        apPDF[i] = ap[i].Average() / sumY;
```

With these preliminaries out of the way, we can now implement the Sample_f() method.

Float 23
HairBxDF::Ap() 612
HairBxDF::h 607
HairBxDF::pMax 606
SafeSqrt() 1034
SampledSpectrum 171
SampledSpectrum::Average() 172
Sqr() 1034

---

10 This approach is applicable since the BSDF's definition includes the product of M_p and N_p and so their joint PDF is separable.

⟨*HairBxDF Method Definitions*⟩ +≡
```
pstd::optional<BSDFSample>
HairBxDF::Sample_f(Vector3f wo, Float uc, Point2f u, TransportMode mode,
                   BxDFReflTransFlags sampleFlags) const {
```
⟨*Compute hair coordinate system terms related to* wo *607*⟩
⟨*Determine which term p to sample for hair scattering* **619**⟩
⟨*Compute* sin θ_o *and* cos θ_o *terms accounting for scales* **617**⟩
⟨*Sample* M_p *to compute* θ_i **619**⟩
⟨*Sample* N_p *to compute* $\Delta\phi$ **619**⟩
⟨*Compute* wi *from sampled hair scattering angles* **620**⟩
⟨*Compute PDF for sampled hair scattering direction* wi **620**⟩
```
    return BSDFSample(f(wo, wi, mode), wi, pdf, Flags());
}
```

Given the PDF over A_p terms, a call to SampleDiscrete() takes care of choosing one. Because we only need to generate one sample from the PDF's distribution, the work to compute an explicit CDF array (for example, by using PiecewiseConstant1D) is not worthwhile. Note that we take advantage of SampleDiscrete()'s optional capability of returning a fresh uniform random sample, overwriting the value in uc. This sample value will be used shortly for sampling N_p.

⟨*Determine which term p to sample for hair scattering*⟩ ≡   **619**
```
pstd::array<Float, pMax + 1> apPDF = ApPDF(cosTheta_o);
int p = SampleDiscrete(apPDF, uc, nullptr, &uc);
```

We can now sample the corresponding M_p term given θ_o to find θ_i. The derivation of this sampling method is fairly involved, so we will include neither the derivation nor the implementation here. This fragment, ⟨*Sample* M_p *to compute* θ_i⟩, consumes both of the sample values u[0] and u[1] and initializes variables sinTheta_i and cosTheta_i according to the sampled direction.

⟨*Sample* M_p *to compute* θ_i⟩ ≡   **619**
```
Float cosTheta = 1 + v[p] * std::log(std::max<Float>(u[0], 1e-5) +
                                     (1 - u[0]) * FastExp(-2 / v[p]));
Float sinTheta = SafeSqrt(1 - Sqr(cosTheta));
Float cosPhi = std::cos(2 * Pi * u[1]);
Float sinTheta_i = -cosTheta * sinThetap_o +
                        sinTheta * cosPhi * cosThetap_o;
Float cosTheta_i = SafeSqrt(1 - Sqr(sinTheta_i));
```

Next we will sample the azimuthal distribution N_p. For terms up to p_{max}, we take a sample from the logistic distribution centered around the exit direction given by $\Phi(p, h)$. For the last term, we sample from a uniform distribution.

⟨*Sample* N_p *to compute* $\Delta\phi$⟩ ≡   **619**
```
⟨Compute γt for refracted ray 610⟩
Float dphi;
if (p < pMax)
    dphi = Phi(p, gamma_o, gamma_t) + SampleTrimmedLogistic(uc, s, -Pi, Pi);
else
    dphi = 2 * Pi * uc;
```

Given θ_i and ϕ_i, we can compute the sampled direction wi. The math is similar to that used in the SphericalDirection() function, but with two important differences. First, because here θ is measured with respect to the plane perpendicular to the cylinder rather than the cylinder axis, we need to compute $\cos(\pi/2 - \theta) = \sin\theta$ for the coordinate with respect to the cylinder axis instead of $\cos\theta$. Second, because the hair shading coordinate system's (θ, ϕ) coordinates are oriented with respect to the $+x$ axis, the order of dimensions passed to the Vector3f constructor is adjusted correspondingly, since the direction returned from Sample_f() should be in the BSDF coordinate system.

⟨*Compute* wi *from sampled hair scattering angles*⟩ ≡   **619**
```
Float phi_i = phi_o + dphi;
Vector3f wi(sinTheta_i, cosTheta_i * std::cos(phi_i),
            cosTheta_i * std::sin(phi_i));
```

Because we could sample directly from the M_p and N_p distributions, the overall PDF is

$$\sum_{p=0}^{p_{max}} M_p(\theta_o, \theta_i)\, \tilde{A}_p(\omega_o) N_p(\phi),$$

where $\tilde{A}_p$ are the normalized PDF terms. Note that θ_o must be shifted to account for hair scales when evaluating the PDF; this is done in the same way (and with the same code fragment) as with BSDF evaluation.

⟨*Compute PDF for sampled hair scattering direction* wi⟩ ≡   **619**
```
Float pdf = 0;
for (int p = 0; p < pMax; ++p) {
    ⟨Compute sin θₒ and cos θₒ terms accounting for scales 617⟩
    ⟨Handle out-of-range cos θₒ from scale adjustment 617⟩
    pdf += Mp(cosTheta_i, cosThetap_o, sinTheta_i, sinThetap_o, v[p]) *
           apPDF[p] * Np(dphi, p, s, gamma_o, gamma_t);
}
pdf += Mp(cosTheta_i, cosTheta_o, sinTheta_i, sinTheta_o, v[pMax]) *
       apPDF[pMax] * (1 / (2 * Pi));
```

The HairBxDF::PDF() method performs the same computation and therefore the implementation is not included here.

9.9.8 HAIR ABSORPTION COEFFICIENTS

The color of hair is determined by how pigments in the cortex absorb light, which in turn is described by the normalized absorption coefficient where distance is measured in terms of the hair diameter. If a specific hair color is desired, there is a non-obvious relationship between the normalized absorption coefficient and the color of hair in a rendered image. Not only does changing the spectral values of the absorption coefficient have an unpredictable connection to the appearance of a single hair, but multiple scattering between collections of many hairs has a significant effect on each one's apparent color. Therefore, pbrt provides implementations of two more intuitive ways to specify hair color.

The first is based on the fact that the color of human hair is determined by the concentration of two pigments. The concentration of eumelanin is the primary factor that causes the difference between black, brown, and blonde hair. (Black hair has the most eumelanin and blonde hair has the least. White hair has none.) The second pigment, pheomelanin, causes hair to be orange or red. The HairBxDF class provides a convenience method that computes an absorption coefficient using the product of user-supplied pigment concentrations and absorption coefficients of the pigments.

Float 23
HairBxDF::Mp() 608
HairBxDF::Np() 615
HairBxDF::pMax 606
HairBxDF::v 609
Pi 1033
Vector3f 86

(a)   (b)

Figure 9.55: The Importance of Multiple Scattering in Blonde Hair. (a) Blonde hair rendered with up to three bounces of light inside the hair. (b) Rendered with up to fifty bounces of light. In light-colored hair, light that has been scattered many times makes an important contribution to its visual appearance. Accurately rendering very blonde or white hair is consequently more computationally intensive than rendering dark hair. *(Hair geometry courtesy of Cem Yuksel.)*

⟨*HairBxDF Method Definitions*⟩ +≡
```
RGBUnboundedSpectrum HairBxDF::SigmaAFromConcentration(Float ce, Float cp) {
    RGB eumelaninSigma_a(0.419f, 0.697f, 1.37f);
    RGB pheomelaninSigma_a(0.187f, 0.4f, 1.05f);
    RGB sigma_a = ce * eumelaninSigma_a + cp * pheomelaninSigma_a;
    return RGBUnboundedSpectrum(*RGBColorSpace::sRGB, sigma_a);
}
```

Eumelanin concentrations of roughly 8, 1.3, and 0.3 give reasonable representations of black, brown, and blonde hair, respectively. Accurately rendering light-colored hair requires simulating many interreflections of light, however; see Figure 9.55.

It is also sometimes useful to specify the desired hair color directly; the `SigmaAFromReflect ance()` method, not included here, is based on a precomputed fit of absorption coefficients to scattered hair color.

FURTHER READING

Hall's (1989) book collected and described the state of the art in physically based surface reflection models for graphics; it remains a seminal reference. It discusses the physics of surface reflection in detail, with many pointers to the original literature.

Microfacet Models

Phong (1975) developed an early empirical reflection model for glossy surfaces in computer graphics. Although neither reciprocal nor energy conserving, it was a cornerstone of the first synthetic images of non-Lambertian objects. The Torrance–Sparrow microfacet model was described by Torrance and Sparrow (1967); it was first introduced to graphics by Blinn (1977), and a variant of it was used by Cook and Torrance (1981, 1982).

The papers by Beckmann and Spizzichino (1963) and Trowbridge and Reitz (1975) introduced two widely used microfacet distribution functions. Kurt et al. (2010) introduced an anisotropic variant of the Beckmann–Spizzichino distribution function; see Heitz (2014) for anisotropic variants of many other microfacet distribution functions. (Early anisotropic BRDF models for computer graphics were developed by Kajiya (1985) and Poulin and Fournier (1990).) Ribardière et al. (2017) applied Student's t-distribution to model microfacet distributions; it provides an additional degree of freedom, which they showed allows a better fit to measured data while subsuming both the Beckmann–Spizzichino and Trowbridge–Reitz distributions. Ribardière et al. (2019) investigated the connection between normal distribution functions (NDFs) and microfacet distributions and also showed how to generate surfaces with distributions described by their model.

The microfacet masking-shadowing function was introduced by Smith (1967), building on the assumption that heights of nearby points on the microfacet surface are uncorrelated. Smith also first derived the normalization constraint in Equation (9.17). Heitz's paper on microfacet masking-shadowing functions (2014) provides a very well-written introduction to microfacet BSDF models in general, with many useful figures and explanations about details of the topic.

The more accurate $G(\omega_i, \omega_o)$ function for Gaussian microfacet surfaces that better accounts for the effects of correlation between the two directions that we have implemented is due to Ross et al. (2005). Our derivation of the $\Lambda(\omega)$ function, Equation (9.19), follows Heitz (2015).

For many decades, Monte Carlo rendering of microfacet models involved generating samples proportional to the microfacet distribution $D(\omega_h)$. Heitz and d'Eon (2014) were the first to demonstrate that it was possible to reduce variance by restricting this sampling process to only consider visible microfacets. Our microfacet sampling implementation in Section 9.6 follows Heitz's improved approach (2018), which showed that sampling the visible area of the Trowbridge–Reitz microfacet distribution corresponds to sampling the projection of a truncated ellipsoid, which in turn can be performed using an approach developed by Walter et al. (2015). See also Heitz (2014) for an overview of traditional techniques that directly sample the microfacet distribution $D(\omega_h)$ without considering visibility.

When dealing with refraction through rough dielectrics, a modified change of variables term is needed to account for the mapping from half vectors to outgoing direction. A model based on this approach was originally developed by Stam (2001); Walter et al. (2007) proposed improvements and provided an elegant geometric justification of the half vector mapping of Equation (9.36). The generalized half-direction vector for refraction used in these models and in Equation (9.34) is due to Sommerfeld and Runge (1911).

One issue with the specular term of the Torrance–Sparrow BRDF presented in Section 9.6.5 is that it only models a single scattering interaction with the microfacet surface, causing a growing portion of the energy to be lost as the roughness increases. In scenes where many subsequent interactions are crucial (e.g., a complex 3D object made from a translucent rough dielectric material), this energy loss can become so conspicuous that standard microfacet models become effectively unusable.

The original model by Torrance and Sparrow (1967) included a diffuse component to simulate light having scattered multiple times. However, a simple diffuse correction is generally unsatisfactory, since the precise amount of energy loss will depend both on the surface roughness and the angle of incidence. Kelemen and Szirmay-Kalos (2001) proposed an improved diffuse-like term that accounts for this dependence. Jakob et al. (2014a) generalized their approach to rough dielectric boundaries in the context of layered structures, where energy losses can be particularly undesirable.

In all of these cases, light is treated as essentially diffuse following scattering by multiple facets. Building on Smith's uncorrelated height assumption, Heitz et al. (2016b) cast a microfacet BRDF model into a volumetric analogue composed of microflakes—that is, a distribution of mirror facets suspended in a 3D space. With this new interpretation, they are able to simulate an arbitrary number of volumetric scattering interactions to evaluate an effective BRDF that is free of energy loss and arguably closer to physical reality.

Analytic solutions may sometimes obviate the need for a stochastic simulation of interreflection. For example, Lee et al. (2018) and Xie and Hanrahan (2018) both derived analytic models for multiple scattering under the assumption of microfacets with a v-groove shape. Efficient approximate models for multiple scattering among microfacets were presented by Kulla and Conty Estevez (2017) and by Turquin (2019).

Microfacet models have provided a foundation for a variety of additional reflection models. Simonot (2009) has developed a model that spans Oren–Nayar's diffuse microfacet model (1994) and Torrance–Sparrow: microfacets are modeled as Lambertian reflectors with a layer above them that ranges from perfectly transmissive to a perfect specular reflector. Conty Estevez and Kulla (2017) have developed a model for cloth. The halo of a softer and wider secondary highlight is often visible with rough surfaces. Barla et al. (2018) described a model for such surfaces with a focus on perceptually meaningful parameters for it.

Weyrich et al. (2009) have developed methods to infer a microfacet distribution that matches a measured or desired reflection distribution. Remarkably, they showed that it is possible to manufacture actual physical surfaces that match a desired reflection distribution fairly accurately.

Layered Materials

Many materials are naturally composed of multiple layers—for example, a metal base surface tarnished with patina, or wood with a varnish coating. Using a specialized BRDF to represent such structures can be vastly more efficient than resolving internal reflections using standard light transport methods.

Hanrahan and Krueger (1993) modeled the layers of skin, accounting for just a single scattering event in each layer, and Dorsey and Hanrahan (1996) rendered layered materials using the Kubelka–Munk theory, which accounts for multiple scattering within layers but assumes that radiance distribution does not vary as a function of direction.

Pharr and Hanrahan (2000) showed that Monte Carlo integration could be used to solve the *adding equations* to efficiently compute BSDFs for layered materials without needing either of these simplifications. The adding equations are integral equations that accurately describe the effect of multiple scattering in layered media; they were derived by van de Hulst (1980) and Twomey et al. (1966).

Weidlich and Wilkie (2007) rendered layered materials more efficiently by making a number of simplifying assumptions. Guo et al. (2018) showed that both unidirectional and bidirectional Monte Carlo random walks through layers led to efficient algorithms for evaluation, sampling, and PDF evaluation. (Their unidirectional approach is implemented in pbrt's LayeredBxDF in Section 14.3.) Xia et al. (2020a) described an improved importance sampling for this approach and Gamboa et al. (2020) showed that bidirectional sampling was unnecessary and described a more efficient approach for multiple layers.

LayeredBxDF 895

Another approach for layered materials is to represent the aggregate scattering behavior of a layered surface using a parametric representation. Examples include Jakob et al. (2014a) and Zeltner and Jakob (2018), who applied the adding equations to discretized scattering matrices describing volumetric layers and rough interfaces. Guo et al. (2017) modeled coated surfaces using a modified microfacet scattering model. Belcour (2018) characterized individual layers' scattering statistically, computed aggregate scattering using the adding equations, and then mapped the result to sums of lobes based on the Trowbridge–Reitz microfacet distribution function. Weier and Belcour (2020) generalized this approach to handle anisotropic reflection from the layer interfaces and Randrianandrasana et al. (2021) further generalized the model to improve accuracy and ensure energy conservation.

It is possible to apply similar approaches to aggregate scattering at other scales. For example, Blumer et al. precomputed the effect of multiple scattering in complex geometry like trees and stored the result in a form that allows for efficient evaluation and sampling (Blumer et al. 2016).

BSDF (Re-)Parameterization and Acquisition

Improvements in data-acquisition technology have led to increasing amounts of detailed real-world BRDF data, even including BRDFs that are spatially varying (sometimes called "bidirectional texture functions," BTFs) (Dana et al. 1999). See Müller et al. (2005) for a survey of work in BRDF measurement until the year 2005 and Guarnera et al. (2016) for a survey through the following decade.

Fitting measured BRDF data to parametric reflection models is a difficult problem. Rusinkiewicz (1998) made the influential observation that reparameterizing the measured data can make it substantially easier to compress or fit to models. The topic of BRDF parameterizations has also been investigated by Stark et al. (2005) and in Marscher's Ph.D. dissertation (1998).

Building on Rusinkiewicz's parameterization, Matusik et al. (2003a, 2003b) designed a BRDF representation and an efficient measurement device that repeatedly photographs a spherical sample to simultaneously acquire BRDF evaluations for many directions. They used this device to assemble a collection of isotropic material measurements that is now known as the MERL BRDF database. Baek et al. (2020) extended this approach with additional optics to capture polarimetric BRDFs, whose evaluation yields 4×4 Mueller matrices that characterize how reflection changes the polarization state of light. Nielsen et al. (2015) analyzed the manifold of MERL BRDFs to show that as few as 10–20 carefully chosen measurements can produce high-quality BRDF approximations.

Dupuy et al. (2015) developed a simple iterative procedure for fitting standard microfacet distributions to measured BRDFs. Dupuy and Jakob (2018) generalized this procedure to arbitrary data-driven microfacet distributions and used the resulting approximation to perform a measurement in reparameterized coordinates, which is the approach underlying the `MeasuredBxDF`. They then used a motorized goniophotometer to spectroscopically acquire a collection of isotropic and anisotropic material samples that can be loaded into pbrt.

While the high-dimensional nature of reflectance functions can pose a serious impediment in any acquisition procedure, the resulting data can often be approximated much more compactly. Bagher et al. (2016) decomposed the MERL database into a set of 1D factors requiring 3.2 KiB per material. Vávra and Filip (2016) showed how lower-dimensional slices can inform a sparse measurement procedure for anisotropic materials.

MeasuredBxDF 592

Hair, Fur, and Fibers

Kajiya and Kay (1989) were the first to develop a reflectance model for hair fibers, observing the characteristic behavior of the underlying cylindrical reflectance geometry. For example, a thin and ideally specular cylinder under parallel illumination will reflect light into a 1D cone of angles. Reflection from a rough cylinder tends to concentrate around the specular 1D cone and decay with increasing angular distance. Kajiya and Kay proposed a phenomenological model combining diffuse and specular terms sharing these properties. For related work, see also the paper by Banks (1994), which discusses basic shading models for 1D primitives like hair. Goldman (1997) developed a probabilistic shading model that models reflection from collections of short hairs. Ward et al.'s survey (2007) has extensive coverage of early research in modeling, animating, and rendering hair.

Marschner et al. (2003) investigated the processes underlying scattering from hair and performed a variety of measurements of scattering from actual hair. They introduced the longitudinal/azimuthal decomposition and the use of the modified index of refraction to hair rendering. They then developed a scattering model where the longitudinal component was derived by first considering perfect specular paths and then allowing roughness by centering a Gaussian around them, and their azimuthal model assumed perfect specular reflections. They showed that this model agreed reasonably well with their measurements. Hery and Ramamoorthi (2012) showed how to sample the first term of this model and Pekelis et al. (2015) developed a more efficient approach to sampling all of its terms.

Zinke and Weber (2007) formalized different ways of modeling scattering from hair and clarified the assumptions underlying each of them. Starting with the *bidirectional fiber scattering distribution function* (BFSDF), which describes reflected differential radiance at a point on a hair as a fraction of incident differential power at another, they showed how assuming homogeneous scattering properties and a far-away viewer and illumination made it possible to simplify the eight-dimensional BFSDF to a four-dimensional *bidirectional curve scattering distribution function* (BCSDF). (Our implementation of the HairBxDF has glossed over some of these subtleties and opted for the simplicity of considering the scattering model as a BSDF.)

Sadeghi et al. (2010) developed a hair scattering model with artist-friendly controls; Ou et al. (2012) showed how to sample from its distribution. Ogaki et al. (2010) created a tabularized model by explicitly modeling hair microgeometry and following random walks through it.

D'Eon et al. (2011, 2013) made a number of improvements to Marschner et al.'s model. They showed that their M_p term was not actually energy conserving and derived a new one that was; this is the model from Equation (9.49) that our implementation uses. (See also d'Eon (2013) for a more numerically stable formulation of M_p for low roughness, as well as Jakob (2012) for notes related to sampling their M_p term in a numerically stable way.) They also introduced a Gaussian to the azimuthal term, allowing for varying azimuthal roughness. A 1D quadrature method was used to integrate the model across the width of the hair h.

The RGB values used for the hair pigments in HairBxDF::SigmaAFromConcentration() were computed by d'Eon et al. (2011), based on a model by Donner and Jensen (2006). The function implemented in the HairBxDF::SigmaAFromReflectance() method is due to Chiang et al. (2016a), who created a cube of hair and rendered it with a variety of absorption coefficients and roughnesses while it was illuminated with a uniform white dome. They then fit a function that mapped from the hair's azimuthal roughness and average color at the center of the front face of the cube to an absorption coefficient.

D'Eon et al. (2014) performed extensive Monte Carlo simulations of scattering from dielectric cylinders with explicitly modeled scales and glossy scattering at the boundary based on

HairBxDF 606

HairBxDF::
SigmaAFromConcentration()
621

HairBxDF::
SigmaAFromReflectance()
621

a Beckmann microfacet distribution. They showed that separable models did not model all the observed effects and that in particular the specular term modeled by M_p varies over the surface of the cylinder and also depends on ϕ. They developed a non-separable scattering model, where both α and β_m vary as a function of h, and showed that it fit their simulations very accurately.

All the scattering models we have described so far have been BCSDFs—they represent the overall scattering across the entire width of the hair in a single model. Such "far field" models assume both that the viewer is far away and that incident illumination is uniform across the hair's width. In practice, both of these assumptions are invalid if one is using path tracing to model multiple scattering inside hair. Two recent models have considered scattering at a single point along the hair's width, making them more suitable for accurately modeling "near field" scattering.

Yan et al. (2015) generalized d'Eon et al.'s model to account for scattering in the medulla, modeling a scattering cylinder in the interior of fur, and validated their model with a variety of measurements of actual animal fur. Subsequent work developed an efficient model that allows both near- and far-field evaluation (Yan et al. 2017a).

Chiang et al. (2016a) showed that eliminating the integral over width from d'Eon et al.'s model works well in practice and that the sampling rates necessary for path tracing also worked well to integrate scattering over the curve width, giving a much more efficient implementation. They also developed the perceptually uniform parameterization of β_m and β_n that we have implemented in the HairBxDF as well as the inverse mapping from reflectance to σ_a used in our HairBxDF::SigmaAFromReflectance() method.

Further recent advances in hair and fur rendering include work by Khungurn and Marschner (2017), who developed a scattering model from elliptical fibers and showed that modeling fibers as elliptical rather than cylindrical gives a closer match to measured data. Benamira and Pattanaik (2021) recently proposed a model that accounts for both elliptical fibers and diffraction effects, which are significant at the scale of human hair.

Modeling and rendering the individual fibers of fabric is closely related to doing so for hair and fur. Recent work includes Zhao et al. (2016), who fit a procedural yarn model to CT-scanned yarn, and Aliaga et al. (2017), who demonstrated the complexity of scattering from a variety of cloth fibers and developed tabularized scattering functions for them using a precomputed simulation.

Glints and Microstructure

The microfacet reflection models in this chapter are all based on the assumption that so many microfacets are visible in a pixel that they can be accurately described by their aggregate statistical behavior. This assumption is not true for many real-world surfaces, where a relatively small number of microfacets may be visible in each pixel; examples of such surfaces include glittery car paint and plastics. Additionally, many types of rough surfaces that aren't considered glittery (e.g., bead-blasted plastic) are characterized by bright high-frequency glints under directionally peaked illumination (e.g., the sun).

A common characteristic of many glint-rendering techniques is that they replace point evaluations of reflectance functions with a directional and/or spatial average covering a small region (e.g., a ray differential). With such an approach, a single sample suffices to find all glints visible within one pixel, which dramatically accelerates the rendering process.

HairBxDF 606

HairBxDF::
  SigmaAFromReflectance()
  621

One approach to rendering glints was introduced by Jakob et al. (2014b), who developed a temporally consistent stochastic process that samples glint positions on the fly during evaluation of a spatio-directional average. Wang et al. (2018) showed that the performance of this method could be improved by a separable approximation of the spatial and directional dimensions. These stochastic methods are compact but also very limited in terms of the glint distributions that can be modeled.

In production rendering systems, fine surface details are often modeled using bump- or normal maps. Glinty surface appearance tends to result when such surfaces have high-resolution detail as well as a specular BRDF, and when they are furthermore subject to sharp (e.g., point or directional) illumination. At the same time, such configurations produce an extremely challenging Monte Carlo integration problem that has motivated numerous specialized methods for rendering normal-mapped specular surfaces.

Yan et al. (2014) proposed a method that organizes the normal maps into a 4D spatio-directional data structure that can be queried to find reflecting surface regions. Yan et al. (2016) drastically reduced the cost of reflectance queries by converting the normal map into a large superposition of 4D Gaussian functions termed a *position-normal distribution*. Though image fidelity is excellent, the overheads of these methods can be significant: slow rendering in the former case, and lengthy preprocessing and storage requirements in the second case. Zhu et al. (2019) addressed both of these issues via clustering and runtime synthesis of normal map detail. Wang et al. (2020a) substantially reduced the storage requirements by using a semi-procedural model that matches the statistics of an input texture. Zeltner et al. (2020) proposed a Newton-like equation-solving iteration that stochastically finds glints within texels of a normal map. Atanasov et al. (2021) developed a multi-level data structure for finding glints around a given half vector.

Other work in this area includes Raymond et al. (2016), who developed methods for rendering scratched surfaces, and Kuznetsov et al., who trained generative adversarial networks to represent microgeometry (Kuznetsov et al. 2019). Chermain et al. (2019) incorporated the effect of multiple scattering among the microstructure facets in such models, and Chermain et al. (2021) proposed a visible normal sampling technique for glint NDF. Loubet et al. recently developed a technique for sampling specular paths that is applicable to rendering caustics as well as rendering glints (2020).

Wave Optics

Essentially all physically based renderers are based on laws that approximate wave-optical behavior geometrically. At a high level, these approximations are sound given the large scale of depicted objects compared to the wavelength of light. At the same time, wave-optical properties tend to make themselves noticeable whenever geometric features occur at scales resembling the wavelength of light, and such features may indeed be present even on objects that are themselves drastically larger.

For example, consider a thin film of oil on a puddle, a tiny scratch on an otherwise smooth metallic surface, or an object with micron-scale surface microstructure. These cases can feature striking structural coloration caused by the interference of light, which a purely geometric simulation would not be able to reproduce. It may be tempting to switch to a full wave-optical simulation of light in such cases, though this line of thought quickly runs into fundamental limits: for example, using the Finite Difference Time Domain (FDTD) method, the simulation domain would need to be discretized at resolutions of < 100 nm and simulated using sub-femtosecond timesteps. This can still work when studying local behavior at the micron scale, but it is practically infeasible for scenes measured in centimeters or even meters. These challenges have motivated numerous specialized methods that reintroduce such wave-optical effects within an otherwise geometric simulation.

Moravec (1981) was the first to apply a wave optics model to computer graphics. Other early work in this area includes Bahar and Chakrabarti (1987) and Stam (1999), who modeled diffraction effects from random and periodic structures. Cuypers et al. (2012) modeled multiple diffraction phenomena using signed BSDFs based on Wigner Distribution Functions.

Musbach et al. (2013) applied the FDTD to obtain a BRDF of the iridescent microstructure of a Morpho butterfly. Their paper provides extensive references to previous work on this topic. Dhillon et al. (2014) developed a model of diffraction from small-scale biological features such as are present in snake skin. Belcour and Barla (2017) modeled thin film iridescence on a rough microfacet surface and showed the importance of this effect for materials such as leather and how the resulting spectral variation can be efficiently calculated in an RGB-based simulation. Werner et al. (2017) developed a model for rendering surfaces with iridescent scratches. Yan et al. (2018) presented a surface microstructure model that integrates over a coherence area to produce iridescent glints, revealing substantial differences between geometric and wave-based modeling. Toisoul and Ghosh (2017) presented a method for capturing and reproducing the appearance of periodic grating-like structures. Xia et al. (2020b) showed that diffraction and interference are meaningful at the scale of fibers and developed a wave optics-based model for scattering from fibers that they validated with measured data.

In contrast to the above applications that reproduce dramatic goniochromatic effects, several works have studied how wave-based modeling can improve modeling of common materials (e.g., rough plastic or conductive surfaces). Löw et al. (2012) proposed and compared geometric and wave-based BRDF models in fits to materials to the MERL database. Dong et al. (2015) measured the surface microstructure of metal samples using a profilometer and used it to construct geometric and wave-based models that they then compared to goniophotometric measurements. Holzschuch and Pacanowski (2017) integrated diffraction effects into a microfacet model and showed that this gives a closer fit to measured data.

Additional Topics

The Lambertian BRDF is an idealized model; as noted earlier, it does not match many real-world BRDFs precisely. Oren and Nayar (1994) proposed an improved model based on Lambertian microfacets that allowed the specification of surface roughness. d'Eon has recently (2021) proposed a model based on scattering Lambertian spheres that matches the appearance of many materials well.

A number of researchers have investigated BRDFs based on modeling the small-scale geometric features of a reflective surface. This work includes the computation of BRDFs from bump maps by Cabral, Max, and Springmeyer (1987); Fournier's normal distribution functions (Fournier 1992); and a technique by Westin, Arvo, and Torrance (1992), who applied Monte Carlo ray tracing to statistically model reflection from microgeometry and represented the resulting BRDFs with spherical harmonics. Wu et al. (2011) developed a system that made it possible to model microgeometry and specify its underlying BRDF while interactively previewing the resulting macro-scale BRDF, and Falster et al. (2020) computed BSDFs of microgeometry, accounting for both multiple scattering and diffraction.

The effect of the polarization of light is not modeled in pbrt, although for some scenes it can be an important effect; see, for example, the paper by Tannenbaum, Tannenbaum, and Wozny (1994) for information about how to extend a renderer to account for this effect. Fluorescence, where light is reflected at different wavelengths than the incident illumination, is also not modeled by pbrt; see Glassner (1994) and Wilkie et al. (2006) for more information on this topic.

Modeling reflection from a variety of specific types of surfaces has received attention from researchers, leading to specialized reflection models. Examples include wood (Marschner, Westin, Arbree, and Moon 2005), car paint (Ergun et al. 2016), paper (Papas et al. 2014), and pearlescent materials (Guillén et al. 2020). Cloth remains a particularly challenging material to render; see the recent survey by Castillo et al. (2019) for comprehensive coverage of work in this area.

Sampling BSDFs well is a key component of efficient image synthesis. Szécsi et al. (2003) evaluated different approaches for sampling BSDFs that are comprised of multiple lobes. It is often only possible to sample some factors of a BSDF (e.g., when sampling the Torrance–Sparrow BRDF using the distribution of visible microfacet normals); Herholz et al. fit parametric sampling distributions to BSDFs in an effort to sample them more effectively (Herholz et al. 2018).

pbrt's test suite uses statistical hypothesis tests to verify the correctness of its BSDF sampling routines. The idea of verifying such graphics-related Monte Carlo sampling routines using statistical tests was introduced by Subr and Arvo (2007a). The χ^2 test variant that is used in pbrt was originally developed as part of the *Mitsuba* renderer by Jakob (2010).

EXERCISES

9.1 A consequence of Fermat's principle from optics is that light traveling from a point p_1 in a medium with index of refraction η_1 to a point p_2 in a medium with index of refraction η_2 will follow a path that minimizes the time to get from the first point to the second point. Snell's law can be shown to follow directly from this fact.

Consider light traveling between two points p_1 and p_2 separated by a planar boundary. The light could potentially pass through the boundary while traveling from p_1 to p_2 at any point on the boundary (see Figure 9.56, which shows two such possible points p' and p''). Recall that the time it takes light to travel between two points in a medium with a constant index of refraction is proportional to the distance between them times the index of refraction in the medium. Using this fact, show that

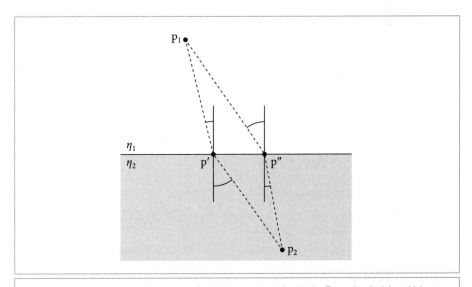

Figure 9.56: Derivation of Snell's Law. Snell's law can be derived using Fermat's principle, which says that light will follow the path that takes the least amount of time to pass between two points. The angle of refraction θ at the boundary between two media can thus be shown to be the one that minimizes the time spent going from p_1 to a point p on the boundary plus the time spent traveling the distance from that point to p_2.

the point p′ on the boundary that minimizes the total time to travel from p_1 to p_2 is the point where $\eta_1 \sin \theta_1 = \eta_2 \sin \theta_2$.

● **9.2**   Read the recent paper by d'Eon (2021) that describes a BRDF based on a model of the aggregate scattering of large collections of spherical particles that are themselves Lambertian. Implement this approach as a new `BxDF` in pbrt and render images comparing its visual appearance to that of the `DiffuseBxDF`.

● **9.3**   Read the paper of Wolff and Kurlander (1990) and the course notes of Wilkie and Weidlich (2012) and apply some of the techniques described to modify pbrt to model the effect of light polarization. (A more in-depth review of the principles of polarization is provided by Collett (1993).) Set up scenes and render images of them that demonstrate a significant difference when polarization is accurately modeled. For this, you will need to implement a polarized version of the Fresnel equations and add BSDFs that model optical elements like linear polarizers and retarders.

● **9.4**   Construct a scene with an actual geometric model of a rough plane with a large number of mirrored microfacets, and illuminate it with an area light source.[11] Place the camera in the scene such that a very large number of microfacets are in each pixel's area, and render images of this scene using hundreds or thousands of pixel samples. Compare the result to using a flat surface with a microfacet-based BRDF model. How well can you get the two approaches to match if you try to tune the microfacet BRDF parameters? Can you construct examples where images rendered with the true microfacets are actually visibly more realistic due to better modeling the effects of masking, self-shadowing, and interreflection between microfacets?

● **9.5**   One shortcoming of the microfacet-based BSDFs in this chapter is that they do not account for multiple scattering among microfacets. Investigate previous work in this area, including the stochastic multiple scattering model of Heitz et al. (2016b) and the analytic models of Lee et al. (2018) and Xie and Hanrahan (2018), and implement one of these approaches in pbrt. Then implement an approximate model for multiple scattering, such as the one presented by Kulla and Conty Estevez (2017) or by Turquin (2019). How do rendered images differ from pbrt's current implementation? How closely do the approximate approaches match the more comprehensive ones? How does execution time compare?

● **9.6**   Review the algorithms for efficiently finding an approximation of a material's normal distribution function and using that to measure BRDFs that are outlined in Section 9.8 and explained in more detail in Dupuy and Jakob (2018). Follow this approach to implement a *virtual gonioreflectometer*, where you provide pbrt with a description of the microgeometry of a complex surface (cloth, velvet, etc.) and its low-level reflection properties and then perform virtual measurements of the BSDF by simulating light paths in the microgeometry.

Store the results of this simulation in the file format used by the `MeasuredBxDFData` and then render images that compare using the tabularized representation to directly rendering the microgeometry. How do the images compare? How much more computationally efficient is using the `MeasuredBxDFData`?

BxDF 538

DiffuseBxDF 546

MeasuredBxDFData 598

---

11 An area light and not a point or directional light is necessary due to subtleties in how lights are seen in specular surfaces. With the light transport algorithms used in pbrt, infinitesimal point sources are never visible in mirrored surfaces. This is a typical limitation of ray-tracing renderers and usually not bothersome in practice.

❷ **9.7** Marschner et al. (2003) note that human hair actually has an elliptical cross section that causes glints in human hair due to caustics; subsequent work by Khungurn and Marschner (2017) proposes a model that accounts for this effect and shows that it matches measurements of scattering from human hair well. Extend the `HairBxDF` implementation here, following their approach. One issue that you will need to address is that the $\partial p/\partial v$ returned by `Curve::Intersect()` is always perpendicular to the incident ray, which leads to different orientations of the azimuthal coordinate system. This is not an issue for the model we have implemented, since it operates only on the difference between angles ϕ in the hair coordinate system. For elliptical hairs, a consistent azimuthal coordinate system is necessary.

❸ **9.8** Read Yan et al.'s paper on fur scattering (2015) and implement their model, which accounts for scattering in the medulla in fur. Render images that show the difference from accounting for this in comparison to the current implementation. You may want to also see Section 4.3 of Chiang et al. (2016a), which discusses extensions for modeling the undercoat (which is shorter and curlier hair underneath the top level) and a more *ad hoc* approach to account for the influence of scattering from the medulla.

❸ **9.9** Read one or more papers from the "Further Reading" section of this chapter on efficiently rendering glints, which are evident when the surface microstructure is large enough or viewed closely enough that the assumption of a continuous distribution of microfacet orientations is no longer valid. Then, choose one such approach and implement it in pbrt. Render images that show off the effects it is capable of producing.

10 TEXTURES AND MATERIALS

The BRDFs and BTDFs introduced in the previous chapter address only part of the problem of describing how a surface scatters light. Although they describe how light is scattered at a particular point on a surface, the renderer needs to determine *which* BRDFs and BTDFs are present at a point on a surface and what their parameters are. In this chapter, we describe a procedural shading mechanism that addresses this issue.

There are two components to pbrt's approach: textures, which describe the spatial variation of some scalar or spectral value over a surface, and materials, which evaluate textures at points on surfaces in order to determine the parameters for their associated BSDFs. Separating the pattern generation responsibilities of textures from the implementations of reflection models via materials makes it easy to combine them in arbitrary ways, thereby making it easier to create a wide variety of appearances.

In pbrt, a *texture* is a fairly general concept: it is a function that maps points in some domain (e.g., a surface's (u, v) parametric space or (x, y, z) object space) to values in some other domain (e.g., spectra or the real numbers). A variety of implementations of texture classes are available in the system. For example, pbrt has textures that represent zero-dimensional functions that return a constant in order to accommodate surfaces that have the same parameter value everywhere. Image map textures are two-dimensional functions that use a 2D array of pixel values to compute texture values at particular points (they are described in Section 10.4). There are even texture functions that compute values based on the values computed by other texture functions.

Textures may be a source of high-frequency variation in the final image. Figure 10.1 shows an image with severe aliasing due to a texture. Although the visual impact of this aliasing can be reduced with the nonuniform sampling techniques from Chapter 8, a better solution to this problem is to implement texture functions that adjust their frequency content based on the rate at which they are being sampled. For many texture functions, computing a reasonable approximation to the frequency content and antialiasing in this manner are not too difficult and are substantially more efficient than reducing aliasing by increasing the image sampling rate.

The first section of this chapter will discuss the problem of texture aliasing and general approaches to solving it. We will then describe the basic texture interface and illustrate its

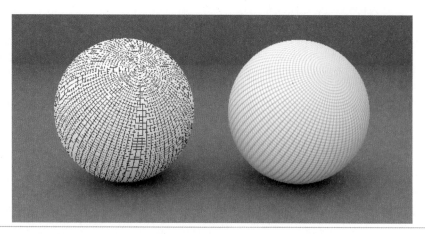

Figure 10.1: Texture Aliasing. Both spheres have the same grid texture applied and each pixel is sampled at its center. No antialiasing is performed on the left sphere; because the texture has higher frequencies than the pixel sampling rate, severe aliasing results. On the right sphere, the texture function has taken into account the image sampling rate to prefilter its function and remove high-frequency detail, giving an antialiased result even with a single sample in each pixel.

use with a variety of texture functions. After the textures have been defined, the last section, 10.5, introduces the Material interface and a number of implementations.

10.1 TEXTURE SAMPLING AND ANTIALIASING

The sampling task from Chapter 8 was a frustrating one since the aliasing problem was known to be unsolvable from the start. The infinite frequency content of geometric edges and hard shadows guarantees aliasing in the final images, no matter how high the image sampling rate. (Our only consolation is that the visual impact of this remaining aliasing can be reduced to unobjectionable levels with a sufficient number of well-placed samples.)

Fortunately, things are not this difficult from the start for textures: either there is often a convenient analytic form of the texture function available, which makes it possible to remove excessively high frequencies before sampling it, or it is possible to be careful when evaluating the function so as not to introduce high frequencies in the first place. When this problem is carefully addressed in texture implementations, as is done through the rest of this chapter, there is usually no need for more than one sample per pixel in order to render an image without texture aliasing. (Of course, sufficiently reducing Monte Carlo noise from lighting calculations may be another matter.)

Two problems must be addressed in order to remove aliasing from texture functions:

1. The sampling rate in texture space must be computed. The screen-space sampling rate is known from the image resolution and pixel sampling rate, but here we need to determine the resulting sampling rate on a surface in the scene in order to find the rate at which the texture function is being sampled.
2. Given the texture sampling rate, sampling theory must be applied to guide the computation of a texture value that does not have higher frequency variation than can be represented by the sampling rate (e.g., by removing excess frequencies beyond the Nyquist limit from the texture function).

These two issues will be addressed in turn throughout the rest of this section.

10.1.1 FINDING THE TEXTURE SAMPLING RATE

Consider an arbitrary texture function that is a function of position, $T(p)$, defined on a surface in the scene. If we ignore the complications introduced by visibility—the possibility that another object may occlude the surface at nearby image samples or that the surface may have a limited extent on the image plane—this texture function can also be expressed as a function over points (x, y) on the image plane, $T(f(x, y))$, where $f(x, y)$ is the function that maps image points to points on the surface. Thus, $T(f(x, y))$ gives the value of the texture function as seen at image position (x, y).

As a simple example of this idea, consider a 2D texture function $T(s, t)$ applied to a quadrilateral that is perpendicular to the z axis and has corners at the world-space points $(0, 0, 0)$, $(1, 0, 0)$, $(1, 1, 0)$, and $(0, 1, 0)$. If an orthographic camera is placed looking down the z axis such that the quadrilateral precisely fills the image plane and if points p on the quadrilateral are mapped to 2D (s, t) texture coordinates by

$$s = p_x \qquad t = p_y,$$

then the relationship between (s, t) and screen (x, y) pixels is straightforward:

$$s = \frac{x}{x_r} \qquad t = \frac{y}{y_r},$$

where the overall image resolution is (x_r, y_r) (Figure 10.2). Thus, given a sample spacing of one pixel in the image plane, the sample spacing in (s, t) texture parameter space is $(1/x_r, 1/y_r)$, and the texture function must remove any detail at a higher frequency than can be represented at that sampling rate.

This relationship between pixel coordinates and texture coordinates, and thus the relationship between their sampling rates, is the key bit of information that determines the maximum frequency content allowable in the texture function. As a slightly more complex example, given a triangle with (u, v) texture coordinates at its vertices and viewed with a perspective projection, it is possible to analytically find the differences in u and v across the sample points

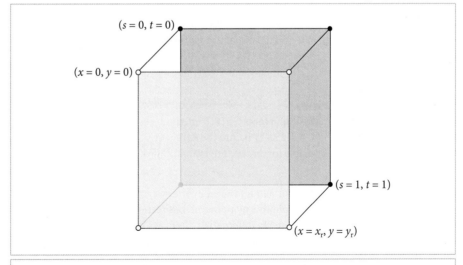

Figure 10.2: If a quadrilateral is viewed with an orthographic perspective such that the quadrilateral precisely fills the image plane, it is easy to compute the relationship between the sampling rate in (x, y) pixel coordinates and the texture sampling rate.

on the image plane. This approach was the basis of texture antialiasing in graphics processors before they became programmable.

For more complex scene geometry, camera projections, and mappings to texture coordinates, it is much more difficult to precisely determine the relationship between image positions and texture parameter values. Fortunately, for texture antialiasing, we do not need to be able to evaluate $f(x, y)$ for arbitrary (x, y) but just need to find the relationship between changes in pixel sample position and the resulting change in texture sample position at a particular point on the image. This relationship is given by the partial derivatives of this function, $\partial f / \partial x$ and $\partial f / \partial y$. For example, these can be used to find a first-order approximation to the value of f,

$$f(x', y') \approx f(x, y) + (x' - x)\frac{\partial f}{\partial x} + (y' - y)\frac{\partial f}{\partial y}.$$

If these partial derivatives are changing slowly with respect to the distances $x' - x$ and $y' - y$, this is a reasonable approximation. More importantly, the values of these partial derivatives give an approximation to the change in texture sample position for a shift of one pixel in the x and y directions, respectively, and thus directly yield the texture sampling rate. For example, in the previous quadrilateral example, $ds/dx = 1/x_r$, $ds/dy = 0$, $dt/dx = 0$, and $dt/dy = 1/y_r$.

The key to finding the values of these derivatives in the general case lies in values from the `RayDifferential` structure, which was defined in Section 3.6.1. This structure is initialized for each camera ray by the `Camera::GenerateRayDifferential()` method; it contains not only the ray being traced through the scene but also two additional rays, one offset horizontally one pixel sample from the camera ray and the other offset vertically by one pixel sample. All the geometric ray intersection routines use only the main camera ray for their computations; the auxiliary rays are ignored (this is easy to do because `RayDifferential` is a subclass of `Ray`).

We can use the offset rays to estimate the partial derivatives of the mapping $p(x, y)$ from image position to world-space position and the partial derivatives of the mappings $u(x, y)$ and $v(x, y)$ from (x, y) to (u, v) parametric coordinates, giving the partial derivatives of rendering-space positions $\partial p / \partial x$ and $\partial p / \partial y$ and the derivatives of (u, v) parametric coordinates du/dx, dv/dx, du/dy, and dv/dy. In Section 10.2, we will see how these can be used to compute the screen-space derivatives of arbitrary quantities based on p or (u, v) and consequently the sampling rates of these quantities. The values of these derivatives at the intersection point are stored in the `SurfaceInteraction` structure.

⟨*SurfaceInteraction Public Members*⟩ +≡   **138**
```
    Vector3f dpdx, dpdy;
    Float dudx = 0, dvdx = 0, dudy = 0, dvdy = 0;
```

The `SurfaceInteraction::ComputeDifferentials()` method computes these values. It is called by `SurfaceInteraction::GetBSDF()` before the `Material`'s `GetBxDF()` method is called so that these values will be available for any texture evaluation routines that are called by the material.

Ray differentials are not available for all rays traced by the system—for example, rays starting from light sources traced for photon mapping or bidirectional path tracing. Further, although we will see how to compute ray differentials after rays undergo specular reflection and transmission in Section 10.1.3, how to compute ray differentials after diffuse reflection is less clear. In cases like those as well as the corner case where one of the differentials' directions is perpendicular to the surface normal, which leads to undefined numerical values in the following, an alternative approach based on approximating the ray differentials of a ray from the camera to the intersection point is used.

⟨*SurfaceInteraction Method Definitions*⟩ ≡
```
void SurfaceInteraction::ComputeDifferentials(const RayDifferential &ray,
        Camera camera, int samplesPerPixel) {
    if (ray.hasDifferentials && Dot(n, ray.rxDirection) != 0 &&
        Dot(n, ray.ryDirection) != 0) {
```
        ⟨*Estimate screen-space change in* p *using ray differentials* **637**⟩
```
    } else {
```
        ⟨*Approximate screen-space change in* p *based on camera projection* **641**⟩
```
    }
```
    ⟨*Estimate screen-space change in* (*u*, *v*) **641**⟩
```
}
```

The key to estimating the derivatives is the assumption that the surface is locally flat with respect to the sampling rate at the point being shaded. This is a reasonable approximation in practice, and it is hard to do much better. Because ray tracing is a point-sampling technique, we have no additional information about the scene in between the rays we have traced. For highly curved surfaces or at silhouette edges, this approximation can break down, though this is rarely a source of noticeable error.

For this approximation, we need the plane through the point p intersected by the main ray that is tangent to the surface. This plane is given by the implicit equation

$$ax + by + cz + d = 0,$$

where $a = \mathbf{n}_x$, $b = \mathbf{n}_y$, $c = \mathbf{n}_z$, and $d = -(\mathbf{n} \cdot \mathbf{p})$. We can then compute the intersection points $\mathbf{p}_x$ and $\mathbf{p}_y$ between the auxiliary rays r_x and r_y and this plane (Figure 10.3). These new points give an approximation to the partial derivatives of position on the surface $\partial p/\partial x$ and $\partial p/\partial y$, based on forward differences:

$$\frac{\partial \mathbf{p}}{\partial x} \approx \mathbf{p}_x - \mathbf{p}, \qquad \frac{\partial \mathbf{p}}{\partial y} \approx \mathbf{p}_y - \mathbf{p}.$$

Because the differential rays are offset one pixel sample in each direction, there is no need to divide these differences by a Δ value, since $\Delta = 1$.

⟨*Estimate screen-space change in* p *using ray differentials*⟩ ≡   **637**
    ⟨*Compute auxiliary intersection points with plane,* px *and* py **638**⟩
```
    dpdx = px - p();
    dpdy = py - p();
```

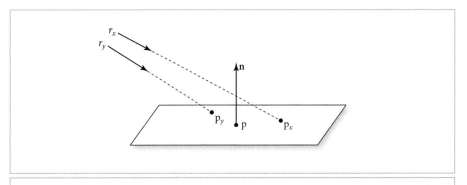

Figure 10.3: By approximating the local surface geometry at the intersection point with the tangent plane through p, approximations to the points at which the auxiliary rays r_x and r_y would intersect the surface can be found by finding their intersection points with the tangent plane $\mathbf{p}_x$ and $\mathbf{p}_y$.

The ray–plane intersection algorithm described in Section 6.1.2 gives the t value where a ray described by origin o and direction $\mathbf{d}$ intersects a plane described by $ax + by + cz + d = 0$:

$$t = \frac{-((a, b, c) \cdot \text{o}) - d}{(a, b, c) \cdot \mathbf{d}}.$$

To compute this value for the two auxiliary rays, the plane's d coefficient is computed first. It is not necessary to compute the a, b, and c coefficients, since they are available in n. We can then apply the formula directly.

⟨*Compute auxiliary intersection points with plane,* px *and* py⟩ ≡   **637**
```
Float d = -Dot(n, Vector3f(p()));
Float tx = (-Dot(n, Vector3f(ray.rxOrigin)) - d) /
           Dot(n, ray.rxDirection);
Point3f px = ray.rxOrigin + tx * ray.rxDirection;
Float ty = (-Dot(n, Vector3f(ray.ryOrigin)) - d) /
           Dot(n, ray.ryDirection);
Point3f py = ray.ryOrigin + ty * ray.ryDirection;
```

For cases where ray differentials are not available, we will add a method to the Camera interface that returns approximate values for $\partial \text{p}/\partial x$ and $\partial \text{p}/\partial y$ at a point on a surface in the scene. These should be a reasonable approximation to the differentials of a ray from the camera that found an intersection at the given point. Cameras' implementations of this method must return reasonable results even for points outside of their viewing volumes for which they cannot actually generate rays.

⟨*Camera Interface*⟩ +≡   **206**
```
void Approximate_dp_dxy(Point3f p, Normal3f n, Float time,
    int samplesPerPixel, Vector3f *dpdx, Vector3f *dpdy) const;
```

CameraBase provides an implementation of an approach to approximating these differentials that is based on the minimum of the camera ray differentials across the entire image. Because all of pbrt's current camera implementations inherit from CameraBase, the following method takes care of all of them.

⟨*CameraBase Public Methods*⟩ +≡   **212**
```
void Approximate_dp_dxy(Point3f p, Normal3f n, Float time,
        int samplesPerPixel, Vector3f *dpdx, Vector3f *dpdy) const {
    ⟨Compute tangent plane equation for ray differential intersections 640⟩
    ⟨Find intersection points for approximated camera differential rays 640⟩
    ⟨Estimate ∂p/∂x and ∂p/∂y in tangent plane at intersection point 641⟩
}
```

This method starts by orienting the camera so that the camera-space z axis is aligned with the vector from the camera position to the intersection point. It then uses lower bounds on the spread of rays over the image that are provided by the camera to find approximate differential rays. It then intersects these rays with the tangent plane at the intersection point. (See Figure 10.4.)

There are a number of sources of error in this approximation. Beyond the fact that it does not account for how light was scattered at intermediate surfaces for multiple-bounce ray paths, there is also the fact that it is based on the minimum of the camera's differentials for all rays. In general, it tries to underestimate those derivatives rather than overestimate them, as we prefer aliasing over blurring here. The former error can at least be addressed with additional pixel samples. In order to give a sense of the impact of some of these approximations,

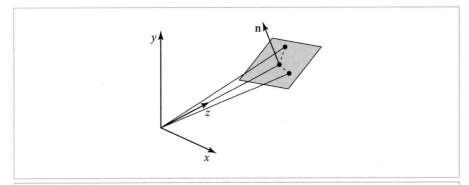

Figure 10.4: `CameraBase::Approximate_dp_dxy()` effectively reorients the camera to point at the provided intersection point. In camera space, the ray to the intersection then has origin $(0, 0, 0)$ and direction $(0, 0, 1)$. The extent of ray differentials on the tangent plane defined by the surface normal at the intersection point can then be found.

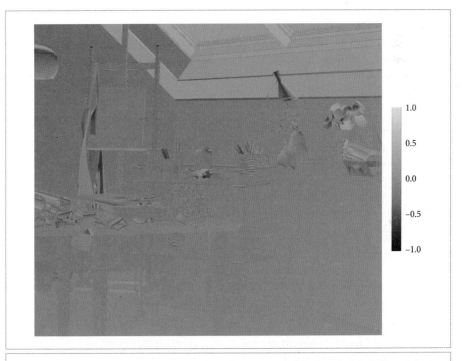

Figure 10.5: Visualization of the Ratio of Filter Areas Estimated by Regular Ray Differentials to Areas Estimated by `CameraBase::Approximate_dp_dxy()`. We represent the filter area as the product $\max(|du/dx|, |du/dy|) \max(|dv/dx|, |dv/dy|)$ and visualize the base 2 logarithm of the ratio of areas computed by the two techniques. Log 2 ratios greater than 0 indicate that the camera-based approximation estimated a larger filter area.

Figure 10.5 has visualization that compares the local area estimated by those derivatives at intersections to the area computed using the actual ray differentials generated by the camera.

CameraBase::
Approximate_dp_dxy()
638

For the first step of the algorithm, we have an intersection point in rendering space p that we would like to transform into a coordinate system where it is along the z axis with the camera at the origin. Transforming to camera space gets us started and an additional rotation that transforms the vector from the origin to the intersection point to be aligned with z

finishes the job. The *d* coefficient of the plane equation can then be found by taking the dot product of the transformed point and surface normal. Because the *x* and *y* components of the transformed point are equal to 0, the dot product can be optimized to be a single multiply.

⟨*Compute tangent plane equation for ray differential intersections*⟩ ≡   **638**
```
Point3f pCamera = CameraFromRender(p, time);
Transform DownZFromCamera =
    RotateFromTo(Normalize(Vector3f(pCamera)), Vector3f(0, 0, 1));
Point3f pDownZ = DownZFromCamera(pCamera);
Normal3f nDownZ = DownZFromCamera(CameraFromRender(n, time));
Float d = nDownZ.z * pDownZ.z;
```

Camera implementations that inherit from CameraBase and use this method must initialize the following member variables with values that are lower bounds on each of the respective position and direction differentials over all the pixels in the image.

⟨*CameraBase Protected Members*⟩ +≡   **212**
```
Vector3f minPosDifferentialX, minPosDifferentialY;
Vector3f minDirDifferentialX, minDirDifferentialY;
```

The main ray in this coordinate system has origin (0, 0, 0) and direction (0, 0, 1). Adding the position and direction differential vectors to those gives the origin and direction of each differential ray. Given those, the same calculation as earlier gives us the *t* values for the ray–plane intersections for the differential rays and thence the intersection points.

⟨*Find intersection points for approximated camera differential rays*⟩ ≡   **638**
```
Ray xRay(Point3f(0,0,0) + minPosDifferentialX,
         Vector3f(0,0,1) + minDirDifferentialX);
Float tx = -(Dot(nDownZ, Vector3f(xRay.o)) - d) / Dot(nDownZ, xRay.d);
Ray yRay(Point3f(0,0,0) + minPosDifferentialY,
         Vector3f(0,0,1) + minDirDifferentialY);
Float ty = -(Dot(nDownZ, Vector3f(yRay.o)) - d) / Dot(nDownZ, yRay.d);
Point3f px = xRay(tx), py = yRay(ty);
```

For an orthographic camera, these differentials can be computed directly. There is no change in the direction vector, and the position differentials are the same at every pixel. Their values are already computed in the OrthographicCamera constructor, so can be used directly to initialize the base class's member variables.

⟨*Compute minimum differentials for orthographic camera*⟩ ≡   **218**
```
minDirDifferentialX = minDirDifferentialY = Vector3f(0, 0, 0);
minPosDifferentialX = dxCamera;
minPosDifferentialY = dyCamera;
```

All the other cameras call FindMinimumDifferentials(), which estimates these values by sampling at many points across the diagonal of the image and storing the minimum of all the differentials encountered. That function is not very interesting, so it is not included here.

⟨*Compute minimum differentials for* PerspectiveCamera⟩ ≡   **220**
```
FindMinimumDifferentials(this);
```

Given the intersection points px and py, $\partial p/\partial x$ and $\partial p/\partial y$ can now be estimated by taking their differences with the main intersection point. To get final estimates of the partial derivatives, these vectors must be transformed back out into rendering space and scaled to account for the actual pixel sampling rate. As with the initial ray differentials that were generated in the ⟨*Scale camera ray differentials based on image sampling rate*⟩ fragment, these are scaled to account for the pixel sampling rate.

⟨*Estimate* ∂p/∂x *and* ∂p/∂y *in tangent plane at intersection point*⟩ ≡   **638**
```
    Float sppScale = GetOptions().disablePixelJitter ? 1 :
        std::max<Float>(.125, 1 / std::sqrt((Float)samplesPerPixel));
    *dpdx = sppScale *
        RenderFromCamera(DownZFromCamera.ApplyInverse(px - pDownZ), time);
    *dpdy = sppScale *
        RenderFromCamera(DownZFromCamera.ApplyInverse(py - pDownZ), time);
```

A call to this method takes care of computing the ∂p/∂x and ∂p/∂y differentials in the `ComputeDifferentials()` method.

⟨*Approximate screen-space change in* p *based on camera projection*⟩ ≡   **637**
```
    camera.Approximate_dp_dxy(p(), n, time, samplesPerPixel, &dpdx, &dpdy);
```

We now have both the partial derivatives ∂p/∂u and ∂p/∂v as well as, one way or another, ∂p/∂x and ∂p/∂y. From them, we would now like to compute du/dx, du/dy, dv/dx, and dv/dy. Using the chain rule, we can find that

$$\frac{\partial \mathrm{p}}{\partial x} = \frac{\partial \mathrm{p}}{\partial u}\frac{\mathrm{d}u}{\mathrm{d}x} + \frac{\partial \mathrm{p}}{\partial v}\frac{\mathrm{d}v}{\mathrm{d}x}. \qquad (10.1)$$

(∂p/∂y has a similar expression with du/dx replaced by du/dy and dv/dx replaced by dv/dy.)

Equation (10.1) can be written as a matrix equation where the two following matrices that include ∂p have three rows, one for each of p's x, y, and z components:

$$\left(\frac{\partial \mathrm{p}}{\partial x} \right) = \left(\frac{\partial \mathrm{p}}{\partial u} \quad \frac{\partial \mathrm{p}}{\partial v} \right) \left(\begin{array}{c} \frac{\mathrm{d}u}{\mathrm{d}x} \\ \frac{\mathrm{d}v}{\mathrm{d}x} \end{array} \right).$$

This is an overdetermined linear system since there are three equations but only two unknowns, du/dx and dv/dx. An effective solution approach in this case is to apply linear least squares, which says that for a linear system of the form $\mathbf{Ax} = \mathbf{b}$ with $\mathbf{A}$ and $\mathbf{b}$ known, the least-squares solution for $\mathbf{x}$ is given by

$$\mathbf{x} = \left(\mathbf{A}^T \mathbf{A} \right)^{-1} \mathbf{A}^T \mathbf{b}. \qquad (10.2)$$

In this case, $\mathbf{A} = (\partial \mathrm{p}/\partial u \quad \partial \mathrm{p}/\partial v)$, $\mathbf{b} = (\partial \mathrm{p}/\partial x)$, and $\mathbf{x} = (\mathrm{d}u/\mathrm{d}x \quad \mathrm{d}v/\mathrm{d}x)^T$.

⟨*Estimate screen-space change in* (u, v)⟩ ≡   **637, 964**
    ⟨*Compute* $\mathbf{A}^T \mathbf{A}$ *and its determinant* **642**⟩
    ⟨*Compute* $\mathbf{A}^T \mathbf{b}$ *for x and y* **642**⟩
    ⟨*Compute u and v derivatives with respect to x and y* **642**⟩
    ⟨*Clamp derivatives of u and v to reasonable values* **642**⟩

$\mathbf{A}^T \mathbf{A}$ is a 2×2 matrix with elements given by dot products of partial derivatives of position:

$$\mathbf{A}^T \mathbf{A} = \begin{pmatrix} \partial \mathrm{p}/\partial u \cdot \partial \mathrm{p}/\partial u & \partial \mathrm{p}/\partial u \cdot \partial \mathrm{p}/\partial v \\ \partial \mathrm{p}/\partial u \cdot \partial \mathrm{p}/\partial v & \partial \mathrm{p}/\partial v \cdot \partial \mathrm{p}/\partial v \end{pmatrix}.$$

Its inverse is

$$\left(\mathbf{A}^T \mathbf{A} \right)^{-1} = \frac{1}{|\mathbf{A}^T \mathbf{A}|} \begin{pmatrix} \partial \mathrm{p}/\partial v \cdot \partial \mathrm{p}/\partial v & -\partial \mathrm{p}/\partial u \cdot \partial \mathrm{p}/\partial v \\ -\partial \mathrm{p}/\partial u \cdot \partial \mathrm{p}/\partial v & \partial \mathrm{p}/\partial u \cdot \partial \mathrm{p}/\partial u \end{pmatrix}. \qquad (10.3)$$

Note that in both matrices the two off-diagonal entries are equal. Thus, the fragment that computes the entries of $\mathbf{A}^T \mathbf{A}$ only needs to compute three values. The inverse of the matrix determinant is computed here as well. If its value is infinite, the linear system cannot be solved; setting invDet to 0 causes the subsequently computed derivatives to be 0, which leads to point-sampled textures, the best remaining option in that case.

⟨*Compute* $\mathbf{A}^T\mathbf{A}$ *and its determinant*⟩ ≡   **641**
```
Float ata00 = Dot(dpdu, dpdu), ata01 = Dot(dpdu, dpdv);
Float ata11 = Dot(dpdv, dpdv);
Float invDet = 1 / DifferenceOfProducts(ata00, ata11, ata01, ata01);
invDet = IsFinite(invDet) ? invDet : 0.f;
```

The $\mathbf{A}^T\mathbf{b}$ portion of the solution is easily computed. For the derivatives with respect to screen-space x, we have the two-element matrix

$$\mathbf{A}^T\mathbf{b} = (\ \partial\mathrm{p}/\partial u \cdot \partial\mathrm{p}/\partial x \quad \partial\mathrm{p}/\partial v \cdot \partial\mathrm{p}/\partial x\ ).\qquad\qquad [10.4]$$

The solution for screen-space y is analogous.

⟨*Compute* $\mathbf{A}^T\mathbf{b}$ *for x and y*⟩ ≡   **641**
```
Float atb0x = Dot(dpdu, dpdx), atb1x = Dot(dpdv, dpdx);
Float atb0y = Dot(dpdu, dpdy), atb1y = Dot(dpdv, dpdy);
```

The solution to Equation (10.2) for each partial derivative can be found by taking the product of Equations (10.3) and (10.4). We will gloss past the algebra; its result can be directly expressed in terms of the values computed so far.

⟨*Compute u and v derivatives with respect to x and y*⟩ ≡   **641**
```
dudx = DifferenceOfProducts(ata11, atb0x, ata01, atb1x) * invDet;
dvdx = DifferenceOfProducts(ata00, atb1x, ata01, atb0x) * invDet;
dudy = DifferenceOfProducts(ata11, atb0y, ata01, atb1y) * invDet;
dvdy = DifferenceOfProducts(ata00, atb1y, ata01, atb0y) * invDet;
```

In certain tricky cases (e.g., with highly distorted (u, v) parameterizations or at object silhouette edges), the estimated partial derivatives may be infinite or have very large magnitudes. It is worth clamping them to reasonable values in that case to prevent overflow and not-a-number values in subsequent computations that are based on them.

⟨*Clamp derivatives of u and v to reasonable values*⟩ ≡   **641**
```
dudx = IsFinite(dudx) ? Clamp(dudx, -1e8f, 1e8f) : 0.f;
dvdx = IsFinite(dvdx) ? Clamp(dvdx, -1e8f, 1e8f) : 0.f;
dudy = IsFinite(dudy) ? Clamp(dudy, -1e8f, 1e8f) : 0.f;
dvdy = IsFinite(dvdy) ? Clamp(dvdy, -1e8f, 1e8f) : 0.f;
```

10.1.2 RAY DIFFERENTIALS AT MEDIUM TRANSITIONS

Now is a good time to take care of another detail related to ray differentials: recall from Section 9.1.5 that materials may return an unset BSDF to indicate an interface between two scattering media that does not itself scatter light. In this case, it is necessary to spawn a new ray in the same direction, but past the intersection on the surface. In this case we would like the effect of the ray differentials to be the same as if no scattering had occurred. This can be achieved by setting the differential origins to the points given by evaluating the ray equation at the intersection t (see Figure 10.6).

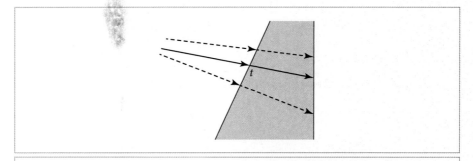

Figure 10.6: When a ray intersects a surface that delineates the boundary between two media, a new ray is spawned on the other side of the boundary. If the origins of this ray's differentials are set by evaluating the ray equation for the original differentials at the intersection t, then the new ray will represent the same footprint as the original one when it subsequently intersects a surface.

⟨*SurfaceInteraction Method Definitions*⟩ +≡
```
void SurfaceInteraction::SkipIntersection(RayDifferential *ray,
                                          Float t) const {
    *((Ray *)ray) = SpawnRay(ray->d);
    if (ray->hasDifferentials) {
        ray->rxOrigin = ray->rxOrigin + t * ray->rxDirection;
        ray->ryOrigin = ray->ryOrigin + t * ray->ryDirection;
    }
}
```

⋆ 10.1.3 RAY DIFFERENTIALS FOR SPECULAR REFLECTION AND TRANSMISSION

Given the effectiveness of ray differentials for finding filter regions for texture antialiasing for camera rays, it is useful to extend the method to make it possible to determine texture-space sampling rates for objects that are seen indirectly via specular reflection or refraction; objects seen in mirrors, for example, should not have texture aliasing, identical to the case for directly visible objects. Igehy (1999) developed an elegant solution to the problem of how to find the appropriate differential rays for specular reflection and refraction, which is the approach used in pbrt.[1]

Figure 10.7 illustrates the difference that proper texture filtering for specular reflection and transmission can make: it shows a glass ball and a mirrored ball on a plane with a texture map containing high-frequency components. Ray differentials ensure that the images of the texture seen via reflection and refraction from the balls are free of aliasing artifacts. Here, ray differentials eliminate aliasing without excessively blurring the texture.

To compute the reflected or transmitted ray differentials at a surface intersection point, we need an approximation to the rays that would have been traced at the intersection points for the two offset rays in the ray differential that hit the surface (Figure 10.8). The new ray for the main ray is found by sampling the BSDF, so here we only need to compute the outgoing rays for the r_x and r_y differentials. This task is handled by another

---

1 Igehy's formulation is slightly different from the one here—he effectively tracked the differences between the main ray and the offset rays, while we store the offset rays explicitly. The mathematics all work out to be the same in the end; we chose this alternative because we believe that it makes the algorithm's operation for camera rays easier to understand.

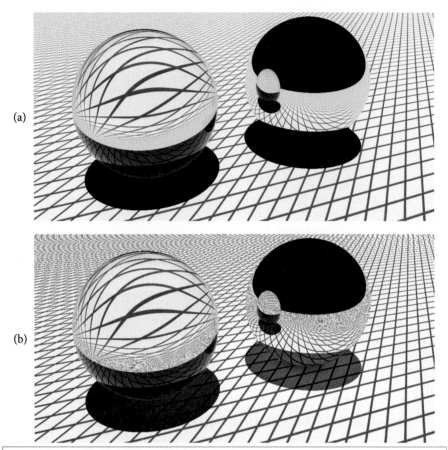

(a)

(b)

Figure 10.7: (a) Tracking ray differentials for reflected and refracted rays ensures that the image map texture seen in the balls is filtered to avoid aliasing. The left ball is glass, exhibiting reflection and refraction, and the right ball is a mirror, just showing reflection. Note that the texture is well filtered over both of the balls. (b) shows the aliasing artifacts that are present if ray differentials are not used.

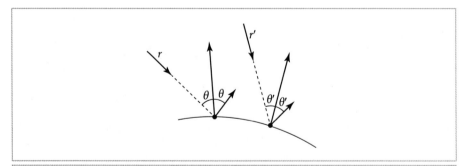

Figure 10.8: The specular reflection formula gives the direction of the reflected ray at a point on a surface. An offset ray for a ray differential r' (dashed line) will generally intersect the surface at a different point and be reflected in a different direction. The new direction is affected by the different surface normal at the point as well as by the offset ray's different incident direction. The computation to find the reflected direction for the offset ray in pbrt estimates the change in reflected direction as a function of image-space position and approximates the ray differential's direction with the main ray's direction added to the estimated change in direction.

SurfaceInteraction::SpawnRay() variant that takes an incident ray differential as well as information about the BSDF and the type of scattering that occurred.

⟨*SurfaceInteraction Method Definitions*⟩ +≡
```
RayDifferential SurfaceInteraction::SpawnRay(
        const RayDifferential &rayi, const BSDF &bsdf, Vector3f wi,
        int flags, Float eta) const {
    RayDifferential rd(SpawnRay(wi));
    if (rayi.hasDifferentials) {
        ⟨Compute ray differentials for specular reflection or transmission 645⟩
    }
    ⟨Squash potentially troublesome differentials⟩
    return rd;
}
```

It is not well defined what the ray differentials should be in the case of non-specular scattering. Therefore, this method handles the two types of specular scattering only; for all other types of rays, approximate differentials will be computed at their subsequent intersection points with Camera::Approximate_dp_dxy().

⟨*Compute ray differentials for specular reflection or transmission*⟩ ≡   **645**
```
    ⟨Compute common factors for specular ray differentials 645⟩
    if (flags == BxDFFlags::SpecularReflection) {
        ⟨Initialize origins of specular differential rays 645⟩
        ⟨Compute differential reflected directions 646⟩
    } else if (flags == BxDFFlags::SpecularTransmission) {
        ⟨Initialize origins of specular differential rays 645⟩
        ⟨Compute differential transmitted directions 646⟩
    }
```

A few variables will be used for both types of scattering, including the partial derivatives of the surface normal with respect to x and y on the image and $\partial\mathbf{n}/\partial x$ and $\partial\mathbf{n}/\partial y$, which are computed using the chain rule.

⟨*Compute common factors for specular ray differentials*⟩ ≡   **645**
```
    Normal3f n = shading.n;
    Normal3f dndx = shading.dndu * dudx + shading.dndv * dvdx;
    Normal3f dndy = shading.dndu * dudy + shading.dndv * dvdy;
    Vector3f dwodx = -rayi.rxDirection - wo, dwody = -rayi.ryDirection - wo;
```

For both reflection and transmission, the origin of each differential ray can be found using the already-computed approximations of how much the surface position changes with respect to (x, y) position on the image plane $\partial\mathbf{p}/\partial x$ and $\partial\mathbf{p}/\partial y$.

⟨*Initialize origins of specular differential rays*⟩ ≡   **645**
```
    rd.hasDifferentials = true;
    rd.rxOrigin = p() + dpdx;
    rd.ryOrigin = p() + dpdy;
```

Finding the directions of these rays is slightly trickier. If we know how much the reflected direction ω_i changes with respect to a shift of a pixel sample in the x and y directions on the image plane, we can use this information to approximate the direction of the offset rays. For example, the direction for the ray offset in x is

$$\omega \approx \omega_i + \frac{\partial\omega_i}{\partial x}.$$

Recall from Equation (9.1) that for a normal $\mathbf{n}$ and outgoing direction ω_o the direction for perfect specular reflection is

$$\omega_i = -\omega_o + 2(\omega_o \cdot \mathbf{n})\mathbf{n}.$$

The partial derivatives of this expression are easily computed:

$$\frac{\partial \omega_i}{\partial x} = \frac{\partial}{\partial x}\left(-\omega_o + 2(\omega_o \cdot \mathbf{n})\mathbf{n}\right)$$

$$= -\frac{\partial \omega_o}{\partial x} + 2\left((\omega_o \cdot \mathbf{n})\frac{\partial \mathbf{n}}{\partial x} + \frac{\partial(\omega_o \cdot \mathbf{n})}{\partial x}\mathbf{n}\right).$$

Using the properties of the dot product, it can further be shown that

$$\frac{\partial(\omega_o \cdot \mathbf{n})}{\partial x} = \frac{\partial \omega_o}{\partial x} \cdot \mathbf{n} + \omega_o \cdot \frac{\partial \mathbf{n}}{\partial x}.$$

The value of $\partial \omega_o / \partial x$ has already been computed from the difference between the direction of the ray differential's main ray and the direction of the r_x offset ray, and all the other necessary quantities are readily available from the SurfaceInteraction.

⟨*Compute differential reflected directions*⟩ ≡   **645**

```
Float dwoDotn_dx = Dot(dwodx, n) + Dot(wo, dndx);
Float dwoDotn_dy = Dot(dwody, n) + Dot(wo, dndy);
rd.rxDirection = wi - dwodx +
    2 * Vector3f(Dot(wo, n) * dndx + dwoDotn_dx * n);
rd.ryDirection = wi - dwody +
    2 * Vector3f(Dot(wo, n) * dndy + dwoDotn_dy * n);
```

A similar process of differentiating the equation for the direction of a specularly transmitted ray, Equation (9.4), gives the equation to find the differential change in the transmitted direction. pbrt computes refracted rays as

$$\omega_i = -\frac{1}{\eta}\omega_o + \left[\frac{1}{\eta}(\omega_o \cdot \mathbf{n}) - \cos\theta_i\right]\mathbf{n},$$

where $\mathbf{n}$ is flipped if necessary to lie in the same hemisphere as ω_o, and where η is the relative index of refraction from ω_o's medium to ω_i's medium.

If we denote the term in brackets by μ, then we have $\omega_i = -(1/\eta)\omega_o + \mu\mathbf{n}$. Taking the partial derivative in x, we have

$$\frac{\partial \omega_i}{\partial x} = -\frac{1}{\eta}\frac{\partial \omega_o}{\partial x} + \mu\frac{\partial \mathbf{n}}{\partial x} + \frac{\partial \mu}{\partial x}\mathbf{n}. \qquad [10.5]$$

Using some of the values found from computing specularly reflected ray differentials, we can find that we already know how to compute all of these values except for $\partial \mu / \partial x$.

⟨*Compute differential transmitted directions*⟩ ≡   **645**

```
⟨Find oriented surface normal for transmission 647⟩
⟨Compute partial derivatives of μ 647⟩
rd.rxDirection = wi - eta * dwodx + Vector3f(mu * dndx + dmudx * n);
rd.ryDirection = wi - eta * dwody + Vector3f(mu * dndy + dmudy * n);
```

Dot() 89
Float 23
Vector3f 86

Before we get to the computation of μ's partial derivatives, we will start by reorienting the surface normal if necessary so that it lies on the same side of the surface as ω_o. This matches pbrt's computation of refracted ray directions.

⟨*Find oriented surface normal for transmission*⟩ ≡   **646**
```
if (Dot(wo, n) < 0) {
    n = -n;
    dndx = -dndx;
    dndy = -dndy;
}
```

Returning to μ and considering $\partial\mu/\partial x$, we have

$$\frac{\partial\mu}{\partial x} = \frac{\partial}{\partial x}\frac{1}{\eta}(\omega_o \cdot \mathbf{n}) - \frac{\partial}{\partial x}\cos\theta_i = \frac{1}{\eta}\frac{\partial(\omega_o \cdot \mathbf{n})}{\partial x} - \frac{\partial\cos\theta_i}{\partial x}.$$

Its first term can be evaluated with already known values. For the second term, we will start with Snell's law, which gives

$$\cos\theta_i = \sqrt{1 - \frac{1 - (\omega_o \cdot \mathbf{n})^2}{\eta^2}}.$$

If we square both sides of the equation and take the partial derivative $\partial/\partial x$, we find

$$2\cos\theta_i\frac{\partial\cos\theta_i}{\partial x} = \frac{\partial}{\partial x}\left(1 - \frac{1 - (\omega_o \cdot \mathbf{n})^2}{\eta^2}\right)$$

$$= \frac{\partial}{\partial x}\left(\frac{(\omega_o \cdot \mathbf{n})^2}{\eta^2}\right) = \frac{2(\omega_o \cdot \mathbf{n})}{\eta^2}\frac{\partial(\omega_o \cdot \mathbf{n})}{\partial x}.$$

We now can solve for $\partial\cos\theta_i/\partial x$:

$$\frac{\partial\cos\theta_i}{\partial x} = \frac{1}{2\cos\theta_i}\frac{2(\omega_o \cdot \mathbf{n})}{\eta^2}\frac{\partial(\omega_o \cdot \mathbf{n})}{\partial x}.$$

Putting it all together and simplifying, we have

$$\frac{\partial\mu}{\partial x} = \frac{\partial(\omega_o \cdot \mathbf{n})}{\partial x}\left(\frac{1}{\eta} + \frac{1}{\eta^2}\frac{(\omega_o \cdot \mathbf{n})}{(\omega_i \cdot \mathbf{n})}\right).$$

The partial derivative in y is analogous and the implementation follows.

⟨*Compute partial derivatives of μ*⟩ ≡   **646**
```
Float dwoDotn_dx = Dot(dwodx, n) + Dot(wo, dndx);
Float dwoDotn_dy = Dot(dwody, n) + Dot(wo, dndy);
Float mu = Dot(wo, n) / eta - AbsDot(wi, n);
Float dmudx = dwoDotn_dx * (1/eta + 1/Sqr(eta) * Dot(wo, n) / Dot(wi, n));
Float dmudy = dwoDotn_dy * (1/eta + 1/Sqr(eta) * Dot(wo, n) / Dot(wi, n));
```

If a ray undergoes many specular bounces, ray differentials sometimes drift off to have very large magnitudes, which can leave a trail of infinite and not-a-number values in their wake when they are used for texture filtering calculations. Therefore, the final fragment in this SpawnRay() method computes the squared length of all the differentials. If any is greater than 10^{16}, the ray differentials are discarded and the RayDifferential hasDifferentials value is set to false. The fragment that handles this, ⟨*Squash potentially troublesome differentials*⟩, is simple and thus not included here.

10.1.4 FILTERING TEXTURE FUNCTIONS

To eliminate texture aliasing, it is necessary to remove frequencies in texture functions that are past the Nyquist limit for the texture sampling rate. The goal is to compute, with as few approximations as possible, the result of the *ideal texture resampling* process, which says that in order to evaluate a texture function T at a point (x, y) on the image without aliasing, we must first band-limit it, removing frequencies beyond the Nyquist limit by convolving it with the sinc filter:

$$T_b(x, y) = \int_{-\infty}^{\infty} \int_{-\infty}^{\infty} \mathrm{sinc}(x') \, \mathrm{sinc}(y') \, T'\big(f(x - x', y - y')\big) \, \mathrm{d}x' \, \mathrm{d}y',$$

where, as in Section 10.1.1, $f(x, y)$ maps pixel locations to points in the texture function's domain. The band-limited function T_b in turn should then be convolved with the pixel filter $g(x, y)$ centered at the (x, y) point on the screen at which we want to evaluate the texture function:

$$T_{\mathrm{ideal}}(x, y) = \int_{-y\mathrm{Width}/2}^{y\mathrm{Width}/2} \int_{-x\mathrm{Width}/2}^{x\mathrm{Width}/2} g(x', y') \, T_b(x - x', y - y') \, \mathrm{d}x' \, \mathrm{d}y'.$$

This gives the theoretically perfect value for the texture as projected onto the screen.[2]

In practice, there are many simplifications that can be made to this process. For example, a box filter may be used for the band-limiting step, and the second step is usually ignored completely, effectively acting as if the pixel filter were a box filter, which makes it possible to do the antialiasing work completely in texture space. (The EWA filtering algorithm in Section 10.4.4 is a notable exception in that it assumes a Gaussian pixel filter.)

Assuming box filters then if, for example, the texture function is defined over parametric (u, v) coordinates, the filtering task is to average it over a region in (u, v):

$$T_{\mathrm{box}}(x, y) = \frac{1}{(u_1 - u_0)(v_1 - v_0)} \int_{v_0}^{v_1} \int_{u_0}^{u_1} T(u', v') \, \mathrm{d}u' \mathrm{d}v'.$$

The extent of the filter region can be determined using the derivatives from the previous sections—for example, setting

$$u_0 = u - -\frac{1}{2} \max\left(\frac{\mathrm{d}u}{\mathrm{d}x}, \frac{\mathrm{d}u}{\mathrm{d}y}\right) \quad \text{and} \quad u_1 = u + -\frac{1}{2} \max\left(\frac{\mathrm{d}u}{\mathrm{d}x}, \frac{\mathrm{d}u}{\mathrm{d}y}\right)$$

and similarly for v_0 and v_1 to conservatively specify the box's extent.

The box filter is easy to use, since it can be applied analytically by computing the average of the texture function over the appropriate region. Intuitively, this is a reasonable approach to the texture filtering problem, and it can be computed directly for many texture functions. Indeed, through the rest of this chapter, we will often use a box filter to average texture function values between samples and informally use the term *filter region* to describe the area being averaged over. This is the most common approach when filtering texture functions.

Even the box filter, with all of its shortcomings, gives acceptable results for texture filtering in many cases. One factor that helps is the fact that a number of samples are usually taken in each pixel. Thus, even if the filtered texture values used in each one are suboptimal, once they are filtered by the pixel reconstruction filter, the end result generally does not suffer too much.

---

2   One simplification that is present in this ideal filtering process is the implicit assumption that the texture function makes a linear contribution to frequency content in the image, so that filtering out its high frequencies removes high frequencies from the image. This is true for many uses of textures—for example, if an image map is used to modulate the diffuse term of a DiffuseMaterial. However, if a texture is used to determine the roughness of a glossy specular object, for example, this linearity assumption is incorrect, since a linear change in the roughness value has a nonlinear effect on the reflected radiance from the microfacet BRDF. We will ignore this issue here, since it is not easily solved in general. The "Further Reading" section has more discussion of this topic.

An alternative to using the box filter to filter texture functions is to use the observation that the effect of the ideal sinc filter is to let frequency components below the Nyquist limit pass through unchanged but to remove frequencies past it. Therefore, if we know the frequency content of the texture function (e.g., if it is a sum of terms, each one with known frequency content), then if we replace the high-frequency terms with their average values, we are effectively doing the work of the sinc prefilter. This approach is known as *clamping*.

Finally, for texture functions where none of these techniques is easily applied, a final option is *supersampling*—the function is evaluated and filtered at multiple locations near the main evaluation point, thus increasing the sampling rate in texture space. If a box filter is used to filter these sample values, this is equivalent to averaging the value of the function. This approach can be expensive if the texture function is complex to evaluate, and as with image sampling, a very large number of samples may be needed to remove aliasing. Although this is a brute-force solution, it is still more efficient than increasing the image sampling rate, since it does not incur the cost of tracing more rays through the scene.

10.2 TEXTURE COORDINATE GENERATION

Almost all the textures in this chapter are functions that take a 2D or 3D coordinate and return a texture value. Sometimes there are obvious ways to choose these texture coordinates; for parametric surfaces, such as the quadrics in Chapter 6, there is a natural 2D (u, v) parameterization of the surface, and for all types of surfaces the shading point p is a natural choice for a 3D coordinate.

In other cases, there is no natural parameterization, or the natural parameterization may be undesirable. For instance, the (u, v) values near the poles of spheres are severely distorted. Therefore, this section introduces classes that provide an interface to different techniques for generating these parameterizations as well as a number of implementations of them.

The Texture implementations later in this chapter store a tagged pointer to a 2D or 3D mapping function as appropriate and use it to compute the texture coordinates at each point at which they are evaluated. Thus, it is easy to add new mappings to the system without having to modify all the Texture implementations, and different mappings can be used for different textures associated with the same surface. In pbrt, we will use the convention that 2D texture coordinates are denoted by (s, t); this helps make clear the distinction between the intrinsic (u, v) parameterization of the underlying surface and the possibly different coordinate values used for texturing.

TextureMapping2D defines the interface for 2D texture coordinate generation. It is defined in the file base/texture.h. The implementations of the texture mapping classes are in textures.h and textures.cpp.

⟨*TextureMapping2D Definition*⟩ ≡
```
class TextureMapping2D
    : public TaggedPointer<UVMapping, SphericalMapping,
                            CylindricalMapping, PlanarMapping> {
  public:
    ⟨TextureMapping2D Interface 650⟩
};
```

The TextureMapping2D interface consists of a single method, Map(). It is given a TextureEval Context that stores relevant geometric information at the shading point and returns a small structure, TexCoord2D, that stores the (s, t) texture coordinates and estimates for the change in (s, t) with respect to pixel x and y coordinates so that textures that use the mapping can determine the (s, t) sampling rate and filter accordingly.

⟨*TextureMapping2D Interface*⟩ ≡   **649**
```
    TexCoord2D Map(TextureEvalContext ctx) const;
```

⟨*TexCoord2D Definition*⟩ ≡
```
    struct TexCoord2D {
        Point2f st;
        Float dsdx, dsdy, dtdx, dtdy;
    };
```

In previous versions of pbrt, the Map() interface was defined to take a complete Surface Interaction; the TextureEvalContext structure did not exist. For this version, we have tightened up the interface to only include specific values that are useful for texture coordinate generation. This change was largely motivated by the GPU rendering path: with the CPU renderer, all the relevant information is already at hand in the functions that call the Map() methods; most likely the SurfaceInteraction is already in the CPU cache. On the GPU, the necessary values have to be read from off-chip memory. TextureEvalContext makes it possible for the GPU renderer to only read the necessary values from memory, which in turn has measurable performance benefits.

TextureEvalContext provides three constructors, not included here. Two initialize the various fields using corresponding values from either an Interaction or a SurfaceInteraction and the third allows specifying them directly.

⟨*TextureEvalContext Definition*⟩ ≡
```
    struct TextureEvalContext {
        ⟨TextureEvalContext Public Methods⟩
        Point3f p;
        Vector3f dpdx, dpdy;
        Normal3f n;
        Point2f uv;
        Float dudx = 0, dudy = 0, dvdx = 0, dvdy = 0;
    };
```

10.2.1 (u, v) MAPPING

UVMapping uses the (u, v) coordinates in the TextureEvalContext to compute the texture coordinates, optionally scaling and offsetting their values in each dimension.

⟨*UVMapping Definition*⟩ ≡
```
    class UVMapping {
      public:
        ⟨UVMapping Public Methods 650⟩
      private:
        Float su, sv, du, dv;
    };
```

⟨*UVMapping Public Methods*⟩ ≡   **650**
```
    UVMapping(Float su = 1, Float sv = 1, Float du = 0, Float dv = 0)
        : su(su), sv(sv), du(du), dv(dv) {}
```

The scale-and-shift computation to compute (s, t) coordinates is straightforward:

⟨*UVMapping Public Methods*⟩ +≡   650
```
  TexCoord2D Map(TextureEvalContext ctx) const {
    ⟨Compute texture differentials for 2D (u, v) mapping⟩
    Point2f st(su * ctx.uv[0] + du, sv * ctx.uv[1] + dv);
    return TexCoord2D{st, dsdx, dsdy, dtdx, dtdy};
  }
```

For a general 2D mapping function $f(u, v) \rightarrow (s, t)$, the screen-space derivatives of s and t are given by the chain rule:

$$\frac{\partial(s, t)}{\partial(x, y)} = \begin{pmatrix} \frac{\partial s}{\partial(u,v)} \cdot \frac{\partial(u,v)}{\partial x} & \frac{\partial s}{\partial(u,v)} \cdot \frac{\partial(u,v)}{\partial y} \\ \frac{\partial t}{\partial(u,v)} \cdot \frac{\partial(u,v)}{\partial x} & \frac{\partial t}{\partial(u,v)} \cdot \frac{\partial(u,v)}{\partial y} \end{pmatrix} = \begin{pmatrix} \frac{ds}{dx} & \frac{ds}{dy} \\ \frac{dt}{dx} & \frac{dt}{dy} \end{pmatrix}. \qquad [10.6]$$

Note that the `TextureEvalContext` provides the values $\partial(u, v)/\partial(x, y)$.

In this case, $f(u, v) = (s_u u + d_u, s_v v + d_v)$ and so

$$\frac{\partial(s, t)}{\partial(x, y)} = \begin{pmatrix} (s_u, 0) \cdot \frac{\partial(u,v)}{\partial x} & (s_u, 0) \cdot \frac{\partial(u,v)}{\partial y} \\ (0, s_v) \cdot \frac{\partial(u,v)}{\partial x} & (0, s_v) \cdot \frac{\partial(u,v)}{\partial y} \end{pmatrix} = \begin{pmatrix} s_u \frac{du}{dx} & s_u \frac{du}{dy} \\ s_v \frac{dv}{dx} & s_v \frac{dv}{dy} \end{pmatrix}. \qquad [10.7]$$

We will skip past the straightforward fragment that implements Equation (10.7) to initialize `dsdx`, `dsdy`, `dtdx`, and `dtdy`.

10.2.2 SPHERICAL MAPPING

Another useful mapping effectively wraps a sphere around the object. Each point is projected along the vector from the sphere's center through the point on to the sphere's surface. Since this mapping is based on spherical coordinates, Equation (3.8) can be applied, with the angles it returns remapped to [0, 1]:

$$f(\mathrm{p}) = \left(\frac{1}{2\pi} \left(\pi + \arctan \frac{\mathrm{p}_y}{\mathrm{p}_x} \right), \frac{1}{\pi} \arccos \frac{\mathrm{p}_z}{\|\mathrm{p}_x^2 + \mathrm{p}_y^2 + \mathrm{p}_z^2\|} \right). \qquad [10.8]$$

Figure 10.9 shows the use of this mapping with an object in the *Kroken* scene.

The `SphericalMapping` further stores a transformation that is applied to points before this mapping is performed; this effectively allows the mapping sphere to be arbitrarily positioned and oriented with respect to the object.

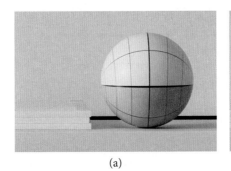

(a)   (b)

Figure 10.9: Use of the `SphericalMapping` in the *Kroken* Scene. (a) Visualization of the resulting (u, v) parameterization. (b) Effect of using the `SphericalMapping` to apply a texture. Note that although the shape is spherical, it is modeled with a triangle mesh, to which the `SphericalMapping` is applied. *(Scene courtesy of Angelo Ferretti.)*

⟨*SphericalMapping Definition*⟩ ≡
```
class SphericalMapping {
  public:
    ⟨SphericalMapping Public Methods 652⟩
  private:
    ⟨SphericalMapping Private Members 652⟩
};
```

⟨*SphericalMapping Private Members*⟩ ≡   652
```
Transform textureFromRender;
```

The Map() function starts by computing the texture-space point pt.

⟨*SphericalMapping Public Methods*⟩ ≡   652
```
TexCoord2D Map(TextureEvalContext ctx) const {
    Point3f pt = textureFromRender(ctx.p);
    ⟨Compute ∂ s/∂ p and ∂ t/∂ p for spherical mapping 652⟩
    ⟨Compute texture coordinate differentials for spherical mapping 652⟩
    ⟨Return (s, t) texture coordinates and differentials based on spherical mapping 653⟩
}
```

For a mapping function based on a 3D point p, the generalization of Equation (10.6) is

$$\frac{\partial(s,\,t)}{\partial(x,\,y)} = \begin{pmatrix} \frac{\partial s}{\partial \mathrm{p}} \cdot \frac{\partial \mathrm{p}}{\partial x} & \frac{\partial s}{\partial \mathrm{p}} \cdot \frac{\partial \mathrm{p}}{\partial y} \\ \frac{\partial t}{\partial \mathrm{p}} \cdot \frac{\partial \mathrm{p}}{\partial x} & \frac{\partial t}{\partial \mathrm{p}} \cdot \frac{\partial \mathrm{p}}{\partial y} \end{pmatrix} = \begin{pmatrix} \frac{ds}{dx} & \frac{ds}{dy} \\ \frac{dt}{dx} & \frac{dt}{dy} \end{pmatrix}. \qquad \text{[10.9]}$$

Taking the partial derivatives of the mapping function, Equation (10.8), we can find

$$\frac{\partial s}{\partial \mathrm{p}} = \frac{1}{2\pi(x^2+y^2)}\,(-y,\,x,\,0)$$

$$\frac{\partial t}{\partial \mathrm{p}} = \frac{1}{\pi(x^2+y^2+z^2)}\left(\frac{xz}{\sqrt{x^2+y^2}},\,\frac{yz}{\sqrt{x^2+y^2}},\,-\sqrt{x^2+y^2}\right). \qquad \text{[10.10]}$$

These quantities are computed using the texture-space position pt.

⟨*Compute ∂ s/∂ p and ∂ t/∂ p for spherical mapping*⟩ ≡   652
```
Float x2y2 = Sqr(pt.x) + Sqr(pt.y);
Float sqrtx2y2 = std::sqrt(x2y2);
Vector3f dsdp = Vector3f(-pt.y, pt.x, 0) / (2 * Pi * x2y2);
Vector3f dtdp = 1 / (Pi * (x2y2 + Sqr(pt.z))) *
    Vector3f(pt.x * pt.z / sqrtx2y2, pt.y * pt.z / sqrtx2y2, -sqrtx2y2);
```

The final differentials are then found using the four dot products from Equation (10.9).

⟨*Compute texture coordinate differentials for spherical mapping*⟩ ≡   652
```
Vector3f dpdx = textureFromRender(ctx.dpdx);
Vector3f dpdy = textureFromRender(ctx.dpdy);
Float dsdx = Dot(dsdp, dpdx), dsdy = Dot(dsdp, dpdy);
Float dtdx = Dot(dtdp, dpdx), dtdy = Dot(dtdp, dpdy);
```

Finally, previously defined spherical geometry utility functions compute the mapping of Equation (10.8).

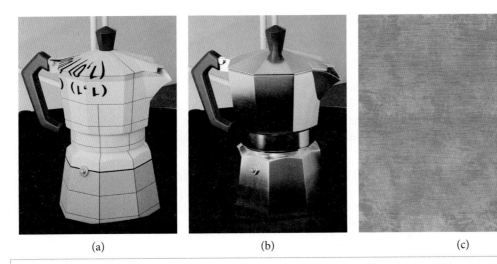

| (a) | (b) | (c) |

Figure 10.10: Use of the Cylindrical Texture Mapping. (a) Visualization of the (u, v) mapping from the `CylindricalMapping`. (b) Kettle with texture maps applied. (c) Scratch texture that is applied using the cylindrical texture mapping. *(Scene courtesy of Angelo Ferretti.)*

⟨*Return (s, t) texture coordinates and differentials based on spherical mapping*⟩ ≡   652
```
Vector3f vec = Normalize(pt - Point3f(0,0,0));
Point2f st(SphericalTheta(vec) * InvPi, SphericalPhi(vec) * Inv2Pi);
return TexCoord2D{st, dsdx, dsdy, dtdx, dtdy};
```

10.2.3 CYLINDRICAL MAPPING

The cylindrical mapping effectively wraps a cylinder around the object and then uses the cylinder's parameterization.

$$f(\mathrm{p}) = \left(\frac{1}{2\pi} \left(\pi + \arctan \frac{\mathrm{p}_y}{\mathrm{p}_x} \right), \mathrm{p}_z \right). \tag{10.11}$$

See Figure 10.10 for an example of its use.

Note that the t texture coordinate it returns is not necessarily between 0 and 1; the mapping should either be scaled in z so that the object being textured has $t \in [0, 1]$ or the texture being used should return results for coordinates outside that range that match the desired result.

⟨*CylindricalMapping Definition*⟩ ≡
```
class CylindricalMapping {
  public:
    ⟨CylindricalMapping Public Methods⟩
  private:
    ⟨CylindricalMapping Private Members 653⟩
};
```

`CylindricalMapping` also supports a transformation to orient the mapping cylinder.

⟨*CylindricalMapping Private Members*⟩ ≡   653
```
Transform textureFromRender;
```

Because the s texture coordinate is computed in the same way as it is with the spherical mapping, the cylindrical mapping's $\partial s/\partial \mathrm{p}$ matches the sphere's in Equation (10.10). The partial derivative in t can easily be seen to be $\partial t/\partial \mathrm{p} = (0, 0, 1)$.

Since the cylindrical mapping function and derivative computation are only slight variations on the spherical mapping's, we will not include the implementation of its `Map()` function here.

10.2.4 PLANAR MAPPING

Another classic mapping method is planar mapping. The point is effectively projected onto a plane; a 2D parameterization of the plane then gives texture coordinates for the point. For example, a point p might be projected onto the $z = 0$ plane to yield texture coordinates given by $s = p_x$ and $t = p_y$.

One way to define such a parameterized plane is with two nonparallel vectors $\mathbf{v}_s$ and $\mathbf{v}_t$ and offsets d_s and d_t. The texture coordinates are given by the coordinates of the point with respect to the plane's coordinate system, which are computed by taking the dot product of the vector from the point to the origin with each vector $\mathbf{v}_s$ and $\mathbf{v}_t$ and then adding the corresponding offset:

$$f(\mathrm{p}) = \big((\mathrm{p} - (0, 0, 0)) \cdot \mathbf{v}_s + d_s, (\mathrm{p} - (0, 0, 0)) \cdot \mathbf{v}_t + d_t\big).$$

⟨*PlanarMapping Definition*⟩ ≡
```
class PlanarMapping {
  public:
    ⟨PlanarMapping Public Methods 654⟩
  private:
    ⟨PlanarMapping Private Members 654⟩
};
```

A straightforward constructor, not included here, initializes the following member variables.

⟨*PlanarMapping Private Members*⟩ ≡   **654**
```
Transform textureFromRender;
Vector3f vs, vt;
Float ds, dt;
```

⟨*PlanarMapping Public Methods*⟩ ≡   **654**
```
TexCoord2D Map(TextureEvalContext ctx) const {
    Vector3f vec(textureFromRender(ctx.p));
    ⟨Initialize partial derivatives of planar mapping (s, t) coordinates 654⟩
    Point2f st(ds + Dot(vec, vs), dt + Dot(vec, vt));
    return TexCoord2D{st, dsdx, dsdy, dtdx, dtdy};
}
```

The planar mapping differentials can be computed directly using the partial derivatives of the mapping function, which are easily found. For example, the partial derivative of the s texture coordinate with respect to screen-space x is just $\partial s / \partial x = (\mathbf{v}_s \cdot \partial \mathrm{p} / \partial x)$.

⟨*Initialize partial derivatives of planar mapping (s, t) coordinates*⟩ ≡   **654**
```
Vector3f dpdx = textureFromRender(ctx.dpdx);
Vector3f dpdy = textureFromRender(ctx.dpdy);
Float dsdx = Dot(vs, dpdx), dsdy = Dot(vs, dpdy);
Float dtdx = Dot(vt, dpdx), dtdy = Dot(vt, dpdy);
```

10.2.5 3D MAPPING

We will also define a `TextureMapping3D` class that defines the interface for generating 3D texture coordinates.

⟨*TextureMapping3D Definition*⟩ ≡

```
class TextureMapping3D : public TaggedPointer<PointTransformMapping> {
  public:
    ⟨TextureMapping3D Interface 655⟩
};
```

The Map() method it specifies returns a 3D point and partial derivative vectors in the form of a TexCoord3D structure.

⟨*TextureMapping3D Interface*⟩ ≡   **655**

```
    TexCoord3D Map(TextureEvalContext ctx) const;
```

TexCoord3D parallels TexCoord2D, storing both the point and its screen-space derivatives.

⟨*TexCoord3D Definition*⟩ ≡

```
struct TexCoord3D {
    Point3f p;
    Vector3f dpdx, dpdy;
};
```

The natural 3D mapping takes the rendering-space coordinate of the point and applies a linear transformation to it. This will often be a transformation that takes the point back to the primitive's object space. Such a mapping is implemented by the PointTransformMapping class.

⟨*PointTransformMapping Definition*⟩ ≡

```
class PointTransformMapping {
  public:
    ⟨PointTransformMapping Public Methods 655⟩
  private:
    Transform textureFromRender;
};
```

Because it applies a linear transformation, the differential change in texture coordinates can be found by applying the same transformation to the partial derivatives of position.

⟨*PointTransformMapping Public Methods*⟩ ≡   **655**

```
    TexCoord3D Map(TextureEvalContext ctx) const {
        return TexCoord3D{textureFromRender(ctx.p), textureFromRender(ctx.dpdx),
                          textureFromRender(ctx.dpdy)};
    }
```

10.3 TEXTURE INTERFACE AND BASIC TEXTURES

Given a variety of ways to generate 2D and 3D texture coordinates, we will now define the general interfaces for texture functions. As mentioned earlier, pbrt supports two types of Textures: scalar Float-valued, and spectral-valued.

For the first, there is FloatTexture, which is defined in base/texture.h. There are currently 14 implementations of this interface in pbrt, which leads to a lengthy list of types for the TaggedPointer template class. Therefore, we have gathered them into a fragment, ⟨*FloatTextures*⟩, that is not included here.

⟨*FloatTexture Definition*⟩ ≡
```
class FloatTexture : public TaggedPointer<⟨FloatTextures⟩> {
  public:
    ⟨FloatTexture Interface 656⟩
};
```

A FloatTexture takes a TextureEvalContext and returns a Float value.

⟨*FloatTexture Interface*⟩ ≡   656
```
Float Evaluate(TextureEvalContext ctx) const;
```

SpectrumTexture plays an equivalent role for spectral textures. It also has so many implementations that we have elided their enumeration from the text. It, too, is defined in base/texture.h.

⟨*SpectrumTexture Definition*⟩ ≡
```
class SpectrumTexture : public TaggedPointer<⟨SpectrumTextures⟩> {
  public:
    ⟨SpectrumTexture Interface 656⟩
};
```

For the reasons that were discussed in Section 4.5.4, the SpectrumTexture evaluation routine does not return a full spectral distribution (e.g., an implementation of the Spectrum interface from Section 4.5.1). Rather, it takes a set of wavelengths of interest and returns the texture's value at just those wavelengths.

⟨*SpectrumTexture Interface*⟩ ≡   656
```
SampledSpectrum Evaluate(TextureEvalContext ctx,
                         SampledWavelengths lambda) const;
```

10.3.1 CONSTANT TEXTURE

The constant textures return the same value no matter where they are evaluated. Because they represent constant functions, they can be accurately reconstructed with any sampling rate and therefore need no antialiasing. Although these two textures are trivial, they are actually quite useful. By providing these classes, all parameters to all Materials can be represented as Textures, whether they are spatially varying or not. For example, a red diffuse object will have a SpectrumConstantTexture that always returns red as the diffuse color of the material. This way, the material system always evaluates a texture to get the surface properties at a point, avoiding the need for separate textured and nontextured versions of materials. Such an approach would grow increasingly unwieldy as the number of material parameters increased.

FloatConstantTexture, like all the following texture implementations, is defined in the files texture.h and texture.cpp.

⟨*FloatConstantTexture Definition*⟩ ≡
```
class FloatConstantTexture {
  public:
    FloatConstantTexture(Float value) : value(value) {}
    Float Evaluate(TextureEvalContext ctx) const { return value; }
  private:
    Float value;
};
```

The spectrum constant texture, SpectrumConstantTexture, is similarly simple. Here is its Evaluate() method; the rest of its structure parallels FloatConstantTexture and so is not included here.

⟨*SpectrumConstantTexture Public Methods*⟩ ≡
```
SampledSpectrum Evaluate(TextureEvalContext ctx,
                         SampledWavelengths lambda) const {
    return value.Sample(lambda);
}
```

10.3.2 SCALE TEXTURE

We have defined the texture interface in a way that makes it easy to use the output of one texture function when computing another. This is useful since it lets us define generic texture operations using any of the other texture types. The FloatScaledTexture takes two Float-valued textures and returns the product of their values.

⟨*FloatScaledTexture Definition*⟩ ≡
```
class FloatScaledTexture {
  public:
    ⟨FloatScaledTexture Public Methods 657⟩
  private:
    FloatTexture tex, scale;
};
```

FloatScaledTexture ignores antialiasing, leaving it to its two subtextures to antialias themselves but not making an effort to antialias their product. While it is easy to show that the product of two band-limited functions is also band limited, the maximum frequency present in the product may be greater than that of either of the two terms individually. Thus, even if the scale and value textures are perfectly antialiased, the result might not be. Fortunately, the most common use of this texture is to scale another texture by a constant, in which case the other texture's antialiasing is sufficient.

One thing to note in the implementation of its Evaluate() method is that it skips evaluating the tex texture if the scale texture returns 0. It is worthwhile to avoid incurring the cost of this computation if it is unnecessary.

⟨*FloatScaledTexture Public Methods*⟩ ≡   **657**
```
Float Evaluate(TextureEvalContext ctx) const {
    Float sc = scale.Evaluate(ctx);
    if (sc == 0) return 0;
    return tex.Evaluate(ctx) * sc;
}
```

SpectrumScaledTexture is the straightforward variant and is therefore not included here. An example of its use is shown in Figure 10.11.

10.3.3 MIX TEXTURES

The mix textures are more general variations of the scale textures. They blend between two textures of the same type based on a scalar blending factor. Note that a constant texture could be used for the blending factor to achieve a uniform blend, or a more complex Texture could be used to blend in a spatially nonuniform way. Figure 10.12 shows the use of the SpectrumMixTexture where an image is used to blend between two constant RGB colors.

(a)   (b)   (c)

(d)

Figure 10.11: Use of the `SpectrumScaledTexture` **in the** *Watercolor* **Scene.** The product of (a) a texture of paint strokes and (b) a mask representing splotches gives (c) colorful splotches. (d) When applied to the surface of a table, a convincing paint spill results. *(Scene courtesy of Angelo Ferretti.)*

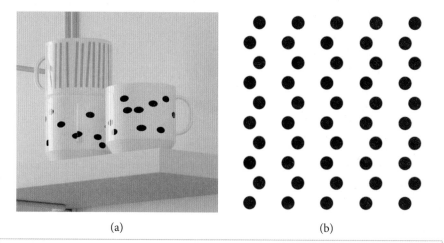

(a)   (b)

Figure 10.12: Use of the Mix Texture in the *Kroken* **Scene.** (a) The `SpectrumMixTexture` is used to find the color at each point on the bottom two cups. (b) Two fixed RGB colors are modulated using this image texture. *(Scene courtesy of Angelo Ferretti.)*

⟨*FloatMixTexture Definition*⟩ ≡
```
class FloatMixTexture {
  public:
    ⟨FloatMixTexture Public Methods 659⟩
  private:
    FloatTexture tex1, tex2;
    FloatTexture amount;
};
```

To evaluate the mixture, the three textures are evaluated and the floating-point value is used to linearly interpolate between the two. When the blend amount amt is zero, the first texture's value is returned, and when it is one the second one's value is returned. The Evaluate() method here makes sure not to evaluate textures unnecessarily if the blending amount implies that only one of their values is necessary. (Section 15.1.1 has further discussion about why the logic for that is written just as it is here, rather than with, for example, cascaded if tests that each directly return the appropriate value.) We will generally assume that amt will be between zero and one, but this behavior is not enforced, so extrapolation is possible as well.

As with the scale textures, antialiasing is ignored, so the introduction of aliasing here is a possibility.

⟨*FloatMixTexture Public Methods*⟩ ≡   **659**
```
Float Evaluate(TextureEvalContext ctx) const {
    Float amt = amount.Evaluate(ctx);
    Float t1 = 0, t2 = 0;
    if (amt != 1) t1 = tex1.Evaluate(ctx);
    if (amt != 0) t2 = tex2.Evaluate(ctx);
    return (1 - amt) * t1 + amt * t2;
}
```

We will not include the implementation of SpectrumMixTexture here, as it parallels that of FloatMixTexture.

It can also be useful to blend between two textures based on the surface's orientation. The FloatDirectionMixTexture and SpectrumDirectionMixTexture use the dot product of the surface normal with a specified direction to compute such a weight. As they are very similar, we will only discuss SpectrumDirectionMixTexture here.

⟨*SpectrumDirectionMixTexture Definition*⟩ ≡
```
class SpectrumDirectionMixTexture {
  public:
    ⟨SpectrumDirectionMixTexture Public Methods 660⟩
  private:
    ⟨SpectrumDirectionMixTexture Private Members 659⟩
};
```

⟨*SpectrumDirectionMixTexture Private Members*⟩ ≡   **659**
```
SpectrumTexture tex1, tex2;
Vector3f dir;
```

Figure 10.13: Use of the `SpectrumDirectionMixTexture` in the *Kroken* Scene. The texture is used to select between one image texture that uses a planar projection to specify the cover image of the magazine and another that uses a different planar projection for its spine. *(Scene courtesy of Angelo Ferretti.)*

If the normal is coincident with the specified direction, tex1 is returned; if it is perpendicular, then tex2 is. Otherwise, the two textures are blended. Figure 10.13 shows an example of the use of this texture.

⟨*SpectrumDirectionMixTexture Public Methods*⟩ ≡   **659**
```
SampledSpectrum Evaluate(TextureEvalContext ctx,
                         SampledWavelengths lambda) const {
    Float amt = AbsDot(ctx.n, dir);
    SampledSpectrum t1, t2;
    if (amt != 0) t1 = tex1.Evaluate(ctx, lambda);
    if (amt != 1) t2 = tex2.Evaluate(ctx, lambda);
    return amt * t1 + (1 - amt) * t2;
}
```

10.4 IMAGE TEXTURE

Image textures store 2D arrays of point-sampled values of a texture function. They use these samples to reconstruct a continuous image function that can be evaluated at an arbitrary (s, t) position.[3] These sample values are often called *texels*, since they are similar to pixels in an image but are used in the context of a texture. Image textures are the most widely used type of texture in computer graphics; digital photographs, scanned artwork, images created with image-editing programs, and images generated by renderers are all extremely useful sources of data for this particular texture representation (Figure 10.14).

---

3   The term *texture map* is often used to refer to this type of texture, although this usage blurs the distinction between the mapping that computes texture coordinates and the texture function itself.

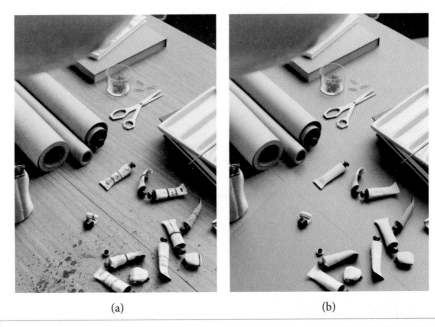

(a)   (b)

Figure 10.14: An Example of Image Textures. Image textures are used throughout the *Watercolor* scene to represent spatially varying surface appearance properties. (a) Scene rendered with image textures. (b) Each image texture has been replaced with its average value. Note how much visual richness is lost. *(Scene courtesy of Angelo Ferretti.)*

As with most of the other types of texture, pbrt provides both Float and spectral variants. Both implementations inherit from ImageTextureBase, which provides some common functionality.

⟨*ImageTextureBase Definition*⟩ ≡
    class ImageTextureBase {
      public:
        ⟨*ImageTextureBase Public Methods* **662**⟩
      protected:
        ⟨*ImageTextureBase Protected Members* **662**⟩
      private:
        ⟨*ImageTextureBase Private Members* **663**⟩
    };

In the following, we will present the implementation of SpectrumImageTexture; FloatImage Texture is analogous and does not add anything new.

ImageTextureBase 661

⟨*SpectrumImageTexture Definition*⟩ ≡
    class SpectrumImageTexture : public ImageTextureBase {
      public:
        ⟨*SpectrumImageTexture Public Methods* **662**⟩
      private:
        ⟨*SpectrumImageTexture Private Members* **662**⟩
    };

10.4.1 TEXTURE MEMORY MANAGEMENT

The caller of SpectrumImageTexture's constructor provides a texture mapping function, the filename of an image, various parameters that control the filtering of the image map, how boundary conditions are managed, and how colors are converted to spectral samples. All the necessary initialization is handled by ImageTextureBase.

⟨*SpectrumImageTexture Public Methods*⟩ ≡   **661**
```
SpectrumImageTexture(TextureMapping2D mapping, std::string filename,
        MIPMapFilterOptions filterOptions, WrapMode wrapMode, Float scale,
        bool invert, ColorEncoding encoding, SpectrumType spectrumType,
        Allocator alloc)
    : ImageTextureBase(mapping, filename, filterOptions, wrapMode,
                        scale, invert, encoding, alloc),
      spectrumType(spectrumType) {}
```

As was discussed in Section 4.6.6, RGB colors are transformed into spectra differently depending on whether or not they represent reflectances. The spectrumType records what type of RGB a texture represents.

⟨*SpectrumImageTexture Private Members*⟩ ≡   **661**
```
SpectrumType spectrumType;
```

The contents of the image file are used to create an instance of the MIPMap class that stores the texels in memory and handles the details of reconstruction and filtering to reduce aliasing.

⟨*ImageTextureBase Public Methods*⟩ ≡   **661**
```
ImageTextureBase(TextureMapping2D mapping, std::string filename,
        MIPMapFilterOptions filterOptions, WrapMode wrapMode, Float scale,
        bool invert, ColorEncoding encoding, Allocator alloc)
    : mapping(mapping), filename(filename), scale(scale), invert(invert) {
    ⟨Get MIPMap from texture cache if present 663⟩
    ⟨Create MIPMap for filename and add to texture cache 663⟩
}
```

A floating-point scale can be specified with each texture; it is applied to the values returned by the Evaluate() method. Further, a true value for the invert parameter causes the texture value to be subtracted from 1 before it is returned. While the same functionality can be achieved with scale and mix textures, it is easy to also provide that functionality directly in the texture here. Doing so can lead to more efficient texture evaluation on GPUs, as is discussed further in Section 15.3.9.

⟨*ImageTextureBase Protected Members*⟩ ≡   **661**
```
TextureMapping2D mapping;
std::string filename;
Float scale;
bool invert;
MIPMap *mipmap;
```

Allocator 40
ColorEncoding 1094
Float 23
ImageTextureBase 661
MIPMap 665
MIPMapFilterOptions 667
SpectrumImageTexture 661
SpectrumType 1125
TextureMapping2D 649
WrapMode 1082

Each MIP map may require a meaningful amount of memory, and a complex scene may have thousands of image textures. Because an on-disk image may be reused for multiple textures in a scene, pbrt maintains a table of MIP maps that have been loaded so far so that they are only loaded into memory once even if they are used in more than one image texture.

pbrt loads textures in parallel after the scene description has been parsed; doing so reduces startup time before rendering begins. Therefore, a mutex is used here to ensure that only one thread accesses the texture cache at a time. Note that if the MIPMap is not found in the cache, the lock is released before it is read so that other threads can access the cache in the meantime.

⟨*Get* MIPMap *from texture cache if present*⟩ ≡   662
```
    TexInfo texInfo(filename, filterOptions, wrapMode, encoding);
    std::unique_lock<std::mutex> lock(textureCacheMutex);
    if (auto iter = textureCache.find(texInfo); iter != textureCache.end()) {
        mipmap = iter->second;
        return;
    }
    lock.unlock();
```

The texture cache itself is managed with a std::map.

⟨*ImageTextureBase Private Members*⟩ ≡   661
```
    static std::mutex textureCacheMutex;
    static std::map<TexInfo, MIPMap *> textureCache;
```

TexInfo is a simple structure that acts as a key for the texture cache std::map. It holds all the specifics that must match for a MIPMap to be reused in another image texture.

⟨*TexInfo Definition*⟩ ≡
```
    struct TexInfo {
        ⟨TexInfo Public Methods 663⟩
        std::string filename;
        MIPMapFilterOptions filterOptions;
        WrapMode wrapMode;
        ColorEncoding encoding;
    };
```

The TexInfo constructor, not included here, sets its member variables with provided values. Its only other method is a comparison operator, which is required by std::map.

⟨*TexInfo Public Methods*⟩ ≡   663
```
    bool operator<(const TexInfo &t) const {
        return std::tie(filename, filterOptions, encoding, wrapMode) <
               std::tie(t.filename, t.filterOptions, t.encoding, t.wrapMode);
    }
```

If the texture has not yet been loaded, a call to CreateFromFile() yields a MIPMap for it. If the file is not found or there is an error reading it, pbrt exits with an error message, so a nullptr return value does not need to be handled here.

⟨*Create* MIPMap *for* filename *and add to texture cache*⟩ ≡   662
```
    mipmap = MIPMap::CreateFromFile(filename, filterOptions, wrapMode,
                                    encoding, alloc);
    lock.lock();
    textureCache[texInfo] = mipmap;
```

10.4.2 IMAGE TEXTURE EVALUATION

Before describing the MIPMap implementation, we will discuss the SpectrumImageTexture Evaluate() method.

⟨*SpectrumImageTexture Method Definitions*⟩ ≡
```
SampledSpectrum SpectrumImageTexture::Evaluate(
        TextureEvalContext ctx, SampledWavelengths lambda) const {
    ⟨Apply texture mapping and flip t coordinate for image texture lookup 664⟩
    ⟨Lookup filtered RGB value in MIPMap 664⟩
    ⟨Return SampledSpectrum for RGB image texture value 664⟩
}
```

It is easy to compute the (*s*, *t*) texture coordinates and their derivatives for filtering with the TextureMapping2D's Map() method. However, the *t* coordinate must be flipped, because pbrt's Image class (and in turn, MIPMap, which is based on it) defines (0, 0) to be the upper left corner of the image, while image textures have (0, 0) at the lower left. (These are the typical conventions for indexing these entities in computer graphics.)

⟨*Apply texture mapping and flip t coordinate for image texture lookup*⟩ ≡   **664**
```
TexCoord2D c = mapping.Map(ctx);
c.st[1] = 1 - c.st[1];
```

The MIPMap's Filter() method provides the filtered value of the image texture over the specified region; any specified scale or inversion is easily applied to the value it returns. A call to ClampZero() here ensures that no negative values are returned after inversion.

⟨*Lookup filtered RGB value in* MIPMap⟩ ≡   **664**
```
RGB rgb = scale * mipmap->Filter<RGB>(c.st, {c.dsdx, c.dtdx},
                                             {c.dsdy, c.dtdy});
rgb = ClampZero(invert ? (RGB(1, 1, 1) - rgb) : rgb);
```

As discussed in Section 4.6.2, an RGB color space is necessary in order to interpret the meaning of an RGB color value. Normally, the code that reads image file formats from disk returns an RGBColorSpace with the read image. Most RGB image formats default to sRGB, and some allow specifying an alternative color space. (For example, OpenEXR allows specifying the primaries of an arbitrary RGB color space in the image file's metadata.) A color space and the value of spectrumType make it possible to create the appropriate type RGB spectrum, and in turn, its Spectrum::Sample() can be called to get the SampledSpectrum that will be returned.

If the MIPMap has no associated color space, the image is assumed to have the same value in all channels and a constant value is returned for all the spectrum samples. This assumption is verified by a DCHECK() call in non-optimized builds.

⟨*Return* SampledSpectrum *for RGB image texture value*⟩ ≡   **664**
```
if (const RGBColorSpace *cs = mipmap->GetRGBColorSpace(); cs) {
    if (spectrumType == SpectrumType::Unbounded)
        return RGBUnboundedSpectrum(*cs, rgb).Sample(lambda);
    else if (spectrumType == SpectrumType::Albedo)
        return RGBAlbedoSpectrum(*cs, Clamp(rgb, 0, 1)).Sample(lambda);
    else
        return RGBIlluminantSpectrum(*cs, rgb).Sample(lambda);
}
DCHECK(rgb[0] == rgb[1] && rgb[1] == rgb[2]);
return SampledSpectrum(rgb[0]);
```

10.4.3 MIP MAPS

As always, if the image texture function has higher frequency detail than can be represented by the texture sampling rate, aliasing will be present in the final image. Any frequencies higher than the Nyquist limit must be removed by prefiltering before the function is evaluated.

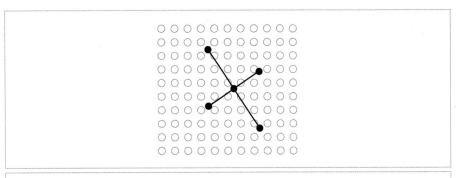

Figure 10.15: Given a point at which to perform an image map lookup (denoted by the solid point in the center) and estimates of the texture-space sampling rate (denoted by adjacent solid points), it may be necessary to filter the contributions of a large number of texels in the image map (denoted by open points).

Figure 10.15 shows the basic problem we face: an image texture has texels that are samples of some image function at a fixed frequency. The filter region for the lookup is given by its (s, t) center point and offsets to the estimated texture coordinate locations for the adjacent image samples. Because these offsets are estimates of the texture sampling rate, we must remove any frequencies higher than twice the distance to the adjacent samples in order to satisfy the Nyquist criterion.

The texture sampling and reconstruction process has a few key differences from the image sampling process discussed in Chapter 8. These differences make it possible to address the antialiasing problem with more effective and less computationally expensive techniques. For example, here it is inexpensive to get the value of a sample—only an array lookup is necessary (as opposed to having to trace a number of rays to compute radiance). Further, because the texture image function is fully defined by the set of samples and there is no mystery about what its highest frequency could be, there is no uncertainty related to the function's behavior between samples. These differences make it possible to remove detail from the texture before sampling, thus eliminating aliasing.

However, the texture sampling rate will typically change from pixel to pixel. The sampling rate is determined by scene geometry and its orientation, the texture coordinate mapping function, and the camera projection and image sampling rate. Because the texture sampling rate is not fixed, texture filtering algorithms need to be able to filter over arbitrary regions of texture samples efficiently.

The `MIPMap` class implements a number of methods for texture filtering with spatially varying filter widths. It can be found in the files `util/mipmap.h` and `util/mipmap.cpp`. The filtering algorithms it offers range from simple point sampling to bilinear interpolation and trilinear interpolation, which is fast and easy to implement and was widely used for texture filtering in early graphics hardware, to elliptically weighted averaging, which is more complex but returns extremely high-quality results. Figure 10.16 compares the result of texture filtering using trilinear interpolation and the EWA algorithm.

⟨*MIPMap Definition*⟩ ≡
```
class MIPMap {
  public:
    ⟨MIPMap Public Methods 667⟩
  private:
    ⟨MIPMap Private Methods⟩
    ⟨MIPMap Private Members 667⟩
};
```

MIPMap 665

Figure 10.16: Filtering the image map properly substantially improves the image. Trilinear interpolation is used for the sphere on the left and the EWA algorithm is used for the sphere on the right. Both of these approaches give a much better result than the unfiltered image map on the sphere on the left in Figure 10.1. Trilinear interpolation is not as effective as EWA at handling strongly anisotropic filter footprints, which is why the lines on the left sphere are blurrier. In regions with highly anisotropic filter footprints such as the pole of the sphere and toward the edges, EWA resolves much more detail.

If an RGB image is provided to the `MIPMap` constructor, its channels should be stored in R, G, B order in memory; for efficiency, the following code assumes that this is the case. All the code that currently uses `MIPMap`s in pbrt ensures that this is so.

⟨*MIPMap Method Definitions*⟩ ≡
```
MIPMap::MIPMap(
        Image image, const RGBColorSpace *colorSpace, WrapMode wrapMode,
        Allocator alloc, const MIPMapFilterOptions &options)
    : colorSpace(colorSpace), wrapMode(wrapMode), options(options) {
    pyramid = Image::GeneratePyramid(std::move(image), wrapMode, alloc);
}
```

To limit the potential number of texels that need to be accessed, these filtering methods use an *image pyramid* of increasingly lower resolution prefiltered versions of the original image to accelerate their operation.[4] The original image texels are at the bottom level of the pyramid, and the image at each level is half the resolution of the previous level, up to the top level, which has a single texel representing the average of all the texels in the original image. This collection of images needs at most 1/3 more memory than storing the most detailed level alone and can be used to quickly find filtered values over large regions of the original image. The basic idea behind the pyramid is that if a large area of texels needs to be filtered, a reasonable approximation is to use a higher level of the pyramid and do the filtering over the same area there, accessing many fewer texels.

The `MIPMap`'s image pyramid is represented by a vector of `Image`s. See Section B.5 for the implementation of `Image` and Section B.5.5 for its `GeneratePyramid()` method, which generates image pyramids.

---

4   The name "MIP map" comes from the Latin *multum in parvo*, which means "much in little," a nod to the image pyramid.

⟨*MIPMap Private Members*⟩ ≡   665
```
pstd::vector<Image> pyramid;
const RGBColorSpace *colorSpace;
WrapMode wrapMode;
MIPMapFilterOptions options;
```

The choice of filtering algorithm and a parameter used by the EWA method are represented by MIPMapFilterOptions.

⟨*MIPMapFilterOptions Definition*⟩ ≡
```
struct MIPMapFilterOptions {
    FilterFunction filter = FilterFunction::EWA;
    Float maxAnisotropy = 8.f;
};
```

⟨*FilterFunction Definition*⟩ ≡
```
enum class FilterFunction { Point, Bilinear, Trilinear, EWA };
```

A few simple utility methods return information about the image pyramid and the MIPMap's color space.

⟨*MIPMap Public Methods*⟩ ≡   665
```
Point2i LevelResolution(int level) const {
    return pyramid[level].Resolution();
}
int Levels() const { return int(pyramid.size()); }
const RGBColorSpace *GetRGBColorSpace() const { return colorSpace; }
const Image &GetLevel(int level) const { return pyramid[level]; }
```

Given the image pyramid, we will define some utility MIPMap methods that retrieve the texel value at a specified pyramid level and discrete integer pixel coordinates. For the RGB variant, there is an implicit assumption that the image channels are laid out in R, G, B (and maybe A) order.

⟨*MIPMap Method Definitions*⟩ +≡
```
template <>
RGB MIPMap::Texel(int level, Point2i st) const {
    if (int nc = pyramid[level].NChannels(); nc == 3 || nc == 4)
        return RGB(pyramid[level].GetChannel(st, 0, wrapMode),
                   pyramid[level].GetChannel(st, 1, wrapMode),
                   pyramid[level].GetChannel(st, 2, wrapMode));
    else {
        Float v = pyramid[level].GetChannel(st, 0, wrapMode);
        return RGB(v, v, v);
    }
}
```

The Float specialization of Texel(), not included here, is analogous.

10.4.4 IMAGE MAP FILTERING

The MIPMap Filter() method returns a filtered image function value at the provided (s, t) coordinates. It takes two derivatives that give the change in (s, t) with respect to image pixel samples.

⟨*MIPMap Method Definitions*⟩ +≡
```
template <typename T>
T MIPMap::Filter(Point2f st, Vector2f dst0, Vector2f dst1) const {
    if (options.filter != FilterFunction::EWA) {
        ⟨Handle non-EWA MIP Map filter 668⟩
    }
    ⟨Compute EWA ellipse axes 670⟩
    ⟨Clamp ellipse vector ratio if too large 671⟩
    ⟨Choose level of detail for EWA lookup and perform EWA filtering 671⟩
}
```

The EWA filtering technique to be described shortly uses both derivatives of (s, t) to compute an *anisotropic filter*—one that filters by different amounts in the different dimensions. The other three use an *isotropic filter* that filters both equally. The isotropic filters are more computationally efficient than the anisotropic filter, though they do not give results that are as good. For them, only a single value is needed to specify the width of the filter. The width here is conservatively chosen to avoid aliasing in both the s and t directions, though this choice means that textures viewed at an oblique angle will appear blurry, since the required sampling rate in one direction will be very different from the sampling rate along the other in this case.

⟨*Handle non-EWA MIP Map filter*⟩ ≡   **668**
```
Float width = 2 * std::max({std::abs(dst0[0]), std::abs(dst0[1]),
                            std::abs(dst1[0]), std::abs(dst1[1])});
⟨Compute MIP Map level for width and handle very wide filter 669⟩
if (options.filter == FilterFunction::Point) {
    ⟨Return point-sampled value at selected MIP level 669⟩
} else if (options.filter == FilterFunction::Bilinear) {
    ⟨Return bilinear-filtered value at selected MIP level 669⟩
} else {
    ⟨Return trilinear-filtered value at selected MIP level 670⟩
}
```

Because filtering over many texels for wide filter widths would be inefficient, this method chooses a MIP map level from the pyramid such that the filter region at that level would cover four texels at that level. Figure 10.17 illustrates this idea.

Since the resolutions of the levels of the pyramid are all powers of two, the resolution of level l is $2^{\text{nLevels}-1-l}$. Therefore, to find the level with a texel spacing width w requires solving

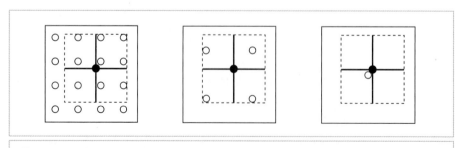

Figure 10.17: Choosing a MIP Map Level for the Triangle Filter. The MIPMap chooses a level such that the filter covers four texels.

$$\frac{1}{w} = 2^{\text{nLevels}-1-l}$$

for l. In general, this will be a floating-point value between two MIP map levels. Values of l greater than the number of pyramid levels correspond to a filter width wider than the image, in which case the single pixel at the top level is returned.

⟨*Compute MIP Map level for* width *and handle very wide filter*⟩ ≡   668
```
int nLevels = Levels();
Float level = nLevels - 1 + Log2(std::max<Float>(width, 1e-8));
if (level >= Levels() - 1)
    return Texel<T>(Levels() - 1, Point2i(0, 0));
int iLevel = std::max(0, int(pstd::floor(level)));
```

For a point-sampled texture lookup, it is only necessary to convert the continuous texture coordinates over [0, 1] to discrete coordinates over the image resolution and to retrieve the appropriate texel value via the MIPMap's Texel() method.

⟨*Return point-sampled value at selected MIP level*⟩ ≡   668
```
Point2i resolution = LevelResolution(iLevel);
Point2i sti(pstd::round(st[0] * resolution[0] - 0.5f),
            pstd::round(st[1] * resolution[1] - 0.5f));
return Texel<T>(iLevel, sti);
```

Bilinear filtering, which is equivalent to filtering using a triangle filter, is easily implemented via a call to Bilerp().

⟨*Return bilinear-filtered value at selected MIP level*⟩ ≡   668
```
return Bilerp<T>(iLevel, st);
```

Bilinear interpolation is provided in a separate method so that it can also be used for trilinear filtering.

⟨*MIPMap Method Definitions*⟩ +≡
```
template <>
RGB MIPMap::Bilerp(int level, Point2f st) const {
    if (int nc = pyramid[level].NChannels(); nc == 3 || nc == 4)
        return RGB(pyramid[level].BilerpChannel(st, 0, wrapMode),
                   pyramid[level].BilerpChannel(st, 1, wrapMode),
                   pyramid[level].BilerpChannel(st, 2, wrapMode));
    else {
        Float v = pyramid[level].BilerpChannel(st, 0, wrapMode);
        return RGB(v, v, v);
    }
}
```

As shown by Figure 10.17, applying a triangle filter to the four texels around the sample point will either filter over too small a region or too large a region (except for very carefully selected filter widths). Therefore, the Trilinear filtering option applies the triangle filter at both of these levels and blends between them according to how close level is to each of them. This helps hide the transitions from one MIP map level to the next at nearby pixels in the final image. While applying a triangle filter to four texels at two levels in this manner does not generally give exactly the same result as applying a triangle filter to the original pixels, the difference is not too bad in practice, and the efficiency of this approach is worth this penalty. In any case, the following elliptically weighted average filtering approach should be used when texture quality is important.

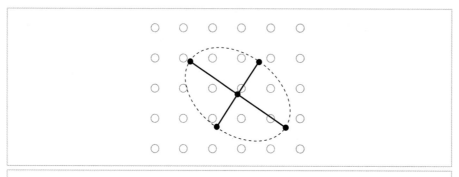

Figure 10.18: The EWA filter applies a Gaussian filter to the texels in an elliptical area around the evaluation point. The extent of the ellipse is such that its edge passes through the positions of the adjacent texture samples as estimated by the texture coordinate partial derivatives.

⟨*Return trilinear-filtered value at selected MIP level*⟩ ≡   **668**
```
if (iLevel == 0)
    return Bilerp<T>(0, st);
else
    return Lerp(level - iLevel, Bilerp<T>(iLevel, st),
                Bilerp<T>(iLevel + 1, st));
```

The elliptically weighted average (EWA) algorithm fits an ellipse to the two differential vectors in texture space and then filters the texture with a Gaussian filter function (Figure 10.18). It is widely regarded as one of the best texture filtering algorithms in graphics and has been carefully derived from the basic principles of sampling theory. Unlike the triangle filter, it can filter over arbitrarily oriented regions of the texture, with different filter extents in different directions. The quality of its results is improved by it being an anisotropic filter, since it can adapt to different sampling rates along the two image axes.

We will not show the full derivation of this filter here, although we do note that it is distinguished by being a *unified resampling filter*: it simultaneously computes the result of a Gaussian filtered texture function convolved with a Gaussian reconstruction filter in image space. This is in contrast to many other texture filtering methods that ignore the effect of the image-space filter or equivalently assume that it is a box. Even if a Gaussian is not being used for filtering the samples for the image being rendered, taking some account of the spatial variation of the image filter improves the results, assuming that the filter being used is somewhat similar in shape to the Gaussian, as the Mitchell and windowed sinc filters are.

The screen-space partial derivatives of the texture coordinates define the ellipse. The lookup method starts out by determining which of the two axes is the longer of the two, swapping them if needed so that dst0 is the longer vector. The length of the shorter vector will be used to select a MIP map level.

⟨*Compute EWA ellipse axes*⟩ ≡   **668**
```
if (LengthSquared(dst0) < LengthSquared(dst1))
    pstd::swap(dst0, dst1);
Float longerVecLength = Length(dst0), shorterVecLength = Length(dst1);
```

Next the ratio of the length of the longer vector to the length of the shorter one is considered. A large ratio indicates a very long and skinny ellipse. Because this method filters texels from a MIP map level chosen based on the length of the shorter differential vector, a large ratio means that a large number of texels need to be filtered. To avoid this expense (and to ensure that any EWA lookup takes a bounded amount of time), the length of the shorter vector may be increased to limit this ratio. The result may be an increase in blurring, although this effect usually is not noticeable in practice.

⟨*Clamp ellipse vector ratio if too large*⟩ ≡   668
```
if (shorterVecLength * options.maxAnisotropy < longerVecLength &&
    shorterVecLength > 0) {
    Float scale = longerVecLength /
        (shorterVecLength * options.maxAnisotropy);
    dst1 *= scale;
    shorterVecLength *= scale;
}
if (shorterVecLength == 0)
    return Bilerp<T>(0, st);
```

Like the triangle filter, the EWA filter uses the image pyramid to reduce the number of texels to be filtered for a particular texture lookup, choosing a MIP map level based on the length of the shorter vector. Given the limited ratio from the clamping above, the total number of texels used is thus bounded. Given the length of the shorter vector, the computation to find the appropriate pyramid level is the same as was used for the triangle filter. Similarly, the implementation here blends between the filtered results at the two levels around the computed level of detail, again to reduce artifacts from transitions from one level to another.

⟨*Choose level of detail for EWA lookup and perform EWA filtering*⟩ ≡   668
```
Float lod = std::max<Float>(0, Levels() - 1 + Log2(shorterVecLength));
int ilod = pstd::floor(lod);
return Lerp(lod - ilod, EWA<T>(ilod, st, dst0, dst1),
            EWA<T>(ilod + 1, st, dst0, dst1));
```

The `MIPMap::EWA()` method actually applies the filter at a particular level.

⟨*MIPMap Method Definitions*⟩ +≡
```
template <typename T>
T MIPMap::EWA(int level, Point2f st, Vector2f dst0, Vector2f dst1) const {
    if (level >= Levels())
        return Texel<T>(Levels() - 1, {0, 0});
    ⟨Convert EWA coordinates to appropriate scale for level 672⟩
    ⟨Find ellipse coefficients that bound EWA filter region 672⟩
    ⟨Compute the ellipse's (s, t) bounding box in texture space 672⟩
    ⟨Scan over ellipse bound and evaluate quadratic equation to filter image 673⟩
}
```

This method first converts from texture coordinates in [0, 1] to coordinates and differentials in terms of the resolution of the chosen MIP map level. It also subtracts 0.5 from the continuous position coordinate to align the sample point with the discrete texel coordinates, as was done in `MIPMap::Bilerp()`.

⟨*Convert EWA coordinates to appropriate scale for level*⟩ ≡   671
```
Point2i levelRes = LevelResolution(level);
st[0] = st[0] * levelRes[0] - 0.5f;
st[1] = st[1] * levelRes[1] - 0.5f;
dst0[0] *= levelRes[0];
dst0[1] *= levelRes[1];
dst1[0] *= levelRes[0];
dst1[1] *= levelRes[1];
```

It next computes the coefficients of the implicit equation for the ellipse centered at the origin that is defined by the vectors (ds0,dt0) and (ds1,dt1). Placing the ellipse at the origin rather than at (s, t) simplifies the implicit equation and the computation of its coefficients and can be easily corrected for when the equation is evaluated later. The general form of the implicit equation for all points (s, t) inside such an ellipse is

$$e(s, t) = As^2 + Bst + Ct^2 < F,$$

although it is more computationally efficient to divide through by F and express this as

$$e(s, t) = \frac{A}{F}s^2 + \frac{B}{F}st + \frac{C}{F}t^2 = A's^2 + B'st + C't^2 < 1.$$

We will not derive the equations that give the values of the coefficients, although the interested reader can easily verify their correctness.[5]

⟨*Find ellipse coefficients that bound EWA filter region*⟩ ≡   671
```
Float A = Sqr(dst0[1]) + Sqr(dst1[1]) + 1;
Float B = -2 * (dst0[0] * dst0[1] + dst1[0] * dst1[1]);
Float C = Sqr(dst0[0]) + Sqr(dst1[0]) + 1;
Float invF = 1 / (A * C - Sqr(B) * 0.25f);
A *= invF;
B *= invF;
C *= invF;
```

The next step is to find the axis-aligned bounding box in discrete integer texel coordinates of the texels that are potentially inside the ellipse. The EWA algorithm loops over all of these candidate texels, filtering the contributions of those that are in fact inside the ellipse. The bounding box is found by determining the minimum and maximum values that the ellipse takes in the s and t directions. These extrema can be calculated by finding the partial derivatives $\partial e/\partial s$ and $\partial e/\partial t$, finding their solutions for $s = 0$ and $t = 0$, and adding the offset to the ellipse center. For brevity, we will not include the derivation for these expressions here.

⟨*Compute the ellipse's (s, t) bounding box in texture space*⟩ ≡   671
```
Float det = -Sqr(B) + 4 * A * C;
Float invDet = 1 / det;
Float uSqrt = SafeSqrt(det * C), vSqrt = SafeSqrt(A * det);
int s0 = pstd::ceil(st[0] - 2 * invDet * uSqrt);
int s1 = pstd::floor(st[0] + 2 * invDet * uSqrt);
int t0 = pstd::ceil(st[1] - 2 * invDet * vSqrt);
int t1 = pstd::floor(st[1] + 2 * invDet * vSqrt);
```

Float 23
MIPMap::LevelResolution() 667
Point2i 92
SafeSqrt() 1034
Sqr() 1034

---

5   Heckbert's thesis has the original derivation (Heckbert 1989b, p. 80): A and C have an extra term of 1 added to them so the ellipse is a minimum of one texel separation wide. This ensures that the ellipse will not fall between the texels when magnifying at the most detailed level.

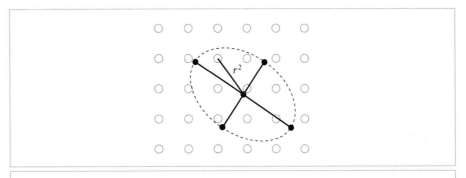

Figure 10.19: Finding the r^2 Ellipse Value for the EWA Filter Table Lookup.

Now that the bounding box is known, the EWA algorithm loops over the texels, transforming each one to the coordinate system where the texture lookup point (s, t) is at the origin with a translation. It then evaluates the ellipse equation to see if the texel is inside the ellipse (Figure 10.19) and computes the filter weight for the texel if so. The final filtered value returned is a weighted sum over texels $T(s', t')$ inside the ellipse, where f is the Gaussian filter function:

$$\frac{\sum f(s' - s, t' - t)T(s', t')}{\sum f(s' - s, t' - t)}.$$

⟨*Scan over ellipse bound and evaluate quadratic equation to filter image*⟩ ≡   671
```
T sum{};
Float sumWts = 0;
for (int it = t0; it <= t1; ++it) {
    Float tt = it - st[1];
    for (int is = s0; is <= s1; ++is) {
        Float ss = is - st[0];
        ⟨Compute squared radius and filter texel if it is inside the ellipse 673⟩
    }
}
return sum / sumWts;
```

A nice feature of the implicit equation $e(s, t)$ is that its value at a particular texel is the squared ratio of the distance from the center of the ellipse to the texel to the distance from the center of the ellipse to the ellipse boundary along the line through that texel (Figure 10.19). This value can be used to index into a precomputed lookup table of Gaussian filter function values.

⟨*Compute squared radius and filter texel if it is inside the ellipse*⟩ ≡   673
```
Float r2 = A * Sqr(ss) + B * ss * tt + C * Sqr(tt);
if (r2 < 1) {
    int index = std::min<int>(r2 * MIPFilterLUTSize, MIPFilterLUTSize - 1);
    Float weight = MIPFilterLUT[index];
    sum += weight * Texel<T>(level, {is, it});
    sumWts += weight;
}
```

The lookup table is precomputed and available as a constant array. Similar to the Gaussian Filter used for image reconstruction, the filter function is offset so that it goes to zero at the end of its extent rather than having an abrupt step. It is

$$e^{-\alpha r^2} - e^{-\alpha}.$$

$\alpha = 2$ was used for the table in pbrt. Because the table is indexed with squared distances from the filter center r^2, each entry stores a value $e^{-\alpha r}$, rather than $e^{-\alpha r^2}$.

⟨*MIPMap EWA Lookup Table Definition*⟩ ≡
```
static constexpr int MIPFilterLUTSize = 128;
static PBRT_CONST Float MIPFilterLUT[MIPFilterLUTSize] = {
    ⟨MIPMap EWA Lookup Table Values⟩
};
```

10.5 MATERIAL INTERFACE AND IMPLEMENTATIONS

With a variety of textures available, we will turn to materials, first introducing the material interface and then a few material implementations. pbrt's materials all follow a similar form, evaluating textures to get parameter values that are used to initialize their particular BSDF model. Therefore, we will only include a few of their implementations in the text here.

The Material interface is defined by the Material class, which can be found in the file base/material.h. pbrt includes the implementations of 11 materials; these are enough that we have collected all of their type names in a fragment that is not included in the text.

⟨*Material Definition*⟩ ≡
```
class Material : public TaggedPointer<⟨Material Types⟩> {
  public:
    ⟨Material Interface 676⟩
};
```

One of the most important methods that Material implementations must provide is GetBxDF(). It has the following signature:

```
template <typename TextureEvaluator>
ConcreteBxDF GetBxDF(TextureEvaluator texEval, MaterialEvalContext ctx,
                     SampledWavelengths &lambda) const;
```

There are a few things to notice in its declaration. First, it is templated based on a type TextureEvaluator. This class is used by materials to, unsurprisingly, evaluate their textures. We will discuss it further in a page or two, as well as MaterialEvalContext, which serves a similar role to TextureEvalContext.

Most importantly, note the return type, ConcreteBxDF. This type is specific to each Material and should be replaced with the actual BxDF type that the material uses. (For example, the DiffuseMaterial returns a DiffuseBxDF.) Different materials thus have different signatures for their GetBxDF() methods. This is unusual for an interface method in C++ and is not usually allowed with regular C++ virtual functions, though we will see shortly how pbrt handles the variety of them.

Each Material is also responsible for defining the type of BxDF that it returns from its GetBxDF() method with a local type definition for the type BxDF. For example, Diffuse Material has

```
using BxDF = DiffuseBxDF;
```

in the body of its definition.

The value of defining the interface in this way is that doing so makes it possible to write generic BSDF evaluation code that is templated on the type of material. Such code can then allocate storage for the BxDF on the stack, for whatever type of BxDF the material uses. pbrt's wavefront renderer, which is described in Chapter 15, takes advantage of this opportunity. (Further details and discussion of its use there are in Section 15.3.9.) A disadvantage of this design is that materials cannot return different BxDF types depending on their parameter values; they are limited to the one that they declare.

The Material class provides a GetBSDF() method that handles the variety of material BxDF return types. It requires some C++ arcana, though it centralizes the complexity of handling the diversity of types returned from the GetBxDF() methods.

Material::GetBSDF() has the same general form of most of the dynamic dispatch method implementations in pbrt. (We have elided almost all of them from the text since most of them are boilerplate code.) Here we define a lambda function, getBSDF, and call the Dispatch() method that Material inherits from TaggedPointer. Recall that Dispatch() uses type information encoded in a 64-bit pointer to determine which concrete material type the Material points to before casting the pointer to that type and passing it to the lambda.

⟨*Material Inline Method Definitions*⟩ ≡
```
template <typename TextureEvaluator>
BSDF Material::GetBSDF(
        TextureEvaluator texEval, MaterialEvalContext ctx,
        SampledWavelengths &lambda, ScratchBuffer &scratchBuffer) const {
    ⟨Define getBSDF lambda function for Material::GetBSDF() 675⟩
    return Dispatch(getBSDF);
}
```

getBSDF is a C++ *generic lambda*: when it is called, the auto mtl parameter will have a concrete type, that of a reference to a pointer to one of the materials enumerated in the ⟨*Material Types*⟩ fragment. Given mtl, then, we can find the concrete type of its material and thence the type of its BxDF. If a material does not return a BxDF, it should use void for its BxDF type definition. In that case, an unset BSDF is returned. (The MixMaterial is the only such Material in pbrt.)

⟨*Define* getBSDF *lambda function for* Material::GetBSDF()⟩ ≡   **675**
```
auto getBSDF = [&](auto mtl) -> BSDF {
    using ConcreteMtl = typename std::remove_reference_t<decltype(*mtl)>;
    using ConcreteBxDF = typename ConcreteMtl::BxDF;
    if constexpr (std::is_same_v<ConcreteBxDF, void>)
        return BSDF();
    else {
        ⟨Allocate memory for ConcreteBxDF and return BSDF for material 676⟩
    }
};
```

The provided ScratchBuffer is used to allocate enough memory to store the material's BxDF; using it is much more efficient than using C++'s new and delete operators here. That memory is then initialized with the value returned by the material's GetBxDF() method before the complete BSDF is returned to the caller.

⟨*Allocate memory for* ConcreteBxDF *and return* BSDF *for material*⟩ ≡   **675**
```
ConcreteBxDF *bxdf = scratchBuffer.Alloc<ConcreteBxDF>();
*bxdf = mtl->GetBxDF(texEval, ctx, lambda);
return BSDF(ctx.ns, ctx.dpdus, bxdf);
```

Materials that incorporate subsurface scattering must define a GetBSSRDF() method that follows a similar form. They must also include a using declaration in their class definition that defines a concrete BSSRDF type. (The code for rendering BSSRDFs is included only in the online edition.)

```
template <typename TextureEvaluator>
ConcreteBSSRDF GetBSSRDF(TextureEvaluator texEval, MaterialEvalContext ctx,
                         SampledWavelengths &lambda) const;
```

The Material class provides a corresponding GetBSSRDF() method that uses the provided ScratchBuffer to allocate storage for the material-specific BSSRDF.

⟨*Material Interface*⟩ ≡   **674**
```
template <typename TextureEvaluator>
BSSRDF GetBSSRDF(TextureEvaluator texEval, MaterialEvalContext ctx,
                 SampledWavelengths &lambda, ScratchBuffer &buf) const;
```

The MaterialEvalContext that GetBxDF() and GetBSSRDF() take plays a similar role to other *EvalContext classes: it encapsulates only the values that are necessary for material evaluation. They are a superset of those that are used for texture evaluation, so it inherits from TextureEvalContext. Doing so has the added advantage that MaterialEvalContexts can be passed directly to the texture evaluation methods.

⟨*MaterialEvalContext Definition*⟩ ≡
```
struct MaterialEvalContext : public TextureEvalContext {
    ⟨MaterialEvalContext Public Methods 676⟩
    Vector3f wo;
    Normal3f ns;
    Vector3f dpdus;
};
```

As before, there is not only a constructor that initializes a MaterialEvalContext from a SurfaceInteraction but also a constructor that takes the values for the members individually (not included here).

⟨*MaterialEvalContext Public Methods*⟩ ≡   **676**
```
MaterialEvalContext() = default;
MaterialEvalContext(const SurfaceInteraction &si)
    : TextureEvalContext(si), wo(si.wo), ns(si.shading.n),
      dpdus(si.shading.dpdu) {}
```

A TextureEvaluator is a class that is able to evaluate some or all of pbrt's texture types. One of its methods takes a set of textures and reports whether it is capable of evaluating them, while others actually evaluate textures. On the face of it, there is no obvious need for such a class: why not allow Materials to call the Texture Evaluate() methods directly? This additional layer of abstraction aids performance with the wavefront integrator; it makes it possible to separate materials into those that have lightweight textures and those with heavyweight textures and to process them separately. Doing so is beneficial to performance on the GPU; see Section 15.3.9 for further discussion.

For now we will only define the UniversalTextureEvaluator, which can evaluate all textures. In practice, the indirection it adds is optimized away by the compiler such that it introduces no runtime overhead. It is used with all of pbrt's integrators other than the one defined in Chapter 15.

⟨*UniversalTextureEvaluator Definition*⟩ ≡
```
class UniversalTextureEvaluator {
  public:
    ⟨UniversalTextureEvaluator Public Methods 677⟩
};
```

TextureEvaluators must provide a CanEvaluate() method that takes lists of FloatTextures and SpectrumTextures. They can then examine the types of the provided textures to determine if they are able to evaluate them. For the universal texture evaluator, the answer is always the same.

⟨*UniversalTextureEvaluator Public Methods*⟩ ≡   677
```
bool CanEvaluate(std::initializer_list<FloatTexture>,
                 std::initializer_list<SpectrumTexture>) const {
    return true;
}
```

TextureEvaluators must also provide operator() method implementations that evaluate a given texture. Thus, given a texture evaluator texEval, material code should use the expression texEval(tex, ctx) rather than tex.Evaluate(ctx). The implementation of this method is again trivial for the universal evaluator. (A corresponding method for spectrum textures is effectively the same and not included here.)

⟨*UniversalTextureEvaluator Method Definitions*⟩ ≡
```
Float UniversalTextureEvaluator::operator()(FloatTexture tex,
                                            TextureEvalContext ctx) {
    return tex.Evaluate(ctx);
}
```

Returning to the Material interface, all materials must provide a CanEvaluateTextures() method that takes a texture evaluator. They should return the result of calling its Can Evaluate() method with all of their textures provided. Code that uses Materials is then responsible for ensuring that a Material's GetBxDF() or GetBSSRDF() method is only called with a texture evaluator that is able to evaluate its textures.

⟨*Material Interface*⟩ +≡   674
```
template <typename TextureEvaluator>
bool CanEvaluateTextures(TextureEvaluator texEval) const;
```

Materials also may modify the shading normals of objects they are bound to, usually in order to introduce the appearance of greater geometric detail than is actually present. The Material interface has two ways that they may do so, normal mapping and bump mapping.

pbrt's normal mapping code, which will be described in Section 10.5.3, takes an image that specifies the shading normals. A nullptr value should be returned by this interface method if no normal map is included with a material.

⟨*Material Interface*⟩ +≡   674
```
const Image *GetNormalMap() const;
```

Alternatively, shading normals may be specified via bump mapping, which takes a displacement function that specifies surface detail with a FloatTexture. A nullptr value should be returned if no such displacement function has been specified.

⟨*Material Interface*⟩ +≡   674
```
FloatTexture GetDisplacement() const;
```

What should be returned by `HasSubsurfaceScattering()` method implementations should be obvious; this method is used to determine for which materials in a scene it is necessary to do the additional processing to model that effect.

⟨*Material Interface*⟩ +≡   674
```
bool HasSubsurfaceScattering() const;
```

10.5.1 MATERIAL IMPLEMENTATIONS

With the preliminaries covered, we will now present a few material implementations. All the `Materials` in pbrt are fairly basic bridges between `Textures` and `BxDFs`, so we will focus here on their basic form and some of the unique details of one of them.

Diffuse Material

`DiffuseMaterial` is the simplest material implementation and is a good starting point for understanding the material requirements.

⟨*DiffuseMaterial Definition*⟩ ≡
```
class DiffuseMaterial {
  public:
    ⟨DiffuseMaterial Type Definitions 678⟩
    ⟨DiffuseMaterial Public Methods 678⟩
  private:
    ⟨DiffuseMaterial Private Members 678⟩
};
```

These are the `BxDF` and `BSSRDF` type definitions for `DiffuseMaterial`. Because this material does not include subsurface scattering, `BSSRDF` can be set to be `void`.

⟨*DiffuseMaterial Type Definitions*⟩ ≡   678
```
using BxDF = DiffuseBxDF;
using BSSRDF = void;
```

The constructor initializes the following member variables with provided values, so it is not included here.

⟨*DiffuseMaterial Private Members*⟩ ≡   678
```
Image *normalMap;
FloatTexture displacement;
SpectrumTexture reflectance;
```

The `CanEvaluateTextures()` method is easy to implement; the various textures used for BSDF evaluation are passed to the given `TextureEvaluator`. Note that the displacement texture is not included here; if present, it is handled separately by the bump mapping code.

⟨*DiffuseMaterial Public Methods*⟩ ≡   678
```
template <typename TextureEvaluator>
bool CanEvaluateTextures(TextureEvaluator texEval) const {
    return texEval.CanEvaluate({}, {reflectance});
}
```

There is also not very much to `GetBxDF()`; it evaluates the reflectance texture, clamping the result to the range of valid reflectances before passing it along to the `DiffuseBxDF` constructor and returning a `DiffuseBxDF`.

⟨*DiffuseMaterial Public Methods*⟩ +≡   **678**
```
template <typename TextureEvaluator>
DiffuseBxDF GetBxDF(TextureEvaluator texEval, MaterialEvalContext ctx,
                    SampledWavelengths &lambda) const {
    SampledSpectrum r = Clamp(texEval(reflectance, ctx, lambda), 0, 1);
    return DiffuseBxDF(r);
}
```

GetNormalMap() and GetDisplacement() return the corresponding member variables and the remaining methods are trivial; see the source code for details.

Dielectric Material

DielectricMaterial represents a dielectric interface.

⟨*DielectricMaterial Definition*⟩ ≡
```
class DielectricMaterial {
  public:
    ⟨DielectricMaterial Type Definitions 679⟩
    ⟨DielectricMaterial Public Methods 679⟩
  private:
    ⟨DielectricMaterial Private Members 679⟩
};
```

It returns a DielectricBxDF and does not include subsurface scattering.

⟨*DielectricMaterial Type Definitions*⟩ ≡   **679**
```
using BxDF = DielectricBxDF;
using BSSRDF = void;
```

DielectricMaterial has a few more parameters than DiffuseMaterial. The index of refraction is specified with a SpectrumTexture so that it may vary with wavelength. Note also that two roughness values are stored, which allows the specification of an anisotropic microfacet distribution. If the distribution is isotropic, this leads to a minor inefficiency in storage and, shortly, texture evaluation, since both are always evaluated.

⟨*DielectricMaterial Private Members*⟩ ≡   **679**
```
Image *normalMap;
FloatTexture displacement;
FloatTexture uRoughness, vRoughness;
bool remapRoughness;
Spectrum eta;
```

GetBxDF() follows a similar form to DiffuseMaterial, evaluating various textures and using their results to initialize the returned DielectricBxDF.

⟨*DielectricMaterial Public Methods*⟩ ≡   **679**
```
template <typename TextureEvaluator>
DielectricBxDF GetBxDF(TextureEvaluator texEval, MaterialEvalContext ctx,
                       SampledWavelengths &lambda) const {
    ⟨Compute index of refraction for dielectric material 680⟩
    ⟨Create microfacet distribution for dielectric material 680⟩
    ⟨Return BSDF for dielectric material 680⟩
}
```

If the index of refraction is the same for all wavelengths, then all wavelengths will follow the same path if a ray is refracted. Otherwise, they will go in different directions—this is dispersion. In that case, pbrt only follows a single ray path according to the first wavelength in SampledWavelengths rather than tracing multiple rays to track each of them, and a call to SampledWavelengths::TerminateSecondary() is necessary. (See Section 4.5.4 for more information.)

DielectricMaterial therefore calls TerminateSecondary() unless the index of refraction is known to be constant, as determined by checking if eta's Spectrum type is a Constant Spectrum. This check does not detect all cases where the sampled spectrum values are all the same, but it catches most of them in practice, and unnecessarily terminating the secondary wavelengths affects performance but not correctness. A bigger shortcoming of the implementation here is that there is no dispersion if light is reflected at a surface and not refracted. In that case, all wavelengths could still be followed. However, how light paths will be sampled at the surface is not known at this point in program execution.

⟨*Compute index of refraction for dielectric material*⟩ ≡   679
```
    Float sampledEta = eta(lambda[0]);
    if (!eta.template Is<ConstantSpectrum>())
        lambda.TerminateSecondary();
```

It can be convenient to specify a microfacet distribution's roughness with a scalar parameter in [0, 1], where values close to zero correspond to near-perfect specular reflection, rather than by specifying α values directly. The RoughnessToAlpha() method performs a mapping that gives a reasonably intuitive control for surface appearance.

⟨*TrowbridgeReitzDistribution Public Methods*⟩ +≡   575
```
    static Float RoughnessToAlpha(Float roughness) {
        return std::sqrt(roughness);
    }
```

The GetBxDF() method then evaluates the roughness textures and remaps the returned values if required.

⟨*Create microfacet distribution for dielectric material*⟩ ≡   679
```
    Float urough = texEval(uRoughness, ctx), vrough = texEval(vRoughness, ctx);
    if (remapRoughness) {
        urough = TrowbridgeReitzDistribution::RoughnessToAlpha(urough);
        vrough = TrowbridgeReitzDistribution::RoughnessToAlpha(vrough);
    }
    TrowbridgeReitzDistribution distrib(urough, vrough);
```

Given the index of refraction and microfacet distribution, it is easy to pull the pieces together to return the final BxDF.

⟨*Return BSDF for dielectric material*⟩ ≡   679
```
    return DielectricBxDF(sampledEta, distrib);
```

Mix Material
The final material implementation that we will describe in the text is MixMaterial, which stores two other materials and uses a Float-valued texture to blend between them.

⟨*MixMaterial Definition*⟩ ≡
```
class MixMaterial {
public:
    ⟨MixMaterial Type Definitions⟩
    ⟨MixMaterial Public Methods 681⟩
private:
    ⟨MixMaterial Private Members 681⟩
};
```

⟨*MixMaterial Private Members*⟩ ≡   **681**
```
FloatTexture amount;
Material materials[2];
```

MixMaterial does not cleanly fit into pbrt's Material abstraction. For example, it is unable to define a single BxDF type that it will return, since its two constituent materials may have different BxDFs, and may themselves be MixMaterials, for that matter. Thus, MixMaterial requires special handling by the code that uses materials. (For example, there is a special case for MixMaterials in the SurfaceInteraction::GetBSDF() method described in Section 10.5.2.)

This is not ideal: as a general point of software design, it would be better to have abstractions that make it possible to provide this functionality without requiring special-case handling in calling code. However, we were unable to find a clean way to do this while still being able to statically reason about the type of BxDF a material will return; that aspect of the Material interface offers enough of a performance benefit that we did not want to change it.

Therefore, when a MixMaterial is encountered, one of its constituent materials is randomly chosen, with probability given by the floating-point amount texture. Thus, a 50/50 mix of two materials is not represented by the average of their respective BSDFs and so forth, but instead by each of them being evaluated half the time. This is effectively the material analog of the stochastic alpha test that was described in Section 7.1.1. The ChooseMaterial() method implements the logic.

⟨*MixMaterial Public Methods*⟩ ≡   **681**
```
template <typename TextureEvaluator>
Material ChooseMaterial(TextureEvaluator texEval,
                        MaterialEvalContext ctx) const {
    Float amt = texEval(amount, ctx);
    if (amt <= 0) return materials[0];
    if (amt >= 1) return materials[1];
    Float u = HashFloat(ctx.p, ctx.wo, materials[0], materials[1]);
    return (amt < u) ? materials[0] : materials[1];
}
```

Stochastic selection of materials can introduce noise in images at low sampling rates; see Figure 10.20. However, a few tens of samples are generally plenty to resolve any visual error. Furthermore, this approach does bring benefits: sampling and evaluation of the resulting BSDF is more efficient than if it was a weighted sum of the BSDFs from the constituent materials.

MixMaterial provides an accessor that makes it possible to traverse all the materials in the scene, including those nested inside a MixMaterial, so that it is possible to perform operations such as determining which types of materials are and are not present in a scene.

⟨*MixMaterial Public Methods*⟩ +≡   **681**
```
Material GetMaterial(int i) const { return materials[i]; }
```

(a)

(b)

Figure 10.20: Effect of Sampling Rate with the `MixMaterial`. In this scene, the `MixMaterial` is used to blend between blue and red diffuse materials for the dragon, using an equal weighting for each. (a) With one sample per pixel, there is visible noise in the corresponding pixels since each pixel only includes one of the two constituent materials. (b) With a sufficient number of samples (here, 128), stochastic selection of materials causes no visual harm. In practice, the pixel sampling rates necessary to reduce other forms of error from simulating light transport are almost always enough to resolve stochastic material sampling.

A fatal error is issued if the `GetBxDF()` method is called. A call to `GetBSSRDF()` is handled similarly, in code not included here.

⟨*MixMaterial Public Methods*⟩ +≡   **681**
```
template <typename TextureEvaluator>
void GetBxDF(TextureEvaluator texEval, MaterialEvalContext ctx,
             SampledWavelengths &lambda) const {
    LOG_FATAL("MixMaterial::GetBxDF() shouldn't be called");
}
```

10.5.2 FINDING THE BSDF AT A SURFACE

Because pbrt's Integrators use the `SurfaceInteraction` class to collect the necessary information associated with each intersection point, we will add a `GetBSDF()` method to this class that handles all the details related to computing the BSDF at its point.

⟨*SurfaceInteraction Method Definitions*⟩ +≡
```
BSDF SurfaceInteraction::GetBSDF(
        const RayDifferential &ray, SampledWavelengths &lambda,
        Camera camera, ScratchBuffer &scratchBuffer, Sampler sampler) {
    ⟨Estimate (u, v) and position differentials at intersection point 683⟩
    ⟨Resolve MixMaterial if necessary 683⟩
```

⟨*Return unset* BSDF *if surface has a null material* **683**⟩
⟨*Evaluate normal or bump map, if present* **683**⟩
⟨*Return BSDF for surface interaction* **684**⟩
}

This method first calls the SurfaceInteraction's ComputeDifferentials() method to compute information about the projected size of the surface area around the intersection on the image plane for use in texture antialiasing.

⟨*Estimate* (*u*, *v*) *and position differentials at intersection point*⟩ ≡   682
    ComputeDifferentials(ray, camera, sampler.SamplesPerPixel());

As described in Section 10.5.1, if there is a MixMaterial at the intersection point, it is necessary to resolve it to be a regular material. A while loop here ensures that nested MixMaterials are handled correctly.

⟨*Resolve* MixMaterial *if necessary*⟩ ≡   682
    while (material.Is<MixMaterial>()) {
        MixMaterial *mix = material.Cast<MixMaterial>();
        material = mix->ChooseMaterial(UniversalTextureEvaluator(), *this);
    }

If the final material is nullptr, it represents a non-scattering interface between two types of participating media. In this case, a default uninitialized BSDF is returned.

⟨*Return unset* BSDF *if surface has a null material*⟩ ≡   682
    if (!material)
        return {};

Otherwise, normal or bump mapping is performed before the BSDF is created.

⟨*Evaluate normal or bump map, if present*⟩ ≡   682
    FloatTexture displacement = material.GetDisplacement();
    const Image *normalMap = material.GetNormalMap();
    if (displacement || normalMap) {
        ⟨*Get shading* ∂p/∂u *and* ∂p/∂v *using normal or bump map* **683**⟩
        Normal3f ns(Normalize(Cross(dpdu, dpdv)));
        SetShadingGeometry(ns, dpdu, dpdv, shading.dndu, shading.dndv, false);
    }

The appropriate utility function for normal or bump mapping is called, depending on which technique is to be used.

⟨*Get shading* ∂p/∂u *and* ∂p/∂v *using normal or bump map*⟩ ≡   683
    Vector3f dpdu, dpdv;
    if (normalMap)
        NormalMap(*normalMap, *this, &dpdu, &dpdv);
    else
        BumpMap(UniversalTextureEvaluator(), displacement, *this, &dpdu, &dpdv);

With differentials both for texture filtering and for shading geometry now settled, the Material::GetBSDF() method can be called. Note that the universal texture evaluator is used both here and previously in the method, as there is no need to distinguish between different texture complexities in this part of the system.

⟨*Return BSDF for surface interaction*⟩ ≡   682
```
      BSDF bsdf = material.GetBSDF(UniversalTextureEvaluator(), *this, lambda,
                                   scratchBuffer);
      if (bsdf && GetOptions().forceDiffuse) {
          ⟨Override bsdf with diffuse equivalent  684⟩
      }
      return bsdf;
```

pbrt provides an option to override all the materials in a scene with equivalent diffuse BSDFs; doing so can be useful for some debugging problems. In this case, the hemispherical–directional reflectance is used to initialize a DiffuseBxDF.

⟨*Override* bsdf *with diffuse equivalent*⟩ ≡   684
```
      SampledSpectrum r = bsdf.rho(wo, {sampler.Get1D()}, {sampler.Get2D()});
      bsdf = BSDF(shading.n, shading.dpdu,
                  scratchBuffer.Alloc<DiffuseBxDF>(r));
```

The SurfaceInteraction::GetBSSRDF() method, not included here, follows a similar path before calling Material::GetBSSRDF().

10.5.3 NORMAL MAPPING

Normal mapping is a technique that maps tabularized surface normals stored in images to surfaces and uses them to specify shading normals in order to give the appearance of fine geometric detail.

With normal maps, one must choose a coordinate system for the stored normals. While any coordinate system may be chosen, one of the most useful is the local shading coordinate system at each point on a surface where the z axis is aligned with the surface normal and tangent vectors are aligned with x and y. (This is the same as the reflection coordinate system described in Section 9.1.1.) When that coordinate system is used, the approach is called *tangent-space normal mapping*. With tangent-space normal mapping, a given normal map can be applied to a variety of shapes, while choosing a coordinate system like object space would closely couple a normal map's encoding to a specific geometric object.

Normal maps are traditionally encoded in RGB images, where red, green, and blue respectively store the x, y, and z components of the surface normal. When tangent-space normal mapping is used, normal map images are typically predominantly blue, reflecting the fact that the z component of the surface normal has the largest magnitude unless the normal has been substantially perturbed. (See Figure 10.21.)

This RGB encoding brings us to an unfortunate casualty from the adoption of spectral rendering in this version of pbrt: while pbrt's SpectrumTextures previously returned RGB colors, they now return point-sampled spectral values. If an RGB image map is used for a spectrum texture, it is not possible to exactly reconstruct the original RGB colors; there will unavoidably be error in the Monte Carlo estimator that must be evaluated to find RGB. Introducing noise in the orientations of surface normals is unacceptable, since it would lead to systemic bias in rendered images. Consider a bumpy shiny object: error in the surface normal would lead to scattered rays intersecting objects that they would never intersect given the correct normals, which could cause arbitrarily large error.

We might avoid that problem by augmenting the SpectrumTexture interface to include a method that returned RGB color, introducing a separate RGBTexture interface and texture implementations, or by introducing a NormalTexture that returned normals directly. Any of

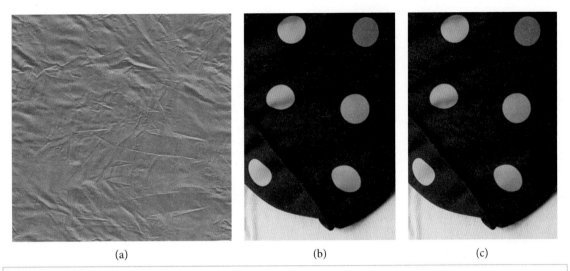

(a)   (b)   (c)

Figure 10.21: (a) A normal map modeling wrinkles for a pillow model. (b) Pillow geometry without normal map. (c) When applied to the pillow, the normal map gives a convincing approximation to more detailed geometry than is actually present. *(Scene courtesy of Angelo Ferretti.)*

these could cleanly support normal mapping, though all would require a significant amount of additional code.

Because the capability of directly looking up RGB values is only needed for normal mapping, the NormalMap() function therefore takes an Image to specify the normal map. It assumes that the first three channels of the image represent red, green, and blue. With this approach we have lost the benefits of being able to scale and mix textures as well as the ability to apply a variety of mapping functions to compute texture coordinates. While that is unfortunate, those capabilities are less often used with normal maps than with other types of textures, and so we prefer not to make the Texture interfaces more complex purely for normal mapping.

⟨*Normal Mapping Function Definitions*⟩ ≡
```
void NormalMap(const Image &normalMap, const NormalBumpEvalContext &ctx,
               Vector3f *dpdu, Vector3f *dpdv) {
    ⟨Get normalized normal vector from normal map 686⟩
    ⟨Transform tangent-space normal to rendering space 686⟩
    ⟨Find ∂p/∂u and ∂p/∂v that give shading normal 687⟩
}
```

Both NormalMap() and BumpMap() take a NormalBumpEvalContext to specify the local geometric information for the point where the shading geometry is being computed.

⟨*NormalBumpEvalContext Definition*⟩ ≡
```
struct NormalBumpEvalContext {
    ⟨NormalBumpEvalContext Public Methods 686⟩
    ⟨NormalBumpEvalContext Public Members 686⟩
};
```

As usual, it has a constructor, not included here, that performs initialization given a Surface Interaction.

⟨*NormalBumpEvalContext Public Members*⟩ ≡   **685**
```
Point3f p;
Point2f uv;
Normal3f n;
struct {
    Normal3f n;
    Vector3f dpdu, dpdv;
    Normal3f dndu, dndv;
} shading;
Float dudx = 0, dudy = 0, dvdx = 0, dvdy = 0;
Vector3f dpdx, dpdy;
```

It also provides a conversion operator to TextureEvalContext, which only needs a subset of the values stored in NormalBumpEvalContext.

⟨*NormalBumpEvalContext Public Methods*⟩ ≡   **685**
```
operator TextureEvalContext() const {
    return TextureEvalContext(p, dpdx, dpdy, n, uv, dudx, dudy,
                              dvdx, dvdy);
}
```

The first step in the normal mapping computation is to read the tangent-space normal vector from the image map. The image wrap mode is hard-coded here since Repeat is almost always the desired mode, though it would be easy to allow the wrap mode to be set via a parameter. Note also that the v coordinate is inverted, again following the image texture coordinate convention discussed in Section 10.4.2.

Normal maps are traditionally encoded in fixed-point image formats with pixel values that range from 0 to 1. This encoding allows the use of compact 8-bit pixel representations as well as compressed image formats that are supported by GPUs. Values read from the image must therefore be remapped to the range $[-1, 1]$ to reconstruct an associated normal vector. The normal vector must be renormalized, as both the quantization in the image pixel format and the bilinear interpolation may have caused it to be non-unit-length.

⟨*Get normalized normal vector from normal map*⟩ ≡   **685**
```
WrapMode2D wrap(WrapMode::Repeat);
Point2f uv(ctx.uv[0], 1 - ctx.uv[1]);
Vector3f ns(2 * normalMap.BilerpChannel(uv, 0, wrap) - 1,
            2 * normalMap.BilerpChannel(uv, 1, wrap) - 1,
            2 * normalMap.BilerpChannel(uv, 2, wrap) - 1);
ns = Normalize(ns);
```

In order to transform the normal to rendering space, a Frame can be used to specify a coordinate system where the original shading normal is aligned with the $+z$ axis. Transforming the tangent-space normal into this coordinate system gives the rendering-space normal.

⟨*Transform tangent-space normal to rendering space*⟩ ≡   **685**
```
Frame frame = Frame::FromZ(ctx.shading.n);
ns = frame.FromLocal(ns);
```

This function returns partial derivatives of the surface that account for the shading normal rather than the shading normal itself. Suitable partial derivatives can be found in two steps. First, a call to GramSchmidt() with the original $\partial p/\partial u$ and the new shading normal $\mathbf{n_s}$ gives the closest vector to $\partial p/\partial u$ that is perpendicular to $\mathbf{n_s}$. $\partial p/\partial v$ is then found by taking the cross product of $\mathbf{n_s}$ and the new $\partial p/\partial v$, giving an orthogonal coordinate system. Both of these vectors are respectively scaled to have the same length as the original $\partial p/\partial u$ and $\partial p/\partial v$ vectors.

⟨*Find $\partial p/\partial u$ and $\partial p/\partial v$ that give shading normal*⟩ ≡   685
```
Float ulen = Length(ctx.shading.dpdu), vlen = Length(ctx.shading.dpdv);
*dpdu = Normalize(GramSchmidt(ctx.shading.dpdu, ns)) * ulen;
*dpdv = Normalize(Cross(ns, *dpdu)) * vlen;
```

10.5.4 BUMP MAPPING

Another way to define shading normals is via a FloatTexture that defines a displacement at each point on the surface: each point p has a displaced point p′ associated with it, defined by $p' = p + d(p)n(p)$, where $d(p)$ is the offset returned by the displacement texture at p and $n(p)$ is the surface normal at p (Figure 10.22). We can use this texture to compute shading normals so that the surface appears as if it actually had been offset by the displacement function, without modifying its geometry. This process is called *bump mapping*. For relatively small displacement functions, the visual effect of bump mapping can be quite convincing.

An example of bump mapping is shown in Figure 10.23, which shows part of the *San Miguel* scene rendered with and without bump mapping. There, the bump map gives the appearance of a substantial amount of detail in the walls and floors that is not actually present in the geometric model. Figure 10.24 shows one of the image maps used to define the bump function in Figure 10.23.

The BumpMap() function is responsible for computing the effect of bump mapping at the point being shaded given a particular displacement texture. Its implementation is based on finding an approximation to the partial derivatives $\partial p/\partial u$ and $\partial p/\partial v$ of the displaced surface and using them in place of the surface's actual partial derivatives to compute the shading normal. Assume that the original surface is defined by a parametric function $p(u, v)$, and the bump offset function is a scalar function $d(u, v)$. Then the displaced surface is given by

$$p'(u, v) = p(u, v) + d(u, v)n(u, v),$$

where $n(u, v)$ is the surface normal at (u, v).

⟨*Bump Mapping Function Definitions*⟩ ≡
```
template <typename TextureEvaluator>
void BumpMap(TextureEvaluator texEval, FloatTexture displacement,
        const NormalBumpEvalContext &ctx, Vector3f *dpdu, Vector3f *dpdv) {
    ⟨Compute offset positions and evaluate displacement texture  689⟩
    ⟨Compute bump-mapped differential geometry  690⟩
}
```

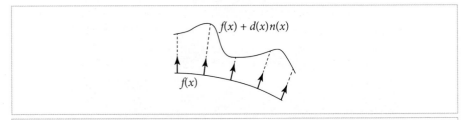

Figure 10.22: A displacement function associated with a material defines a new surface based on the old one, offset by the displacement amount along the normal at each point. pbrt does not compute a geometric representation of this displaced surface in the BumpMap() function, but instead uses it to compute shading normals for bump mapping.

(a)

(b)

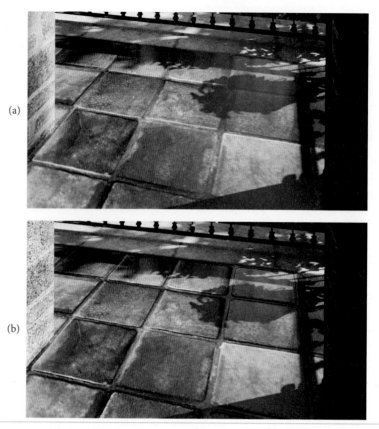

Figure 10.23: Detail of the *San Miguel* scene, rendered (a) without bump mapping and (b) with bump mapping. Bump mapping substantially increases the apparent geometric complexity of the model, without the increased rendering time and memory use that would result from a geometric representation with the equivalent amount of small-scale detail. *(Scene courtesy of Guillermo M. Leal Llaguno.)*

Figure 10.24: The image used as a bump map for the tiles in the *San Miguel* rendering in Figure 10.23.

The partial derivatives of p' can be found using the chain rule. For example, the partial derivative in u is

$$\frac{\partial p'}{\partial u} = \frac{\partial p(u, v)}{\partial u} + \frac{\partial d(u, v)}{\partial u}\mathbf{n}(u, v) + d(u, v)\frac{\partial \mathbf{n}(u, v)}{\partial u}. \tag{10.12}$$

We have already computed the value of $\partial p(u, v)/\partial u$; it is $\partial p/\partial u$ and is available in the TextureEvalContext structure, which also stores the surface normal $\mathbf{n}(u, v)$ and the partial derivative $\partial \mathbf{n}(u, v)/\partial u = \partial \mathbf{n}/\partial u$. The displacement function $d(u, v)$ can be readily evaluated, which leaves $\partial d(u, v)/\partial u$ as the only remaining term.

There are two possible approaches to finding the values of $\partial d(u, v)/\partial u$ and $\partial d(u, v)/\partial v$. One option would be to augment the FloatTexture interface with a method to compute partial derivatives of the underlying texture function. For example, for image map textures mapped to the surface directly using its (u, v) parameterization, these partial derivatives can be computed by subtracting adjacent texels in the u and v directions. However, this approach is difficult to extend to complex procedural textures like some of the ones defined earlier in this chapter. Therefore, pbrt directly computes these values with forward differencing, without modifying the FloatTexture interface.

Recall the definition of the partial derivative:

$$\frac{\partial d(u, v)}{\partial u} = \lim_{\Delta_u \to 0} \frac{d(u + \Delta_u, v) - d(u, v)}{\Delta_u}.$$

Forward differencing approximates the value using a finite value of Δ_u and evaluating $d(u, v)$ at two positions. Thus, the final expression for $\partial p'/\partial u$ is the following (for simplicity, we have dropped the explicit dependence on (u, v) for some of the terms):

$$\frac{\partial p'}{\partial u} \approx \frac{\partial p}{\partial u} + \frac{d(u + \Delta_u, v) - d(u, v)}{\Delta_u}\mathbf{n} + d(u, v)\frac{\partial \mathbf{n}}{\partial u}.$$

Interestingly enough, most bump-mapping implementations ignore the final term under the assumption that $d(u, v)$ is expected to be relatively small. (Since bump mapping is mostly useful for approximating small perturbations, this is a reasonable assumption.) The fact that many renderers do not compute the values $\partial \mathbf{n}/\partial u$ and $\partial \mathbf{n}/\partial v$ may also have something to do with this simplification. An implication of ignoring the last term is that the magnitude of the displacement function then does not affect the bump-mapped partial derivatives; adding a constant value to it globally does not affect the final result, since only differences of the bump function affect it. pbrt computes all three terms since it has $\partial \mathbf{n}/\partial u$ and $\partial \mathbf{n}/\partial v$ readily available, although in practice this final term rarely makes a visually noticeable difference.

⟨*Compute offset positions and evaluate displacement texture*⟩ ≡   687
    TextureEvalContext shiftedCtx = ctx;
    ⟨*Shift* shiftedCtx du *in the u direction* 690⟩
    Float uDisplace = texEval(displacement, shiftedCtx);
    ⟨*Shift* shiftedCtx dv *in the v direction*⟩
    Float vDisplace = texEval(displacement, shiftedCtx);
    Float displace = texEval(displacement, ctx);

One remaining issue is how to choose the offsets Δ_u and Δ_v for the finite differencing computations. They should be small enough that fine changes in $d(u, v)$ are captured but large enough so that available floating-point precision is sufficient to give a good result. Here, we will choose Δ_u and Δ_v values that lead to an offset that is about half the image-space pixel sample spacing and use them to update the appropriate member variables in the TextureEvalContext to reflect a shift to the offset position.

Float 23
TextureEvalContext 650

⟨*Shift* shiftedCtx du *in the u direction*⟩ ≡   **689**
```
    Float du = .5f * (std::abs(ctx.dudx) + std::abs(ctx.dudy));
    if (du == 0) du = .0005f;
    shiftedCtx.p = ctx.p + du * ctx.shading.dpdu;
    shiftedCtx.uv = ctx.uv + Vector2f(du, 0.f);
```

The ⟨*Shift* shiftedCtx dv *in the v direction*⟩ fragment is nearly the same as the fragment that shifts du, so it is not included here.

Given the new positions and the displacement texture's values at them, the partial derivatives can be computed directly using Equation (10.12):

⟨*Compute bump-mapped differential geometry*⟩ ≡   **687**
```
    *dpdu = ctx.shading.dpdu +
            (uDisplace - displace) / du * Vector3f(ctx.shading.n) +
            displace * Vector3f(ctx.shading.dndu);
    *dpdv = ctx.shading.dpdv +
            (vDisplace - displace) / dv * Vector3f(ctx.shading.n) +
            displace * Vector3f(ctx.shading.dndv);
```

FURTHER READING

Ray Footprints

The cone-tracing method of Amanatides (1984) was one of the first techniques for automatically estimating filter footprints for ray tracing. The beam-tracing algorithm of Heckbert and Hanrahan (1984) was another early extension of ray tracing to incorporate an area associated with each image sample rather than just an infinitesimal ray. The pencil-tracing method of Shinya et al. (1987) is another approach to this problem. Other related work on the topic of associating areas or footprints with rays includes Mitchell and Hanrahan's paper (1992) on rendering caustics and Turkowski's technical report (1993).

Collins (1994) estimated the ray footprint by keeping a tree of all rays traced from a given camera ray, examining corresponding rays at the same level and position. The ray differentials used in pbrt are based on Igehy's (1999) formulation, which was extended by Suykens and Willems (2001) to handle glossy reflection in addition to perfect specular reflection. Belcour et al. (2017) applied Fourier analysis to the light transport equation in order to accurately and efficiently track ray footprints after scattering.

Twelve floating-point values are required to store ray differentials, and Belcour et al.'s approach has similar storage requirements. This poses no challenge in a CPU ray tracer that only operates on one or a few rays at a time, but can add up to a considerable amount of storage (and consequently, bandwidth consumption) on the GPU. To address this issue, Akenine-Möller et al. (2019) developed a number of more space-efficient alternatives and showed their effectiveness for antialiasing that was further improved in subsequent work (Akenine-Möller et al. 2021; Boksansky et al. 2021). The approach we have implemented in CameraBase::Approximate_dp_dxy() was described by Li (2018).

Worley's chapter in *Texturing and Modeling* (Ebert et al. 2003) on computing differentials for filter regions presents an approach similar to ours. See Elek et al. (2014) for an extension of ray differentials to include wavelength, which can improve results with spectral rendering.

Image Texture Maps

Two-dimensional texture mapping with images was first introduced to graphics by Blinn and Newell (1976). Ever since Crow (1977) identified aliasing as the source of many errors in images in graphics, much work has been done to find efficient and effective ways of antialiasing image maps. Dungan, Stenger, and Sutty (1978) were the first to suggest creating a pyramid of prefiltered texture images; they used the nearest texture sample at the appropriate level when looking up texture values, using supersampling in screen space to antialias the result. Feibush, Levoy, and Cook (1980) investigated a spatially varying filter function, rather than a simple box filter. (Blinn and Newell were aware of Crow's results and used a box filter for their textures.)

Williams (1983) used a MIP map image pyramid for texture filtering with trilinear interpolation. Shortly thereafter, Crow (1984) introduced summed area tables, which make it possible to efficiently filter over axis-aligned rectangular regions of texture space. Summed area tables handle anisotropy better than Williams's method, although only for primarily axis-aligned filter regions. Heckbert (1986) wrote a good survey of early texture mapping algorithms.

Greene and Heckbert (1986) originally developed the elliptically weighted average technique, and Heckbert's master's thesis (1989b) put the method on a solid theoretical footing. Fournier and Fiume (1988) developed an even higher-quality texture filtering method that focuses on using a bounded amount of computation per lookup. Nonetheless, their method appears to be less efficient than EWA overall. Lansdale's master's thesis (1991) has an extensive description of EWA and Fournier and Fiume's method, including implementation details.

A number of researchers have investigated generalizing Williams's original method using a series of trilinear MIP map samples in an effort to increase quality without having to pay the price for the general EWA algorithm. By taking multiple samples from the MIP map, anisotropy is handled well while preserving the computational efficiency. Examples include Barkans's (1997) description of texture filtering in the Talisman architecture, McCormack et al.'s (1999) Feline method, and Cant and Shrubsole's (2000) technique. Manson and Schaefer (2013, 2014) have shown how to accurately approximate a variety of filter functions with a fixed small number of bilinearly interpolated sample values. An algorithm to convert an arbitrary filter into a set of bilinear lookups over multiple passes subject to a specified performance target was given by Schuster et al. (2020). These sorts of approaches are particularly useful on GPUs, where hardware-accelerated bilinear interpolation is available.

For scenes with many image textures where reading them all into memory simultaneously has a prohibitive memory cost, an effective approach can be to allocate a fixed amount of memory for image maps (a *texture cache*), load textures into that memory on demand, and discard the image maps that have not been accessed recently when the memory fills up (Peachey 1990). To enable good performance with small texture caches, image maps should be stored in a *tiled* format that makes it possible to load in small square regions of the texture independently of each other. Tiling techniques like these are used in graphics hardware to improve the performance of their texture memory caches (Hakura and Gupta 1997; Igehy et al. 1998, 1999). High-performance texture caching with parallel execution can be challenging because the cache contents may be frequently updated; it is desirable to minimize mutual exclusion in the cache implementation so that threads do not stall while others are updating the cache. For an effective approach to this problem, see Pharr (2017), who applied the *read-copy update* technique (McKenney and Slingwine 1998) to accomplish this.

Smith's (2002) website and document on audio resampling gives a good overview of resampling signals in one dimension. Heckbert's (1989a) zoom source code is the canonical reference for image resampling. His implementation carefully avoids feedback without using auxiliary storage.

A variety of *texture synthesis* algorithms have been developed that take an example texture image and then synthesize larger texture images that appear similar to the original texture while not being exactly the same. Survey articles by Wei et al. (2009) and Barnes and Zhang (2017) summarize work in this area. Convolutional neural networks have been applied to this task (Gatys et al. 2015; Sendik and Cohen-Or 2017), giving impressive results, and Frühstück et al. (2019) have showed the effectiveness of generative adversarial networks for this problem.

Solid Texturing and Noise Functions

Three-dimensional solid texturing was originally developed by Gardner (1984, 1985), Perlin (1985a), and Peachey (1985). Norton, Rockwood, and Skolmoski (1982) developed the *clamping* method that is widely used for antialiasing textures based on solid texturing. The general idea of procedural texturing, where texture is generated via computation rather than via looking up values from images, was introduced by Cook (1984), Perlin (1985a), and Peachey (1985).

Noise functions, which randomly vary while still having limited frequency content, have been a key ingredient for many procedural texturing techniques. Perlin (1985a) introduced the first such noise function, and later revised it to correct a number of subtle shortcomings (Perlin 2002). (See also Kensler et al. (2008) for further improvements.) Many more noise functions have been developed; see Lagae et al. (2010) for a survey of work up to that year. Tricard et al. (2019) recently introduced a noise function ("phasor noise") that can be filtered anisotropically and allows control of the orientation, frequency, and contrast of the noise function. Their paper also includes citations to other recent work on this topic.

In recent years, the *Shadertoy* website, *shadertoy.com*, has become a hub of creative application of procedural modeling and texturing, all of it running interactively in web browsers. *Shadertoy* was developed by Quilez and Jeremias (2021).

Shading Languages

The first languages and systems that supported the idea of user-supplied procedural shaders were developed by Cook (1984) and Perlin (1985a). (The texture composition model in this chapter is similar to Cook's shade trees.) The *RenderMan* shading language, described in a paper by Hanrahan and Lawson (1990), remains the classic shading language in graphics, though a more modern shading language is available in *Open Shading Language* (OSL) (Gritz et al. 2010), which is open source and increasingly used for production rendering. It follows pbrt's model of the shader returning a representation of the material rather than a final color value. See also Karrenberg et al. (2010), who introduced the *AnySL* shading language, which was designed for high performance as well as portability across multiple rendering systems (including pbrt).

See Ebert et al. (2003) and Apodaca and Gritz (2000) for techniques for writing procedural shaders; both of those have excellent discussions of issues related to antialiasing in procedural shaders.

Normal Mapping, Bump Mapping, and Shading Normals

Blinn (1978) invented the bump-mapping technique. Kajiya (1985) generalized the idea of bump mapping the normal to *frame mapping*, which also perturbs the surface's primary tangent vector and is useful for controlling the appearance of anisotropic reflection models. Normal mapping was introduced by Cohen et al. (1998).

Mikkelsen's thesis (2008) carefully investigates a number of the assumptions underlying bump mapping and normal mapping, proposes generalizations, and addresses a number of subtleties with respect to its application to real-time rendering.

One visual shortcoming of normal and bump mapping is that those techniques do not naturally account for self-shadowing, where bumps cast shadows on the surface and prevent light from reaching nearby points. These shadows can have a significant impact on the appearance of rough surfaces. Max (1988) developed the *horizon mapping* technique, which efficiently accounts for this effect through precomputed information about each bump map. More recently, Conty Estevez et al. and Chiang et al. have introduced techniques based on microfacet shadowing functions to improve the visual fidelity of bump-mapped surfaces at shadow terminators (Conty Estevez et al. 2019, Chiang et al. 2019).

Another challenging issue is that antialiasing bump and normal maps that have higher-frequency detail than can be represented in the image is quite difficult. In particular, it is not enough to remove high-frequency detail from the underlying function, but in general the BSDF needs to be modified to account for this detail. Fournier (1992) applied normal distribution functions to this problem, where the surface normal was generalized to represent a distribution of normal directions. Becker and Max (1993) developed algorithms for blending between bump maps and BRDFs that represented higher-frequency details. Schilling (1997, 2001) investigated this issue particularly for application to graphics hardware.

Effective approaches to filtering bump maps were developed by Han et al. (2007) and Olano and Baker (2010). Both Dupuy et al. (2013) and Hery et al. (2014) developed techniques that convert displacements into anisotropic distributions of Beckmann microfacets. Further improvements to these approaches were introduced by Kaplanyan et al. (2016), Tokuyoshi and Kaplanyan (2019), and Wu et al. (2019).

A number of researchers have looked at the issue of antialiasing surface reflection functions. Early work in this area was done by Amanatides, who developed an algorithm to detect specular aliasing for a specific BRDF model (Amanatides 1992). Van Horn and Turk (2008) developed an approach to automatically generate MIP maps of reflection functions that represent the characteristics of shaders over finite areas in order to antialias them. Bruneton and Neyret (2012) surveyed the state of the art in this area, and Jarabo et al. (2014b) also considered perceptual issues related to filtering inputs to these functions. See also Heitz et al. (2014) for further work on this topic.

Displacement Mapping

An alternative to bump mapping is displacement mapping, where the bump function is used to actually modify the surface geometry, rather than just perturbing the normal (Cook 1984; Cook et al. 1987). Advantages of displacement mapping include geometric detail on object silhouettes and the possibility of accounting for self-shadowing. Patterson and collaborators described an innovative algorithm for displacement mapping with ray tracing where the geometry is unperturbed, but the ray's direction is modified such that the intersections that are found are the same as would be found with the displaced geometry (Patterson, Hoggar, and Logie 1991; Logie and Patterson 1994). Heidrich and Seidel (1998) developed a technique for computing direct intersections with procedurally defined displacement functions.

One approach for displacement mapping has been to use an implicit function to define the displaced surface and to then take steps along rays until a zero crossing with the implicit function is found—this point is an intersection. This approach was first introduced by Hart

(1996); see Donnelly (2005) for information about using this approach for displacement mapping on the GPU. (This approach was more recently popularized by Quilez (2015) on the *Shadertoy* website.)

Another option is to finely tessellate the scene geometry and displace its vertices to define high-resolution meshes. Pharr and Hanrahan (1996) described an approach to this problem based on geometry caching, and Wang et al. (2000) described an adaptive tessellation algorithm that reduces memory requirements. Smits, Shirley, and Stark (2000) lazily tessellate individual triangles, saving a substantial amount of memory.

Measuring fine-scale surface geometry of real surfaces to acquire bump or displacement maps can be challenging. Johnson et al. (2011) developed a novel handheld system that can measure detail down to a few microns, which more than suffices for these uses.

Material Models

Burley's (2012) course notes describe a material model developed at Disney for feature films. This write-up includes extensive discussion of features of real-world reflection functions that can be observed in Matusik et al.'s (2003b) measurements of one hundred BRDFs and analyzes the ways that existing BRDF models do and do not fit these features well. These insights are then used to develop an "artist-friendly" material model that can express a wide range of surface appearances. The model describes reflection with a single color and ten scalar parameters, all of which are in the range [0, 1] and have fairly predictable effects on the appearance of the resulting material. An earlier material model designed to have intuitive parameters for artistic control was developed by Strauss (1990).

The *bidirectional texture function* (BTF) is a generalization of the BRDF that was introduced by Dana et al. (1999). (BTFs are also referred to as spatially varying BRDFs (SVBRDFs).) It is a six-dimensional reflectance function that adds two dimensions to account for spatial variation to the BSDF. pbrt's material model can thus be seen as imposing a particular factorization of the BTF where variation due to the spatial dimension is incorporated into textures that in turn provide values for a parametric BSDF that defines the directional distribution. The BTF representation is especially useful for material acquisition, as it does not impose a particular representation or specific factorization of the six dimensions. The survey articles on BTF acquisition and representation by Müller et al. (2005) and Filip and Haindl (2009) have good coverage of earlier work in this area.

Rainer et al. (2019) recently trained a neural network to represent a given BTF; network evaluation took the position and lighting directions as parameters and returned the corresponding BTF value. This work was subsequently generalized with a technique based on training a single network that provides a parameterization to which given BTFs can easily be mapped (Rainer et al. 2020). Kuznetsov et al. (2021) also used a neural approach, developing a compact representation that allowed 7D queries of position, two directions, and a filter size.

EXERCISES

⊘ **10.1** Read the papers by Manson and Schaefer (2013, 2014) on approximating high-quality filters with MIP maps and a small number of bilinear samples. Add an option to use their method for texture filtering in place of the EWA implementation currently in pbrt. Compare image quality for a number of scenes that use textures. How does running time compare? You may also find it beneficial to use a profiler to compare the amount of time it takes to run texture filtering code for each of the two approaches.

⊘ 10.2 An additional advantage of properly antialiased image map lookups is that they improve cache performance. Consider, for example, the situation of undersampling a high-resolution image map: nearby samples on the screen will access widely separated parts of the image map, such that there is low probability that texels fetched from main memory for one texture lookup will already be in the cache for texture lookups at adjacent pixel samples. Modify pbrt so that it always does image texture lookups from the finest level of the MIPMap, being careful to ensure that the same number of texels are still being accessed. How does performance change? What do cache-profiling tools report about the overall change in effectiveness of the CPU cache?

⊘ 10.3 Read Worley's paper that describes a noise function with substantially different visual characteristics than Perlin noise (Worley 1996). Implement this cellular noise function, and add Textures to pbrt that are based on it.

⊖ 10.4 Read some of the papers on filtering bump maps referenced in the "Further Reading" section of this chapter, choose one of the techniques described there, and implement it in pbrt. Show the visual artifacts from bump map aliasing without the technique you implement, as well as examples of how well your implementation addresses them.

⊖ 10.5 Modify pbrt to support a shading language to allow user-written programs to compute texture values. Unless you are also interested in writing your own compiler, *OSL* (Gritz et al. 2010) is a good choice.

CHAPTER ELEVEN

11 VOLUME SCATTERING

We have assumed so far that scenes are made up of collections of surfaces in a vacuum, which means that radiance is constant along rays between surfaces. However, there are many real-world situations where this assumption is inaccurate: fog and smoke attenuate and scatter light, and scattering from particles in the atmosphere makes the sky blue and sunsets red. This chapter introduces the mathematics that describe how light is affected as it passes through *participating media*—large numbers of very small particles distributed throughout a region of 3D space. These volume scattering models in computer graphics are based on the assumption that there are so many particles that scattering is best modeled as a probabilistic process rather than directly accounting for individual interactions with particles. Simulating the effect of participating media makes it possible to render images with atmospheric haze, beams of light through clouds, light passing through cloudy water, and subsurface scattering, where light exits a solid object at a different place than where it entered.

This chapter first describes the basic physical processes that affect the radiance along rays passing through participating media, including the phase function, which characterizes the distribution of light scattered at a point in space. (It is the volumetric analog to the BSDF.) It then introduces transmittance, which describes the attenuation of light in participating media. Computing unbiased estimates of transmittance can be tricky, so we then discuss null scattering, a mathematical formalism that makes it easier to sample scattering integrals like the one that describes transmittance. Next, the Medium interface is defined; it is used for representing the properties of participating media in a region of space. Medium implementations provide information about the scattering properties at points in their extent. This chapter does not cover techniques related to computing lighting and the effect of multiple scattering in volumetric media; the associated Monte Carlo integration algorithms and implementations of Integrators that handle volumetric effects will be the topic of Chapter 14.

11.1 VOLUME SCATTERING PROCESSES

There are three main physical processes that affect the distribution of radiance in an environment with participating media:

- *Absorption*: the reduction in radiance due to the conversion of light to another form of energy, such as heat.

Figure 11.1: Dragon Illuminated by a Spotlight through Fog. Light scattering from particles in the medium back toward the camera makes the spotlight's illumination visible even in pixels where there are no visible surfaces that reflect it. The dragon blocks light, casting a volumetric shadow on the right side of the image. *(Dragon model courtesy of the Stanford Computer Graphics Laboratory.)*

- *Emission*: radiance that is added to the environment from luminous particles.
- *Scattering*: radiance heading in one direction that is scattered to other directions due to collisions with particles.

The characteristics of all of these properties may be *homogeneous* or *inhomogeneous*. Homogeneous properties are constant throughout some region of space, while inhomogeneous properties vary throughout space. Figure 11.1 shows a simple example of volume scattering, where a spotlight shining through a homogeneous participating medium illuminates particles in the medium and casts a volumetric shadow.

All of these processes may have different behavior at different wavelengths of light. While wavelength-dependent emission can be handled in the same way that it is from surface emitters, wavelength-dependent absorption and scattering require special handling in Monte Carlo estimators. We will gloss past those details in this chapter, deferring discussion of them until Section 14.2.2.

Physically, these processes all happen discretely: a photon is absorbed by some particle or it is not. We will nevertheless model all of these as continuous processes, following the same assumptions as underlie our use of radiometry to model light in pbrt (Section 4.1). However, as we apply Monte Carlo to solve the integrals that describe this process, we will end up considering the effect of these processes at particular points in the scene, which we will term *scattering events*. Note that "scattering events" is a slight misnomer, since absorption is a possibility as well as scattering.

All the models in this chapter are based on the assumption that the positions of the particles are uncorrelated—in other words, that although their density may vary spatially, their positions are otherwise independent. (In the context of the colors of noise introduced in Section 8.1.6, the assumption is a white noise distribution of their positions.) This assumption does not hold for many types of physical media; for example, it is not possible for two particles to both be in the same point in space and so a true white noise distribution is not possible. See the "Further Reading" section at the end of the chapter for pointers to recent work in relaxing this assumption.

11.1.1 ABSORPTION

Consider thick black smoke from a fire: the smoke obscures the objects behind it because its particles absorb light traveling from the object to the viewer. The thicker the smoke, the more light is absorbed. Figure 11.2 shows this effect with a realistic cloud model.

Absorption is described by the medium's *absorption coefficient*, σ_a, which is the probability density that light is absorbed per unit distance traveled in the medium. (Note that the medium absorption is distinct from the absorption coefficient used in specifying indices of refraction of conductors, as introduced in Section 9.3.6.) It is usually a spectrally varying quantity, though we will neglect the implications of that detail in this chapter and return to them in Section 14.2.2. Its units are reciprocal distance (m^{-1}), which means that σ_a can take

Figure 11.2: If a participating medium primarily absorbs light passing through it, it will have a dark appearance, as shown here. (a) A relatively dense medium leads to a more apparent boundary as well as a darker result. (b) A less dense medium gives a softer look, as more light makes it through the medium. *(Cloud model courtesy of Walt Disney Animation Studios.)*

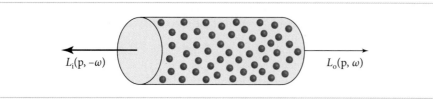

Figure 11.3: Absorption reduces the amount of radiance along a ray through a participating medium. Consider a ray carrying incident radiance at a point p from direction $-\omega$. If the ray passes through a differential cylinder filled with absorbing particles, the change in radiance due to absorption by those particles is $dL_o(p, \omega) = -\sigma_a(p, \omega)L_i(p, -\omega)dt$.

on any nonnegative value; it is not required to be between 0 and 1, for instance. In general, the absorption coefficient may vary with both position p and direction ω, although the volume scattering code in pbrt models it as purely a function of position. We will therefore sometimes simplify notation by not including ω in the use of σ_a and other related scattering properties, though it is easy enough to reintroduce when it is relevant.

Figure 11.3 shows the effect of absorption along a very short segment of a ray. Some amount of radiance $L_i(p, -\omega)$ is arriving at point p, and we would like to find the exitant radiance $L_o(p, \omega)$ after absorption in the differential volume. This change in radiance along the differential ray length dt is described by the differential equation[1]

$$L_o(p, \omega) - L_i(p, -\omega) = dL_o(p, \omega) = -\sigma_a(p, \omega)\, L_i(p, -\omega)\, dt,$$

which says that the differential reduction in radiance along the beam is a linear function of its initial radiance. (This is another instance of the linearity assumption in radiometry: the fraction of light absorbed does not vary based on the ray's radiance, but is always a fixed fraction.)

This differential equation can be solved to give the integral equation describing the total fraction of light absorbed for a ray. If we assume that the ray travels a distance d in direction ω through the medium starting at point p, the surviving portion of the original radiance is given by

$$e^{-\int_0^d \sigma_a(p+t\omega,\omega)\, dt}.$$

11.1.2 EMISSION

While absorption reduces the amount of radiance along a ray as it passes through a medium, emission increases it due to chemical, thermal, or nuclear processes that convert energy into visible light. Figure 11.4 shows emission in a differential volume, where we denote emitted radiance added to a ray per unit distance at a point p in direction ω by $\sigma_a(p, \omega)L_e(p, \omega)$. Figure 11.5 shows the effect of emission with a data set from a physical simulation of an explosion.

The differential equation that gives the change in radiance due to emission is

$$dL_o(p, \omega) = \sigma_a(p, \omega)\, L_e(p, \omega)\, dt. \tag{11.1}$$

The presence of σ_a on the right hand side stems from the connection between how efficiently an object absorbs light and how efficiently it emits it, as was introduced in Section 4.4.1. That

---

1   The position for the L_i functions should actually be $p + dt\omega$, though in a slight abuse of notation we will here and elsewhere use p.

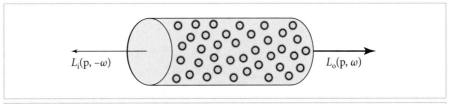

Figure 11.4: The volume emission function $L_e(p, \omega)$ gives the change in radiance along a ray as it passes through a differential volume of emissive particles. The change in radiance due to emission per differential distance is given by Equation (11.1).

Figure 11.5: A Participating Medium Where the Dominant Volumetric Effect Is Emission. *(Scene courtesy of Jim Price.)*

factor also ensures that the corresponding term has units of radiance when the differential equation is converted to an integral equation.

Note that this equation incorporates the assumption that the emitted light L_e is not dependent on the incoming light L_i. This is always true under the linear optics assumptions that pbrt is based on.

11.1.3 OUT SCATTERING AND ATTENUATION

The third basic light interaction in participating media is scattering. As a ray passes through a medium, it may collide with particles and be scattered in different directions. This has two effects on the total radiance that the beam carries. It reduces the radiance exiting a differential region of the beam because some of it is deflected to different directions. This effect is called

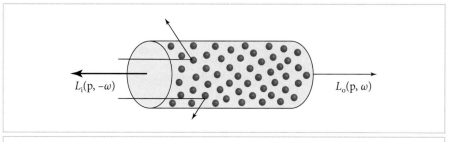

Figure 11.6: Like absorption, out scattering also reduces the radiance along a ray. Light that hits particles may be scattered in another direction such that the radiance exiting the region in the original direction is reduced.

out scattering (Figure 11.6) and is the topic of this section. However, radiance from other rays may be scattered into the path of the current ray; this *in-scattering* process is the subject of the next section. We will sometimes say that these two forms of scattering are *real scattering*, to distinguish them from null scattering, which will be introduced in Section 11.2.1.

The probability of an out-scattering event occurring per unit distance is given by the *scattering coefficient*, σ_s. Similar to absorption, the reduction in radiance along a differential length dt due to out scattering is given by

$$dL_o(\mathrm{p}, \omega) = -\sigma_s(\mathrm{p}, \omega)\, L_i(\mathrm{p}, -\omega)\, dt.$$

The total reduction in radiance due to absorption and out scattering is given by the sum $\sigma_a + \sigma_s$. This combined effect of absorption and out scattering is called *attenuation* or *extinction*. The sum of these two coefficients is denoted by the attenuation coefficient σ_t:

$$\sigma_t(\mathrm{p}, \omega) = \sigma_a(\mathrm{p}, \omega) + \sigma_s(\mathrm{p}, \omega).$$

Two values related to the attenuation coefficient will be useful in the following. The first is the *single-scattering albedo*, which is defined as

$$\rho(\mathrm{p}, \omega) = \frac{\sigma_s(\mathrm{p}, \omega)}{\sigma_t(\mathrm{p}, \omega)}.$$

Under the assumptions of radiometry, the single-scattering albedo is always between 0 and 1. It describes the probability of scattering (versus absorption) at a scattering event. The second is the *mean free path*, $1/\sigma_t(\mathrm{p}, \omega)$, which gives the average distance that a ray travels in a medium with attenuation coefficient $\sigma_t(\mathrm{p}, \omega)$ before interacting with a particle.

11.1.4 IN SCATTERING

While out scattering reduces radiance along a ray due to scattering in different directions, *in scattering* accounts for increased radiance due to scattering from other directions (Figure 11.7). Figure 11.8 shows the effect of in scattering with the cloud model. There is no absorption there, corresponding to a single scattering albedo of 1. Light thus scatters many times inside the cloud, giving it a very different appearance.

Assuming that the separation between particles is at least a few times the lengths of their radii, it is possible to ignore inter-particle interactions when describing scattering at a particular location. Under this assumption, the *phase function* $p(\omega, \omega')$ describes the angular distribution of scattered radiation at a point; it is the volumetric analog to the BSDF. The BSDF analogy is not exact, however. For example, phase functions have a normalization constraint: for all ω, the condition

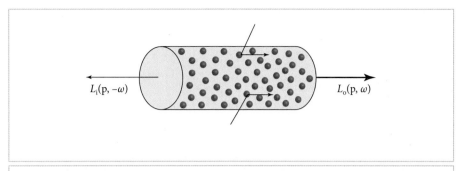

Figure 11.7: In scattering accounts for the increase in radiance along a ray due to scattering of light from other directions. Radiance from outside the differential volume is scattered along the direction of the ray and added to the incoming radiance.

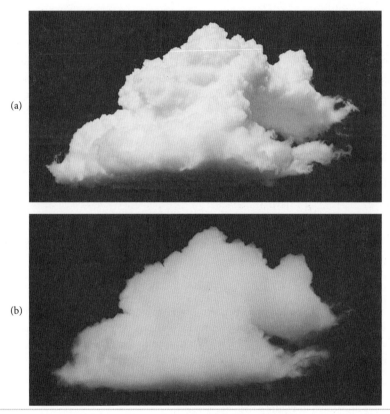

(a)

(b)

Figure 11.8: In Scattering with the Cloud Model. For these scenes, there is no absorption and only scattering, which gives a substantially different result than the clouds in Figure 11.2. (a) Relatively dense cloud. (b) Thinner cloud. *(Cloud model courtesy of Walt Disney Animation Studios.)*

$$\int_{\mathbb{S}^2} p(\omega, \omega')\, d\omega' = 1 \qquad\qquad [11.2]$$

must hold.[2] This constraint means that phase functions are probability distributions for scattering in a particular direction.

---

2   This difference is purely due to convention; the phase function could have equally well been defined to include the albedo, like the BSDF.

The total added radiance per unit distance due to in scattering is given by the *source function* L_s:

$$dL_o(p, \omega) = \sigma_t(p, \omega)\, L_s(p, \omega)\, dt.$$

It accounts for both volume emission and in scattering:

$$L_s(p, \omega) = \frac{\sigma_a(p, \omega)}{\sigma_t(p, \omega)} L_e(p, \omega) + \frac{\sigma_s(p, \omega)}{\sigma_t(p, \omega)} \int_{S^2} p(p, \omega_i, \omega)\, L_i(p, \omega_i)\, d\omega_i. \qquad [11.3]$$

The in-scattering portion of the source function is the product of the albedo and the amount of added radiance at a point, which is given by the spherical integral of the product of incident radiance and the phase function. Note that the source function is very similar to the scattering equation, Equation (4.14); the main difference is that there is no cosine term since the phase function operates on radiance rather than differential irradiance.

11.2 TRANSMITTANCE

The scattering processes in Section 11.1 are all specified in terms of their local effect at points in space. However, in rendering, we are usually interested in their aggregate effects on radiance along a ray, which usually requires transforming the differential equations to integral equations that can be solved using Monte Carlo. The reduction in radiance between two points on a ray due to extinction is a quantity that will often be useful; for example, we will need to estimate this value to compute the attenuated radiance from a light source that is incident at a point on a surface in scenes with participating media.

Given the attenuation coefficient σ_t, the differential equation that describes extinction,

$$\frac{dL_o(p, \omega)}{dt} = -\sigma_t(p, \omega)\, L_i(p, -\omega), \qquad [11.4]$$

can be solved to find the *beam transmittance* T_r, which gives the fraction of radiance that is transmitted between two points:

$$T_r(p \to p') = e^{-\int_0^d \sigma_t(p+t\omega, \omega)\, dt}, \qquad [11.5]$$

where $d = \|p - p'\|$ is the distance between p and p', and ω is the normalized direction vector between them. Note that the transmittance is always between 0 and 1. Thus, if exitant radiance from a point p on a surface in a given direction ω is given by $L_o(p, \omega)$, then after accounting for extinction the incident radiance at another point p' in direction $-\omega$ is

$$T_r(p \to p')\, L_o(p, \omega).$$

This idea is illustrated in Figure 11.9.

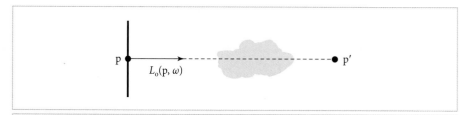

Figure 11.9: The beam transmittance $T_r(p \to p')$ gives the fraction of light transmitted from one point to another, accounting for absorption and out scattering, but ignoring emission and in scattering. Given exitant radiance at a point p in direction ω (e.g., reflected radiance from a surface), the radiance visible at another point p' along the ray is $T_r(p \to p')L_o(p, \omega)$.

Figure 11.10: Shadow-Casting Volumetric Bunny. The bunny, which is modeled entirely with partici-pating media, casts a shadow on the ground plane because it attenuates light from the sun (which is to the left) on its way to the ground. *(Bunny courtesy of the Stanford Computer Graphics Laboratory; volumetric enhancement courtesy of the OpenVDB sample model repository.)*

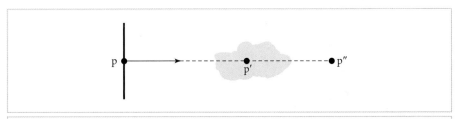

Figure 11.11: A useful property of beam transmittance is that it is multiplicative: the transmittance between points p and p'' on a ray like the one shown here is equal to the transmittance from p to p' times the transmittance from p' to p'' for all points p' between p and p''.

Not only is transmittance useful for modeling the attenuation of light within participating media, but accounting for transmittance along shadow rays makes it possible to accurately model shadowing on surfaces due to the effect of media; see Figure 11.10.

Two useful properties of beam transmittance are that transmittance from a point to itself is 1, $T_r(p \to p) = 1$, and in a vacuum $\sigma_t = 0$ and so $T_r(p \to p') = 1$ for all p'. Furthermore, if the attenuation coefficient satisfies the directional symmetry $\sigma_t(\omega) = \sigma_t(-\omega)$ or does not vary with direction ω and only varies as a function of position, then the transmittance between two points is the same in both directions:

$$T_r(p \to p') = T_r(p' \to p).$$

This property follows directly from Equation (11.5).

Another important property, true in all media, is that transmittance is multiplicative along points on a ray:

$$T_r(p \to p'') = T_r(p \to p') \, T_r(p' \to p''),\tag{11.6}$$

for all points p' between p and p'' (Figure 11.11). This property is useful for volume scattering implementations, since it makes it possible to incrementally compute transmittance at mul-tiple points along a ray: transmittance from the origin to a point $T_r(o \to p)$ can be computed by taking the product of transmittance to a previous point $T_\mathrm{r}(\mathrm{o} \to \mathrm{p}')$ and the transmittance of the segment between the previous and the current point $T_\mathrm{r}(\mathrm{p}' \to \mathrm{p})$.

The negated exponent in the definition of T_r in Equation (11.5) is called the *optical thickness* between the two points. It is denoted by the symbol τ:

$$\tau(\mathrm{p} \to \mathrm{p}') = \int_0^d \sigma_\mathrm{t}(\mathrm{p} + t\omega, \omega)\, \mathrm{d}t.$$

In a homogeneous medium, σ_t is a constant, so the integral that defines τ is trivially evaluated, giving *Beer's law:*

$$T_\mathrm{r}(\mathrm{p} \to \mathrm{p}') = \mathrm{e}^{-\sigma_\mathrm{t} d}. \tag{11.7}$$

It may appear that a straightforward application of Monte Carlo could be used to compute the beam transmittance in inhomogeneous media. Equation (11.5) consists of a 1D integral over a ray's parametric t position that is then exponentiated; given a method to sample distances along the ray t' according to some distribution p, one could evaluate the estimator:

$$\mathrm{e}^{-\int_0^d \sigma_\mathrm{t}(\mathrm{p}+t\omega,\omega)\, \mathrm{d}t} \approx \mathrm{e}^{-\left[\frac{\sigma_\mathrm{t}(\mathrm{p}+t'\omega,\omega)}{p(t')}\right]}. \tag{11.8}$$

However, even if the estimator in square brackets is an unbiased estimator of the optical thickness along the ray, the estimate of transmittance is *not* unbiased and will actually underestimate its value: $E[\mathrm{e}^{-X}] \neq \mathrm{e}^{-E[X]}$. (This state of affairs is explained by *Jensen's inequality* and the fact that e^{-x} is a convex function.)

The error introduced by estimators of the form of Equation (11.8) decreases as error in the estimate of the beam transmittance decreases. For many applications, this error may be acceptable—it is still widespread practice in graphics to estimate τ in some manner, e.g., via a Riemann sum, and then to compute the transmittance that way. However, it is possible to derive an alternative equation for transmittance that allows unbiased estimation; that is the approach used in pbrt.

First, we will consider the change in radiance between two points p and p' along the ray. Integrating Equation (11.4) and dropping the directional dependence of σ_t for notational simplicity, we can find that

$$\int_0^d \frac{\mathrm{d}L(\mathrm{p} + t\omega)}{\mathrm{d}t}\, \mathrm{d}t = L(\mathrm{p}') - L(\mathrm{p}) = \int_0^d -\sigma_\mathrm{t}(\mathrm{p} + t\omega)\, L(\mathrm{p} + t\omega)\, \mathrm{d}t, \tag{11.9}$$

where, as before, d is the distance between p and p' and ω is the normalized vector from p to p'.

The transmittance is the fraction of the original radiance, and so $T_\mathrm{r}(\mathrm{p} \to \mathrm{p}') = L(\mathrm{p}')/L(\mathrm{p})$. Thus, if we divide Equation (11.9) by $L(\mathrm{p})$ and rearrange terms, we can find that

$$T_\mathrm{r}(\mathrm{p} \to \mathrm{p}') = 1 - \int_0^d \sigma_\mathrm{t}(\mathrm{p} + t\omega)\, T_\mathrm{r}(\mathrm{p} + t\omega \to \mathrm{p}')\, \mathrm{d}t. \tag{11.10}$$

We have found ourselves with transmittance defined recursively in terms of an integral that includes transmittance in the integrand; although this may seem to be making the problem more complex than it was before, this definition makes it possible to apply Monte Carlo to the integral and to compute unbiased estimates of transmittance. However, it is difficult to sample this integrand well; in practice, estimates of it will have high variance. Therefore, the following section will introduce an alternative formulation of it that is amenable to sampling and makes a number of efficient solution techniques possible.

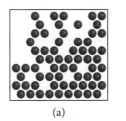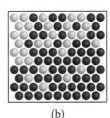

(a)   (b)

Figure 11.12: If the null-scattering coefficient is defined using a majorant σ_{maj} as in Equation (11.11), then it can be interpreted as taking (a) an inhomogeneous medium (dark circles) and (b) filling it with fictitious particles (light circles) until it reaches a uniform density.

11.2.1 NULL SCATTERING

The key idea that makes it possible to derive a more easily sampled transmittance integral is an approach known as *null scattering*. Null scattering is a mathematical formalism that can be interpreted as introducing an additional type of scattering that does not correspond to any type of physical scattering process but is specified so that it has no effect on the distribution of light. In doing so, null scattering makes it possible to treat inhomogeneous media as if they were homogeneous, which makes it easier to apply sampling algorithms to inhomogeneous media. (In Chapter 14, we will see that it is a key foundation for volumetric light transport algorithms beyond transmittance estimation.)

We will start by defining the *null-scattering coefficient* σ_n. Similar to the other scattering coefficients, it gives the probability of a null-scattering event per unit distance traveled in the medium. Here, we will define $\sigma_n(p)$ via a constant *majorant* σ_{maj} that is greater than or equal to $\sigma_a + \sigma_s$ at all points in the medium:[3]

$$\sigma_n(p, \omega) = \sigma_{maj} - \sigma_t(p, \omega).\qquad\text{[11.11]}$$

Thus, the total scattering coefficient $\sigma_a + \sigma_s + \sigma_n = \sigma_{maj}$ is uniform throughout the medium. (This idea is illustrated in Figure 11.12.)

With this definition of σ_n, we can rewrite Equation (11.4) in terms of the majorant and the null-scattering coefficient:

$$\frac{dL_o(p, \omega)}{dt} = -(\sigma_{maj} - \sigma_n(p, \omega))\, L_i(p, -\omega).\qquad\text{[11.12]}$$

We will not include the full derivation here, but just as with Equation (11.10), this equation can be integrated over the segment of a ray and divided by the initial radiance $L(p)$ to find an equation for the transmittance. The result is:

$$T_r(p \to p') = e^{-\sigma_{maj}d} + \int_0^d e^{-\sigma_{maj}t}\, \sigma_n(p + t\omega)\, T_r(p + t\omega \to p')\, dt.\qquad\text{[11.13]}$$

Note that with this expression of transmittance and a homogeneous medium, $\sigma_n = 0$ and the integral disappears. The first term then corresponds to Beer's law. For inhomogeneous

---

3   The attentive reader will note that for some of the following Monte Carlo estimators based on null scattering, there is no mathematical requirement that σ_n must be positive and that thus, the so-called majorant is not necessarily greater than or equal to $\sigma_a + \sigma_s$. It turns out that Monte Carlo estimators that include negative σ_n values tend to have high variance, so in practice actual majorants are used.

media, the first term can be seen as computing an underestimate of the true transmittance, where the integral then accounts for the rest of it.

To compute Monte Carlo estimates of Equation (11.13), we would like to sample a distance t' from some distribution that is proportional to the integrand and then apply the regular Monte Carlo estimator. A convenient sampling distribution is the probability density function (PDF) of the exponential distribution that is derived in Section A.4.2. In this case, the PDF associated with $e^{-\sigma_{\text{maj}}t}$ is

$$p_{\text{maj}}(t) = \sigma_{\text{maj}}\, e^{-\sigma_{\text{maj}}t}$$

and a corresponding sampling recipe is available via the `SampleExponential()` function.

Because p_{maj} is nonzero over the range $[0, \infty)$, the sampling algorithm will sometimes generate samples $t' > d$, which may seem to be undesirable. However, although we could define a PDF for the exponential function limited to $[0, d]$, sampling from p_{maj} leads to a simple way to terminate the recursive evaluation of transmittance. To see why, consider rewriting the second term of Equation (11.13) as the sum of two integrals that cover the range $[0, \infty)$:

$$\int_0^d e^{-\sigma_{\text{maj}}t}\, \sigma_{\text{n}}(\mathrm{p} + t\omega)\, T_{\text{r}}(\mathrm{p} + t\omega \to \mathrm{p}')\, \mathrm{d}t + \int_d^\infty 0\, \mathrm{d}t. \qquad [11.14]$$

If the Monte Carlo estimator is applied to this sum, we can see that the value of t' with respect to d determines which integrand is evaluated and thus that sampling $t' > d$ can be conveniently interpreted as a condition for ending the recursive estimation of Equation (11.13).

Given the decision to sample from p_{maj}, perhaps the most obvious approach for estimating the value of Equation (11.13) is to sample t' in this way and to directly apply the Monte Carlo estimator, which gives

$$T_{\text{r}}(\mathrm{p} \to \mathrm{p}') \approx e^{-\sigma_{\text{maj}}d} + \begin{cases} \frac{\sigma_{\text{n}}(\mathrm{p}+t'\omega)}{\sigma_{\text{maj}}}\, T_{\text{r}}(\mathrm{p} + t'\omega \to \mathrm{p}') & t' < d \\ 0 & \text{otherwise.} \end{cases} \qquad [11.15]$$

This estimator is known as the *next-flight estimator*. It has the advantage that it has zero variance for homogeneous media, although interestingly it is often not as efficient as other estimators for inhomogeneous media.

Other estimators randomly choose between the two terms of Equation (11.13) and only evaluate one of them. If we define p_{e} as the discrete probability of evaluating the first term, transmittance can be estimated by

$$T_{\text{r}}(\mathrm{p} \to \mathrm{p}') \approx \begin{cases} \frac{e^{-\sigma_{\text{maj}}d}}{p_{\text{e}}} & \text{with probability } p_{\text{e}} \\ \frac{1}{1-p_{\text{e}}} \int_0^d e^{-\sigma_{\text{maj}}t}\, \sigma_{\text{n}}(\mathrm{p} + t\omega)\, T_{\text{r}}(\mathrm{p} + t\omega \to \mathrm{p}')\, \mathrm{d}t & \text{otherwise.} \end{cases}$$

$$[11.16]$$

The *ratio tracking* estimator is the result from setting $p_{\text{e}} = e^{-\sigma_{\text{maj}}d}$. Then, the first case of Equation (11.16) yields a value of 1. We can further combine the choice between the two cases with sampling t' using the fact that the probability that $t' > d$ is equal to $e^{-\sigma_{\text{maj}}d}$. (This can be seen using p_{maj}'s cumulative distribution function (CDF), Equation (A.1).) After simplifying, the resulting estimator works out to be:

$$T_{\text{r}}(\mathrm{p} \to \mathrm{p}') \approx \begin{cases} 1 & t' > d \\ \frac{\sigma_{\text{n}}(\mathrm{p}+t'\omega)}{\sigma_{\text{maj}}}\, T_{\text{r}}(\mathrm{p} + t'\omega \to \mathrm{p}') & \text{otherwise.} \end{cases} \qquad [11.17]$$

`SampleExponential()` 1003

If the recursive evaluations are expanded out, ratio tracking leads to an estimator of the form

$$T_{\mathrm{r}}(\mathrm{p} \to \mathrm{p}') \approx \prod_{i}^{n} \frac{\sigma_{\mathrm{n}}(p + t_i \omega)}{\sigma_{\mathrm{maj}}},$$

where t_i are the series of t values that are sampled from p_{maj} and where successive t_i values are sampled starting from the previous one until one is sampled past the endpoint. Ratio tracking is the technique that is implemented to compute transmittance in pbrt's light transport routines in Chapter 14.

A disadvantage of ratio tracking is that it continues to sample the medium even after the transmittance has become very small. Russian roulette can be used to terminate recursive evaluation to avoid this problem. If the Russian roulette termination probability at each sampled point is set to be equal to the ratio of σ_{n} and σ_{maj}, then the scaling cancels and the estimator becomes

$$T_{\mathrm{r}}(\mathrm{p} \to \mathrm{p}') \approx \begin{cases} 1 & t' > d \\ T_{\mathrm{r}}(\mathrm{p} + t'\omega \to \mathrm{p}') & t' \le d \text{ and with probability } \frac{\sigma_{\mathrm{n}}(\mathrm{p}+t'\omega)}{\sigma_{\mathrm{maj}}} \\ 0 & \text{otherwise.} \end{cases} \qquad [11.18]$$

Thus, recursive estimation of transmittance continues either until termination due to Russian roulette or until the sampled point is past the endpoint. This approach is the *track-length transmittance estimator*, also known as *delta tracking*.

A physical interpretation of delta tracking is that it randomly decides whether the ray interacts with a true particle or a fictitious particle at each scattering event. Interactions with fictitious particles (corresponding to null scattering) are ignored and the algorithm continues, restarting from the sampled point. Interactions with true particles cause extinction, in which case 0 is returned. If a ray makes it through the medium without extinction, the value 1 is returned.

Delta tracking can also be used to sample positions t along a ray with probability proportional to $\sigma_{\mathrm{t}}(t)T_{\mathrm{r}}(t)$. The algorithm is given by the following pseudocode, which assumes that the function u() generates a uniform random number between 0 and 1 and where the recursion has been transformed into a loop:

```
optional<Point> DeltaTracking(Point p, Vector w, Float sigma_maj, Float d) {
    Float t = SampleExponential(u(), sigma_maj);
    while (t < d) {
        Float sigma_n = /* evaluate sigma_n at p + t * w */;
        if (u() < sigma_n / sigma_maj)
            t += SampleExponential(u(), sigma_maj);
        else
            return p + t * w;
    }
    return {}; /* no sample before d */
}
```

11.3 PHASE FUNCTIONS

SampleExponential() 1003

Just as there is a wide variety of BSDF models that describe scattering from surfaces, many phase functions have also been developed. These range from parameterized models (which can be used to fit a function with a small number of parameters to measured data) to analytic models that are based on deriving the scattered radiance distribution that results from particles with known shape and material (e.g., spherical water droplets).

In most naturally occurring media, the phase function is a 1D function of the angle θ between the two directions ω_o and ω_i; these phase functions are often written as $p(\cos\theta)$. Media with this type of phase function are called *isotropic* or *symmetric* because their response to incident illumination is (locally) invariant under rotations. In addition to being normalized, an important property of naturally occurring phase functions is that they are *reciprocal*: the two directions can be interchanged and the phase function's value remains unchanged. Note that symmetric phase functions are trivially reciprocal because $\cos(-\theta) = \cos(\theta)$.

In *anisotropic* media that consist of particles arranged in a coherent structure, the phase function can be a 4D function of the two directions, which satisfies a more involved kind of reciprocity relation. Examples of this are crystals or media made of coherently oriented fibers; the "Further Reading" discusses these types of media further.

In a slightly confusing overloading of terminology, phase functions themselves can be isotropic or anisotropic as well. Thus, we might have an anisotropic phase function in an isotropic medium. An isotropic phase function describes equal scattering in all directions and is thus independent of either of the two directions. Because phase functions are normalized, there is only one such function:

$$p(\omega_o, \omega_i) = \frac{1}{4\pi}.$$

The PhaseFunction class defines the PhaseFunction interface. Only a single phase function is currently provided in pbrt, but we have used the TaggedPointer machinery to make it easy to add others. Its implementation is in the file base/medium.h.

⟨*PhaseFunction Definition*⟩ ≡
```
class PhaseFunction : public TaggedPointer<HGPhaseFunction> {
  public:
    ⟨PhaseFunction Interface 710⟩
};
```

The p() method returns the value of the phase function for the given pair of directions. As with BSDFs, pbrt uses the convention that the two directions both point away from the point where scattering occurs; this is a different convention from what is usually used in the scattering literature (Figure 11.13).

⟨*PhaseFunction Interface*⟩ ≡   710
```
Float p(Vector3f wo, Vector3f wi) const;
```

It is also useful to be able to draw samples from the distribution described by a phase function. PhaseFunction implementations therefore must provide a Sample_p() method, which

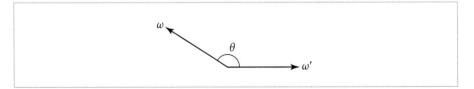

Figure 11.13: Phase functions in pbrt are implemented with the convention that both the incident direction and the outgoing direction point away from the point where scattering happens. This is the same convention that is used for BSDFs in pbrt but is different from the convention in the scattering literature, where the incident direction generally points toward the scattering point. The angle between the two directions is denoted by θ.

samples an incident direction ω_i given the outgoing direction ω_o and a sample value in $[0, 1)^2$.

⟨*PhaseFunction Interface*⟩ +≡   710
```
pstd::optional<PhaseFunctionSample> Sample_p(Vector3f wo, Point2f u) const;
```

Phase function samples are returned in a structure that stores the phase function's value p, the sampled direction wi, and the PDF pdf.

⟨*PhaseFunctionSample Definition*⟩ ≡
```
struct PhaseFunctionSample {
    Float p;
    Vector3f wi;
    Float pdf;
};
```

An accompanying PDF() method returns the value of the phase function sampling PDF for the provided directions.

⟨*PhaseFunction Interface*⟩ +≡   710
```
Float PDF(Vector3f wo, Vector3f wi) const;
```

11.3.1 THE HENYEY–GREENSTEIN PHASE FUNCTION

A widely used phase function was developed by Henyey and Greenstein (1941). This phase function was specifically designed to be easy to fit to measured scattering data. A single parameter g (called the *asymmetry parameter*) controls the distribution of scattered light:[4]

$$p_{HG}(\cos\theta) = \frac{1}{4\pi}\frac{1 - g^2}{(1 + g^2 + 2g(\cos\theta))^{3/2}}.$$

The HenyeyGreenstein() function implements this computation.

⟨*Scattering Inline Functions*⟩ +≡
```
Float HenyeyGreenstein(Float cosTheta, Float g) {
    Float denom = 1 + Sqr(g) + 2 * g * cosTheta;
    return Inv4Pi * (1 - Sqr(g)) / (denom * SafeSqrt(denom));
}
```

The asymmetry parameter g in the Henyey–Greenstein model has a precise meaning. It is the integral of the product of the given phase function and the cosine of the angle between ω' and ω and is referred to as the *mean cosine*. Given an arbitrary phase function p, the value of g can be computed as[5]

$$g = \int_{\mathcal{S}^2} p(-\omega, \omega')(\omega \cdot \omega') \, d\omega' = 2\pi \int_0^\pi p(-\cos\theta) \, \cos\theta \, \sin\theta \, d\theta.\qquad [11.19]$$

Thus, an isotropic phase function gives $g = 0$, as expected.

Any number of phase functions can satisfy this equation; the g value alone is not enough to uniquely describe a scattering distribution. Nevertheless, the convenience of being able to easily convert a complex scattering distribution into a simple parameterized model is often more important than this potential loss in accuracy.

Float 23
Inv4Pi 1033
PhaseFunctionSample 711
Point2f 92
SafeSqrt() 1034
Sqr() 1034
Vector3f 86

---

4   Note that the sign of the $2g(\cos\theta)$ term in the denominator is the opposite of the sign used in the scattering literature. This difference is due to our use of the same direction convention for BSDFs and phase functions.

5   Once more, there is a sign difference compared to the radiative transfer literature: the first argument to p is negated due to our use of the same direction convention for BSDFs and phase functions.

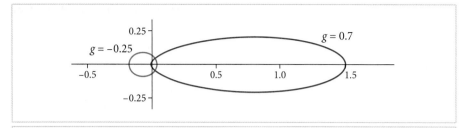

Figure 11.14: Plots of the Henyey–Greenstein Phase Function for Asymmetry g **Parameters** -0.25 **and 0.7.** Negative g values describe phase functions that primarily scatter light back in the incident direction, and positive g values describe phase functions that primarily scatter light forward in the direction it was already traveling (here, along the $+x$ axis).

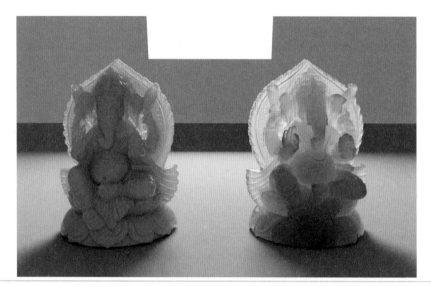

Figure 11.15: Ganesha model filled with participating media rendered with (left) strong backward scattering ($g = -0.9$) and (right) strong forward scattering ($g = 0.9$). Because most of the light comes from a light source behind the objects, forward scattering leads to more light reaching the camera in this case.

More complex phase functions that are not described well with a single asymmetry parameter can often be modeled by a weighted sum of phase functions like Henyey–Greenstein, each with different parameter values:

$$p(\omega, \omega') = \sum_{i=1}^{n} w_i \, p_i(\omega \to \omega'),$$

where the weights w_i sum to one to maintain normalization. This generalization is not provided in pbrt but would be easy to add.

Figure 11.14 shows plots of the Henyey–Greenstein phase function with varying asymmetry parameters. The value of g for this model must be in the range $(-1, 1)$. Negative values of g correspond to *back-scattering*, where light is mostly scattered back toward the incident direction, and positive values correspond to forward-scattering. The greater the magnitude of g, the more scattering occurs close to the ω or $-\omega$ directions (for back-scattering and forward-scattering, respectively). See Figure 11.15 to compare the visual effect of forward- and back-scattering.

The HGPhaseFunction class implements the Henyey–Greenstein model in the context of the PhaseFunction interface.

⟨*HGPhaseFunction Definition*⟩ ≡
```
class HGPhaseFunction {
  public:
    ⟨HGPhaseFunction Public Methods 713⟩
  private:
    ⟨HGPhaseFunction Private Members 713⟩
};
```

Its only parameter is g, which is provided to the constructor and stored in a member variable.

⟨*HGPhaseFunction Public Methods*⟩ ≡   713
```
HGPhaseFunction(Float g) : g(g) {}
```

⟨*HGPhaseFunction Private Members*⟩ ≡   713
```
Float g;
```

Evaluating the phase function is a simple matter of calling the HenyeyGreenstein() function.

⟨*HGPhaseFunction Public Methods*⟩ +≡   713
```
Float p(Vector3f wo, Vector3f wi) const {
    return HenyeyGreenstein(Dot(wo, wi), g);
}
```

It is possible to sample directly from the Henyey–Greenstein phase function's distribution. This operation is provided via a stand-alone utility function. Because the sampling algorithm is exact and because the Henyey–Greenstein phase function is normalized, the PDF is equal to the phase function's value for the sampled direction.

⟨*Sampling Function Definitions*⟩ +≡
```
Vector3f SampleHenyeyGreenstein(Vector3f wo, Float g,
                                Point2f u, Float *pdf) {
    ⟨Compute cos θ for Henyey–Greenstein sample 713⟩
    ⟨Compute direction wi for Henyey–Greenstein sample 714⟩
    if (pdf) *pdf = HenyeyGreenstein(cosTheta, g);
    return wi;
}
```

The PDF for the Henyey–Greenstein phase function is separable into θ and ϕ components, with $p(\phi) = 1/(2\pi)$ as usual. The main task is to sample $\cos \theta$. With pbrt's convention for the orientation of direction vectors, the distribution for θ is

$$\cos \theta = -\frac{1}{2g} \left(1 + g^2 - \left(\frac{1 - g^2}{1 + g - 2g\xi} \right)^2 \right)$$

if $g \neq 0$; otherwise, $\cos \theta = 1 - 2\xi$ gives a uniform sampling over the sphere of directions.

⟨*Compute cos θ for Henyey–Greenstein sample*⟩ ≡   713
```
Float cosTheta;
if (std::abs(g) < 1e-3f)
    cosTheta = 1 - 2 * u[0];
else
    cosTheta = -1 / (2 * g) *
               (1 + Sqr(g) - Sqr((1 - Sqr(g)) / (1 + g - 2 * g * u[0])));
```

The $(\cos\theta, \phi)$ values specify a direction with respect to a coordinate system where wo is along the $+z$ axis. Therefore, it is necessary to transform the sampled vector to wo's coordinate system before returning it.

⟨*Compute direction* wi *for Henyey–Greenstein sample*⟩ ≡   713
```
Float sinTheta = SafeSqrt(1 - Sqr(cosTheta));
Float phi = 2 * Pi * u[1];
Frame wFrame = Frame::FromZ(wo);
Vector3f wi = wFrame.FromLocal(SphericalDirection(sinTheta, cosTheta, phi));
```

The HGPhaseFunction sampling method is now easily implemented.

⟨*HGPhaseFunction Public Methods*⟩ +≡   713
```
pstd::optional<PhaseFunctionSample> Sample_p(Vector3f wo, Point2f u) const {
    Float pdf;
    Vector3f wi = SampleHenyeyGreenstein(wo, g, u, &pdf);
    return PhaseFunctionSample{pdf, wi, pdf};
}
```

Because sampling is exact and phase functions are normalized, its PDF() method just evaluates the phase function for the given directions.

⟨*HGPhaseFunction Public Methods*⟩ +≡   713
```
Float PDF(Vector3f wo, Vector3f wi) const { return p(wo, wi); }
```

11.4 MEDIA

Implementations of the Medium interface provide various representations of volumetric scattering properties in a region of space. In a complex scene, there may be multiple Medium instances, each representing different types of scattering in different parts of the scene. For example, an outdoor lake scene might have one Medium to model atmospheric scattering, another to model mist rising from the lake, and a third to model particles suspended in the water of the lake.

The Medium interface is also defined in the file base/media.h.

⟨*Medium Definition*⟩ ≡
```
class Medium : public TaggedPointer<⟨Medium Types 714⟩> {
  public:
    ⟨Medium Interface 717⟩
    ⟨Medium Public Methods⟩
};
```

pbrt provides five medium implementations. The first three will be discussed in the book, but CloudMedium is only included in the online edition of the book and the last, NanoVDBMedium, will not be presented at all. (It provides support for using volumes defined in the *NanoVDB* format in pbrt. As elsewhere, we avoid discussion of the use of third-party APIs in the book text.)

⟨*Medium Types*⟩ ≡   714
```
HomogeneousMedium, GridMedium, RGBGridMedium, CloudMedium, NanoVDBMedium
```

Before we get to the specification of the methods in the interface, we will describe a few details related to how media are represented in pbrt.

The spatial distribution and extent of media in a scene is defined by associating Medium instances with the camera, lights, and primitives in the scene. For example, Cameras store a Medium that represents the medium that the camera is inside. Rays leaving the camera then have the Medium associated with them. In a similar fashion, each Light stores a Medium representing its medium. A nullptr value can be used to indicate a vacuum (where no volumetric scattering occurs).

In pbrt, the boundary between two different types of scattering media is always represented by the surface of a primitive. Rather than storing a single Medium like lights and cameras each do, primitives may store a MediumInterface, which stores the medium on each side of the primitive's surface.

⟨*MediumInterface Definition*⟩ ≡
```
struct MediumInterface {
    ⟨MediumInterface Public Methods 715⟩
    ⟨MediumInterface Public Members 715⟩
};
```

MediumInterface holds two Mediums, one for the interior of the primitive and one for the exterior.

⟨*MediumInterface Public Members*⟩ ≡   715
```
Medium inside, outside;
```

Specifying the extent of participating media in this way does allow the user to specify impossible or inconsistent configurations. For example, a primitive could be specified as having one medium outside of it, and the camera could be specified as being in a different medium without there being a MediumInterface between the camera and the surface of the primitive. In this case, a ray leaving the primitive toward the camera would be treated as being in a different medium from a ray leaving the camera toward the primitive. In turn, light transport algorithms would be unable to compute consistent results. For pbrt's purposes, we think it is reasonable to expect that the user will be able to specify a consistent configuration of media in the scene and that the added complexity of code to check this is not worthwhile.

A MediumInterface can be initialized with either one or two Medium values. If only one is provided, then it represents an interface with the same medium on both sides.

⟨*MediumInterface Public Methods*⟩ ≡   715
```
MediumInterface(Medium medium) : inside(medium), outside(medium) {}
MediumInterface(Medium inside, Medium outside)
    : inside(inside), outside(outside) {}
```

The IsMediumTransition() method indicates whether a particular MediumInterface instance marks a transition between two distinct media.

⟨*MediumInterface Public Methods*⟩ +≡   715
```
bool IsMediumTransition() const { return inside != outside; }
```

With this context in hand, we can now provide a missing piece in the implementation of the SurfaceInteraction::SetIntersectionProperties() method—the implementation of the ⟨*Set medium properties at surface intersection*⟩ fragment. (Recall that this method is called by Primitive Intersect() methods when an intersection has been found.)

Instead of simply copying the value of the primitive's MediumInterface into the Surface Interaction, it follows a slightly different approach and only uses this MediumInterface if it specifies a proper transition between participating media. Otherwise, the Ray::medium field takes precedence. Setting the SurfaceInteraction's mediumInterface field in this way greatly simplifies the specification of scenes containing media: in particular, it is not necessary to provide corresponding Mediums at every scene surface that is in contact with a medium. Instead, only non-opaque surfaces that have different media on each side require an explicit medium interface. In the simplest case where a scene containing opaque objects is filled with a participating medium (e.g., haze), it is enough for the camera and light sources to have their media specified accordingly.

⟨*Set medium properties at surface intersection*⟩ ≡   398
```
if (primMediumInterface && primMediumInterface->IsMediumTransition())
    mediumInterface = primMediumInterface;
else
    medium = rayMedium;
```

Once mediumInterface or medium is set, it is possible to implement methods that return information about the local media. For surface interactions, a direction w can be specified to select a side of the surface. If a MediumInterface has been stored, the dot product with the surface normal determines whether the inside or outside medium should be returned. Otherwise, medium is returned.

⟨*Interaction Public Methods*⟩ +≡   136
```
Medium GetMedium(Vector3f w) const {
    if (mediumInterface)
        return Dot(w, n) > 0 ? mediumInterface->outside :
                               mediumInterface->inside;
    return medium;
}
```

For interactions that are known to be inside participating media, another variant of Get Medium() that does not take the irrelevant outgoing direction vector is available. In this case, if a MediumInterface * has been stored, it should point to the same medium for both "inside" and "outside."

⟨*Interaction Public Methods*⟩ +≡   136
```
Medium GetMedium() const {
    return mediumInterface ? mediumInterface->inside : medium;
}
```

Primitives associated with shapes that represent medium boundaries generally have a Material associated with them. For example, the surface of a lake might use an instance of DielectricMaterial to describe scattering at the lake surface, which also acts as the boundary between the rising mist's Medium and the lake water's Medium. However, sometimes we only need the shape for the boundary surface that it provides to delimit a participating medium boundary and we do not want to see the surface itself. For example, the medium representing a cloud might be bounded by a box made of triangles where the triangles are only there to delimit the cloud's extent and should not otherwise affect light passing through them.

While such a surface that disappears and does not affect ray paths could be accurately described by a BTDF that represents perfect specular transmission with the same index of refraction on both sides, dealing with such surfaces places extra burden on the Integrators (not all of which handle this type of specular light transport well). Therefore, pbrt allows such surfaces to have a Material that is nullptr, indicating that they do not affect light passing through them; in turn, SurfaceInteraction::GetBSDF() will return an unset BSDF. The light transport routines then do not worry about light scattering from such surfaces and only

DielectricMaterial 679

Interaction::medium 138

Interaction::mediumInterface 138

Material 674

Medium 714

MediumInterface::inside 715

MediumInterface:: IsMediumTransition() 715

MediumInterface::outside 715

SurfaceInteraction 138

SurfaceInteraction::GetBSDF() 682

Vector3f 86

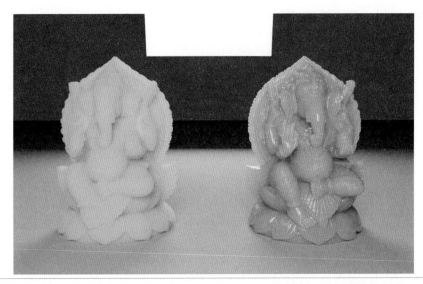

Figure 11.16: Scattering Media inside the Ganesha. Both models have the same isotropic homogeneous scattering media inside of them. On the left, the `Material` is `nullptr`, which indicates that the surface should be ignored by rays and is only used to delineate a participating medium's extent. On the right, the model's surface has a dielectric interface that both makes the interface visible and scatters some of the incident light, making the interior darker.

account for changes in the current medium at them. For an example of the difference that scattering at the surface makes, see Figure 11.16, which has two instances of the Ganesha model filled with scattering media; one has a scattering surface at the boundary and the other does not.

11.4.1 Medium INTERFACE

`Medium` implementations must include three methods. The first is `IsEmissive()`, which indicates whether they include any volumetric emission. This method is used solely so that pbrt can check if a scene has been specified without any light sources and print an informative message if so.

⟨*Medium Interface*⟩ ≡   714
```
bool IsEmissive() const;
```

The `SamplePoint()` method returns information about the scattering and emission properties of the medium at a specified rendering-space point in the form of a `MediumProperties` object.

⟨*Medium Interface*⟩ +≡   714
```
MediumProperties SamplePoint(Point3f p,
                             const SampledWavelengths &lambda) const;
```

`MediumProperties` is a simple structure that wraps up the values that describe scattering and emission at a point inside a medium. When initialized to their default values, its member variables together indicate no scattering or emission. Thus, implementations of `SamplePoint()` can directly return a `MediumProperties` with no further initialization if the specified point is outside of the medium's spatial extent.

⟨*MediumProperties Definition*⟩ ≡
```
struct MediumProperties {
    SampledSpectrum sigma_a, sigma_s;
    PhaseFunction phase;
    SampledSpectrum Le;
};
```

The third method that `Medium` implementations must implement is `SampleRay()`, which provides information about the medium's majorant σ_{maj} along the ray's extent. It does so using one or more `RayMajorantSegment` objects. Each describes a constant majorant over a segment of a ray.

⟨*RayMajorantSegment Definition*⟩ ≡
```
struct RayMajorantSegment {
    Float tMin, tMax;
    SampledSpectrum sigma_maj;
};
```

Some `Medium` implementations have a single medium-wide majorant (e.g., `Homogeneous Medium`), though for media where the scattering coefficients vary significantly over their extent, it is usually better to have distinct local majorants that bound σ_t over smaller regions. These tighter majorants can improve rendering performance by reducing the frequency of null scattering when sampling interactions along a ray.

The number of segments along a ray is variable, depending on both the ray's geometry and how the medium discretizes space. However, we would not like to return variable-sized arrays of `RayMajorantSegment`s from `SampleRay()` method implementations. Although dynamic memory allocation to store them could be efficiently handled using a `ScratchBuffer`, another motivation not to immediately return all of them is that often not all the `RayMajorant Segment`s along the ray are needed; if the ray path terminates or scattering occurs along the ray, then any additional `RayMajorantSegment`s past the corresponding point would be unused and their initialization would be wasted work.

Therefore, the `RayMajorantIterator` interface provides a mechanism for `Medium` implementations to return `RayMajorantSegment`s one at a time as they are needed. There is a single method in this interface: `Next()`. Implementations of it should return majorant segments from the front to the back of the ray with no overlap in t between segments, though it may skip over ranges of t corresponding to regions of space where there is no scattering. (See Figure 11.17.) After it has returned all segments along the ray, an unset `optional` value should be returned. Thanks to this interface, different `Medium` implementations can generate `RayMajorantSegment`s in different ways depending on their internal medium representation.

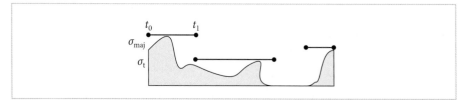

Figure 11.17: `RayMajorantIterator` implementations return a series of segments in parametric t along a ray where each segment has a majorant that is an upper bound of the medium's σ_t value along the segment. Implementations are free to specify segments of varying lengths and to skip regions of space with no scattering, though they must provide segments in front-to-back order.

⟨*RayMajorantIterator Definition*⟩ ≡
```
class RayMajorantIterator : public TaggedPointer<HomogeneousMajorantIterator,
                                                 DDAMajorantIterator> {
  public:
    pstd::optional<RayMajorantSegment> Next();
};
```

Turning back now to the SampleRay() interface method: in Chapters 14 and 15 we will find it useful to know the type of RayMajorantIterator that is associated with a specific Medium type. We can then declare the iterator as a local variable that is stored on the stack, which improves efficiency both from avoiding dynamic memory allocation for it and from allowing the compiler to more easily store it in registers. Therefore, pbrt requires that Medium implementations include a local type definition for MajorantIterator in their class definition that gives the type of their RayMajorantIterator. Their SampleRay() method itself should then directly return their majorant iterator type. Concretely, a Medium implementation should include declarations like the following in its class definition, with the ellipsis replaced with its RayMajorantIterator type.

```
using MajorantIterator = ...;
MajorantIterator SampleRay(Ray ray, Float tMax,
                           const SampledWavelengths &lambda) const;
```

(The form of this type and method definition is similar to the Material::GetBxDF() methods in Section 10.5.)

For cases where the medium's type is not known at compile time, the Medium class itself provides the implementation of a different SampleRay() method that takes a ScratchBuffer, uses it to allocate the appropriate amount of storage for the medium's ray iterator, and then calls the Medium's SampleRay() method implementation to initialize it. The returned RayMajorantIterator can then be used to iterate over the majorant segments.

The implementation of this method uses the same trick that Material::GetBSDF() does: the TaggedPointer's dynamic dispatch capabilities are used to automatically generate a separate call to the provided lambda function for each medium type, with the medium parameter specialized to be of the Medium's concrete type.

⟨*Medium Sampling Function Definitions*⟩ ≡
```
RayMajorantIterator Medium::SampleRay(Ray ray, Float tMax,
        const SampledWavelengths &lambda, ScratchBuffer &buf) const {
    auto sample = [ray,tMax,lambda,&buf](auto medium) {
        ⟨Return RayMajorantIterator for medium's majorant iterator  720⟩
    };
    return DispatchCPU(sample);
}
```

The Medium passed to the lambda function arrives as a reference to a pointer to the medium type; those are easily removed to get the basic underlying type. From it, the iterator type follows from the MajorantIterator type declaration in the associated class. In turn, storage can be allocated for the iterator type and it can be initialized. Since the returned value is of the RayMajorantIterator interface type, the caller can proceed without concern for the actual type.

⟨*Return* RayMajorantIterator *for medium's majorant iterator*⟩ ≡   **719**
```
    using ConcreteMedium = typename std::remove_reference_t<decltype(*medium)>;
    using Iter = typename ConcreteMedium::MajorantIterator;
    Iter *iter = (Iter *)buf.Alloc(sizeof(Iter), alignof(Iter));
    *iter = medium->SampleRay(ray, tMax, lambda);
    return RayMajorantIterator(iter);
```

11.4.2 HOMOGENEOUS MEDIUM

The HomogeneousMedium is the simplest possible medium. It represents a region of space with constant σ_a, σ_s, and L_e values throughout its extent. It uses the Henyey–Greenstein phase function to represent scattering in the medium, also with a constant g. Its definition is in the files media.h and media.cpp. This medium was used for the images in Figures 11.15 and 11.16.

⟨*HomogeneousMedium Definition*⟩ ≡
```
    class HomogeneousMedium {
      public:
        ⟨HomogeneousMedium Public Type Definitions 720⟩
        ⟨HomogeneousMedium Public Methods 720⟩
      private:
        ⟨HomogeneousMedium Private Data 720⟩
    };
```

Its constructor (not included here) initializes the following member variables from provided parameters. It takes spectral values in the general form of Spectrums but converts them to the form of DenselySampledSpectrums. While this incurs a memory cost of a kilobyte or so for each one, it ensures that sampling the spectrum will be fairly efficient and will not require, for example, the binary search that PiecewiseLinearSpectrum uses. It is unlikely that there will be enough distinct instances of HomogeneousMedium in a scene that this memory cost will be significant.

⟨*HomogeneousMedium Private Data*⟩ ≡   **720**
```
    DenselySampledSpectrum sigma_a_spec, sigma_s_spec, Le_spec;
    HGPhaseFunction phase;
```

Implementation of the IsEmissive() interface method is straightforward.

⟨*HomogeneousMedium Public Methods*⟩ ≡   **720**
```
    bool IsEmissive() const { return Le_spec.MaxValue() > 0; }
```

SamplePoint() just needs to sample the various constant scattering properties at the specified wavelengths.

⟨*HomogeneousMedium Public Methods*⟩ +≡   **720**
```
    MediumProperties SamplePoint(Point3f p,
                                 const SampledWavelengths &lambda) const {
        SampledSpectrum sigma_a = sigma_a_spec.Sample(lambda);
        SampledSpectrum sigma_s = sigma_s_spec.Sample(lambda);
        SampledSpectrum Le = Le_spec.Sample(lambda);
        return MediumProperties{sigma_a, sigma_s, &phase, Le};
    }
```

SampleRay() uses the HomogeneousMajorantIterator class for its RayMajorantIterator.

⟨*HomogeneousMedium Public Type Definitions*⟩ ≡   **720**
```
    using MajorantIterator = HomogeneousMajorantIterator;
```

There is no need for null scattering in a homogeneous medium and so a single `RayMajorant` `Segment` for the ray's entire extent suffices. `HomogeneousMajorantIterator` therefore stores such a segment directly.

⟨*HomogeneousMajorantIterator Definition*⟩ ≡
```
class HomogeneousMajorantIterator {
  public:
    ⟨HomogeneousMajorantIterator Public Methods 721⟩
  private:
    RayMajorantSegment seg;
    bool called;
};
```

Its default constructor sets `called` to true and stores no segment; in this way, the case of a ray missing a medium and there being no valid segment can be handled with a default-initialized `HomogeneousMajorantIterator`.

⟨*HomogeneousMajorantIterator Public Methods*⟩ ≡   **721**
```
HomogeneousMajorantIterator() : called(true) {}
HomogeneousMajorantIterator(Float tMin, Float tMax,
                            SampledSpectrum sigma_maj)
    : seg{tMin, tMax, sigma_maj}, called(false) {}
```

If a segment was specified, it is returned the first time `Next()` is called. Subsequent calls return an unset value, indicating that there are no more segments.

⟨*HomogeneousMajorantIterator Public Methods*⟩ +≡   **721**
```
pstd::optional<RayMajorantSegment> Next() {
    if (called) return {};
    called = true;
    return seg;
}
```

The implementation of `HomogeneousMedium::SampleRay()` is now trivial. Its only task is to compute the majorant, which is equal to $\sigma_t = \sigma_a + \sigma_s$.

⟨*HomogeneousMedium Public Methods*⟩ +≡   **720**
```
HomogeneousMajorantIterator SampleRay(
        Ray ray, Float tMax, const SampledWavelengths &lambda) const {
    SampledSpectrum sigma_a = sigma_a_spec.Sample(lambda);
    SampledSpectrum sigma_s = sigma_s_spec.Sample(lambda);
    return HomogeneousMajorantIterator(0, tMax, sigma_a + sigma_s);
}
```

11.4.3 DDA MAJORANT ITERATOR

Before moving on to the remaining two `Medium` implementations, we will describe another `RayMajorantIterator` that is much more efficient than the `HomogeneousMajorantIterator` when the medium's scattering coefficients vary over its extent. To understand the problem with a single majorant in this case, recall that the mean free path is the average distance between scattering events. It is one over the attenuation coefficient and so the average t step returned by a call to `SampleExponential()` given a majorant σ_{maj} will be $1/\sigma_{maj}$. Now consider a medium that has a $\sigma_t = 1$ almost everywhere but has $\sigma_t = 100$ in a small region. If $\sigma_{maj} = 100$ everywhere, then in the less dense region 99% of the sampled distances will be null-scattering events and the ray will take steps that are 100 times shorter than it would take if σ_{maj} was 1. Rendering performance suffers accordingly.

This issue motivates using a data structure to store spatially varying majorants, which allows tighter majorants and more efficient sampling operations. A variety of data structures have been used for this problem; the "Further Reading" section has details. The remainder of pbrt's Medium implementations all use a simple grid where each cell stores a majorant over the corresponding region of the volume. In turn, as a ray passes through the medium, it is split into segments through this grid and sampled based on the local majorant.

More precisely, the local majorant is found with the combination of a regular grid of voxels of scalar densities and a SampledSpectrum σ_t value. The majorant in each voxel is given by the product of σ_t and the voxel's density. The MajorantGrid class stores that grid of voxels.

⟨*MajorantGrid Definition*⟩ ≡
```
struct MajorantGrid {
    ⟨MajorantGrid Public Methods 722⟩
    ⟨MajorantGrid Public Members 722⟩
};
```

MajorantGrid just stores an axis-aligned bounding box for the grid, its voxel values, and its resolution in each dimension.

⟨*MajorantGrid Public Members*⟩ ≡   722
```
Bounds3f bounds;
pstd::vector<Float> voxels;
Point3i res;
```

The voxel array is indexed in the usual manner, with x values laid out consecutively in memory, then y, and then z. Two simple methods handle the indexing math for setting and looking up values in the grid.

⟨*MajorantGrid Public Methods*⟩ ≡   722
```
Float Lookup(int x, int y, int z) const {
    return voxels[x + res.x * (y + res.y * z)];
}
void Set(int x, int y, int z, Float v) {
    voxels[x + res.x * (y + res.y * z)] = v;
}
```

Next, the VoxelBounds() method returns the bounding box corresponding to the specified voxel in the grid. Note that the returned bounds are with respect to $[0, 1]^3$ and not the bounds member variable.

⟨*MajorantGrid Public Methods*⟩ +≡   722
```
Bounds3f VoxelBounds(int x, int y, int z) const {
    Point3f p0(Float(x)   / res.x, Float(y)   / res.y, Float(z)   / res.z);
    Point3f p1(Float(x+1) / res.x, Float(y+1) / res.y, Float(z+1) / res.z);
    return Bounds3f(p0, p1);
}
```

Efficiently enumerating the voxels that the ray passes through can be done with a technique that is similar in spirit to Bresenham's classic line drawing algorithm, which incrementally finds series of pixels that a line passes through using just addition and comparisons to step from one pixel to the next. (This type of algorithm is known as a *digital differential analyzer* (DDA)—hence the name of the DDAMajorantIterator.) The main difference between the ray stepping algorithm and Bresenham's is that we would like to find *all* of the voxels that the ray passes through, while Bresenham's algorithm typically only turns on one pixel per row or column that a line passes through.

⟨*DDAMajorantIterator Definition*⟩ ≡
```
class DDAMajorantIterator {
  public:
    ⟨DDAMajorantIterator Public Methods 723⟩
  private:
    ⟨DDAMajorantIterator Private Members 723⟩
};
```

After copying parameters passed to it to member variables, the constructor's main task is to compute a number of values that represent the DDA's state.

⟨*DDAMajorantIterator Public Methods*⟩ ≡   **723**
```
DDAMajorantIterator(Ray ray, Float tMin, Float tMax,
                    const MajorantGrid *grid, SampledSpectrum sigma_t)
    : tMin(tMin), tMax(tMax), grid(grid), sigma_t(sigma_t) {
    ⟨Set up 3D DDA for ray through the majorant grid 724⟩
}
```

The tMin and tMax member variables store the parametric range of the ray for which majorant segments are yet to be generated; tMin is advanced after each step. Their default values specify a degenerate range, which causes a default-initialized DDAMajorantIterator to return no segments when its Next() method is called.

⟨*DDAMajorantIterator Private Members*⟩ ≡   **723**
```
SampledSpectrum sigma_t;
Float tMin = Infinity, tMax = -Infinity;
const MajorantGrid *grid;
```

Grid voxel traversal is handled by an incremental algorithm that tracks the current voxel and the parametric t where the ray enters the next voxel in each direction. It successively takes a step in the direction that has the smallest such t until the ray exits the grid or traversal is halted. The values that the algorithm needs to keep track of are the following:

1. The integer coordinates of the voxel currently being considered, voxel.
2. The parametric t position along the ray where it makes its next crossing into another voxel in each of the x, y, and z directions, nextCrossingT (Figure 11.18).
3. The change in the current voxel coordinates after a step in each direction (1 or −1), stored in step.
4. The parametric distance along the ray between voxels in each direction, deltaT.
5. The coordinates of the voxel after the last one the ray passes through when it exits the grid, voxelLimit.

The first two values are updated as the ray steps through the grid, while the last three are constant for each ray. All are stored in member variables.

⟨*DDAMajorantIterator Private Members*⟩ +≡   **723**
```
Float nextCrossingT[3], deltaT[3];
int step[3], voxelLimit[3], voxel[3];
```

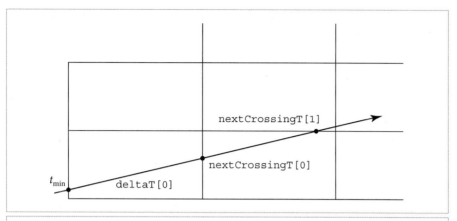

Figure 11.18: Stepping a Ray through a Voxel Grid. The parametric distance along the ray to the point where it crosses into the next voxel in the x direction is stored in nextCrossingT[0], and similarly for the y and z directions (not shown). When the ray crosses into the next x voxel, for example, it is immediately possible to update the value of nextCrossingT[0] by adding a fixed value, the voxel width in x divided by the ray's x direction, deltaT[0].

For the DDA computations, we will transform the ray to a coordinate system where the grid spans $[0, 1]^3$, giving the ray rayGrid. Working in this space simplifies some of the calculations related to the DDA.[6]

⟨*Set up 3D DDA for ray through the majorant grid*⟩ ≡   **723**
```
Vector3f diag = grid->bounds.Diagonal();
Ray rayGrid(Point3f(grid->bounds.Offset(ray.o)),
            Vector3f(ray.d.x / diag.x, ray.d.y / diag.y, ray.d.z / diag.z));
Point3f gridIntersect = rayGrid(tMin);
for (int axis = 0; axis < 3; ++axis) {
    ⟨Initialize ray stepping parameters for axis 724⟩
}
```

Some of the DDA state values for each dimension are always computed in the same way, while others depend on the sign of the ray's direction in that dimension.

⟨*Initialize ray stepping parameters for* axis⟩ ≡   **724**
```
⟨Compute current voxel for axis and handle negative zero direction 725⟩
if (rayGrid.d[axis] >= 0) {
    ⟨Handle ray with positive direction for voxel stepping 725⟩
} else {
    ⟨Handle ray with negative direction for voxel stepping 725⟩
}
```

The integer coordinates of the initial voxel are easily found using the grid intersection point. Because it is with respect to the $[0, 1]^3$ cube, all that is necessary is to scale by the resolution in each dimension and take the integer component of that value. It is, however, important to clamp this value to the valid range in case round-off error leads to an out-of-bounds value.

---

6   If you are wondering why it is correct to use the value of tMin that was computed using ray with rayGrid to find the point gridIntersect, review Section 6.1.4 and carefully consider how the components of rayGrid are initialized.

Next, deltaT is found by dividing the voxel width, which is one over its resolution since we are working in $[0, 1]^3$, by the absolute value of the ray's direction component for the current axis. (The absolute value is taken since t only increases as the DDA visits successive voxels.)

Finally, a rare and subtle case related to the IEEE floating-point representation must be handled. Recall from Section 6.8.1 that both "positive" and "negative" zero values can be represented as floats. Normally there is no need to distinguish between them as the distinction is mostly not evident—for example, comparing a negative zero to a positive zero gives a true result. However, the fragment after this one will take advantage of the fact that it is legal to compute $1 \oslash 0$ in floating point, which gives an infinite value. There, we would always like the positive infinity, and thus negative zeros are cleaned up here.

⟨*Compute current voxel for axis and handle negative zero direction*⟩ ≡ 724

```
voxel[axis] = Clamp(gridIntersect[axis] * grid->res[axis],
                    0, grid->res[axis] - 1);
deltaT[axis] = 1 / (std::abs(rayGrid.d[axis]) * grid->res[axis]);
if (rayGrid.d[axis] == -0.f)
    rayGrid.d[axis] = 0.f;
```

The parametric t value where the ray exits the current voxel, nextCrossingT[axis], is found with the ray–slab intersection algorithm from Section 6.1.2, using the plane that passes through the corresponding voxel face. Given a zero-valued direction component, nextCrossingT ends up with the positive floating-point ∞ value. The voxel stepping logic will always decide to step in one of the other directions and will correctly never step in this direction.

For positive directions, rays exit at the upper end of a voxel's extent and therefore advance plus one voxel in each dimension. Traversal completes when the upper limit of the grid is reached.

⟨*Handle ray with positive direction for voxel stepping*⟩ ≡ 724

```
Float nextVoxelPos = Float(voxel[axis] + 1) / grid->res[axis];
nextCrossingT[axis] = tMin + (nextVoxelPos - gridIntersect[axis]) /
                             rayGrid.d[axis];
step[axis] = 1;
voxelLimit[axis] = grid->res[axis];
```

Similar expressions give these values for rays with negative direction components.

⟨*Handle ray with negative direction for voxel stepping*⟩ ≡ 724

```
Float nextVoxelPos = Float(voxel[axis]) / grid->res[axis];
nextCrossingT[axis] = tMin + (nextVoxelPos - gridIntersect[axis]) /
                             rayGrid.d[axis];
step[axis] = -1;
voxelLimit[axis] = -1;
```

The Next() method takes care of generating the majorant segment for the current voxel and taking a step to the next using the DDA. Traversal terminates when the remaining parametric range $[t_{min}, t_{max}]$ is degenerate.

⟨*DDAMajorantIterator Public Methods*⟩ +≡   **723**
```
    pstd::optional<RayMajorantSegment> Next() {
        if (tMin >= tMax) return {};
        ⟨Find stepAxis for stepping to next voxel and exit point tVoxelExit 726⟩
        ⟨Get maxDensity for current voxel and initialize RayMajorantSegment, seg 726⟩
        ⟨Advance to next voxel in maximum density grid  727⟩
        return seg;
    }
```

The first order of business when Next() executes is to figure out which axis to step along to visit the next voxel. This gives the t value at which the ray exits the current voxel, tVoxelExit. Determining this axis requires finding the smallest of three numbers—the parametric t values where the ray enters the next voxel in each dimension, which is a straightforward task. However, in this case an optimization is possible because we do not care about the *value* of the smallest number, just its corresponding index in the nextCrossingT array. It is possible to compute this index in straight-line code without any branches, which can be beneficial to performance.

The following tricky bit of code determines which of the three nextCrossingT values is the smallest and sets stepAxis accordingly. It encodes this logic by setting each of the three low-order bits in an integer to the results of three comparisons between pairs of nextCrossingT values. It then uses a table (cmpToAxis) to map the resulting integer to the direction with the smallest value.

⟨*Find* stepAxis *for stepping to next voxel and exit point* tVoxelExit⟩ ≡   **726**
```
    int bits = ((nextCrossingT[0] < nextCrossingT[1]) << 2) +
               ((nextCrossingT[0] < nextCrossingT[2]) << 1) +
               ((nextCrossingT[1] < nextCrossingT[2]));
    const int cmpToAxis[8] = {2, 1, 2, 1, 2, 2, 0, 0};
    int stepAxis = cmpToAxis[bits];
    Float tVoxelExit = std::min(tMax, nextCrossingT[stepAxis]);
```

Computing the majorant for the current voxel is a matter of multiplying sigma_t with the maximum density value over the voxel's volume.

⟨*Get* maxDensity *for current voxel and initialize* RayMajorantSegment, seg⟩ ≡   **726**
```
    SampledSpectrum sigma_maj = sigma_t *
                        grid->Lookup(voxel[0], voxel[1], voxel[2]);
    RayMajorantSegment seg{tMin, tVoxelExit, sigma_maj};
```

With the majorant segment initialized, the method finishes by updating the DDAMajorant Iterator's state to reflect stepping to the next voxel in the ray's path. That is easy to do given that the ⟨*Find* stepAxis *for stepping to next voxel and exit point* tVoxelExit⟩ fragment has already set stepAxis to the dimension with the smallest t step that advances to the next voxel. First, tMin is tentatively set to correspond to the current voxel's exit point, though if stepping causes the ray to exit the grid, it is advanced to tMax. This way, the if test at the start of the Next() method will return immediately the next time it is called.

Otherwise, the DDA steps to the next voxel coordinates and increments the chosen direction's nextCrossingT by its deltaT value so that future traversal steps will know how far it is necessary to go before stepping in this direction again.

726

⟨*Advance to next voxel in maximum density grid*⟩ ≡
```
tMin = tVoxelExit;
if (nextCrossingT[stepAxis] > tMax) tMin = tMax;
voxel[stepAxis] += step[stepAxis];
if (voxel[stepAxis] == voxelLimit[stepAxis]) tMin = tMax;
nextCrossingT[stepAxis] += deltaT[stepAxis];
```

Although the grid can significantly improve the efficiency of volume sampling by providing majorants that are a better fit to the local medium density and thence reducing the number of null-scattering events, it also introduces the overhead of additional computations for stepping through voxels with the DDA. Too low a grid resolution and the majorants may not fit the volume well; too high a resolution and too much time will be spent walking through the grid. Figure 11.19 has a graph that illustrates these trade-offs, plotting voxel grid resolution versus execution time when rendering the cloud model used in Figures 11.2 and 11.8. We can see that the performance characteristics are similar on both the CPU and the GPU, with both exhibiting good performance with grid resolutions that span roughly 64 through 256 voxels on a side. Figure 11.20 shows the extinction coefficient and the majorant

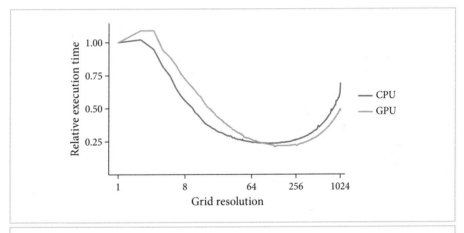

Figure 11.19: Rendering Performance versus Maximum Density Grid Resolution. Performance is measured when rendering the cloud model in Figure 11.8 on both the CPU and the GPU; results are normalized to the performance on the corresponding processor with a single-voxel grid. Low-resolution grids give poor performance from many null-scattering events due to loose majorants, while high-resolution grids harm performance from grid traversal overhead.

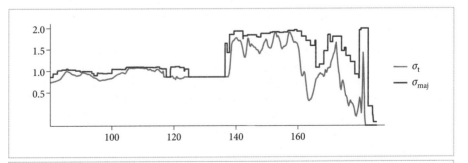

Figure 11.20: Extinction Coefficient and Majorant along a Ray. These quantities are plotted for a randomly selected ray that was traced when rendering the image in Figure 11.8. The majorant grid resolution was 256 voxels on a side, which leads to a good fit to the actual extinction coefficient along the ray.

along a randomly selected ray that was traced when rendering the cloud scene; we can see that the majorants end up fitting the extinction coefficient well.

11.4.4 UNIFORM GRID MEDIUM

The GridMedium stores medium densities and (optionally) emission at a regular 3D grid of positions, similar to the way that the image textures represent images with a 2D grid of samples.

⟨*GridMedium Definition*⟩ ≡
```
class GridMedium {
  public:
    ⟨GridMedium Public Type Definitions 730⟩
    ⟨GridMedium Public Methods 729⟩
  private:
    ⟨GridMedium Private Members 728⟩
};
```

The constructor takes a 3D array that stores the medium's density and values that define emission as well as the medium space bounds of the grid and a transformation matrix that goes from medium space to rendering space. Most of its work is direct initialization of member variables, which we have elided here. Its one interesting bit is in the fragment ⟨*Initialize* majorantGrid *for* GridMedium⟩, which we will see in a few pages.

⟨*GridMedium Private Members*⟩ ≡   728
```
Bounds3f bounds;
Transform renderFromMedium;
```

Two steps give the σ_a and σ_s values for the medium at a point: first, baseline spectral values of these coefficients, sigma_a_spec and sigma_s_spec, are sampled at the specified wavelengths to give SampledSpectrum values for them. These are then scaled by the interpolated density from densityGrid. The phase function in this medium is uniform and parameterized only by the Henyey–Greenstein g parameter.

⟨*GridMedium Private Members*⟩ +≡   728
```
DenselySampledSpectrum sigma_a_spec, sigma_s_spec;
SampledGrid<Float> densityGrid;
HGPhaseFunction phase;
```

The GridMedium allows volumetric emission to be specified in one of two ways. First, a grid of temperature values may be provided; these are interpreted as blackbody emission temperatures specified in degrees Kelvin (Section 4.4.1). Alternatively, a single general spectral distribution may be provided. Both are then scaled by values from the LeScale grid. Even though spatially varying general spectral distributions are not supported, these representations make it possible to specify a variety of emissive effects; Figure 11.5 uses blackbody emission and Figure 11.21 uses a scaled spectrum. An exercise at the end of the chapter outlines how this representation might be generalized.

⟨*GridMedium Private Members*⟩ +≡   728
```
pstd::optional<SampledGrid<Float>> temperatureGrid;
DenselySampledSpectrum Le_spec;
SampledGrid<Float> LeScale;
```

Figure 11.21: Volumetric Emission Specified with a Spectrum. The emission inside the globe is specified using a fixed spectrum that represents a purple color that is then scaled by a spatially varying factor. *(Scene courtesy of Jim Price.)*

A Boolean, isEmissive, indicates whether any emission has been specified. It is initialized in the GridMedium constructor, which makes the implementation of the IsEmissive() interface method easy.

⟨*GridMedium Public Methods*⟩ ≡   **728**
```
bool IsEmissive() const { return isEmissive; }
```

⟨*GridMedium Private Members*⟩ +≡   **728**
```
bool isEmissive;
```

The medium's properties at a given point are found by interpolating values from the appropriate grids.

⟨*GridMedium Public Methods*⟩ +≡   **728**
```
MediumProperties SamplePoint(Point3f p,
                             const SampledWavelengths &lambda) const {
```
⟨*Sample spectra for grid medium σ_a and σ_s* **729**⟩
⟨*Scale scattering coefficients by medium density at* p **730**⟩
⟨*Compute grid emission* Le *at* p **730**⟩
```
    return MediumProperties{sigma_a, sigma_s, &phase, Le};
}
```

Initial values of σ_a and σ_s are found by sampling the baseline values.

⟨*Sample spectra for grid medium σ_a and σ_s*⟩ ≡   **729, 731**
```
SampledSpectrum sigma_a = sigma_a_spec.Sample(lambda);
SampledSpectrum sigma_s = sigma_s_spec.Sample(lambda);
```

Next, σ_a and σ_s are scaled by the interpolated density at p. The provided point must be transformed from rendering space to the medium's space and then remapped to $[0, 1]^3$ before the grid's Lookup() method is called to interpolate the density.

⟨*Scale scattering coefficients by medium density at* p⟩ ≡   **729**
```
p = renderFromMedium.ApplyInverse(p);
p = Point3f(bounds.Offset(p));
Float d = densityGrid.Lookup(p);
sigma_a *= d;
sigma_s *= d;
```

If emission is present, the emitted radiance at the point is computed using whichever of the methods was used to specify it. The implementation here goes through some care to avoid calls to Lookup() when they are unnecessary, in order to improve performance.

⟨*Compute grid emission* Le *at* p⟩ ≡   **729**
```
SampledSpectrum Le(0.f);
if (isEmissive) {
    Float scale = LeScale.Lookup(p);
    if (scale > 0) {
        ⟨Compute emitted radiance using temperatureGrid or Le_spec 730⟩
    }
}
```

Given a nonzero scale, whichever method is being used to specify emission is queried to get the SampledSpectrum.

⟨*Compute emitted radiance using* temperatureGrid *or* Le_spec⟩ ≡   **730**
```
if (temperatureGrid) {
    Float temp = temperatureGrid->Lookup(p);
    Le = scale * BlackbodySpectrum(temp).Sample(lambda);
} else
    Le = scale * Le_spec.Sample(lambda);
```

As mentioned earlier, GridMedium uses DDAMajorantIterator to provide its majorants rather than using a single grid-wide majorant.

⟨*GridMedium Public Type Definitions*⟩ ≡   **728**
```
using MajorantIterator = DDAMajorantIterator;
```

The GridMedium constructor concludes with the following fragment, which initializes a MajorantGrid with its majorants. Doing so is just a matter of iterating over all the majorant cells, computing their bounds, and finding the maximum density over them. The maximum density is easily found with a convenient SampledGrid method.

⟨*Initialize* majorantGrid *for* GridMedium⟩ ≡
```
for (int z = 0; z < majorantGrid.res.z; ++z)
    for (int y = 0; y < majorantGrid.res.y; ++y)
        for (int x = 0; x < majorantGrid.res.x; ++x) {
            Bounds3f bounds = majorantGrid.VoxelBounds(x, y, z);
            majorantGrid.Set(x, y, z, densityGrid.MaxValue(bounds));
        }
```

⟨*GridMedium Private Members*⟩ +≡   **728**
```
MajorantGrid majorantGrid;
```

The implementation of the SampleRay() Medium interface method is now easy. We can find the overlap of the ray with the medium using a straightforward fragment, not included here, and compute the baseline σ_t value. With that, we have enough information to initialize the DDAMajorantIterator.

⟨*GridMedium Public Methods*⟩ +≡   **728**
```
    DDAMajorantIterator SampleRay(Ray ray, Float raytMax,
                                  const SampledWavelengths &lambda) const {
```
    ⟨*Transform ray to medium's space and compute bounds overlap*⟩
    ⟨*Sample spectra for grid medium σ_a and σ_s* **729**⟩
```
        SampledSpectrum sigma_t = sigma_a + sigma_s;
        return DDAMajorantIterator(ray, tMin, tMax, &majorantGrid, sigma_t);
    }
```

11.4.5 RGB GRID MEDIUM

The last Medium implementation that we will describe is the RGBGridMedium. It is a variant of GridMedium that allows specifying the absorption and scattering coefficients as well as volumetric emission via RGB colors. This makes it possible to render a variety of colorful volumetric effects; an example is shown in Figure 11.22.

⟨*RGBGridMedium Definition*⟩ ≡
```
    class RGBGridMedium {
      public:
        ⟨RGBGridMedium Public Type Definitions 733⟩
        ⟨RGBGridMedium Public Methods 732⟩
      private:
        ⟨RGBGridMedium Private Members 731⟩
    };
```

Its constructor, not included here, is similar to that of GridMedium in that most of what it does is to directly initialize member variables with values passed to it. As with GridMedium, the medium's extent is jointly specified by a medium space bounding box and a transformation from medium space to rendering space.

⟨*RGBGridMedium Private Members*⟩ ≡   **731**
```
    Bounds3f bounds;
    Transform renderFromMedium;
```

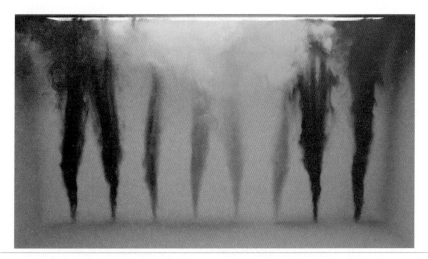

Figure 11.22: Volumetric Scattering Properties Specified Using RGB Coefficients. The RGBGridMedium class makes it possible to specify colorful participating media like the example shown here. *(Scene courtesy of Jim Price.)*

Emission is specified by the combination of an optional SampledGrid of RGBIlluminant Spectrum values and a scale factor. The RGBGridMedium reports itself as emissive if the grid is present and the scale is nonzero. This misses the case of a fully zero LeGrid, though we assume that case to be unusual.

⟨*RGBGridMedium Public Methods*⟩ ≡   731
```
bool IsEmissive() const { return LeGrid && LeScale > 0; }
```

⟨*RGBGridMedium Private Members*⟩ +≡   731
```
pstd::optional<SampledGrid<RGBIlluminantSpectrum>> LeGrid;
Float LeScale;
```

Sampling the medium at a point is mostly a matter of converting the various RGB values to SampledSpectrum values and trilinearly interpolating them to find their values at the lookup point p.

⟨*RGBGridMedium Public Methods*⟩ +≡   731
```
MediumProperties SamplePoint(Point3f p,
                             const SampledWavelengths &lambda) const {
    p = renderFromMedium.ApplyInverse(p);
    p = Point3f(bounds.Offset(p));
    ⟨Compute σa and σs for RGBGridMedium 732⟩
    ⟨Find emitted radiance Le for RGBGridMedium 733⟩
    return MediumProperties{sigma_a, sigma_s, &phase, Le};
}
```

As with earlier Medium implementations, the phase function is uniform throughout this medium.

⟨*RGBGridMedium Private Members*⟩ +≡   731
```
HGPhaseFunction phase;
```

The absorption and scattering coefficients are stored using the RGBUnboundedSpectrum class. However, this class does not support the arithmetic operations that are necessary to perform trilinear interpolation in the SampledGrid::Lookup() method. For such cases, SampledGrid allows passing a callback function that converts the in-memory values to another type that does support them. Here, the implementation provides one that converts to SampledSpectrum, which does allow arithmetic and matches the type to be returned in MediumProperties as well.

⟨*Compute σa and σs for RGBGridMedium*⟩ ≡   732
```
auto convert = [=] (RGBUnboundedSpectrum s) { return s.Sample(lambda); };
SampledSpectrum sigma_a = sigmaScale *
    (sigma_aGrid ? sigma_aGrid->Lookup(p, convert) : SampledSpectrum(1.f));
SampledSpectrum sigma_s = sigmaScale *
    (sigma_sGrid ? sigma_sGrid->Lookup(p, convert) : SampledSpectrum(1.f));
```

Because sigmaScale is applied to both σ_a and σ_s, it provides a convenient way to fine-tune the density of a medium without needing to update all of its individual RGB values.

⟨*RGBGridMedium Private Members*⟩ +≡   731
```
pstd::optional<SampledGrid<RGBUnboundedSpectrum>> sigma_aGrid, sigma_sGrid;
Float sigmaScale;
```

Volumetric emission is handled similarly, with a lambda function that converts the RGB IlluminantSpectrum values to SampledSpectrums for trilinear interpolation in the Lookup() method.

⟨*Find emitted radiance* Le *for* RGBGridMedium⟩ ≡   732
```
SampledSpectrum Le(0.f);
if (LeGrid && LeScale > 0) {
    auto convert =
        [=] (RGBIlluminantSpectrum s) { return s.Sample(lambda); };
    Le = LeScale * LeGrid->Lookup(p, convert);
}
```

The DDAMajorantIterator provides majorants for the RGBGridMedium as well.

⟨*RGBGridMedium Public Type Definitions*⟩ ≡   731
```
using MajorantIterator = DDAMajorantIterator;
```

The MajorantGrid that is used by the DDAMajorantIterator is initialized by the following fragment, which runs at the end of the RGBGridMedium constructor.

⟨*Initialize* majorantGrid *for* RGBGridMedium⟩ ≡
```
for (int z = 0; z < majorantGrid.res.z; ++z)
    for (int y = 0; y < majorantGrid.res.y; ++y)
        for (int x = 0; x < majorantGrid.res.x; ++x) {
            Bounds3f bounds = majorantGrid.VoxelBounds(x, y, z);
            ⟨Initialize majorantGrid voxel for RGB σ_a and σ_s 734⟩
        }
```

Before explaining how the majorant grid voxels are initialized, we will discuss why RGB UnboundedSpectrum values are stored in rgbDensityGrid rather than the more obvious choice of RGB values. The most important reason is that the RGB to spectrum conversion approach from Section 4.6.6 does not guarantee that the spectral distribution's value will always be less than or equal to the maximum of the original RGB components. Thus, storing RGB and setting majorants using bounds on RGB values would not give bounds on the eventual SampledSpectrum values that are computed.

One might nevertheless try to store RGB, convert those RGB values to spectra when initializing the majorant grid, and then bound those spectra to find majorants. That approach would also be unsuccessful, since when two RGB values are linearly interpolated, the corresponding RGBUnboundedSpectrum does not vary linearly between the RGBUnboundedSpectrum distributions of the two original RGB values.

Thus, RGBGridMedium stores RGBUnboundedSpectrum values at the grid sample points and linearly interpolates their SampledSpectrum values at lookup points. With that approach, we can guarantee that bounds on RGBUnboundedSpectrum values in a region of space (and then a bit more, given trilinear interpolation) give bounds on the sampled spectral values that are returned by SampledGrid::Lookup() in the SamplePoint() method, fulfilling the requirement for the majorant grid.

To compute the majorants, we use a SampledGrid method that returns its maximum value over a region of space and takes a lambda function that converts its underlying type to another—here, Float for the MajorantGrid.

One nit in how the majorants are computed is that the following code effectively assumes that the values in the σ_a and σ_s grids are independent. Although it computes a valid majorant, it is unable to account for cases like the two being defined such that $\sigma_s = c - \sigma_a$ for some constant c. Then, the bound will be looser than it could be.

⟨*Initialize* majorantGrid *voxel for RGB* σ_a *and* σ_s⟩ ≡   **733**
```
auto max = [] (RGBUnboundedSpectrum s) { return s.MaxValue(); };
Float maxSigma_t = (sigma_aGrid ? sigma_aGrid->MaxValue(bounds, max) : 1) +
                   (sigma_sGrid ? sigma_sGrid->MaxValue(bounds, max) : 1);
majorantGrid.Set(x, y, z, sigmaScale * maxSigma_t);
```

⟨*RGBGridMedium Private Members*⟩ +≡   **731**
```
MajorantGrid majorantGrid;
```

With the majorant grid initialized, the SampleRay() method's implementation is trivial. (See Exercise 11.3 for a way in which it might be improved, however.)

⟨*RGBGridMedium Public Methods*⟩ +≡   **731**
```
DDAMajorantIterator SampleRay(Ray ray, Float raytMax,
                              const SampledWavelengths &lambda) const {
    ⟨Transform ray to medium's space and compute bounds overlap⟩
    SampledSpectrum sigma_t(1);
    return DDAMajorantIterator(ray, tMin, tMax, &majorantGrid, sigma_t);
}
```

FURTHER READING

The books written by van de Hulst (1980) and Preisendorfer (1965, 1976) are excellent introductions to volume light transport. The seminal book by Chandrasekhar (1960) is another excellent resource, although it is mathematically challenging. d'Eon's book (2016) has rigorous coverage of this topic and includes extensive references to work in the area. Novák et al.'s report (2018) provides a comprehensive overview of research in volumetric light transport for rendering through 2018; see also the "Further Reading" section of Chapter 14 for more references on this topic.

The Henyey–Greenstein phase function was originally described by Henyey and Greenstein (1941). Detailed discussion of scattering and phase functions, along with derivations of phase functions that describe scattering from independent spheres, cylinders, and other simple shapes, can be found in van de Hulst's book (1981). Extensive discussion of the Mie and Rayleigh scattering models is also available there. Hansen and Travis's survey article is also a good introduction to the variety of commonly used phase functions (Hansen and Travis 1974); see also d'Eon's book (2016) for a catalog of useful phase functions and associated sampling techniques.

While the Henyey–Greenstein model often works well, there are many media that it cannot represent accurately. Gkioulekas et al. (2013a) showed that sums of Henyey–Greenstein and von Mises-Fisher lobes are more accurate for representing scattering in many materials than Henyey–Greenstein alone and derived a 2D parameter space that allows for intuitive control of translucent appearance.

The paper by Raab et al. (2006) introduced many important sampling building-blocks for rendering participating media to graphics, including the delta-tracking algorithm for inhomogeneous media. Delta tracking has been independently invented in a number of fields; see both Kutz et al. (2017) and Kettunen et al. (2021) for further details of this history.

The ratio tracking algorithm was introduced to graphics by Novák et al. (2014), though see the discussion in Novák et al. (2018) for the relationship of this approach to previously developed estimators in neutron transport. Novák et al. (2014) also introduced *residual ratio tracking*, which makes use of lower bounds on a medium's density to analytically integrate part of the beam transmittance. Kutz et al. (2017) extended this approach to distance sampling and introduced the integral formulation of transmittance due to Galtier et al. (2013). Our derivation of the integral transmittance equations (11.10) and (11.13) follows Georgiev et al. (2019), as does our discussion of connections between those equations and various transmittance estimators. Georgiev at al. also developed a number of additional estimators for transmittance that can give significantly lower error than the ratio tracking estimator that pbrt uses.

Kettunen et al. (2021) recently developed a significantly improved transmittance estimator with much lower error than previous approaches. Remarkably, their estimator is effectively a combination of uniform ray marching with a correction term that removes bias.

For media with substantial variation in density, delta tracking can be inefficient—many small steps must be taken to get through the optically thin sections. Danskin and Hanrahan (1992) presented a technique for efficient volume ray marching using a hierarchical data structure. Another way of addressing this issue was presented by Szirmay-Kalos et al. (2011), who used a grid to partition scattering volumes in cells and applied delta tracking using the majorant of each cell as the ray passed through them. This is effectively the approach implemented in pbrt's DDAMajorantIterator. The grid cell traversal algorithm implemented there is due to Cleary and Wyvill (1988) and draws from Bresenham's line drawing algorithm (Bresenham 1965). Media stored in grids are sometimes tabulated in the camera's projective space, making it possible to have more detail close to the camera and less detail farther away. Gamito has recently developed an algorithm for DDA traversal in this case (Gamito 2021).

Yue et al. (2010) used a kd-tree to store majorants, which was better able to adapt to spatially varying densities than a grid. In follow-on work, they derived an approach to estimate the efficiency of spatial partitionings and used it to construct them more effectively (Yue et al. 2011).

Because scattering may be sampled rarely in optically thin media, many samples may be necessary to achieve low error. To address this issue, Villemin et al. proposed increasing the sampling density in such media (Villemin et al. 2018).

Kulla and Fajardo (2012) noted that techniques based on sampling according to transmittance ignore another important factor: spatial variation in the scattering coefficient. They developed a method based on computing a tabularized 1D sampling distribution for each ray passing through participating media based on the product of beam transmittance and scattering coefficient at a number of points along it. They then drew samples from this distribution, showing good results.

A uniform grid of sample values as is implemented in GridMedium and RGBGridMedium may consume an excessive amount of memory, especially for media that have not only large empty regions of space but also fine detail in some regions. This issue is addressed by Museth's VDB format (2013) as well as the Field3D system that was described by Wrenninge (2015), both of which use adaptive hierarchical grids to reduce storage requirements. pbrt's NanoVDBMedium is based on NanoVDB (Museth 2021), which is a lighterweight version of VDB.

Just as procedural modeling of textures is an effective technique for shading surfaces, procedural modeling of volume densities can be used to describe realistic-looking volumetric objects like clouds and smoke. Perlin and Hoffert (1989) described early work in this area, and the book by Ebert et al. (2003) has a number of sections devoted to this topic, including further references. More recently, accurate physical simulation of the dynamics of smoke and fire has led to extremely realistic volume data sets, including the ones used in this chapter; for early work in this area, see for example Fedkiw, Stam, and Jensen (2001). The book by Wrenninge (2012) has further information about modeling participating media, with particular focus on techniques used in modern feature film production.

For media that are generated through simulations, it may be desirable to account for the variation in the medium over time in order to include the effect of motion blur. Clinton and Elendt (2009) described an approach to do so based on deforming the vertices of the grid that stores the medium, and Kulla and Fajardo (2012) applied Eulerian motion blur, where each grid cell also stores a velocity vector that is used to shift the lookup point based on its time. Wrenninge described a more efficient approach that instead stores the scattering properties in each cell as a compact time-varying function (Wrenninge 2016).

In this chapter, we have ignored all issues related to sampling and antialiasing of volume density functions that are represented by samples in a 3D grid, although these issues should be considered, especially in the case of a volume that occupies just a few pixels on the screen. Furthermore, we have used a simple triangle filter to reconstruct densities at intermediate positions, which is suboptimal for the same reasons that the triangle filter is not a high-quality image reconstruction filter. Marschner and Lobb (1994) presented the theory and practice of sampling and reconstruction for 3D data sets, applying ideas similar to those in Chapter 8. See also the paper by Theußl, Hauser, and Gröller (2000) for a comparison of a variety of windowing functions for volume reconstruction with the sinc function and a discussion of how to derive optimal parameters for volume reconstruction filter functions.

Hofmann et al. (2021) noted that sample reconstruction may have a significant performance cost, even with trilinear filtering. They suggested *stochastic sample filtering*, where a single volume sample is chosen with probability given by its filter weight, and showed performance benefits. However, this approach does introduce bias if a nonlinear function is applied to the sample value (as is the case when estimating transmittance, for example).

Acquiring volumetric scattering properties of real-world objects is particularly difficult, requiring a solution to the inverse problem of determining the values that lead to the measured result. See Jensen et al. (2001b), Goesele et al. (2004), Narasimhan et al. (2006), and Peers et al. (2006) for work on acquiring scattering properties for subsurface scattering. More recently, Gkioulekas et al. (2013b) produced accurate measurements of a variety of media. Hawkins et al. (2005) have developed techniques to measure properties of media like smoke, acquiring measurements in real time. Another interesting approach to this problem was introduced by Frisvad et al. (2007), who developed methods to compute these properties from a lower-level characterization of the scattering properties of the medium. A comprehensive survey of work in this area was presented by Frisvad et al. (2020). (See also the discussion of inverse rendering techniques in Section 16.3.1 for additional approaches to these problems.)

Acquiring the volumetric density variation of participating media is also challenging. See work by Fuchs et al. (2007), Atcheson et al. (2008), and Gu et al. (2013a) for a variety of approaches to this problem, generally based on illuminating the medium in particular ways while photographing it from one or more viewpoints.

EXERCISES

● **11.1** The `GridMedium` and `RGBGridMedium` classes use a relatively large amount of memory for complex volume densities. Determine their memory requirements when used with complex medium densities and modify their implementations to reduce memory use. One approach might be to detect regions of space with constant (or relatively constant) density values using an octree data structure and to only refine the octree in regions where the densities are changing. Another possibility is to use less memory to record each density value—for example, by computing the minimum and maximum densities and then using 8 or 16 bits per density value to interpolate between them. What sorts of errors appear when either of these approaches is pushed too far?

② 11.2 Improve `GridMedium` to allow specifying grids of arbitrary `Spectrum` values to define emission. How much more memory does your approach use for blackbody emission distributions than the current implementation, which only stores floating-point temperatures in that case? How much memory does it use when other spectral representations are provided? Can you find ways of reducing memory use—for example, by detecting equal spectra and only storing them in memory once?

③ 11.3 One shortcoming of the majorants computed by the `RGBGridMedium` is that they do not account for spectral variation in the scattering coefficients—although conservative, they may give a loose bound for wavelengths where the coefficients are much lower than the maximum values. Computing tighter majorants is not straightforward in a spectral renderer: in a renderer that used RGB color for rendering, it is easy to maintain a majorant grid of RGB values instead of `Float`s, though doing so is more difficult with a spectral renderer, for reasons related to why `RGBUnboundedSpectrum` values are stored in the grids for σ_a and σ_s and not RGB. (See the discussion of this topic before the ⟨*Initialize* `majorantGrid` *voxel for RGB* σ_a *and* σ_s⟩ fragment.)

Investigate this issue and develop an approach that better accounts for spectral variation in the scattering coefficients to return wavelength-varying majorants when `RGBGridMedium::SampleRay()` is called. You might, for example, find a way to compute `RGBUnboundedSpectrum` values that bound the maximum of two or more others. How much overhead does your representation introduce? How much is rendering time improved for scenes with colored media due to more efficient sampling when it is used?

② 11.4 The `Medium` implementations that use the `MajorantGrid` all currently use fixed grid resolutions for it, regardless of the amount of variation in density in their underlying media. Read the paper by Yue et al. (2011) and use their approach to choose those resolutions adaptively. Then, measure performance over a sweep of grid sizes with a variety of volume densities. Are there any cases where there is a significant performance benefit from a different grid resolution? Considering their assumptions and pbrt's implementation, can you explain any discrepancies between grid sizes set with their heuristics versus the most efficient resolution in pbrt?

② 11.5 Read Wrenninge's paper (2016) on a time-varying density representation for motion blur in volumes and implement this approach in pbrt. One challenge will be to generate volumes in this representation; you may need to implement a physical simulation system in order to make some yourself.

CHAPTER TWELVE

12 LIGHT SOURCES

In order for objects in a scene to be visible, there must be a source of illumination so that some light is reflected from them to the camera sensor. To that end, this chapter first presents the `Light` interface, which allows specification of a variety of types of light sources. (Before reading this chapter, you may wish to review Section 4.4, which describes the physical processes underlying light emission.)

The implementations of a number of useful light sources follow. Because the implementations of different types of lights are all hidden behind a carefully designed interface, the light transport routines in Chapters 13 through 15 can generally operate without knowing which particular types of lights are in the scene, similar to how acceleration structures can hold collections of different types of primitives without needing to know the details of their actual representations.

A wide variety of light source models are introduced in this chapter, although the variety is slightly limited by pbrt's physically based design. Many non-physical light source models have been developed for computer graphics, incorporating control over properties like the rate at which the light falls off with distance, which objects are illuminated by the light, which objects cast shadows from the light, and so on. These sorts of controls are incompatible with physically based light transport algorithms and thus cannot be provided in the models here.

As an example of the problems such lighting controls pose, consider a light that does not cast shadows: the total energy arriving at surfaces in the scene increases without bound as more surfaces are added. Consider a series of concentric shells of spheres around such a light; if occlusion is ignored, each added shell increases the total received energy. This directly violates the principle that the total energy arriving at surfaces illuminated by the light cannot be greater than the total energy emitted by the light.

In scenes with many lights, it is impractical to account for the illumination from all of them at each point being shaded. Fortunately, this issue is yet another that can be handled stochastically. Given a suitable weighting factor, an unbiased estimate of the effect of illumination from all the lights can be computed by considering just a few of them, or even just one. The last section of this chapter therefore introduces the `LightSampler`, which defines an interface for choosing such light sources as well as a number of implementations of it.

12.1 LIGHT INTERFACE

The Light class defines the interface that light sources must implement. It is defined in the file base/light.h and all the light implementations in the following sections are in the files lights.h and lights.cpp.

⟨*Light Definition*⟩ ≡
```
class Light : public TaggedPointer<⟨Light Source Types 740⟩> {
  public:
    ⟨Light Interface 740⟩
};
```

This chapter will describe all 9 of the following types of light source.

⟨*Light Source Types*⟩ ≡   **740**
```
    PointLight, DistantLight, ProjectionLight, GoniometricLight, SpotLight,
    DiffuseAreaLight, UniformInfiniteLight, ImageInfiniteLight,
    PortalImageInfiniteLight
```

All lights must be able to return their total emitted power, Φ. Among other things, this makes it possible to sample lights according to their relative power in the forthcoming PowerLightSampler. Devoting more samples to the lights that make the largest contribution can significantly improve rendering efficiency.

⟨*Light Interface*⟩ ≡   **740**
```
    SampledSpectrum Phi(SampledWavelengths lambda) const;
```

The Light interface does not completely abstract away all the differences among different types of light source. While doing so would be desirable in principle, in practice pbrt's integrators sometimes need to handle different types of light source differently, both for efficiency and for correctness. We have already seen an example of this issue in the RandomWalk Integrator in Section 1.3.6. There, "infinite" lights received special handling since they must be considered for rays that escape the scene without hitting any geometry.

Another example is that the Monte Carlo algorithms that sample illumination from light sources need to be aware of which lights are described by delta distributions, since this affects some of their computations. Lights therefore categorize themselves into one of a few different types; the Type() method returns which one a light is.

⟨*Light Interface*⟩ +≡   **740**
```
    LightType Type() const;
```

There are four different light categories:

- DeltaPosition: lights that emit solely from a single point in space. ("Delta" refers to the fact that such lights can be described by Dirac delta distributions.)
- DeltaDirection: lights that emit radiance along a single direction.
- Area: lights that emit radiance from the surface of a geometric shape.
- Infinite: lights "at infinity" that do not have geometry associated with them but provide radiance to rays that escape the scene.

⟨*LightType Definition*⟩ ≡
```
    enum class LightType { DeltaPosition, DeltaDirection, Area, Infinite };
```

A helper function checks if a light is defined using a Dirac delta distribution.

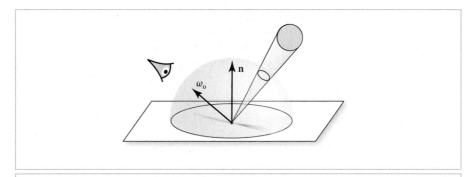

Figure 12.1: An effective sampling strategy for choosing an incident direction from a point for direct lighting computations is to allow the light source to define a distribution of directions with respect to solid angle at the point. Here, a small spherical light source is illuminating the point. The cone of directions that the sphere subtends is a much better sampling distribution to use than a uniform distribution over the hemisphere, for example.

⟨*Light Inline Functions*⟩ ≡
```
bool IsDeltaLight(LightType type) {
    return (type == LightType::DeltaPosition ||
            type == LightType::DeltaDirection);
}
```

Being able to sample directions at a point where illumination may be incident is an important sampling operation for rendering. Consider a diffuse surface illuminated by a small spherical area light source (Figure 12.1): sampling directions using the BSDF's sampling distribution is likely to be very inefficient because the light is only visible within a small cone of directions from the point. A much better approach is to instead use a sampling distribution that is based on the light source. In this case, the sampling routine should choose from among only those directions where the sphere is potentially visible.

This important task is the responsibility of implementations of the SampleLi() method. Its caller passes a LightSampleContext that provides information about a reference point in the scene, and the light optionally returns a LightLiSample that encapsulates incident radiance, information about where it is being emitted from, and the value of the probability density function (PDF) for the sampled point. If it is impossible for light to reach the reference point or if there is no valid light sample associated with u, an invalid sample can be returned. Finally, allowIncompletePDF indicates whether the sampling routine may skip generating samples for directions where the light's contribution is small. This capability is used by integrators that apply MIS compensation (Section 2.2.3).

⟨*Light Interface*⟩ +≡   740
```
pstd::optional<LightLiSample>
SampleLi(LightSampleContext ctx, Point2f u, SampledWavelengths lambda,
        bool allowIncompletePDF = false) const;
```

The LightSampleContext takes the usual role of encapsulating just as much information about the point receiving illumination as the various sampling routines need.

⟨*LightSampleContext Definition*⟩ ≡
```
class LightSampleContext {
public:
    ⟨LightSampleContext Public Methods 742⟩
    ⟨LightSampleContext Public Members 742⟩
};
```

The context just stores a point in the scene, a surface normal, and a shading normal. The point is provided as a `Point3fi` that makes it possible to include error bounds around the computed ray intersection point. Some of the following sampling routines will need this information as part of their sampling process. If the point is in a scattering medium and not on a surface, the two normals are left at their default (0, 0, 0) values.

Note that the context does not include a time—pbrt's light sources do not support animated transformations. An exercise at the end of the chapter discusses issues related to extending them to do so.

⟨*LightSampleContext Public Members*⟩ ≡   741
```
Point3fi pi;
Normal3f n, ns;
```

As with the other `Context` classes, a variety of constructors make it easy to create a `Light SampleContext`.

⟨*LightSampleContext Public Methods*⟩ ≡   741
```
LightSampleContext(const SurfaceInteraction &si)
    : pi(si.pi), n(si.n), ns(si.shading.n) {}
LightSampleContext(const Interaction &intr) : pi(intr.pi) {}
LightSampleContext(Point3fi pi, Normal3f n, Normal3f ns)
    : pi(pi), n(n), ns(ns) {}
```

A convenience method provides the point as a regular `Point3f` for the routines that would prefer to access it as such.

⟨*LightSampleContext Public Methods*⟩ +≡   741
```
Point3f p() const { return Point3f(pi); }
```

Light samples are bundled up into instances of the `LightLiSample` structure. The radiance `L` is the amount of radiance leaving the light toward the receiving point; it does not include the effect of extinction due to participating media or occlusion, if there is an object between the light and the receiver. `wi` gives the direction along which light arrives at the point that was specified via the `LightSampleContext` (see Figure 12.2) and the point from which light is being emitted is provided by `pLight`. Finally, the PDF value for the light sample is returned in `pdf`. This PDF should be measured with respect to solid angle at the receiving point.

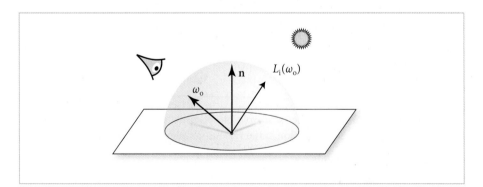

Interaction 136
Light::SampleLi() 741
LightSampleContext 741
LightSampleContext::pi 742
Normal3f 94
Point3f 92
Point3fi 1061
SurfaceInteraction 138

Figure 12.2: The `Light::SampleLi()` method returns incident radiance from the light at a point and also returns the direction vector ω_i that gives the direction from which radiance is arriving.

⟨*LightLiSample Definition*⟩ ≡
```
struct LightLiSample {
    ⟨LightLiSample Public Methods⟩
    SampledSpectrum L;
    Vector3f wi;
    Float pdf;
    Interaction pLight;
};
```

Just as we saw for perfect specular reflection and transmission with BSDFs, light sources that are defined in terms of delta distributions fit naturally into this sampling framework, although they require care on the part of the routines that call their sampling methods, since there are implicit delta distributions in the radiance and PDF values that they return. For the most part, these delta distributions naturally cancel out when estimators are evaluated, although multiple importance sampling code must be aware of this case, just as with BSDFs. For samples taken from delta distribution lights, the pdf value in the returned LightLiSample should be set to 1.

Related to this, the PDF_Li() method returns the value of the PDF for sampling the given direction wi from the point represented by ctx. This method is particularly useful in the context of multiple importance sampling (MIS) where, for example, the BSDF may have sampled a direction and we need to compute the PDF for the light's sampling that direction in order to compute the MIS weight. Implementations of this method may assume that a ray from ctx in direction wi has already been found to intersect the light source, and as with SampleLi(), the PDF should be measured with respect to solid angle. Here, the returned PDF value should be 0 if the light is described by a Dirac delta distribution.

⟨*Light Interface*⟩ +≡   740
```
Float PDF_Li(LightSampleContext ctx, Vector3f wi,
             bool allowIncompletePDF = false) const;
```

If a ray happens to intersect an area light source, it is necessary to find the radiance that is emitted back along the ray. This task is handled by the L() method, which takes local information about the intersection point and the outgoing direction. This method should never be called for any light that does not have geometry associated with it.

⟨*Light Interface*⟩ +≡   740
```
SampledSpectrum L(Point3f p, Normal3f n, Point2f uv, Vector3f w,
                  const SampledWavelengths &lambda) const;
```

Another interface method that only applies to some types of lights is Le(). It enables infinite area lights to contribute radiance to rays that do not hit any geometry in the scene. This method should only be called for lights that report their type to be LightType::Infinite.

⟨*Light Interface*⟩ +≡   740
```
SampledSpectrum Le(const Ray &ray, const SampledWavelengths &lambda) const;
```

Finally, the Light interface includes a Preprocess() method that is invoked prior to rendering. It takes the rendering space bounds of the scene as an argument. Some light sources need to know these bounds and they are not available when lights are initially created, so this method makes the bounds available to them.

⟨*Light Interface*⟩ +≡   740
```
void Preprocess(const Bounds3f &sceneBounds);
```

There are three additional light interface methods that will be defined later, closer to the code that uses them. `Light::Bounds()` provides information that bounds the light's spatial and directional emission distribution; one use of it is to build acceleration hierarchies for light sampling, as is done in Section 12.6.3. `Light::SampleLe()` and `Light::PDF_Le()` are used to sample rays leaving light sources according to their distribution of emission. They are cornerstones of bidirectional light transport algorithms and are defined in the online edition of the book along with algorithms that use them.

12.1.1 PHOTOMETRIC LIGHT SPECIFICATION

pbrt uses radiometry as the basis of its model of light transport. However, light sources are often described using photometric units—a light bulb package might report that it emits 1,000 lumens of light, for example. Beyond their familiarity, one advantage of photometric descriptions of light emission is that they also account for the variation of human visual response with wavelength. It is also more intuitive to describe lights in terms of the visible power that they emit rather than the power they consume in the process of doing so. (Related to this topic, recall the discussion of luminous efficacy in Section 4.4.)

Therefore, light sources in pbrt's scene description files can be specified in terms of the luminous power that they emit. These specifications are then converted to radiometric quantities in the code that initializes the scene representation. Radiometric values are then passed to the constructors of the `Light` implementations in this chapter, often in the form of a base spectral distribution and a scale factor that is applied to it.

12.1.2 THE LightBase CLASS

As there was with classes like `CameraBase` and `FilmBase` for `Camera` and `Film` implementations, there is a `LightBase` class that all of pbrt's light sources inherit from. `LightBase` stores a number of values that are common to all of pbrt's lights and is thus able to implement some of the `Light` interface methods. It is not required that a `Light` in pbrt inherit from `LightBase`, but lights must provide implementations of a few more `Light` methods if they do not.

⟨*LightBase Definition*⟩ ≡
```
class LightBase {
  public:
    ⟨LightBase Public Methods 745⟩
  protected:
    ⟨LightBase Protected Methods⟩
    ⟨LightBase Protected Members 745⟩
};
```

The following three values are passed to the `LightBase` constructor, which stores them in these member variables:

- type characterizes the light's type.
- renderFromLight is a transformation that defines the light's coordinate system with respect to rendering space. As with shapes, it is often handy to be able to implement a light assuming a particular coordinate system (e.g., that a spotlight is always located at the origin of its light space, shining down the $+z$ axis). The rendering-from-light transformation makes it possible to place such lights at arbitrary positions and orientations in the scene.
- A `MediumInterface` describes the participating medium on the inside and the outside of the light source. For lights that do not have "inside" and "outside" (e.g., a point light), the `MediumInterface` stores the same `Medium` on both sides.

⟨*LightBase Protected Members*⟩ ≡   744
```
LightType type;
Transform renderFromLight;
MediumInterface mediumInterface;
```

LightBase can thus take care of providing an implementation of the Type() interface method.

⟨*LightBase Public Methods*⟩ ≡   744
```
LightType Type() const { return type; }
```

It also provides default implementations of L() and Le() so that lights that are not respectively area or infinite lights do not need to implement these themselves.

⟨*LightBase Public Methods*⟩ +≡   744
```
SampledSpectrum L(Point3f p, Normal3f n, Point2f uv, Vector3f w,
                  const SampledWavelengths &lambda) const {
    return SampledSpectrum(0.f);
}
```

⟨*LightBase Public Methods*⟩ +≡   744
```
SampledSpectrum Le(const Ray &, const SampledWavelengths &) const {
    return SampledSpectrum(0.f);
}
```

Most of the following Light implementations take a Spectrum value in their constructor to specify the light's spectral emission but then convert it to a DenselySampledSpectrum to store in a member variable. By doing so, they enjoy the benefits of efficient sampling operations from tabularizing the spectrum and a modest performance benefit from not requiring dynamic dispatch to call Spectrum methods.

However, a DenselySampledSpectrum that covers the visible wavelengths uses approximately 2 kB of storage; for scenes with millions of light sources, the memory required may be significant. Therefore, LightBase provides a LookupSpectrum() method that helps reduce memory use by eliminating redundant copies of the same DenselySampledSpectrum. It uses the InternCache from Section B.4.2 to do so, only allocating storage for a single instance of each DenselySampledSpectrum provided. If many lights have the same spectral emission profile, the memory savings may be significant.

⟨*LightBase Method Definitions*⟩ ≡
```
const DenselySampledSpectrum *LightBase::LookupSpectrum(Spectrum s) {
    ⟨Initialize spectrumCache on first call⟩
    ⟨Return unique DenselySampledSpectrum from intern cache for s 746⟩
}
```

The ⟨*Initialize* spectrumCache *on first call*⟩ fragment, not included here, handles the details of initializing the spectrumCache, including ensuring mutual exclusion if multiple threads have called LookupSpectrum() concurrently and using an appropriate memory allocator—notably, one that allocates memory on the GPU if GPU rendering has been enabled.

LookupSpectrum() then calls the InternCache::Lookup() method that takes a callback function to create the object that is stored in the cache. In this way, it is able to pass the provided allocator to the DenselySampledSpectrum constructor, which in turn ensures that it is used to allocate the storage needed for its spectral samples.

⟨*Return unique* DenselySampledSpectrum *from intern cache for* s⟩ ≡   745
```
    auto create = [](Allocator alloc, const DenselySampledSpectrum &s) {
        return alloc.new_object<DenselySampledSpectrum>(s, alloc);
    };
    return spectrumCache->Lookup(DenselySampledSpectrum(s), create);
```

⟨*LightBase Protected Members*⟩ +≡   744
```
    static InternCache<DenselySampledSpectrum> *spectrumCache;
```

12.2 POINT LIGHTS

A number of interesting lights can be described in terms of emission from a single point in space with some possibly angularly varying distribution of outgoing light. This section describes the implementation of a number of them, starting with PointLight, which represents an isotropic point light source that emits the same amount of light in all directions. (Figure 12.3 shows a scene rendered with a point light source.) Building on this base, a number of more complex lights based on point sources will then be introduced, including spotlights and a light that projects an image into the scene.

⟨*PointLight Definition*⟩ ≡
```
    class PointLight : public LightBase {
      public:
        ⟨PointLight Public Methods 747⟩
      private:
        ⟨PointLight Private Members 747⟩
    };
```

PointLights are positioned at the origin in the light coordinate system. To place them elsewhere, the rendering-from-light transformation should be set accordingly. In addition to passing the common light parameters to LightBase, the constructor supplies LightType::

Figure 12.3: Scene Rendered with a Point Light Source. Notice the hard shadow boundaries from this type of light. *(Dragon model courtesy of the Stanford Computer Graphics Laboratory.)*

DeltaPosition for its light type, since point lights represent singularities that only emit light from a single position. The constructor also stores the light's intensity (Section 4.1.1).

⟨*PointLight Public Methods*⟩ ≡   746
```
PointLight(Transform renderFromLight, MediumInterface mediumInterface,
        Spectrum I, Float scale)
    : LightBase(LightType::DeltaPosition, renderFromLight, mediumInterface),
      I(LookupSpectrum(I)), scale(scale) {}
```

As HomogeneousMedium and GridMedium did with spectral scattering coefficients, PointLight uses a DenselySampledSpectrum rather than a Spectrum for the spectral intensity, trading off storage for more efficient spectral sampling operations.

⟨*PointLight Private Members*⟩ ≡   746
```
const DenselySampledSpectrum *I;
Float scale;
```

Strictly speaking, it is incorrect to describe the light arriving at a point due to a point light source using units of radiance. Radiant intensity is instead the proper unit for describing emission from a point light source, as explained in Section 4.1. In the light source interfaces here, however, we will abuse terminology and use SampleLi() methods to report the illumination arriving at a point for all types of light sources, dividing radiant intensity by the squared distance to the point p to convert units. In the end, the correctness of the computation does not suffer from this fudge, and it makes the implementation of light transport algorithms more straightforward by not requiring them to use different interfaces for different types of lights.

Point lights are described by a delta distribution such that they only illuminate a receiving point from a single direction. Thus, the sampling problem is deterministic and makes no use of the random sample u. We find the light's position p in the rendering coordinate system and sample its spectral emission at the provided wavelengths. Note that a PDF value of 1 is returned in the LightLiSample: there is implicitly a Dirac delta distribution in both the radiance and the PDF that cancels when the Monte Carlo estimator is evaluated.

⟨*PointLight Public Methods*⟩ +≡   746
```
pstd::optional<LightLiSample>
SampleLi(LightSampleContext ctx, Point2f u, SampledWavelengths lambda,
        bool allowIncompletePDF) const {
    Point3f p = renderFromLight(Point3f(0, 0, 0));
    Vector3f wi = Normalize(p - ctx.p());
    SampledSpectrum Li = scale * I->Sample(lambda) /
                            DistanceSquared(p, ctx.p());
    return LightLiSample(Li, wi, 1, Interaction(p, &mediumInterface));
}
```

Due to the delta distribution, the PointLight::PDF_Li() method returns 0. This value reflects the fact that there is no chance for some other sampling process to randomly generate a direction that would intersect an infinitesimal light source.

⟨*PointLight Public Methods*⟩ +≡   746
```
Float PDF_Li(LightSampleContext, Vector3f, bool allowIncompletePDF) const {
    return 0;
}
```

The total power emitted by the light source can be found by integrating the intensity over the entire sphere of directions:

$$\Phi = \int_{\mathcal{S}^2} I \; d\omega = I \int_{\mathcal{S}^2} d\omega = 4\pi I.$$

Radiant power is returned by the Phi() method and not the luminous power that may have been used to specify the light source.

⟨*PointLight Method Definitions*⟩ ≡
```
SampledSpectrum PointLight::Phi(SampledWavelengths lambda) const {
    return 4 * Pi * scale * I->Sample(lambda);
}
```

12.2.1 SPOTLIGHTS

Spotlights are a handy variation on point lights; rather than shining illumination in all directions, they emit light in a cone of directions from their position. For simplicity, we will define the spotlight in the light coordinate system to always be at position $(0, 0, 0)$ and pointing down the $+z$ axis. To place or orient it elsewhere in the scene, the rendering-from-light transformation should be set accordingly. Figure 12.4 shows a rendering of the same scene as Figure 12.3, illuminated with a spotlight instead of a point light.

⟨*SpotLight Definition*⟩ ≡
```
class SpotLight : public LightBase {
  public:
    ⟨SpotLight Public Methods 749⟩
  private:
    ⟨SpotLight Private Members 749⟩
};
```

There is not anything interesting in the SpotLight constructor, so it is not included here. It is given angles that set the extent of the SpotLight's cone—the overall angular width of the cone

Figure 12.4: Scene Rendered with a Spotlight. The spotlight cone smoothly cuts off illumination past a user-specified angle from the light's central axis. *(Dragon model courtesy of the Stanford Computer Graphics Laboratory.)*

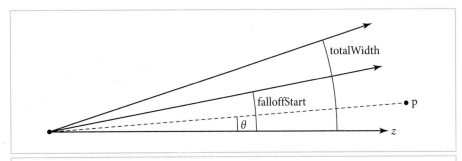

Figure 12.5: Spotlights are defined by two angles, falloffStart and totalWidth, that are measured with respect to the *z* axis in light space. Objects inside the inner cone of angles, up to *falloffStart*, are fully illuminated by the light. The directions between *falloffStart* and *totalWidth* are a transition zone that ramps down from full illumination to no illumination, such that points outside the *totalWidth* cone are not illuminated at all. The cosine of the angle *θ* between the vector to a point p and the spotlight axis can easily be computed with a dot product.

and the angle at which falloff starts (Figure 12.5)—but it stores the cosines of these angles, which are more useful to have at hand in the SpotLight's methods.

⟨*SpotLight Private Members*⟩ ≡   **748**
```
const DenselySampledSpectrum *Iemit;
Float scale, cosFalloffStart, cosFalloffEnd;
```

The SpotLight::SampleLi() method is of similar form to that of PointLight::SampleLi(), though an unset sample is returned if the receiving point is outside of the spotlight's outer cone and thus receives zero radiance.

⟨*SpotLight Public Methods*⟩ ≡   **748**
```
pstd::optional<LightLiSample>
SampleLi(LightSampleContext ctx, Point2f u, SampledWavelengths lambda,
         bool allowIncompletePDF) const {
    Point3f p = renderFromLight(Point3f(0, 0, 0));
    Vector3f wi = Normalize(p - ctx.p());
    ⟨Compute incident radiance Li for SpotLight 749⟩
    if (!Li) return {};
    return LightLiSample(Li, wi, 1, Interaction(p, &mediumInterface));
}
```

The I() method computes the distribution of light accounting for the spotlight cone. This computation is encapsulated in a separate method since other SpotLight methods will need to perform it as well.

⟨*Compute incident radiance* Li *for* SpotLight⟩ ≡   **749**
```
Vector3f wLight = Normalize(renderFromLight.ApplyInverse(-wi));
SampledSpectrum Li = I(wLight, lambda) / DistanceSquared(p, ctx.p());
```

As with point lights, the SpotLight's PDF_Li() method always returns zero. It is not included here.

To compute the spotlight's strength for a direction leaving the light, the first step is to compute the cosine of the angle between that direction and the vector along the center of the spotlight's cone. Because the spotlight is oriented to point down the +*z* axis, the CosTheta() function can be used to do so.

The SmoothStep() function is then used to modulate the emission according to the cosine of the angle: it returns 0 if the provided value is below cosFalloffEnd, 1 if it is above cosFalloffStart, and it interpolates between 0 and 1 for intermediate values using a cubic curve. (To understand its usage, keep in mind that for $\theta \in [0, \pi]$, as is the case here, if $\theta > \theta'$, then $\cos \theta < \cos \theta'$.)

⟨*SpotLight Method Definitions*⟩ ≡
```
SampledSpectrum SpotLight::I(Vector3f w, SampledWavelengths lambda) const {
    return SmoothStep(CosTheta(w), cosFalloffEnd, cosFalloffStart) *
            scale * Iemit->Sample(lambda);
}
```

To compute the power emitted by a spotlight, it is necessary to integrate the falloff function over the sphere. In spherical coordinates, θ and ϕ are separable, so we just need to integrate over θ and scale the result by 2π. For the part that lies inside the inner cone of full power, we have

$$\int_0^{\theta_{\text{start}}} \sin \theta \; d\theta = 1 - \cos \theta_{\text{start}}.$$

The falloff region works out simply, thanks in part to SmoothStep() being a polynomial.

$$\int_{\theta_{\text{start}}}^{\theta_{\text{end}}} \text{smoothstep}(\cos \theta, \theta_{\text{end}}, \theta_{\text{start}}) \sin \theta \; d\theta = \frac{\cos \theta_{\text{start}} - \cos \theta_{\text{end}}}{2}.$$

⟨*SpotLight Method Definitions*⟩ +≡
```
SampledSpectrum SpotLight::Phi(SampledWavelengths lambda) const {
    return scale * Iemit->Sample(lambda) * 2 * Pi *
            ((1 - cosFalloffStart) + (cosFalloffStart - cosFalloffEnd) / 2);
}
```

12.2.2 TEXTURE PROJECTION LIGHTS

Another useful light source acts like a slide projector; it takes an image map and projects its image out into the scene. The ProjectionLight class uses a projective transformation to project points in the scene onto the light's projection plane based on the field of view angle given to the constructor (Figure 12.6).

The use of this light in the lighting example scene is shown in Figure 12.7.

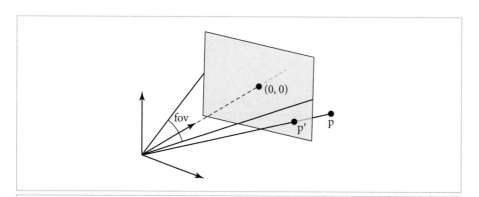

Figure 12.6: The Basic Setting for Projection Light Sources. A point p in the light's coordinate system is projected onto the plane of the image using the light's projection matrix.

Figure 12.7: Scene Rendered with a Projection Light Using a Grid Image. The projection light acts like a slide projector, projecting an image onto objects in the scene. *(Dragon model courtesy of the Stanford Computer Graphics Laboratory.)*

⟨*ProjectionLight Definition*⟩ ≡
```
class ProjectionLight : public LightBase {
  public:
    ⟨ProjectionLight Public Methods⟩
  private:
    ⟨ProjectionLight Private Members 751⟩
};
```

This light could use a Texture to represent the light projection distribution so that procedural projection patterns could be used. However, having a tabularized representation of the projection function makes it easier to sample with probability proportional to the projection function. Therefore, the Image class is used to specify the projection pattern.

⟨*ProjectionLight Method Definitions*⟩ ≡
```
ProjectionLight::ProjectionLight(
        Transform renderFromLight, MediumInterface mediumInterface,
        Image im, const RGBColorSpace *imageColorSpace, Float scale,
        Float fov, Allocator alloc)
    : LightBase(LightType::DeltaPosition, renderFromLight, mediumInterface),
        image(std::move(im)), imageColorSpace(imageColorSpace), scale(scale),
        distrib(alloc) {
    ⟨ProjectionLight constructor implementation 752⟩
}
```

A color space for the image is stored so that it is possible to convert image RGB values to spectra.

⟨*ProjectionLight Private Members*⟩ ≡   751
```
Image image;
const RGBColorSpace *imageColorSpace;
Float scale;
```

The constructor has more work to do than the ones we have seen so far, including initializing a projection matrix and computing the area of the projected image on the projection plane.

⟨ProjectionLight *constructor implementation*⟩ ≡   751
    ⟨*Initialize* ProjectionLight *projection matrix* 752⟩
    ⟨*Compute projection image area* A 752⟩
    ⟨*Compute sampling distribution for* ProjectionLight⟩

First, similar to the PerspectiveCamera, the ProjectionLight constructor computes a projection matrix and the screen space extent of the projection on the $z = 1$ plane.

⟨*Initialize* ProjectionLight *projection matrix*⟩ ≡   752
```
Float aspect = Float(image.Resolution().x) / Float(image.Resolution().y);
if (aspect > 1)
    screenBounds = Bounds2f(Point2f(-aspect, -1), Point2f(aspect, 1));
else
    screenBounds = Bounds2f(Point2f(-1, -1/aspect), Point2f(1, 1/aspect));
screenFromLight = Perspective(fov, hither, 1e30f /* yon */);
lightFromScreen = Inverse(screenFromLight);
```

Since there is no particular need to keep ProjectionLights compact, both of the screen–light transformations are stored explicitly, which makes code in the following that uses them more succinct.

⟨ProjectionLight *Private Members*⟩ +≡   751
```
Bounds2f screenBounds;
Float hither = 1e-3f;
Transform screenFromLight, lightFromScreen;
```

For a number of the following methods, we will need the light-space area of the image on the $z = 1$ plane. One way to find this is to compute half of one of the two rectangle edge lengths using the projection's field of view and to use the fact that the plane is a distance of 1 from the camera's position. Doubling that gives one edge length and the other can be found using a factor based on the aspect ratio; see Figure 12.8.

⟨*Compute projection image area* A⟩ ≡   752
```
Float opposite = std::tan(Radians(fov) / 2);
A = 4 * Sqr(opposite) * (aspect > 1 ? aspect : (1 / aspect));
```

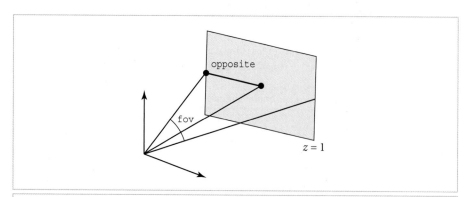

Figure 12.8: The first step of computing the light-space area of the image on the $z = 1$ projection plane is to compute the length opposite illustrated here. It is easily found using basic trigonometry.

⟨*ProjectionLight Private Members*⟩ +≡   751
    Float A;

The ProjectionLight::SampleLi() follows the same form as SpotLight::SampleLi() except that it uses the following I() method to compute the spectral intensity of the projected image. We will therefore skip over its implementation here. We will also not include the PDF_Li() method's implementation, as it, too, returns 0.

The direction passed to the I() method should be normalized and already transformed into the light's coordinate system.

⟨*ProjectionLight Method Definitions*⟩ +≡
    SampledSpectrum ProjectionLight::I(Vector3f w,
        const SampledWavelengths &lambda) const {
      ⟨*Discard directions behind projection light* 753⟩
      ⟨*Project point onto projection plane and compute RGB* 753⟩
      ⟨*Return scaled wavelength samples corresponding to RGB* 754⟩
    }

Because the projective transformation has the property that it projects points behind the center of projection to points in front of it, it is important to discard points with a negative z value. Therefore, the projection code immediately returns no illumination for projection points that are behind the hither plane for the projection. If this check were not done, then it would not be possible to know if a projected point was originally behind the light (and therefore not illuminated) or in front of it.

⟨*Discard directions behind projection light*⟩ ≡   753
    if (w.z < hither)
        return SampledSpectrum(0.f);

After being projected to the projection plane, points with coordinate values outside the screen window are discarded. Points that pass this test are transformed to get texture coordinates inside $[0, 1]^2$ for the lookup in the image.

One thing to note is that a "nearest" lookup is used rather than, say, bilinear interpolation of the image samples. Although bilinear interpolation would lead to smoother results, especially for low-resolution image maps, in this way the projection function will exactly match the piecewise-constant distribution that is used for importance sampling in the light emission sampling methods. Further, the code here assumes that the image stores red, green, and blue in its first three channels; the code that creates ProjectionLights ensures that this is so.

⟨*Project point onto projection plane and compute RGB*⟩ ≡   753
    Point3f ps = screenFromLight(Point3f(w));
    if (!Inside(Point2f(ps.x, ps.y), screenBounds))
        return SampledSpectrum(0.f);
    Point2f uv = Point2f(screenBounds.Offset(Point2f(ps.x, ps.y)));
    RGB rgb;
    for (int c = 0; c < 3; ++c)
        rgb[c] = image.LookupNearestChannel(uv, c);

It is important to use an RGBIlluminantSpectrum to convert the RGB value to spectral samples rather than, say, an RGBUnboundedSpectrum. This ensures that, for example, a (1, 1, 1) RGB value corresponds to the color space's illuminant and not a constant spectral distribution.

⟨*Return scaled wavelength samples corresponding to RGB*⟩ ≡   **753**
```
RGBIlluminantSpectrum s(*imageColorSpace, ClampZero(rgb));
return scale * s.Sample(lambda);
```

The total emitted power is given by integrating radiant intensity over the sphere of directions (Equation (4.2)), though here the projection function is tabularized over a planar 2D area. Power can thus be computed by integrating over the area of the image and applying a change of variables factor $d\omega/dA$:

$$\Phi = \int_{\mathbb{S}^2} I(\omega) \, d\omega = \int_A I(p) \, \frac{d\omega}{dA} \, dA.$$

⟨*ProjectionLight Method Definitions*⟩ +≡
```
SampledSpectrum ProjectionLight::Phi(SampledWavelengths lambda) const {
    SampledSpectrum sum(0.f);
    for (int y = 0; y < image.Resolution().y; ++y)
        for (int x = 0; x < image.Resolution().x; ++x) {
            ⟨Compute change of variables factor dwdA for projection light pixel 754⟩
            ⟨Update sum for projection light pixel 755⟩
        }
    ⟨Return final power for projection light 755⟩
}
```

Recall from Section 4.2.3 that differential area dA is converted to differential solid angle $d\omega$ by multiplying by a $\cos\theta$ factor and dividing by the squared distance. Because the plane we are integrating over is at $z = 1$, the distance from the origin to a point on the plane is equal to $1/\cos\theta$ and thus the aggregate factor is $\cos^3\theta$; see Figure 12.9.

⟨*Compute change of variables factor* dwdA *for projection light pixel*⟩ ≡   **754**
```
Point2f ps = screenBounds.Lerp(Point2f((x + 0.5f) / image.Resolution().x,
                                       (y + 0.5f) / image.Resolution().y));
Vector3f w = Vector3f(lightFromScreen(Point3f(ps.x, ps.y, 0)));
w = Normalize(w);
Float dwdA = Pow<3>(CosTheta(w));
```

For the same reasons as in the Project() method, an RGBIlluminantSpectrum is used to convert each RGB value to spectral samples.

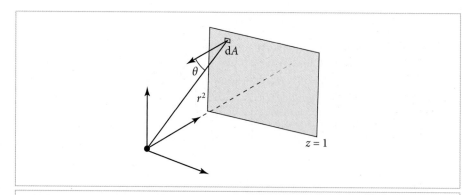

Figure 12.9: To find the power of a point light source, we generally integrate radiant intensity over directions around the light. For the ProjectionLight, we instead integrate over the $z = 1$ plane, in which case we need to account for the change of variables, applying both a $\cos\theta$ and a $1/r^2$ factor.

⟨*Update* sum *for projection light pixel*⟩ ≡   754
```
RGB rgb;
for (int c = 0; c < 3; ++c)
    rgb[c] = image.GetChannel({x, y}, c);
RGBIlluminantSpectrum s(*imageColorSpace, ClampZero(rgb));
sum += s.Sample(lambda) * dwdA;
```

The final integrated value includes a factor of the area that was integrated over, A, and is divided by the total number of pixels.

⟨*Return final power for projection light*⟩ ≡   754
```
return scale * A * sum / (image.Resolution().x * image.Resolution().y);
```

12.2.3 GONIOPHOTOMETRIC DIAGRAM LIGHTS

A *goniophotometric diagram* describes the angular distribution of luminance from a point light source; it is widely used in illumination engineering to characterize lights. Figure 12.10 shows an example of a goniophotometric diagram in two dimensions. In this section, we will implement a light source that uses goniophotometric diagrams encoded in 2D image maps to describe the emission distribution lights.

Figure 12.11 shows a few goniophotometric diagrams encoded as image maps and Figure 12.12 shows a scene rendered with a light source that uses one of these images to modulate

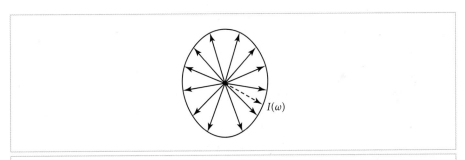

Figure 12.10: An Example of a Goniophotometric Diagram Specifying an Outgoing Light Distribution from a Point Light Source in 2D. The emitted intensity is defined in a fixed set of directions on the unit sphere, and the intensity for a given outgoing direction ω is found by interpolating the intensities of the adjacent samples.

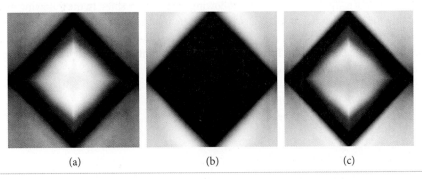

(a)   (b)   (c)

Figure 12.11: Goniophotometric Diagrams for Real-World Light Sources. These images are encoded using an equal-area parameterization (Section 3.8.3). (a) A light that mostly illuminates in its up direction, with only a small amount of illumination in the down direction. (b) A light that mostly illuminates in the down direction. (c) A light that casts illumination both above and below.

Figure 12.12: Scene Rendered Using the Goniophotometric Diagram from Figure 12.11(b). Even though a point light source is the basis of this light, including the directional variation of a realistic light improves the visual realism of the rendered image. *(Dragon model courtesy of the Stanford Computer Graphics Laboratory.)*

its directional distribution of illumination. The GoniometricLight uses the equal-area parameterization of the sphere that was introduced in Section 3.8.3, so the center of the image corresponds to the "up" direction.

⟨*GoniometricLight Definition*⟩ ≡
```
class GoniometricLight : public LightBase {
  public:
    ⟨GoniometricLight Public Methods 757⟩
  private:
    ⟨GoniometricLight Private Members 756⟩
};
```

The GoniometricLight constructor takes a base intensity, an image map that scales the intensity based on the angular distribution of light, and the usual transformation and medium interface; these are stored in the following member variables. In the following methods, only the first channel of the image map will be used to scale the light's intensity: the GoniometricLight does not support specifying color via the image. It is the responsibility of calling code to convert RGB images to luminance or some other appropriate scalar value before passing the image to the constructor here.

⟨*GoniometricLight Private Members*⟩ ≡   **756**
```
const DenselySampledSpectrum *Iemit;
Float scale;
Image image;
```

The SampleLi() method follows the same form as that of SpotLight and ProjectionLight, so it is not included here. It uses the following method to compute the radiant intensity for a given direction.

```
SampledSpectrum I(Vector3f w, const SampledWavelengths &lambda) const {
    Point2f uv = EqualAreaSphereToSquare(w);
    return scale * Iemit->Sample(lambda) * image.LookupNearestChannel(uv, 0);
}
```

Because it uses an equal-area mapping from the image to the sphere, each pixel in the image subtends an equal solid angle and the change of variables factor for integrating over the sphere of directions is the same for all pixels. Its value is 4π, the ratio of the area of the unit sphere to the unit square.

⟨*GoniometricLight Method Definitions*⟩ ≡
```
SampledSpectrum GoniometricLight::Phi(SampledWavelengths lambda) const {
    Float sumY = 0;
    for (int y = 0; y < image.Resolution().y; ++y)
        for (int x = 0; x < image.Resolution().x; ++x)
            sumY += image.GetChannel({x, y}, 0);
    return scale * Iemit->Sample(lambda) * 4 * Pi * sumY /
            (image.Resolution().x * image.Resolution().y);
}
```

12.3 DISTANT LIGHTS

Another useful light source type is the *distant light*, also known as a *directional light*. It describes an emitter that deposits illumination from the same direction at every point in space. Such a light is also called a point light "at infinity," since, as a point light becomes progressively farther away, it acts more and more like a directional light. For example, the sun (as considered from Earth) can be thought of as a directional light source. Although it is actually an area light source, the illumination effectively arrives at Earth in nearly parallel beams because it is so far away.

⟨*DistantLight Definition*⟩ ≡
```
class DistantLight : public LightBase {
  public:
    ⟨DistantLight Public Methods 757⟩
  private:
    ⟨DistantLight Private Members 757⟩
};
```

The DistantLight constructor does not take a MediumInterface parameter; the only reasonable medium for a distant light to be in is a vacuum—if it was itself in a medium that absorbed any light at all, then all of its emission would be absorbed, since it is modeled as being infinitely far away.

⟨*DistantLight Public Methods*⟩ ≡   757
```
DistantLight(const Transform &renderFromLight, Spectrum Lemit,
             Float scale)
    : LightBase(LightType::DeltaDirection, renderFromLight, {}),
      Lemit(LookupSpectrum(Lemit)), scale(scale) {}
```

⟨*DistantLight Private Members*⟩ ≡   757
```
const DenselySampledSpectrum *Lemit;
Float scale;
```

Some of the `DistantLight` methods need to know the bounds of the scene. Because pbrt creates lights before the scene geometry, these bounds are not available when the `DistantLight` constructor executes. Therefore, `DistantLight` implements the optional `Preprocess()` method where it converts the scene's `Bounds3f` to a bounding sphere, which will be an easier representation to work with in the following.

⟨*DistantLight Public Methods*⟩ +≡   757
```
void Preprocess(const Bounds3f &sceneBounds) {
    sceneBounds.BoundingSphere(&sceneCenter, &sceneRadius);
}
```

⟨*DistantLight Private Members*⟩ +≡   757
```
Point3f sceneCenter;
Float sceneRadius;
```

The incident radiance at a point p due to a distant light can be described using a Dirac delta distribution,

$$L_i(p, \omega) = L_e \, \delta(\omega - \omega_l),$$

where the light's direction is ω_l. Given this definition, the implementation of the `SampleLi()` method is straightforward: the incident direction and radiance are always the same. The only interesting bit is the initialization of the `Interaction` that provides the second point for the future shadow ray. It is set along the distant light's incident direction at a distance of twice the radius of the scene's bounding sphere, guaranteeing a second point that is outside of the scene's bounds (Figure 12.13).

⟨*DistantLight Public Methods*⟩ +≡   757
```
pstd::optional<LightLiSample>
SampleLi(LightSampleContext ctx, Point2f u, SampledWavelengths lambda,
        bool allowIncompletePDF) const {
    Vector3f wi = Normalize(renderFromLight(Vector3f(0, 0, 1)));
    Point3f pOutside = ctx.p() + wi * (2 * sceneRadius);
    return LightLiSample(scale * Lemit->Sample(lambda), wi, 1,
                         Interaction(pOutside, nullptr));
}
```

Bounds3::BoundingSphere()
  103
Bounds3f 97
DenselySampledSpectrum::
  Sample()
  167
DistantLight::Lemit 757
DistantLight::scale 757
DistantLight::sceneCenter
  758
DistantLight::sceneRadius
  758
Float 23
Interaction 136
LightBase::renderFromLight
  745
LightLiSample 743
LightSampleContext 741
LightSampleContext::p() 742
Normalize() 88
Point2f 92
Point3f 92
SampledWavelengths 173
Transform::operator() 130
Vector3f 86

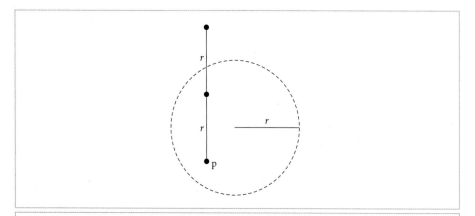

Figure 12.13: Computing the Second Point for a `DistantLight` Shadow Ray. Given a sphere that bounds the scene (dashed line) with radius *r* and given some point in the scene p, if we then move a distance of 2*r* along any vector from p, the resulting point must be outside of the scene's bound. If a shadow ray to such a point is unoccluded, then we can be certain that the point p receives illumination from a distant light along the vector's direction.

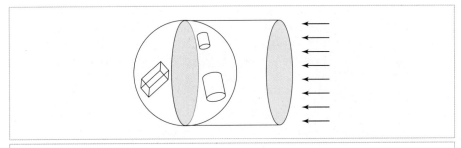

Figure 12.14: An approximation of the power emitted by a distant light into a given scene can be obtained by finding the sphere that bounds the scene, computing the area of an inscribed disk, and computing the power that arrives on the surface of that disk.

The distant light is different than the lights we have seen so far in that the amount of power it emits is related to the spatial extent of the scene. In fact, it is proportional to the area of the scene receiving light. To see why this is so, consider a disk of area A being illuminated by a distant light with emitted radiance L where the incident light arrives along the disk's normal direction. The total power reaching the disk is $\Phi = AL$. As the size of the receiving surface varies, power varies proportionally.

To find the emitted power for a `DistantLight`, it is impractical to compute the total surface area of the objects that are visible to the light. Instead, we will approximate this area with a disk inside the scene's bounding sphere oriented in the light's direction (Figure 12.14). This will always overestimate the actual area but is sufficient for the needs of code elsewhere in the system.

⟨*DistantLight Method Definitions*⟩ ≡
```
SampledSpectrum DistantLight::Phi(SampledWavelengths lambda) const {
    return scale * Lemit->Sample(lambda) * Pi * Sqr(sceneRadius);
}
```

12.4 AREA LIGHTS

Area lights are defined by the combination of a `Shape` and a directional distribution of radiance at each point on its surface. In general, computing radiometric quantities related to area lights requires computing integrals over the surface of the light that often cannot be computed in closed form, though they are well suited to Monte Carlo integration. The reward for this complexity (and computational expense) is soft shadows and more realistic lighting effects, rather than the hard shadows and stark lighting that come from point lights. (See Figure 12.15, which shows the effect of varying the size of an area light source used to illuminate the dragon; compare its soft look to illumination from a point light in Figure 12.3.)

The `DiffuseAreaLight` class defines an area light where emission at each point on the surface has a uniform directional distribution.

⟨*DiffuseAreaLight Definition*⟩ ≡
```
class DiffuseAreaLight : public LightBase {
  public:
    ⟨DiffuseAreaLight Public Methods 761⟩
  private:
    ⟨DiffuseAreaLight Private Members 761⟩
    ⟨DiffuseAreaLight Private Methods 762⟩
};
```

(a)

(b)

Figure 12.15: Dragon Model Illuminated by Disk Area Lights. (a) The disk's radius is relatively small; the shadow has soft penumbrae, but otherwise the image looks similar to the one with a point light. (b) The effect of using a much larger disk: not only have the penumbrae become much larger, to the point of nearly eliminating the shadow of the tail, for example, but note also how the shading on the body is smoother, with the specular highlights less visible due to illumination coming from a wider range of directions. *(Dragon model courtesy of the Stanford Computer Graphics Laboratory.)*

Its constructor, not included here, sets the following member variables from the parameters provided to it. If an `alpha` texture has been associated with the shape to cut away parts of its surface, it is used here so that there is no illumination from those parts of the shape.[1] (Recall that alpha masking was introduced in Section 7.1.1.) The area of the emissive Shape is needed in a number of the following methods and so is cached in a member variable.

---

1   As a special case, pbrt also (reluctantly) supports the trick of creating an invisible light source by specifying a light with a zero-valued alpha texture. Though non-physical, such lights can be useful for artistic purposes. In code not included in the text here, the `DiffuseAreaLight` constructor characterizes them as being of `LightType::DeltaPosition`, which leads to their being handled correctly in the lighting integration routines even though rays can never intersect them.

⟨*DiffuseAreaLight Private Members*⟩ ≡   759
```
Shape shape;
FloatTexture alpha;
Float area;
```

A number of parameters specify emission from DiffuseAreaLights. By default, emission is only on one side of the surface, where the surface normal is outward-facing. A scaling transform that flips the normal or the ReverseOrientation directive in the scene description file can be used to cause emission to be on the other side of the surface. If twoSided is true, then the light emits on both sides.

Emission that varies over the surface can be defined using an Image; if one is provided to the constructor, the surface will have spatially varying emission defined by its color values. Otherwise, spatially uniform emitted spectral radiance is given by a provided Lemit spectrum. For both methods of specifying emission, an additional scale factor in scale is applied to the returned radiance.

⟨*DiffuseAreaLight Private Members*⟩ +≡   759
```
bool twoSided;
const DenselySampledSpectrum *Lemit;
Float scale;
Image image;
const RGBColorSpace *imageColorSpace;
```

Recall from Section 12.1 that the Light interface includes an L() method that area lights must implement to provide the emitted radiance at a specified point on their surface. This method is called if a ray happens to intersect an emissive surface, for example. DiffuseAreaLight's implementation starts by checking a few cases in which there is no emitted radiance before calculating emission using the Image, if provided, and otherwise the specified constant radiance.

⟨*DiffuseAreaLight Public Methods*⟩ ≡   759
```
SampledSpectrum L(Point3f p, Normal3f n, Point2f uv, Vector3f w,
                  const SampledWavelengths &lambda) const {
    ⟨Check for zero emitted radiance from point on area light 761⟩
    if (image) {
        ⟨Return DiffuseAreaLight emission using image 762⟩
    } else
        return scale * Lemit->Sample(lambda);
}
```

Two cases allow immediately returning no emitted radiance: the first is if the light is one-sided and the outgoing direction ω faces away from the surface normal and the second is if the point on the light's surface has been cut away by an alpha texture.

⟨*Check for zero emitted radiance from point on area light*⟩ ≡   761
```
if (!twoSided && Dot(n, w) < 0)
    return SampledSpectrum(0.f);
if (AlphaMasked(Interaction(p, uv)))
    return SampledSpectrum(0.f);
```

The AlphaMasked() method performs a stochastic alpha test for a point on the light.

⟨*DiffuseAreaLight Private Methods*⟩ ≡   759
```
bool AlphaMasked(const Interaction &intr) const {
    if (!alpha) return false;
    Float a = UniversalTextureEvaluator()(alpha, intr);
    if (a >= 1) return false;
    if (a <= 0) return true;
    return HashFloat(intr.p()) > a;
}
```

If an `Image` has been provided to specify emission, then the emitted radiance is found by looking up an RGB value and converting it to the requested spectral samples. Note that the v coordinate is inverted before being passed to `BilerpChannel()`; in this way, the parameterization matches the image texture coordinate conventions that were described in Section 10.4.2. (See Figure 6.26 for a scene with an area light source with emission defined using an image.)

⟨*Return* `DiffuseAreaLight` *emission using image*⟩ ≡   761
```
RGB rgb;
uv[1] = 1 - uv[1];
for (int c = 0; c < 3; ++c)
    rgb[c] = image.BilerpChannel(uv, c);
RGBIlluminantSpectrum spec(*imageColorSpace, ClampZero(rgb));
return scale * spec.Sample(lambda);
```

For convenience, we will add a method to the `SurfaceInteraction` class that makes it easy to compute the emitted radiance at a surface point intersected by a ray.

⟨*SurfaceInteraction Method Definitions*⟩ +≡
```
SampledSpectrum SurfaceInteraction::Le(Vector3f w,
        const SampledWavelengths &lambda) const {
    return areaLight ? areaLight.L(p(), n, uv, w, lambda)
                     : SampledSpectrum(0.f);
}
```

All the `SampleLi()` methods so far have been deterministic: because all the preceding light models have been defined in terms of Dirac delta distributions of either position or direction, there has only been a single incident direction along which illumination arrives at any point. This is no longer the case with area lights and we will finally make use of the uniform 2D sample u.

⟨*DiffuseAreaLight Method Definitions*⟩ ≡
```
pstd::optional<LightLiSample>
DiffuseAreaLight::SampleLi(LightSampleContext ctx, Point2f u,
        SampledWavelengths lambda, bool allowIncompletePDF) const {
    ⟨Sample point on shape for DiffuseAreaLight 763⟩
    ⟨Check sampled point on shape against alpha texture, if present 763⟩
    ⟨Return LightLiSample for sampled point on shape 763⟩
}
```

The second variant of `Shape::Sample()`, which takes a receiving point and returns a point on the shape and PDF expressed with respect to solid angle at the receiving point, is an exact match for the `Light SampleLi()` interface. Therefore, the implementation starts by calling that method.

The astute reader will note that if an image is being used to define the light's emission, leaving the sampling task to the shape alone may not be ideal. Yet, extending the Shape's sampling interface to optionally take a reference to an Image or some other representation of spatially varying emission would be a clunky addition. pbrt's solution to this problem is that BilinearPatch shapes (but no others) allow specifying an image to use for sampling. To have to specify this information twice in the scene description is admittedly not ideal, but it suffices to make the common case of a quadrilateral emitter with an image work out.

⟨*Sample point on shape for* DiffuseAreaLight⟩ ≡   762
```
ShapeSampleContext shapeCtx(ctx.pi, ctx.n, ctx.ns, 0 /* time */);
pstd::optional<ShapeSample> ss = shape.Sample(shapeCtx, u);
if (!ss || ss->pdf == 0 || LengthSquared(ss->intr.p() - ctx.p()) == 0)
    return {};
ss->intr.mediumInterface = &mediumInterface;
```

If the sampled point has been masked by the alpha texture, an invalid sample is returned.

⟨*Check sampled point on shape against alpha texture, if present*⟩ ≡   762
```
if (AlphaMasked(ss->intr))
    return {};
```

If the shape has generated a valid sample, the next step is to compute the emitted radiance at the sample point. If that is a zero-valued spectrum, then an unset sample value is returned; calling code can then avoid the expense of tracing an unnecessary shadow ray.

⟨*Return* LightLiSample *for sampled point on shape*⟩ ≡   762
```
Vector3f wi = Normalize(ss->intr.p() - ctx.p());
SampledSpectrum Le = L(ss->intr.p(), ss->intr.n, ss->intr.uv, -wi, lambda);
if (!Le) return {};
return LightLiSample(Le, wi, ss->pdf, ss->intr);
```

The PDF for sampling a given direction from a receiving point is also easily handled, again thanks to Shape providing a corresponding method.

⟨*DiffuseAreaLight Method Definitions*⟩ +≡
```
Float DiffuseAreaLight::PDF_Li(LightSampleContext ctx, Vector3f wi,
                              bool allowIncompletePDF) const {
    ShapeSampleContext shapeCtx(ctx.pi, ctx.n, ctx.ns, 0 /* time */);
    return shape.PDF(shapeCtx, wi);
}
```

Emitted power from an area light with uniform emitted radiance over the surface can be computed in closed form: from Equation (4.1) it follows that it is π times the surface area times the emitted radiance. If an image has been specified for the emission, its average value is computed in a fragment that is not included here. That computation neglects the effect of any alpha texture and effectively assumes that there is no distortion in the surface's (u, v) parameterization. If these are not the case, there will be error in the Φ value.

⟨*DiffuseAreaLight Method Definitions*⟩ +≡
```
SampledSpectrum DiffuseAreaLight::Phi(SampledWavelengths lambda) const {
    SampledSpectrum L(0.f);
    if (image) {
        ⟨Compute average light image emission⟩
    } else
        L = Lemit->Sample(lambda) * scale;
    return Pi * (twoSided ? 2 : 1) * area * L;
}
```

(a)

(b)

(c)

Figure 12.16: Car model (a) illuminated with a few area lights, (b) illuminated with midday skylight from an environment map, (c) using a sunset environment map. *(Model courtesy of Yasutoshi Mori.)*

12.5 INFINITE AREA LIGHTS

Another useful kind of light is an infinitely far-away area light source that surrounds the entire scene. One way to visualize this type of light is as an enormous sphere that casts light into the scene from every direction. One important use of infinite area lights is for *environment lighting*, where an image of the illumination in an environment is used to illuminate synthetic objects as if they were in that environment. Figure 12.16 compares illuminating a car model with standard area lights to illuminating it with two environment maps that simulate illumination from the sky at different times of day. The increase in realism is striking.

pbrt provides three implementations of infinite area lights of progressive complexity. The first describes an infinite light with uniform emitted radiance; the second instead takes an image that represents the directional distribution of emitted radiance, and the third adds capabilities for culling parts of such images that are occluded at the reference point, which can substantially improve sampling efficiency.

12.5.1 UNIFORM INFINITE LIGHTS

A uniform infinite light source is fairly easy to implement; some of the details will be helpful for understanding the infinite light variants to follow.

⟨*UniformInfiniteLight Definition*⟩ ≡
```
class UniformInfiniteLight : public LightBase {
  public:
    ⟨UniformInfiniteLight Public Methods⟩
  private:
    ⟨UniformInfiniteLight Private Members 765⟩
};
```

Emitted radiance is specified as usual by both a spectrum and a separate scale. (The straight-forward constructor that initializes these is not included in the text.)

⟨*UniformInfiniteLight Private Members*⟩ ≡   **765**
```
const DenselySampledSpectrum *Lemit;
Float scale;
```

All the infinite light sources, including `UniformInfiniteLight`, store a bounding sphere of the scene that they use when computing their total power and for sampling rays leaving the light.

⟨*UniformInfiniteLight Private Members*⟩ +≡   **765**
```
Point3f sceneCenter;
Float sceneRadius;
```

Infinite lights must implement the following `Le()` method to return their emitted radiance for a given ray. Since the `UniformInfiniteLight` emits the same amount for all rays, the implementation is trivial.

⟨*UniformInfiniteLight Method Definitions*⟩ ≡
```
SampledSpectrum
UniformInfiniteLight::Le(const Ray &ray,
                         const SampledWavelengths &lambda) const {
    return scale * Lemit->Sample(lambda);
}
```

We can see the use of the `allowIncompletePDF` parameter for the first time in the `SampleLi()` method. If it is true, then `UniformInfiniteLight` immediately returns an unset sample. (And its `PDF_Li()` method, described a bit later, will return a PDF of zero for all directions.) To understand why it is implemented in this way, consider the direct lighting integral

$$\int_{\mathcal{S}^2} f(\mathrm{p}, \omega_\mathrm{o}, \omega_\mathrm{i})\, L_\mathrm{i}(\mathrm{p}, \omega_\mathrm{i})\, |\cos\theta_\mathrm{i}|\, d\omega_\mathrm{i}.$$

For a uniform infinite light, the incident radiance function is a constant times the visibility term; the constant can be pulled out of the integral, leaving

$$c \int_{\mathcal{S}^2} f(\mathrm{p}, \omega_\mathrm{o}, \omega_\mathrm{i})\, |\cos\theta_\mathrm{i}|\, d\omega_\mathrm{i}.$$

There is no reason for the light to participate in sampling this integral, since BSDF sampling accounts for the remaining factors well. Furthermore, recall from Section 2.2.3 that multiple importance sampling (MIS) can increase variance when one of the sampling techniques is much more effective than the others. This is such a case, so as long as calling code is sampling the BSDF and using MIS, samples should not be generated here. (This is an application of MIS compensation, which was introduced in Section 2.2.3.)

⟨*UniformInfiniteLight Method Definitions*⟩ +≡
```
    pstd::optional<LightLiSample>
    UniformInfiniteLight::SampleLi(LightSampleContext ctx, Point2f u,
            SampledWavelengths lambda, bool allowIncompletePDF) const {
        if (allowIncompletePDF) return {};
        ⟨Return uniform spherical sample for uniform infinite light 766⟩
    }
```

If sampling is to be performed, the light generates a sample so that valid Monte Carlo estimates can still be computed. This task is easy—all directions are sampled with uniform probability. Note that the endpoint of the shadow ray is set in the same way as it was by the DistantLight: by computing a point that is certainly outside of the scene's bounds.

⟨*Return uniform spherical sample for uniform infinite light*⟩ ≡   766
```
    Vector3f wi = SampleUniformSphere(u);
    Float pdf = UniformSpherePDF();
    return LightLiSample(scale * Lemit->Sample(lambda), wi, pdf,
        Interaction(ctx.p() + wi * (2 * sceneRadius), &mediumInterface));
```

The PDF_Li() method must account for the value of allowIncompletePDF so that the PDF values it returns are consistent with its sampling method.

⟨*UniformInfiniteLight Method Definitions*⟩ +≡
```
    Float UniformInfiniteLight::PDF_Li(LightSampleContext ctx, Vector3f w,
                                bool allowIncompletePDF) const {
        if (allowIncompletePDF) return 0;
        return UniformSpherePDF();
    }
```

The total power from an infinite light can be found by taking the product of the integral of the incident radiance over all directions times an integral over the area of the disk, along the lines of DistantLight::Phi().

⟨*UniformInfiniteLight Method Definitions*⟩ +≡
```
    SampledSpectrum
    UniformInfiniteLight::Phi(SampledWavelengths lambda) const {
        return 4 * Pi * Pi * Sqr(sceneRadius) * scale * Lemit->Sample(lambda);
    }
```

12.5.2 IMAGE INFINITE LIGHTS

ImageInfiniteLight is a useful infinite light variation that uses an Image to define the directional distribution of emitted radiance. Given an image that represents the distribution of incident radiance in a real-world environment (sometimes called an *environment map*), this light can be used to render objects under the same illumination, which is particularly useful for applications like visual effects for movies, where it is often necessary to composite rendered objects with film footage. (See the "Further Reading" section for information about techniques for capturing this lighting data from real-world environments.) Figure 12.17 shows the image radiance maps used in Figure 12.16.

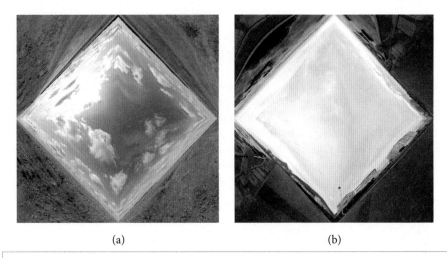

Figure 12.17: Environment Maps Used for Illumination in Figure 12.16. All use the octahedral mapping and equal-area parameterization of the sphere from Section 3.8.3. (a) Midday and (b) sunset sky. *(Midday environment map courtesy of Sergej Majboroda, sunset environment map courtesy of Greg Zaal, both via Poly Haven.)*

⟨*ImageInfiniteLight Definition*⟩ ≡
```
class ImageInfiniteLight : public LightBase {
  public:
    ⟨ImageInfiniteLight Public Methods 768⟩
  private:
    ⟨ImageInfiniteLight Private Methods 769⟩
    ⟨ImageInfiniteLight Private Members 767⟩
};
```

The image that specifies the emission distribution should use the equal-area octahedral parameterization of directions that was defined in Section 3.8.3. The LightBase::renderFrom Light transformation can be used to orient the environment map.

⟨*ImageInfiniteLight Private Members*⟩ ≡   767
```
Image image;
const RGBColorSpace *imageColorSpace;
Float scale;
```

Like UniformInfiniteLights, ImageInfiniteLights also need the scene bounds; here again, the Preprocess() method (this one not included in the text) stores the scene's bounding sphere after all the scene geometry has been created.

⟨*ImageInfiniteLight Private Members*⟩ +≡   767
```
Point3f sceneCenter;
Float sceneRadius;
```

The ImageInfiniteLight constructor contains a fair amount of boilerplate code that we will skip past. (For example, it verifies that the provided image has channels named "R," "G," and "B" and issues an error if it does not.) The interesting parts of it are gathered in the following fragment.

⟨*ImageInfiniteLight constructor implementation*⟩ ≡
    ⟨*Initialize sampling PDFs for image infinite area light* 768⟩
    ⟨*Initialize compensated PDF for image infinite area light* 768⟩

The image maps used with ImageInfiniteLights often have substantial variation along different directions: consider, for example, an environment map of the sky during daytime, where the relatively small number of directions that the sun subtends are thousands of times brighter than the rest of the directions. Therefore, implementing a sampling method for ImageInfiniteLights that matches the illumination distribution can significantly reduce variance in rendered images compared to sampling directions uniformly. To this end, the constructor initializes a PiecewiseConstant2D distribution that is proportional to the image pixel values.

⟨*Initialize sampling PDFs for image infinite area light*⟩ ≡   768
    Array2D<Float> d = image.GetSamplingDistribution();
    Bounds2f domain = Bounds2f(Point2f(0, 0), Point2f(1, 1));
    distribution = PiecewiseConstant2D(d, domain, alloc);

⟨*ImageInfiniteLight Private Members*⟩ +≡   767
    PiecewiseConstant2D distribution;

A second sampling distribution is computed based on a thresholded version of the image where the average pixel value is subtracted from each pixel's sampling weight. The use of both of these sampling distributions will be discussed in more detail shortly, with the implementation of the SampleLi() method.

⟨*Initialize compensated PDF for image infinite area light*⟩ ≡   768
    Float average = std::accumulate(d.begin(), d.end(), 0.) / d.size();
    for (Float &v : d)
        v = std::max<Float>(v - average, 0);
    compensatedDistribution = PiecewiseConstant2D(d, domain, alloc);

⟨*ImageInfiniteLight Private Members*⟩ +≡   767
    PiecewiseConstant2D compensatedDistribution;

Before we get to the sampling methods, we will provide an implementation of the Le() method that is required by the Light interface for infinite lights. After computing the 2D coordinates of the provided ray's direction in image coordinates, it defers to the ImageLe() method.

⟨*ImageInfiniteLight Public Methods*⟩ ≡   767
    SampledSpectrum Le(const Ray &ray, const SampledWavelengths &lambda) const {
        Vector3f wLight = Normalize(renderFromLight.ApplyInverse(ray.d));
        Point2f uv = EqualAreaSphereToSquare(wLight);
        return ImageLe(uv, lambda);
    }

ImageLe() returns the emitted radiance for a given point in the image.

⟨ImageInfiniteLight Private Methods⟩ ≡   767
```
SampledSpectrum ImageLe(Point2f uv,
                           const SampledWavelengths &lambda) const {
    RGB rgb;
    for (int c = 0; c < 3; ++c)
        rgb[c] = image.LookupNearestChannel(uv, c,
                                            WrapMode::OctahedralSphere);
    RGBIlluminantSpectrum spec(*imageColorSpace, ClampZero(rgb));
    return scale * spec.Sample(lambda);
}
```

There is a bit more work to do for sampling an incident direction at a reference point according to the light's emitted radiance.

⟨ImageInfiniteLight Public Methods⟩ +≡   767
```
pstd::optional<LightLiSample>
SampleLi(LightSampleContext ctx, Point2f u, SampledWavelengths lambda,
        bool allowIncompletePDF) const {
    ⟨Find (u, v) sample coordinates in infinite light texture  769⟩
    ⟨Convert infinite light sample point to direction  769⟩
    ⟨Compute PDF for sampled infinite light direction  770⟩
    ⟨Return radiance value for infinite light direction  770⟩
}
```

The first step is to generate an image sample with probability proportional to the image pixel values, which is a task that is handled by the PiecewiseConstant2D Sample() method. If SampleLi() is called with allowIncompletePDF being true, then the second sampling distribution that was based on the thresholded image is used. The motivation for doing so is the same as when UniformInfiniteLight::SampleLi() does not generate samples at all in that case: here, there is no reason to spend samples in parts of the image that have a relatively low contribution. It is better to let other sampling techniques (e.g., BSDF sampling) generate samples in those directions when they are actually important for the full function being integrated. Light samples are then allocated to the bright parts of the image, where they are more useful.

⟨Find (u, v) sample coordinates in infinite light texture⟩ ≡   769
```
Float mapPDF = 0;
Point2f uv;
if (allowIncompletePDF)
    uv = compensatedDistribution.Sample(u, &mapPDF);
else
    uv = distribution.Sample(u, &mapPDF);
if (mapPDF == 0)
    return {};
```

It is a simple matter to convert from image coordinates to a rendering space direction wi.

⟨Convert infinite light sample point to direction⟩ ≡   769
```
Vector3f wLight = EqualAreaSquareToSphere(uv);
Vector3f wi = renderFromLight(wLight);
```

The PDF returned by `PiecewiseConstant2D::Sample()` is with respect to the image's $[0, 1]^2$ domain. To find the corresponding PDF with respect to direction, the change of variables factor for going from the unit square to the unit sphere $1/(4\pi)$ must be applied.

⟨*Compute PDF for sampled infinite light direction*⟩ ≡   **769**
```
Float pdf = mapPDF / (4 * Pi);
```

Finally, as with the `DistantLight` and `UniformInfiniteLight`, the second point for the shadow ray is found by offsetting along the `wi` direction far enough until that resulting point is certainly outside of the scene's bounds.

⟨*Return radiance value for infinite light direction*⟩ ≡   **769**
```
return LightLiSample(ImageLe(uv, lambda), wi, pdf,
    Interaction(ctx.p() + wi * (2 * sceneRadius), &mediumInterface));
```

Figure 12.18 illustrates how much error is reduced by sampling image infinite lights well. It compares three images of a dragon model illuminated by the morning skylight environment map from Figure 12.17. The first image was rendered using a simple uniform spherical sampling distribution for selecting incident illumination directions, the second used the full image-based sampling distribution, and the third used the compensated distribution— all rendered with 32 samples per pixel. For the same number of samples taken and with negligible additional computational cost, both importance sampling methods give a much better result with much lower variance.

Most of the work to compute the PDF for a provided direction is handled by the `Piecewise Constant2D` distribution. Here as well, the PDF value it returns is divided by 4π to account for the area of the unit sphere.

⟨*ImageInfiniteLight Method Definitions*⟩ ≡
```
Float ImageInfiniteLight::PDF_Li(LightSampleContext ctx, Vector3f w,
                                 bool allowIncompletePDF) const {
    Vector3f wLight = renderFromLight.ApplyInverse(w);
    Point2f uv = EqualAreaSphereToSquare(wLight);
    Float pdf = 0;
    if (allowIncompletePDF)
        pdf = compensatedDistribution.PDF(uv);
    else
        pdf = distribution.PDF(uv);
    return pdf / (4 * Pi);
}
```

The `ImageInfiniteLight::Phi()` method, not included here, integrates incident radiance over the sphere by looping over all the image pixels and summing them before multiplying by a factor of 4π to account for the area of the unit sphere as well as by the area of a disk of radius `sceneRadius`.

★ 12.5.3 PORTAL IMAGE INFINITE LIGHTS

`ImageInfiniteLights` provide a handy sort of light source, though one shortcoming of that class's implementation is that it does not account for visibility in its sampling routines. Samples that it generates that turn out to be occluded are much less useful than those that do carry illumination to the reference point. While the expense of ray tracing is necessary to fully account for visibility, accounting for even some visibility effects in light sampling can significantly reduce error.

(a)

(b)

(c)

Figure 12.18: Dragon Model Illuminated by the Morning Skylight Environment Map. All images were rendered with 32 samples per pixel. (a) Rendered using a uniform sampling distribution. (b) Rendered with samples distributed according to environment map image pixels. (c) Rendered using the compensated distribution that skips sampling unimportant parts of the image. All images took essentially the same amount of time to render, though (b) has over 38,000 times lower MSE than (a), and (c) further improves MSE by a factor of 1.52. *(Dragon model courtesy of the Stanford Computer Graphics Laboratory.)*

ImageInfiniteLight 767

Consider the scene shown in Figure 12.19, where all the illumination is coming from a skylight environment map that is visible only through the windows. Part of the scene is directly illuminated by the sun, but much of it is not. Those other parts are still illuminated, but by much less bright regions of blue sky. Yet because the sun is so bright, the ImageInfiniteLight ends up taking many samples in its direction, though all the ones where the sun is not visible

(a)

(b)

Figure 12.19: *Watercolor* **Scene Illuminated by a Daytime Sky Environment Map.** This is a challenging scene to render since the direct lighting calculation only finds illumination when it samples a ray that passes through the window. (a) When rendered with the `ImageInfiniteLight` and 16 samples per pixel, error is high because the environment map includes a bright sun, though it does not illuminate all parts of the room. For such points, none of the many samples taken toward the sun has any contribution. (b) When rendered using the `PortalImageInfiniteLight`, results are much better with the same number of samples because the light is able to sample just the part of the environment map that is visible through the window. In this case, MSE is reduced by a factor of 2.82. *(Scene courtesy of Angelo Ferretti.)*

through the window will be wasted. In those regions of the scene, light sampling will occasionally choose a part of the sky that is visible through the window and occasionally BSDF sampling will find a path to the light through the window, so that the result is still correct in expectation, but many samples may be necessary to achieve a high-quality result.

The PortalImageInfiniteLight is designed to handle this situation more effectively. Given a user-specified *portal*, a quadrilateral region through which the environment map is potentially visible, it generates a custom sampling distribution at each point being shaded so that it can draw samples according to the region of the environment map that is visible through the portal. For an equal number of samples, this can be much more effective than the ImageInfiniteLight's approach, as shown in Figure 12.19(b).

⟨*PortalImageInfiniteLight Definition*⟩ ≡
```
class PortalImageInfiniteLight : public LightBase {
  public:
    ⟨PortalImageInfiniteLight Public Methods⟩
  private:
    ⟨PortalImageInfiniteLight Private Methods 775⟩
    ⟨PortalImageInfiniteLight Private Members 776⟩
};
```

Given a portal and a point in the scene, there is a set of directions from that point that pass through the portal. If we can find the corresponding region of the environment map, then our task is to sample from it according to the environment map's emission. This idea is illustrated in Figure 12.20. With the equal-area mapping, the shape of the visible region of the environment map seen from a given point can be complex. The problem is illustrated in Figure 12.21(a), which visualizes the visible regions from two points in the scene from Figure 12.19.

The PortalImageInfiniteLight therefore uses a different parameterization of directions that causes the visible region seen through a portal to always be rectangular. Later in this section, we will see how this property makes efficient sampling possible.

The directional parameterization used by the PortalImageInfiniteLight is based on a coordinate system where the x and y axes are aligned with the edges of the portal. Note that the position of the portal is not used in defining this coordinate system—only the directions of its edges. As a first indication that this idea is getting us somewhere, consider the vectors from a point in the scene to the four corners of the portal, transformed into this coordinate system.

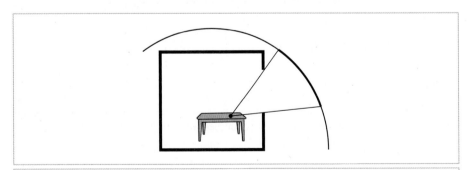

Figure 12.20: Given a scene with a portal (opening in the box), for each point in the scene we can find the set of directions that pass through the portal. To sample illumination efficiently, we would like to only sample from the corresponding visible region of the environment map (thick segment on the sphere).

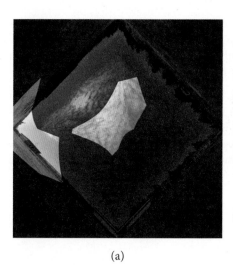

(a)   (b)

Figure 12.21: Shapes of Visible Regions of an Environment Map as Seen through a Portal. These images illustrate the visible regions of the environment map as seen through the window for a point on the floor and a point on one of the paintings on the wall for the scene in Figure 12.19. (a) The equal-area mapping used by the ImageInfiniteLight is convenient for sampling the entire environment map, but it leads to the portal-visible regions having complex shapes. (b) With the directional parameterization used by the PortalImageInfiniteLight, the visible region is always rectangular, which makes it feasible to sample from just that part of it. *(Environment map courtesy of Sergej Majboroda, via Poly Haven.)*

It should be evident that in this coordinate system, vectors to adjacent vertices of the portal only differ in one of their x or y coordinate values and that the four directions thus span a rectangular region in xy. (If this is not clear, it is a detail worth pausing to work through.) We will term directional representations that have this property as *rectified*.

The xy components of vectors in this coordinate system still span $(-\infty, \infty)$, so it is necessary to map them to a finite 2D domain if the environment map is to be represented using an image. It is important that this mapping does not interfere with the axis-alignment of the portal edges and that rectification is preserved. This requirement rules out a number of possibilities, including both the equirectangular and equal-area mappings. Even normalizing a vector and taking the x and y coordinates of the resulting unit vector is unsuitable given this requirement.

A mapping that does work is based on the angles α and β that the x and y coordinates of the vector respectively make with the z axis, as illustrated in Figure 12.22. These angles are given by

$$(\alpha, \beta) = \left(\arctan \frac{x}{z}, \arctan \frac{y}{z} \right).$$ [12.1]

We can ignore vectors with negative z components in the rectified coordinate system: they face away from the portal and thus do not receive any illumination. Each of α and β then spans the range $[-\pi/2, \pi/2]$ and the pair of them can be easily mapped to $[0, 1]^2$ (u, v) image coordinates. The environment map resampled into this parameterization is shown in Figure 12.21(b), with the visible regions for the same two points in the scene indicated.

We will start the implementation of the PortalImageInfiniteLight with its ImageFromRender() method, which applies this mapping to a vector in the rendering coordinate system wRender. (We will come to the initialization of the portalFrame member variable in the PortalImageInfiniteLight constructor later in this section.) It uses pstd::optional for the

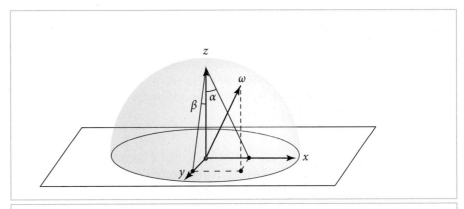

Figure 12.22: Vectors in the portal's coordinate system can be represented by a pair of angles (α, β) that measure the angle made by the x or y component, respectively, with the z axis.

return value in order to be able to return an invalid result in the case that the vector is coplanar with the portal or facing away from it.

⟨*PortalImageInfiniteLight Private Methods*⟩ ≡   773
```
    pstd::optional<Point2f> ImageFromRender(Vector3f wRender,
                                            Float *duv_dw = nullptr) const {
        Vector3f w = portalFrame.ToLocal(wRender);
        if (w.z <= 0) return {};
        ⟨Compute Jacobian determinant of mapping d(u, v)/dω if needed 775⟩
        Float alpha = std::atan2(w.x, w.z), beta = std::atan2(w.y, w.z);
        return Point2f(Clamp((alpha + Pi / 2) / Pi, 0, 1),
                    Clamp((beta + Pi / 2) / Pi, 0, 1));
    }
```

We will find it useful to be able to convert sampling densities from the (u, v) parameterization of the image to be with respect to solid angle on the unit sphere. The appropriate factor can be found following the usual approach of computing the determinant of the Jacobian of the mapping function, which is based on Equation (12.1), and then rescaling the coordinates to image coordinates in $[0, 1]^2$. The result is a simple expression when expressed in terms of ω:

$$\frac{\mathrm{d}(u, v)}{\mathrm{d}\omega} = \pi^2 \frac{(1 - \omega_x^2)(1 - \omega_y^2)}{\omega_z}.$$

If a non-nullptr duv_dw parameter is passed to this method, this factor is returned.

⟨*Compute Jacobian determinant of mapping* d(u, v)/dω *if needed*⟩ ≡   775, 776
```
    if (duv_dw)
        *duv_dw = Sqr(Pi) * (1 - Sqr(w.x)) * (1 - Sqr(w.y)) / w.z;
```

The inverse transformation can be found by working in reverse. It is implemented in RenderFromImage(), which also optionally returns the same change of variables factor.

⟨*PortalImageInfiniteLight Private Methods*⟩ +≡   773

```
Vector3f RenderFromImage(Point2f uv, Float *duv_dw = nullptr) const {
    Float alpha = -Pi / 2 + uv[0] * Pi, beta = -Pi / 2 + uv[1] * Pi;
    Float x = std::tan(alpha), y = std::tan(beta);
    Vector3f w = Normalize(Vector3f(x, y, 1));
    ⟨Compute Jacobian determinant of mapping d(u, v)/dω if needed  775⟩
    return portalFrame.FromLocal(w);
}
```

Because the mapping is rectified, we can find the image-space bounding box of the visible region of the environment map from a given point using the coordinates of two opposite portal corners. This method also returns an optional value, for the same reasons as for `ImageFromRender()`.

⟨*PortalImageInfiniteLight Private Methods*⟩ +≡   773

```
pstd::optional<Bounds2f> ImageBounds(Point3f p) const {
    pstd::optional<Point2f> p0 = ImageFromRender(Normalize(portal[0] - p));
    pstd::optional<Point2f> p1 = ImageFromRender(Normalize(portal[2] - p));
    if (!p0 || !p1) return {};
    return Bounds2f(*p0, *p1);
}
```

Most of the `PortalImageInfiniteLight` constructor consists of straightforward initialization of member variables from provided parameter values, checking that the provided image has RGB channels, and so forth. All of that has not been included in this text. We will, however, discuss the following three fragments, which run at the end of the constructor.

⟨*PortalImageInfiniteLight constructor conclusion*⟩ ≡

```
    ⟨Compute frame for portal coordinate system  776⟩
    ⟨Resample environment map into rectified image  777⟩
    ⟨Initialize sampling distribution for portal image infinite light  778⟩
```

The portal itself is specified by four vertices, given in the rendering coordinate system. Additional code, not shown here, checks to ensure that they describe a planar quadrilateral. A Frame for the portal's coordinate system can be found from two normalized adjacent edge vectors of the portal using the `Frame::FromXY()` method.

⟨*Compute frame for portal coordinate system*⟩ ≡   776

```
Vector3f p01 = Normalize(portal[1] - portal[0]);
Vector3f p03 = Normalize(portal[3] - portal[0]);
portalFrame = Frame::FromXY(p03, p01);
```

⟨*PortalImageInfiniteLight Private Members*⟩ ≡   773

```
pstd::array<Point3f, 4> portal;
Frame portalFrame;
```

The constructor also resamples a provided equal-area image into the rectified representation at the same resolution. Because the rectified image depends on the geometry of the portal, it is better to take an equal-area image and resample it in the constructor than to require the user to provide an already-rectified image. In this way, it is easy for the user to change the portal specification just by changing the portal's coordinates in the scene description file.

⟨*Resample environment map into rectified image*⟩ ≡   776
```
    image = Image(PixelFormat::Float, equalAreaImage.Resolution(),
                  {"R", "G", "B"}, equalAreaImage.Encoding(), alloc);
    ParallelFor(0, image.Resolution().y, [&](int y) {
        for (int x = 0; x < image.Resolution().x; ++x) {
            ⟨Resample equalAreaImage to compute rectified image pixel (x, y) 777⟩
        }
    });
```

⟨*PortalImageInfiniteLight Private Members*⟩ +≡   773
```
    Image image;
```

At each rectified image pixel, the implementation first computes the corresponding light-space direction and looks up a bilinearly interpolated value from the equal-area image. No further filtering is performed. A better implementation would use a spatially varying filter here in order to ensure that there was no risk of introducing aliasing due to undersampling the source image.

⟨*Resample* equalAreaImage *to compute rectified image pixel* (x, y)⟩ ≡   777
```
    ⟨Find (u, v) coordinates in equal-area image for pixel 777⟩
    for (int c = 0; c < 3; ++c) {
        Float v = equalAreaImage.BilerpChannel(uvEqui, c,
                                               WrapMode::OctahedralSphere);
        image.SetChannel({x, y}, c, v);
    }
```

The image coordinates in the equal-area image can be found by determining the direction vector corresponding to the current pixel in the rectified image and then finding the equal-area image coordinates that this direction maps to.

⟨*Find* (u, v) *coordinates in equal-area image for pixel*⟩ ≡   777
```
    Point2f uv((x + 0.5f) / image.Resolution().x,
               (y + 0.5f) / image.Resolution().y);
    Vector3f w = RenderFromImage(uv);
    w = Normalize(renderFromLight.ApplyInverse(w));
    Point2f uvEqui = EqualAreaSphereToSquare(w);
```

Given the rectified image, the next step is to initialize an instance of the WindowedPiecewiseConstant2D data structure, which performs the sampling operation. (It is defined in Section A.5.6.) As its name suggests, it generalizes the functionality of the PiecewiseConstant2D class to allow a caller-specified window that limits the sampling region.

It is worthwhile to include the change of variables factor $d(u, v)/d\omega$ at each pixel in the image sampling distribution. Doing so causes the weights associated with image samples to be more uniform, as this factor will nearly cancel the same factor when a sample's PDF is computed. (The cancellation is not exact, as the factor here is computed at the center of each pixel while in the PDF it is computed at the exact sample location.)

⟨*Initialize sampling distribution for portal image infinite light*⟩ ≡   **776**
```
    auto duv_dw = [&](Point2f p) {
        Float duv_dw;
        (void)RenderFromImage(p, &duv_dw);
        return duv_dw;
    };
    Array2D<Float> d = image.GetSamplingDistribution(duv_dw);
    distribution = WindowedPiecewiseConstant2D(d, alloc);
```

⟨*PortalImageInfiniteLight Private Members*⟩ +≡   **773**
```
    WindowedPiecewiseConstant2D distribution;
```

The light's total power can be found by integrating radiance over the hemisphere of directions that can be seen through the portal and then multiplying by the portal's area, since all light that reaches the scene passes through it. The corresponding `PortalImageInfiniteLight::Phi()` method is not included here, as it boils down to being a matter of looping over the pixels, applying the change of variables factor to account for integration over the unit sphere, and then multiplying the integrated radiance by the portal's area.

In order to compute the radiance for a ray that has left the scene, the (u, v) coordinates in the image corresponding to the ray's direction are computed first. The radiance corresponding to those coordinates is returned if they are inside the portal bounds for the ray origin, and a zero-valued spectrum is returned otherwise. (In principle, the `Le()` method should only be called for rays that have left the scene, so that the portal check should always pass, but it is worth including for the occasional ray that escapes the scene due to a geometric error in the scene model. This way, those end up carrying no radiance rather than causing a light leak.)

⟨*PortalImageInfiniteLight Method Definitions*⟩ ≡
```
    SampledSpectrum
    PortalImageInfiniteLight::Le(const Ray &ray,
                                 const SampledWavelengths &lambda) const {
        pstd::optional<Point2f> uv = ImageFromRender(Normalize(ray.d));
        pstd::optional<Bounds2f> b = ImageBounds(ray.o);
        if (!uv || !b || !Inside(*uv, *b))
            return SampledSpectrum(0.f);
        return ImageLookup(*uv, lambda);
    }
```

The `ImageLookup()` method returns the radiance at the given image (u, v) and wavelengths. We encapsulate this functionality in its own method, as it will be useful repeatedly in the remainder of the light's implementation.

⟨*PortalImageInfiniteLight Method Definitions*⟩ +≡
```
    SampledSpectrum PortalImageInfiniteLight::ImageLookup(
            Point2f uv, const SampledWavelengths &lambda) const {
        RGB rgb;
        for (int c = 0; c < 3; ++c)
            rgb[c] = image.LookupNearestChannel(uv, c);
        RGBIlluminantSpectrum spec(*imageColorSpace, ClampZero(rgb));
        return scale * spec.Sample(lambda);
    }
```

As before, the image's color space must be known in order to convert its RGB values to spectra.

⟨*PortalImageInfiniteLight Private Members*⟩ +≡   **773**
```
const RGBColorSpace *imageColorSpace;
Float scale;
```

SampleLi() is able to take advantage of the combination of the rectified image representation and the ability of WindowedPiecewiseConstant2D to sample a direction from the specified point that passes through the portal, according to the directional distribution of radiance over the portal.

⟨*PortalImageInfiniteLight Method Definitions*⟩ +≡
```
pstd::optional<LightLiSample>
PortalImageInfiniteLight::SampleLi(LightSampleContext ctx, Point2f u,
        SampledWavelengths lambda, bool allowIncompletePDF) const {
    ⟨Sample (u, v) in potentially visible region of light image 779⟩
    ⟨Convert portal image sample point to direction and compute PDF 779⟩
    ⟨Compute radiance for portal light sample and return LightLiSample 779⟩
}
```

WindowedPiecewiseConstant2D's Sample() method takes a Bounds2f to specify the sampling region. This is easily provided using the ImageBounds() method. It may not be able to generate a valid sample—for example, if the point is on the outside of the portal or lies on its plane. In this case, an unset sample is returned.

⟨*Sample (u, v) in potentially visible region of light image*⟩ ≡   **779**
```
pstd::optional<Bounds2f> b = ImageBounds(ctx.p());
if (!b) return {};
Float mapPDF;
pstd::optional<Point2f> uv = distribution.Sample(u, *b, &mapPDF);
if (!uv) return {};
```

After image (u, v) coordinates are converted to a direction, the method computes the sampling PDF with respect to solid angle at the reference point represented by ctx. Doing so just requires the application of the change of variables factor returned by RenderFromImage().

⟨*Convert portal image sample point to direction and compute PDF*⟩ ≡   **779**
```
Float duv_dw;
Vector3f wi = RenderFromImage(*uv, &duv_dw);
if (duv_dw == 0) return {};
Float pdf = mapPDF / duv_dw;
```

The remaining pieces are easy at this point: ImageLookup() provides the radiance for the sampled direction and the endpoint of the shadow ray is found in the same way that is done for the other infinite lights.

⟨*Compute radiance for portal light sample and return LightLiSample*⟩ ≡   **779**
```
SampledSpectrum L = ImageLookup(*uv, lambda);
Point3f pl = ctx.p() + 2 * sceneRadius * wi;
return LightLiSample(L, wi, pdf, Interaction(pl, &mediumInterface));
```

Also as with the other infinite lights, the radius of the scene's bounding sphere is stored when the Preprocess() method, not included here, is called.

⟨*PortalImageInfiniteLight Private Members*⟩ +≡   **773**
```
Float sceneRadius;
```

Finding the PDF for a specified direction follows the way in which the PDF was calculated in the sampling method.

⟨*PortalImageInfiniteLight Method Definitions*⟩ +≡
```
Float PortalImageInfiniteLight::PDF_Li(LightSampleContext ctx, Vector3f w,
                                       bool allowIncompletePDF) const {
    ⟨Find image (u, v) coordinates corresponding to direction w 780⟩
    ⟨Return PDF for sampling (u, v) from reference point 780⟩
}
```

First, `ImageFromRender()` gives the (u, v) coordinates in the portal image for the specified direction.

⟨*Find image (u, v) coordinates corresponding to direction w*⟩ ≡ 　　　　　　**780**
```
Float duv_dw;
pstd::optional<Point2f> uv = ImageFromRender(w, &duv_dw);
if (!uv || duv_dw == 0) return 0;
```

Following its `Sample()` method, the `WindowedPiecewiseConstant2D::PDF()` method also takes a 2D bounding box to window the function. The PDF value it returns is normalized with respect to those bounds and a value of zero is returned if the given point is outside of them. Application of the change of variables factor gives the final PDF with respect to solid angle.

⟨*Return PDF for sampling (u, v) from reference point*⟩ ≡ 　　　　　　**780**
```
pstd::optional<Bounds2f> b = ImageBounds(ctx.p());
if (!b) return 0;
Float pdf = distribution.PDF(*uv, *b);
return pdf / duv_dw;
```

12.6 LIGHT SAMPLING

Due to the linearity assumption in radiometry, illumination at a point in a scene with multiple light sources can be computed by summing the independent contributions of each light. As we have seen before, however, correctness alone is not always sufficient—if it were, we might have sampled `ImageInfiniteLights` uniformly with the suggestion that one take thousands of samples per pixel until error has been reduced sufficiently. Especially in scenes with thousands or more independent light sources, considering all of them carries too much of a performance cost.

Fortunately, here, too, is a setting where stochastic sampling can be applied. An unbiased estimator for a sum of terms f_i is given by

$$\sum_i^n f_i \approx \frac{f_j}{p(j)},$$ 　　　　　　(12.2)

where the probability mass function (PMF) $p(j) > 0$ for any term where f_j is nonzero and where $j \sim p$. This is the discrete analog to the integral Monte Carlo estimator, Equation (2.7). Therefore, we can replace any sum over all the scene's light sources with a sum over just one or a few of them, where the contributions are weighted by one over the probability of sampling the ones selected.

Figure 12.23 is a rendered image of a scene with 8,878 light sources. A few observations motivate some of the light sampling algorithms to come. At any given point in the scene, some lights are facing away and others are occluded. Ideally, such lights would be given a zero

Figure 12.23: *Zero Day* Scene, with 8,878 Light Sources. It is infeasible to consider every light when computing reflected radiance at a point on a surface, and therefore light sampling methods from this section are necessary to render this scene efficiently. *(Scene courtesy of Beeple.)*

sampling probability. Furthermore, often many lights are both far away from a given point and have relatively low power; such lights should have a low probability of being sampled. (Consider, for example, the small yellow lights inset in the machinery.) Of course, even a small and dim light is important to points close to it. Therefore, the most effective light sampling probabilities will vary across the scene depending on position, surface normal, the BSDF, and so forth.

The LightSampler class defines the LightSampler interface for sampling light sources.[2] It is defined in the file base/lightsampler.h. LightSampler implementations can be found in lightsamplers.h and lightsamplers.cpp.

⟨*LightSampler Definition*⟩ ≡
```
class LightSampler :
    public TaggedPointer<UniformLightSampler, PowerLightSampler,
                         BVHLightSampler> {
  public:
    ⟨LightSampler Interface 781⟩
};
```

The key LightSampler method is Sample(), which takes a uniform 1D sample and information about a reference point in the form of a LightSampleContext. When sampling is successful, a SampledLight is returned. Otherwise, the optional value is left unset, as may happen if the light sampler is able to determine that no lights illuminate the provided point.

⟨*LightSampler Interface*⟩ ≡   781
```
    pstd::optional<SampledLight> Sample(const LightSampleContext &ctx,
                                        Float u) const;
```

SampledLight just wraps up a light and the discrete probability for it having been sampled.

---

2   Our use of the term "sampling light sources" is admittedly overloaded: it can refer to both sampling a point on the surface of a light or a direction toward it, as well as choosing an individual light source. The intended meaning should always be clear in context.

⟨SampledLight Definition⟩ ≡
```
struct SampledLight {
    Light light;
    Float p = 0;
};
```

In order to compute the MIS weighting term when a ray happens to hit a light source, it is necessary to be able to find the value of the probability mass function for sampling a particular light. This task is handled by PMF() method implementations.

⟨LightSampler Interface⟩ +≡   **781**
```
    Float PMF(const LightSampleContext &ctx, Light light) const;
```

LightSamplers must also provide methods to sample a light and return the corresponding probability independent of a specific point being illuminated. These methods are useful for light transport algorithms like bidirectional path tracing that start paths at the light sources.

⟨LightSampler Interface⟩ +≡   **781**
```
    pstd::optional<SampledLight> Sample(Float u) const;
    Float PMF(Light light) const;
```

12.6.1 UNIFORM LIGHT SAMPLING

UniformLightSampler is the simplest possible light sampler: it samples all lights with uniform probability. In practice, more sophisticated sampling algorithms are usually much more effective, but this one is easy to implement and provides a useful baseline for comparing light sampling techniques.

⟨UniformLightSampler Definition⟩ ≡
```
    class UniformLightSampler {
      public:
        ⟨UniformLightSampler Public Methods 782⟩
      private:
        ⟨UniformLightSampler Private Members 782⟩
    };
```

As with all light samplers, an array of all the lights in the scene is provided to the constructor; UniformLightSampler makes a copy of them in a member variable.

⟨UniformLightSampler Public Methods⟩ ≡   **782**
```
    UniformLightSampler(pstd::span<const Light> lights, Allocator alloc)
        : lights(lights.begin(), lights.end(), alloc) {}
```

⟨UniformLightSampler Private Members⟩ ≡   **782**
```
    pstd::vector<Light> lights;
```

Since the light sampling probabilities do not depend on the lookup point, we will only include the variants of Sample() and PMF() that do not take a LightSampleContext here. The versions of these methods that do take a context just call these variants. For sampling, a light is chosen by scaling the provided uniform sample by the array size and returning the corresponding light.

⟨*UniformLightSampler Public Methods*⟩ +≡   **782**
```
pstd::optional<SampledLight> Sample(Float u) const {
    if (lights.empty()) return {};
    int lightIndex = std::min<int>(u * lights.size(), lights.size() - 1);
    return SampledLight{lights[lightIndex], 1.f / lights.size()};
}
```

Given uniform sampling probabilities, the value of the PMF is always one over the number of lights.

⟨*UniformLightSampler Public Methods*⟩ +≡   **782**
```
Float PMF(Light light) const {
    if (lights.empty()) return 0;
    return 1.f / lights.size();
}
```

12.6.2 POWER LIGHT SAMPLER

PowerLightSampler sets the probability for sampling each light according to its power. Doing so generally gives better results than sampling uniformly, but the lack of spatial variation in sampling probabilities limits its effectiveness. (We will return to this topic at the end of this section where some comparisons between the two techniques are presented.)

⟨*PowerLightSampler Definition*⟩ ≡
```
class PowerLightSampler {
  public:
    ⟨PowerLightSampler Public Methods 784⟩
  private:
    ⟨PowerLightSampler Private Members 783⟩
};
```

Its constructor also makes a copy of the provided lights but initializes some additional data structures as well.

⟨*PowerLightSampler Method Definitions*⟩ ≡
```
PowerLightSampler::PowerLightSampler(pstd::span<const Light> lights,
                                     Allocator alloc)
    : lights(lights.begin(), lights.end(), alloc), lightToIndex(alloc),
      aliasTable(alloc) {
    if (lights.empty()) return;
    ⟨Initialize lightToIndex hash table 783⟩
    ⟨Compute lights' power and initialize alias table 784⟩
}
```

⟨*PowerLightSampler Private Members*⟩ ≡   **783**
```
pstd::vector<Light> lights;
```

To efficiently return the value of the PMF for a given light, it is necessary to be able to find the index in the lights array of a given light. Therefore, the constructor also initializes a hash table that maps from Lights to indices.

⟨*Initialize lightToIndex hash table*⟩ ≡   **783**
```
for (size_t i = 0; i < lights.size(); ++i)
    lightToIndex.Insert(lights[i], i);
```

⟨*PowerLightSampler Private Members*⟩ +≡   783
```
    HashMap<Light, size_t> lightToIndex;
```

The `PowerLightSampler` uses an `AliasTable` for sampling. It is initialized here with weights based on the emitted power returned by each light's `Phi()` method. Note that if the light's emission distribution is spiky (e.g., as with many fluorescent lights), there is a risk of underestimating its power if a spike is missed. We have not found this to be a problem in practice, however.

⟨*Compute lights' power and initialize alias table*⟩ ≡   783
```
    pstd::vector<Float> lightPower;
    SampledWavelengths lambda = SampledWavelengths::SampleVisible(0.5f);
    for (const auto &light : lights) {
        SampledSpectrum phi = SafeDiv(light.Phi(lambda), lambda.PDF());
        lightPower.push_back(phi.Average());
    }
    aliasTable = AliasTable(lightPower, alloc);
```

⟨*PowerLightSampler Private Members*⟩ +≡   783
```
    AliasTable aliasTable;
```

Given the alias table, sampling is easy.

⟨*PowerLightSampler Public Methods*⟩ ≡   783
```
    pstd::optional<SampledLight> Sample(Float u) const {
        if (!aliasTable.size()) return {};
        Float pmf;
        int lightIndex = aliasTable.Sample(u, &pmf);
        return SampledLight{lights[lightIndex], pmf};
    }
```

To evaluate the PMF, the hash table gives the mapping to an index in the array of lights. In turn, the PMF returned by the alias table for the corresponding entry is the probability of sampling the light.

⟨*PowerLightSampler Public Methods*⟩ +≡   783
```
    Float PMF(Light light) const {
        if (!aliasTable.size()) return 0;
        return aliasTable.PMF(lightToIndex[light]);
    }
```

As with the `UniformLightSampler`, the `Sample()` and `PMF()` methods that do take a `LightSampleContext` just call the corresponding methods that do not take one.

Sampling lights based on their power usually works well. Figure 12.24 compares both sampling methods using the *Zero Day* scene. For this scene, noise is visibly reduced when sampling according to power, and mean squared error (MSE) is improved by a factor of 12.4.

Although sampling according to power generally works well, it is not optimal. Like uniform sampling, it is hindered by not taking the geometry of emitters and the relationship between emitters and the receiving point into account. Relatively dim light sources may make the greatest visual contribution in a scene, especially if the bright ones are far away, mostly occluded, or not visible at all.

As an extreme example of this problem with sampling according to power, consider a large triangular light source that emits a small amount of radiance. The triangle's emitted power

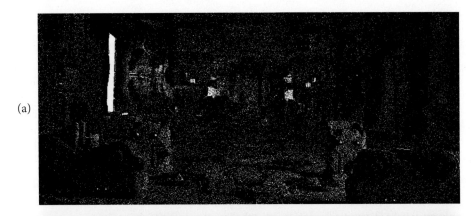

Figure 12.24: **Sampling Lights Uniformly versus by Emitted Power with the *Zero Day* Scene.**
(a) Rendered with uniform light sampling. (b) Rendered with lights sampled according to power. Both images are rendered with 16 samples per pixel and rendering time is nearly the same. Sampling lights according to power reduces MSE by a factor of 12.4 for this scene. *(Scene courtesy of Beeple.)*

can be made arbitrarily large by scaling it to increase its total area. However, at any point in the scene the triangle can do no more than subtend a hemisphere, which limits its effect on the total incident radiance at a point. Sampling by power can devote far too many samples to such lights.

★ 12.6.3 BVH LIGHT SAMPLING

Varying the light sampling probabilities based on the point being shaded can be an effective light sampling strategy, though if there are more than a handful of lights, some sort of data structure is necessary to do this without having to consider every light at each point being shaded. One widely used approach is to construct a hierarchy over the light sources with the effect of multiple lights aggregated into the higher nodes of the hierarchy. This representation makes it possible to traverse the hierarchy to find the important lights near a given point.

Given a good light hierarchy, it is possible to render scenes with hundreds of thousands or even millions of light sources nearly as efficiently as a scene with just one light. In this section, we will describe the implementation of the BVHLightSampler, which applies bounding volume hierarchies to this task.

BVHLightSampler 796

Bounding Lights

When bounding volume hierarchies (BVHs) were used for intersection acceleration structures in Section 7.3, it was necessary to abstract away the details of the various types of primitives and underlying shapes that they stored so that the BVHAggregate did not have to be explicitly aware of each of them. There, the primitives' rendering-space bounding boxes were used for building the hierarchy. Although there were cases where the quality of the acceleration structure might have been improved using shape-specific information (e.g., if the acceleration structure was aware of skinny diagonal triangles with large bounding boxes with respect to the triangle's area), the BVHAggregate's implementation was substantially simplified with that approach.

We would like to have a similar decoupling for the BVHLightSampler, though it is less obvious what the right abstraction should be. For example, we might want to know that a spotlight only emits light in a particular cone, so that the sampler does not choose it for points outside the cone. Similarly, we might want to know that a one-sided area light only shines light on one side of a particular plane. For all sorts of lights, knowing their total power would be helpful so that brighter lights can be sampled preferentially to dimmer ones. Of course, power does not tell the whole story, as the light's spatial extent and relationship to a receiving point affect how much power is potentially received at that point.

The LightBounds structure provides the abstraction used by pbrt for these purposes. It stores a variety of values that make it possible to represent the emission distribution of a variety of types of light.

⟨*LightBounds Definition*⟩ ≡
```
class LightBounds {
public:
    ⟨LightBounds Public Methods 787⟩
    ⟨LightBounds Public Members 786⟩
};
```

It is evident that the spatial bounds of the light and its emitted power will be useful quantities, so those are included in LightBounds. However, this representation excludes light sources at infinity such as the DistantLight and the various infinite lights. That limitation is fine, however, since it is unclear how such light sources would be stored in a BVH anyway. (The BVHLightSampler therefore handles these types of lights separately.)

⟨*LightBounds Public Members*⟩ ≡   786
```
Bounds3f bounds;
Float phi = 0;
```

As suggested earlier, bounding a light's directional emission distribution is important for sampling lights effectively. The representation used here is based on a unit vector ω that specifies a principal direction for the emitter's surface normal and two angles that specify its variation. First, θ_o specifies the maximum deviation of the emitter's surface normal from the principal normal direction ω. Second, θ_e specifies the angle beyond θ_o up to which there may be emission (see Figure 12.25). Thus, directions that make an angle up to $\theta_o + \theta_e$ with ω may receive illumination from a light and those that make a greater angle certainly do not.

While this representation may seem overly specialized for emissive shapes alone, it works well for all of pbrt's (noninfinite) light types. For example, a point light can be represented with an arbitrary average normal ω and an angle of π for θ_o. A spotlight can use the direction it is facing for ω, its central cone angle for θ_o, and the angular width of its falloff region for θ_e.

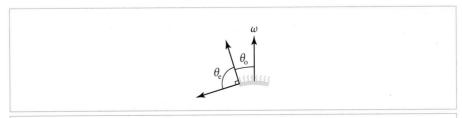

Figure 12.25: Specification of Potential Emission Directions for a Light. Lights specify a principal direction of their distribution of surface normals ω as well as two angles, θ_o and θ_e. The first angle bounds the variation in surface normals from ω and the second gives the additional angle beyond which emission is possible.

Our implementation stores the cosine of these angles rather than the angles themselves; this representation will make it possible to avoid the expense of evaluating a number of trigonometric functions in the following.

⟨*LightBounds Public Members*⟩ +≡   786
```
Vector3f w;
Float cosTheta_o, cosTheta_e;
```

The last part of the emission bounds for a light is a twoSided flag, which indicates whether the direction ω should be negated to specify a second cone that uses the same pair of angles.

⟨*LightBounds Public Members*⟩ +≡   786
```
bool twoSided;
```

The LightBounds constructor takes corresponding parameters and initializes the member variables. The implementation is straightforward, and so is not included here.

⟨*LightBounds Public Methods*⟩ ≡   786
```
LightBounds(const Bounds3f &b, Vector3f w, Float phi, Float cosTheta_o,
            Float cosTheta_e, bool twoSided);
```

To cluster lights into a hierarchy, we will need to be able to find the bounds that encompass two specified LightBounds objects. This capability is provided by the Union() function.

⟨*LightBounds Inline Methods*⟩ ≡
```
LightBounds Union(const LightBounds &a, const LightBounds &b) {
    ⟨If one LightBounds has zero power, return the other 787⟩
    ⟨Find average direction and updated angles for LightBounds 788⟩
    ⟨Return final LightBounds union 788⟩
}
```

It is worthwhile to start out by checking for the easy case of one or the other specified LightBounds having zero power. In this case, the other can be returned immediately.

⟨*If one* LightBounds *has zero power, return the other*⟩ ≡   787
```
if (a.phi == 0) return b;
if (b.phi == 0) return a;
```

Otherwise, a new average normal direction and updated angles θ_o and θ_e must be computed. Most of the work involved is handled by the DirectionCone's Union() method, which takes a pair of cones of directions and returns one that bounds the two of them. The cosine of the new angle θ_o is then given by the cosine of the spread angle of that cone.

The value of θ_e should be the maximum of the θ_e values for the two cones. However, because LightBounds stores the cosines of the angles and because the cosine function is monotonically decreasing over the range of possible θ values, $[0, \pi]$, we take the minimum cosine of the two angles.

⟨*Find average direction and updated angles for* LightBounds⟩ ≡   787
```
    DirectionCone cone = Union(DirectionCone(a.w, a.cosTheta_o),
                               DirectionCone(b.w, b.cosTheta_o));
    Float cosTheta_o = cone.cosTheta;
    Float cosTheta_e = std::min(a.cosTheta_e, b.cosTheta_e);
```

The remainder of the parameter values for the LightBounds constructor are easily computed from the two LightBounds that were provided.

⟨*Return final* LightBounds *union*⟩ ≡   787
```
    return LightBounds(Union(a.bounds, b.bounds), cone.w, a.phi + b.phi,
                       cosTheta_o, cosTheta_e, a.twoSided | b.twoSided);
```

A utility method returns the centroid of the spatial bounds; this value will be handy when building the light BVH.

⟨*LightBounds Public Methods*⟩ +≡   786
```
    Point3f Centroid() const { return (bounds.pMin + bounds.pMax) / 2; }
```

The Importance() method provides the key LightBounds functionality: it returns a scalar value that estimates the contribution of the light or lights represented in the LightBounds at a given point. If the provided normal is nondegenerate, it is assumed to be the surface normal at the receiving point. Scattering points in participating media pass a zero-valued Normal3f.

⟨*LightBounds Method Definitions*⟩ ≡
```
    Float LightBounds::Importance(Point3f p, Normal3f n) const {
        ⟨Return importance for light bounds at reference point 788⟩
    }
```

It is necessary to make a number of assumptions in order to estimate the amount of light arriving at a point given a LightBounds. While it will be possible to make use of principles such as the received power falling off with the squared distance from the emitter or the incident irradiance at a surface varying according to Lambert's law, some approximations are inevitable, given the loss of specifics that comes with adopting the LightBounds representation.

⟨*Return importance for light bounds at reference point*⟩ ≡   788, 796
    ⟨*Compute clamped squared distance to reference point* 789⟩
    ⟨*Define cosine and sine clamped subtraction lambdas* 789⟩
    ⟨*Compute sine and cosine of angle to vector* w, θ_w 790⟩
    ⟨*Compute* cos θ_b *for reference point* 790⟩
    ⟨*Compute* cos θ' *and test against* cos θ_e 790⟩
    ⟨*Return final importance at reference point* 791⟩

Even computing the squared distance for the falloff of received power is challenging if bounds is not degenerate: to which point in bounds should the distance be computed? It may seem that finding the minimum distance from the point p to the bounds would be a safe choice, though this would imply a very small distance for a point close to the bounds and a zero distance for a point inside it. Either of these would lead to a very large $1/r^2$ factor and potentially high error due to giving too much preference to such a LightBounds. Further, choosing between the two child LightBounds of a node when a point is inside both would be impossible, given infinite weights for each.

Therefore, our first fudge is to compute the distance from the center of the bounding box but further to ensure that the squared distance is not too small with respect to the length of the diagonal of the bounding box. Thus, for larger bounding boxes with corresponding uncertainty about what the actual spatial distribution of emission is, the inverse squared distance factor cannot become too large.

⟨*Compute clamped squared distance to reference point*⟩ ≡   788
```
Point3f pc = (bounds.pMin + bounds.pMax) / 2;
Float d2 = DistanceSquared(p, pc);
d2 = std::max(d2, Length(bounds.Diagonal()) / 2);
```

In the following computations, we will need to produce a series of values of the form $\cos(\max(0, \theta_a - \theta_b))$ and $\sin(\max(0, \theta_a - \theta_b))$. Given the sine and cosine of θ_a and θ_b, it is possible to do so without evaluating any trigonometric functions. To see how, consider the cosine: $\theta_a - \theta_b < 0$ implies that $\theta_a < \theta_b$ and that therefore $\cos \theta_a > \cos \theta_b$. We thus start by checking that case and returning $\cos 0 = 1$ if it is true. We are otherwise left with $\cos(\theta_a - \theta_b)$, which can be expressed in terms of the sines and cosines of the two angles using a trigonometric identity, $\cos \theta_a \cos \theta_b + \sin \theta_a \sin \theta_b$. The case for sine follows analogously.

Two simple lambda functions provide these capabilities. (Only the one for cosine is included in the text, as sinSubClamped follows a similar form.)

⟨*Define cosine and sine clamped subtraction lambdas*⟩ ≡   788
```
auto cosSubClamped = [](Float sinTheta_a, Float cosTheta_a,
                        Float sinTheta_b, Float cosTheta_b) -> Float {
    if (cosTheta_a > cosTheta_b)
        return 1;
    return cosTheta_a * cosTheta_b + sinTheta_a * sinTheta_b;
};
```

There are a number of angles involved in the importance computation. In addition to the ones that specify the directional emission bounds, θ_o and θ_e, we will start by computing the sine and cosine of θ_w, the angle between the principal normal direction and the vector from the center of the light bounds to the reference point (Figure 12.26(a)).

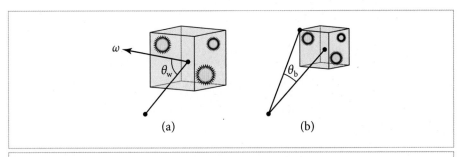

Figure 12.26: (a) θ_w measures the angle between the principal normal direction ω and the vector from the center of the bounding box to the reference point. (b) θ_b is the angle that the LightBounds's bounding box, **bounds**, subtends with respect to the reference point.

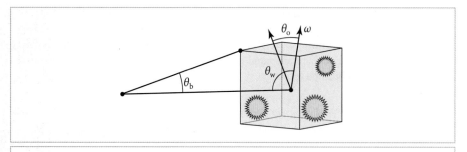

Figure 12.27: θ' is the minimum angle between the emitter and the vector to the reference point.

⟨*Compute sine and cosine of angle to vector w, θ_w*⟩ ≡   788
```
Vector3f wi = Normalize(p - pc);
Float cosTheta_w = Dot(Vector3f(w), wi);
if (twoSided)
    cosTheta_w = std::abs(cosTheta_w);
Float sinTheta_w = SafeSqrt(1 - Sqr(cosTheta_w));
```

To bound the variation of various angles across the extent of the bounding box, we will also make use of the angle that the bounding box subtends with respect to the reference point (see Figure 12.26(b)). We will denote this angle θ_b. The preexisting DirectionCone::Bound SubtendedDirections() function takes care of computing its cosine. Its sine follows directly.

⟨*Compute* $\cos \theta_b$ *for reference point*⟩ ≡   788
```
Float cosTheta_b = BoundSubtendedDirections(bounds, p).cosTheta;
Float sinTheta_b = SafeSqrt(1 - Sqr(cosTheta_b));
```

The last angle we will use is the minimum angle between the emitter's normal and the vector to the reference point. We will denote it by θ', and it is given by

$$\theta' = \max(0, \theta_w - \theta_o - \theta_b);$$

see Figure 12.27. As with the other angles, we only need its sine and cosine, which can be computed one subtraction at a time.

If this angle is greater than θ_e (or, here, if its cosine is less than $\cos \theta_e$), then it is certain that the lights represented by the bounds do not illuminate the reference point and an importance value of 0 can be returned immediately.

⟨*Compute* $\cos \theta'$ *and test against* $\cos \theta_e$⟩ ≡   788
```
Float sinTheta_o = SafeSqrt(1 - Sqr(cosTheta_o));
Float cosTheta_x =
    cosSubClamped(sinTheta_w, cosTheta_w, sinTheta_o, cosTheta_o);
Float sinTheta_x =
    sinSubClamped(sinTheta_w, cosTheta_w, sinTheta_o, cosTheta_o);
Float cosThetap =
    cosSubClamped(sinTheta_x, cosTheta_x, sinTheta_b, cosTheta_b);
if (cosThetap <= cosTheta_e)
    return 0;
```

The importance value can now be computed. It starts with the product of the power of the lights, the $\cos \theta'$ factor that accounts for the cosine at the emitter, and the inverse squared distance.

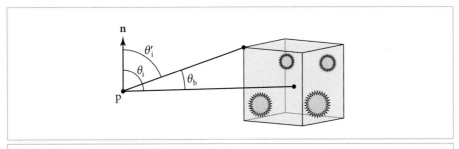

Figure 12.28: An angle θ_i' that gives a lower bound on the angle between the incident lighting direction and the surface normal can be found by subtracting θ_b, the angle that the bounding box subtends with respect to the reference point p, from θ_i, the angle between the surface normal and the vector to the center of the box.

⟨*Return final importance at reference point*⟩ ≡   **788**
```
Float importance = phi * cosThetap / d2;
```
⟨*Account for* cos θ_i *in importance at surfaces* **791**⟩
```
return importance;
```

At a surface, the importance also accounts for a conservative estimate of the incident cosine factor there. We have wi, the unit vector from the reference point to the center of the LightBounds, but would like to conservatively set the importance based on the maximum value of the incident cosine over the entire bounding box. The corresponding minimum angle with the surface normal is given by $\max(0, \theta_i - \theta_b)$ (see Figure 12.28).

Our implementation of this computation uses the cosSubClamped() lambda function introduced earlier to compute the cosine of the angle θ_i' directly using the sines and cosines of the two contributing angles.

⟨*Account for* cos θ_i *in importance at surfaces*⟩ ≡   **791**
```
if (n != Normal3f(0, 0, 0)) {
    Float cosTheta_i = AbsDot(wi, n);
    Float sinTheta_i = SafeSqrt(1 - Sqr(cosTheta_i));
    Float cosThetap_i = cosSubClamped(sinTheta_i, cosTheta_i,
                                      sinTheta_b, cosTheta_b);
    importance *= cosThetap_i;
}
```

Bounds for Light Implementations

Given the definition of LightBounds, we will add another method to the Light interface to allow lights to return bounds on their emission.

⟨*Light Interface*⟩ +≡   **740**
```
pstd::optional<LightBounds> Bounds() const;
```

Lights at infinity return an unset optional value. Here, for example, is the implementation of this method for ImageInfiniteLight. The other infinite lights and the DistantLight do likewise.

⟨*ImageInfiniteLight Public Methods*⟩ +≡   **767**
```
pstd::optional<LightBounds> Bounds() const { return {}; }
```

The PointLight's implementation is just a few lines of code, as befitting the simplicity of that type of light source. The spatial bounds are given by the light's rendering space position and the total emitted power is easily computed following the approach in PointLight::Phi().

Because this light shines in all directions, the average normal direction is arbitrary and θ_o is π, corresponding to the full sphere of directions.

⟨*PointLight Method Definitions*⟩ +≡
```
pstd::optional<LightBounds> PointLight::Bounds() const {
    Point3f p = renderFromLight(Point3f(0, 0, 0));
    Float phi = 4 * Pi * scale * I->MaxValue();
    return LightBounds(Bounds3f(p, p), Vector3f(0, 0, 1), phi, std::cos(Pi),
                       std::cos(Pi / 2), false);
}
```

The SpotLight's bounding method is a bit more interesting: now the average normal vector is relevant; it is set here to be the light's direction. The θ_o range is set to be the angular width of the inner cone of the light and θ_e corresponds to the width of its falloff at the edges. While this falloff does not exactly match the cosine-weighted falloff used in the LightBounds::Importance() method, it is close enough for these purposes.

There is a subtlety in the computation of phi for this light: it is computed as if the light source was an isotropic point source and is not affected by the spotlight's cone angle, like the computation in SpotLight::Phi() is. To understand the reason for this, consider two spotlights with the same radiant intensity, one with a very narrow cone and one with a wide cone, both illuminating some point in the scene. The total power emitted by the former is much less than the latter, though for a point inside both of their cones, both should be sampled with equal probability—effectively, the cone is accounted for in the light importance function and so should not be included in the phi value supplied here.

⟨*SpotLight Method Definitions*⟩ +≡
```
pstd::optional<LightBounds> SpotLight::Bounds() const {
    Point3f p = renderFromLight(Point3f(0, 0, 0));
    Vector3f w = Normalize(renderFromLight(Vector3f(0, 0, 1)));
    Float phi = scale * Iemit->MaxValue() * 4 * Pi;
    Float cosTheta_e = std::cos(std::acos(cosFalloffEnd) -
                                std::acos(cosFalloffStart));
    return LightBounds(Bounds3f(p, p), w, phi, cosFalloffStart,
                       cosTheta_e, false);
}
```

We will skip past the implementations of the ProjectionLight and GoniometricLight Bounds() methods, which are along similar lines.

The DiffuseAreaLight's Bounds() implementation is different than the previous ones. The utility of the Shape::NormalBounds() method may now be better appreciated; the cone of directions that it returns gives the average normal direction ω and its spread angle θ_o. For area lights, $\theta_e = \pi/2$, since illumination is emitted in the entire hemisphere around each surface normal.

⟨*DiffuseAreaLight Method Definitions*⟩ +≡
```
pstd::optional<LightBounds> DiffuseAreaLight::Bounds() const {
    ⟨Compute phi for diffuse area light bounds 794⟩
    DirectionCone nb = shape.NormalBounds();
    return LightBounds(shape.Bounds(), nb.w, phi, nb.cosTheta,
                       std::cos(Pi / 2), twoSided);
}
```

(a)

(b)

Figure 12.29: Simple Scene with Two Area Lights. The quadrilateral on the right emits light from both sides, while the one on the left only emits from the front side. (a) If the `DiffuseAreaLight::Bounds()` method includes an additional factor of 2 for the two-sided light's importance, then it receives more samples than it should. (b) Without this factor, the light importance values are more accurate, which in turn gives a visible reduction in error. The MSE improvement is a factor of 1.42.

The phi value is found by integrating over the light's area. For lights that use an Image for spatially varying emission, the ⟨*Compute average* `DiffuseAreaLight` *image channel value*⟩ fragment, not included here, computes its average value. Because LightBounds accounts for whether the emitter is one- or two-sided, it is important not to double the shape's area if it is two-sided; that factor is already included in the importance computation. (This subtlety is similar to the one for the SpotLight's phi value.) See Figure 12.29 for an illustration of how this detail makes a difference.

DiffuseAreaLight::Bounds()
  792
Image 1079
LightBounds 786

⟨*Compute* phi *for diffuse area light bounds*⟩ ≡ 　　　　　　　　　　　　　　　　**792**
```
    Float phi = 0;
    if (image) {
        ⟨Compute average DiffuseAreaLight image channel value⟩
    } else
        phi = Lemit->MaxValue();
    phi *= scale * area * Pi;
```

Compactly Bounding Lights

The LightBounds class uses 52 bytes of storage. This is not a problem as far as the total amount of memory consumed for the lights in the scene, but it does affect performance from the amount of space it uses in the cache. For scenes with thousands of lights, multiple instances of the LightBounds will be accessed when traversing the light BVH, and so minimizing its storage requirements improves cache performance and thus overall performance. (This is especially the case on the GPU, since many threads run concurrently on each processor and each will generally follow a different path through the light BVH and thus access different LightBounds instances.)

Therefore, we have also implemented a CompactLightBounds class, which applies a number of techniques to reduce storage requirements for the LightBounds information. It uses just 24 bytes of storage. We use both classes in pbrt: the uncompressed LightBounds is convenient for lights to return from their Bounds() methods and is also a good representation to use when building the light BVH. CompactLightBounds is used solely in the in-memory representation of light BVH nodes, where minimizing size is beneficial to performance.

⟨*CompactLightBounds Definition*⟩ ≡
```
    class CompactLightBounds {
    public:
        ⟨CompactLightBounds Public Methods 794⟩
    private:
        ⟨CompactLightBounds Private Methods 795⟩
        ⟨CompactLightBounds Private Members 795⟩
    };
```

Its constructor takes both a LightBounds instance and a bounding box allb that must completely bound LightBounds::bounds. This bounding box is used to compute quantized bounding box vertex positions to reduce their storage requirements.

⟨*CompactLightBounds Public Methods*⟩ ≡ 　　　　　　　　　　　　　　　　　**794**
```
    CompactLightBounds(const LightBounds &lb, const Bounds3f &allb)
        : w(Normalize(lb.w)), phi(lb.phi),
          qCosTheta_o(QuantizeCos(lb.cosTheta_o)),
          qCosTheta_e(QuantizeCos(lb.cosTheta_e)), twoSided(lb.twoSided) {
        ⟨Quantize bounding box into qb 795⟩
    }
```

The OctahedralVector class from Section 3.8.3 stores a unit vector in 4 bytes, saving 8 from the Vector3 used in LightBounds. Then, the two cosines and the twoSided flag are packed into another 4 bytes using a bitfield, saving another 8. We have left phi alone, since the various compactions already implemented are sufficient for pbrt's current requirements.

⟨*CompactLightBounds Private Members*⟩ ≡   794
```
OctahedralVector w;
Float phi = 0;
struct {
    unsigned int qCosTheta_o: 15;
    unsigned int qCosTheta_e: 15;
    unsigned int twoSided: 1;
};
```

QuantizeCos() maps the provided value (which is expected to be the cosine of an angle and thus between -1 and 1) to a 15-bit unsigned integer. After being remapped to be in $[0, 1]$, multiplying by the largest representable 15-bit unsigned integer, $2^{15} - 1 = 32{,}767$, gives a value that spans the valid range.

Note the use of pstd::floor() to round the quantized cosine value down before returning it: this is preferable to, say, rounding to the nearest integer, since it ensures that any quantization error serves to slightly increase the corresponding angle rather than decreasing it. (Decreasing it could lead to inadvertently determining that the light did not illuminate a point that it actually did.)

⟨*CompactLightBounds Private Methods*⟩ ≡   794
```
static unsigned int QuantizeCos(Float c) {
    return pstd::floor(32767.f * ((c + 1) / 2));
}
```

The bounding box corners are also quantized. Each coordinate of each corner gets 16 bits, all of them stored in the qb member variable. This brings the storage for the bounds down to 12 bytes, from 24 before. Here the quantization is also conservative, rounding down at the lower end of the extent and rounding up at the upper end.

⟨*Quantize bounding box into qb*⟩ ≡   794
```
for (int c = 0; c < 3; ++c) {
    qb[0][c] = pstd::floor(QuantizeBounds(lb.bounds[0][c],
                                   allb.pMin[c], allb.pMax[c]));
    qb[1][c] = pstd::ceil(QuantizeBounds(lb.bounds[1][c],
                                   allb.pMin[c], allb.pMax[c]));
}
```

⟨*CompactLightBounds Private Members*⟩ +≡   794
```
uint16_t qb[2][3];
```

QuantizeBounds() remaps a coordinate value c between min and max to the range $[0, 2^{16} - 1]$, the range of values that an unsigned 16-bit integer can store.

⟨*CompactLightBounds Private Methods*⟩ +≡   794
```
static Float QuantizeBounds(Float c, Float min, Float max) {
    if (min == max) return 0;
    return 65535.f * Clamp((c - min) / (max - min), 0, 1);
}
```

A few convenience methods make the values of various member variables available. For the two quantized cosines, the inverse computation of QuantizeCos() is performed.

⟨*CompactLightBounds Public Methods*⟩ +≡   **794**
```
    bool TwoSided() const { return twoSided; }
    Float CosTheta_o() const { return 2 * (qCosTheta_o / 32767.f) - 1; }
    Float CosTheta_e() const { return 2 * (qCosTheta_e / 32767.f) - 1; }
```

The `Bounds()` method returns the `Bounds3f` for the `CompactLightBounds`. It must be passed the same `Bounds3f` as was originally passed to its constructor for the correct result to be returned.

⟨*CompactLightBounds Public Methods*⟩ +≡   **794**
```
    Bounds3f Bounds(const Bounds3f &allb) const {
        return {Point3f(Lerp(qb[0][0] / 65535.f, allb.pMin.x, allb.pMax.x),
                        Lerp(qb[0][1] / 65535.f, allb.pMin.y, allb.pMax.y),
                        Lerp(qb[0][2] / 65535.f, allb.pMin.z, allb.pMax.z)),
                Point3f(Lerp(qb[1][0] / 65535.f, allb.pMin.x, allb.pMax.x),
                        Lerp(qb[1][1] / 65535.f, allb.pMin.y, allb.pMax.y),
                        Lerp(qb[1][2] / 65535.f, allb.pMin.z, allb.pMax.z))};
    }
```

Finally, `CompactLightBounds()` also provides an `Importance()` method. Its implementation also requires that the original `Bounds3f` be provided so that the `Bounds()` method can be called. Given the unquantized bounds and cosines made available in appropriately named local variables, the remainder of the implementation can share the same fragments as were used in the implementation of `LightBounds::Importance()`.

⟨*CompactLightBounds Public Methods*⟩ +≡   **794**
```
    Float Importance(Point3f p, Normal3f n, const Bounds3f &allb) const {
        Bounds3f bounds = Bounds(allb);
        Float cosTheta_o = CosTheta_o(), cosTheta_e = CosTheta_e();
        ⟨Return importance for light bounds at reference point 788⟩
    }
```

Light Bounding Volume Hierarchies

Given a way of bounding lights as well as a compact representation of these bounds, we can turn to the implementation of the `BVHLightSampler`. This light sampler is the default for most of the integrators in pbrt. Not only is it effective at efficiently sampling among large collections of lights, it even reduces error in simple scenes with just a few lights. Figures 12.30 and 12.31 show two examples.

⟨*BVHLightSampler Definition*⟩ ≡
```
    class BVHLightSampler {
      public:
        ⟨BVHLightSampler Public Methods 802⟩
      private:
        ⟨BVHLightSampler Private Methods 800⟩
        ⟨BVHLightSampler Private Members 797⟩
    };
```

Its constructor starts by making a copy of the provided array of lights before proceeding to initialize the BVH and additional data structures.

(a)

(b)

Figure 12.30: A Simple Scene with Two Light Sources. (a) Rendered with 1 sample per pixel using the `PowerLightSampler`. (b) Rendered with 1 sample per pixel using the `BVHLightSampler`. Even with a small number of lights, error is visibly lower with a sampler that uses spatially varying sampling probabilities due to being able to choose nearby bright lights with higher probability. In this case, MSE is improved by a factor of 2.72.

⟨*BVHLightSampler Method Definitions*⟩ ≡
```
BVHLightSampler::BVHLightSampler(pstd::span<const Light> lights,
                                 Allocator alloc)
    : lights(lights.begin(), lights.end(), alloc), infiniteLights(alloc),
      nodes(alloc), lightToBitTrail(alloc) {
    ⟨Initialize infiniteLights array and light BVH 798⟩
}
```

⟨*BVHLightSampler Private Members*⟩ ≡   **796**
```
pstd::vector<Light> lights;
```

(a)

(b)

Figure 12.31: *Zero Day* **Scene, with 8,878 Area Lights.** (a) Rendered with the `PowerLightSampler`. (b) Rendered with the `BVHLightSampler`. Both images are rendered with 16 samples per pixel. For a scene of this complexity, an effective light sampling algorithm is crucial. The `BVHLightSampler` gives an MSE improvement of 2.37× with only a 5.8% increase in rendering time. Monte Carlo efficiency is improved by a factor of 2.25. *(Scene courtesy of Beeple.)*

Because the BVH cannot store lights at infinity, the first step is to partition the lights into those that can be stored in the BVH and those that cannot. This is handled by a loop over all the provided lights after which the BVH is constructed.

⟨*Initialize* infiniteLights *array and light BVH*⟩ ≡   **797**
```
    std::vector<std::pair<int, LightBounds>> bvhLights;
    for (size_t i = 0; i < lights.size(); ++i) {
        ⟨Store ith light in either infiniteLights or bvhLights 799⟩
    }
    if (!bvhLights.empty())
        buildBVH(bvhLights, 0, bvhLights.size(), 0, 0);
```

Lights that are not able to provide a `LightBounds` are added to the `infiniteLights` array and are sampled independently of the lights stored in the BVH. As long as they have nonzero emitted power, the rest are added to the `bvhLights` array, which is used during BVH construction. Along the way, a bounding box that encompasses all the BVH lights' bounding boxes is maintained in `allLightBounds`; this is the bounding box that will be passed to the `CompactLightBounds` for quantizing the spatial bounds of individual lights.

⟨*Store ith light in either* infiniteLights *or* bvhLights⟩ ≡   798
```
Light light = lights[i];
pstd::optional<LightBounds> lightBounds = light.Bounds();
if (!lightBounds)
    infiniteLights.push_back(light);
else if (lightBounds->phi > 0) {
    bvhLights.push_back(std::make_pair(i, *lightBounds));
    allLightBounds = Union(allLightBounds, lightBounds->bounds);
}
```

⟨*BVHLightSampler Private Members*⟩ +≡   796
```
pstd::vector<Light> infiniteLights;
Bounds3f allLightBounds;
```

The light BVH is represented using an instance of the LightBVHNode structure for each tree node, both interior and leaf. It uses a total of 28 bytes of storage, adding just 4 to the 24 used by CompactLightBounds, though its declaration specifies 32-byte alignment, ensuring that 2 of them fit neatly into a typical 64-byte cache line on a CPU, and 4 of them fit into a 128-byte GPU cache line.

⟨*LightBVHNode Definition*⟩ ≡
```
struct alignas (32) LightBVHNode {
    ⟨LightBVHNode Public Methods 799⟩
    ⟨LightBVHNode Public Members 799⟩
};
```

Naturally, each LightBVHNode stores the CompactLightBounds for either a single light or a collection of them. Like the BVHAggregate's BVH, the light BVH is laid out in memory so that the first child of each interior node is immediately after it. Therefore, it is only necessary to store information about the second child's location in the LightBVHNode. The BVHLightSampler stores all nodes in a contiguous array, so an index suffices; a full pointer is unnecessary.

⟨*LightBVHNode Public Members*⟩ ≡   799
```
CompactLightBounds lightBounds;
struct {
    unsigned int childOrLightIndex:31;
    unsigned int isLeaf:1;
};
```

⟨*BVHLightSampler Private Members*⟩ +≡   796
```
pstd::vector<LightBVHNode> nodes;
```

Two object-creation methods return a LightBVHNode of the specified type.

⟨*LightBVHNode Public Methods*⟩ ≡   799
```
static LightBVHNode MakeLeaf(unsigned int lightIndex,
                             const CompactLightBounds &cb) {
    return LightBVHNode{cb, {lightIndex, 1}};
}
```

⟨*LightBVHNode Public Methods*⟩ +≡   799

```
static LightBVHNode MakeInterior(unsigned int child1Index,
                                 const CompactLightBounds &cb) {
    return LightBVHNode{cb, {child1Index, 0}};
}
```

The `buildBVH()` method constructs the BVH by recursively partitioning the lights until it reaches a single light, at which point a leaf node is constructed. Its implementation closely follows the approach implemented in the `BVHAggregate::buildRecursive()` method: along each dimension, the light bounds are assigned to a fixed number of buckets according to their centroids. Next, a cost model is evaluated for splitting the lights at each bucket boundary. The minimum cost split is chosen and the lights are partitioned into two sets, each one passed to a recursive invocation of `buildBVH()`.

Because these two methods are so similar, here we will only include the fragments where the `BVHLightSampler` substantially diverges—in how nodes are initialized and in the cost model used to evaluate candidate splits.

⟨*BVHLightSampler Private Methods*⟩ ≡   796

```
std::pair<int, LightBounds> buildBVH(
    std::vector<std::pair<int, LightBounds>> &bvhLights, int start, int end,
    uint32_t bitTrail, int depth);
```

When this method is called with a range corresponding to a single light, a leaf node is initialized and the recursion terminates. A `CompactLightBounds` is created using the bounding box of all lights' bounds to initialize its quantized bounding box coordinates and the BVH tree node can be added to the `nodes` array.

⟨*Initialize leaf node if only a single light remains*⟩ ≡

```
if (end - start == 1) {
    int nodeIndex = nodes.size();
    CompactLightBounds cb(bvhLights[start].second, allLightBounds);
    int lightIndex = bvhLights[start].first;
    nodes.push_back(LightBVHNode::MakeLeaf(lightIndex, cb));
    lightToBitTrail.Insert(lights[lightIndex], bitTrail);
    return {nodeIndex, bvhLights[start].second};
}
```

In order to implement the `PMF()` method, it is necessary to follow a path through the BVH from the root down to the leaf node for the given light. We encode these paths using *bit trails*, integers where each bit encodes which of the two child nodes should be visited at each level of the tree in order to reach the light's leaf node. The lowest bit indicates which child should be visited after the root node, and so forth. These values are computed while the BVH is built and stored in a hash table that uses `Light`s as keys.

⟨*BVHLightSampler Private Members*⟩ +≡   796

```
HashMap<Light, uint32_t> lightToBitTrail;
```

When there are multiple lights to consider, the `EvaluateCost()` method is called to evaluate the cost model for the two `LightBounds` for each split candidate. In addition to the `LightBounds` for which to compute the cost, it takes the bounding box of all the lights passed to the current invocation of `buildBVH()` as well as the dimension in which the split is being performed.

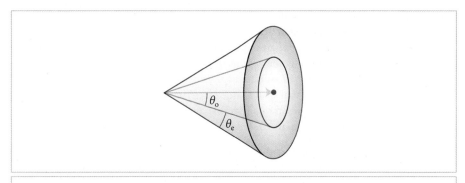

Figure 12.32: The direction bounds measure is found by integrating to find the solid angle of the center cone up to θ_o and then applying a cosine weighting over the additional angle of θ_e.

⟨*BVHLightSampler Private Methods*⟩ +≡   796
```
Float EvaluateCost(const LightBounds &b, const Bounds3f &bounds,
                   int dim) const {
    ⟨Evaluate direction bounds measure for LightBounds 801⟩
    ⟨Return complete cost estimate for LightBounds 802⟩
}
```

The principal surface normal direction and the angles θ_o and θ_e that are stored in LightBounds are worthwhile to include in the light BVH cost function. Doing so can encourage partitions of primitives into groups that emit light in different directions, which can be helpful for culling groups of lights that do not illuminate a given receiving point. To compute these costs, pbrt uses a weighted measure of the solid angle of directions that the direction bounds subtend. A weight of 1 is used for all directions inside the center cone up to θ_o and then the remainder of directions up to θ_e are cosine-weighted, following the importance computation earlier. (See Figure 12.32.) Integrating over the relevant directions gives us the direction bounds measure,

$$M_\Omega = 2\pi \left(\int_0^{\theta_o} \sin\theta' \, d\theta' + \int_{\theta_o}^{\min(\theta_o+\theta_e,\pi)} \cos(\theta'-\theta_o) \, \sin\theta' \, d\theta' \right).$$

The first term integrates to $1 - \cos\theta_o$ and the second has a simple analytic form that is evaluated in the second term of M_omega's initializer below.

⟨*Evaluate direction bounds measure for LightBounds*⟩ ≡   801
```
Float theta_o = std::acos(b.cosTheta_o), theta_e = std::acos(b.cosTheta_e);
Float theta_w = std::min(theta_o + theta_e, Pi);
Float sinTheta_o = SafeSqrt(1 - Sqr(b.cosTheta_o));
Float M_omega = 2 * Pi * (1 - b.cosTheta_o) +
    Pi / 2 * (2 * theta_w * sinTheta_o - std::cos(theta_o - 2 * theta_w) -
              2 * theta_o * sinTheta_o + b.cosTheta_o);
```

Three other factors go into the full cost estimate:

- The power estimate phi: in general, the higher the power of the lights in a LightBounds, the more important it is to minimize factors like the spatial and direction bounds.
- A regularization factor Kr that discourages long and thin bounding boxes.
- The surface area of the LightBounds's bounding box.

The use of surface area in the cost metric deserves note: with the BVHAggregate, the surface area heuristic was grounded in geometric probability, as the surface area of a convex object is proportional to the probability of a random ray intersecting it. In this case, no rays are being traced. Arguably, minimizing the volume of the bounds would be a more appropriate approach in this case. In practice, the surface area seems to be more effective—one reason is that it penalizes bounding boxes that span a large extent in two dimensions but little or none in the third. Such bounding boxes are undesirable as they may subtend large solid angles, adding more uncertainty to importance estimates.

⟨*Return complete cost estimate for* LightBounds⟩ ≡   **801**
```
Float Kr = MaxComponentValue(bounds.Diagonal()) / bounds.Diagonal()[dim];
return b.phi * M_omega * Kr * b.bounds.SurfaceArea();
```

Once the lights have been partitioned, two fragments take care of recursively initializing the child nodes and then initializing the interior node. The first step is to take a spot in the nodes array for the interior node; this spot must be claimed before the children are initialized in order to ensure that the first child is the successor of the interior node in the array. Two recursive calls to buildBVH() then initialize the children. The main thing to note in them is the maintenance of the bitTrail value passed down into each one. For the first child, the corresponding bit should be set to zero. bitTrail is zero-initialized in the initial call to buildBVH(), so it has this value already and there is nothing to do. For the second call, the bit for the current tree depth is set to 1.

⟨*Allocate interior* LightBVHNode *and recursively initialize children*⟩ ≡
```
int nodeIndex = nodes.size();
nodes.push_back(LightBVHNode());
std::pair<int, LightBounds> child0 =
    buildBVH(bvhLights, start, mid, bitTrail, depth + 1);
std::pair<int, LightBounds> child1 =
    buildBVH(bvhLights, mid, end, bitTrail | (1u << depth), depth + 1);
```

The interior node can be initialized after the children have been. Its light bounds are given by the union of its children's, which allows initializing a CompactLightBounds and then the LightBVHNode itself.

⟨*Initialize interior node and return node index and bounds*⟩ ≡
```
LightBounds lb = Union(child0.second, child1.second);
CompactLightBounds cb(lb, allLightBounds);
nodes[nodeIndex] = LightBVHNode::MakeInterior(child1.first, cb);
return {nodeIndex, lb};
```

Given the BVH, we can now implement the Sample() method, which samples a light given a reference point in a LightSampleContext.

⟨*BVHLightSampler Public Methods*⟩ ≡   **796**
```
pstd::optional<SampledLight>
Sample(const LightSampleContext &ctx, Float u) const {
    ⟨Compute infinite light sampling probability pInfinite 803⟩
    if (u < pInfinite) {
        ⟨Sample infinite lights with uniform probability 803⟩
    } else {
        ⟨Traverse light BVH to sample light 804⟩
    }
}
```

The first choice to make is whether an infinite light should be sampled or whether the light BVH should be used to choose a noninfinite light. The BVHLightSampler gives equal probability to sampling each infinite light and to sampling the BVH, from which the probability of sampling an infinite light follows directly.

⟨*Compute infinite light sampling probability* pInfinite⟩ ≡   802, 805
```
    Float pInfinite = Float(infiniteLights.size()) /
        Float(infiniteLights.size() + (nodes.empty() ? 0 : 1));
```

If an infinite light is to be sampled, then the random sample u is rescaled to provide a new uniform random sample that is used to index into the infiniteLights array.

⟨*Sample infinite lights with uniform probability*⟩ ≡   802
```
    u /= pInfinite;
    int index = std::min<int>(u * infiniteLights.size(),
                              infiniteLights.size() - 1);
    Float pmf = pInfinite / infiniteLights.size();
    return SampledLight{infiniteLights[index], pmf};
```

Otherwise a light is sampled by traversing the BVH. At each interior node, probabilities are found for sampling each of the two children using importance values returned by the LightBounds for the reference point. A child node is then randomly chosen according to these probabilities. In the end, the probability of choosing a leaf node is equal to the product of probabilities along the path from the root to the leaf (see Figure 12.33). With this traversal scheme, there is no need to maintain a stack of nodes to be processed as the BVHAggregate does—a single path is taken down the tree from the root to a leaf.

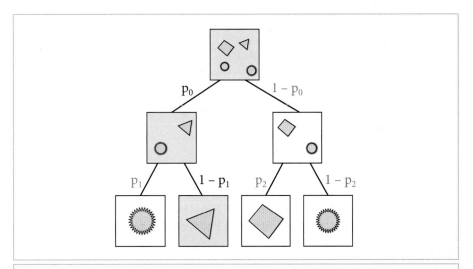

Figure 12.33: Sampling a Light BVH. At each non-leaf node of the tree, we compute discrete probabilities p_i and $1 - p_i$ for sampling each child node and then randomly choose a child accordingly. The probability of sampling each leaf node is the product of probabilities along the path from the root of the tree down to it. Here, the nodes that are visited and the associated probabilities for sampling the triangular light source are highlighted.

⟨*Traverse light BVH to sample light*⟩ ≡   **802**

```
if (nodes.empty())
    return {};
```
⟨*Declare common variables for light BVH traversal* **804**⟩
```
while (true) {
```
    ⟨*Process light BVH node for light sampling* **804**⟩
```
}
```

A few values will be handy in the following traversal of the BVH. Among them are the uniform sample u, which is remapped to a new uniform random sample in $[0, 1)$. pmf starts out with the probability of sampling the BVH in the first place; each time a child node of the tree is randomly sampled, it will be multiplied by the discrete probability of that sampling choice so that in the end it stores the complete probability for sampling the light.

⟨*Declare common variables for light BVH traversal*⟩ ≡   **804**

```
Point3f p = ctx.p();
Normal3f n = ctx.ns;
u = std::min<Float>((u - pInfinite) / (1 - pInfinite), OneMinusEpsilon);
int nodeIndex = 0;
Float pmf = 1 - pInfinite;
```

At each interior node, a child node is randomly sampled. Given a leaf node, we have reached the sampled light.

⟨*Process light BVH node for light sampling*⟩ ≡   **804**

```
LightBVHNode node = nodes[nodeIndex];
if (!node.isLeaf) {
    ⟨Compute light BVH child node importances 804⟩
    ⟨Randomly sample light BVH child node 805⟩
} else {
    ⟨Confirm light has nonzero importance before returning light sample 805⟩
}
```

The first step at an interior node is to compute the importance values for the two child nodes. It may be the case that both of them are 0, indicating that neither child illuminates the reference point. That we may end up in this situation may be surprising: in that case, why would we have chosen to visit this node in the first place? This state of affairs is a natural consequence of the accuracy of light bounds improving on the way down the tree, which makes it possible for them to better differentiate regions that their respective subtrees do and do not illuminate.

⟨*Compute light BVH child node importances*⟩ ≡   **804**

```
const LightBVHNode *children[2] = {&nodes[nodeIndex + 1],
                                   &nodes[node.childOrLightIndex] };
Float ci[2] = { children[0]->lightBounds.Importance(p, n, allLightBounds),
                children[1]->lightBounds.Importance(p, n, allLightBounds)};
if (ci[0] == 0 && ci[1] == 0)
    return {};
```

Given at least one nonzero importance value, SampleDiscrete() takes care of choosing a child node. The sampling PMF it returns is incorporated into the running pmf product. We further use its capability for remapping the sample u to a new uniform sample in $[0, 1)$, which allows the reuse of the u variable in subsequent loop iterations.

⟨*Randomly sample light BVH child node*⟩ ≡   804
```
Float nodePMF;
int child = SampleDiscrete(ci, u, &nodePMF, &u);
pmf *= nodePMF;
nodeIndex = (child == 0) ? (nodeIndex + 1) : node.childOrLightIndex;
```

When a leaf node is reached, we have found a light. The light should only be returned if it has a nonzero importance value, however: if the importance is zero, then it is better to return no light than to return one and cause the caller to go through some additional work to sample it before finding that it has no contribution. Most of the time, we have already determined that the node's light bounds have a nonzero importance value by dint of sampling the node while traversing the BVH in the first place. It is thus only in the case of a single-node BVH with a single light stored in it that this test must be performed here.

⟨*Confirm light has nonzero importance before returning light sample*⟩ ≡   804
```
if (nodeIndex > 0 ||
    node.lightBounds.Importance(p, n, allLightBounds) > 0)
    return SampledLight{lights[node.childOrLightIndex], pmf};
return {};
```

Computing the PMF for sampling a specified light follows a set of computations similar to those of the sampling method: if the light is an infinite light, the infinite light sampling probability is returned and otherwise the BVH is traversed to compute the light's sampling probability. In this case, BVH traversal is not stochastic, but is specified by the bit trail for the given light, which encodes the path to the leaf node that stores it.

⟨*BVHLightSampler Public Methods*⟩ +≡   796
```
Float PMF(const LightSampleContext &ctx, Light light) const {
    ⟨Handle infinite light PMF computation 805⟩
    ⟨Initialize local variables for BVH traversal for PMF computation 805⟩
    ⟨Compute light's PMF by walking down tree nodes to the light 806⟩
}
```

If the given light is not in the bit trail hash table, then it is not stored in the BVH and therefore must be an infinite light. The probability of sampling it is one over the total number of infinite lights plus one if there is a light BVH.

⟨*Handle infinite light PMF computation*⟩ ≡   805
```
if (!lightToBitTrail.HasKey(light))
    return 1.f / (infiniteLights.size() + (nodes.empty() ? 0 : 1));
```

A number of values will be useful as the tree is traversed, including the bit trail that points the way to the correct leaf, the PMF of the path taken so far, and the index of the current node being visited, starting here at the root.

⟨*Initialize local variables for BVH traversal for PMF computation*⟩ ≡   805
```
uint32_t bitTrail = lightToBitTrail[light];
Point3f p = ctx.p();
Normal3f n = ctx.ns;
⟨Compute infinite light sampling probability pInfinite 803⟩
Float pmf = 1 - pInfinite;
int nodeIndex = 0;
```

For a light that is stored in the BVH, the probability of sampling it is again computed as the product of each discrete probability of sampling the child node that leads to its leaf node.

⟨*Compute light's PMF by walking down tree nodes to the light*⟩ ≡   805
```
while (true) {
    const LightBVHNode *node = &nodes[nodeIndex];
    if (node->isLeaf)
        return pmf;
    ⟨Compute child importances and update PMF for current node 806⟩
    ⟨Use bitTrail to find next node index and update its value 806⟩
}
```

The lowest bit of bitTrail encodes which of the two children of the node is visited on a path down to the light's leaf node. In turn, it is possible to compute the probability of sampling that node given the two child nodes' importance values.

⟨*Compute child importances and update PMF for current node*⟩ ≡   806
```
const LightBVHNode *child0 = &nodes[nodeIndex + 1];
const LightBVHNode *child1 = &nodes[node->childOrLightIndex];
Float ci[2] = { child0->lightBounds.Importance(p, n, allLightBounds),
                child1->lightBounds.Importance(p, n, allLightBounds) };
pmf *= ci[bitTrail & 1] / (ci[0] + ci[1]);
```

The low-order bit of bitTrail also points us to which node to visit next on the way down the tree. After nodeIndex is updated, bitTrail is shifted right by one bit so that the low-order bit encodes the choice to make at the next level of the tree.

⟨*Use bitTrail to find next node index and update its value*⟩ ≡   806
```
nodeIndex = (bitTrail & 1) ? node->childOrLightIndex : (nodeIndex + 1);
bitTrail >>= 1;
```

The basic Sample() and PMF() methods for when a reference point is not specified sample all the lights uniformly and so are not included here, as they parallel the implementations in the UniformLightSampler.

FURTHER READING

Light Emission Descriptions

Warn (1983) developed early models of light sources with nonisotropic emission distributions, including the spotlight model used in this chapter. Verbeck and Greenberg (1984) also described a number of techniques for modeling light sources that are now classic parts of the light modeling toolbox. Barzel (1997) described a highly parameterized model for light sources, including multiple parameters for controlling rate of falloff, the area of space that is illuminated, and so on. Bjorke (2001) described a number of additional techniques for shaping illumination for artistic effect. (Many parts of the Barzel and Bjorke approaches are not physically based, however.)

The goniophotometric light source approximation is widely used to model area light sources in the field of illumination engineering. The rule of thumb there is that once a reference point is five times an area light source's radius away from it, a point light approximation has sufficient accuracy for most applications. File format standards have been developed for encoding goniophotometric diagrams for these applications (Illuminating Engineering Society of North America 2002). Many lighting fixture manufacturers provide data in these formats on their websites.

Ashdown (1993) proposed a more sophisticated light source model than goniophotometric; he measured the directional distribution of emitted radiance at a large number of points around a light source and described how to use the resulting 4D table to compute the received radiance distribution at other points. Another generalization of goniometric lights was suggested by Heidrich et al. (1998), who represented light sources as a 4D exitant *lightfield*—essentially a function of both position and direction—and showed how to use this representation for rendering. Additional work in this area was done by Goesele et al. (2003) and Mas et al. (2008), who introduced a more space-efficient representation and improved rendering efficiency.

Peters (2021a) has developed efficient techniques for sampling lights defined by lines (i.e., infinitesimally thin cylinders) and shown how to sample the product of lighting and the BRDF using linearly transformed cosines (Heitz et al. 2016a).

Real-world light sources are often fairly complex, including carefully designed systems of mirrors and lenses to shape the distribution of light emitted by the light source. (Consider, for example, the headlights on a car, where it is important to evenly illuminate the surface of the road without shining too much light in the eyes of approaching drivers.) All the corresponding specular reflection and transmission is challenging for light transport algorithms. It can therefore be worthwhile to do some precomputation to create a representation of light sources' final emission distributions after all of this scattering that is then used as the light source model for rendering. To this end, Kniep et al. (2009) proposed tracing the paths of photons leaving the light's filament until they hit a bounding surface around the light. They then recorded the position and direction of outgoing photons and used this information when computing illumination at points in the scene. Velázquez-Armendáriz et al. (2015) showed how to compute a set of point lights with directionally varying emission distributions to model emitted radiance from complex light sources. They then approximated the radiance distribution in the light interior using spherical harmonics. More recently, Zhu et al. (2021) applied a neural representation to complex lights, encoding lights' radiance distributions and view-dependent sampling distributions and opacities in neural networks.

Illumination from Environment Maps

Blinn and Newell (1976) first introduced the idea of environment maps and their use for simulating illumination, although they only considered illumination of specular objects. Greene (1986) further refined these ideas, considering antialiasing and different representations for environment maps. Nishita and Nakamae (1986) developed algorithms for efficiently rendering objects illuminated by hemispherical skylights and generated some of the first images that showed off that distinctive lighting effect. Miller and Hoffman (1984) were the first to consider using arbitrary environment maps to illuminate objects with diffuse and glossy BRDFs. Debevec (1998) later extended this work and investigated issues related to capturing images of real environments.

Representing illumination from the sun and sky is a particularly important application of infinite light sources; the "Further Reading" section in Chapter 14 includes a number of references related to simulating skylight scattering. Directly measuring illumination from the sky is also an effective way to find accurate skylight illumination; see Kider et al. (2014) for details of a system built to do this.

pbrt's infinite area light source models incident radiance from the light as purely a function of direction. Especially for indoor scenes, this assumption can be fairly inaccurate; position matters as well. Unger et al. (2003) captured the incident radiance as a function of direction at many different locations in a real-world scene and used this representation for rendering. Unger et al. (2008) improved on this work and showed how to decimate the samples to reduce storage requirements without introducing too much error. Lu et al. (2015) developed techniques for efficiently importance sampling these light sources.

The use of the `allowIncompletePDF` parameter to avoid generating low-probability samples from infinite light sources in the presence of multiple importance sampling is an application of MIS compensation, which was developed by Karlík et al. (2019).

Subr and Arvo (2007b) developed an efficient technique for sampling environment map light sources that not only accounts for the $\cos\theta$ term from the scattering equation but also only generates samples in the hemisphere around the surface normal. More recently, Conty Estevez and Lecocq (2018) introduced a technique for sampling according to the product of the BSDF and the environment map based on discretizing the environment map into coarse grids of pixels, conservatively evaluating the maximum of the BSDF over the corresponding sets of directions, and then choosing a region of the environment map according to the product of BSDF and pixel values. Given a selected grid cell, conventional environment map sampling is applied. (See also the "Further Reading" section in Chapter 13 for further references to light and BSDF product sampling algorithms.)

When environment maps are used for illuminating indoor scenes, many incident directions may be blocked by the building structure. Bitterli et al. (2015) developed the environment map rectification approach to this problem that we have implemented in the `PortalImageInfiniteLight`. One shortcoming of Bitterli et al.'s approach is that the image must be rectified for each plane in which there is a portal. Ogaki (2020) addresses this issue by building a BVH over the portals using Conty Estevez and Kulla's light BVH (2018) and then decomposing portals into triangles to sample a specific direction according to the environment map.

Sampling-based approaches can also be used to account for environment map visibility. Bashford-Rogers et al. (2013) developed a two-pass algorithm where a first pass from the camera finds directions that reach the environment map; this information is used to create sampling distributions for use in a second rendering pass. Atanasov et al. (2018) also applied a two-pass algorithm to the task, furthermore discretizing regions of the scene in order to account for different parts of the environment map being visible in different regions of the scene.

Optimizing Visibility Testing

As discussed in Chapter 6, one way to reduce the time spent tracing shadow rays is to have methods like `Shape::IntersectP()` and `Primitive::IntersectP()` that just check for any occlusion along a ray without bothering to compute the geometric information at the intersection point.

Another approach for optimizing ray tracing for shadow rays is the *shadow cache*, where each light stores a pointer to the last primitive that occluded a shadow ray to the light. That primitive is checked first to see if it occludes subsequent shadow rays before the ray is passed to the acceleration structure (Haines and Greenberg 1986). Pearce (1991) pointed out that the shadow cache does not work well if the scene has finely tessellated geometry; it may be better to cache the BVH node that held the last occluder, for instance. (The shadow cache can similarly be defeated when multiple levels of reflection and refraction are present or when Monte Carlo ray-tracing techniques are used.) Hart et al. (1999) developed a generalization of the shadow cache that tracks which objects block light from particular light sources and clips their geometry against the light-source geometry so that shadow rays do not need to be traced toward the parts of the light that are certain to be occluded.

A related technique, described by Haines and Greenberg (1986), is the *light buffer* for point light sources, where the light discretizes the directions around it and determines which objects are visible along each set of directions (and are thus potential occluding objects for shadow rays). A related optimization is *shaft culling*, which takes advantage of coherence among groups of rays traced in a similar set of directions (e.g., shadow rays from a single point to points on an area light source). With shaft culling, a shaft that bounds a collection of rays is computed and then the objects in the scene that penetrate the shaft are found. For all the rays in the shaft, it is only necessary to check for intersections with those objects that intersect the shaft, and the expense of ray intersection acceleration structure traversal for each of the rays is avoided (Haines and Wallace 1994).

Woo and Amanatides (1990) classified which lights are visible, not visible, and partially visible in different parts of the scene and stored this information in a voxel-based 3D data structure, using the information to save shadow ray tests. Fernandez, Bala, and Greenberg (2002) developed a similar approach based on spatial decomposition that stores references to important blockers in each voxel and also builds up this information on demand during rendering. A related approach to reducing the cost of shadow rays is visibility caching, where the point-to-point visibility function's value is cached for clusters of points on surfaces in the scene (Clarberg and Akenine-Möller 2008b; Popov et al. 2013).

For complex models, simplified versions of their geometry can be used for shadow ray intersections. For example, the simplification envelopes described by Cohen et al. (1996) can create a simplified mesh that bounds a given mesh from both the inside and the outside. If a ray misses the mesh that bounds a complex model from the outside or intersects the mesh that bounds it from the inside, then no further shadow processing is necessary. Only the uncertain remaining cases need to be intersected against the full geometry. A related technique is described by Lukaszewski (2001), who uses the Minkowski sum to effectively expand primitives (or bounds of primitives) in the scene so that intersecting one ray against one of these primitives can determine if any of a collection of rays might have intersected the actual primitives.

The expense of tracing shadow rays to light sources can be significant; a number of techniques have been developed to improve the efficiency of this part of the rendering computation. Billen et al. (2013) tested only a random subset of potential occluders for intersections; a compensation term ensured that the result was unbiased. Following work showed how to use simplified geometry for some shadow tests while still computing the correct result overall (Billen et al. 2014).

Many-Light Sampling

A number of approaches have been developed to efficiently render scenes with hundreds or thousands of light sources. Early work on this problem was done by Ward (1991) and Shirley et al. (1996).

Wald et al. (2003) suggested rendering an image with path tracing and a very low sampling rate (e.g., one path per pixel), recording information about which of the light sources made some contribution to the image. This information is then used to set probabilities for sampling each light. Donikian et al. (2006) adaptively found PDFs for sampling lights through an iterative process of taking a number of light samples, noting which ones were effective, and reusing this information at nearby pixels. The "lightcuts" algorithm, described in the "Further Reading" section of Chapter 13, also addresses this problem.

Tokuyoshi and Harada (2016) organized lights in trees of bounding spheres and stochastically culled them when shading. Conty Estevez and Kulla (2018) organized lights in BVHs and introduced effective approaches for building light BVHs and sampling lights stored in them. pbrt's BVHLightSampler is directly based on their approach. (The *Iray* renderer uses a BVH in a similar fashion for light sampling (Keller et al. 2017).) Conty Estevez and Kulla's approach was subsequently improved by Liu et al. (2019b), who incorporated the BSDF in the sampling weight computations.

BVHLightSampler 796

Incorporating light visibility into the sampling process can substantially improve the results. Vévoda et al. (2018) clustered lights and tracked visibility to them, applying Bayesian regression to learn how to effectively sample lights. Guo et al. (2020) cached information about voxel-to-voxel visibility in a discretization of the scene, which can either be used for Russian roulette or for light importance sampling. Bitterli et al. (2020) showed how to apply spatial and temporal resampling of light samples that include visibility in order to achieve high-quality results with few shadow rays per pixel.

The "bit trail" technique used to encode the path from the root to each light at the leaves of pbrt's BVHLightSampler is due to Laine (2010).

EXERCISES

12.1 The functionality of the SpotLight could be replicated by using a suitable image in conjunction with the ProjectionLight or GoniometricLight. Discuss the advantages and disadvantages of providing this specific functionality separately with the SpotLight class.

12.2 Modify the ProjectionLight to also support orthographic projections. This variant is particularly useful even without an image map, since it gives a directional light source with a beam of user-defined extent.

12.3 The current light source implementations do not support animated transformations. Modify pbrt to include this functionality and render images showing off the effect of animating light positions. Note that if you would like to use the BVHLightSampler with animated light sources, it will require substantial modifications.

12.4 Implement an area light that generalizes the DiffuseAreaLight to support directionally varying emitted radiance. You might, for example, allow focusing the light by computing the cosine of the outgoing direction and the surface normal and raising it to some power. Derive a model such that the total power of the light is left unchanged as the directional distribution of emitted radiance varies and update the light's SampleLe() methods for sampling rays leaving the light to account for the emission distribution. Discuss the implications of your approach for sampling via SampleLi(); should that method be aware of the changed directional distribution?

12.5 Read some of the papers in the "Further Reading" section that discuss the shadow cache, and add this optimization to pbrt. Measure how much it speeds up the system for a variety of scenes. What techniques can you come up with that make it work better in the presence of multiple levels of reflection?

12.6 One of the advantages of the linearity assumption in radiometry is that the final image of a scene is the same as the sum of individual images that account for each light source's contribution (assuming a floating-point image file format is used that does not clip pixel radiance values). An implication of this property is that if a renderer creates a separate image for each light source, it is possible to write interactive lighting design tools that make it possible to quickly see the effects of scaling the contributions of individual lights in the scene without needing to re-render it from scratch. Instead, a light's individual image can be scaled and the final image regenerated by summing all the light images again. (This technique was first applied for opera lighting design by Dorsey, Sillion, and Greenberg (1991).) Modify pbrt to output a separate image for each of the lights in the scene, and write an interactive lighting design tool that uses them in this manner.

⊚ 12.7 Read the paper by Velázquez-Armendáriz et al. (2015), and implement their method for efficiently rendering scenes with complex light sources. Create or find models of a few complex lights that include many shapes that exhibit specular reflection or transmission in order to evaluate your implementation.

⊚ 12.8 Generalize the PortalImageInfiniteLight to allow the specification of multiple portals. Note that multiple coplanar portals can be supported without resampling the environment map, but non-coplanar portals will require multiple copies of it. As noted by Bitterli et al. (2015), the summed area table representation makes it easy to compute the total power passing through a portal given a receiving point. Modify your implementation to use the relative power of multiple portals as a sampling distribution to choose which portal to sample. Render images that show the benefit of this improvement.

⊚ 12.9 Sampling wavelengths according to the XYZ matching functions is a reasonable approach for many scenes, though if the light sources in the scene have highly peaked spectra (as, for example, many fluorescent lights do), error may be reduced by instead sampling wavelengths according to the lights' spectral distributions. Implement this approach and compare the results to pbrt's current wavelength sampling implementation using a variety of spectral emission profiles. How much does the alternative sampling strategy help in the best case versus the worst case? Can you find a way to improve the results further by applying multiple importance sampling?

⊚ 12.10 The BVHLightSampler is missing a number of features in the BVH sampling scheme described by Conty Estevez and Kulla (2018), including an importance factor specialized for participating media and adaptive splitting, where multiple lights may be returned from the sampling operation when it is difficult to determine which child node is a better choice at the upper levels of the tree. Read their paper and improve pbrt's implementation. What is the change in Monte Carlo efficiency? Does the reduction in error justify the increase in computation?

⊚ 12.11 Another shortcoming of the current BVHLightSampler implementation is that it does not account for the BSDF at the reference point but instead effectively assumes a diffuse surface. Read the paper by Liu et al. (2019b) and improve the BVH light sampler's implementation by using their approach to account for this factor. Measure the change in MSE for a variety of scenes with this improvement.

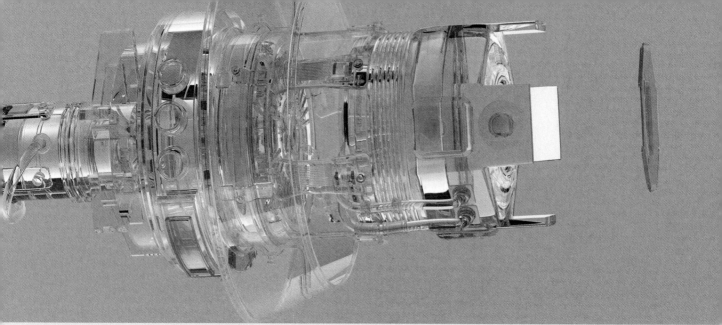

CHAPTER THIRTEEN

13 LIGHT TRANSPORT I: SURFACE REFLECTION

This chapter brings together the ray-tracing algorithms, radiometric concepts, and Monte Carlo sampling algorithms of the previous chapters to implement two different integrators that compute scattered radiance from surfaces in the scene. These integrators are much more effective than the RandomWalkIntegrator from the first chapter; with them, some scenes are rendered with hundreds of times lower error.

We start by deriving the light transport equation, which was first introduced in Section 1.2.6. We can then formally introduce the path-tracing algorithm, which applies Monte Carlo integration to solve that equation. We will then describe the implementation of the SimplePath Integrator, which provides a pared-down implementation of path tracing that is useful for understanding the basic algorithm and for debugging sampling algorithms. The chapter concludes with the PathIntegrator, which is a more complete path tracing implementation.

Both of these integrators find light-carrying paths starting from the camera, accounting for scattering from shapes' surfaces. Chapter 14 will extend path tracing to include the effects of participating media. (The online edition of this book also includes a chapter that describes bidirectional methods for constructing light-carrying paths starting both from the camera and from light sources.)

13.1 THE LIGHT TRANSPORT EQUATION

The light transport equation (LTE) is the governing equation that describes the equilibrium distribution of radiance in a scene. It gives the total reflected radiance at a point on a surface in terms of emission from the surface, its BSDF, and the distribution of incident illumination arriving at the point. For now we will continue to only consider the case where there are no participating media in the scene, saving those complexities for Chapter 14.

The detail that makes evaluating the LTE difficult is the fact that incident radiance at a point is affected by the geometry and scattering properties of all the objects in the scene. For example, a bright light shining on a red object may cause a reddish tint on nearby objects in the scene, or glass may focus light into caustic patterns on a tabletop. Rendering algorithms that account for this complexity are often called *global illumination* algorithms, to differentiate them from *local illumination* algorithms that use only information about the local surface properties in their shading computations.

In this section, we will first derive the LTE and describe some approaches for manipulating the equation to make it easier to solve numerically. We will then describe two generalizations of the LTE that make some of its key properties more clear and serve as the foundation for integrators that implement sophisticated light transport algorithms.

13.1.1 BASIC DERIVATION

The light transport equation depends on the basic assumptions we have already made in choosing to use radiometry to describe light—that wave optics effects are unimportant and that the distribution of radiance in the scene is in equilibrium.

The key principle underlying the LTE is *energy balance*. Any change in energy has to be "charged" to some process, and we must keep track of all the energy. Since we are assuming that lighting is a linear process, the difference between the amount of energy going out of a system and the amount of energy coming in must also be equal to the difference between energy emitted and energy absorbed. This idea holds at many levels of scale. On a macro level we have conservation of power:

$$\Phi_o - \Phi_i = \Phi_e - \Phi_a.$$

The difference between the power leaving an object, Φ_o, and the power entering it, Φ_i, is equal to the difference between the power it emits and the power it absorbs, $\Phi_e - \Phi_a$.

To enforce energy balance at a surface, exitant radiance L_o must be equal to emitted radiance plus the fraction of incident radiance that is scattered. Emitted radiance is given by L_e, and scattered radiance is given by the scattering equation, which gives

$$L_o(\mathrm{p}, \omega_o) = L_e(\mathrm{p}, \omega_o) + \int_{g^2} f(\mathrm{p}, \omega_o, \omega_i)\, L_i(\mathrm{p}, \omega_i)\, |\cos\theta_i|\, d\omega_i.$$

Because we have assumed for now that no participating media are present, radiance is constant along rays through the scene. We can therefore relate the incident radiance at p to the outgoing radiance from another point p′, as shown by Figure 13.1. If we define the *ray-casting function* $t(\mathrm{p}, \omega)$ as a function that computes the first surface point p′ intersected by a ray from p in the direction ω, we can write the incident radiance at p in terms of outgoing radiance at p′:

$$L_i(\mathrm{p}, \omega) = L_o(t(\mathrm{p}, \omega), -\omega).$$

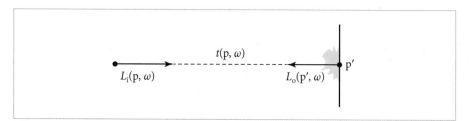

Figure 13.1: Radiance along a Ray through Free Space Is Unchanged. Therefore, to compute the incident radiance along a ray from point p in direction ω, we can find the first surface the ray intersects and compute exitant radiance in the direction $-\omega$ there. The ray-casting function $t(\mathrm{p}, \omega)$ gives the point p′ on the first surface that the ray (p, ω) intersects.

In case the scene is not closed, we will define the ray-casting function to return a special value Λ if the ray (p, ω) does not intersect any object in the scene, such that $L_o(\Lambda, \omega)$ is always 0.

Dropping the subscripts from L_o for brevity, this relationship allows us to write the LTE as

$$L(\text{p}, \omega_o) = L_e(\text{p}, \omega_o) + \int_{\mathcal{S}^2} f(\text{p}, \omega_o, \omega_i)\, L(t(\text{p}, \omega_i), -\omega_i)\, |\cos\theta_i|\, d\omega_i. \qquad [13.1]$$

The key to the above representation is that there is only *one* quantity of interest, exitant radiance from points on surfaces. Of course, it appears on both sides of the equation, so our task is still not simple, but it is certainly easier. It is important to keep in mind that we were able to arrive at this equation simply by enforcing energy balance in our scene.

13.1.2 ANALYTIC SOLUTIONS TO THE LTE

The brevity of the LTE belies the fact that it is impossible to solve analytically other than in very simple cases. The complexity that comes from physically based BSDF models, arbitrary scene geometry, and the intricate visibility relationships among objects all conspire to mandate a numerical solution technique. Fortunately, the combination of ray-tracing algorithms and Monte Carlo integration gives a powerful pair of tools that can handle this complexity without needing to impose restrictions on various components of the LTE (e.g., requiring that all BSDFs be Lambertian or substantially limiting the geometric representations that are supported).

It is possible to find analytic solutions to the LTE in very simple settings. While this is of little help for general-purpose rendering, it can help with debugging the implementations of integrators. If an integrator that is supposed to solve the complete LTE does not compute a solution that matches an analytic solution, then clearly there is a bug in the integrator. As an example, consider the interior of a sphere where all points on the surface of the sphere have a Lambertian BRDF, $f(\text{p}, \omega_o, \omega_i) = c$, and also emit a constant amount of radiance in all directions. We have

$$L(\text{p}, \omega_o) = L_e + c \int_{\mathcal{H}^2(\mathbf{n})} L(t(\text{p}, \omega_i), -\omega_i)\, |\cos\theta_i|\, d\omega_i.$$

The outgoing radiance distribution at any point on the sphere interior must be the same as at any other point; nothing in the environment introduces any variation among different points. Therefore, the incident radiance distribution must be the same at all points, and the cosine-weighted integral of incident radiance must be the same everywhere as well. As such, we can replace the radiance functions with constants and simplify, writing the LTE as

$$L = L_e + c\pi L.$$

While we could immediately solve this equation for L, it is interesting to consider successive substitution of the right hand side into the L term on the right hand side. If we also replace πc with ρ_{hh}, the reflectance of a Lambertian surface, we have

$$L = L_e + \rho_{hh}(L_e + \rho_{hh}(L_e + \cdots$$
$$= \sum_{i=0}^{\infty} L_e \rho_{hh}^i.$$

In other words, exitant radiance is equal to the emitted radiance at the point plus light that has been scattered by a BSDF once after emission, plus light that has been scattered twice, and so forth.

Because $\rho_{hh} < 1$ due to conservation of energy, the series converges and the reflected radiance at all points in all directions is

$$L = \frac{L_e}{1 - \rho_{hh}}.$$

(This series is called a *Neumann series*.)

This process of repeatedly substituting the LTE's right hand side into the incident radiance term in the integral can be instructive in more general cases.[1] For example, only accounting for direct illumination effectively computes the result of making a single substitution:

$$L(p, \omega_o) = L_e(p, \omega_o) + \int_{s^2} f(p, \omega_o, \omega_i) L_d(p, \omega_i) |\cos \theta_i| \, d\omega_i,$$

where

$$L_d(p, \omega_i) = L_e(t(p, \omega_i), -\omega_i)$$

and further scattering is ignored.

Over the next few pages, we will see how performing successive substitutions in this manner and then regrouping the results expresses the LTE in a more natural way for developing rendering algorithms.

13.1.3 THE SURFACE FORM OF THE LTE

One reason the LTE as written in Equation (13.1) is complex is that the relationship between geometric objects in the scene is implicit in the ray-tracing function $t(p, \omega)$. Making the behavior of this function explicit in the integrand will shed some light on the structure of this equation. To do this, we will rewrite Equation (13.1) as an integral over *area* instead of an integral over directions on the sphere.

First, we define exitant radiance from a point p' to a point p by

$$L(p' \to p) = L(p', \omega)$$

if p' and p are mutually visible and $\omega = \widehat{p - p'}$. We can also write the BSDF at p' as

$$f(p'' \to p' \to p) = f(p', \omega_o, \omega_i),$$

where $\omega_i = \widehat{p'' - p'}$ and $\omega_o = \widehat{p - p'}$ (Figure 13.2). This is sometimes called the *three-point form* of the BSDF.

Rewriting the terms in the LTE in this manner is not quite enough, however. We also need to multiply by the Jacobian that relates solid angle to area in order to transform the LTE from an integral over direction to one over surface area. Recall that this is $|\cos \theta'|/r^2$.

We will combine this change-of-variables term, the original $|\cos \theta|$ term from the LTE, and a binary visibility function V ($V = 1$ if the two points are mutually visible, and $V = 0$ otherwise) into a single geometric coupling term, $G(p \leftrightarrow p')$:

$$G(p \leftrightarrow p') = V(p \leftrightarrow p') \frac{|\cos \theta| \, |\cos \theta'|}{\| p - p' \|^2}. \tag{13.2}$$

---

[1] Indeed, this sort of series expansion and inversion can be used in the general case, where quantities like the BSDF are expressed in terms of general operators that map incident radiance functions to exitant radiance functions. This approach forms the foundation for applying sophisticated tools from analysis to the light transport problem. See Arvo's thesis (Arvo 1995a) and Veach's thesis (Veach 1997) for further information.

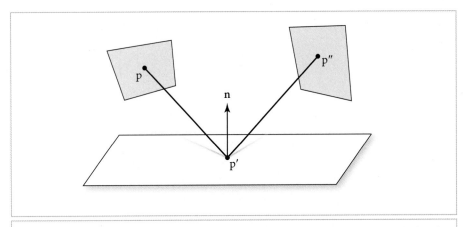

Figure 13.2: The three-point form of the light transport equation converts the integral to be over the domain of points on surfaces in the scene, rather than over directions on the sphere. It is a key transformation for deriving the path integral form of the light transport equation.

Substituting these into the light transport equation and converting to an area integral, we have the three-point form of the LTE,

$$L(\mathrm{p}' \to \mathrm{p}) = L_\mathrm{e}(\mathrm{p}' \to \mathrm{p}) + \int_A f(\mathrm{p}'' \to \mathrm{p}' \to \mathrm{p})\, L(\mathrm{p}'' \to \mathrm{p}')\, G(\mathrm{p}'' \leftrightarrow \mathrm{p}')\, \mathrm{d}A(\mathrm{p}''),$$

[13.3]

where A is all the surfaces of the scene.

Although Equations (13.1) and (13.3) are equivalent, they represent two different ways of approaching light transport. To evaluate Equation (13.1) with Monte Carlo, we would sample directions from a distribution of directions on the sphere and cast rays to evaluate the integrand. For Equation (13.3), however, we would sample points on surfaces according to a distribution over surface area and compute the coupling between those points to evaluate the integrand, tracing rays to evaluate the visibility term $V(\mathrm{p} \leftrightarrow \mathrm{p}')$.

13.1.4 INTEGRAL OVER PATHS

With the area integral form of Equation (13.3), we can derive a more flexible form of the LTE known as the *path integral* formulation of light transport, which expresses radiance as an integral over paths that are themselves points in a high-dimensional *path space*. One of the main motivations for using path space is that it provides an expression for the value of a measurement as an explicit integral over paths, as opposed to the unwieldy recursive definition resulting from the energy balance equation, (13.1).

The explicit form allows for considerable freedom in how these paths are found—essentially any technique for randomly choosing paths can be turned into a workable rendering algorithm that computes the right answer given a sufficient number of samples. This form of the LTE provides the foundation for bidirectional light transport algorithms.

To go from the area integral to a sum over path integrals involving light-carrying paths of different lengths, we can start to expand the three-point light transport equation, repeatedly substituting the right hand side of the equation into the $L(\mathrm{p}'' \to \mathrm{p}')$ term inside the integral. Here are the first few terms that give incident radiance at a point p_0 from another point p_1, where p_1 is the first point on a surface along the ray from p_0 in direction $\mathrm{p}_1 - \mathrm{p}_0$:

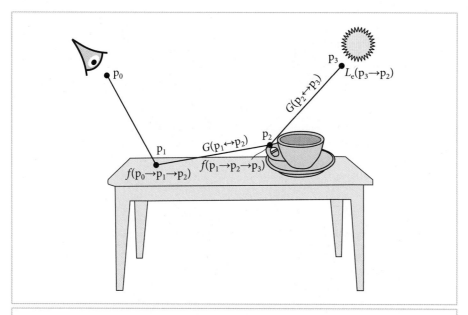

Figure 13.3: The integral over all points p_2 and p_3 on surfaces in the scene given by the light transport equation gives the total contribution of two bounce paths to radiance leaving p_1 in the direction of p_0. The components of the product in the integrand are shown here: the emitted radiance from the light, L_e; the geometric terms between vertices, G; and scattering from the BSDFs, f.

$$L(p_1 \to p_0) = L_e(p_1 \to p_0)$$
$$+ \int_A L_e(p_2 \to p_1) f(p_2 \to p_1 \to p_0)\, G(p_2 \leftrightarrow p_1)\, dA(p_2)$$
$$+ \int_A \int_A L_e(p_3 \to p_2) f(p_3 \to p_2 \to p_1)\, G(p_3 \leftrightarrow p_2)$$
$$\times f(p_2 \to p_1 \to p_0)\, G(p_2 \leftrightarrow p_1)\, dA(p_3)\, dA(p_2) + \cdots$$

Each term on the right side of this equation represents a path of increasing length. For example, the third term is illustrated in Figure 13.3. This path has four vertices, connected by three segments. The total contribution of all such paths of length four (i.e., a vertex at the camera, two vertices at points on surfaces in the scene, and a vertex on a light source) is given by this term. Here, the first two vertices of the path, p_0 and p_1, are predetermined based on the camera ray origin and the point that the camera ray intersects, but p_2 and p_3 can vary over all points on surfaces in the scene. The integral over all such p_2 and p_3 gives the total contribution of paths of length four to radiance arriving at the camera.

This infinite sum can be written compactly as

$$L(p_1 \to p_0) = \sum_{n=1}^{\infty} P(\bar{p}_n). \tag{13.4}$$

$P(\bar{p}_n)$ gives the amount of radiance scattered over a path $\bar{p}_n$ with $n+1$ vertices,

$$\bar{p}_n = p_0, p_1, \ldots, p_n,$$

where p_0 is on the film plane or front lens element and p_n is on a light source, and

$$P(\bar{\mathrm{p}}_n) = \underbrace{\int_A \int_A \cdots \int_A}_{n-1} L_e(\mathrm{p}_n \to \mathrm{p}_{n-1})$$

$$\times \left(\prod_{i=1}^{n-1} f(\mathrm{p}_{i+1} \to \mathrm{p}_i \to \mathrm{p}_{i-1}) \, G(\mathrm{p}_{i+1} \leftrightarrow \mathrm{p}_i) \right) \, dA(\mathrm{p}_2) \cdots dA(\mathrm{p}_n). \qquad [13.5]$$

Before we move on, we will define one additional term that will be helpful in the subsequent discussion. The product of a path's BSDF and geometry terms is called the *throughput* of the path; it describes the fraction of radiance from the light source that arrives at the camera after all the scattering at vertices between them. We will denote it by

$$T(\bar{\mathrm{p}}_n) = \prod_{i=1}^{n-1} f(\mathrm{p}_{i+1} \to \mathrm{p}_i \to \mathrm{p}_{i-1}) \, G(\mathrm{p}_{i+1} \leftrightarrow \mathrm{p}_i), \qquad [13.6]$$

so

$$P(\bar{\mathrm{p}}_n) = \underbrace{\int_A \int_A \cdots \int_A}_{n-1} L_e(\mathrm{p}_n \to \mathrm{p}_{n-1}) \, T(\bar{\mathrm{p}}_n) \, dA(\mathrm{p}_2) \cdots dA(\mathrm{p}_n).$$

Given Equation (13.4) and a particular length n, all that we need to do to compute a Monte Carlo estimate of the radiance arriving at p_0 due to paths of length n is to sample a set of vertices with an appropriate sampling density, $\bar{\mathrm{p}}_n \sim p$, to generate a path and then to evaluate an estimate of $P(\bar{\mathrm{p}}_n)$ using those vertices:

$$L(\mathrm{p}_1 \to \mathrm{p}_0) \approx \sum_{n=1}^{\infty} \frac{P(\bar{\mathrm{p}}_n)}{p(\bar{\mathrm{p}}_n)}.$$

Whether we generate those vertices by starting a path from the camera, starting from the light, starting from both ends, or starting from a point in the middle is a detail that only affects how the path probability $p(\bar{\mathrm{p}}_n)$ is computed. We will see how this formulation leads to practical light transport algorithms throughout this and the following chapters.

13.1.5 DELTA DISTRIBUTIONS IN THE INTEGRAND

Delta functions may be present in $P(\bar{\mathrm{p}}_i)$ terms due not only to certain types of light sources (e.g., point lights and directional lights) but also to BSDF components described by delta distributions. If present, these distributions need to be handled explicitly by the light transport algorithm. For example, it is impossible to randomly choose an outgoing direction from a point on a surface that would intersect a point light source; instead, it is necessary to explicitly choose the single direction from the point to the light source if we want to be able to include its contribution. (The same is true for sampling BSDFs with delta components.) While handling this case introduces some additional complexity to the integrators, it is generally welcome because it reduces the dimensionality of the integral to be evaluated, turning parts of it into a plain sum.

For example, consider the direct illumination term, $P(\bar{\mathrm{p}}_2)$, in a scene with a single point light source at point $\mathrm{p}_{\text{light}}$ described by a delta distribution:

$$P(\bar{\mathrm{p}}_2) = \int_A L_e(\mathrm{p}_2 \to \mathrm{p}_1) \, f(\mathrm{p}_2 \to \mathrm{p}_1 \to \mathrm{p}_0) \, G(\mathrm{p}_2 \leftrightarrow \mathrm{p}_1) \, dA(\mathrm{p}_2)$$

$$= \frac{\delta(\mathrm{p}_{\text{light}} - \mathrm{p}_2) \, L_e(\mathrm{p}_{\text{light}} \to \mathrm{p}_1)}{p(\mathrm{p}_{\text{light}})} f(\mathrm{p}_2 \to \mathrm{p}_1 \to \mathrm{p}_0) \, G(\mathrm{p}_2 \leftrightarrow \mathrm{p}_1).$$

In other words, p_2 must be the light's position in the scene; the delta distribution in the numerator cancels out due to an implicit delta distribution in $p(p_{light})$ (recall the discussion of sampling Dirac delta distributions in Section 12.1), and we are left with terms that can be evaluated directly, with no need for Monte Carlo. An analogous situation holds for BSDFs with delta distributions in the path throughput $T(\bar{p}_n)$; each one eliminates an integral over area from the estimate to be computed.

13.1.6 PARTITIONING THE INTEGRAND

Many rendering algorithms have been developed that are particularly good at solving the LTE under some conditions but do not work well (or at all) under others. For example, Whitted's original ray-tracing algorithm only handles specular reflection from delta distribution BSDFs and ignores multiply scattered light from diffuse and glossy BSDFs.

Because we would like to be able to derive correct light transport algorithms that account for all possible modes of scattering without ignoring any contributions and without double-counting others, it is important to pay attention to which parts of the LTE a particular solution method accounts for. A nice way of approaching this problem is to partition the LTE in various ways. For example, we might expand the sum over paths to

$$L(p_1 \rightarrow p_0) = P(\bar{p}_1) + P(\bar{p}_2) + \sum_{i=3}^{\infty} P(\bar{p}_i),$$

where the first term is trivially evaluated by computing the emitted radiance at p_1, the second term is solved with an accurate direct lighting solution technique, but the remaining terms in the sum are handled with a faster but less accurate approach. If the contribution of these additional terms to the total reflected radiance is relatively small for the scene we are rendering, this may be a reasonable approach to take. The only detail is that it is important to be careful to ignore $P(\bar{p}_1)$ and $P(\bar{p}_2)$ with the algorithm that handles $P(\bar{p}_3)$ and beyond (and similarly with the other terms).

It is also useful to partition individual $P(\bar{p}_n)$ terms. For example, we might want to split the emission term into emission from small light sources, $L_{e,s}$, and emission from large light sources, $L_{e,l}$, giving us two separate integrals to estimate:

$$P(\bar{p}_n) = \int_{A^{n-1}} (L_{e,s}(p_n \rightarrow p_{n-1}) + L_{e,l}(p_n \rightarrow p_{n-1})) \, T(\bar{p}_n) \, dA(p_2) \cdots dA(p_n)$$

$$= \int_{A^{n-1}} L_{e,s}(p_n \rightarrow p_{n-1}) \, T(\bar{p}_n) \, dA(p_2) \cdots dA(p_n)$$

$$+ \int_{A^{n-1}} L_{e,l}(p_n \rightarrow p_{n-1}) \, T(\bar{p}_n) \, dA(p_2) \cdots dA(p_n).$$

The two integrals can be evaluated independently, possibly using completely different algorithms or different numbers of samples, selected in a way that handles the different conditions well. As long as the estimate of the $L_{e,s}$ integral ignores any emission from large lights, the estimate of the $L_{e,l}$ integral ignores emission from small lights, and all lights are categorized as either "large" or "small," the correct result is computed in the end.

Finally, the BSDF terms can be partitioned as well (in fact, this application was the reason BSDF categorization with BxDFFlags values was introduced in Section 9.1.2). For example, if f_Δ denotes components of the BSDF described by delta distributions and $f_{\neg\Delta}$ denotes the remaining components,

(a)   (b)

Figure 13.4: *Kroken* Scene Rendered with Path Tracing. (a) Rendered with path tracing with 8192 samples per pixel. (b) Rendered with just 8 samples per pixel, giving the characteristic grainy noise that is the hallmark of variance. Although the second image appears darker, the average pixel values of both are actually the same; very large values in some of its pixels cannot be displayed in print. *(Scene courtesy of Angelo Ferretti.)*

$$P(\bar{p}_n) = \int_{A^{n-1}} L_e(p_n \to p_{n-1})$$

$$\times \prod_{i=1}^{n-1} \left(f_\Delta(p_{i+1} \to p_i \to p_{i-1}) + f_{\neg\Delta}(p_{i+1} \to p_i \to p_{i-1}) \right)$$

$$\times G(p_{i+1} \leftrightarrow p_i)\, dA(p_2) \cdots dA(p_n).$$

Note that because there are $n - 1$ BSDF terms in the product, it is important to be careful not to count only terms with just f_Δ components or just $f_{\neg\Delta}$ components; all the mixed terms like $f_\Delta f_{\neg\Delta} f_{\neg\Delta}$ must be accounted for as well if a partitioning scheme like this is used.

13.2 PATH TRACING

Now that we have derived the path integral form of the light transport equation, we will show how it can be used to derive the *path-tracing* light transport algorithm and will present a path-tracing integrator. Figure 13.4 compares images of a scene rendered with different numbers of pixel samples using the path-tracing integrator. In general, hundreds or thousands of samples per pixel may be necessary for high-quality results.

Path tracing was the first general-purpose unbiased Monte Carlo light transport algorithm used in graphics. Kajiya (1986) introduced it in the same paper that first described the light transport equation. Path tracing incrementally generates paths of scattering events starting at the camera and ending at light sources in the scene.

Although it is slightly easier to derive path tracing directly from the basic light transport equation, we will instead approach it from the path integral form, which helps build understanding of the path integral equation and makes the generalization to bidirectional path sampling algorithms easier to understand.

13.2.1 OVERVIEW

Given the path integral form of the LTE, we would like to estimate the value of the exitant radiance from the camera ray's intersection point p_1,

$$L(p_1 \to p_0) = \sum_{i=1}^{\infty} P(\bar{p}_i),$$

for a given camera ray from p_0 that first intersects the scene at p_1. We have two problems that must be solved in order to compute this estimate:

1. How do we estimate the value of the sum of the infinite number of $P(\bar{p}_i)$ terms with a finite amount of computation?
2. Given a particular $P(\bar{p}_i)$ term, how do we generate one or more paths $\bar{p}$ in order to compute a Monte Carlo estimate of its multidimensional integral?

For path tracing, we can take advantage of the fact that for physically valid scenes, paths with more vertices scatter less light than paths with fewer vertices overall (this is not necessarily true for any particular pair of paths, just in the aggregate). This is a natural consequence of conservation of energy in BSDFs. Therefore, we will always estimate the first few terms $P(\bar{p}_i)$ and will then start to apply Russian roulette to stop sampling after a finite number of terms without introducing bias. (Recall that Section 2.2.4 showed how to use Russian roulette to probabilistically stop computing terms in a sum as long as the terms that are not skipped are reweighted appropriately.) For example, if we always computed estimates of $P(\bar{p}_1)$, $P(\bar{p}_2)$, and $P(\bar{p}_3)$ but stopped without computing more terms with probability q, then an unbiased estimate of the sum would be

$$P(\bar{p}_1) + P(\bar{p}_2) + P(\bar{p}_3) + \frac{1}{1-q} \sum_{i=4}^{\infty} P(\bar{p}_i).$$

Using Russian roulette in this way does not solve the problem of needing to evaluate an infinite sum but has pushed it a bit farther out.

If we take this idea a step further and instead randomly consider terminating evaluation of the sum at each term with probability q_i,

$$\frac{1}{1-q_1} \left(P(\bar{p}_1) + \frac{1}{1-q_2} \left(P(\bar{p}_2) + \frac{1}{1-q_3} \left(P(\bar{p}_3) + \cdots \right. \right. \right.,$$

we will eventually stop continued evaluation of the sum. Yet, because for any particular value of i there is greater than zero probability of evaluating the term $P(\bar{p}_i)$ and because it will be weighted appropriately if we do evaluate it, the final result is an unbiased estimate of the sum.

13.2.2 PATH SAMPLING

Given this method for evaluating only a finite number of terms of the infinite sum, we also need a way to estimate the contribution of a particular term $P(\bar{p}_i)$. We need $i + 1$ vertices to specify the path, where the last vertex p_i is on a light source and the first vertex p_0 is a point on the camera film or lens (Figure 13.5). Looking at the form of $P(\bar{p}_i)$, a multiple integral over surface area of objects in the scene, the most natural thing to do is to sample vertices p_i according to the surface area of objects in the scene, such that all points on surfaces in the scene are sampled with equal probability. (We do not actually use this approach in the integrator implementations in this chapter for reasons that will be described later, but this sampling technique could possibly be used to improve the efficiency of our basic implementation and helps to clarify the meaning of the path integral LTE.)

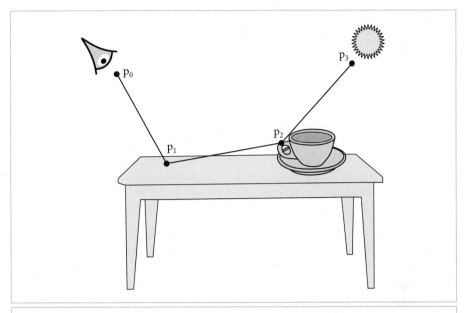

Figure 13.5: A path $\bar{p}_i$ of $i + 1$ vertices from the camera at p, intersecting a series of positions on surfaces in the scene, to a point on the light p_i. Scattering according to the BSDF occurs at each path vertex from p_1 to p_{i-1} such that the radiance estimate at the camera due to this path is given by the product of the path throughput $T(\bar{p}_i)$ and the emitted radiance from the light divided by the path sampling weights.

With this sampling approach, we might define a discrete probability over the n objects in the scene. If each has surface area A_i, then the probability of sampling a path vertex on the surface of the ith object should be

$$p_i = \frac{A_i}{\sum_j A_j}.$$

Then, given a method to sample a point on the ith object with uniform probability, the probability density function (PDF) for sampling any particular point on object i is $1/A_i$. Thus, the overall probability density for sampling the point is

$$\frac{A_i}{\sum_j A_j} \frac{1}{A_i},$$

and all samples p_i have the same PDF value:

$$p_A(p_i) = \frac{1}{\sum_j A_j}.$$

It is reassuring that they all have the same weight, since our intent was to choose among all points on surfaces in the scene with equal probability.

Given the set of vertices $p_0, p_1, \ldots, p_{i-1}$ sampled in this manner, we can then sample the last vertex p_i on a light source in the scene, defining its PDF in the same way. Although we could use the same technique used for sampling path vertices to sample points on lights, this would usually lead to high variance, since for all the paths where p_i was not on the surface of an emitter, the path would have zero value. The expected value would still be the correct value of the integral, but convergence would be extremely slow. A better approach is to sample over the areas of only the emitting objects with probabilities updated accordingly. Given a complete path, we have all the information we need to compute the estimate of $P(\bar{\mathrm{p}}_i)$; it is just a matter of evaluating each of the terms.

It is easy to be more creative about how we set the sampling probabilities with this general approach. For example, if we knew that indirect illumination from a few objects contributed to most of the lighting in the scene, we could assign a higher probability to generating path vertices p_i on those objects, updating the sample weights appropriately.

However, there are two interrelated problems with sampling paths in this manner. The first can lead to high variance, while the second can lead to incorrect results. The first problem is that many of the paths will have no contribution if they have pairs of adjacent vertices that are not mutually visible. Consider applying this area sampling method in a complex building model: adjacent vertices in the path will almost always have a wall or two between them, giving no contribution for the path and high variance in the estimate.

The second problem is that if the integrand has delta functions in it (e.g., a point light source or a perfect specular BSDF), this sampling technique will never be able to choose path vertices such that the delta distributions are nonzero. Even if there are no delta distributions, as the BSDFs become increasingly glossy almost all the paths will have low contributions since the points in $f(\mathrm{p}_{i+1} \to \mathrm{p}_i \to \mathrm{p}_{i-1})$ will cause the BSDF to have a small or zero value, and again we will suffer from high variance.

13.2.3 INCREMENTAL PATH CONSTRUCTION

A solution that solves both of these problems is to construct the path incrementally, starting from the vertex at the camera p_0. At each vertex, the BSDF is sampled to generate a new direction; the next vertex p_{i+1} is found by tracing a ray from p_i in the sampled direction and finding the closest intersection. We are effectively trying to find a path with a large overall contribution by making a series of choices that find directions with important local contributions. While one can imagine situations where this approach could be ineffective, it is generally a good strategy.

Because this approach constructs the path by sampling BSDFs according to solid angle, and because the path integral LTE is an integral over surface area in the scene, we need to apply the correction to convert from the probability density according to solid angle p_ω to a density according to area p_A (Section 4.2). If ω_{i-1} is the normalized direction sampled at p_{i-1}, it is:

$$p_A(\mathrm{p}_i) = p_\omega(\omega_{i-1}) \frac{|\cos \theta_i|}{\|\mathrm{p}_{i-1} - \mathrm{p}_i\|^2}.$$

This correction causes all the factors of the corresponding geometric function $G(\mathrm{p}_{i+1} \leftrightarrow \mathrm{p}_i)$ to cancel out of $P(\bar{\mathrm{p}}_i)$ except for the $\cos \theta_{i+1}$ term. Furthermore, we already know that p_{i-1} and p_i must be mutually visible since we traced a ray to find p_i, so the visibility term is trivially equal to 1. An alternative way to think about this is that ray tracing provides an operation to importance sample the visibility component of G.

With path tracing, the last vertex of the path, which is on the surface of a light source, gets special treatment. Rather than being sampled incrementally, it is sampled from a distribution that is just over the surfaces of the lights. (Sampling the last vertex in this way is often referred to as *next event estimation* (NEE), after a Monte Carlo technique with that name.) For now we will assume there is such a sampling distribution p_e over the emitters, though in Section 13.4 we will see that a more effective estimator can be constructed using multiple importance sampling.

With this approach, the value of the Monte Carlo estimate for a path is

$$P(\bar{p}_i) \approx \frac{L_e(p_i \to p_{i-1}) f(p_i \to p_{i-1} \to p_{i-2}) \, G(p_i \leftrightarrow p_{i-1})}{p_e(p_i)}$$

$$\times \left(\prod_{j=1}^{i-2} \frac{f(p_{j+1} \to p_j \to p_{j-1}) \, |\cos\theta_j|}{p_\omega(\omega_j)} \right). \qquad [13.7]$$

Because this sampling scheme reuses vertices of the path of length $i - 1$ (except the vertex on the emitter) when constructing the path of length i, it does introduce correlation among the $P(\bar{p}_i)$ terms. This does not affect the unbiasedness of the Monte Carlo estimator, however. In practice this correlation is more than made up for by the improved efficiency from tracing fewer rays than would be necessary to make the $P(\bar{p}_i)$ terms independent.

Relationship to the RandomWalkIntegrator

With this derivation of the foundations of path tracing complete, the implementation of the RandomWalkIntegrator from Chapter 1 can now be understood more formally: at each path vertex, uniform spherical sampling is used for the distribution p_ω—and hence the division by $1/(4\pi)$, corresponding to the uniform spherical PDF. The factor in parentheses in Equation (13.7) is effectively computed via the product of beta values through recursive calls to RandomWalkIntegrator::LiRandomWalk(). Emissive surfaces contribute to the radiance estimate whenever a randomly sampled path hits a surface with a nonzero L_e; because directions are sampled with respect to solid angle, the $p_e(p_i)$ factor in Equation (13.7) is not over emissive geometry but is the uniform directional probability p_ω. Most of the remaining G factor then cancels out due to the change of variables from integrating over area to integrating over solid angle.

13.3 A SIMPLE PATH TRACER

The path tracing estimator in Equation (13.7) makes it possible to apply the BSDF and light sampling techniques that were respectively defined in Chapters 9 and 12 to rendering. As shown in Figure 13.6, more effective importance sampling approaches than the uniform sampling in the RandomWalkIntegrator significantly reduce error. Although the SimplePathIntegrator takes longer to render an image at equal sample counts, most of that increase is because paths often terminate early with the RandomWalkIntegrator; because it samples outgoing directions at intersections uniformly over the sphere, half of the sampled directions lead to path termination at non-transmissive surfaces. The overall improvement in Monte Carlo efficiency from the SimplePathIntegrator is 12.8×.

The "simple" in the name of this integrator is meaningful: PathIntegrator, which will be introduced shortly, adds a number of additional sampling improvements and should be used in preference to SimplePathIntegrator if rendering efficiency is important. This integrator is still useful beyond pedagogy, however; it is also useful for debugging and for validating the implementation of sampling algorithms. For example, it can be configured to use BSDFs' sampling methods or to use uniform directional sampling; given a sufficient number of samples, both approaches should converge to the same result (assuming that the BSDF is not perfect specular). If they do not, the error is presumably in the BSDF sampling code. Light sampling techniques can be tested in a similar fashion.

(a)   (b)

Figure 13.6: **Comparison of the** `RandomWalkIntegrator` **and the** `SimplePathIntegrator`. (a) Scene rendered with 64 pixel samples using the `RandomWalkIntegrator`. (b) Rendered with 64 pixel samples and the `SimplePathIntegrator`. The `SimplePathIntegrator` gives an image that is visibly much improved, thanks to using more effective BSDF and light sampling techniques. Here, mean squared error (MSE) is reduced by a factor of 101. Even though rendering time was $7.8\times$ longer, the overall improvement in Monte Carlo efficiency was still $12.8\times$. *(Scene courtesy of Angelo Ferretti.)*

⟨*SimplePathIntegrator Definition*⟩ ≡
```
class SimplePathIntegrator : public RayIntegrator {
  public:
    ⟨SimplePathIntegrator Public Methods⟩
  private:
    ⟨SimplePathIntegrator Private Members  827⟩
};
```

The constructor sets the following member variables from provided parameters, so it is not included here. Similar to the `RandomWalkIntegrator`, `maxDepth` caps the maximum path length.[2]

The `sampleLights` member variable determines whether lights' `SampleLi()` methods should be used to sample direct illumination or whether illumination should only be found by rays randomly intersecting emissive surfaces, as was done in the `RandomWalkIntegrator`. In a similar fashion, `sampleBSDF` determines whether BSDFs' `Sample_f()` methods should be used to sample directions or whether uniform directional sampling should be used. Both are `true` by default. A `UniformLightSampler` is always used for sampling a light; this, too, is an instance where this integrator opts for simplicity and a lower likelihood of bugs in exchange for lower efficiency.

---

2   "Depth" is something of a misnomer in that this integrator constructs the path iteratively rather than recursively as the `RandomWalkIntegrator` did. Nevertheless, here and in the following integrators, we will continue to describe the path length in this way.

⟨*SimplePathIntegrator Private Members*⟩ ≡   826
```
int maxDepth;
bool sampleLights, sampleBSDF;
UniformLightSampler lightSampler;
```

As a RayIntegrator, this integrator provides a Li() method that returns an estimate of the radiance along the provided ray. It does not provide the capability of initializing a VisibleSurface at the first intersection point, so the corresponding parameter is ignored.

⟨*SimplePathIntegrator Method Definitions*⟩ ≡
```
SampledSpectrum SimplePathIntegrator::Li(RayDifferential ray,
        SampledWavelengths &lambda, Sampler sampler,
        ScratchBuffer &scratchBuffer, VisibleSurface *) const {
    ⟨Estimate radiance along ray using simple path tracing 827⟩
}
```

A number of variables record the current state of the path. L is the current estimated scattered radiance from the running total of $\sum P(\bar{p}_i)$ and ray is updated after each surface intersection to be the next ray to be traced. specularBounce records if the last outgoing path direction sampled was due to specular reflection; the need to track this will be explained shortly.

The beta variable holds the *path throughput weight*, which is defined as the factors of the throughput function $T(\bar{p}_{i-1})$—that is, the product of the BSDF values and cosine terms for the vertices generated so far, divided by their respective sampling PDFs:

$$\beta = \prod_{j=1}^{i-2} \frac{f(p_{j+1} \to p_j \to p_{j-1}) \, |\cos \theta_j|}{p_\omega(\omega_j)}. \tag{13.8}$$

Thus, the product of beta with scattered light from direct lighting from the final vertex of the path gives the contribution for a path. (This quantity will reoccur many times in the following few chapters, and we will consistently refer to it as beta.) Because the effect of earlier path vertices is aggregated in this way, there is no need to store the positions and BSDFs of all the vertices of the path—only the last one.

⟨*Estimate radiance along ray using simple path tracing*⟩ ≡   827
```
SampledSpectrum L(0.f), beta(1.f);
bool specularBounce = true;
int depth = 0;
while (beta) {
    ⟨Find next SimplePathIntegrator vertex and accumulate contribution 827⟩
}
return L;
```

Each iteration of the while loop accounts for an additional segment of a path, corresponding to a term of $P(\bar{p}_i)$'s sum.

⟨*Find next SimplePathIntegrator vertex and accumulate contribution*⟩ ≡   827
```
⟨Intersect ray with scene 828⟩
⟨Account for infinite lights if ray has no intersection 828⟩
⟨Account for emissive surface if light was not sampled 828⟩
⟨End path if maximum depth reached 829⟩
⟨Get BSDF and skip over medium boundaries 828⟩
⟨Sample direct illumination if sampleLights is true 829⟩
⟨Sample outgoing direction at intersection to continue path 830⟩
```

The first step is to find the intersection of the ray for the current segment with the scene geometry.

⟨*Intersect ray with scene*⟩ ≡   **827**
```
pstd::optional<ShapeIntersection> si = Intersect(ray);
```

If there is no intersection, then the ray path comes to an end. Before the accumulated path radiance estimate can be returned, however, in some cases radiance from infinite light sources is added to the path's radiance estimate, with contribution scaled by the accumulated beta factor.

If sampleLights is false, then emission is only found when rays happen to intersect emitters, in which case the contribution of infinite area lights must be added to rays that do not intersect any geometry. If it is true, then the integrator calls the Light SampleLi() method to estimate direct illumination at each path vertex. In that case, infinite lights have already been accounted for, except in the case of a specular BSDF at the previous vertex. Then, SampleLi() is not useful since only the specular direction scatters light. Therefore, specularBounce records whether the last BSDF was perfect specular, in which case infinite area lights must be included here after all.

⟨*Account for infinite lights if ray has no intersection*⟩ ≡   **827**
```
if (!si) {
    if (!sampleLights || specularBounce)
        for (const auto &light : infiniteLights)
            L += beta * light.Le(ray, lambda);
    break;
}
```

If the ray hits an emissive surface, similar logic governs whether its emission is added to the path's radiance estimate.

⟨*Account for emissive surface if light was not sampled*⟩ ≡   **827**
```
SurfaceInteraction &isect = si->intr;
if (!sampleLights || specularBounce)
    L += beta * isect.Le(-ray.d, lambda);
```

The next step is to find the BSDF at the intersection point. A special case arises when an unset BSDF is returned by the SurfaceInteraction's GetBSDF() method. In that case, the current surface should have no effect on light. pbrt uses such surfaces to represent transitions between participating media, whose boundaries are themselves optically inactive (i.e., they have the same index of refraction on both sides). Since the SimplePathIntegrator ignores media, it simply skips over such surfaces without counting them as scattering events in the depth counter.

⟨*Get BSDF and skip over medium boundaries*⟩ ≡   **827, 834, 884**
```
BSDF bsdf = isect.GetBSDF(ray, lambda, camera, scratchBuffer, sampler);
if (!bsdf) {
    isect.SkipIntersection(&ray, si->tHit);
    continue;
}
```

Otherwise we have a valid surface intersection and can go ahead and increment depth. The path is then terminated if it has reached the maximum depth.

⟨*End path if maximum depth reached*⟩ ≡   827, 834
```
if (depth++ == maxDepth)
    break;
```

If explicit light sampling is being performed, then the first step is to use the UniformLight
Sampler to choose a single light source. (Recall from Section 12.6 that sampling only one of
the scene's light sources can still give a valid estimate of the effect of all of them, given suitable
weighting.)

⟨*Sample direct illumination if* sampleLights *is true*⟩ ≡   827
```
Vector3f wo = -ray.d;
if (sampleLights) {
    pstd::optional<SampledLight> sampledLight =
        lightSampler.Sample(sampler.Get1D());
    if (sampledLight) {
        ⟨Sample point on sampledLight to estimate direct illumination 829⟩
    }
}
```

Given a light source, a call to SampleLi() yields a sample on the light. If the light sample is
valid, a direct lighting calculation is performed.

⟨*Sample point on* sampledLight *to estimate direct illumination*⟩ ≡   829
```
Point2f uLight = sampler.Get2D();
pstd::optional<LightLiSample> ls =
    sampledLight->light.SampleLi(isect, uLight, lambda);
if (ls && ls->L && ls->pdf > 0) {
    ⟨Evaluate BSDF for light and possibly add scattered radiance 829⟩
}
```

Returning to the path tracing estimator in Equation (13.7), we have the path throughput
weight in beta, which corresponds to the term in parentheses there. A call to SampleLi()
yields a sample on the light. Because the light sampling methods return samples that are
with respect to solid angle and not area, yet another Jacobian correction term is necessary,
and the estimator becomes

$$P(\bar{p}_i) = \frac{L_e(p_i \to p_{i-1}) f(p_i \to p_{i-1} \to p_{i-2}) |\cos \theta_i| V(p_i \leftrightarrow p_{i-1})}{p_l(\omega_i) \, p(l)} \beta,$$ [13.9]

where p_l is the solid angle density that the chosen light l would use to sample the direction
ω_i and $p(l)$ is the discrete probability of sampling the light l (recall Equation (12.2)). Their
product gives the full probability of the light sample.

Before tracing the shadow ray to evaluate the visibility factor V, it is worth checking if
the BSDF is zero for the sampled direction, in which case that computational expense is
unnecessary.

⟨*Evaluate BSDF for light and possibly add scattered radiance*⟩ ≡   829
```
Vector3f wi = ls->wi;
SampledSpectrum f = bsdf.f(wo, wi) * AbsDot(wi, isect.shading.n);
if (f && Unoccluded(isect, ls->pLight))
    L += beta * f * ls->L / (sampledLight->p * ls->pdf);
```

Unoccluded() is a convenience method provided in the Integrator base class.

⟨*Integrator Public Methods*⟩ +≡   22
```
bool Unoccluded(const Interaction &p0, const Interaction &p1) const {
    return !IntersectP(p0.SpawnRayTo(p1), 1 - ShadowEpsilon);
}
```

To sample the next path vertex, the direction of the ray leaving the surface is found either by calling the BSDF's sampling method or by sampling uniformly, depending on the sampleBSDF parameter.

⟨*Sample outgoing direction at intersection to continue path*⟩ ≡   827
```
if (sampleBSDF) {
    ⟨Sample BSDF for new path direction 830⟩
} else {
    ⟨Uniformly sample sphere or hemisphere to get new path direction⟩
}
```

If BSDF sampling is being used to sample the new direction, the Sample_f() method gives a direction and the associated BSDF and PDF values. beta can then be updated according to Equation (13.8).

⟨*Sample BSDF for new path direction*⟩ ≡   830
```
Float u = sampler.Get1D();
pstd::optional<BSDFSample> bs = bsdf.Sample_f(wo, u, sampler.Get2D());
if (!bs)
    break;
beta *= bs->f * AbsDot(bs->wi, isect.shading.n) / bs->pdf;
specularBounce = bs->IsSpecular();
ray = isect.SpawnRay(bs->wi);
```

Otherwise, the fragment ⟨*Uniformly sample sphere or hemisphere to get new path direction*⟩ uniformly samples a new direction for the ray leaving the surface. It goes through more care than the RandomWalkIntegrator did: for example, if the surface is reflective but not transmissive, it makes sure that the sampled direction is in the hemisphere where light is scattered. We will not include that fragment here, as it has to handle a number of such cases, but there is not much that is interesting about how it does so.

13.4 A BETTER PATH TRACER

The PathIntegrator is based on the same path tracing approach as the SimplePathIntegrator but incorporates a number of improvements. They include these:

- The direct lighting calculation is performed by sampling both the BSDF and the sampled light source and weighting both samples using multiple importance sampling. This approach can substantially reduce variance compared to sampling the light alone.
- Any LightSampler can be used, which makes it possible to use effective light sampling algorithms like the one implemented in BVHLightSampler to choose lights.
- It initializes the VisibleSurface when it is provided, giving geometric information about the first intersection point to Film implementations like GBufferFilm.
- Russian roulette is used to terminate paths, which can significantly boost the integrator's efficiency.
- A technique known as *path regularization* can be applied in order to reduce variance from difficult-to-sample paths.

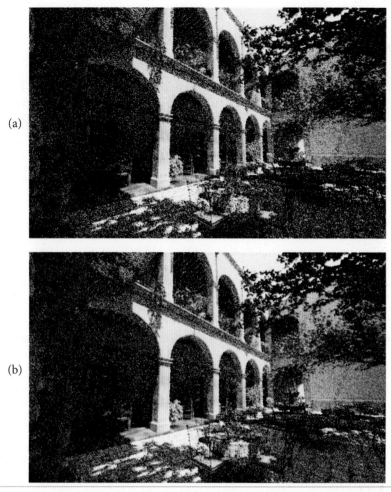

(a)

(b)

Figure 13.7: Comparison of the `SimplePathIntegrator` **and the** `PathIntegrator`. (a) Rendered using the `SimplePathIntegrator` with 64 samples per pixel. (b) The `PathIntegrator`, also with 64 samples per pixel. Once again, improving the underlying sampling algorithms leads to a substantial reduction in error. Not only is MSE improved by a factor of 1.97, but execution time is 4.44× faster, giving an overall efficiency improvement of 8.75×. *(Scene courtesy of Guillermo M. Leal Llaguno.)*

While these additions make its implementation more complex, they also substantially improve efficiency; see Figure 13.7 for a comparison of the two.

The most important of these differences is how the direct lighting calculation is performed. In the `SimplePathIntegrator`, a light was chosen with uniform probability and then that light sampled a direction; the corresponding estimator was given by Equation (13.9). More generally, the path contribution estimator can be expressed in terms of an arbitrary directional probability distribution p, which gives

$$P(\bar{p}_i) \approx \frac{L_e(p_i \to p_{i-1}) f(p_i \to p_{i-1} \to p_{i-2}) |\cos \theta_i| V(p_i \leftrightarrow p_{i-1})}{p(\omega_i)} \beta.$$

It may seem that using only a sampling PDF that matches the L_e factor to sample these directions, as done by the `SimplePathIntegrator`, would be a good strategy; after all, the radiance L_e can then be expected to be nonzero for the sampled direction. If we instead

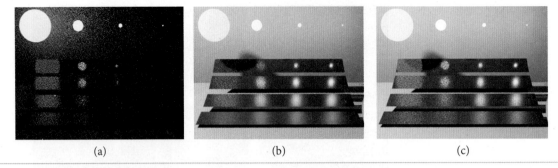

(a)   (b)   (c)

Figure 13.8: Four surfaces ranging from very smooth (top) to very rough (bottom) illuminated by spherical light sources of decreasing size and rendered with different sampling techniques (modeled after a scene by Eric Veach). (a) BSDF sampling, (b) light sampling, and (c) both techniques combined using MIS. Sampling the BSDF is generally more effective for highly specular materials and large light sources, as illumination is coming from many directions, but the BSDF's value is large for only a few of them (top left reflection). The converse is true for small sources and rough materials (bottom right reflection), where sampling the light source is more effective.

drew samples using the BSDF's sampling distribution, we might choose directions that did not intersect a light source at all, finding no emitted radiance after incurring the expense of tracing a ray in the hope of intersecting a light.

However, there are cases where sampling the BSDF can be the more effective strategy. For a very smooth surface, the BSDF is nonzero for a small set of directions. Sampling the light source will be unlikely to find directions that have a significant effect on scattering from the surface, especially if the light source is large and close by. Even worse, when such a light sample happens to lie in the BSDF lobe, an estimate with large magnitude will be the result due to the combination of a high contribution from the numerator and a small value for the PDF in the denominator. The estimator has high variance.

Figure 13.8 shows a variety of cases where each of these sampling methods is much better than the other. In this scene, four rectangular surfaces ranging from very smooth (top) to very rough (bottom) are illuminated by spherical light sources of decreasing size. Figures 13.8(a) and (b) show the BSDF and light sampling strategies on their own. As the example illustrates, sampling the BSDF is much more effective when it takes on large values on a narrow set of directions that is much smaller than the set of directions that would be obtained by sampling the light sources. This case is most visible in the top left reflection of a large light source in a low-roughness surface. On the other hand, sampling the light sources can be considerably more effective in the opposite case—when the light source is small and the BSDF lobe is less concentrated (this case is most visible in the bottom right reflection).

Taking a single sample with each sampling technique and averaging the estimators would be of limited benefit. The resulting estimator would still have high variance in cases where one of the sampling strategies was ineffective and that strategy happened to sample a direction with nonzero contribution.

This situation is therefore a natural for the application of multiple importance sampling—we have multiple sampling techniques, each of which is sometimes effective and sometimes not. That approach is used in the PathIntegrator with one light sample $\omega_l \sim p_l$ and one BSDF sample $\omega_b \sim p_b$, giving the estimator

$$P(\bar{p}_i) \approx w_l(\omega_l) \frac{L_e(p_l \to p_{i-1}) f(p_l \to p_{i-1} \to p_{i-2}) |\cos\theta_l|\, V(p_l \leftrightarrow p_{i-1})}{p_l(\omega_l)} \beta +$$

$$w_b(\omega_b) \frac{L_e(p_b \to p_{i-1}) f(p_b \to p_{i-1} \to p_{i-2}) |\cos\theta_b|\, V(p_b \leftrightarrow p_{i-1})}{p_b(\omega_b)} \beta,$$

[13.10]

PathIntegrator 833

where the surface intersection points corresponding to the two sampled directions are respectively denoted p_l and p_b and each term includes a corresponding multiple importance sampling (MIS) weight w_l or w_b that can be computed, for example, using the balance heuristic from Equation (2.14) or the power heuristic from Equation (2.15). Figure 13.8(c) shows the effectiveness of combining these two sampling techniques with multiple importance sampling.

With that context established, we can start the implementation of the PathIntegrator. It is another RayIntegrator.

⟨*PathIntegrator Definition*⟩ ≡
```
class PathIntegrator : public RayIntegrator {
  public:
    ⟨PathIntegrator Public Methods⟩
  private:
    ⟨PathIntegrator Private Methods⟩
    ⟨PathIntegrator Private Members 833⟩
};
```

Three member variables affect the PathIntegrator's operation: a maximum path depth; the lightSampler used to sample a light source; and regularize, which controls whether path regularization is used.

⟨*PathIntegrator Private Members*⟩ ≡   833
```
int maxDepth;
LightSampler lightSampler;
bool regularize;
```

The form of the Li() method is similar to SimplePathIntegrator::Li().

⟨*PathIntegrator Method Definitions*⟩ ≡
```
SampledSpectrum PathIntegrator::Li(RayDifferential ray,
        SampledWavelengths &lambda, Sampler sampler,
        ScratchBuffer &scratchBuffer, VisibleSurface *visibleSurf) const {
    ⟨Declare local variables for PathIntegrator::Li() 833⟩
    ⟨Sample path from camera and accumulate radiance estimate 834⟩
}
```

The L, beta, and depth variables play the same role as the corresponding variables did in the SimplePathIntegrator.

⟨*Declare local variables for PathIntegrator::Li()*⟩ ≡   833
```
SampledSpectrum L(0.f), beta(1.f);
int depth = 0;
```

Also similarly, each iteration of the while loop traces a ray to find its closest intersection and its BSDF. Note that a number of code fragments from the SimplePathIntegrator are reused here and in what follows to define the body of the while loop. The loop continues until either the maximum path length is reached or the path is terminated via Russian roulette.

⟨*Sample path from camera and accumulate radiance estimate*⟩ ≡   **833**
```
while (true) {
    ⟨Trace ray and find closest path vertex and its BSDF  834⟩
    ⟨End path if maximum depth reached  829⟩
    ⟨Sample direct illumination from the light sources  835⟩
    ⟨Sample BSDF to get new path direction  837⟩
    ⟨Possibly terminate the path with Russian roulette  840⟩
}
return L;
```

We will defer discussing the implementation of the first fragment used below, ⟨*Add emitted light at intersection point or from the environment*⟩, until later in this section after more details of the implementation of the MIS direct lighting calculation have been introduced.

⟨*Trace ray and find closest path vertex and its BSDF*⟩ ≡   **834**
```
pstd::optional<ShapeIntersection> si = Intersect(ray);
⟨Add emitted light at intersection point or from the environment  838⟩
SurfaceInteraction &isect = si->intr;
⟨Get BSDF and skip over medium boundaries  828⟩
⟨Initialize visibleSurf at first intersection  834⟩
⟨Possibly regularize the BSDF  842⟩
```

If the Film being used takes a VisibleSurface, then a non-nullptr VisibleSurface * is passed to the Li() method. It is initialized at the first intersection.

⟨*Initialize visibleSurf at first intersection*⟩ ≡   **834, 884**
```
if (depth == 0 && visibleSurf) {
    ⟨Estimate BSDF's albedo  834⟩
    *visibleSurf = VisibleSurface(isect, albedo, lambda);
}
```

The only quantity that is not immediately available from the SurfaceInteraction is the albedo of the surface, which is computed here as the hemispherical-directional reflectance, Equation (4.12). Recall that the BSDF::rho() method estimates this value using Monte Carlo integration. Here, a set of 16 precomputed Owen-scrambled Halton points in arrays ucRho and uRho, not included in the text, are used for the estimate.

The use of Monte Carlo with this many samples is somewhat unsatisfying. The computed albedo is most commonly used for image-space denoising algorithms after rendering; most of these start by dividing the final color at each pixel by the first visible surface's albedo in order to approximate the incident illumination alone. It is therefore important that the albedo value itself not have very much error. However, the albedo can be computed analytically for some BSDFs (e.g., the ideal Lambertian BRDF). In those cases, executing both the BSDF sampling and evaluation algorithms repeatedly is wasteful. An exercise at the end of the chapter discusses this matter further.

⟨*Estimate BSDF's albedo*⟩ ≡   **834**
```
⟨Define sample arrays ucRho and uRho for reflectance estimate⟩
SampledSpectrum albedo = bsdf.rho(isect.wo, ucRho, uRho);
```

The next task is to sample a light source to find a direction ω_i to use to estimate the first term of Equation (13.10). However, if the BSDF is purely specular, there is no reason to do this work, since the value of the BSDF for a sampled point on a light will certainly be zero.

⟨*Sample direct illumination from the light sources*⟩ ≡   **834**
```
if (IsNonSpecular(bsdf.Flags())) {
    SampledSpectrum Ld = SampleLd(isect, &bsdf, lambda, sampler);
    L += beta * Ld;
}
```

Although `SampleLd()` is only called once and thus could be expanded inline in the `Li()` method, there are multiple points along the way where it may return early. We therefore prefer a function here, as it avoids deeply nested `if` statements that would be needed otherwise.

⟨*PathIntegrator Method Definitions*⟩ +≡
```
SampledSpectrum PathIntegrator::SampleLd(
        const SurfaceInteraction &intr, const BSDF *bsdf,
        SampledWavelengths &lambda, Sampler sampler) const {
    ⟨Initialize LightSampleContext for light sampling  835⟩
    ⟨Choose a light source for the direct lighting calculation  836⟩
    ⟨Sample a point on the light source for direct lighting  836⟩
    ⟨Evaluate BSDF for light sample and check light visibility  836⟩
    ⟨Return light's contribution to reflected radiance  837⟩
}
```

A `LightSampleContext` is necessary both for choosing a specific light source and for sampling a point on it. One is initialized using the constructor that takes a `SurfaceInteraction`.

⟨*Initialize LightSampleContext for light sampling*⟩ ≡   **835**
```
LightSampleContext ctx(intr);
⟨Try to nudge the light sampling position to correct side of the surface  836⟩
```

If the surface is purely reflective or purely transmissive, then the reference point used for sampling pi is shifted slightly so that it lies on the side of the surface from which the outgoing ray will leave the intersection point toward the light. Doing so helps avoid a subtle error that is the result of the combination of floating-point round-off error in the computed intersection point and a ray that intersects an emitter that does not have a completely absorbing BSDF. The problem is illustrated in Figure 13.9.

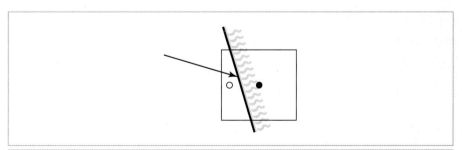

Figure 13.9: The `LightSampleContext` stores the error bounds around the computed intersection point `pi`. Typically, the center of these bounds (filled circle) is used as the reference point for sampling a point on the light source. If a ray intersects the non-emissive side of a one-sided light, the light's BSDF is nonzero, and if the center of the pi bounds is on the emissive side of the light, then it may seem that the intersection point is illuminated by the light. The result is an occasional bright pixel on the back side of light sources. Offsetting the reference point to the side of the surface from which the outgoing ray will leave (open circle) works around this problem.

⟨*Try to nudge the light sampling position to correct side of the surface*⟩ ≡   835, 886
```
BxDFFlags flags = bsdf->Flags();
if (IsReflective(flags) && !IsTransmissive(flags))
    ctx.pi = intr.OffsetRayOrigin(intr.wo);
else if (IsTransmissive(flags) && !IsReflective(flags))
    ctx.pi = intr.OffsetRayOrigin(-intr.wo);
```

Next, the LightSampler selects a light. One thing to note in the implementation here is that two more dimensions are consumed from the Sampler even if the LightSampler does not return a valid light. This is done in order to keep the allocation of Sampler dimensions consistent across all the pixel samples. (Recall the discussion of this issue in Section 8.3.)

⟨*Choose a light source for the direct lighting calculation*⟩ ≡   835
```
Float u = sampler.Get1D();
pstd::optional<SampledLight> sampledLight = lightSampler.Sample(ctx, u);
Point2f uLight = sampler.Get2D();
if (!sampledLight) return {};
```

Sampling a direction with the light proceeds using Light::SampleLi(), though here a true value is passed for its allowIncompletePDF parameter. Because we will use a second sampling technique, BSDF sampling, for the estimator in Equation (13.10), and that technique has nonzero probability of sampling all directions ω_i where the integrand is nonzero, the light sampling distribution may not include directions where the light's emission is relatively low. (The motivation for this was discussed in Section 2.2.3 in the context of MIS compensation.)

Given a light sample, it is worth checking for various cases that require no further processing here. As an example, consider a spotlight where the intersection point is outside of its emission cone; the LightLiSample will have a zero radiance value in that case. It is worthwhile to find that there is no incident radiance before incurring the cost of evaluating the BSDF.

⟨*Sample a point on the light source for direct lighting*⟩ ≡   835
```
Light light = sampledLight->light;
pstd::optional<LightLiSample> ls = light.SampleLi(ctx, uLight, lambda, true);
if (!ls || !ls->L || ls->pdf == 0)
    return {};
```

A shadow ray is only traced if the BSDF for the sampled direction is nonzero. It is not unusual for the BSDF to be zero here: for example, given a surface that is reflective but not transmissive, any sampled direction that is on the other side of the surface than the incident ray will have zero contribution.

⟨*Evaluate BSDF for light sample and check light visibility*⟩ ≡   835
```
Vector3f wo = intr.wo, wi = ls->wi;
SampledSpectrum f = bsdf->f(wo, wi) * AbsDot(wi, intr.shading.n);
if (!f || !Unoccluded(intr, ls->pLight))
    return {};
```

The light sample's contribution can now be computed; recall that the returned value corresponds to the first term of Equation (13.10), save for the β factor. The case of a light that is described by a delta distribution receives special treatment here; recall from Section 12.1 that in that case there is an implied delta distribution in the emitted radiance value returned from SampleLi() as well as the PDF and that they cancel out when the estimator is evaluated. Further, BSDF sampling is unable to generate a light sample and therefore we must not try to apply multiple importance sampling but should evaluate the standard estimator, Equation (13.9), instead. If we do not have a delta distribution light source, then the value of

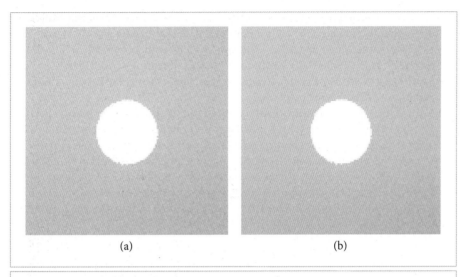

$$(a) \qquad\qquad\qquad\qquad (b)$$

Figure 13.10: Comparison of the Balance and Power Heuristics for Direct Lighting. A zoomed-in region of Figure 13.8 is shown here. (a) Rendered using the balance heuristic to weight BSDF and light samples in the direct lighting calculation. (b) Rendered using the power heuristic. The pixels behind the light source have a visible reduction in noise.

the BSDF's PDF for sampling the direction ω_i is found by calling BSDF::PDF() and the MIS weight is computed using the power heuristic. (See Figure 13.10 for a comparison between the balance heuristic and power heuristic for this computation.)

⟨*Return light's contribution to reflected radiance*⟩ ≡   **835**

```
    Float p_l = sampledLight->p * ls->pdf;
    if (IsDeltaLight(light.Type()))
        return ls->L * f / p_l;
    else {
        Float p_b = bsdf->PDF(wo, wi);
        Float w_l = PowerHeuristic(1, p_l, 1, p_b);
        return w_l * ls->L * f  / p_l;
    }
```

Returning now to the Li() method implementation, the next step is to sample the BSDF at the intersection to get an outgoing direction for the next ray to trace. That ray will be used to sample indirect illumination as well as for the BSDF sample for the direct lighting estimator.

⟨*Sample BSDF to get new path direction*⟩ ≡   **834**

```
    Vector3f wo = -ray.d;
    Float u = sampler.Get1D();
    pstd::optional<BSDFSample> bs = bsdf.Sample_f(wo, u, sampler.Get2D());
    if (!bs)
        break;
    ⟨Update path state variables after surface scattering 838⟩
    ray = isect.SpawnRay(ray, bsdf, bs->wi, bs->flags, bs->eta);
```

In addition to the path throughput weight beta, a number of additional values related to the path are maintained, as follows:

- p_b is the PDF for sampling the direction bs->wi; this value is needed for the MIS-based direct lighting estimate. One nit comes from BSDFs like the LayeredBxDF that return a BSDFSample where the f and pdf are only proportional to their true values. In that case, an explicit call to BSDF::PDF() is required to get an estimate of the true PDF.
- As in the SimplePathIntegrator, specularBounce tracks whether the last scattering event was from a perfect specular surface.
- anyNonSpecularBounces tracks whether any scattering event along the ray's path has been non-perfect specular. This value is used for path regularization if it is enabled.
- etaScale is the accumulated product of scaling factors that have been applied to beta due to rays being transmitted between media of different indices of refraction—a detail that is discussed in Section 9.5.2. This value will be used in the Russian roulette computation.
- Finally, prevIntrCtx stores geometric information about the intersection point from which the sampled ray is leaving. This value is also used in the MIS computation for direct lighting.

⟨*Update path state variables after surface scattering*⟩ ≡   837
```
beta *= bs->f * AbsDot(bs->wi, isect.shading.n) / bs->pdf;
p_b = bs->pdfIsProportional ? bsdf.PDF(wo, bs->wi) : bs->pdf;
specularBounce = bs->IsSpecular();
anyNonSpecularBounces |= !bs->IsSpecular();
if (bs->IsTransmission())
    etaScale *= Sqr(bs->eta);
prevIntrCtx = si->intr;
```

⟨*Declare local variables for* PathIntegrator::Li()⟩ +≡   833
```
Float p_b, etaScale = 1;
bool specularBounce = false, anyNonSpecularBounces = false;
LightSampleContext prevIntrCtx;
```

The new ray will account for indirect illumination at the intersection point in the following execution of the while loop.

Returning now to the ⟨*Add emitted light at intersection point or from the environment*⟩ fragment at the start of the loop, we can see how the ray from the previous iteration of the while loop can take care of the BSDF sample in Equation (13.10). The ray's direction was chosen by sampling the BSDF, and so if it happens to hit a light source, then we have everything we need to evaluate the second term of the estimate other than the MIS weight $w_b(\omega)$. If the ray does not hit a light source, then that term is zero for the BSDF sample and there is no further work to do.

There are two cases to handle: infinite lights for rays that do not intersect any geometry, and surface emission for rays that do. In the first case, the ray path can terminate once lights have been considered.

⟨*Add emitted light at intersection point or from the environment*⟩ ≡   834
```
if (!si) {
    ⟨Incorporate emission from infinite lights for escaped ray 839⟩
    break;
}
⟨Incorporate emission from surface hit by ray⟩
```

For the initial ray from the camera or after a perfect specular scattering event, emitted radiance should be included in the path without any MIS weighting, since light sampling was not performed at the previous vertex of the path. At this point in execution, beta already includes the BSDF, cosine factor, and PDF value from the previous scattering event, so multiplying beta by the emitted radiance gives the correct contribution.

⟨*Incorporate emission from infinite lights for escaped ray*⟩ ≡   838
```
for (const auto &light : infiniteLights) {
    SampledSpectrum Le = light.Le(ray, lambda);
    if (depth == 0 || specularBounce)
        L += beta * Le;
    else {
        ⟨Compute MIS weight for infinite light 839⟩
        L += beta * w_b * Le;
    }
}
```

Otherwise, it is necessary to compute the MIS weight w_b. p_b gives us the BSDF's PDF from the previous scattering event, so all we need is the PDF for the ray's direction from sampling the light. This value is given by the product of the probability of sampling the light under consideration times the probability the light returns for sampling the direction.

Note that the PDF_Li() method is passed a true value for allowIncompletePDF here, again reflecting the fact that because BSDF sampling is capable of sampling all valid directions, it is not required that light sampling do so as well.

⟨*Compute MIS weight for infinite light*⟩ ≡   839
```
Float p_l = lightSampler.PMF(prevIntrCtx, light) *
    light.PDF_Li(prevIntrCtx, ray.d, true);
Float w_b = PowerHeuristic(1, p_b, 1, p_l);
```

The code for the case of a ray hitting an emissive surface is in the fragment ⟨*Incorporate emission from surface hit by ray*⟩. It is almost the same as the infinite light case, so we will not include it here.

The final issue is Russian roulette–based path termination. As outlined in Section 13.2.1, the task is easy: we compute a termination probability q however we like, make a random choice as to whether to terminate the path, and update beta if the path is not terminated so that all subsequent $P(\bar{p}_i)$ terms will be scaled appropriately.

However, the details of how q is set can make a big difference.[3] In general, it is a good idea for the termination probability to be based on the path throughput weight; in this way, if the BSDF's value is small, it is more likely that the path will be terminated. Further, if the path is not terminated, then the scaling factor will generally cause beta to have a value around 1. Thus, all rays that are traced tend to make the same contribution to the image, which improves efficiency.

Another issue is that it is best if the beta value used to compute q does not include radiance scaling due to refraction. Consider a ray that passes through a glass object with a relative index of refraction of 1.5: when it enters the object, beta will pick up a factor of $1/1.5^2 \approx 0.44$, but when it exits, that factor will cancel and beta will be back to 1. For ray paths that would exit, to have terminated them after the first refraction would be the wrong decision. Therefore, etaScale tracks those factors in beta so that they can be removed. The image in Figure 13.11 shows the increase in noise if this effect is not corrected for.

---

3   By this we mean that this is a place where the current version of pbrt does markedly better than previous ones.

(a)

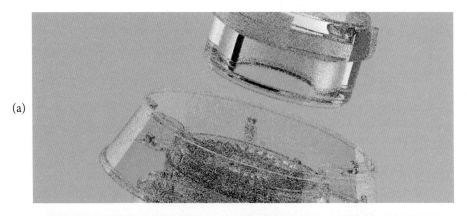

(b)

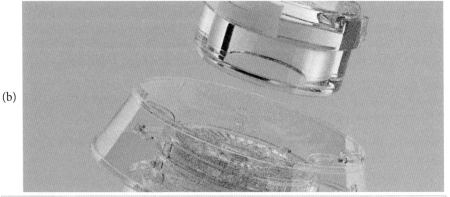

Figure 13.11: The Effect of Including Radiance Scaling Due to Transmission in the Russian Roulette Probability q. (a) If `etaScale` is not included in the probability, then some rays that would have passed through the glass object are terminated unnecessarily, leading to noise in the corresponding parts of the image. (b) Including `etaScale` in the computation of q fixes this issue. *(Transparent Machines scene courtesy of Beeple.)*

Finally, note that the termination probability is set according to the maximum component value of `rrBeta` rather than, for example, its average. Doing so gives better results when surface reflectances are highly saturated and some of the wavelength samples have much lower beta values than others, since it prevents any of the beta components from going above 1 due to Russian roulette.

⟨*Possibly terminate the path with Russian roulette*⟩ ≡   **834**
```
SampledSpectrum rrBeta = beta * etaScale;
if (rrBeta.MaxComponentValue() < 1 && depth > 1) {
    Float q = std::max<Float>(0, 1 - rrBeta.MaxComponentValue());
    if (sampler.Get1D() < q)
        break;
    beta /= 1 - q;
}
```

Float 23

SampledSpectrum 171

SampledSpectrum::
  MaxComponentValue()
  172

Sampler::Get1D() 470

Recall that Russian roulette only increases variance. Because it terminates some paths, this must be so, as the final image includes less information when it is applied. However, it can improve efficiency by allowing the renderer to focus its efforts on tracing rays that make the greatest contribution to the final image. Table 13.1 presents measurements of efficiency improvements from Russian roulette for a number of scenes.

Table 13.1: Monte Carlo Efficiency Benefits from Russian Roulette. Measurements of MSE and rendering time when using Russian roulette. All values reported are relative to rendering the same scene without Russian roulette. As expected, MSE increases to varying degrees due to ray termination, but the performance benefit more than makes up for it, leading to an increase in Monte Carlo efficiency.

Scene	MSE	Time	Efficiency
Kroken (Figure 13.4)	1.31	0.261	2.92
Watercolor (Figure 13.6)	1.19	0.187	4.51
San Miguel (Figure 13.7)	1.00	0.239	4.17
BMW M6 (Figure 13.12)	1.00	0.801	1.25

Figure 13.12: Image with High Variance Due to Difficult-to-Sample Indirect Lighting. The environment map illuminating the scene includes the sun, which is not only bright but also subtends a small solid angle. When an indirect lighting sample hits a specular surface and reflects to the sun's direction, variance spikes in the image result because its contribution is not sampled well. *(Car model courtesy of tyrant monkey, via Blend Swap.)*

13.4.1 PATH REGULARIZATION

Scenes with concentrated indirect lighting can pose a challenge to the path-tracing algorithm: the problem is that if the incident indirect radiance at a point has substantial variation but BSDF sampling is being used to generate the direction of indirect rays, then the sampling distribution may be a poor match for the integrand. Variance spikes then occur when the ratio $f(x)/p(x)$ in the Monte Carlo estimator is large.

Figure 13.12 shows an example of this issue. The car is illuminated by a sky environment map where a bright sun occupies a small number of pixels. Consider sampling indirect lighting at a point on the ground near one of the wheels: the ground material is fairly diffuse, so any direction will be sampled with equal (cosine-weighted) probability. Rarely, a direction will be sampled that both hits the highly specular wheel and then also reflects to a direction where the sun is visible. This is the cause of the bright pixels on the ground. (The lighting in the

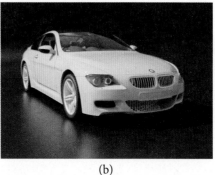

(a)   (b)

Figure 13.13: Scene from Figure 13.12 with Roughened BSDFs. (a) Increasing the roughness of all the BSDFs eliminates the variance spikes by allowing the use of MIS at all indirect ray intersection points, though this substantially changes the appearance of the scene. (Note that the car paint is duller and the window glass and headlight covers have the appearance of frosted glass.) (b) Roughening BSDFs only after the first non-specular scattering event along the path preserves visual detail while reducing the error from difficult light paths. *(Car model courtesy of tyrant monkey, via Blend Swap.)*

car interior is similarly difficult to sample, since the glass prevents light source sampling; the variance spikes there follow.)

Informally, the idea behind path regularization is to blur the function being integrated in the case that it cannot be sampled effectively (or cannot be sampled in the first place). See Figure 13.13, which shows the same scene, but with all the BSDFs made more rough: perfect specular surfaces are glossy specular, and glossy specular surfaces are more diffuse. Although the overall characteristics of the image are quite different, the high variance on the ground has been eliminated: when an indirect lighting ray hits one of the wheels, it is now possible to use a lower variance MIS-based direct lighting calculation in place of following whichever direction is dictated by the law of specular reflection.

Blurring all the BSDFs in this way is an undesirable solution, but there is no need to do so for the camera rays or for rays that have only undergone perfect specular scattering: in those cases, we would like to leave the scene as it was specified. We can consider non-specular scattering itself to be a sort of blurring of the incident light, such that blurring the scene that is encountered after it occurs is less likely to be objectionable—thus the motivation to track this case via the anyNonSpecularBounces variable.

⟨Possibly regularize the BSDF⟩ ≡   834, 884
```
    if (regularize && anyNonSpecularBounces)
        bsdf.Regularize();
```

The BSDF class provides a Regularize() method that forwards the request on to its BxDF.

⟨BSDF Public Methods⟩ +≡   544
```
    void Regularize() { bxdf.Regularize(); }
```

The BxDF interface in turn requires the implementation of a Regularize() method. For BxDFs that are already fairly broad (e.g., the DiffuseBxDF), the corresponding method implementation is empty.

⟨BxDF Interface⟩ +≡   538
```
    void Regularize();
```

However, both the `DielectricBxDF` and `ConductorBxDF` can be nearly specular or perfect specular, depending on how smooth their microfacet distribution is. Therefore, their `Regularize()` method implementations do adjust their scattering properties, through a call to yet one more method named `Regularize()`, this one implemented by the `TrowbridgeReitz Distribution`.

⟨*DielectricBxDF Public Methods*⟩ +≡   563
```
void Regularize() { mfDistrib.Regularize(); }
```

Unless the surface is already fairly rough, the `TrowbridgeReitzDistribution`'s `Regularize()` method doubles the α parameters and then clamps them—to ensure both that perfect specular surfaces with a roughness of zero become non-perfect specular and that surfaces are not excessively roughened.

⟨*TrowbridgeReitzDistribution Public Methods*⟩ +≡   575
```
void Regularize() {
    if (alpha_x < 0.3f) alpha_x = Clamp(2 * alpha_x, 0.1f, 0.3f);
    if (alpha_y < 0.3f) alpha_y = Clamp(2 * alpha_y, 0.1f, 0.3f);
}
```

FURTHER READING

The first application of Monte Carlo to global illumination for creating synthetic images that we are aware of was described in Tregenza's paper on lighting design (Tregenza 1983). Cook's distribution ray-tracing algorithm computed glossy reflections, soft shadows from area lights, motion blur, and depth of field with Monte Carlo sampling (Cook et al. 1984; Cook 1986), although the general form of the light transport equation was not stated until papers by Kajiya (1986) and Immel, Cohen, and Greenberg (1986).

Kajiya (1986) introduced the general-purpose path-tracing algorithm. Other important early work on Monte Carlo in rendering includes Shirley's Ph.D. thesis (1990) and a paper by Kirk and Arvo (1991) on sources of bias in rendering algorithms.

Fundamental theoretical work on light transport has been done by Arvo (1993, 1995a), who investigated the connection between rendering algorithms in graphics and previous work in *transport theory*, which applies classical physics to particles and their interactions to predict their overall behavior. Our description of the path integral form of the LTE follows the framework in Veach's Ph.D. thesis, which has thorough coverage of different forms of the LTE and its mathematical structure (Veach 1997).

The next event estimation technique that corresponds to the direct lighting computation in path tracing was first introduced by Coveyou et al. (1967), in the context of neutron transport.

Russian roulette was introduced to graphics by Arvo and Kirk (1990). Hall and Greenberg (1983) had previously suggested adaptively terminating ray trees by not tracing rays with less than some minimum contribution. Arvo and Kirk's technique is unbiased, although in some situations bias and less noise may be the more desirable artifact.

The Russian roulette termination probability computed in the `PathIntegrator` is largely determined by the albedo of the surface at the last scattering event; that approach was first introduced by Szecsi et al. (2003). This is a reasonable way to set the probability, but better is to set the termination probability that also accounts for the incident lighting at a point: it would be better to terminate paths more aggressively in darker parts of the scene and less aggressively in brighter parts. Vorba and Křivánek described an approach for doing so based on an approximation of the lighting in the scene (Vorba and Křivánek 2016). They further applied splitting to the problem, increasing the number of paths in important regions.

Control variates is a Monte Carlo technique based on finding an approximation to the integrand that is efficient to evaluate and then applying Monte Carlo to integrate the difference between the approximation and the true integrand. The variance of the resulting estimator then is dependent on the difference. This approach was first applied to rendering by Lafortune and Willems (1994, 1995). Recent work in this area includes Rousselle et al. (2016), who made use of correlations between nearby pixels to define control variates. (Their paper also has comprehensive coverage of other applications of control variates to rendering after Lafortune and Willems's work.) Müller et al. (2020) have demonstrated the effectiveness of neural networks for computing control variates for rendering. Crespo et al. (2021) fit polynomials to the samples taken in each pixel and used them as control variates, showing reduction in error in pixels where the integrand was smooth.

One approach to improving the performance of path tracing is to reuse computation across nearby points in the scene. Irradiance caching (Ward et al. 1988; Ward 1994) is one such technique. It is based on storing the irradiance due to indirect illumination at a sparse set of points on surfaces in the scene; because indirect lighting is generally slowly changing, irradiance can often be safely interpolated. Tabellion and Lamorlette (2004) described a number of additional improvements to irradiance caching that made it viable for rendering for movie productions.

Křivánek and collaborators generalized irradiance caching to *radiance caching*, where a more complex directional distribution of incident radiance is stored, so that more accurate shading from glossy surfaces is possible (Křivánek et al. 2005). Schwarzhaupt et al. have proposed a better way of assessing the validity of a cache point using a second-order expansion of the incident lighting (Schwarzhaupt et al. 2012) and Zhao et al. (2019) have developed a number of improvements that are especially useful for glossy scenes. Ren et al. (2013) first applied neural networks to represent the radiance distribution in a scene for rendering; more recently, Müller et al. (2021) trained a fully connected 7-layer network to represent radiance during rendering and demonstrated both high performance and accurate indirect illumination.

Improved Estimators and Sampling Algorithms

A number of approaches have been developed to sample from the product distribution of the BSDF and light source for direct lighting (Burke et al. 2005; Cline et al. 2006). Product sampling can give better results than MIS-weighted light and BSDF samples when neither of those distributions matches the true product well. Clarberg, Rousselle, and collaborators developed techniques based on representing BSDFs and illumination in the wavelet basis and efficiently sampling from their product (Clarberg et al. 2005; Rousselle et al. 2008; Clarberg and Akenine-Möller 2008a). Efficiency of the direct lighting calculation can be further improved by sampling from the *triple product* distribution of BSDF, illumination, and visibility; this issue was investigated by Ghosh and Heidrich (2006) and Clarberg and Akenine-Möller (2008b). Wang and Åkerlund (2009) introduced an approximation to the indirect illumination that is used in the light sampling distribution with these approaches. More recently, Belcour et al. (2018) derived approaches for integrating the spherical harmonics over polygonal domains and demonstrated their application to product sampling. Hart et al. (2020) showed how simple warps of uniform random samples can be used for product sampling. Peters (2021b) has shown use of linearly transformed cosines (Heitz et al. 2016a) with a new algorithm for sampling polygonal light sources to perform product sampling.

Subr et al. (2014) analyzed the combination of multiple importance sampling and jittered sampling for direct lighting calculations and proposed techniques that improve convergence rates.

Heitz et al. (2018) applied ratio estimators to direct illumination computations, which allows the use of analytic techniques for computing unshadowed direct illumination and then computing the correct result in expectation after tracing a shadow ray. They showed the effectiveness of this approach with sophisticated models for analytic illumination from area lights (Heitz et al. 2016a; Dupuy et al. 2017) and noted a number of benefits of this formulation in comparison to control variates. Another approach for applying analytic techniques to direct lighting was described by Billen and Dutré (2016) and Salesin and Jarosz (2019), who integrated one dimension of the integral analytically.

Path regularization was introduced by Kaplanyan and Dachsbacher (2013). Our implementation applies an admittedly *ad hoc* roughening to all non-diffuse BSDFs, while they only applied regularization to Dirac delta distributions and replaced them with a function designed to not lose energy, as ours may. See also Bouchard et al. (2013), who incorporated regularization as one of the sampling strategies to use with MIS. A principled approach to regularization for microfacet-based BSDFs was developed by Jendersie and Grosch (2019). Weier et al. (2021) have recently developed a path regularization approach based on learning regularization parameters with a variety of scenes and differentiable rendering.

A number of specialized sampling techniques have been developed for especially tricky scattering problems. Wang et al. (2020b) developed methods to render scattering paths that exclusively exhibit specular light transport, including those that start at pinhole cameras and end at point light sources. Such light-carrying paths cannot be sampled directly using the incremental path sampling approach used in `pbrt`. Loubet et al. (2020) showed how to efficiently render caustics in a path tracer by constructing a data structure that records which triangles may cast caustics in a region of space and then directly sampling a specular light path from the light to the triangle to a receiving point. Zeltner et al. (2020) found caustic paths using a equation-solving iteration with random initialization, which requires precautions when reasoning about the probability of a generated sample.

Path Guiding

The `PathIntegrator` samples the BSDF in order to sample indirect illumination, though for scenes where the indirect illumination varies significantly as a function of direction, this is not an ideal approach. A family of approaches that have come to be known as *path guiding* have been developed to address this problem; all share the idea of building a data structure that represents the indirect illumination in the scene and then using it to draw samples. Early work in this area was done by Lafortune and Willems (1995), who used a 5D tree to represent the scene radiance distribution, and Jensen (1995), who traced samples from the light sources ("photons") and used them to do the same. Hey and Purgathofer (2002a) developed an improved approach based on photons and Pegoraro et al. (2008a) applied the theory of sequential Monte Carlo to this problem. An early path guiding technique based on adapting the distribution of uniform random samples to better sample important paths was described by Cline et al. (2008).

Vorba et al. (2014) applied a parametric representation based on Gaussian mixture models (GMMs) that are learned over the course of rendering for path guiding and Herholz et al. (2016) also included the BRDF in GMMs, demonstrating better performance in scenes with non-diffuse BSDFs. Ruppert et al. (2020) described a number of further improvements,

PathIntegrator 833

applying the von Mises–Fisher distribution for their parametric model, improving the robustness of the fitting algorithm, and accounting for parallax, which causes the directional distribution of incident radiance to vary over volumes of space.

A path guiding technique developed by Müller and collaborators (Müller et al. 2017; Müller 2019) has seen recent adoption. It is based on an adaptive spatial decomposition using an octree where each octree leaf node stores an adaptive directional decomposition of incident radiance. Both of these decompositions are refined as more samples are taken and are used for sampling ray directions. This approach was generalized to include product sampling with the BSDF by Diolatzis et al. (2020), who used Heitz et al.'s (2016a) linearly transformed cosines representation to do so.

A challenge with path guiding is that the Monte Carlo estimator generally includes variance due to factors not accounted for by the path guiding algorithm. Rath et al. (2020) considered this issue and developed an approach for accounting for this variance in the function that is learned for guiding.

Reibold et al. (2018) described a path guiding method based on storing entire ray paths and then defining a PDF for path guiding using Gaussian distributions around them in path space.

Machine learning approaches have also been applied to path guiding: Dahm and Keller (2017) investigated the connections between light transport and reinforcement learning and Müller et al. and Zheng and Zwicker both used neural nets to learn the illumination in the scene and applied them to importance sampling (Müller et al. 2019; Zheng and Zwicker 2019). A scene-independent approach was described by Bako et al. (2019), who trained a neural net to take a local neighborhood of sample values and reconstruct the incident radiance function to use for path guiding. Deep reinforcement learning has been applied to this problem by Huo et al. (2020). Zhu et al. (2021) recently introduced a path guiding approach based on storing directional samples in a quadtree and applying a neural network to generate sampling distributions from such quadtrees. They further generated quadtree samples using paths both from the camera and from the light sources and showed that doing so further reduces error in challenging lighting scenarios.

Photon Mapping

The general idea of tracing light-carrying paths from light sources was first investigated by Arvo (1986), who stored light in texture maps on surfaces and rendered caustics. Heckbert (1990b) built on this approach to develop a general ray-tracing-based global illumination algorithm, and Dutré et al. (1993) and Pattanaik and Mudur (1995) developed early particle-tracing techniques. Christensen (2003) surveyed applications of adjoint functions and importance to solving the LTE and related problems.

Jensen (1995) developed the photon mapping algorithm, which introduced the key innovation of storing light contributions in a general 3D data structure. Important early improvements to the photon mapping method are described in follow-up papers and a book by Jensen (1996, 1997, 2001).

Herzog et al. (2007) described an approach based on storing all the visible points as seen from the camera and splatting photon contributions to them. Hachisuka et al. (2008) developed the progressive photon mapping algorithm, which builds on that representation; stochastic progressive photon mapping (SPPM) was subsequently developed by Hachisuka and Jensen (2009). (The online edition of this book includes an implementation of the SPPM algorithm.)

The question of how to find the most effective set of photons for photon mapping is an important one: light-driven particle-tracing algorithms do not work well for all scenes (consider, for example, a complex building model with lights in every room but where the camera sees only a single room). Recent techniques for improved photon sampling include the work of Grittmann et al., who adapted the primary sample space distribution of samples in order to more effectively generate photon paths (Grittmann et al. 2018). Conty Estevez and Kulla described an adaptive photon shooting algorithm that has been used in production (2020). Both papers survey previous work in that area.

Bidirectional Path Tracing

Bidirectional path tracing constructs paths starting both from the camera and from the lights and then forms connections between them. Doing so can be an effective way to sample some light-carrying paths. This technique was independently developed by Lafortune and Willems (1993) and Veach and Guibas (1994). The development of multiple importance sampling was integral to the effectiveness of bidirectional path tracing (Veach and Guibas 1995). Lafortune and Willems (1996) showed how to apply bidirectional path tracing to rendering participating media. (An implementation of bidirectional path tracing is included in the online edition of the book; many additional references to related work are included there.)

Simultaneous work by Hachisuka et al. (2012) and Georgiev et al. (2012) provided a unified framework for both photon mapping and bidirectional path tracing. (This approach is often called either *unified path sampling* (UPS) or *vertex connection and merging* (VCM), after respective terminology in those two papers.) Their approaches allowed photon mapping to be included in the path space formulation of the light transport equation, which in turn made it possible to derive light transport algorithms that use both approaches to generate paths and combine them using multiple importance sampling.

Metropolis Sampling

Veach and Guibas (1997) first applied the Metropolis sampling algorithm to solving the light transport equation. They demonstrated how this method could be applied to image synthesis and showed that the result was a light transport algorithm that was robust to traditionally difficult lighting configurations (e.g., light shining through a slightly ajar door). Pauly, Kollig, and Keller (2000) generalized the Metropolis light transport (MLT) algorithm to include volume scattering. Pauly's thesis (Pauly 1999) described the theory and implementation of bidirectional and Metropolis-based algorithms for volume light transport.

MLT algorithms generally are unable to take advantage of the superior convergence rates offered by well-distributed sample values. Bitterli and Jarosz present a hybrid light transport algorithm that uses path tracing by default but with the integrand partitioned so that only high-variance samples are handled instead by Metropolis sampling (Bitterli and Jarosz 2019). In this way, the benefits of both algorithms are available, with Metropolis available to sample tricky paths and path tracing with well-distributed sample points efficiently taking care of the rest.

Kelemen et al. (2002) developed the "primary sample space MLT" formulation of Metropolis light transport, which is much easier to implement than Veach and Guibas's original formulation. That approach is implemented in the online edition of this book, including the "multiplexed MLT" improvement developed by Hachisuka et al. (2014).

Inverting the sampling functions that convert primary sample space samples to light paths makes it possible to develop MLT algorithms that operate both in primary sample space and in path space, the basis of Veach and Guibas's original formulation of MLT. Pantaleoni (2017) used such inverses to improve the distribution of samples and to develop new light transport algorithms, and Otsu et al. (2017) developed a novel approach that applies mutations in both spaces. Bitterli et al. (2018a) used this approach to apply reversible jump Markov chain Monte Carlo to light transport and to develop new sampling techniques.

See Šik and Křivánek's article for a comprehensive survey of the application of Markov chain sampling algorithms to light transport (Šik and Křivánek 2018).

Other Rendering Approaches

A number of algorithms have been developed based on a first phase of computation that traces paths from the light sources to create so-called virtual lights, where these lights are then used to approximate indirect illumination during a second phase. The principles behind this approach were first introduced by Keller's work on *instant radiosity* (Keller 1997). The more general *instant global illumination* algorithm was developed by Wald, Benthin, and collaborators (Wald et al. 2002, 2003; Benthin et al. 2003). See Dachsbacher et al.'s survey (2014) for a summary of work in this area.

Building on the virtual point lights concept, Walter and collaborators (2005, 2006) developed *lightcuts*, which are based on creating thousands of virtual point lights and then building a hierarchy by progressively clustering nearby ones together. When a point is being shaded, traversal of the light hierarchy is performed by computing bounds on the error that would result from using clustered values to illuminate the point versus continuing down the hierarchy, leading to an approach with both guaranteed error bounds and good efficiency. A similar hierarchy is used by Yuksel and Yuksel (2017) for determining the illumination from volumetric emitters. Bidirectional lightcuts (Walter et al. 2012) trace longer subpaths from the camera to obtain a family of light connection strategies; combining the strategies using multiple importance sampling eliminates bias artifacts that are commonly produced by virtual point light methods.

Jakob and Marschner (2012) expressed light transport involving specular materials as an integral over a high-dimensional manifold embedded in path space. A single light path corresponds to a point on the manifold, and nearby paths are found using a local parameterization that resembles Newton's method; they applied a Metropolis-type method through this parameterization to explore the neighborhood of challenging specular and near-specular configurations.

Hanika et al. (2015a) applied an improved version of the local path parameterization in a pure Monte Carlo context to estimate the direct illumination through one or more dielectric boundaries; this leads to significantly better convergence when rendering glass-enclosed objects or surfaces covered with water droplets.

Kaplanyan et al. (2014) observed that the path contribution function is close to being separable when paths are parameterized using the endpoints and the half-direction vectors at intermediate vertices, which are equal to the microfacet normals in the context of microfacet reflectance models. Performing Metropolis sampling in this half-vector domain leads to a method that is particularly good at rendering glossy interreflection. An extension by Hanika et al. (2015b) improves the robustness of this approach and proposes an optimized scheme to select mutation sizes to reduce sample clumping in image space.

Another interesting approach was developed by Lehtinen and collaborators, who considered rendering from the perspective of computing gradients of the image (Lehtinen et al. 2013, Manzi et al. 2014). Their insight was that, ideally, most samples from the path space should be taken around discontinuities and not in smooth regions of the image. They then developed a measurement contribution function for Metropolis sampling that focused samples on gradients and then reconstructed high-quality final images from horizontal and vertical gradient images and a coarse, noisy image. More recently, Kettunen et al. (2015) showed how this approach could be applied to regular path tracing without Metropolis sampling. Manzi et al. (2015) showed its application to bidirectional path tracing and Sun et al. (2017) applied it to vertex connection and merging. Petitjean et al. (2018) used gradient domain techniques to improve spectral rendering. Hua et al. (2019) have written a comprehensive survey of work in this area.

Hair is particularly challenging to render; not only is it extremely geometrically complex but multiple scattering among hair also makes a significant contribution to its final appearance. Traditional light transport algorithms often have difficulty handling this case well. See the papers by Moon and Marschner (2006), Moon et al. (2008), and Zinke et al. (2008) for recent work in specialized rendering algorithms for hair. Yan et al. (2017b) have recently demonstrated the effectiveness of models based on diffusion in addressing this problem.

While the rendering problem as discussed so far has been challenging enough, Jarabo et al. (2014a) showed the extension of the path integral to not include the steady-state assumption—that is, accounting for the noninfinite speed of light. Time ends up being extremely high frequency, which makes rendering challenging; they showed successful application of density estimation to this problem.

EXERCISES

② 13.1 To further improve efficiency, Russian roulette can be applied to skip tracing many of the shadow rays that make a low contribution to the final image: to implement this approach, tentatively compute the potential contribution of each shadow ray to the final overall radiance value before tracing the ray. If the contribution is below some threshold, apply Russian roulette to possibly skip tracing the ray. Measure the effect your scheme has on Monte Carlo efficiency for a number of test scenes.

② 13.2 Read Veach's description of efficiency-optimized Russian roulette, which adaptively chooses a threshold for applying Russian roulette (Veach 1997; Section 10.4.1). Implement this algorithm in pbrt, and evaluate its effectiveness in comparison to manually setting these thresholds.

② 13.3 If a scene has an object with a material that causes all but one of the wavelengths in SampledWavelengths to be terminated (e.g., due to dispersion), then rays may often undergo a number of scattering events before they hit such an object. In pbrt's current implementation, the path's radiance estimate is divided by the wavelength PDF values once, in the PixelSensor::ToSensorRGB() method. An implication of this design is that all the lighting calculations along the path are affected by the termination of wavelengths, and not just the ones after it happens. The result is an increase in color noise in such images.

Modify one or more integrators to instead perform this division by the current set of wavelength PDFs each time the radiance estimate being calculated is updated and not in PixelSensor::ToSensorRGB(). Verify that the same image is computed for scenes without wavelength termination (other than minor differences due to round-off error). Is there any change in performance? Find a scene where this change improves the result and measure the reduction in MSE.

② 13.4 Measure how much time is spent in Monte Carlo evaluation in the BSDF::rho() method when VisibleSurfaces are being initialized in the PathIntegrator. Do so for both simple and complex scenes that include a variety of BSDF models. Then, improve the BSDF interface so that each BxDF can provide its own rho()

implementation, possibly returning either an approximation or the closed-form reflectance. How much does performance improve as a result of your changes?

⊗ **13.5** Implement a technique for generating samples from the product of the light and BSDF distributions; see for example the papers by Burke et al. (2005), Cline et al. (2006), Clarberg et al. (2005), Rousselle et al. (2008), and Hart et al. (2020). Compare the effectiveness of the approach you implement to the direct lighting calculation currently implemented in pbrt. Investigate how scene complexity (and, thus, how expensive shadow rays are to trace) affects the Monte Carlo efficiency of the two techniques.

⊗ **13.6** Clarberg and Akenine-Möller (2008b) and Popov et al. (2013) both described algorithms that perform visibility caching—computing and interpolating information about light source visibility at points in the scene. Implement one of these methods and use it to improve the direct lighting calculation in pbrt. What sorts of scenes is it particularly effective for? Are there scenes for which it does not help?

⊗ **13.7** Modify pbrt so that the user can flag certain objects in the scene as being important sources of indirect lighting, and modify the PathIntegrator to sample points on those surfaces according to dA to generate some of the vertices in the paths it generates. Use multiple importance sampling to compute weights for the path samples, incorporating the probability that they would have been sampled both with BSDF sampling and with this area sampling. How much can this approach reduce variance and improve efficiency for scenes with substantial indirect lighting? How much can it hurt if the user flags surfaces that make little or no contribution or if multiple importance sampling is not used? Investigate generalizations of this approach that learn which objects are important sources of indirect lighting as rendering progresses so that the user does not need to supply this information ahead of time.

⊗ **13.8** Implement a path guiding algorithm such as the one developed by Müller and collaborators (Müller et al. 2017; Müller 2019) or Reibold et al. (2018). How much does your approach reduce error for scenes with highly varying indirect lighting? What is its effect on scenes with smoother lighting?

PathIntegrator 833

CHAPTER FOURTEEN

14 LIGHT TRANSPORT II: VOLUME RENDERING

The abstractions for representing participating media that were introduced in Chapter 11 describe how media scatter light but they do not provide the capability of simulating the global effects of light transport in a scene. The situation is similar to that with BSDFs: they describe local effects, but it was necessary to start to introduce integrators in Chapter 13 that accounted for direct lighting and interreflection in order to render images. This chapter does the same for volumetric scattering.

We begin with the introduction of the equation of transfer, which generalizes the light transport equation to describe the equilibrium distribution of radiance in scenes with participating media. Like the transmittance equations in Section 11.2, the equation of transfer has a null-scattering generalization that allows sampling of heterogeneous media for unbiased integration. We will also introduce a path integral formulation of it that generalizes the surface path integral from Section 13.1.4.

Following sections discuss implementations of solutions to the equation of transfer. Section 14.2 introduces two Integrators that use Monte Carlo integration to solve the full equation of transfer, making it possible to render scenes with complex volumetric effects. Section 14.3 then describes the implementation of LayeredBxDF, which solves a 1D specialization of the equation of transfer to model scattering from layered materials at surfaces.

14.1 THE EQUATION OF TRANSFER

The equation of transfer is the fundamental equation that governs the behavior of light in a medium that absorbs, emits, and scatters radiation. It accounts for all the volume scattering processes described in Chapter 11—absorption, emission, in scattering, and out scattering—to give an equation that describes the equilibrium distribution of radiance. The light transport equation is in fact a special case of it, simplified by the lack of participating media and specialized for scattering from surfaces. (We will equivalently refer to the equation of transfer as the *volumetric light transport equation*.)

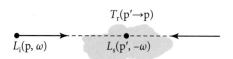

Figure 14.1: The equation of transfer gives the incident radiance at point $L_i(p, \omega)$ accounting for the effect of participating media. At each point p' along the ray, the source function $L_s(p', -\omega)$ gives the differential radiance added at the point due to scattering and emission. This radiance is then attenuated by the beam transmittance $T_r(p' \to p)$ from the point p' to the ray's origin.

In its most basic form, the equation of transfer is an integro-differential equation that describes how the radiance along a beam changes at a point in space. It can be derived by subtracting the effects of the scattering processes that reduce energy along a beam (absorption and out scattering) from the processes that increase energy along it (emission and in scattering).

To start, recall the source function L_s from Section 11.1.4: it gives the change in radiance at a point p in a direction ω due to emission and in-scattered light from other points in the medium:

$$L_s(p, \omega) = \frac{\sigma_a(p, \omega)}{\sigma_t(p, \omega)} L_e(p, \omega) + \frac{\sigma_s(p, \omega)}{\sigma_t(p, \omega)} \int_{S^2} p(p, \omega_i, \omega) L_i(p, \omega_i) \, d\omega_i.$$

The source function accounts for all the processes that add radiance to a ray.

The attenuation coefficient, $\sigma_t(p, \omega)$, accounts for all processes that reduce radiance at a point: absorption and out scattering. The differential equation that describes its effect, Equation (11.4), is

$$dL_o(p, \omega) = -\sigma_t(p, \omega) L_i(p, -\omega) \, dt.$$

The overall differential change in radiance at a point $p' = p + t\omega$ along a ray is found by adding these two effects together to get the integro-differential form of the equation of transfer:[1]

$$\frac{\partial}{\partial t} L_o(p', \omega) = -\sigma_t(p', \omega) L_i(p', -\omega) + \sigma_t(p', \omega) L_s(p', \omega). \tag{14.1}$$

(The σ_t modulation of the source function accounts for the medium's density at the point.)

With suitable boundary conditions, this equation can be transformed to a pure integral equation that describes the effect of participating media from the infinite number of points along a ray. For example, if we assume that there are no surfaces in the scene so that the rays are never blocked and have an infinite length, the integral equation of transfer is

$$L_i(p, \omega) = \int_0^\infty T_r(p' \to p) \, \sigma_t(p', \omega) \, L_s(p', -\omega) \, dt.$$

(See Figure 14.1.) The meaning of this equation is reasonably intuitive: it just says that the radiance arriving at a point from a given direction is determined by accumulating the radiance added at all points along the ray. The amount of added radiance at each point along the ray that reaches the ray's origin is reduced by the beam transmittance to the point.

---

1   It is an integro-differential equation due to the integral over the sphere in the source function.

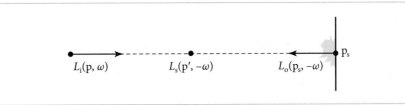

Figure 14.2: For a finite ray that intersects a surface, the incident radiance, $L_i(p, \omega)$, is equal to the outgoing radiance from the surface, $L_o(p_s, -\omega)$, times the beam transmittance to the surface plus the added radiance from all points along the ray from p to p_s.

More generally, if there are reflecting or emitting surfaces in the scene, rays do not necessarily have infinite length and the first surface that a ray hits affects its radiance, adding outgoing radiance from the surface at the point and preventing radiance from points along the ray beyond the intersection point from contributing to radiance at the ray's origin. If a ray (p, ω) intersects a surface at some point p_s at a parametric distance t along the ray, then the integral equation of transfer is

$$L_i(p, \omega) = T_r(p_s \to p)L_o(p_s, -\omega) + \int_0^t T_r(p' \to p)\, \sigma_t(p', \omega)\, L_s(p', -\omega)\, dt', \qquad [14.2]$$

where $p' = p + t'\omega$ are points along the ray (Figure 14.2).

This equation describes the two effects that contribute to radiance along the ray. First, reflected radiance back along the ray from the surface is given by the L_o term, which gives the emitted and reflected radiance from the surface. This radiance may be attenuated by the participating media; the beam transmittance from the ray origin to the point p_s accounts for this. The second term accounts for the added radiance along the ray due to volumetric scattering and emission up to the point where the ray intersects the surface; points beyond that one do not affect the radiance along the ray.

14.1.1 NULL-SCATTERING EXTENSION

In Section 11.2.1 we saw the value of null scattering, which made it possible to sample from a modified transmittance equation and to compute unbiased estimates of the transmittance between two points using algorithms like delta tracking and ratio tracking. Null scattering can be applied in a similar way to the equation of transfer, giving similar benefits.

In order to simplify notation in the following, we will assume that the various scattering coefficients σ do not vary as a function of direction. As before, we will also assume that the null-scattering coefficient σ_n is nonnegative and has been set to homogenize the medium's density to a fixed majorant $\sigma_{maj} = \sigma_n + \sigma_t$. Neither of these simplifications affect the course of the following derivations; both generalizations could be easily reintroduced.

A null-scattering generalization of the equation of transfer can be found using the relationship $\sigma_t = \sigma_{maj} - \sigma_n$ from Equation (11.11). If that substitution is made in the integro-differential equation of transfer, Equation (14.1), and the boundary condition of a surface at distance t along the ray is applied, then the result can be transformed into the pure integral equation

$$L_i(p, \omega) = T_{maj}(p_s \to p)L_o(p_s, -\omega)$$

$$+ \sigma_{maj} \int_0^t T_{maj}(p' \to p)\, L_n(p', -\omega)\, dt', \qquad [14.3]$$

where $p' = p + t'\omega$, as before, and we have introduced T_{maj} to denote the *majorant transmittance* that accounts for both regular attenuation and null scattering. Using the same convention as before that $d = \|p - p'\|$ is the distance between points p and p', it is

$$T_{maj}(p' \to p) = e^{\int_0^d -(\sigma_t(p+t\omega)+\sigma_n(p+t\omega))\,dt} = e^{-\sigma_{maj}d}. \qquad [14.4]$$

The null-scattering source function L_n is the source function L_s from Equation (11.3) plus a new third term:

$$L_n(p, \omega) = \frac{\sigma_a(p)}{\sigma_{maj}} L_e(p, \omega) + \frac{\sigma_s(p)}{\sigma_{maj}} \int_{\mathbb{S}^2} p(p, \omega_i, \omega) L_i(p, \omega_i)\,d\omega_i$$
$$+ \frac{\sigma_n(p)}{\sigma_{maj}} L_i(p, \omega). \qquad [14.5]$$

Because it includes attenuation due to null scattering, T_{maj} is always less than or equal to the actual transmittance. Thus, the product $T_{maj}L_o$ in Equation (14.3) may be less than the actual contribution of radiance leaving the surface, $T_r L_o$. However, any such deficiency is made up for by the last term of Equation (14.5).

14.1.2 EVALUATING THE EQUATION OF TRANSFER

The T_{maj} factor in the null-scattering equation of transfer gives a convenient distribution for sampling distances t along the ray in the medium that leads to the volumetric path-tracing algorithm, which we will now describe. (The algorithm we will arrive at is sometimes described as using delta tracking to solve the equation of transfer, since that is the sampling technique it uses for finding the locations of absorption and scattering events.)

If we assume for now that there is no geometry in the scene, then the null-scattering equation of transfer, Equation (14.3), simplifies to

$$L_i(p, \omega) = \sigma_{maj} \int_0^\infty T_{maj}(p' \to p) L_n(p', -\omega)\,dt'.$$

Thanks to null scattering having made the majorant medium homogeneous, $\sigma_{maj}T_{maj}$ can be sampled exactly. The first step in the path-tracing algorithm is to sample a point p' from its distribution, giving the estimator

$$L_i(p, \omega) \approx \frac{\sigma_{maj}T_{maj}(p' \to p) L_n(p', -\omega)}{p(p')}.$$

From Section A.4.2, we know that the probability density function (PDF) for sampling a distance t from the exponential distribution $e^{-\sigma_{maj}t}$ is $p(t) = \sigma_{maj}e^{-\sigma_{maj}t}$, and so the estimator simplifies to

$$L_i(p, \omega) \approx L_n(p', -\omega). \qquad [14.6]$$

What is left is to evaluate L_n.

Because $\sigma_{maj} = \sigma_a + \sigma_s + \sigma_n$, the initial σ factors in each term of Equation (14.5) can be considered to be three probabilities that sum to 1. If one of the three terms is randomly selected according to its probability and the rest of the term is evaluated without that factor, the expected value of the result is equal to L_n. Considering how to evaluate each of the terms:

- If the σ_a term is chosen, then the emission at $L_e(p', \omega)$ is returned and sampling terminates.
- For the σ_s term, the integral over the sphere of directions must be estimated. A direction ω' is sampled from some distribution and recursive evaluation of $L_i(p', \omega')$ then pro-

ceeds, weighted by the ratio of the phase function and the probability of sampling the direction ω'.

- If the null-scattering term is selected, $L_i(p', \omega)$ is to be evaluated, which can be handled recursively as well.

For the full equation of transfer that includes scattering from surfaces, both the surface-scattering term and the integral over the ray's extent lead to recursive evaluation of the equation of transfer. In the context of path tracing, however, we would like to only evaluate one of the terms in order to avoid an exponential increase in work. We will therefore start by defining a probability q of estimating the surface-scattering term; volumetric scattering is evaluated otherwise. Given such a q, the Monte Carlo estimator

$$
L_i(p, \omega) \approx
\begin{cases}
\frac{T_{\text{maj}}(p_s \to p) L_o(p_s, -\omega)}{q}, & \text{with probability } q \\
\frac{\sigma_{\text{maj}} \int_0^t T_{\text{maj}}(p' \to p)\, L_n(p', -\omega)\, dt'}{1-q}, & \text{otherwise}
\end{cases}
$$

gives $L_i(p, \omega)$ in expectation.

A good choice for q is that it be equal to $T_{\text{maj}}(p_s \to p)$. Surface scattering is then evaluated with a probability proportional to the transmittance to the surface and the ratio T_{maj}/q is equal to 1, leaving just the L_o factor. Furthermore, a sampling trick can be used to choose between the two terms: if a sample $t' \in [0, \infty)$ is taken from $\sigma_{\text{maj}} T_{\text{maj}}$'s distribution, then the probability that $t' > t$ is equal to $T_{\text{maj}}(p_s \to p)$. (This can be shown by integrating T_{maj}'s PDF to find its cumulative distribution function (CDF) and then considering the value of its CDF at t.) Using this technique and then making the same simplifications that brought us to Equation (14.6), we arrive at the estimator

$$
L_i(p, \omega) \approx
\begin{cases}
L_o(p_s, \omega), & \text{if } t' > t \\
L_n(p', -\omega), & \text{otherwise.}
\end{cases}
\tag{14.7}
$$

From this point, outgoing radiance from a surface can be estimated using techniques that were introduced in Chapter 13, and L_n can be estimated as described earlier.

14.1.3 SAMPLING THE MAJORANT TRANSMITTANCE

We have so far presented volumetric path tracing with the assumption that σ_{maj} is constant along the ray and thus that T_{maj} is a single exponential function. However, those assumptions are not compatible with the segments of piecewise-constant majorants that `Medium` implementations provide with their `RayMajorantIterator`s. We will now resolve this incompatibility.

Figure 14.3 shows example majorants along a ray, the optical thickness that they integrate to, and the resulting majorant transmittance function. The transmittance function is continuous and strictly decreasing, though at a rate that depends on the majorant at each point along the ray. If integration starts from $t = 0$, and we denote the ith segment's majorant as σ_{maj}^i and its endpoint as p_i, the transmittance can be written as

$$
T_{\text{maj}}(p \to p') = T_{\text{maj}}^1(p \to p_1)\, T_{\text{maj}}^2(p_1 \to p_2) \cdots T_{\text{maj}}^n(p_{n-1} \to p')
$$

where T_{maj}^i is the transmittance function for the ith segment and the point p' is the endpoint of the nth segment. (This relationship uses the multiplicative property of transmittance from Equation (11.6).)

Given the general task of estimating an integral of the form

Medium 714

$$
\int_0^t \sigma_{\text{maj}}(p')\, T_{\text{maj}}(p \to p')\, f(p')\, dt'
$$

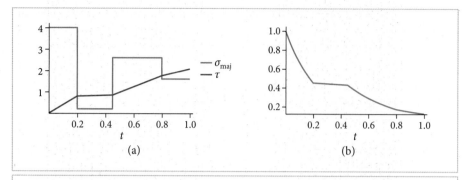

Figure 14.3: (a) Given piecewise-constant majorants defined over segments along a ray, the corresponding optical thickness τ is a piecewise-linear function. (b) Exponentiating the negative optical thickness gives the transmittance at each point along the ray. The transmittance function is continuous and decreasing, but has a first derivative discontinuity at transitions between segments.

with $p' = p + t'\omega$ and $\omega = \widehat{p' - p}$, it is useful to rewrite the integral to be over the individual majorant segments, which gives

$$\sigma_{maj}^1 \int_0^{t_1} T_{maj}^1(p \to p')\, f(p')\, dt'$$

$$+ \sigma_{maj}^1 T_{maj}^1(p \to p_1)\, \sigma_{maj}^2 \int_{t_1}^{t_2} T_{maj}^2(p_1 \to p')\, f(p')\, dt' \qquad [14.8]$$

$$+ \sigma_{maj}^1 T_{maj}^1(p \to p_1)\, \sigma_{maj}^2 T_{maj}^2(p_1 \to p_2) \int_{t_2}^{t_3} T_{maj}^3(p_2 \to p')\, f(p')\, dt' + \cdots .$$

Note that each term's contribution is modulated by the transmittances and majorants from the previous segments.

The form of Equation (14.8) hints at a sampling strategy: we start by sampling a value t'_1 from T_{maj}^1's distribution p_1; if t'_1 is less than t_1, then we evaluate the estimator at the sampled point p':

$$\frac{\sigma_{maj}^1 T_{maj}^1(p \to p')\, f(p')}{p_1(t'_1)} = f(p').$$

Applying the same ideas that led to Equation (14.7), we otherwise continue and consider the second term, drawing a sample t'_2 from T_{maj}^2's distribution, starting at t_1. If the sampled point is before the segment's endpoint, $t'_2 < t_2$, then we have the estimator

$$\frac{\sigma_{maj}^1 T_{maj}^1(p \to p_1)\, \sigma_{maj}^2 T_{maj}^2(p_1 \to p')\, f(p')}{\Pr\{t'_1 > t_1\}\, p_2(t'_2)} .$$

Because the probability that $t'_1 > t$ is equal to $\sigma_{maj}^1 T_{maj}^1(p \to p_1)$, the estimator for the second term again simplifies to $f(p')$. Otherwise, following this sampling strategy for subsequent segments similarly leads to the same simplified estimator in the end. It can furthermore be shown that the probability that no sample is generated in any of the segments is equal to the full majorant transmittance from 0 to t, which is exactly the probability required for the surface/volume estimator of Equation (14.7).

The `SampleT_maj()` function implements this sampling strategy, handling the details of iterating over `RayMajorantSegments` and sampling them. Its functionality will be used repeatedly in the following volumetric integrators.

⟨*Medium Sampling Functions*⟩ ≡
```
template <typename F>
SampledSpectrum SampleT_maj(Ray ray, Float tMax, Float u,
    RNG &rng, const SampledWavelengths &lambda, F callback);
```

In addition to a ray and an endpoint along it specified by `tMax`, `SampleT_maj()` takes a single uniform sample and an `RNG` to use for generating any necessary additional samples. This allows it to use a well-distributed value from a `Sampler` for the first sampling decision along the ray while it avoids consuming a variable and unbounded number of sample dimensions if more are needed (recall the discussion of the importance of consistency in sample dimension consumption in Section 8.3).

The provided `SampledWavelengths` play their usual role, though the first of them has additional meaning: for media with scattering properties that vary with wavelength, the majorant at the first wavelength is used for sampling. The alternative would be to sample each wavelength independently, though that would cause an explosion in samples to be evaluated in the context of algorithms like path tracing. Sampling a single wavelength can work well for evaluating all wavelengths' contributions if multiple importance sampling (MIS) is used; this topic is discussed further in Section 14.2.2.

A callback function is the last parameter passed to `SampleT_maj()`. This is a significant difference from pbrt's other sampling methods, which all generate a single sample (or sometimes, no sample) each time they are called. When sampling media that has null scattering, however, often a succession of samples are needed along the same ray. (Delta tracking, described in Section 11.2.1, is an example of such an algorithm.) The provided callback function is therefore invoked by `SampleT_maj()` each time a sample is taken. After the callback processes the sample, it should return a Boolean value that indicates whether sampling should recommence starting from the provided sample. With this implementation approach, `SampleT_maj()` can maintain state like the `RayMajorantIterator` between samples along a ray, which improves efficiency.

The signature of the callback function should be the following:

```
bool callback(Point3f p, MediumProperties mp, SampledSpectrum sigma_maj,
              SampledSpectrum T_maj)
```

Each invocation of the callback is passed a sampled point along the ray, the associated `MediumProperties` and σ_{maj} for the medium at that point, and the majorant transmittance T_{maj}. The first time `callback` is invoked, the majorant transmittance will be from the ray origin to the sample; any subsequent invocations give the transmittance from the previous sample to the current one.

After sampling concludes, `SampleT_maj()` returns the majorant transmittance T_{maj} from the last sampled point in the medium (or the ray origin, if no samples were generated) to the ray's endpoint (see Figure 14.4).

As if all of this was not sufficiently complex, the implementation of `SampleT_maj()` starts out with some tricky C++ code. There is a second variant of `SampleT_maj()` we will introduce shortly that is templated based on the concrete type of `Medium` being sampled. In order to call the appropriate template specialization, we must determine which type of `Medium` the ray is

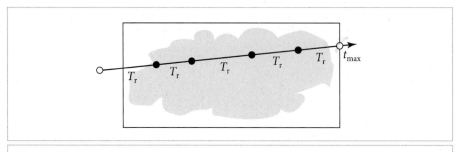

Figure 14.4: In addition to calling a provided callback function at sampled points in the medium, shown here as filled circles, the SampleT_maj() function returns the majorant transmittance T_{maj} from the last sampled point to the provided t_{max} value.

passing through. Conceptually, we would like to do something like the following, using the TaggedPointer::Is() method:

```
if (ray.medium.Is<HomogeneousMedium>())
    SampleT_maj<HomogeneousMedium>(ray, tMax, u,rng, lambda, func);
else if (ray.medium.Is<UniformGridMedium>())
    .
    .
    .
```

However, enumerating all the media that are implemented in pbrt in the SampleT_maj() function is undesirable: that would add an unexpected and puzzling additional step for users who wanted to extend the system with a new Medium. Therefore, the first SampleT_maj() function uses the dynamic dispatch capability of the Medium's TaggedPointer along with a generic lambda function, sample, to determine the Medium's type. TaggedPointer::Dispatch() ends up passing the Medium pointer back to sample; because the parameter is declared as auto, it then takes on the actual type of the medium when it is invoked. Thus, the following function has equivalent functionality to the code above but naturally handles all the media that are listed in the Medium class declaration without further modification.

⟨*Medium Sampling Function Definitions*⟩ +≡
```
template <typename F>
SampledSpectrum SampleT_maj(Ray ray, Float tMax, Float u, RNG &rng,
                           const SampledWavelengths &lambda, F callback) {
    auto sample = [&](auto medium) {
        using M = typename std::remove_reference_t<decltype(*medium)>;
        return SampleT_maj<M>(ray, tMax, u, rng, lambda, callback);
    };
    return ray.medium.Dispatch(sample);
}
```

With the concrete type of the medium available, we can proceed with the second instance of SampleTmaj(), which can now be specialized based on that type.

⟨*Medium Sampling Function Definitions*⟩ +≡
```
template <typename ConcreteMedium, typename F>
SampledSpectrum SampleT_maj(Ray ray, Float tMax, Float u, RNG &rng,
                            const SampledWavelengths &lambda, F callback) {
    ⟨Normalize ray direction and update tMax accordingly  861⟩
    ⟨Initialize MajorantIterator for ray majorant sampling  861⟩
    ⟨Generate ray majorant samples until termination  861⟩
}
```

The function starts by normalizing the ray's direction so that parametric distance along the ray directly corresponds to distance from the ray's origin. This simplifies subsequent transmittance computations in the remainder of the function. Since normalization scales the direction's length, the tMax endpoint must also be updated so that it corresponds to the same point along the ray.

⟨*Normalize ray direction and update* tMax *accordingly*⟩ ≡   **860**
```
tMax *= Length(ray.d);
ray.d = Normalize(ray.d);
```

Since the actual type of the medium is known and because all Medium implementations must define a MajorantIterator type (recall Section 11.4.1), the medium's iterator type can be directly declared as a stack-allocated variable. This gives a number of benefits: not only is the expense of dynamic allocation avoided, but subsequent calls to the iterator's Next() method in this function are regular method calls that can even be expanded inline by the compiler; no dynamic dispatch is necessary for them. An additional benefit of knowing the medium's type is that the appropriate SampleRay() method can be called directly without incurring the cost of dynamic dispatch here.

⟨*Initialize* MajorantIterator *for ray majorant sampling*⟩ ≡   **860**
```
ConcreteMedium *medium = ray.medium.Cast<ConcreteMedium>();
typename ConcreteMedium::MajorantIterator iter =
    medium->SampleRay(ray, tMax, lambda);
```

With an iterator initialized, sampling along the ray can proceed. The T_maj variable declared here tracks the accumulated majorant transmittance from the ray origin or the previous sample along the ray (depending on whether a sample has yet been generated).

⟨*Generate ray majorant samples until termination*⟩ ≡   **860**
```
SampledSpectrum T_maj(1.f);
bool done = false;
while (!done) {
    ⟨Get next majorant segment from iterator and sample it 861⟩
}
return SampledSpectrum(1.f);
```

If the iterator has no further majorant segments to provide, then sampling is complete. In this case, it is important to return any majorant transmittance that has accumulated in T_maj; that represents the remaining transmittance to the ray's endpoint. Otherwise, a few details are attended to before sampling proceeds along the segment.

⟨*Get next majorant segment from iterator and sample it*⟩ ≡   **861**
```
pstd::optional<RayMajorantSegment> seg = iter.Next();
if (!seg)
    return T_maj;
⟨Handle zero-valued majorant for current segment 862⟩
⟨Generate samples along current majorant segment 862⟩
```

If the majorant has the value 0 in the first wavelength, then there is nothing to sample along the segment. It is important to handle this case, since otherwise the subsequent call to SampleExponential() in this function would return an infinite value that would subsequently lead to not-a-number values. Because the other wavelengths may not themselves have zero-valued majorants, we must still update T_maj for the segment's majorant transmittance even though the transmittance for the first wavelength is unchanged.

⟨*Handle zero-valued majorant for current segment*⟩ ≡   **861**
```
    if (seg->sigma_maj[0] == 0) {
        Float dt = seg->tMax - seg->tMin;
        ⟨Handle infinite dt for ray majorant segment 862⟩
        T_maj *= FastExp(-dt * seg->sigma_maj);
        continue;
    }
```

One edge case must be attended to before the exponential function is called. If tMax holds the IEEE floating-point infinity value, then dt will as well; it then must be bumped down to the largest finite Float. This is necessary because with floating-point arithmetic, zero times infinity gives a not-a-number value (whereas any nonzero value times infinity gives infinity). Otherwise, for any wavelengths with zero-valued sigma_maj, not-a-number values would be passed to FastExp().

⟨*Handle infinite* dt *for ray majorant segment*⟩ ≡   **862**
```
    if (IsInf(dt))
        dt = std::numeric_limits<Float>::max();
```

The implementation otherwise tries to generate a sample along the current segment. This work is inside a while loop so that multiple samples may be generated along the segment.

⟨*Generate samples along current majorant segment*⟩ ≡   **861**
```
    Float tMin = seg->tMin;
    while (true) {
        ⟨Try to generate sample along current majorant segment 862⟩
    }
```

In the usual case, a distance is sampled according to the PDF $\sigma_{\mathrm{maj}}e^{-\sigma_{\mathrm{maj}}t}$. Separate cases handle a sample that is within the current majorant segment and one that is past it.

One detail to note in this fragment is that as soon as the uniform sample u has been used, a replacement is immediately generated using the provided RNG. In this way, the method maintains the invariant that u is always a valid independent sample value. While this can lead to a single excess call to RNG::Uniform() each time SampleT_maj() is called, it ensures the initial u value provided to the method is used only once.

⟨*Try to generate sample along current majorant segment*⟩ ≡   **862**
```
    Float t = tMin + SampleExponential(u, seg->sigma_maj[0]);
    u = rng.Uniform<Float>();
    if (t < seg->tMax) {
        ⟨Call callback function for sample within segment 863⟩
    } else {
        ⟨Handle sample past end of majorant segment 863⟩
    }
```

For a sample within the segment's extent, the final majorant transmittance to be passed to the callback is found by accumulating the transmittance from tMin to the sample point. The rest of the necessary medium properties can be found using SamplePoint(). If the callback function returns false to indicate that sampling should conclude, then we have a doubly nested while loop to break out of; a break statement takes care of the inner one, and setting done to true causes the outer one to terminate.

FastExp() 1036
Float 23
IsInf() 363
RayMajorantSegment::sigma_maj
  718
RayMajorantSegment::tMax 718
RayMajorantSegment::tMin 718
RNG::Uniform<Float>() 1056
SampleExponential() 1003

If true is returned by the callback, indicating that sampling should restart at the sample that was just generated, then the accumulated transmittance is reset to 1 and tMin is updated to be at the just-taken sample's position.

⟨*Call callback function for sample within segment*⟩ ≡   862
```
T_maj *= FastExp(-(t - tMin) * seg->sigma_maj);
MediumProperties mp = medium->SamplePoint(ray(t), lambda);
if (!callback(ray(t), mp, seg->sigma_maj, T_maj)) {
    done = true;
    break;
}
T_maj = SampledSpectrum(1.f);
tMin = t;
```

If the sampled distance *t* is past the end of the segment, then there is no medium interaction along it and it is on to the next segment, if any. In this case, majorant transmittance up to the end of the segment must be accumulated into T_maj so that the complete majorant transmittance along the ray is provided with the next valid sample (if any).

⟨*Handle sample past end of majorant segment*⟩ ≡   862
```
Float dt = seg->tMax - tMin;
T_maj *= FastExp(-dt * seg->sigma_maj);
break;
```

⋆ 14.1.4 GENERALIZED PATH SPACE

Just as it was helpful to express the light transport equation (LTE) as a sum over paths of scattering events, it is also helpful to express the null-scattering integral equation of transfer in this form. Doing so makes it possible to apply variance reduction techniques like multiple importance sampling and is a prerequisite for constructing participating medium-aware bidirectional integrators.

Recall how, in Section 13.1.4, the surface form of the LTE was repeatedly substituted into itself to derive the path space contribution function for a path of length *n*

$$P(\bar{\mathrm{p}}_n) = \underbrace{\int_A \int_A \cdots \int_A}_{n-1} L_e(\mathrm{p}_n \to \mathrm{p}_{n-1})\, T(\bar{\mathrm{p}}_n)\, \mathrm{d}A(\mathrm{p}_2) \cdots \mathrm{d}A(\mathrm{p}_n),$$

where the throughput $T(\bar{\mathrm{p}}_n)$ was defined as

$$T(\bar{\mathrm{p}}_n) = \prod_{i=1}^{n-1} f(\mathrm{p}_{i+1} \to \mathrm{p}_i \to \mathrm{p}_{i-1})\, G(\mathrm{p}_{i+1} \leftrightarrow \mathrm{p}_i).$$

This previous definition only works for surfaces, but using a similar approach of substituting the integral equation of transfer, a medium-aware path integral can be derived. The derivation is laborious and we will just present the final result here. (The "Further Reading" section has a pointer to the full derivation.)

FastExp() 1036
Float 23
Medium::SamplePoint() 717
MediumProperties 718
RayMajorantSegment::sigma_maj
  718
RayMajorantSegment::tMax 718
SampledSpectrum 171

Previously, integration occurred over a Cartesian product of surface locations A^n. Now, we will need a formal way of writing down an integral over an arbitrary sequence of each of 2D surface locations A, 3D positions in a participating medium V where actual scattering occurs, and 3D positions in a participating medium $V_\emptyset$ where null scattering occurs. (The two media V and $V_\emptyset$ represent the same volume of space with the same scattering properties, but we will find it handy to distinguish between them in the following.)

First, we will focus only on a specific arrangement of n surface and medium vertices encoded in a configuration vector $\mathbf{c}$. The associated set of paths is given by a Cartesian product of surface locations and medium locations,

$$\mathcal{P}_n^{\mathbf{c}} = \underset{i=1}{\overset{n}{\times}} \begin{cases} A, & \text{if } c_i = 0 \\ V, & \text{if } c_i = 1 \\ V_\emptyset, & \text{if } c_i = 2. \end{cases}$$

The set of all paths of length n is the union of the above sets over all possible configuration vectors:

$$\mathcal{P}_n = \bigcup_{\mathbf{c} \in \{0,1,2\}^n} \mathcal{P}_n^{\mathbf{c}}.$$

Next, we define a *measure*, which provides an abstract notion of the volume of a subset $D \subseteq \mathcal{P}_n$ that is essential for integration. The measure we will use simply sums up the product of surface area and volume associated with the individual vertices in each of the path spaces of specific configurations.

$$\mu_n(D) = \sum_{\mathbf{c} \in \{0,1\}^n} \mu_n^{\mathbf{c}}(D \cap \mathcal{P}_n^{\mathbf{c}}) \quad \text{where } \mu_n^{\mathbf{c}}(D) = \int_D \prod_{i=1}^{n} \begin{cases} dA(\mathrm{p}_i), & \text{if } c_i = 0 \\ dV(\mathrm{p}_i), & \text{if } c_i = 1 \\ dV_\emptyset(\mathrm{p}_i), & \text{if } c_i = 2. \end{cases}$$

The measure for null-scattering vertices $dV_\emptyset$ incorporates a Dirac delta distribution to limit integration to be along the line between successive real-scattering vertices.

The generalized path contribution $\hat{P}(\bar{\mathrm{p}}_n)$ can now be written as

$$\hat{P}(\bar{\mathrm{p}}_n) = \int_{\mathcal{P}_{n-1}} \hat{L}_e(\mathrm{p}_n \to \mathrm{p}_{n-1}) \, \hat{T}(\bar{\mathrm{p}}_n) \, d\mu_{n-1}(\mathrm{p}_2, \ldots, \mathrm{p}_n), \qquad [14.9]$$

where

$$\hat{L}_e(\mathrm{p}_n \to \mathrm{p}_{n-1}) = \begin{cases} L_e(\mathrm{p}_n \to \mathrm{p}_{n-1}) & \text{if } \mathrm{p}_n \in A, \\ \sigma_a(\mathrm{p}_n) L_e(\mathrm{p}_n \to \mathrm{p}_{n-1}) & \text{if } \mathrm{p}_n \in V. \end{cases} \qquad [14.10]$$

Due to the measure defined earlier, the generalized path contribution is a sum of many integrals considering all possible sequences of surface, volume, and null-scattering events.

The full set of path vertices p_i include both null- and real-scattering events. We will find it useful to use r_i to denote the subset of them that represent real scattering (see Figure 14.5). Note a given real-scattering vertex r_i will generally have a different index value in the full path.

The path throughput function $\hat{T}(\bar{\mathrm{p}}_n)$ can then be defined as:

$$\hat{T}(\bar{\mathrm{p}}_n) = \left(\prod_{i=1}^{n-1} \hat{f}(\mathrm{p}_{i+1} \to \mathrm{p}_i \to \mathrm{p}_{i-1}) \right) \left(\prod_{i=0}^{n-1} T_{\mathrm{maj}}(\mathrm{p}_i \to \mathrm{p}_{i+1}) \right)$$
$$\times \left(\prod_{i=1}^{m-1} \hat{G}(\mathrm{r}_i \leftrightarrow \mathrm{r}_{i+1}) \right) \qquad [14.11]$$

It now refers to a generalized scattering distribution function $\hat{f}$ and generalized geometric term $\hat{G}$. The former simply falls back to the BSDF, phase function (multiplied by σ_s), or a factor that enforces the ordering of null-scattering vertices, depending on the type of the vertex p_i. Note that the first two products in Equation (14.11) are over all vertices but the third is only over real-scattering vertices.

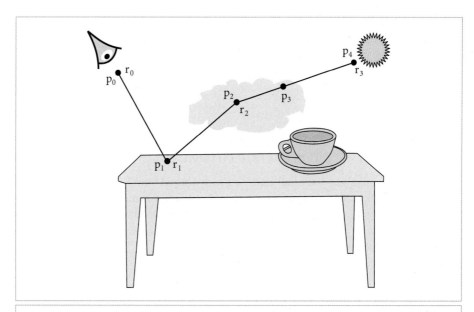

Figure 14.5: In the path space framework, a path is defined by a set of *n* vertices p_i that have an emitter at one endpoint and a sensor at the other, where intermediate vertices represent scattering events, including null scattering. The subset of *m* vertices that represent real scattering events are labeled r_i.

The scattering distribution function $\hat{f}$ is defined by

$$\hat{f}(p_{i+1} \to p_i \to p_{i-1}) = \begin{cases} f(p_{i+1} \to p_i \to p_{i-1}), & \text{if } p_i \in A \\ \sigma_s(p_i)\, p\,(p_{i+1} \to p_i \to p_{i-1}), & \text{if } p_i \in V \\ \sigma_n(p_i)\, H((p_i - p_{i+1}) \cdot (p_{i-1} - p_i)), & \text{if } p_i \in V_\emptyset. \end{cases} \quad [14.12]$$

Here, H is the Heaviside function, which is 1 if its parameter is positive and 0 otherwise.

Equation (13.2) in Section 13.1.3 originally defined the geometric term G as

$$G(p \leftrightarrow p') = V(p \leftrightarrow p') \frac{|\cos\theta|\,|\cos\theta'|}{\|p - p'\|^2}.$$

A generalized form of this geometric term is given by

$$\hat{G}(p \leftrightarrow p') = V(p \leftrightarrow p') \frac{C_p(p, p')\, C_{p'}(p', p)}{\|p - p'\|^2}, \quad [14.13]$$

where

$$C_p(p, p') = \begin{cases} \left| n_p \cdot \dfrac{p - p'}{\|p - p'\|} \right|, & \text{if } p \in A \\ 1, & \text{if } p \in V \end{cases}$$

incorporates the absolute angle cosine between the connection segment and the normal direction when the underlying vertex p is located on a surface. Note that C_p is only evaluated for real-scattering vertices r_i, so the case of $p \in V_\emptyset$ does not need to be considered.

Similar to integrating over the path space for surface scattering, the Monte Carlo estimator for the path contribution function $\hat{P}$ can be defined for a path $\bar{p}_n$ of n path vertices p_i. The resulting Monte Carlo estimator is

$$\hat{P}(\bar{p}_n) = \frac{\hat{T}(\bar{p}_n)\, \hat{L}_e(p_n \to p_{n-1})}{p(\bar{p}_n)}, \quad [14.14]$$

where $p(\bar{p}_n)$ is the probability of sampling the path $\bar{p}_n$ with respect to the generalized path space measure.

Following Equation (13.8), we will also find it useful to define the volumetric path through-put weight

$$\beta(\bar{p}_n) = \frac{\hat{T}(\bar{p}_n)}{p(\bar{p}_n)}. \qquad (14.15)$$

⋆ 14.1.5 EVALUATING THE VOLUMETRIC PATH INTEGRAL

The Monte Carlo estimator of the null-scattering path integral from Equation (14.14) allows sampling path vertices in a variety of ways; it is not necessary to sample them incrementally from the camera as in path tracing, for example. We will now reconsider sampling paths via path tracing under the path integral framework to show its use. For simplicity, we will consider scenes that have only volumetric scattering here.

The volumetric path-tracing algorithm from Section 14.1.2 is based on three sampling operations: sampling a distance along the current ray to a scattering event, choosing which type of interaction happens at that point, and then sampling a new direction from that point if the path has not been terminated. We can write the corresponding Monte Carlo estimator for the generalized path contribution function $\hat{P}$ from Equation (14.14) with the path probability $p(\bar{p}_n)$ expressed as the product of three probabilities:

- $p_{\mathrm{maj}}(p_{i+1}|p_i, \omega_i)$: the probability of sampling the point p_{i+1} along the direction ω_i from the point p_i.
- $p_{\mathrm{e}}(p_i)$: the discrete probability of sampling the type of scattering event—absorption, real-, or null-scattering—that was chosen at p_i.
- $p_\omega(\omega'|r_i, \omega_i)$: the probability of sampling the direction ω' after a regular scattering event at point r_i with incident direction ω_i.

For an n vertex path with m real-scattering vertices, the resulting estimator is

$$\frac{\hat{T}(\bar{p}_n)\,\hat{L}_{\mathrm{e}}(p_n \to p_{n-1})}{\left(\prod_{i=0}^{n-1} p_{\mathrm{maj}}(p_{i+1}|p_i, \omega_i)\right)\left(\prod_{i=1}^{n} p_{\mathrm{e}}(p_i)\right)\left(\prod_{i=1}^{m-1} p_\omega(\omega_{i+1}|r_i, \omega_i)\,\hat{G}(r_i \leftrightarrow r_{i+1})\right)}, \qquad (14.16)$$

where ω_i denotes the direction from p_i to p_{i+1} and where the $\hat{G}$ factor in the denominator accounts for the change of variables from sampling with respect to solid angle to sampling with respect to the path space measure.

We consider each of the three sampling operations in turn, starting with distance sampling, which has density p_{maj}. Assuming a single majorant σ_{maj}, we find that p_{maj} has density $\sigma_{\mathrm{maj}}e^{-\sigma_{\mathrm{maj}}t}$, and the exponential factors cancel out the T_{maj} factors in $\hat{T}$, each one leaving behind a $1/\sigma_{\mathrm{maj}}$ factor. Expanding out $\hat{T}$ and simplifying, including eliminating the $\hat{G}$ factors, all of which also cancel out, we have the estimator

$$\hat{P}(\bar{p}_n) = \frac{\left(\prod_{i=1}^{n-1}\hat{f}(p_{i+1} \to p_i \to p_{i-1})\right)\hat{L}_{\mathrm{e}}(p_n \to p_{n-1})}{(\sigma_{\mathrm{maj}})^n\left(\prod_{i=1}^{n} p_{\mathrm{e}}(p_i)\right)\left(\prod_{i=1}^{m-1} p_\omega(\omega_{i+1}|r_i, \omega_i)\right)}. \qquad (14.17)$$

Consider next the discrete choice among the three types of scattering event. The probabilities p_{e} are all of the form $\sigma_{\{a,s,n\}}/\sigma_{\mathrm{maj}}$, according to which type of scattering event was chosen at each vertex. The $(\sigma_{\mathrm{maj}})^n$ factor in Equation (14.17) cancels, leaving us with

$$\hat{P}(\bar{\mathrm{p}}_n) = \frac{\left(\prod\limits_{i=1}^{n-1} \hat{f}(\mathrm{p}_{i+1} \to \mathrm{p}_i \to \mathrm{p}_{i-1})\right) \hat{L}_e(\mathrm{p}_n \to \mathrm{p}_{n-1})}{\left(\prod\limits_{i=1}^{n} \sigma_{\{a,s,n\}_i}(\mathrm{p}_i)\right) \left(\prod\limits_{i=1}^{m-1} p_\omega(\omega_{i+1}|\mathrm{r}_i, \omega_i)\right)}.$$

The first $n-1$ $\sigma_{\{a,s,n\}}$ factors must be either real or null scattering, and the last must be σ_a, given how the path was sampled. Thus, the estimator is equivalent to

$$\hat{P}(\bar{\mathrm{p}}_n) = \frac{\left(\prod\limits_{i=1}^{n-1} \hat{f}(\mathrm{p}_{i+1} \to \mathrm{p}_i \to \mathrm{p}_{i-1})\right) \hat{L}_e(\mathrm{p}_n \to \mathrm{p}_{n-1})}{\left(\prod\limits_{i=1}^{n-1} \sigma_{\{s,n\}_i}(\mathrm{p}_i)\right) \sigma_a(\mathrm{p}_n) \left(\prod\limits_{i=1}^{m-1} p_\omega(\omega_{i+1}|\mathrm{r}_i, \omega_i)\right)}. \qquad [14.18]$$

Because we are for now neglecting surface scattering, $\hat{f}$ represents either regular volumetric scattering or null scattering. Recall from Equation (14.12) that $\hat{f}$ includes a σ_s or σ_n factor in those respective cases, which cancels out all the corresponding factors in the $\sigma_{\{s,n\}}$ product in the denominator. Further, note that the Heaviside function for null scattering's $\hat{f}$ function is always 1 given how vertices are sampled with path tracing, so we can also restrict ourselves to the remaining m real-scattering events in the numerator. Our estimator simplifies to

$$\hat{P}(\bar{\mathrm{p}}_n) = \left(\prod\limits_{i=1}^{m-1} \frac{p(\mathrm{r}_{i-1} \to \mathrm{r}_i \to \mathrm{r}_{i+1})}{p_\omega(\omega_{i+1}|\mathrm{r}_i, \omega_i)}\right) \frac{\hat{L}_e(\mathrm{p}_n \to \mathrm{p}_{n-1})}{\sigma_a(\mathrm{p}_n)}. \qquad [14.19]$$

The σ_a factor in the path space emission function, Equation (14.10), cancels the remaining $\sigma_a(\mathrm{p}_n)$. We are left with the emission $L_e(\mathrm{p}_n \to \mathrm{p}_{n-1})$ at the last vertex scaled by the product of ratios of phase function values and sampling probabilities as the estimator's value, just as we saw in Section 14.1.2.

14.2 VOLUME SCATTERING INTEGRATORS

The path space expression of the null-scattering equation of transfer allows a variety of sampling techniques to be applied to the light transport problem. This section defines two integrators that are based on path tracing starting from the camera.

First is the SimpleVolPathIntegrator, which uses simple sampling techniques, giving an implementation that is short and easily verified. This integrator is particularly useful for computing ground-truth results when debugging more sophisticated volumetric sampling and integration algorithms.

The VolPathIntegrator is defined next. This integrator is fairly complex, but it applies state-of-the-art sampling techniques to volume light transport while handling surface scattering similarly to the PathIntegrator. It is pbrt's default integrator and is also the template for the wavefront integrator in Chapter 15.

14.2.1 A SIMPLE VOLUMETRIC INTEGRATOR

The SimpleVolPathIntegrator implements a basic volumetric path tracer, following the sampling approach described in Section 14.1.2. Its Li() method is under 100 lines of code, none of them too tricky. However, with this simplicity comes a number of limitations. First, like the RandomWalkIntegrator, it does not perform any explicit light sampling, so it requires that

Figure 14.6: Explosion Rendered Using the `SimpleVolPathIntegrator`. With 256 samples per pixel, this integrator gives a reasonably accurate rendering of the volumetric model, though there are variance spikes in some pixels (especially visible toward the bottom of the volume) due to error from the integrator not directly sampling the scene's light sources. The `VolPathIntegrator`, which uses more sophisticated sampling strategies, renders this scene with 1,288 times lower MSE; it is discussed in Section 14.2.2. *(Scene courtesy of Jim Price.)*

rays are able to randomly intersect the lights in the scene. Second, it does not handle scattering from surfaces. An error message is therefore issued if it is used with a scene that contains delta distribution light sources or has surfaces with nonzero-valued BSDFs. (These defects are all addressed in the `VolPathIntegrator` discussed in Section 14.2.2.) Nevertheless, this integrator is capable of rendering complex volumetric effects; see Figure 14.6.

⟨*SimpleVolPathIntegrator Definition*⟩ ≡
```
class SimpleVolPathIntegrator : public RayIntegrator {
  public:
    ⟨SimpleVolPathIntegrator Public Methods⟩
  private:
    ⟨SimpleVolPathIntegrator Private Members 869⟩
};
```

This integrator's only parameter is the maximum path length, which is set via a value passed to the constructor (not included here).

⟨*SimpleVolPathIntegrator Private Members*⟩ ≡   868
```
    int maxDepth;
```

The general form of the Li() method follows that of the PathIntegrator.

⟨*SimpleVolPathIntegrator Method Definitions*⟩ ≡
```
    SampledSpectrum SimpleVolPathIntegrator::Li(RayDifferential ray,
            SampledWavelengths &lambda, Sampler sampler, ScratchBuffer &buf,
            VisibleSurface *) const {
        ⟨Declare local variables for delta tracking integration 869⟩
        ⟨Terminate secondary wavelengths before starting random walk 869⟩
        while (true) {
            ⟨Estimate radiance for ray path using delta tracking 870⟩
        }
        return L;
    }
```

A few familiar variables track the path state, including L to accumulate the radiance estimate for the path. For this integrator, beta, which tracks the path throughput weight, is just a single Float value, since the product of ratios of phase function values and sampling PDFs from Equation (14.19) is a scalar value.

⟨*Declare local variables for delta tracking integration*⟩ ≡   869
```
    SampledSpectrum L(0.f);
    Float beta = 1.f;
    int depth = 0;
```

Media with scattering properties that vary according to wavelength introduce a number of complexities in sampling and evaluating Monte Carlo estimators. We will defer addressing them until we cover the VolPathIntegrator. The SimpleVolPathIntegrator instead estimates radiance at a single wavelength by terminating all but the first wavelength sample.

Here is a case where we have chosen simplicity over efficiency for this integrator's implementation: we might instead have accounted for all wavelengths until the point that spectrally varying scattering properties were encountered, enjoying the variance reduction benefits of estimating all of them for scenes where doing so is possible. However, doing this would have led to a more complex integrator implementation.

⟨*Terminate secondary wavelengths before starting random walk*⟩ ≡   869
```
    lambda.TerminateSecondary();
```

The first step in the loop is to find the ray's intersection with the scene geometry, if any. This gives the parametric distance t beyond which no samples should be taken for the current ray, as the intersection either represents a transition to a different medium or a surface that occludes farther-away points.

The scattered and terminated variables declared here will allow the lambda function that is passed to SampleT_maj() to report back the state of the path after sampling terminates.

⟨*Estimate radiance for ray path using delta tracking*⟩ ≡   **869**

```
pstd::optional<ShapeIntersection> si = Intersect(ray);
bool scattered = false, terminated = false;
if (ray.medium) {
```
      ⟨*Initialize* RNG *for sampling the majorant transmittance* **870**⟩
      ⟨*Sample medium using delta tracking* **870**⟩
```
}
```
   ⟨*Handle terminated and unscattered rays after medium sampling* **872**⟩

An RNG is required for the call to the SampleT_maj() function. We derive seeds for it based on two random values from the sampler, hashing them to convert Floats into integers.

⟨*Initialize* RNG *for sampling the majorant transmittance*⟩ ≡   **870, 880**

```
uint64_t hash0 = Hash(sampler.Get1D());
uint64_t hash1 = Hash(sampler.Get1D());
RNG rng(hash0, hash1);
```

With that, a call to SampleT_maj() starts the generation of samples according to $\sigma_{\mathrm{maj}} T_{\mathrm{maj}}$. The Sampler is used to generate the first uniform sample u that is passed to the method; recall from Section 14.1.3 that subsequent ones will be generated using the provided RNG. In a similar fashion, the Sampler is used for the initial value of uMode here. It will be used to choose among the three types of scattering event at the first sampled point. For uMode as well, the RNG will provide subsequent values.

In this case, the transmittance that SampleT_maj() returns for the final segment is unneeded, so it is ignored.

⟨*Sample medium using delta tracking*⟩ ≡   **870**

```
Float tMax = si ? si->tHit : Infinity;
Float u = sampler.Get1D();
Float uMode = sampler.Get1D();
SampleT_maj(ray, tMax, u, rng, lambda,
    [&](Point3f p, MediumProperties mp, SampledSpectrum sigma_maj,
        SampledSpectrum T_maj) {
```
        ⟨*Compute medium event probabilities for interaction* **870**⟩
        ⟨*Randomly sample medium scattering event for delta tracking* **871**⟩
```
    });
```

Float 23
Hash() 1042
Infinity 361
Integrator::Intersect() 23
MediumProperties 718
MediumProperties::sigma_a 718
MediumProperties::sigma_s 718
Point3f 92
Ray::medium 95
RNG 1054
SampledSpectrum 171
Sampler 469
Sampler::Get1D() 470
SampleT_maj() 859
ShapeIntersection 266
ShapeIntersection::tHit 266

For each sample returned by SampleT_maj(), it is necessary to select which type of scattering it represents. The first step is to compute the probability of each possibility. Because we have specified σ_{n} such that it is nonnegative and $\sigma_a + \sigma_s + \sigma_n = \sigma_{\mathrm{maj}}$, the null-scattering probability can be found as one minus the other two probabilities. A call to std::max() ensures that any slightly negative values due to floating-point round-off error are clamped at zero.

⟨*Compute medium event probabilities for interaction*⟩ ≡   **870, 880**

```
Float pAbsorb = mp.sigma_a[0] / sigma_maj[0];
Float pScatter = mp.sigma_s[0] / sigma_maj[0];
Float pNull = std::max<Float>(0, 1 - pAbsorb - pScatter);
```

A call to SampleDiscrete() then selects one of the three terms of L_{n} using the specified probabilities.

⟨*Randomly sample medium scattering event for delta tracking*⟩ ≡   870

```
int mode = SampleDiscrete({pAbsorb, pScatter, pNull}, uMode);
if (mode == 0) {
    ⟨Handle absorption event for medium sample 871⟩
} else if (mode == 1) {
    ⟨Handle regular scattering event for medium sample 871⟩
} else {
    ⟨Handle null-scattering event for medium sample 872⟩
}
```

If absorption is chosen, the path terminates. Any emission is added to the radiance estimate, and evaluation of Equation (14.19) is complete. The fragment therefore sets `terminated` to indicate that the path is finished and returns `false` from the lambda function so that no further samples are generated along the ray.

⟨*Handle absorption event for medium sample*⟩ ≡   871

```
L += beta * mp.Le;
terminated = true;
return false;
```

For a scattering event, `beta` is updated according to the ratio of phase function and its directional sampling probability from Equation (14.19).

⟨*Handle regular scattering event for medium sample*⟩ ≡   871

```
⟨Stop path sampling if maximum depth has been reached 871⟩
⟨Sample phase function for medium scattering event 871⟩
⟨Update state for recursive evaluation of Lᵢ 872⟩
```

The counter for the number of scattering events is only incremented for real-scattering events; we do not want the number of null-scattering events to affect path termination. If this scattering event causes the limit to be reached, the path is terminated.

⟨*Stop path sampling if maximum depth has been reached*⟩ ≡   871, 882

```
if (depth++ >= maxDepth) {
    terminated = true;
    return false;
}
```

If the path is not terminated, then a new direction is sampled from the phase function's distribution.

⟨*Sample phase function for medium scattering event*⟩ ≡   871

```
Point2f u{rng.Uniform<Float>(), rng.Uniform<Float>()};
pstd::optional<PhaseFunctionSample> ps = mp.phase.Sample_p(-ray.d, u);
if (!ps) {
    terminated = true;
    return false;
}
```

Given a sampled direction, the beta factor must be updated. Volumetric path-tracing implementations often assume that the phase function sampling distribution matches the phase function's actual distribution and dispense with `beta` entirely since it is always equal to 1. This variation is worth pausing to consider: in that case, emitted radiance at the end of the path is always returned, unscaled. All of the effect of transmittance, phase functions, and so forth is entirely encapsulated in the distribution of how often various terms are evaluated and in the distribution of scattered ray directions. pbrt does not impose the requirement on phase functions that their importance sampling technique be perfect, though this is the case for the Henyey–Greenstein phase function in pbrt.

Be it with beta or without, there is no need to do any further work along the current ray after a scattering event, so after the following code updates the path state to account for scattering, it too returns false to direct that no further samples should be taken along the ray.

⟨*Update state for recursive evaluation of L_i*⟩ ≡   871
```
beta *= ps->p / ps->pdf;
ray.o = p;
ray.d = ps->wi;
scattered = true;
return false;
```

Null-scattering events are ignored, so there is nothing to do but to return true to indicate that additional samples along the current ray should be taken. Similar to the real-scattering case, this can be interpreted as starting a recursive evaluation of Equation (14.3) from the current sampled position without incurring the overhead of actually doing so. Since this is the only case that may lead to another invocation of the lambda function, uMode must be refreshed with a new uniform sample value in case another sample is generated.

⟨*Handle null-scattering event for medium sample*⟩ ≡   871
```
uMode = rng.Uniform<Float>();
return true;
```

If the path was terminated due to absorption, then there is no more work to do in the Li() method; the final radiance value can be returned. Further, if the ray was scattered, then there is nothing more to do but to restart the while loop and start sampling the scattered ray. Otherwise, the ray either underwent no scattering events or only underwent null scattering.

⟨*Handle terminated and unscattered rays after medium sampling*⟩ ≡   870
```
if (terminated) return L;
if (scattered) continue;
⟨Add emission to surviving ray 872⟩
⟨Handle surface intersection along ray path 873⟩
```

If the ray is unscattered and unabsorbed, then any emitters it interacts with contribute radiance to the path. Either surface emission or emission from infinite light sources is accounted for, depending on whether an intersection with a surface was found. Further, if the ray did not intersect a surface, then the path is finished and the radiance estimate can be returned.

⟨*Add emission to surviving ray*⟩ ≡   872
```
if (si)
    L += beta * si->intr.Le(-ray.d, lambda);
else {
    for (const auto &light : infiniteLights)
        L += beta * light.Le(ray, lambda);
    return L;
}
```

It is still necessary to consider surface intersections, even if scattering from them is not handled by this integrator. There are three cases to consider:

- If the surface has no BSDF, it represents a transition between different types of participating media. A call to SkipIntersection() moves the ray past the intersection and updates its medium appropriately.

- If there is a valid BSDF and that BDSF also returns a valid sample from `Sample_f()`, then we have a BSDF that scatters; an error is issued and rendering stops.
- A valid but zero-valued BSDF is allowed; such a BSDF should be assigned to area light sources in scenes to be rendered using this integrator.

⟨*Handle surface intersection along ray path*⟩ ≡   872
```
BSDF bsdf = si->intr.GetBSDF(ray, lambda, camera, buf, sampler);
if (!bsdf)
    si->intr.SkipIntersection(&ray, si->tHit);
else {
    ⟨Report error if BSDF returns a valid sample⟩
}
```

★ 14.2.2 IMPROVING THE SAMPLING TECHNIQUES

The `VolPathIntegrator` adds three significant improvements to the approach implemented in `SimpleVolPathIntegrator`: it supports scattering from surfaces as well as from volumes; it handles spectrally varying medium scattering properties without falling back to sampling a single wavelength; and it samples lights directly, using multiple importance sampling to reduce variance when doing so. The first improvement—including surface scattering—is mostly a matter of applying the ideas of Equation (14.7), sampling distances in volumes but then choosing surface scattering if the sampled distance is past the closest intersection. For the other two, we will here discuss the underlying foundations before turning to their implementation.

Chromatic Media

We have thus far glossed over some of the implications of spectrally varying medium properties. Because pbrt uses point-sampled spectra, they introduce no complications in terms of evaluating things like the modified path throughput $\hat{T}(\bar{p}_n)$ or the path throughput weight $\beta(\bar{p}_n)$: given a set of path vertices, such quantities can be evaluated for all the wavelength samples simultaneously using the `SampledSpectrum` class.

The problem with spectrally varying medium properties comes from sampling. Consider a wavelength-dependent function $f_\lambda(x)$ that we would like to integrate at n wavelengths λ_i. If we draw samples $x \sim p_{\lambda_1}$ from a wavelength-dependent PDF based on the first wavelength and then evaluate f at all the wavelengths, we have the estimators

$$\frac{\left[f_{\lambda_1}(x),\, f_{\lambda_2}(x),\, \dots,\, f_{\lambda_n}(x) \right]}{p_{\lambda_1}(x)}.$$

Even if the PDF p_{λ_1} that was used for sampling matches f_{λ_1} well, it may be a poor match for f at the other wavelengths. It may not even be a valid PDF for them, if it is zero-valued where the function is nonzero. However, falling back to integrating a single wavelength at a time would be unfortunately inefficient, as shown in Section 4.5.4.

This problem of a single sampling PDF possibly mismatched with a wavelength-dependent function comes up repeatedly in volumetric path tracing. For example, sampling the majorant transmittance at one wavelength may be a poor approach for sampling it at others. That could be handled by selecting a majorant that bounds all wavelengths' extinction coefficients, but such a majorant would lead to many null-scattering events at wavelengths that could have used a much lower majorant, which would harm performance.

The path tracer's choice among absorption, real scattering, and null scattering at a sampled point cannot be sidestepped in a similar way: different wavelengths may have quite different probabilities for each of these types of medium interaction, yet with path tracing the integrator must choose only one of them. Splitting up the computation to let each wavelength choose individually would be nearly as inefficient as only considering a single wavelength at a time.

However, if a single type of interaction is chosen based on a single wavelength and we evaluate the modified path contribution function $\hat{P}$ for all wavelengths, we could have arbitrarily high variance in the other wavelengths. To see why, note how all the $\sigma_{\{s,n\}}$ factors that came from the $p_e(p_i)$ factors in Equation (14.18) canceled out to give the delta-tracking estimator, Equation (14.19). In the spectral case, if, for example, real scattering is chosen based on a wavelength λ's scattering coefficient σ_s and if a wavelength λ' has scattering coefficient σ_s', then the final estimator for λ' will include a factor of σ_s'/σ_s that can be arbitrarily large.

The fact that SampleT_maj() nevertheless samples according to a single wavelength's majorant transmittance suggests that there is a solution to this problem. That solution, yet again, is multiple importance sampling. In this case, we are using a single sampling technique rather than MIS-weighting multiple techniques, so we use the single-sample MIS estimator from Equation (2.16), which here gives

$$\frac{w_{\lambda_1}(x)}{q} \frac{\left[f_{\lambda_1}(x), f_{\lambda_2}(x), \ldots, f_{\lambda_n}(x)\right]}{p_{\lambda_1}(x)},$$

where q is the discrete probability of sampling using the wavelength λ_1, here uniform at $1/n$ with n the number of spectral samples.

The balance heuristic is optimal for single-sample MIS. It gives the MIS weight

$$w_{\lambda_1}(x) = \frac{p_{\lambda_1}(x)}{\sum_i^n p_{\lambda_i}(x)},$$

which gives the estimator

$$\frac{p_{\lambda_1}(x)}{\frac{1}{n}\sum_i^n p_{\lambda_i}(x)} \frac{\left[f_{\lambda_1}(x), f_{\lambda_2}(x), \ldots, f_{\lambda_n}(x)\right]}{p_{\lambda_1}(x)} = \frac{\left[f_{\lambda_1}(x), f_{\lambda_2}(x), \ldots, f_{\lambda_n}(x)\right]}{\frac{1}{n}\sum_i^n p_{\lambda_i}(x)}. \tag{14.20}$$

See Figure 14.7 for an example that shows the benefits of MIS for chromatic media.

Direct Lighting

Multiple importance sampling is also at the heart of how the VolPathIntegrator samples direct illumination. As with the PathIntegrator, we would like to combine the strategies of sampling the light sources with sampling the BSDF or phase function to find light-carrying paths and then to weight the contributions of each sampling technique using MIS. Doing so is more complex than it is in the absence of volumetric scattering, however, because not only does the sampling distribution used at the last path vertex differ (as before) but the VolPathIntegrator also uses ratio tracking to estimate the transmittance along the shadow ray. That is a different distance sampling technique than the delta-tracking approach used when sampling ray paths, and so it leads to a different path PDF.

In the following, we will say that the two path-sampling techniques used in the VolPath Integrator are *unidirectional path sampling* and *light path sampling*; we will write their respective path PDFs as p_u and p_l. The first corresponds to the sampling approach from Section 14.1.5, with delta tracking used to find real-scattering vertices and with the phase function or BSDF sampled to find the new direction at each vertex. Light path sampling follows the same approach up to the last real-scattering vertex before the light vertex; there, the

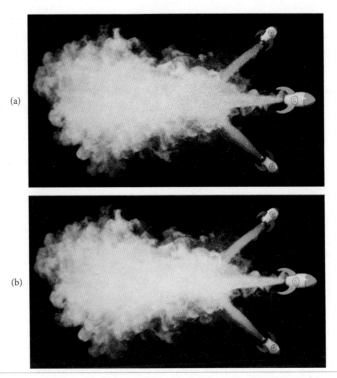

(a)

(b)

Figure 14.7: Chromatic Volumetric Media. (a) When rendered without spectral MIS, variance is high. (b) Results are much better with spectral MIS, as implemented in the `VolPathIntegrator`. For this scene, MSE is reduced by a factor of 149. *(Scene courtesty of Jim Price.)*

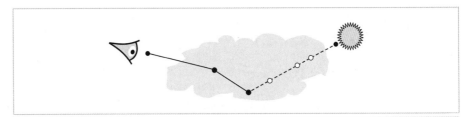

Figure 14.8: In the direct lighting calculation, at each path vertex a point is sampled on a light source and a shadow ray (dotted line) is traced. The `VolPathIntegrator` uses ratio tracking to compute the transmittance along the ray by accumulating the product σ_n/σ_{maj} at sampled points along the ray (open circles). For the MIS weight, it is necessary to be able not only to compute the PDF for sampling the corresponding direction at the last path vertex but also to compute the probability of generating these samples using delta tracking, since that is how the path would be sampled with unidirectional path sampling.

light selects the direction and then ratio tracking gives the transmittance along the last path segment. (See Figure 14.8.) Given a path $\bar{p}_{n-1}$, both approaches share the same path throughput weight β up to the vertex p_{n-1} and the same path PDF up to that vertex, $p_u(\bar{p}_{n-1})$.[2]

For the full PDF for unidirectional path sampling, at the last scattering vertex we have the probability of scattering, $\sigma_s(p_{n-1})/\sigma_{maj}$ times the directional probability for sampling the

2   Strictly speaking, two such paths ending at the same point on a light may have a different number of vertices due to different numbers of null-scattering vertices along the last segment. To simplify notation, we will here describe both as n vertex paths with p_n the point on the light and p_{n-1} the scattering vertex immediately before it; we will index intermediate vertices on the last segment independently.

new direction $p_\omega(\omega_n)$, which is given by the sampling strategy used for the BSDF or phase function. Then, for the path to find an emitter at the vertex p_n, it must have only sampled null-scattering vertices between p_{n-1} and p_n; absorption or a real-scattering vertex preclude making it to p_n.

Using the results from Section 14.1.5, we can find that the path PDF between two points p_i and p_j with m intermediate null-scattering vertices indexed by k is given by the product of

$$p_e(p_{i+k}) = \frac{\sigma_n(p_{i+k})}{\sigma_{maj}} \text{ and}$$

$$p_{maj}(p_{i+k}) = \sigma_{maj} T_{maj}(p_{i+k-1} \to p_{i+k})$$

for all null-scattering vertices. The σ_{maj} factors cancel and the null-scattering path probability is

$$p_{null}(p_i, p_j) = \left(\prod_{k=1}^{m} \sigma_n(p_{i+k})\, T_{maj}(p_{i+k-1} \to p_{i+k}) \right) T_{maj}(p_{i+m} \to p_j).$$

The full unidirectional path probability is then given by

$$p_u(\bar{p}_n) = p_u(\bar{p}_{n-1}) \frac{\sigma_s(p_{n-1})}{\sigma_{maj}} p_\omega(\omega_n)\, p_{null}(p_{n-1}, p_n). \qquad \text{[14.21]}$$

For light sampling, we again have the discrete probability $\sigma_s(p_{n-1})/\sigma_{maj}$ for scattering at p_{n-1} but the directional PDF at the vertex is determined by the light's sampling distribution, which we will denote by $p_{l,\omega}(\omega_n)$. The only missing piece is the PDF of the last segment (the shadow ray), where ratio tracking is used. In that case, points are sampled according to the majorant transmittance and so the PDF for a path sampled between points p_i and p_j with m intermediate vertices is

$$p_{ratio}(p_i, p_j) = \left(\prod_{k=1}^{m} T_{maj}(p_{i+k-1} \to p_{i+k})\, \sigma_{maj} \right), T_{maj}(p_{i+m} \to p_j), \qquad \text{[14.22]}$$

and the full light sampling path PDF is given by

$$p_l(\bar{p}_n) = p_u(\bar{p}_{n-1}) \frac{\sigma_s(p_{n-1})}{\sigma_{maj}} p_{l,\omega}(\omega_n)\, p_{ratio}(p_{n-1}, p_n). \qquad \text{[14.23]}$$

The VolPathIntegrator samples both types of paths according to the first wavelength λ_1 but evaluates these PDFs at all wavelengths so that MIS over wavelengths can be used. Given the path $\bar{p}_n$ sampled using unidirectional path sampling and then the path $\bar{p}'_n$ sampled using light path sampling, the two-sample MIS estimator is

$$w_u(\bar{p}_n) \frac{\hat{T}(\bar{p}_n)\, L_e(p_n \to p_{n-1})}{p_{u,\lambda_1}(\bar{p}_n)} + w_l(\bar{p}'_n) \frac{\hat{T}(\bar{p}'_n)\, L_e(p' \to p'_{n-1})}{p_{l,\lambda_1}(\bar{p}'_n)}. \qquad \text{[14.24]}$$

Note that because the paths share the same vertices for all of $\bar{p}_{n-1}$, not only do the two $\hat{T}$ factors share common factors, but $p_{u,\lambda_1}(\bar{p}_n)$ and $p_{l,\lambda_1}(\bar{p}'_n)$ do as well, following Equations (14.21) and (14.23).

In this case, the MIS weights can account not only for the differences between unidirectional and light path sampling but also for the different per-wavelength probabilities for each sampling strategy. For example, with the balance heuristic, the MIS weight for the unidirectional strategy works out to be

VolPathIntegrator 877

$$w_{\mathrm{u}}(\bar{\mathrm{p}}_n) = \frac{p_{\mathrm{u},\lambda_1}(\bar{\mathrm{p}}_n)}{\frac{1}{m}\left(\sum_i^m p_{\mathrm{u},\lambda_i}(\bar{\mathrm{p}}_n) + \sum_i^m p_{\mathrm{l},\lambda_i}(\bar{\mathrm{p}}_n)\right)}, \qquad [14.25]$$

with m the number of spectral samples. The MIS weight for light sampling is equivalent, but with the p_{u,λ_1} function in the numerator replaced with p_{l,λ_1}.

★ 14.2.3 IMPROVED VOLUMETRIC INTEGRATOR

The VolPathIntegrator pulls together all of these ideas to robustly handle both surface and volume transport. See Figures 14.9 and 14.10 for images rendered with this integrator that show off the visual complexity that comes from volumetric emission, chromatic media, and multiple scattering in participating media.

⟨*VolPathIntegrator Definition*⟩ ≡
```
class VolPathIntegrator : public RayIntegrator {
  public:
    ⟨VolPathIntegrator Public Methods⟩
  private:
    ⟨VolPathIntegrator Private Methods⟩
    ⟨VolPathIntegrator Private Members 877⟩
};
```

As with the other Integrator constructors that we have seen so far, the VolPathIntegrator constructor does not perform any meaningful computation, but just initializes member variables with provided values. These three are all equivalent to their parallels in the Path Integrator.

⟨*VolPathIntegrator Private Members*⟩ ≡   877
```
int maxDepth;
LightSampler lightSampler;
bool regularize;
```

Figure 14.9: Volumetric Emission inside Lightbulbs. The flames in each lightbulb are modeled with participating media and rendered with the VolPathIntegrator. *(Scene courtesy of Jim Price.)*

Figure 14.10: Volumetric Scattering in Liquid. Scattering in the paint-infused water is modeled with participating media and rendered with the `VolPathIntegrator`. *(Scene courtesy of Angelo Ferretti.)*

⟨*VolPathIntegrator Method Definitions*⟩ ≡
```
    SampledSpectrum VolPathIntegrator::Li(RayDifferential ray,
            SampledWavelengths &lambda, Sampler sampler,
            ScratchBuffer &scratchBuffer, VisibleSurface *visibleSurf) const {
        ⟨Declare state variables for volumetric path sampling 879⟩
        while (true) {
            ⟨Sample segment of volumetric scattering path 879⟩
        }
        return L;
    }
```

There is a common factor of $p_{\mathrm{u},\lambda_1}(\bar{\mathrm{p}}_n)$ in the denominator of the first term of the two-sample MIS estimator, Equation (14.24), and the numerator of the MIS weights, Equation (14.25). There is a corresponding p_{l,λ_1} factor in the second term of the estimator and in the w_l weight. It is tempting to cancel these out; in that case, the path state to be tracked by the integrator would consist of $\hat{T}(\bar{\mathrm{p}}_n)$ and the wavelength-dependent probabilities $p_\mathrm{u}(\bar{\mathrm{p}}_n)$ and $p_\mathrm{l}(\bar{\mathrm{p}}_n)$. Doing so is mathematically valid and would provide all the quantities necessary to evaluate Equation (14.24), but suffers from the problem that the quantities involved may overflow or underflow the range of representable floating-point values.

To understand the problem, consider a highly specular surface—the BSDF will have a large value for directions around its peak, but the PDF for sampling those directions will also be large. That causes no problems in the PathIntegrator, since its beta variable tracks their ratio, which ends up being close to 1. However, with $\hat{T}(\bar{p}_n)$ maintained independently, a series of specular bounces could lead to overflow. (Many null-scattering events along a path can cause similar problems.)

Therefore, the VolPathIntegrator tracks the path throughput weight for the sampled path

$$\beta(\bar{p}_n) = \frac{\hat{T}(\bar{p}_n)}{p_{u,\lambda_1}(\bar{p}_n)},$$

which is numerically well behaved. Directly tracking the probabilities $p_u(\bar{p}_n)$ and $p_l(\bar{p}_n)$ would also stress the range of floating-point numbers, so instead it tracks the *rescaled path probabilities*

$$r_{u,\lambda_i}(\bar{p}_n) = \frac{p_{u,\lambda_i}(\bar{p}_n)}{p_{path}(\bar{p}_n)} \qquad \text{and} \qquad r_{l,\lambda_i}(\bar{p}_n) = \frac{p_{l,\lambda_i}(\bar{p}_n)}{p_{path}(\bar{p}_n)}, \qquad [14.26]$$

where $p_{path}(\bar{p}_n)$ is the probability for sampling the current path. It is equal to the light path probability p_{l,λ_1} for paths that end with a shadow ray from light path sampling and the unidirectional path probability otherwise. (Later in the implementation, we will take advantage of the fact that these two probabilities are the same until the last scattering vertex, which in turn implies that whichever of them is chosen for p_{path} does not affect the values of $r_{u,\lambda_i}(\bar{p}_{n-1})$ and $r_{l,\lambda_i}(\bar{p}_{n-1})$.)

These rescaled path probabilities are all easily incrementally updated during path sampling. If $p_{path} = p_{u,\lambda_1}$, then MIS weights like those in Equation (14.25) can be found with

$$w_u(\bar{p}_n) = \frac{1}{\frac{1}{m}\left(\sum_i^m r_{u,\lambda_i}(\bar{p}_n) + \sum_i^m r_{l,\lambda_i}(\bar{p}_n)\right)}, \qquad [14.27]$$

and similarly for w_l when $p_{path} = p_{l,\lambda_1}$.

The remaining variables in the following fragment have the same function as the variables of the same names in the PathIntegrator.

⟨*Declare state variables for volumetric path sampling*⟩ ≡   878
```
SampledSpectrum L(0.f), beta(1.f), r_u(1.f), r_l(1.f);
bool specularBounce = false, anyNonSpecularBounces = false;
int depth = 0;
Float etaScale = 1;
```

The while loop for each ray segment starts out similarly to the corresponding loop in the SimpleVolPathIntegrator: the integrator traces a ray to find a t_{max} value at the closest surface intersection before sampling the medium, if any, between the ray origin and the intersection point.

⟨*Sample segment of volumetric scattering path*⟩ ≡   878
```
pstd::optional<ShapeIntersection> si = Intersect(ray);
if (ray.medium) {
    ⟨Sample the participating medium 880⟩
}
⟨Handle surviving unscattered rays 884⟩
```

The form of the fragment for sampling the medium is similar as well: tMax is set using the ray intersection t, if available, and an RNG is prepared before medium sampling proceeds. If the path is terminated or undergoes real scattering in the medium, then no further work is done to sample surface scattering at a ray intersection point.

⟨*Sample the participating medium*⟩ ≡   879
```
bool scattered = false, terminated = false;
Float tMax = si ? si->tHit : Infinity;
⟨Initialize RNG for sampling the majorant transmittance 870⟩
SampledSpectrum T_maj = SampleT_maj(ray, tMax, sampler.Get1D(), rng, lambda,
        [&](Point3f p, MediumProperties mp, SampledSpectrum sigma_maj,
            SampledSpectrum T_maj) {
            ⟨Handle medium scattering event for ray 880⟩
        });
⟨Handle terminated, scattered, and unscattered medium rays 883⟩
```

Given a sampled point p' in the medium, the lambda function's task is to evaluate the L_n source function, taking care of the second case of Equation (14.7).

⟨*Handle medium scattering event for ray*⟩ ≡   880
```
⟨Add emission from medium scattering event 880⟩
⟨Compute medium event probabilities for interaction 870⟩
⟨Sample medium scattering event type and update path 881⟩
```

A small difference from the SimpleVolPathIntegrator is that volumetric emission is added at every point that is sampled in the medium rather than only when the absorption case is sampled. There is no reason not to do so, since emission is already available via the MediumProperties passed to the lambda function.

⟨*Add emission from medium scattering event*⟩ ≡   880
```
if (depth < maxDepth && mp.Le) {
    ⟨Compute β' at new path vertex 880⟩
    ⟨Compute rescaled path probability for absorption at path vertex 881⟩
    ⟨Update L for medium emission 881⟩
}
```

In the following, we will sometimes use the notation $[\bar{p}_n + p']$ to denote the path $\bar{p}_n$ with the vertex p' appended to it. Thus, for example, $\bar{p}_n = [\bar{p}_{n-1} + p_n]$. The estimator that gives the contribution for volumetric emission at p' is then

$$\beta([\bar{p}_n + p'])\, \sigma_a(p')\, L_e(p' \to p_n). \tag{14.28}$$

beta holds $\beta(\bar{p}_n)$, so we can incrementally compute $\beta([\bar{p}_n + p'])$ by

$$\beta([\bar{p}_n + p']) = \frac{\beta(\bar{p}_n)\, T_{maj}(p_n \to p')}{p_e(p')\, p_{maj}(p'|p_n, \omega)}.$$

From Section 14.1.5, we know that $p_{maj}(p_{i+1}|p_i, \omega) = \sigma_{maj}e^{-\sigma_{maj}t}$. Because we are always sampling absorption (at least as far as including emission goes), p_e is 1 here.

⟨*Compute β' at new path vertex*⟩ ≡   880
```
Float pdf = sigma_maj[0] * T_maj[0];
SampledSpectrum betap = beta * T_maj / pdf;
```

Even though this is the only sampling technique for volumetric emission, different wavelengths may sample this vertex with different probabilities, so it is worthwhile to apply MIS over the wavelengths' probabilities. With r_u storing the rescaled unidirectional probabilities up to the previous path vertex, the rescaled path probabilities for sampling the emissive vertex, r_e, can be found by multiplying r_u by the per-wavelength p_{maj} probabilities and dividing by the probability for the wavelength that was used for sampling p′, which is already available in pdf. (Note that in monochromatic media, these ratios are all 1.)

⟨*Compute rescaled path probability for absorption at path vertex*⟩ ≡   880
    SampledSpectrum r_e = r_u * sigma_maj * T_maj / pdf;

Here we have a single-sample MIS estimator with balance heuristic weights given by

$$w_e([\bar{p}_n + p']) = \frac{1}{\frac{1}{m}\sum_i^m r_{e,\lambda_i}([\bar{p}_n + p'])}.$$ [14.29]

The absorption coefficient and emitted radiance for evaluating Equation (14.28) are available in MediumProperties and the SampledSpectrum::Average() method conveniently computes the average of rescaled probabilities in the denominator of Equation (14.29).

⟨*Update* L *for medium emission*⟩ ≡   880
    if (r_e)
        L += betap * mp.sigma_a * mp.Le / r_e.Average();

Briefly returning to the initialization of betap and r_e in the previous fragments: it may seem tempting to cancel out the T_maj factors from them, but note how the final estimator does not perform a component-wise division of these two quantities but instead divides by the average of the rescaled probabilities when computing the MIS weight. Thus, performing such cancellations would lead to incorrect results.[3]

After emission is handled, the next step is to determine which term of L_n to evaluate; this follows the same approach as in the SimpleVolPathIntegrator.

⟨*Sample medium scattering event type and update path*⟩ ≡   880
    Float um = rng.Uniform<Float>();
    int mode = SampleDiscrete({pAbsorb, pScatter, pNull}, um);
    if (mode == 0) {
        ⟨*Handle absorption along ray path* **881**⟩
    } else if (mode == 1) {
        ⟨*Handle scattering along ray path* **882**⟩
    } else {
        ⟨*Handle null scattering along ray path* **883**⟩
    }

As before, the ray path is terminated in the event of absorption. Since any volumetric emission at the sampled point has already been added, there is nothing to do but handle the details associated with ending the path.

⟨*Handle absorption along ray path*⟩ ≡   881
    terminated = true;
    return false;

For a real-scattering event, a shadow ray is traced to a light to sample direct lighting, and the path state is updated to account for the new ray. A false value returned from the lambda function prevents further sample generation along the current ray.

---

3   This misconception periodically played a role in our initial development of this integrator.

⟨*Handle scattering along ray path*⟩ ≡   881
    ⟨*Stop path sampling if maximum depth has been reached* 871⟩
    ⟨*Update* beta *and* r_u *for real-scattering event* 882⟩
    `if (beta && r_u) {`
        ⟨*Sample direct lighting at volume-scattering event* 882⟩
        ⟨*Sample new direction at real-scattering event* 882⟩
    `}`
    `return false;`

The PDF for real scattering at this vertex is the product of the PDF for sampling its distance along the ray, $\sigma_{\mathrm{maj}}\, e^{-\sigma_{\mathrm{maj}}t}$, and the probability for sampling real scattering, $\sigma_s(\mathrm{p}')/\sigma_{\mathrm{maj}}$. The σ_{maj} values cancel.

Given the PDF value, beta can be updated to include T_{maj} along the segment up to the new vertex divided by the PDF. The rescaled probabilities are computed in the same way as the path sampling PDF before being divided by it, following Equation (14.26). The rescaled light path probabilities will be set shortly, after a new ray direction is sampled.

⟨*Update* beta *and* r_u *for real-scattering event*⟩ ≡   882
```
Float pdf = T_maj[0] * mp.sigma_s[0];
beta *= T_maj * mp.sigma_s / pdf;
r_u *= T_maj * mp.sigma_s / pdf;
```

Direct lighting is handled by the `SampleLd()` method, which we will defer until later in this section.

⟨*Sample direct lighting at volume-scattering event*⟩ ≡   882
```
MediumInteraction intr(p, -ray.d, ray.time, ray.medium, mp.phase);
L += SampleLd(intr, nullptr, lambda, sampler, beta, r_u);
```

Sampling the phase function gives a new direction at the scattering event.

⟨*Sample new direction at real-scattering event*⟩ ≡   882
```
Point2f u = sampler.Get2D();
pstd::optional<PhaseFunctionSample> ps = intr.phase.Sample_p(-ray.d, u);
if (!ps || ps->pdf == 0)
    terminated = true;
else {
    ⟨Update ray path state for indirect volume scattering  883⟩
}
```

There is a bit of bookkeeping to take care of after a real-scattering event. We can now incorporate the phase function value into beta, which completes the contribution of $\hat{f}$ from Equation (14.12). Because both unidirectional path sampling and light path sampling use the same set of sampling operations up to a real-scattering vertex, an initial value for the rescaled light path sampling probabilities r_l comes from the value of the rescaled unidirectional probabilities before scattering. It is divided by the directional PDF from p_{u,λ_1} for this vertex here. The associated directional PDF for light sampling at this vertex will be incorporated into r_l later. There is no need to update r_u here, since the scattering direction's probability is the same for all wavelengths and so the update factor would always be 1.

At this point, the integrator also updates various variables that record the scattering history and updates the current ray.

⟨*Update ray path state for indirect volume scattering*⟩ ≡   882
```
beta *= ps->p / ps->pdf;
r_l = r_u / ps->pdf;
prevIntrContext = LightSampleContext(intr);
scattered = true;
ray.o = p;
ray.d = ps->wi;
specularBounce = false;
anyNonSpecularBounces = true;
```

If the ray intersects a light source, the LightSampleContext from the previous path vertex will be needed to compute MIS weights; prevIntrContext is updated to store it after each scattering event, whether in a medium or on a surface.

⟨*Declare state variables for volumetric path sampling*⟩ +≡   878
```
LightSampleContext prevIntrContext;
```

If null scattering is selected, the updates to beta and the rescaled path sampling probabilities follow the same form as we have seen previously: the former is given by Equation (14.11) and the latter with a $p_e = \sigma_n / \sigma_{maj}$ factor where, as with real scattering, the σ_{maj} cancels with a corresponding factor from the p_{maj} probability (Section 14.1.5).

In this case, we also must update the rescaled path probabilities for sampling this path vertex via light path sampling, which samples path vertices according to p_{maj}.

This fragment concludes the implementation of the lambda function that is passed to the SampleT_maj() function.

⟨*Handle null scattering along ray path*⟩ ≡   881
```
SampledSpectrum sigma_n = ClampZero(sigma_maj - mp.sigma_a - mp.sigma_s);
Float pdf = T_maj[0] * sigma_n[0];
beta *= T_maj * sigma_n / pdf;
if (pdf == 0) beta = SampledSpectrum(0.f);
r_u *= T_maj * sigma_n / pdf;
r_l *= T_maj * sigma_maj / pdf;
return beta && r_u;
```

Returning to the Li() method immediately after the SampleT_maj() call, if the path terminated due to absorption, it is only here that we can break out and return the radiance estimate to the caller of the Li() method. Further, it is only here that we can jump back to the start of the while loop for rays that were scattered in the medium.

⟨*Handle terminated, scattered, and unscattered medium rays*⟩ ≡   880
```
if (terminated || !beta || !r_u) return L;
if (scattered) continue;
```

With those cases taken care of, we are left with rays that either underwent no scattering events in the medium or only underwent null scattering. For those cases, both the path throughput weight β and the rescaled path probabilities must be updated. β takes a factor of T_{maj} to account for the transmittance from either the last null-scattering event or the ray's origin to the ray's t_{max} position. The rescaled unidirectional and light sampling probabilities also take the same T_{maj}, which corresponds to the final factors outside of the parenthesis in the definitions of p_{null} and p_{ratio}.

⟨*Handle terminated, scattered, and unscattered medium rays*⟩ +≡   880
```
    beta *= T_maj / T_maj[0];
    r_u *= T_maj / T_maj[0];
    r_l *= T_maj / T_maj[0];
```

There is much more to do for rays that have either escaped the scene or have intersected a surface without medium scattering or absorption. We will defer discussion of the first following fragment, ⟨*Add emitted light at volume path vertex or from the environment*⟩, until later in the section when we discuss the direct lighting calculation. A few of the others are implemented reusing fragments from earlier integrators.

⟨*Handle surviving unscattered rays*⟩ ≡   879
    ⟨*Add emitted light at volume path vertex or from the environment* 890⟩
    ⟨*Get BSDF and skip over medium boundaries* 828⟩
    ⟨*Initialize* visibleSurf *at first intersection* 834⟩
    ⟨*Terminate path if maximum depth reached* 884⟩
    ⟨*Possibly regularize the BSDF* 842⟩
    ⟨*Sample illumination from lights to find attenuated path contribution* 884⟩
    ⟨*Sample BSDF to get new volumetric path direction* 884⟩
    ⟨*Account for attenuated subsurface scattering, if applicable*⟩
    ⟨*Possibly terminate volumetric path with Russian roulette* 885⟩

As with the PathIntegrator, path termination due to reaching the maximum depth only occurs after accounting for illumination from any emissive surfaces that are intersected.

⟨*Terminate path if maximum depth reached*⟩ ≡   884
```
    if (depth++ >= maxDepth)
        return L;
```

Sampling the light source at a surface intersection is handled by the same SampleLd() method that is called for real-scattering vertices in the medium. As with medium scattering, the LightSampleContext corresponding to this scattering event is recorded for possible later use in MIS weight calculations.

⟨*Sample illumination from lights to find attenuated path contribution*⟩ ≡   884
```
    if (IsNonSpecular(bsdf.Flags()))
        L += SampleLd(isect, &bsdf, lambda, sampler, beta, r_u);
    prevIntrContext = LightSampleContext(isect);
```

The logic for sampling scattering at a surface is very similar to the corresponding logic in the PathIntegrator.

⟨*Sample BSDF to get new volumetric path direction*⟩ ≡   884
```
    Vector3f wo = isect.wo;
    Float u = sampler.Get1D();
    pstd::optional<BSDFSample> bs = bsdf.Sample_f(wo, u, sampler.Get2D());
    if (!bs) break;
    ⟨Update beta and rescaled path probabilities for BSDF scattering 885⟩
    ⟨Update volumetric integrator path state after surface scattering 885⟩
```

Given a BSDF sample, β is first multiplied by the value of the BSDF, which takes care of $\hat{f}$ from Equation (14.12). This is also a good time to incorporate the cosine factor from the C_p factor of the generalized geometric term, Equation (14.13).

BSDF::Flags() 544
BSDF::Sample_f() 545
BSDFSample 541
BxDFFlags::IsNonSpecular() 539
Float 23
Interaction::wo 137
LightSampleContext 741
PathIntegrator 833
Sampler::Get1D() 470
Sampler::Get2D() 470
Vector3f 86
VolPathIntegrator::maxDepth 877
VolPathIntegrator::SampleLd() 886

Updates to the rescaled path probabilities follow how they were done for medium scattering: first, there is no need to update r_u since the probabilities are the same over all wavelengths. The rescaled light path sampling probabilities are also initialized from r_u, here also with only the $1/p_{u,\lambda_1}$ factor included. The other factors in r_l will only be computed and included if the ray intersects an emitter; otherwise r_l is unused.

One nit in updating r_l is that the BSDF and PDF value returned in the BSDFSample may only be correct up to a (common) scale factor. This case comes up with sampling techniques like the random walk used by the LayeredBxDF that is described in Section 14.3.2. In that case, a call to BSDF::PDF() gives an independent value for the PDF that can be used.

⟨*Update* beta *and rescaled path probabilities for BSDF scattering*⟩ ≡   884
```
    beta *= bs->f * AbsDot(bs->wi, isect.shading.n) / bs->pdf;
    if (bs->pdfIsProportional)
        r_l = r_u / bsdf.PDF(wo, bs->wi);
    else
        r_l = r_u / bs->pdf;
```

A few additional state variables must be updated after surface scattering, as well.

⟨*Update volumetric integrator path state after surface scattering*⟩ ≡   884
```
    specularBounce = bs->IsSpecular();
    anyNonSpecularBounces |= !bs->IsSpecular();
    if (bs->IsTransmission())
        etaScale *= Sqr(bs->eta);
    ray = isect.SpawnRay(ray, bsdf, bs->wi, bs->flags, bs->eta);
```

Russian roulette follows the same general approach as before, though we scale beta by the accumulated effect of radiance scaling for transmission that is encoded in etaScale and use the balance heuristic over wavelengths. If the Russian roulette test passes, beta is updated with a factor that accounts for the survival probability, 1 - q.

⟨*Possibly terminate volumetric path with Russian roulette*⟩ ≡   884
```
    SampledSpectrum rrBeta = beta * etaScale / r_u.Average();
    Float uRR = sampler.Get1D();
    if (rrBeta.MaxComponentValue() < 1 && depth > 1) {
        Float q = std::max<Float>(0, 1 - rrBeta.MaxComponentValue());
        if (uRR < q) break;
        beta /= 1 - q;
    }
```

Estimating Direct Illumination

All that remains in the VolPathIntegrator's implementation is direct illumination. We will start with the SampleLd() method, which is called to estimate scattered radiance due to direct illumination by sampling a light source, both at scattering points in media and on surfaces. (It is responsible for computing the second term of Equation (14.24).) The purpose of most of its parameters should be evident. The last, r_p, gives the rescaled path probabilities up to the vertex intr. (A separate variable named r_u will be used in the function's implementation, so a new name is needed here.)

⟨*VolPathIntegrator Method Definitions*⟩ +≡
```
    SampledSpectrum VolPathIntegrator::SampleLd(const Interaction &intr,
            const BSDF *bsdf, SampledWavelengths &lambda, Sampler sampler,
            SampledSpectrum beta, SampledSpectrum r_p) const {
        ⟨Estimate light-sampled direct illumination at intr 886⟩
    }
```

The overall structure of this method's implementation is similar to the PathIntegrator's SampleLd() method: a light source and a point on it are sampled, the vertex's scattering function is evaluated, and then the light's visibility is determined. Here we have the added complexity of needing to compute the transmittance between the scattering point and the point on the light rather than finding a binary visibility factor, as well as the need to compute spectral path sampling weights for MIS.

⟨*Estimate light-sampled direct illumination at* intr⟩ ≡   886
```
    ⟨Initialize LightSampleContext for volumetric light sampling 886⟩
    ⟨Sample a light source using lightSampler 886⟩
    ⟨Sample a point on the light source 887⟩
    ⟨Evaluate BSDF or phase function for light sample direction 887⟩
    ⟨Declare path state variables for ray to light source 887⟩
    while (lightRay.d != Vector3f(0, 0, 0)) {
        ⟨Trace ray through media to estimate transmittance 888⟩
    }
    ⟨Return path contribution function estimate for direct lighting 890⟩
```

Because it is called for both surface and volumetric scattering path vertices, SampleLd() takes a plain Interaction to represent the scattering point. Some extra care is therefore needed when initializing the LightSampleContext: if scattering is from a surface, it is important to interpret that interaction as the SurfaceInteraction that it is so that the shading normal is included in the LightSampleContext. This case also presents an opportunity, as was done in the PathIntegrator, to shift the light sampling point to avoid incorrectly sampling self-illumination from area lights.

⟨*Initialize* LightSampleContext *for volumetric light sampling*⟩ ≡   886
```
    LightSampleContext ctx;
    if (bsdf) {
        ctx = LightSampleContext(intr.AsSurface());
        ⟨Try to nudge the light sampling position to correct side of the surface 836⟩
    }
    else ctx = LightSampleContext(intr);
```

Sampling a point on the light follows in the usual way. Note that the implementation is careful to consume the two sample dimensions from the Sampler regardless of whether sampling a light was successful, in order to keep the association of sampler dimensions with integration dimensions fixed across pixel samples.

⟨*Sample a light source using* lightSampler⟩ ≡   886
```
    Float u = sampler.Get1D();
    pstd::optional<SampledLight> sampledLight = lightSampler.Sample(ctx, u);
    Point2f uLight = sampler.Get2D();
    if (!sampledLight)
        return SampledSpectrum(0.f);
    Light light = sampledLight->light;
```

The light samples a direction from the reference point in the usual manner. The true value passed for the allowIncompletePDF parameter of Light::SampleLi() indicates the use of MIS here.

⟨*Sample a point on the light source*⟩ ≡   886
```
pstd::optional<LightLiSample> ls =
    light.SampleLi(ctx, uLight, lambda, true);
if (!ls || !ls->L || ls->pdf == 0)
    return SampledSpectrum(0.f);
Float lightPDF = sampledLight->p * ls->pdf;
```

As in PathIntegrator::SampleLd(), it is worthwhile to evaluate the BSDF or phase function before tracing the shadow ray: if it turns out to be zero-valued for the direction to the light source, then it is possible to exit early and perform no further work.

⟨*Evaluate BSDF or phase function for light sample direction*⟩ ≡   886
```
Float scatterPDF;
SampledSpectrum f_hat;
Vector3f wo = intr.wo, wi = ls->wi;
if (bsdf) {
    ⟨Update f_hat and scatterPDF accounting for the BSDF 887⟩
} else {
    ⟨Update f_hat and scatterPDF accounting for the phase function 887⟩
}
if (!f_hat) return SampledSpectrum(0.f);
```

The f_hat variable that holds the value of the scattering function is slightly misnamed: it also includes the cosine factor for scattering from surfaces and does not include the σ_s for scattering from participating media, as that has already been included in the provided value of beta.

⟨*Update f_hat and scatterPDF accounting for the BSDF*⟩ ≡   887
```
f_hat = bsdf->f(wo, wi) * AbsDot(wi, intr.AsSurface().shading.n);
scatterPDF = bsdf->PDF(wo, wi);
```

⟨*Update f_hat and scatterPDF accounting for the phase function*⟩ ≡   887
```
PhaseFunction phase = intr.AsMedium().phase;
f_hat = SampledSpectrum(phase.p(wo, wi));
scatterPDF = phase.PDF(wo, wi);
```

A handful of variables keep track of some useful quantities for the ray-tracing and medium sampling operations that are performed to compute transmittance. T_ray holds the transmittance along the ray and r_u and r_l respectively hold the rescaled path probabilities for unidirectional sampling and light sampling, though only along the ray. Maintaining these values independently of the full path contribution and PDFs facilitates the use of Russian roulette in the transmittance computation.

⟨*Declare path state variables for ray to light source*⟩ ≡   886
```
Ray lightRay = intr.SpawnRayTo(ls->pLight);
SampledSpectrum T_ray(1.f), r_l(1.f), r_u(1.f);
RNG rng(Hash(lightRay.o), Hash(lightRay.d));
```

SampleLd() successively intersects the shadow ray with the scene geometry, returning zero contribution if an opaque surface is found and otherwise sampling the medium to estimate the transmittance up to the intersection. For intersections that represent transitions between different media, this process repeats until the ray reaches the light source.

For some scenes, it could be more efficient to instead first check that there are no intersections with opaque surfaces before sampling the media to compute the transmittance. With the current implementation, it is possible to do wasted work estimating transmittance before finding an opaque surface farther along the ray.

⟨*Trace ray through media to estimate transmittance*⟩ ≡   886
```
    pstd::optional<ShapeIntersection> si = Intersect(lightRay, 1-ShadowEpsilon);
```
    ⟨*Handle opaque surface along ray's path* 888⟩
    ⟨*Update transmittance for current ray segment* 888⟩
    ⟨*Generate next ray segment or return final transmittance* 889⟩

If an intersection is found with a surface that has a non-`nullptr` `Material`, the visibility term is zero and the method can return immediately.

⟨*Handle opaque surface along ray's path*⟩ ≡   888
```
    if (si && si->intr.material)
        return SampledSpectrum(0.f);
```

Otherwise, if participating media is present, `SampleT_maj()` is called to sample it along the ray up to whichever is closer—the surface intersection or the sampled point on the light.

⟨*Update transmittance for current ray segment*⟩ ≡   888
```
    if (lightRay.medium) {
        Float tMax = si ? si->tHit : (1 - ShadowEpsilon);
        Float u = rng.Uniform<Float>();
        SampledSpectrum T_maj = SampleT_maj(lightRay, tMax, u, rng, lambda,
                [&](Point3f p, MediumProperties mp, SampledSpectrum sigma_maj,
                    SampledSpectrum T_maj) {
                    ⟨Update ray transmittance estimate at sampled point  888⟩
                });
        ⟨Update transmittance estimate for final segment  889⟩
    }
```

For each sampled point in the medium, the transmittance and rescaled path probabilities are updated before Russian roulette is considered.

⟨*Update ray transmittance estimate at sampled point*⟩ ≡   888
```
    ⟨Update T_ray and PDFs using ratio-tracking estimator  889⟩
    ⟨Possibly terminate transmittance computation using Russian roulette  889⟩
    return true;
```

In the context of the equation of transfer, using ratio tracking to compute transmittance can be seen as sampling distances along the ray according to the majorant transmittance and then only including the null-scattering component of the source function L_n to correct any underestimate of transmittance from T_{maj}. Because only null-scattering vertices are sampled along transmittance rays, the logic for updating the transmittance and rescaled path probabilities at each vertex exactly follows that in the ⟨*Handle null scattering along ray path*⟩ fragment.

⟨*Update* T_ray *and PDFs using ratio-tracking estimator*⟩ ≡   888

```
SampledSpectrum sigma_n = ClampZero(sigma_maj - mp.sigma_a - mp.sigma_s);
Float pdf = T_maj[0] * sigma_maj[0];
T_ray *= T_maj * sigma_n / pdf;
r_l *= T_maj * sigma_maj / pdf;
r_u *= T_maj * sigma_n / pdf;
```

Russian roulette is used to randomly terminate rays with low transmittance. A natural choice might seem to be setting the survival probability equal to the transmittance—along the lines of how Russian roulette is used for terminating ray paths from the camera according to β. However, doing so would effectively transform ratio tracking to delta tracking, with the transmittance always equal to zero or one. The implementation therefore applies a less aggressive termination probability, only to highly attenuated rays.

In the computation of the transmittance value used for the Russian roulette test, note that an MIS weight that accounts for both the unidirectional and light sampling strategies is used, along the lines of Equation (14.27).

⟨*Possibly terminate transmittance computation using Russian roulette*⟩ ≡   888

```
SampledSpectrum Tr = T_ray / (r_l + r_u).Average();
if (Tr.MaxComponentValue() < 0.05f) {
    Float q = 0.75f;
    if (rng.Uniform<Float>() < q)
        T_ray = SampledSpectrum(0.);
    else
        T_ray /= 1 - q;
}
```

After the SampleT_maj() call returns, the transmittance and rescaled path probabilities all must be multiplied by the T_maj returned from SampleT_maj() for the final ray segment. (See the discussion for the earlier ⟨*Handle terminated, scattered, and unscattered medium rays*⟩ fragment for why each is updated as it is.)

⟨*Update transmittance estimate for final segment*⟩ ≡   888

```
T_ray *= T_maj / T_maj[0];
r_l *= T_maj / T_maj[0];
r_u *= T_maj / T_maj[0];
```

If the transmittance is zero (e.g., due to Russian roulette termination), it is possible to return immediately. Furthermore, if there is no surface intersection, then there is no further medium sampling to be done and we can move on to computing the scattered radiance from the light. Alternatively, if there is an intersection, it must be with a surface that represents the boundary between two media; the SpawnRayTo() method call returns the continuation ray on the other side of the surface, with its medium member variable set appropriately.

⟨*Generate next ray segment or return final transmittance*⟩ ≡   888

```
if (!T_ray) return SampledSpectrum(0.f);
if (!si) break;
lightRay = si->intr.SpawnRayTo(ls->pLight);
```

After the while loop terminates, we can compute the final rescaled path probabilities, compute MIS weights, and return the final estimate of the path contribution function for the light sample.

The r_p variable passed in to SampleLd() stores the rescaled path probabilities for unidirectional sampling of the path up to the vertex where direct lighting is being computed—though here, r_u and r_l have been rescaled using the light path sampling probability, since that is how the vertices were sampled along the shadow ray. However, recall from Equations (14.21) and (14.23) that $p_{u,\lambda_1}(\bar{p}_n) = p_{l,\lambda_1}(\bar{p}_n)$ for the path up to the scattering vertex. Thus, r_p can be interpreted as being rescaled using $1/p_{l,\lambda_1}$. This allows multiplying r_l and r_u by r_p to compute final rescaled path probabilities.

If the light source is described by a delta distribution, only the light sampling technique is applicable; there is no chance of intersecting such a light via sampling the BSDF or phase function. In that case, we still apply MIS using all the wavelengths' individual path PDFs in order to reduce variance in chromatic media.

For area lights, we are able to use both light source and the scattering function samples, giving two primary sampling strategies, each of which has a separate weight for each wavelength.

⟨*Return path contribution function estimate for direct lighting*⟩ ≡   886
```
r_l *= r_p * lightPDF;
r_u *= r_p * scatterPDF;
if (IsDeltaLight(light.Type()))
    return beta * f_hat * T_ray * ls->L / r_l.Average();
else
    return beta * f_hat * T_ray * ls->L / (r_l + r_u).Average();
```

With SampleLd() implemented, we will return to the fragments in the Li() method that handle the cases where a ray escapes from the scene and possibly finds illumination from infinite area lights, as well as where a ray intersects an emissive surface. These handle the first term in the direct lighting MIS estimator, Equation (14.24).

⟨*Add emitted light at volume path vertex or from the environment*⟩ ≡   884
```
if (!si) {
    ⟨Accumulate contributions from infinite light sources 890⟩
    break;
}
SurfaceInteraction &isect = si->intr;
if (SampledSpectrum Le = isect.Le(-ray.d, lambda); Le) {
    ⟨Add contribution of emission from intersected surface⟩
}
```

As with the PathIntegrator, if the previous scattering event was due to a delta-distribution scattering function, then sampling the light is not a useful strategy. In that case, the MIS weight is only based on the per-wavelength PDFs for the unidirectional sampling strategy.

⟨*Accumulate contributions from infinite light sources*⟩ ≡   890
```
for (const auto &light : infiniteLights) {
    if (SampledSpectrum Le = light.Le(ray, lambda); Le) {
        if (depth == 0 || specularBounce)
            L += beta * Le / r_u.Average();
        else {
            ⟨Add infinite light contribution using both PDFs with MIS 891⟩
        }
    }
}
```

Otherwise, the MIS weight should account for both sampling techniques. At this point, r_1 has everything but the probabilities for sampling the light itself. (Recall that we deferred that when initializing r_1 at the real-scattering vertex earlier.) After incorporating that factor, all that is left is to compute the final weight, accounting for both sampling strategies.

⟨*Add infinite light contribution using both PDFs with MIS*⟩ ≡   890
```
Float lightPDF = lightSampler.PMF(prevIntrContext, light) *
                 light.PDF_Li(prevIntrContext, ray.d, true);
r_1 *= lightPDF;
L += beta * Le / (r_u + r_1).Average();
```

The work done in the ⟨*Add contribution of emission from intersected surface*⟩ fragment is very similar to that done for infinite lights, so it is not included here.

14.3 SCATTERING FROM LAYERED MATERIALS

In addition to describing scattering from larger-scale volumetric media like clouds or smoke, the equation of transfer can be used to model scattering at much smaller scales. The Layered BxDF applies it to this task, implementing a reflection model that accounts for scattering from two interfaces that are represented by surfaces with independent BSDFs and with a medium between them. Monte Carlo can be applied to estimating the integrals that describe the aggregate scattering behavior, in a way similar to what is done in light transport algorithms. This approach is effectively the generalization of the technique used to sum up aggregate scattering from a pair of perfectly smooth dielectric interfaces in the ThinDielectricBxDF in Section 9.5.1.

Modeling surface reflectance as a composition of layers makes it possible to describe a variety of surfaces that are not well modeled by the BSDFs presented in Chapter 9. For example, automobile paint generally has a smooth reflective "clear coat" layer applied on top of it; the overall appearance of the paint is determined by the combination of light scattering from the layer's interface as well as light scattering from the paint. (See Figure 14.11.) Tarnished metal can be modeled by an underlying metal BRDF with a thin scattering medium on top of it; it is again the aggregate result of a variety of light scattering paths that determines the overall appearance of the surface.

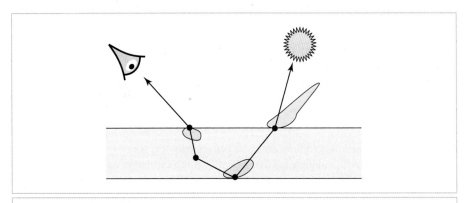

Figure 14.11: Scattering from Layered Surfaces. Surface reflection can be modeled with a series of layers, where each interface between media is represented with a BSDF and where the media between layers may itself both absorb and scatter light. The aggregate scattering from such a configuration can be determined by finding solutions to the equation of transfer.

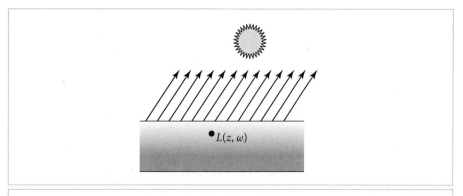

Figure 14.12: Setting for the One-Dimensional Equation of Transfer. If the properties of the medium only vary in one dimension and if the incident illumination is uniform over its boundary, then the equilibrium radiance distribution varies only with depth z and direction ω and a 1D specialization of the equation of transfer can be used.

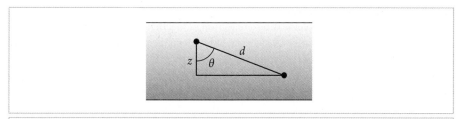

Figure 14.13: Transmittance in 1D. The distance between two depths d is given by the z distance between them divided by the cosine of the ray's angle with respect to the z axis, θ. The transmittance follows.

With general layered media, light may exit the surface at a different point than that at which it entered it. The LayeredBxDF does not model this effect but instead assumes that light enters and exits at the same point on the surface. (As a BxDF, it is unable to express any other sort of scattering, anyway.) This is a reasonable approximation if the distance between the two interfaces is relatively small. This approximation makes it possible to use a simplified 1D version of the equation of transfer. After deriving this variant, we will show its application to evaluating and sampling such BSDFs.

14.3.1 THE ONE-DIMENSIONAL EQUATION OF TRANSFER

Given *plane-parallel* 3D scattering media where the scattering properties are homogeneous across planes and only vary in depth, and where the incident illumination does not vary as a function of position over the medium's planar boundary, the equations that describe scattering can be written in terms of 1D functions over depth (see Figure 14.12).

In this setting, the various quantities are more conveniently expressed as functions of depth z rather than of distance t along a ray. For example, if the extinction coefficient is given by $\sigma_t(z)$, then the transmittance between two depths z_0 and z_1 for a ray with direction ω is

$$T_r(z_0 \rightarrow z_1, \omega) = e^{-\int_{z_0}^{z_1} \sigma_t(z')/|\cos\theta|\, \mathrm{d}z'} = e^{-\int_{z_0}^{z_1} \sigma_t(z')/|\omega_z|\, \mathrm{d}z'}.$$

BxDF 538

See Figure 14.13. This definition uses the fact that if a ray with direction ω travels a distance t, then the change in z is $t\omega_z$.

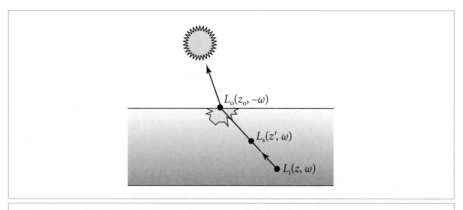

Figure 14.14: The 1D specialization of the equation of transfer from Equation (14.31) expresses the incident radiance L_i at a depth z as the sum of attenuated radiance L_o from the interface that is visible along the ray and the transmission-modulated source function L_s integrated over z.

In the case of a homogeneous medium,

$$T_r(z_0 \to z_1, \omega) = e^{-\sigma_t \left| \frac{z_0 - z_1}{\omega_z} \right|}.$$ (14.30)

The 1D equation of transfer can be found in a similar fashion. It says that at points inside the medium the incident radiance at a depth z in direction ω is given by

$$L_i(z, \omega) = T_r(z \to z_i, \omega) L_o(z_i, -\omega) + \int_z^{z_i} \frac{T_r(z \to z', \omega) L_s(z', -\omega)}{|\omega_z|} \, dz',$$ (14.31)

where z_i is the depth of the medium interface that the ray from z in direction ω intersects. (See Figure 14.14.) At boundaries, the incident radiance function is given by Equation (14.31) for directions ω that point into the medium. For directions that point outside it, incident radiance is found by integrating illumination from the scene.

The scattering from an interface at a boundary of the medium is given by the incident radiance modulated by the boundary's BSDF,

$$L_o(z, \omega_o) = \int_{\mathbb{S}^2} f_z(\omega_o, \omega') \, L_i(z, \omega') \, |\cos\theta'| \, d\omega'.$$ (14.32)

If we also assume there is no volumetric emission (as we will do in the LayeredBxDF), the source function in Equation (14.31) simplifies to

$$L_s(z, \omega) = \frac{\sigma_s}{\sigma_t} \int_{\mathbb{S}^2} p(\omega', \omega) \, L_i(z, \omega') \, d\omega'.$$ (14.33)

The LayeredBxDF further assumes that σ_t is constant over all wavelengths in the medium, which means that null scattering is not necessary for sampling distances in the medium. Null scattering is easily included in the 1D simplification of the equation of transfer if necessary, though we will not do so here. For similar reasons, we will also not derive its path integral form in 1D, though it too can be found with suitable simplifications to the approach that was used in Section 14.1.4. The "Further Reading" section has pointers to more details.

14.3.2 LAYERED BxDF

LayeredBxDF 895

The equation of transfer describes the equilibrium distribution of radiance, though our interest here is in evaluating and sampling the BSDF that represents all the scattering from the

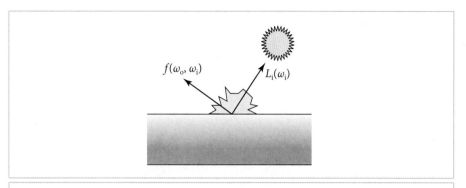

Figure 14.15: If a medium is illuminated with a virtual light source of the form of Equation (14.34), then the radiance leaving the surface in the direction ω_o is equivalent to the layered surface's BSDF, $f(\omega_o, \omega_i)$.

layered medium. Fortunately, these two things can be connected. If we would like to evaluate the BSDF for a pair of directions ω_o and ω_i, then we can define an incident radiance function from a virtual light source from ω_i as

$$L_i(\omega) = \frac{\delta(\omega - \omega_i)}{|\cos \theta_i|}. \qquad [14.34]$$

If a 1D medium is illuminated by such a light, then the outgoing radiance $L_o(\omega_o)$ at the medium's interface is equivalent to the value of the BSDF, $f(\omega_o, \omega_i)$ (see Figure 14.15). One way to understand why this is so is to consider using such a light with the surface reflection equation:

$$L_o(\omega_o) = \int_{\mathcal{S}^2} f(\omega_o, \omega)\, L_i(\omega)\, |\cos \theta|\, d\omega = \int_{\mathcal{S}^2} f(\omega_o, \omega)\, \delta(\omega - \omega_i)\, d\omega = f(\omega_o, \omega_i).$$

Thus, integrating the equation of transfer with such a light allows us to evaluate and sample the corresponding BSDF. However, this means that unlike all the BxDF implementations from Chapter 9, the values that LayeredBxDF returns from methods like f() and PDF() are stochastic. This is perfectly fine in the context of all of pbrt's Monte Carlo–based techniques and does not affect the correctness of other estimators that use these values; it is purely one more source of error that can be controlled in a predictable way by increasing the number of samples.

The LayeredBxDF allows the specification of only two interfaces and a homogeneous participating medium between them. Figure 14.16 illustrates the geometric setting. Surfaces with more layers can be modeled using a LayeredBxDF where one or both of its layers are themselves LayeredBxDFs. (An exercise at the end of the chapter discusses a more efficient approach for supporting additional layers.)

The types of BxDFs at both interfaces can be provided as template parameters. While the user of a LayeredBxDF is free to provide a BxDF for both of these types (in which case pbrt's regular dynamic dispatch mechanism will be used), performance is better if they are specific BxDFs and the compiler can generate a specialized implementation. This approach is used for the CoatedDiffuseBxDF and the CoatedConductorBxDF that are defined in Section 14.3.3. (The meaning of the twoSided template parameter will be explained in a few pages, where it is used.)

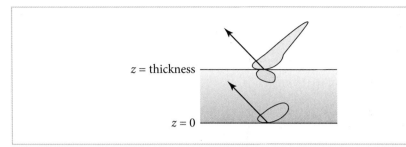

Figure 14.16: Geometric Setting for the LayeredBxDF. Scattering is specified by two interfaces with associated BSDFs where the bottom one is at $z = 0$ and there is a medium of user-specified thickness between the two interfaces.

(a)   (b)   (c)

Figure 14.17: Effect of Varying Medium Thickness with the LayeredBxDF. (a) Dragon with surface reflectance modeled by a smooth conductor base layer and a dielectric interface above it. (b) With a scattering layer with albedo 0.7 and thickness 0.15 between the interface and the conductor, the reflection of the conductor is slightly dimmed. (c) With a thicker scattering layer of thickness 0.5, the conductor is much more attenuated and the overall reflection is more diffuse. *(Dragon model courtesy of the Stanford Computer Graphics Laboratory.)*

⟨*LayeredBxDF Definition*⟩ ≡
```
template <typename TopBxDF, typename BottomBxDF, bool twoSided>
class LayeredBxDF {
  public:
    ⟨LayeredBxDF Public Methods 897⟩
  private:
    ⟨LayeredBxDF Private Methods 896⟩
    ⟨LayeredBxDF Private Members 895⟩
};
```

In addition to BxDFs for the two interfaces, the LayeredBxDF maintains member variables that describe the medium between them. Rather than have the user specify scattering coefficients, which can be unintuitive to set manually, it assumes a medium with $\sigma_t = 1$ and leaves it to the user to specify both the thickness of the medium and its scattering albedo. Figure 14.17 shows the effect of varying the thickness of the medium between a conductor base layer and a dielectric interface.

⟨*LayeredBxDF Private Members*⟩ ≡   **895**
```
TopBxDF top;
BottomBxDF bottom;
Float thickness, g;
SampledSpectrum albedo;
```

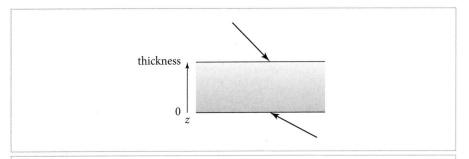

Figure 14.18: If the incident ray intersects the layer at $z = \text{thickness}$, then the top layer is the same as is specified in the `LayeredBxDF::top` member variable. However, if it intersects the surface from the other direction at $z = 0$, we will find it useful to treat the $z = 0$ layer as the top one and the other as the bottom. The `TopOrBottomBxDF` class helps with related bookkeeping.

Two parameters control the Monte Carlo estimates. `maxDepth` has its usual role in setting a maximum number of scattering events along a path and `nSamples` controls the number of independent samples of the estimators that are averaged. Because additional samples in this context do not require tracing more rays or evaluating textures, it is more efficient to reduce any noise due to the stochastic BSDF by increasing this sampling rate rather than increasing the pixel sampling rate if a higher pixel sampling rate is not otherwise useful.

⟨*LayeredBxDF Private Members*⟩ +≡   **895**
```
int maxDepth, nSamples;
```

We will find it useful to have a helper function `Tr()` that returns the transmittance for a ray segment in the medium with given direction `w` that passes through a distance `dz` in z, following Equation (14.30) with $\sigma_t = 1$.

⟨*LayeredBxDF Private Methods*⟩ ≡   **895**
```
static Float Tr(Float dz, Vector3f w) {
    return FastExp(-std::abs(dz / w.z));
}
```

Although the `LayeredBxDF` is specified in terms of top and bottom interfaces, we will find it useful to exchange the "top" and "bottom" as necessary to have the convention that the interface that the incident ray intersects is defined to be the top one. (See Figure 14.18.) A helper class, `TopOrBottomBxDF`, manages the logic related to these possibilities. As its name suggests, it stores a pointer to one (and only one) of two `BxDF` types that are provided as template parameters.

⟨*TopOrBottomBxDF Definition*⟩ ≡
```
template <typename TopBxDF, typename BottomBxDF>
class TopOrBottomBxDF {
  public:
    ⟨TopOrBottomBxDF Public Methods 897⟩
  private:
    const TopBxDF *top = nullptr;
    const BottomBxDF *bottom = nullptr;
};
```

`TopOrBottomBxDF` provides the implementation of a number of `BxDF` methods like `f()`, where it calls the corresponding method of whichever of the two `BxDF` types has been provided.

In addition to f(), it has similar straightforward Sample_f(), PDF(), and Flags() methods, which we will not include here.

⟨*TopOrBottomBxDF Public Methods*⟩ ≡   896
```
SampledSpectrum f(Vector3f wo, Vector3f wi, TransportMode mode) const {
    return top ? top->f(wo, wi, mode) : bottom->f(wo, wi, mode);
}
```

BSDF Evaluation

The BSDF evaluation method f() can now be implemented; it returns an average of the specified number of independent samples.

⟨*LayeredBxDF Public Methods*⟩ ≡   895
```
SampledSpectrum f(Vector3f wo, Vector3f wi, TransportMode mode) const {
    SampledSpectrum f(0.);
    ⟨Estimate LayeredBxDF value f using random sampling 897⟩
    return f / nSamples;
}
```

There is some preliminary computation that is independent of each sample taken to estimate the BSDF's value. A few fragments take care of it before the random estimation begins.

⟨*Estimate* LayeredBxDF *value* f *using random sampling*⟩ ≡   897
```
⟨Set wi and wi for layered BSDF evaluation 898⟩
⟨Determine entrance interface for layered BSDF 898⟩
⟨Determine exit interface and exit z for layered BSDF 898⟩
⟨Account for reflection at the entrance interface 898⟩
⟨Declare RNG for layered BSDF evaluation 899⟩
for (int s = 0; s < nSamples; ++s) {
    ⟨Sample random walk through layers to estimate BSDF value 899⟩
}
```

With this BSDF, layered materials can be specified as either one- or two-sided via the twoSided template parameter. If a material is one-sided, then the shape's surface normal is used to determine which interface an incident ray enters. If it is in the same hemisphere as the surface normal, it enters the top interface and otherwise it enters the bottom. This configuration is especially useful when both interfaces are transmissive and have different BSDFs.

For two-sided materials, the ray always enters the top interface. This option is useful when the bottom interface is opaque as is the case with the CoatedDiffuseBxDF, for example. In this case, it is usually desirable for scattering from both layers to be included, no matter which side the ray intersects.

One way to handle these options in the f() method would be to negate both directions and make a recursive call to f() if ω_o points below the surface and the material is two-sided. However, that solution is not a good one for the GPU, where it is likely to introduce thread divergence. (This topic is discussed in more detail in Section 15.1.1.) Therefore, both directions are negated at the start of the method and no recursive call is made in this case, which gives an equivalent result.

⟨*Set* wi *and* wi *for layered BSDF evaluation*⟩ ≡   **897**
```
if (twoSided && wo.z < 0) {
    wo = -wo;
    wi = -wi;
}
```

The next step is to determine which of the two BxDFs is the one that is encountered first by the incident ray. The sign of ω_o's z component in the reflection coordinate system gives the answer.

⟨*Determine entrance interface for layered BSDF*⟩ ≡   **897**
```
TopOrBottomBxDF<TopBxDF, BottomBxDF> enterInterface;
bool enteredTop = twoSided || wo.z > 0;
if (enteredTop) enterInterface = &top;
else            enterInterface = &bottom;
```

It is also necessary to determine which interface ω_i exits. This is determined both by which interface ω_o enters and by whether ω_o and ω_i are in the same hemisphere. We end up with an unusual case where the EXCLUSIVE-OR operator comes in handy. Along the way, the method also stores which interface is the one that ω_i does not exit from. As random paths are sampled through the layers and medium, the implementation will always choose reflection from this interface and not transmission, as choosing the latter would end the path without being able to scatter out in the ω_i direction. The same logic then covers determining the z depth at which the ray path will exit the surface.

⟨*Determine exit interface and exit z for layered BSDF*⟩ ≡   **897**
```
TopOrBottomBxDF<TopBxDF, BottomBxDF> exitInterface, nonExitInterface;
if (SameHemisphere(wo, wi) ^ enteredTop) {
    exitInterface = &bottom;
    nonExitInterface = &top;
} else {
    exitInterface = &top;
    nonExitInterface = &bottom;
}
Float exitZ = (SameHemisphere(wo, wi) ^ enteredTop) ? 0 : thickness;
```

If both directions are on the same side of the surface, then part of the BSDF's value is given by reflection at the entrance interface. This can be evaluated directly by calling the interface's BSDF's f() method. The resulting value must be scaled by the total number of samples taken to estimate the BSDF in this method, since the final returned value is divided by nSamples.

⟨*Account for reflection at the entrance interface*⟩ ≡   **897**
```
if (SameHemisphere(wo, wi))
    f = nSamples * enterInterface.f(wo, wi, mode);
```

pbrt's BxDF interface does not include any uniform sample values as parameters to the f() method; there is no need for them for any of the other BxDFs in the system. In any case, an unbounded number of uniform random numbers are required for sampling operations when evaluating layered BSDFs. Therefore, f() initializes an RNG and defines a convenience lambda function that returns uniform random sample values. This does mean that the benefits of sampling with well-distributed point sets are not present here; an exercise at the end of the chapter returns to this issue.

The RNG is seeded carefully: it is important that calls to f() with different directions have different seeds so that there is no risk of errors due to correlation between the RNGs used for

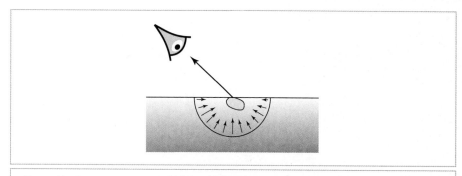

Figure 14.19: The effect of light that scatters between the interface layers is found by integrating the product of the cosine-weighted BTDF at the entrance interface with the incident radiance from the medium, Equation (14.35).

multiple samples in a pixel or across nearby pixels. However, we would also like the samples to be deterministic so that any call to f() with the same two directions always has the same set of random samples. This sort of reproducibility is important for debugging so that errors appear consistently across multiple runs of the program. Hashing the two provided directions along with the system-wide seed addresses all of these concerns.

⟨*Declare* RNG *for layered BSDF evaluation*⟩ ≡   897
```
RNG rng(Hash(GetOptions().seed, wo), Hash(wi));
auto r = [&rng]() { return std::min<Float>(rng.Uniform<Float>(),
                                           OneMinusEpsilon); };
```

In order to find the radiance leaving the interface in the direction ω_o, we need to integrate the product of the cosine-weighted BTDF at the interface with the incident radiance from inside the medium,

$$\int_{\mathcal{H}_t^2} f_t(\omega_o, \omega') \, L_i(z, \omega') \, |\cos \theta'| \, d\omega',$$ (14.35)

where $\mathcal{H}_t^2$ is the hemisphere inside the medium (see Figure 14.19). The implementation uses the standard Monte Carlo estimator, taking a sample ω' from the BTDF and then proceeding to estimate L_i.

⟨*Sample random walk through layers to estimate BSDF value*⟩ ≡   897
```
    ⟨Sample transmission direction through entrance interface 900⟩
    ⟨Sample BSDF for virtual light from wi 900⟩
    ⟨Declare state for random walk through BSDF layers 901⟩
    for (int depth = 0; depth < maxDepth; ++depth) {
        ⟨Sample next event for layered BSDF evaluation random walk 901⟩
    }
```

Sampling the direction ω' is a case where it is useful to be able to specify to Sample_f() that only transmission should be sampled.

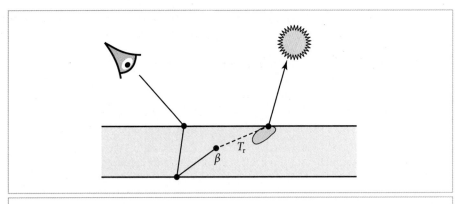

Figure 14.20: Illumination Contribution from the Virtual Light Source. At a path vertex, the contribution of the virtual light source is given by the product of the path throughput weight β that accounts for previous scattering along the path, the scattering at the vertex, the transmittance T_r to the exit interface, and the effect of the BTDF at the interface.

⟨*Sample transmission direction through entrance interface*⟩ ≡   **899**
```
    Float uc = r();
    pstd::optional<BSDFSample> wos =
        enterInterface.Sample_f(wo, uc, Point2f(r(), r()), mode,
                            BxDFReflTransFlags::Transmission);
    if (!wos || !wos->f || wos->pdf == 0 || wos->wi.z == 0)
        continue;
```

The task now is to compute a Monte Carlo estimate of the 1D equation of transfer, Equation (14.31). Before discussing how it is sampled, however, we will first consider some details related to the lighting calculation with the virtual light source. At each vertex of the path, we will want to compute the incident illumination due to the light. As shown in Figure 14.20, there are three factors in the light's contribution: the value of the phase function or interface BSDF for a direction ω, the transmittance between the vertex and the exit interface, and the value of the interface's BTDF for the direction from $-\omega$ to ω_i.

Each of these three factors could be used for sampling; as before, one may sometimes be much more effective than the others. The LayeredBxDF implementation uses two of the three—sampling the phase function or BRDF at the current path vertex (as appropriate) and sampling the BTDF at the exit interface—and then weights the results using MIS.

There is no reason to repeatedly sample the exit interface BTDF at each path vertex since the direction ω_i is fixed. Therefore, the following fragment samples it once and holds on to the resulting BSDFSample. Note that the negation of the TransportMode parameter value mode is taken for the call to Sample_f(), which is important to reflect the fact that this sampling operation is following the reverse path with respect to sampling in terms of ω_o. This is an important detail so that the underlying BxDF can correctly account for non-symmetric scattering; see Section 9.5.2.

⟨*Sample BSDF for virtual light from* wi⟩ ≡   **899**
```
    uc = r();
    pstd::optional<BSDFSample> wis =
        exitInterface.Sample_f(wi, uc, Point2f(r(), r()), !mode,
                            BxDFReflTransFlags::Transmission);
    if (!wis || !wis->f || wis->pdf == 0 || wis->wi.z == 0)
        continue;
```

Moving forward to the random walk estimation of the equation of transfer, the implementation maintains the current path throughput weight beta, the depth z of the last scattering event, and the ray direction w.

⟨*Declare state for random walk through BSDF layers*⟩ ≡   899
```
SampledSpectrum beta = wos->f * AbsCosTheta(wos->wi) / wos->pdf;
Float z = enteredTop ? thickness : 0;
Vector3f w = wos->wi;
HGPhaseFunction phase(g);
```

We can now move to the body of the inner loop over scattering events along the path. After a Russian roulette test, a distance is sampled along the ray to determine the next path vertex either within the medium or at whichever interface the ray intersects.

⟨*Sample next event for layered BSDF evaluation random walk*⟩ ≡   899
```
⟨Possibly terminate layered BSDF random walk with Russian roulette 901⟩
⟨Account for media between layers and possibly scatter 901⟩
⟨Account for scattering at appropriate interface 903⟩
```

It is worth considering terminating the path as the path throughput weight becomes low, though here the termination probability is set less aggressively than it was in the Path Integrator and VolPathIntegrator. This reflects the fact that each bounce here is relatively inexpensive, so doing more work to improve the accuracy of the estimate is worthwhile.

⟨*Possibly terminate layered BSDF random walk with Russian roulette*⟩ ≡   901
```
if (depth > 3 && beta.MaxComponentValue() < 0.25f) {
    Float q = std::max<Float>(0, 1 - beta.MaxComponentValue());
    if (r() < q) break;
    beta /= 1 - q;
}
```

The common case of no scattering in the medium is handled separately since it is much simpler than the case where volumetric scattering must be considered.

⟨*Account for media between layers and possibly scatter*⟩ ≡   901
```
if (!albedo) {
    ⟨Advance to next layer boundary and update beta for transmittance 901⟩
} else {
    ⟨Sample medium scattering for layered BSDF evaluation 902⟩
}
```

If there is no medium scattering, then only the first term of Equation (14.31) needs to be evaluated. The path vertices alternate between the two interfaces. Here beta is multiplied by the transmittance for the ray segment through the medium; the L_o factor is found by estimating Equation (14.32), which will be handled shortly.

⟨*Advance to next layer boundary and update* beta *for transmittance*⟩ ≡   901
```
z = (z == thickness) ? 0 : thickness;
beta *= Tr(thickness, w);
```

If the medium is scattering, we only sample one of the two terms of the 1D equation of transfer, choosing between taking a sample inside the medium and scattering at the other interface. A change in depth Δz can be perfectly sampled from the 1D beam transmittance, Equation (14.30). Since $\sigma_t = 1$, the PDF is

$$p(\Delta z) = \frac{1}{|\omega_z|} e^{-\frac{\Delta z}{|\omega_z|}}.$$

Given a depth z' found by adding or subtracting Δz from the current depth z according to the ray's direction, medium scattering is chosen if z' is inside the medium and surface scattering is chosen otherwise. (The sampling scheme is thus similar to how the VolPathIntegrator chooses between medium and surface scattering.) In the case of scattering from an interface, the Clamp() call effectively forces z to lie on whichever of the two interfaces the ray intersects next.

⟨*Sample medium scattering for layered BSDF evaluation*⟩ ≡   **901**
```
    Float sigma_t = 1;
    Float dz = SampleExponential(r(), sigma_t / std::abs(w.z));
    Float zp = w.z > 0 ? (z + dz) : (z - dz);
    if (0 < zp && zp < thickness) {
        ⟨Handle scattering event in layered BSDF medium 902⟩
        continue;
    }
    z = Clamp(zp, 0, thickness);
```

If z' is inside the medium, we have the estimator

$$\frac{T_{\mathrm{r}}(z \to z')\, L_s(z', -\omega)}{p(\Delta z)\, |\omega_z|}.$$

Both the exponential factors and $|\omega_z|$ factors in T_{r} and $p(\Delta z)$ cancel, and we are left with simply the source function $L_s(z', -\omega)$, which should be scaled by the path throughput. The following fragment adds an estimate of its value to the sum in f.

⟨*Handle scattering event in layered BSDF medium*⟩ ≡   **902**
```
    ⟨Account for scattering through exitInterface using wis 902⟩
    ⟨Sample phase function and update layered path state 903⟩
    ⟨Possibly account for scattering through exitInterface 903⟩
```

For a scattering event inside the medium, it is necessary to add the contribution of the virtual light source to the path radiance estimate and to sample a new direction to continue the path. For the MIS lighting sample based on sampling the interface's BTDF, the outgoing direction from the path vertex is predetermined by the BTDF sample wis; all the factors of the path contribution are easily evaluated and the MIS weight is found using the PDF for the other sampling technique, sampling the phase function.

⟨*Account for scattering through exitInterface using wis*⟩ ≡   **902**
```
    Float wt = 1;
    if (!IsSpecular(exitInterface.Flags()))
        wt = PowerHeuristic(1, wis->pdf, 1, phase.PDF(-w, -wis->wi));
    f += beta * albedo * phase.p(-w, -wis->wi) * wt * Tr(zp - exitZ, wis->wi) *
        wis->f / wis->pdf;
```

The second sampling strategy for the virtual light is based on sampling the phase function and then connecting to the virtual light source through the exit interface. Doing so shares some common work with sampling a new direction for the path, so the implementation takes the opportunity to update the path state after sampling the phase function here.

⟨*Sample phase function and update layered path state*⟩ ≡   902
```
Point2f u{r(), r()};
pstd::optional<PhaseFunctionSample> ps = phase.Sample_p(-w, u);
if (!ps || ps->pdf == 0 || ps->wi.z == 0)
    continue;
beta *= albedo * ps->p / ps->pdf;
w = ps->wi;
z = zp;
```

There is no reason to try connecting through the exit interface if the current ray direction is pointing away from it or if its BSDF is perfect specular.

⟨*Possibly account for scattering through* exitInterface⟩ ≡   902
```
if (((z < exitZ && w.z > 0) || (z > exitZ && w.z < 0)) &&
    !IsSpecular(exitInterface.Flags())) {
    ⟨Account for scattering through exitInterface 903⟩
}
```

If there is transmission through the interface, then because beta has already been updated to include the effect of scattering at z', only the transmittance to the exit, MIS weight, and BTDF value need to be evaluated to compute the light's contribution. One important detail in the following code is the ordering of arguments to the call to f() in the first line: due to the non-reciprocity of BTDFs, swapping these would lead to incorrect results.[4]

⟨*Account for scattering through* exitInterface⟩ ≡   903
```
SampledSpectrum fExit = exitInterface.f(-w, wi, mode);
if (fExit) {
    Float exitPDF =
        exitInterface.PDF(-w, wi, mode, BxDFReflTransFlags::Transmission);
    Float wt = PowerHeuristic(1, ps->pdf, 1, exitPDF);
    f += beta * Tr(zp - exitZ, ps->wi) * fExit * wt;
}
```

If no medium scattering event was sampled, the next path vertex is at an interface. In this case, the transmittance along the ray can be ignored: as before, the probability of evaluating the first term of Equation (14.31) has probability equal to T_r and thus the two T_r factors cancel, leaving us only needing to evaluate scattering at the boundary, Equation (14.32). The details differ depending on which interface the ray intersected.

⟨*Account for scattering at appropriate interface*⟩ ≡   901
```
if (z == exitZ) {
    ⟨Account for reflection at exitInterface 904⟩
} else {
    ⟨Account for scattering at nonExitInterface⟩
}
```

If the ray intersected the exit interface, then it is only necessary to update the path throughput: no connection is made to the virtual light source since transmission through the exit interface to the light is accounted for by the lighting computation at the previous vertex. This fragment samples only the reflection component of the path here, since a ray that was transmitted outside the medium would end the path.

---

4   As was learned, painfully, during the implementation of this BxDF.

⟨*Account for reflection at* `exitInterface`⟩ ≡   903

```
    Float uc = r();
    pstd::optional<BSDFSample> bs = exitInterface.Sample_f(
        -w, uc, Point2f(r(), r()), mode, BxDFReflTransFlags::Reflection);
    if (!bs || !bs->f || bs->pdf == 0 || bs->wi.z == 0)
        break;
    beta *= bs->f * AbsCosTheta(bs->wi) / bs->pdf;
    w = bs->wi;
```

The ⟨*Account for scattering at* `nonExitInterface`⟩ fragment handles scattering from the other interface. It applies MIS to compute the contribution of the virtual light and samples a new direction with a form very similar to the case of scattering within the medium, just with the phase function replaced by the BRDF for evaluation and sampling. Therefore, we have not included its implementation here.

BSDF Sampling

The implementation of `Sample_f()` is generally similar to `f()`, so we will not include its implementation here, either. Its task is actually simpler: given the initial direction ω_o at one of the layer's boundaries, it follows a random walk of scattering events through the layers and the medium, maintaining both the path throughput and the product of PDFs for each of the sampling decisions. When the random walk exits the medium, the outgoing direction is the sampled direction that is returned in the `BSDFSample`.

With this approach, it can be shown that the ratio of the path throughput to the PDF is equal to the ratio of the actual value of the BSDF and its PDF for the sampled direction (see the "Further Reading" section for details). Therefore, when the weighted path throughput is multiplied by the ratio of `BSDFSample::f` and `BSDFSample::pdf`, the correct weighting term is applied. (Review, for example, the fragment ⟨*Update path state variables after surface scattering*⟩ in the `PathIntegrator`.)

However, an implication of this is that the PDF value returned by `Sample_f()` cannot be used to compute the multiple importance sampling weight if the sampled ray hits an emissive surface; in that case, an independent estimate of the PDF must be computed via a call to the `PDF()` method. The `BSDFSample::pdfIsProportional` member variable flags this case and is set by `Sample_f()` here.

PDF Evaluation

The PDF $p(\omega_o, \omega_i)$ that corresponds to a `LayeredBxDF`'s BSDF can be expressed as an infinite sum. For example, consider the case of having a bottom layer that reflects light with BRDF f_r^- and a top layer that both reflects light with BRDF f_r^+ and transmits it with BTDF f_t^+, with an overall BSDF $f^+ = f_r^+ + f_t^+$. If those BSDFs have associated PDFs p and if scattering in the medium is neglected, then the overall PDF is

$$p(\omega_o, \omega_i) = p_r^+(\omega_o, \omega_i)$$
$$+ \int_{\mathbb{S}^2} \int_{\mathbb{S}^2} p_t^+(\omega_o, \omega')\, p_r^-(-\omega', \omega'')\, p_t^+(-\omega'', \omega_i)\, d\omega' d\omega'' + \cdots. \tag{14.36}$$

The first term gives the contribution for the PDF at the top interface and the second is the PDF for directions ω_i that were sampled via transmission through the top interface, scattering at the bottom, and then transmission back out in direction ω_i. Note the coupling of directions between the PDF factors in the integrand: the negation of the initial transmitted direction ω' gives the first direction for evaluation of the base PDF p_r^-, and so forth (see Figure 14.21). Subsequent terms of this sum account for light that is reflected back downward

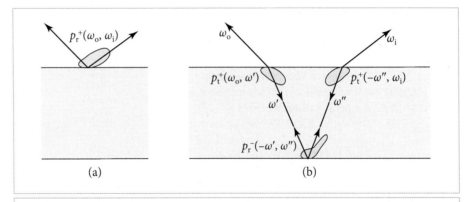

Figure 14.21: The First Two Terms of the Infinite Sum that Give a Layered BSDF's PDF. (a) The PDF of the reflection component of the interface's BSDF accounts for light that scatters without entering the layers. (b) The second term is given by a double integral over directions. A direction ω' pointing into the medium is sampled; it gives the second direction for the interface's BTDF PDF p_t^+ and its negation gives one of the two directions for p_r^-. A second direction ω'' is used for p_r^- as well as for a second evaluation of p_t^+.

at the top interface instead of exiting the layers, and expressions of a similar form can be found for the PDF if the base layer is also transmissive.

It is possible to compute a stochastic estimate of the PDF by applying Monte Carlo to the integrals and by terminating the infinite sum using Russian roulette. For example, for the integral in Equation (14.36), we have the estimator

$$\frac{p_t^+(\omega_o, \omega')\ p_r^-(-\omega', \omega'')\ p_t^+(-\omega'', \omega_i)}{p_1(\omega')\ p_2(\omega'')},$$ (14.37)

where ω' is sampled from some distribution p_1 and ω'' from a distribution p_2. There is great freedom in choosing the distributions p_1 and p_2. However, as with algorithms like path tracing, care must be taken if some of the PDFs are Dirac delta distributions. For example, if the bottom layer is perfect specular, then $p_r^-(-\omega', \omega'')$ will always be zero unless ω'' was sampled according to its PDF.

Consider what happens if ω' is sampled using f_t^+'s sampling method, conditioned on ω_o, and if ω'' is sampled using f_t^+'s sampling method, conditioned on ω_i: the first and last probabilities in the numerator cancel with the probabilities in the denominator, and we are left simply with $p_r^-(-\omega', \omega'')$ as the estimate; the effect of f_t^+ in the PDF is fully encapsulated by the distribution of directions used to evaluate p_r^-.

A stochastic estimate of the PDF can be computed by following a random walk in a manner similar to the `f()` method, just with phase function and BSDF evaluation replaced with evaluations of the corresponding PDFs. However, because the `PDF()` method is only called to compute PDF values that are used for computing MIS weights, the implementation here will return an approximate PDF; doing so does not invalidate the MIS estimator.[5]

---

5   It is admittedly unfriendly to provide an implementation of a method with a name that very clearly indicates that it should return a valid PDF and yet does not in fact do that, and to justify this with the fact that doing so is fine due to the current usage of the function. This represents a potentially gnarly bug lying in wait for someone in the future who might not expect this when extending the system. For that, our apologies in advance.

⟨*LayeredBxDF Public Methods*⟩ +≡   895
```
    Float PDF(Vector3f wo, Vector3f wi, TransportMode mode,
             BxDFReflTransFlags sampleFlags = BxDFReflTransFlags::All) const {
        ⟨Set wo and wi for layered BSDF evaluation⟩
        ⟨Declare RNG for layered PDF evaluation 906⟩
        ⟨Update pdfSum for reflection at the entrance layer 906⟩
        for (int s = 0; s < nSamples; ++s) {
            ⟨Evaluate layered BSDF PDF sample 906⟩
        }
        ⟨Return mixture of PDF estimate and constant PDF 908⟩
    }
```

It is important that the RNG for the PDF() method is seeded differently than it is for the f() method, since it will often be called with the same pair of directions as are passed to f(), and we would like to be certain that there is no correlation between the results returned by the two of them.

⟨*Declare* RNG *for layered PDF evaluation*⟩ ≡   906
```
    RNG rng(Hash(GetOptions().seed, wi), Hash(wo));
    auto r = [&rng]() { return std::min<Float>(rng.Uniform<Float>(),
                                               OneMinusEpsilon); };
```

If both directions are on the same side of the surface, then part of the full PDF is given by the PDF for reflection at the interface (this was the first term of Equation (14.36)). This component can be evaluated non-stochastically, assuming that the underlying PDF() methods are not themselves stochastic.

⟨*Update* pdfSum *for reflection at the entrance layer*⟩ ≡   906
```
    bool enteredTop = twoSided || wo.z > 0;
    Float pdfSum = 0;
    if (SameHemisphere(wo, wi)) {
        auto reflFlag = BxDFReflTransFlags::Reflection;
        pdfSum += enteredTop ?
                  nSamples * top.PDF(wo, wi, mode, reflFlag) :
                  nSamples * bottom.PDF(wo, wi, mode, reflFlag);
    }
```

The more times light has been scattered, the more isotropic its directional distribution tends to become. We can take advantage of this fact by evaluating only the first term of the stochastic PDF estimate and modeling the remaining terms with a uniform distribution. We further neglect the effect of scattering in the medium, again under the assumption that if it is significant, a uniform distribution will be a suitable approximation.

⟨*Evaluate layered BSDF PDF sample*⟩ ≡   906
```
    if (SameHemisphere(wo, wi)) {
        ⟨Evaluate TRT term for PDF estimate 907⟩
    } else {
        ⟨Evaluate TT term for PDF estimate⟩
    }
```

If both directions are on the same side of the interface, then the remaining PDF integral is the double integral of the product of three PDFs that we considered earlier. We use the shorthand "TRT" for this case, corresponding to transmission, then reflection, then transmission.

⟨*Evaluate TRT term for PDF estimate*⟩ ≡   906
```
TopOrBottomBxDF<TopBxDF, BottomBxDF> rInterface, tInterface;
if (enteredTop) {
    rInterface = &bottom;  tInterface = &top;
} else {
    rInterface = &top;       tInterface = &bottom;
}
```
⟨*Sample* tInterface *to get direction into the layers* 907⟩
⟨*Update* pdfSum *accounting for TRT scattering events* 907⟩

We will apply two sampling strategies. The first is sampling both directions via tInterface, once conditioned on ω_o and once on ω_i—effectively a bidirectional approach. The second is sampling one direction via tInterface conditioned on ω_o and the other via rInterface conditioned on the first sampled direction. These are then combined using multiple importance sampling. After canceling factors and introducing an MIS weight $w(\omega'')$, Equation (14.37) simplifies to

$$w(\omega'') \frac{p_r^-(-\omega', \omega'') \, p_t^+(-\omega'', \omega_i)}{p(\omega'')},$$ [14.38]

which is the estimator for both strategies.

Both sampling methods will use the wos sample while only one uses wis.

⟨*Sample* tInterface *to get direction into the layers*⟩ ≡   907
```
auto trans = BxDFReflTransFlags::Transmission;
pstd::optional<BSDFSample> wos, wis;
wos = tInterface.Sample_f(wo, r(), {r(), r()}, mode, trans);
wis = tInterface.Sample_f(wi, r(), {r(), r()}, !mode, trans);
```

If tInterface is perfect specular, then there is no need to try sampling p_r^- or to apply MIS. The p_r^- PDF is all that remains from Equation (14.38).

⟨*Update* pdfSum *accounting for TRT scattering events*⟩ ≡   907
```
if (wos && wos->f && wos->pdf > 0 && wis && wis->f && wis->pdf > 0) {
    if (!IsNonSpecular(tInterface.Flags()))
        pdfSum += rInterface.PDF(-wos->wi, -wis->wi, mode);
    else {
        ⟨Use multiple importance sampling to estimate PDF product 907⟩
    }
}
```

Otherwise, we sample from p_r^- as well. If that sample is from a perfect specular component, then again there is no need to use MIS and the estimator is just $p_t^+(-\omega'', \omega_i)$.

⟨*Use multiple importance sampling to estimate PDF product*⟩ ≡   907
```
pstd::optional<BSDFSample> rs =
    rInterface.Sample_f(-wos->wi, r(), {r(), r()}, mode);
if (rs && rs->f && rs->pdf > 0) {
    if (!IsNonSpecular(rInterface.Flags()))
        pdfSum += tInterface.PDF(-rs->wi, wi, mode);
    else {
        ⟨Compute MIS-weighted estimate of Equation (14.38) 908⟩
    }
}
```

If neither interface has a specular sample, then both are combined. For the first sampling technique, the second p_t^+ factor cancels out as well and the estimator is $p_r^-(-\omega', -\omega'')$ times the MIS weight.

⟨*Compute MIS-weighted estimate of Equation (14.38)*⟩ ≡   907
```
Float rPDF = rInterface.PDF(-wos->wi, -wis->wi, mode);
Float wt = PowerHeuristic(1, wis->pdf, 1, rPDF);
pdfSum += wt * rPDF;
```

Similarly, for the second sampling technique, we are left with a p_t^+ PDF to evaluate and then weight using MIS.

⟨*Compute MIS-weighted estimate of Equation (14.38)*⟩ +≡   907
```
Float tPDF = tInterface.PDF(-rs->wi, wi, mode);
wt = PowerHeuristic(1, rs->pdf, 1, tPDF);
pdfSum += wt * tPDF;
```

The ⟨*Evaluate TT term for PDF estimate*⟩ fragment is of a similar form, so it is not included here.

The final returned PDF value has the PDF for uniform spherical sampling, $1/4\pi$, mixed with the estimate to account for higher-order terms.

⟨*Return mixture of PDF estimate and constant PDF*⟩ ≡   906
```
return Lerp(0.9f, 1 / (4 * Pi), pdfSum / nSamples);
```

14.3.3 COATED DIFFUSE AND COATED CONDUCTOR MATERIALS

Adding a dielectric interface on top of both diffuse materials and conductors is often useful to model surface reflection. For example, plastic can be modeled by putting such an interface above a diffuse material, and coated metals can be modeled by adding such an interface as well. In both cases, introducing a scattering layer can model effects like tarnish or weathering. Figure 14.22 shows the dragon model with a few variations of these.

pbrt provides both the CoatedDiffuseBxDF and the CoatedConductorBxDF for such uses. There is almost nothing to their implementations other than a public inheritance from LayeredBxDF with the appropriate types for the two interfaces.

⟨*CoatedDiffuseBxDF Definition*⟩ ≡
```
class CoatedDiffuseBxDF :
    public LayeredBxDF<DielectricBxDF, DiffuseBxDF, true> {
  public:
    ⟨CoatedDiffuseBxDF Public Methods⟩
};
```

⟨*CoatedConductorBxDF Definition*⟩ ≡
```
class CoatedConductorBxDF :
    public LayeredBxDF<DielectricBxDF, ConductorBxDF, true> {
  public:
    ⟨CoatedConductorBxDF Public Methods⟩
};
```

There are also corresponding Material implementations, CoatedDiffuseMaterial and CoatedConductorMaterial. Their implementations follow the familiar pattern of evaluating textures and then initializing the corresponding BxDF, and they are therefore not included here.

(a)   (b)   (c)

Figure 14.22: A Variety of Effects That Can Be Achieved Using Layered Materials. (a) Dragon model with a blue diffuse BRDF. (b) The effect of adding a smooth dielectric interface on top of the diffuse BRDF. In addition to the specular highlights, note how the color has become more saturated, which is due to multiple scattering from paths that reflected back into the medium from the exit interface. (c) The effect of roughening the interface. The surface appears less shiny, but the blue remains more saturated. *(Dragon model courtesy of the Stanford Computer Graphics Laboratory.)*

FURTHER READING

Lommel (1889) first derived the equation of transfer. Not only did he derive this equation, but he also solved it in some simplified cases in order to estimate reflection functions from real-world surfaces (including marble and paper), and he compared his solutions to measured reflectance data from these surfaces. The equation of transfer was independently found by Khvolson (1890) soon afterward; see Mishchenko (2013) for a history of early work in the area.

Seemingly unaware of Lommel's work, Schuster (1905) was the next researcher in radiative transfer to consider the effect of multiple scattering. He used the term *self-illumination* to describe the fact that each part of the medium is illuminated by every other part of the medium, and he derived differential equations that described reflection from a slab along the normal direction, assuming the presence of isotropic scattering. The conceptual framework that he developed remains essentially unchanged in the field of radiative transfer.

Soon thereafter, Schwarzschild (1906) introduced the concept of radiative equilibrium, and Jackson (1910) expressed Schuster's equation in integral form, also noting that "the obvious physical mode of solution is Liouville's method of successive substitutions" (i.e., a Neumann series solution). Finally, King (1913) completed the rediscovery of the equation of transfer by expressing it in the general integral form.

Books by Chandrasekhar (1960), Preisendorfer (1965, 1976), and van de Hulst (1980) cover volume light transport in depth. D'Eon's book (2016) extensively discusses scattering problems, including both analytic and Monte Carlo solutions, and contains many references to related work in other fields.

The equation of transfer was introduced to graphics by Kajiya and Von Herzen (1984). Arvo (1993) made essential connections between previous formalizations of light transport in graphics and the equation of transfer as well as to the field of radiative transfer in general. Pauly et al. (2000) derived the generalization of the path integral form of the light transport equation for the volume-scattering case; see also Chapter 3 of Jakob's Ph.D. thesis (2013) for a full derivation.

The integral null-scattering volume light transport equation was derived by Galtier et al. (2013) in the field of radiative transfer; Eymet et al. (2013) described the generalization to include scattering from surfaces. This approach was introduced to graphics by Novák et al. (2014). Miller et al. (2019) derived its path integral form, which made it possible to apply powerful variance reduction techniques based on multiple importance sampling.

Volumetric Path Tracing

von Neumann's original description of the Monte Carlo algorithm was in the context of neutron transport problems (Ulam et al. 1947); his technique included the algorithm for sampling distances from an exponential distribution (our Equation (A.2)), uniformly sampling 3D directions via uniform sampling of $\cos\theta$ (as implemented in `SampleUniformSphere()`), and randomly choosing among scattering events as described in Section 14.1.2.

Rushmeier (1988) was the first to use Monte Carlo to solve the volumetric light transport equation in a general setting.

Szirmay-Kalos et al. (2005) precomputed interactions between sample points in the medium in order to more quickly compute multiple scattering. Kulla and Fajardo (2012) proposed a specialized sampling technique that is effective for light sources inside participating media. (This technique was first introduced in the field of neutron transport by Kalli and Cashwell (1977).) Georgiev et al. (2013) made the observation that incremental path sampling can generate particularly bad paths in participating media. They proposed new multi-vertex sampling methods that better account for all the relevant terms in the equation of transfer.

Sampling direct illumination from lights at points inside media surrounded by an interface is challenging; traditional direct lighting algorithms are not applicable at points inside the medium, as refraction through the interface will divert the shadow ray's path. Walter et al. (2009) considered this problem and developed algorithms to efficiently find paths to lights accounting for this refraction. More recent work on this topic was done by Holzschuch (2015) and Koerner et al. (2016). Weber et al. (2017) developed an approach for more effectively sampling direct lighting in forward scattering media by allowing multiple scattering events along the path to the light.

Szirmay-Kalos et al. (2017) first showed the use of the integral null-scattering volume light transport equation for rendering scattering inhomogeneous media. Kutz et al. (2017) subsequently applied it to efficient rendering of spectral media and Szirmay-Kalos et al. (2018) developed improved algorithms for sampling multiple scattering. After deriving the path integral formulation, Miller et al. (2019) used it to show the effectiveness of combining a variety of sampling techniques using multiple importance scattering, including bidirectional path tracing.

The visual appearance of high-albedo objects like clouds is striking, but many bounces may be necessary for good results. Wrenninge et al. (2013) described an approximation where after the first few bounces, the scattering coefficient, the attenuation coefficient for shadow rays, and the eccentricity of the phase function are all progressively reduced. Kallweit et al. (2017) applied neural networks to store precomputed multiple scattering solutions for use in rendering highly scattering clouds.

Pegoraro et al. (2008b) developed a Monte Carlo sampling approach for rendering participating media that used information from previous samples to guide future sampling. More recent work in volumetric path guiding by Herholz et al. applied product sampling based on the phase function and an approximation to the light distribution in the medium (Herholz et al. 2019). Wrenninge and Villemin (2020) developed a volumetric product sampling approach based on adapting the majorant to account for important regions of the integrand and then randomly selecting among candidate samples based on weights that account for

SampleUniformSphere() 1016

factors beyond transmittance. Villeneuve et al. (2021) have also developed algorithms for product sampling in media, accounting for the surface normal at area light sources, transmittance along the ray, and the phase function.

Volumetric emission is not handled efficiently by the VolPathIntegrator, as there is no specialized sampling technique to account for it. Villemin and Hery (2013) precomputed tabularized CDFs for sampling volumetric emission, and Simon et al. (2017) developed further improvements, including integrating emission along rays and using the sampled point in the volume solely to determine the initial sampling direction, which gives better results in dense media.

The one-dimensional volumetric light transport algorithms implemented in LayeredBxDF are based on Guo et al.'s approach (2018).

Other Light Transport Algorithms

Blinn (1982b) first used basic volume scattering algorithms for computer graphics. Rushmeier and Torrance (1987) used finite-element methods for rendering participating media. Other early work in volume scattering for computer graphics includes work by Max (1986); Nishita, Miyawaki, and Nakamae (1987); Bhate and Tokuta's approach based on spherical harmonics (Bhate and Tokuta 1992), and Blasi et al.'s two-pass Monte Carlo algorithm, where the first pass shoots energy from the lights and stores it in a grid and the second pass does final rendering using the grid to estimate illumination at points in the scene (Blasi, Saëc, and Schlick 1993). Glassner (1995) provided a thorough overview of this topic and early applications of it in graphics, and Max's survey article (Max 1995) also covers early work well. See Cerezo et al. (2005) for an extensive survey of approaches to rendering participating media up through 2005.

One important application of volume scattering algorithms in computer graphics has been simulating atmospheric scattering. Work in this area includes early papers by Klassen (1987) and Preetham et al. (1999), who introduced a physically rigorous and computationally efficient atmospheric and sky-lighting model. Haber et al. (2005) described a model for twilight, and Hošek and Wilkie (2012, 2013) developed a comprehensive model for sky- and sunlight. Bruneton evaluated the accuracy and efficiency of a number of models for atmospheric scattering (Bruneton 2017). A sophisticated model that accurately accounts for polarization, observers at arbitrary altitudes, and the effect of atmospheric scattering for objects at finite distances was recently introduced by Wilkie et al. (2021).

Jarosz et al. (2008a) first extended the principles of irradiance caching to participating media. Marco et al. (2018) described a state-of-the-art algorithm for volumetric radiance caching based on Schwarzhaupt et al.'s surface-based second-order derivatives (Schwarzhaupt et al. 2012).

Jensen and Christensen (1998) were the first to generalize the photon-mapping algorithm to participating media. Knaus and Zwicker (2011) showed how to render participating media using stochastic progressive photon mapping (SPPM). Jarosz et al. (2008b) had the important insight that expressing the scattering integral over a beam through the medium as the measurement to be evaluated could make photon mapping's rate of convergence much higher than if a series of point photon estimates was instead taken along each ray. Section 5.6 of Hachisuka's thesis (2011) and Jarosz et al. (2011a, 2011b) showed how to apply this approach progressively. For another representation, see Jakob et al. (2011), who fit a sum of anisotropic Gaussians to the equilibrium radiance distribution in participating media.

LayeredBxDF 895
VolPathIntegrator 877

Many of the other bidirectional light transport algorithms discussed in the "Further Reading" section of Chapter 13 also have generalizations to account for participating media. See also Jarosz's thesis (2008), which has extensive background on this topic and includes a number of important contributions.

Some researchers have had success in deriving closed-form expressions that describe scattering along unoccluded ray segments in participating media; these approaches can be substantially more efficient than integrating over a series of point samples. See Sun et al. (2005), Pegoraro and Parker (2009), and Pegoraro et al. (2009, 2010, 2011) for examples of such methods. (Remarkably, Pegoraro and collaborators' work provides a closed-form expression for scattering from a point light source along a ray passing through homogeneous participating media with anisotropic phase functions.)

Subsurface Scattering

Subsurface scattering models based on volumetric light transport were first introduced to graphics by Hanrahan and Krueger (1993), although their approach did not attempt to simulate light that entered the object at points other than at the point being shaded. Dorsey et al. (1999) applied photon maps to simulating subsurface scattering that did include this effect, and Pharr and Hanrahan (2000) introduced an approach based on computing BSSRDFs for arbitrary scattering media with an integral over the medium's depth.

The *diffusion approximation* has been shown to be an effective way to model highly scattering media for rendering. It was first introduced to graphics by Kajiya and Von Herzen (1984), though Stam (1995) was the first to clearly identify many of its advantages for rendering.

A solution of the diffusion approximation based on dipoles was developed by Farrell et al. (1992); that approach was applied to BSSRDF modeling for rendering by Jensen et al. (2001b). Subsequent work by Jensen and Buhler (2002) improved the efficiency of that method. A more accurate solution based on *photon beam diffusion* was developed by Habel et al. (2013). (The online edition of this book includes the implementation of a BSSRDF model based on photon beam diffusion as well as many more references to related work.)

Rendering realistic human skin is a challenging problem; this problem has driven the development of a number of new methods for rendering subsurface scattering after the initial dipole work as issues of modeling the layers of skin and computing more accurate simulations of scattering between layers have been addressed. For a good overview of these issues, see Igarashi et al.'s (2007) survey on the scattering mechanisms inside skin and approaches for measuring and rendering skin. Notable research in this area includes papers by Donner and Jensen (2006), d'Eon et al. (2007), Ghosh et al. (2008), and Donner et al. (2008). Donner's thesis includes a discussion of the importance of accurate spectral representations for high-quality skin rendering (Donner 2006, Section 8.5). See Gitlina et al. (2020) for recent work in the measurement of the scattering properties of skin and fitting it to a BSSRDF model.

An alternative to BSSRDF-based approaches to subsurface scattering is to apply the same volumetric Monte Carlo path-tracing techniques that are used for other scattering media. This approach is increasingly used in production (Chiang et al. 2016b). See Wrenninge et al. (2017) for a discussion of such a model designed for artistic control and expressiveness.

Křivánek and d'Eon introduced the theory of zero-variance random walks for path-traced subsurface scattering, applying Dwivedi's sampling technique (1982a; 1982b) to guide paths to stay close to the surface while maintaining an unbiased estimator (Křivánek and d'Eon 2014). Meng et al. (2016) developed further improvements to this approach, including strategies that handle back-lit objects more effectively. More recent work on zero-variance theory by d'Eon and Křivánek (2020) includes improved results with isotropic scattering and new sampling schemes that further reduce variance.

Leonard et al. (2021) applied machine learning to subsurface scattering, training conditional variational auto-encoders to sample scattering, to model absorption probabilities, and to sample the positions of ray paths in spherical regions. They then used these capabilities to implement an efficient sphere-tracing algorithm.

Generalizations

Moon et al. (2007) made the important observation that some of the assumptions underlying the use of the equation of transfer—that the scattering particles in the medium are not too close together so that scattering events can be considered to be statistically independent—are not in fact true for interesting scenes that include small crystals, ice, or piles of many small glass objects. They developed a new light transport algorithm for these types of *discrete random media* based on composing precomputed scattering solutions. (See also concurrent work by Lee and O'Sullivan (2007) on composing scattering solutions.) Further work on rendering such materials was done by Müller et al. (2016), Guo et al. (2019), and Zhang and Zhao (2020).

Non-exponential media have distributions of interactions that are not described by an exponential distribution. They arise from media that have correlation in the distribution of their particles. The assumption of uncorrelated media that we adopted in Chapter 11 and have used throughout this chapter can immediately be understood to be at minimum not quite right by considering the fact that there must be a minimum distance between any two particles; thus, the distribution cannot be perfectly uncorrelated. In practice, media with even more significant correlations are common; a variety of physical effects that lead to them are described by Bitterli et al. (2018b). Both d'Eon (2018) and Jarabo et al. (2018) developed generalizations of the equation of transfer that allow non-exponential media. Bitterli et al. (2018b) presented a more general path integral form of it that maintains reciprocity and allows heterogeneous media.

Jakob et al. (2010) derived a generalized transfer equation that describes scattering by distributions of oriented particles. They proposed a *microflake* scattering model as a specific example of a particle distribution (where a microflake is the volumetric analog of a microfacet on a surface) and showed a number of ways of solving this equation based on Monte Carlo, finite elements, and a dipole model. More recently, Heitz et al. (2015) derived a generalized microflake distribution, which is considerably more efficient to sample and evaluate. Their model quantifies the local scattering properties using projected areas observed from different directions, which adds a well-defined notion of volumetric level of detail. Zhao et al. (2016) and Loubet and Neyret (2018) developed techniques for downsampling microflake distributions while still maintaining their visual appearance.

The equation of transfer assumes that the index of refraction of a medium will only change at discrete boundaries, though many actual media have continuously varying indices of refraction. Ament et al. (2014) derived a variant of the equation of transfer that allows for this case and applied photon mapping to render images with it. Pediredla et al. (2020) further investigated this topic and developed an unbiased rendering algorithm for such media based on path tracing.

Handling fluorescence in the context of volumetric scattering introduces a number of complexities discussed by Mojzík et al. (2018), who also derived a fluorescence-aware sampling algorithm.

EXERCISES

⊘ **14.1**   Replace ratio tracking in the `VolPathIntegrator::SampleLd()` method with delta tracking. After you confirm that your changes converge to the correct result, measure the difference in performance and MSE in order to compare the Monte Carlo efficiency of the two approaches for a variety of volumetric data sets. Do you find any cases where delta tracking is more efficient? If so, can you explain why?

⊘ **14.2**   *Residual ratio tracking* can compute transmittance more efficiently than ratio tracking in dense media; it is based on finding lower bounds of σ_t in regions of space, analytically computing that portion of the transmittance, and then using ratio tracking for the remaining variation (Novák et al. 2014). Implement this approach in pbrt and measure its effectiveness. Note that you will need to make modifications to both the `Medium`'s `RayMajorantSegment` representation and the implementation of the `VolPathIntegrator` in order to do so.

⊘ **14.3**   The current implementation of `SampleT_maj()` consumes a new uniform random value for each `RayMajorantSegment` returned by the medium's iterator. Its sampling operation can alternatively be implemented using a single uniform value to sample a total optical thickness and then finding the point along the ray where that optical thickness has been accumulated. Modify `SampleT_maj()` to implement that approach and measure rendering performance. Is there a benefit compared to the current implementation?

⊘ **14.4**   It is not possible to directly sample emission in volumes with the current `Medium` interface. Thus, integrators are left to include emission only when their random walk through a medium happens to find a part of it that is emissive. This approach can be quite inefficient, especially for localized bright emission. Add methods to the `Medium` interface that allow for sampling emission and modify the direct lighting calculation in the `VolPathIntegrator` to use them. For inspiration, it may be worthwhile to read the papers by Villemin and Hery (2013) and Simon et al. (2017) on Monte Carlo sampling of 3D emissive volumes. Measure the improvement in efficiency with your approach. Are there any cases where it hurts performance?

⊘ **14.5**   While sampling distances in participating media according to the majorant is much more effective than sampling uniformly, it does not account for other factors that vary along the ray, such as the scattering coefficient and phase function or variation in illumination from light sources. Implement the approach described by Wrenninge and Villemin (2020) on product sampling based on adapting the majorant to account for multiple factors in the integrand and then randomly selecting among weighted sample points. (You may find weighted reservoir sampling (Section A.2) a useful technique to apply in order to avoid the storage costs of maintaining the candidate samples.) Measure the performance of your implementation as well as how much it improves image quality for tricky volumetric scenes.

⊘ **14.6**   Add the capability to specify a bump or normal map for the bottom interface in the `LayeredBxDF`. (The current implementation applies bump mapping at the top interface only.) Render images that show the difference between perturbing the normal at the top interface and having a smooth bottom interface and vice versa.

⊘ **14.7**   Investigate the effect of improving the sampling patterns used in the `LayeredBxDF`—for example, by replacing the uniform random numbers used with low-discrepancy points. You may need to pass further information through the BSDF evaluation routines to do so, such as the current pixel, pixel sample, and current ray depth.

Measure how much error is reduced by your changes as well as their performance impact.

⬤ **14.8** Generalize the `LayeredBxDF` to allow the specification of an arbitrary number of layers with different media between them. You may want to review the improved sampling techniques for this case that were introduced by Gamboa et al. (2020). Verify that your implementation gives equivalent results to nested application of the `LayeredBxDF` and measure the efficiency difference between the two approaches.

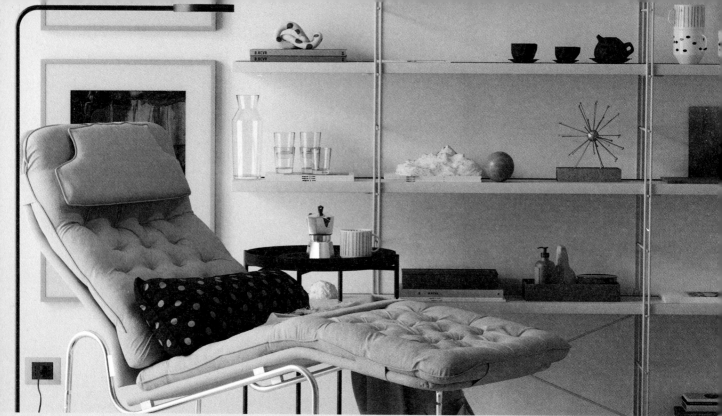

CHAPTER FIFTEEN

★ 15 WAVEFRONT RENDERING ON GPUS

One of the major changes in pbrt for this edition of the book is the addition of support for rendering on GPUs as well as on CPUs. Between the substantial computational capabilities that GPUs offer and the recent availability of custom hardware units for efficient ray intersection calculations, the GPU is a compelling target for ray tracing. For example, the image in Figure 15.1 takes 318.6 seconds to render with pbrt on a 2020-era high-end GPU at 1500×1500 resolution with 2048 samples per pixel. On an 8-core CPU, it takes 11,983 seconds to render with the same settings—over 37 times longer. Even on a high-end 32-core CPU, it takes 2,669 seconds to render (still over 8 times longer).[1]

pbrt's GPU rendering path offers only a single integration algorithm: volumetric path tracing, following the algorithms used in the CPU-based VolPathIntegrator described in Section 14.2.3. It otherwise supports all of pbrt's functionality, using the same classes and functions that have been presented in the preceding 14 chapters. This chapter will therefore not introduce any new rendering algorithms but instead will focus on topics like parallelism and data layout in memory that are necessary to achieve good performance on GPUs.

The integrator described in this chapter, WavefrontPathIntegrator, is structured using a *wavefront* architecture—effectively, many rays are processed simultaneously, with rendering work organized in queues that collect related tasks to be processed together. ("Wavefront" in this context will be defined more precisely in Section 15.1.2.)

Some of the code discussed in this chapter makes more extensive use of advanced C++ features than we have generally used in previous chapters. While we have tried not to use such features unnecessarily, we will see that in some cases they make it possible to generate highly specialized code that runs much more efficiently than if their capabilities are not used. We had previously sidestepped many low-level optimizations due to their comparatively

VolPathIntegrator 877

WavefrontPathIntegrator 939

---

1 For these measurements, the GPU was an NVIDIA RTX 3090. The 8-core CPU was a 3.6GHz Intel Core i9, and the 32-core CPU was a 3.7GHz AMD Ryzen Threadripper 3970X.

Figure 15.1: Scene Used for CPU versus GPU Ray Tracing Performance Comparison. *(Scene courtesy of Angelo Ferretti.)*

small impact on CPUs. Such implementation-level decisions can, however, change rendering performance by orders of magnitude when targeting GPUs.

The WavefrontPathIntegrator imposes three requirements on a GPU platform:

1. It must support a *unified address space*, where the CPU and GPU can both access the GPU's memory, using pointers that are consistent on both types of processor. This capability is integral to being able to parse the scene description and initialize the scene representation on the CPU, including initializing pointer-based data structures there, before the same data structures are then used in code that runs on the GPU.
2. The GPU compilation infrastructure must be compatible with C++17, the language that the rest of pbrt is implemented in. This makes it possible to use the same class and function implementations on both types of processors.
3. The GPU must have support for ray tracing, either in hardware or in vendor-supplied software. (pbrt's existing acceleration structures would not be efficient on the GPU in their present form.)

The attentive reader will note that CPUs themselves fulfill all of those requirements, the third potentially via pbrt's acceleration structures from Chapter 7. Therefore, pbrt makes it possible to execute the WavefrontPathIntegrator on CPUs as well; it is used if the --wavefront

WavefrontPathIntegrator 939

command-line option is provided. However, the wavefront organization is usually not a good fit for CPUs and performance is almost always worse than if the VolPathIntegrator is used instead. Nonetheless, the CPU wavefront path is useful for debugging and testing the WavefrontPathIntegrator implementation on systems that do not have suitable GPUs.

At this writing, the only GPUs that provide all three of these capabilities are based on NVIDIA's CUDA platform, so NVIDIA's GPUs are the only ones that pbrt currently supports. We hope that it will be possible to support others in the future. Around two thousand lines of platform-specific code are required to handle low-level details like allocating unified memory, launching work on the GPU, and performing ray intersections on the GPU. As usual, we will not include platform-specific code in the book, but see the gpu/ directory in the pbrt source code distribution for its implementation.

15.1 MAPPING PATH TRACING TO THE GPU

Achieving good performance on GPUs requires some care in how computation is organized and how data is laid out in memory. We will start with an overview of how GPUs work and the ways in which they differ from CPUs. This foundation makes it possible to discuss the design space of GPU ray tracers. After summarizing some of the alternatives, we give an overview of the design of the wavefront path integrator, which subsequent sections will delve into more deeply.

15.1.1 BASIC GPU ARCHITECTURE

The performance difference between CPUs and GPUs stems from a fundamental difference in the computations that they are designed for. CPUs have long been designed to minimize *latency*—to run a single thread of computation as efficiently as possible, finishing its work as quickly as possible. (This has somewhat changed with the advent of multicore CPUs, though each core remains latency optimized.) In contrast, GPUs target *throughput*: they are designed to work on many computations in parallel and finish all of them quickly, which is a different thing than finishing any one of them as quickly as possible.

The focus on throughput allows GPUs to devote much less space on the chip for caches, branch prediction hardware, out-of-order execution units, and other features that have been invented to improve single-thread performance on CPUs. Thus, given a fixed amount of chip area, GPUs are able to provide many more of the arithmetic logic units (ALUs) that actually perform computation than a CPU provides. Yet, more ALUs do not necessarily deliver more performance: they must be kept occupied doing useful work.

An ALU cannot perform computation if the input values it requires are not available. On current processors, reading a value from memory consumes a few hundred processor cycles, and so it is important to avoid the situation where a processor remains idle while it waits for the completion of such read operations—substantial amounts of potential computation might be lost. CPUs and GPUs approach this problem quite differently. Understanding each helps illuminate their philosophical differences.

CPUs apply a barrage of techniques to this task. They feature a relatively large amount of on-chip memory in the form of caches; if a memory request targets a location that is already present in a cache, the result can be returned much more quickly than reading from dynamic random access memory (DRAM). Cache memory access typically takes from a handful of cycles to at most a few tens of them. When it is necessary to wait for a memory read, CPUs also use out-of-order execution, continuing to execute the program's instructions past the read instruction. Dependencies are carefully tracked during this process, and operations that are

VolPathIntegrator 877
WavefrontPathIntegrator 939

independent of pending computations can execute out of order. The CPU may also execute instructions speculatively, ready to roll back their effects if it turns out they should not have run. If all of that does not suffice, another thread may be available, ready to start executing—modern CPUs generally use *hyperthreading* to switch to another thread in the event of a stall. This thread switch can be performed without any overhead, which is much better than the thousands of processor cycles it takes for the operating system to perform a context switch.

GPUs instead focus on a single mechanism to address such latencies: much more aggressive thread switching, over many more threads than are used for hyperthreading on CPUs. If one thread reads from memory, a GPU will just switch to another, saving all of the complexity and chip area required for out-of-order execution logic. If that other thread issues a read, then yet another is scheduled. Given enough threads and computation between memory accesses, such an approach is sufficient to keep the ALUs fed with useful work while avoiding long periods of inactivity.

An implication of this design is that GPUs require much more parallelism than CPUs to run at their peak potential. While tens of threads—or at most a few hundred—suffice to fully utilize a modern multicore CPU, a GPU may require tens of thousands of them. Path tracing fortunately involves millions of independent calculations (one per pixel sample), which makes it a good fit for throughput-oriented architectures like GPUs.

Thread Execution

GPUs contain an array of independent processors, numbered from the tens up to nearly a hundred at writing. We will not often need to consider these in the following, but will denote them as *processors* when we do.[2] Each one typically executes 32 or 64 threads concurrently, with as many as a thousand threads available to be scheduled.

The execution model of GPUs centers around the concept of a *kernel*, which refers to a GPU-targeted function that is executed by a specified number of threads. Parameters passed to the kernel are forwarded to each thread; a *thread index* provides the information needed to distinguish one thread from another. *Launching* a kernel refers to the operation that informs the GPU that a particular kernel function should be executed concurrently. This differs from an ordinary function call in the sense that the kernel will complete asynchronously at some later point. Frameworks like CUDA provide extensive API functionality to wait for the conclusion of such asynchronous computation, or to enforce ordering constraints between multiple separate kernel launches. Launching vast numbers of threads on the GPU is extremely efficient, so there is no need to amortize this cost using a thread pool, as is done in pbrt's ThreadPool class for CPU parallelism.

Kernels may be launched both from the CPU and from the GPU, though pbrt only does the former. In contrast to an ordinary function call, a kernel launch cannot return any values to the caller. Kernels therefore must write their results to memory before exiting.

An important hardware simplification that distinguishes CPUs and GPUs is that GPUs bundle multiple threads into what we will refer to as a *thread group*.[3] This group (32 threads on most current GPUs) executes instructions together, which means that a single instruction decoder can be shared by the group instead of requiring one for each executing thread. Consequently, silicon die area that would ordinarily be needed for instruction decoding can be dedicated to improving parallelism in the form of additional ALUs. Most GPU programming

---

ThreadPool 1102

2   These correspond to *compute units* on AMD GPUs, *execution units* on Intel GPUs, and *streaming multiprocessors* on NVIDIA GPUs.

3   This term corresponds to a *subgroup* in OpenCL and Vulkan, a *warp* in CUDA's model, and a *wavefront* on AMD GPUs.

models further organize thread groups into larger aggregations—though these are not used in pbrt's GPU implementation, so we will not discuss them further here.

While the hardware simplifications enabled by thread groups allow for additional parallelism, the elimination of per-thread instruction decoders also brings limitations that can have substantial performance implications. Efficient GPU implementation of algorithms requires a thorough understanding of them. Although the threads in a thread group are free to work independently, just as the threads on different CPU cores are, the more that they follow similar paths through the program, the better performance will be achieved. This is a different performance model than for CPUs and can be a subtle point to consider when optimizing code: performance is not just a consequence of the computation performed by an individual thread, but also how often that same computation is performed at the same time with other threads within the same group.

For example, consider this simple block of code:

```
if (condition) a();
else b();
```

Executed on a CPU, the processor will test the condition and then execute either a() or b() depending on the condition's value. On a GPU, the situation is more complex: if all the threads in a thread group follow the same control flow path, then execution proceeds as it does on a CPU. However, if some threads need to evaluate a() and some b(), then the GPU will execute both functions' instructions with a subset of the threads disabled for each one. These disabled threads represent a wasted opportunity to perform useful work.

In the worst case, a computation could be serialized all the way down to the level of individual threads, resulting in a $32\times$ loss of performance that would largely negate the benefits of the GPU. Algorithms like path tracing are especially susceptible to this type of behavior, which is a consequence of the physical characteristics of light: when a beam of light interacts with an object, it will tend to spread out and eventually reach every part of the environment with nonzero probability. Suppose that a bundle of rays is processed by a thread group: due to this property, an initially coherent computation could later encounter many different shapes and materials that are implemented in different parts of the system. Additional work is necessary to reorder computation into coherent groups to avoid such degenerate behavior.

The implementation of the FloatMixTexture::Evaluate() method from Section 10.3.3 can be better understood with thread groups in mind. Its body was:

```
Float amt = amount.Evaluate(ctx);
Float t1 = 0, t2 = 0;
if (amt != 1) t1 = tex1.Evaluate(ctx);
if (amt != 0) t2 = tex2.Evaluate(ctx);
return (1 - amt) * t1 + amt * t2;
```

A more natural implementation might have been the following, which computes the same result in the end:

```
Float amt = amount.Evaluate(ctx);
if (amt == 0) return tex1.Evaluate(ctx);
if (amt == 1) return tex2.Evaluate(ctx);
return (1 - amt) * tex1.Evaluate(ctx) + amt * tex2.Evaluate(ctx);
```

FloatMixTexture::Evaluate()
659

Considered under the lens of GPU execution, we can see the benefit of the first implementation. If some of the threads have a value of 0 for amt, some have a value of 1, and the rest have a value in between, then the second implementation will execute the code for evaluating tex1

Table 15.1: Key Properties of a Representative Modern CPU and GPU. This CPU and GPU have approximately the same cost at time of writing but provide their computational capabilities using very different architectures. This table summarizes some of their most important characteristics.

	AMD 3970x CPU	NVIDIA 3090 RTX GPU
Processors	32	82
Peak single-precision TFLOPS	3.8	36
Peak memory bandwidth	$\sim$ 100 GiB/s	936 GiB/s

and tex2 twice, for a different subset of threads for each time.[4] With the first implementation, all of the threads that need to evaluate tex1 do so together, and similarly for tex2.

We will say that execution across a thread group is *converged* when all of the threads follow the same control flow path through the program, and that it has become *divergent* at points in the program execution where some threads follow one path and others follow another through the program code. Some divergence is inevitable, but the less there is the better. Convergence can be improved both by writing individual blocks of code to minimize the number of separate control paths and by sorting work so that all of the threads in a thread block do the same thing. This latter idea will come up repeatedly in Section 15.3 when we discuss the set of kernels that the WavefrontPathIntegrator executes.

One implication of thread groups is that techniques like Russian roulette may have a different performance impact on a CPU than on a GPU. With pbrt's CPU integrators, if a ray path is terminated with Russian roulette, the CPU thread can immediately go on to start work on a new path. Depending on how the rendering computation is mapped to threads on a GPU, terminating one ray path may not have the same benefit if it just leads to an idle thread being carried along with an otherwise still-active thread group.

Memory Hierarchy

Large differences in the memory system architectures of CPUs and GPUs further affect how a system should be structured to run efficiently on each type of processor. Table 15.1 summarizes some relevant quantities for a representative modern CPU and GPU that at the time of this writing have roughly the same cost.

Two differences are immediately apparent: the peak memory bandwidth and number of TFLOPS (trillions of floating point operations per second) are both approximately ten times higher on the GPU. It is also clear that neither processor is able to reach its peak performance solely by operating on values stored in memory. For example, the 3.8 TFLOPS that the CPU is capable of would require 15.2 TB/s of memory bandwidth if each 4-byte floating-point value operated on was to be read from memory. Consequently, we can see that the performance of a computation such as iterating over a large array, reading each value, squaring it, and writing the result back to memory would not be limited by the processor's computational capabilities but would be limited by the memory bandwidth. We say that such computations are *bandwidth limited*.

A useful measurement of a computation is its *arithmetic intensity*, which is usually measured as the number of floating-point operations performed per byte of memory accessed. Dividing peak TFLOPS by peak memory bandwidth gives a measurement of how much arithmetic

---

4   This assumes that the compiler is unable to automatically restructure the code in the way that we have done manually. It might, but it might not; our experience has been that it is best not to expect too much of compilers in such ways, lest they disappoint.

Table 15.2: Key Properties of the Example CPU and GPU Processors. This table summarizes a few relevant per-processor quantities for the CPU and GPU in Table 15.1. For the CPU, "maximum available threads" is the number that can be switched to without incurring the cost of an operating system thread switch. Furthermore, the number of CPU registers here is the total available for out-of-order execution, which is many more than are visible through the instruction set. The L2 cache on the GPU is shared across all processors and the L3 cache on the CPU is shared across four processors; here we report those cache sizes divided by the number of processors that share them.

	AMD 3970x CPU	NVIDIA 3090 RTX GPU
Concurrently executing threads	1	32
Maximum available threads	2	1,024
`float` operations per cycle & thread	32	2
Registers	160 (`float`)	65,536
L1 cache	32 KiB (data)	128 KiB
L2 cache	512 KiB	~ 75 KiB
L3 cache	4 MiB	none

intensity a processor requires to achieve its peak performance. For this CPU, we can see that it is roughly 38 floating-point operations (FLOPS) per byte, or 152 FLOPS for every 4-byte `float` read from memory. For the GPU, the values are 38.5 and 154, respectively— remarkably, almost exactly the same. Given such arithmetic intensity requirements, it is easy to become bandwidth limited.

Therefore, there must be some combination of reuse of each value read from memory and reuse of intermediate computed values that are stored in on-chip memory in order to reach peak floating-point performance. Both the processors' register files and cache hierarchies are integral to keeping them working productively by making some values available from faster on-chip memory, though their effect is quite different on the two types of architecture. See Table 15.2, which presents additional quantities related to the individual processors on the example CPU and GPU.

To understand the differences, it is illuminating to compare the two in terms of their cache size with respect to the number of threads that they are running. (Space in the caches is not explicitly allocated to threads, though this is still a useful thought exercise.) This CPU runs one thread at a time on each core, with a second ready for hyperthreading, giving 16 KiB of L1 cache, 256 KiB of L2, and 2 MiB of L3 cache for each of the two threads. This is enough memory to give a fairly wide window for the reuse of previous values and is enough that, for example, we do not need to worry about how big the SurfaceInteraction structure is (it is just under 256 bytes); it fits comfortably in the caches close to the processor. These generous cache hierarchies can be a great help to programmers, leaving them with the task of making sure their programs have some locality in their memory accesses but often allowing them not to worry over it too much further.

The GPU runs thread groups of 32 threads, with as many as 31 additional thread groups ready to switch to, for a total of 1,024 threads afoot. We are left with 128 bytes of L1 cache and 75 bytes of L2 per thread, meaning factors of 128× and 3500× less than the CPU, respectively. If the GPU threads are accessing independent memory locations, we are left with a very small window of potential data reuse that can be served by the caches. Thus, structuring GPU computation so that threads access the same locations in memory as much as possible can significantly improve performance by making the caches more effective.

SurfaceInteraction 138

GPUs partially make up for their small caches with large register files; for the one in this comparison there are 65,536 32-bit registers for each GPU processor, giving 64 or more for each thread. (Note that this register file actually has twice as much total storage as the processor's L1 cache.) If a computation can be structured such that it fits into its allocation of registers and has limited memory traffic (especially reads that are different than other threads'), then its computation can achieve high performance on the GPU.

The allocation of registers to a kernel must be determined at compile time; this presents a balance for the compiler to strike. On one hand, allocating more registers to a kernel gives it more on-chip storage and, in turn, generally reduces the amount of memory bandwidth that it requires. However, the more registers that are allocated to a kernel, the fewer threads can be scheduled on a processor. For the example GPU, allocating 64 registers for each thread of a kernel means that 1,024 threads can run on a processor at once. 128 registers per thread means just 512 threads, and so forth. The fewer threads that are running, the more difficult it is to hide memory latency via thread switching, and performance may suffer when all threads are stalled waiting for memory reads.

The effect of these constraints is that reducing the size of objects can significantly improve performance on the GPU: doing so reduces the amount of bandwidth consumed when reading them from memory (and so may improve performance if a computation is bandwidth limited) and can reduce the number of registers consumed to store them after they have been loaded, potentially allowing more threads and thus more effective latency hiding. This theme will come up repeatedly later in the chapter.

The coherence of the memory locations accessed by the threads in a thread group affects performance as well. A reasonable model for thinking about this is in terms of the processor's cache lines. A common GPU cache line size is 128 bytes. The cost of a memory access by the threads in a thread group is related to the total number of cache lines that the threads access. The best case is that they all access the same cache line, for a location that is already in the cache. (Thus with a 128-byte cache line size, 32 threads accessing successive cache line–aligned 4-byte values such as floats access a single cache line.) Performance remains reasonable if the locations accessed correspond to a small number of cache lines that are already in the cache.

An entire cache line must be read for a cache miss. Here as well, the coherence of the locations accessed by the threads has a big impact on performance: if all locations are in a single cache line, then a single memory read can be performed. If all 32 threads access locations that lie in different cache lines, then 32 independent memory reads are required; not only is there a significant bandwidth cost to reading so much data, but there is much more memory latency—likely more than can be effectively hidden. Thus, another important theme in the following implementation will be organizing data structures and computation in order to improve the coherence of memory locations accessed by the threads in a thread group.

A final issue related to memory performance arises due to the various different types of memory that can be referenced by a computation. The GPU has its own *device memory*, distinct from the *host memory* used by the CPU. Each GPU processor offers a small high-performance *shared memory* that can be used by the threads running on it.[5] It is best interpreted as a manually managed cache. Shared memory and L1 and L2 caches provide much higher bandwidth and lower latency than device memory, while host memory is the most expensive for the GPU to access: any read or write must be encapsulated into a transaction that is sent over the comparably slow PCI Express bus connecting the CPU and GPU. Optimally placing and, if necessary, moving data in memory during multiple phases of a computation requires expertise and extra engineering effort.

---

5   Shared memory corresponds to local memory in OpenCL, thread group shared memory in DirectX Compute, and shared memory in CUDA.

pbrt sidesteps this issue using *managed memory*, which exists in a unified address space that can be accessed from both CPU and GPU. Its physical location is undecided and can migrate on demand to improve performance. This automatic migration comes at a small additional performance cost, but this is well worth the convenience of not having to micromanage memory allocations. In pbrt, the CPU initializes the scene in managed memory, and this migration cost is paid once when rendering on the GPU begins. There is then a small cost to read back the final image from the Film at the end. In the following implementation, as CPU code is launching kernels on the GPU, it is important that it does not inadvertently access GPU memory, which would harm performance.

15.1.2 STRUCTURING RENDERING COMPUTATION

With these factors that affect GPU performance in mind, we can consider various ways of structuring pbrt's rendering computation so that it is suitable for the GPU. First, consider applying the same parallelism decomposition that is used in the ImageTileIntegrator: assigning each tile of the image to a thread that is then responsible for evaluating its pixel samples. Such an approach is hopeless from the start. Not only is it unlikely to provide a sufficient number of threads to fill the GPU, but the effect of the load imbalance among tiles is exacerbated when the threads execute in groups. (Recall Figure 1.17, the histogram of time spent rendering image tiles in Figure 1.11.) Since a thread group continues executing until all of its threads have finished, performance is worse if the long-running threads are spread across many different thread groups versus all together in fewer.

Another natural approach might be to assign each pixel sample to a thread, launching as many threads as there are pixel samples, and to have each thread execute the same code as runs on the CPU to evaluate a pixel sample. Each thread's task then would be to generate a camera ray, find the closest intersection, evaluate the material and textures at the intersection point, and so forth. This is known as the *megakernel* approach, since a single large kernel is responsible for all rendering computation for a ray. This approach provides more than sufficient parallelism to the GPU, but suffers greatly from execution divergence. While the computation may remain converged until intersections are found, if different rays hit objects with different materials, or the same material but with different textures, their execution will diverge and performance will quickly deteriorate.

Even if the camera rays all hit objects with the same material, coherence will generally be lost with tracing the first batch of indirect rays: some may find no intersection and leave the scene, others may hit objects with various materials, and yet others may end up scattering in participating media. Each different case leads to execution divergence. Even if all the threads end up sampling a light BVH, for instance, they may not do so at the same time and thus that code may be executed multiple times, just as was the case for the inferior approach of implementing the FloatMixTexture Evaluate() method. We can expect that over time all of the threads will fully diverge, leading to processing that is less efficient than it could be by a factor of the number of threads in a thread group.

The performance of a megakernel ray tracer can be improved with the addition of work scheduling and reordering within the executing kernels. Such a megakernel ray tracer can be seen as what is effectively a thread group–wide state machine that successively chooses an operation to perform: "generate camera rays," "find closest intersections," "evaluate and sample diffuse BSDFs," "sample the light BVH," and so forth. It might choose among operations based on how many threads would like to perform the corresponding operation.

This approach can greatly improve execution convergence. For example, if only a single thread is waiting to evaluate and sample diffuse BSDFs, that work can be deferred while other threads trace rays and do other rendering work. Perhaps some of those rays will intersect diffuse surfaces, adding themselves to the tally of threads that need to do that operation. When that operation is eventually selected, it can be done for the benefit of more threads, redundant executions saved.

Direct implementation of the megakernel approach does have disadvantages. The megakernels themselves may be comprised of a large amount of code (effectively, everything that the renderer needs to do), which can lead to long compilation times depending on the sophistication of the ray tracer. They are further limited to finding shared work among the threads in a thread group or, at most, the threads running on a single GPU processor. It therefore may not be possible to achieve an optimal degree of thread convergence. Nevertheless, the approach is a good one, and is the most common one for real-time ray tracers today.

The other main GPU ray tracer architecture is termed *wavefront*. A wavefront ray tracer separates the main operations into separate kernels, each one operating on many pixel samples in parallel: for example, there might be one kernel that generates camera rays, another that finds ray intersections, perhaps one to evaluate diffuse materials and another to evaluate dielectrics, and so forth. The kernels are organized in a dataflow architecture, where each one may enqueue additional work to be performed in one or more subsequent kernels.

A significant advantage of the wavefront approach is that execution in each kernel can start out fully converged: the diffuse-material kernel is invoked for only the intersection points with a diffuse material, and so forth. While the execution may diverge within the kernel, regularly starting out with converged execution can greatly aid performance, especially for systems with a wide variety of materials, BSDFs, lights, and so forth.

Another advantage of the wavefront approach is that different numbers of registers can be allocated to different kernels. Thus, simple kernels can use fewer registers and reap benefits in more effective latency hiding, and it is only the more complex kernels that incur the costs of that trade-off. In contrast, the register allocation for a megakernel must be made according to the worst case across the entire set of rendering computation.

However, wavefront ray tracers pay a cost in bandwidth. Because data does not persist on-chip between kernel launches, each kernel must read all of its inputs from memory and then write its results back to it. In contrast, megakernels can often keep intermediate information on-chip. The performance of a wavefront ray tracer is more likely than a megakernel to be limited by the amount of memory bandwidth and not the GPU's computational capabilities. This is an undesirable state of affairs since it is projected that bandwidth will continue to grow more slowly than computation in future processor architectures.

The recent addition of hardware ray-tracing capabilities to GPUs has led to the development of graphics programming interfaces that allow the user to specify which kernels to run at various stages of ray tracing. This gives an alternative to the megakernel and wavefront approaches that avoids many of their respective disadvantages. With these APIs, the user not only provides single kernels for operations like generating initial rays, but can also specify multiple kernels to run at ray intersection points—where the kernel that runs at a given point might be determined based on an object's material, for example. Scheduling computation and orchestrating the flow of data between stages is not the user's concern, and the GPU's hardware and software has the opportunity to schedule work in a way that is tuned to the hardware architecture. (The semantics of these APIs are discussed further in Section 15.3.6.)

15.1.3 SYSTEM OVERVIEW

This version of pbrt adopts the wavefront approach for its GPU rendering path, although some of its kernels fuse together multiple stages of the ray-tracing computation in order to

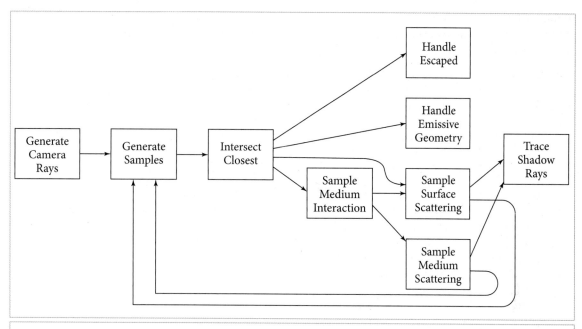

Figure 15.2: Overview of Kernels Used in the Wavefront Integrator. Arrows correspond to queues on which kernels may enqueue work for subsequent kernels. After camera rays have been generated, the subsequent kernels execute one time for each ray depth up to the maximum depth.

reduce the amount of memory traffic that is used. We found this approach to be a good fit given the variety of materials, BxDFs, and light sources that pbrt supports. Further, rendering features like volume scattering fit in nicely: we can skip the corresponding kernels entirely if the scene does not include those effects.

As with the CPU-targeted Integrators, a BasicScene parses the scene description and stores various entities that represent scene components. When the wavefront integrator is being used, the parsed scene is then passed to the RenderWavefront() function, which is defined in the file wavefront/wavefront.cpp. Beyond some housekeeping, its main task is to allocate an instance of the WavefrontPathIntegrator class and to call its Render() method. Since the housekeeping is not very interesting, we will not include its implementation here.

The WavefrontPathIntegrator constructor converts many of the entities in the BasicScene to pbrt objects in the same way as is done for the CPU renderer: all the lights are converted to corresponding instances of the Light classes, and similarly for the camera, film, sampler, light sampler, media, materials, and textures. One important difference, however, is that the Allocator that is provided for them allocates managed memory so that it can be initialized on the CPU and accessed by the GPU. Another difference is that only some shapes are handled with pbrt's Shape implementations. Shapes like triangles that have native support from the GPU's ray intersection hardware are instead handled using that hardware. Finally, image map textures use a specialized implementation that uses the GPU's texturing hardware for texture lookups.

Once the scene representation is ready, a call to WavefrontPathIntegrator::Render() starts the rendering process. The details of the implementation of that method will be the subject of the following sections of this chapter, but Figure 15.2 gives an overview of the kernels that

it launches.[6] The sequence of computations is similar to that of the VolPathIntegrator::Li()
method, though decomposed into kernels. Queues are used to buffer work between kernels:
each kernel can push work onto one or more queues to be processed in subsequent kernels.

Rendering starts with a kernel that generates camera rays for a number of pixel samples
(typically, a million or so). Given camera rays, the loop up to the maximum ray depth can
begin. Each time through the loop, the following kernels are executed:

- First, samples for use with the ray are generated using the Sampler and stored in memory
  for use in later kernels.
- The closest intersection of each ray is found with the scene geometry. The kernel that
  finds these intersections pushes work onto a variety of queues to be processed by other
  kernels, including a queue for rays that escape the scene, one for rays that hit emissive
  geometry, and another for rays that pass through participating media. Rays that intersect
  surfaces are pushed onto queues that partition work based on material types.
- Rays passing through participating media are then processed, possibly leading to a
  shadow ray and an indirect ray being enqueued if the ray scatters. Unscattered rays that
  were earlier found to have intersected a surface are pushed on to the same variety of
  queues as are used in the intersection kernel for rays not passing through media.
- Rays that have intersected emissive geometry and rays that have left the scene are handled by two kernels that both update rays' radiance estimates to incorporate the effect of
  emission found by such rays.
- Each material is then handled individually, with separate kernels specialized based on
  the material type. Textures are evaluated to initialize a BSDF and a light is sampled. This,
  too, leads to indirect and shadow rays being enqueued.
- A final kernel traces shadow rays and incorporates their contributions into the rays' radiance estimates, including accounting for absorption along rays in participating media.

Until the maximum ray depth, the loop then starts again with the queued indirect rays
replacing the camera rays as the rays to trace next.

15.2 IMPLEMENTATION FOUNDATIONS

Before we discuss the implementation of the wavefront integrator and the details of its
kernels, we will start by discussing some of the lower-level capabilities that it is built upon, as
well as the abstractions that we use to hide the details of platform-specific APIs.

15.2.1 EXECUTION AND MEMORY SPACE SPECIFICATION

If you have perused the pbrt source code, you will have noticed that the signatures of many
functions include a PBRT_CPU_GPU. We have elided all of these from the book text thus far in
the interests of avoiding distraction. Now we must pay closer attention to them.

When pbrt is compiled with GPU support, the compiler must know whether each function
in the system is intended for CPU execution only, GPU execution only, or execution on both
types of processor. In some cases, a function may only be able to run on one of the two—for
example, if it uses low-level functionality that the other type of processor does not support.
In other cases, it may be possible for it to run on both, though it may not make sense to do so.

BSDF 544

Sampler 469

VolPathIntegrator::Li() 878

---

6   In describing the WavefrontPathIntegrator in the remainder of this chapter, we will frequently use the terminology
    of "launching kernels" to describe its operation, even though when it is running on the CPU, "launch" is just a
    function call, and a kernel is a regular class method.

For example, an object constructor that does extensive serial processing would be unsuited to the GPU.

PBRT_CPU_GPU hides the platform-specific details of how these characteristics are indicated. (With CUDA, it turns into a __host__ __device__ specifier.) There is also a PBRT_GPU macro, which signifies that a function can only be called from GPU code. These macros are all defined in the file pbrt.h. If no specifier is provided, a function can only be called from code that is running on the CPU.

These specifiers can be used with variable declarations as well, to similar effect. pbrt only makes occasional use of them for that, mostly using managed memory for such purposes. (There is also a PBRT_CONST variable qualifier that is used to define large constant arrays in a way that makes them accessible from both CPU and GPU.)

In addition to informing the compiler of which processors to compile functions for, having these specifiers in the signatures of functions allows the compiler to determine whether a function call is valid: a CPU-only function that directly calls a GPU-only function, or vice versa, leads to a compile time error.

15.2.2 LAUNCHING KERNELS ON THE GPU

pbrt also provides functions that abstract the platform-specific details of launching kernels on the GPU. These are all defined in the files gpu/util.h and gpu/util.cpp.

The most important of them is GPUParallelFor(), which launches a specified number of GPU threads and invokes the provided kernel function for each one, passing it an index ranging from zero up to the total number of threads. The index values passed always span a contiguous range for all of the threads in a thread group. This is an important property in that, for example, indexing into a float array using the index leads to contiguous memory accesses.

This function is the GPU analog to ParallelFor(), with the differences that it always starts iteration from zero, rather than taking a 1D range, and that it takes a description string that describes the kernel's functionality. Its implementation includes code that tracks the total time each kernel spends executing on the GPU, which makes it possible to print a performance breakdown after rendering completes using the provided description string.

⟨*GPU Launch Function Declarations*⟩ ≡
```
template <typename F>
void GPUParallelFor(const char *description, int nItems, F func);
```

Similar to ParallelFor(), all the work from one call to GPUParallelFor() finishes before any work from a subsequent call to GPUParallelFor() begins, and it, too, is also generally used with lambda functions. A simple example of its usage is below: the callback function func is invoked with a single integer argument, corresponding to the item index that it is responsible for. Note also that a PBRT_GPU specifier is necessary for the lambda function to indicate that it will be invoked from GPU code.

```
float *array = /* allocate managed memory */;
GPUParallelFor("Initialize array", 100,
               [=] PBRT_GPU (int i) { array[i] = i; });
```

GPUParallelFor() 929
ParallelFor() 1107

We provide a macro for specifying lambda functions for GPUParallelFor() and related functions that adds the PBRT_GPU specifier and also hides some platform-system specific details (which are not included in the text here).

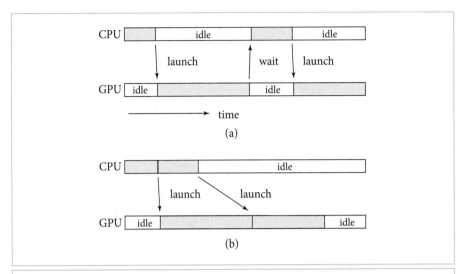

Figure 15.3: Comparison of Synchronous and Asynchronous CPU/GPU Execution. (a) If the two processors are synchronous, only one is ever executing. The CPU stalls after launching a kernel on the GPU, and then the GPU is idle after a kernel finishes until the CPU resumes and launches another one. (b) With the asynchronous model, the CPU continues execution after launching each kernel and is able to enqueue more of them while the GPU is working on earlier ones. In turn, the GPU does not need to wait for the next batch of work to do.

⟨*GPU Macro Definitions*⟩ ≡
```
#define PBRT_CPU_GPU_LAMBDA(...) [=] PBRT_CPU_GPU (__VA_ARGS__)
```

We do not provide a variant analogous to `ParallelFor2D()` for iterating over a 2D array, though it would be easy to do so; pbrt just has no need for such functionality.

Although execution is serialized between successive calls to `GPUParallelFor()`, it is important to be aware that the execution of the CPU and GPU are decoupled. When a call to `GPUParallelFor()` returns on the CPU, the corresponding threads on the GPU often will not even have been launched, let alone completed. Work on the GPU proceeds asynchronously. While this execution model thus requires explicit synchronization operations between the two processors, it is important for achieving high performance. Consider the two alternatives illustrated in Figure 15.3; automatically synchronizing execution of the two processors would mean that only one of them could be running at a given time.

An implication of this model is that the CPU must be careful about when it reads values from managed memory that were computed on the GPU. For example, if the implementation had code that tried to read the final image immediately after launching the last rendering kernel, it would almost certainly read an incomplete result. We therefore require a mechanism so that the CPU can wait for all the previous kernel launches to complete. This capability is provided by `GPUWait()`. Again, the implementation is not included here, as it is based on platform-specific functionality.

⟨*GPU Synchronization Function Declarations*⟩ ≡
```
void GPUWait();
```

15.2.3 STRUCTURE-OF-ARRAYS LAYOUT

ParallelFor2D() 1108
PBRT_CPU_GPU 928

As discussed earlier, the thread group execution model of GPUs affects the pattern of memory accesses that program execution generates. A consequence is that the way in which data is

Figure 15.4: Memory Layout of an Array of SimpleRay Structures. The elements of each ray are consecutive in memory.

laid out in memory can have a meaningful effect on performance. To understand the issue, consider the following definition of a ray structure:

```
struct SimpleRay {
    Point3f o;
    Vector3f d;
};
```

Now consider a kernel that takes a queue of SimpleRays as input. Such a kernel might be responsible for finding the closest intersection along each ray, for example. A natural representation of the queue would be an array of SimpleRays. (This layout is termed *array of structures*, and is sometimes abbreviated as *AOS*.) Such a queue would be laid out in memory as shown in Figure 15.4, where each SimpleRay occupies a contiguous region of memory with its elements stored in consecutive locations in memory.

Now consider what happens when the threads in a thread group read their corresponding ray into memory. If the pointer to the array is rays and the index passed to each thread's lambda function is i, then each thread might start out by reading its ray using code like

```
SimpleRay r = rays[i];
```

The generated code would typically load each component of the origins and directions individually. Figure 15.5(a) illustrates the distribution of memory locations accessed when each thread in a thread group loads the x component of its ray origin. The locations span many cache lines, which in turn incurs a performance cost.

An alternative layout is termed *structure of arrays*, or *SOA*. The idea behind this approach is to effectively transpose the layout of the object in memory, storing all the origins' x components contiguously in an array of Floats, then all of its origins' y components in another Float array, and so forth. We might declare a specialized structure to represent arrays of SimpleRays laid out like this:

```
struct SimpleRayArray {
    Float *ox, *oy, *oz;
    Float *dx, *dy, *dz;
};
```

In turn, if the threads in a thread group want to load the x component of their ray's origin, the expression rays.ox[i] suffices to load that value. The locations accessed are contiguous in memory and span many fewer cache lines[7] (Figure 15.5(b)).

---

7   Another alternative, *array of structures of arrays*, or *AOSOA*, offers a middle ground between AOS and SOA by repeatedly applying SOA with fixed-size (e.g., 32-element) arrays, collecting those in structures. This provides many of SOA's benefits while further improving memory access locality.

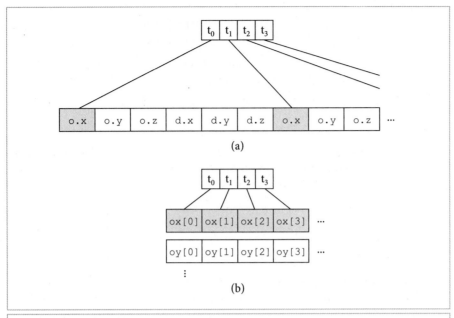

Figure 15.5: Effect of Memory Layout on Read Coherence. (a) When the threads in a thread group t_i load the x component of their ray origin with an array of structures layout, each thread reads from a memory location that is offset by `sizeof(SimpleRay)` from the previous one; in this case, 24 bytes, assuming 4-byte `Float`s. Consequently, multiple cache lines must be accessed, with corresponding performance cost. (b) With structure of arrays layout, the threads in a thread group access contiguous locations to read the x component, corresponding to 1 or at most 2 cache-line accesses, depending on the alignment of the array. Performance is generally much better.

However, this performance benefit comes at a cost of making the code more unwieldy. Loading an entire ray with this approach requires indexing into each of the constituent arrays—for example,

```
SimpleRay r(Point3f(rays.ox[i], rays.oy[i], rays.oz[i]),
            Vector3f(rays.dx[i], rays.dy[i], rays.dz[i]));
```

Even more verbose manual indexing is required for the task of writing a ray out to memory in SOA format; the cleanliness of the AOS array syntax has been lost.

In order to avoid such complexity, the code in the remainder of this chapter makes extensive use of SOA template types that make it possible to work with SOA data using syntax that is the same as array indexing with an array of structures data layout. For any type that has an SOA template specialization (e.g., pbrt's regular Ray class), we are able to write code like the following:

```
SOA<Ray> rays(1024, Allocator());
int index = ...;
Ray r = rays[index];
Transform transform = ...;
rays[index] = transform(r);
```

Both loads from and stores to the array are expressed using regular C++ array indexing syntax.

While it is straightforward programming to implement such SOA classes, doing so is rather tedious, especially if one has many types to lay out in SOA. Therefore, pbrt includes a small utility program, soac (*structure of arrays compiler*), that automates this process. Its source code is in the file cmd/soac.cpp in the pbrt distribution. There is not much to be proud of in its implementation, so we will not discuss that here, but we will describe its usage as well as the form of the SOA type definitions that it generates.

soac takes structure specifications in a custom format of the following form:

```
flat Float;
soa Point2f { Float x, y; };
```

Here, flat specifies that the following type should be stored directly in arrays, while soa specifies a structure. Although not shown here, soa structures can themselves hold other soa structure types. See the files pbrt.soa and wavefront/workitems.soa in the pbrt source code for more examples.

This format is easy to parse and is sufficient to provide the information necessary to generate pbrt's SOA type definitions. A more bulletproof solution (and one that would avoid the need for writing the code to parse a custom format) would be to modify a C++ compiler to optionally emit SOA type definitions for types it has already parsed. Of course, that is a more complex approach to implement than soac was.

When pbrt is compiled, soac is invoked to generate header files based on the *.soa specifications. For example, pbrt.soa is turned into pbrt_soa.h, which can be found in pbrt's build directory after the system has been compiled. For each soa type defined in a specification file, soac generates an SOA template specialization. Here is the one for Point2f. (Here we have taken automatically generated code and brought it into the book text for dissection, which is the opposite flow from all the other code in the text.)

⟨*Point2f* SOA *Definition*⟩ ≡
```
template <> struct SOA<Point2f> {
    ⟨Point2f SOA Types 934⟩
    ⟨Point2f SOA Public Methods 933⟩
    ⟨Point2f SOA Public Members 933⟩
};
```

The constructor uses a provided allocator to allocate space for individual arrays for the class member variables. The use of the this-> syntax for initializing the member variables may seem gratuitous, though it ensures that if one of the member variables has the same name as one of the constructor parameters, it is still initialized correctly.

⟨*Point2f* SOA *Public Methods*⟩ ≡   933
```
SOA(int n, Allocator alloc) : nAlloc(n) {
    this->x = alloc.allocate_object<Float>(n);
    this->y = alloc.allocate_object<Float>(n);
}
```

The SOA class's members store the array size and the individual member pointers. The PBRT_RESTRICT qualifier informs the compiler that no other pointer will point to these arrays, which can allow it to generate more efficient code.

⟨*Point2f* SOA *Public Members*⟩ ≡   933
```
int nAlloc;
Float * PBRT_RESTRICT x;
Float * PBRT_RESTRICT y;
```

It is easy to generate a method that allows indexing into the SOA arrays to read values. Note that the generated code requires that the class has a default constructor and that it can directly initialize the class's member variables. In the event that they are private, the class should use a `friend` declaration to make them available to its SOA specialization.

⟨*Point2f* SOA *Public Methods*⟩ +≡   933
```
Point2f operator[](int i) const {
    Point2f r;
    r.x = this->x[i];
    r.y = this->y[i];
    return r;
}
```

It is less obvious how to support assignment of values using the regular array indexing syntax. soac provides this capability through the indirection of an auxiliary class, `GetSetIndirector`. When `operator[]` is called with a non-const SOA object, it returns an instance of that class. It records not only a pointer to the SOA object but also the index value.

⟨*Point2f* SOA *Public Methods*⟩ +≡   933
```
GetSetIndirector operator[](int i) {
    return GetSetIndirector{this, i};
}
```

Assignment is handled by the `GetSetIndirector`'s `operator=` method. Given a `Point2f` value, it is able to perform the appropriate assignments using the SOA * and the index.

⟨*Point2f* SOA *Types*⟩ ≡   933
```
struct GetSetIndirector {
    void operator=(const Point2f &a) {
        soa->x[i] = a.x;
        soa->y[i] = a.y;
    }
    SOA *soa;
    int i;
};
```

Variables of type `GetSetIndirector` should never be declared explicitly. Rather, the role of this structure is to cause an assignment of the form `p[i] = Point2f(...)` to correspond to the following code, where the initial parenthesized expression corresponds to invoking the SOA class's `operator[]` to get a temporary `GetSetIndirector` and where the assignment is then handled by its `operator=` method.

```
(p.operator[](i)).operator=(Point2f(...));
```

`GetSetIndirector` also provides an `operator Point2f()` conversion operator (not included here) that handles the case of an SOA array read with a non-const SOA object.

We conclude with a caveat: SOA layout is effective if access is coherent, but can be detrimental if it is not. If threads are accessing an array of some structure type in an incoherent fashion, then AOS may be a better choice: in that case, although each thread's initial access to the structure may incur a cache miss, its subsequent accesses may be efficient if nearby values in the structure are still in the cache. Conversely, incoherent access to SOA data may incur a miss for each access to each structure member, polluting the cache by bringing in many unnecessary values that are not accessed by any other threads.

15.2.4 WORK QUEUES

Our last bit of groundwork before getting back into rendering will be to define two classes that manage the input and output of kernels in the ray-tracing pipeline. Both are defined in the file wavefront/workqueue.h.

First is WorkQueue, which represents a queue of objects of a specified type, WorkItem. The items in the queue are stored in SOA layout; this is achieved by publicly inheriting from the SOA template class for the item type. This inheritance also allows the items in the work queue to be indexed using regular array indexing syntax, via the SOA public methods.

⟨*WorkQueue Definition*⟩ ≡
```
template <typename WorkItem>
class WorkQueue : public SOA<WorkItem> {
  public:
    ⟨WorkQueue Public Methods 935⟩
  protected:
    ⟨WorkQueue Protected Methods 936⟩
  private:
    ⟨WorkQueue Private Members 935⟩
};
```

The constructor takes the maximum number of objects that can be stored in the queue as well as an allocator, but leaves the actual allocation to the SOA base class.

⟨*WorkQueue Public Methods*⟩ ≡   935
```
WorkQueue(int n, Allocator alloc) : SOA<WorkItem>(n, alloc) {}
```

There is only a single private member variable: the number of objects stored in the queue. It is represented using a platform-specific atomic type. When WorkQueues are used on the CPU, a std::atomic is sufficient; that case is shown here.

⟨*WorkQueue Private Members*⟩ ≡   935
```
std::atomic<int> size{0};
```

Simple methods return the size of the queue and reset it so that it stores no items.

⟨*WorkQueue Public Methods*⟩ +≡   935
```
int Size() const {
    return size.load(std::memory_order_relaxed);
}
void Reset() {
    size.store(0, std::memory_order_relaxed);
}
```

An item is added to the queue by finding a slot for it via a call to AllocateEntry(). We implement that functionality separately so that WorkQueue subclasses can implement their own methods for adding items to the queue if further processing is needed when doing so. In this case, all that needs to be done is to store the provided value in the specified spot using the SOA indexing operator.

⟨*WorkQueue Public Methods*⟩ +≡   **935**
```
int Push(WorkItem w) {
    int index = AllocateEntry();
    (*this)[index] = w;
    return index;
}
```

When a slot is claimed for a new item in the queue, the `size` member variable is incremented using an atomic operation, and so it is fine if multiple threads are concurrently adding items to the queue without any further coordination.

Returning to how threads access memory, we would do well to allocate consecutive slots for all of the threads in a thread group that are adding entries to a queue. Given the SOA layout of the queue, such an allocation leads to writes to consecutive memory locations, with corresponding performance benefits. Our use of `fetch_add` here does not provide that guarantee, since each thread calls it independently. However, a common way to implement atomic addition in the presence of thread groups is to aggregate the operation over all the active threads in the group and to perform a single addition for all of them, doling out corresponding individual results back to the individual threads. Our code here assumes such an implementation; on a platform where the assumption is incorrect, it would be worthwhile to use a different mechanism that did give that result.

⟨*WorkQueue Protected Methods*⟩ ≡   **935**
```
int AllocateEntry() {
    return size.fetch_add(1, std::memory_order_relaxed);
}
```

`ForAllQueued()` makes it easy to apply a function to all of the items stored in a `WorkQueue()` in parallel. The provided callback function is passed the `WorkItem` that it is responsible for.

⟨*WorkQueue Inline Functions*⟩ ≡
```
template <typename F, typename WorkItem>
void ForAllQueued(const char *desc, const WorkQueue<WorkItem> *q,
                  int maxQueued, F &&func) {
    if (Options->useGPU) {
        ⟨Launch GPU threads to process q using func 937⟩
    } else {
        ⟨Process q using func with CPU threads 937⟩
    }
}
```

If the GPU is being used, a thread is launched for the maximum number of items that could be stored in the queue, rather than only for the number that are actually stored there. This stems from the fact that kernels are launched from the CPU but the number of objects actually in the queue is stored in managed memory. Not only would it be inefficient to read the actual size of the queue back from GPU memory to the CPU for the call to `GPUParallelFor()`, but retrieving the correct value would require synchronization with the GPU, which would further harm performance.

Therefore, a number of threads certain to be sufficient are launched and those that do not have an item to process exit immediately. Because thread creation is so inexpensive on GPUs, this approach does not introduce a meaningful amount of overhead. If it was a problem, it is also possible to launch kernels directly from the GPU, in which case exactly the correct number of threads could be launched. In this case, we adopt the greater simplicity of always launching kernels from the CPU.

⟨*Launch GPU threads to process* q *using* func⟩ ≡   **936**
```
GPUParallelFor(desc, maxQueued, [=] PBRT_GPU (int index) mutable {
    if (index >= q->Size())
        return;
    func((*q)[index]);
});
```

For CPU processing, there are no concerns about reading the size field, so precisely the right number of items to process can be passed to ParallelFor().

⟨*Process* q *using* func *with CPU threads*⟩ ≡   **936**
```
ParallelFor(0, q->Size(), [&](int index) { func((*q)[index]); });
```

We will also find it useful to have work queues that support multiple types of objects and maintain separate queues, one for each type. This functionality is provided by the MultiWorkQueue.

⟨*MultiWorkQueue Definition*⟩ ≡
```
template <typename T> class MultiWorkQueue;
```

The definition of this class is a *variadic template* specialization that takes all of the types Ts it is to manage using a TypePack.

⟨*MultiWorkQueue Definition*⟩ +≡
```
template <typename... Ts> class MultiWorkQueue<TypePack<Ts...>> {
public:
    ⟨MultiWorkQueue Public Methods 937⟩
private:
    ⟨MultiWorkQueue Private Members 937⟩
};
```

The MultiWorkQueue internally expands to a set of per-type WorkQueue instances that are stored in a tuple.

⟨*MultiWorkQueue Private Members*⟩ ≡   **937**
```
pstd::tuple<WorkQueue<Ts>...> queues;
```

Note the ellipsis (...) in the code fragment above, which is a C++ *template pack expansion*. Such an expansion is only valid when it contains a template pack (Ts in this case), and it simply inserts the preceding element once for each specified template argument while replacing Ts with the corresponding type. For example, a hypothetical MultiWorkQueue<TypePack<A, B>> would contain a tuple of the form pstd::tuple<WorkQueue<A>, WorkQueue<B>>. This and the following template-based transformations significantly reduce the amount of repetitive code that would otherwise be needed to implement equivalent functionality.

The following template method returns a queue for a particular work item that must be one of the MultiWorkQueue template arguments. The search through tuple items is resolved at compile time and so incurs no additional runtime cost.

⟨*MultiWorkQueue Public Methods*⟩ ≡   **937**
```
template <typename T>
WorkQueue<T> *Get() {
    return &pstd::get<WorkQueue<T>>(queues);
}
```

The MultiWorkQueue constructor takes the maximum number of items to store in the queue and an allocator. The third argument is a span of Boolean values that indicates whether each type is actually present. Saving memory for types that are not required in a given execution of the renderer is worthwhile when both the maximum number of items is large and the work item types themselves are large.

⟨*MultiWorkQueue Public Methods*⟩ +≡   **937**
```
MultiWorkQueue(int n, Allocator alloc, pstd::span<const bool> haveType) {
    int index = 0;
    ((*Get<Ts>() = WorkQueue<Ts>(haveType[index++] ? n : 1, alloc)), ...);
}
```

Once more, note the use of the ellipsis in the above fragment, which is a more advanced case of a template pack expansion following the pattern ((expr), ...). As before, this expansion will simply repeat the element (expr) preceding the ellipsis once for every Ts with appropriate substitutions. In contrast to the previous case, we are now expanding expressions rather than types. The actual values of these expressions are ignored because they will be joined by the comma operator that ignores the value of the preceding expression. Finally, the actual expression being repeated has side effects: it initializes each tuple entry with a suitable instance, and it also advances a counter index that is used to access corresponding elements of the haveType span.

The Size() method returns the size of a queue, and Push() appends an element. Both methods require that the caller specify the concrete type T of work item, which allows it to directly call the corresponding method of the appropriate queue.

⟨*MultiWorkQueue Public Methods*⟩ +≡   **937**
```
template <typename T>
int Size() const { return Get<T>()->Size(); }
template <typename T>
int Push(const T &value) { return Get<T>()->Push(value); }
```

Finally, all queues are reset via a call to Reset(). Once again, template pack expansion generates calls to all the individual queues' Reset() methods via the following terse code.

⟨*MultiWorkQueue Public Methods*⟩ +≡   **937**
```
void Reset() { (Get<Ts>()->Reset(), ...); }
```

15.3 PATH TRACER IMPLEMENTATION

With these utility classes in hand, we can turn to the WavefrontPathIntegrator class implementation. As mentioned earlier, its functionality matches that of the VolPathIntegrator, restructured to run with a wavefront architecture.

The WavefrontPathIntegrator class declaration is in the file wavefront/integrator.h and some of its implementation is in wavefront/integrator.cpp, though a number of its method implementations are distributed across separate source files in the wavefront/ directory. While this is a different organization than we have used elsewhere in pbrt (where all the non-inline method definitions for a class defined in a file named file.h are in file.cpp), distributing them in this way reduces the time necessary to compile pbrt, since many of the methods make use of C++ features that can lead to long compile times. Spreading them out across multiple files allows multiple CPU cores to compile their implementations in parallel.

⟨*WavefrontPathIntegrator Definition*⟩ ≡
```
class WavefrontPathIntegrator {
  public:
    ⟨WavefrontPathIntegrator Public Methods 939⟩
    ⟨WavefrontPathIntegrator Member Variables 939⟩
};
```

The constructor converts the provided BasicScene into the objects that represent the scene for rendering. We will skip over the majority of its implementation here, however, as most of it just calls all the appropriate object Create() methods to allocate and initialize the corresponding objects (see Section C.3). All allocations are performed with Allocators that use the provided memory resource. When rendering on the GPU, this leads to the use of managed memory.

⟨*WavefrontPathIntegrator Public Methods*⟩ ≡   939
```
WavefrontPathIntegrator(pstd::pmr::memory_resource *memoryResource,
                        BasicScene &scene);
```

⟨*WavefrontPathIntegrator Member Variables*⟩ ≡   939
```
pstd::pmr::memory_resource *memoryResource;
```

These are some of the key scene objects that are initialized in the constructor. As with the CPU-based Integrators, the infinite lights are stored independently so that they can be efficiently iterated over for rays that escape the scene.

⟨*WavefrontPathIntegrator Member Variables*⟩ +≡   939
```
Filter filter;
Film film;
Sampler sampler;
Camera camera;
pstd::vector<Light> *infiniteLights;
LightSampler lightSampler;
```

There are a few additional member variables to store what should now be familiar configuration options.

⟨*WavefrontPathIntegrator Member Variables*⟩ +≡   939
```
int maxDepth, samplesPerPixel;
bool regularize;
```

In order to limit memory use, this integrator places a limit on the number of pixel samples that it works on at once. All told, each active pixel sample requires roughly 1,000 bytes of additional storage for its state variables and to ensure that all the queues have sufficient space for the work to be done for the ray. (The actual amount of storage varies based on the scene, as the constructor is careful not to allocate work queues for the volume scattering kernels if there is no participating media in the scene, for example.)

The following fragment from the WavefrontPathIntegrator constructor therefore sets a maximum number of active samples and then determines how many scanlines of pixels that corresponds to. That value in turn determines how many passes (of rendering that many scanlines) are necessary to cover the full image resolution. Finally, scanlinesPerPass is set with a new value that evens out the number of scanlines rendered in each pass. This can help with load balancing by avoiding having a small number of scanlines in the final pass.

⟨*Compute number of scanlines to render per pass*⟩ ≡
```
    Vector2i resolution = film.PixelBounds().Diagonal();
    int maxSamples = 1024 * 1024;
    scanlinesPerPass = std::max(1, maxSamples / resolution.x);
    int nPasses = (resolution.y + scanlinesPerPass - 1) / scanlinesPerPass;
    scanlinesPerPass = (resolution.y + nPasses - 1) / nPasses;
    maxQueueSize = resolution.x * scanlinesPerPass;
```

All the queues that are allocated to buffer work between kernels are also allocated to be able to store `maxQueueSize` individual work items. Thus, all queues are able to store one work item for each of the active pixel samples. This is a sufficient number, as none of the kernels in the current implementation ever push more than one item on a queue for each item processed. However, it may waste a substantial amount of memory. For example, there is a work queue for rays that hit emissive surfaces in the scene. It is rare that all the rays will hit emissive objects, yet there must be storage for all in case of that eventuality. The alternative, dynamically increasing the size of the queues when necessary, would be difficult to implement efficiently in the context of the massive parallelism on GPUs.

⟨*WavefrontPathIntegrator Member Variables*⟩ +≡   **939**
```
    int scanlinesPerPass, maxQueueSize;
```

The `WavefrontPathIntegrator` does not use only queues to provide values to kernels and to communicate results. While the queue model is elegant, it can be inefficient if some values are computed early and not used until much later. For example, consider the `VisibleSurface` structure that is provided to `Film` implementations like the `GBufferFilm`: it is initialized at the first intersection after the camera, but then its value is not used again until the full ray path has been traced and the `Film::AddSample()` method is called at the end. `VisibleSurface` is, further, a relatively large structure. In a purely queue-based model, a substantial amount of memory bandwidth would be consumed passing it along from kernel to kernel until the end.

Therefore, the `PixelSampleState` structure is used for storing all such values. Various member variables will be added to it in what follows.

⟨*PixelSampleState Definition*⟩ ≡
```
    struct PixelSampleState {
        ⟨PixelSampleState Public Members 945⟩
    };
```

The `WavefrontPathIntegrator` maintains an SOA-arranged array of `PixelSampleStates`, allocated to have `maxQueueSize` entries. Each sample's index into this array is carried through the rendering computation so that it is easy to determine which entry corresponds to a pixel sample being processed.

⟨*WavefrontPathIntegrator Member Variables*⟩ +≡   **939**
```
    SOA<PixelSampleState> pixelSampleState;
```

15.3.1 WORK LAUNCH

Because the `WavefrontPathIntegrator` may be running either on the CPU or on the GPU, it provides methods for launching work that use the appropriate processor. Each selects the appropriate type of processor based on the renderer's configuration.

The first, `ParallelFor()`, selects between the types of two parallel for loops.

⟨*WavefrontPathIntegrator Public Methods*⟩ +≡   939

```
template <typename F>
void ParallelFor(const char *description, int nItems, F &&func) {
    if (Options->useGPU)
        GPUParallelFor(description, nItems, func);
    else
        pbrt::ParallelFor(0, nItems, func);
}
```

The Do() method executes the provided function in a single thread. On the CPU, it is no different than a regular function call; on the GPU, however, it executes the provided function using GPUParallelFor() with a single-item loop. For reasons that should be clear by now, this not a good way to do a meaningful amount of work on the GPU, but this capability is necessary for resetting counters, clearing queues, and the like.

⟨*WavefrontPathIntegrator Public Methods*⟩ +≡   939

```
template <typename F>
void Do(const char *description, F &&func) {
    if (Options->useGPU)
        GPUParallelFor(description, 1,
                       [=] PBRT_GPU (int) mutable { func(); });
    else
        func();
}
```

15.3.2 THE Render() METHOD

Rendering is initiated by a call to Render(). (Recall Figure 15.2 in Section 15.1.3, which summarizes the kernels that this method launches.) Similar to earlier integrators, it progressively takes more samples in all pixels until the requested number of samples have been taken. This method tracks how long rendering takes and returns the number of elapsed seconds; we have not included here the straightforward few lines of code that handle that.

One subtlety is that the initialization of the pixelBounds variable at the start is important for rendering performance. It will be necessary to have this value later on in the implementation of Render()—though because the Film is stored in managed memory, calling the PixelBounds() method after GPU kernels have been launched could incur the overhead of copying data back to the CPU.

⟨*WavefrontPathIntegrator Method Definitions*⟩ ≡

```
Float WavefrontPathIntegrator::Render() {
    Bounds2i pixelBounds = film.PixelBounds();
    Vector2i resolution = pixelBounds.Diagonal();
    ⟨Loop over sample indices and evaluate pixel samples 942⟩
}
```

By default, the number of samples taken in each pixel is the number determined by the Sampler; the value returned by its SamplesPerPixel() method is cached in a member variable for the same reason as pixelBounds is cached above. It is possible to limit rendering to a single specified sample index using the --debugstart command line option; the code to set firstSampleIndex and lastSampleIndex in that case is not included here.

⟨*Loop over sample indices and evaluate pixel samples*⟩ ≡   **941**
```
int firstSampleIndex = 0, lastSampleIndex = samplesPerPixel;
for (int sampleIndex = firstSampleIndex; sampleIndex < lastSampleIndex;
     ++sampleIndex) {
    ⟨Render image for sample sampleIndex 942⟩
}
```

Given a sample index, the next step is to loop over the one or more chunks of scanlines and to evaluate a sample in each of their pixels. This code is also similar to the corresponding code in the VolPathIntegrator: evaluating each sample starts with generating a camera ray and then following it through multiple intersections until it is terminated or the maximum depth is reached. The key difference is that, here, these tasks are being performed for as many as a million or so pixel samples at a time.

⟨*Render image for sample* sampleIndex⟩ ≡   **942**
```
for (int y0 = pixelBounds.pMin.y; y0 < pixelBounds.pMax.y;
     y0 += scanlinesPerPass) {
    ⟨Generate camera rays for current scanline range 942⟩
    ⟨Trace rays and estimate radiance up to maximum ray depth 948⟩
    UpdateFilm();
}
```

Before the rays are generated, it is necessary to reset the work queue that will store them. We will need to maintain more than one ray queue: one for the set of rays currently being traced and another for the indirect rays that have been spawned to be traced at the next depth. The CurrentRayQueue() method, defined shortly, returns the queue for the specified depth.

When the GPU is being used for rendering, it is critically important that the Reset() method is called from the GPU and not the CPU; Do() is thus used here. Not only could resetting it from the CPU be inefficient, as doing so would involve the CPU writing to managed memory, but—given the asynchronous execution of the GPU—it would almost certainly be incorrect, potentially resetting a queue that was still in use by the code that was executing on the GPU.

⟨*Generate camera rays for current scanline range*⟩ ≡   **942**
```
RayQueue *cameraRayQueue = CurrentRayQueue(0);
Do("Reset ray queue", PBRT_CPU_GPU_LAMBDA () {
                          cameraRayQueue->Reset();
                      });
GenerateCameraRays(y0, sampleIndex);
```

The RayQueue class adds a few convenience methods to WorkQueue that we will discuss in the following pages. (RayWorkItem will also be defined in a few pages, closer to where it is first used.)

⟨*RayQueue Definition*⟩ ≡
```
class RayQueue : public WorkQueue<RayWorkItem> {
  public:
    ⟨RayQueue Public Methods 947⟩
};
```

The WavefrontPathIntegrator maintains a pair of ray queues, rather than allocating one for each ray depth up to the maximum. It manages them using *double buffering*: one stores the current active set of rays and should only be read from, while the other stores the rays enqueued to trace at the next depth and should only be written to. At each successive ray depth, the roles of the two queues are switched.

⟨*WavefrontPathIntegrator Member Variables*⟩ +≡   **939**
    RayQueue *rayQueues[2];

Two convenience methods return pointers to the RayQueues given a depth. The double buffering logic is effectively encapsulated in their implementations.

⟨*WavefrontPathIntegrator Public Methods*⟩ +≡   **939**
```
    RayQueue *CurrentRayQueue(int wavefrontDepth) {
        return rayQueues[wavefrontDepth & 1];
    }
    RayQueue *NextRayQueue(int wavefrontDepth) {
        return rayQueues[(wavefrontDepth + 1) & 1];
    }
```

15.3.3 GENERATING CAMERA RAYS

The two methods related to generating camera rays are implemented in the file wavefront/ camera.cpp, not in wavefront/integrator.cpp, because we have used C++ templates to generate multiple specialized instances of the methods, each one specialized based on some of the object types involved. As mentioned earlier, techniques like this can cause lengthy compile times, so it is worthwhile to isolate the camera method implementations in their own source file.

There are two GenerateCameraRays() methods. The first, which is called by WavefrontPath Integrator::Render(), determines the concrete type of the Sampler being used and then calls the second GenerateCameraRays() method, which is templated on the type of the Sampler. This idea is something that we will see again in other methods: CPU code making a runtime determination of the types of objects involved in a computation, which allows the execution of code that is specialized for those types. This is especially beneficial to performance when running on the GPU.

The first method defines a lambda function, generateRays, and then invokes the Tagged Pointer's dynamic dispatch mechanism, which will end up calling the lambda function using the concrete type of the Sampler. (In this case, we use the DispatchCPU() variant, which must be used for code that can only execute on the CPU.)

⟨*WavefrontPathIntegrator Camera Ray Methods*⟩ ≡
```
    void WavefrontPathIntegrator::GenerateCameraRays(int y0, int sampleIndex) {
        ⟨Define generateRays lambda function 944⟩
        sampler.DispatchCPU(generateRays);
    }
```

Using auto in the parameter declaration for the following lambda function causes it to be parameterized by the type of sampler, like a template function. (C++20 provides a less obscure syntax for templated lambda functions, though this version of pbrt limits itself to C++17.) Thus, the type of sampler will be a concrete instance of one of the sampler types provided in the Sampler declaration in Section 8.3.

There is a nit in that sampler is passed as a reference to a pointer to the specific Sampler type; a bit of work in the using declaration gives us the actual Sampler type. A second nit is that we must filter out the MLTSampler, which is only used by the MLTIntegrator, and DebugMLTSampler, a variant of it that is used for debugging. Those classes use vector methods like push_back() that are not supported in GPU code, and therefore we must make clear to the compiler what we know in any case: those samplers will not be used here.

With the concrete sampler type in hand, the second `GenerateCameraRays()` method can be called, with the sampler type provided for the template specialization.

⟨*Define* `generateRays` *lambda function*⟩ ≡   **943**
```
auto generateRays = [=](auto sampler) {
    using ConcreteSampler = std::remove_reference_t<decltype(*sampler)>;
    if constexpr (!std::is_same_v<ConcreteSampler, MLTSampler> &&
                  !std::is_same_v<ConcreteSampler, DebugMLTSampler>)
        GenerateCameraRays<ConcreteSampler>(y0, sampleIndex);
};
```

We can now move on to the second `GenerateCameraRays()` method, which calls `Wavefront PathIntegrator::ParallelFor()` to generate all of the rays in parallel.

⟨*WavefrontPathIntegrator Camera Ray Methods*⟩ +≡
```
template <typename ConcreteSampler>
void WavefrontPathIntegrator::GenerateCameraRays(int y0, int sampleIndex) {
    RayQueue *rayQueue = CurrentRayQueue(0);
    ParallelFor("Generate camera rays", maxQueueSize,
        PBRT_CPU_GPU_LAMBDA (int pixelIndex) {
            ⟨Enqueue camera ray and set pixel state for sample 944⟩
        });
}
```

The sequence of operations performed for each camera ray again generally matches what we have seen before: after computing the pixel coordinates for the provided loop index, samples are generated, a set of wavelengths are sampled, and then the Camera generates the ray.

⟨*Enqueue camera ray and set pixel state for sample*⟩ ≡   **944**
  ⟨*Compute pixel coordinates for* `pixelIndex` **944**⟩
  ⟨*Test pixel coordinates against pixel bounds* **945**⟩
  ⟨*Initialize* `Sampler` *for current pixel and sample* **945**⟩
  ⟨*Sample wavelengths for ray path* **945**⟩
  ⟨*Generate* `CameraSample` *and corresponding ray* **946**⟩
  ⟨*Initialize remainder of* `PixelSampleState` *for ray* **946**⟩
  ⟨*Enqueue camera ray for intersection tests* **946**⟩

Given the pixel bounds of the film, the `pixelIndex` value is mapped to pixel coordinates, starting from the (x, y) lower bound given by the pixel bounds and `y0` value, respectively. Threads are then assigned to pixels in scanline order. Because the `PBRT_GPU_LAMBDA` macro includes `*this` in the lambda capture, various `WavefrontPathIntegrator` member variables such as `film`, which is used here, can be directly accessed in the lambda function.

The pixel coordinates are then stored in `PixelSampleState`. Note that if we are just setting a single member variable of an SOA structure rather than assigning an entire structure value, then the member variable must be indexed and not the `pixelSampleState` structure itself; our automatically generated SOA classes are not able to provide the same syntax as would be used for an array of structures layout in that case.

⟨*Compute pixel coordinates for* `pixelIndex`⟩ ≡   **944**
```
Bounds2i pixelBounds = film.PixelBounds();
int xResolution = pixelBounds.pMax.x - pixelBounds.pMin.x;
Point2i pPixel(pixelBounds.pMin.x + pixelIndex % xResolution,
               y0 + pixelIndex / xResolution);
pixelSampleState.pPixel[pixelIndex] = pPixel;
```

The pixel coordinates corresponding to a sample are our first addition to the PixelSample State structure.

⟨*PixelSampleState Public Members*⟩ ≡   **940**
    Point2i pPixel;

If the image has been split into multiple spans of scanlines, then the number of parallel loop iterations in the final pass may be a few more than there are pixels left to be sampled. Rather than worry about this when specifying the number of threads to launch in the call to WavefrontPathIntegrator::ParallelFor(), we just check this condition in the kernel. Indices for out of bounds pixels return after initializing PixelSampleState::pPixel and do not enqueue any rays.

⟨*Test pixel coordinates against pixel bounds*⟩ ≡   **944**
    if (!InsideExclusive(pPixel, pixelBounds))
        return;

Next, samples are needed to generate the camera ray. Here we can see the value of specializing this method based on the ConcreteSampler type. The following fragment is perhaps best understood by reading it with the ConcreteSampler in the following replaced with, say, HaltonSampler in your head. pixelSampler then is a stack-allocated HaltonSampler, and the TaggedPointer::Cast() call gives us a pointer of that type; dereferencing it lets each thread initialize its own sampler from the exemplar of the one that the WavefrontPathIntegrator stores. All threads access the same memory locations, so reading the Sampler from memory does not consume much bandwidth.

The benefit from this approach comes from having the sampler allocated on the stack. On the GPU, its member variables can be stored directly in registers, giving high performance when executing its methods. As an additional bonus, there is no overhead for dynamic dispatch in the StartPixelSample() call: the sampler's type is known, so the appropriate method can be called directly. It will usually be expanded inline at the call site.

⟨*Initialize* Sampler *for current pixel and sample*⟩ ≡   **944**
    ConcreteSampler pixelSampler = *sampler.Cast<ConcreteSampler>();
    pixelSampler.StartPixelSample(pPixel, sampleIndex, 0);

Wavelengths are sampled in precisely the same way as they are in most of the other integrators.

⟨*Sample wavelengths for ray path*⟩ ≡   **944**
    Float lu = pixelSampler.Get1D();
    SampledWavelengths lambda = film.SampleWavelengths(lu);

The CameraSample can be initialized in the usual way and then it is on to call Camera:: GenerateRay(). In this case, this method call is also resolved using pbrt's usual dynamic dispatch system, just as it is in all the other integrators. An alternative implementation approach would be to further specialize the GenerateCameraRays() method based on the type of the Camera being used; after all, it is the same for all pixel samples and so it is somewhat wasteful for all threads to perform the same computations for dynamic dispatch. We have found that in practice that alternative gives a negligible performance benefit, and so our implementation here remains based on dynamic dispatch.

One other thing to note is that the wavefront integrator path generates regular Rays here and not RayDifferentials. Approximate differentials for filtering will be computed later, trading off superior antialiasing quality in exchange for higher performance from reduced memory bandwidth due to having less information associated with each ray. An exercise at the end of the chapter revisits this choice.

⟨*Generate* CameraSample *and corresponding ray*⟩ ≡   944
```
    CameraSample cameraSample = GetCameraSample(pixelSampler, pPixel, filter);
    pstd::optional<CameraRay> cameraRay =
        camera.GenerateRay(cameraSample, lambda);
```

A few additional values that are stored in PixelSampleState can now be set. We avoid initializing the heavyweight VisibleSurface member if it is not going to be used by the Film; the initializeVisibleSurface member variable is set in the WavefrontPathIntegrator constructor to record whether it is needed. Saving this memory bandwidth when possible is worth this easy check.

⟨*Initialize remainder of* PixelSampleState *for ray*⟩ ≡   944
```
    pixelSampleState.L[pixelIndex] = SampledSpectrum(0.f);
    pixelSampleState.lambda[pixelIndex] = lambda;
    pixelSampleState.filterWeight[pixelIndex] = cameraSample.filterWeight;
    if (initializeVisibleSurface)
        pixelSampleState.visibleSurface[pixelIndex] = VisibleSurface();
```

Of these member variables, we will see L most often in what follows. It stores the accumulated radiance estimate for the ray path. After the path terminates, its value will be provided to the Film.

⟨*PixelSampleState Public Members*⟩ +≡   940
```
    SampledSpectrum L;
    SampledWavelengths lambda;
    Float filterWeight;
    VisibleSurface visibleSurface;
```

If the Camera successfully generated a ray, it is pushed into the RayQueue along with its wavelengths and associated pixel index, which allows subsequent kernels to be able to index into WavefrontPathIntegrator::pixelSampleState to retrieve values there that are associated with this ray.

⟨*Enqueue camera ray for intersection tests*⟩ ≡   944
```
    if (cameraRay) {
        rayQueue->PushCameraRay(cameraRay->ray, lambda, pixelIndex);
        pixelSampleState.cameraRayWeight[pixelIndex] = cameraRay->weight;
    } else
        pixelSampleState.cameraRayWeight[pixelIndex] = SampledSpectrum(0);
```

⟨*PixelSampleState Public Members*⟩ +≡   940
```
    SampledSpectrum cameraRayWeight;
```

Some of the work queues provide specialized methods for pushing work on to them; RayQueue is one of them. It provides a PushCameraRay() method for camera rays and Push IndirectRay() for scattered rays that sample indirect lighting. Doing so not only makes the code where work is pushed on to the queue slightly cleaner, but it also makes it possible to set some of the forthcoming RayWorkItem member variables to default values for camera rays without needing to specify default values here. (For example, RayWorkItem carries path sampling PDFs that are initialized to 1 for camera rays.) We will pass over the implementation of this method here, as it is all setting member variables, either from passed-in values or from defaults.

⟨*RayQueue Public Methods*⟩ ≡   942
```
int PushCameraRay(const Ray &ray, const SampledWavelengths &lambda,
                  int pixelIndex);
```

We will start the definition of the `RayWorkItem` structure here.

⟨*RayWorkItem Definition*⟩ ≡
```
struct RayWorkItem {
    ⟨RayWorkItem Public Members 947⟩
};
```

As would be expected from the parameters passed to `PushCameraRay()`, `RayWorkItem` stores a ray, its wavelengths, and an index into the `WavefrontPathIntegrator`'s `pixelSampleState` array from which additional data associated with the ray can be found.

⟨*RayWorkItem Public Members*⟩ ≡   947
```
Ray ray;
int depth;
SampledWavelengths lambda;
int pixelIndex;
```

The reader may have noted that `lambda` is both pushed to the ray queue and stored in the `PixelSampleState`, which is admittedly redundant, though there are good reasons for both. Its value must be stored in the `PixelSampleState` structure, as it is required for updating the film, which is not scheduled using work queues but via a loop over the `PixelSampleState` values; see further discussion of this design in Section 15.3.11.

However, if other kernels along the way accessed `lambda` via `PixelSampleState`, performance would be poor, since the initial correlation between the value of `pixelIndex` and threads in a thread group quickly becomes shuffled up over the course of rendering. Thus, reads from `PixelSampleState` would be highly incoherent. Because it is used in just about every kernel, `lambda` is also passed along throughout the queues of the wavefront integrator. Since it is in work queues, the loads and stores to read and save its value are coherent across the thread group, giving good performance.

15.3.4 LOOP OVER RAY DEPTHS

With the camera having seeded the ray queue with an initial set of rays, we can now turn to the loop that executes once for each successive set of ray intersection tests and shading calculations up until the maximum ray path length. One subtlety is that this loop is over "wavefront depth," which is different than the ray depth that has been tracked in other integrators. Here, the wavefront depth reflects the number of times that this loop has executed, tracing a batch of rays and processing their intersections. Each ray tracks its own depth, which is usually the same as the wavefront depth, though the depth of rays that hit invisible surfaces that delineate the boundaries between volumetric media is not incremented at those intersections (as in other integrators).

This loop always runs on the CPU; when the GPU is used for rendering, it is responsible for launching the appropriate kernels to perform the rendering computation. An implication of this design and the decoupling of the CPU and GPU is that the CPU has no visibility into the state of the ray-tracing calculations on the GPU. For example, if all rays terminate after the first intersection, the CPU will continue submitting kernel launches to execute the ray-tracing pipeline even though no work is passing through it. All the kernels would exit immediately, though there would be a cost from launching all of them and their determining that there is no work to be done. For many scenes this is not a problem, but it can harm this integrator's performance with high maximum ray depths. An exercise at the end of the chapter outlines some design alternatives.

⟨*Trace rays and estimate radiance up to maximum ray depth*⟩ ≡   942
```
for (int wavefrontDepth = 0; true; ++wavefrontDepth) {
    ⟨Reset queues before tracing rays 948⟩
    ⟨Follow active ray paths and accumulate radiance estimates 948⟩
}
```

All the work queues except for the RayQueue holding the current set of rays must be cleared at the start of each iteration. The following fragment clears the RayQueue for the next set of indirect rays and adds a fragment for the rest of the queues. We will add additional Reset() calls to this fragment for the various other queues along with the code that defines and uses them.

⟨*Reset queues before tracing rays*⟩ ≡   948
```
RayQueue *nextQueue = NextRayQueue(wavefrontDepth);
Do("Reset queues before tracing rays",
    PBRT_CPU_GPU_LAMBDA () {
        nextQueue->Reset();
        ⟨Reset queues before tracing next batch of rays 958⟩
    });
```

Once the queues are cleared, rendering proceeds mostly following the same steps as the VolPathIntegrator. First, the Sampler computes sample values for all of the rays and stores them in memory.

⟨*Follow active ray paths and accumulate radiance estimates*⟩ ≡   948
```
GenerateRaySamples(wavefrontDepth, sampleIndex);
```

The closest intersection with a surface, if any, is then found for each ray.

⟨*Follow active ray paths and accumulate radiance estimates*⟩ +≡   948
```
⟨Find closest intersections along active rays 952⟩
```

Before surface scattering or emission is considered, the medium (if any) is sampled. If the medium scatters or absorbs the ray, then any surface intersection will be ignored.

⟨*Follow active ray paths and accumulate radiance estimates*⟩ +≡   948
```
SampleMediumInteraction(wavefrontDepth);
```

Only after medium sampling are rays that left the scene taken care of. In this way, rays passing through participating media that do not interact with it and then leave the scene can be processed at the same time as rays that left the scene but did not pass through media.

⟨*Follow active ray paths and accumulate radiance estimates*⟩ +≡   948
```
HandleEscapedRays();
```

The contribution of emissive surfaces to a sample's radiance value is also only added after medium sampling, since it should not be included if the medium scattered or absorbed the ray.

⟨*Follow active ray paths and accumulate radiance estimates*⟩ +≡   948
```
HandleEmissiveIntersection();
```

The loop over wavefront depth can only be terminated after emissive surfaces have been accounted for, since the MIS-based direct lighting calculation accounts for their contribution.

⟨*Follow active ray paths and accumulate radiance estimates*⟩ +≡   948
```
    if (wavefrontDepth == maxDepth)
        break;
```

If the loop does not terminate, only now are surface intersections handled, with the Materials evaluating their textures and returning BSDFs, lights sampled, and indirect rays enqueued.

⟨*Follow active ray paths and accumulate radiance estimates*⟩ +≡   948
```
    EvaluateMaterialsAndBSDFs(wavefrontDepth);
```

Next, the shadow rays enqueued by the material evaluation kernel are traced; the radiance contributions of the unoccluded ones are accumulated in PixelSampleState.

⟨*Follow active ray paths and accumulate radiance estimates*⟩ +≡   948
```
    TraceShadowRays(wavefrontDepth);
```

The following sections go into these steps in more detail.

15.3.5 SAMPLE GENERATION

The first step in each loop iteration is to generate values for all the sample dimensions that may be required for sampling lighting if a scattering event is found along the ray, either in a participating medium or on a surface. Generating all of these samples ahead of time in a separate kernel allows for specializing that kernel based on the sampler type, giving the same performance benefits as were found in GenerateCameraRays().

The GenerateRaySamples() method is defined in the file wavefront/samples.cpp. Similar to camera rays, there is an initial GenerateRaySamples() method called in the main rendering loop that determines the actual Sampler type and invokes the appropriate specialization. Because this dispatch method is nearly the same as the analog in GenerateCameraRays(), we omit it here and turn directly to the specialized method.

⟨*WavefrontPathIntegrator Sampler Methods*⟩ ≡
```
    template <typename ConcreteSampler>
    void WavefrontPathIntegrator::GenerateRaySamples(int wavefrontDepth,
                                                     int sampleIndex) {
        ⟨Generate description string desc for ray sample generation⟩
        RayQueue *rayQueue = CurrentRayQueue(wavefrontDepth);
        ForAllQueued(desc.c_str(), rayQueue, maxQueueSize,
            PBRT_CPU_GPU_LAMBDA (const RayWorkItem w) {
                ⟨Generate samples for ray segment at current sample index  950⟩
        });
    }
```

Unlike the CPU-only integrators, where sample dimensions are allocated implicitly based on the runtime sequence of Get1D() and Get2D() method calls, here dimensions are explicitly allocated, ensuring that unique dimensions are assigned to different uses of samples. Doing so imposes a coupling between this kernel and the use of samples in following ones and also means that samples may be generated that are not actually used (e.g., if a perfect specular surface is intersected). These costs are worth paying in return for the performance benefits of generating samples in a specialized kernel.

⟨Generate samples for ray segment at current sample index⟩ ≡   **949**
    ⟨Find first sample dimension 950⟩
    ⟨Initialize Sampler *for pixel, sample index, and dimension 950⟩*
    ⟨Initialize RaySamples *structure with sample values 950⟩*
    ⟨Store RaySamples *in pixel sample state 951⟩*

The first task is to find the first dimension to allocate for this ray's samples. The first 5 sample dimensions are used to generate the camera ray, and then 1 is used to sample the wavelengths. At least 7 samples are needed for each ray depth: 3 for the call to BSDF::Sample_f(), 1 to sample a light source and then 2 to sample a position on it, and then 1 more for Russian roulette for the indirect ray. Two additional dimensions are consumed for sampling participating media. (The haveMedia WavefrontPathIntegrator member variable is set in its constructor based on the scene.)

⟨Find first sample dimension⟩ ≡   **950**
```
int dimension = 6 + 7 * w.depth;
if (haveMedia)
    dimension += 2 * w.depth;
```

This kernel uses the same trick to get a stack-allocated Sampler as was done for camera rays. In this case, figuring out which pixel the ray is associated with requires a read from the PixelSampleState.

⟨Initialize Sampler *for pixel, sample index, and dimension⟩ ≡*   **950**
```
ConcreteSampler pixelSampler = *sampler.Cast<ConcreteSampler>();
Point2i pPixel = pixelSampleState.pPixel[w.pixelIndex];
pixelSampler.StartPixelSample(pPixel, sampleIndex, dimension);
```

The RaySamples structure bundles up the samples needed for a ray. A series of Get1D() and Get2D() calls initializes its member variables. We omit the fragment that initializes the indirect samples, as it is more of the same. We have carefully ordered the sample generation method calls below to match their use in the VolPathIntegrator so that the two integrators use the same sample values for their sampling tasks at each pixel sample.

⟨Initialize RaySamples *structure with sample values⟩ ≡*   **950**
```
RaySamples rs;
rs.direct.uc = pixelSampler.Get1D();
rs.direct.u = pixelSampler.Get2D();
```
    ⟨Initialize remaining samples in rs⟩

⟨RaySamples Definition⟩ ≡
```
struct RaySamples {
    ⟨RaySamples Public Members  950⟩
};
```

The three sample dimensions for sampling the light source are available in the direct substructure.

⟨RaySamples Public Members⟩ ≡   **950**
```
struct {
    Point2f u;
    Float uc;
} direct;
```

Similarly, the dimensions for BSDF sampling and Russian roulette are available in indirect.

⟨*RaySamples Public Members*⟩ +≡   **950**
```
struct {
    Float uc, rr;
    Point2f u;
} indirect;
```

`haveMedia` indicates whether medium samples have been stored, which makes it possible to save bandwidth when they are unset.

⟨*RaySamples Public Members*⟩ +≡   **950**
```
bool haveMedia;
struct {
    Float uDist, uMode;
} media;
```

Sample values are squirreled away in `PixelSampleState` rather than being passed along via work queues. This does mean that both storing sample values here and reading them in subsequent kernels is not done with coherent memory accesses, since a thread group's `pixelIndex` values will not necessarily be contiguous after the initial camera rays. However, because they are not used in many kernels, passing them along through work queues would entail multiple instances of reading them from one queue just to write them to another, which would be a waste of bandwidth. We have found that the current approach gives marginally better performance in practice.

⟨*Store* RaySamples *in pixel sample state*⟩ ≡   **950**
```
pixelSampleState.samples[w.pixelIndex] = rs;
```

⟨*PixelSampleState Public Members*⟩ +≡   **940**
```
RaySamples samples;
```

One shortcoming of the approach implemented in this section is that samples are still generated for rays that do not intersect anything. A more optimized implementation might try to defer sample generation until the specific samples required were known, though the benefits are likely to be marginal: on the GPU, if the samples needed vary over the rays in a thread group, then—given the GPU's thread group execution model—there may be no savings from skipping the work for some threads if it is still needed by others. Further, sample generation is normally just a few percent of overall rendering time, and so anything more sophisticated is not worth bothering with, at least for pbrt's requirements.

15.3.6 INTERSECTION TESTING

Ray intersections are handled differently depending on whether the wavefront integrator is running on the CPU or the GPU. On the CPU, the ray queues are consumed using `ParallelFor()` calls and pbrt's regular acceleration structures from Chapter 7 are used to find intersections. On the GPU, platform-specific functionality is used to do so. In order to abstract the differences between these approaches (and to make it easier to add support for additional GPU architectures), ray intersection work done by the `WavefrontPathIntegrator` is handled by an implementation of the `WavefrontAggregate` class, which defines an interface that reflects the integrator's needs.

⟨*WavefrontAggregate Definition*⟩ ≡
```
class WavefrontAggregate {
public:
    ⟨WavefrontAggregate Interface 952⟩
};
```

The `WavefrontPathIntegrator` stores a `WavefrontAggregate` in its aggregate member variable. The CPU implementation, `CPUAggregate`, is found in the source files `wavefront/aggregate.h` and `wavefront/aggregate.cpp`. The implementation for NVIDIA GPUs, `OptiXAggregate`, is found in `gpu/aggregate.h` and `gpu/aggregate.cpp`.

⟨*WavefrontPathIntegrator Member Variables*⟩ +≡   939
    `WavefrontAggregate *aggregate = nullptr;`

All `WavefrontAggregate`s must provide a method that returns the bounds of the entire scene.

⟨*WavefrontAggregate Interface*⟩ ≡   951
    `virtual Bounds3f Bounds() const = 0;`

`IntersectClosest()` traces a set of rays and finds their closest surface intersections. Beyond the queue that provides the rays to be traced, a number of additional queues must be provided to it. Further work for a ray may be added to multiple queues depending on the specifics of its surface intersection.

⟨*WavefrontAggregate Interface*⟩ +≡   951
    `virtual void IntersectClosest(int maxRays, const RayQueue *rayQ,`
        `EscapedRayQueue *escapedRayQ, HitAreaLightQueue *hitAreaLightQ,`
        `MaterialEvalQueue *basicMtlQ, MaterialEvalQueue *universalMtlQ,`
        `MediumSampleQueue *mediumSampleQ, RayQueue *nextRayQ) const = 0;`

The `WavefrontPathIntegrator`'s call to `IntersectClosest()` mostly passes the corresponding queues from its member variables, though calls to `GetCurrentQueue()` and `NextRayQueue()` are necessary to get the appropriate instances of those queues.

⟨*Find closest intersections along active rays*⟩ ≡   948
    `aggregate->IntersectClosest(maxQueueSize, CurrentRayQueue(wavefrontDepth),`
        `escapedRayQueue, hitAreaLightQueue, basicEvalMaterialQueue,`
        `universalEvalMaterialQueue, mediumSampleQueue,`
        `NextRayQueue(wavefrontDepth));`

In order to discuss the responsibilities of `IntersectClosest()` implementations, we will focus on its implementation in `CPUAggregate`. Rather than once again repeating the unwieldy list of arguments here, we will proceed directly to the method implementation, which starts with a parallel for loop over the items in the queue.

⟨*CPUAggregate::IntersectClosest() method implementation*⟩ ≡
    `ParallelFor(0, rayQueue->Size(), [=] (int index) {`
        `const RayWorkItem r = (*rayQueue)[index];`
        ⟨*Intersect r's ray with the scene and enqueue resulting work* **952**⟩
    `});`

A regular aggregate stored in `CPUAggregate` handles the ray intersection test, with different cases afterward for rays that have an intersection with a surface and rays that do not.

⟨*Intersect r's ray with the scene and enqueue resulting work*⟩ ≡   952
    `pstd::optional<ShapeIntersection> si = aggregate.Intersect(r.ray);`
    `if (!si)`
        `EnqueueWorkAfterMiss(r, mediumSampleQueue, escapedRayQueue);`
    `else`
        `EnqueueWorkAfterIntersection(r, r.ray.medium, si->tHit, si->intr,`
            `mediumSampleQueue, nextRayQueue, hitAreaLightQueue,`
            `basicEvalMaterialQueue, universalEvalMaterialQueue);`

The details of enqueuing further work for rays that have no intersections are handled by the EnqueueWorkAfterMiss() function, which is defined in the file wavefront/intersect.h. That header file provides a number of functions that are used by both the CPU- and GPU-based ray intersection code. Gathering them there allows a single implementation to be used by both, which in turn reduces the complexity of those WavefrontAggregate implementations.

Unlike many of the other functions in wavefront/intersect.h, EnqueueWorkAfterMiss() is simple enough that it barely merits its own function—if the ray is passing through participating media, it is enqueued for medium sampling, and otherwise it is enqueued for evaluating infinite light sources' contribution to its radiance, if there are any in the scene.

⟨*Wavefront Ray Intersection Enqueuing Functions*⟩ ≡
```
void EnqueueWorkAfterMiss(RayWorkItem r,
                          MediumSampleQueue *mediumSampleQueue,
                          EscapedRayQueue *escapedRayQueue) {
    if (r.ray.medium)
        mediumSampleQueue->Push(r, Infinity);
    else if (escapedRayQueue)
        escapedRayQueue->Push(r);
}
```

For rays that do intersect a surface, there is more to be done. The EnqueueWorkAfterIntersection() function, which is not included in the text, handles all the following details.

If the ray is passing through participating media, it is enqueued for medium sampling. Only if the ray is not absorbed or scattered in the medium sampling kernel is work then queued for the surface intersection to be processed.

If a ray with an associated intersection is not scattered or absorbed by participating media and hits an emissive surface, it is added to a queue so that the surface's scattered radiance will be added to the ray's radiance estimate. Rays hitting surfaces are also sorted by the surfaces' materials and the complexity of their textures into basicEvalMaterialQueue or universalEvalMaterialQueue, both of which are MultiWorkQueues. (Section 15.3.9 describes how the material queues are organized.) Finally, rays that hit surfaces with no materials that represent medium transitions are pushed on to the nextRayQueue to be continued in the next iteration, on the other side of the surface intersection with their medium member variable updated accordingly.

GPU Ray Intersections

Following our custom of not including platform-specific code in the book text, we will not discuss the details of pbrt's use of CUDA and the OptiX API for its GPU ray-tracing implementation, but we will summarize the abstractions currently used for GPU ray tracing. See the files gpu/optix.h and gpu/optix.cu for details, however.

Current GPU ray intersection APIs follow a different model than the CPU-focused accelerators in Chapter 7. Those accelerators provide a fully procedural model, where the user calls functions that take a single ray and execute synchronously before returning their results. GPU ray tracing is based on a programmable pipeline, where some functionality is provided by the GPU vendor (either in hardware or in software), and some is provided by the user in the form of code that is executed at particular points in the pipeline.

The user-supplied code is in the form of a series of *shaders*, each of which is a function that is invoked in specific cases. In practice, many instances of these shaders run concurrently, following the GPU's thread group execution model. Ray tracing starts with a *ray generation shader* that is responsible for generating a ray and submitting it to the GPU ray-tracing function. In pbrt's implementation, the ray generation shader retrieves the ray from the RayQueue.

GPUs currently only have native support for intersecting rays with triangles. If a scene has no other types of shapes, then the intersection tests are handled entirely by the GPU's ray-tracing implementation. For other types of shapes, custom *intersection shaders* can be provided by the user. The user specifies a shape's axis-aligned bounding box and associates an intersection shader with it. When a ray intersects that box, the intersection shader is invoked to determine if there is an intersection. If there is, both the parametric *t* value along the ray and a handful of additional user-defined values can be returned to associate with the intersection.

pbrt uses custom intersection shaders for all the quadric shapes as well as for the Bilinear Patch. All follow the same pattern. For example, for bilinear patches, the intersection shader calls the previously defined IntersectBilinearPatch() function. Recall that in the event of an intersection, it returns a BilinearIntersection, not a full SurfaceInteraction. This design is intentional, as a BilinearIntersection is much smaller—just 3 Floats. Returning a small representation of the intersection is beneficial for performance, as it reduces how much information must be written to memory.

Alpha testing adds an additional complication to intersection testing (recall the discussion of alpha textures in Section 7.1.1). An *any hit shader* is applied to any primitives with alpha textures, such as leaves with alpha masks. The any hit shader executes for all intersections with such primitives, before it is known if an intersection is the closest. Our implementation uses the any hit shader to evaluate the alpha texture and apply a stochastic test, just like the ⟨*Possibly ignore intersection based on stochastic alpha test*⟩ fragment in the GeometricPrimitive class used by the CPU. If the test fails, then the GPU is instructed to ignore the intersection completely.

Once ray intersection testing has been completed, one of two shaders is invoked. For rays that have no intersections, a *miss shader* is called. Otherwise, a *closest hit shader* is invoked for processing at the intersection point. Now a full SurfaceInteraction is needed. All the shapes that are handled with custom intersection shaders have a method that converts their compact intersection representation to a SurfaceInteraction; for example, it is BilinearPatch::InteractionFromIntersection() for bilinear patches. The GPU reports the barycentric coordinates of triangle intersections, which are sufficient for the Triangle:: InteractionFromIntersection() method to do its work.

Given final intersections (or the determination that a ray does not intersect anything), additional work is enqueued using functions from wavefront/intersection.h, as is the case for the wavefront CPU ray-tracing aggregate.

15.3.7 PARTICIPATING MEDIA

In the interest of space, we will not walk through the code for the kernels launched by the medium sampling method, SampleMediumInteraction(). Algorithmically, it matches the corresponding code in VolPathIntegrator, so we will just summarize the queues and types of work involved.

For any ray with a non-nullptr Medium, the ray intersection code enqueues a MediumSample WorkItem in the mediumSampleQueue. A first medium-related kernel processes all the entries on this queue. Its task is to call the ray medium's SampleT_maj() method, adding emission at each sampled point before sampling one of absorption, real scattering, or null scattering. Absorption causes path termination; real scattering causes work to be added to another queue, mediumScatterQueue, that holds MediumScatterWorkItems; and null scattering causes medium sampling to continue. The path throughput $\hat{T}$ and path sampling PDFs are updated along the way. In the end, if the ray is neither scattered nor absorbed, then work is added to queues in the same manner as for rays that are not passing through media in the closest hit shader.

A second kernel is then launched to process all the medium scattering events in the `medium ScatterQueue`. The usual sampling process ensues: a light and then a point on it are sampled, path sampling PDFs are computed, and a shadow ray is enqueued. Next, the phase function is sampled to generate an indirect ray direction. Work for that ray is then added to the next wavefront depth's `RayQueue` via a call to `PushIndirectRay()`.

15.3.8 RAY-FOUND EMISSION

Two kernels handle rays that may add emission to their radiance estimates due to their interaction with emissive entities. The first processes rays that have left the scene and the second handles rays that intersect emissive surfaces.

`escapedRayQueue` is only allocated if the scene has one or more infinite area lights; there is otherwise no work to be done for such rays.

⟨*WavefrontPathIntegrator Member Variables*⟩ +≡   **939**
```
    EscapedRayQueue *escapedRayQueue = nullptr;
```

Note that `HandleEscapedRays()` returns immediately if there is no queue and thus no infinite area lights, saving the cost of an unnecessary kernel launch in that case.

⟨*WavefrontPathIntegrator Method Definitions*⟩ +≡
```
    void WavefrontPathIntegrator::HandleEscapedRays() {
        if (!escapedRayQueue) return;
        ForAllQueued("Handle escaped rays", escapedRayQueue, maxQueueSize,
            PBRT_CPU_GPU_LAMBDA (const EscapedRayWorkItem w) {
                ⟨Compute weighted radiance for escaped ray 956⟩
                ⟨Update pixel radiance if ray's radiance is nonzero 956⟩
            });
    }
```

`EscapedRayQueue`, not included here, is a `WorkQueue` of `EscapedRayWorkItems`. It provides a `Push()` method that takes a `RayWorkItem` and copies the values from it that are needed in the kernel.

⟨*EscapedRayWorkItem Definition*⟩ ≡
```
    struct EscapedRayWorkItem {
        ⟨EscapedRayWorkItem Public Members 955⟩
    };
```

The work item for escaped rays stores the ray origin, direction, and depth as well as its wavelengths. The ray's associated pixel index makes it possible to add any found emission to its radiance estimate.

⟨*EscapedRayWorkItem Public Members*⟩ ≡   **955**
```
    Point3f rayo;
    Vector3f rayd;
    int depth;
    SampledWavelengths lambda;
    int pixelIndex;
```

The kernel's implementation parallels the ⟨*Accumulate contributions from infinite light sources*⟩ fragment in the VolPathIntegrator, just using the information about the ray from the EscapedRayWorkItem.

⟨*Compute weighted radiance for escaped ray*⟩ ≡   955
```
SampledSpectrum L(0.f);
for (const auto &light : *infiniteLights) {
    if (SampledSpectrum Le = light.Le(Ray(w.rayo, w.rayd), w.lambda); Le) {
        ⟨Compute path radiance contribution from infinite light 956⟩
    }
}
```

The final result is then added to the ray's associated PixelSampleState::L value, so long as L is nonzero. If it is zero, skipping the unnecessary update may not lead to fewer instructions being executed, given the GPU's execution model, but it will save memory bandwidth, which can be just as important to performance.

⟨*Update pixel radiance if ray's radiance is nonzero*⟩ ≡   955
```
if (L) {
    L += pixelSampleState.L[w.pixelIndex];
    pixelSampleState.L[w.pixelIndex] = L;
}
```

For infinite area lights that are directly visible or are encountered through specular reflection, MIS is performed using only the unidirectional path PDF, since that is the only way the path could have been sampled.

⟨*Compute path radiance contribution from infinite light*⟩ ≡   956
```
if (w.depth == 0 || w.specularBounce) {
    L += w.beta * Le / w.r_u.Average();
} else {
    ⟨Compute MIS-weighted radiance contribution from infinite light 956⟩
}
```

The path throughput beta is needed to weight the light's contribution. Further, whether or not the previous bounce was due to specular reflection must be tracked. Note that this value only requires a single bit; using a full 32-bit int is wasteful. A more optimized implementation might save some bandwidth by stealing one of the bits from pixelIndex, which does not need all 32 of them.

⟨*EscapedRayWorkItem Public Members*⟩ +≡   955
```
SampledSpectrum beta;
int specularBounce;
```

If other types of scattering preceded the ray's escape, MIS weights are computed using both the light and unidirectional sampling PDFs, following the same approach as is implemented in the ⟨*Add infinite light contribution using both PDFs with MIS*⟩ fragment in the VolPathIntegrator.

⟨*Compute MIS-weighted radiance contribution from infinite light*⟩ ≡   956
```
LightSampleContext ctx = w.prevIntrCtx;
Float lightChoicePDF = lightSampler.PMF(ctx, light);
SampledSpectrum r_l = w.r_l * lightChoicePDF *
    light.PDF_Li(ctx, w.rayd, true);
L += w.beta * Le / (w.r_u + r_l).Average();
```

In order to compute MIS weights, the `EscapedRayWorkItem` must provide not only rescaled path probabilities but also geometric information about the previous path scattering vertex.

⟨*EscapedRayWorkItem Public Members*⟩ +≡   955
```
SampledSpectrum r_u, r_l;
LightSampleContext prevIntrCtx;
```

The second kernel handles rays that intersect emissive surfaces.

⟨*WavefrontPathIntegrator Method Definitions*⟩ +≡
```
void WavefrontPathIntegrator::HandleEmissiveIntersection() {
    ForAllQueued("Handle emitters hit by indirect rays", hitAreaLightQueue,
            maxQueueSize,
        PBRT_CPU_GPU_LAMBDA (const HitAreaLightWorkItem w) {
            ⟨Find emitted radiance from surface that ray hit 957⟩
            ⟨Compute area light's weighted radiance contribution to the path 958⟩
            ⟨Update L in PixelSampleState for area light's radiance 958⟩
        });
}
```

The `HitAreaLightQueue` stores `HitAreaLightWorkItem`s.

⟨*HitAreaLightQueue Definition*⟩ ≡
```
using HitAreaLightQueue = WorkQueue<HitAreaLightWorkItem>;
```

⟨*WavefrontPathIntegrator Member Variables*⟩ +≡   939
```
HitAreaLightQueue *hitAreaLightQueue = nullptr;
```

⟨*HitAreaLightWorkItem Definition*⟩ ≡
```
struct HitAreaLightWorkItem {
    ⟨HitAreaLightWorkItem Public Members 958⟩
};
```

The first step in the kernel is to compute the emitted radiance at the ray's intersection point. If there is none, the kernel can return immediately. Note that it thus could be beneficial if a `Light` method was added that did a quick conservative test for this case. Such a method could make it possible not to pay the cost of enqueuing work for cases such as a one-sided light source that was intersected on its non-emissive side. With the current implementation, that case is detected only here, costing both bandwidth for the queue work and execution divergence from the threads that return. (Such a method should be simple, deferring more complex tasks like performing texture lookups for surfaces that use image maps to modulate their emission, in order not to harm performance.)

We also note that the call to `Light::L()` would be a potential source of execution divergence if pbrt had more than one `Light` implementation that could be used for emissive surfaces. Currently, there is only `DiffuseAreaLight`, so this is not a concern, but if there were more, it might be worthwhile to have a separate queue for each type of area light in order to avoid this divergence.

⟨*Find emitted radiance from surface that ray hit*⟩ ≡   957
```
SampledSpectrum Le = w.areaLight.L(w.p, w.n, w.uv, w.wo, w.lambda);
if (!Le)
    return;
```

The following `HitAreaLightWorkItem` member variables provide the information necessary to compute the emitted radiance from the intersection point back along the ray.

⟨*HitAreaLightWorkItem Public Members*⟩ ≡   957
```
Light areaLight;
Point3f p;
Normal3f n;
Point2f uv;
Vector3f wo;
SampledWavelengths lambda;
```

The final path contribution is found similarly to how it is for escaped rays and infinite area lights.

⟨*Compute area light's weighted radiance contribution to the path*⟩ ≡   957
```
SampledSpectrum L(0.f);
if (w.depth == 0 || w.specularBounce) {
    L = w.beta * Le / w.r_u.Average();
} else {
    ⟨Compute MIS-weighted radiance contribution from area light⟩
}
```

Once again, the `specularBounce` member could be packed in elsewhere in order to save storage and reduce bandwidth requirements.

⟨*HitAreaLightWorkItem Public Members*⟩ +≡   957
```
int depth;
SampledSpectrum beta, r_u, r_l;
LightSampleContext prevIntrCtx;
int specularBounce;
int pixelIndex;
```

We will not include the ⟨*Compute MIS-weighted radiance contribution from area light*⟩ fragment here, which closely parallels the corresponding case in the `VolPathIntegrator` as well as the earlier fragment ⟨*Compute MIS-weighted radiance contribution from infinite light*⟩.

The final weighted radiance value is then accumulated in the ray's `PixelSampleState`.

⟨*Update* L *in* PixelSampleState *for area light's radiance*⟩ ≡   957
```
L += pixelSampleState.L[w.pixelIndex];
pixelSampleState.L[w.pixelIndex] = L;
```

The queues for both of these kernels need to be reset at the start of each ray depth iteration, so we will add the corresponding Reset() calls to the queue-resetting fragment defined earlier.

⟨*Reset queues before tracing next batch of rays*⟩ ≡   948
```
if (escapedRayQueue) escapedRayQueue->Reset();
hitAreaLightQueue->Reset();
```

Having seen these two kernels, it is fair to ask: why not handle these cases immediately in the ray intersection and medium sampling kernels, rather than incurring the bandwidth costs of queuing up work there and then consuming it here? This is yet another trade-off of bandwidth versus execution convergence. Doing this work in separate kernels for only the cases where it is required means that the kernels both start execution fully converged, with all threads doing useful work. In the intersection and medium scattering kernels, we would generally expect that only a subset of the rays would leave the scene or intersect emissive surfaces. In that case, we would have control divergence and all rays in the thread group that did not intersect an emissive surface would incur a performance cost if even one of the others did. The optimal trade-off depends on both the complexity of the computation to be done in those cases and the amount of bandwidth offered by the GPU.

15.3.9 SURFACE SCATTERING

With the WavefrontPathIntegrator, the majority of rendering time is usually spent in the kernels responsible for surface scattering. These kernels are specialized by the surfaces' materials and, in turn, the type of BxDF that each material uses for the BSDF it returns. Starting from a ray–shape intersection, a surface-scattering kernel handles everything from normal and bump mapping to material evaluation, light and BSDF sampling, and queuing up shadow and indirect rays for later processing.

All of this starts with the Render() method calling EvaluateMaterialsAndBSDFs(), which is implemented in wavefront/surfscatter.cpp. With this method's implementation, we encounter a new idiom that orchestrates the kernel launches: a call to ForEachType(). In its use here, that function iterates over all of the types that a Material could be and calls a callback function for each one of them. Thus, if pbrt is extended with an additional material, adding that one to the list of materials that Material passes to the TaggedPointer that it inherits from in its declaration in base/material.h automatically leads to a specialized kernel for that material being generated here.

⟨*WavefrontPathIntegrator Surface Scattering Methods*⟩ ≡
```
void WavefrontPathIntegrator::EvaluateMaterialsAndBSDFs(
        int wavefrontDepth) {
    ForEachType(EvaluateMaterialCallback{wavefrontDepth, this},
            Material::Types());
}
```

A lambda function is not sufficient to pass to ForEachType(), as it does not pass a value of the given type to the callback but instead invokes its function call operator, passing the type for use in a template specialization. Therefore, we wrap the values needed for the material evaluation method call in a small structure.

⟨*EvaluateMaterialCallback Definition*⟩ ≡
```
struct EvaluateMaterialCallback {
    int wavefrontDepth;
    WavefrontPathIntegrator *integrator;
    ⟨EvaluateMaterialCallback Public Methods 959⟩
};
```

ForEachType() invokes the following method for each type of material. We skip over the MixMaterial here, since all instances of it are resolved to one of the other material types before being enqueued for the surface-shading kernels. (See Section 10.5.1 for a discussion of this detail of MixMaterial's usage.)

⟨*EvaluateMaterialCallback Public Methods*⟩ ≡   **959**
```
template <typename ConcreteMaterial>
void operator()() {
    if constexpr (!std::is_same_v<ConcreteMaterial, MixMaterial>)
        integrator->EvaluateMaterialAndBSDF<ConcreteMaterial>(wavefrontDepth);
}
```

The EvaluateMaterialAndBSDF() method does not yet bring us to the point of launching kernels—two considerations are handled beforehand. First, the implementation skips launching the specialized EvaluateMaterialAndBSDF() method for any material types that are not present in the scene. Such work queues will have no entries, so there is no reason to bother with them. This is handled using two arrays, haveBasicEvalMaterial and haveUniversalEvalMaterial, that are initialized in the WavefrontPathIntegrator constructor. (The two further distinguish the materials based on the complexity of their textures, which is a topic that will be discussed immediately after the following fragment.) Both arrays are indexed using the TaggedPointer TypeIndex() method, which returns an integer index for each representable type.

⟨*WavefrontPathIntegrator Surface Scattering Methods*⟩ +≡
```
template <typename ConcreteMaterial>
void WavefrontPathIntegrator::EvaluateMaterialAndBSDF(int wavefrontDepth) {
    int index = Material::TypeIndex<ConcreteMaterial>();
    if (haveBasicEvalMaterial[index])
        EvaluateMaterialAndBSDF<ConcreteMaterial, BasicTextureEvaluator>(
                            basicEvalMaterialQueue, wavefrontDepth);
    if (haveUniversalEvalMaterial[index])
        EvaluateMaterialAndBSDF<ConcreteMaterial, UniversalTextureEvaluator>(
                            universalEvalMaterialQueue, wavefrontDepth);
}
```

The WavefrontPathIntegrator maintains two work queues for materials, partitioning them based on the complexity of their textures. Each queue is a MultiWorkQueue with one entry for each material type.

⟨*WavefrontPathIntegrator Member Variables*⟩ +≡   939
```
MaterialEvalQueue *basicEvalMaterialQueue = nullptr;
MaterialEvalQueue *universalEvalMaterialQueue = nullptr;
```

These give two more queues to add to the ones that are reset at the start of tracing rays at each wavefront depth.

⟨*Reset queues before tracing next batch of rays*⟩ +≡   948
```
basicEvalMaterialQueue->Reset();
universalEvalMaterialQueue->Reset();
```

Before continuing into the EvaluateMaterialAndBSDF() template specialization, we will detour to discuss texture evaluation in the wavefront integrator in more detail. Recall that when the Material interface was introduced in Section 10.5, it included the notion of a TextureEvaluator. Methods like GetBxDF() and GetBSSRDF() were templated on this type, took an instance of it as a parameter, and used it to evaluate textures rather than calling their Evaluate() methods directly.

There was no point in doing that for CPU rendering: there, a UniversalTextureEvaluator is always used. It immediately forwards texture evaluation requests on to the textures. pbrt's full set of textures spans a wide range of complexity, however, ranging from trivial constant textures that return a fixed value to complex textures that evaluate noise functions to ones like SpectrumMixTexture that themselves recursively evaluate other textures.

Not only do more complex textures require more registers on the GPU, but the potential for unbounded recursion from the mixture textures requires that the compiler allocate resources to be prepared for that case. In turn, the performance of evaluating the simpler textures can be harmed due to choices the compiler has made for the more complex ones. Because the simpler textures are common, it is thus worthwhile to separate materials according to the complexity of their textures and to have separate kernels for the materials that only use the simpler ones.[8] Doing so can give further benefits from reducing control flow divergence. The following BasicTextureEvaluator class helps with this task.

⟨*BasicTextureEvaluator Definition*⟩ ≡
```
class BasicTextureEvaluator {
  public:
    ⟨BasicTextureEvaluator Public Methods 961⟩
};
```

We will categorize constant textures and plain image map textures as "basic." Thus, the BasicTextureEvaluator's CanEvaluate() method iterates over all provided textures and checks that each is one of those types. When material evaluation work is to be enqueued in the EnqueueWorkAfterIntersection() function, the material's Material::CanEvaluate Textures() method is called with a BasicTextureEvaluator to determine whether the work is valid for the basic material evaluation queues. If not, it goes on the appropriate universalEval MaterialQueue.

⟨*BasicTextureEvaluator Public Methods*⟩ ≡   961
```
bool CanEvaluate(std::initializer_list<FloatTexture> ftex,
                 std::initializer_list<SpectrumTexture> stex) const {
    ⟨Return false if any FloatTextures cannot be evaluated 961⟩
    ⟨Return false if any SpectrumTextures cannot be evaluated⟩
    return true;
}
```

The texture types are easily checked with the TaggedPointer::Is() method. (The scene initialization code creates instances of GPUFloatImageTexture in place of FloatImageTextures when GPU rendering is being used. That class uses platform-specific functionality to perform filtered texture look-ups more efficiently than executing Image methods would. GPUSpectrum ImageTexture follows equivalently.)

⟨*Return* false *if any* FloatTextures *cannot be evaluated*⟩ ≡   961
```
for (FloatTexture f : ftex)
    if (f && !f.Is<FloatConstantTexture>() && !f.Is<FloatImageTexture>() &&
        !f.Is<GPUFloatImageTexture>())
        return false;
```

The corresponding fragment for SpectrumTextures is equivalent and is therefore not included here.

The implementation of the TextureEvaluator evaluation method is key to the efficiency benefits provided by this approach. It would do no good to sort materials based on their textures but to then use pbrt's regular dynamic dispatch mechanism for texture evaluation: in that case, the compiler would have no insight into the fact that the texture being passed to it must be one of the simple types accepted by CanEvaluate().

Therefore, the evaluation method instead tries casting the texture to each of the supported types until it finds the correct one. It then calls the corresponding evaluation method directly. In this way, the compiler can easily tell that the only texture evaluation methods that might be called are those for FloatConstantTexture, FloatImageTexture, and GPUFloatImageTexture,

---

8   We have found that this partitioning of texture evaluation work can give as much as a 20% improvement in rendering performance on current GPUs.

and it does not need to worry about resource allocation for evaluating the more complex texture types.

⟨*BasicTextureEvaluator Public Methods*⟩ +≡   **961**
```
Float operator()(FloatTexture tex, TextureEvalContext ctx) {
    if (tex.Is<FloatConstantTexture>())
        return tex.Cast<FloatConstantTexture>()->Evaluate(ctx);
    else if (tex.Is<FloatImageTexture>())
        return tex.Cast<FloatImageTexture>()->Evaluate(ctx);
    else if (tex.Is<GPUFloatImageTexture>())
        return tex.Cast<GPUFloatImageTexture>()->Evaluate(ctx);
    else
        return 0.f;
}
```

The evaluation method for spectrum textures is similar and therefore not included here.

With the motivation for the BasicTextureEvaluator explained, it is possible to better understand why ImageTextureBase in Section 10.4.1 offers scale and invert parameters even though scale and mix textures could be used to achieve the same results. With that capability directly available in textures that can be evaluated by the BasicTextureEvaluator, the UniversalTextureEvaluator can be invoked less often. pbrt actually has a texture rewriting pass that, for example, converts a scale texture with a constant scale applied to an image texture to just an image texture, configured to apply that scale itself. (See, for example, the SpectrumScaledTexture::Create() method implementation for details.)

The following definition of the MaterialEvalQueue type is admittedly complex. However, it is another key to pbrt's extensibility. For material and BSDF evaluation, we would like to have a MultiWorkQueue where there is a separate queue for each type of Material that pbrt supports, where the type of the work items is the template class MaterialEvalWorkItem, specialized with each material type. While we could enumerate all the currently supported materials in template parameters, to do so would mean that adding a new material to the system would require editing an obscure part of the wavefront integrator implementation for it to be available there as well.

Therefore, we go through some gymnastics in order to define the type of the MultiWorkQueue automatically. First, the TaggedPointer type that Material inherits from includes a type declaration, Types, that holds a TypePack of all types that the pointer can represent. We then use the MapType functionality from Section B.4.3 to wrap each material type inside the forthcoming MaterialEvalWorkItem template class. This gives us the final TypePack of types to provide to MultiWorkQueue.

⟨*MaterialEvalQueue Definition*⟩ ≡
```
using MaterialEvalQueue =
    MultiWorkQueue<typename MapType<MaterialEvalWorkItem,
                          typename Material::Types>::type>;
```

⟨*MaterialEvalWorkItem Definition*⟩ ≡
```
template <typename ConcreteMaterial>
struct MaterialEvalWorkItem {
    ⟨MaterialEvalWorkItem Public Methods⟩
    ⟨MaterialEvalWorkItem Public Members 963⟩
};
```

It is crucial to have a pointer to the material in `MaterialEvalWorkItem`. Note that this can be a pointer to a concrete material type such as `DiffuseMaterial` due to `MaterialEvalWorkItem` being a template class on the `ConcreteMaterial` type. (We will introduce the rest of the member variables of the `MaterialEvalWorkItem` as they are used in code in the remainder of the section.)

⟨*MaterialEvalWorkItem Public Members*⟩ ≡   962
```
const ConcreteMaterial *material;
```

With this context in hand, we can proceed to the implementation of the `EvaluateMaterial` `AndBSDF()` method. It is parameterized both by the concrete type of material that is being evaluated and by a `TextureEvaluator`, which allows us to generate specializations based not only on material but also on the two types of `TextureEvaluator`.

⟨*WavefrontPathIntegrator Surface Scattering Methods*⟩ +≡
```
template <typename ConcreteMaterial, typename TextureEvaluator>
void WavefrontPathIntegrator::EvaluateMaterialAndBSDF(
        MaterialEvalQueue *evalQueue, int wavefrontDepth) {
    ⟨Get BSDF for items in evalQueue and sample illumination 963⟩
}
```

After some initialization work that includes getting a pointer to the `WorkQueue` for material evaluation of `ConcreteMaterial`, the work items in the queue are processed in parallel.

⟨*Get BSDF for items in* evalQueue *and sample illumination*⟩ ≡   963
```
⟨Construct desc for material/texture evaluation kernel⟩
RayQueue *nextRayQueue = NextRayQueue(wavefrontDepth);
auto queue = evalQueue->Get<MaterialEvalWorkItem<ConcreteMaterial>>();
ForAllQueued(desc.c_str(), queue, maxQueueSize,
    PBRT_CPU_GPU_LAMBDA (const MaterialEvalWorkItem<ConcreteMaterial> w) {
        ⟨Evaluate material and BSDF for ray intersection 963⟩
    });
```

The structure of the material evaluation and sampling kernel parallels that of the surface-scattering–focused part of `VolPathIntegrator::Li()`.

⟨*Evaluate material and BSDF for ray intersection*⟩ ≡   963
```
TextureEvaluator texEval;
⟨Compute differentials for position and (u, v) at intersection point 964⟩
⟨Compute shading normal if bump or normal mapping is being used 964⟩
⟨Get BSDF at intersection point 965⟩
⟨Regularize BSDF, if appropriate 966⟩
⟨Initialize VisibleSurface at first intersection if necessary⟩
⟨Sample BSDF and enqueue indirect ray at intersection point 966⟩
⟨Sample light and enqueue shadow ray at intersection point 968⟩
```

One difference from the `VolPathIntegrator` is that the wavefront integrator does not carry ray differentials with the rays it traces. Therefore, in order to compute filter widths for texture filtering, the `Camera`'s `Approximate_dp_dxy()` method is used to compute approximate differentials at the intersection point. While the resulting filter width estimates are less accurate if there has been specular reflection or transmission from curved surfaces, they usually work well in practice. Note that by declaring local variables `dpdu` and `dpdv` at the end of this fragment that store the surface's partial derivatives, we are able to reuse the earlier fragment ⟨*Estimate screen-space change in* (u, v)⟩ to compute the (u, v) texture derivatives.

⟨*Compute differentials for position and* (u, v) *at intersection point*⟩ ≡   **963**
```
Vector3f dpdx, dpdy;
Float dudx = 0, dudy = 0, dvdx = 0, dvdy = 0;
camera.Approximate_dp_dxy(Point3f(w.pi), w.n, w.time, samplesPerPixel,
                          &dpdx, &dpdy);
Vector3f dpdu = w.dpdu, dpdv = w.dpdv;
```
⟨*Estimate screen-space change in* (u, v) **641**⟩

MaterialEvalWorkItem also carries a variety of information about the local geometry of the ray–shape intersection that is copied from the SurfaceInteraction when material evaluation work is enqueued.

⟨*MaterialEvalWorkItem Public Members*⟩ +≡   **962**
```
Point3fi pi;
Normal3f n;
Vector3f dpdu, dpdv;
Float time;
int depth;
```

Before any further work is done, the effect of normal or bump mapping on the local shading geometry is found, if appropriate.

⟨*Compute shading normal if bump or normal mapping is being used*⟩ ≡   **963**
```
Normal3f ns = w.ns;
Vector3f dpdus = w.dpdus;
FloatTexture displacement = w.material->GetDisplacement();
const Image *normalMap = w.material->GetNormalMap();
if (normalMap) {
    ⟨Call NormalMap() to find shading geometry 965⟩
} else if (displacement) {
    ⟨Call BumpMap() to find shading geometry⟩
}
```

MaterialEvalWorkItem carries along information about the initial shading geometry from the intersected shape for a starting point for calls to NormalMap() or BumpMap() and for direct use if there is no normal or bump mapping at the intersection point.

⟨*MaterialEvalWorkItem Public Members*⟩ +≡   **962**
```
Normal3f ns;
Vector3f dpdus, dpdvs;
Normal3f dndus, dndvs;
Point2f uv;
```

As before, all work related to normal mapping is performed in the NormalMap() function and bump mapping is handled by BumpMap(). Note that here we are able to avoid dynamic dispatch in the calling of the material's GetDisplacement() and GetNormalMap() methods thanks to ConcreteMaterial being a known specific material type. If a displacement texture or normal map is present, the NormalBumpEvalContext for the call to BumpMap() comes from a MaterialEvalWorkItem utility function that we do not include here; it just initializes a NormalBumpEvalContext using appropriate values from its member variables.

On the GPU, there are a few ways that there may be execution divergence here. First, if some of the threads in the thread group have normal maps or displacement textures and some do not, then all of them will pay the cost of executing the NormalMap() and BumpMap() functions. Second, some threads may have displacement textures and others may have normal maps, which will lead to execution divergence. Finally, the types of the FloatTextures used for defining displacements may vary across the threads. Each of these factors could be used to sort work more finely, though we have not found this divergence to be too much of a problem in practice.

⟨*Call* NormalMap() *to find shading geometry*⟩ ≡   964
```
NormalBumpEvalContext bctx = w.GetNormalBumpEvalContext(dudx, dudy,
                                                        dvdx, dvdy);

Vector3f dpdvs;
NormalMap(*normalMap, bctx, &dpdus, &dpdvs);
ns = Normal3f(Normalize(Cross(dpdus, dpdvs)));
ns = FaceForward(ns, w.n);
```

The fragment that calls BumpMap() for bump mapping parallels the one for normal mapping, so it is not included here.

The BSDF is initialized here in a different way than in the VolPathIntegrator. Because the EvaluateMaterialAndBSDF() method is specialized on the material type, and because Materials in pbrt must provide a type definition for their associated BxDF, it is possible to stack-allocate the BxDF here rather than use an instance of the ScratchBuffer class to allocate space for it. It is then possible to call the material's GetBxDF() method directly rather than using dynamic dispatch through a call to Material::GetBSDF() to do so.

The benefit from avoiding use of the ScratchBuffer for BxDFs is significant: just as stack-allocating the concrete Sampler type in the camera ray generation and sample generation kernels made it possible for the Sampler's member variables to be stored in GPU registers, this approach does the same for the BxDF, giving a substantial performance benefit compared to storing them in device memory.

The MaterialEvalWorkItem GetMaterialEvalContext() method, which is also not included here, initializes a MaterialEvalContext from its corresponding member variables.

⟨*Get BSDF at intersection point*⟩ ≡   963
```
SampledWavelengths lambda = w.lambda;
MaterialEvalContext ctx = w.GetMaterialEvalContext(dudx, dudy, dvdx, dvdy,
                                                   ns, dpdus);
using ConcreteBxDF = typename ConcreteMaterial::BxDF;
ConcreteBxDF bxdf = w.material->GetBxDF(texEval, ctx, lambda);
BSDF bsdf(ctx.ns, ctx.dpdus, &bxdf);
```
⟨*Handle terminated secondary wavelengths after BSDF creation* **965**⟩

⟨*MaterialEvalWorkItem Public Members*⟩ +≡   962
```
SampledWavelengths lambda;
```

The call to GetBxDF() above may cause secondary wavelengths to be terminated—for example, in case of dispersion. It is therefore important that the stack-allocated lambda value both be used here in this kernel and also be passed along to subsequent rendering kernels, rather than the initial SampledWavelengths value from the MaterialEvalWorkItem. If the secondary wavelengths in lambda have been terminated, the copy of the SampledWavelengths for the path in PixelSampleState must be updated. Note that the implementation here may end up writing lambda multiple times redundantly at subsequent intersections in that case.

⟨*Handle terminated secondary wavelengths after BSDF creation*⟩ ≡   965
```
if (lambda.SecondaryTerminated())
    pixelSampleState.lambda[w.pixelIndex] = lambda;
```

⟨*MaterialEvalWorkItem Public Members*⟩ +≡   962
```
int pixelIndex;
```

BSDF regularization proceeds as before, only happening if the option has been enabled and a ray has undergone a non-specular scattering event.

⟨*Regularize BSDF, if appropriate*⟩ ≡   963
```
if (regularize && w.anyNonSpecularBounces)
    bsdf.Regularize();
```

The `anyNonSpecularBounces` member variable is yet another single-bit quantity taking up 32 bits. A more bandwidth-efficient implementation would pack this value into a free bit elsewhere in the `MaterialEvalWorkItem`.

⟨*MaterialEvalWorkItem Public Members*⟩ +≡   962
```
int anyNonSpecularBounces;
```

We will omit the fragment that initializes the `VisibleSurface` at the first intersection, as it is not especially interesting or different than the corresponding code in the CPU-based rendering path.

There are two new things to see in the fragment that samples the BSDF. First, the sample values used come from the `RaySamples` object rather than from `Sampler` method calls. Second, because the `ConcreteBxDF` type is known here at compile time, it is possible to call the templated `BSDF::Sample_f()` variant that takes the BxDF type and thus avoids dynamic dispatch, calling the appropriate BxDF method implementation directly.

⟨*Sample BSDF and enqueue indirect ray at intersection point*⟩ ≡   963
```
Vector3f wo = w.wo;
RaySamples raySamples = pixelSampleState.samples[w.pixelIndex];
pstd::optional<BSDFSample> bsdfSample =
    bsdf.Sample_f<ConcreteBxDF>(wo, raySamples.indirect.uc,
                                raySamples.indirect.u);
if (bsdfSample) {
    ⟨Compute updated path throughput and PDFs and enqueue indirect ray 966⟩
}
```

⟨*MaterialEvalWorkItem Public Members*⟩ +≡   962
```
Vector3f wo;
```

The path throughput and rescaled path probabilities are updated in the same manner as in the `VolPathIntegrator` ⟨*Update volumetric integrator path state after surface scattering*⟩ fragment.

⟨*Compute updated path throughput and PDFs and enqueue indirect ray*⟩ ≡   966
```
Vector3f wi = bsdfSample->wi;
SampledSpectrum beta = w.beta * bsdfSample->f * AbsDot(wi, ns)/bsdfSample->pdf;
SampledSpectrum r_u = w.r_u, r_l;
⟨Update r_u based on BSDF sample PDF 967⟩
⟨Update etaScale accounting for BSDF scattering 967⟩
⟨Apply Russian roulette to indirect ray based on weighted path throughput⟩
if (beta) {
    ⟨Initialize spawned ray and enqueue for next ray depth 967⟩
}
```

Only the unidirectional rescaled path probability needs to be passed in to this kernel, since the light path probability is initialized during its execution.

⟨*MaterialEvalWorkItem Public Members*⟩ +≡   962
```
SampledSpectrum beta, r_u;
```

The logic for updating the unidirectional rescaled path probability also follows that of the VolPathIntegrator, including how proportional BSDF samples such as those from the LayeredBxDF are handled. The call to the BSDF::PDF() method presents another opportunity to avoid dynamic dispatch given a compile-time known BxDF, however.

⟨*Update r_u based on BSDF sample PDF*⟩ ≡   966
```
if (bsdfSample->pdfIsProportional)
    r_l = r_u / bsdf.PDF<ConcreteBxDF>(wo, bsdfSample->wi);
else
    r_l = r_u / bsdfSample->pdf;
```

The etaScale factor used in Russian roulette is also updated in the same manner as before.

⟨*Update* etaScale *accounting for BSDF scattering*⟩ ≡   966
```
Float etaScale = w.etaScale;
if (bsdfSample->IsTransmission())
    etaScale *= Sqr(bsdfSample->eta);
```

⟨*MaterialEvalWorkItem Public Members*⟩ +≡   962
```
Float etaScale;
```

We will omit the ⟨*Apply Russian roulette to indirect ray based on weighted path throughput*⟩ fragment, which is almost exactly the same as the VolPathIntegrator's ⟨*Possibly terminate volumetric path with Russian roulette*⟩, other than the fact that in this case the sample value for the Russian roulette test comes from RaySamples.indirect.rr.

For indirect rays, a ray is initialized and pushed on to the RayQueue for the next level of the ray tree. (We omit the implementation of the RayQueue::PushIndirectRay() method, which stores the provided values in the corresponding member variables.)

⟨*Initialize spawned ray and enqueue for next ray depth*⟩ ≡   966
```
Ray ray = SpawnRay(w.pi, w.n, w.time, wi);
```
⟨*Initialize ray medium if media are present 967*⟩
```
bool anyNonSpecularBounces = !bsdfSample->IsSpecular() ||
                             w.anyNonSpecularBounces;
LightSampleContext ctx(w.pi, w.n, ns);
nextRayQueue->PushIndirectRay(
    ray, w.depth + 1, ctx, beta, r_u, r_l, lambda,
    etaScale, bsdfSample->IsSpecular(), anyNonSpecularBounces, w.pixelIndex);
```

The medium member of the Ray must be set manually based on which side of the surface the ray starts in.

⟨*Initialize ray medium if media are present*⟩ ≡   967, 968
```
if (haveMedia)
    ray.medium = Dot(ray.d, w.n) > 0 ? w.mediumInterface.outside
                                     : w.mediumInterface.inside;
```

The MediumInterface at the intersection point is thus needed in MaterialEvalWorkItem.

⟨*MaterialEvalWorkItem Public Members*⟩ +≡   962
```
MediumInterface mediumInterface;
```

Indirect rays require a few additions to the RayWorkItem class including the current path throughput β, rescaled path probabilities, and the information necessary to compute MIS weights if the ray encounters emission.

⟨*RayWorkItem Public Members*⟩ +≡   947
```
    SampledSpectrum beta, r_u, r_l;
    LightSampleContext prevIntrCtx;
    Float etaScale;
    int specularBounce;
    int anyNonSpecularBounces;
```

The direct lighting calculation follows a similar path as in the VolPathIntegrator.

⟨*Sample light and enqueue shadow ray at intersection point*⟩ ≡   963
```
    BxDFFlags flags = bsdf.Flags();
    if (IsNonSpecular(flags)) {
        ⟨Choose a light source using the LightSampler⟩
        ⟨Sample light source and evaluate BSDF for direct lighting⟩
        ⟨Compute path throughput and path PDFs for light sample 968⟩
        ⟨Enqueue shadow ray with tentative radiance contribution 968⟩
    }
```

We will omit the ⟨*Choose a light source using the* LightSampler⟩ and ⟨*Sample light source and evaluate BSDF for direct lighting*⟩ fragments, as they are essentially the same as corresponding fragments that we have seen in earlier integrators. The first fragment gives us the sampledLight variable that stores a SampledLight and the second calls Light::SampleLi() with that light, giving an ls variable that stores the LightLiSample.

The path throughput and path sampling weights are computed in the same way as they are in the VolPathIntegrator::SampleLd() method, though here it is again possible to use the templated BSDF::PDF() method that avoids the dynamic dispatch overhead to compute the BSDF's PDF.

⟨*Compute path throughput and path PDFs for light sample*⟩ ≡   968
```
    SampledSpectrum beta = w.beta * f * AbsDot(wi, ns);
    Float lightPDF = ls->pdf * sampledLight->p;
    Float bsdfPDF = IsDeltaLight(light.Type()) ? 0.f
                                      : bsdf.PDF<ConcreteBxDF>(wo, wi);
    SampledSpectrum r_u = w.r_u * bsdfPDF;
    SampledSpectrum r_l = w.r_u * lightPDF;
```

We go ahead and compute Ld, which is the final weighted contribution that the shadow ray would give to the pixel sample's radiance estimate if it is unoccluded. If the ray is unoccluded and there are participating media in the scene, Ld may still be reduced due to the effect of extinction along the shadow ray; that factor is handled when the shadow ray is traced.

⟨*Enqueue shadow ray with tentative radiance contribution*⟩ ≡   968
```
    SampledSpectrum Ld = beta * ls->L;
    Ray ray = SpawnRayTo(w.pi, w.n, w.time, ls->pLight.pi, ls->pLight.n);
    ⟨Initialize ray medium if media are present 967⟩
    shadowRayQueue->Push(ShadowRayWorkItem{ray, 1 - ShadowEpsilon, lambda, Ld,
                                     r_u, r_l, w.pixelIndex});
```

15.3.10 SHADOW RAYS

The set of shadow rays to be traced after material evaluation and the direct lighting calculation in the EvaluateMaterialAndBSDF() method are stored in a ShadowRayQueue.

⟨*ShadowRayQueue Definition*⟩ ≡
```
using ShadowRayQueue = WorkQueue<ShadowRayWorkItem>;
```

A single ShadowRayQueue is maintained by the WavefrontPathIntegrator.

⟨*WavefrontPathIntegrator Member Variables*⟩ +≡   **939**
```
ShadowRayQueue *shadowRayQueue = nullptr;
```

The work items in the queue store values that include the ray to be traced, its wavelengths, and tentative contribution Ld, as well as the rescaled path probabilities up to the ray's origin.

⟨*ShadowRayWorkItem Definition*⟩ ≡
```
struct ShadowRayWorkItem {
    Ray ray;
    Float tMax;
    SampledWavelengths lambda;
    SampledSpectrum Ld, r_u, r_l;
    int pixelIndex;
};
```

The WavefrontAggregate interface includes two methods for tracing shadow rays: Intersect Shadow(), which is called for scenes that have no participating media where only a binary visibility test is needed, and IntersectShadowTr() for scenes that do have media and where transmittance must be computed. A call to the WavefrontPathIntegrator::TraceShadowRays() method leads to a call of the appropriate method; the shadow ray queue is reset immediately afterward.

⟨*WavefrontAggregate Interface*⟩ +≡   **951**
```
virtual void IntersectShadow(int maxRays, ShadowRayQueue *shadowRayQueue,
    SOA<PixelSampleState> *pixelSampleState) const = 0;
virtual void IntersectShadowTr(int maxRays, ShadowRayQueue *shadowRayQueue,
    SOA<PixelSampleState> *pixelSampleState) const = 0;
```

The CPU implementation of IntersectShadow() processes items from the queue in parallel and calls its aggregate's IntersectP() method to determine if each ray is occluded. A call to RecordShadowRayResult(), another utility function shared by both CPU and GPU aggregates that is defined in wavefront/intersect.h, takes care of the additional work to be done after the intersection test has been resolved.

⟨*CPUAggregate Method Definitions*⟩ ≡
```
void CPUAggregate::IntersectShadow(
        int maxRays, ShadowRayQueue *shadowRayQueue,
        SOA<PixelSampleState> *pixelSampleState) const {
    ⟨Intersect shadow rays from shadowRayQueue in parallel 970⟩
}
```

⟨*Intersect shadow rays from* shadowRayQueue *in parallel*⟩ ≡   **969**
```
    ParallelFor(0, shadowRayQueue->Size(),
                [=] (int index) {
                    const ShadowRayWorkItem w = (*shadowRayQueue)[index];
                    bool hit = aggregate.IntersectP(w.ray, w.tMax);
                    RecordShadowRayResult(w, pixelSampleState, hit);
                });
```

If the ray was occluded, then no further work is necessary. Otherwise, the final MIS-weighted radiance is found by dividing by the two rescaled path probabilities and is then added to the running sum of the radiance estimate in the PixelSampleState for the ray.

⟨*Wavefront Ray Intersection Enqueuing Functions*⟩ +≡
```
    void RecordShadowRayResult(const ShadowRayWorkItem w,
            SOA<PixelSampleState> *pixelSampleState, bool foundIntersection) {
        if (foundIntersection)
            return;
        SampledSpectrum Ld = w.Ld / (w.r_u + w.r_l).Average();
        SampledSpectrum Lpixel = pixelSampleState->L[w.pixelIndex];
        pixelSampleState->L[w.pixelIndex] = Lpixel + Ld;
    }
```

In the presence of participating media, there is more work to do for shadow rays. The computation proceeds just as in the latter two thirds of the VolPathIntegrator::SampleLd() method: the ray is successively intersected against the scene geometry, terminating if it hits an opaque surface. Otherwise a call to SampleT_maj() samples the medium, so that transmittance can be estimated using ratio tracking just as in ⟨*Update transmittance for current ray segment*⟩ in that method. Given the close similarities, we will not include that code for the wavefront integrator here.

15.3.11 UPDATING THE FILM

Each pixel sample's value is provided to the Film only after all of them are finished. One might wonder: why not push samples on to a queue whenever their ray paths terminate and add film samples sooner by periodically running a kernel that processes the items on the queue? There are two costs to such an approach: the first is that samples would be added to the film in an arbitrary order, so the accesses to values like PixelSampleState::L would be irregular across threads in thread groups, which could harm performance.

The second cost is the unnecessary bandwidth that would be used to push work onto the queue and to process it. We know that every pixel sample taken at the start of tracing each path will eventually be added to the film, so there is no need to separately enumerate them. For both of these reasons, it is more efficient to use a plain GPUParallelFor() loop and process the PixelSampleState structures in order.

⟨*WavefrontPathIntegrator Film Methods*⟩ ≡
```
    void WavefrontPathIntegrator::UpdateFilm() {
        ParallelFor("Update film", maxQueueSize,
            PBRT_CPU_GPU_LAMBDA (int pixelIndex) {
                ⟨Check pixel against film bounds 971⟩
                ⟨Compute final weighted radiance value 971⟩
                ⟨Provide sample radiance value to film 971⟩
            });
    }
```

Recall that the GenerateCameraRays() method sets the PixelSampleState::pPixel coordinates for all the threads, but that it then exits immediately for threads corresponding to extra scanlines beyond the end of the image. Therefore, we must perform the same check of the pixel coordinates against the film bounds here, and not do any further processing for such pixels.

⟨*Check pixel against film bounds*⟩ ≡ 970

```
Point2i pPixel = pixelSampleState.pPixel[pixelIndex];
if (!InsideExclusive(pPixel, film.PixelBounds()))
    return;
```

The final radiance value is scaled by the camera ray weight returned by the Camera before it is provided to the Film.[9]

⟨*Compute final weighted radiance value*⟩ ≡ 970

```
SampledSpectrum Lw = SampledSpectrum(pixelSampleState.L[pixelIndex]) *
                            pixelSampleState.cameraRayWeight[pixelIndex];
```

A few more values read from pixelSampleState and we have everything that we need to call the Film's AddSample() method. The implementation uses the initializeVisibleSurface member variable, set in the constructor, to distinguish between Film implementations that make use of the VisibleSurface and those that do not in order to save the memory bandwidth of reading it if it will not be used.

⟨*Provide sample radiance value to film*⟩ ≡ 970

```
SampledWavelengths lambda = pixelSampleState.lambda[pixelIndex];
Float filterWeight = pixelSampleState.filterWeight[pixelIndex];
if (initializeVisibleSurface) {
    ⟨Call Film::AddSample() with VisibleSurface for pixel sample 971⟩
} else
    film.AddSample(pPixel, Lw, lambda, nullptr, filterWeight);
```

One interesting detail is that the VisibleSurface must be loaded from SOA format into the regular VisibleSurface structure layout so that a pointer to it can be passed to the AddSample() method; a pointer to its current in-memory representation does not correspond to the layout that this method expects.

⟨*Call Film::AddSample() with VisibleSurface for pixel sample*⟩ ≡ 971

```
VisibleSurface visibleSurface = pixelSampleState.visibleSurface[pixelIndex];
film.AddSample(pPixel, Lw, lambda, &visibleSurface, filterWeight);
```

FURTHER READING

Purcell et al. (2002, 2003) and Carr, Hall, and Hart (2002) were the first to map general-purpose ray tracers to graphics processors.

A classic paper by Aila and Laine (2009) carefully analyzed the performance of ray tracing on contemporary GPUs and developed improved traversal algorithms based on their insights. Follow-on work by Laine et al. (2013) discussed the benefits of the wavefront architecture for

---

9   The explicit SampledSpectrum cast of the L value read from pixelSampleState is an unfortunate artifact of the GetSetIndirector used in the SOA classes. If the value read from the array is not immediately converted to a SampledSpectrum, then the compiler is left with what seems to be an attempt to multiply a GetSetIndirector type with a SampledSpectrum, leading to a syntax error.

rendering systems that support a wide variety of materials, textures, and lights. (The use of a wavefront approach for the path tracer described in this chapter is motivated by Laine et al.'s insights.)

Most work in performance optimization for GPU ray tracers analyzes the balance between improving thread execution and memory convergence versus the cost of reordering work to do so.[10] Influential early work includes Hoberock et al. (2009), who re-sorted a large number of intersection points to create coherent collections of work before executing their surface shaders. Novák et al. (2010) introduced *path regeneration* to start tracing new ray paths in threads that are otherwise idle due to ray termination. Wald (2011) and van Antwerpen (2011) both applied compaction, densely packing the active threads in thread groups.

Lier et al. (2018b) considered the unconventional approach of distributing the work for a single ray across multiple GPU threads and showed performance benefits for incoherent rays. (This approach parallels how computation is often mapped to CPU SIMD units for high-performance ray tracing.)

Reordering the rays to be traced can also improve performance by improving the coherence of memory accesses performed during intersection tests. Early work in this area was done by Garanzha and Loop (2010) and Costa et al. (2015). Meister et al. (2020) have recently examined ray reordering in the context of a GPU with hardware-accelerated intersection testing and found benefits from using it.

An alternative to taking an arbitrary set of rays and finding structure in them is to generate rays that are inherently coherent in the first place. Examples include the algorithms of Szirmay-Kalos and Purgathofer (1998) and Hachisuka (2005), which select a single direction for all indirect rays at each level, allowing the use of a rasterizer with parallel projection to trace them. More generally, adding structure to the sample values used for importance sampling can lead to coherence in the rays that are traced. Keller and Heidrich (2001) developed interleaved sampling patterns that reuse sample values at separated pixels in order to trade off sample coherence and variation, and Sadeghi et al. (2009) investigated the combination of interleaved sampling and using the same pseudo-random sequence at nearby pixels to increase ray coherence. Dufay et al. (2016) randomized samples using small random offsets so that nearby pixels still have similar sample values.

Efficient GPU-based construction of acceleration structures is challenging due to the degree of parallelism required; there has been much research on this topic. See Zhou et al. (2008), Lauterbach et al. (2009), Pantaleoni and Luebke (2010), Garanzha et al. (2011), Karras and Aila (2013), Domingues and Pedrini (2015), and Vinkler et al. (2016) for techniques for building kd-trees and BVHs on GPUs. See also the "Further Reading" section in Chapter 7 for additional discussion of algorithms for constructing and traversing acceleration structures on the GPU.

The relatively limited amount of on-chip memory that GPUs have can make it challenging to efficiently implement light transport algorithms that require more than a small amount of storage for each ray. (For example, even storing all the vertices of a pair of subpaths for a bidirectional path-tracing algorithm is much more than a thread could ask to keep on-chip.) The paper by Davidovič et al. (2014) gives a thorough overview of these issues and previous work and includes a discussion of implementations of a number of sophisticated light transport algorithms on the GPU.

---

10 Similar issues apply with packet or stream tracing on the CPU; see Section 16.2.3 for discussion of work on that topic.

Zellmann and Lang used compile time polymorphism in C++ to improve the performance of a GPU ray tracer (Zellmann and Lang 2017); our implementation in this chapter is based on similar ideas. Zhang et al. (2021) compared a number of approaches for dynamic function dispatch on GPUs and evaluated their performance.

Fewer papers have been written about the design of full ray-tracing–based rendering systems on the GPU than on the CPU. Notable papers in this area include Pantaleoni et al.'s (2010) description of *PantaRay*, which was used to compute occlusion and lighting by Weta Digital, and Keller et al.'s (2017) discussion of the architecture of the *Iray* rendering system. Bikker and van Schijndel (2013) described *Brigade*, which targets path-traced games, balancing work between the CPU and GPU and adapting the workload to maintain the desired frame rate.

Ray-Tracing Hardware

While all the stages of ray-tracing calculations—construction of the acceleration hierarchy, traversal of the hierarchy, and ray–primitive intersections, as well as shading, lighting, and integration calculations—can be implemented in software on GPUs, there has long been interest in designing specialized hardware for ray–primitive intersection tests and construction and traversal of the acceleration hierarchy for better performance. Deng et al.'s survey article has thorough coverage of hardware acceleration of ray tracing through 2017 (Deng et al. 2017); here, we will focus on early work and more recent developments.

Early published work in this area includes a paper by Woop et al. (2005), who described the design of a "ray processing unit" (RPU). Aila and Karras (2010) described general architectural issues related to handling incoherent rays, as are common with global illumination algorithms. More recently, Shkurko et al. (2017) and Vasiou et al. (2019) have described a hardware architecture that is based on reordering ray intersection computation so that it exhibits predictable streaming memory accesses.

Doyle et al. (2013) did early work on SAH BVH construction using specialized hardware. Viitanen et al. (2017, 2018) have done additional work in this area, designing architectures for efficient HLBVH construction for animated scenes and for high-quality SAH-based BVH construction.

Imagination Technologies announced a mobile GPU that would use a ray-tracing architecture from Caustic (McCombe 2013), though it never shipped in volume. The NVIDIA Turing architecture (NVIDIA 2018) is the first GPU with hardware-accelerated ray tracing that has seen widespread adoption. The details of its ray-tracing hardware architecture are not publicly documented, though Sanzharov et al. (2020) have applied targeted benchmarks to measure its performance characteristics in order to develop hypotheses about its implementation.

EXERCISES

● **15.1** Modify soac so that the code it generates leaves objects in AOS layout in memory and recompile pbrt. (You will need to manually update a few places in the WavefrontPathIntegrator that only access a single field of a structure, as well.) How is performance affected by this change?

❷ **15.2** pbrt's SampledWavelengths class stores two Floats for each wavelength: one for the wavelength value and one for its PDF. This class is passed along between almost all kernels. Render a scene on the GPU and work out an estimate of the amount of bandwidth consumed in communicating these values between kernels. (You may need to make some assumptions to do so.)

Then, implement an alternative SOA representation for `SampledWavelengths` that stores only two values: the `Float` sample used to originally sample the wavelengths and a Boolean value that indicates whether the secondary wavelengths have been terminated. You might use the sign bit to encode the Boolean value, or you might even try a 16-bit encoding, with the [0, 1) sample value quantized to 15 bits and the 16th used to indicate termination. Write code to encode `SampledWavelengths` to this representation when they are pushed to a queue and to decode this representation back to `SampledWavelengths` when work is read from the queue via a call to `Film::SampleWavelengths()` and then possibly a call to `SampledWavelengths::TerminateSecondary()`. Estimate how much bandwidth your improved representation saves. How is runtime performance affected? Can you draw any conclusions about whether your GPU is memory or bandwidth limited when running these kernels?

⚫ **15.3**   The direct lighting code in the `EvaluateMaterialsAndBSDFs()` kernel may suffer from divergence in the `Light::SampleLi()` call if the scene has a variety of types of light source. Construct such a scene and then experiment with moving light sampling into a separate kernel, using a work queue to supply work to it and where the light samples are pushed on to a queue for the rest of the direct lighting computation. What is the effect on performance for your test scene? Is performance negatively impacted for scenes with just a single type of light?

⚫ **15.4**   Add support for ray differentials to the `WavefrontPathIntegrator`, including both generating them for camera rays and computing updated differentials for reflected and refracted rays. (You will likely want to repurpose the code in the implementation of the `SurfaceInteraction SpawnRay()` method in Section 10.1.3.)

After ensuring that texture filtering results match `pbrt` running on the CPU, measure the performance impact of your changes. How much performance is lost from the bandwidth used in passing ray differentials between kernels? Do any kernels have better performance? If so, can you explain why?

Next, implement one of the more space-efficient techniques for representing derivative information with rays that are described by Akenine-Möller et al. (2019). How do performance and filtering quality compare to ray differentials?

⚫ **15.5**   The `WavefrontPathIntegrator`'s performance can suffer from scenes with very high maximum ray depths when there are few active rays remaining at high depths and, in turn, insufficient parallelism for the GPU to reach its peak capabilities. One approach to address this problem is *path regeneration*, which was described by Novák et al. (2010).

Following this approach, modify `pbrt` so that each ray traced handles its termination individually when it reaches the maximum depth. Execute a modified camera ray generation kernel each time through the main rendering loop so that additional pixel samples are taken and camera rays are generated until the current `RayQueue` is filled or there are no more samples to take. Note that you will have to handle `Film` updates in a different way than the current implementation—for example, via a work queue when rays terminate. You may also have to handle the case of multiple threads updating the same pixel sample. Finally, implement a mechanism for the GPU to notify the CPU when all rays have terminated so that it knows when to stop launching kernels.

With all that taken care of, measure pbrt's performance for a scene with a high maximum ray depth. (Scenes that include volumetric scattering with media with very high albedos are a good choice for this measurement.) How much is performance improved with your approach? How is performance affected for easier scenes with lower maximum depths that do not suffer from this problem?

⑨ 15.6 In pbrt's current implementation, the wavefront path tracer is usually slower than the VolPathIntegrator when running on the CPU. Render a few scenes using both approaches and benchmark pbrt's performance. Are any opportunities to improve the performance of the wavefront approach on the CPU evident?

Next, measure how performance changes as you increase or decrease the queue sizes (and consequently, the number of pixel samples that are evaluated in parallel). Performance may be suboptimal with the current value of WavefrontPathIntegrator:: maxQueueSize, which leads to queues much larger than can fit in the on-chip caches. However, too small a queue size may offer insufficient parallelism or may lead to too little work being done in each ParallelFor() call, which may also hurt performance. Are there better default queue sizes for the CPU than the ones used currently?

⑨ 15.7 When the WavefrontPathIntegrator runs on the CPU, there is currently minimal performance benefit from organizing work in queues. However, the queues offer the possibility of making it easier to use SIMD instructions on the CPU: kernels might remove 8 work items at a time, for example, processing them together using the 8 elements of a 256-bit SIMD register. Implement this approach and investigate pbrt's performance. (You may want to consider using a language such as ispc (Pharr and Mark 2012) to avoid the challenges of manually writing code using SIMD intrinsics.)

⑨ 15.8 Implement a GPU ray tracer that is based on pbrt's class implementations from previous chapters but uses the GPU's ray-tracing API for scheduling rendering work instead of the wavefront-based architecture used in this chapter. (You may want to start by supporting only a subset of the full functionality of the WavefrontPath Integrator.) Measure the performance of the two implementations and discuss their differences. You may find it illuminating to use a profiler to measure the bandwidth consumed by each implementation. Can you find cases where the wavefront integrator's performance is limited by available memory bandwidth but yours is not?

ParallelFor() 1107

VolPathIntegrator 877

WavefrontPathIntegrator::
  maxQueueSize
  940

CHAPTER SIXTEEN

16 RETROSPECTIVE AND THE FUTURE

In this concluding chapter, we begin with a review of how pbrt has changed over the years and discuss how improvements in computer hardware have affected its design and performance. We then outline some alternative architectures for rendering systems before we conclude with a brief retrospective of the system's adoption and impact.

16.1 pbrt OVER THE YEARS

Over four editions of this book and the four versions of pbrt that have accompanied them, much has changed: while path tracing has been present since the start, it was not the default integration technique until the third edition. Furthermore, the first two editions devoted many pages to techniques like irradiance caching that reuse indirect lighting computation across nearby points in order to reduce rendering time. All of those techniques but for photon mapping are gone now, as sampling algorithms have improved and computers have become much faster, making path tracing and related approaches the most appropriate focus today.

There have been numerous improvements throughout the system over time—we have adopted more effective algorithms as they have been developed and as we ourselves have learned more about how to write a good renderer; notably, the techniques used for generating sampling patterns and for importance sampling BSDFs and light sources are substantially better now than they were at the start. Those improvements have brought added complexity: pbrt-v1, the first version of the system, was roughly 20,000 lines of code, excluding tabularized data and automatically generated source files for parsing. This version is just over 60,000 lines of code measured the same way, though some of the increase is due to the addition of a variety of new features, like subsurface scattering, volumetric light transport, the `RealisticCamera`, and the `Curve` and `BilinearPatch` shapes.

Through all the improvements to the underlying algorithms, the bones of the system have not changed very much—`Integrator`s have always been at the core of solving the light transport equation, and many of the core interface types like `Shape`s, `Light`s, `Camera`s, `Filter`s, and `Sampler`s have all been there throughout with the same responsibilities, though there have

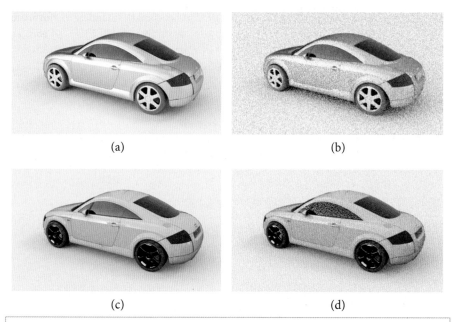

(a)   (b)

(c)   (d)

Figure 16.1: Audi TT Car Model Lit by an Environment Map. (a) Reference image, rendered with `pbrt-v1` with 64k samples per pixel. (b) Rendered with `pbrt-v1` with 16 samples per pixel. (c) Reference image, rendered with `pbrt-v4` with 64k samples per pixel. (d) Rendered with `pbrt-v4` with 16 samples per pixel. (Some image differences due to changes in material models since `pbrt-v1` are expected.) The reduction in noise from (b) to (d) is notable; all of it is due to improvements in sampling and Monte Carlo integration algorithms over `pbrt`'s lifetime. *(Car model courtesy of Marko Dabrovic and Mihovil Odak.)*

been changes to their interfaces and operation along the way. Looking back at `pbrt-v1` now, we can find plenty of snippets of code that are still present, unchanged since the start.

To quantify the algorithmic improvements to `pbrt`, we resurrected `pbrt-v1` and compared it to the version of `pbrt` described in this book, rendering the scene shown in Figure 16.1.[1] The latest version of `pbrt` takes $1.47\times$ longer than `pbrt-v1` to render this scene using path tracing, but mean squared error (MSE) with respect to reference images is improved by over $4.42\times$. The net is a $3.05\times$ improvement in Monte Carlo efficiency purely due to algorithmic improvements.

The changes in computers' computational capabilities since `pbrt-v1` have had even more of an impact on rendering performance. Much of the early development of `pbrt` in the late 1990s was on laptop computers that had a single-core 366 MHz Pentium II CPU. Some of the development of the latest version has been on a system that has 32 CPU cores, each one running at ten times the clock rate, 3.7 GHz.

A tenfold increase in processor clock speed does not tell the whole story about a CPU core's performance: there have been many microarchitectural improvements over the years such as better branch predictors, more aggressive out-of-order execution, and multi-issue pipelines. Caches have grown larger and compilers have improved as well. Data gathered by Rupp (2020) provides one measure of the aggregate improvement: from 1999 to late 2019, single-

---

1   This is an inexact comparison for many reasons. Among them: `pbrt` is now a spectral renderer, while before it used RGB for lighting calculations; materials like `CoatedDiffuseMaterial` now require stochastic evaluation; its sampling algorithms are much better, but more computationally intensive; and improvements to the geometric robustness of ray intersection computations have imposed some performance cost (Section 6.8.8). Nevertheless, we believe that the results are directionally valid.

CoatedDiffuseMaterial 909

thread CPU performance as measured by the SPECInt benchmark (Standard Performance Evaluation Corporation 2006) has improved by over 40×. Though SPECInt and pbrt are not the same, we still estimate that, between improvements in single-thread performance and having 32× more cores available, the overall difference in performance between the two computers is well over a factor of 1,000.

The impact of a 1,000× speedup is immense. It means that what took an hour to render on that laptop we can now render in around three seconds. Conversely, a painfully slow hour-long rendering computation on the 32-core system today would take an intolerable 42 days on the laptop. Lest the reader feel sympathy for our having suffered with such slow hardware at the start, consider the IBM 4341 that Kajiya used for the first path-traced images: its floating-point performance was roughly 250× slower than that of our laptop's CPU: around 0.2 MFLOPS for the 4341 (Dongarra 1984) versus around 50 for the Pentium II (Longbottom 2017). If we consider ray tracing on the GPU, where pbrt is generally 10–20× faster than on the 32-core CPU, we could estimate that we are now able to path trace images around 2,500,000× faster than Kajiya could—in other words, that pbrt on the GPU today can render in roughly ten seconds what his computer could do over the course of a year.

16.2 DESIGN ALTERNATIVES

pbrt represents a single point in the space of rendering system designs. The basic decisions we made early on—that ray tracing would be the geometric visibility algorithm used, that physical correctness would be a cornerstone of the system, that Monte Carlo would be the main approach used for numerical integration—all had pervasive implications for the system's design.

There are many ways to write a renderer, and the best approach depends on many factors: is portability important, or can the system target a single type of computer system? Is inter-action a requirement, or is the renderer a batch-mode system? Is time a constraint (e.g., a requirement to maintain a fixed frame rate), or must rendering continue until a particular quality level is reached? Must the system be able to render any scene no matter how complex, or can it impose limitations on the input?

Throughout the book, we have tried to always add an exercise at the end of the chapter when we have known that there was an important design alternative or where we made an implementation trade-off that would likely be made differently in a rendering system with different goals than pbrt. It is therefore worth reading the exercises even if you do not plan to do them. Going beyond the exercises, we will discuss a number of more radical design alternatives for path tracing–based rendering systems that are good to be aware of if you are designing a renderer yourself.

16.2.1 OUT-OF-CORE RENDERING

Given well-built acceleration structures, a strength of ray tracing is that the time spent on ray–primitive intersections grows slowly with added scene complexity. As such, the max-imum complexity that a ray tracer can handle may be limited more by memory than by computation. Because rays may pass through many different regions of the scene over a short period of time, virtual memory often performs poorly when ray tracing complex scenes due to the resulting incoherent memory access patterns.

One way to increase the potential complexity that a renderer is capable of handling is to reduce the memory used to store the scene. For example, pbrt currently uses approximately 3.3 GB of memory to store the 24 million triangles and the BVHs in the landscape scene in Figure 7.2. This works out to an average of 148 bytes per triangle. We have previously written ray tracers that managed an average of 40 bytes per triangle for scenes like these, which represents a 3.7× reduction. Reducing memory overhead requires careful attention to memory use throughout the system. For example, in the aforementioned system, we had three different `Triangle` implementations, one using 8-bit `uint8_ts` to store vertex indices, one using 16-bit `uint16_ts`, and one using 32-bit `uint32_ts`. The smallest index size that was sufficient for the range of vertex indices in the mesh was chosen at run time. Deering's paper on geometry compression (Deering 1995) and Ward's packed color format (Ward 1992) are both good inspirations for thinking along these lines. See the "Further Reading" section in Chapter 7 for information about more memory-efficient representations of acceleration structures.

On-demand loading of geometry and textures can also reduce memory requirements if some parts of the scene are never needed when rendering from a particular viewpoint. An additional advantage of this approach is that rendering can often start more quickly than it would otherwise. Taking that a step further, one might cache textures (Peachey 1990) or geometry (Pharr and Hanrahan 1996), holding a fixed amount of it in memory and discarding that which has not been accessed recently when the cache is full. This approach is especially useful for scenes with much tessellated geometry, where a compact higher-level shape representation like a subdivision surface can explode into a large number of triangles: when available memory is low, some of this geometry can be discarded and regenerated later if needed. With the advent of economical flash memory storage offering gigabytes per second of read bandwidth, this approach is even more attractive.

The performance of such caches can be substantially improved by reordering the rays that are traced in order to improve their spatial and thus memory coherence (Pharr et al. 1997). An easier-to-implement and more effective approach to improving the cache's behavior was described by Christensen et al. (2003), who wrote a ray tracer that uses simplified representations of the scene geometry in a geometry cache. More recently, Yoon et al. (2006), Budge et al. (2009), Moon et al. (2010), and Hanika et al. (2010) have developed improved approaches to this problem. See Rushmeier, Patterson, and Veerasamy (1993) for an early example of how to use simplified scene representations when computing indirect illumination.

Disney's *Hyperion* renderer is an example of a renderer for feature films that maintains a large collection of active rays and then sorts them in order to improve the coherence of geometry and texture cache access. See the papers by Eisenacher et al. (2013) and Burley et al. (2018) for details of its implementation.

16.2.2 PRESHADED MICROPOLYGON GRIDS

Another form of complexity that is required for feature film production is in the form of surface shading; in contrast to pbrt's fairly simple texture blending capabilities, production renderers typically provide procedural shading languages that make it possible to compute material parameters by combining multiple image maps and procedural patterns such as those generated by noise functions in user-provided shader programs. Evaluating these shaders can be a major component of rendering cost.

An innovative solution to this challenge has been implemented in Weta Digital's *Manuka* renderer, which is described in a paper by Fascione et al. (2018). In a first rendering phase, *Manuka* tessellates all the scene geometry into grids of *micropolygons*, subpixel-sized triangles. (This approach is inspired by the Reyes rendering algorithm (Cook et al. 1987).) Procedural shaders are then evaluated at the polygon vertices and the resulting material parameters are stored.

Triangle 301

Path tracing then proceeds using these micropolygons. At each intersection point, no shader evaluation is necessary and the material parameters are interpolated from nearby vertices in order to instantiate a BSDF. Because micropolygons are subpixel sized, there is no visible error from not evaluating the surface shader at the actual intersection point.

If the total number of ray intersections to be shaded during rendering is larger than the number of micropolygons, this approach is generally beneficial. It offers additional benefits from exhibiting coherent texture image map accesses and from simultaneous evaluation of shaders at many vertices during the first phase, which makes the workload amenable to SIMD processing. Downsides of this approach include the issue that if a substantial amount of the scene's geometry is occluded and never accessed during rendering, then the work to generate those micropolygon grids will have been wasted. It also causes startup time to increase due to the first phase of computation and thus a longer wait before initial pixel values can be displayed. Caching preshaded micropolygon grids can help.

A related approach is described by Munkberg et al. (2016), who cache shaded results in surface textures during rendering. These cached values can then be reused over multiple frames of an animation and used to accelerate rendering effects like depth of field.

16.2.3 PACKET TRACING

Early work on parallel tracing focused on multiprocessors (Cleary et al. 1983; Green and Paddon 1989; Badouel and Priol 1989) and clusters of computers (Parker et al. 1999; Wald et al. 2001a, 2001b, 2002, 2003).

More recently, as multi-core CPUs have become the norm and as CPUs have added computational capability through wider SIMD vector units, high-performance CPU ray-tracing research has focused on effectively using both multi-core and SIMD vector parallelism. Parallelizing ray tracing over multiple CPU cores in a single computer is not too difficult; the screen-space decomposition that pbrt uses is a common approach. Making good use of SIMD units is trickier; this is something that pbrt does not try to do in the interests of avoiding the corresponding code complexity.

SIMD widths of 8 to 16 32-bit floats are typical on current CPUs. Achieving the full potential performance of CPUs therefore requires using SIMD effectively. Achieving excellent utilization of SIMD vector units generally requires that the entire computation be expressed in a *data parallel* manner, where the same computation is performed on many data elements simultaneously. A natural way to extract data parallelism in a ray tracer is to have each processing core responsible for tracing n rays at a time, where n is at least the SIMD width. Each SIMD vector lane is then responsible for just a single ray, and each vector instruction performs a single scalar computation for each of the rays it is responsible for. Thus, high SIMD utilization comes naturally, at least until some rays require different computations than others.

This approach, *packet tracing*, was first introduced by Wald et al. (2001a). It has since seen wide adoption. In a packet tracer, acceleration structure traversal algorithms are implemented so that they visit a node if *any* of the rays in the packet passes through it; primitives in the leaves are tested for intersection with all the rays in the packet, and so forth.

Reshetov et al. (2005) generalized packet tracing, showing that gathering up many rays from a single origin into a frustum and then using the frustum for acceleration structure traversal could lead to very high-performance ray tracing; they refined the frusta into subfrusta and eventually the individual rays as they reached lower levels of the tree. Reshetov (2007) later introduced a technique for efficiently intersecting a collection of rays against a collection of triangles in acceleration structure leaf nodes by generating a frustum around the rays and using it for first-pass culling. See Benthin and Wald (2009) for a technique to use ray frusta and packets for efficient shadow rays.

While packet tracing is effective for coherent collections of rays that mostly follow the same path through acceleration structures, it is much less effective for incoherent collections of rays, which are common with global illumination algorithms. To address this issue, Christensen et al. (2006), Ernst and Greiner (2008), Wald et al. (2008), and Dammertz et al. (2008) proposed only traversing a single ray through the acceleration structure at once but improving SIMD efficiency by simultaneously testing each ray against a number of bounding boxes at each step in the hierarchy. Fuetterling et al. extended such approaches to the 16-wide SIMD units that are available on some recent CPUs (Fuetterling et al. 2017).

Embree, described in a paper by Wald et al. (2014), is a high-performance open source rendering system that supports both packet tracing and highly efficient traversal of single rays on the CPU. See also the paper by Benthin et al. (2011) on the topic of finding a balance between these two approaches.

Another approach to the ray incoherence problem is to reorder small batches of incoherent rays to improve SIMD efficiency; representative work in this area includes papers by Mansson et al. (2007), Boulos et al. (2008), Gribble and Ramani (2008), and Tsakok (2009). More recently, Barringer and Akenine-Möller (2014) developed a SIMD ray-traversal algorithm that delivered substantial performance improvements given large numbers of rays.

Effectively applying SIMD to the rest of the rendering computation often requires sorting work to improve coherence; see for example Áfra et al.'s approach for sorting materials between pipeline stages to improve SIMD utilization (Áfra et al. 2016). Many of the same principles used for efficient GPU ray tracing discussed in the "Further Reading" section of Chapter 15 also apply.

These algorithms are often implemented with the SIMD vectorization made explicit: intersection functions are written to explicitly take some number of rays as a parameter rather than just a single ray, and so forth. In contrast, as we saw in Chapter 15, the parallelism in programs written for GPUs is generally implicit: code is written as if it operates on a single ray at a time, but the underlying hardware actually executes it in parallel.

It is possible to use the implicit model on CPUs as well. Parker et al.'s (2007) ray-tracing shading language is an example of compiling an implicitly data-parallel language to a SIMD instruction set on CPUs. See also Georgiev and Slusallek's (2008) work, where generic programming techniques are used in C++ to implement a high-performance ray tracer with details like packets well hidden. ispc, described in a paper by Pharr and Mark (2012), provides a general-purpose "single program multiple data" (SPMD) language for CPU vector units that also provides this model. The *MoonRay* rendering system, which was developed at DreamWorks, uses ispc to target CPU SIMD units. The paper by Lee et al. (2017) describes its implementation and also discusses the important issue of maintaining data parallel computation when evaluating surface shaders.

If a rendering system can provide many rays for intersection tests at once, a variety of alternatives beyond packet tracing are possible. For example, Keller and Wächter (2011) and Mora (2011) described algorithms for intersecting a large number of rays against the scene geometry where there is no acceleration structure at all. Instead, primitives and rays are both recursively partitioned until small collections of rays and small collections of primitives remain, at which point intersection tests are performed. Improvements to this approach were described by Áfra (2012) and Nabata et al. (2013).

16.2.4 INTERACTIVE AND ANIMATION RENDERING

pbrt is very much a one-frame-at-a-time rendering system. Renderers that specifically target animation or allow the user to interact with the scene being rendered operate under a substantially different set of constraints, which leads to different designs.

Interactive rendering systems have the additional challenge that the scene to be rendered may not be known until shortly before it is time to render it, since the user is able to make changes to it. Fast algorithms for building or refitting acceleration structures are critical, and it may be necessary to limit the number of rays traced in order to reach a desired frame rate. The task, then, is to make the best image possible using a fixed number of rays, which requires the ability to allocate rays from a budget. As current hardware is generally not able to trace enough rays to generate noise-free path-traced images at real-time rates, such systems generally have denoising algorithms deeply integrated into their display pipeline as well.

A system that renders a sequence of images for an animation has the opportunity to reuse information temporally across frames, ranging from pixel values themselves to data structures that represent the distribution of light in the scene. An early application of this idea was described by Ghosh et al. (2006), who applied it to rendering glossy surfaces lit by environment light sources. Scherzer et al. (2011) provided a comprehensive survey of work in this area until 2011.

More recent examples of techniques that apply temporal reuse include the SVGF denoising algorithm (Schied et al. 2017, 2018), which reuses reprojected pixel colors across frames when appropriate, and the ReSTIR direct lighting technique (Bitterli et al. 2020), which reuses light samples across nearby pixels and frames of an animation to substantially improve the quality of direct lighting in scenes with many light sources. Other recent work in this area includes Dittebrandt et al.'s temporal sample reuse approach (2020), Hasselgren et al.'s temporal adaptive sampling and denoising algorithm (2020), and the extension of ReSTIR to path-traced indirect illumination by Ouyang et al. (2021).

16.2.5 SPECIALIZED COMPILATION

OptiX, which was described by Parker et al. (2010), has an interesting system structure: it is a combination of built-in functionality (e.g., for building acceleration structures and traversing rays through them) that can be extended by user-supplied code (e.g., for shape intersections and surface shading). Many renderers over the years have allowed user extensibility of this sort, usually through some kind of plug-in architecture. OptiX is distinctive in that it is built using a runtime compilation system that brings all of this code together before optimizing it.

Because the compiler has a view of the entire system when generating the final code, the resulting custom renderer can be automatically specialized in a variety of ways. For example, if the surface-shading code never uses the (u, v) texture coordinates, the code that computes them in the triangle shape intersection test can be optimized out as dead code. Or, if the ray's time field is never accessed, then both the code that sets it and even the structure member itself can be eliminated. This approach allows a degree of specialization (and resulting performance) that would be difficult to achieve manually, at least for more than a single system variant.

An even more aggressive specialization approach is implemented in the *Rodent* system, which is described in a paper by Pérard-Gayot et al. (2019), who also cover previous work in specialization for graphics computations. *Rodent* specializes the entire renderer based on the provided scene description, eliminating unnecessary logic in order to improve performance.

16.3 EMERGING TOPICS

Rendering research continues to be a vibrant field, as should be evident by the length of the "Further Reading" sections at the conclusions of the previous chapters. In addition to the topics discussed earlier, there are two important emerging areas of rendering research that we have not covered in this book—inverse and differentiable rendering and the use of machine learning techniques in image synthesis. Work in these areas is progressing rapidly, and so we believe that it would be premature to include implementations of associated techniques in pbrt and to discuss them in the book text; whichever algorithms we chose would likely be obsolete in a year or two. However, given the amount of activity in these areas, we will briefly summarize the landscape of each.

16.3.1 INVERSE AND DIFFERENTIABLE RENDERING

This book has so far focused on *forward* rendering, in which rendering algorithms convert an input scene description ("x") into a synthetic image ("y") taken in the corresponding virtual world. Assuming that the underlying computation is consistent across runs, we can think of the entire process as the evaluation of an intricate function $f : \mathcal{X} \to \mathcal{Y}$ satisfying $f(x) = y$. The main appeal of physically based forward-rendering methods is that they account for global light transport effects, which improves the visual realism of the output y.

However, many applications instead require an *inverse* $f^{-1}(y) = x$ to infer a scene description x that is consistent with a given image y, which may be a real-world photograph. Examples of disciplines where such inverses are needed include autonomous driving, robotics, biomedical imaging, microscopy, architectural design, and many others.

Evaluating f^{-1} is a surprisingly difficult and ambiguous problem: for example, a bright spot on a surface could be alternatively explained by texture or shape variation, illumination from a light source, focused reflection from another object, or simply shadowing at all other locations. Resolving this ambiguity requires multiple observations of the scene and reconstruction techniques that account for the interconnected nature of light transport and scattering. In other words, physically based methods are not just desirable—they are a prerequisite.

Directly inverting f is possible in some cases, though doing so tends to involve drastic simplifying assumptions: consider measurements taken by an X-ray CT scanner, which require further processing to reveal a specimen's interior structure. (X-rays are electromagnetic radiation just like visible light that are simply characterized by much shorter wavelengths in the 0.1–10nm range.) Standard methods for this reconstruction assume a purely absorbing medium, in which case a 3D density can be found using a single pass over all data. However, this approximate inversion leads to artifacts when dense bone or metal fragments reflect some of the X-rays.

The function f that is computed by a physically based renderer like pbrt is beyond the reach of such an explicit inversion. Furthermore, a scene that perfectly reproduces images seen from a given set of viewpoints may not exist at all. Inverse rendering methods therefore pursue a relaxed minimization problem of the form

$$x^* = \underset{x \in \mathcal{X}}{\operatorname{argmin}} \, g(f(x)), \qquad\qquad \text{[16.1]}$$

where $g : \mathcal{Y} \to \mathbb{R}$ refers to a *loss function* that quantifies the quality of a rendered image of the scene x. For example, the definition $g(y') = \|y' - y\|$ could be used to measure the L_2 distance to a reference image y. This type of optimization is often called *analysis-by-synthesis* due to the reliance on repeated simulation (synthesis) to gain understanding about an inverse problem. The approach easily generalizes to simultaneous optimization of multiple view-points. An extra *regularization* term $R(x)$ depending only on the scene parameters is often added on the right hand side to encode prior knowledge about reasonable parameter ranges. Composition with further computation is also possible: for example, we could alternatively optimize $g(f(N(w)))$, where $x = N(w)$ is a neural network that produces the scene x from learned parameters w.

Irrespective of such extensions, the nonlinear optimization problem in Equation (16.1) remains too challenging to solve in one step and must be handled using iterative methods. The usual caveats about their use apply here: iterative methods require a starting guess and may not converge to the optimal solution. This means that selecting an initial configuration and incorporating prior information (valid parameter ranges, expected smoothness of the solution, etc.) are both important steps in any inverse rendering task. The choice of loss $g : \mathcal{Y} \to \mathbb{R}$ and parameterization of the scene can also have a striking impact on the convexity of the optimization task (for example, direct optimization of triangle meshes tends to be particularly fragile, while implicit surface representations are better behaved).

Realistic scene descriptions are composed of millions of floating-point values that together specify the shapes, BSDFs, textures, volumes, light sources, and cameras. Each value contributes a degree of freedom to an extremely high-dimensional optimization domain (for example, a quadrilateral with a 768×768 RGB image map texture adds roughly 1.7 million dimensions to $\mathcal{X}$). Systematic exploration of a space with that many dimensions is not possible, making gradient-based optimization the method of choice for this problem. The gradient is invaluable here because it provides a direction of steepest descent that can guide the optimization toward higher-quality regions of the scene parameter space.

Let us consider the most basic gradient descent update equation for this problem:

$$x \leftarrow x - \alpha \frac{\partial}{\partial x} g(f(x)), \tag{16.2}$$

where α denotes the step size. A single iteration of this optimization can be split into four individually simpler steps via the chain rule:

$$
\begin{aligned}
y &\leftarrow f(x), \\
\delta_y &\leftarrow J_g(y), \\
\delta_x &\leftarrow \delta_y \cdot J_f(x), \\
x &\leftarrow x + \alpha\, \delta_x,
\end{aligned}
\tag{16.3}
$$

where $J_f \in \mathbb{R}^{m \times n}$ and $J_g \in \mathbb{R}^{1 \times m}$ are the Jacobian matrices of the rendering algorithm and loss function, and n and m respectively denote the number of scene parameters and rendered pixels. These four steps correspond to:

1. Rendering an image of the scene x.
2. Differentiating the loss function to obtain an image-space gradient vector δ_y. (A positive component in this vector indicates that increasing the value of the associated pixel in the rendered image would reduce the loss; the equivalent applies for a negative component.)
3. Converting the image-space gradient δ_y into a parameter-space gradient δ_x.
4. Taking a gradient step.

In practice, more sophisticated descent variants than the one in Equation (16.3) are often used for step 4—for example, to introduce per-variable momentum and track the variance of gradients, as is done in the commonly used *Adam* (Kingma and Ba 2014) optimizer. Imposing a metric on the optimization domain to pre-condition gradient steps can substantially accelerate convergence, as demonstrated by Nicolet et al. (2021) in the case of differentiable mesh optimization.

The third step evaluates the vector-matrix product $\delta_y \cdot J_f$, which is the main challenge in this sequence. At size $m \times n$, the Jacobian J_f of the rendering algorithm is far too large to store or even compute, as both n and m could be in the range of multiple millions of elements. Methods in the emerging field of *differentiable rendering* therefore directly evaluate this product without ever constructing the matrix J_f. The remainder of this subsection reviews the history and principles of these methods.

For completeness, we note that a great variety of techniques have used derivatives to improve or accelerate the process of physically based rendering; these are discussed in "Further Reading" sections throughout the book. In the following, we exclusively focus on parametric derivatives for inverse problems.

Inverse problems are of central importance in computer vision, and so it should be of no surprise that the origins of differentiable rendering as well as many recent advances can be found there: following pioneering work on *OpenDR* by Loper and Black (2014), a number of approximate differentiable rendering techniques have been proposed and applied to challenging inversion tasks. For example, Rhodin et al. (2015) reconstructed the pose of humans by optimizing a translucent medium composed of Gaussian functions. Kato et al. (2018) and Liu et al. (2019a) proposed different ways of introducing smoothness into the traditional rasterization pipeline. Laine et al. (2020) recently proposed a highly efficient modular GPU-accelerated rasterizer based on deferred shading followed by a differentiable antialiasing step. While rasterization-based methods can differentiate the rendering of directly lit objects, they cannot easily account for effects that couple multiple scene objects like shadows or interreflection.

Early work that used physically based differentiable rendering focused on the optimization of a small number of parameters, where there is considerable flexibility in how the differentiation is carried out. For example, Gkioulekas et al. (2013b) used stochastic gradient descent to reconstruct homogeneous media represented by a low-dimensional parameterization. Khungurn et al. (2015) differentiated a transport simulation to fit fabric parameters to the appearance in a reference photograph. Hašan and Ramamoorthi (2013) used volumetric derivatives to enable near-instant edits of path-traced heterogeneous media. Gkioulekas et al. (2016) studied the challenges of differentiating local properties of heterogeneous media, and Zhao et al. (2016) performed local gradient-based optimization to drastically reduce the size of heterogeneous volumes while preserving their appearance.

Besides the restriction to volumetric representations, a shared limitation of these methods is that they cannot efficiently differentiate a simulation with respect to the full set of scene parameters, particularly when n and m are large (in other words, they are not practical choices for the third step of the previous procedure). Subsequent work has adopted *reverse-mode differentiation*, which can simultaneously propagate derivatives to an essentially arbitrarily large number of parameters. (The same approach also powers training of neural networks, where it is known as *backpropagation*.)

Of particular note is the groundbreaking work by Li et al. (2018) along with their *redner* reference implementation, which performs reverse-mode derivative propagation using a hand-crafted implementation of the necessary derivatives. In the paper, the authors make the important observation that 3D scenes are generally riddled with visibility-induced discontinuities at object silhouettes, where the radiance function undergoes sudden changes. These are normally no problem in a Monte Carlo renderer, but they cause a severe problem following differentiation. To see why, consider a hypothetical integral that computes the average incident illumination at some position p. When computing the derivative of such a calculation, it is normally fine to exchange the order of differentiation and integration:

$$\frac{\partial}{\partial x} \int_{\mathcal{S}^2} L_i(p, \omega) \, d\omega = \int_{\mathcal{S}^2} \frac{\partial}{\partial x} L_i(p, \omega) \, d\omega. \qquad [16.4]$$

The left hand side is the desired answer, while the right hand side represents the result of differentiating the simulation code. Unfortunately, the equality generally no longer holds when $L_i(p, \omega)$ is discontinuous in the ω argument being integrated. Li et al. recognized that an extra correction term must be added to account for how perturbations of the scene parameters x cause the discontinuities to shift. They resolved primary visibility by integrating out discontinuities via the pixel reconstruction filter and used a hierarchical data structure to place additional edge samples on silhouettes to correct for secondary visibility.

Building on the Reynolds transport theorem, Zhang et al. (2019) generalized this approach into a more general theory of differential transport that also accounts for participating media. (In that framework, the correction by Li et al. (2018) can also be understood as an application of the Reynolds transport theorem to a simpler 2D integral.) Zhang et al. also studied further sources of problematic discontinuities such as open boundaries and shading discontinuities and showed how they can also be differentiated without bias.

Gkioulekas et al. (2016) and Azinović et al. (2019) observed that the gradients produced by a differentiable renderer are generally biased unless extra care is taken to decorrelate the forward and differential computation (i.e., steps 1 and 3)—for example, by using different random seeds.

Manual differentiation of simulation code can be a significant development and maintenance burden. This problem can be addressed using tools for *automatic differentiation* (AD), in which case derivatives are obtained by mechanically transforming each step of the forward simulation code. See the excellent book by Griewank and Walther (2008) for a review of AD techniques. A curious aspect of differentiation is that the computation becomes unusually dynamic and problem-dependent: for example, derivative propagation may only involve a small subset of the program variables, which may not be known until the user launches the actual optimization.

Mirroring similar developments in the machine learning world, recent work on differentiable rendering has therefore involved combinations of AD with *just-in-time* (JIT) compilation to embrace the dynamic nature of this problem and take advantage of optimization opportunities. There are several noteworthy differences between typical machine learning and rendering workloads: the former tend to be composed of a relatively small number of arithmetically intense operations like matrix multiplications and convolutions, while the latter use vast numbers of simple arithmetic operations. Besides this difference, ray-tracing operations and polymorphism are ubiquitous in rendering code; polymorphism refers to the property that function calls (e.g., texture evaluation or BSDF sampling) can indirectly branch to many different parts of a large codebase. These differences have led to tailored AD/JIT frameworks for differentiable rendering.

The *Mitsuba 2* system described by Nimier-David et al. (2019) traces the flow of computation in rendering algorithms while applying forward- or reverse-mode AD; the resulting code is then JIT-compiled into wavefront-style GPU kernels. Later work on the underlying *Enoki* just-in-time compiler added more flexibility: in addition to wavefront-style execution, the system can also generate megakernels with reduced memory usage. Polymorphism-aware optimization passes simplify the resulting kernels, which are finally compiled into vectorized machine code that runs on the CPU or GPU.

A fundamental issue of any method based on reverse-mode differentiation (whether using AD or hand-written derivatives) is that the backpropagation step requires access to certain intermediate values computed by the forward simulation. The sequence of accesses to these values occurs in reverse order compared to the original program execution, which is inconvenient because they must either be stored or recomputed many times. The intermediate state needed to differentiate a realistic simulation can easily exhaust the available system memory, limiting performance and scalability.

Nimier-David et al. (2020) and Stam (2020) observed that differentiating a light transport simulation can be interpreted as a simulation in its own right, where a differential form of radiance propagates through the scene. This derivative radiation is "emitted" from the camera, reflected by scene objects, and eventually "received" by scene objects with differentiable parameters. This idea, termed *radiative backpropagation*, can drastically improve the scalability limitation mentioned above (the authors report speedups of up to $1000\times$ compared to naive AD). Following this idea, costly recording of program state followed by reverse-mode differentiation can be replaced by a Monte Carlo simulation of the "derivative radiation." The runtime complexity of the original radiative backpropagation method is quadratic in the length of the simulated light paths, which can be prohibitive in highly scattering media. Vicini et al. (2021) addressed this flaw and enabled backpropagation in linear time by exploiting two different flavors of reversibility: the physical reciprocity of light and the mathematical invertibility of deterministic computations in the rendering code.

We previously mentioned how visibility-related discontinuities can bias computed gradients unless precautions are taken. A drawback of the original silhouette edge sampling approach by Li et al. (2018) was relatively poor scaling with geometric complexity. Zhang et al. (2020) extended differentiable rendering to Veach's path space formulation, which brings unique benefits in such challenging situations: analogous to how path space forward-rendering methods open the door to powerful sampling techniques, differential path space methods similarly enable access to previously infeasible ways of generating silhouette edges. For example, instead of laboriously searching for silhouette edges that are visible from a specific scene location, we can start with any triangle edge in the scene and simply trace a ray to find suitable scene locations. Zhang et al. (2021b) later extended this approach to a larger path space including volumetric scattering interactions.

Loubet et al. (2019) made the observation that discontinuous integrals themselves are benign: it is the fact that they move with respect to scene parameter perturbations that causes problems under differentiation. They therefore proposed a reparameterization of all spherical integrals that has the curious property that it moves along with each discontinuity. The integrals are then static in the new coordinates, which makes differentiation under the integral sign legal.

Bangaru et al. (2020) differentiated the rendering equation and applied the divergence theorem to convert a troublesome boundary integral into a more convenient interior integral, which they subsequently showed to be equivalent to a reparameterization. They furthermore identified a flaw in Loubet et al.'s method that causes bias in computed gradients and proposed a construction that finally enables unbiased differentiation of discontinuous integrals.

Differentiating under the integral sign changes the integrand, which means that sampling strategies that were carefully designed for a particular forward computation may no longer be appropriate for its derivative. Zeltner et al. (2021) investigated the surprisingly large space of differential rendering algorithms that results from differentiating standard constructions like importance sampling and MIS in different ways (for example, differentiation followed by importance sampling is not the same as importance sampling followed by differentiation). They also proposed a new sampling strategy specifically designed for the differential transport simulation. In contrast to ordinary rendering integrals, their differentiated counterparts also contain both positive and negative-valued regions, which means that standard sampling approaches like the inversion method are no longer optimal from the viewpoint of minimizing variance. Zhang et al. (2021a) applied antithetic sampling to reduce gradient variance involving challenging cases that arise when optimizing the geometry of objects in scenes with glossy interreflection.

While differentiable rendering still remains challenging, fragile, and computationally expensive, steady advances continue to improve its practicality over time, leading to new applications made possible by this capability.

16.3.2 MACHINE LEARNING AND RENDERING

As noted by Hertzmann (2003) in a prescient early paper, machine learning offers effective approaches to many important problems in computer graphics, including regression and clustering. Yet until recently, application of ideas from that field was limited. However, just as in other areas of computer science, machine learning and deep neural networks have recently become an important component of many techniques at the frontiers of rendering research.

This work can be (roughly) organized into three broad categories that are progressively farther afield from the topics discussed in this book:

1. Application of *learned data structures*, typically based on neural networks, to replace traditional data structures in traditional rendering algorithms.
2. Using machine learning–based algorithms (often deep convolutional neural networks) to improve images generated by traditional rendering algorithms.
3. Directly synthesizing photorealistic images using deep neural networks.

Early work in the first category includes Nowrouzezahrai et al. (2009), who used neural networks to encode spherical harmonic coefficients that represented the reflectance of dynamic objects; Dachsbacher (2011), who used neural networks to represent inter-object visibility; and Ren et al. (2013), who encoded scenes' radiance distributions using neural networks.

Previous chapters' "Further Reading" sections have discussed many techniques based on learned data structures, including approaches that use neural networks to represent complex materials (Rainer et al. 2019, 2020; Kuznetsov et al. 2021), complex light sources (Zhu et al. 2021), and the scene's radiance distribution to improve sampling (Müller et al. 2019, 2020, 2021). Many other techniques based on caching and interpolating radiance in the scene can be viewed through the lens of learned data structures, spanning Vorba et al.'s (2014) use of Gaussian mixture models even to techniques like irradiance caching (Ward et al. 1988).

One challenge in using learned data structures with traditional rendering algorithms is that the ability to just evaluate a learned function is often not sufficient, since effective Monte Carlo integration generally requires the ability to draw samples from a matching distribution and to quantify their density. Another challenge is that *online learning* is often necessary, where the learned data structure is constructed while rendering proceeds rather than being initialized ahead of time. For interactive rendering of dynamic scenes, incrementally updating learned representations can be especially beneficial.

More broadly, it may be desirable to represent an entire scene with a neural representation; there is no requirement that the abstractions of meshes, BRDFs, textures, lights, and media be separately and explicitly encoded. Furthermore, learning the parameters to such representations in inverse rendering applications can be challenging due to the ambiguities noted earlier. At writing, *neural radiance fields* (NeRF) (Mildenhall et al. 2020) are seeing widespread adoption as a learned scene representation due to the effectiveness and efficiency of the approach. NeRF is a volumetric representation that gives radiance and opacity at a given point and viewing direction. Because it is based on volume rendering, it has the additional advantage that it avoids the challenges of discontinuities in the light transport integral discussed in the previous section.

In rendering, work in the second category—using machine learning to improve conventionally rendered images—began with neural denoising algorithms, which are discussed in the "Further Reading" section at the end of Chapter 5. These algorithms can be remarkably effective; as with many areas of computer vision, deep convolutional neural networks have rapidly become much more effective at this problem than previous non-learned techniques.

Figure 16.2 shows an example of the result of using such a denoiser. Given a noisy image rendered with 32 samples per pixel as well as two auxiliary images that encode the surface albedo and surface normal, the denoiser is able to produce a noise-free image in a few tens of milliseconds. Given such results, the alternative of paying the computational cost of rendering a clean image by taking thousands of pixel samples is unappealing; doing so would take much longer, especially given that Monte Carlo error only decreases at a rate $O(n^{-1/2})$ in the number of samples n. Furthermore, neural denoisers are usually effective at eliminating the noise from spiky high-variance pixels, which otherwise would require enormous numbers of samples to achieve acceptable error.

Most physically based renderers today are therefore used with denoisers. This leads to an important question: *what is the role of the renderer, if its output is to be consumed by a neural network?* Given a denoiser, the renderer's task is no longer to try to make the most accurate or visually pleasing image for a human observer, but is to generate output that is most easily converted by the neural network to the desired final representation. This question has deep implications for the design of both renderers and denoisers and is likely to see much attention in coming years. (For an example of recent work in this area, see the paper by Cho et al. (2021), who improved denoising by incorporating information directly from the paths traced by the renderer and not just from image pixels.)

The question of the renderer's role is further provoked by neural post-rendering approaches that do much more than denoise images; a recent example is *GANcraft*, which converts low-fidelity blocky images of *Minecraft* scenes to be near-photorealistic (Hao et al. 2021). A space of techniques lies in between this extreme and less intrusive post-processing approaches like denoising: *deep shading* (Nalbach et al. 2017) synthesizes expensive effects starting from a cheaply computed set of G-buffers (normals, albedo, etc.). Granskog et al. (2020) improved shading inference using additional view-independent context extracted from a set of high-quality reference images. More generally, *neural style transfer* algorithms (Gatys et al. 2016) can be an effective way to achieve a desired visual style without fully simulating it in a renderer. Providing nuanced artistic control to such approaches remains an open problem, however.

In the third category, a number of researchers have investigated training deep neural networks to encode a full rendering algorithm that goes from a scene description to an image. See Hermosilla et al. (2019) and Chen et al. (2021) for recent work in this area. Images may also be synthesized without using conventional rendering algorithms at all, but solely from characteristics learned from real-world images. A recent example of such a *generative model* is *StyleGAN*, which was developed by Karras et al. (2018, 2020); it is capable of generating high-resolution and photorealistic images of a variety of objects, including human faces,

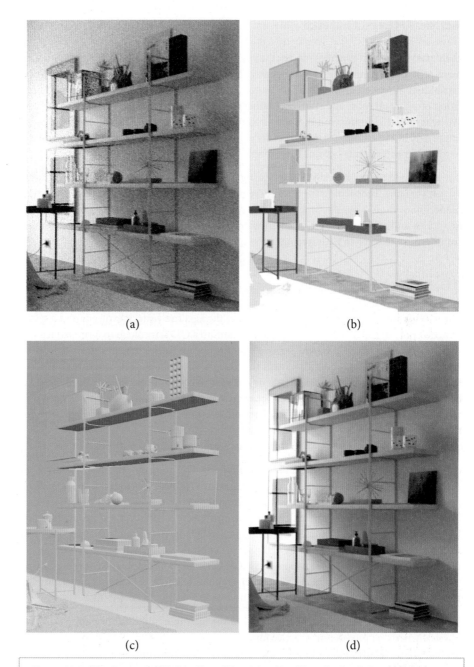

(a)

(b)

(c)

(d)

Figure 16.2: **Effectiveness of Modern Neural Denoising Algorithms for Rendering.** (a) Noisy image rendered with 32 samples per pixel. (b) Feature buffer with the average surface albedo at each pixel. (c) Feature buffer with the surface normal at each pixel. (d) Denoised image. *(Image denoised with the NVIDIA OptiX 7.3 denoiser.)*

cats, cars, and interior scenes. Techniques based on *segmentation maps* (Chen and Koltun 2017; Park et al. 2019) allow a user to denote that regions of an image should be of general categories like "sky," "water," "mountain," or "car" and then synthesize a realistic image that follows those categories. See the report by Tewari et al. (2020) for a comprehensive summary of recent work in such areas.

16.4 THE FUTURE

Even after the massive increase in computational capability over the past two decades and many algorithmic improvements, rendering still remains far from a solved problem. Greater capabilities of renderers have translated into more complex scenes and more accurate simulation of light transport and scattering rather than rendering the same old thing, just faster. We believe that innovation in sampling and rendering algorithms will become increasingly important in the coming years, especially as further performance benefits from computer hardware improvements become increasingly hard-won as Moore's law slows.

The recent addition of specialized ray-tracing hardware to GPUs has opened a new chapter for path tracing, broadening the set of developers who are able to consider using the technique. Innovation generally progresses at a rate related to the number of people working in an area and so we very much look forward to the new ideas that the real-time graphics community will bring to path tracing in the coming years.

16.5 CONCLUSION

The idea for pbrt was born in October 1999. Over the next five years, it evolved from a system designed only to support the students taking Stanford's CS348b course to a robust, feature-rich, extensible rendering system. Since its inception, we have learned a great deal about what it takes to build a rendering system that does not just make pretty pictures but is one that other people enjoy using and modifying as well. What has been most difficult, however, is designing a large piece of software that others might enjoy *reading*. This has been a far more challenging (and rewarding) task than implementing any of the rendering algorithms themselves.

After its first publication, the book enjoyed widespread adoption in advanced graphics courses worldwide, which we found very gratifying. We were unprepared, however, for the impact that pbrt has had on rendering research. Writing a ray tracer from scratch is a formidable task (as so many students in undergraduate graphics courses can attest), and creating a robust physically based renderer is much harder still. We are proud that pbrt has lowered the barrier to entry for aspiring researchers in rendering, making it easier for researchers to experiment with and demonstrate the value of new ideas in rendering. We continue to be delighted to see papers in SIGGRAPH, the Eurographics Rendering Symposium, High Performance Graphics, and other graphics research venues that either build on pbrt to achieve their goals, or compare their images to pbrt as "ground truth."

More recently, we have been delighted again to see the rapid adoption of path tracing and physically based approaches in practice for offline rendering and, recently as of this writing, games and interactive applications. Though we are admittedly unusual folk, it is a particular delight to see incredible graphics on a screen and marvel at the billions of pseudo-random (or quasi-random) samples taken, billions of rays traced, and the complex mathematics that went into each image passing by.

We would like to sincerely thank everyone who has built upon this work for their own research, to build a new curriculum, to create amazing movies or games, or just to learn more about rendering. We hope that this new edition continues to serve the graphics community in the same way that its predecessors have.

A SAMPLING ALGORITHMS

Chapter 2 provided an introduction to the principles of sampling and Monte Carlo integration that are most widely used in pbrt. However, a number of additional sampling techniques—the alias method, reservoir sampling, and rejection sampling—that are used only occasionally were not described there. This appendix introduces each of those techniques and then concludes with two sections that further apply the inversion method to derive sampling techniques for a variety of useful distributions.

A.1 THE ALIAS METHOD

If many samples need to be generated from a discrete distribution, using the approach implemented in the SampleDiscrete() function would be wasteful: each generated sample would require $O(n)$ computation. That approach could be improved to $O(\log n)$ time by computing a cumulative distribution function (CDF) table once and then using binary search to generate each sample, but there is another option that is even more efficient, requiring just $O(1)$ time for each sample; that approach is the *alias method*.[1]

To understand how the alias method works, first consider the task of sampling from n discrete outcomes, each with equal probability. In that case, computing the value $\lfloor n\xi \rfloor$ gives a uniformly distributed index between 0 and $n-1$ and the corresponding outcome can be selected—no further work is necessary. The alias method allows a similar searchless sampling method if the outcomes have arbitrary probabilities p_i.

The alias method is based on creating n bins, one for each outcome. Bins are sampled uniformly and then two values stored in each bin are used to generate the final sample: if the ith bin was sampled, then q_i gives the probability of sampling the ith outcome, and otherwise the *alias* is chosen; it is the index of a single alternative outcome. Though we will not include the proof here, it can be shown that this representation—the ith bin associated with the ith outcome and no more than a single alias per bin—is sufficient to represent arbitrary discrete probability distributions.

SampleDiscrete() 70

---

1 Note that the use of "alias" in this context is unrelated to the aliasing in images that is discussed in Section 8.1.3.

Table A.1: A Simple Alias Table. This alias table makes it possible to generate samples from the distribution of discrete probabilities $\{1/2, 1/4, 1/8, 1/8\}$. To generate a sample, an entry is first chosen with uniform probability. Given an entry i, its corresponding sample is chosen with probability q_i and the sample corresponding to its alias index is chosen with probability $1 - q_i$.

Index	q_i	Alias Index
1	1	n/a
2	0.5	1
3	0.5	1
4	0.5	2

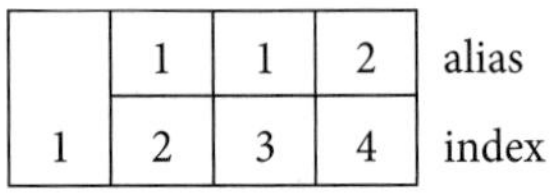

Figure A.1: Graphical Representation of the Alias Table in Table A.1. One bin is allocated for each outcome and is filled by the outcome's probability, up to $1/n$. Excess probability is allocated to other bins that have probabilities less than $1/n$ and thus extra space.

With the alias method, if the probabilities are all the same, then each bin's probability q_i is one, and it reduces to the earlier example with uniform probabilities. Otherwise, for outcomes i where the associated probability p_i is greater than the average probability, the outcome i will be stored as the alias in one or more of the other bins. For outcomes i where the associated p_i is less than the average probability, q_i will be less than one and the alias will point to one of the higher-probability outcomes.

For a specific example, consider the probabilities $p_i = \{1/2, 1/4, 1/8, 1/8\}$. A corresponding alias table is shown in Table A.1. It is possible to see that, for example, the first sample is chosen with probability $1/2$: there is a $1/4$ probability of choosing the first table entry, in which case the first sample is always chosen. Otherwise, there is a $1/4$ probability of choosing the second and third table entries, and for each, there is a $1/2$ chance of choosing the alias, giving in sum an additional $1/4$ probability of choosing the first sample. The other probabilities can be verified similarly.

One way to interpret an alias table is that each bin represents $1/n$ of the total probability mass function. If outcomes are first allocated to their corresponding bins, then the probability mass of outcomes that are greater than $1/n$ must be distributed to other bins that have associated probabilities less than $1/n$. This idea is illustrated in Figure A.1, which corresponds to the example of Table A.1.

The `AliasTable` class implements algorithms for generating and sampling from alias tables. As with the other sampling code, its implementation is found in `util/sampling.h` and `util/sampling.cpp`.

⟨*AliasTable Definition*⟩ ≡
```
class AliasTable {
  public:
    ⟨AliasTable Public Methods 997⟩
  private:
    ⟨AliasTable Private Members 995⟩
};
```

Its constructor takes an array of weights, not necessarily normalized, that give the relative probabilities for the possible outcomes.

⟨*AliasTable Method Definitions*⟩ ≡

```
AliasTable::AliasTable(pstd::span<const Float> weights, Allocator alloc)
    : bins(weights.size(), alloc) {
    ⟨Normalize weights to compute alias table PDF 995⟩
    ⟨Create alias table work lists 995⟩
    ⟨Process under and over work item together 996⟩
    ⟨Handle remaining alias table work items⟩
}
```

The `Bin` structure represents an alias table bin. It stores the probability q, the corresponding outcome's probability p, and an alias.

⟨*AliasTable Private Members*⟩ ≡   994

```
struct Bin {
    Float q, p;
    int alias;
};
pstd::vector<Bin> bins;
```

We have found that with large numbers of outcomes, especially when the magnitudes of their weights vary significantly, it is important to use double precision to compute their sum so that the alias table initialization algorithm works correctly. Therefore, here `std::accumulate` takes the double-precision value `0.` as its initial value, which in turn causes all its computation to be in double precision. Given the sum of weights, the normalized probabilities can be computed.

⟨*Normalize* weights *to compute alias table PDF*⟩ ≡   995

```
Float sum = std::accumulate(weights.begin(), weights.end(), 0.);
for (size_t i = 0; i < weights.size(); ++i)
    bins[i].p = weights[i] / sum;
```

The first stage of the alias table initialization algorithm is to split the outcomes into those that have probability less than the average and those that have probability higher than the average. Two `std::vectors` of the `Outcome` structure are used for this.

⟨*Create alias table work lists*⟩ ≡   995

```
struct Outcome {
    Float pHat;
    size_t index;
};
std::vector<Outcome> under, over;
for (size_t i = 0; i < bins.size(); ++i) {
    ⟨Add outcome i to an alias table work list 996⟩
}
```

Here and in the remainder of the initialization phase, we will scale the individual probabilities by the number of bins n, working in terms of $\hat{p}_i = p_i\, n$. Thus, the average $\hat{p}$ value is 1, which will be convenient in the following.

⟨*Add outcome* i *to an alias table work list*⟩ ≡   **995**
```
    Float pHat = bins[i].p * bins.size();
    if (pHat < 1)
        under.push_back(Outcome{pHat, i});
    else
        over.push_back(Outcome{pHat, i});
```

To initialize the alias table, one outcome is taken from under and one is taken from over. Together, they make it possible to initialize the element of bins that corresponds to the outcome from under. After that bin has been initialized, the outcome from over will still have some excess probability that is not yet reflected in bins. It is added to the appropriate work list and the loop executes again until under and over are empty. This algorithm runs in $O(n)$ time.

It is not immediately obvious that this approach will successfully initialize the alias table, or that it will necessarily terminate. We will not rigorously show that here, but informally, we can see that at the start, there must be at least one item in each work list unless they all have the same probability (in which case, initialization is trivial). Then, each time through the loop, we initialize one bin, which consumes $\hat{p} = 1$ worth of probability mass. With one less bin to initialize and that much less probability to distribute, we have the same average probability over the remaining bins. That brings us to the same setting as the starting condition: some of the remaining items in the list must be above the average and some must be below, unless they are all equal to it.

⟨*Process under and over work item together*⟩ ≡   **995**
```
    while (!under.empty() && !over.empty()) {
```
⟨*Remove items* un *and* ov *from the alias table work lists* **996**⟩
⟨*Initialize probability and alias for* un **996**⟩
⟨*Push excess probability on to work list* **996**⟩
```
    }
```

⟨*Remove items* un *and* ov *from the alias table work lists*⟩ ≡   **996**
```
    Outcome un = under.back(), ov = over.back();
    under.pop_back();
    over.pop_back();
```

The probability $\hat{p}_{un}$ of un must be less than one. We can initialize its bin's q with $\hat{p}_{un}$, as that is equal to the probability it should be sampled if its bin is chosen. In order to allocate the remainder of the bin's probability mass, the alias is set to ov. Because $\hat{p}_{ov} \geq 1$, it certainly has enough probability to fill the remainder of the bin—we just need $1 - \hat{p}_{un}$ of it.

⟨*Initialize probability and alias for* un⟩ ≡   **996**
```
    bins[un.index].q = un.pHat;
    bins[un.index].alias = ov.index;
```

In initializing bins[un.index], we have consumed $\hat{p} = 1$ worth of the scaled probability mass. The remainder, un.pHat + ov.pHat - 1, is the as-yet unallocated probability for ov.index; it is added to the appropriate work list based on how much is left.

⟨*Push excess probability on to work list*⟩ ≡   **996**
```
    Float pExcess = un.pHat + ov.pHat - 1;
    if (pExcess < 1)
        under.push_back(Outcome{pExcess, ov.index});
    else
        over.push_back(Outcome{pExcess, ov.index});
```

Due to floating-point round-off error, there may be work items remaining on either of the two work lists with the other one empty. These items have probabilities slightly less than or slightly greater than one and should be given probability $q = 1$ in the alias table. The fragment that handles this, ⟨*Handle remaining alias table work items*⟩, is not included in the book.

Given an initialized alias table, sampling is easy. As described before, an entry is chosen with uniform probability and then either the corresponding sample or its alias is returned. As with the SampleDiscrete() function, a new uniform random sample derived from the original one is optionally returned.

⟨*AliasTable Method Definitions*⟩ +≡
```
int AliasTable::Sample(Float u, Float *pmf, Float *uRemapped) const {
    ⟨Compute alias table offset and remapped random sample up 997⟩
    if (up < bins[offset].q) {
        ⟨Return sample for alias table at offset 997⟩
    } else {
        ⟨Return sample for alias table at alias[offset] 997⟩
    }
}
```

The index for the chosen entry is found by multiplying the random sample by the number of entries. Because u was only used for the discrete sampling decision of selecting an initial entry, it is possible to derive a new uniform random sample from it. That computation is done here to get an independent uniform sample up that is used to decide whether to sample the alias at the current entry.

⟨*Compute alias table* offset *and remapped random sample* up⟩ ≡   997
```
int offset = std::min<int>(u * bins.size(), bins.size() - 1);
Float up = std::min<Float>(u * bins.size() - offset, OneMinusEpsilon);
```

If the initial entry is selected, the various return values are easily computed.

⟨*Return sample for alias table at* offset⟩ ≡   997
```
if (pmf)
    *pmf = bins[offset].p;
if (uRemapped)
    *uRemapped = std::min<Float>(up / bins[offset].q, OneMinusEpsilon);
return offset;
```

Otherwise the appropriate values for the alias are returned.

⟨*Return sample for alias table at* alias[offset]⟩ ≡   997
```
int alias = bins[offset].alias;
if (pmf)
    *pmf = bins[alias].p;
if (uRemapped)
    *uRemapped =
        std::min<Float>((up - bins[offset].q) /
                        (1 - bins[offset].q), OneMinusEpsilon);
return alias;
```

Beyond sampling, it is useful to be able to query the size of the table and the probability of a given outcome. These two operations are easily provided.

⟨*AliasTable Public Methods*⟩ ≡   994
```
size_t size() const { return bins.size(); }
Float PMF(int index) const { return bins[index].p; }
```

A.2 RESERVOIR SAMPLING

To perform the sampling operation, both `SampleDiscrete()` and alias tables require the number of outcomes being sampled from as well as all their probabilities to be stored in memory. Often this is not a problem, but for cases where we would like to draw a sample from a large number of events, or cases where each event requires a large amount of memory, it is useful to be able to generate samples without storing all of them at once.

A family of algorithms based on a technique called *reservoir sampling* makes this possible, by taking a stream of candidate samples one at a time and randomly keeping just one of them in a way that ensures that the sample that is kept is from the distribution defined by the samples that have been seen so far. Reservoir sampling algorithms date to the early days of computer tape drives, where data could only be accessed sequentially and there was often more of it than could be stored in main memory. Reservoir sampling made it possible to draw random samples from data stored on tape while only reading the tape once.

The basic reservoir sampling algorithm is easily expressed. Each candidate sample is stored in the reservoir with probability equal to one over the number of candidates that have been considered:

$$\text{reservoir} \leftarrow \emptyset, n \leftarrow 0$$
$$\text{while sample} \leftarrow \text{GetSample}() :$$
$$\quad n \leftarrow n + 1$$
$$\quad \text{if } \xi < 1/n$$
$$\qquad \text{reservoir} \leftarrow \text{sample}$$

The correctness of this algorithm can be shown using induction. For the base case, it is clear that if there is a single sample, it will be stored in the reservoir, and the reservoir has successfully drawn a sample with the appropriate probability from the sample distribution.

Now consider the case where n samples have been considered and assume that the sample stored in the reservoir has been kept with probability $1/n$. When a new sample is considered, it will be kept with probability $1/(n + 1)$, which is clearly the correct probability for it. The existing sample is kept with probability $n/(n + 1)$; the product of the probability of keeping the existing sample and its probability of being stored in the reservoir gives the correct probability, $1/(n + 1)$, as well.

Weighted reservoir sampling algorithms generalize the basic algorithm by making it possible to associate a nonnegative weight with each sample. Samples are then kept with probability given by the ratio of their weight to the sum of weights of all of the candidate samples that have been seen so far. The `WeightedReservoirSampler` class implements this algorithm. It is parameterized by the type of object being sampled `T`.

⟨*WeightedReservoirSampler Definition*⟩ ≡
```
template <typename T>
class WeightedReservoirSampler {
  public:
    ⟨WeightedReservoirSampler Public Methods 999⟩
  private:
    ⟨WeightedReservoirSampler Private Members 999⟩
};
```

RNG 1054
SampleDiscrete() 70

`WeightedReservoirSampler` stores an `RNG` object that provides the random numbers that are used in deciding whether to add each sample to the reservoir. The constructor correspondingly takes a seed value that is passed on to the `RNG`.

⟨*WeightedReservoirSampler Public Methods*⟩ ≡   998
```
WeightedReservoirSampler() = default;
WeightedReservoirSampler(uint64_t rngSeed) : rng(rngSeed) {}
```

⟨*WeightedReservoirSampler Private Members*⟩ ≡   998
```
RNG rng;
```

If an array of WeightedReservoirSamplers is allocated, then the default constructor runs instead. In that case, the RNGs in individual samplers can be seeded via the Seed() method.

⟨*WeightedReservoirSampler Public Methods*⟩ +≡   998
```
void Seed(uint64_t seed) { rng.SetSequence(seed); }
```

The Add() method takes a single sample and a nonnegative weight value and updates the reservoir so that the stored sample is from the expected distribution.

⟨*WeightedReservoirSampler Public Methods*⟩ +≡   998
```
void Add(const T &sample, Float weight) {
    weightSum += weight;
    ⟨Randomly add sample to reservoir 999⟩
}
```

⟨*WeightedReservoirSampler Private Members*⟩ +≡   998
```
Float weightSum = 0;
```

The probability p for storing the sample candidate in the reservoir is easily found given weightSum.

⟨*Randomly add* sample *to reservoir*⟩ ≡   999
```
Float p = weight / weightSum;
if (rng.Uniform<Float>() < p) {
    reservoir = sample;
    reservoirWeight = weight;
}
```

The weight of the sample stored in the reservoir is stored in reservoirWeight; it is needed to compute the value of the probability mass function (PMF) for the sample that is kept.

⟨*WeightedReservoirSampler Private Members*⟩ +≡   998
```
Float reservoirWeight = 0;
T reservoir;
```

A second Add() method takes a callback function that returns a sample. This function is only called when the sample is to be stored in the reservoir. This variant is useful in cases where the sample's weight can be computed independently of its value and where its value is relatively expensive to compute. The fragment that contains its implementation, ⟨*Process weighted reservoir sample via callback*⟩, otherwise follows the same structure as the first Add() method, so it is not included here.

⟨*WeightedReservoirSampler Public Methods*⟩ +≡   998
```
template <typename F>
void Add(F func, Float weight) {
    ⟨Process weighted reservoir sample via callback⟩
}
```

A number of methods provide access to the sample and the probability that it was stored in the reservoir.

⟨*WeightedReservoirSampler Public Methods*⟩ +≡   **998**
```
    int HasSample() const { return weightSum > 0; }
    const T &GetSample() const { return reservoir; }
    Float SampleProbability() const { return reservoirWeight / weightSum; }
    Float WeightSum() const { return weightSum; }
```

It is sometimes useful to reset a `WeightedReservoirSampler` and restart from scratch with a new stream of samples; the `Reset()` method handles this task.

⟨*WeightedReservoirSampler Public Methods*⟩ +≡   **998**
```
    void Reset() { reservoirWeight = weightSum = 0; }
```

Remarkably, it is possible to merge two reservoirs into one in such a way that the stored sample is kept with the same probability as if a single reservoir had considered all of the samples seen by the two. Merging two reservoirs is a matter of randomly taking the sample stored by the second reservoir with probability defined by its sum of sample weights divided by the sum of both reservoirs' sums of sample weights, which in turn is exactly what the `Add()` method does.

⟨*WeightedReservoirSampler Public Methods*⟩ +≡   **998**
```
    void Merge(const WeightedReservoirSampler &wrs) {
        if (wrs.HasSample())
            Add(wrs.reservoir, wrs.weightSum);
    }
```

A.3 THE REJECTION METHOD

Many functions cannot be integrated in order to normalize them to find their PDFs. Even given a PDF, it is often not possible to invert the associated CDF to generate samples using the inversion method. In such cases, the *rejection method* can be useful: it is a technique for generating samples according to a function's distribution without needing to do either of these steps. Assume that we want to draw samples from some function $f(x)$ where we have some PDF $p(x)$ that satisfies $f(x) < c\, p(x)$ for a constant c, and suppose that we do know how to sample from p. The rejection method is then:

> loop forever:
>> sample $X \sim p$
>> if $\xi < f(X)/(c\, p(X))$ then
>>> return X

This procedure repeatedly chooses a pair of random variables (X, ξ). If the point $(X, \xi\, c\, p(X))$ lies under $f(X)$, then the sample X is accepted. Otherwise, it is rejected and a new sample pair is chosen. This idea is illustrated in Figure A.2; it works in any number of dimensions. It should be evident that the efficiency of this scheme depends on how tightly $c\, p(x)$ bounds $f(x)$.

For example, suppose we want to select a uniformly distributed point inside a unit disk. Using the rejection method, we simply select a random (x, y) position inside the circumscribed square and return it if it falls inside the disk. This process is shown in Figure A.3.

The function `RejectionSampleDisk()` implements this algorithm. A similar approach will work to generate uniformly distributed samples on the inside of any complex shape as long as it has an inside–outside test.

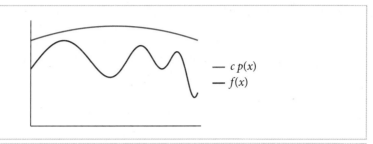

Figure A.2: Rejection sampling generates samples according to the distribution of a function $f(x)$ even if f's PDF is unknown or its CDF cannot be inverted. If some distribution $p(x)$ and a scalar constant c are known such that $f(x) < c\, p(x)$, then samples can be drawn from $p(x)$ and randomly accepted in a way that causes the accepted samples to be from f's distribution. The closer the fit of $c\, p(x)$ to $f(x)$, the more efficient this process is.

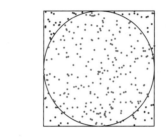

Figure A.3: Rejection Sampling a Disk. One approach to finding uniform points in the unit disk is to sample uniform random points in the unit square and reject all that lie outside the disk (red points). The remaining points will be uniformly distributed within the disk.

⟨*Sampling Function Definitions*⟩ +≡
```
Point2f RejectionSampleDisk(RNG &rng) {
    Point2f p;
    do {
        p.x = 1 - 2 * rng.Uniform<Float>();
        p.y = 1 - 2 * rng.Uniform<Float>();
    } while (Sqr(p.x) + Sqr(p.y) > 1);
    return p;
}
```

In general, the efficiency of rejection sampling depends on the percentage of samples that are expected to be rejected. For `RejectionSampleDisk()`, this is easy to compute. It is the area of the disk divided by the area of the square: $\frac{\pi}{4} \approx 78.5\%$. If the method is applied to generate samples in hyperspheres in the general n-dimensional case, however, the volume of an n-dimensional hypersphere goes to 0 as n increases, and this approach becomes increasingly inefficient.

Rejection sampling is not used in any of the Monte Carlo algorithms currently implemented in pbrt. We will normally prefer to find distributions that are similar to the function that can be sampled directly, so that well-distributed sample points in $[0, 1)^n$ can be mapped to sample points that are in turn well distributed. Nevertheless, rejection sampling is an important technique to be aware of, particularly when debugging Monte Carlo implementations.

For example, if one suspects the presence of a bug in code that draws samples from some distribution using the inversion method, then one can replace it with a straightforward implementation based on the rejection method and see if the Monte Carlo estimator converges to the same value. Of course, it is necessary to take many samples in situations like these, so that variance in the estimates does not mask errors.

A.4 SAMPLING 1D FUNCTIONS

Throughout the implementation of pbrt we have found it useful to draw samples from a wide variety of functions. This section therefore presents the implementations of additional functions for sampling in 1D to augment the ones in Section 2.3.2. All are based on the inversion method and most introduce useful tricks for sampling that are helpful to know when deriving new sampling algorithms.

A.4.1 SAMPLING THE TENT FUNCTION

SampleTent() uses SampleLinear() to sample the "tent" function with radius r,

$$f(x) = \begin{cases} r - |x| & |x| < r \\ 0 & \text{otherwise.} \end{cases}$$

The sampling algorithm first uses the provided uniform sample u with the SampleDiscrete() function to choose whether to sample a value greater than or less than zero, with each possibility having equal probability. Note the use of SampleDiscrete()'s capability of returning a new uniform random sample here, overwriting u's original value. In turn, one of the two linear functions is sampled, with the result scaled so that the interval $[-r, r]$ is sampled.

One thing to note in this function is that the cases and expressions have been carefully crafted so that u==0 maps to -r and then as u increases, the sampled value increases monotonically until u==1 maps to r, without any jumps or reversals. This property is helpful for preserving well-distributed sample points (e.g., if they have low discrepancy).

⟨*Sampling Inline Functions*⟩ +≡
```
Float SampleTent(Float u, Float r) {
    if (SampleDiscrete({0.5f, 0.5f}, u, nullptr, &u) == 0)
        return -r + r * SampleLinear(u, 0, 1);
    else
        return r * SampleLinear(u, 1, 0);
}
```

The tent function is easily normalized to find its PDF.

⟨*Sampling Inline Functions*⟩ +≡
```
Float TentPDF(Float x, Float r) {
    if (std::abs(x) >= r)
        return 0;
    return 1 / r - std::abs(x) / Sqr(r);
}
```

The inversion function is based on InvertLinearSample().

⟨*Sampling Inline Functions*⟩ +≡
```
inline Float InvertTentSample(Float x, Float r) {
    if (x <= 0)
        return (1 - InvertLinearSample(-x / r, 1, 0)) / 2;
    else
        return 0.5f + InvertLinearSample(x / r, 1, 0) / 2;
}
```

A.4.2 SAMPLING EXPONENTIAL DISTRIBUTIONS

Sampling the transmittance function when rendering images with participating media often requires samples from a distribution $p(x) \propto e^{-ax}$. As before, the first step is to find a constant c that normalizes this distribution so that it integrates to one. In this case, we will assume for now that the range of values x we'd like the generated samples to cover is $[0, \infty)$ rather than $[0, 1]$, so

$$c \int_0^\infty e^{-ax}\, dx = -\left.\frac{c}{a}e^{-ax}\right|_0^\infty = \frac{c}{a} = 1.$$

Thus, $c = a$ and our PDF is $p(x) = ae^{-ax}$.

⟨*Sampling Inline Functions*⟩ +≡
```
Float ExponentialPDF(Float x, Float a) {
    return a * std::exp(-a * x);
}
```

We can integrate to find $P(x)$:

$$P(x) = \int_0^x ae^{-ax'}\, dx' = 1 - e^{-ax}, \tag{A.1}$$

which gives a function that is easy to invert:

$$P^{-1}(x) = -\frac{\ln(1-x)}{a}.$$

Therefore, we can draw samples using

$$X = -\frac{\ln(1-\xi)}{a}. \tag{A.2}$$

⟨*Sampling Inline Functions*⟩ +≡
```
Float SampleExponential(Float u, Float a) {
    return -std::log(1 - u) / a;
}
```

It may be tempting to simplify the log term from $\ln(1 - \xi)$ to $\ln \xi$, under the theory that because $\xi \in [0, 1)$, these are effectively the same and a subtraction can thus be saved. The problem with this idea is that ξ may have the value 0 but never has the value 1. With the simplification, it is possible that we would try to take the logarithm of 0, which is undefined; this danger is avoided with the first formulation.[2] While a ξ value of 0 may seem very unlikely, it is possible, especially in the world of floating-point arithmetic and not the real numbers. Sample generation algorithms based on the radical inverse function (Section 8.6.1) are particularly prone to generating the value 0.

Float 23
InvertLinearSample() 73

---

2   This is a subtlety that the authors did not appreciate in the first two editions of the book.

As before, the inverse sampling function is given by evaluating $P(x)$.

⟨*Sampling Inline Functions*⟩ +≡
```
Float InvertExponentialSample(Float x, Float a) {
    return 1 - std::exp(-a * x);
}
```

A.4.3 SAMPLING THE GAUSSIAN

The Gaussian function is parameterized by its center μ and standard deviation σ:

$$g(x) = \frac{1}{\sqrt{2\pi\sigma^2}} e^{-\frac{(x-\mu)^2}{2\sigma^2}}. \qquad \text{[A.3]}$$

The probability distribution it defines is called the *normal distribution*. The Gaussian is already normalized, so the PDF follows directly.

⟨*Sampling Inline Functions*⟩ +≡
```
Float NormalPDF(Float x, Float mu = 0, Float sigma = 1) {
    return Gaussian(x, mu, sigma);
}
```

However, the Gaussian's CDF cannot be expressed with elementary functions. It is

$$P(x) = \frac{1}{2}\left(1 + \mathrm{erf}\left(\frac{x - \mu}{\sigma\sqrt{2}}\right)\right),$$

where $\mathrm{erf}(x)$ is the error function. If we equate $\xi = P(x)$ and solve, we find that:

$$x = \mu + \sqrt{2}\sigma\,\mathrm{erf}^{-1}(2\xi - 1).$$

The inverse error function erf^{-1} can be well approximated with a polynomial, which in turn gives a sampling technique.

⟨*Sampling Inline Functions*⟩ +≡
```
Float SampleNormal(Float u, Float mu = 0, Float sigma = 1) {
    return mu + Sqrt2 * sigma * ErfInv(2 * u - 1);
}
```

InvertNormalSample(), not included here, evaluates $P(x)$.

The *Box-Muller transform* is an alternative sampling technique for the normal distribution; it takes a pair of random samples and returns a pair of normally distributed samples. It makes use of the fact that if two normally distributed variables are considered as a 2D point and transformed to 2D polar coordinates (r, θ), then $r^2 = -2\ln\xi_1$ and $\theta = 2\pi\xi_2$.

⟨*Sampling Inline Functions*⟩ +≡
```
Point2f SampleTwoNormal(Point2f u, Float mu = 0, Float sigma = 1) {
    Float r2 = -2 * std::log(1 - u[0]);
    return {mu + sigma * std::sqrt(r2 * std::cos(2 * Pi * u[1])),
            mu + sigma * std::sqrt(r2 * std::sin(2 * Pi * u[1]))};
}
```

A.4.4 SAMPLING THE LOGISTIC FUNCTION

The *logistic function* is shaped similarly to the Gaussian, but can be sampled directly. It is therefore useful in cases where a distribution similar to the Gaussian is useful but an exact

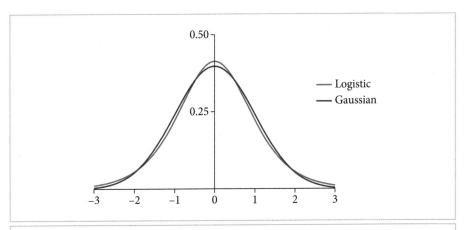

Figure A.4: Plots of the logistic function, Equation (A.4) with $s = 0.603$, and the Gaussian, Equation (A.3), with $\sigma = 1$. (s was found via a least-squares fit to minimize error over the domain of the plot.)

Gaussian is not needed. (It is used, for example, in the implementation of pbrt's scattering model for hair.) The logistic function centered at the origin is

$$f(x) = \frac{e^{-|x|/s}}{s(1 + e^{-|x|/s})^2},$$

(A.4)

where s is a parameter that controls its rate of falloff similar to σ in the Gaussian. Figure A.4 shows a plot of the logistic and Gaussian functions with parameter values that lead to curves with similar shapes.

The logistic function is normalized by design, so the PDF evaluation function follows directly.

⟨*Sampling Inline Functions*⟩ +≡
```
Float LogisticPDF(Float x, Float s) {
    x = std::abs(x);
    return std::exp(-x / s) / (s * Sqr(1 + std::exp(-x / s)));
}
```

Its CDF,

$$P(x) = \frac{1}{1 + e^{-x/s}},$$

is easily found, and can be inverted to derive a sampling routine. The result is implemented in SampleLogistic().

⟨*Sampling Inline Functions*⟩ +≡
```
Float SampleLogistic(Float u, Float s) {
    return -s * std::log(1 / u - 1);
}
```

As usual in 1D, the sample inversion method is performed by evaluating the CDF.

⟨*Sampling Inline Functions*⟩ +≡
```
Float InvertLogisticSample(Float x, Float s) {
    return 1 / (1 + std::exp(-x / s));
}
```

A.4.5 SAMPLING A FUNCTION OVER AN INTERVAL

It is sometimes useful to sample from a function's distribution over a specified interval $[a, b]$. It turns out that this is easy to do if we are able to evaluate the function's CDF. We will use the logistic function as an example here, though the underlying technique applies more generally.

First consider the task of finding the PDF of the function limited to the interval, $p_{[a,b]}(x)$: we need to renormalize it. Doing so requires being able to integrate $p(x)$, which is otherwise known as finding its CDF:

$$
\begin{aligned}
p_{[a,b]}(x) &= \frac{p(x)}{\int_a^b p(x)\,dx} \\
&= \frac{p(x)}{P(b) - P(a)}.
\end{aligned}
$$

[A.5]

The function to evaluate the PDF follows directly. Here we have wrapped a call to `Invert LogisticSample()` in a simple lambda expression in order to make the relationship to Equation (A.5) more clear.

⟨*Sampling Inline Functions*⟩ +≡
```
Float TrimmedLogisticPDF(Float x, Float s, Float a, Float b) {
    if (x < a || x > b) return 0;
    auto P = [&](Float x) { return InvertLogisticSample(x, s); };
    return Logistic(x, s) / (P(b) - P(a));
}
```

Next, consider sampling using the inversion method. Following the definition of $p_{[a,b]}(x)$, we can see that the CDF associated with $p_{[a,b]}(x)$ is

$$
P_{[a,b]}(x) = \int_a^x p_{[a,b]}(x')\,dx' = \frac{P(x) - P(a)}{P(b) - P(a)}.
$$

[A.6]

Setting $\xi = P_{[a,b]}(X)$ and solving for X, we have

$$
X = P^{-1}\left(\xi(P(b) - P(a)) + P(a)\right).
$$

Thus, if we compute a new ξ value (that, in a slight abuse of notation, is not between 0 and 1) by using ξ to linearly interpolate between $P(a)$ and $P(b)$ and then apply the original sampling algorithm, we will generate a sample from the distribution over the interval $[a, b]$.

⟨*Sampling Inline Functions*⟩ +≡
```
Float SampleTrimmedLogistic(Float u, Float s, Float a, Float b) {
    auto P = [&](Float x) { return InvertLogisticSample(x, s); };
    u = Lerp(u, P(a), P(b));
    Float x = SampleLogistic(u, s);
    return Clamp(x, a, b);
}
```

The inversion routine follows directly from Equation (A.6).

⟨*Sampling Inline Functions*⟩ +≡
```
Float InvertTrimmedLogisticSample(Float x, Float s, Float a, Float b) {
    auto P = [&](Float x) { return InvertLogisticSample(x, s); };
    return (P(x) - P(a)) / (P(b) - P(a));
}
```

A.4.6 SAMPLING NON-INVERTIBLE CDFS

It was not possible to invert the normal distribution's CDF to derive a sampling technique, so there we used a polynomial approximation of the inverse CDF. In cases like that, another option is to use numerical root–finding techniques. We will demonstrate that approach using the *smoothstep* function as an example.

Smoothstep defines an s-shaped curve based on a third-degree polynomial that goes from zero to one starting at a point a and ending at a point b. It is zero for values $x < a$ and one for values $x > b$. Otherwise, it is defined as

$$f(x) = 3t^2 - 2t^3,$$

with $t = (x - a)/(b - a)$. In pbrt the smoothstep function is used to define the falloff at the edges of a spotlight.

We will consider the task of sampling the function within the range $[a, b]$. First, it is easy to show that the PDF is

$$p(x) = \frac{2f(x)}{b - a}.$$

⟨Sampling Inline Functions⟩ $+\equiv$
```
Float SmoothStepPDF(Float x, Float a, Float b) {
    if (x < a || x > b) return 0;
    return (2 / (b - a)) * SmoothStep(x, a, b);
}
```

Integrating the PDF is also easy; the resulting CDF is

$$P(x) = \frac{2t^3 - t^4}{b - a}.$$

The challenge in sampling f is evident: doing so requires solving a fourth-degree polynomial.

The sampling task can be expressed as a zero-finding problem: to apply the inversion method, we would like to solve $\xi = P(X)$ for X. Doing so is equivalent to finding the value X such that $P(X) - \xi = 0$. The SampleSmoothStep() function below uses a Newton-bisection solver that is defined in Section B.2.10 to do this. That function takes a callback that returns the value of the function and its derivative at a given point; these values are easily computed given the equations derived so far.

⟨Sampling Inline Functions⟩ $+\equiv$
```
Float SampleSmoothStep(Float u, Float a, Float b) {
    auto cdfMinusU = [=](Float x) -> std::pair<Float, Float> {
        Float t = (x - a) / (b - a);
        Float P = 2 * Pow<3>(t) - Pow<4>(t);
        Float PDeriv = SmoothStepPDF(x, a, b);
        return {P - u, PDeriv};
    };
    return NewtonBisection(a, b, cdfMinusU);
}
```

Sample inversion can be performed following the same approach as was used earlier in Equation (A.6) for the logistic over an interval.

⟨*Sampling Inline Functions*⟩ +≡

```
Float InvertSmoothStepSample(Float x, Float a, Float b) {
    Float t = (x - a) / (b - a);
    auto P = [&](Float x) { return 2 * Pow<3>(t) - Pow<4>(t); };
    return (P(x) - P(a)) / (P(b) - P(a));
}
```

A.4.7 SAMPLING PIECEWISE-CONSTANT 1D FUNCTIONS

The inversion method can also be applied to tabularized functions; in this section, we will consider piecewise-constant functions defined over [0, 1]. The algorithms described here will provide the foundation for sampling piecewise-constant 2D functions, used in multiple parts of pbrt to sample from distributions defined by images.

Assume that the 1D function's domain is split into n equal-sized pieces of size $\Delta = 1/n$. These regions start and end at points $x_i = i\Delta$, where i ranges from 0 to n, inclusive. Within each region, the value of the function $f(x)$ is a constant (Figure A.5(a)).

The value of $f(x)$ is then

$$f(x) = \begin{cases} v_0 & x_0 \le x < x_1 \\ v_1 & x_1 \le x < x_2 \\ \vdots \end{cases}.$$

The function need not always be positive, though its PDF must be. Therefore, the absolute value of the function is taken to define its PDF. The integral $\int |f(x)|\,dx$ is

$$c = \int_0^1 |f(x)|\,dx = \sum_{i=0}^{n-1} |v_i|\Delta = \sum_{i=0}^{n-1} \frac{|v_i|}{n}, \tag{A.7}$$

and so it is easy to construct the PDF $p(x)$ for $f(x)$ as $|f(x)|/c$. By direct application of the relevant formulae, the CDF $P(x)$ is a piecewise-linear function defined at points x_i by

$$P(x_0) = 0$$

$$P(x_1) = \int_{x_0}^{x_1} p(x)\,dx = \frac{|v_0|}{cn} = P(x_0) + \frac{|v_0|}{cn}$$

$$P(x_2) = \int_{x_0}^{x_2} p(x)\,dx = \int_{x_0}^{x_1} p(x)\,dx + \int_{x_1}^{x_2} p(x)\,dx = P(x_1) + \frac{|v_1|}{cn}$$

$$P(x_i) = P(x_{i-1}) + \frac{|v_{i-1}|}{cn}.$$

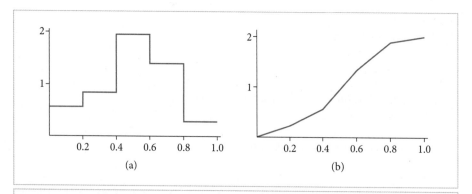

(a) (b)

Float 23

Figure A.5: (a) Probability density function for a piecewise-constant 1D function and (b) cumulative distribution function defined by this PDF.

Between two points x_i and x_{i+1}, the CDF is linearly increasing with slope $|v_i|/c$.

Recall that in order to sample $f(x)$ we need to invert the CDF to find the value x such that

$$\xi = \int_0^x p(x')\,\mathrm{d}x' = P(x).$$

Because the CDF is monotonically increasing, the value of x must be between the x_i and x_{i+1} such that $P(x_i) \leq \xi < P(x_{i+1})$. Given an array of CDF values, this pair of $P(x_i)$ values can be efficiently found with a binary search.

The PiecewiseConstant1D class brings these ideas together to provide methods for efficient sampling and PDF evaluation of this class of functions.

⟨*PiecewiseConstant1D Definition*⟩ ≡
```
class PiecewiseConstant1D {
  public:
    ⟨PiecewiseConstant1D Public Methods 1009⟩
    ⟨PiecewiseConstant1D Public Members 1009⟩
};
```

The PiecewiseConstant1D constructor takes n values of a piecewise-constant function f defined over a range [min, max]. (The generalization to a non-[0, 1] interval simply requires remapping returned samples to the specified range and renormalizing the PDF based on its extent.)

⟨*PiecewiseConstant1D Public Methods*⟩ ≡   1009
```
PiecewiseConstant1D(pstd::span<const Float> f, Float min, Float max,
                    Allocator alloc = {})
    : func(f.begin(), f.end(), alloc), cdf(f.size() + 1, alloc),
      min(min), max(max) {
    ⟨Take absolute value of func 1009⟩
    ⟨Compute integral of step function at xi 1010⟩
    ⟨Transform step function integral into CDF 1010⟩
}
```

The constructor makes its own copy of the function values and computes the function's CDF. Note that the constructor allocates n+1 Floats for the cdf array because if $f(x)$ has n step values, then there are $n + 1$ values $P(x_i)$ that define the CDF. Storing the final CDF value of 1 is redundant but simplifies the sampling code later.

⟨*PiecewiseConstant1D Public Members*⟩ ≡   1009
```
pstd::vector<Float> func, cdf;
Float min, max;
```

Because the specified function may be negative, the absolute value of it is taken here first. (There is no further need for the original function in the PiecewiseConstant1D implementation.)

⟨*Take absolute value of func*⟩ ≡   1009
```
for (Float &f : func) f = std::abs(f);
```

Next, the integral of $|f(x)|$ at each point x_i is computed using Equation (A.7), with the result stored in the cdf array for now.

⟨*Compute integral of step function at x_i*⟩ ≡   **1009**
```
cdf[0] = 0;
size_t n = f.size();
for (size_t i = 1; i < n + 1; ++i)
    cdf[i] = cdf[i - 1] + func[i - 1] * (max - min) / n;
```

With the value of the integral stored in cdf[n], this value can be copied into funcInt and the CDF can be normalized by dividing through all entries by this value. The case of a zero-valued function is handled by defining a linear CDF, which leads to uniform sampling. That case occurs more frequently than one might expect due to the use of this class when sampling piecewise-constant 2D functions; when that is used with images, images with zero-valued scanlines lead to zero-valued functions here.

⟨*Transform step function integral into CDF*⟩ ≡   **1009**
```
funcInt = cdf[n];
if (funcInt == 0)
    for (size_t i = 1; i < n + 1; ++i)
        cdf[i] = Float(i) / Float(n);
else
    for (size_t i = 1; i < n + 1; ++i)
        cdf[i] /= funcInt;
```

⟨*PiecewiseConstant1D Public Members*⟩ +≡   **1009**
```
Float funcInt = 0;
```

The integral of the absolute value of the function is made available via a method and the size() method returns the number of tabularized values.

⟨*PiecewiseConstant1D Public Methods*⟩ +≡   **1009**
```
Float Integral() const { return funcInt; }
size_t size() const { return func.size(); }
```

The PiecewiseConstant1D::Sample() method uses the given random sample u to sample from its distribution. It returns the corresponding value x and the value of the PDF $p(x)$. If the optional offset parameter is not nullptr, it returns the offset into the array of function values of the largest index where the CDF was less than or equal to u. (In other words, cdf[*offset] <= u < cdf[*offset+1].)

⟨*PiecewiseConstant1D Public Methods*⟩ +≡   **1009**
```
Float Sample(Float u, Float *pdf = nullptr, int *offset = nullptr) const {
    ⟨Find surrounding CDF segments and offset 1010⟩
    ⟨Compute offset along CDF segment 1011⟩
    ⟨Compute PDF for sampled offset 1011⟩
    ⟨Return x corresponding to sample 1011⟩
}
```

Mapping u to an interval matching the above criterion is carried out using the efficient binary search implemented in FindInterval().

⟨*Find surrounding CDF segments and offset*⟩ ≡   **1010**
```
int o = FindInterval((int)cdf.size(),
                     [&](int index) { return cdf[index] <= u; });
if (offset)
    *offset = o;
```

Given the pair of CDF values that straddle u, we can compute x. First, we determine how far u is between cdf[o] and cdf[o+1]. We denote this value with du, where du is 0 if u == cdf[o] and goes up to 1 if u == cdf[o+1]. Because the CDF is piecewise-linear, the sample value x is the same offset between x_i and x_{i+1} (Figure A.5(b)).

⟨*Compute offset along CDF segment*⟩ ≡   1010
```
Float du = u - cdf[o];
if (cdf[o + 1] - cdf[o] > 0)
    du /= cdf[o + 1] - cdf[o];
```

The PDF for this sample $p(x)$ is easily computed since we have the function's integral in funcInt. (Note that the offset o into the CDF array has been computed in a way so that func[o] gives the value of the function in the CDF range that the sample landed in.)

⟨*Compute PDF for sampled offset*⟩ ≡   1010
```
if (pdf)
    *pdf = (funcInt > 0) ? func[o] / funcInt : 0;
```

Finally, the appropriate value of x is computed and returned. Here is where the sampled value in [0, 1) is remapped to the user-specified range [min, max).

⟨*Return x corresponding to sample*⟩ ≡   1010
```
return Lerp((o + du) / size(), min, max);
```

As with the other sampling routines so far, PiecewiseConstant1D provides an inversion method that takes a point x in the range [min, max] and returns the [0, 1) sample value that maps to it. As before, this is a matter of evaluating the CDF $P(x)$ at the given position.

⟨*PiecewiseConstant1D Public Methods*⟩ +≡   1009
```
pstd::optional<Float> Invert(Float x) const {
    ⟨Compute offset to CDF values that bracket x 1011⟩
    ⟨Linearly interpolate between adjacent CDF values to find sample value 1011⟩
}
```

Because the CDF is tabularized at regular steps over [min, max], if we remap x to lie within [0, 1), scale by the number of CDF values, and take the floor of that value, we have the offset to the entry in the cdf array that precedes x.

⟨*Compute offset to CDF values that bracket x*⟩ ≡   1011
```
if (x < min || x > max)
    return {};
Float c = (x - min) / (max - min) * func.size();
int offset = Clamp(int(c), 0, func.size() - 1);
```

Given those two points, we linearly interpolate between their values to evaluate the CDF.

⟨*Linearly interpolate between adjacent CDF values to find sample value*⟩ ≡   1011
```
Float delta = c - offset;
return Lerp(delta, cdf[offset], cdf[offset + 1]);
```

A.5 SAMPLING MULTIDIMENSIONAL FUNCTIONS

Multidimensional sampling is also common in pbrt, most frequently when sampling points on the surfaces of shapes and sampling directions after scattering at points. This section therefore works through the derivations and implementations of algorithms for sampling in a number of useful multidimensional domains. Some of them involve separable PDFs where each dimension can be sampled independently, while others use the approach of sampling from marginal and conditional density functions that was introduced in Section 2.4.2.

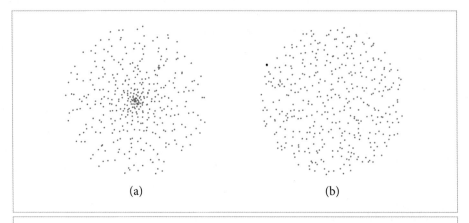

(a)   (b)

Figure A.6: (a) When the obvious but incorrect mapping of uniform random variables to points on the disk is used, the resulting distribution is not uniform and the samples are more likely to be near the center of the disk. (b) The correct mapping gives a uniform distribution of points.

A.5.1 SAMPLING A UNIT DISK

Uniformly sampling a unit disk can be tricky because it has an incorrect intuitive solution. The wrong approach is the seemingly obvious one of sampling its polar coordinates uniformly: $r = \xi_1$, $\theta = 2\pi\xi_2$. Although the resulting point is both random and inside the disk, it is *not* uniformly distributed; it actually clumps samples near the center of the disk. Figure A.6(a) shows a plot of samples on the unit disk when this mapping was used for a set of uniform random samples (ξ_1, ξ_2). Figure A.6(b) shows uniformly distributed samples resulting from the following correct approach.

Since we would like to sample uniformly with respect to area, the PDF $p(x, y)$ must be a constant. By the normalization constraint, $p(x, y) = 1/\pi$. If we transform into polar coordinates, we have $p(r, \theta) = r/\pi$ given the relationship between probability densities in Cartesian coordinates and polar coordinates that was derived in Section 2.4.1, Equation (2.22).

We can now compute the marginal and conditional densities:

$$p(r) = \int_0^{2\pi} p(r, \theta)\, d\theta = 2r$$
$$p(\theta|r) = \frac{p(r, \theta)}{p(r)} = \frac{1}{2\pi}.$$

The fact that $p(\theta|r)$ is a constant should make sense because of the symmetry of the disk. Integrating and inverting to find $P(r)$, $P^{-1}(r)$, $P(\theta)$, and $P^{-1}(\theta)$, we can find that the correct solution to generate uniformly distributed samples on a disk is

$$r = \sqrt{\xi_1}$$
$$\theta = 2\pi\xi_2.$$

Taking the square root of ξ_1 effectively pushes the samples back toward the edge of the disk, counteracting the clumping referred to earlier.

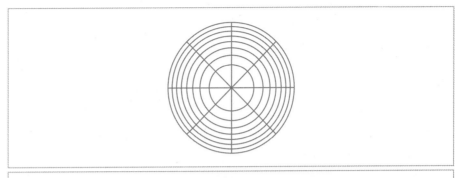

Figure A.7: The mapping from 2D random samples to points on the disk implemented in `SampleUniform DiskPolar()` distorts areas substantially. Each section of the disk here has equal area and represents $\frac{1}{8}$ of the unit square of uniform random samples in each direction. In general, we would prefer a mapping that did a better job at mapping nearby (ξ_1, ξ_2) values to nearby points on the disk.

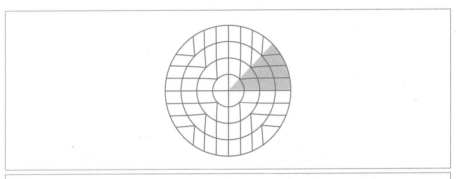

Figure A.8: The concentric mapping maps squares to circles, giving a less distorted mapping than the first method shown for uniformly sampling points on the unit disk. It is based on mapping triangular wedges of the unit square to pie-shaped wedges of the disk, as shown here.

⟨*Sampling Inline Functions*⟩ $+\equiv$

```
Point2f SampleUniformDiskPolar(Point2f u) {
    Float r = std::sqrt(u[0]);
    Float theta = 2 * Pi * u[1];
    return {r * std::cos(theta), r * std::sin(theta)};
}
```

The inversion method, `InvertUniformDiskPolarSample()`, is straightforward and is not included here.

Although this mapping solves the problem at hand, it distorts areas on the disk; areas on the unit square are elongated or compressed when mapped to the disk (Figure A.7). This distortion can reduce the effectiveness of stratified sampling patterns by making the strata less compact. A better approach that avoids this problem is a "concentric" mapping from the unit square to the unit disk. The concentric mapping takes points in the square $[-1, 1]^2$ to the unit disk by uniformly mapping concentric squares to concentric circles (Figure A.8).

The mapping turns wedges of the square into slices of the disk. For example, points in the shaded area in Figure A.8 are mapped to (r, θ) by

$$r = x$$
$$\theta = \frac{y}{x}\frac{\pi}{4}.$$

Float 23
Pi 1033
Point2f 92
SampleUniformDiskPolar()
    1013

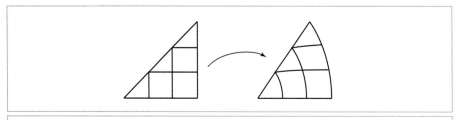

Figure A.9: Triangular wedges of the square are mapped into (r, θ) pairs in pie-shaped slices of the disk in the `SampleUniformDiskConcentric()` function.

See Figure A.9. The other seven wedges are handled analogously.

⟨*Sampling Inline Functions*⟩ +≡
```
Point2f SampleUniformDiskConcentric(Point2f u) {
    ⟨Map u to [−1, 1]² and handle degeneracy at the origin  1014⟩
    ⟨Apply concentric mapping to point  1014⟩
}
```

For the following, the random samples are mapped to the $[-1, 1]^2$ square. The $(0, 0)$ point is then handled specially so that the following code does not need to avoid dividing by zero.

⟨*Map* u *to* $[-1, 1]^2$ *and handle degeneracy at the origin*⟩ ≡   **1014**
```
Point2f uOffset = 2 * u - Vector2f(1, 1);
if (uOffset.x == 0 && uOffset.y == 0)
    return {0, 0};
```

All the other points are transformed using the mapping from square wedges to disk slices by way of computing (r, θ) polar coordinates for them. The following implementation is carefully crafted so that the mapping is continuous across adjacent slices.

⟨*Apply concentric mapping to point*⟩ ≡   **1014**
```
Float theta, r;
if (std::abs(uOffset.x) > std::abs(uOffset.y)) {
    r = uOffset.x;
    theta = PiOver4 * (uOffset.y / uOffset.x);
} else {
    r = uOffset.y;
    theta = PiOver2 - PiOver4 * (uOffset.x / uOffset.y);
}
return r * Point2f(std::cos(theta), std::sin(theta));
```

The corresponding inversion function, `InvertUniformDiskConcentricSample()`, is not included in the text here.

A.5.2 UNIFORMLY SAMPLING HEMISPHERES AND SPHERES

The area of a unit hemisphere is 2π, and thus the PDF for uniform sampling must be $p(\omega) = 1/(2\pi)$.

We will use spherical coordinates to derive a sampling algorithm. Using Equation (2.23) from Section 2.4.1, we have $p(\theta, \phi) = \sin\theta/(2\pi)$. This density function is separable. Because ϕ ranges from 0 to 2π and must have a constant PDF, $p(\phi) = 1/(2\pi)$ and therefore $p(\theta) = \sin\theta$. The two CDFs follow:

Float 23
PiOver2 1033
PiOver4 1033
Point2f 92
Vector2f 86

$$P(\theta) = \int_0^\theta \sin \theta' \, d\theta' = 1 - \cos \theta$$

$$P(\phi) = \int_0^\phi \frac{1}{2\pi} \, d\phi' = \frac{\phi}{2\pi}.$$

Inverting these functions is straightforward, and in this case we can tidy the result by replacing $1 - \xi$ with ξ, giving

$$\theta = \cos^{-1} \xi_1$$

$$\phi = 2\pi \xi_2.$$

Converting back to Cartesian coordinates, we get the final sampling formulae:

$$x = \sin \theta \cos \phi = \cos\left(2\pi \xi_2\right) \sqrt{1 - \xi_1^2}$$

$$y = \sin \theta \sin \phi = \sin\left(2\pi \xi_2\right) \sqrt{1 - \xi_1^2} \qquad \text{(A.8)}$$

$$z = \cos \theta = \xi_1.$$

This sampling strategy is implemented in the following code. Two uniform random numbers are provided in u, and a vector on the hemisphere is returned.

⟨*Sampling Inline Functions*⟩ +≡
```
Vector3f SampleUniformHemisphere(Point2f u) {
    Float z = u[0];
    Float r = SafeSqrt(1 - Sqr(z));
    Float phi = 2 * Pi * u[1];
    return {r * std::cos(phi), r * std::sin(phi), z};
}
```

For each PDF evaluation function, it is important to be clear which PDF is being evaluated—for example, we have already seen directional probabilities expressed both in terms of solid angle and in terms of (θ, ϕ). For hemispheres (and all other directional sampling in pbrt), these functions return probability with respect to solid angle. Thus, the uniform hemisphere PDF function is trivial and does not require that the direction be passed to it.

⟨*Sampling Inline Functions*⟩ +≡
```
Float UniformHemispherePDF() { return Inv2Pi; }
```

The inverse sampling method can be derived starting from Equation (A.8).

⟨*Sampling Inline Functions*⟩ +≡
```
Point2f InvertUniformHemisphereSample(Vector3f w) {
    Float phi = std::atan2(w.y, w.x);
    if (phi < 0)
        phi += 2 * Pi;
    return Point2f(w.z, phi / (2 * Pi));
}
```

Float 23
Inv2Pi 1033
Pi 1033
Point2f 92
SafeSqrt() 1034
Sqr() 1034
Vector3f 86

Sampling the full sphere uniformly over its area follows almost exactly the same derivation, which we omit here. The end result is

$$x = \cos(2\pi \xi_2)\sqrt{1 - z^2} = \cos(2\pi \xi_2) 2\sqrt{\xi_1(1 - \xi_1)}$$

$$y = \sin(2\pi \xi_2)\sqrt{1 - z^2} = \sin(2\pi \xi_2) 2\sqrt{\xi_1(1 - \xi_1)}$$

$$z = 1 - 2\xi_1.$$

⟨*Sampling Inline Functions*⟩ +≡
```
Vector3f SampleUniformSphere(Point2f u) {
    Float z = 1 - 2 * u[0];
    Float r = SafeSqrt(1 - Sqr(z));
    Float phi = 2 * Pi * u[1];
    return {r * std::cos(phi), r * std::sin(phi), z};
}
```

The PDF is $1/(4\pi)$, one over the surface area of the unit sphere.

⟨*Sampling Inline Functions*⟩ +≡
```
Float UniformSpherePDF() { return Inv4Pi; }
```

The sampling inversion method also follows directly.

⟨*Sampling Inline Functions*⟩ +≡
```
Point2f InvertUniformSphereSample(Vector3f w) {
    Float phi = std::atan2(w.y, w.x);
    if (phi < 0)
        phi += 2 * Pi;
    return Point2f((1 - w.z) / 2, phi / (2 * Pi));
}
```

A.5.3 COSINE-WEIGHTED HEMISPHERE SAMPLING

As we saw in the discussion of importance sampling (Section 2.2.2), it is often useful to sample from a distribution that has a shape similar to that of the integrand being estimated. Many light transport integrals include a cosine factor, and therefore it is useful to have a method that generates directions according to a cosine-weighted distribution on the hemisphere. Such a method gives samples that are more likely to be close to the top of the hemisphere, where the cosine term has a large value, rather than near the bottom, where the cosine term is small.

Mathematically, this means that we would like to sample directions ω from a PDF

$$p(\omega) \propto \cos \theta.$$

Normalizing as usual,

$$\int_{\mathcal{H}^2} p(\omega) \, d\omega = 1$$

$$\int_0^{2\pi} \int_0^{\frac{\pi}{2}} c \cos \theta \sin \theta \, d\theta \, d\phi = 1$$

$$c \, 2\pi \int_0^{\pi/2} \cos \theta \sin \theta \, d\theta = 1$$

$$c = \frac{1}{\pi}.$$

Thus,

$$p(\theta, \phi) = \frac{1}{\pi} \cos \theta \sin \theta.$$

We could compute the marginal and conditional densities as before, but instead we can use a technique known as *Malley's method* to generate these cosine-weighted points. The idea behind Malley's method is that if we choose points uniformly from the unit disk and then

Float 23
Inv4Pi 1033
Pi 1033
Point2f 92
SafeSqrt() 1034
Sqr() 1034
Vector3f 86

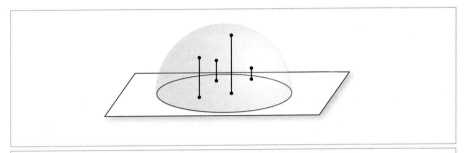

Figure A.10: Malley's Method. To sample direction vectors from a cosine-weighted distribution, uniformly sample points on the unit disk and project them up to the unit hemisphere.

generate directions by projecting the points on the disk up to the hemisphere above it, the result will have a cosine-weighted distribution of directions (Figure A.10).

Why does this work? Let (r, ϕ) be the polar coordinates of the point chosen on the disk (note that we are using ϕ instead of the usual θ for the polar angle here). From Section A.5.1, we know that the joint density $p(r, \phi) = r/\pi$ gives the density of a point sampled on the disk.

Now, we map this point to the hemisphere. The vertical projection gives $\sin \theta = r$, which is easily seen from Figure A.10. To complete the $(r, \phi) = (\sin \theta, \phi) \rightarrow (\theta, \phi)$ transformation, we need the determinant of the Jacobian

$$|J_T| = \begin{vmatrix} \cos \theta & 0 \\ 0 & 1 \end{vmatrix} = \cos \theta.$$

Therefore,

$$p(\theta, \phi) = |J_T| \, p(r, \phi) = \cos \theta \frac{r}{\pi} = \frac{\cos \theta \sin \theta}{\pi},$$

which is exactly what we wanted! We have used the transformation method to prove that Malley's method generates directions with a cosine-weighted distribution. Note that this technique works with any uniform disk sampling approach, so we can use the earlier concentric mapping just as well as the simpler $(r, \theta) = (\sqrt{\xi_1}, 2\pi\xi_2)$ method.

⟨*Sampling Inline Functions*⟩ +≡
```
Vector3f SampleCosineHemisphere(Point2f u) {
    Point2f d = SampleUniformDiskConcentric(u);
    Float z = SafeSqrt(1 - Sqr(d.x) - Sqr(d.y));
    return Vector3f(d.x, d.y, z);
}
```

Because directional PDFs in pbrt are defined with respect to solid angle, the PDF function returns the value $\cos \theta / \pi$.

⟨*Sampling Inline Functions*⟩ +≡
```
Float CosineHemispherePDF(Float cosTheta) {
    return cosTheta * InvPi;
}
```

Finally, a directional sample can be inverted purely from its (x, y) coordinates on the disk.

⟨*Sampling Inline Functions*⟩ +≡
```
Point2f InvertCosineHemisphereSample(Vector3f w) {
    return InvertUniformDiskConcentricSample({w.x, w.y});
}
```

A.5.4 SAMPLING WITHIN A CONE

It is sometimes useful to be able to uniformly sample rays in a cone of directions. This distribution is separable in (θ, ϕ), with $p(\phi) = 1/(2\pi)$, and so we therefore need to derive a method to sample a direction θ up to the maximum angle of the cone, θ_{max}. Incorporating the $\sin \theta$ term from the measure on the unit sphere from Equation (4.8), we have

$$1 = c \int_0^{\theta_{max}} \sin \theta \, d\theta$$

$$= c(1 - \cos \theta_{max}).$$

So $p(\theta) = \sin \theta / (1 - \cos \theta_{max})$ and $p(\omega) = 1/(2\pi(1 - \cos \theta_{max}))$.

⟨*Sampling Inline Functions*⟩ +≡
```
Float UniformConePDF(Float cosThetaMax) {
    return 1 / (2 * Pi * (1 - cosThetaMax));
}
```

The PDF can be integrated to find the CDF and the sampling technique for θ follows:

$$\cos \theta = (1 - \xi) + \xi \cos \theta_{max}.$$

The following code samples a canonical cone around the (0, 0, 1) axis; the sample can be transformed to cones with other orientations using the Frame class.

⟨*Sampling Inline Functions*⟩ +≡
```
Vector3f SampleUniformCone(Point2f u, Float cosThetaMax) {
    Float cosTheta = (1 - u[0]) + u[0] * cosThetaMax;
    Float sinTheta = SafeSqrt(1 - Sqr(cosTheta));
    Float phi = u[1] * 2 * Pi;
    return SphericalDirection(sinTheta, cosTheta, phi);
}
```

The inversion function, InvertUniformConeSample(), is not included here.

A.5.5 PIECEWISE-CONSTANT 2D DISTRIBUTIONS

Building on the approach for sampling piecewise-constant 1D distributions in Section A.4.7, we can apply the marginal-conditional approach to sample from piecewise-constant 2D distributions. We will consider the case of a 2D function defined over a user-specified domain by a 2D array of $n_u \times n_v$ sample values. This case is particularly useful for generating samples from distributions defined by image maps and environment maps.

Consider a 2D function $f(u, v)$ defined by a set of $n_u \times n_v$ values $f[u_i, v_j]$ where $u_i \in [0, 1, \ldots, n_u - 1]$, $v_j \in [0, 1, \ldots, n_v - 1]$, and $f[u_i, v_j]$ gives the constant value of f over the range $[i/n_u, (i + 1)/n_u) \times [j/n_v, (j + 1)/n_v)$. Given continuous values (u, v), we will use $(\tilde{u}, \tilde{v})$ to denote the corresponding discrete (u_i, v_j) indices, with $\tilde{u} = \lfloor n_u u \rfloor$ and $\tilde{v} = \lfloor n_v v \rfloor$ so that $f(u, v) = f[\tilde{u}, \tilde{v}]$.

Integrals of f are sums of $f[u_i, v_j]$, so that, for example, the integral of f over the domain is

$$I_f = \iint f(u, v) \, du \, dv = \frac{1}{n_u n_v} \sum_{i=0}^{n_u-1} \sum_{j=0}^{n_v-1} f[u_i, v_j].$$

Using the definition of the PDF and the integral of f, we can find f's PDF,

$$p(u, v) = \frac{f(u, v)}{\iint f(u, v) \, du \, dv} = \frac{f[\tilde{u}, \tilde{v}]}{1/(n_u n_v) \sum_{i=0}^{n_u-1} \sum_{j=0}^{n_v-1} f[u_i, v_j]}.$$

Recalling Equation (2.24), the marginal density $p(v)$ can be computed as a sum of $f[u_i, v_j]$ values

$$p(v) = \int p(u, v) \, du = \frac{(1/n_u) \sum_{i=0}^{n_u-1} f[u_i, \tilde{v}]}{I_f}. \tag{A.9}$$

Because this function only depends on $\tilde{v}$, it is thus itself a piecewise-constant 1D function, $p[\tilde{v}]$, defined by n_v values. The 1D sampling machinery from Section A.4.7 can be applied to sampling from its distribution.

Given a v sample, the conditional density $p(u|v)$ is then

$$p(u|v) = \frac{p(u, v)}{p(v)} = \frac{f[\tilde{u}, \tilde{v}]/I_f}{p[\tilde{v}]}. \tag{A.10}$$

Note that, given a particular value of $\tilde{v}$, $p[\tilde{u}|\tilde{v}]$ is a piecewise-constant 1D function of $\tilde{u}$ that can be sampled with the usual 1D approach. There are n_v such distinct 1D conditional densities, one for each possible value of $\tilde{v}$.

Putting this all together, the PiecewiseConstant2D class provides functionality similar to PiecewiseConstant1D, except that it generates samples from piecewise-constant 2D distributions.

⟨*PiecewiseConstant2D Definition*⟩ ≡
```
class PiecewiseConstant2D {
  public:
      ⟨PiecewiseConstant2D Public Methods 1019⟩
  private:
      ⟨PiecewiseConstant2D Private Members 1019⟩
};
```

Its constructor has two tasks. First, it computes a 1D conditional sampling density $p[\tilde{u}|\tilde{v}]$ for each of the n_v individual $\tilde{v}$ values using Equation (A.10). It then computes the marginal sampling density $p[\tilde{v}]$ with Equation (A.9). (PiecewiseConstant2D provides a variety of additional constructors, not included here, including ones that take an Array2D to specify the values. See the pbrt source code for details.)

⟨*PiecewiseConstant2D Public Methods*⟩ ≡   1019
```
PiecewiseConstant2D(pstd::span<const Float> func, int nu, int nv,
                    Bounds2f domain, Allocator alloc = {})
  : domain(domain), pConditionalV(alloc), pMarginal(alloc) {
    for (int v = 0; v < nv; ++v)
        ⟨Compute conditional sampling distribution for ṽ 1020⟩
    ⟨Compute marginal sampling distribution p[ṽ] 1020⟩
}
```

⟨*PiecewiseConstant2D Private Members*⟩ ≡   1019
```
Bounds2f domain;
```

PiecewiseConstant1D can directly compute the $p[\tilde{u}|\tilde{v}]$ distributions from each of the n_v rows of n_u function values, since they are laid out linearly in memory. The I_f and $p[\tilde{v}]$ terms from Equation (A.10) do not need to be included in the values passed to PiecewiseConstant1D since they have the same value for all the n_u values and are thus just a constant scale that does not affect the normalized distribution that PiecewiseConstant1D computes.

⟨*Compute conditional sampling distribution for $\tilde{v}$*⟩ ≡   1019
```
pConditionalV.emplace_back(func.subspan(v * nu, nu), domain.pMin[0],
                           domain.pMax[0], alloc);
```

⟨*PiecewiseConstant2D Private Members*⟩ +≡   1019
```
pstd::vector<PiecewiseConstant1D> pConditionalV;
```

Given the conditional densities for each $\tilde{v}$ value, we can find the 1D marginal density for sampling each one, $p[\tilde{v}]$. Because the PiecewiseConstant1D class has a method that provides the integral of its function, it is just necessary to copy these values to the marginalFunc buffer so they are stored linearly in memory for the PiecewiseConstant1D constructor.

⟨*Compute marginal sampling distribution $p[\tilde{v}]$*⟩ ≡   1019
```
pstd::vector<Float> marginalFunc;
for (int v = 0; v < nv; ++v)
    marginalFunc.push_back(pConditionalV[v].Integral());
pMarginal = PiecewiseConstant1D(marginalFunc, domain.pMin[1],
                                domain.pMax[1], alloc);
```

⟨*PiecewiseConstant2D Private Members*⟩ +≡   1019
```
PiecewiseConstant1D pMarginal;
```

The integral of the function over the $[0, 1]^2$ domain is made available via the Integral() method. Because the marginal distribution is the integral of one dimension, its integral gives the function's full integral.

⟨*PiecewiseConstant2D Public Methods*⟩ +≡   1019
```
Float Integral() const { return pMarginal.Integral(); }
```

As described previously, in order to sample from the 2D distribution, first a sample is drawn from the $p[\tilde{v}]$ marginal distribution in order to find the v coordinate of the sample. The offset of the sampled function value gives the integer $\tilde{v}$ value that determines which of the precomputed conditional distributions should be used for sampling the u value. Figure A.11 illustrates this idea using a low-resolution image as an example.

⟨*PiecewiseConstant2D Public Methods*⟩ +≡   1019
```
Point2f Sample(Point2f u, Float *pdf = nullptr,
               Point2i *offset = nullptr) const {
    Float pdfs[2];
    Point2i uv;
    Float d1 = pMarginal.Sample(u[1], &pdfs[1], &uv[1]);
    Float d0 = pConditionalV[uv[1]].Sample(u[0], &pdfs[0], &uv[0]);
    if (pdf)
        *pdf = pdfs[0] * pdfs[1];
    if (offset)
        *offset = uv;
    return Point2f(d0, d1);
}
```

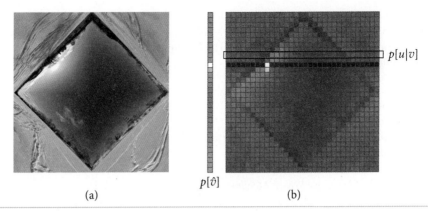

$$p[\hat{v}] \qquad\qquad p[u|v]$$

(a) (b)

Figure A.11: The Piecewise-Constant Sampling Distribution for a High-Dynamic-Range Environment Map. (a) The original environment map. (b) A low-resolution version of the marginal density function $p[\hat{v}]$ and the conditional distributions for rows of the image. First the marginal 1D distribution is used to select a v value, giving a row of the image to sample. Rows with bright pixels are more likely to be sampled. Then, given a row, a value u is sampled from that row's 1D distribution.

The value of the PDF for a given sample value is computed as the product of the conditional and marginal PDFs for sampling it.

⟨*PiecewiseConstant2D Public Methods*⟩ +≡   **1019**
```
Float PDF(Point2f pr) const {
    Point2f p = Point2f(domain.Offset(pr));
    int iu = Clamp(int(p[0] * pConditionalV[0].size()), 0,
                   pConditionalV[0].size() - 1);
    int iv = Clamp(int(p[1] * pMarginal.size()), 0, pMarginal.size() - 1);
    return pConditionalV[iv].func[iu] / pMarginal.Integral();
}
```

The Invert() method, not included here, inverts the provided sample by inverting the v sample using the marginal distribution and then inverting u via the appropriate conditional distribution.

A.5.6 WINDOWED PIECEWISE-CONSTANT 2D DISTRIBUTIONS

WindowedPiecewiseConstant2D generalizes the PiecewiseConstant2D class to allow the caller to specify a window that limits the sampling domain to a given rectangular subset of it. (This capability was key for the implementation of the PortalImageInfiniteLight in Section 12.5.3.) Before going into its implementation, we will start with the SummedAreaTable class, which provides some capabilities that make it easier to implement. We have encapsulated them in a stand-alone class, as they can be useful in other settings as well.

In 2D, a *summed-area table* is a 2D array where each element (x, y) stores a sum of values from another array a:

$$s(x,\,y) = \sum_{x'=0}^{x-1} \sum_{y'=0}^{y-1} a(x',\,y'), \qquad\qquad \text{[A.11]}$$

where here we have used C++'s zero-based array indexing convention.

Summed-area tables can be used to compute the sum of array values over rectangular regions of the original array in constant time. If the array a is interpreted as samples of a function, a summed-area table can efficiently compute integrals over arbitrary rectangular regions in a similar fashion. (Summed-area tables are therefore sometimes referred to as *integral images*.) They have a straightforward generalization to higher dimensions, though two of them suffice for pbrt's needs.

⟨*SummedAreaTable Definition*⟩ ≡
```
class SummedAreaTable {
  public:
    ⟨SummedAreaTable Public Methods 1022⟩
  private:
    ⟨SummedAreaTable Private Methods 1023⟩
    ⟨SummedAreaTable Private Members 1022⟩
};
```

The constructor takes a 2D array of values that are used to initialize its sum array, which holds the corresponding sums. The first entry is easy: it is just the $(0, 0)$ entry from the provided values array.

⟨*SummedAreaTable Public Methods*⟩ ≡   1022
```
SummedAreaTable(const Array2D<Float> &values, Allocator alloc = {})
    : sum(values.XSize(), values.YSize(), alloc) {
  sum(0, 0) = values(0, 0);
  ⟨Compute sums along first row and column 1022⟩
  ⟨Compute sums for the remainder of the entries 1022⟩
}
```

⟨*SummedAreaTable Private Members*⟩ ≡   1022
```
Array2D<double> sum;
```

All the remaining entries in sum can be computed incrementally. It is easiest to start out by computing sums as x varies with $y = 0$ and vice versa.

⟨*Compute sums along first row and column*⟩ ≡   1022
```
for (int x = 1; x < sum.XSize(); ++x)
    sum(x, 0) = values(x, 0) + sum(x - 1, 0);
for (int y = 1; y < sum.YSize(); ++y)
    sum(0, y) = values(0, y) + sum(0, y - 1);
```

The remainder of the sums are computed incrementally by adding the corresponding value from the provided array to two of the previous sums and subtracting a third. It is possible to use the definition from Equation (A.11) to verify that this expression gives the desired value, but it can also be understood geometrically; see Figure A.12.

⟨*Compute sums for the remainder of the entries*⟩ ≡   1022
```
for (int y = 1; y < sum.YSize(); ++y)
    for (int x = 1; x < sum.XSize(); ++x)
        sum(x, y) = (values(x, y) + sum(x - 1, y) + sum(x, y - 1) -
                     sum(x - 1, y - 1));
```

We will find it useful to be able to treat the sum as a continuous function defined over $[0, 1]^2$. In doing so, our implementation effectively treats the originally provided array of values as the specification of a piecewise-constant function. Under this interpretation, the stored sum values effectively represent the function's value at the upper corners of the box-shaped regions that the domain has been discretized into. (See Figure A.13.)

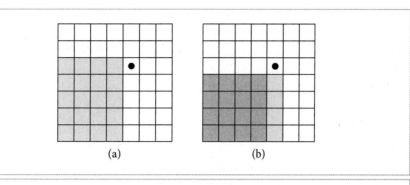

Figure A.12: Computing a Value in a Summed-Area Table Based on Previous Sums. (a) A starting value for the sum at a location (x, y) (filled circle) is given by the sum at $(x - 1, y)$ (shaded region). To this value, we need to add the provided array's value at (x, y). (b) What is left is the sum of values in the column beneath (x, y) (lighter shaded region); that value can be found by taking the sum at $(x, y - 1)$ and subtracting the sum at $(x - 1, y - 1)$ (darker shaded region).

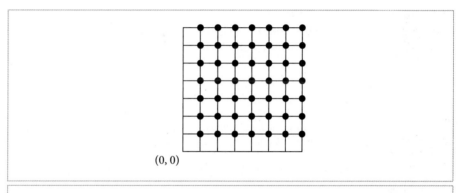

$(0, 0)$

Figure A.13: Interpretation of sum Array Values. If the sample array values is interpreted as defining a piecewise-constant function over $[0, 1]^2$, then the values stored in sum represent the sums at the upper-right corner of each piecewise-constant region. The sums along $x = 0$ and $y = 0$, all of which are 0, are not stored.

This Lookup() method returns the interpolated sum at the given continuous coordinate values.

⟨*SummedAreaTable Private Methods*⟩ ≡   **1022**
```
Float Lookup(Float x, Float y) const {
    ⟨Rescale (x, y) to table resolution and compute integer coordinates 1023⟩
    ⟨Bilinearly interpolate between surrounding table values 1024⟩
}
```

It is more convenient to work with coordinates that are with respect to the array's dimensions and so this method starts by scaling the provided coordinates accordingly. Note that an offset of 0.5 is not included in this remapping, as is done when indexing pixel values (recall the discussion of this topic in Section 8.1.4); this is due to the fact that sum defines function values at the upper corners of the discretized regions rather than at their center.

Array2D::XSize() 1070
Array2D::YSize() 1070
Float 23

⟨*Rescale (x, y) to table resolution and compute integer coordinates*⟩ ≡   **1023**
```
x *= sum.XSize();
y *= sum.YSize();
int x0 = (int)x, y0 = (int)y;
```

Bilinear interpolation of the four values surrounding the lookup point proceeds as usual, using `LookupInt()` to look up values of the sum at provided integer coordinates.

⟨*Bilinearly interpolate between surrounding table values*⟩ ≡   1023
```
Float v00 = LookupInt(x0, y0), v10 = LookupInt(x0 + 1, y0);
Float v01 = LookupInt(x0, y0 + 1), v11 = LookupInt(x0 + 1, y0 + 1);
Float dx = x - int(x), dy = y - int(y);
return (1 - dx) * (1 - dy) * v00 + (1 - dx) * dy * v01 +
        dx  * (1 - dy) * v10 +        dx *  dy * v11;
```

`LookupInt()` returns the value of the sum for provided integer coordinates. In particular, it is responsible for handling the details related to the sum array storing the sum at the upper corners of the domain strata.

⟨*SummedAreaTable Private Methods*⟩ +≡   1022
```
Float LookupInt(int x, int y) const {
    ⟨Return zero at lower boundaries  1024⟩
    ⟨Reindex (x, y) and return actual stored value  1024⟩
}
```

If either coordinate is zero-valued, the lookup point is along one of the lower edges of the domain (or is at the origin). In this case, a sum value of 0 is returned.

⟨*Return zero at lower boundaries*⟩ ≡   1024
```
if (x == 0 || y == 0)
    return 0;
```

Otherwise, one is subtracted from each coordinate so that indexing into the sum array accounts for the zero sums at the lower edges not being stored in sum.

⟨*Reindex (x, y) and return actual stored value*⟩ ≡   1024
```
x = std::min(x - 1, sum.XSize() - 1);
y = std::min(y - 1, sum.YSize() - 1);
return sum(x, y);
```

Summed-area tables compute sums and integrals over arbitrary rectangular regions in a similar way to how the interior sum values were originally initialized. Here it is also possible to verify this computation algebraically, but the geometric interpretation may be more intuitive; see Figure A.14.

The `SummedAreaTable` class provides this capability through its `Integral()` method, which returns the integral of the piecewise-constant function over a 2D bounding box. Here, the sum of function values over the region is converted to an integral by dividing by the size of the function strata over the domain. We have used double precision here to compute the final sum in order to improve its accuracy: especially if there are thousands of values in each dimension, the sums may have large magnitudes and thus taking their differences can lead to catastrophic cancellation.

⟨*SummedAreaTable Public Methods*⟩ +≡   1022
```
Float Integral(Bounds2f extent) const {
    double s = (((double)Lookup(extent.pMax.x, extent.pMax.y) -
                 (double)Lookup(extent.pMin.x, extent.pMax.y)) +
                ((double)Lookup(extent.pMin.x, extent.pMin.y) -
                 (double)Lookup(extent.pMax.x, extent.pMin.y)));
    return std::max<Float>(s / (sum.XSize() * sum.YSize()), 0);
}
```

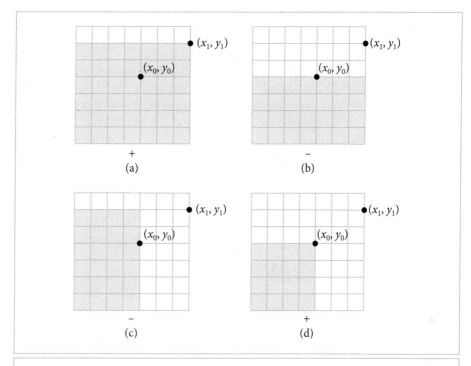

Figure A.14: Computing the Sum of an Arbitrary Rectangular Region. Given two points (x_0, y_0) and (x_1, y_1) representing the corners of a rectangular region, the sum of values inside the rectangular region can be found in terms of sums of subregions. (a) The sum at (x_1, y_1) gives the desired result and then much more. (b) Subtracting the (x_0, y_1) sum eliminates some of the excess, leaving the region underneath the region to be removed. (c) Subtracting the (x_1, y_0) sum takes care of the excess and then some; the shaded region has now been removed twice. (d) Adding the shaded region's sum, which is the sum at (x_0, y_0), rectifies the excess subtraction and leaves us with the desired result.

Given SummedAreaTable's capability of efficiently evaluating integrals over rectangular regions of a piecewise-constant function's domain, the WindowedPiecewiseConstant2D class is able to provide sampling and PDF evaluation functions that operate over arbitrary caller-specified regions.

⟨*WindowedPiecewiseConstant2D Definition*⟩ ≡
```
class WindowedPiecewiseConstant2D {
  public:
    ⟨WindowedPiecewiseConstant2D Public Methods 1025⟩
  private:
    ⟨WindowedPiecewiseConstant2D Private Methods 1027⟩
    ⟨WindowedPiecewiseConstant2D Private Members 1026⟩
};
```

The constructor both copies the provided function values and initializes a summed-area table with them.

⟨*WindowedPiecewiseConstant2D Public Methods*⟩ ≡   **1025**
```
WindowedPiecewiseConstant2D(Array2D<Float> f, Allocator alloc = {})
    : sat(f, alloc), func(f, alloc) {}
```

⟨*WindowedPiecewiseConstant2D Private Members*⟩ ≡   **1025**
```
SummedAreaTable sat;
Array2D<Float> func;
```

With the `SummedAreaTable` in hand, it is now possible to bring the pieces together to implement the `Sample()` method. Because it is possible that there is no valid sample inside the
specified bounds (e.g., if the function's value is zero), an optional return value is used in
order to be able to indicate such cases.

⟨*WindowedPiecewiseConstant2D Public Methods*⟩ +≡   **1025**
```
pstd::optional<Point2f> Sample(Point2f u, Bounds2f b, Float *pdf) const {
    ⟨Handle zero-valued function for windowed sampling 1026⟩
    ⟨Define lambda function Px for marginal cumulative distribution 1026⟩
    ⟨Sample marginal windowed function in x 1027⟩
    ⟨Sample conditional windowed function in y 1027⟩
    ⟨Compute PDF and return point sampled from windowed function 1028⟩
}
```

The first step is to check whether the function's integral is zero over the specified bounds.
This may happen due to a degenerate `Bounds2f` or due to a plain old zero-valued function
over the corresponding part of its domain. In this case, it is not possible to return a valid
sample.

⟨*Handle zero-valued function for windowed sampling*⟩ ≡   **1026**
```
if (sat.Integral(b) == 0)
    return {};
```

As discussed in Section 2.4.2, multidimensional distributions can be sampled by first integrating out all of the dimensions but one, sampling the resulting function, and then
using that sample value in sampling the corresponding conditional distribution. `Windowed`
`PiecewiseConstant2D` applies that very same idea, taking advantage of the fact that the
summed-area table can efficiently evaluate the necessary integrals as needed.

For a 2D continuous function $f(x, y)$ defined over a rectangular domain from (x_0, y_0) to
(x_1, y_1), the marginal distribution in x is defined by

$$p(x) = \frac{\int_{y_0}^{y_1} f(x, y') \, dy'}{\int_{x_0}^{x_1} \int_{y_0}^{y_1} f(x', y') \, dx' \, dy'},$$

and the marginal's cumulative distribution is

$$P(x) = \frac{\int_{x_0}^{x} \int_{y_0}^{y_1} f(x', y') \, dx' dy'}{\int_{x_0}^{x_1} \int_{y_0}^{y_1} f(x', y') \, dx' \, dy'}.$$

The integrals in both the numerator and denominator of $P(x)$ can be evaluated using a
summed-area table. The following lambda function evaluates $P(x)$, using a cached normalization factor for the denominator in `bInt` to improve performance, as it will be necessary to
repeatedly evaluate `Px` in order to sample from the distribution.

⟨*Define lambda function Px for marginal cumulative distribution*⟩ ≡   **1026**
```
Float bInt = sat.Integral(b);
auto Px = [&, this](Float x) -> Float {
    Bounds2f bx = b;
    bx.pMax.x = x;
    return sat.Integral(bx) / bInt;
};
```

Sampling is performed using a separate utility method, `SampleBisection()`, that will also be useful for sampling the conditional density in y.

⟨*Sample marginal windowed function in x*⟩ ≡   1026
```
Point2f p;
p.x = SampleBisection(Px, u[0], b.pMin.x, b.pMax.x, func.XSize());
```

`SampleBisection()` draws a sample from the density described by the provided CDF P by applying the bisection method to solve $u = P(x)$ for x over a specified range [min, max]. (It expects $P(x)$ to have the value 0 at min and 1 at max.) This function has the built-in assumption that the CDF is piecewise-linear over n equal-sized segments over [0, 1]. This fits `SummedAreaTable` perfectly, though it means that `SampleBisection()` would need modification to be used in other contexts.

⟨*WindowedPiecewiseConstant2D Private Methods*⟩ ≡   1025
```
template <typename CDF>
static Float SampleBisection(CDF P, Float u, Float min, Float max, int n) {
    ⟨Apply bisection to bracket u 1027⟩
    ⟨Find sample by interpolating between min and max 1027⟩
}
```

The initial min and max values bracket the solution. Therefore, bisection can proceed by successively evaluating P at their midpoint and then updating one or the other of them to maintain the bracket. This process continues until both endpoints lie inside one of the function discretization strata of width $1/n$.

⟨*Apply bisection to bracket u*⟩ ≡   1027
```
while (pstd::ceil(n * max) - pstd::floor(n * min) > 1) {
    Float mid = (min + max) / 2;
    if (P(mid) > u) max = mid;
    else min = mid;
}
```

Once both endpoints are in the same stratum, it is possible to take advantage of the fact that P is known to be piecewise-linear and to find the value of x in closed form.

⟨*Find sample by interpolating between min and max*⟩ ≡   1027
```
Float t = (u - P(min)) / (P(max) - P(min));
return Clamp(Lerp(t, min, max), min, max);
```

Given the sample x, we now need to draw a sample from the conditional distribution

$$p(y|x) = \frac{f(x, y)}{\int_{y_0}^{y_1} f(x, y')\, dy'},$$

which has CDF

$$P(y|x) = \frac{\int_{y_0}^{y} f(x, y')\, dy'}{\int_{y_0}^{y_1} f(x, y')\, dy'}.$$

Although the `SummedAreaTable` class does not provide the capability to evaluate 1D integrals directly, because the function is piecewise-constant we can equivalently evaluate a 2D integral where the x range spans only the stratum of the sampled x value.

⟨*Sample conditional windowed function in y*⟩ ≡   1026
```
⟨Compute 2D bounds bCond for conditional sampling 1028⟩
⟨Define lambda function for conditional distribution and sample y 1028⟩
```

bCond stores the bounding box that spans the range of potential y values and the stratum of the x sample. It is necessary to check for a zero function integral over these bounds: this should not be possible mathematically, but may be the case due to floating-point round-off error. In that rare case, conditional sampling is not possible and an invalid sample must be returned.

⟨*Compute 2D bounds* bCond *for conditional sampling*⟩ ≡   1027
```
int nx = func.XSize();
Bounds2f bCond(Point2f(pstd::floor(p.x * nx) / nx, b.pMin.y),
               Point2f(pstd::ceil(p.x * nx) / nx, b.pMax.y));
if (bCond.pMin.x == bCond.pMax.x) bCond.pMax.x += 1.f / nx;
if (sat.Integral(bCond) == 0)
    return {};
```

Similar to the marginal CDF $P(x)$, we can define a lambda function to evaluate the conditional CDF $P(y|x)$. Again precomputing the normalization factor is worthwhile, as Py will be evaluated multiple times in the course of the sampling operation.

⟨*Define lambda function for conditional distribution and sample y*⟩ ≡   1027
```
Float condIntegral = sat.Integral(bCond);
auto Py = [&, this](Float y) -> Float {
    Bounds2f by = bCond;
    by.pMax.y = y;
    return sat.Integral(by) / condIntegral;
};
p.y = SampleBisection(Py, u[1], b.pMin.y, b.pMax.y, func.YSize());
```

The PDF value is computed by evaluating the function at the sampled point p and normalizing with its integral over b, which is already available in bInt.

⟨*Compute PDF and return point sampled from windowed function*⟩ ≡   1026
```
*pdf = Eval(p) / bInt;
return p;
```

The Eval() method wraps up the details of looking up the function value corresponding to the provided 2D point.

⟨*WindowedPiecewiseConstant2D Private Methods*⟩ +≡   1025
```
Float Eval(Point2f p) const {
    Point2i pi(std::min<int>(p[0] * func.XSize(), func.XSize() - 1),
               std::min<int>(p[1] * func.YSize(), func.YSize() - 1));
    return func[pi];
}
```

The PDF method implements the same computation that is used to compute the PDF in the Sample() method.

⟨*WindowedPiecewiseConstant2D Public Methods*⟩ +≡   1025
```
Float PDF(Point2f p, const Bounds2f &b) const {
    Float funcInt = sat.Integral(b);
    if (funcInt == 0)
        return 0;
    return Eval(p) / funcInt;
}
```

FURTHER READING

Rejection sampling was developed by von Neumann (1951) shortly after the Monte Carlo method was invented.

The alias method was introduced by Walker (1974, 1977). The algorithm that we have implemented to generate alias tables in the `AliasTable` class is due to Vose (1991). See Schwarz's article (2011) for extensive information about implementing alias tables and related techniques.

A number of algorithms for reservoir sampling were described by Vitter (1985), though he credits the basic algorithm we outlined at the start of Section A.2 to Alan Waterman. The weighted reservoir sampling algorithm in pbrt's `WeightedReservoirSampler` class is due to Chao (1982).

The square to disk mapping in Section A.5.1 was described by Shirley and Chiu (1997). The implementation here benefits by observations in Shirley's 2011 blog by Dave Cline and the commenter "franz" that the logic could be simplified considerably from the original algorithm (Shirley 2011). Articles by Shirley and collaborators describe a number of useful recipes for warping uniform random numbers to useful distributions for rendering (Shirley 1992; Shirley et al. 2019).

The summed-area table data structure was introduced by Crow (1984). Its use for efficiently sampling arbitrary rectangluar regions of images was demonstrated by Bitterli et al. (2015).

A number of additional sampling techniques have been developed for tabularized multi-dimensional distributions. Steigleder and McCool (2003) linearized 2D and higher dimensional domains into 1D using a Hilbert curve and then sampled using 1D samples over the 1D domain, which still maintains desirable stratification properties of the sampling distribution thanks to the spatial coherence preserving properties of the Hilbert curve. McCool and Harwood (1997) as well as Clarberg et al. (2005) described an approach for sampling images based on quadtrees that repeatedly transforms uniform sample values until they match a target distribution.

Lawrence et al. (2005) described an adaptive representation for tabularized CDFs, where the CDF is approximated with a piecewise-linear function with fewer, irregularly spaced vertices than the given CDF. This approach can substantially reduce storage requirements and improve lookup efficiency, taking advantage of the fact that large ranges of the CDF may be efficiently approximated with a single linear function.

The time spent searching the CDF when sampling from a tabularized distribution can be reduced with auxiliary data structures. Chen and Asau (1974) suggested the *guide table method*, where an additional array of offsets into the table gives a starting point for the search. Cline et al. (2009) introduced this approach to graphics and also presented a method based on approximating the inverse CDF as a piecewise-linear function of ξ, thus enabling constant-time lookups at a cost of some accuracy. Binder and Keller (2020) presented algorithms for building and sampling from tabularized distributions that run efficiently on GPUs. Another innovative approach to sampling from such CDFs was described by Morrical and Zellmann (2021), who showed how hardware ray tracing capabilities could be used for this task. Vitsas et al. (2021) fit Gaussian mixture models to the sampling distribution of clear sky environment maps and showed a significant reduction in memory use with a sampling algorithm that does not require table search.

Arithmetic coding offers another interesting way to approach sampling from distributions (MacKay 2003, p. 118; Piponi 2012). If we have a discrete set of probabilities from which we would like to generate samples, one way to approach the problem is to encode the CDF as a binary tree where each node splits the $[0, 1)$ interval at some point and where, given a random sample ξ, we determine which sample value it corresponds to by traversing the tree until we reach the leaf node for its sample value. Ideally, we would like leaf nodes that represent higher probabilities to be higher up in the tree, so that it takes fewer traversal steps to find them (and thus those more frequently generated samples can be found more quickly). Looking at the problem from this perspective, it can be shown that the optimal structure of such a tree is given by Huffman coding, which is normally used for compression.

EXERCISES

● **A.1**   Show that the `WeightedReservoirSampler::Merge()` method leaves the resulting reservoir with a sample that indeed is stored with probability equal to its weight divided by the sums of weights for all the samples in the two reservoirs.

● **A.2**   Modify the `PiecewiseConstant1D` implementation to use the adaptive CDF representation described by Lawrence et al. (2005), and experiment with how much more compact the CDF representation can be made without causing image artifacts. (Good test scenes include those that use `ImageInfiniteLights`, which use the `PiecewiseConstant2D` and, thus, `PiecewiseConstant1D` for sampling.) Can you measure an improvement in rendering speed due to more efficient searches through the approximated CDF?

● **A.3**   Extend `SummedAreaTable` to provide methods that efficiently compute 1D integrals along each dimension and then modify the `WindowedPiecewiseConstant2D` class's `Sample()` method to use this capability for sampling the conditional CDF $P(y|x)$. How is overall rendering performance affected by your change when rendering a scene that uses the `PortalImageInfiniteLight`? Profile pbrt and measure the change in performance of the `Sample()` method with your changes. What conclusions can you draw from your results?

⬛ UTILITIES

In addition to all the graphics-related code presented thus far, pbrt makes use of a number of general utility routines and classes. Although these are key to pbrt's operation, it is not necessary to understand their implementation in detail in order to work with the rest of the system. This appendix describes the interfaces to these routines, including those that handle mathematical foundations, error reporting, memory management, support for parallel execution on multiple CPU cores, and other basic infrastructure. The implementations of some of this functionality—the parts that are interesting enough to be worth delving into—are also discussed.

B.1 SYSTEM STARTUP, CLEANUP, AND OPTIONS

Two structures that are defined in the options.h header represent various user-specified options that are generally not part of the scene description file but are instead specified using command-line arguments to pbrt. pbrt's main() function allocates the structure and then overrides its default values as appropriate.

BasicPBRTOptions stores the options that are used in both the CPU and GPU rendering pipelines. How most of them are used should be self-evident, though seed deserves note: any time an RNG is initialized in pbrt, the seed value in the options should be incorporated in the seed passed to its constructor. In this way, the renderer will generate independent images if the user specifies different --seed values using command-line arguments.

⟨*BasicPBRTOptions Definition*⟩ ≡
```
struct BasicPBRTOptions {
    int seed = 0;
    bool quiet = false;
    bool disablePixelJitter = false, disableWavelengthJitter = false;
    bool disableTextureFiltering = false;
    bool forceDiffuse = false;
    bool useGPU = false;
    bool wavefront = false;
    RenderingCoordinateSystem renderingSpace =
        RenderingCoordinateSystem::CameraWorld;
};
```

RenderingCoordinateSystem 1032

RNG 1054

⟨*RenderingCoordinateSystem Definition*⟩ ≡
```
enum class RenderingCoordinateSystem { Camera, CameraWorld, World };
```

The PBRTOptions structure, not included here, inherits from BasicPBRTOptions and adds a number of additional options that are mostly used when processing the scene description and not during rendering. A number of these options are std::strings that are not accessible in GPU code. Splitting the options in this way allows GPU code to access a BasicPBRTOptions instance to get the particular option values that are relevant to it.

The options are passed to InitPBRT(), which should be called before any of pbrt's other classes or interfaces are used. It handles system-wide initialization and configuration. When rendering completes, CleanupPBRT() should be called so that the system can gracefully shut down. Both of these functions are defined in the file pbrt.cpp.

⟨*Initialization and Cleanup Function Declarations*⟩ ≡
```
void InitPBRT(const PBRTOptions &opt);
void CleanupPBRT();
```

In code that only runs on the CPU, the options can be accessed via a global variable.

⟨*Options Global Variable Declaration*⟩ ≡
```
extern PBRTOptions *Options;
```

For code that runs on both the CPU and GPU, options must be accessed through the GetOptions() function, which returns a copy of the options that is either stored in CPU or GPU memory, depending on which type of processor the code is executing.

⟨*Options Inline Functions*⟩ ≡
```
const BasicPBRTOptions &GetOptions();
```

B.2 MATHEMATICAL INFRASTRUCTURE

pbrt uses a wide range of mathematical routines. Much of this functionality is implemented in the files util/math.h and util/math.cpp; everything in this section is found there, with a few exceptions that will be noted when they are encountered.

A table of the first 1,000 prime numbers is provided via a global variable. Its main use in pbrt is for determining bases to use for the radical inverse based low-discrepancy points in Chapter 8.

⟨*Prime Table Declarations*⟩ ≡
```
static constexpr int PrimeTableSize = 1000;
extern PBRT_CONST int Primes[PrimeTableSize];
```

NextPrime() returns the next prime number after the provided one.

⟨*Math Function Declarations*⟩ ≡
```
int NextPrime(int x);
```

B.2.1 BASIC ALGEBRAIC FUNCTIONS

Clamp() clamps the given value to lie between the values low and high. For convenience, it allows the types of the values giving the extent to be different than the type being clamped (but its implementation requires that implicit conversion among the types involved is legal). By being implemented this way rather than requiring all to have the same type, the implementation allows calls like Clamp(floatValue, 0, 1) that would otherwise be disallowed by C++'s template type resolution rules.

⟨*Math Inline Functions*⟩ +≡
```
template <typename T, typename U, typename V>
constexpr T Clamp(T val, U low, V high) {
    if (val < low)        return T(low);
    else if (val > high) return T(high);
    else                  return val;
}
```

`Mod()` computes the remainder of a/b. pbrt has its own version of this (rather than using %) in order to provide the behavior that the modulus of a negative number is always positive or zero. Starting with C++11, the behavior of % has been specified to return a negative value or zero in this case, so that the identity `(a/b)*b + a%b == a` holds.

⟨*Math Inline Functions*⟩ +≡
```
template <typename T>
T Mod(T a, T b) {
    T result = a - (a / b) * b;
    return (T)((result < 0) ? result + b : result);
}
```

A specialization for `Float`s calls the corresponding standard library function.

⟨*Math Inline Functions*⟩ +≡
```
template <>
Float Mod(Float a, Float b) { return std::fmod(a, b); }
```

It can be useful to be able to invert the bilinear interpolation function, Equation (2.25). Because there are two unknowns in the result, values with at least two dimensions must be bilinearly interpolated in order to invert it. In that case, two equations with two unknowns can be formed, which in turn leads to a quadratic equation.

⟨*Point2 Inline Functions*⟩ ≡
```
Point2f InvertBilinear(Point2f p, pstd::span<const Point2f> v);
```

A number of constants, most of them related to π, are used enough that it is worth having them easily available.

⟨*Mathematical Constants*⟩ +≡
```
constexpr Float Pi      = 3.14159265358979323846;
constexpr Float InvPi   = 0.31830988618379067154;
constexpr Float Inv2Pi  = 0.15915494309189533577;
constexpr Float Inv4Pi  = 0.07957747154594766788;
constexpr Float PiOver2 = 1.57079632679489661923;
constexpr Float PiOver4 = 0.78539816339744830961;
constexpr Float Sqrt2   = 1.41421356237309504880;
```

Two simple functions convert from angles expressed in degrees to radians, and vice versa:

⟨*Math Inline Functions*⟩ +≡
```
Float Radians(Float deg) { return (Pi / 180) * deg; }
Float Degrees(Float rad) { return (180 / Pi) * rad; }
```

It is often useful to blend between two values using a smooth curve that does not have the first derivative discontinuities that a linear interpolant would. `SmoothStep()` takes a range $[a, b]$ and a value x, returning 0 if $x \le a$, 1 if $x \ge b$, and smoothly blends between 0 and 1 for intermediate values of x using a cubic polynomial. Among other uses in the system, the SpotLight uses SmoothStep() to model the falloff to its edge.

⟨*Math Inline Functions*⟩ +≡
```
Float SmoothStep(Float x, Float a, Float b) {
    if (a == b) return (x < a) ? 0 : 1;
    Float t = Clamp((x - a) / (b - a), 0, 1);
    return t * t * (3 - 2 * t);
}
```

Finally, SafeSqrt() returns the square root of the given value, clamping it to zero in case of rounding errors being the cause of a slightly negative value. A second variant for doubles is effectively the same and is therefore not included here.

⟨*Math Inline Functions*⟩ +≡
```
float SafeSqrt(float x) { return std::sqrt(std::max(0.f, x)); }
```

B.2.2 INTEGER POWERS AND POLYNOMIALS

Sqr() squares the provided value. Though it is not much work to write this operation out directly, we have often found this function to be helpful in making the implementations of formulae more succinct.

⟨*Math Inline Functions*⟩ +≡
```
template <typename T>
constexpr T Sqr(T v) { return v * v; }
```

Pow() efficiently raises a value to a power if the power is a compile-time constant. Note that the total number of multiply operations works out to be logarithmic in the power n.

⟨*Math Inline Functions*⟩ +≡
```
template <int n>
constexpr float Pow(float v) {
    if constexpr (n < 0) return 1 / Pow<-n>(v);
    float n2 = Pow<n / 2>(v);
    return n2 * n2 * Pow<n & 1>(v);
}
```

Specializations for $n = 1$ and $n = 0$ terminate the template function recursion.

⟨*Math Inline Functions*⟩ +≡
```
template <>
constexpr float Pow<1>(float v) { return v; }
template <>
constexpr float Pow<0>(float v) { return 1; }
```

EvaluatePolynomial() evaluates a provided polynomial using Horner's method, which is based on the equivalence

$$c_0 + c_1 x + c_2 x^2 + \cdots = c_0 + x(c_1 + x(c_2 + \cdots.$$

This formulation both gives good numerical accuracy and is amenable to use of fused multiply add operations.

⟨*Math Inline Functions*⟩ +≡
```
template <typename Float, typename C>
constexpr Float EvaluatePolynomial(Float t, C c) { return c; }
```

Clamp() 1033
Float 23
Pow() 1034
SpotLight 748

⟨*Math Inline Functions*⟩ +≡
```
template <typename Float, typename C, typename... Args>
constexpr Float EvaluatePolynomial(Float t, C c, Args... cRemaining) {
    return FMA(t, EvaluatePolynomial(t, cRemaining...), c);
}
```

B.2.3 TRIGONOMETRIC FUNCTIONS

The function $\sin(x)/x$ is used in multiple places in pbrt, including in the implementation of the LanczosSincFilter. It is undefined at $x = 0$ and suffers from poor numerical accuracy if directly evaluated at nearby values. A robust computation of its value is possible by considering the power series expansion

$$\frac{\sin x}{x} = 1 - \frac{x^2}{3!} + \frac{x^4}{5!} - \cdots.$$

If x is small and $1 - x^2/3!$ rounds to 1, then $\sin(x)/x$ also rounds to 1. The following function uses a slightly more conservative variant of that test, which is close enough for our purposes.

⟨*Math Inline Functions*⟩ +≡
```
Float SinXOverX(Float x) {
    if (1 - x * x == 1)
        return 1;
    return std::sin(x) / x;
}
```

Similar to SafeSqrt(), pbrt also provides "safe" versions of the inverse sine and cosine functions so that if the provided value is slightly outside of the legal range $[-1, 1]$, a reasonable result is returned rather than a not-a-number value. In debug builds, an additional check is performed to make sure that the provided value is not too far outside the valid range.

⟨*Math Inline Functions*⟩ +≡
```
float SafeASin(float x) { return std::asin(Clamp(x, -1, 1)); }
float SafeACos(float x) { return std::acos(Clamp(x, -1, 1)); }
```

B.2.4 LOGARITHMS AND EXPONENTIATION

Because the math library does not provide a base-2 logarithm function, we provide one here, using the identity $\log_2(x) = \log x/\log 2$.

⟨*Math Inline Functions*⟩ +≡
```
Float Log2(Float x) {
    const Float invLog2 = 1.442695040888963387004650940071;
    return std::log(x) * invLog2;
}
```

If only the integer component of the base-2 logarithm of a float is needed, then the result is available (nearly) in the exponent of the floating-point representation. In the implementation below, we augment that approach by testing the significand of the provided value to the midpoint of significand values between the current exponent and the next one up, using the result to determine whether rounding the exponent up or rounding it down gives a more accurate result. A corresponding function for doubles is not included here.

⟨*Math Inline Functions*⟩ +≡
```
int Log2Int(float v) {
    if (v < 1) return -Log2Int(1 / v);
    // midsignif = Significand(std::pow(2., 1.5))
    const uint32_t midsignif = 0b00000000000110101000010011110011;
    return Exponent(v) + ((Significand(v) >= midsignif) ? 1 : 0);
}
```

It is also often useful to be able to compute the base-2 logarithm of an integer. Rather than computing an expensive floating-point logarithm and converting to an integer, it is much more efficient to count the number of leading zeros up to the first one in the 32-bit binary representation of the value and then subtract this value from 31, which gives the index of the first bit set, which is in turn the integer base-2 logarithm. (This efficiency comes in part from the fact that most processors have an instruction to count these zeros.)

Though we generally eschew including target-specific code in the book text, we will make an exception here just as an illustration of the messiness that often results when it is necessary to leave the capabilities of the standard libraries to access features that have different interfaces on different targets.

⟨*Math Inline Functions*⟩ +≡
```
int Log2Int(uint32_t v) {
#ifdef PBRT_IS_GPU_CODE
    return 31 - __clz(v);
#elif defined(PBRT_HAS_INTRIN_H)
    unsigned long lz = 0;
    if (_BitScanReverse(&lz, v))
        return lz;
    return 0;
#else
    return 31 - __builtin_clz(v);
#endif
}
```

It is occasionally useful to compute the base-4 logarithm of an integer value. This is easily done using the identity $\log_4 x = (\log_2 x)/2$.

⟨*Math Inline Functions*⟩ +≡
```
template <typename T>
int Log4Int(T v) { return Log2Int(v) / 2; }
```

An efficient approximation to the exponential function e^x comes in handy, especially for volumetric light transport algorithms where such values need to be computed frequently. Like Log2Int(), this value can be computed efficiently by taking advantage of the floating-point representation.

⟨*Math Inline Functions*⟩ +≡
```
float FastExp(float x) {
    ⟨Compute x' such that eˣ = 2^{x'} 1037⟩
    ⟨Find integer and fractional components of x' 1037⟩
    ⟨Evaluate polynomial approximation of 2^f 1037⟩
    ⟨Scale 2^f by 2^i and return final result 1037⟩
}
```

The first step is to convert the problem into one to compute a base-2 exponential; a factor of $1/\log 2$ does so. This step makes it possible to take advantage of computers' native floating-point representation.

⟨*Compute x' such that $e^x = 2^{x'}$*⟩ ≡   1036
```
    float xp = x * 1.442695041f;
```

Next, the function splits the exponent into an integer $i = \lfloor x' \rfloor$ and a fractional part $f = x' - i$, giving $2^{x'} = 2^{i+f} = 2^i 2^f$.

⟨*Find integer and fractional components of x'*⟩ ≡   1036
```
    float fxp = pstd::floor(xp), f = xp - fxp;
    int i = (int)fxp;
```

Because f is between 0 and 1, 2^f can be accurately approximated with a polynomial. We have fit a cubic polynomial to this function using a constant term of 1 so that 2^0 is exact. The following coefficients give a maximum absolute error of less than 0.0002 over the range of f.

⟨*Evaluate polynomial approximation of 2^f*⟩ ≡   1036
```
    float twoToF = EvaluatePolynomial(f, 1.f, 0.695556856f,
                                 0.226173572f, 0.0781455737f);
```

The last task is to apply the 2^i scale. This can be done by directly operating on the exponent in the twoToF value. It is necessary to make sure that the resulting exponent fits in the valid exponent range of 32-bit floats; if it does not, then the computation has either underflowed to 0 or overflowed to infinity. If the exponent is valid, then the existing exponent bits are cleared so that final exponent can be stored. (For the source of the value of 127 that is added to the exponent, see Equation (6.17).)

⟨*Scale 2^f by 2^i and return final result*⟩ ≡   1036
```
    int exponent = Exponent(twoToF) + i;
    if (exponent < -126) return 0;
    if (exponent > 127) return Infinity;
    uint32_t bits = FloatToBits(twoToF);
    bits &= 0b10000000011111111111111111111111u;
    bits |= (exponent + 127) << 23;
    return BitsToFloat(bits);
```

B.2.5 TRANSCENDENTAL AND SPECIAL FUNCTIONS

Gaussian() evaluates the Gaussian function

$$g(x, \mu, \sigma) = \frac{1}{\sqrt{2\pi\sigma^2}} e^{-\frac{(x-\mu)^2}{2\sigma^2}} .$$

⟨*Math Inline Functions*⟩ +≡
```
    Float Gaussian(Float x, Float mu = 0, Float sigma = 1) {
        return 1 / std::sqrt(2 * Pi * sigma * sigma) *
               FastExp(-Sqr(x - mu) / (2 * sigma * sigma));
    }
```

The integral of the Gaussian over a range $[x_0, x_1]$ can be expressed in terms of the error function, which is available from the standard library.

⟨*Math Inline Functions*⟩ +≡
```
Float GaussianIntegral(Float x0, Float x1, Float mu = 0, Float sigma = 1) {
    Float sigmaRoot2 = sigma * Float(1.414213562373095);
    return 0.5f * (std::erf((mu - x0) / sigmaRoot2) -
                   std::erf((mu - x1) / sigmaRoot2));
}
```

The logistic distribution takes a scale factor s, which controls its width:

$$l(x, s) = \frac{e^{-x/s}}{s(1 + e^{-x/s})^2}.$$

It has a generally similar shape to the Gaussian—it is symmetric and smoothly falls off from its peak—but it can be integrated in closed form. Evaluating the logistic is straightforward, though it is worth taking the absolute value of x to avoid numerical instability for when the ratio x/s is relatively large. (The function is symmetric around the origin, so this is mathematically equivalent.)

⟨*Math Inline Functions*⟩ +≡
```
Float Logistic(Float x, Float s) {
    x = std::abs(x);
    return std::exp(-x / s) / (s * Sqr(1 + std::exp(-x / s)));
}
```

The logistic function is normalized so it is its own probability density function (PDF). Its cumulative distribution function (CDF) can be easily found via integration.

⟨*Math Inline Functions*⟩ +≡
```
Float LogisticCDF(Float x, Float s) { return 1 / (1 + std::exp(-x / s)); }
```

The trimmed logistic function is the logistic limited to an interval $[a, b]$ and then renormalized using the technique introduced in Section A.4.5.

⟨*Math Inline Functions*⟩ +≡
```
Float TrimmedLogistic(Float x, Float s, Float a, Float b) {
    return Logistic(x, s) / (LogisticCDF(b, s) - LogisticCDF(a, s));
}
```

ErfInv() is the inverse to the error function std:erf(), implemented via a polynomial approximation. I0() evaluates the modified Bessel function of the first kind and LogI0() returns its logarithm.

⟨*Math Inline Functions*⟩ +≡
```
Float ErfInv(Float a);
Float I0(Float x);
Float LogI0(Float x);
```

B.2.6 INTERVAL SEARCH

FindInterval() is a helper function that emulates the behavior of std::upper_bound() but uses a function object to get values at various indices instead of requiring access to an actual array. This way, it becomes possible to bisect arrays that are procedurally generated, such as those interpolated from point samples.

It generally returns the index i such that pred(i) is true and pred($i + 1$) is false. However, since this function is primarily used to locate an interval $(i, i + 1)$ for linear interpolation, it applies the following boundary conditions to prevent out-of-bounds accesses and to deal with predicates that evaluate to true or false over the entire domain:

- The returned index i is no larger than sz-2, so that it is always legal to access both of the elements i and $i + 1$.
- If there is no index such that the predicate is true, 0 is returned.
- If there is no index such that the predicate is false, sz-2 is returned.

⟨*Math Inline Functions*⟩ +≡

```
template <typename Predicate>
size_t FindInterval(size_t sz, const Predicate &pred) {
    using ssize_t = std::make_signed_t<size_t>;
    ssize_t size = (ssize_t)sz - 2, first = 1;
    while (size > 0) {
        ⟨Evaluate predicate at midpoint and update first and size 1039⟩
    }
    return (size_t)Clamp((ssize_t)first - 1, 0, sz - 2);
}
```

⟨*Evaluate predicate at midpoint and update* first *and* size⟩ ≡   1039

```
size_t half = (size_t)size >> 1, middle = first + half;
bool predResult = pred(middle);
first = predResult ? middle + 1 : first;
size = predResult ? size - (half + 1) : half;
```

B.2.7 BIT OPERATIONS

There are clever tricks that can be used to efficiently determine if a given integer is an exact power of 2, or round an integer up to the next higher (or equal) power of 2. (It is worthwhile to take a minute and work through for yourself how these two functions work.)

⟨*Math Inline Functions*⟩ +≡

```
template <typename T>
bool IsPowerOf2(T v) { return v && !(v & (v - 1)); }
```

⟨*Math Inline Functions*⟩ +≡

```
int32_t RoundUpPow2(int32_t v) {
    v--;
    v |= v >> 1;
    v |= v >> 2;
    v |= v >> 4;
    v |= v >> 8;
    v |= v >> 16;
    return v + 1;
}
```

A variant of RoundUpPow2() for int64_t is also provided but is not included in the text here.

The bits of an integer quantity can be efficiently reversed with a series of bitwise operations. The first line of the ReverseBits32() function, which reverses the bits of a 32-bit integer, swaps the lower 16 bits with the upper 16 bits of the value. The next line simultaneously swaps the first 8 bits of the result with the second 8 bits and the third 8 bits with the fourth. This process continues until the last line, which swaps adjacent bits. To understand this code, it is helpful to write out the binary values of the various hexadecimal constants. For example, 0xff00ff00 is 11111111000000001111111100000000 in binary; it is then easy to see that a bitwise OR with this value masks off the first and third 8-bit quantities.

⟨*Bit Operation Inline Functions*⟩ ≡
```
inline uint32_t ReverseBits32(uint32_t n) {
    n = (n << 16) | (n >> 16);
    n = ((n & 0x00ff00ff) << 8) | ((n & 0xff00ff00) >> 8);
    n = ((n & 0x0f0f0f0f) << 4) | ((n & 0xf0f0f0f0) >> 4);
    n = ((n & 0x33333333) << 2) | ((n & 0xcccccccc) >> 2);
    n = ((n & 0x55555555) << 1) | ((n & 0xaaaaaaaa) >> 1);
    return n;
}
```

The bits of a 64-bit value can then be reversed by reversing the two 32-bit components individually and then interchanging them.

⟨*Bit Operation Inline Functions*⟩ +≡
```
inline uint64_t ReverseBits64(uint64_t n) {
    uint64_t n0 = ReverseBits32((uint32_t)n);
    uint64_t n1 = ReverseBits32((uint32_t)(n >> 32));
    return (n0 << 32) | n1;
}
```

Morton Indexing

To be able to compute 3D Morton codes, which were introduced in Section 7.3.3, we will first define a helper function: LeftShift3() takes a 32-bit value and returns the result of shifting the ith bit to be at the $3i$th bit, leaving zeros in other bits. Figure B.1 illustrates this operation.

The most obvious approach to implement this operation, shifting each bit value individually, is not the most efficient. (It would require a total of 9 shifts, along with bitwise OR operations to compute the final value.) Instead, we can decompose each bit's shift into multiple shifts of power-of-two size that together shift the bit's value to its final position. Then, all the bits that need to be shifted a given power-of-two number of places can be shifted together. The LeftShift3() function implements this computation, and Figure B.2 shows how it works.

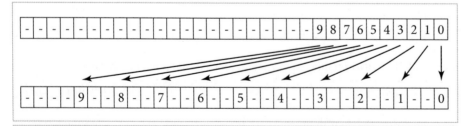

Figure B.1: Bit Shifts to Compute 3D Morton Codes. The LeftShift3() function takes a 32-bit integer value and for the bottom 10 bits, shifts the ith bit to be in position $3i$—in other words, shifts it $2i$ places to the left. All other bits are set to zero.

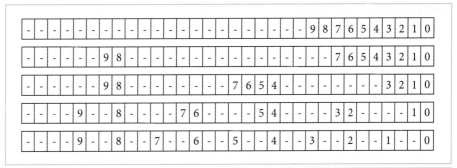

Figure B.2: Power-of-Two Decomposition of Morton Bit Shifts. The bit shifts to compute the Morton code for each 3D coordinate are performed in a series of shifts of power-of-two size. First, bits 8 and 9 are shifted 16 places to the left. This places bit 8 in its final position. Next bits 4 through 7 are shifted 8 places. After shifts of 4 and 2 places (with appropriate masking so that each bit is shifted the right number of places in the end), all bits are in the proper position. This computation is implemented by the LeftShift3() function.

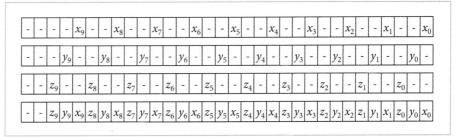

Figure B.3: Final Interleaving of Coordinate Values. Given interleaved values for x, y, and z computed by LeftShift3(), the final Morton-encoded value is computed by shifting y and z one and two places, respectively, and then computing the bitwise OR of the results.

⟨*Bit Operation Inline Functions*⟩ +≡
```
inline uint32_t LeftShift3(uint32_t x) {
    if (x == (1 << 10))
        --x;
    x = (x | (x << 16)) & 0b00000011000000000000000011111111;
    x = (x | (x << 8))  & 0b00000011000000001111000000001111;
    x = (x | (x << 4))  & 0b00000011000011000011000011000011;
    x = (x | (x << 2))  & 0b00001001001001001001001001001001;
    return x;
}
```

EncodeMorton3() takes a 3D coordinate value where each component is a floating-point value between 0 and 2^{10}. It converts these values to integers and then computes the Morton code by expanding the three 10-bit quantized values so that their ith bits are at position $3i$, then shifting the y bits over one more, the z bits over two more, and computing the bitwise OR of the result (Figure B.3).

⟨*Bit Operation Inline Functions*⟩ +≡

```
uint32_t EncodeMorton3(float x, float y, float z) {
    return (LeftShift3(z) << 2) | (LeftShift3(y) << 1) | LeftShift3(x);
}
```

Support for 2D Morton encoding is provided by the `EncodeMorton2()` function, which takes a pair of 32-bit integer values and follows an analogous approach. It is not included here.

B.2.8 HASHING AND RANDOM PERMUTATIONS

A handful of hashing functions are provided. Their implementations are in the file `util/hash.h`.

The first, `MixBits()`, takes an integer value and applies a so-called *finalizer*, which is commonly found at the end of hash function implementations. A good hash function has the property that flipping a single bit in the input causes each of the bits in the result to flip with probability 1/2; a finalizer takes values where this may not be the case and shuffles them around in a way that increases this likelihood.

`MixBits()` is particularly handy for tasks like computing unique seeds for a pseudo-random number generator at each pixel: depending on the RNG implementation, the naive approach of converting the pixel coordinates into an index and giving the RNG successive integer values as seeds may lead to correlation between values it generates at nearby pixels. Running such an index through `MixBits()` first is good protection against this.

⟨*Hashing Inline Functions*⟩ ≡
```
uint64_t MixBits(uint64_t v);
```

There are also complete hash functions for arbitrary data. `HashBuffer()` hashes a region of memory of given size using *MurmurHash64A*, which is an efficient and high-quality hash function.

⟨*Hashing Inline Functions*⟩ +≡
```
template <typename T>
uint64_t HashBuffer(const T *ptr, size_t size, uint64_t seed = 0) {
    return MurmurHash64A((const unsigned char *)ptr, size, seed);
}
```

For convenience, pbrt also provides a `Hash()` function that can be passed an arbitrary sequence of values, all of which are hashed together.

⟨*Hashing Inline Functions*⟩ +≡
```
template <typename... Args>
uint64_t Hash(Args... args);
```

It is sometimes useful to convert a hash to a floating-point value between 0 and 1; the `HashFloat()` function handles the details of doing so.

⟨*Hashing Inline Functions*⟩ +≡
```
template <typename... Args>
Float HashFloat(Args... args) { return uint32_t(Hash(args...)) * 0x1p-32f; }
```

`PermutationElement()` returns the `i`th element of a random permutation of `n` values based on the provided seed. Remarkably, it is able to do so without needing to explicitly represent the permutation. The key idea underlying its implementation is the insight that any invertible hash function of n bits represents a permutation of the values from 0 to $2^n - 1$—otherwise, it would not be invertible.

Such a hash function can be used to define a permutation over a non-power-of-two number of elements n using the permutation for the next power-of-two number of elements and then repermuting any values greater than n until a valid one is reached.

Float 23
Hash() 1042

⟨*Permutation Inline Function Declarations*⟩ ≡
```
int PermutationElement(uint32_t i, uint32_t n, uint32_t seed);
```

⋆ B.2.9 ERROR-FREE TRANSFORMATIONS

It is possible to increase the accuracy of some floating-point calculations using an approach known as *error-free transformations* (EFT). The idea of them is to maintain the accumulated error that is in a computed floating-point value and to then make use of that error to correct later computations. For example, we know that the rounded floating-point value $a \otimes b$ is in general not equal to the true product $a \times b$. Using EFTs, we also compute an error term e such that

$$a \otimes b = (a \times b) + e.$$

A clever use of fused multiply add (FMA) makes it possible to compute e without resorting to higher-precision floating-point numbers. Consider the computation `FMA(-a, b, a * b)`: on the face of it, it computes zero, adding the negated product of a and b to itself. In the context of the FMA operation, however, it gives the rounding error, since the product of $-a$ and b is not rounded before $a \otimes b$, which is rounded, is added to it.

`TwoProd()` multiplies two numbers and determines the error, returning both results using the `CompensatedFloat` structure.

⟨*Math Inline Functions*⟩ +≡
```
CompensatedFloat TwoProd(Float a, Float b) {
    Float ab = a * b;
    return {ab, FMA(a, b, -ab)};
}
```

`CompensatedFloat` is a small wrapper class that holds the results of EFT-based computations.

⟨*CompensatedFloat Definition*⟩ ≡
```
struct CompensatedFloat {
  public:
    ⟨CompensatedFloat Public Methods 1043⟩
    Float v, err;
};
```

It provides the expected constructor and conversion operators, which are qualified with `explicit` to force callers to express their intent to use them.

⟨*CompensatedFloat Public Methods*⟩ ≡   **1043**
```
CompensatedFloat(Float v, Float err = 0) : v(v), err(err) {}
explicit operator float() const { return v + err; }
explicit operator double() const { return double(v) + double(err); }
```

It is also possible to compute a compensation term e for floating-point addition of two values: $a \oplus b = (a + b) + e$.

⟨*Math Inline Functions*⟩ +≡
```
CompensatedFloat TwoSum(Float a, Float b) {
    Float s = a + b, delta = s - a;
    return {s, (a - (s - delta)) + (b - delta)};
}
```

It is not in general possible to compute exact compensation terms for sums or products of more than two values. However, maintaining them anyway, even if they carry some rounding error, makes it possible to implement various algorithms with lower error than if they were not used.

A similar trick based on FMA can be applied to the difference-of-products calculation of the form $a \times b - c \times d$. To understand the challenge involved in this computation, consider computing this difference as FMA(a, b, $-c \otimes d$). There are two rounding operations, one after computing $c \times d$ and then another after the FMA.[1] If, for example, all of a, b, c, and d are positive and the products $a \times b$ and $c \times d$ are of similar magnitudes, then catastrophic cancellation may result: the rounding error from $c \otimes d$, though small with respect to the product $c \times d$, may be large with respect to the final result.

The following DifferenceOfProducts() function uses FMA in a similar manner to TwoProd(), finding an initial value for the difference of products as well as the rounding error from $c \otimes d$. The rounding error is then added back to the value that is returned, thus fixing up catastrophic cancellation after the fact. It has been shown that this gives a result within 1.5 ulps of the correct value; see the "Further Reading" section for details.

⟨*Math Inline Functions*⟩ +≡
```
template <typename Ta, typename Tb, typename Tc, typename Td>
inline auto DifferenceOfProducts(Ta a, Tb b, Tc c, Td d) {
    auto cd = c * d;
    auto differenceOfProducts = FMA(a, b, -cd);
    auto error = FMA(-c, d, cd);
    return differenceOfProducts + error;
}
```

pbrt also provides a SumOfProducts() function that reliably computes $a \times b + c \times d$ in a similar manner.

Compensation can also be used to compute a sum of numbers more accurately than adding them together directly. An algorithm to do so is implemented in the CompensatedSum class.

⟨*CompensatedSum Definition*⟩ ≡
```
template <typename Float>
class CompensatedSum {
  public:
    ⟨CompensatedSum Public Methods 1044⟩
  private:
    Float sum = 0, c = 0;
};
```

The value added to the sum, delta, is the difference between the value provided and the accumulated error in c. After the addition is performed, the compensation term is updated appropriately.

⟨*CompensatedSum Public Methods*⟩ ≡   1044
```
CompensatedSum &operator+=(Float v) {
    Float delta = v - c;
    Float newSum = sum + delta;
    c = (newSum - sum) - delta;
    sum = newSum;
    return *this;
}
```

---

[1] The following argument applies equivalently to computing the value as FMA($-c$, d, a $\otimes$ b).

⟨*CompensatedSum Public Methods*⟩ +≡   **1044**
```
explicit operator Float() const { return sum; }
```

B.2.10 FINDING ZEROS

The `Quadratic()` function finds solutions of the quadratic equation $at^2 + bt + c = 0$; the Boolean return value indicates whether solutions were found.

⟨*Math Inline Functions*⟩ +≡
```
bool Quadratic(float a, float b, float c, float *t0, float *t1) {
    ⟨Handle case of a = 0 for quadratic solution 1045⟩
    ⟨Find quadratic discriminant 1045⟩
    ⟨Compute quadratic t values 1046⟩
    return true;
}
```

If a is zero, then the caller has actually specified a linear function. That case is handled first to avoid not-a-number values being generated via the usual execution path. (Our implementation does not handle the case of all coefficients being equal to zero, in which case there are an infinite number of solutions.)

⟨*Handle case of a = 0 for quadratic solution*⟩ ≡   **1045**
```
if (a == 0) {
    if (b == 0) return false;
    *t0 = *t1 = -c / b;
    return true;
}
```

The discriminant $b^2 - 4ac$ is computed using `DifferenceOfProducts()`, which improves the accuracy of the computed value compared to computing it directly using floating-point multiplication and subtraction. If the discriminant is negative, then there are no real roots and the function returns `false`.

⟨*Find quadratic discriminant*⟩ ≡   **1045**
```
float discrim = DifferenceOfProducts(b, b, 4 * a, c);
if (discrim < 0)
    return false;
float rootDiscrim = std::sqrt(discrim);
```

The usual version of the quadratic equation can give poor numerical accuracy when $b \approx \pm\sqrt{b^2 - 4ac}$ due to cancellation error. It can be rewritten algebraically into a more stable form:

$$t_0 = \frac{q}{a}$$

$$t_1 = \frac{c}{q},$$

where

$$q = \begin{cases} -\frac{1}{2}(b - \sqrt{b^2 - 4ac}) & b < 0, \\ -\frac{1}{2}(b + \sqrt{b^2 - 4ac}) & \text{otherwise.} \end{cases}$$

The implementation uses `pstd::copysign()` in place of an `if` test for the condition on b, setting the sign of the square root of the discriminant to be the same as the sign of b, which is equivalent. This micro-optimization does not meaningfully affect pbrt's performance, but it is a trick that is worth being aware of.

⟨*Compute quadratic* t *values*⟩ ≡   **1045**

```
float q = -0.5f * (b + pstd::copysign(rootDiscrim, b));
*t0 = q / a;
*t1 = c / q;
if (*t0 > *t1)
    pstd::swap(*t0, *t1);
```

NewtonBisection() finds a zero of an arbitrary function $f(x)$ over a specified range $[x_0, x_1]$ using an iterative root-finding technique that is guaranteed to converge to the solution so long as $[x_0, x_1]$ brackets a root and $f(x_0)$ and $f(x_1)$ differ in sign.

In each iteration, bisection search splits the interval into two parts and discards the subinterval that does not bracket the solution—in this way, it can be interpreted as a continuous extension of binary search. The method's robustness is clearly desirable, but its relatively slow (linear) convergence can still be improved. We therefore use *Newton-bisection*, which is a combination of the quadratically converging but potentially unsafe[2] Newton's method with the safety of bisection search as a fallback.

The provided function f should return a std::pair<Float, Float> where the first value is the function's value and the second is its derivative. Two "epsilon" values control the accuracy of the result: xEps gives a minimum distance between the x values that bracket the root, and fEps specifies how close to zero is sufficient for $f(x)$.

⟨*Math Inline Functions*⟩ +≡

```
template <typename Func>
Float NewtonBisection(Float x0, Float x1, Func f, Float xEps = 1e-6f,
                      Float fEps = 1e-6f) {
    ⟨Check function endpoints for roots 1046⟩
    ⟨Set initial midpoint using linear approximation of f 1047⟩
    while (true) {
        ⟨Fall back to bisection if xMid is out of bounds 1047⟩
        ⟨Evaluate function and narrow bracket range [x0, x1] 1047⟩
        ⟨Stop the iteration if converged 1047⟩
        ⟨Perform a Newton step 1047⟩
    }
}
```

Before the iteration begins, a check is performed to see if one of the endpoints is a zero. (For example, this case comes up if a zero-valued function is specified.) If so, there is no need to do any further work.

⟨*Check function endpoints for roots*⟩ ≡   **1046**

```
Float fx0 = f(x0).first, fx1 = f(x1).first;
if (std::abs(fx0) < fEps) return x0;
if (std::abs(fx1) < fEps) return x1;
bool startIsNegative = fx0 < 0;
```

The number of required Newton-bisection iterations can be reduced by starting the algorithm with a good initial guess. The function uses a heuristic that assumes that the function is linear and finds the zero crossing of the line between the two endpoints.

Float 23

---

2   Newton's method can exhibit oscillatory or divergent behavior and is only guaranteed to converge when started sufficiently close to the solution. In practice, it is usually hard to provide such a guarantee; hence we prefer the unconditionally safe combination with bisection search.

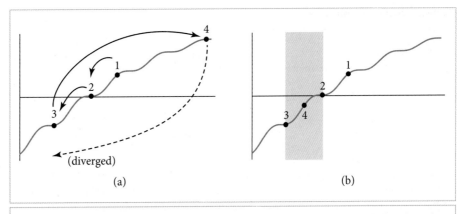

Figure B.4: The Robustness of Newton-Bisection. (a) This function increases monotonically and contains a single root on the shown interval, but a naive application of Newton's method diverges. (b) The bisection feature of the robust root-finder enables recovery from the third Newton step, which jumps far away from the root (the bisection interval is highlighted). The method converges a few iterations later.

⟨*Set initial midpoint using linear approximation of* f⟩ ≡   1046
```
Float xMid = x0 + (x1 - x0) * -fx0 / (fx1 - fx0);
```

The first fragment in the inner loop checks if the current proposed midpoint is inside the bracketing interval $[x_0, x_1]$. Otherwise, it is reset to the interval center, resulting in a standard bisection step (Figure B.4).

⟨*Fall back to bisection if* xMid *is out of bounds*⟩ ≡   1046
```
if (!(x0 < xMid && xMid < x1))
    xMid = (x0 + x1) / 2;
```

The function can now be evaluated and the bracket range can be refined. Either x0 or x1 is set to xMid in a way that maintains the invariant that the function has different signs at $f(x_0)$ and $f(x_1)$.

⟨*Evaluate function and narrow bracket range* [x0, x1]⟩ ≡   1046
```
std::pair<Float, Float> fxMid = f(xMid);
if (startIsNegative == (fxMid.first < 0))
    x0 = xMid;
else
    x1 = xMid;
```

The iteration stops either if the function value is close to 0 or if the bracketing interval has become sufficiently small.

⟨*Stop the iteration if converged*⟩ ≡   1046
```
if ((x1 - x0) < xEps || std::abs(fxMid.first) < fEps)
    return xMid;
```

If the iteration is to continue, an updated midpoint is computed using a Newton step. The next loop iteration will detect the case of this point being outside the bracket interval.

Float 23

⟨*Perform a Newton step*⟩ ≡   1046
```
xMid -= fxMid.first / fxMid.second;
```

B.2.11 ROBUST VARIANCE ESTIMATION

One problem with computing the sample variance using Equation (2.11) is that doing so requires storing all the samples X_i. The storage requirements for this may be unacceptable—for example, for a Film implementation that is estimating per-pixel variance with thousands of samples per pixel. Equation (2.9) suggests another possibility: if we accumulate estimates of both $\bar{X}$ and $\sum X_i^2$, then the sample variance could be estimated as

$$\frac{1}{n-1} \left(\sum_{i=1}^{n} X_i^2 - \bar{X}^2 \right),$$

which only requires storing two values. This approach is numerically unstable, however, due to $\sum X_i^2$ having a much larger magnitude than $\bar{X}$. Therefore, the following Variance Estimator class, which computes an online estimate of variance without storing all the samples, uses *Welford's algorithm*, which is numerically stable. Its implementation in pbrt is parameterized by a floating-point type so that, for example, double precision can be used even when pbrt is built to use single-precision Floats.

```
⟨VarianceEstimator Definition⟩ ≡
    template <typename Float = Float>
    class VarianceEstimator {
      public:
        ⟨VarianceEstimator Public Methods 1049⟩
      private:
        ⟨VarianceEstimator Private Members 1048⟩
    };
```

Welford's algorithm computes two quantities: the sample mean $\bar{X}$ and the sum of squares of differences between the samples and the sample mean, $S = \sum (X_i - \bar{X})^2$. In turn, $S/(n-1)$ gives the sample variance.

```
⟨VarianceEstimator Private Members⟩ ≡                                    1048
    Float mean = 0, S = 0;
    int64_t n = 0;
```

Both of these quantities can be computed incrementally. First, if $\bar{X}_{n-1}$ is the sample mean of the first $n-1$ samples, then given an additional sample X_n, the updated sample mean $\bar{X}_n$ is

$$\bar{X}_n = \frac{\bar{X}_{n-1}(n-1) + X_n}{n} = \bar{X}_{n-1} + \frac{X_n - \bar{X}_{n-1}}{n}. \tag{B.1}$$

Next, if S_n is the sum of squares of differences from the current mean,

$$S_n = \sum_{i=1}^{n} (X_i - \bar{X}_n)^2,$$

then consider the difference $M_n = S_n - S_{n-1}$, which is the quantity that when added to S_{n-1} gives S_n:

$$M_n = S_n - S_{n-1} = \sum_{i=1}^{n} (X_i - \bar{X}_n)^2 - \sum_{i=1}^{n-1} (X_i - \bar{X}_{n-1})^2.$$

After some algebraic manipulation, this can be found to be equal to

Float 23

$$M_n = (X_n - \bar{X}_n)(X_i - \bar{X}_{n-1}), \tag{B.2}$$

which is comprised of quantities that are all readily available. The implementation of the VarianceEstimator Add() method is then just a matter of applying Equations (B.1) and (B.2).

⟨*VarianceEstimator Public Methods*⟩ ≡   **1048**
```
void Add(Float x) {
    ++n;
    Float delta = x - mean;
    mean += delta / n;
    Float delta2 = x - mean;
    S += delta * delta2;
}
```

Given these two quantities, VarianceEstimator can provide a number of useful statistical quantities.

⟨*VarianceEstimator Public Methods*⟩ +≡   **1048**
```
Float Mean() const { return mean; }
Float Variance() const { return (n > 1) ? S / (n - 1) : 0; }
Float RelativeVariance() const {
    return (n < 1 || mean == 0) ? 0 : Variance() / Mean();
}
```

It is also possible to merge two VarianceEstimators so that the result stores the same mean and variance estimates (modulo minor floating-point rounding error) as if a single VarianceEstimator had processed all the values seen by the two of them. This capability is particularly useful in parallel implementations, where separate threads may separately compute sample statistics that are merged later.

The Merge() method implements this operation, which we will not include here; see the "Further Reading" section for details of its derivation.

B.2.12 SQUARE MATRICES

The SquareMatrix class provides a representation of square matrices with dimensionality set at compile time via the template parameter N. It is an integral part of both the Transform class and pbrt's color space conversion code.

⟨*SquareMatrix Definition*⟩ ≡
```
template <int N>
class SquareMatrix {
  public:
    ⟨SquareMatrix Public Methods 1050⟩
  private:
    Float m[N][N];
};
```

The default constructor initializes the identity matrix. Other constructors (not included here) allow providing the values of the matrix directly or via a two-dimensional array of values. Alternatively, Zero() can be used to get a zero-valued matrix or Diag() can be called with N values to get the corresponding diagonal matrix.

⟨*SquareMatrix Public Methods*⟩ ≡   **1049**
```
static SquareMatrix Zero() {
    SquareMatrix m;
    for (int i = 0; i < N; ++i)
        for (int j = 0; j < N; ++j)
            m.m[i][j] = 0;
    return m;
}
```

All the basic arithmetic operations between matrices are provided, including multiplying them or dividing them by scalar values. Here is the implementation of the method that adds two matrices together.

⟨*SquareMatrix Public Methods*⟩ +≡   **1049**
```
SquareMatrix operator+(const SquareMatrix &m) const {
    SquareMatrix r = *this;
    for (int i = 0; i < N; ++i)
        for (int j = 0; j < N; ++j)
            r.m[i][j] += m.m[i][j];
    return r;
}
```

The IsIdentity() checks whether the matrix is the identity matrix via a simple loop over its elements.

⟨*SquareMatrix Public Methods*⟩ +≡   **1049**
```
bool IsIdentity() const;
```

Indexing operators are provided as well. Because these methods return spans, the syntax for multidimensional indexing is the same as it is for regular C++ arrays: m[i][j].

⟨*SquareMatrix Public Methods*⟩ +≡   **1049**
```
pstd::span<const Float> operator[](int i) const { return m[i]; }
pstd::span<Float> operator[](int i) { return pstd::span<Float>(m[i]); }
```

The SquareMatrix class provides a matrix–vector multiplication function based on template classes to define the types of both the vector that is operated on and the result. It only requires that the result type has a default constructor and that both types allow element indexing via operator[]. Thus it can, for example, be used in pbrt's color space conversion code to convert from RGB to XYZ via a call of the form Mul<XYZ>(m, rgb), where m is a 3 × 3 SquareMatrix and rgb is of type RGB.

⟨*SquareMatrix Inline Functions*⟩ ≡
```
template <typename Tresult, int N, typename T>
Tresult Mul(const SquareMatrix<N> &m, const T &v) {
    Tresult result;
    for (int i = 0; i < N; ++i) {
        result[i] = 0;
        for (int j = 0; j < N; ++j)
            result[i] += m[i][j] * v[j];
    }
    return result;
}
```

Float 23
RGB 182
SquareMatrix 1049
SquareMatrix::m 1049
XYZ 178

The `Determinant()` function returns the value of the matrix's determinant using the standard formula. Specializations for 3×3 and 4×4 matrices are carefully written to use `DifferenceOfProducts()` for intermediate calculations of matrix minors in order to maximize accuracy in the result for those common cases.

⟨*SquareMatrix Inline Functions*⟩ +≡
```
template <int N>
Float Determinant(const SquareMatrix<N> &m);
```

Finally, there are both `Transpose()` and `Inverse()` functions. Like `Determinant()`, `Inverse()` has specializations for `N` up to 4 and then a general implementation for matrices of larger dimensionality.

⟨*SquareMatrix Inline Functions*⟩ +≡
```
template <int N>
SquareMatrix<N> Transpose(const SquareMatrix<N> &m);
template <int N>
pstd::optional<SquareMatrix<N>> Inverse(const SquareMatrix<N> &);
```

The regular `Inverse()` function returns an unset `optional` value if the matrix has no inverse. If no recovery is possible in that case, `InvertOrExit()` can be used, allowing calling code to directly access the matrix result.

⟨*SquareMatrix Inline Functions*⟩ +≡
```
template <int N>
SquareMatrix<N> InvertOrExit(const SquareMatrix<N> &m) {
    pstd::optional<SquareMatrix<N>> inv = Inverse(m);
    CHECK(inv.has_value());
    return *inv;
}
```

Given the `SquareMatrix` definition, it is easy to implement a `LinearLeastSquares()` function that finds a matrix **M** that minimizes the least squares error of a mapping from one set of vectors to another. This function is used as part of pbrt's infrastructure for modeling camera response curves.

⟨*Math Inline Functions*⟩ +≡
```
template <int N> pstd::optional<SquareMatrix<N>>
LinearLeastSquares(const Float A[][N], const Float B[][N], int rows);
```

B.2.13 BÉZIER CURVES

Bézier curves, first introduced in Section 6.7 with the `Curve` shape, are polynomial functions that are widely used in graphics. They are specified by a number of control points p_i that have the useful property that the curve passes through the first and last of them. Cubic Béziers, which are specified by four control points, are commonly used. pbrt's functions for working with them are defined in the file `util/splines.h`.

They are commonly defined using polynomial basis functions called the *Bernstein basis functions*, though here we will focus on them through an approach called *blossoming*. The blossom $b(u_0, u_1, u_2)$ of a cubic Bézier is defined by three stages of linear interpolation, starting with the original control points p_i:

$$a_i = (1 - u_0)p_i + u_0\, p_{i+1} \quad i \in [0, 1, 2]$$
$$b_j = (1 - u_1)a_j + u_1\, a_{j+1} \quad j \in [0, 1]$$
$$b(u_0, u_1, u_2) = (1 - u_2)b_0 + u_2\, b_1.$$

[B.3]

`BlossomBezier()` implements this computation, which we will see has a variety of uses. The type `P` of the control point is a template parameter, which makes it possible to call this function with any type for which a `Lerp()` function is defined.

⟨*Bezier Inline Functions*⟩ ≡
```
template <typename P>
P BlossomCubicBezier(pstd::span<const P> p, Float u0, Float u1, Float u2) {
    P a[3] = { Lerp(u0, p[0], p[1]), Lerp(u0, p[1], p[2]),
               Lerp(u0, p[2], p[3]) };
    P b[2] = { Lerp(u1, a[0], a[1]), Lerp(u1, a[1], a[2]) };
    return Lerp(u2, b[0], b[1]);
}
```

The blossom $p(u, u, u)$ gives the curve's value at position u. (To verify this for yourself, expand Equation (B.3) using $u_i = u$, simplify, and compare to Equation (6.16).) Thus, implementation of the `EvaluateCubicBezier()` function is trivial. It too is a template function of the type of control point.

⟨*Bezier Inline Functions*⟩ +≡
```
template <typename P>
P EvaluateCubicBezier(pstd::span<const P> cp, Float u) {
    return BlossomCubicBezier(cp, u, u, u);
}
```

A second variant of `EvaluateCubicBezier()` also optionally returns the curve's derivative at the evaluation point. This and the following Bézier functions could also be template functions based on the type of control point; for pbrt's uses, however, only `Point3f` variants are required. We therefore implement them in terms of `Point3f`, if only to save the verbosity and slight obscurity of the templated variants.

⟨*Bezier Inline Functions*⟩ +≡
```
Point3f EvaluateCubicBezier(pstd::span<const Point3f> cp, Float u,
                            Vector3f *deriv) {
    Point3f cp1[3] = { Lerp(u, cp[0], cp[1]), Lerp(u, cp[1], cp[2]),
                       Lerp(u, cp[2], cp[3]) };
    Point3f cp2[2] = { Lerp(u, cp1[0], cp1[1]), Lerp(u, cp1[1], cp1[2]) };
    if (deriv) {
        ⟨Compute Bézier curve derivative at u 1052⟩
    }
    return Lerp(u, cp2[0], cp2[1]);
}
```

With blossoming, the final two control points that are linearly interpolated to compute the curve value define a line that is tangent to the curve.

One edge case must be handled here: if, for example, the first three control points are coincident, then the derivative of the curve is legitimately 0 at $u = 0$. However, returning a zero-valued derivative in that case would be problematic since pbrt uses the derivative to compute the tangent vector of the curve. Therefore, this function returns the difference between the first and last control points in such cases.

⟨*Compute Bézier curve derivative at u*⟩ ≡   1052
```
if (LengthSquared(cp2[1] - cp2[0]) > 0)
    *deriv = 3 * (cp2[1] - cp2[0]);
else
    *deriv = cp[3] - cp[0];
```

`SubdivideCubicBezier()` splits a Bézier curve into two Bézier curves that together are equivalent to the original curve. The last control point of the first subdivided curve is the same as the first control point of the second one and the 7 total control points are specified by the blossoms $(0, 0, 0)$, $(0, 0, 1/2)$, $(0, 1/2, 1/2)$, $(1/2, 1/2, 1/2)$, $(1/2, 1/2, 1)$, $(1/2, 1, 1)$, and $(1, 1, 1)$. There is no need to call `BlossomCubicBezier()` to evaluate them, however, as each one works out to be a simple combination of existing control points.

⟨*Bezier Inline Functions*⟩ +≡
```
pstd::array<Point3f, 7> SubdivideCubicBezier(pstd::span<const Point3f> cp) {
    return {cp[0],
            (cp[0] + cp[1]) / 2,
            (cp[0] + 2 * cp[1] + cp[2]) / 4,
            (cp[0] + 3 * cp[1] + 3 * cp[2] + cp[3]) / 8,
            (cp[1] + 2 * cp[2] + cp[3]) / 4,
            (cp[2] + cp[3]) / 2,
            cp[3]};
}
```

More generally, the four control points for the curve segment over the range u_{min} to u_{max} are given by the blossoms:

$$
\begin{aligned}
p_0 &= p(u_{min}, u_{min}, u_{min}) \\
p_1 &= p(u_{min}, u_{min}, u_{max}) \\
p_2 &= p(u_{min}, u_{max}, u_{max}) \\
p_3 &= p(u_{max}, u_{max}, u_{max})
\end{aligned}
\tag{B.4}
$$

(see Figure B.5). `CubicBezierControlPoints()` implements this computation.

⟨*Bezier Inline Functions*⟩ +≡
```
pstd::array<Point3f, 4>
CubicBezierControlPoints(pstd::span<const Point3f> cp, Float uMin,
                         Float uMax) {
    return { BlossomCubicBezier(cp, uMin, uMin, uMin),
             BlossomCubicBezier(cp, uMin, uMin, uMax),
             BlossomCubicBezier(cp, uMin, uMax, uMax),
             BlossomCubicBezier(cp, uMax, uMax, uMax) };
}
```

Bounding boxes of `Curve`s can be efficiently computed by taking advantage of the *convex hull property*, a property of Bézier curves that says that they must lie within the convex hull of their control points. Therefore, the bounding box of the control points gives a conservative

BlossomCubicBezier() 1052

Float 23

Point3f 92

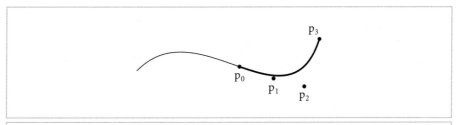

Figure B.5: Blossoming to Find Control Points for a Segment of a Bézier Curve. The four blossoms in Equation (B.4) give the control points for the curve from u_{min} to u_{max}. Blossoming provides an elegant method to compute the Bézier control points of the curve that represent a subset of the overall curve.

bound of the underlying curve. This bounding box is returned by the BoundCubicBezier() function.

⟨*Bezier Inline Functions*⟩ +≡
```
Bounds3f BoundCubicBezier(pstd::span<const Point3f> cp) {
    return Union(Bounds3f(cp[0], cp[1]), Bounds3f(cp[2], cp[3]));
}
```

A second variant of this function bounds a Bézier curve over a specified parametric range via a call to CubicBezierControlPoints().

⟨*Bezier Inline Functions*⟩ +≡
```
Bounds3f BoundCubicBezier(pstd::span<const Point3f> cp, Float uMin,
                          Float uMax) {
    if (uMin == 0 && uMax == 1)
        return BoundCubicBezier(cp);
    auto cpSeg = CubicBezierControlPoints(cp, uMin, uMax);
    return BoundCubicBezier(pstd::span<const Point3f>(cpSeg));
}
```

B.2.14 PSEUDO-RANDOM NUMBER GENERATION

pbrt uses an implementation of the PCG pseudo-random number generator (O'Neill 2014) to generate pseudo-random numbers. This generator not only passes a variety of rigorous statistical tests of randomness, but its implementation is also extremely efficient.

We wrap its implementation in a small random number generator class, RNG, which can be found in the files util/rng.h and util/rng.cpp. Random number generator implementation is an esoteric art; therefore, we will not include or discuss the implementation here but will describe the interfaces provided.

⟨*RNG Definition*⟩ ≡
```
class RNG {
  public:
    ⟨RNG Public Methods 1054⟩
  private:
    ⟨RNG Private Members⟩
};
```

The RNG class provides three constructors. The first, which takes no arguments, sets the internal state to reasonable defaults. The others allow providing values that seed its state. The PCG random number generator actually allows the user to provide two 64-bit values to configure its operation: one chooses from one of 2^{63} different sequences of 2^{64} random numbers, while the second effectively selects a starting point within such a sequence. Many pseudo-random number generators only allow this second form of configuration, which alone is not as useful: having independent non-overlapping sequences of values rather than different starting points in a single sequence provides greater nonuniformity in the generated values.

⟨*RNG Public Methods*⟩ ≡   **1054**
```
RNG() : state(PCG32_DEFAULT_STATE), inc(PCG32_DEFAULT_STREAM) {}
RNG(uint64_t seqIndex, uint64_t offset) { SetSequence(seqIndex, offset); }
RNG(uint64_t seqIndex) { SetSequence(seqIndex); }
```

RNGs should not be used in `pbrt` without either providing an initial sequence index via the constructor or a call to the `SetSequence()` method; otherwise, there is risk that different parts of the system will inadvertently use correlated sequences of pseudo-random values, which in turn could cause surprising errors.

⟨*RNG Public Methods*⟩ +≡   **1054**
```
void SetSequence(uint64_t sequenceIndex, uint64_t offset);
void SetSequence(uint64_t sequenceIndex) {
    SetSequence(sequenceIndex, MixBits(sequenceIndex));
}
```

The `RNG` class defines a template method `Uniform()` that returns a uniformly distributed random value of the specified type. A variety of specializations of this method are provided for basic arithmetic types.

⟨*RNG Public Methods*⟩ +≡   **1054**
```
template <typename T>
T Uniform();
```

The default implementation of `Uniform()` attempts to ensure that a useful error message is issued if it is invoked with an unsupported type.

⟨*RNG Inline Method Definitions*⟩ ≡
```
template <typename T>
T RNG::Uniform() { return T::unimplemented; }
```

A specialization for `uint32_t` uses the PCG algorithm to generate a 32-bit value. We will not include its implementation here, as it would be impenetrable without an extensive discussion of the details of the pseudo-random number generation approach it implements.

⟨*RNG Inline Method Definitions*⟩ +≡
```
template <>
uint32_t RNG::Uniform<uint32_t>();
```

Given a source of pseudo-randomness, a variety of other specializations of `Uniform()` can be provided. For example, a uniform 64-bit unsigned integer can be generated by using the bits from two 32-bit random numbers.

⟨*RNG Inline Method Definitions*⟩ +≡
```
template <>
uint64_t RNG::Uniform<uint64_t>() {
    uint64_t v0 = Uniform<uint32_t>(), v1 = Uniform<uint32_t>();
    return (v0 << 32) | v1;
}
```

Generating a uniformly distributed signed 32-bit integer requires surprisingly tricky code. The issue is that in C++, it is undefined behavior to assign a value to a signed integer that is larger than it can represent. Undefined behavior does not just mean that the result is undefined, but that, in principle, no further guarantees are made about correct program execution after it occurs. Therefore, the following code is carefully written to avoid integer overflow. In practice, a good compiler can be expected to optimize away the extra work.

⟨*RNG Inline Method Definitions*⟩ +≡
```
template <>
int32_t RNG::Uniform<int32_t>() {
    uint32_t v = Uniform<uint32_t>();
    if (v <= (uint32_t)std::numeric_limits<int32_t>::max())
        return int32_t(v);
    return int32_t(v - std::numeric_limits<int32_t>::min()) +
            std::numeric_limits<int32_t>::min();
}
```

A similar method returns pseudo-random int64_t values.

It is often useful to generate a value that is uniformly distributed in the range $[0, b-1]$ given a bound b. The first two versions of pbrt effectively computed Uniform<int32_t>() % b to do so. That approach is subtly flawed—in the case that b does not evenly divide 2^{32}, there is higher probability of choosing any given value in the sub-range $[0, 2^{32} \bmod b - 1]$.

Therefore, the implementation here first computes the above remainder $2^{32} \bmod b$ efficiently using 32-bit arithmetic and stores it in the variable threshold. Then, if the value returned by Uniform() is less than threshold, it is discarded and a new value is generated. The resulting distribution of values has a uniform distribution after the modulus operation, giving a uniformly distributed sample value.

The tricky declaration of the return value ensures that this variant of Uniform() is only available for integral types.

⟨*RNG Public Methods*⟩ +≡   1054
```
template <typename T>
typename std::enable_if_t<std::is_integral_v<T>, T> Uniform(T b) {
    T threshold = (~b + 1u) % b;
    while (true) {
        T r = Uniform<T>();
        if (r >= threshold)
            return r % b;
    }
}
```

A specialization of Uniform() for floats generates a pseudo-random floating-point number in the half-open interval $[0, 1)$ by multiplying a 32-bit random value by 2^{-32}. Mathematically, this value is always less than one; it can be at most $(2^{32} - 1)/2^{32}$. However, some values still round to 1 when computed using floating-point arithmetic. That case is handled here by clamping to the largest representable float less than one. Doing so introduces a tiny bias, but not one that is meaningful for rendering applications.

⟨*RNG Inline Method Definitions*⟩ +≡
```
template <>
float RNG::Uniform<float>() {
    return std::min<float>(OneMinusEpsilon, Uniform<uint32_t>() * 0x1p-32f);
}
```

An equivalent method for doubles is provided but is not included here.

With this random number generator, it is possible to step forward or back to a different spot in the sequence without generating all the intermediate values. The Advance() method provides this functionality.

OneMinusEpsilon 470

⟨*RNG Public Methods*⟩ +≡   **1054**
```
void Advance(int64_t idelta);
```

B.2.15 INTERVAL ARITHMETIC

Interval arithmetic is a technique that can be used to reason about the range of a function over some range of values and also to bound the round-off error introduced by a series of floating-point calculations. The Interval class provides functionality for both of these uses.

To understand the basic idea of interval arithmetic, consider, for example, the function $f(x) = 2x$. If we have an interval of values $[a, b] \subset \mathbb{R}$, then we can see that, over the interval, the range of f is the interval $[2a, 2b]$. In other words, $f([a, b]) \subset [2a, 2b]$. More generally, all the basic operations of arithmetic have *interval extensions* that describe how they operate on intervals of values. For example, given two intervals $[a, b]$ and $[c, d]$,

$$[a, b] + [c, d] \subset [a + c, b + d].$$

In other words, if we add together two values where one is in the range $[a, b]$ and the second is in $[c, d]$, then the result must be in the range $[a + c, b + d]$. Interval arithmetic has the important property that the intervals that it gives are conservative. For example, if $f([a, b]) \subset [c, d]$ and if $c > 0$, then we know for sure that no value in $[a, b]$ causes f to be negative.

When implemented in floating-point arithmetic, interval operations can be defined so that they result in intervals that bound the true value. Given a function RoundDown that rounds a value that cannot exactly be represented as a floating-point value down to the next lower floating-point value and RoundUp that similarly rounds up, interval addition can be defined as

$$[a, b] \oplus [c, d] \subset [\mathrm{RoundDown}(a + c), \mathrm{RoundUp}(c + d)]. \tag{B.5}$$

Performing a series of floating-point calculations in this manner is the basis of running error analysis, which was described in Section 6.8.1.

pbrt uses interval arithmetic to compute error bounds for ray intersections with quadrics and also uses the interval-based Point3i class to store computed ray intersection points on surfaces. The zero-finding method used to find the extrema of moving bounding boxes in AnimatedTransform::BoundPointMotion() (included in the online edition) is also based on interval arithmetic.

The Interval class provides interval arithmetic capabilities using operator overloading to make it fairly easy to switch existing regular floating-point computations over to be interval-based.

⟨*Interval Definition*⟩ ≡
```
class Interval {
  public:
     ⟨Interval Public Methods 1058⟩
  private:
     ⟨Interval Private Members 1058⟩
};
```

Before we go further with Interval, we will define some supporting utility functions for performing basic arithmetic with specified rounding. Recall that the default with floating-point arithmetic is that results are rounded to the nearest representable floating-point value, with ties being rounded to the nearest even value (i.e., with a zero-valued low bit in its significand). However, in order to compute conservative intervals like those in Equation (B.5), it is necessary to specify different rounding modes for different operations, rounding down when computing the value at the lower range of the interval and rounding up at the upper range.

The IEEE floating-point standard requires capabilities to control the rounding mode, but unfortunately it is expensive to change it on modern CPUs. Doing so generally requires a flush of the execution pipeline, which may cost many tens of cycles. Therefore, pbrt provides utility functions that perform various arithmetic operations where the final value is then nudged up or down to the next representable float. This will lead to intervals that are slightly too large, sometimes nudging when it is not necessary, but for pbrt's purposes it is preferable to paying the cost of changing the rounding mode.

Some GPUs provide intrinsic functions to perform these various operations directly, with the rounding mode specified as part of the instruction and with no performance cost. Alternative implementations of these functions, not included here, use those when they are available.

⟨*Floating-point Inline Functions*⟩ +≡
```
Float AddRoundUp(Float a, Float b) {
    return NextFloatUp(a + b);
}
Float AddRoundDown(Float a, Float b) {
    return NextFloatDown(a + b);
}
```

Beyond addition, there are equivalent methods that are not included here for subtraction, multiplication, division, the square root, and FMA.

An interval can be initialized with a single value or a pair of values that specify an interval with nonzero width.

⟨*Interval Public Methods*⟩ ≡   1057
```
explicit Interval(Float v) : low(v), high(v) {}
Interval(Float low, Float high)
    : low(std::min(low, high)), high(std::max(low, high)) {}
```

⟨*Interval Private Members*⟩ ≡   1057
```
Float low, high;
```

It can also be specified by a value and an error bound. Note that the implementation uses rounded arithmetic functions to ensure a conservative interval.

⟨*Interval Public Methods*⟩ +≡   1057
```
static Interval FromValueAndError(Float v, Float err) {
    Interval i;
    if (err == 0)
        i.low = i.high = v;
    else {
        i.low = SubRoundDown(v, err);
        i.high = AddRoundUp(v, err);
    }
    return i;
}
```

A number of accessor methods provide information about the interval. An implementation of operator[], not included here, allows indexing the two bounding values.

⟨*Interval Public Methods*⟩ +≡   1057
```
    Float UpperBound() const { return high; }
    Float LowerBound() const { return low; }
    Float Midpoint() const { return (low + high) / 2; }
    Float Width() const { return high - low; }
```

An interval can be converted to a Float approximation to it, but only through an explicit cast, which ensures that intervals are not accidentally reduced to Floats in the middle of a computation, thus causing an inaccurate final interval.

⟨*Interval Public Methods*⟩ +≡   1057
```
    explicit operator Float() const { return Midpoint(); }
```

InRange() method implementations check whether a given value is in the interval and whether two intervals overlap.

⟨*Interval Inline Functions*⟩ ≡
```
    bool InRange(Float v, Interval i) {
        return v >= i.LowerBound() && v <= i.UpperBound();
    }
    bool InRange(Interval a, Interval b) {
        return a.LowerBound() <= b.UpperBound() &&
                a.UpperBound() >= b.LowerBound();
    }
```

Negation of an interval is straightforward, as it does not require any rounding.

⟨*Interval Public Methods*⟩ +≡   1057
```
    Interval operator-() const { return {-high, -low}; }
```

The addition operator just requires implementing Equation (B.5) with the appropriate rounding.

⟨*Interval Public Methods*⟩ +≡   1057
```
    Interval operator+(Interval i) const {
        return {AddRoundDown(low, i.low), AddRoundUp(high, i.high)};
    }
```

The subtraction operator and the += and -= operators follow the same pattern, so they are not included in the text.

Interval multiplication and division are slightly more involved: which of the low and high bounds of each of the two intervals is used to determine each of the bounds of the result depends on the signs of the values involved. Rather than incur the overhead of working out exactly which pairs to use, Interval's implementation of the multiply operator computes all of them and then takes the minimum and maximum.

⟨*Interval Public Methods*⟩ +≡   1057
```
    Interval operator*(Interval i) const {
        Float lp[4] = { MulRoundDown(low, i.low),  MulRoundDown(high, i.low),
                        MulRoundDown(low, i.high), MulRoundDown(high, i.high)};
        Float hp[4] = { MulRoundUp(low, i.low),  MulRoundUp(high, i.low),
                        MulRoundUp(low, i.high), MulRoundUp(high, i.high)};
        return {std::min({lp[0], lp[1], lp[2], lp[3]}),
                std::max({hp[0], hp[1], hp[2], hp[3]})};
    }
```

The division operator follows a similar form, though it must check to see if the divisor interval spans zero. If so, an infinite interval must be returned.

The interval Sqr() function is more than a shorthand; it is sometimes able to compute a tighter bound than would be found by multiplying an interval by itself using operator*. To see why, consider two independent intervals that both happen to have the range $[-2, 3]$. Multiplying them together results in the interval $[-6, 9]$. However, if we are multiplying an interval by itself, we know that there is no way that squaring it would result in a negative value. Therefore, if an interval with the bounds $[-2, 3]$ is multiplied by itself, it is possible to return the tighter interval $[0, 9]$ instead.

⟨*Interval Inline Functions*⟩ +≡
```
Interval Sqr(Interval i) {
    Float alow = std::abs(i.LowerBound()), ahigh = std::abs(i.UpperBound());
    if (alow > ahigh)
        pstd::swap(alow, ahigh);
    if (InRange(0, i))
        return Interval(0, MulRoundUp(ahigh, ahigh));
    return Interval(MulRoundDown(alow, alow), MulRoundUp(ahigh, ahigh));
}
```

A variety of additional arithmetic operations are provided by the Interval class, including Abs(), Min(), Max(), Sqrt(), Floor(), Ceil(), Quadratic(), and assorted trigonometric functions. See the pbrt source code for their implementations.

pbrt provides 3D vector and point classes that use Interval for the coordinate values. Here, the "fi" at the end of Vector3fi denotes "float interval." These classes are easily defined thanks to the templated definition of the Vector3 and Point3 classes and the underlying Tuple3 class from Section 3.2.

⟨*Vector3fi Definition*⟩ ≡
```
class Vector3fi : public Vector3<Interval> {
  public:
    ⟨Vector3fi Public Methods 1060⟩
};
```

In addition to the usual constructors, Vector3fi can be initialized by specifying a base vector and a second one that gives error bounds for each component.

⟨*Vector3fi Public Methods*⟩ ≡   **1060**
```
Vector3fi(Vector3f v, Vector3f e)
    : Vector3<Interval>(Interval::FromValueAndError(v.x, e.x),
                        Interval::FromValueAndError(v.y, e.y),
                        Interval::FromValueAndError(v.z, e.z)) {}
```

Helper methods return error bounds for the vector components and indicate if the value stored has empty intervals.

⟨*Vector3fi Public Methods*⟩ +≡   **1060**
```
Vector3f Error() const {
    return {x.Width() / 2, y.Width() / 2, z.Width() / 2};
}
bool IsExact() const {
    return x.Width() == 0 && y.Width() == 0 && z.Width() == 0;
}
```

The `Point3fi` class, not included here, similarly provides the capabilities of a `Point3` using intervals for its coordinate values. It, too, provides `Error()` and `IsExact()` methods.

B.3 USER INTERACTION

A number of functions and classes are useful to mediate communicating information to the user. In addition to consolidating functionality like printing progress bars, hiding user communication behind a small API like the one here also permits easy modification of the communication mechanisms. For example, if `pbrt` were embedded in an application that had a graphical user interface, errors might be reported via a dialog box or a routine provided by the parent application. If `printf()` calls were strewn throughout the system, it would be more difficult to make the two systems work together well.

B.3.1 WORKING WITH FILES

A few utility routines make it easy to read and write files from disk. `ReadFileContents()` returns the contents of a file as a string and `ReadDecompressedFileContents()` does the same for files that are compressed using the *gzip* algorithm, decompressing them before returning their contents. `WriteFileContents()` writes the contents of a string to a file. Note that the use of `std::string` does not impose the requirement that the file contents be text: binary data, including null characters, can be stored in a `std::string`.

⟨*File and Filename Function Declarations*⟩ ≡
```
std::string ReadFileContents(std::string filename);
std::string ReadDecompressedFileContents(std::string filename);
bool WriteFileContents(std::string filename, const std::string &contents);
```

A number of parts of `pbrt` need to read text files that store floating-point values. Examples include the code that reads measured spectral distributions. The `ReadFloatFile()` function is available for such uses; it parses text files of white space-separated numbers, returning the values found in a `vector`. The parsing code ignores all text after a hash mark (#) to the end of its line to allow comments.

⟨*File and Filename Function Declarations*⟩ +≡
```
std::vector<Float> ReadFloatFile(std::string filename);
```

B.3.2 CHARACTER ENCODING AND UNICODE

As a rendering system, `pbrt` is relatively unconcerned with text processing. Yet the scene description is provided as text and the user can configure the system by specifying text command-line arguments, including those that specify scene description files to be parsed and the filename for the final rendered image. Previous versions of `pbrt` have implicitly assumed that all text is encoded in ASCII, where each character is represented using a single byte. There are 95 printable ASCII characters. In hexadecimal, their values range from 20_{16}, a blank space, to $7e_{16}$, a tilde.

Adopting ASCII implied that the only letters that can be used in this text are the Latin letters from A to Z. No accented letters were allowed, nor was text written in Chinese, Japanese, or the Devanagari script used for Hindi. (Emoji were also not possible, though we are unsure whether being able to directly render an image named 🚒.exr is a feature worth devoting attention to.)

Float 23
Point3 92

This version of `pbrt` uses Unicode (Unicode Consortium 2020) to represent text. At writing, Unicode allows the representation of nearly 150,000 characters, drawn from scripts that cover a wide variety of languages. (In Unicode, a *script* is a collection of letters and symbols used in the writing system for a language.) Fortunately, most of the code that handles text in pbrt was minimally affected by the change to Unicode, though it is important to understand the underlying principles if one is to read or modify code in pbrt that works with character strings.

Unicode associates a unique numeric *code point* with each character; code points are denoted by U+*n*, where *n* is a hexadecimal integer.[3] The code points for ASCII characters match the ASCII encoding, so "~" corresponds to both ASCII $7e_{16}$ and U+007e. The letter ü is represented by U+00fc, and the Chinese character 充 is U+5149.

Unicode also defines a number of *encodings* that map code points to sequences of byte values. The simplest is UTF-32, which uses 4 bytes (32 bits) to represent each code point. UTF-32 has the advantage that all code points use the same amount of storage, which makes it easy to perform operations like finding the *n*th code point in a string, though it uses four times more storage for ASCII characters than ASCII does, which is a disadvantage if text is mostly ASCII.

UTF-8 uses a variable number of bytes to represent each code point. ASCII characters are represented with a single byte equal to their code point's value and thus pure ASCII text is by construction UTF-8 encoded. Code points after U+007f are encoded using 2, 3, or 4 bytes depending on their magnitude. Therefore, finding the *n*th code point requires scanning from the start of a string in the absence of auxiliary data structures. (That operation is not important in pbrt, however.)

UTF-16 occupies an awkward middle ground; it uses two bytes to encode most code points, though it requires four for the ones that cannot fit in two. It offers the disadvantages of UTF-32 (wasted space if text is primarily ASCII), with few advantages in return. UTF-16 is used in the Windows APIs, however, which requires us to be aware of it.

Rather than supporting multiple encodings, pbrt standardizes on UTF-8. It uses std:: strings to represent UTF-8-encoded strings, which poses no problems since, in C++, std::strings are just arrays of bytes. It is, however, important to keep in mind that indexing to the *n*th element in a std::string does not necessarily return the *n*th character of the string and that the size() method returns the number of bytes stored in the string and not necessarily the number of characters it holds.

Given the choice of UTF-8, we must ensure that any input from the user in a different encoding is converted to UTF-8 and that any use of strings in calls to system library functions is converted to the character encoding they use. For example, OSX and most versions of Linux now set the system locale to use a UTF-8 encoding. This causes command shells to encode programs' command-line arguments as UTF-8. On those systems, pbrt therefore assumes that the argv parameters passed to the main() function are already UTF-8 encoded. On Windows, however, command-line arguments are available in ASCII or UTF-16; pbrt takes the latter and converts them to UTF-8.

The GetCommandLineArguments() function handles these details, returning the provided command-line arguments in a vector of std::strings that use the UTF-8 encoding.

---

3   For those already familiar with Unicode, we admit that our use of the word "character" in this section is informal; Unicode differentiates between *abstract characters*, *coded characters*, and *user-perceived characters*, each with distinct definitions, and none of them the same as a *glyph*, which is a shape defined by a font for display. We will generally equate code points with characters here, with the caveat that this equivalence is not always so.

⟨*Command-line Argument Utility Functions*⟩ ≡
```
std::vector<std::string> GetCommandLineArguments(char *argv[]);
```

pbrt provides two functions that convert both ways between the UTF-8 and UTF-16 encodings, where strings of 16-bit values, `std::u16string`, are used for UTF-16. These are both thin wrappers around functionality provided by the C++ standard library.

⟨*String Utility Function Declarations*⟩ ≡
```
std::string UTF8FromUTF16(std::u16string str);
std::u16string UTF16FromUTF8(std::string str);
```

Windows introduces the additional complication of using the type `std::wchar_t` for the elements of UTF-16-encoded strings. On Windows, this type is 16 bits, though the C++ standard does not specify its size. Therefore, pbrt provides additional functions on Windows to convert to and from UTF-16-encoded `std::wstrings`, which store elements using `std::wchar_t`.

⟨*String Utility Function Declarations*⟩ +≡
```
#ifdef PBRT_IS_WINDOWS
std::wstring WStringFromUTF8(std::string str);
std::string UTF8FromWString(std::wstring str);
#endif // PBRT_IS_WINDOWS
```

Filenames also require attention. On Linux, filenames can be any string of bytes, other than the forward slash "/", which separates path components, and U+0000, which is the end of string marker in C. Thus, UTF-8 encoded filenames (slash notwithstanding) are supported with no further effort, though filenames that are not valid UTF-8 strings are also allowed. Both OSX and Windows use Unicode for filenames, with the UTF-8 and UTF-16 encodings, respectively.

Both the `ReadFileContents()` and `WriteFileContents()` functions introduced earlier therefore handle converting filenames to UTF-16 on Windows, allowing callers to directly pass UTF-8 encoded strings to them. pbrt further provides `FOpenRead()` and `FOpenWrite()` functions that wrap the functionality of `fopen()`. On Windows, they perform the UTF-16 filename conversion and then call `_wfopen()` in place of `fopen()`.

Few further changes were needed for Unicode support in pbrt thanks to a key component of the UTF-8 design: not only are the ASCII characters represented in UTF-8 with a single byte and with the same value, but it is also guaranteed that no byte used to encode a non-ASCII code point will be equal to an ASCII value. (Effectively, this means that because the high bit of 8-bit ASCII values is unset, the high bit of any byte used for a non-ASCII Unicode character in UTF-8 is always set.)

To see the value of this part of the design of UTF-8, consider parsing the scene description in pbrt. If for example the parser has encountered an opening double quotation mark ", it then copies all subsequent bytes until the closing quote into a `std::string` and issues an error if a newline is encountered before the closing quote. In UTF-8, the quotation mark U+0022 is encoded as 22_{16} and newline U+000a as $0a_{16}$. Because the byte values 22_{16} and $0a_{16}$ are not used to encode any other code points, the parser can be oblivious to Unicode, copying bytes into a string just as it did before until it encounters a 22_{16} byte. It makes no difference to the parsing code whether the byte values in the string represent plain ASCII or characters from other scripts.

More generally, because pbrt does not use any non-ASCII characters in the definition of its scene description format, the parser can continue to operate one byte at a time, without being concerned whether each one is part of a multi-byte UTF-8 character.

B.3.3 PRINTING AND FORMATTING STRINGS

Printf() and StringPrintf() respectively provide improvements to C's printf() and sprintf() functions. Both support all the formatting directives of printf() and sprintf(), but with the following improvements:

- When %f is used, floating-point values are printed out with a sufficient number of digits to exactly specify their value. This is, unfortunately, not the default behavior of C's routines.
- The %d directive works directly for all integer types; there is no need for additional qualifiers for int64_t or size_t values, etc.
- %s can be used for any class that provides a ToString() method, as almost all of pbrt's classes do. (It can also be used for std::strings and many of the container classes in the C++ standard library.)

We have found the last of these three capabilities to be particularly useful for debugging and tracing the system's operation. These functions are implemented in util/print.h and util/print.cpp.

StringPrintf() has the added enhancement that it returns its result directly as a std::string, freeing the caller from needing to worry about allocating a sufficient amount of memory for the result.

⟨*Printing Function Declarations*⟩ ≡
```
template <typename... Args>
void Printf(const char *fmt, Args &&... args);
template <typename... Args>
std::string StringPrintf(const char *fmt, Args &&... args);
```

B.3.4 ERROR REPORTING

A few functions are available for communicating with the user, provided via the files util/error.h and util/error.cpp. These should be used for things like reporting errors in scene description files or warnings for cases like scene descriptions that lack any light sources. Each of them takes a FileLoc pointer; this is the structure that the parser uses to record which file and line number a particular token is from. These are passed through to object creation routines as the scene description is being initialized so that error messages can include that information.

⟨*Error Reporting Function Declarations*⟩ ≡
```
void Warning(const FileLoc *loc, const char *message);
void Error(const FileLoc *loc, const char *message);
[[noreturn]] void ErrorExit(const FileLoc *loc, const char *message);
```

There are variants of all of these that call StringPrintf() so that printf-style formatting strings can be used to print the values of additional arguments. Here is the one for Warning():

⟨*Error Reporting Inline Functions*⟩ ≡
```
template <typename... Args>
void Warning(const FileLoc *loc, const char *fmt, Args &&... args) {
    Warning(loc, StringPrintf(fmt, std::forward<Args>(args)...).c_str());
}
```

FileLoc 1120
StringPrintf() 1064

For cases where a `FileLoc *` is not available, there are corresponding warning and error functions that take just a format string and arguments. (Alternatively, `nullptr` can be passed for the `FileLoc *` to the methods declared above.)

⟨*Error Reporting Function Declarations*⟩ +≡
```
template <typename... Args>
void Warning(const char *fmt, Args &&... args);
template <typename... Args>
void Error(const char *fmt, Args &&... args);
template <typename... Args>
[[noreturn]] void ErrorExit(const char *fmt, Args &&... args);
```

B.3.5 LOGGING

Mechanisms for logging program execution are provided in the files `util/log.h` and `util/log.cpp`. These are intended to be used for debugging and other programmer-focused tasks; when printed, they include information such as the source file and line number of the logging call, the date and time that it was made, and which thread made it.

The most important of them are `LOG_VERBOSE()`, `LOG_ERROR()`, and `LOG_FATAL()`. Each takes a formatting string with `printf`-style formatting directives and then a variable number of arguments to provide values. Their implementations all end up calling `StringPrintf()`, so all the additional capabilities it provides can be used.

Which messages are printed can be controlled by the `--log-level` command line option to pbrt. The specified logging level is represented with the `LogLevel` enumeration, an enumerator of which is stored in a global variable. If the `--log-file` option is used, a `FILE *` is opened to store the logging messages.

⟨*LogLevel Definition*⟩ ≡
```
enum class LogLevel { Verbose, Error, Fatal, Invalid };
```

⟨*LogLevel Global Variable Declaration*⟩ ≡
```
namespace logging {
extern LogLevel logLevel;
extern FILE *logFile;
} // namespace logging
```

Here is the implementation of `LOG_VERBOSE()`; the other two are similar. There is one trick to note: the macro is carefully written using the short-circuit `&&` operator so that not only does it expand to a single statement, making it safe to use after an `if` statement without braces, but the arguments after the formatting string are also not evaluated if verbose logging has not been specified. In this way, it is safe to write logging code that calls functions that may do meaningful amounts of computation for the parameter values while not paying the cost for them if their results are unneeded.

⟨*Logging Macros*⟩ ≡
```
#define LOG_VERBOSE(...)                                            \
    (pbrt::LogLevel::Verbose >= logging::logLevel &&                \
     (pbrt::Log(LogLevel::Verbose, __FILE__, __LINE__, __VA_ARGS__), \
      true))
```

LogLevel 1065
StringPrintf() 1064

The underlying `Log()` function handles the details of formatting the log entry and storing logging messages in a buffer in memory during GPU execution; in that case, messages are eventually copied back to the CPU to be printed.

B.3.6 ASSERTIONS AND RUNTIME ERROR CHECKING

A few capabilities are provided for checking for unexpected values at runtime, all defined in the file util/check.h. pbrt uses these in place of the system-provided assert() macro as they provide more information about which values led to assertion failures, when they occur. These should only be used for errors that the system cannot recover from and only for errors that are due to the system's implementation: errors in user input and such should be detected and reported using the more friendly mechanisms of the Warning() and Error() functions.

First, CHECK() replaces assert(), issuing a fatal error if the specified condition is not true. A DCHECK() macro, not included here, performs similar functionality, though only in debug builds.

⟨*CHECK Macro Definitions*⟩ ≡
```
#define CHECK(x) (!(!(x) && (LOG_FATAL("Check failed: %s", #x), true)))
```

A common use of assertions is to check a relationship between two values (e.g., that they are equal, or that one is strictly less than another). These operations are performed by the following macros, which dispatch to another one that they all share. (There are similarly D-prefixed variants of these for debug builds only.)

⟨*CHECK Macro Definitions*⟩ +≡
```
#define CHECK_EQ(a, b) CHECK_IMPL(a, b, ==)
#define CHECK_NE(a, b) CHECK_IMPL(a, b, !=)
#define CHECK_GT(a, b) CHECK_IMPL(a, b, >)
#define CHECK_GE(a, b) CHECK_IMPL(a, b, >=)
#define CHECK_LT(a, b) CHECK_IMPL(a, b, <)
#define CHECK_LE(a, b) CHECK_IMPL(a, b, <=)
```

There are three things to see in CHECK_IMPL(). First, it is careful to evaluate the provided expressions only once, storing their values in the va and vb variables. This ensures that they do not introduce unexpected behavior if they are invoked with an expression that includes side effects (e.g., var++). Second, when the check fails, the error message includes not just the source code form of the check, but also the values that caused the failure. This additional information alone is sometimes enough to debug an issue. Finally, it is implemented in terms of a single iteration do/while loop; in this way, it is a single C++ statement and therefore can be used with if statements without braces.

⟨*CHECK_IMPL Macro Definition*⟩ ≡
```
#define CHECK_IMPL(a, b, op)                                        \
    do {                                                            \
        auto va = a;                                                \
        auto vb = b;                                                \
        if (!(va op vb))                                            \
            LOG_FATAL("Check failed: %s " #op " %s with %s = %s, %s = %s",\
                      #a, #b, #a, va, #b, vb);                      \
    } while (false) /* swallow semicolon */
```

When a CHECK fails, not only is the error message printed, but pbrt also prints a stack trace that shows some context of the program's state of execution at that point. In addition, the CheckCallbackScope class can be used to provide additional information about the current program state that is printed upon a CHECK failure.

The error handling system keeps a list of active CheckCallbackScope objects. For each one, it calls the provided callback to get an error string if a CHECK fails.

Error() 1064

Warning() 1064

⟨*CheckCallbackScope Public Methods*⟩ ≡
```
CheckCallbackScope(std::function<std::string(void)> callback);
```

Thus, it might be used as

```
Point2i currentPixel; /* Variable that is updated during rendering */
CheckCallbackScope callbackScope([&]() {
    return StringPrintf("The current pixel is %s", currentPixel);
});
// Render...
```

to include the current pixel coordinates in the error output. The expectation is that `Check CallbackScope` objects will be stack-allocated, such that when a function returns, for example, then a `CheckCallbackScope` that it declared will go out of scope and thence be removed from the active callback scopes by its destructor.

Especially in systems that extensively use stochastic sampling, there may be unusual conditions that are allowed to happen rarely, but where their frequent occurrence would be a bug. (One example that comes up in the implementation of microfacet distributions is when the incident and outgoing directions are exactly opposite, in which case the half angle vector is degenerate. The renderer needs to handle this case when it happens, but it should only happen rarely.) pbrt therefore also provides a `CHECK_RARE(freq, cond)` macro that takes a maximum frequency of failure and a condition to check. An error is issued at the end of program execution for any of them where the condition occurred too frequently.

B.3.7 DISPLAYING IMAGES

pbrt supports a simple socket-based protocol that allows it to communicate with external programs that can display images, both on the same machine and on a remote system from the one that pbrt is running on.[4] This is the mechanism that is invoked when the `--display-server` option is provided on the command line.

If a connection has been made with such a display program, there are a number of functions that make it easy to visualize arbitrary image data using it. This can be especially useful for debugging or for understanding pbrt's execution.

`DisplayStatic()` causes an image of the specified size to be displayed. The number of specified image channel names determines the number of channels in the image. The provided callback will be called repeatedly for tiles of the overall image, where each call is provided a separate buffer for each specified image channel. These buffers should be filled with values for the given tile bounds in scanline order.

⟨*DisplayServer Function Declarations*⟩ ≡
```
void DisplayStatic(std::string title, Point2i resolution,
    std::vector<std::string> channelNames,
    std::function<void(Bounds2i, pstd::span<pstd::span<Float>>)> getValues);
```

Bounds2i 97
CheckCallbackScope 1066
Float 23
Point2i 92

`DisplayDynamic()` is similar, but the callback will be called repeatedly during program execution to get the latest values for dynamic data.

---

4   Thomas Müller's tev image viewer, available from *https://github.com/Tom94/tev*, supports this protocol.

⟨*DisplayServer Function Declarations*⟩ +≡
```
void DisplayDynamic(std::string title, Point2i resolution,
    std::vector<std::string> channelNames,
    std::function<void(Bounds2i, pstd::span<pstd::span<Float>>)> getValues);
```

There are additional convenience functions that take Images for both static and dynamic display. Their implementations take care of providing the necessary callback routines to copy data from the image to the provided buffers.

⟨*DisplayServer Function Declarations*⟩ +≡
```
void DisplayStatic(std::string title, const Image &image,
                   pstd::optional<ImageChannelDesc> channelDesc = {});
void DisplayDynamic(std::string title, const Image &image,
                   pstd::optional<ImageChannelDesc> channelDesc = {});
```

B.3.8 REPORTING PROGRESS

The ProgressReporter class gives the user feedback about how much of a task has been completed and how much longer it is expected to take. For example, implementations of the various Integrator::Render() methods generally use a ProgressReporter to show rendering progress. The implementation prints a row of plus signs, the elapsed time, and the estimated remaining time.

⟨*ProgressReporter Definition*⟩ ≡
```
class ProgressReporter {
  public:
    ⟨ProgressReporter Public Methods 1068⟩
  private:
    ⟨ProgressReporter Private Methods⟩
    ⟨ProgressReporter Private Members⟩
};
```

The constructor takes the total number of units of work to be done (e.g., the total number of camera rays that will be traced) and a short string describing the task being performed. If the gpu parameter is true, then execution on the GPU is tracked. In that case, the implementation must handle the fact that CPU and GPU operation is asynchronous, which it does by adding events to the GPU command stream at each Update() call and then periodically determining which events have been completed to report the appropriate degree of progress. See the source code for details.

⟨*ProgressReporter Public Methods*⟩ ≡   **1068**
```
ProgressReporter(int64_t totalWork, std::string title, bool quiet,
                 bool gpu = false);
```

Once the ProgressReporter has been created, each call to its Update() method signifies that one unit of work has been completed. An optional integer value can be passed to indicate that multiple units have been done. A call to Done() indicates that all work has been completed. Finally, the elapsed time since the ProgressReporter was created is available via the ElapsedSeconds() method. This quantity must be tracked for the progress updates and is often useful to have available.

⟨*ProgressReporter Public Methods*⟩ +≡   **1068**
```
void Update(int64_t num = 1);
void Done();
double ElapsedSeconds() const;
```

B.4 CONTAINERS AND MEMORY MANAGEMENT

A variety of container data structures that extend those made available by the standard library are provided in the file util/containers.h.

First, there is InlinedVector. We will not describe its implementation here, but note that it is an extended version of std::vector that has storage for a handful of vector elements preallocated in its class definition. Thus, for short vectors, it can be used without incurring the cost of dynamic memory allocation. It is used extensively in the Image class, for example.

Its class declaration is of the form:

```
template <typename T, int N, class Allocator = /* ... */>
class InlinedVector;
```

The value of N specifies the number of elements to handle via the inline allocation in the class definition.

Even though the C++ standard library provides a hash table via std::unordered_map, pbrt additionally provides a HashMap, also not included here. There are two reasons it exists: first, the hash table in the standard library is specified such that pointers to elements in the hash table will not change even if the table is resized, which in turn requires dynamic memory allocation for each element. Second, the GPU rendering path requires a hash table that can be used from GPU code. Its class declaration is of the form:

```
template <typename Key, typename Value, typename Hash = std::hash<Key>,
          typename Allocator = /* ... */>
class HashMap;
```

Its main methods have the following signatures:

```
void Insert(const Key &key, const Value &value);
bool HasKey(const Key &key) const;
const Value &operator[](const Key &key) const;
```

B.4.1 2D ARRAYS

While it is not difficult to index into a 1D memory buffer that represents a 2D array of values, having a template class that handles this task helps make code elsewhere in the system less verbose and easier to verify. Array2D fills this role in pbrt.

⟨*Array2D Definition*⟩ ≡
```
template <typename T> class Array2D {
  public:
    ⟨Array2D Type Definitions⟩
    ⟨Array2D Public Methods 1070⟩
  private:
    ⟨Array2D Private Members 1069⟩
};
```

The array is defined over a 2D region specified by extent; its lower bounds do not necessarily need to be at (0, 0).

⟨*Array2D Private Members*⟩ ≡   **1069**
```
Bounds2i extent;
Allocator allocator;
T *values;
```

Allocator 40
Bounds2i 97
Image 1079

Array2D provides a variety of constructors, including ones that initialize its entries with a constant value or via a start and ending iterator. Here is the one that default-initializes the entries.

⟨*Array2D Public Methods*⟩ ≡   1069
```
Array2D(Bounds2i extent, Allocator allocator = {})
    : extent(extent), allocator(allocator) {
    int n = extent.Area();
    values = allocator.allocate_object<T>(n);
    for (int i = 0; i < n; ++i)
        allocator.construct(values + i);
}
```

The array can be indexed using a Point2i, which should be inside the specified extent. After translating the point by the origin of the bounds, the usual indexing computation is performed to find the value. Array2D also provides a const version of this method as well as an operator() that takes a pair of integers.

⟨*Array2D Public Methods*⟩ +≡   1069
```
T &operator[](Point2i p) {
    DCHECK(InsideExclusive(p, extent));
    p.x -= extent.pMin.x;
    p.y -= extent.pMin.y;
    return values[p.x + (extent.pMax.x - extent.pMin.x) * p.y];
}
```

A few methods give the total size and sizes of individual dimensions of the array.

⟨*Array2D Public Methods*⟩ +≡   1069
```
int size() const { return extent.Area(); }
int XSize() const { return extent.pMax.x - extent.pMin.x; }
int YSize() const { return extent.pMax.y - extent.pMin.y; }
```

It is also possible to iterate over elements of the array directly.

⟨*Array2D Public Methods*⟩ +≡   1069
```
iterator begin() { return values; }
iterator end() { return begin() + size(); }
```

B.4.2 INTERNED OBJECTS

If many instances of the same object are stored in memory, especially if the objects are large, the *interning* technique can be helpful. With it, a single copy of each unique object is stored and all uses of it refer to that copy. (The technique is thus generally only useful for read-only data.) pbrt uses interning both for transformations found in the scene description and for strings in the scene entity objects defined in Section C.2.1. For complex scenes, the memory savings from eliminating redundant copies can be large.

The InternCache class manages such caches. It is a template class based on the type being managed and its hash function. Types managed by it must provide an equality operator so that it can find matches.

```
template <typename T, typename Hash = std::hash<T>>
class InternCache;
```

Beyond the constructor, InternCache provides two variations of a single method, Lookup(). Their signatures are below. Both store a single copy of provided objects in a hash table, using a mutex to allow concurrent access by multiple threads. The first `Lookup()` method allocates memory for the object itself using the allocator passed to the `InternCache` constructor and copies the provided item to initialize the object stored in the cache. The second takes a user-provided creation callback function with the signature shown below. This allows for more complex object initialization—as is used in the `LightBase::LookupSpectrum()` method, for example.

```
const T *Lookup(const T &item);

/* F: T *create(Allocator alloc, const T &item) */
template <typename F> const T *Lookup(const T &item, F create);
```

Note that the `Lookup()` methods return a pointer to the shared instance of the object. They always return the same pointer for equal objects, so a pointer equality test can be used to test for equality with values returned by the cache. For large or complex objects, more efficient equality tests can be a further benefit of interning.

`InternedString` is a convenience class for strings stored in an `InternCache`. Using it makes it clear that a string pointer refers to an interned string, which helps clarify code.

⟨*InternedString Definition*⟩ ≡
```
class InternedString {
public:
    ⟨InternedString Public Methods 1071⟩
private:
    const std::string *str = nullptr;
};
```

It also provides an automatic conversion operator to `std::string`, saving users from needing to dereference the pointer themselves. Comparison operators with strings and `const char *`s are also available.

⟨*InternedString Public Methods*⟩ ≡   **1071**
```
    InternedString(const std::string *str) : str(str) {}
    operator const std::string &() const { return *str; }
```

⋆ B.4.3 COLLECTIONS OF TYPES

In pbrt's wavefront rendering path, it was useful to perform various operations on collections of types (e.g., to instantiate a template function for each of the possible `Material` types). There is no direct support for such operations in C++, but with some application of template programming it is possible to provide these capabilities.

First, we define `TypePack`, a structure that holds no non-`static` data. Its purpose is to define a type that represents a collection of types—those provided in the template parameter pack. It also provides a handy `count` member variable that gives the number of types.

⟨*TypePack Definition*⟩ ≡
```
    template <typename... Ts>
    struct TypePack {
        static constexpr size_t count = sizeof...(Ts);
    };
```

`IndexOf` provides the index of a given type among the types in a `TypePack`. Here is the declaration of the structure for its general template, which will only be instantiated if the given type is not in fact one of the types in a type pack. We can use a C++ trick to ensure a reasonable error message is printed in this case: because the following static_assert's condition can only be evaluated at compile time given a concrete type T (even though it will clearly always be false), the error message is thus only printed if this version of IndexOf is instantiated.

⟨*TypePack Operations*⟩ ≡
```
template <typename T, typename... Ts>
struct IndexOf {
    static constexpr int count = 0;
    static_assert(!std::is_same_v<T, T>, "Type not present in TypePack");
};
```

A first template specialization handles the case where the first type in the TypePack matches the given type T. In this case, the index is zero.

⟨*TypePack Operations*⟩ +≡
```
template <typename T, typename... Ts>
struct IndexOf<T, TypePack<T, Ts...>> {
    static constexpr int count = 0;
};
```

Another template specialization handles the case where T is not the first type. One is added to the final count, and a recursive template instantiation checks the next type. Note that because all the types involved are known at compile time, the final value is a compile-time constant (as evidenced by the constexpr qualifier).

⟨*TypePack Operations*⟩ +≡
```
template <typename T, typename U, typename... Ts>
struct IndexOf<T, TypePack<U, Ts...>> {
    static constexpr int count = 1 + IndexOf<T, TypePack<Ts...>>::count;
};
```

We will find it useful to be able to wrap a template class around each of a set of types. This operation is provided by MapType. The base case is a single-element type pack.

⟨*TypePack Operations*⟩ +≡
```
template <template <typename> class M, typename T>
struct MapType<M, TypePack<T>> {
    using type = TypePack<M<T>>;
};
```

Larger numbers of types are handled recursively. Prepend, not included here, gives the TypePack that results from prepending a given type to a TypePack of others.

⟨*TypePack Operations*⟩ +≡
```
template <template <typename> class M, typename T, typename... Ts>
struct MapType<M, TypePack<T, Ts...>> {
    using type = typename Prepend<M<T>,
        typename MapType<M, TypePack<Ts...>>::type>::type;
};
```

Finally, we will define a ForEachType() function, which calls the provided function (which is assumed to be a template function) once for each of the types in a TypePack. The general case peels off the first type, calls the provided function, and then proceeds with a recursive call with the remainder of types in the TypePack. In this case, the recursion is expressed in a slightly different manner, via a temporary instance of a TypePack-typed variable that is used purely to record the types yet to be handled.

⟨*TypePack Operations*⟩ +≡
```
template <typename F, typename T, typename... Ts>
void ForEachType(F func, TypePack<T, Ts...>) {
    func.template operator()<T>();
    ForEachType(func, TypePack<Ts...>());
}
```

The base case of an empty TypePack ends the recursion.

⟨*TypePack Operations*⟩ +≡
```
template <typename F> void ForEachType(F func, TypePack<>) {}
```

B.4.4 TAGGED POINTERS

The TaggedPointer class is at the heart of how pbrt handles polymorphic types. It takes the pointer to an object of known type and uses excess bits in its pointer to encode the object's actual type (i.e., to *tag* it). When dynamic dispatch or other type-specific operations are needed, the object's type can be extracted from the pointer.[5] This class's implementation is in the file util/taggedptr.h.

TaggedPointer is a template class that requires all the types it may represent to be provided at compile time. Note that this approach thus precludes runtime loading of additional class definitions of new types, as would be possible with the usual approach to polymorphism based on virtual functions.

⟨*TaggedPointer Definition*⟩ ≡
```
template <typename... Ts>
class TaggedPointer {
  public:
    ⟨TaggedPointer Public Types 1073⟩
    ⟨TaggedPointer Public Methods 1074⟩
  private:
    ⟨TaggedPointer Private Members 1074⟩
};
```

All the possible types for a tagged pointer are provided via a public type definition.

⟨*TaggedPointer Public Types*⟩ ≡   1073
```
using Types = TypePack<Ts...>;
```

Modern processors ubiquitously use 64-bit pointers, which allow addressing 2^{64} bytes of memory. Memory sizes of tens to hundreds of gigabytes are common now, which is a far cry from the *billions* of gigabytes that a 64-bit pointer can address. Therefore, processors specify the size of their addressable memory space in terms of a smaller number of bits. Until recently, a 48-bit address space was common on CPUs, though that has recently increased to 57 bits. While it is still unimaginable for a single system to have 2^{57} bytes of RAM, large address spaces can be useful for cluster computing where many machines present a unified address space or for mapping pointers to data in offline storage.

TaggedPointer therefore steals the upper bits of pointers in order to encode types. Even with 57-bit address spaces, there are still 7 bits left, which allows 2^7 types, far more than pbrt needs.

TypePack 1071

---

5   Our TaggedPointer implementation is derived from DiscriminatedPtr in Facebook's open source *folly* library.

⟨*TaggedPointer Private Members*⟩ ≡   1073
```
static constexpr int tagShift = 57;
static constexpr int tagBits = 64 - tagShift;
```

`tagMask` is a bitmask that extracts the type tag's bits, and `ptrMask` extracts the original pointer.

⟨*TaggedPointer Private Members*⟩ +≡   1073
```
static constexpr uint64_t tagMask = ((1ull << tagBits) - 1) << tagShift;
static constexpr uint64_t ptrMask = ~tagMask;
```

We can now implement the primary `TaggedPointer` constructor. Given a pointer of known type T, it uses the `TypeIndex()` method to get an integer index for its type. In turn, the `bits` member is set by combining the original pointer with the integer type, shifted up into the unused bits of the pointer value.

⟨*TaggedPointer Public Methods*⟩ ≡   1073
```
template <typename T>
TaggedPointer(T *ptr) {
    uintptr_t iptr = reinterpret_cast<uintptr_t>(ptr);
    constexpr unsigned int type = TypeIndex<T>();
    bits = iptr | ((uintptr_t)type << tagShift);
}
```

⟨*TaggedPointer Private Members*⟩ +≡   1073
```
uintptr_t bits = 0;
```

Most of the work for the `TypeIndex()` method is done by the `IndexOf` structure defined in the previous section. One more index is needed to represent a null pointer, however, so an index of 0 is used for it and the rest have one added to them.

⟨*TaggedPointer Public Methods*⟩ +≡   1073
```
template <typename T>
static constexpr unsigned int TypeIndex() {
    using Tp = typename std::remove_cv_t<T>;
    if constexpr (std::is_same_v<Tp, std::nullptr_t>) return 0;
    else return 1 + pbrt::IndexOf<Tp, Types>::count;
}
```

`Tag()` returns a `TaggedPointer`'s tag by extracting the relevant bits. In turn, the `Is()` method performs a runtime check of whether a `TaggedPointer` represents a particular type.

⟨*TaggedPointer Public Methods*⟩ +≡   1073
```
unsigned int Tag() const { return ((bits & tagMask) >> tagShift); }
template <typename T>
bool Is() const { return Tag() == TypeIndex<T>(); }
```

The maximum value of a tag is equal to the number of represented types.

⟨*TaggedPointer Public Methods*⟩ +≡   1073
```
static constexpr unsigned int MaxTag() { return sizeof...(Ts); }
```

A pointer of a specified type is returned by `CastOrNullptr()`. As the name suggests, it returns `nullptr` if the `TaggedPointer` does not in fact hold an object of type T. In addition to this method, `TaggedPointer` also provides a `const` variant that returns a `const T *` as well as unsafe `Cast()` methods that always return a pointer of the given type. Those should only be used when there is no question about the underlying type held by a `TaggedPointer`.

⟨*TaggedPointer Public Methods*⟩ +≡   **1073**
```
template <typename T>
T *CastOrNullptr() {
    if (Is<T>()) return reinterpret_cast<T *>(ptr());
    else return nullptr;
}
```

For cases where the original pointer is needed but void pointer will suffice, the ptr() method is available. It has a const variant as well.

⟨*TaggedPointer Public Methods*⟩ +≡   **1073**
```
void *ptr() { return reinterpret_cast<void *>(bits & ptrMask); }
```

The most interesting TaggedPointer method is Dispatch(), which is at the heart of pbrt's dynamic dispatch mechanism for polymorphic types. Its task is to determine which type of object a TaggedPointer points to and then call the provided function, passing it the object's pointer, cast to the correct type. (See the Spectrum::operator() method, which calls TaggedPointer::Dispatch(); details about the operation of the function that is provided to Dispatch() are discussed with its implementation.)

Most of the work is done by standalone Dispatch() functions that are defined in a detail namespace, signifying that although they are defined in a header file, they should not be used by code outside of the header. Those functions require the return type of the provided function, which is determined by the ReturnType helper template. We will not include ReturnType's implementation here; it uses C++ template pack expansion to find the return type of func when called with each of the types that the TaggedPointer can hold, issues a compile time error if they are not all the same, and provides the return type via its definition of type.[6]

⟨*TaggedPointer Public Methods*⟩ +≡   **1073**
```
template <typename F>
PBRT_CPU_GPU decltype(auto) Dispatch(F &&func) {
    using R = typename detail::ReturnType<F, Ts...>::type;
    return detail::Dispatch<F, R, Ts...>(func, ptr(), Tag() - 1);
}
```

detail::Dispatch() may be called with an arbitrary number of types to handle, depending on how many a TaggedPointer manages. This is handled by providing a number of template specializations for different numbers of such types.

Early in the development of this version of pbrt, we implemented a dispatch mechanism that applied binary search, making a series of recursive function calls based on the type index until the corresponding type was found. That had equivalent performance to the approach implemented here and entailed fewer lines of code. However, we found that it cluttered call stacks, which was a nuisance when debugging. With the current approach, dynamic dispatch only imposes a single function call.

As an example of a Dispatch() function, here is the implementation of the one that handles three types; it is parameterized by the type of the callback function F and its return type R

---

6 About the decltype(auto) specifying Dispatch()'s return type: this syntax is unfortunately necessary in C++ for *perfect forwarding*, which ensures that reference types are returned as references and not converted to their underlying value type if a plain auto was used.

as well. All that there is to it is a `switch` statement to call the function with the appropriate pointer type based on the index passed in from `TaggedPointer::Dispatch()`.

⟨*TaggedPointer Helper Templates*⟩ ≡
```
template <typename F, typename R, typename T0, typename T1, typename T2>
R Dispatch(F &&func, void *ptr, int index) {
    switch (index) {
      case 0:  return func((T0 *)ptr);
      case 1:  return func((T1 *)ptr);
      default: return func((T2 *)ptr);
    }
}
```

There are implementations of `detail::Dispatch()` for up to 8 types. If more are provided, a fallback implementation handles the first 8 and then makes a recursive call to `detail::Dispatch()` with the rest of them for larger indices. For pbrt's uses, where there are at most 10 or so types, this approach works well.

`TaggedPointer` also includes a `const`-qualified dispatch method as well as `DispatchCPU()`, which is necessary for methods that are only able to run on the CPU. (The default `Dispatch()` method requires that the method be callable from both CPU or GPU code, which is the most common use case in pbrt.) These both have corresponding dispatch functions in the `detail` namespace.

B.4.5 3D SAMPLED DATA

`SampledGrid` represents a point-sampled function over the $[0, 1]^3$ domain. It is in a sense the 3D generalization of the `Image` class, though it offers far fewer capabilities. Its main use in pbrt is as a representation for the `GridMedium` used to represent volumetric media. It is templated on a type `T` that represents the point-sampled values.

⟨*SampledGrid Definition*⟩ ≡
```
template <typename T>
class SampledGrid {
  public:
    ⟨SampledGrid Public Methods 1077⟩
  private:
    ⟨SampledGrid Private Members 1076⟩
};
```

It offsets a few constructors, not included here, that initialize a vector of values at specified sampling rates nx, ny, and nz in each dimension.

⟨*SampledGrid Private Members*⟩ ≡   **1076**
```
pstd::vector<T> values;
int nx, ny, nz;
```

`Lookup()` takes a point and a function that can be used to convert from the type stored in memory to another type that is returned from the method. (This capability is used, for example, by the `RGBGridMedium`, which stores a grid of RGB values that are represented using the `RGBUnboundedSpectrum` class but then wants a corresponding `SampledSpectrum` at specific wavelengths to be returned from `Lookup()`.)

⟨*SampledGrid Public Methods*⟩ ≡   **1076**
```
template <typename F>
auto Lookup(Point3f p, F convert) const {
    ⟨Compute voxel coordinates and offsets for p 1077⟩
    ⟨Return trilinearly interpolated voxel values 1077⟩
}
```

For the convenience of cases where the in-memory type T is the one that should be returned, a second implementation of Lookup(), not included here, provides a default identity implementation of the conversion function.

SampledGrid follows the same conventions as were used for discrete and continuous coordinates for pixel indexing, defined in Section 8.1.4. Here the discrete coordinates for the lower corner of the 8 samples are computed.

⟨*Compute voxel coordinates and offsets for* p⟩ ≡   **1077**
```
Point3f pSamples(p.x * nx - .5f, p.y * ny - .5f, p.z * nz - .5f);
Point3i pi = (Point3i)Floor(pSamples);
Vector3f d = pSamples - (Point3f)pi;
```

A sequence of linear interpolations gives the trilinearly interpolated sample value. They use a second Lookup() method, not included here, that returns a voxel sample given integer coordinates. Out-of-bounds indices result in a default-initialized value being returned, which is generally the zero value for the type.

Note that SampledGrid is able to represent any class for which an appropriate Lerp() function is defined for the type returned by the conversion function. Further, note the use of auto, which allows this method to be implemented without worrying about what type is returned by convert.

⟨*Return trilinearly interpolated voxel values*⟩ ≡   **1077**
```
auto d00 = Lerp(d.x, Lookup(pi, convert),
                     Lookup(pi + Vector3i(1, 0, 0), convert));
auto d10 = Lerp(d.x, Lookup(pi + Vector3i(0, 1, 0), convert),
                     Lookup(pi + Vector3i(1, 1, 0), convert));
auto d01 = Lerp(d.x, Lookup(pi + Vector3i(0, 0, 1), convert),
                     Lookup(pi + Vector3i(1, 0, 1), convert));
auto d11 = Lerp(d.x, Lookup(pi + Vector3i(0, 1, 1), convert),
                     Lookup(pi + Vector3i(1, 1, 1), convert));
return Lerp(d.z, Lerp(d.y, d00, d10), Lerp(d.y, d01, d11));
```

Finally, the MaxValue() method, also not included here, returns a bound on the maximum value of the interpolated function over the given bounds, computed by looping over all of the sample values that contribute to grid lookups inside those bounds. It takes a function that converts the in-memory type to a Float; the maximum of all such Floats is then returned.

B.4.6 EFFICIENT TEMPORARY MEMORY ALLOCATIONS

For small objects with short lifetimes, C++'s traditional new and delete memory allocation operators may impose undesirable overhead from maintenance of their internal data structures. A custom allocation technique that has proved to be useful in such cases is *arena-based allocation*, which allocates objects from a large contiguous region of memory. In this scheme, individual objects are never explicitly freed; instead, the entire region of memory is released when the lifetime of all the allocated objects ends.

The ScratchBuffer class implements this approach. It is used for dynamic allocation of BxDFs, BSSRDFs, and RayMajorantIterators as rays are being traced through the scene. Some of its efficiency comes from its not allowing multiple threads to use a single ScratchBuffer instance concurrently; instead, pbrt's ThreadLocal capability should be used to allocate a separate ScratchBuffer for each thread that needs one.

One important detail in its definition is the use of alignas, which helps improve CPU cache performance by preventing multiple threads from accessing the same cache line. (For details, see the discussion of false sharing in Section B.6.3.)

⟨*ScratchBuffer Definition*⟩ ≡
```
class alignas(PBRT_L1_CACHE_LINE_SIZE) ScratchBuffer {
  public:
    ⟨ScratchBuffer Public Methods 1078⟩
  private:
    ⟨ScratchBuffer Private Methods 1079⟩
    ⟨ScratchBuffer Private Members 1078⟩
};
```

The ScratchBuffer hands out pointers to memory from a single preallocated block. If the block's size is insufficient, it will be replaced with a larger one; this allows a small default block size, though the caller can specify a larger one if the default is known to be too little.

⟨*ScratchBuffer Public Methods*⟩ ≡   1078
```
ScratchBuffer(int size = 256) : allocSize(size) {
    ptr = (char *)Allocator().allocate_bytes(size, align);
}
```

offset maintains the offset after ptr where free memory begins.

⟨*ScratchBuffer Private Members*⟩ ≡   1078
```
static constexpr int align = PBRT_L1_CACHE_LINE_SIZE;
char *ptr = nullptr;
int allocSize = 0, offset = 0;
```

To service an allocation request, the allocation routine first advances offset as necessary so that the returned address meets the specified memory alignment. (It is thus required that ptr has at minimum that alignment.) If the allocation would go past the end of the allocated buffer, Realloc() takes care of allocating a new, larger buffer. With the usual case of long-lived ScratchBuffers, this should happen rarely. Given sufficient space, the pointer can be returned and offset incremented to account for the allocation.

⟨*ScratchBuffer Public Methods*⟩ +≡   1078
```
void *Alloc(size_t size, size_t align) {
    if ((offset % align) != 0)
        offset += align - (offset % align);
    if (offset + size > allocSize)
        Realloc(size);
    void *p = ptr + offset;
    offset += size;
    return p;
}
```

ScratchBuffer provides two additional Alloc() methods that are not included here. Both are templated on the type of object being allocated. One allocates a single object, passing along provided parameters to its constructor. The other allocates an array of objects of a specified length, running the default constructor for each one.

If a larger buffer is needed, Realloc() holds on to a pointer to the current buffer and its size in smallBuffers. The current buffer cannot be freed until the user later calls ScratchBuffer's Reset() method, but it should be returned to the system then, as ScratchBuffer will henceforth have no need for it.

⟨*ScratchBuffer Private Methods*⟩ ≡   1078
```
void Realloc(size_t minSize) {
    smallBuffers.push_back(std::make_pair(ptr, allocSize));
    allocSize = std::max(2 * minSize, allocSize + minSize);
    ptr = (char *)Allocator().allocate_bytes(allocSize, align);
    offset = 0;
}
```

⟨*ScratchBuffer Private Members*⟩ +≡   1078
```
std::list<std::pair<char *, size_t>> smallBuffers;
```

A call to Reset() is lightweight, usually just resetting offset to 0. Note that, lacking the necessary information to be able to do so, it does not run the destructors of the allocated objects.

⟨*ScratchBuffer Public Methods*⟩ +≡   1078
```
void Reset() {
    for (const auto &buf : smallBuffers)
        Allocator().deallocate_bytes(buf.first, buf.second, align);
    smallBuffers.clear();
    offset = 0;
}
```

B.5 IMAGES

The Image class stores a 2D array of pixel values, where each pixel stores a fixed number of scalar-valued *channels*. (For example, an image storing RGB color would have three channels.) It provides a variety of operations ranging from looking up or interpolating pixel values to image-wide operations like resizing. It is at the core of both the FloatImageTexture and SpectrumImageTexture classes and is used for lights such as the ImageInfiniteLight and ProjectionLight. Furthermore, both of pbrt's Film implementations make use of its capabilities for writing images to disk in a variety of file formats.

⟨*Image Definition*⟩ ≡
```
class Image {
  public:
    ⟨Image Public Methods 1080⟩
  private:
    ⟨Image Private Methods⟩
    ⟨Image Private Members 1080⟩
};
```

Image is defined in the files util/image.h and util/image.cpp.

The Image class provides a number of constructors as well as a method (which will be discussed in Section B.5.3) that reads an image from a file. We will only describe the operation of its most general-purpose constructor here; see the class definition for the remainder of them.

This Image constructor takes the in-memory format to use for storing pixel data, format, the overall image resolution, and names for all of the channels. Optionally, both a ColorEncoding and an Allocator can be provided; the former specifies a technique for encoding fixed-precision pixel values and will be discussed in Section B.5.6.

⟨*Image Public Methods*⟩ ≡   **1079**
```
Image(PixelFormat format, Point2i resolution,
      pstd::span<const std::string> channelNames,
      ColorEncoding encoding = nullptr, Allocator alloc = {});
```

Three in-memory formats are supported for pixel channel values. Note that Image uses the same encoding for all channels; it is not possible to mix and match. The first of them, U256, specifies an unsigned 8-bit encoding of values between 0 and 1 using integers ranging from 0 to 255. This is a memory-efficient encoding and is widely used in image file formats, but it provides limited range. Half uses 16-bit floating-point values (which were described in Section 6.8.1) to provide much more dynamic range than U256, while still being memory efficient. Finally, Float specifies full 32-bit floats. It would not be difficult to generalize Image to also support double-precision floating-point storage, though we have not found a need to do so for pbrt's uses of this class.

⟨*PixelFormat Definition*⟩ ≡
```
enum class PixelFormat { U256, Half, Float };
```

A few helper functions test whether a given PixelFormat uses a specified amount of storage. Isolating these tests in this way makes it easier, for example, to extend Image to also provide a 16-bit integer representation without needing to update logic that purely relates to memory allocation.

⟨*PixelFormat Inline Functions*⟩ ≡
```
bool Is8Bit(PixelFormat format) { return format == PixelFormat::U256; }
bool Is16Bit(PixelFormat format) { return format == PixelFormat::Half; }
bool Is32Bit(PixelFormat format) { return format == PixelFormat::Float; }
```

The size of the provided channelNames parameter determines the number of channels the image stores at each pixel. The Image class does not impose any semantics on the channels or attempt to interpret their meaning but instead just stores values and performs the operations on them specified by the caller.

⟨*Image Private Members*⟩ ≡   **1079**
```
PixelFormat format;
Point2i resolution;
pstd::vector<std::string> channelNames;
ColorEncoding encoding = nullptr;
```

Because these values are stored as private member variables, Image provides corresponding accessor methods.

⟨*Image Public Methods*⟩ +≡   **1079**
```
PixelFormat Format() const { return format; }
Point2i Resolution() const { return resolution; }
int NChannels() const { return channelNames.size(); }
std::vector<std::string> ChannelNames() const;
const ColorEncoding Encoding() const { return encoding; }
```

Image allows the specification of an image with no pixels; operator bool provides a quick check for whether an image is nonempty.

⟨*Image Public Methods*⟩ +≡   **1079**
```
operator bool() const { return resolution.x > 0 && resolution.y > 0; }
```

One of the following member variables stores the pixel values. Which one is used is determined by the specified PixelFormat.

⟨*Image Private Members*⟩ +≡   **1079**
```
pstd::vector<uint8_t> p8;
pstd::vector<Half> p16;
pstd::vector<float> p32;
```

The PixelOffset() method returns the offset into the pixel value array for given integer pixel coordinates. In debug builds, a DCHECK() call, not included here, checks that the provided coordinates are between 0 and the image resolution in each dimension.

A few factors determine the following indexing computation: first, the coordinate system for images has (0, 0) at the upper left corner of the image; images are then laid out in *x* scanline order, and each pixel's channel values are laid out successively in memory.

⟨*Image Public Methods*⟩ +≡   **1079**
```
size_t PixelOffset(Point2i p) const {
    return NChannels() * (p.y * resolution.x + p.x);
}
```

An alternative memory layout would first store all the pixels' first channel values contiguously in memory, then the second channel values, and so forth. In pbrt, the most common uses of Image involve accessing all the channels in a pixel, so the layout we have chosen gives better memory access coherence, which generally leads to better cache performance.

B.5.1 WORKING WITH PIXEL VALUES

The GetChannel() method returns the floating-point value for a single image channel, taking care of both addressing pixels and converting the in-memory value to a Float. Note that if this method is used, it is the caller's responsibility to keep track of what is being stored in each channel.

⟨*Image Public Methods*⟩ +≡   **1079**
```
Float GetChannel(Point2i p, int c,
                 WrapMode2D wrapMode = WrapMode::Clamp) const {
    ⟨Remap provided pixel coordinates before reading channel 1082⟩
    switch (format) {
    case PixelFormat::U256:  { ⟨Return U256-encoded pixel channel value 1082⟩ }
    case PixelFormat::Half:  { ⟨Return Half-encoded pixel channel value 1082⟩ }
    case PixelFormat::Float: { ⟨Return Float-encoded pixel channel value 1082⟩ }
    }
}
```

Like all the upcoming methods that return pixel values, the lookup point p that is passed to GetChannel() is not required to be inside the image bounds. This is a convenience for code that calls these methods and saves them from all needing to handle boundary conditions themselves.

WrapMode and WrapMode2D specify how out-of-bounds coordinates should be handled. The first three options are widely used in texture mapping, and are respectively to return a black (zero-valued) result, to clamp out-of-bounds coordinates to the valid bounds, and to take them modulus the image resolution, which effectively repeats the image infinitely. The last option, OctahedralSphere, accounts for the layout of the octahedron used in the definition of equi-area spherical mapping (see Section 3.8.3) and should be used when looking up values in images that are based on that parameterization.

⟨*WrapMode Definitions*⟩ ≡
```
enum class WrapMode { Black, Clamp, Repeat, OctahedralSphere };
struct WrapMode2D {
    pstd::array<WrapMode, 2> wrap;
};
```

The RemapPixelCoords() function handles modifying the pixel coordinates as needed according to the WrapMode for each dimension. If an out-of-bounds coordinate has been provided and WrapMode::Black has been specified, it returns a false value, which is handled here by returning 0. The implementation of this function is not included here.

⟨*Remap provided pixel coordinates before reading channel*⟩ ≡   1081
```
if (!RemapPixelCoords(&p, resolution, wrapMode))
    return 0;
```

Given a valid pixel coordinate, PixelOffset() gives the offset to the first channel for that pixel. A further offset by the channel index c is all that is left to get to the channel value. For U256 images, this value is decoded into a Float using the specified color encoding (discussed in Section B.5.6).

⟨*Return U256-encoded pixel channel value*⟩ ≡   1081
```
Float r;
encoding.ToLinear({&p8[PixelOffset(p) + c], 1}, {&r, 1});
return r;
```

For Half images, the Half class's Float conversion operator is invoked to get the return value.

⟨*Return Half-encoded pixel channel value*⟩ ≡   1081
```
return Float(p16[PixelOffset(p) + c]);
```

And for Float images, the task is trivial.

⟨*Return Float-encoded pixel channel value*⟩ ≡   1081
```
return p32[PixelOffset(p) + c];
```

The Image class also provides a LookupNearestChannel() method, which returns the specified channel value for the pixel sample nearest a provided coordinate with respect to $[0, 1]^2$. It is a simple wrapper around GetChannel(), so it is not included here.

Slightly more interesting in its implementation is BilerpChannel, which uses bilinear interpolation between four image pixels to compute the channel value. (This is equivalent to filtering with a pixel-wide triangle filter.)

⟨*Image Public Methods*⟩ +≡   1079
```
Float BilerpChannel(Point2f p, int c,
                    WrapMode2D wrapMode = WrapMode::Clamp) const {
    ⟨Compute discrete pixel coordinates and offsets for p 1083⟩
    ⟨Load pixel channel values and return bilinearly interpolated value 1083⟩
}
```

The first step is to scale the provided coordinates p by the image resolution, turning them into continuous pixel coordinates. Because these are continuous coordinates and the pixels in the image are defined at discrete pixel coordinates, it is important to carefully convert into a common representation (Section 8.1.4). Here, the work is performed using discrete coordinates, with the continuous pixel coordinates mapped to the discrete space.

For example, consider the 1D case with a continuous texture coordinate of 2.4: this coordinate is a distance of 0.1 below the discrete texel coordinate 2 (which corresponds to a continuous coordinate of 2.5) and is 0.9 above the discrete coordinate 1 (continuous coordinate 1.5). Thus, if we subtract 0.5 from the continuous coordinate 2.4, giving 1.9, we can correctly compute the correct distances to the discrete coordinates 1 and 2 by subtracting.

⟨*Compute discrete pixel coordinates and offsets for* p⟩ ≡   1082
```
Float x = p[0] * resolution.x - 0.5f, y = p[1] * resolution.y - 0.5f;
int xi = pstd::floor(x), yi = pstd::floor(y);
Float dx = x - xi, dy = y - yi;
```

After the distances are found in each dimension to the pixel at the last integer before the given coordinates, dx and dy, the four pixels are bilinearly interpolated.

⟨*Load pixel channel values and return bilinearly interpolated value*⟩ ≡   1082
```
pstd::array<Float, 4> v = {GetChannel({xi,     yi},     c, wrapMode),
                           GetChannel({xi + 1, yi},     c, wrapMode),
                           GetChannel({xi,     yi + 1}, c, wrapMode),
                           GetChannel({xi + 1, yi + 1}, c, wrapMode)};
return ((1 - dx) * (1 - dy) * v[0] + dx * (1 - dy) * v[1] +
        (1 - dx) *      dy  * v[2] + dx *      dy  * v[3]);
```

The SetChannel() method, the implementation of which is not included in the book, sets the value of a channel in a specified pixel.

⟨*Image Public Methods*⟩ +≡   1079
```
void SetChannel(Point2i p, int c, Float value);
```

A few methods return multiple pixel channel values all at once. Doing so can be more efficient than repeatedly calling methods like GetChannel() or BilerpChannel(), as various common computations like handling the wrapMode can be done just once.

GetChannels() returns all the channel values for a given pixel all at once. (There are also LookupNearest() and Bilerp() methods that similarly perform the corresponding lookup on all channels and return the result using ImageChannelValues.)

⟨*Image Public Methods*⟩ +≡   1079
```
ImageChannelValues GetChannels(Point2i p,
                               WrapMode2D wrapMode = WrapMode::Clamp) const;
```

GetChannels() returns the channel values using an instance of the ImageChannelValues class, the definition of which is not included here. ImageChannelValues can be operated on more or less as if it were a std::vector, though it is based on the InlinedVector class that was described in Section B.4. It is thus able to avoid the cost of the dynamic memory allocations that std::vector would otherwise require if a small number of channel values were being returned.

It is also possible to specify a particular subset of the channels for these sorts of operations. GetChannelDesc() takes one or more image channel names and returns an instance of the ImageChannelDesc class. This class is opaque to the caller, but tracks which channel index each of the requested channels corresponds to. It includes an `operator bool()` method that can be called to check whether the requested channels were in fact present in the image.

⟨*Image Public Methods*⟩ +≡   **1079**
```
ImageChannelDesc GetChannelDesc(
    pstd::span<const std::string> channels) const;
```

All the methods that we have seen in this section also have variants that take an `ImageChannel Desc` and then return values for just the specified channels, in the order they were requested in the call to `GetChannelDesc()`. Here is the one for `GetChannels()`:

⟨*Image Public Methods*⟩ +≡   **1079**
```
ImageChannelValues GetChannels(Point2i p, const ImageChannelDesc &desc,
                               WrapMode2D wrapMode = WrapMode::Clamp) const;
```

B.5.2 IMAGE-WIDE OPERATIONS

The `Image` class also provides a number of operations that operate on the entire image, again agnostic to the semantics of the values an image stores.

`SelectChannels()` returns a new image that includes only the specified channels of the original image, and `Crop()` returns an image that contains the specified subset of pixels of the original.

⟨*Image Public Methods*⟩ +≡   **1079**
```
Image SelectChannels(const ImageChannelDesc &desc,
                     Allocator alloc = {}) const;
Image Crop(const Bounds2i &bounds, Allocator alloc = {}) const;
```

`CopyRectOut()` and `CopyRectIn()` copy the specified rectangular regions of the image to and from the provided buffers. For some performance-sensitive image processing operations, it is helpful to incur the overhead of converting the in-memory image format to `float`s just once so that subsequent operations can operate directly on `float` values.

⟨*Image Public Methods*⟩ +≡   **1079**
```
void CopyRectOut(const Bounds2i &extent, pstd::span<float> buf,
                 WrapMode2D wrapMode = WrapMode::Clamp) const;
void CopyRectIn(const Bounds2i &extent, pstd::span<const float> buf);
```

A number of methods compute aggregate statistics about the image. `Average()` returns the average value of each specified channel across the entire image.

⟨*Image Public Methods*⟩ +≡   **1079**
```
ImageChannelValues Average(const ImageChannelDesc &desc) const;
```

Two methods respectively check for pixels with infinite or not-a-number values.

⟨*Image Public Methods*⟩ +≡   **1079**
```
bool HasAnyInfinitePixels() const;
bool HasAnyNaNPixels() const;
```

Three methods measure error, comparing the image to a provided reference image, which should have the same resolution and named channels. Each takes a set of channels to include in the error computation and returns the error with respect to the specified metric. Optionally, they return an `Image` where each pixel stores its error.

`MAE()` computes mean absolute error—the absolute value of the difference with the reference image. `MSE()` computes mean squared error, and `MRSE()` computes mean relative squared error, which is based on dividing the squared error by the reference value.

⟨*Image Public Methods*⟩ +≡   1079
```
    ImageChannelValues MAE(const ImageChannelDesc &desc, const Image &ref,
                           Image *errorImage = nullptr) const;
    ImageChannelValues MSE(const ImageChannelDesc &desc, const Image &ref,
                           Image *mseImage = nullptr) const;
    ImageChannelValues MRSE(const ImageChannelDesc &desc, const Image &ref,
                            Image *mrseImage = nullptr) const;
```

Finally, GetSamplingDistribution() returns a 2D array of scalar weights for use in importance sampling. The weights are not normalized, but are suitable to be directly passed to the PiecewiseConstant2D class's constructor. The caller can optionally specify the domain of the image as well as a function that returns a change of variables factor if the final sampling domain is not uniform and over $[0, 1]^2$. This factor is then included in the sampling distribution.

⟨*Image Public Methods*⟩ +≡   1079
```
    template <typename F>
    Array2D<Float> GetSamplingDistribution(
        F dxdA, const Bounds2f &domain = Bounds2f(Point2f(0, 0), Point2f(1, 1)),
        Allocator alloc = {});
    Array2D<Float> GetSamplingDistribution() {
        return GetSamplingDistribution([](Point2f) { return Float(1); });
    }
```

B.5.3 READING AND WRITING IMAGES

Many image file formats have been developed over the years and it is worthwhile to support a variety of them, especially for the convenience of scene specification. pbrt is able to read a variety of other image formats, including JPG, TGA, BMP, GIF, PFM, HDR, and OpenEXR.[7]

For pbrt's image output requirements, we are mainly interested in those that support imagery represented by floating-point pixel values. In particular, the images generated by pbrt will often have a large dynamic range; such formats are crucial for being able to store the computed radiance values directly. Legacy image file formats that store 8 bits of data for red, green, and blue components to represent colors in the range [0, 1] are not a good fit for physically based rendering.

pbrt supports reading and writing two floating-point image file formats: OpenEXR and PFM. (Support for both reading and writing PNGs is also provided, though that format has limited dynamic range.) OpenEXR is a floating-point file format originally designed at Industrial Light and Magic for use in movie productions (Kainz et al. 2004). We chose this format because it has a clean design, is easy to use, and has first-class support for floating-point image data. Libraries that read and write OpenEXR images are freely available, and support for the format is available in many other tools.

PFM is a floating-point format based on an extension to the PPM file format; it is very easily read and written, though it is not as widely supported as OpenEXR. Unlike OpenEXR, it does not support compression, so files may be fairly large.

Allocator 40
Array2D 1069
Bounds2f 97
Float 23
Image 1079
ImageChannelDesc 1083
ImageChannelValues 1083
PiecewiseConstant2D 1019
Point2f 92

---

7   pbrt's PNG support is provided by Lode Vandevenne's *lodepng* library, PFM support is thanks to code from Jiawen Chen, and JPG, TGA, BMP, GIF, and HDR are thanks to Sean Barrett's *stb_image.h* library.

The Image Read() method attempts to read an image from the given file. It uses the suffix at the end of the filename to determine which image file format reader to use.

⟨*Image Public Methods*⟩ +≡   **1079**
```
static ImageAndMetadata Read(std::string filename, Allocator alloc = {},
                             ColorEncoding encoding = nullptr);
```

Image::Read() returns an instance of the ImageAndMetadata structure. In the event of an error reading the image, it issues an error message and exits immediately, so no error handling is required of the caller.

⟨*ImageAndMetadata Definition*⟩ ≡
```
struct ImageAndMetadata {
    Image image;
    ImageMetadata metadata;
};
```

Some image formats can store additional metadata beyond the pixel values; ImageMetadata is pbrt's container for this information. OpenEXR is particularly flexible in this regard: the user is free to add arbitrary named metadata using a variety of data types.

⟨*ImageMetadata Definition*⟩ ≡
```
struct ImageMetadata {
    ⟨ImageMetadata Public Methods⟩
    ⟨ImageMetadata Public Members 1086⟩
};
```

If the image has the corresponding metadata, pbrt's image reading routines initialize the following fields.

⟨*ImageMetadata Public Members*⟩ ≡   **1086**
```
pstd::optional<float> renderTimeSeconds;
pstd::optional<SquareMatrix<4>> cameraFromWorld, NDCFromWorld;
pstd::optional<Bounds2i> pixelBounds;
pstd::optional<Point2i> fullResolution;
pstd::optional<int> samplesPerPixel;
pstd::optional<const RGBColorSpace *> colorSpace;
```

The Write() method writes an image in one of the supported formats, based on the extension of the filename passed to it. It stores as much of the provided metadata as possible given the image format used.

⟨*Image Public Methods*⟩ +≡   **1079**
```
bool Write(std::string name, const ImageMetadata &metadata = {}) const;
```

B.5.4 RESIZING IMAGES

Image resizing involves application of the sampling and reconstruction theory from Chapter 8: we have an image function that has been sampled at one sampling rate, and we would like to reconstruct a continuous image function from the original samples to resample at a new set of sample positions. In this section, we will discuss the Image's FloatResizeUp() method, which resamples an image to a higher resolution. Because this represents an increase in the sampling rate from the original rate, we do not have to worry about introducing aliasing due to undersampling high-frequency components in this step; we only need to reconstruct and directly resample the new function. Figure B.6 illustrates this task in 1D.

A separable reconstruction filter is used for this task; recall from Section 8.8 that separable filters can be written as the product of 1D filters: $f(x, y) = f(x)f(y)$. One advantage of

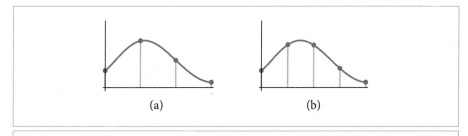

Figure B.6: To increase an image's resolution, the Image class performs two 1D resampling steps with a separable reconstruction filter. (a) A 1D function reconstructed from four samples, denoted by dots. (b) To represent the same image function with more samples, we only need to reconstruct the continuous function and evaluate it at the new positions.

a separable filter is that if we are using one to resample an image from one resolution (x, y) to another (x', y'), then we can implement the resampling as two 1D resampling steps, first resampling in x to create an image of resolution (x', y) and then resampling that image to create the final image of resolution (x', y'). Resampling the image via two 1D steps in this manner simplifies implementation and makes the number of pixels accessed for each pixel in the final image a linear function of the filter width, rather than a quadratic one.

Reconstructing the original image function and sampling it at a new pixel's position are mathematically equivalent to centering the reconstruction filter kernel at the new pixel's position and weighting the nearby pixels in the original image appropriately. Thus, each new pixel is a weighted average of a small number of pixels in the original image.

The Image::ResampleWeights() method utility determines which original pixels contribute to each new pixel and what the values are of the contribution weights for each new pixel. It returns the values in an array of ResampleWeight structures for all the pixels in a 1D row or column of the image. Because this information is the same for all rows of the image when resampling in x and all columns when resampling in y, it is more efficient to compute it once for each of the two passes and then reuse it many times for each one.

For the reconstruction filter used here, no more than four of the original pixels will contribute to each new pixel after resizing, so ResampleWeight only needs to hold four weights. Because the four pixels are contiguous, we only store the offset to the first one.

⟨*ResampleWeight Definition*⟩ ≡
```
struct ResampleWeight {
    int firstPixel;
    Float weight[4];
};
```

⟨*Image Method Definitions*⟩ ≡
```
std::vector<ResampleWeight> Image::ResampleWeights(int oldRes, int newRes) {
    std::vector<ResampleWeight> wt(newRes);
    Float filterRadius = 2, tau = 2;
    for (int i = 0; i < newRes; ++i) {
        ⟨Compute image resampling weights for ith pixel 1088⟩
        ⟨Normalize filter weights for pixel resampling 1088⟩
    }
    return wt;
}
```

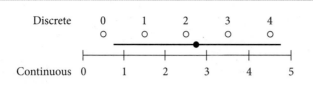

Figure B.7: The computation to find the first pixel inside a reconstruction filter's support is slightly tricky. Consider a filter centered around continuous coordinate 2.75 with radius 2, as shown here. The filter's support covers the range [0.75, 4.75], although pixel zero is outside the filter's support: adding 0.5 to the lower end before taking the floor to find the discrete pixel gives the correct starting pixel, number one.

Here is another instance where it is important to distinguish between discrete and continuous pixel coordinates. For each pixel in the resampled image, this function starts by computing its continuous coordinates in terms of the source image's pixel coordinates. This value is stored in center, because it is the center of the reconstruction filter for the new pixel. Next, it is necessary to find the offset to the first pixel that contributes to the new pixel. This is a slightly tricky calculation—after subtracting the filter width to find the start of the filter's nonzero range, it is necessary to add an extra 0.5 offset to the continuous coordinate before taking the floor to find the discrete coordinate. Figure B.7 illustrates why this offset is needed.

Starting from that first contributing pixel, this function loops over four pixels, computing each one's offset to the center of the filter kernel and the corresponding filter weight.

⟨*Compute image resampling weights for* ith *pixel*⟩ ≡   **1087**
```
Float center = (i + .5f) * oldRes / newRes;
wt[i].firstPixel = pstd::floor((center - filterRadius) + 0.5f);
for (int j = 0; j < 4; ++j) {
    Float pos = wt[i].firstPixel + j + .5f;
    wt[i].weight[j] = WindowedSinc(pos - center, filterRadius, tau);
}
```

The four filter weights generally do not sum to one. Therefore, to ensure that the resampled image will not be any brighter or darker than the original image, the weights are normalized here.

⟨*Normalize filter weights for pixel resampling*⟩ ≡   **1087**
```
Float invSumWts = 1 / (wt[i].weight[0] + wt[i].weight[1] +
                       wt[i].weight[2] + wt[i].weight[3]);
for (int j = 0; j < 4; ++j)
    wt[i].weight[j] *= invSumWts;
```

Given ResampleWeights(), we can continue to FloatResizeUp(), which resizes an image to a higher resolution and returns the result, with pixels stored as Floats in memory, regardless of the input image format.

⟨*Image Method Definitions*⟩ +≡
```
Image Image::FloatResizeUp(Point2i newRes, WrapMode2D wrapMode) const {
    Image resampledImage(PixelFormat::Float, newRes, channelNames);
    ⟨Compute x and y resampling weights for image resizing 1089⟩
    ⟨Resize image in parallel, working by tiles 1089⟩
    return resampledImage;
}
```

⟨*Compute x and y resampling weights for image resizing*⟩ ≡   1088
```
std::vector<ResampleWeight> xWeights, yWeights;
xWeights = ResampleWeights(resolution[0], newRes[0]);
yWeights = ResampleWeights(resolution[1], newRes[1]);
```

Given filter weights, the image is resized in parallel, where threads work on tiles of the output image. Although this parallelism scheme leads to some redundant work among threads from the need to compute extra pixel values at the boundaries of tiles, it has the advantage that the second filtering operation in y has a more compact memory access pattern, which gives a performance benefit from better cache coherence.

⟨*Resize image in parallel, working by tiles*⟩ ≡   1088
```
ParallelFor2D(Bounds2i({0, 0}, newRes), [&](Bounds2i outExtent) {
    ⟨Determine extent in source image and copy pixel values to inBuf 1089⟩
    ⟨Resize image in the x dimension  1089⟩
    ⟨Resize image in the y dimension⟩
    ⟨Copy resampled image pixels out into resampledImage 1090⟩
});
```

The first step copies all the pixel values that will be needed from the source image to compute the pixels in outExtent into a local buffer, inBuf. There are two reasons for doing this (versus accessing pixel values as needed from the input image): first, CopyRectOut() is generally more efficient than accessing the pixel channel values individually since not only are boundary conditions handled just once, but any necessary format conversion to Float is also done once for each pixel channel and in bulk. Second, the pixel channel values that will be accessed for subsequent filtering computations end up being contiguous in memory, which also improves cache coherence.

⟨*Determine extent in source image and copy pixel values to inBuf*⟩ ≡   1089
```
Bounds2i inExtent(Point2i(xWeights[outExtent.pMin.x].firstPixel,
                          yWeights[outExtent.pMin.y].firstPixel),
                  Point2i(xWeights[outExtent.pMax.x - 1].firstPixel + 4,
                          yWeights[outExtent.pMax.y - 1].firstPixel + 4));
std::vector<float> inBuf(NChannels() * inExtent.Area());
CopyRectOut(inExtent, pstd::span<float>(inBuf), wrapMode);
```

After allocating a temporary buffer for the x-resampled image, the following loops iterate over all its pixels to compute their resampled channel values.

⟨*Resize image in the x dimension*⟩ ≡   1089
```
⟨Compute image extents and allocate xBuf 1090⟩
int xBufOffset = 0;
for (int yOut = inExtent.pMin.y; yOut < inExtent.pMax.y; ++yOut) {
    for (int xOut = outExtent.pMin.x; xOut < outExtent.pMax.x; ++xOut) {
        ⟨Resample image pixel (xOut, yOut) 1090⟩
    }
}
```

The result of the x resampling step will be stored in xBuf. Note that it is necessary to perform the x resampling across all the scanlines in inExtent's y range, as the x-resampled instances of them will be needed for the y resampling step.

⟨*Compute image extents and allocate* xBuf⟩ ≡   **1089**
```
int nxOut = outExtent.pMax.x - outExtent.pMin.x;
int nyOut = outExtent.pMax.y - outExtent.pMin.y;
int nxIn = inExtent.pMax.x - inExtent.pMin.x;
int nyIn = inExtent.pMax.y - inExtent.pMin.y;
std::vector<float> xBuf(NChannels() * nyIn * nxOut);
```

Once all the values are lined up, the actual resampling operation is straightforward—effectively just the inner product of the normalized filter weights and pixel channel values.

⟨*Resample image pixel* (xOut, yOut)⟩ ≡   **1089**
```
const ResampleWeight &rsw = xWeights[xOut];
```
⟨*Compute* inOffset *into* inBuf *for* (xOut, yOut) **1090**⟩
```
for (int c = 0; c < NChannels(); ++c, ++xBufOffset, ++inOffset)
    xBuf[xBufOffset] = rsw.weight[0] * inBuf[inOffset] +
                       rsw.weight[1] * inBuf[inOffset + NChannels()] +
                       rsw.weight[2] * inBuf[inOffset + 2 * NChannels()] +
                       rsw.weight[3] * inBuf[inOffset + 3 * NChannels()];
```

The (xOut, yOut) pixel coordinate is with respect to the overall final resampled image. However, only the necessary input pixels for the tile have been copied to inBuf. Therefore, some reindexing is necessary to compute the offset into inBuf that corresponds to the first pixel that will be accessed to compute (xOut, yOut)'s *x*-resized value.

⟨*Compute* inOffset *into* inBuf *for* (xOut, yOut)⟩ ≡   **1090**
```
int xIn = rsw.firstPixel - inExtent.pMin.x;
int yIn = yOut - inExtent.pMin.y;
int inOffset = NChannels() * (xIn + yIn * nxIn);
```

The fragment ⟨*Resize image in the y dimension*⟩ follows a similar approach but filters along *y*, going from xBuf into outBuf. It is therefore not included here.

Given resampled pixels for outExtent, they can be copied in bulk to the output image via CopyRectIn().

⟨*Copy resampled image pixels out into* resampledImage⟩ ≡   **1089**
```
resampledImage.CopyRectIn(outExtent, outBuf);
```

B.5.5 IMAGE PYRAMIDS

The GeneratePyramid() method generates an image pyramid, which stores a source image, first resized if necessary to have power-of-two resolution in each dimension, at its base. Higher levels of the pyramid are successively found by downsampling the next lower level by a factor of two in each dimension. Image pyramids are widely used for accelerating image filtering operations and are a cornerstone of MIP mapping, which is implemented in pbrt's MIPMap class, defined in Section 10.4.3.

⟨*Image Method Definitions*⟩ +≡
```
pstd::vector<Image> Image::GeneratePyramid(Image image, WrapMode2D wrapMode,
                                           Allocator alloc) {
    PixelFormat origFormat = image.format;
    int nChannels = image.NChannels();
    ColorEncoding origEncoding = image.encoding;
    ⟨Prepare image for building pyramid 1091⟩
```

⟨*Initialize levels of pyramid from* image **1091**⟩
⟨*Initialize top level of pyramid and return it* **1093**⟩
}

Implementation of an image pyramid is easier if the resolution of the original image is an exact power of two in each direction; this ensures that there is a direct relationship between the level of the pyramid and the number of texels at that level. If the user has provided an image where the resolution in one or both of the dimensions is not a power of two, then the GeneratePyramid() method calls FloatResizeUp() to resize the image up to the next power-of-two resolution greater than the original resolution before constructing the pyramid. (Exercise B.1 at the end of the chapter describes an approach for building image pyramids with non-power-of-two resolutions.)

Otherwise, if the provided image does not use 32-bit floats for its in-memory format, it is converted to that representation. This helps avoid errors in the image pyramid due to insufficient precision being used for the inputs to the filtering computations. (In the end, however, the returned pyramid will have images in the format of the original image so that memory use is not unnecessarily increased.)

These two operations motivate taking the Image as a parameter to a static method, as GeneratePyramid() is, rather than being a non-static member function. Thus, a new image can easily be reassigned to image as necessary.

⟨*Prepare* image *for building pyramid*⟩ ≡   1090
```
if (!IsPowerOf2(image.resolution[0]) || !IsPowerOf2(image.resolution[1]))
    image = image.FloatResizeUp(Point2i(RoundUpPow2(image.resolution[0]),
                                        RoundUpPow2(image.resolution[1])),
                                wrapMode);
else if (!Is32Bit(image.format))
    image = image.ConvertToFormat(PixelFormat::Float);
```

Once we have a floating-point image with resolutions that are powers of two, the levels of the MIP map can be initialized, starting from the bottom (finest) level. Each higher level is found by filtering the texels from the previous level.

⟨*Initialize levels of pyramid from* image⟩ ≡   1090
```
int nLevels = 1 + Log2Int(std::max(image.resolution[0],
                                   image.resolution[1]));
pstd::vector<Image> pyramid(alloc);
for (int i = 0; i < nLevels - 1; ++i) {
    ⟨Initialize i + 1st level from ith level and copy ith into pyramid 1091⟩
}
```

Each time through this loop, image starts out as the already-filtered image for the ith level that will be downsampled to generate the image for the $i + 1$st level. A new entry is added to the image pyramid for image, though using the original pixel format.

⟨*Initialize* $i + 1$*st level from* i*th level and copy* i*th into pyramid*⟩ ≡   1091
```
pyramid.push_back(Image(origFormat, image.resolution, image.channelNames,
                        origEncoding, alloc));
```
⟨*Initialize* nextImage *for* $i + 1$*st level* **1092**⟩
⟨*Compute offsets from pixels to the 4 pixels used for downsampling* **1092**⟩
⟨*Downsample* image *to create next level and update* pyramid **1092**⟩

For non-square images, the resolution in one direction must be clamped to 1 for the upper levels of the image pyramid, where there is still downsampling to do in the larger of the two resolutions. This is handled by the following std::max() calls:

⟨*Initialize* nextImage *for i* + 1*st level*⟩ ≡   **1091**
```
    Point2i nextResolution(std::max(1, image.resolution[0] / 2),
                           std::max(1, image.resolution[1] / 2));
    Image nextImage(image.format, nextResolution, image.channelNames,
                    origEncoding);
```

GeneratePyramid() uses a simple box filter to average four texels from the previous level to find the value at the current texel. Using the Lanczos filter here would give a slightly better result for this computation, although this modification is left for Exercise B.2 at the end of the chapter.

With the box filter, each pixel (x, y) in nextImage is given by the average of the pixels $(2x, 2y)$, $(2x + 1, 2y)$, $(2x, 2y + 1)$, and $(2x + 1, 2y + 1)$. Here we compute the corresponding offsets from a pixel in the source image to those four pixels; doing this here saves some math in pixel indexing when downsampling. These offsets are based on the scanline-based layout of Image data in memory; referring to the implementation of Image::PixelOffset() may make their operation more clear.

Here is also a good chance to handle images with single pixel resolution in one dimension; in that case the offsets are set so that valid pixels are used twice, and the downsampling loop can be written to always assume four values.

⟨*Compute offsets from pixels to the 4 pixels used for downsampling*⟩ ≡   **1091**
```
    int srcDeltas[4] = {0, nChannels, nChannels * image.resolution[0],
                        nChannels * (image.resolution[0] + 1)};
    if (image.resolution[0] == 1) {
        srcDeltas[1] = 0;
        srcDeltas[3] -= nChannels;
    }
    if (image.resolution[1] == 1) {
        srcDeltas[2] = 0;
        srcDeltas[3] -= nChannels * image.resolution[0];
    }
```

The work for the current level is performed in parallel since each output pixel's value is independent of the others. For scenes with many textures, MIP map generation may be a meaningful amount of pbrt's startup time, so it is worthwhile to try to optimize this work done by this method so that rendering can begin more quickly. When the work for each level is finished, the image for the next level is assigned to image so that the loop can proceed once again.

⟨*Downsample* image *to create next level and update* pyramid⟩ ≡   **1091**
```
    ParallelFor(0, nextResolution[1], [&](int64_t y) {
        ⟨Loop over pixels in scanline y and downsample for the next pyramid level 1093⟩
        ⟨Copy two scanlines from image out to its pyramid level 1093⟩
    });
    image = std::move(nextImage);
```

The following fragment computes a scanline's worth of downsampled pixel values in next Image. It makes extensive use of the fact that the channels for each pixel are laid out consecutively in memory and that pixels are stored in scanline order in memory. Thus, it can compute offsets into the pixel arrays for the y scanline starting at $x = 0$ and efficiently incrementally update them for each image channel and each pixel. Note also that the offsets to the neighboring pixels from srcDeltas are used to efficiently find the necessary pixel values from image.

⟨*Loop over pixels in scanline y and downsample for the next pyramid level*⟩ ≡   1092
```
int srcOffset = image.PixelOffset(Point2i(0, 2 * int(y)));
int nextOffset = nextImage.PixelOffset(Point2i(0, int(y)));
for (int x = 0; x < nextResolution[0]; ++x, srcOffset += nChannels)
    for (int c = 0; c < nChannels; ++c, ++srcOffset, ++nextOffset)
        nextImage.p32[nextOffset] =
            (image.p32[srcOffset] + image.p32[srcOffset + srcDeltas[1]] +
             image.p32[srcOffset + srcDeltas[2]] +
             image.p32[srcOffset + srcDeltas[3]]) / 4;
```

We will take advantage of the fact that processing is happening in parallel here to also copy pixel values from image into their place in the pyramid. Doing so here has the added benefit that the pixel values should already be in the cache from their use as inputs to the downsampling computation.

Because the ParallelFor() loop is over scanlines in the lower-resolution image, two scanlines from image are copied here except in the edge case of a single-scanline-high image from a non-square-input image. The Image CopyRectIn() method copies the pixels inside the provided bounds, taking care of converting them to the format of the destination image pixels if necessary.

⟨*Copy two scanlines from image out to its pyramid level*⟩ ≡   1092
```
int yStart = 2 * y;
int yEnd = std::min(2 * int(y) + 2, image.resolution[1]);
int offset = image.PixelOffset({0, yStart});
size_t count = (yEnd - yStart) * nChannels * image.resolution[0];
pyramid[i].CopyRectIn(Bounds2i({0, yStart}, {image.resolution[0], yEnd}),
                      pstd::span<const float>(image.p32.data() + offset, count));
```

After the loop terminates, we are left with a 1×1 image to copy into the top level of the image pyramid before it can be returned.

⟨*Initialize top level of pyramid and return it*⟩ ≡   1090
```
pyramid.push_back(Image(origFormat, {1, 1}, image.channelNames,
                        origEncoding, alloc));
pyramid[nLevels - 1].CopyRectIn(Bounds2i({0, 0}, {1, 1}),
                      pstd::span<const float>(image.p32.data(), nChannels));
return pyramid;
```

B.5.6 COLOR ENCODINGS

Color spaces often define a *transfer function* that is used to encode color component values that are stored in the color space. Transfer functions date to cathode ray tube (CRT) displays, which had a nonlinear relationship between display intensity and the voltage V of the electron gun, which was modeled with a gamma curve V^γ. With CRTs, doubling the RGB color components stored at a pixel did not lead to a doubling of displayed intensity, an undesirable nonlinearity at the end of a rendering process that is built on an assumption of linearity. It was therefore necessary to apply *gamma correction* to image pixels using the inverse of the gamma curve so that the image on the screen had a linear relationship between intensity and pixel values.

While modern displays no longer use electron guns, it is still worthwhile to use a nonlinear mapping with colors that are stored in quantized representations (e.g., 8-bit pixel components). One reason to do so is suggested by *Weber's law*, which is based on the observation that an increase of 1% of a stimulus value (e.g., displayed color) is generally required before a human observer notices a change—this is the *just noticeable difference*. In turn, a pixel encoding that allocates multiple values to invisible differences is inefficient, at least for display. Weber's law also suggests a power law–based encoding, along the lines of gamma correction.

pbrt does most of its computation using floating-point color values, for which there is no need to apply a color encoding. (And indeed, such an encoding would need to be inverted any time a computation was performed with such a color value.) However, it is necessary to support color encodings to decode color values from non-floating-point image formats like PNG as well as to encode them before writing images in such formats.

The ColorEncoding class defines the ColorEncoding interface, which handles both encoding and decoding color in various ways.

⟨*ColorEncoding Definitions*⟩ ≡
```
class ColorEncoding
    : public TaggedPointer<LinearColorEncoding, sRGBColorEncoding,
                           GammaColorEncoding> {
  public:
    ⟨ColorEncoding Interface 1094⟩
};
```

The two main methods that ColorEncodings must provide are ToLinear(), which takes a set of encoded 8-bit color values and converts them to linear Floats, and FromLinear(), which does the reverse. Both of these take buffers of potentially many values to convert at once, which saves dynamic dispatch overhead compared to invoking them for each value independently.

⟨*ColorEncoding Interface*⟩ ≡   **1094**
```
void ToLinear(pstd::span<const uint8_t> vin,
              pstd::span<Float> vout) const;
void FromLinear(pstd::span<const Float> vin,
                pstd::span<uint8_t> vout) const;
```

It is sometimes useful to decode values with greater than 8-bit precision (e.g., some image formats like PNG are able to store 16-bit color channels). Such cases are handled by ToFloatLinear(), which takes a single encoded value stored as a Float and decodes it.

⟨*ColorEncoding Interface*⟩ +≡   **1094**
```
Float ToFloatLinear(Float v) const;
```

The LinearColorEncoding class is trivial: it divides 8-bit values by 255 to convert them to Floats and does the reverse to convert back. pbrt also provides GammaColorEncoding, which applies a plain gamma curve of specified exponent. Neither of these are included in the text here.

sRGBColorEncoding implements the encoding specified by the sRGB color space. It combines a linear segment for small values with a power curve for larger ones.

⟨*ColorEncoding Definitions*⟩ +≡
```
class sRGBColorEncoding {
  public:
    ⟨sRGBColorEncoding Public Methods⟩
};
```

A linear value x is converted to an sRGB-encoded value x_e by

$$x_e = \begin{cases} 12.92x & x \leq 0.0031308 \\ 1.055x^{1/2.4} - 0.055 & \text{otherwise.} \end{cases}$$

The work of conversion is handled by the `LinearToSRGB8()` function, which is not included here. It uses a rational polynomial approximation to avoid the cost of a `std::pow()` call in computing the encoded value.

⟨*ColorEncoding Method Definitions*⟩ ≡
```
void sRGBColorEncoding::FromLinear(pstd::span<const Float> vin,
                                   pstd::span<uint8_t> vout) const {
    for (size_t i = 0; i < vin.size(); ++i)
        vout[i] = LinearToSRGB8(vin[i]);
}
```

The inverse transformation is

$$x = \begin{cases} \frac{x_e}{12.92} & x_e \leq 0.04045 \\ \left(\frac{x_e + 0.055}{1.055}\right)^{2.4} & \text{otherwise.} \end{cases}$$

For 8-bit encoded values, the `SRGB8ToLinear()` function uses a precomputed 256-entry lookup table. A separate `SRGBToLinear()` uses a rational polynomial approximation for arbitrary floating-point values between 0 and 1.

⟨*ColorEncoding Method Definitions*⟩ +≡
```
void sRGBColorEncoding::ToLinear(pstd::span<const uint8_t> vin,
                                 pstd::span<Float> vout) const {
    for (size_t i = 0; i < vin.size(); ++i)
        vout[i] = SRGB8ToLinear(vin[i]);
}
```

The linear and sRGB encodings are widely used in the system, so they are made available via `static` member variables in the `ColorEncoding` class.

⟨*ColorEncoding Interface*⟩ +≡   1094
```
static ColorEncoding Linear;
static ColorEncoding sRGB;
```

B.6 PARALLELISM

As improvements in the performance of single processing cores have slowed over the past fifteen years, it has become increasingly important to write parallel programs in order to reach the full computational capabilities of a system. Fortunately, ray tracing offers abundant independent work, which makes it easier to distribute work across processing cores. This section discusses some important principles of parallelism, focusing on CPUs, and introduces assorted classes and functions that pbrt uses for parallelism. (See Section 15.1 for discussion of parallelism on GPUs and how pbrt is parallelized on those processors.)

ColorEncoding 1094
Float 23
LinearToSRGB8() 1095

One of the biggest challenges with parallel ray tracing is the impact of nonparallel phases of computation. For example, it is not as easy to effectively parallelize the construction of many types of acceleration structure while the scene is being constructed as it is to parallelize rendering. While this may seem like a minor issue, *Amdahl's law*, which describes the speedup of a workload that has both serial and parallel phases, points to the challenge. Given n cores performing computation and a workload where the fraction s of its overall computation is inherently serial, the maximum speedup then possible is

$$\frac{1}{s + \frac{1}{n}(1 - s)}.$$

Thus, even with an infinite number of cores, the maximum speedup is $1/s$. If, for example, a seemingly innocuous 5% of the run time is spent in a serial phase of parsing the scene file and building acceleration structures, the maximum speedup possible is $1/0.05 = 20\times$, no matter how quickly the parallel phase executes.

We experienced the impact of Amdahl's law as we brought pbrt's GPU rendering path to life: it was often the case that it took longer to parse the scene description and to prepare the scene for rendering than it took to render the image, even at high sampling rates! This led to more attention to parallelizing parsing and creating the objects that represent the scene. (See Section C.3 for further discussion of this topic.)

B.6.1 DATA RACES AND COORDINATION

When pbrt is running on the CPU, we assume that the computation is running on processors that provide *coherent shared memory*. The main idea of coherent shared memory is that all threads can read and write to a common set of memory locations and that changes to memory made by one thread will eventually be seen by other threads. These properties greatly simplify the implementation of the system, as there is no need to explicitly communicate data between cores.

Although coherent shared memory relieves the need for separate threads to explicitly communicate data with each other, they still need to *coordinate* their access to shared data; a danger of coherent shared memory is *data races*. If two threads modify the same memory location without coordination between the two of them, the program will almost certainly compute incorrect results or even crash. Consider the example of two processors simultaneously running the following innocuous-looking code, where globalCounter starts with a value of two:

```
extern int globalCounter;
if (--globalCounter == 0)
    printf("done\n");
```

Because the two threads do not coordinate their reading and writing of globalCounter, it is possible that "done" will be printed zero, one, or even two times. For example, if both threads simultaneously load globalCounter, decrement it in a local register, and then write the result simultaneously, both will write a value of 1 and "done" will never be printed.[8]

Two main mechanisms are used for this type of synchronization: mutual exclusion and atomic operations. Mutual exclusion is implemented with std::mutex objects in pbrt. A

8　More generally, C++ defines such uncoordinated access to be "undefined behavior," which in turn means that what happens in subsequent program execution is completely undefined.

`std::mutex` can be used to protect access to some resource, ensuring that only one thread can access it at a time:

```
extern int globalCounter;
extern std::mutex globalCounterMutex;
globalCounterMutex.lock();
if (--globalCounter == 0)
    printf("done\n");
globalCounterMutex.unlock();
```

Atomic memory operations (or *atomics*) are the other option for correctly performing this type of memory update with multiple threads. Atomics are machine instructions that guarantee that their respective memory updates will be performed in a single transaction. (*Atomic* in this case refers to the notion that the memory updates are indivisible.) The implementations of atomic operations in pbrt are from the C++ standard library. Using atomics, the computation above could be written to use the `std::atomic<int>` type, which has overloaded add, subtract, increment, and decrement operations, as below:

```
extern std::atomic<int> globalCounter;
if (--globalCounter == 0)
    printf("done\n");
```

The `std::atomic --` operator subtracts one from the given variable, `globalCounter`, and returns the new value of the variable. Using an atomic operation ensures that if two threads simultaneously try to update the variable, then not only will the final value of the variable be the expected value, but each thread will be returned the value of the variable after its update alone. In this example, then, `globalCounter` will end up with a value of zero, as expected, with one thread guaranteed to have the value one returned from the atomic subtraction and the other thread guaranteed to have zero returned.

Another useful atomic operation is "compare and swap," which is also provided by the C++ standard library. It takes a memory location and the value that the caller believes the location currently stores. If the memory location still holds that value when the atomic compare and swap executes, then a new value is stored and `true` is returned; otherwise, memory is left unchanged and `false` is returned.

Compare and swap is a building block that can be used to build many other atomic operations. For example, the code below could be executed by multiple threads to compute the maximum of values computed by all the threads. (For this particular case, the specialized atomic maximum function would be a better choice, but this example helps convey the usage.)

```
std::atomic<int> maxValue;
int localMax = ...;
int currentMax = maxValue;
while (localMax > currentMax) {
    if (maxValue.compare_exchange_weak(currentMax, localMax))
        break;
}
```

If only a single thread is trying to update the memory location and the local value is larger, the loop is successful the first time through; the value loaded into `currentMax` is still the value stored by `maxValue` when `compare_exchange_weak()` executes and so `localMax` is successfully stored and `true` is returned.[9] If multiple threads are executing concurrently, then another thread may update the value in `maxValue` between the thread's read of `maxValue` and the execution of `compare_exchange_weak()`. In that case, the compare and swap fails, memory is not updated, and another pass is taken through the loop to try again. In the case of a failure, `compare_exchange_weak()` updates `currentMax` with the new value of `maxValue`.

An important application of atomic compare and swap is for the construction of data structures. Consider, for example, a tree data structure where each node has child node pointers initially set to `nullptr`. If code traversing the tree wants to create a new child at a node, code could be written like:

```
// atomic<Type *> node->firstChild
if (!node->firstChild) {
    Type *newChild = new Type ...
    Type *current = nullptr;
    if (node->firstChild.compare_exchange_weak(current, newChild) == false)
        delete newChild;
}
// node->firstChild != nullptr now
```

The idea is that if the child has the value `nullptr`, the thread speculatively creates and fully initializes the child node into a local variable, not yet visible to the other threads. Atomic compare and swap is then used to try to initialize the child pointer; if it still has the value `nullptr`, then the new child is stored and made available to all threads. If the child pointer no longer has the value `nullptr`, then another thread has initialized the child in the time between the current thread first seeing that it was `nullptr` and later trying to update it. In this case, the work done in the current thread turns out to have been wasted, but it can delete the locally created child node and continue execution, using the node created by the other thread.

This method of tree construction is an example of a *lock-free* algorithm. This approach has a few advantages compared to, for example, using a single mutex to manage updating the tree. First, there is no overhead of acquiring the mutex for regular tree traversal. Second, multiple threads can naturally concurrently update different parts of the tree. The "Further Reading" section at the end of this appendix has pointers to more information about lock-free algorithms.

B.6.2 ATOMIC FLOATING-POINT VALUES

The `std::atomic` template cannot be used with floating-point types. One of the main reasons that atomic operations are not supported with it is that floating-point operations are generally not associative: as discussed in Section 6.8.1, when computed in floating-point, the value of the sum `(a+b)+c` is not necessarily equal to the sum `a+(b+c)`. In turn, if a multi-threaded computation used atomic floating-point addition operations to compute some value, then the result computed would not be the same across multiple program executions. (In contrast, with integer types all the supported operations are associative, and so atomic operations give consistent results no matter which order threads perform them in.)

For pbrt's needs, these inconsistencies are generally tolerable, and being able to use atomic operations on `Float`s is preferable in some cases to using a lock. (One example is splatting

9 The "weak" in the compare/exchange instruction refers to the shared memory model required of the underlying hardware. For our purposes, the lesser requirement of "weak" is fine, as it can be much more efficient than a strongly ordered memory model on some architectures. In return for this choice, the compare and exchange may occasionally fail incorrectly, so it requires a retry loop as we have implemented here.

pixel contributions in the `RGBFilm::AddSplat()` and `GBufferFilm::AddSplat()` methods.) For these purposes, we provide a small `AtomicFloat` class.

⟨*AtomicFloat Definition*⟩ ≡
```
class AtomicFloat {
  public:
    ⟨AtomicFloat Public Methods 1099⟩
  private:
    ⟨AtomicFloat Private Members 1099⟩
};
```

An `AtomicFloat` can be initialized from a provided floating-point value. In the implementation here, floating-point values are actually represented as their unsigned integer bitwise values, as returned by the `FloatToBits()` function.

⟨*AtomicFloat Public Methods*⟩ ≡   1099
```
explicit AtomicFloat(float v = 0) {
    bits = FloatToBits(v);
}
```

Using an integer type to represent the value allows us to use a `std::atomic` type to store it in memory, which in turn allows the compiler to be aware that the value in memory is being updated atomically.

⟨*AtomicFloat Private Members*⟩ ≡   1099
```
std::atomic<FloatBits> bits;
```

Assigning the value or returning it as a `Float` is just a matter of converting to or from the unsigned integer representation.

⟨*AtomicFloat Public Methods*⟩ +≡   1099
```
operator float() const {
    return BitsToFloat(bits);
}
Float operator=(float v) {
    bits = FloatToBits(v);
    return v;
}
```

Atomic floating-point addition is implemented via an atomic compare and exchange operation. In the do loop below, we convert the in-memory bit representation of the value to a `Float`, add the provided difference in v, and attempt to atomically store the resulting bits. If the in-memory value has been changed by another thread since the value from `bits` was read from memory, the implementation continues retrying until the value in memory matches the expected value (in `oldBits`), at which point the atomic update succeeds.

⟨*AtomicFloat Public Methods*⟩ +≡   1099
```
void Add(float v) {
    FloatBits oldBits = bits, newBits;
    do {
        newBits = FloatToBits(BitsToFloat(oldBits) + v);
    } while (!bits.compare_exchange_weak(oldBits, newBits));
}
```

pbrt does not currently need to perform any other operations on `AtomicFloats`, so we do not provide any additional methods. An `AtomicDouble` class, not included here, provides an equivalent `Add()` method for atomic addition with `doubles`.

B.6.3 MEMORY COHERENCE MODELS AND PERFORMANCE

Cache coherence is a feature of all modern multicore CPUs; with it, memory writes by one processor are automatically visible to other processors. This is an incredibly useful feature; being able to assume it in the implementation of a system like pbrt is extremely helpful to the programmer. Understanding the subtleties and performance characteristics of this feature is important, however.

One potential issue is that other processors may not see writes to memory in the same order that the processor that performed the writes issued them. This can happen for two main reasons: the compiler's optimizer may have reordered write operations to improve performance, and the CPU hardware may write values to memory in a different order than the stream of executed machine instructions. When only a single thread is running, both of these are innocuous; by design, the compiler and hardware, respectively, ensure that it is impossible for a single thread of execution running the program to detect when these cases happen. This guarantee is not provided for multi-threaded code, however; doing so would impose a significant performance penalty, so hardware architectures leave requiring such ordering, when it matters, to software.

Memory barrier instructions can be used to ensure that all write instructions before the barrier are visible in memory before any subsequent instructions execute. In practice, we generally do not need to issue memory barrier instructions explicitly, since both C++ atomic and the thread synchronization calls used to build multi-threaded algorithms can include them in their operation.

Although cache coherence is helpful to the programmer, it can sometimes impose a substantial performance penalty for data that is frequently modified and accessed by multiple processors. Read-only data has little penalty; copies of it can be stored in the local caches of all the processors that are accessing it, allowing all of them the same performance benefits from the caches as in the single-threaded case. To understand the downside of taking too much advantage of cache coherence for read–write data, it is useful to understand how cache coherence is typically implemented on processors.

CPUs implement a *cache coherence protocol*, which is responsible for tracking the memory transactions issued by all the processors in order to provide cache coherence. A classic such protocol is *MESI*, where the acronym represents the four states that each cache line can be in. Each processor stores the current state for each cache line in its local caches:

- *Modified*—The current processor has written to the memory location, but the result is only stored in the cache—it is *dirty* and has not been written to main memory. No other processor has the location in its cache.
- *Exclusive*—The current processor is the only one with the data from the corresponding memory location in its cache. The value in the cache matches the value in memory.
- *Shared*—Multiple processors have the corresponding memory location in their caches, but they have only performed read operations.
- *Invalid*—The cache line does not hold valid data.

At system startup time, the caches are empty and all cache lines are in the invalid state. The first time a processor reads a memory location, the data for that location is loaded into cache and its cache line marked as being in the "exclusive" state. If another processor performs a memory read of a location that is in the "exclusive" state in another cache, then both caches record the state for the corresponding memory location to instead be "shared."

When a processor writes to a memory location, the performance of the write depends on the state of the corresponding cache line. If it is in the "exclusive" state and already in the writing processor's cache, then the write is cheap; the data is modified in the cache and the cache line's state is changed to "modified." (If it was already in the "modified" state, then the write is similarly efficient.) In these cases, the value will eventually be written to main memory, at which point the corresponding cache line returns to the "exclusive" state.

However, if a processor writes to a memory location that is in the "shared" state in its cache or is in the "modified" or "exclusive" state in another processor's cache, then expensive communication between the cores is required. All of this is handled transparently by the hardware, though it still has a performance impact. In this case, the writing processor must issue a *read for ownership* (RFO), which marks the memory location as invalid in the caches of any other processors; RFOs can cause stalls of tens or hundreds of cycles—a substantial penalty for a single memory write.

In general, we would therefore like to avoid the situation of multiple processors concurrently writing to the same memory location as well as unnecessarily reading memory that another processor is writing to. An important case to be aware of is "false sharing," where a single cache line holds some read-only data and some data that is frequently modified. In this case, even if only a single processor is writing to the part of the cache line that is modified but many are reading from the read-only part, the overhead of frequent RFO operations will be unnecessarily incurred. pbrt uses alignas in the declaration of classes that are modified during rendering and are susceptible to false sharing in order to ensure that they take entire cache lines for themselves. A macro makes the system's cache line size available.

⟨*Define Cache Line Size Constant*⟩ ≡
```
#ifdef PBRT_BUILD_GPU_RENDERER
#define PBRT_L1_CACHE_LINE_SIZE 128
#else
#define PBRT_L1_CACHE_LINE_SIZE 64
#endif
```

8.6.4 THREAD POOLS AND PARALLEL JOBS

Although C++ provides a portable abstraction for CPU threads via its std::thread class, creating and then destroying threads each time there is parallel work to do is usually not a good approach. Thread creation requires calls to the operating system, which must allocate and update data structures to account for each thread; this work consumes processing cycles that we would prefer to devote to rendering. Further, unchecked creation of threads can overwhelm the processor with many more threads than it is capable of executing concurrently. Flooding it with more work than it can handle may be detrimental to its ability to get through it.

A widely used solution to both of these issues is *thread pools*. With a thread pool, a fixed number of threads are launched at system startup time. They persist throughout the program's execution, waiting for parallel work to help out with and sleeping when there is no work for them to do. In pbrt, the call to InitPBRT() creates a pool of worker threads (generally, one for each available CPU core). A further advantage of this implementation approach is that providing work to the threads is a fairly lightweight operation, which encourages the use of the thread pool even for fine-grained tasks.

InitPBRT() 1032

PBRT_L1_CACHE_LINE_SIZE 1101

⟨*ThreadPool Definition*⟩ ≡
```
class ThreadPool {
  public:
    ⟨ThreadPool Public Methods⟩
  private:
    ⟨ThreadPool Private Methods⟩
    ⟨ThreadPool Private Members 1102⟩
};
```

pbrt's main thread of execution also participates in executing parallel work, so the ThreadPool constructor launches one fewer than the requested number of threads.

⟨*ThreadPool Method Definitions*⟩ ≡
```
ThreadPool::ThreadPool(int nThreads) {
    for (int i = 0; i < nThreads - 1; ++i)
        threads.push_back(std::thread(&ThreadPool::Worker, this));
}
```

⟨*ThreadPool Private Members*⟩ ≡   **1102**
```
std::vector<std::thread> threads;
```

The worker threads all run the ThreadPool's Worker() method, which acquires a mutex and calls WorkOrWait() until system shutdown, at which point shutdownThreads will be set to true to signal the worker threads to exit. When we get to the implementation of WorkOrWait(), we will see that this mutex is only held briefly, until the thread is able to determine whether or not there is more work for it to perform.

⟨*ThreadPool Method Definitions*⟩ +≡
```
void ThreadPool::Worker() {
    std::unique_lock<std::mutex> lock(mutex);
    while (!shutdownThreads)
        WorkOrWait(&lock, false);
}
```

⟨*ThreadPool Private Members*⟩ +≡   **1102**
```
mutable std::mutex mutex;
bool shutdownThreads = false;
```

Before we get to the implementation of the WorkOrWait() method, we will discuss the ParallelJob class, which specifies an abstract interface for work that is executed by the thread pool and defines a few member variables that the ThreadPool will use to keep track of work. Because it is only used for CPU parallelism and is not used on the GPU, we will use regular virtual functions for dynamic dispatch in its implementation.

⟨*ParallelJob Definition*⟩ ≡
```
class ParallelJob {
  public:
    ⟨ParallelJob Public Methods 1103⟩
    ⟨ParallelJob Public Members 1103⟩
  private:
    ⟨ParallelJob Private Members 1103⟩
};
```

All the parallel work in pbrt is handled by a single thread pool managed by ParallelJob.

ThreadPool 1102
ThreadPool::mutex 1102
ThreadPool::shutdownThreads 1102
ThreadPool::threads 1102
ThreadPool::Worker() 1102
ThreadPool::WorkOrWait() 1104

⟨*ParallelJob Public Members*⟩ ≡   **1102**
```
static ThreadPool *threadPool;
```

Each job may consist of one or more independent tasks. The two key methods that `Parallel`
`Job` implementations must provide are `HaveWork()` and `RunStep()`. The former indicates
whether there is any remaining work that has not yet commenced, and when the latter is
called, some of the remaining work should be done. The implementation can assume that
none of its methods will be called concurrently by multiple threads—in other words, that
the calling code uses a mutex to ensure mutual exclusion.

`RunStep()` is further passed a pointer to a lock that is already held when the method is called.
It should be unlocked at its return.

⟨*ParallelJob Public Methods*⟩ ≡   **1102**
```
virtual bool HaveWork() const = 0;
virtual void RunStep(std::unique_lock<std::mutex> *lock) = 0;
```

`ParallelJob` carries along a few member variables that are purely for the use of the `Thread`
`Pool`. Including them in the `ParallelJob` class here saves the thread pool from needing to
dynamically allocate any per-job storage. One is `activeWorkers`, which the thread pool uses
to track how many threads are currently working on the job.

⟨*ParallelJob Private Members*⟩ ≡   **1102**
```
friend class ThreadPool;
int activeWorkers = 0;
```

In turn, a job is only finished if there is no more work to be handed out and if no threads are
currently working on it.

⟨*ParallelJob Public Methods*⟩ +≡   **1102**
```
bool Finished() const { return !HaveWork() && activeWorkers == 0; }
```

Returning to the `ThreadPool` implementation now, we will consider how work to be done is
managed. The `ThreadPool` maintains a doubly linked list of jobs where its `jobList` member
variable points to the list's head. `ThreadPool::mutex` must always be held when accessing
`jobList` or values stored in the `ParallelJob` objects held in it.

⟨*ThreadPool Private Members*⟩ +≡   **1102**
```
ParallelJob *jobList = nullptr;
```

The link pointers are stored as `ParallelJob` member variables that are just for the use of the
`ThreadPool` and should not be accessed by the `ParallelJob` implementation.

⟨*ParallelJob Private Members*⟩ +≡   **1102**
```
ParallelJob *prev = nullptr, *next = nullptr;
```

`AddToJobList()` acquires the mutex and adds the provided job to the work list before using
a condition variable to signal the worker threads so that they wake up and start taking work
from the list. The mutex lock is returned to the caller so that it can do any further job-related
setup, assured that work will not start until it releases the lock.

⟨*ThreadPool Method Definitions*⟩ +≡

```
std::unique_lock<std::mutex> ThreadPool::AddToJobList(ParallelJob *job) {
    std::unique_lock<std::mutex> lock(mutex);
    ⟨Add job to head of jobList 1104⟩
    jobListCondition.notify_all();
    return lock;
}
```

Jobs are added to the front of the work list. In this way, if some parallel work enqueues additional work, the additional work will be processed before more is done on the initial work. This corresponds to depth-first processing of the work if dependent jobs are considered as a tree, which can avoid an explosion in the number of items in the work list.

⟨*Add* job *to head of* jobList⟩ ≡   **1104**

```
if (jobList)
    jobList->prev = job;
job->next = jobList;
jobList = job;
```

When there is no available work, worker threads wait on the jobListCondition condition variable.

⟨*ThreadPool Private Members*⟩ +≡   **1102**

```
std::condition_variable jobListCondition;
```

We can finally return to the WorkOrWait() method that all threads execute. The lock provided to it is of the mutex member variable, so it is safe to access other ThreadPool members as long as it is held. Its second parameter, isEnqueuingThread, is used when the thread pool has been temporarily disabled to ensure that only the thread that submits work performs computation in that case. (That capability is needed for an arcane situation in the implementation of some of pbrt's GPU code, so it is not discussed further here.)

The method implementation starts by walking through the job list in search of a ParallelJob that still has work left.

⟨*ThreadPool Method Definitions*⟩ +≡

```
void ThreadPool::WorkOrWait(std::unique_lock<std::mutex> *lock,
                            bool isEnqueuingThread) {
    ⟨Return if this is a worker thread and the thread pool is disabled⟩
    ParallelJob *job = jobList;
    while (job && !job->HaveWork())
        job = job->next;
    if (job) {
        ⟨Execute work for job 1104⟩
    } else
        ⟨Wait for new work to arrive or the job to finish 1105⟩
}
```

If an unfinished job is found, then its active worker count is incremented and its RunStep() method is called with the lock passed along.

⟨*Execute work for* job⟩ ≡   **1104**

```
job->activeWorkers++;
job->RunStep(lock);
⟨Handle post-job-execution details 1105⟩
```

Recall that RunStep() methods should release the lock before they do their actual work, so the lock will not be held by this thread after that call returns. Thus, the lock must be reacquired before this thread can update activeWorkers and check to see if the job is completed. If it is, the condition variable must be signaled again: the thread that initially spawned the work may be waiting on the condition variable for other threads to finish their work on the job.

⟨*Handle post-job-execution details*⟩ ≡   1104
```
lock->lock();
job->activeWorkers--;
if (job->Finished())
    jobListCondition.notify_all();
```

Threads wait on the condition variable if there is no work to be done. The semantics of condition variables are such that the lock is released upon the call to wait(), but when the call returns due to the thread having been woken up, it will again hold the lock.

⟨*Wait for new work to arrive or the job to finish*⟩ ≡   1104
```
jobListCondition.wait(*lock);
```

Removing a job from the list just requires rewiring the pointers of adjacent list nodes, if present, and updating the list head pointer if the job is at the head.

⟨*ThreadPool Method Definitions*⟩ +≡
```
void ThreadPool::RemoveFromJobList(ParallelJob *job) {
    if (job->prev)
        job->prev->next = job->next;
    else
        jobList = job->next;
    if (job->next)
        job->next->prev = job->prev;
}
```

The ThreadPool::WorkOrReturn() method is very similar to WorkOrWait() with the differences that it acquires a lock to the mutex itself rather than expecting it to be passed in and that it returns if there is no work available. (Its implementation is therefore elided.) This method will be useful with the forthcoming AsyncJob class, which opportunistically helps out with parallel work when it would otherwise be blocked.

The thread pool also provides a ForEachThread() function that takes a function to be executed on each of the threads in the thread pool as well as the main thread. In pbrt, it is used by the statistics system to collect statistics that are stored in per-thread variables.

B.6.5 PARALLEL for LOOPS

Much of the multi-core parallelism when pbrt is running on the CPU is expressed through parallel for loops using the ParallelFor() and ParallelFor2D() functions, which implement the ParallelJob interface.[10] These functions take the loop body in the form of a function that is called for each iteration as well as a count of the total number of loop iterations to execute. Multiple iterations can thus run in parallel on different CPU cores. Calls to these functions return only after all the loop iterations have finished.

---

10 Our implementation is based on the parallel for loop implementation in *Halide* written by Jonathan Ragan-Kelley, Andrew Adams, and Zalman Stern.

Here is an example of using ParallelFor(). The first two arguments give the range of values for the loop index and a C++ lambda expression is used to define the loop body; the loop index is passed to it as an argument. The lambda has access to the local array variable and doubles each array element in its body.

```
Float array[1024] = { ... };
ParallelFor(0, 1024, [array](int index) { array[index] *= 2; });
```

While it is also possible to pass a function pointer to ParallelFor(), lambdas are generally much more convenient, given their ability to capture locally visible variables and make them available in their body.

ParallelForLoop1D implements the ParallelJob interface, for use in the ParallelFor() functions.

⟨*ParallelForLoop1D Definition*⟩ ≡
```
class ParallelForLoop1D : public ParallelJob {
  public:
    ⟨ParallelForLoop1D Public Methods 1106⟩
  private:
    ⟨ParallelForLoop1D Private Members 1106⟩
};
```

In addition to the callback function for the loop body, the constructor takes the range of values the loop should cover via the startIndex and endIndex parameters. For loops with relatively large iteration counts where the work done per iteration is small, it can be worthwhile to have the threads running loop iterations do multiple iterations before getting more work. (Doing so helps amortize the overhead of determining which iterations should be assigned to a thread.) Therefore, ParallelFor() also takes an optional chunkSize parameter that controls the granularity of the mapping of loop iterations to processing threads.

⟨*ParallelForLoop1D Public Methods*⟩ ≡   **1106**
```
ParallelForLoop1D(int64_t startIndex, int64_t endIndex, int chunkSize,
                  std::function<void(int64_t, int64_t)> func)
    : func(std::move(func)), nextIndex(startIndex), endIndex(endIndex),
      chunkSize(chunkSize) {}
```

The nextIndex member variable tracks the next loop index to be executed. It is incremented by workers as they claim loop iterations to execute in their threads.

⟨*ParallelForLoop1D Private Members*⟩ ≡   **1106**
```
std::function<void(int64_t, int64_t)> func;
int64_t nextIndex, endIndex;
int chunkSize;
```

The HaveWork() method is easily implemented.

⟨*ParallelForLoop1D Public Methods*⟩ +≡   **1106**
```
bool HaveWork() const { return nextIndex < endIndex; }
```

RunStep() determines which loop iterations to run and does some housekeeping before releasing the provided lock and executing loop iterations.

⟨*ParallelForLoop1D Method Definitions*⟩ ≡
```
void ParallelForLoop1D::RunStep(std::unique_lock<std::mutex> *lock) {
    ⟨Determine the range of loop iterations to run in this step 1107⟩
    ⟨Remove job from list if all work has been started 1107⟩
    ⟨Release lock and execute loop iterations in [indexStart, indexEnd) 1107⟩
}
```

Recall that the ThreadPool ensures that no other threads will concurrently call any of the other ParallelForLoop1D methods as long as the provided lock is held. Therefore, the method implementation here is free to access and modify member variables without needing to worry about mutual exclusion or atomic updates. Here, it is a simple matter to determine the range of iterations to run next, given a starting iteration and the chunk size. Note, however, that it is important to copy the nextIndex member variable into a local variable here while the lock is held, as that value will be accessed later when the lock is not held.

⟨*Determine the range of loop iterations to run in this step*⟩ ≡   1107
```
int64_t indexStart = nextIndex;
int64_t indexEnd = std::min(indexStart + chunkSize, endIndex);
nextIndex = indexEnd;
```

If all the work for a job has begun, there is no need for it to be in the list of unfinished jobs that the ThreadPool maintains. Therefore, we immediately remove it from the list in that case. Note that just because a job is not in the work list does not mean that its work is completed.

⟨*Remove job from list if all work has been started*⟩ ≡   1107
```
if (!HaveWork())
    threadPool->RemoveFromJobList(this);
```

Finally, the thread can release the lock and get to work executing the specified loop iterations.

⟨*Release lock and execute loop iterations in* [indexStart, indexEnd)⟩ ≡   1107
```
lock->unlock();
func(indexStart, indexEnd);
```

The ParallelFor() function pulls all the pieces together to create a ParallelForLoop1D object, provide it to the thread pool, and then execute loop iterations in the thread that specified the loop. This function does not return until all the specified loop iterations are complete.

⟨*Parallel Function Definitions*⟩ ≡
```
void ParallelFor(int64_t start, int64_t end,
                 std::function<void(int64_t, int64_t)> func) {
    if (start == end) return;
    ⟨Compute chunk size for parallel loop 1108⟩
    ⟨Create and enqueue ParallelForLoop1D for this loop 1108⟩
    ⟨Help out with parallel loop iterations in the current thread 1108⟩
}
```

ParallelForLoop1D::chunkSize 1106

ParallelForLoop1D::endIndex 1106

ParallelForLoop1D::func 1106

ParallelForLoop1D::HaveWork() 1106

ParallelForLoop1D::nextIndex 1106

ThreadPool 1102

ThreadPool::RemoveFromJobList() 1105

The first step is to compute the chunk size—how many loop iterations are performed each time a thread gets another block of work to do. On one hand, the larger this value is, the less often threads will need to acquire the mutex to get more work. If its value is too small, parallel speedup may be inhibited by worker threads being stalled while they wait for other threads to release the mutex. On the other hand, if it is too large, then load balancing may be poor: all the threads but one may have finished the available work and be stalled, waiting for the last thread still working. Here the value is set inversely proportional to the number of threads in an effort to balance these two factors.

⟨*Compute chunk size for parallel loop*⟩ ≡   1107
```
int64_t chunkSize =
    std::max<int64_t>(1, (end - start) / (8 * RunningThreads()));
```

(The `RunningThreads()` function, which is not included in the book, returns the total number of available threads for pbrt.)

A `ParallelForLoop1D` object can now be initialized and provided to the thread pool. Because this `ParallelFor()` call does not return until all work for the loop is done, it is safe to allocate `loop` on the stack—no dynamic memory allocation is required.

⟨*Create and enqueue* `ParallelForLoop1D` *for this loop*⟩ ≡   1107
```
ParallelForLoop1D loop(start, end, chunkSize, std::move(func));
std::unique_lock<std::mutex> lock =
    ParallelJob::threadPool->AddToJobList(&loop);
```

After adding the job, the thread that called `ParallelFor()` (be it the main thread or one of the worker threads) starts work on the loop. By finishing the loop before allowing the thread that submitted it to do any more work, the implementation keeps the amount of enqueued work limited and allows subsequent code in the caller to proceed knowing the loop's work is done after its call to `ParallelFor()` returns.

Because a held lock to the `ThreadPool`'s mutex is returned from the call to `AddToJobList()`, it is safe to call both `Finished()` and `WorkOrWait()`.

⟨*Help out with parallel loop iterations in the current thread*⟩ ≡   1107
```
while (!loop.Finished())
    ParallelJob::threadPool->WorkOrWait(&lock, true);
```

There is a second variant of `ParallelFor()` that calls a callback that only takes a single loop index. This saves a line or two of code in implementations that do not care to know about the chunk's [start, end) range.

⟨*Parallel Inline Functions*⟩ ≡
```
void ParallelFor(int64_t start, int64_t end,
                 std::function<void(int64_t)> func) {
    ParallelFor(start, end, [&func](int64_t start, int64_t end) {
        for (int64_t i = start; i < end; ++i)
            func(i);
    });
}
```

`ParallelFor2D()`, not included here, takes a `Bounds2i` to specify the loop domain and then calls a function that either takes a `Bounds2i` or one that takes a `Point2i`, along the lines of the two `ParallelFor()` variants.

B.6.6 ASYNCHRONOUS JOBS

Parallel for loops are useful when the parallel work is easily expressed as a loop of independent iterations; it is just a few lines of changed code to parallelize an existing for loop. The fact that `ParallelFor()` and `ParallelFor2D()` ensure that all loop iterations have finished before they return is also helpful since subsequent code can proceed knowing any values set in the loop are available.

However, not all work fits that form. Sometimes one thread of execution may produce independent work that could be done concurrently by a different thread. In this case, we would like to be able to provide that work to the thread pool and then continue on in the current thread, harvesting the result of the independent work some time later. pbrt therefore provides a second mechanism for parallel execution in the form of *asynchronous jobs* that execute a given function (often, a lambda function). The following code shows an example of their use.

```
extern Result func(float x);
AsyncJob<Result> *job = RunAsync(func, 0.5f);
...
Result r = job->GetResult();
```

The RunAsync() function takes a function as its first parameter as well as any arguments that the function takes. It returns an AsyncJob to the caller, which can then continue execution. When the AsyncJob's GetResult() method is subsequently called, the call will only return after the asynchronous function has executed, be it by another thread in the thread pool or by the calling thread. The value returned by the asynchronous function is then returned to the caller.

The AsyncJob class implements the ParallelJob interface. It is templated on the return type of the function it manages.

⟨*AsyncJob Definition*⟩ ≡
```
template <typename T>
class AsyncJob : public ParallelJob {
public:
    ⟨AsyncJob Public Methods 1109⟩
private:
    ⟨AsyncJob Private Members 1109⟩
};
```

The constructor, not included here, takes the asynchronous function and stores it in the func member variable. started is used to record whether some thread has begun running the function.

⟨*AsyncJob Private Members*⟩ ≡   1109
```
std::function<T(void)> func;
bool started = false;
```

An AsyncJob represents a single quantum of work; only one thread can help, so once one has started running the function, there is nothing for any other thread to do. Implementation of the HaveWork() method for the ParallelJob interface follows.

⟨*AsyncJob Public Methods*⟩ ≡   1109
```
bool HaveWork() const { return !started; }
```

The RunStep() method starts with some minor bookkeeping before calling the provided function; it is worth removing the AsyncJob from the job list at this point, as there is no reason for other threads to consider it when they iterate through the list.

⟨*AsyncJob Public Methods*⟩ +≡   1109
```
void RunStep(std::unique_lock<std::mutex> *lock) {
    threadPool->RemoveFromJobList(this);
    started = true;
    lock->unlock();
    ⟨Execute asynchronous work and notify waiting threads of its completion 1110⟩
}
```

The asynchronous function is called without the `AsyncJob`'s mutex being held so that its execution does not stall other threads that may want to quickly check whether the function has finished running; the mutex is only acquired when a value is available to store in `result`. Note also the use of a condition variable after `result` is set: other threads that are waiting for the result wait on this condition variable, so it is important that they be notified.

⟨*Execute asynchronous work and notify waiting threads of its completion*⟩ ≡   1109
```
T r = func();
std::unique_lock<std::mutex> ul(mutex);
result = r;
cv.notify_all();
```

Using `optional` to store the function's result simplifies keeping track of whether the function has been executed.

⟨*AsyncJob Private Members*⟩ +≡   1109
```
pstd::optional<T> result;
mutable std::mutex mutex;
std::condition_variable cv;
```

A convenience `IsReady()` method that indicates whether the function has run and its result is available is easily implemented.

⟨*AsyncJob Public Methods*⟩ +≡   1109
```
bool IsReady() const {
    std::lock_guard<std::mutex> lock(mutex);
    return result.has_value();
}
```

The `GetResult()` method starts by calling `Wait()`, which only returns once the function's return value is available. The value of `*result` can therefore then be returned with no further checks.

⟨*AsyncJob Public Methods*⟩ +≡   1109
```
T GetResult() {
    Wait();
    std::lock_guard<std::mutex> lock(mutex);
    return *result;
}
```

`AsyncJob` also provides a `TryGetResult()` method that takes an already-locked `std::mutex` as a parameter. It then returns the asynchronous function's return value if it is available, with the lock still held, or unlocks the lock, performs some work via a call to `DoParallelWork()`, and then relocks the mutex. (The definition of `DoParallelWork()` is not included in the text; it takes a single work item from the parallel job queue, performs the associated work, and then returns.) This variant is useful when multiple threads are waiting for the value returned by an asynchronous function, since it allows them to perform other useful work rather than stalling as they wait.

So long as the asynchronous function has not yet finished, `Wait()` calls `DoParallelWork()` to help out with work enqueued in the thread pool (including, at some point, the current `AsyncJob`, if another thread has not yet taken care of it). If the result is not available and there is no work to run, then some other thread must be running the asynchronous job; the current thread then waits for the condition variable to be signaled.

1109

⟨*AsyncJob Public Methods*⟩ +≡

```
void Wait() {
    while (!IsReady() && DoParallelWork())
        ;
    std::unique_lock<std::mutex> lock(mutex);
    if (!result.has_value())
        cv.wait(lock, [this]() { return result.has_value(); });
}
```

For the simplicity of the AsyncJob implementation, there is some complexity in RunAsync(), which takes care of creating an AsyncJob and making it available to the thread pool. That complexity starts with the function using a variadic template to capture the function's argument values.

⟨*Asynchronous Task Launch Function Definitions*⟩ ≡

```
template <typename F, typename... Args>
auto RunAsync(F func, Args &&...args) {
    ⟨Create AsyncJob for func and args 1111⟩
    ⟨Enqueue job or run it immediately 1111⟩
    return job;
}
```

The AsyncJob class assumes that the function to execute does not take any arguments, though RunAsync() allows the provided function to take arguments. Therefore, it starts by using std::bind() to create a new callable object with the arguments bound and no arguments remaining. An alternative design might generalize AsyncJob to allow arguments, though at a cost of added complexity that we think is better left to std::bind. Given the new function fvoid, its return type R can be found, which allows for creating an AsyncJob of the correct type. Dynamic allocation is necessary for the AsyncJob here since it must outlast the call to RunAsync().

⟨*Create* AsyncJob *for* func *and* args⟩ ≡   1111

```
auto fvoid = std::bind(func, std::forward<Args>(args)...);
using R = typename std::invoke_result_t<F, Args...>;
AsyncJob<R> *job = new AsyncJob<R>(std::move(fvoid));
```

If there is no thread pool (e.g., due to the user specifying that no additional threads should be used), then the work is performed immediately via a call to DoWork() (the implementation of which is not included here), which immediately invokes the function and saves its result in AsyncJob::result. Otherwise, it is added to the job list.

⟨*Enqueue* job *or run it immediately*⟩ ≡   1111

```
std::unique_lock<std::mutex> lock;
if (RunningThreads() == 1)
    job->DoWork();
else
    lock = ParallelJob::threadPool->AddToJobList(job);
```

B.6.7 THREAD-LOCAL VARIABLES

It is often useful to have local data associated with each executing thread that it can access without concern of mutual exclusion with other threads. For example, per-thread Samplers and ScratchBuffers were used by the ImageTileIntegrator in Section 1.3.4. The ThreadLocal template class handles the details of such cases, creating per-thread instances of a managed object type T on demand as threads require them.

⟨*ThreadLocal Definition*⟩ ≡
```
template <typename T>
class ThreadLocal {
public:
    ⟨ThreadLocal Public Methods 1112⟩
private:
    ⟨ThreadLocal Private Members⟩
};
```

ThreadLocal uses a hash table to manage the objects. It allocates a fixed-size array for the hash table in order to avoid the complexity of resizing the hash table at runtime. For pbrt's use, where the number of running threads is fixed, this is a reasonable simplification. If the caller provides a function that returns objects of the type T, then it is used to create them; otherwise, the object's default constructor is called.

⟨*ThreadLocal Public Methods*⟩ ≡   1112
```
ThreadLocal()
    : hashTable(4 * RunningThreads()), create([]() { return T(); }) {}
ThreadLocal(std::function<T(void)> &&c)
    : hashTable(4 * RunningThreads()), create(c) {}
```

The Get() method returns the instance of the object that is associated with the calling thread. It takes care of allocating the object and inserting it into the hash table when needed.

⟨*ThreadLocal Public Methods*⟩ +≡   1112
```
T &Get();
```

It is useful to be able to iterate over all the per-thread objects managed by ThreadLocal. That capability is provided by the ForAll() method.

⟨*ThreadLocal Public Methods*⟩ +≡   1112
```
template <typename F>
void ForAll(F &&func);
```

B.7 STATISTICS

Collecting data about the runtime behavior of the system can provide a substantial amount of insight into its behavior and opportunities for improving its performance. For example, we might want to track the average number of primitive intersection tests performed for all the rays; if this number is surprisingly high, then there may be a latent bug somewhere in the system. pbrt's statistics system makes it possible to measure and aggregate this sort of data in a variety of ways. The statistics system is only available with the CPU renderer; an exercise at the end of this appendix discusses how it might be brought to the GPU.

It is important to make it as easy as possible to add new measurements to track the system's runtime behavior; the easier it is to do this, the more measurements end up being added to the system, and the more likely that "interesting" data will be discovered, leading to new insights and improvements. Therefore, it is fairly easy to add new measurements to pbrt. For example, the following lines declare two counters that can be used to record how many times the corresponding events happen.

RunningThreads() 1108
ThreadLocal 1112

```
STAT_COUNTER("Integrator/Regular ray intersection tests", nIsectTests);
STAT_COUNTER("Integrator/Shadow ray intersection tests", nShadowTests);
```

As appropriate, counters can be incremented with simple statements like

```
++nIsectTests;
```

With no further intervention from the developer, the preceding is enough for the statistics system to be able to automatically print out nicely formatted results like the following when rendering completes:

```
Integrator
    Regular ray intersection tests           752982
    Shadow ray intersection tests            4237165
```

The statistics system supports the following aggregate measurements:

- STAT_COUNTER("name", var): A count of the number of instances of an event. The counter variable var can be updated as if it was a regular integer variable; for example, ++var and var += 10 are both valid.
- STAT_MEMORY_COUNTER("name", var): A specialized counter for recording memory usage. In particular, the values reported at the end of rendering are in terms of kilobytes, megabytes, or gigabytes, as appropriate. The counter is updated the same way as a regular counter: var += count * sizeof(MyStruct) and so forth.
- STAT_INT_DISTRIBUTION("name", dist): Tracks the distribution of some value; at the end of rendering, the minimum, maximum, and average of the supplied values are reported. Call dist << value to include value in the distribution.
- STAT_PERCENT("name", num, denom): Tracks how often a given event happens; the aggregate value is reported as the percentage num/denom when statistics are printed. Both num and denom can be incremented as if they were integers—for example, one might write if (event) ++num; or ++denom.
- STAT_RATIO("name", num, denom): This tracks how often an event happens but reports the result as a ratio num/denom rather than a percentage. This is often a more useful presentation if num is often greater than denom. (For example, we might record the percentage of ray–triangle intersection tests that resulted in an intersection but the ratio of triangle intersection tests to the total number of rays traced.)

In addition to statistics that are aggregated over the entire rendering, pbrt can also measure statistics at each pixel and generate images with their values. Two variants are supported: STAT_PIXEL_COUNTER and STAT_PIXEL_RATIO, which are used in the same way as the corresponding aggregate statistics. Per-pixel statistics are only measured if the --pixelstats command line option is provided to pbrt. Figure B.8 shows an image generated using STAT_PIXEL_COUNTER.

All the macros to define statistics trackers can only be used at file scope and should only be used in *.cpp files (for reasons that will become apparent as we dig into their implementations). They specifically should not be used in header files or function or class definitions.

Note also that the string names provided for each measurement should be of the form "category/statistic." When values are reported, everything under the same category is reported together (as in the preceding example).

B.7.1 IMPLEMENTATION

There are a number of challenges in making the statistics system both efficient and easy to use. The efficiency challenges stem from pbrt being multi-threaded: if there was not any parallelism, we could associate regular integer or floating-point variables with each measurement and just update them like regular variables. In the presence of multiple concurrent threads of

Figure B.8: Visualization of Average Path Length at Each Pixel. Each pixel's value is based on the number of rays traced to compute the pixel's shaded value. Not only it is evident that longer paths are traced at pixels with specular surfaces like the glasses on the tables, but it is also possible to see the effect of Russian roulette terminating paths more quickly at darker surfaces. This image was generated using `STAT_PIXEL_COUNTER` and only required adding two lines of code to an integrator. *(Scene courtesy of Guillermo M. Leal Llaguno.)*

execution, however, we need to ensure that two threads do not try to modify these variables at the same time (recall the discussion of mutual exclusion in Section B.6.1).

While atomic operations like those described in Section B.6.1 could be used to safely increment counters without using a mutex, there would still be a performance impact from multiple threads modifying the same location in memory. Recall from Section B.6.3 that the cache coherence protocols can introduce substantial overhead in this case. Because the statistics measurements are updated so frequently during the course of rendering, we found that an atomics-based implementation caused the renderer to be 10–15% slower than the following implementation, which avoids the overhead of multiple threads frequently modifying the same memory location.

The implementation here is based on having separate counters for each running thread, allowing the counters to be updated without atomics and without cache coherence overhead (since each thread increments its own counters). This approach means that in order to report statistics, it is necessary to merge all of these per-thread counters into final aggregate values, which we will see is possible with a bit of trickiness.

To see how this all works, we will dig into the implementation for regular counters; the other types of measurements are all along similar lines. First, here is the `STAT_COUNTER` macro, which packs three different things into its definition.

⟨*Statistics Macros*⟩ ≡
```
#define STAT_COUNTER(title, var)                                    \
    static thread_local int64_t var;                                \
    static StatRegisterer STATS_REG##var([](StatsAccumulator &accum) { \
        accum.ReportCounter(title, var);                            \
        var = 0;                                                    \
    });
```

First, and most obviously, the macro defines a 64-bit integer variable named `var`, the second argument passed to the macro. The variable definition has the `thread_local` qualifier, which indicates that there should be a separate copy of the variable for each executing thread. This variable can then be incremented directly as appropriate to report results. However, given these per-thread instances, we need to be able to sum together the per-thread values and to aggregate all the individual counters into the final program output.

To this end, the macro next defines a static variable of type `StatRegisterer`, giving it a (we hope!) unique name derived from `var`. A lambda function is passed to the `StatRegisterer` constructor, which stores a copy of it. When called, the lambda passes the current thread's counter value to a `ReportCounter()` method and then resets the counter. Evidently, all that is required is for this lambda to be called by each thread and for `ReportCounter()` to sum up the values provided and then report them. (We will gloss over the implementation of the `StatsAccumulator` class and methods like `ReportCounter()`, as there is nothing very interesting about them.)

Recall that in C++, constructors of global `static` objects run when program execution starts; thus, each `static` instance of the `StatRegisterer` class runs its constructor before `main()` starts running. This constructor, which is not included here, adds the lambda passed to it to a `std::vector` that holds all such lambdas for all the statistics.

At the end of rendering, the `ForEachThread()` function is used to cause each thread to loop over the registered lambdas and call each of them. In turn, the `StatsAccumulator` will have all the aggregate values when they are done. The `PrintStats()` function can then be called to print all the statistics that have been accumulated in `StatsAccumulator`.

FURTHER READING

Hacker's Delight (Warren 2006) is a delightful and thought-provoking exploration of bit-twiddling algorithms like those used in some of the utility routines in this appendix. Sean Anderson (2004) has a Web page filled with a collection of bit-twiddling techniques like the ones in `IsPowerOf2()` and `RoundUpPow2()` at *graphics.stanford.edu/~seander/bithacks.html*.

The MurmurHash hashing function that is wrapped by pbrt's `Hash()` and `HashBuffer()` functions is due to Appleby (2011) and the implementation of `MixBits()` is due to Stafford (2011), who found the various constant values used in the implementation via search.

The inverse bilinear interpolation function implemented in `InvertBilinear()` is due to Quilez (2010) and `SinXOverX()` is thanks to Hatch (2003).

The algorithm implemented in `TwoSum()` is due to Møller (1965) and Knuth (1969), and the FMA-based `TwoProd()` was developed by Ogita et al. (2005). The approach used in the `CompensatedSum` class is due to Kahan (1965). The approach used in `DifferenceOfProducts()` is also attributed to Kahan; its error was analyzed by Jeannerod et al. (2013).

Welford (1962) developed the algorithm that is implemented in the `VarianceEstimator` class. Its `Merge()` method is based on an algorithm developed by Chan et al. (1979).

Atkinson's book (1993) on numerical analysis discusses algorithms for matrix inversion and solving linear systems. See Moore's book (1966) for an introduction to interval arithmetic.

Farin's book (2001) is a good introduction to splines. The blossoming approach was introduced by Ramshaw (1987); his report remains a readable introduction to the topic. A subsequent publication drew further connections to polar forms and related work (Ramshaw 1989).

The PCG random number generator was developed by O'Neill (2014). The paper describing its implementation is well written and also features extensive discussion of a range of previous pseudo-random number generators and the challenges that they have faced in passing rigorous tests of their quality (L'Ecuyer and Simard 2007).

The article "UTF-8 Everywhere" by Radzivilovsky et al. (2012) is a good introduction to Unicode and also makes a strong case for adopting the UTF-8 representation. pbrt follows the approach they propose for interoperating with Windows's UTF-16-based APIs. At over 1,000 pages, the length of the official Unicode specification gives some sense of the complexities in representing multi-lingual text (Unicode Consortium 2020).

Gamma correction has a long history in computer graphics. Poynton (2002a, 2002b) has written comprehensive FAQs on issues related to color representation and gamma correction. The sRGB encoding was described by the International Electrotechnical Commission (1999). See Gritz and d'Eon (2008) for a detailed discussion of the implications of gamma correction for rendering and how to correctly account for it in rendering systems.

McKenney's book on parallel programming is wonderfully written and has comprehensive coverage of the underlying issues, as well as many useful techniques for high-performance parallel programming on CPUs (2021). Drepper's paper (2007) is a useful resource for understanding performance issues related to caches, cache coherence, and main memory access, particularly in multicore systems.

Boehm's paper "Threads Cannot Be Implemented as a Library" (2005) makes the remarkable (and disconcerting) observation that multi-threading cannot be reliably implemented without the compiler having explicit knowledge of the fact that multi-threaded execution is expected. Boehm presented a number of examples that demonstrate the corresponding dangers in 2005-era compilers and language standards like C and C++ that did not have awareness of threading. Fortunately, the C++11 and C11 standards addressed the issues that he identified.

pbrt's parallel for loop–based approach to multi-threading is a widely used technique for multi-threaded programming; the OpenMP standard supports a similar construct (and much more) (OpenMP Architecture Review Board 2013). A slightly more general model for multi-core parallelism is available from *task systems*, where computations are broken up into a set of independent tasks that can be executed concurrently. That model is supported through RunAsync(). Blumofe et al. (1996) described the task scheduler in Cilk, and Blumofe and Leiserson (1999) described the work-stealing algorithm that is the mainstay of many current high-performance task systems.

EXERCISES

⊘ **B.1** It is possible to use image pyramids and MIP mapping with images that have non-power-of-two resolutions—the details are explained by Guthe and Heckbert (2005). Implementing this approach can save a substantial amount of memory: in the worst case, the resampling that pbrt's MIPMap implementation performs can increase memory requirements by a factor of four. (Consider a 513 × 513 texture that is resampled to be 1024 × 1024.) Implement this approach in pbrt, and compare the amount of memory used to store texture data for a variety of texture-heavy scenes.

⊘ **B.2** Improve the filtering algorithm used in the Image::GeneratePyramid() method to initialize the pyramid levels using the Lanczos filter instead of the box filter. How

Image::GeneratePyramid() 1090

MIPMap 665

RunAsync() 1111

do the sphere test images in Figure 10.16 change after your modifications? Do you see a difference in other scenes that use image textures?

⊘ **B.3** Try a few alternative implementations of the statistics system described in Section B.7 to get a sense of the performance trade-offs with various approaches. You might try using atomic operations to update single counters that are shared across threads, or you might try using a mutex to allow safe updates to shared counters by multiple threads. Measure the performance compared to pbrt's current implementation and discuss possible explanations for your results.

⊛ **B.4** Generalize the statistics system (including the per-pixel statistics) so that it is also available in the GPU rendering path. You will likely want to pursue an approach based on atomic variables rather than the thread_local approach that is used for the CPU. Measure the performance of your implementation and compare to the system before your changes. Is performance meaningfully affected?

ⴻ PROCESSING THE SCENE DESCRIPTION

In the discussion of pbrt's main() function in Section 1.3.2 at the start of the book, we wrote that after the command-line arguments are processed, the scene description is parsed and converted into corresponding Shapes, Lights, Materials, and so forth. Thereafter, as we have discussed the implementations of those classes, we have not worried about when they are created or where the parameter values for their constructors come from. This appendix fills in that gap and explains the path from human-readable scene description files to corresponding C++ objects in memory.

The scene description is processed in three stages, each of which is described in successive sections of this appendix:

- The text file format that describes the scene is parsed. Each statement in the file causes a corresponding method to be called in a ParserTarget class implementation.
- An instance of the BasicSceneBuilder class, which implements the ParserTarget interface, tracks graphics state such as the current material and transformation matrix as the file is parsed. For each entity in the scene (the camera, each light and shape, etc.), it produces a single object that represents the entity and its parameters.
- A BasicScene instance collects the objects produced by the BasicSceneBuilder and creates the corresponding object types that are used for rendering.

Once the BasicScene is complete, it is passed to either the RenderCPU() or RenderWavefront() function, as appropriate. Those functions then create the final representation of the scene that they will use for rendering. For most types of scene objects (e.g., the Sampler), both call a BasicScene method that returns the object that corresponds to what was specified in the scene description. Those two functions diverge in how they represent the intersectable scene geometry. In RenderCPU() as well as when the wavefront renderer is running on the CPU, the primitives and accelerators defined in Chapter 7 are used to represent it. With GPU rendering, shapes are converted to the representation expected by the GPU's ray-tracing API.

C.1 TOKENIZING AND PARSING

Two functions expose pbrt's scene-parsing capabilities, one taking one or more names of files to process in sequence, and the other taking a string that holds a scene description. All of pbrt's parsing code is in the files parser.h and parser.cpp.

⟨*Scene Parsing Declarations*⟩ ≡
```
void ParseFiles(ParserTarget *target,
                pstd::span<const std::string> filenames);
void ParseString(ParserTarget *target, std::string str);
```

Rather than directly returning an object that represents the parsed scene, the parsing functions call methods of the provided ParserTarget to convey what they have found. Parser Target is an abstract interface class that defines nearly 40 pure virtual functions, each one corresponding to a statement in a pbrt scene description file.

⟨*ParserTarget Definition*⟩ ≡
```
class ParserTarget {
  public:
    ⟨ParserTarget Interface 1120⟩
  protected:
    ⟨ParserTarget Protected Methods⟩
};
```

For example, given the statement

```
    Scale 2 2 4
```

in a scene description file, the parsing code will call its ParserTarget's Scale() method.

⟨*ParserTarget Interface*⟩ ≡   **1120**
```
virtual void Scale(Float sx, Float sy, Float sz, FileLoc loc) = 0;
```

The provided FileLoc records the location of the corresponding statement in a file. If it is passed to the Warning(), Error(), and ErrorExit() functions, the resulting message includes this information so that it is easier for users to fix errors in their scene files.

⟨*FileLoc Definition*⟩ ≡
```
struct FileLoc {
    std::string_view filename;
    int line = 1, column = 0;
};
```

Specifying ParserTarget as an abstract base class makes it easy to do a variety of things while parsing pbrt scene descriptions. For example, there is a FormattingParserTarget implementation of the ParserTarget interface that pretty-prints scene files and can upgrade scene files from the previous version of pbrt to conform to the current implementation's syntax. (FormattingParserTarget is not described any further in the book.) Section C.2 will describe the BasicSceneBuilder class, which also inherits from ParserTarget and builds an in-memory representation of the parsed scene.

pbrt's scene description is easy to convert into tokens.[1] Its salient properties are:

---

1   See the *pbrt.org* website for more information about the text file format used to describe pbrt scenes.

- Individual tokens are separated by whitespace.
- Strings are delimited using double quotes.
- One-dimensional arrays of values can be specified using square brackets: [ ].
- Comments start with a hash character, #, and continue to the end of the current line.

We have not included pbrt's straightforward tokenizer in the book text. (See the `Tokenizer` class in `parser.h` and `parser.cpp` for its implementation.)

Given a stream of tokens, the next task is parsing them. Some scene file statements have a fixed format (e.g., `Scale`, which expects three numeric values to follow). For each of those, the parser has fixed logic that looks for the expected number of values and checks that they have the correct types, issuing an error message if they are deficient. Other statements take lists of named parameters and values:

```
Shape "sphere" "float radius" 10 "float zmin" 0
```

Such named parameter lists are encoded by the parser in instances of the `ParsedParameter` `Vector` class that are passed to `ParserTarget` interface methods. For example, the signature for the `Shape()` interface method is:

⟨*ParserTarget Interface*⟩ +≡   **1120**
```
virtual void Shape(const std::string &name,
                   ParsedParameterVector params, FileLoc loc) = 0;
```

One might ask: why tokenize and parse the files using a custom implementation and not use lexer and parser generators like `flex`, `bison`, or `antlr`? In fact, previous versions of pbrt did use `flex` and `bison`. However, when investigating pbrt's performance in loading multi-gigabyte scene description files when rendering Disney's *Moana Island* scene (Walt Disney Animation Studios 2018), we found that a substantial fraction of execution time was spent in the mechanics of parsing. Replacing that part of the system with a custom implementation substantially improved parsing performance. A secondary advantage of not using those tools is that doing so makes it easier to build pbrt on a variety of systems by eliminating the requirement of ensuring that they are installed.

`ParsedParameterVector` uses `InlinedVector` to store a vector of parameters, avoiding the performance cost of dynamic allocation that comes with `std::vector` in the common case of a handful of parameters.

⟨*ParsedParameterVector Definition*⟩ ≡
```
using ParsedParameterVector = InlinedVector<ParsedParameter *, 8>;
```

⟨*ParsedParameter Definition*⟩ ≡
```
class ParsedParameter {
  public:
    ⟨ParsedParameter Public Methods⟩
    ⟨ParsedParameter Public Members 1122⟩
};
```

FileLoc 1120
InlinedVector 1069
ParsedParameter 1121
ParsedParameterVector 1121
ParserTarget 1120

`ParsedParameter` provides the parameter type and name as strings as well as the location of the parameter in the scene description file. For the first parameter in the sphere example above, `type` would store "float" and `name` would store "radius". Note that the parser makes no effort to ensure that the type is valid or that the parameter name is used by the corresponding statement; those checks are handled subsequently.

⟨*ParsedParameter Public Members*⟩ ≡   **1121**
```
std::string type, name;
FileLoc loc;
```

Parameter values are provided in one of four formats, corresponding to the basic types used for parameter values in scene description files. (Values for higher-level parameter types like point3 are subsequently constructed from the corresponding basic type.) Exactly one of the following vectors will be non-empty in each provided ParsedParameter.

As before, the parser makes no effort to validate these—for example, if the user has provided string values for a parameter with "float" type, those values will be provided in strings with no complaint (yet).

⟨*ParsedParameter Public Members*⟩ +≡   **1121**
```
pstd::vector<Float> floats;
pstd::vector<int> ints;
pstd::vector<std::string> strings;
pstd::vector<uint8_t> bools;
```

The lookedUp member variable is provided for the code related to extracting parameter values. It makes it easy to issue an error message if any provided parameters were not actually used by pbrt, which generally indicates a misspelling or other user error.

⟨*ParsedParameter Public Members*⟩ +≡   **1121**
```
mutable bool lookedUp = false;
```

We will not discuss the remainder of the methods in the ParserTarget interface here, though we will see more of them in the BasicSceneBuilder methods that implement them in Sections C.2.3 and C.2.4.

C.2 MANAGING THE SCENE DESCRIPTION

pbrt's scene description files allow the user to specify various properties that then apply to the definition of subsequent objects in the scene. One example is a current material. Once the current material is set, all subsequent shapes are assigned that material until it is changed. In addition to the material, the current transformation matrix, RGB color space, an area light specification, and the current media are similarly maintained. We will call this collective information the *graphics state*. Tracking graphics state provides the advantage that it is not necessary to specify a material with every shape in the scene description, but it imposes the requirement that the scene processing code keep track of the current graphics state while the scene description is being parsed.

Managing this graphics state is the primary task of the BasicSceneBuilder, which implements the interface defined by ParserTarget. Its implementation is in the files scene.h and scene.cpp. An initial BasicSceneBuilder is allocated at the start of parsing the scene description. Typically, it handles graphics state management for the provided scene description files. However, pbrt's scene description format supports an Import directive that indicates that a file can be parsed in parallel with the file that contains it. (Import effectively discards any changes to the graphics state at the end of an imported file, which allows parsing of the current file to continue concurrently without needing to wait for the imported file.) A new BasicSceneBuilder is allocated for each imported file; it makes a copy of the current graphics state before parsing begins.

⟨*BasicSceneBuilder Definition*⟩ ≡
```
class BasicSceneBuilder : public ParserTarget {
  public:
    ⟨BasicSceneBuilder Public Methods⟩
  private:
    ⟨BasicSceneBuilder::GraphicsState Definition 1128⟩
    ⟨BasicSceneBuilder Private Methods 1131⟩
    ⟨BasicSceneBuilder Private Members 1123⟩
};
```

As the entities in the scene are fully specified, they are passed along to an instance of the BasicScene class, which will be described in the next section. When parsing is being performed in parallel with multiple BasicSceneBuilders, all share a single BasicScene.

⟨*BasicSceneBuilder Private Members*⟩ ≡   1123
```
BasicScene *scene;
```

In addition to storing a pointer to a BasicScene, the BasicSceneBuilder constructor sets a few default values so that if, for example, no camera is specified in the scene description, a basic 90 degree perspective camera is used. The fragment that sets these values is not included here.

⟨*BasicSceneBuilder Method Definitions*⟩ ≡
```
BasicSceneBuilder::BasicSceneBuilder(BasicScene *scene)
    : scene(scene) {
  ⟨Set scene defaults⟩
}
```

pbrt scene descriptions are split into sections by the WorldBegin statement. Before WorldBegin is encountered, it is legal to specify global rendering options including the camera, film, sampler, and integrator, but shapes, lights, textures, and materials cannot yet be specified. After WorldBegin, all of that flips: things like the camera specification are fixed, and the rest of the scene can be specified. Some scene description statements, like those that modify the current transformation or specify participating media, are allowed in both contexts.

This separation of information can help simplify the implementation of the renderer. For example, consider a spline patch shape that tessellates itself into triangles. This shape might compute the size of its triangles based on the area of the screen that it covers. If the camera's position and the image resolution are fixed when the shape is created, then the shape can tessellate itself immediately at creation time.

An enumeration records which part of the scene description is currently being specified. Two macros that are not included here, VERIFY_OPTIONS() and VERIFY_WORLD(), check the current block against the one that is expected and issue an error if there is a mismatch.

⟨*BasicSceneBuilder Private Members*⟩ +≡   1123
```
enum class BlockState { OptionsBlock, WorldBlock };
BlockState currentBlock = BlockState::OptionsBlock;
```

C.2.1 SCENE ENTITIES

Before further describing the BasicSceneBuilder's operation, we will start by describing the form of its output, which is a high-level representation of the parsed scene. In this representation, all the objects in the scene are represented by various *Entity classes.

`SceneEntity` is the simplest of them; it records the name of the entity (e.g., "rgb" or "gbuffer" for the film), the file location of the associated statement in the scene description, and any user-provided parameters. It is used for the film, sampler, integrator, pixel filter, and accelerator, and is also used as a base class for some of the other scene entity types.

⟨*SceneEntity Definition*⟩ ≡
```
    struct SceneEntity {
        ⟨SceneEntity Public Methods⟩
        ⟨SceneEntity Public Members 1124⟩
    };
```

All the scene entity objects use `InternedStrings` for any string member variables to save memory when strings are repeated. (Often many are, including frequently used shape names like "trianglemesh" and the names of object instances that are used repeatedly.)

⟨*SceneEntity Public Members*⟩ ≡   1124
```
    InternedString name;
    FileLoc loc;
    ParameterDictionary parameters;
```

A single `InternCache` defined as a public static member in `SceneEntity` is used for all string interning in this part of the system.

⟨*SceneEntity Public Members*⟩ +≡   1124
```
    static InternCache<std::string> internedStrings;
```

Other entity types include the `CameraSceneEntity`, `LightSceneEntity`, `TextureSceneEntity`, `MediumSceneEntity`, `ShapeSceneEntity`, and `AnimatedShapeSceneEntity`. All have the obvious roles. There is furthermore an `InstanceDefinitionSceneEntity`, which represents an instance definition, and `InstanceSceneEntity`, which represents the use of an instance definition. We will not include the definitions of these classes in the text as they are all easily understood from their definitions in the source code.

C.2.2 PARAMETER DICTIONARIES

Most of the scene entity objects store lists of associated parameters from the scene description file. While the `ParsedParameter` is a convenient representation for the parser to generate, it does not provide capabilities for checking the validity of parameters or for easily extracting parameter values. To that end, `ParameterDictionary` adds both semantics and convenience to vectors of `ParsedParameters`. Thus, it is the class that is used for `SceneEntity::parameters`.

⟨*ParameterDictionary Definition*⟩ ≡
```
    class ParameterDictionary {
      public:
        ⟨ParameterDictionary Public Methods 1124⟩
      private:
        ⟨ParameterDictionary Private Methods⟩
        ⟨ParameterDictionary Private Members 1125⟩
    };
```

Its constructor takes both a `ParsedParameterVector` and an `RGBColorSpace` that defines the color space of any RGB-valued parameters.

⟨*ParameterDictionary Public Methods*⟩ ≡   1124
```
    ParameterDictionary(ParsedParameterVector params,
                        const RGBColorSpace *colorSpace);
```

It directly stores the provided ParsedParameterVector; no preprocessing of it is performed in the constructor—for example, to sort the parameters by name or to validate that the parameters are valid. An implication of this is that the following methods that look up parameter values have $O(n)$ time complexity in the total number of parameters. For the small numbers of parameters that are provided in practice, this inefficiency is not a concern.

⟨*ParameterDictionary Private Members*⟩ ≡   1124
```
    ParsedParameterVector params;
    const RGBColorSpace *colorSpace = nullptr;
```

A ParameterDictionary can hold eleven types of parameters: Booleans, integers, floating-point values, points (2D and 3D), vectors (2D and 3D), normals, spectra, strings, and the names of Textures that are used as parameters for Materials and other Textures. An enumeration of these types will be useful in the following.

⟨*ParameterType Definition*⟩ ≡
```
    enum class ParameterType {
        Boolean,  Float,     Integer,  Point2f, Vector2f, Point3f,
        Vector3f, Normal3f, Spectrum, String,   Texture
    };
```

For each parameter type, there is a method for looking up parameters that have a single data value. Here are the declarations of a few:

⟨*ParameterDictionary Public Methods*⟩ +≡   1124
```
    Float GetOneFloat(const std::string &name, Float def) const;
    int GetOneInt(const std::string &name, int def) const;
    bool GetOneBool(const std::string &name, bool def) const;
    std::string GetOneString(const std::string &name,
                             const std::string &def) const;
```

These methods all take the name of the parameter and a default value. If the parameter is not found, the default value is returned. This makes it easy to write initialization code like:

```
    Point3f center = params.GetOnePoint3f("center", Point3f(0, 0, 0));
```

The single value lookup methods for the other types follow the same form and so their declarations are not included here.

In contrast, if calling code wants to detect a missing parameter and issue an error, it should instead use the corresponding parameter array lookup method, which returns an empty vector if the parameter is not present. (Those methods will be described in a few pages.)

For parameters that represent spectral distributions, it is necessary to specify if the spectrum represents an illuminant, a reflectance that is bounded between 0 and 1, or is an arbitrary spectral distribution (e.g., a scattering coefficient). In turn, if a parameter has been specified using RGB color, the appropriate one of RGBIlluminantSpectrum, RGBAlbedoSpectrum, or RGBUnboundedSpectrum is used for the returned Spectrum.

⟨*ParameterDictionary Public Methods*⟩ +≡   1124
```
    Spectrum GetOneSpectrum(const std::string &name,
        Spectrum def, SpectrumType spectrumType, Allocator alloc) const;
```

⟨*SpectrumType Definition*⟩ ≡
```
    enum class SpectrumType { Illuminant, Albedo, Unbounded };
```

The parameter lookup methods make use of C++ type traits, which make it possible to associate additional information with specific types that can then be accessed at compile time via templates. This approach allows succinct implementations of the lookup methods. Here we will discuss the corresponding implementation for Point3f-valued parameters; the other types are analogous.

The implementation of GetOnePoint3f() requires a single line of code to forward the request on to the lookupSingle() method.

⟨*ParameterDictionary Method Definitions*⟩ ≡
```
    Point3f ParameterDictionary::GetOnePoint3f(const std::string &name,
                                               Point3f def) const {
        return lookupSingle<ParameterType::Point3f>(name, def);
    }
```

The following signature of the lookupSingle() method alone has brought us into the realm of template-based type information. lookupSingle() is itself a template method, parameterized by an instance of the ParameterType enumeration. In turn, we can see that another template class, ParameterTypeTraits, not yet defined, is expected to provide the type ReturnType, which is used for both lookupSingle's return type and the provided default value.

⟨*ParameterDictionary Method Definitions*⟩ +≡
```
    template <ParameterType PT>
    typename ParameterTypeTraits<PT>::ReturnType
    ParameterDictionary::lookupSingle(const std::string &name,
            typename ParameterTypeTraits<PT>::ReturnType defaultValue) const {
        ⟨Search params for parameter name 1127⟩
        return defaultValue;
    }
```

Each of the parameter types in the ParameterType enumeration has a ParameterTypeTraits template specialization. Here is the one for Point3f:

⟨*Point3f ParameterTypeTraits Definition*⟩ ≡
```
    template <>
    struct ParameterTypeTraits<ParameterType::Point3f> {
        ⟨ParameterType::Point3f Type Traits 1126⟩
    };
```

All the specializations provide a type definition for ReturnType. Naturally, the Parameter Type::Point3f specialization uses Point3f for ReturnType.

⟨*ParameterType::Point3f Type Traits*⟩ ≡   1126
```
    using ReturnType = Point3f;
```

Type traits also provide the string name for each type.

⟨*ParameterType::Point3f Type Traits*⟩ +≡   1126
```
    static constexpr char typeName[] = "point3";
```

In turn, the search for a parameter checks not only for the specified parameter name but also for a matching type string.

⟨*Search* params *for parameter* name⟩ ≡   1126
```
    using traits = ParameterTypeTraits<PT>;
    for (const ParsedParameter *p : params) {
        if (p->name != name || p->type != traits::typeName)
            continue;
        ⟨Extract parameter values from p 1127⟩
        ⟨Issue error if an incorrect number of parameter values were provided  1127⟩
        ⟨Return parameter values as ReturnType 1127⟩
    }
```

A static GetValues() method in each type traits template specialization returns a reference to one of the floats, ints, strings, or bools ParsedParameter member variables. Note that using auto for the declaration of values makes it possible for this code in lookupSingle() to work with any of those.

⟨*Extract parameter values from* p⟩ ≡   1127
```
    const auto &values = traits::GetValues(*p);
```

For Point3f parameters, the parameter values are floating-point.

⟨*ParameterType::Point3f Type Traits*⟩ +≡   1126
```
    static const auto &GetValues(const ParsedParameter &param) {
        return param.floats;
    }
```

Another trait, nPerItem, provides the number of individual values associated with each parameter. In addition to making it possible to check that the right number of values were provided in the GetOne*() methods, this value is also used when parsing arrays of parameter values.

⟨*Issue error if an incorrect number of parameter values were provided*⟩ ≡   1127
```
    if (values.empty())
        ErrorExit(&p->loc, "No values provided for parameter \"%s\".", name);
    if (values.size() != traits::nPerItem)
        ErrorExit(&p->loc, "Expected %d values for parameter \"%s\".",
                  traits::nPerItem, name);
```

For each Point3f, three values are expected.

⟨*ParameterType::Point3f Type Traits*⟩ +≡   1126
```
    static constexpr int nPerItem = 3;
```

Finally, a static Convert() method in the type traits specialization takes care of converting from the raw values to the returned parameter type. At this point, the fact that the parameter was in fact used is also recorded.

⟨*Return parameter values as* ReturnType⟩ ≡   1127
```
    p->lookedUp = true;
    return traits::Convert(values.data(), &p->loc);
```

The Convert() method converts the parameter values, starting at a given location, to the return type. When arrays of values are returned, this method is called once per returned array element, with the pointer incremented after each one by the type traits nPerItem value. The current FileLoc is passed along to this method in case any errors need to be reported.

⟨*ParameterType::Point3f Type Traits*⟩ +≡ **1126**
```
static Point3f Convert(const Float *f, const FileLoc *loc) {
    return Point3f(f[0], f[1], f[2]);
}
```

Implementing the parameter lookup methods via type traits is more complex than implementing each one directly would be. However, this approach has the advantage that each additional parameter type effectively only requires defining an appropriate ParameterType Traits specialization, which is just a few lines of code. Further, that additional code is mostly declarative, which in turn is easier to verify as correct than multiple independent implementations of parameter processing logic.

The second set of parameter lookup functions returns an array of values. An empty vector is returned if the parameter is not found, so no default value need be provided by the caller. Here are the declarations of a few of them. The rest are equivalent, though GetSpectrumArray() also takes a SpectrumType and an Allocator to use for allocating any returned Spectrum values.

⟨*ParameterDictionary Public Methods*⟩ +≡ **1124**
```
std::vector<Float> GetFloatArray(const std::string &name) const;
std::vector<int> GetIntArray(const std::string &name) const;
std::vector<uint8_t> GetBoolArray(const std::string &name) const;
```

We will not include the implementations of any of the array lookup methods or the type traits for the other parameter types here. We also note that the methods corresponding to Spectrum parameters are more complex than the other ones, since spectral distributions may be specified in a number of different ways, including as RGB colors, blackbody emission temperatures, and spectral distributions stored in files; see the source code for details.

Finally, because the user may misspell parameter names in the scene description file, the ParameterDictionary also provides a ReportUnused() function that issues an error if any of the parameters present were never looked up; the assumption is that in that case the user has provided an incorrect parameter. (This check is based on the values of the ParsedParameter:: lookedUp member variables.)

⟨*ParameterDictionary Public Methods*⟩ +≡ **1124**
```
void ReportUnused() const;
```

C.2.3 TRACKING GRAPHICS STATE

All the graphics state managed by the BasicSceneBuilder is stored in an instance of the GraphicsState class.

⟨*BasicSceneBuilder::GraphicsState Definition*⟩ ≡ **1123**
```
struct GraphicsState {
    ⟨GraphicsState Public Methods 1130⟩
    ⟨GraphicsState Public Members 1129⟩
};
```

A GraphicsState instance is maintained in a member variable.

⟨*BasicSceneBuilder Private Members*⟩ +≡ **1123**
```
GraphicsState graphicsState;
```

There is usually not much to do when a statement that modifies the graphics state is encountered in a scene description file. Here, for example, is the implementation of the method that is called when the ReverseOrientation statement is parsed. This statement is only valid in the world block, so that state is checked before the graphics state's corresponding variable is updated.

⟨*BasicSceneBuilder Method Definitions*⟩ +≡
```
void BasicSceneBuilder::ReverseOrientation(FileLoc loc) {
    VERIFY_WORLD("ReverseOrientation");
    graphicsState.reverseOrientation = !graphicsState.reverseOrientation;
}
```

⟨*GraphicsState Public Members*⟩ ≡   **1128**
```
bool reverseOrientation = false;
```

The current RGB color space can be specified in both the world and options blocks, so there is no need to check the value of currentBlock in the corresponding method.

⟨*BasicSceneBuilder Method Definitions*⟩ +≡
```
void BasicSceneBuilder::ColorSpace(const std::string &name, FileLoc loc) {
    if (const RGBColorSpace *cs = RGBColorSpace::GetNamed(name))
        graphicsState.colorSpace = cs;
    else
        Error(&loc, "%s: color space unknown", name);
}
```

⟨*GraphicsState Public Members*⟩ +≡   **1128**
```
const RGBColorSpace *colorSpace = RGBColorSpace::sRGB;
```

Many of the other method implementations related to graphics state management are similarly simple, so we will only include a few of the interesting ones in the following.

Managing Transformations

The *current transformation matrix* (CTM) is a widely used part of the graphics state. Initially the identity matrix, the CTM is modified by statements like Translate and Scale in scene description files. When objects like shapes and lights are defined, the CTM gives the transformation between their object coordinate system and world space.

The current transformation matrix is actually a pair of transformation matrices, each one specifying a transformation at a specific time. If the transformations are different, then they describe an animated transformation. A number of methods are available to modify one or both of the CTMs as well as to specify the time associated with each one.

GraphicsState stores these two CTMs in a ctm member variable. They are represented by a TransformSet, which is a simple utility class that stores an array of transformations and provides some routines for managing them. Its methods include an operator[] for indexing into the Transforms, an Inverse() method that returns a TransformSet that is the inverse, and IsAnimated(), which indicates whether the two Transforms differ from each other.

The activeTransformBits member variable is a bit-vector indicating which of the CTMs are active; the active Transforms are updated when the transformation-related API calls are made, while the others are unchanged. This mechanism allows the user to selectively modify the CTMs in order to define animated transformations.

⟨*GraphicsState Public Members*⟩ +≡   **1128**
```
TransformSet ctm;
uint32_t activeTransformBits = AllTransformsBits;
```

⟨*BasicSceneBuilder Private Members*⟩ +≡   **1123**

```
static constexpr int StartTransformBits = 1 << 0;
static constexpr int EndTransformBits = 1 << 1;
static constexpr int AllTransformsBits = (1 << MaxTransforms) - 1;
```

Only two transformations are currently supported. An exercise at the end of this appendix is based on relaxing this constraint.

⟨*MaxTransforms Definition*⟩ ≡

```
constexpr int MaxTransforms = 2;
```

The methods that are called when a change to the current transformation is specified in the scene description are all simple. Because the CTM is used for both the rendering options and the scene description sections, there is no need to check the value of `currentBlock` in them. Here is the method called for the `Identity` statement, which sets the CTM to the identity transform.

⟨*BasicSceneBuilder Method Definitions*⟩ +≡

```
void BasicSceneBuilder::Identity(FileLoc loc) {
    graphicsState.ForActiveTransforms(
        [](auto t) { return pbrt::Transform(); });
}
```

`ForActiveTransforms()` is a convenience method that encapsulates the logic for determining which of the CTMs is active and for passing their current value to a provided function that returns the updated transformation.

⟨*GraphicsState Public Methods*⟩ ≡   **1128**

```
template <typename F>
void ForActiveTransforms(F func) {
    for (int i = 0; i < MaxTransforms; ++i)
        if (activeTransformBits & (1 << i)) ctm[i] = func(ctm[i]);
}
```

`Translate()` postmultiplies the active CTMs with specified translation transformation.

⟨*BasicSceneBuilder Method Definitions*⟩ +≡

```
void BasicSceneBuilder::Translate(Float dx, Float dy, Float dz,
                                  FileLoc loc) {
    graphicsState.ForActiveTransforms(
        [=](auto t) { return t * pbrt::Translate(Vector3f(dx, dy, dz)); });
}
```

The rest of the transformation methods are similarly defined, so we will not show their definitions here.

`RenderFromObject()` is a convenience method that returns the rendering-from-object transformation for the specified transformation index. It is called, for example, when a shape is specified. In the world specification block, the CTM specifies the world-from-object transformation, but because pbrt performs rendering computation in a separately defined rendering coordinate system (recall Section 5.1.1), the rendering-from-world transformation must be included to get the full transformation.

⟨*BasicSceneBuilder Private Methods*⟩ ≡   1123
```
class Transform RenderFromObject(int index) const {
    return pbrt::Transform((renderFromWorld *
                            graphicsState.ctm[index]).GetMatrix());
}
```

The camera-from-world transformation is given by the CTM when the camera is specified in the scene description. renderFromWorld is therefore set in the BasicSceneBuilder::Camera() method (not included here), via a call to the CameraTransform::RenderFromWorld() method with the CameraTransform for the camera.

⟨*BasicSceneBuilder Private Members*⟩ +≡   1123
```
class Transform renderFromWorld;
```

A second version of RenderFromObject returns an AnimatedTransform that includes both transformations.

⟨*BasicSceneBuilder Private Methods*⟩ +≡   1123
```
AnimatedTransform RenderFromObject() const {
    return {RenderFromObject(0), graphicsState.transformStartTime,
            RenderFromObject(1), graphicsState.transformEndTime};
}
```

GraphicsState also maintains the starting and ending times for the specified transformations.

⟨*GraphicsState Public Members*⟩ +≡   1128
```
Float transformStartTime = 0, transformEndTime = 1;
```

A final issue related to Transforms is minimizing their storage costs. In the usual case of using 32-bit floats for pbrt's Float type, each Transform class instance uses 128 bytes of memory. Because the same transformation may be applied to many objects in the scene, it is worthwhile to reuse the same Transform for all of them when possible. The InternCache class helps with this task, allocating and storing a single Transform for each unique transformation that is passed to its Lookup() method. In turn, classes like Shape implementations are able to save memory by storing just a const Transform * rather than a full Transform.

⟨*BasicSceneBuilder Private Members*⟩ +≡   1123
```
InternCache<class Transform> transformCache;
```

Hierarchical Graphics State

When specifying the scene, it is useful to be able to make a set of changes to the graphics state, instantiate some scene objects, and then roll back to an earlier graphics state. For example, one might want to specify a base transformation to position a car model in a scene and then to use additional transformations relative to the initial one to place the wheels, the seats, and so forth. A convenient way to do this is via a stack of saved GraphicsState objects: the user can specify that the current graphics state should be copied and pushed on the stack and then later specify that the current state should be replaced with the state on the top of the stack.

This stack is managed by the AttributeBegin and AttributeEnd statements in pbrt's scene description files. The former saves the current graphics state and the latter restores the most recent saved state. Thus, a scene description file might contain the following:

```
Material "diffuse"
AttributeBegin
  Material "dielectric"
  Translate 5 0 0
  Shape "sphere" "float radius" [ 1 ]
AttributeEnd
Shape "sphere" "float radius" [ 1 ]
```

The first sphere is affected by the translation and is bound to the dielectric material, while the second sphere is diffuse and is not translated.

BasicSceneBuilder maintains a vector of GraphicsStates for this stack.

⟨*BasicSceneBuilder Method Definitions*⟩ +≡
```
void BasicSceneBuilder::AttributeBegin(FileLoc loc) {
    VERIFY_WORLD("AttributeBegin");
    pushedGraphicsStates.push_back(graphicsState);
}
```

⟨*BasicSceneBuilder Private Members*⟩ +≡   **1123**
```
std::vector<GraphicsState> pushedGraphicsStates;
```

The AttributeEnd() method also checks to see if the stack is empty and issues an error if there was no matching AttributeBegin() call earlier.

⟨*BasicSceneBuilder Method Definitions*⟩ +≡
```
void BasicSceneBuilder::AttributeEnd(FileLoc loc) {
    VERIFY_WORLD("AttributeEnd");
    ⟨Issue error on unmatched AttributeEnd⟩
    graphicsState = std::move(pushedGraphicsStates.back());
    pushedGraphicsStates.pop_back();
}
```

C.2.4 CREATING SCENE ELEMENTS

As soon as an entity in the scene is fully specified, BasicSceneBuilder passes its specification on to the BasicScene. It is thus possible to immediately begin construction of the associated object that is used for rendering even as parsing the rest of the scene description continues. For brevity, in this section and in Section C.3 we will only discuss how this process works for Samplers and for the Medium objects that represent participating media. (Those two are representative of how the rest of the scene objects are handled.)

When a Sampler statement is parsed in the scene description, the following Sampler() method is called by the parser. All that needs to be done is to record the sampler's name and parameters; because the sampler may be changed by a subsequent Sampler statement in the scene description, it should not immediately be passed along to the BasicScene.

⟨*BasicSceneBuilder Method Definitions*⟩ +≡
```
void BasicSceneBuilder::Sampler(const std::string &name,
        ParsedParameterVector params, FileLoc loc) {
    ParameterDictionary dict(std::move(params), graphicsState.colorSpace);
    VERIFY_OPTIONS("Sampler");
    sampler = SceneEntity(name, std::move(dict), loc);
}
```

BasicSceneBuilder holds on to a SceneEntity for the sampler in a member variable until its value is known to be final.

⟨*BasicSceneBuilder Private Members*⟩ +≡   **1123**
```
SceneEntity sampler;
```

Once the WorldBegin statement is parsed, the sampler, camera, film, pixel filter, accelerator, and integrator are all set; they cannot be subsequently changed. Thus, when the parser calls the WorldBegin() method of BasicSceneBuilder, each corresponding SceneEntity can be passed along to the BasicScene. (This method also does some maintenance of the graphics state, resetting the CTM to the identity transformation and handling other details; that code is not included here.)

⟨*BasicSceneBuilder Method Definitions*⟩ +≡
```
void BasicSceneBuilder::WorldBegin(FileLoc loc) {
    VERIFY_OPTIONS("WorldBegin");
    ⟨Reset graphics state for WorldBegin⟩
    ⟨Pass pre-WorldBegin entities to scene 1133⟩
}
```

All the entities are passed with a single method call; as we will see in the implementation of the SetOptions() method, having all of them at hand simultaneously makes it easier to start creating the corresponding objects for rendering.

⟨*Pass pre-WorldBegin entities to scene*⟩ ≡   **1133**
```
scene->SetOptions(filter, film, camera, sampler, integrator, accelerator);
```

There is not much more to do for media. MakeNamedMedium() begins with a check to make sure that a medium with the given name has not already been specified.

⟨*BasicSceneBuilder Method Definitions*⟩ +≡
```
void BasicSceneBuilder::MakeNamedMedium(const std::string &name,
        ParsedParameterVector params, FileLoc loc) {
    ⟨Issue error if medium name is multiply defined⟩
    ⟨Create ParameterDictionary for medium and call AddMedium() 1133⟩
}
```

Assuming the medium is not multiply defined, all that is to be done is to pass along a MediumSceneEntity to the BasicScene. This can be done immediately in this case, as there is no way for it to be subsequently changed during parsing.

⟨*Create ParameterDictionary for medium and call AddMedium()*⟩ ≡   **1133**
```
ParameterDictionary dict(std::move(params), graphicsState.mediumAttributes,
                         graphicsState.colorSpace);
scene->AddMedium(MediumSceneEntity(name, std::move(dict), loc,
                                   RenderFromObject()));
```

The other object specification methods follow the same general form, though the BasicScene Builder::Shape() method is more complex than the others. Not only does it need to check to see if an AreaLight specification is active and call BasicScene::AddAreaLight() if so, but it also needs to distinguish between shapes with animated transformations and those without, creating an AnimatedShapeSceneEntity or a ShapeSceneEntity as appropriate.

C.3 BasicScene AND FINAL OBJECT CREATION

The responsibilities of the BasicScene are straightforward: it takes scene entity objects and provides methods that convert them into objects for rendering. However, there are two factors that make its implementation not completely trivial. First, as discussed in Section C.2, if the Import directive is used in the scene specification, there may be multiple BasicSceneBuilders that are concurrently calling BasicScene methods. Therefore, the implementation must use mutual exclusion to ensure correct operation.

The second consideration is performance: we would like to minimize the time spent in the execution of BasicScene methods, as time spent in them delays parsing the remainder of the scene description. System startup time is a facet of performance that is worth attending to, and so BasicScene uses the asynchronous job capabilities introduced in Section B.6.6 to create scene objects while parsing proceeds when possible.

⟨*BasicScene Definition*⟩ ≡
```
class BasicScene {
  public:
    ⟨BasicScene Public Methods 1136⟩
    ⟨BasicScene Public Members 1134⟩
  private:
    ⟨BasicScene Private Methods⟩
    ⟨BasicScene Private Members 1135⟩
};
```

⟨*BasicScene Method Definitions*⟩ ≡
```
void BasicScene::SetOptions(SceneEntity filter, SceneEntity film,
                            CameraSceneEntity camera, SceneEntity sampler,
                            SceneEntity integ, SceneEntity accel) {
    ⟨Store information for specified integrator and accelerator 1134⟩
    ⟨Immediately create filter and film⟩
    ⟨Enqueue asynchronous job to create sampler 1135⟩
    ⟨Enqueue asynchronous job to create camera⟩
}
```

When SetOptions() is called, the specifications of the geometry and lights in the scene have not yet been parsed. Therefore, it is not yet possible to create the integrator (which needs the lights) or the acceleration structure (which needs the geometry). Therefore, their specification so far is saved in member variables for use when parsing is finished.

⟨*Store information for specified integrator and accelerator*⟩ ≡   1134
```
integrator = integ;
accelerator = accel;
```

⟨*BasicScene Public Members*⟩ ≡   1134
```
SceneEntity integrator, accelerator;
```

However, it is possible to start work on creating the Sampler, Camera, Filter, and Film. While they could all be created in turn in the SetOptions() method, we instead use RunAsync() to launch multiple jobs to take care of them. Thus, the SetOptions() method can return quickly, allowing parsing to resume, and creation of those objects can proceed in parallel as parsing proceeds if there are available CPU cores. Although these objects usually take little time to initialize, sometimes they do not: the RealisticCamera requires a second or so on a current

CPU to compute exit pupil bounds and the HaltonSampler takes approximately 0.1 seconds to initialize its random permutations. If that work can be done concurrently with parsing the scene, rendering can begin that much more quickly.

⟨*Enqueue asynchronous job to create sampler*⟩ ≡   1134
```
samplerJob = RunAsync([sampler, this]() {
    Allocator alloc = threadAllocators.Get();
    Point2i res = this->film.FullResolution();
    return Sampler::Create(sampler.name, sampler.parameters, res,
                           &sampler.loc, alloc);
});
```

The AsyncJob * returned by RunAsync() is held in a member variable. The BasicScene constructor also initializes threadAllocators so that appropriate memory allocators are available depending on whether the scene objects should be stored in CPU memory or GPU memory.

⟨*BasicScene Private Members*⟩ ≡   1134
```
AsyncJob<Sampler> *samplerJob = nullptr;
mutable ThreadLocal<Allocator> threadAllocators;
```

Briefly diverting from the BasicScene implementation, we will turn to the Sampler::Create() method that is called in the job that creates the Sampler. (This method is defined in the file samplers.cpp with the rest of the Sampler code.) It checks the provided sampler name against all the sampler names it is aware of, calling the appropriate object-specific creation method when it finds a match and issuing an error if no match is found. Thus, if the system is to be extended with an additional sampler, this is a second place in the code where the existence of the new sampler must be registered.

Most of the values that are passed to the object constructors are extracted from the Parameter Dictionary in the object-specific Create() methods, though some that are not in the available parameter list (like here, the uncropped image resolution) are directly passed as parameters to the Create() methods.

⟨*Sampler Method Definitions*⟩ ≡
```
Sampler Sampler::Create(const std::string &name,
        const ParameterDictionary &parameters, Point2i fullRes,
        const FileLoc *loc, Allocator alloc) {
    Sampler sampler = nullptr;
    if (name == "zsobol")
        sampler = ZSobolSampler::Create(parameters, fullRes, loc, alloc);
    ⟨Create remainder of Sampler types⟩
    return sampler;
}
```

The fragment that handles the remainder of types of samplers, ⟨*Create remainder of* Sampler *types*⟩, is not included here.

All the other base interface classes like Light, Shape, Camera, and so forth provide corresponding Create() methods, all of which have the same general form.

BasicScene also provides methods that return these asynchronously created objects. All have a similar form, acquiring a mutex before harvesting the result from the asynchronous job if needed. Calling code should delay calling these methods as long as possible, doing as much independent work as it can to increase the likelihood that the asynchronous job has completed and that the `AsyncJob::GetResult()` calls do not stall.

⟨*BasicScene Public Methods*⟩ ≡   **1134**
```
Sampler GetSampler() {
    samplerJobMutex.lock();
    while (!sampler) {
        pstd::optional<Sampler> s = samplerJob->TryGetResult(&samplerJobMutex);
        if (s)
            sampler = *s;
    }
    samplerJobMutex.unlock();
    return sampler;
}
```

⟨*BasicScene Private Members*⟩ +≡   **1134**
```
std::mutex samplerJobMutex;
Sampler sampler;
```

`Medium` creation is also based on `RunAsync()`'s asynchronous job capabilities, though in that case a `std::map` of jobs is maintained, one for each medium. Note that it is important that a mutex be held when storing the `AsyncJob *` returned by `RunAsync()` in `mediumJobs`, since multiple threads may call this method concurrently if `Import` statements are used for multi-threaded parsing.

⟨*BasicScene Method Definitions*⟩ +≡
```
void BasicScene::AddMedium(MediumSceneEntity medium) {
    ⟨Define create lambda function for Medium creation 1136⟩
    std::lock_guard<std::mutex> lock(mediaMutex);
    mediumJobs[medium.name] = RunAsync(create);
}
```

⟨*BasicScene Private Members*⟩ +≡   **1134**
```
std::mutex mediaMutex;
std::map<std::string, AsyncJob<Medium> *> mediumJobs;
```

Creation of each `Medium` follows a similar form to `Sampler` creation, though here the type of medium to be created is found from the parameter list; the `MediumSceneEntity::name` member variable holds the user-provided name to associate with the medium.

⟨*Define* create *lambda function for* Medium *creation*⟩ ≡   **1136**
```
auto create = [medium, this]() {
    std::string type = medium.parameters.GetOneString("type", "");
    ⟨Check for missing medium "type" or animated medium transform⟩
    return Medium::Create(type, medium.parameters,
                          medium.renderFromObject.startTransform,
                          &medium.loc, threadAllocators.Get());
};
```

All the media specified in the scene are provided to callers via a map from names to `Medium` objects.

⟨*BasicScene Method Definitions*⟩ +≡
```
std::map<std::string, Medium> BasicScene::CreateMedia() {
    mediaMutex.lock();
    if (!mediumJobs.empty()) {
        ⟨Consume results for asynchronously created Medium objects 1137⟩
    }
    mediaMutex.unlock();
    return mediaMap;
}
```

The asynchronously created `Medium` objects are consumed using calls to `AsyncJob::TryGet Result()`, which returns the result if it is available and otherwise unlocks the mutex, does some of the enqueued parallel work, and then relocks it before returning. Thus, there is no risk of deadlock from one thread holding `mediaMutex`, finding that the result is not ready and working on enqueued parallel work that itself ends up trying to acquire `mediaMutex`.

⟨*Consume results for asynchronously created* Medium *objects*⟩ ≡   1137
```
for (auto &m : mediumJobs) {
    while (mediaMap.find(m.first) == mediaMap.end()) {
        pstd::optional<Medium> med = m.second->TryGetResult(&mediaMutex);
        if (med)
            mediaMap[m.first] = *med;
    }
}
mediumJobs.clear();
```

⟨*BasicScene Private Members*⟩ +≡   1134
```
std::map<std::string, Medium> mediaMap;
```

As much as possible, other scene objects are created similarly using `RunAsync()`. Light sources are easy to handle, and it is especially helpful to start creating image textures during parsing, as reading image file formats from disk can be a bottleneck for scenes with many such textures. However, extra attention is required due to the cache of images already read for textures (Section 10.4.1). If an image file on disk is used in multiple textures, `BasicScene` takes care not to have multiple jobs redundantly reading the same image. Instead, only one reads it and the rest wait. When those textures are then created, the image they need can be efficiently returned from the cache.

In return for the added complexity of this asynchronous object creation, we have found that for complex scenes it is not unusual for this version of pbrt to be able to start rendering 4 times more quickly than the previous version.

C.4 ADDING NEW OBJECT IMPLEMENTATIONS

To sum up various details that have been spread across multiple chapters, three main steps are required in order to add a new implementation of one of pbrt's interface types:

1. The source files containing its implementation need to be added to the appropriate places in pbrt's top-level `CMakeLists.txt` file, or they should be added to an appropriate preexisting source file so that they are compiled into the pbrt binary.
2. The name of the type should be added to the list of types provided to the `TaggedPointer` that the corresponding interface type inherits from; this can be done by editing the appropriate header file in the base/ directory.

3. The interface type's `Create()` method should be modified to create an instance of the new type when it has been specified in the scene description.

It is probably a good idea to implement a `static Create()` method in the new type that takes a `ParameterDictionary` and such, to specify the object's parameters in the same way that the existing classes do, but doing so is not a requirement.

FURTHER READING

pbrt's scene file format is custom, which has allowed us to tailor it to present all the system's capabilities, though it makes it more challenging to import scenes from other systems, requiring a conversion step. (See the pbrt website for links to a number of such converters.)

There has been little standardization in these file formats; many 3D graphics file formats have been developed, in part due to the needs of graphics systems changing over time and in part due to lack of standardization on material and texture models. In addition to its own text format, pbrt does support the PLY format for specifying polygon meshes, which was originally developed by Greg Turk in the 1990s. PLY provides both text and binary encodings; the latter can be parsed fairly efficiently. Pixar's *RenderMan* interface (Upstill 1989; Apodaca and Gritz 2000) saw some adoption in past decades, and the ambitiously named *Universal Scene Description* (USD) format is currently widely used in film production (Pixar Animation Studios 2020).

EXERCISES

❸ **C.1** An advantage of the way that pbrt separates parsing, graphics state management, and the creation of scene objects is that it is easier to replace or extend those components of the system than it might be if all those responsibilities were in a single class. Investigate pbrt's parsing performance with scenes that have multi-gigabyte `*.pbrt` scene description files (Disney's *Moana Island* scene (Walt Disney Animation Studios 2018) is a good choice) and develop a scene description format for pbrt that is more efficient to parse. You might, for example, consider a compact binary format.

Take advantage of the `ParserTarget` interface to write a converter from pbrt's current scene file format to your format and then implement new parsing routines that call `ParserTarget` interface methods. Use a profiler to measure how much time is spent in parsing before and after your changes. What is the performance benefit from your representation? How much smaller are file sizes?

❸ **C.2** Generalize pbrt's mechanism for specifying animation; the current implementation only allows the user to provide two transformation matrices, at the start and end of a fixed time range. For specifying more complex motion, a more flexible approach may be useful. One improvement is to allow the user to specify an arbitrary number of *keyframe* transformations, each associated with an arbitrary time.

More generally, the system could be extended to support transformations that are explicit functions of time. For example, a rotation could be described with an expression of the form `Rotate (time * 2 + 1) 0 0 1` to describe a time-varying rotation about the z axis. Extend pbrt to support a more general matrix animation scheme, and render images showing results that are not possible with the current

ParameterDictionary 1124
ParserTarget 1120

implementation. Is there a performance cost due to your changes for scenes with animated objects that do not need the generality of your improvements?

● **C.3** Extend pbrt to have some retained mode semantics so that animated sequences of images can be rendered without needing to respecify the entire scene for each frame. Make sure that it is possible to remove some objects from the scene, add others, modify objects' materials and transformations from frame to frame, and so on. Measure the performance benefit from your approach versus the current implementation. How is the benefit affected by how fast rendering is?

● **C.4** In pbrt's current implementation, a unique TransformedPrimitive is created for each Shape with an animated transformation when the CPU is used for rendering. If many shapes have exactly the same animated transformation, this turns out to be a poor choice. Consider the difference between a million-triangle mesh with an animated transformation versus a million independent triangles, all of which happen to have the same animated transformation.

In the first case, all the triangles in the mesh are stored in a single instance of a TransformedPrimitive with an animated transformation. If a ray intersects the bounding box that encompasses all the object's motion over the frame time, then it is transformed to the mesh's object space according to the interpolated transformation at the ray's time. At this point, the intersection computation is no different from the intersection test with a static primitive; the only overhead due to the animation is from the larger bounding box and rays that hit the bounding box but not the animated primitive and the extra computation for matrix interpolation and transforming each ray once, according to its time.

In the second case, each triangle is stored in its own TransformedPrimitive, all of which happen to have the same AnimatedTransform. Each instance of Transformed Primitive will have a large bounding box to encompass each triangle's motion, giving the acceleration structure a difficult set of inputs to deal with: many primitives with substantially overlapping bounding boxes. The impact on ray–primitive intersection efficiency will be high: the ray will be redundantly transformed many times by what happens to be the same recomputed interpolated transformation, and many intersection tests will be performed due to the large bounding boxes. Performance will be much worse than the first case.

To address this case, modify the code that creates primitives so that if independent shapes are provided with the same animated transformation, they are all collected into a single acceleration structure with a single animated transformation. What is the performance improvement for the worst case outlined above? Are there cases where the current implementation is a better choice?

References

Adams, A., and M. Levoy. 2007. General linear cameras with finite aperture. In *Rendering Techniques (Proceedings of the 2007 Eurographics Symposium on Rendering)*, 121–26.

Áfra, A. 2012. Incoherent ray tracing without acceleration structures. *Eurographics 2012 Short Papers*.

Áfra, A. T., C. Benthin, I. Wald, and J. Munkberg. 2016. Local shading coherence extraction for SIMD-efficient path tracing on CPUs. *Proceedings of High Performance Graphics (HPG '16)*, 119–28.

Ahmed, A., T. Niese, H. Huang, and O. Deussen. 2017. An adaptive point sampler on a regular lattice. *ACM Transactions on Graphics (Proceedings of SIGGRAPH) 36* (4), 138:1–13.

Ahmed, A., H. Perrier, D. Coeurjolly, V. Ostromoukhov, J. Guo, D. Yan, H. Huang, and O. Deussen. 2016. Low-discrepancy blue noise sampling. *ACM Transactions on Graphics (Proceedings of SIGGRAPH Asia) 35* (6), 247:1–13.

Ahmed, A. G. M., and P. Wonka. 2020. Screen-space blue-noise diffusion of Monte Carlo sampling error via hierarchical ordering of pixels. *ACM Transactions on Graphics (Proceedings of SIGGRAPH Asia) 39* (6), 244:1–15.

Ahmed, A. G. M., and P. Wonka. 2021. Optimizing dyadic nets. *ACM Transactions on Graphics (Proceedings of SIGGRAPH) 40* (4), 141:1–17.

Aila, T., and T. Karras. 2010. Architecture considerations for tracing incoherent rays. In *Proceedings of High Performance Graphics 2010*, 113–22.

Aila, T., T. Karras, and S. Laine. 2013. On quality metrics of bounding volume hierarchies. In *Proceedings of High Performance Graphics 2013*, 101–7.

Aila, T., and S. Laine. 2009. Understanding the efficiency of ray traversal on GPUs. In *Proceedings of High Performance Graphics 2009*, 145–50.

Akalin, F. 2015. Sampling the visible sphere. *https://www.akalin.com/sampling-visible-sphere*.

Akenine-Möller, T., C. Crassin, J. Boksansky, L. Belcour, A. Panteleev, and O. Wright. 2021. Improved shader and texture level of detail using ray cones. *Journal of Computer Graphics Techniques (JCGT) 10* (1), 1–24.

Akenine-Möller, T., E. Haines, N. Hoffman, A. Peesce, M. Iwanicki, and S. Hillaire. 2018. *Real-Time Rendering* (4th ed.). Boca Raton, FL: CRC Press.

Akenine-Möller, T., J. Nilsson., M. Andersson, C. Barré-Brisebois, R. Toth, and T. Karras. 2019. Texture level of detail strategies for real-time ray tracing. In E. Haines and T. Akenine-Möller (ed.), *Ray Tracing Gems*, 321–45. Berkeley: Apress.

Aliaga, C., C. Castillo, D. Gutiérrez, M. A. Otaduy, J. Lopez-Moreno, and A. Jarabo. 2017. An appearance model for textile fibers. *Computer Graphics Forum 36* (4), 35–45.

Alim, U. R. 2013. Rendering in shift-invariant spaces. In *Proceedings of Graphics Interface 2013*, 189–96.

Amanatides, J. 1984. Ray tracing with cones. *Computer Graphics (SIGGRAPH '84 Proceedings) 18* (3), 129–35.

Amanatides, J. 1992. Algorithms for the detection and elimination of specular aliasing. In *Proceedings of Graphics Interface 1992*, 86–93.

Amanatides, J., and D. P. Mitchell. 1990. Some regularization problems in ray tracing. In *Proceedings of Graphics Interface 1990*, 221–28.

Amanatides, J., and A. Woo. 1987. A fast voxel traversal algorithm for ray tracing. In *Proceedings of Eurographics '87*, 3–10.

Ament, M., C. Bergmann, and D. Weiskopf. 2014. Refractive radiative transfer equation. *ACM Transactions on Graphics (Proceedings of SIGGRAPH 2014) 33* (2), 17:1–22.

Anderson, L., T.-M. Li, J. Lehtinen, and F. Durand. 2017. Aether: An embedded domain specific sampling language for Monte Carlo rendering. *ACM Transactions on Graphics (Proceedings of SIGGRAPH 2017) 36* (4), 99:1–16.

Anderson, S. 2004. Bit twiddling hacks. *graphics.stanford.edu/~seander/bithacks.html*.

Antonov, I. A., and V. M. Saleev. 1979. An economic method of computing LP_τ sequences. *Zh. Vychisl. Mat. Mat. Fiz. 19* (1), 243–45. (*U.S.S.R. Computational Mathematics and Mathematical Physics 19* (1), 252–56.)

Apodaca, A. A., and L. Gritz. 2000. *Advanced RenderMan: Creating CGI for Motion Pictures*. San Francisco: Morgan Kaufmann.

Appel, A. 1968. Some techniques for shading machine renderings of solids. In *AFIPS 1968 Spring Joint Computer Conference 32*, 37–45.

Appleby, A. 2011. MurmurHash3. *https://sites.google.com/site/murmurhash/*.

Arnaldi, B., T. Priol, and K. Bouatouch. 1987. A new space subdivision method for ray tracing CSG modeled scenes. *The Visual Computer 3* (2), 98–108.

Arvo, J. 1986. Backward ray tracing. In *Developments in Ray Tracing, SIGGRAPH '86 Course Notes*, 259–63.

Arvo, J. 1988. Linear-time voxel walking for octrees. *Ray Tracing News 1* (5).

Arvo, J. 1990. Transforming axis-aligned bounding boxes. In A. S. Glassner (ed.), *Graphics Gems I*, 548–50. San Diego: Academic Press.

Arvo, J. 1993. Transfer equations in global illumination. In *Global Illumination, SIGGRAPH '93 Course Notes*, Volume 42, 1:1–30.

Arvo, J. 1995a. Analytic methods for simulated light transport. Ph.D. thesis, Yale University.

Arvo, J. 1995b. Stratified sampling of spherical triangles. In *Proceedings of SIGGRAPH 1995*, 437–38.

Arvo, J. 2001a. Stratified sampling of 2-manifolds. In *SIGGRAPH 2001 Course Notes 29*, 1–34.

Arvo, J. 2001b. SphTri.h and SphTri.C. *Jim Arvo's Software and Data Archive, https://web.archive.org/web/20050216002912/http://www.cs.caltech.edu/~arvo/code/SphTri.C*.

Arvo, J., and D. Kirk. 1987. Fast ray tracing by ray classification. *Computer Graphics (SIGGRAPH '87 Proceedings) 21* (4), 55–64.

Arvo, J., and D. Kirk. 1990. Particle transport and image synthesis. *Computer Graphics (SIGGRAPH '90 Proceedings) 24* (4), 63–66.

Arvo, J., and K. Novins. 2007. Stratified sampling of convex quadrilaterals. *Journal of Graphics, GPU, and Game Tools 12* (2), 1–12.

Ashdown, I. 1993. Near-field photometry: A new approach. *Journal of the Illuminating Engineering Society 22* (1), 163–80.

Ashdown, I. 1994. *Radiosity: A Programmer's Perspective.* New York: John Wiley & Sons.

Atanasov, A., V. Koylazov, B. Taskov, A. Soklev, V. Chizhov, and J. Křivánek. 2018. Adaptive environment sampling on CPU and GPU. In *ACM SIGGRAPH 2018 Talks*, 68:1–2.

Atanasov, A., A. Wilkie, V. Koylazov, and J. Křivánek. 2021. A multiscale microfacet model based on inverse bin mapping. *Computer Graphics Forum (Proceedings of Eurographics) 40* (2), 103–13.

Atcheson, B., I. Ihrke, W. Heidrich, A. Tevs, D. Bradley, M. Magnor, and H.-P. Seidel. 2008. Time-resolved 3d capture of non-stationary gas flows. *ACM Transactions on Graphics (Proceedings of SIGGRAPH Asia) 27* (5), 132:1–9.

Atkinson, K. 1993. *Elementary Numerical Analysis.* New York: John Wiley & Sons.

Azinović, D., T.-M. Li, A. Kaplanyan, and M. Nießner. 2019. Inverse path tracing for joint material and lighting estimation. In *IEEE Conference on Computer Vision and Pattern Recognition*, 2442–51.

Badouel, D., and T. Priol. 1990. An efficient parallel ray tracing scheme for highly parallel architectures. In *Proceedings of the Fifth Eurographics conference on Advances in Computer Graphics Hardware: Rendering, Ray Tracing and Visualization Systems (EGGH '90)*, 93–106.

Baek, S.-H., T. Zeltner, H. J. Ku, I. Hwang, X. Tong, W. Jakob, and M. H. Kim. 2020. Image-based acquisition and modeling of polarimetric reflectance. *ACM Transactions on Graphics (Proceedings of SIGGRAPH) 39* (4), 139:1–14.

Bagher, M. M., J. M. Snyder, and D. Nowrouzezahrai. 2016. A non-parametric factor microfacet model for isotropic BRDFs. *ACM Transactions on Graphics 35* (5), 159:1–16.

Bahar, E., and S. Chakrabarti. 1987. Full-wave theory applied to computer-aided graphics for 3D objects. *IEEE Computer Graphics and Applications 7* (7), 46–60.

Bako, S., M. Meyer, T. DeRose, and P. Sen. 2019. Offline deep importance sampling for Monte Carlo path tracing. *Computer Graphics Forum 38* (7), 527–42.

Bako, S., T. Vogels, B. McWilliams, M. Meyer, J. Novák, A. Harvill, P. Sen, T. DeRose, and F. Rousselle. 2017. Kernel-predicting convolutional networks for denoising Monte Carlo renderings. *ACM Transactions on Graphics (Proceedings of SIGGRAPH) 36* (4), 97:1–14.

Bangaru, S., T.-M. Li, and F. Durand. 2020. Unbiased warped-area sampling for differentiable rendering. *ACM Transactions on Graphics (Proceedings of SIGGRAPH Asia) 39* (6), 245:1–18.

Banks, D. C. 1994. Illumination in diverse codimensions. In *Proceedings of SIGGRAPH '94*, Computer Graphics Proceedings, Annual Conference Series, 327–34.

Barequet, G., and G. Elber. 2005. Optimal bounding cones of vectors in three dimensions. *Information Processing Letters 93* (2), 83–89.

Barkans, A. C. 1997. High-quality rendering using the Talisman architecture. In *1997 SIGGRAPH/Eurographics Workshop on Graphics Hardware*, 79–88.

Barla, P., R. Pacanowski, and P. Vangorp. 2018. A composite BRDF model for hazy gloss. *Computer Graphics Forum 37* (4), 55–66.

Barnes, C., and F.-L. Zhang. 2017. A survey of the state-of-the-art in patch-based synthesis. *Computational Visual Media 3*, 3–20.

Barnes, T. 2014. Exact bounding boxes for spheres/ellipsoids. *https://tavianator.com/2014/ellipsoid_bounding_boxes.html*.

Barringer, R., and T. Akenine-Möller. 2014. Dynamic ray stream traversal. *ACM Transactions on Graphics (Proceedings of SIGGRAPH 2014) 33* (4), 151:1–9.

Barzel, R. 1997. Lighting controls for computer cinematography. *Journal of Graphics Tools 2* (1), 1–20.

Bashford-Rogers, T., K. Debattista, and A. Chalmers. 2013. Importance driven environment map sampling. *IEEE Transactions on Visualization and Computer Graphics 20* (6), 907–18.

Basu, K., and A. B. Owen. 2015. Low discrepancy constructions in the triangle. *SIAM Journal on Numerical Analysis 53* (2), 743–61.

Basu, K., and A. B. Owen. 2016. Transformations and Hardy–Krause variation. *SIAM Journal on Numerical Analysis 54* (3), 1946–66.

Basu, K., and A. B. Owen. 2017. Scrambled geometric net integration over general product spaces. *Foundations of Computational Mathematics 17*, 467–96.

Bauszat, P., M. Eisemann, and M. Magnor. 2010. The minimal bounding volume hierarchy. *Vision, Modeling, and Visualization (2010)*, 227–34.

Becker, B. G., and N. L. Max. 1993. Smooth transitions between bump rendering algorithms. In *Proceedings of SIGGRAPH '93*, Computer Graphics Proceedings, Annual Conference Series, 183–90.

Beckmann, P., and A. Spizzichino. 1963. *The Scattering of Electromagnetic Waves from Rough Surfaces*. New York: Pergamon.

Belcour, L. 2018. Efficient rendering of layered materials using an atomic decomposition with statistical operators. *ACM Transactions on Graphics (Proceedings of SIGGRAPH) 37* (4), 73:1–15.

Belcour, L., and P. Barla. 2017. A practical extension to microfacet theory for the modeling of varying iridescence. *ACM Transactions on Graphics (Proceedings of SIGGRAPH) 36* (4), 65:1–14.

Belcour, L., C. Soler, K. Subr, N. Holzschuch, and F. Durand. 2013. 5D covariance tracing for efficient defocus and motion blur. *ACM Transactions on Graphics 32* (3), 31:1–18.

Belcour, L., G. Xie, C. Hery, M. Meyer, W. Jarosz, and D. Nowrouzezahrai. 2018. Integrating clipped spherical harmonics expansions. *ACM Transactions on Graphics 37* (2), 19:1–12.

Belcour, L., L.-Q. Yan, R. Ramamoorthi, and D. Nowrouzezahrai. 2017. Antialiasing complex global illumination effects in path-space. *ACM Transactions on Graphics 36* (1), 9:1–13.

Benamira, A., and S. Pattanaik. 2021. A combined scattering and diffraction model for elliptical hair rendering. *Computer Graphics Forum (Proceedings of EGSR 2021) 40* (4), 163–75.

Benthin, C. 2006. Realtime ray tracing on current CPU architectures. Ph.D. thesis, Saarland University.

Benthin, C., S. Boulos, D. Lacewell, and I. Wald. 2007. Packet-based ray tracing of Catmull–Clark subdivision surfaces. *SCI Institute Technical Report, No. UUSCI-2007-011*. University of Utah.

Benthin, C., and I. Wald. 2009. Efficient ray traced soft shadows using multi-frusta tracing. In *Proceedings of High Performance Graphics 2009*, 135–44.

Benthin, C., I. Wald, and P. Slusallek. 2003. A scalable approach to interactive global illumination. In *Computer Graphics Forum 22* (3), 621–30.

Benthin, C., I. Wald, and P. Slusallek. 2006. Techniques for interactive ray tracing of Bézier surfaces. *Journal of Graphics, GPU, and Game Tools 11* (2), 1–16.

Benthin, C., I. Wald, S. Woop, and A. T. Áfra. 2018. Compressed-leaf bounding volume hierarchies. *Proceedings of High Performance Graphics (HPG '18)*, 6:1–4.

Benthin, C., I. Wald, S. Woop, M. Ernst, and W. R. Mark. 2011. Combining single and packet ray tracing for arbitrary ray distributions on the Intel® MIC architecture. *IEEE Transactions on Visualization and Computer Graphics 18* (9), 1438–48.

Benthin, C., S. Woop, M. Nießner, K. Selgrad, and I. Wald. 2015. Efficient ray tracing of subdivision surfaces using tessellation caching. *Proceedings of the 7th Conference on High Performance Graphics (HPG '15)*, 5–12.

Benthin, C., S. Woop, I. Wald, and A. T. Áfra. 2017. Improved two-level BVHs using partial re-braiding. *Proceedings of High Performance Graphics (HPG '17)*, 7:1–8.

Betrisey, C., J. F. Blinn, B. Dresevic, B. Hill, G. Hitchcock, B. Keely, D. P. Mitchell, J. C. Platt, and T. Whitted. 2000. Displaced filtering for patterned displays. *Society for Information Display International Symposium. Digest of Technical Papers 31*, 296–99.

Bhate, N., and A. Tokuta. 1992. Photorealistic volume rendering of media with directional scattering. In *Proceedings of the Third Eurographics Rendering Workshop*, 227–45.

Bigler, J., A. Stephens, and S. Parker. 2006. Design for parallel interactive ray tracing systems. *IEEE Symposium on Interactive Ray Tracing*, 187–95.

Bikker, J., and J. van Schijndel. 2013. The Brigade renderer: A path tracer for real-time games. *International Journal of Computer Games Technology*, Volume 8.

Billen, N., and P. Dutré. 2016. Line sampling for direct illumination. *Computer Graphics Forum 35* (4), 45–55.

Billen, N., B. Engelen, A. Lagae, and P. Dutré. 2013. Probabilistic visibility evaluation for direct illumination. *Computer Graphics Forum (Proceedings of the 2013 Eurographics Symposium on Rendering) 32* (4), 39–47.

Billen, N., A. Lagae, and P. Dutré. 2014. Probabilistic visibility evaluation using geometry proxies. *Computer Graphics Forum (Proceedings of the 2014 Eurographics Symposium on Rendering) 33* (4), 143–52.

Binder, N., and A. Keller. 2016. Efficient stackless hierarchy traversal on GPUs with backtracking in constant time. *Proceedings of High Performance Graphics*, 41–50.

Binder, N., and A. Keller. 2018. Fast, high precision ray/fiber intersection using tight, disjoint bounding volumes. arXiv:1811.03374 [cs.GR].

Binder, N., and A. Keller. 2020. Massively parallel construction of radix tree forests for the efficient sampling of discrete or piecewise constant probability distributions. *Monte Carlo and Quasi-Monte Carlo Methods (MCQMC 2018)*. arXiv: 1902.05942 [cs].

Bitterli, B., W. Jakob, J. Novák, and W. Jarosz. 2018a. Reversible jump Metropolis light transport using inverse mappings. *ACM Transactions on Graphics 37* (1), 1:1–12.

Bitterli, B., and W. Jarosz. 2019. Selectively Metropolised Monte Carlo light transport simulation. *ACM Transactions on Graphics (Proceedings of SIGGRAPH Asia) 38* (6), 153:1–10.

Bitterli, B., J. Novák, and W. Jarosz. 2015. Portal-masked environment map sampling. *Computer Graphics Forum (Proceedings of the 2015 Eurographics Symposium on Rendering) 34* (4), 13–19.

Bitterli, B., S. Ravichandran, T. Müller, M. Wrenninge, J. Novák, S. Marschner, and W. Jarosz. 2018b. A radiative transfer framework for non-exponential media. *ACM Transactions on Graphics (Proceedings of SIGGRAPH Asia) 37* (6), 225:1–17.

Bitterli, B., F. Rousselle, B. Moon, J. A. Iglesias-Guitián, D. Adler, K. Mitchell, W. Jarosz, and J. Novák. 2016. Nonlinearly weighted first-order regression for denoising Monte Carlo renderings. *Computer Graphics Forum 35* (4), 107–17.

Bitterli, B., C. Wyman, M. Pharr, P. Shirley, A. Lefohn, and W. Jarosz. 2020. Spatiotemporal reservoir resampling for real-time ray tracing with dynamic direct lighting. *ACM Transactions on Graphics (Proceedings of SIGGRAPH) 39* (4), 148:1–17.

Bittner, J., M. Hapala, and V. Havran. 2013. Fast insertion-based optimization of bounding volume hierarchies. *Computer Graphics Forum 32* (1), 85–100.

Bittner, J., M. Hapala, and V. Havran. 2014. Incremental BVH construction for ray tracing. *Computers & Graphics 47*, 135–44.

Bjorke, K. 2001. Using Maya with RenderMan on Final Fantasy: The Spirits Within. *SIGGRAPH 2001 RenderMan Course Notes.*

Blakey, E. 2012. Ray tracing—computing the incomputable? *Developments in Computational Models*, 32–40.

Blasi, P., B. L. Saëc, and C. Schlick. 1993. A rendering algorithm for discrete volume density objects. *Computer Graphics Forum (Proceedings of Eurographics '93) 12* (3), 201–10.

Blinn, J. F. 1977. Models of light reflection for computer synthesized pictures. *Computer Graphics (SIGGRAPH '77 Proceedings) 11*, 192–98.

Blinn, J. F. 1978. Simulation of wrinkled surfaces. In *Computer Graphics (SIGGRAPH '78 Proceedings) 12*, 286–92.

Blinn, J. F. 1982a. A generalization of algebraic surface drawing. *ACM Transactions on Graphics 1* (3), 235–56.

Blinn, J. F. 1982b. Light reflection functions for simulation of clouds and dusty surfaces. *Computer Graphics 16* (3), 21–29.

Blinn, J. F., and M. E. Newell. 1976. Texture and reflection in computer generated images. *Communications of the ACM 19*, 542–46.

Blumer, A., J. Novák, R. Habel, D. Nowrouzezahrai, and W. Jarosz. 2016. Reduced aggregate scattering operators for path tracing. *Computer Graphics Forum 35* (7), 461–73.

Blumofe, R., C. Joerg, B. Kuszmaul, C. Leiserson, K. Randall, and Y. Zhou. 1996. Cilk: An efficient multithreaded runtime system. *Journal of Parallel and Distributed Computing 37* (1), 55–69.

Blumofe, R., and C. Leiserson. 1999. Scheduling multithreaded computations by work stealing. *Journal of the ACM 46* (5), 720–48.

Boehm, H.-J. 2005. Threads cannot be implemented as a library. *ACM SIGPLAN Notices 40* (6), 261–68.

Boksansky, J., C. Crassin, and T. Akenine-Möller. 2021. Refraction ray cones for texture level of detail. In Marrs, A., P. Shirley, and I. Wald (eds.), *Ray Tracing Gems II*. Berkeley: Apress, 127–38.

Borges, C. 1991. Trichromatic approximation for computer graphics illumination models. *Computer Graphics (Proceedings of SIGGRAPH '91) 25*, 101–4.

Bouchard, G., J.-C. Iehl, V. Ostromoukhov, and P. Poulin. 2013. Improving robustness of Monte-Carlo global illumination with directional regularization. In *SIGGRAPH Asia 2013 Technical Briefs*, 22:1–4.

Boughida, M., and T. Boubekeur. 2017. Bayesian collaborative denoising for Monte Carlo rendering. *Computer Graphics Forum 36* (4), 137–53.

Boulos, S., and E. Haines. 2006. Ray–box sorting. *Ray Tracing News 19* (1), www.realtimerendering.com/resources/RTNews/html/rtnv19n1.html.

Boulos, S., I. Wald, and C. Benthin. 2008. Adaptive ray packet reordering. In *Proceedings of IEEE Symposium on Interactive Ray Tracing*, 131–38.

Braaten, E., and G. Weller. 1979. An improved low-discrepancy sequence for multidimensional quasi-Monte Carlo integration. *Journal of Computational Physics 33* (2), 249–58.

Bracewell, R. N. 2000. *The Fourier Transform and Its Applications*. New York: McGraw-Hill.

Bratley, P., and B. L. Fox. 1988. Algorithm 659: Implementing Sobol's quasirandom sequence generator. *ACM Transactions on Mathematical Software 14* (1), 88–100.

Bresenham, J. E. 1965. Algorithm for computer control of a digital plotter. *IBM Systems Journal 4* (1), 25–30.

Bronsvoort, W. F., and F. Klok. 1985. Ray tracing generalized cylinders. *ACM Transactions on Graphics 4* (4), 291–303.

Bruneton, E. 2017. A qualitative and quantitative evaluation of 8 clear sky models. *IEEE Transactions on Visualization and Computer Graphics 23* (12), 2641–55.

Bruneton, E., and F. Neyret. 2012. A survey of nonlinear prefiltering methods for efficient and accurate surface shading. *IEEE Transactions on Visualization and Computer Graphics 18* (2), 242–60.

Buck, R. C. 1978. *Advanced Calculus*. New York: McGraw-Hill.

Budge, B., T. Bernardin, J. Stuart, S. Sengupta, K. Joy, and J. D. Owens. 2009. Out-of-core data management for path tracing on hybrid resources. *Computer Graphics Forum (Proceedings of Eurographics 2009) 28* (2), 385–96.

Budge, B., D. Coming, D. Norpchen, and K. Joy. 2008. Accelerated building and ray tracing of restricted BSP trees. *2008 IEEE Symposium on Interactive Ray Tracing*, 167–74.

Buisine, J., S. Delepoulle, and C. Renaud. 2021. Firefly removal in Monte Carlo rendering with adaptive Median of meaNs. *Proceedings of the Eurographics Symposium on Rendering*, 121–32.

Burke, D., A. Ghosh, and W. Heidrich. 2005. Bidirectional importance sampling for direct illumination. In *Rendering Techniques 2005: 16th Eurographics Workshop on Rendering*, 147–56.

Burley, B. 2012. Physically-based shading at Disney. *Physically Based Shading in Film and Game Production, SIGGRAPH 2012 Course Notes*.

Burley, B. 2020. Hash-based Owen scrambling. *Journal of Computer Graphics Techniques (JCGT) 9* (4), 1–20.

Burley, B., D. Adler, M. J-Y. Chiang, H. Driskill, R. Habel, P. Kelly, P. Kutz, Y. K. Li, and D. Teece. 2018. The design and evolution of Disney's Hyperion renderer. *ACM Transactions on Graphics 37* (3), 33:1–22.

Cabral, B., N. Max, and R. Springmeyer. 1987. Bidirectional reflection functions from surface bump maps. *Computer Graphics (SIGGRAPH '87 Proceedings) 21*, 273–81.

Cant, R. J., and P. A. Shrubsole. 2000. Texture potential MIP mapping, a new high-quality texture antialiasing algorithm. *ACM Transactions on Graphics 19* (3), 164–84.

Carr, N., J. D. Hall, and J. Hart. 2002. The ray engine. In *Proceedings of ACM SIGGRAPH Workshop on Graphics Hardware 2002*, 37–46.

Castillo, C., J. López-Moreno, and C. Aliaga. 2019. Recent advances in fabric appearance reproduction. *Computers & Graphics 84*, 103–21.

Catmull, E., and J. Clark. 1978. Recursively generated B-spline surfaces on arbitrary topological meshes. *Computer-Aided Design 10*, 350–55.

Cazals, F., G. Drettakis, and C. Puech. 1995. Filtering, clustering and hierarchy construction: A new solution for ray-tracing complex scenes. *Computer Graphics Forum 14* (3), 371–82.

Celarek, A., W. Jakob, M. Wimmer, and J. Lehtinen. 2019. Quantifying the error of light transport algorithms. *Computer Graphics Forum 38* (4), 111–21.

Cerezo, E., F. Perez-Cazorla, X. Pueyo, F. Seron, and F. Sillion. 2005. A survey on participating media rendering techniques. *The Visual Computer 21* (5), 303–28.

Chaitanya, C. R. A., A. S. Kaplanyan, C. Schied, M. Salvi, A. Lefohn, D. Nowrouzezahrai, and T. Aila. 2017. Interactive reconstruction of Monte Carlo image sequences using a recurrent denoising autoencoder. *ACM Transactions on Graphics (Proceedings of SIGGRAPH) 36* (4), 98:1–12.

Chan, T. F., G. Golub, R. J. LeVeque. 1979. Updating formulae and a pairwise algorithm for computing sample variances. *Technical Report STAN-CS-79-773*, Department of Computer Science, Stanford University.

Chandrasekhar, S. 1960. *Radiative Transfer*. New York: Dover Publications. Originally published by Oxford University Press, 1950.

Chao, M. T. 1982. A general purpose unequal probability sampling plan. *Biometrika 69* (3), 653–56.

Chen, J., K. Venkataraman, D. Bakin, B. Rodricks, R. Gravelle, P. Rao, and Y. Ni. 2009. Digital camera imaging system simulation. *IEEE Transactions on Electron Devices 56* (11), 2496–505.

Chen, H. C., and Y. Asau. 1974. On generating random variates from an empirical distribution. *AIIE Transactions 6* (2), 163–66.

Chen, Q., and V. Koltun. 2017. Photographic image synthesis with cascaded refinement networks. *IEEE/CVF International Conference on Computer Vision (ICCV)*, 1511–20. arXiv:1707:09405 [cs.CV].

Chen, X., D. Cohen-Or, B. Chen, and N. J. Mitra. 2021. Towards a neural graphics pipeline for controllable image generation. *Computer Graphics Forum 40* (2), 127–40.

Chermain, X., F. Claux, and S. Mérillou. 2019. Glint rendering based on a multiple-scattering patch BRDF. *Computer Graphics Forum 38* (4), 27–37.

Chermain, X., B. Sauvage, J.-M. Dischler, and C. Dachsbacher. 2021. Importance sampling of glittering BSDFs based on finite mixture distributions. *Proceedings of the Eurographics Symposium on Rendering*, 45–53.

Chiang, M. J.-Y., B. Bitterli, C. Tappan, and B. Burley. 2016a. A practical and controllable hair and fur model for production path tracing. *Computer Graphics Forum (Proceedings of Eurographics 2016) 35* (2), 275–83.

Chiang, M. J.-Y., P. Kutz, and B. Burley. 2016b. Practical and controllable subsurface scattering for production path tracing. *ACM SIGGRAPH 2016 Talks*, 49:1–2.

Chiang, M. J.-Y., Y. K. Li, and B. Burley. 2019. Taming the shadow terminator. *ACM SIGGRAPH 2019 Talks*, 71:1–2.

Chiu, K., P. Shirley, and C. Wang. 1994. Multi-jittered sampling. In P. Heckbert (ed.), *Graphics Gems IV*, 370–74. San Diego: Academic Press.

Cho, I.-Y., Y. Huo, and S.-E. Yoon. 2021. Weakly-supervised contrastive learning in path manifold for Monte Carlo image reconstruction. *ACM Transactions on Graphics (Proceedings of SIGGRAPH 2021) 40* (4), 38:1–14.

Choi, B., B. Chang, and I. Ihm. 2013. Improving memory space efficiency of kd-tree for real-time ray tracing. *Computer Graphics Forum 32* (7), 335–44.

Choi, B., R. Komuravelli, V. Lu, H. Sung, R. L. Bocchino, S. V. Adve, and J. C. Hart. 2010. Parallel SAH k-D tree construction. In *Proceedings of High Performance Graphics 2010*, 77–86.

Christensen, P. 2015. The path-tracing revolution in the movie industry. *ACM SIGGRAPH 2015 Course*, 24:1–7.

Christensen, P. 2018. Progressive sampling strategies for disk light sources. *Pixar Animation Studios Technical Memo 18-02.*

Christensen, P., J. Fong, J. Shade, W. Wooten, B. Schubert, A. Kensler, S. Friedman, C. Kilpatrick, C. Ramshaw, M. Bannister, B. Rayner, J. Brouillat, and M. Liani. 2018.

RenderMan: An advanced path-tracing architecture for movie rendering. *ACM Transactions on Graphics 37* (3), 30:1–21.

Christensen, P., A. Kensler, and C. Kilpatrick. 2018. Progressive multi-jittered sample sequences. *Computer Graphics Forum 37* (4), 21–33.

Christensen, P. H. 2003. Adjoints and importance in rendering: An overview. *IEEE Transactions on Visualization and Computer Graphics 9* (3), 329–40.

Christensen, P. H., J. Fong, D. M. Laur, and D. Batali. 2006. Ray tracing for the movie *Cars*. In *Proceedings of the IEEE Symposium on Interactive Ray Tracing*, 1–6.

Christensen, P. H., D. M. Laur, J. Fong, W. L. Wooten, and D. Batali. 2003. Ray differentials and multiresolution geometry caching for distribution ray tracing in complex scenes. In *Computer Graphics Forum (Eurographics 2003 Conference Proceedings) 22* (3), 543–52.

CIE Technical Report. 2004. Colorimetry. *Publication 15:2004 (3rd ed.)*, CIE Central Bureau, Vienna.

Ciechanowski, B. 2019. Color spaces. *https://ciechanow.ski/color-spaces/.*

Cigolle, Z. H., S. Donow, D. Evangelakos, M. Mara, M. McGuire, and Q. Meyer. 2014. Survey of efficient representations for independent unit vectors. *Journal of Computer Graphics Techniques (JCGT) 3* (2), 1–30.

Clarberg, P. 2008. Fast equal-area mapping of the (hemi)sphere using SIMD. *Journal of Graphics Tools 13* (3), 53–68.

Clarberg, P., and T. Akenine-Möller. 2008a. Practical product importance sampling for direct illumination. *Computer Graphics Forum (Proceedings of Eurographics 2008) 27* (2), 681–90.

Clarberg, P., and T. Akenine-Möller. 2008b. Exploiting visibility correlation in direct illumination. *Computer Graphics Forum (Proceedings of the 2008 Eurographics Symposium on Rendering) 27* (4), 1125–36.

Clarberg, P., W. Jarosz, T. Akenine-Möller, and H. W. Jensen. 2005. Wavelet importance sampling: Efficiently evaluating products of complex functions. *ACM Transactions on Graphics (Proceedings of SIGGRAPH 2005) 24* (3), 1166–75.

Clark, J. H. 1976. Hierarchical geometric models for visible surface algorithms. *Communications of the ACM 19* (10), 547–54.

Cleary, J. G., B. M. Wyvill, R. Vatti, and G. M. Birtwistle. 1983. Design and analysis of a parallel ray tracing computer. In *Proceedings of Graphics Interface 1983*, 33–38.

Cleary, J. G., and G. Wyvill. 1988. Analysis of an algorithm for fast ray tracing using uniform space subdivision. *The Visual Computer 4* (2), 65–83.

Cline, D., D. Adams, and P. Egbert. 2008. Table-driven adaptive importance sampling. *Computer Graphics Forum (Proceedings of the 2008 Eurographics Symposium on Rendering) 27* (4), 1115–23.

Cline, D., P. Egbert, J. Talbot, and D. Cardon. 2006. Two stage importance sampling for direct lighting. *Rendering Techniques 2006: 17th Eurographics Workshop on Rendering*, 103–14.

Cline, D., A. Razdan, and P. Wonka. 2009. A comparison of tabular PDF inversion methods. *Computer Graphics Forum 28* (1), 154–60.

Clinton, A., and M. Elendt. 2009. Rendering volumes with microvoxels. *SIGGRAPH 2009 Talks*, 47:1.

Cohen, J., M. Olano, and D. Manocha. 1998. Appearance-preserving simplification. In *Proceedings of SIGGRAPH '98*, Computer Graphics Proceedings, Annual Conference Series, 115–22.

Cohen, J., A. Varshney, D. Manocha, G. Turk, H. Weber, P. Agarwal, F. P. Brooks Jr., and W. Wright. 1996. Simplification envelopes. In *Proceedings of SIGGRAPH '96*, Computer Graphics Proceedings, Annual Conference Series, 119–28.

Cohen, M., and D. P. Greenberg. 1985. The hemi-cube: A radiosity solution for complex environments. *SIGGRAPH Computer Graphics 19* (3), 31–40.

Cohen, M., and J. Wallace. 1993. *Radiosity and Realistic Image Synthesis*. San Diego: Academic Press Professional.

Collett, E. 1993. *Polarized Light: Fundamentals and Applications*. New York: Marcel Dekker.

Collins, S. 1994. Adaptive splatting for specular to diffuse light transport. In *Fifth Eurographics Workshop on Rendering*, 119–35.

Conty Estevez, A., and C. Kulla. 2017. Production friendly microfacet sheen BRDF. *SIGGRAPH 2017 Talks*.

Conty Estevez, A., and C. Kulla. 2018. Importance sampling of many lights with adaptive tree splitting. *Proceedings of the ACM on Computer Graphics and Interactive Techniques 1* (2), 25:1–17.

Conty Estevez, A., and C. Kulla. 2020. Adaptive caustics rendering in production with photon guiding. *EGSR Industry Track*.

Conty Estevez, A., and P. Lecocq. 2018. Fast product importance sampling of environment maps. *ACM SIGGRAPH 2018 Talks* 69, 1–2.

Conty Estevez, A., P. Lecocq, and C. Stein. 2019. A microfacet-based shadowing function to solve the bump terminator problem. In E. Haines and T. Akenine-Möller (eds.), *Ray Tracing Gems*, 149–58. Berkeley: Apress.

Cook, R. L. 1984. Shade trees. *Computer Graphics (SIGGRAPH '84 Proceedings) 18*, 223–31.

Cook, R. L. 1986. Stochastic sampling in computer graphics. *ACM Transactions on Graphics 5* (1), 51–72.

Cook, R. L., L. Carpenter, and E. Catmull. 1987. The Reyes image rendering architecture. *Computer Graphics (Proceedings of SIGGRAPH '87) 21* (4), 95–102.

Cook, R. L., T. Porter, and L. Carpenter. 1984. Distributed ray tracing. *Computer Graphics (SIGGRAPH '84 Proceedings) 18*, 137–45.

Cook, R. L., and K. E. Torrance. 1981. A reflectance model for computer graphics. *Computer Graphics (SIGGRAPH '81 Proceedings) 15*, 307–16.

Cook, R. L., and K. E. Torrance. 1982. A reflectance model for computer graphics. *ACM Transactions on Graphics 1* (1), 7–24.

Costa, V., J. M. Pereira, and J. A. Jorge. 2015. Accelerating occlusion rendering on a GPU via ray classification. *International Journal of Creative Interfaces and Computer Graphics 6* (2), 1–17.

Coveyou, R. R., V. R. Cain, and K. J. Yost. 1967. Adjoint and importance in Monte Carlo application. *Nuclear Science and Engineering 27* (2), 219–34.

Crespo, M., A. Jarabo, and A. Muñoz. 2021. Primary-space adaptive control variates using piecewise-polynomial approximations. *ACM Transactions on Graphics (Proceedings of SIGGRAPH) 40* (3), 25:1–15.

Crow, F. C. 1977. The aliasing problem in computer-generated shaded images. *Communications of the ACM 20* (11), 799–805.

Crow, F. C. 1984. Summed-area tables for texture mapping. *Computer Graphics (Proceedings of SIGGRAPH '84) 18*, 207–12.

Cuypers, T., T. Haber, P. Bekaert, S. B. Oh, and R. Raskar. 2012. Reflectance model for diffraction. *ACM Transactions on Graphics 31* (5), 122:1–11.

Dachsbacher, C. 2011. Analyzing visibility configurations. *IEEE Transactions on Visualization and Computer Graphics 17* (4), 475–86.

Dachsbacher, C., J. Křivánek, M. Hašan, A. Arbree, B. Walter, and J. Novák. 2014. Scalable realistic rendering with many-light methods. *Computer Graphics Forum 33* (1), 88–104.

Dahm, K., and A. Keller. 2017. Learning light transport the reinforced way. arXiv:1701.07403 [cs.LG].

Dammertz, H., J. Hanika, and A. Keller. 2008. Shallow bounding volume hierarchies for fast SIMD ray tracing of incoherent rays. *Computer Graphics Forum 27* (4), 1225–33.

Dammertz, H., and A. Keller. 2006. Improving ray tracing precision by object space intersection computation. *IEEE Symposium on Interactive Ray Tracing*, 25–31.

Dammertz, H., and A. Keller. 2008a. The edge volume heuristic—robust triangle subdivision for improved BVH performance. In *IEEE Symposium on Interactive Ray Tracing*, 155–58.

Dammertz, H., D. Sewtz, J. Hanika, and H. P. A. Lensch. 2010. Edge-avoiding À-Trous wavelet transform for fast global illumination filtering. *Proceedings of High Performance Graphics (HPG '10)*, 67–75.

Dammertz, S., and A. Keller. 2008b. Image synthesis by rank-1 lattices. *Monte Carlo and Quasi-Monte Carlo Methods 2006*, 217–36.

Dana, K. J., B. van Ginneken, S. K. Nayar, and J. J. Koenderink. 1999. Reflectance and texture of real-world surfaces. *ACM Transactions on Graphics 18* (1), 1–34.

Danskin, J., and P. Hanrahan. 1992. Fast algorithms for volume ray tracing. In *1992 Workshop on Volume Visualization*, 91–98.

Daumas, M., and G. Melquiond. 2010. Certification of bounds on expressions involving rounded operators. *ACM Transactions on Mathematical Software 37* (1), 2:1–20.

Davidovič, T., J. Křivánek, M. Hašan, and P. Slusallek. 2014. Progressive light transport simulation on the GPU: Survey and improvements. *ACM Transactions on Graphics 33* (3), 29:1–19.

de Voogt, E., A. van der Helm, and W. F. Bronsvoort. 2000. Ray tracing deformed generalized cylinders. *The Visual Computer 16* (3–4), 197–207.

Debevec, P. 1998. Rendering synthetic objects into real scenes: Bridging traditional and image-based graphics with global illumination and high dynamic range photography. In *Proceedings of SIGGRAPH '98*, 189–98.

DeCoro, C., T. Weyrich, and S. Rusinkiewicz. 2010. Density-based outlier rejection in Monte Carlo rendering. *Computer Graphics Forum (Proceedings of Pacific Graphics) 29* (7), 2119–25.

Deering, M. F. 1995. Geometry compression. In *Proceedings of SIGGRAPH '95*, Computer Graphics Proceedings, Annual Conference Series, 13–20.

Deng, Y., Y. Ni, Z. Li, S. Mu, and W. Zhang. 2017. Toward real-time ray tracing: A survey on hardware acceleration and microarchitecture techniques. *ACM Computing Surveys 50* (4), 58:1–41.

d'Eon, E. 2013. Notes on *An energy-conserving hair reflectance model*.

d'Eon, E. 2016. *A Hitchhiker's Guide to Multiple Scattering*. http://www.eugenedeon.com/hitchhikers.

d'Eon, E. 2018. A reciprocal formulation of non-exponential radiative transfer. 1: Sketch and motivation. arXiv:1803.03259 [physics.comp-ph].

d'Eon, E. 2021. An analytic BRDF for materials with spherical Lambertian scatterers. *Computer Graphics Forum (Proceedings of EGSR) 40* (4), 153–61.

d'Eon, E., G. Francois, M. Hill, J. Letteri, and J.-M. Aubry. 2011. An energy-conserving hair reflectance model. *Computer Graphics Forum 30* (4), 1181–87.

d'Eon, E., and J. Křivánek. 2020. Zero-variance theory for efficient subsurface scattering. *SIGGRAPH 2020 Course: Advances in Monte Carlo rendering: The legacy of Jaroslav Křivánek*, 3:1–366.

d'Eon, E., D. Luebke, and E. Enderton. 2007. Efficient rendering of human skin. In *Rendering Techniques 2007: 18th Eurographics Workshop on Rendering*, 147–58.

d'Eon, E., S. Marschner, and J. Hanika. 2013. Importance sampling for physically-based hair fiber models. *SIGGRAPH Asia 2013 Technical Briefs*, 25:1–4.

d'Eon, E., S. Marschner, and J. Hanika. 2014. A fiber scattering model with non-separable lobes—supplemental report. In *SIGGRAPH 2014 Talks*, 46:1.

DeRose, T. D. 1989. *A Coordinate-Free Approach to Geometric Programming*. Math for SIGGRAPH, SIGGRAPH Course Notes #23. Also available as Technical Report No. 89-09-16, Department of Computer Science and Engineering, University of Washington, Seattle.

Deussen, O., P. M. Hanrahan, B. Lintermann, R. Mech, M. Pharr, and P. Prusinkiewicz. 1998. Realistic modeling and rendering of plant ecosystems. In *Proceedings of SIGGRAPH '98*, Computer Graphics Proceedings, Annual Conference Series, 275–86.

Devlin, K., A. Chalmers, A. Wilkie, and W. Purgathofer. 2002. Tone reproduction and physically based spectral rendering. *Proceedings of Eurographics 2002*, 101–23.

Dhillon, D. S., J. Teyssier, M. Single, I. Gaponenko, M. C. Milinkovitch, and M. Zwicker. 2014. Interactive diffraction from biological nanostructures. *Computer Graphics Forum 33* (8), 177–88.

Dick, J., and F. Pillichshammer. 2010. *Digital Nets and Sequences: Discrepancy Theory and Quasi-Monte Carlo Integration*. Cambridge: Cambridge University Press.

Diolatzis, S., A. Gruson, W. Jakob, D. Nowrouzezahrai, and G. Drettakis. 2020. Practical product path guiding using linearly transformed cosines. *Computer Graphics Forum 39* (4), 23–33.

Dippé, M. A. Z., and E. H. Wold. 1985. Antialiasing through stochastic sampling. *Computer Graphics (SIGGRAPH '85 Proceedings) 19*, 69–78.

Dittebrandt, A., J. Hanika, and C. Dachsbacher. 2020. Temporal sample reuse for next event estimation and path guiding for real-time path tracing. *Eurographics Symposium on Rendering*, 1–13.

Dobkin, D. P., D. Eppstein, and D. P. Mitchell. 1996. Computing the discrepancy with applications to supersampling patterns. *ACM Transactions on Graphics 15* (4), 354–76.

Dobkin, D. P., and D. P. Mitchell. 1993. Random-edge discrepancy of supersampling patterns. In *Proceedings of Graphics Interface 1993*, Toronto, Ontario, 62–69. Canadian Information Processing Society.

Domingues, L. R., and H. Pedrini. 2015. Bounding volume hierarchy optimization through agglomerative treelet restructuring. *Proceedings of High Performance Graphics (HPG '15)*, 13–20.

Dong, Z., B. Walter, S. Marschner, and D. P. Greenberg. 2015. Predicting appearance from measured microgeometry of metal surfaces. *ACM Transactions on Graphics 35* (1), 9:1–13.

Dongarra, J. J. 1984. Performance of various computers using standard linear equations software in a Fortran environment. *ACM SIGNUM Newsletter 19* (1), 23–26.

Donikian, M., B. Walter, K. Bala, S. Fernandez, and D. P. Greenberg. 2006. Accurate direct illumination using iterative adaptive sampling. *IEEE Transactions on Visualization and Computer Graphics 12* (3), 353–64.

Donnay, J. D. H. 1945. *Spherical Trigonometry after the Cesàro Method*. New York, NY: Interscience Publishers.

Donnelly, W. 2005. Per-pixel displacement mapping with distance functions. In M. Pharr (ed.), *GPU Gems 2*, 123–35. Reading, Massachusetts: Addison-Wesley.

Donner, C. 2006. Towards realistic image synthesis of scattering materials. Ph.D. thesis, University of California, San Diego.

Donner, C., and H. W. Jensen. 2006. A spectral BSSRDF for shading human skin. *Rendering Techniques 2006: 17th Eurographics Workshop on Rendering*, 409–17.

Donner, C., T. Weyrich, E. d'Eon, R. Ramamoorthi, and S. Rusinkiewicz. 2008. A layered, heterogeneous reflectance model for acquiring and rendering human skin. *ACM Transactions on Graphics (Proceedings of ACM SIGGRAPH Asia 2008) 27* (5), 140:1–12.

Doo, D., and M. Sabin. 1978. Behaviour of recursive division surfaces near extraordinary points. *Computer-Aided Design 10* (6), 356–60.

Dorsey, J., A. Edelman, J. Legakis, H. W. Jensen, and H. K. Pedersen. 1999. Modeling and rendering of weathered stone. In *Proceedings of SIGGRAPH '99*, Computer Graphics Proceedings, Annual Conference Series, 225–34.

Dorsey, J. O., F. X. Sillion, and D. P. Greenberg. 1991. Design and simulation of opera lighting and projection effects. In *Computer Graphics (Proceedings of SIGGRAPH '91) 25*, 41–50.

Dorsey, J., and P. Hanrahan. 1996. Modeling and rendering of metallic patinas. In *Proceedings of SIGGRAPH '96*, 387–96.

Doyle, M. J., C. Fowler, and M. Manzke. 2013. A hardware unit for fast SAH-optimised BVH construction. *ACM Transactions on Graphics (Proceedings of SIGGRAPH 2013) 32* (4), 139:1–10.

Drepper, U. 2007. What every programmer should know about memory. *people.redhat.com/drepper/cpumemory.pdf*.

Drew, M., and G. Finlayson. 2003. Multispectral rendering without spectra. *Journal of the Optical Society of America A 20* (7), 1181–93.

Driemeyer, T., and R. Herken. 2002. *Programming mental ray*. Wien: Springer-Verlag.

Dufay, D., P. Lecocq, R. Pacanowski, J.-E. Marvie, and X. Granier. 2016. Cache-friendly micro-jittered sampling. *SIGGRAPH 2016 Talks*, 36:1–2.

Duff, T. 1985. Compositing 3-D rendered images. *Computer Graphics (Proceedings of SIGGRAPH '85) 19*, 41–44.

Duff, T., J. Burgess, P. Christensen, C. Hery, A. Kensler, M. Liani, and R. Villemin. 2017. Building an orthonormal basis, revisited. *Journal of Computer Graphics Techniques (JCGT) 6* (1), 1–8.

Dungan, W. Jr., A. Stenger, and G. Sutty. 1978. Texture tile considerations for raster graphics. *Computer Graphics (Proceedings of SIGGRAPH '78) 12*, 130–34.

Dupuy, J., E. Heitz, and L. Belcour. 2017. A spherical cap preserving parameterization for spherical distributions. *ACM Transactions on Graphics (Proceedings of SIGGRAPH) 36* (4), 139:1–12.

Dupuy, J., E. Heitz, J.-C. Iehl, P. Poulin, F. Neyret, and V. Ostromoukhov. 2013. Linear efficient antialiased displacement and reflectance mapping. *ACM Transactions on Graphics 32* (6), 211:1–11.

Dupuy, J., E. Heitz, J.-C. Iehl, P. Poulin, and V. Ostromoukhov. 2015. Extracting microfacet-based BRDF parameters from arbitrary materials with power iterations. *Computer Graphics Forum (Proceedings of the 2015 Eurographics Symposium on Rendering) 34* (4), 21–30.

Dupuy, J., and W. Jakob. 2018. An adaptive parameterization for efficient material acquisition and rendering. *ACM Transactions on Graphics (Proceedings of SIGGRAPH Asia) 37* (6), 274:1–14.

Durand, F. 2011. A frequency analysis of Monte-Carlo and other numerical integration schemes. *MIT CSAIL Technical Report 2011-052*.

Durand, F., N. Holzschuch, C. Soler, E. Chan, and F. X. Sillion. A frequency analysis of light transport. 2005. *ACM Transactions on Graphics (Proceedings of SIGGRAPH 2005) 24* (3), 1115–26.

Dutré, P., E. P. Lafortune, and Y. D. Willems. 1993. Monte Carlo light tracing with direct computation of pixel intensities. *3rd International Conference on Computational Graphics and Visualisation Techniques*, 128–37.

Dwivedi, S. 1982a. A new importance biasing scheme for deep-penetration Monte Carlo. *Annals of Nuclear Energy 9* (7), 359–68.

Dwivedi, S. R. 1982b. Zero variance biasing schemes for Monte Carlo calculations of neutron and radiation transport. *Nuclear Science and Engineering 80* (1), 172–78.

Eberly, D. H. 2001. *3D Game Engine Design: A Practical Approach to Real-Time Computer Graphics*. San Francisco: Morgan Kaufmann.

Ebert, D., F. K. Musgrave, D. Peachey, K. Perlin, and S. Worley. 2003. *Texturing and Modeling: A Procedural Approach*. San Francisco: Morgan Kaufmann.

Egan, K., Y.-T. Tseng, N. Holzschuch, F. Durand, and R. Ramamoorthi. 2009. Frequency analysis and sheared reconstruction for rendering motion blur. *ACM Transactions on Graphics (Proceedings of SIGGRAPH 2009) 28* (3), 93:1–13.

Eilertsen, G., R. K. Mantiuk, and J. Unger. 2017. A comparative review of tone-mapping algorithms for high dynamic range video. *Computer Graphics Forum (Eurographics State of the Art Report) 36* (2), 565–92.

Eisemann, M., M. Magnor, T. Grosch, and S. Müller. 2007. Fast ray/axis-aligned bounding box overlap tests using ray slopes. *Journal of Graphics, GPU, and Game Tools 12* (4), 35–46.

Eisenacher, C., G. Nichols, A. Selle, and B. Burley. 2013. Sorted deferred shading for production path tracing. *Computer Graphics Forum (Proceedings of the 2013 Eurographics Symposium on Rendering) 32* (4), 125–32.

Eldar, Y. C., and T. Michaeli. 2009. Beyond bandlimited sampling. *IEEE Signal Processing Magazine 26* (3), 48–68.

Elek, O., P. Bauszat, T. Ritschel, M. Magnor, and H.-P. Seidel. Spectral ray differentials. 2014. *Computer Graphics Forum (Proceedings of the 2014 Eurographics Symposium on Rendering) 33* (4), 113–22.

Enderton, E., E. Sintorn, P. Shirley, and D. Luebke. 2010. Stochastic transparency. *Proceedings of the 2010 ACM SIGGRAPH Symposium on Interactive 3D Graphics and Games (I3D '10)*, 157–64.

Ergun, S., S. Önel, and A. Ozturk. 2016. A general micro-flake model for predicting the appearance of car paint. *Eurographics Symposium on Rendering—Experimental Ideas and Implementations*, 65–71.

Ericson, C. 2004. *Real-Time Collision Detection*. Morgan Kaufmann Series in Interactive 3D Technology. San Francisco: Morgan Kaufmann.

Ernst, M., and G. Greiner. 2007. Early split clipping for bounding volume hierarchies. *IEEE Symposium on Interactive Ray Tracing*, 73–78.

Ernst, M., and G. Greiner. 2008. Multi bounding volume hierarchies. In *Proceedings of the IEEE Symposium on Interactive Ray Tracing 2008*, 35–40.

Ernst, M., M. Stamminger, and G. Greiner. 2006. Filter importance sampling. *IEEE Symposium on Interactive Ray Tracing*, 125–32.

Evans, G., and M. McCool. 1999. Stratified wavelength clusters for efficient spectral Monte Carlo rendering. *Proceedings of Graphics Interface 1999*, 42–49.

Eymet, V., D. Poitou, M. Galtier, M. El-Hafi, G. Terrée, and R. Fournier. 2013. Null-collision meshless Monte-Carlo—Application to the validation of fast radiative transfer solvers embedded in combustion simulators. *Journal of Quantitative Spectroscopy and Radiative Transfer 129*, 145–57.

Fabianowski, B., C. Fowler, and J. Dingliana. 2009. A cost metric for scene-interior ray origins. *Short Paper Proceedings of the 30th Annual Conference of the European Association for Computer Graphics (Eurographics 2009)*, 49–50.

Falster, V., A. Jarabo, and J. R. Frisvad. 2020. Computing the bidirectional scattering of a microstructure using scalar diffraction theory and path tracing. *Computer Graphics Forum 39* (7), 231–42.

Fante, R. L. 1981. Relationship between radiative-transport theory and Maxwell's equations in dielectric media. *Journal of the Optical Society of America 71* (4), 460–68.

Faridul, H. S., T. Pouli, C. Chamaret, J. Stauder, E. Reinhard, D. Kuzovkin, and A. Tremeau. 2016. Colour mapping: A review of recent methods, extensions and applications. *Computer Graphics Forum 35* (1), 59–88.

Farin, G. 2001. *Curves and Surfaces for CAGD: A Practical Guide* (5th ed.). San Francisco: Morgan Kaufmann.

Farmer, D. F. 1981. Comparing the 4341 and M80/40. *Computerworld 15* (6), 9–20.

Farrell, T., M. Patterson, and B. Wilson. 1992. A diffusion theory model of spatially resolved, steady-state diffuse reflectance for the noninvasive determination of tissue optical properties *in vivo*. *Med. Phys. 19* (4), 879–88.

Fascione, L., J. Hanika, M. Leone, M. Droske, J. Schwarzhaupt, T. Davidovič, A. Weidlich, and J. Meng. 2018. Manuka: A batch-shading architecture for spectral path tracing in movie production. *ACM Transactions on Graphics 37* (3), 31:1–18.

Faure, H. 1992. Good permutations for extreme discrepancy. *Journal of Number Theory 42* (1), 47–56.

Faure, H., and C. Lemieux. 2009. Generalized Halton sequences in 2008: A comparative study. *ACM Transactions on Modeling and Computer Simulation 19* (4), 15:1–31.

Fedkiw, R., J. Stam, and H. W. Jensen. 2001. Visual simulation of smoke. *Proceedings of ACM SIGGRAPH 2001*, Computer Graphics Proceedings, Annual Conference Series, 15–22.

Feibush, E. A., M. Levoy, and R. L. Cook. 1980. Synthetic texturing using digital filters. *Computer Graphics (Proceedings of SIGGRAPH '80) 14*, 294–301.

Fernandez, S., K. Bala, and D. P. Greenberg. 2002. Local illumination environments for direct lighting acceleration. *Rendering Techniques 2002: 13th Eurographics Workshop on Rendering*, 7–14.

Ferwerda, J. A. 2001. Elements of early vision for computer graphics. *IEEE Computer Graphics and Applications 21* (5), 22–33.

Fichet, A., R. Pacanowski, and A. Wilkie. 2021. An OpenEXR layout for spectral images. *Journal of Computer Graphics Techniques 10* (3), 1–18.

Filip, J., and M. Haindl. 2009. Bidirectional texture function modeling: A state of the art survey. *IEEE Transactions on Pattern Analysis and Machine Intelligence 31* (11), 1921–40.

Fishman, G. S. 1996. *Monte Carlo: Concepts, Algorithms, and Applications*. New York: Springer-Verlag.

Foley, T., and J. Sugerman. 2005. KD-tree acceleration structures for a GPU raytracer. *Proceedings of the ACM SIGGRAPH/EUROGRAPHICS Conference on Graphics Hardware*, 15–22.

Fournier, A. 1992. Normal distribution functions and multiple surfaces. *Graphics Interface '92 Workshop on Local Illumination*, 45–52.

Fournier, A., and E. Fiume. 1988. Constant-time filtering with space-variant kernels. *Computer Graphics (SIGGRAPH '88 Proceedings) 22* (4), 229–38.

Fournier, A., D. Fussel, and L. Carpenter. 1982. Computer rendering of stochastic models. *Communications of the ACM 25* (6), 371–84.

Fraser, C., and D. Hanson. 1995. *A Retargetable C Compiler: Design and Implementation*. Reading, Massachusetts: Addison-Wesley.

Friedel, I., and A. Keller. 2002. Fast generation of randomized low-discrepancy point sets. *Monte Carlo and Quasi–Monte Carlo Methods 2000*, 257–73.

Frisvad, J., N. Christensen, and H. W. Jensen. 2007. Computing the scattering properties of participating media using Lorenz-Mie theory. *ACM Transactions on Graphics (Proceedings of SIGGRAPH 2007) 26* (3), 60:1–10.

Frisvad, J. R. 2012. Building an orthonormal basis from a 3d unit vector without normalization. *Journal of Graphics Tools 16* (3), 151–159.

Frisvad, J. R., S. A. Jensen, J. S. Madsen, A. Correia, L. Yang, S. K. S. Gregersen, Y. Meuret, and P.-E. Hansen. 2020. Survey of models for acquiring the optical properties of translucent materials. *Computer Graphics Forum (Eurographics State of the Art Report) 39* (2), 729–55.

Frühstück, A., I. Alhashim, and P. Wonka. 2019. TileGAN: Synthesis of large-scale non-homogeneous textures. *ACM Transactions on Graphics (Proceedings of SIGGRAPH) 38* (4), 58:1–11.

Fuchs, C., T. Chen, M. Goesele, H. Theisel, and H.-P. Seidel. 2007. Density estimation for dynamic volumes. *Computers and Graphics 31* (2), 205–11.

Fuetterling, V., C. Lojewski, F.-J. Pfreundt, B. Hamann, and A. Ebert. 2017. Accelerated single ray tracing for wide vector units. *Proceedings of High Performance Graphics (HPG '17)*, 6:1–9.

Fujimoto, A., T. Tanaka, and K. Iwata. 1986. Arts: Accelerated ray-tracing system. *IEEE Computer Graphics and Applications 6* (4), 16–26.

Galtier, M., S. Blanco, C. Caliot, C. Coustet, J. Dauchet, M. El Hafi, V. Eymet, R. Fournier, J. Gautrais, A. Khuong, B. Piaud, and G. Terrée. 2013. Integral formulation of null-collision Monte Carlo algorithms. *Journal of Quantitative Spectroscopy and Radiative Transfer 125*, 57–68.

Gamboa, L. E., A. Gruson, and D. Nowrouzezahrai. 2020. An efficient transport estimator for complex layered materials. *Computer Graphics Forum 39* (2), 363–71.

Gamito, M. N. 2016. Solid angle sampling of disk and cylinder lights. *Computer Graphics Forum 35* (4), 25–36.

Gamito, M. N. 2021. Ray traversal of OpenVDB frustum grids. *Journal of Computer Graphics Techniques 10* (1), 49–63.

Ganestam, P., and M. Doggett. 2016. SAH guided spatial split partitioning for fast BVH construction. *Computer Graphics Forum 35* (2), 285–93.

Garanzha, K. 2009. The use of precomputed triangle clusters for accelerated ray tracing in dynamic scenes. *Computer Graphics Forum (Proceedings of the 2009 Eurographics Symposium on Rendering) 28* (4), 1199–206.

Garanzha, K., and C. Loop. 2010. Fast ray sorting and breadth-first packet traversal for GPU ray tracing. *Computer Graphics Forum 29* (2), 289–98.

Garanzha, K., J. Pantaleoni, D. McAllister. 2011. Simpler and faster HLBVH with work queues. *Proceedings of High Performance Graphics 2011*, 59–64.

Gardner, G. Y. 1984. Simulation of natural scenes using textured quadric surfaces. *Computer Graphics (SIGGRAPH '84 Proceedings) 18* (3), 11–20.

Gardner, G. Y. 1985. Visual simulation of clouds. *Computer Graphics (Proceedings of SIGGRAPH '85) 19*, 297–303.

Gardner, R. P., H. K. Choi, M. Mickael, A. M. Yacout, Y. Yin, and K. Verghese. 1987. Algorithms for forcing scattered radiation to spherical, planar circular, and right circular cylindrical detectors for Monte Carlo simulation. *Nuclear Science and Engineering 95*, 245–56.

Gatys, L. A., A. S. Ecker, and M. Bethge. 2015. Texture synthesis using convolutional neural networks. *Proceedings of the 28th International Conference on Neural Information Processing Systems*, Volume 1, 262–70.

Gatys, L. A., A. S. Ecker, and M. Bethge. 2016. Image style transfer using convolutional neural networks. *Proceedings of the IEEE Conference on Computer Vision and Pattern Recognition (CVPR)*, 2414–23.

Geisler, D., I. Yoon, A. Kabra, H. He, Y. Sanders, and A. Sampson. 2020. Geometry types for graphics programming. *Proceedings of the ACM on Programming Languages (OOPSLA 2020) 4*, 173:1–25.

Georgiev, I., and M. Fajardo. 2016. Blue-noise dithered sampling. *ACM SIGGRAPH 2016 Talks (SIGGRAPH '16)* 35:1.

Georgiev, I., T. Ize, M. Farnsworth, R. Montoya-Vozmediano, A. King, B. Van Lommel, A. Jimenez, O. Anson, S. Ogaki, E. Johnston, A. Herubel, D. Russell, F. Servant, and M. Fajardo. 2018. Arnold: A brute-force production path tracer. *ACM Transactions on Graphics 37* (3), 32:1–12.

Georgiev, I., J. Křivánek, T. Davidovič, and P. Slusallek. 2012. Light transport simulation with vertex connection and merging. *ACM Transactions on Graphics (Proceedings of SIGGRAPH Asia 2012) 31* (6), 192:1–10.

Georgiev, I., J. Křivánek, T. Hachisuka, D. Nowrouzezahrai, and W. Jarosz. 2013. Joint importance sampling of low-order volumetric scattering. *ACM Transactions on Graphics (Proceedings of SIGGRAPH Asia 2013) 32* (6), 164:1–14.

Georgiev, I., Z. Misso, T. Hachisuka, D. Nowrouzezahrai, J. Křivánek, and W. Jarosz. 2019. Integral formulations of volumetric transmittance. *ACM Transactions on Graphics (Proceedings of SIGGRAPH Asia) 38* (6), 154:1–17.

Georgiev, I., and P. Slusallek. 2008. RTfact: Generic concepts for flexible and high performance ray tracing. In *Proceedings of IEEE Symposium on Interactive Ray Tracing*, 115–22.

Gershun, A. 1939. The light field. *Journal of Mathematics and Physics 18* (1-4), 51–151.

Gharbi, M., T.-M. Li, M. Aittala, J. Lehtinen, and F. Durand. 2019. Sample-based Monte Carlo denoising using a kernel-splatting network. *ACM Transactions on Graphics (Proceedings of SIGGRAPH) 38* (4), 125:1–12.

Ghosh, A., A. Doucet, and W. Heidrich. 2006. Sequential sampling for dynamic environment map illumination. *Proceedings of the Eurographics Symposium on Rendering*, 115–26.

Ghosh, A., T. Hawkins, P. Peers, S. Frederiksen, and P. Debevec. 2008. Practical modeling and acquisition of layered facial reflectance. *ACM Transactions on Graphics (Proceedings of ACM SIGGRAPH Asia 2008) 27* (5), 139:1–10.

Ghosh, A., and W. Heidrich. 2006. Correlated visibility sampling for direct illumination. *The Visual Computer 22* (9–10), 693–701.

Gijsenij, A., T. Gevers, and J. van de Weijer. 2011. Computational color constancy: Survey and experiments. *IEEE Transactions on Image Processing 20* (9), 2475–89.

Gitlina, Y., G. C. Guarnera, D. D. Singh, J. Hansen, A. Lattas, D. Pai, and A. Ghosh. 2020. Practical measurement and reconstruction of spectral skin reflectance. *Computer Graphics Forum 39* (4), 75–89.

Gkioulekas, I., A. Levin, and T. Zickler. 2016. An evaluation of computational imaging techniques for heterogeneous inverse scattering. *European Conference on Computer Vision (Proceedings of ECCV 2016)*, 685–701.

Gkioulekas, I., B. Xiao, S. Zhao, E. H. Adelson, T. Zickler, and K. Bala. 2013a. Understanding the role of phase function in translucent appearance. *ACM Transactions on Graphics 32* (5), 147:1–19.

Gkioulekas, I., S. Zhao, K. Bala, T. Zickler, and A. Levin. 2013b. Inverse volume rendering with material dictionaries. *ACM Transactions on Graphics (Proceedings of SIGGRAPH Asia 2013) 32* (6), 162:1–13.

Glassner, A. 1984. Space subdivision for fast ray tracing. *IEEE Computer Graphics and Applications 4* (10), 15–22.

Glassner, A. 1988. Spacetime ray tracing for animation. *IEEE Computer Graphics & Applications 8* (2), 60–70.

Glassner, A. (ed.) 1989a. *An Introduction to Ray Tracing*. San Diego: Academic Press.

Glassner, A. 1989b. How to derive a spectrum from an RGB triplet. *IEEE Computer Graphics and Applications 9* (4), 95–99.

Glassner, A. 1993. Spectrum: An architecture for image synthesis, research, education, and practice. *Developing Large-Scale Graphics Software Toolkits, SIGGRAPH '93 Course Notes, 3*, 1:14–43.

Glassner, A. 1994. A model for fluorescence and phosphorescence. *Proceedings of the Fifth Eurographics Workshop on Rendering*, 57–68.

Glassner, A. 1995. *Principles of Digital Image Synthesis*. San Francisco: Morgan Kaufmann.

Glassner, A. 1999. An open and shut case. *IEEE Computer Graphics and Applications 19* (3), 82–92.

Goesele, M., X. Granier, W. Heidrich, and H.-P. Seidel. 2003. Accurate light source acquisition and rendering. *ACM Transactions on Graphics (Proceedings of SIGGRAPH 2003) 22* (3), 621–30.

Goesele, M., H. Lensch, J. Lang, C. Fuchs, and H.-P. Seidel. 2004. DISCO—Acquisition of translucent objects. *ACM Transactions on Graphics (Proceedings of SIGGRAPH 2004) 23* (3), 844–53.

Goldberg, D. 1991. What every computer scientist should know about floating-point arithmetic. *ACM Computing Surveys 23* (1), 5–48.

Goldman, D. B. 1997. Fake fur rendering. *Proceedings of SIGGRAPH '97*, Computer Graphics Proceedings, Annual Conference Series, 127–34.

Goldman, R. 1985. Illicit expressions in vector algebra. *ACM Transactions on Graphics 4* (3), 223–43.

Goldsmith, J., and J. Salmon. 1987. Automatic creation of object hierarchies for ray tracing. *IEEE Computer Graphics and Applications 7* (5), 14–20.

Goldstein, R. A., and R. Nagel. 1971. 3-D visual simulation. *Simulation 16* (1), 25–31.

Goral, C. M., K. E. Torrance, D. P. Greenberg, and B. Battaile. 1984. Modeling the interaction of light between diffuse surfaces. *Proceedings of the 11th Annual Conference on Computer Graphics and Interactive Techniques (SIGGRAPH '84) 18* (3), 213–22.

Gortler, S. J., R. Grzeszczuk, R. Szeliski, and M. F. Cohen. 1996. The lumigraph. *Proceedings of SIGGRAPH '96*, Computer Graphics Proceedings, Annual Conference Series, 43–54.

Granskog, J., F. Rousselle, M. Papas, and J. Novák. 2020. Compositional neural scene representations for shading inference. *ACM Transactions on Graphics 39* (4), 135:1–13.

Gray, A. 1993. *Modern Differential Geometry of Curves and Surfaces*. Boca Raton, Florida: CRC Press.

Green, S. A., and D. J. Paddon. 1989. Exploiting coherence for multiprocessor ray tracing. *IEEE Computer Graphics and Applications 9* (6), 12–26.

Greenberg, D. P., K. E. Torrance, P. S. Shirley, J. R. Arvo, J. A. Ferwerda, S. Pattanaik, E. P. F. Lafortune, B. Walter, S.-C. Foo, and B. Trumbore. 1997. A framework for realistic image synthesis. *Proceedings of SIGGRAPH '97*, Computer Graphics Proceedings, Annual Conference Series, 477–94.

Greene, N. 1986. Environment mapping and other applications of world projections. *IEEE Computer Graphics and Applications 6* (11), 21–29.

Greene, N., and P. S. Heckbert. 1986. Creating raster Omnimax images from multiple perspective views using the elliptical weighted average filter. *IEEE Computer Graphics and Applications 6* (6), 21–27.

Gribble, C., and K. Ramani. 2008. Coherent ray tracing via stream filtering. *Proceedings of IEEE Symposium on Interactive Ray Tracing*, 59–66.

Gribel, C. J., and T. Akenine-Möller. 2017. Time-continuous quasi-Monte Carlo ray tracing. *Computer Graphics Forum 36* (6), 354–67.

Griewank, A., and A. Walther. 2008. *Evaluating derivatives: Principles and techniques of algorithmic differentiation* (2nd ed.). Society for Industrial and Applied Mathematics.

Grittmann, P., I. Georgiev, and P. Slusallek. 2021. Correlation-aware multiple importance sampling for bidirectional rendering algorithms. *Computer Graphics Forum (Proceedings of Eurographics) 40* (2), 231–38.

Grittmann, P., I. Georgiev, P. Slusallek, and J. Křivánek. 2019. Variance-aware multiple importance sampling. *ACM Transactions on Graphics (Proceedings of SIGGRAPH Asia 2019) 38* (6), 152:1–9.

Grittmann, P., A. Pérard-Gayot, P. Slusallek, and J. Křivánek. 2018. Efficient caustic rendering with lightweight photon mapping. *Computer Graphics Forum 37* (4), 133–42.

Gritz, L., and E. d'Eon. 2008. The importance of being linear. In H. Nguyen (ed.), *GPU Gems 3*, 529–42. Boston, Massachusetts: Addison-Wesley.

Gritz, L., and J. K. Hahn. 1996. BMRT: A global illumination implementation of the RenderMan standard. *Journal of Graphics Tools 1* (3), 29–47.

Gritz, L., C. Stein, C. Kulla, and A. Conty. 2010. Open Shading Language. *SIGGRAPH 2010 Talks*, 3:1.

Grünschloß, L., J. Hanika, R. Schwede, and A. Keller. 2008. (t, m, s)-nets and maximized minimum distance. In *Monte Carlo and Quasi-Monte Carlo Methods 2006*, 397–412. Berlin: Springer Verlag.

Grünschloß, L., and A. Keller. 2009. (t, m, s)-nets and maximized minimum distance, part II. In *Monte Carlo and Quasi-Monte Carlo Methods 2008*, 395–409. Berlin: Springer Verlag.

Grünschloß, L., M. Raab, and A. Keller. 2012. Enumerating quasi-Monte Carlo point sequences in elementary intervals. In *Monte Carlo and Quasi-Monte Carlo Methods 2010*, 399–408. Berlin: Springer Verlag.

Grünschloß, L., M. Stich, S. Nawaz, and A. Keller. 2011. MSBVH: An efficient acceleration data structure for ray traced motion blur. *Proceedings of High Performance Graphics 2011*, 65–70.

Gu, J., S. K. Nayar, E. Grinspun, P. N. Belhumeur, and R. Ramamoorthi. 2013a. Compressive structured light for recovering inhomogeneous participating media. *IEEE Transactions on Pattern Analysis and Machine Intelligence 35* (3), 845–58.

Gu, Y., Y. He, and G. E. Blelloch. 2015. Ray specialized contraction on bounding volume hierarchies. *Computer Graphics Forum 34* (7), 309–18.

Gu, Y., Y. He, K. Fatahalian, and G. Blelloch. 2013b. Efficient BVH construction via approximate agglomerative clustering. *Proceedings of High Performance Graphics 2013*, 81–88.

Guarnera, D., G. Guarnera, A. Ghosh, C. Denk, and M. Glencross. 2016. BRDF representation and acquisition. *Computer Graphics Forum (Eurographics State of the Art Report) 35* (2), 625–50.

Guennebaud, G., B. Jacob, and others. 2010. Eigen v3. *http://eigen.tuxfamily.org*.

Guillén, I., J. Marco, D. Gutierrez, W. Jakob, and A. Jarabo. 2020. A general framework for pearlescent materials. *ACM Transactions on Graphics (Proceedings of SIGGRAPH Asia) 39* (6), 253:1–15.

Guillén, I., C. Ureña, A. King, M. Fajardo, I. Georgiev, J. López-Moreno, and A. Jarabo. 2017. Area-preserving parameterizations for spherical ellipses. *Computer Graphics Forum 36* (4), 179–87.

Günther, J., S. Popov, H. P. Seidel, and P. Slusallek. 2007. Realtime ray tracing on GPU with BVH-based packet traversal. *IEEE Symposium on Interactive Ray Tracing*, 113–18.

Guo, J., Y. Chen, B. Hu, L.-Q. Yan, Y. Guo, and Y. Liu. 2019. Fractional Gaussian fields for modeling and rendering of spatially-correlated media. *ACM Transactions on Graphics (Proceedings of SIGGRAPH) 38* (4), 45:1–13.

Guo, J., J. Qian, Y. Guo. and J. Pan. 2017. Rendering thin transparent layers with extended normal distribution functions. *IEEE Transactions on Visualization & Computer Graphics 23* (9), 2108–19.

Guo, J. J., M. Eisemann, and E. Eisemann. 2020. Next event estimation++: Visibility mapping for efficient light transport simulation. *Computer Graphics Forum 39* (7), 205–17.

Guo, Y., M. Hašan, and S. Zhao. 2018. Position-free Monte Carlo simulation for arbitrary layered BSDFs. *ACM Transactions on Graphics (Proceedings of SIGGRAPH Asia) 37* (6), 279:1–14.

Guthe, S., and P. Heckbert 2005. Non-power-of-two Mipmap creation. *NVIDIA Technical Report*.

Habel, R., P. H. Christensen, and W. Jarosz. 2013. Photon beam diffusion: A hybrid Monte Carlo method for subsurface scattering. *Computer Graphics Forum (Proceedings of the 2013 Eurographics Symposium on Rendering) 32* (4), 27–37.

Haber, J., M. Magnor, and H.-P. Seidel. 2005. Physically-based simulation of twilight phenomena. *ACM Transactions on Graphics 24* (4), 1353–73.

Hachisuka, T. 2005. High-quality global illumination rendering using rasterization. In M. Pharr (ed.), *GPU Gems II: Programming Techniques for High-Performance Graphics and General-Purpose Computation*, 615–34. Reading, Massachusetts: Addison-Wesley.

Hachisuka, T. 2011. Robust light transport simulation using progressive density estimation. Ph.D. thesis, University of California, San Diego.

Hachisuka, T., and H. W. Jensen. 2009. Stochastic progressive photon mapping. *ACM Transactions on Graphics (Proceedings of SIGGRAPH Asia 2009) 28* (5), 141:1–8.

Hachisuka, T., A. S. Kaplanyan, and C. Dachsbacher. 2014. Multiplexed Metropolis light transport. *ACM Transactions on Graphics (Proceedings of SIGGRAPH 2014) 33* (4), 100:1–10.

Hachisuka, T., S. Ogaki, and H. W. Jensen. 2008. Progressive photon mapping. *ACM Transactions on Graphics (Proceedings of SIGGRAPH Asia 2008) 27* (5), 130:1–8.

Hachisuka, T., J. Pantaleoni, and H. W. Jensen. 2012. A path space extension for robust light transport simulation. *ACM Transactions on Graphics (Proceedings of SIGGRAPH Asia 2012) 31* (6), 191:1–10.

Haines, E., J. Günther, and T. Akenine-Möller. 2019. Precision improvements for ray/sphere intersection. In E. Haines and T. Akenine-Möller (eds.), *Ray Tracing Gems*, 7–14. Berkeley: Apress.

Haines, E. A. 1989. Essential ray tracing algorithms. In A. Glassner (ed.), *An Introduction to Ray Tracing*, 33–78. San Diego: Academic Press.

Haines, E. A. 1994. Point in polygon strategies. In P. Heckbert (ed.), *Graphics Gems IV*, 24–46. San Diego: Academic Press.

Haines, E. A., and D. P. Greenberg. 1986. The light buffer: A shadow testing accelerator. *IEEE Computer Graphics and Applications 6* (9), 6–16.

Haines, E. A., and J. R. Wallace. 1994. Shaft culling for efficient ray-traced radiosity. *Second Eurographics Workshop on Rendering (Photorealistic Rendering in Computer Graphics)*, 122–38. Also in *SIGGRAPH 1991 Frontiers in Rendering Course Notes*.

Hakura, Z. S., and A. Gupta. 1997. The design and analysis of a cache architecture for texture mapping. *Proceedings of the 24th International Symposium on Computer Architecture*, 108–20.

Hall, R. 1989. *Illumination and Color in Computer Generated Imagery*. New York: Springer-Verlag.

Hall, R. 1999. Comparing spectral color computation methods. *IEEE Computer Graphics and Applications 19* (4), 36–46.

Hall, R. A., and D. P. Greenberg. 1983. A testbed for realistic image synthesis. *IEEE Computer Graphics and Applications 3* (8), 10–20.

Hammersley, J., and D. Handscomb. 1964. *Monte Carlo Methods*. New York: John Wiley.

Han, C., B. Sun, R. Ramamoorthi, and E. Grinspun. 2007. Frequency domain normal map filtering. *ACM Transactions on Graphics (Proceedings of SIGGRAPH 2007) 26* (3), 28:1–11.

Han, M., I. Wald, W. Usher, Q. Wu, F. Wang, V. Pascucci, C. D. Hansen, and C. R. Johnson. 2019. Ray tracing generalized tube primitives: Method and applications. *Computer Graphics Forum 38* (3), 467–78.

Hanika, J., and C. Dachsbacher. 2014. Efficient Monte Carlo rendering with realistic lenses. *Computer Graphics Forum (Proceedings of Eurographics 2014) 33* (2), 323–32.

Hanika, J., M. Droske, and L. Fascione. 2015a. Manifold next event estimation. *Computer Graphics Forum (Proceedings of the 2015 Eurographics Symposium on Rendering) 34* (4), 87–97.

Hanika, J., A. Kaplanyan, and C. Dachsbacher. 2015b. Improved half vector space light transport. *Computer Graphics Forum (Proceedings of the 2015 Eurographics Symposium on Rendering) 34* (4), 65–74.

Hanika, J., A. Keller, and H. P. A. Lensch. 2010. Two-level ray tracing with reordering for highly complex scenes. *Proceedings of Graphics Interface 2010*, 145–52.

Hanrahan, P. 1983. Ray tracing algebraic surfaces. *Computer Graphics (Proceedings of SIGGRAPH '83) 17*, 83–90.

Hanrahan, P., and W. Krueger. 1993. Reflection from layered surfaces due to subsurface scattering. *Computer Graphics (SIGGRAPH '93 Proceedings)*, 165–74.

Hanrahan, P., and J. Lawson. 1990. A language for shading and lighting calculations. *Computer Graphics (SIGGRAPH '90 Proceedings) 24*, 289–98.

Hansen, J. E., and L. D. Travis. 1974. Light scattering in planetary atmospheres. *Space Science Reviews 16*, 527–610.

Hanson, D. R. 1996. *C Interfaces and Implementations: Techniques for Creating Reusable Software*. Boston, Massachusetts: Addison-Wesley Longman.

Hao, Z., A. Mallya, S. Belongie, and M.-Y. Liu. 2021. GANcraft: Unsupervised 3D neural rendering of Minecraft worlds. *IEEE/CVF International Conference on Computer Vision (ICCV)*. arXiv:2104.07659 [cs.CV].

Hart, D., P. Dutré, and D. P. Greenberg. 1999. Direct illumination with lazy visibility evaluation. *Proceedings of SIGGRAPH '99*, Computer Graphics Proceedings, Annual Conference Series, 147–54.

Hart, D., M. Pharr, T. Müller, W. Lopes, M. McGuire, and P. Shirley. 2020. Practical product sampling by fitting and composing warps. *Computer Graphics Forum 39* (4), 149–58.

Hart, J. C. 1996. Sphere tracing: A geometric method for the antialiased ray tracing of implicit surfaces. *The Visual Computer 12* (9), 527–45.

Hart, J. C., D. J. Sandin, and L. H. Kauffman. 1989. Ray tracing deterministic 3-D fractals. *Computer Graphics (Proceedings of SIGGRAPH '89) 23*, 289–96.

Hašan, M., and R. Ramamoorthi. 2013. Interactive albedo editing in path-traced volumetric materials. *ACM Transactions on Graphics 32* (2), 11:1–11.

Hasinoff, S. W., and K. N. Kutulakos. 2011. Light-efficient photography. *IEEE Transactions on Pattern Analysis and Machine Intelligence 33* (11), 2203–14.

Hasselgren, J., J. Munkberg, A. Patney, M. Salvi, and A. Lefohn. 2020. Neural temporal adaptive sampling and denoising. *Computer Graphics Forum 39* (2), 147–55.

Hatch, D. 2003. The right way to calculate stuff. *http://www.plunk.org/~hatch/rightway.html*.

Havran, V. 2000. Heuristic ray shooting algorithms. Ph.D. thesis, Czech Technical University.

Havran, V., and J. Bittner. 2002. On improving kd-trees for ray shooting. In *Proceedings of WSCG 2002 Conference*, 209–17.

Havran, V., R. Herzog, and H.-P. Seidel. 2006. On the fast construction of spatial hierarchies for ray tracing. In *IEEE Symposium on Interactive Ray Tracing*, 71–80.

Hawkins, T., P. Einarsson, and P. Debevec. 2005. Acquisition of time-varying participating media. *ACM Transactions on Graphics (Proceedings of SIGGRAPH 2005) 24* (3), 812–15.

Hearn, D. D., and M. P. Baker. 2004. *Computer Graphics with OpenGL* (3rd ed.). Boston: Pearson.

Hecht, E. 2002. *Optics*. Reading, Massachusetts: Addison-Wesley.

Heckbert, P. S. 1984. *The Mathematics of Quadric Surface Rendering and SOID*. 3-D Technical Memo, New York Institute of Technology Computer Graphics Lab.

Heckbert, P. S. 1986. Survey of texture mapping. *IEEE Computer Graphics and Applications 6* (11), 56–67.

Heckbert, P. S. 1989a. Image zooming source code. *http://www.cs.cmu.edu/~ph/src/zoom/*.

Heckbert, P. S. 1989b. Fundamentals of texture mapping and image warping. M.S. thesis, Department of Electrical

Engineering and Computer Science, University of California, Berkeley.

Heckbert, P. S. 1990a. What are the coordinates of a pixel? In A. S. Glassner (ed.), *Graphics Gems I*, 246–48. San Diego: Academic Press.

Heckbert, P. S. 1990b. Adaptive radiosity textures for bidirectional ray tracing. *Computer Graphics (Proceedings of SIGGRAPH '90) 24*, 145–54.

Heckbert, P. S., and P. Hanrahan. 1984. Beam tracing polygonal objects. In *Computer Graphics (Proceedings of SIGGRAPH '84) 18*, 119–27.

Heidrich, W., J. Kautz, P. Slusallek, and H.-P. Seidel. 1998. Canned lightsources. In *Rendering Techniques '98: Proceedings of the Eurographics Rendering Workshop*, 293–300.

Heidrich, W., and H.-P. Seidel. 1998. Ray-tracing procedural displacement shaders. In *Proceedings of Graphics Interface 1998*, 8–16.

Heitz, E. 2014. Understanding the masking-shadowing function in microfacet-based BRDFs. *Journal of Computer Graphics Techniques (JCGT) 3* (2), 32–91.

Heitz, E. 2015. Derivation of the microfacet $\Lambda(\omega)$ function. Personal communication.

Heitz, E. 2018. Sampling the GGX distribution of visible normals. *Journal of Computer Graphics Techniques (JCGT) 7* (4), 1–13.

Heitz, E. 2019. A low-distortion map between triangle and square. *Technical Report*.

Heitz, E. 2020. Can't invert the CDF? The triangle-cut parameterization of the region under the curve. *Computer Graphics Forum 39* (4), 121–32.

Heitz, E., and L. Belcour. 2019. Distributing Monte Carlo errors as a blue noise in screen space by permuting pixel seeds between frames. *Computer Graphics Forum 38* (4), 149–58.

Heitz, E., L. Belcour, V. Ostromoukhov, D. Coeurjolly, and J.-C. Iehl. 2019. A low-discrepancy sampler that distributes Monte Carlo errors as a blue noise in screen space. *SIGGRAPH '19 Talks*, 68:1–2.

Heitz, E., and E. d'Eon. 2014. Importance sampling microfacet-based BSDFs using the distribution of visible normals. *Computer Graphics Forum (Proceedings of the 2014 Eurographics Symposium on Rendering) 33* (4), 103–12.

Heitz, E., J. Dupuy, C. Crassin, and C. Dachsbacher. 2015. The SGGX microflake distribution. *ACM Transactions on Graphics (Proceedings of SIGGRAPH 2015) 34* (4), 48:1–11.

Heitz, E., J. Dupuy, S. Hill, and D. Neubelt. 2016a. Real-time polygonal-light shading with linearly transformed cosines. *ACM Transactions on Graphics (Proceedings of SIGGRAPH) 35* (4), 41:1–8.

Heitz, E., J. Hanika, E. d'Eon, and C. Dachsbacher. 2016b. Multiple-scattering microfacet BSDFs with the Smith model. *ACM Transactions on Graphics (Proceedings of SIGGRAPH) 35* (4), 58:1–14.

Heitz, E., S. Hill, and M. McGuire. 2018. Combining analytic direct illumination and stochastic shadows. *Proceedings of the ACM SIGGRAPH Symposium on Interactive 3D Graphics and Games*, 2:1–11.

Heitz, E., D. Nowrouzezahrai, P. Poulin, and F. Neyret. 2014. Filtering non-linear transfer functions on surfaces. *IEEE Transactions on Visualization and Computer Graphics 20* (7), 996–1008.

Helmer, A., P. Christensen, and A. Kensler. 2021. Stochastic generation of (t,s) sample sequences. *Proceedings of the Eurographics Symposium on Rendering*, 21–33.

Hendrich, J., D. Meister, and J. Bittner. 2017. Parallel BVH construction using progressive hierarchical refinement. *Computer Graphics Forum 36* (2), 487–94.

Hendrich, J., A. Pospíšil, D. Meister, and J. Bittner. 2019. Ray classification for accelerated BVH traversal. *Computer Graphics Forum 38* (4), 49–56.

Henyey, L. G., and J. L. Greenstein. 1941. Diffuse radiation in the galaxy. *Astrophysical Journal 93*, 70–83.

Herholz, S., O. Elek, J. Schindel, J. Křivánek, and H. P. A. Lensch. 2018. A unified manifold framework for efficient BRDF sampling based on parametric mixture models. *Eurographics Symposium on Rendering—Experimental Ideas and Implementations*, 41–52.

Herholz, S., O. Elek, J. Vorba, H. Lensch, and J. Křivánek. 2016. Product importance sampling for light transport path guiding. *Computer Graphics Forum 35* (4), 67–77.

Herholz, S., Y. Zhao, O. Elek, D. Nowrouzezahrai, H. P. A. Lensch, and J. Křivánek. 2019. Volume path guiding based on zero-variance random walk theory. *ACM Transactions on Graphics (Proceedings of SIGGRAPH) 38* (3), 25:1–19.

Hermosilla, P., S. Maisch, T. Ritschel, and T. Ropinski. 2019. Deep-learning the latent space of light transport. *Computer Graphics Forum 38* (4), 207–17.

Hertzmann, A. 2003. Machine learning for computer graphics: A manifesto and tutorial. *Proceedings of the 11th Pacific Conference on Computer Graphics and Applications (PG '03)*.

Hery, C., M. Kass, and J. Ling. 2014. Geometry into shading. *Pixar Technical Memo 14-04*.

Hery, C., and R. Ramamoorthi. 2012. Importance sampling of reflection from hair fibers. *Journal of Computer Graphics Techniques (JCGT) 1* (1), 1–17.

Herzog, R., V. Havran, S. Kinuwaki, K. Myszkowski, and H.-P. Seidel. 2007. Global illumination using photon ray splatting. *Computer Graphics Forum (Proceedings of Eurographics 2007) 26* (3), 503–13.

Hey, H., and P. Purgathofer. 2002a. Importance sampling with hemispherical particle footprints. In *Spring Conference on Computer Graphics*, 107–14.

Higham, N. J. 2002. *Accuracy and Stability of Numerical Algorithms* (2nd ed.). Philadelphia: Society for Industrial and Applied Mathematics.

Hoberock, J., V. Lu, Y. Jia, J. Hart. 2009. Stream compaction for deferred shading. In *Proceedings of High Performance Graphics 2009*, 173–80.

Hoffmann, C. M. 1989. *Geometric and Solid Modeling: An Introduction*. San Francisco: Morgan Kaufmann.

Hofmann, N., J. Hasselgren, P. Clarberg, and J. Munkberg. 2021. Interactive path tracing and reconstruction of sparse volumes. *Proceedings of the ACM on Computer Graphics and Interactive Techniques 4* (1), 5:1–19.

Holzschuch, N. 2015. Accurate computation of single scattering in participating media with refractive boundaries. *Computer Graphics Forum 34* (6), 48–59.

Holzschuch, N., and R. Pacanowski. 2017. A two-scale microfacet reflectance model combining reflection and diffraction. *ACM Transactions on Graphics (Proceedings of SIGGRAPH) 36* (4), 66:1–12.

Hošek, L., and A. Wilkie. 2012. An analytic model for full spectral sky-dome radiance. *ACM Transactions on Graphics (Proceedings of SIGGRAPH 2012) 31* (4), 95:1–9.

Hošek, L., and A. Wilkie. 2013. Adding a solar-radiance function to the Hošek–Wilkie skylight model. *IEEE Computer Graphics and Applications 33* (3), 44–52.

Hua, B.-S., A. Gruson, V. Petitjean, M. Zwicker, D. Nowrouzezahrai, E. Eisemann, and T. Hachisuka. 2019. A survey on gradient-domain rendering. *Computer Graphics Forum (Eurographics State of the Art Report) 38* (2), 455–72.

Hughes, J. F. 2021. Personal communication.

Hullin, M. B., J. Hanika, and W. Heidrich. 2012. Polynomial optics: A construction kit for efficient ray-tracing of lens systems. *Computer Graphics Forum (Proceedings of the 2012 Eurographics Symposium on Rendering) 31* (4), 1375–83.

Hunt, W. 2008. Corrections to the surface area metric with respect to mail-boxing. In *IEEE Symposium on Interactive Ray Tracing*, 77–80.

Hunt, W., and B. Mark. 2008a. Ray-specialized acceleration structures for ray tracing. In *IEEE Symposium on Interactive Ray Tracing*, 3–10.

Hunt, W., and B. Mark. 2008b. Adaptive acceleration structures in perspective space. In *IEEE Symposium on Interactive Ray Tracing*, 111–17.

Hunt, W., W. Mark, and G. Stoll. 2006. Fast kd-tree construction with an adaptive error-bounded heuristic. In *IEEE Symposium on Interactive Ray Tracing*, 81–88.

Huo, Y., R. Wang, R. Zheng, H. Xu, H. Bao, and S.-E. Yoon. 2020. Adaptive incident radiance field sampling and reconstruction using deep reinforcement learning. *ACM Transactions on Graphics 39* (1), 6:1–17.

Hurley, J., A. Kapustin, A. Reshetov, and A. Soupikov. 2002. Fast ray tracing for modern general purpose CPU. In *Proceedings of GraphiCon 2002*.

Igarashi, T., K. Nishino, and S. K. Nayar. 2007. The appearance of human skin: A survey. *Foundations and Trends in Computer Graphics and Vision 3* (1), 1–95.

Igehy, H. 1999. Tracing ray differentials. In *Proceedings of SIGGRAPH '99*, Computer Graphics Proceedings, Annual Conference Series, 179–86.

Igehy, H., M. Eldridge, and P. Hanrahan. 1999. Parallel texture caching. In *1999 SIGGRAPH/Eurographics Workshop on Graphics Hardware*, 95–106.

Igehy, H., M. Eldridge, and K. Proudfoot. 1998. Prefetching in a texture cache architecture. In *1998 SIGGRAPH/Eurographics Workshop on Graphics Hardware*, 133–42.

Illuminating Engineering Society of North America. 2002. IESNA standard file format for electronic transfer of photometric data. BSR/IESNA Publication LM-63-2002. *www.iesna.org*.

Immel, D. S., M. F. Cohen, and D. P. Greenberg. 1986. A radiosity method for non-diffuse environments. In *Computer Graphics (SIGGRAPH '86 Proceedings)*, Volume 20, 133–42.

Institute of Electrical and Electronic Engineers. 1985. IEEE standard 754-1985 for binary floating-point arithmetic. Reprinted in *SIGPLAN 22* (2), 9–25.

Institute of Electrical and Electronic Engineers. 2008. IEEE standard 754-2008 for binary floating-point arithmetic.

International Electrotechnical Commission (IEC). 1999. Multimedia systems and equipment—Colour measurement and management—Part 2-1: Colour management—Default RGB colour space—sRGB. IEC Standard 61966-2-1.

Ize, T. 2013. Robust BVH ray traversal. *Journal of Computer Graphics Techniques (JCGT) 2* (2), 12–27.

Ize, T., and C. Hansen. 2011. RTSAH traversal order for occlusion rays. *Computer Graphics Forum (Proceedings of Eurographics 2011) 30* (2), 295–305.

Ize, T., P. Shirley, and S. Parker. 2007. Grid creation strategies for efficient ray tracing. In *IEEE Symposium on Interactive Ray Tracing*, 27–32.

Ize, T., I. Wald, and S. Parker. 2008. Ray tracing with the BSP tree. In *IEEE Symposium on Interactive Ray Tracing*, 159–66.

Ize, T., I. Wald, C. Robertson, and S. G. Parker. 2006. An evaluation of parallel grid construction for ray tracing dynamic scenes. *IEEE Symposium on Interactive Ray Tracing*, 47–55.

Jackson, W. H. 1910. The solution of an integral equation occurring in the theory of radiation. *Bulletin of the American Mathematical Society 16*, 473–75.

Jacobs, D. E., J. Baek, and M. Levoy. 2012. Focal stack compositing for depth of field control. *Stanford Computer Graphics Laboratory Technical Report*, CSTR 2012-1.

Jakob, W. 2010. Mitsuba renderer. *http://www.mitsuba-renderer.org*.

Jakob, W. 2012. Numerically stable sampling of the von Mises Fisher distribution on S^2 (and other tricks). *https://www.mitsuba-renderer.org/~wenzel/files/vmf.pdf*.

Jakob, W. 2013. Light transport on path-space manifolds. Ph.D. thesis, Cornell University.

Jakob, W., A. Arbree, J. T. Moon, K. Bala, and M. Steve. 2010. A radiative transfer framework for rendering materials with anisotropic structure. *ACM Transactions on Graphics (Proceedings of SIGGRAPH 2010) 29* (4), 53:1–13.

Jakob, W., E. d'Eon, O. Jakob, and S. Marschner. 2014a. A comprehensive framework for rendering layered materials. *ACM Transactions on Graphics 33* (4), 118:1–14.

Jakob, W., and J. Hanika. 2019. A low-dimensional function space for efficient spectral upsampling. *Computer Graphics Forum (Proceedings of Eurographics) 38* (2), 147–55.

Jakob, W., M. Hašan, L.-Q. Yan, J. Lawrence, R. Ramamoorthi, and S. Marschner. 2014b. Discrete stochastic microfacet models. *ACM Transactions on Graphics 33* (4), 115:1–10.

Jakob, W., and S. Marschner. 2012. Manifold exploration: A Markov chain Monte Carlo technique for rendering scenes with difficult specular transport. *ACM Transactions on Graphics (Proceedings of SIGGRAPH 2012) 31* (4), 58:1–13.

Jakob, W., C. Regg, and W. Jarosz. 2011. Progressive expectation-maximization for hierarchical volumetric photon mapping. *Computer Graphics Forum (Proceedings of the 2011 Eurographics Symposium on Rendering) 30* (4), 1287–97.

Jansen, F. W. 1986. Data structures for ray tracing. In *Data Structures for Raster Graphics, Workshop Proceedings*, 57–73. New York: Springer-Verlag.

Jarabo, A., C. Aliaga, and D. Gutierrez. 2018. A radiative transfer framework for spatially-correlated materials. *ACM Transactions on Graphics (Proceedings of SIGGRAPH) 37* (4), 177:1–10.

Jarabo, A., J. Marco, A. Muñoz, R. Buisan, W. Jarosz, and D. Gutierrez. A framework for transient rendering. 2014a. *ACM Transactions on Graphics (Proceedings of SIGGRAPH Asia 2014) 33* (6), 177:1–10.

Jarabo, A., H. Wu, J. Dorsey, H. Rushmeier, and D. Gutierrez. 2014b. Effects of approximate filtering on the appearance of bidirectional texture functions. *IEEE Transactions on Visualization and Computer Graphics 20* (6), 880–92.

Jarosz, W. 2008. Efficient Monte Carlo methods for light transport in scattering media. Ph.D. thesis, UC San Diego.

Jarosz, W., C. Donner, M. Zwicker, and H. W. Jensen. 2008a. Radiance caching for participating media. *ACM Transactions on Graphics 27* (1), 7:1–11.

Jarosz, W., A. Enayet, A. Kensler, C. Kilpatrick, and P. Christensen. 2019. Orthogonal array sampling for Monte Carlo rendering. *Computer Graphics Forum 38* (4), 135–47.

Jarosz, W., D. Nowrouzezahrai, I. Sadeghi, and H. W. Jensen. 2011a. A comprehensive theory of volumetric radiance estimation using photon points and beams. *ACM Transactions on Graphics 30* (1), 5:1–19.

Jarosz, W., D. Nowrouzezahrai, R. Thomas, P.-P. Sloan, and M. Zwicker. 2011b. Progressive photon beams. *ACM Transactions on Graphics (Proceedings of SIGGRAPH Asia 2011) 30* (6), 181:1–12.

Jarosz, W., M. Zwicker, and H. W. Jensen. 2008b. The beam radiance estimate for volumetric photon mapping. *Computer Graphics Forum (Proceedings of Eurographics 2008) 27* (2), 557–66.

Jeannerod, C.-P., N. Louvet, and J.-M. Muller. 2013. Further analysis of Kahan's algorithm for the accurate computation of 2×2 determinants. *Mathematics of Computation 82* (284), 2245–64.

Jendersie, J., and T. Grosch. 2019. Microfacet model regularization for robust light transport. *Computer Graphics Forum 38* (4), 39–47.

Jensen, H. W. 1995. Importance driven path tracing using the photon map. In *Eurographics Rendering Workshop 1995*, 326–35.

Jensen, H. W. 1996. Global illumination using photon maps. In *Eurographics Rendering Workshop 1996*, 21–30.

Jensen, H. W. 1997. Rendering caustics on non-Lambertian surfaces. *Computer Graphics Forum 16* (1), 57–64.

Jensen, H. W. 2001. *Realistic Image Synthesis Using Photon Mapping*. Natick, Massachusetts: A. K. Peters.

Jensen, H. W., J. Arvo, P. Dutré, A. Keller, A. Owen, M. Pharr, and P. Shirley. 2003. Monte Carlo ray tracing. In *SIGGRAPH 2003 Courses*, San Diego.

Jensen, H. W., J. Arvo, M. Fajardo, P. Hanrahan, D. Mitchell, M. Pharr, and P. Shirley. 2001a. State of the art in

Monte Carlo ray tracing for realistic image synthesis. In *SIGGRAPH 2001 Course 29*, Los Angeles.

Jensen, H. W., and J. Buhler. 2002. A rapid hierarchical rendering technique for translucent materials. *ACM Transactions on Graphics 21* (3), 576–81.

Jensen, H. W., and N. Christensen. 1995. Optimizing path tracing using noise reduction filters. In *Proceedings of WSCG*, 134–42.

Jensen, H. W., and P. H. Christensen. 1998. Efficient simulation of light transport in scenes with participating media using photon maps. In *SIGGRAPH '98 Conference Proceedings*, Annual Conference Series, 311–20.

Jensen, H. W., S. R. Marschner, M. Levoy, and P. Hanrahan. 2001b. A practical model for subsurface light transport. In *Proceedings of ACM SIGGRAPH 2001*, Computer Graphics Proceedings, Annual Conference Series, 511–18.

Jevans, D., and B. Wyvill. 1989. Adaptive voxel subdivision for ray tracing. In *Proceedings of Graphics Interface 1989*, 164–72.

Joe, S., and F.-Y. Kuo. 2008. Constructing Sobol′ sequences with better two-dimensional projections. *SIAM J. Sci. Comput. 30*, 2635–54.

Johnson, G. M., and M. D. Fairchild. 1999. Full spectral color calculations in realistic image synthesis. *IEEE Computer Graphics and Applications 19* (4), 47–53.

Johnson, M. K., F. Cole, A. Raj, and E. H. Adelson. 2011. Microgeometry capture using an elastomeric sensor. *ACM Transactions on Graphics (Proceedings of SIGGRAPH 2011) 30* (4), 46:1–8.

Joo, H., S. Kwon, S. Lee, E. Eisemann, and S. Lee. 2016. Efficient ray tracing through aspheric lenses and imperfect Bokeh synthesis. *Computer Graphics Forum 35* (4), 99–105.

Judd, D. B., D. L. MacAdam, and G. Wyszecki. 1964. Spectral distribution of typical daylight as a function of correlated color temperature. *Journal of the Optical Society of America 54* (8), 1031–40.

Jung, A., J. Hanika, and C. Dachsbacher. 2020. Detecting bias in Monte Carlo renderers using Welch's t-test. *Journal of Computer Graphics Techniques (JCGT) 9* (2), 1–25.

Jung, A., A. Wilkie, J. Hanika, W. Jakob, and C. Dachsbacher. 2019. Wide gamut spectral upsampling with fluorescence. *Computer Graphics Forum 38* (4), 87–96.

Kahan, W. 1965. Further remarks on reducing truncation errors. *Communications of the ACM 8* (1), 40.

Kainz, F., R. Bogart, and D. Hess. 2004. The OpenEXR File Format. In R. Fernando (ed.), *GPU Gems*, 425–44. Reading, Massachusetts: Addison-Wesley.

Kajiya, J., and M. Ullner. 1981. Filtering high quality text for display on raster scan devices. In *Computer Graphics (Proceedings of SIGGRAPH '81)*, 7–15.

Kajiya, J. T. 1982. Ray tracing parametric patches. In *Computer Graphics (SIGGRAPH 1982 Conference Proceedings)*, 245–54.

Kajiya, J. T. 1983. New techniques for ray tracing procedurally defined objects. In *Computer Graphics (Proceedings of SIGGRAPH '83) 17*, 91–102.

Kajiya, J. T. 1985. Anisotropic reflection models. *Computer Graphics (Proceedings of SIGGRAPH '85) 19*, 15–21.

Kajiya, J. T. 1986. The rendering equation. In *Computer Graphics (SIGGRAPH '86 Proceedings) 20*, 143–50.

Kajiya, J. T., and T. L. Kay. 1989. Rendering fur with three dimensional textures. *Computer Graphics (Proceedings of SIGGRAPH '89) 23*, 271–80.

Kajiya, J. T., and B. P. Von Herzen. 1984. Ray tracing volume densities. In *Computer Graphics (Proceedings of SIGGRAPH '84)*, Volume 18, 165–74.

Kalantari, N. K., S. Bako, and P. Sen. 2015. A machine learning approach for filtering Monte Carlo noise. *ACM Transactions on Graphics (Proceedings of SIGGRAPH 2015) 34* (4), 122:1–12.

Kalli, H. J., and E. D. Cashwell. 1977. Evaluation of three Monte Carlo estimation schemes for flux at a point. *LA-6865-MS*, Los Alamos National Laboratory.

Kallweit, S., T. Müller, B. McWilliams, M. Gross, and J. Novák. 2017. Deep scattering: Rendering atmospheric clouds with radiance-predicting neural networks. *ACM Transactions on Graphics (Proceedings of SIGGRAPH Asia) 36* (6), 231:1–11.

Kalos, M. H., and P. A. Whitlock. 1986. *Monte Carlo Methods: Volume I: Basics*. New York: Wiley.

Kalra, D., and A. H. Barr. 1989. Guaranteed ray intersections with implicit surfaces. In *Computer Graphics (Proceedings of SIGGRAPH '89)*, Volume 23, 297–306.

Kammaje, R., and B. Mora. 2007. A study of restricted BSP trees for ray tracing. In *IEEE Symposium on Interactive Ray Tracing*, 55–62.

Kaplan, M. R. 1985. The uses of spatial coherence in ray tracing. In *ACM SIGGRAPH Course Notes 11*.

Kaplanyan, A. S., and C. Dachsbacher. 2013. Path space regularization for holistic and robust light transport. *Computer Graphics Forum (Proceedings of Eurographics 2013) 32* (2), 63–72.

Kaplanyan, A. S., J. Hanika, and C. Dachsbacher. 2014. The natural-constraint representation of the path space for efficient light transport simulation. *ACM Transactions on Graphics (Proceedings of SIGGRAPH 2014) 33* (4), 102:1–13.

Kaplanyan, A. S., S. Hill, A. Patney, and A. Lefohn. 2016. Filtering distributions of normals for shading antialiasing. In *Proceedings of High Performance Graphics (HPG '16)*.

Karlík, O., M. Šik, P. Vévoda, T. Skřivan, and J. Křivánek. 2019. MIS compensation: Optimizing sampling techniques in multiple importance sampling. *ACM Transactions on Graphics (Proceedings of SIGGRAPH Asia) 38* (6), 151:1–12.

Karras, T., and T. Aila. 2013. Fast parallel construction of high-quality bounding volume hierarchies. In *Proceedings of High Performance Graphics 2013*, 89–99.

Karras, T., S. Laine, and T. Aila. 2018. A style-based generator architecture for generative adversarial networks. *Computer Vision and Pattern Recognition*, 4396–405.

Karras, T., S. Laine, M. Aittala, J. Hellsten, J. Lehtinen, and T. Aila. 2020. Analyzing and improving the image quality of StyleGAN. *Computer Vision and Pattern Recognition*, 8110–19.

Karrenberg, R., D. Rubinstein, P. Slusallek, and S. Hack. 2010. AnySL: Efficient and portable shading for ray tracing. In *Proceedings of High Performance Graphics 2010*, 97–105.

Kato, H., Y. Ushiku, and T. Harada. 2018. Neural 3D mesh renderer. *IEEE Conference on Computer Vision and Pattern Recognition*, 3907–16.

Kay, D. S., and D. P. Greenberg. 1979. Transparency for computer synthesized images. In *Computer Graphics (SIGGRAPH '79 Proceedings)*, Volume 13, 158–64.

Kay, T., and J. Kajiya. 1986. Ray tracing complex scenes. In *Computer Graphics (SIGGRAPH '86 Proceedings)*, Volume 20, 269–78.

Kelemen, C., and L. Szirmay-Kalos. 2001. A microfacet based coupled specular-matte BRDF model with importance sampling. *Eurographics 2001—Short Presentations*.

Kelemen, C., L. Szirmay-Kalos, G. Antal, and F. Csonka. 2002. A simple and robust mutation strategy for the Metropolis light transport algorithm. *Computer Graphics Forum 21* (3), 531–40.

Keller, A. 1996. Quasi-Monte Carlo radiosity. In *Eurographics Rendering Workshop 1996*, 101–10.

Keller, A. 1997. Instant radiosity. In *Proceedings of SIGGRAPH '97*, Computer Graphics Proceedings, Annual Conference Series, 49–56.

Keller, A. 1998. Quasi-Monte Carlo methods for photorealistic image synthesis. Ph.D. thesis, Shaker Verlag Aachen.

Keller, A. 2001. Strictly deterministic sampling methods in computer graphics. *mental images Technical Report*. Also in *SIGGRAPH 2003 Monte Carlo Course Notes*.

Keller, A. 2004. Stratification by rank-1 lattices. *Monte Carlo and Quasi-Monte Carlo Methods 2002*, 299–313. Berlin: Springer-Verlag.

Keller, A. 2012. Quasi-Monte Carlo image synthesis in a nutshell. In *Monte Carlo and Quasi-Monte Carlo Methods 2012*, 213–49. Berlin: Springer-Verlag.

Keller, A., and W. Heidrich. 2001. Interleaved sampling. *Proceedings of the 12th Eurographics Workshop on Rendering Techniques*, 269–76.

Keller, A., and C. Wächter. 2011. Efficient ray tracing without auxiliary acceleration data structure. *High Performance Graphics 2011 Poster*.

Keller, A., C. Wächter, M. Raab, D. Seibert, D. van Antwerpen, J. Korndörfer, and L. Kettner. 2017. The Iray light transport simulation and rendering system. arXiv:1705.01263 [cs.GR].

Kensler, A. 2008. Tree rotations for improving bounding volume hierarchies. In *IEEE Symposium on Interactive Ray Tracing*, 73–76.

Kensler, A. 2013. Correlated multi-jittered sampling. *Pixar Technical Memo 13-01*.

Kensler, A. 2021. Tilt-shift rendering using a thin lens model. In Marrs, A., P. Shirley, and I. Wald (eds.), *Ray Tracing Gems II*, 499–513. Berkeley: Apress.

Kensler, A., A. Knoll, and P. Shirley. 2008. Better gradient noise. *Technical Report UUSCI-2008-001*, SCI Institute, University of Utah.

Kensler, A., and P. Shirley. 2006. Optimizing ray-triangle intersection via automated search. In *IEEE Symposium on Interactive Ray Tracing*, 33–38.

Kettunen, M., E. d'Eon, J. Pantaleoni, and J. Novák. 2021. An unbiased ray-marching transmittance estimator. *ACM Transactions on Graphics (Proceedings of SIGGRAPH) 40* (4), 137:1–20.

Kettunen, M., M. Manzi, M. Aittala, J. Lehtinen, F. Durand, and M. Zwicker. 2015. Gradient-domain path tracing. *ACM Transactions on Graphics (Proceedings of SIGGRAPH 2015) 34* (4), 123:1–13.

Khungurn, P., and S. Marschner. 2017. Azimuthal scattering from elliptical hair fibers. *ACM Transactions on Graphics 36* (2), 13:1–23.

Khungurn, P., D. Schroeder, S. Zhao, K. Bala, and S. Marschner. 2015. Matching real fabrics with microappearance models. *ACM Transactions on Graphics (Proceedings of SIGGRAPH 2015) 35* (1), 1:1–26.

Khvolson, O. D. 1890. Grundzüge einer matematischen Theorie der inneren Diffusion des Lichtes. *Izv. Peterburg. Academii Nauk 33*, 221–65.

Kider Jr., J. T., D. Knowlton, J. Newlin, Y. K. Li, and D. P. Greenberg. 2014. A framework for the experimental comparison of solar and skydome illumination. *ACM Transactions on Graphics (Proceedings of SIGGRAPH Asia 2014) 33* (6), 180:1–12.

King, L. V. 1913. On the scattering and absorption of light in gaseous media, with applications to the intensity of sky radiation. *Philosophical Transactions of the Royal Society of*

London. Series A. Mathematical and Physical Sciences 212, 375–433.

Kingma, D. P., and J. Ba. 2014. Adam: A method for stochastic optimization. *3rd International Conference on Learning Representations, (ICLR)*. San Diego, CA, USA. arXIV:1412.6980 [cs.LG].

Kirk, D., and J. Arvo. 1988. The ray tracing kernel. In *Proceedings of Ausgraph '88*, 75–82.

Kirk, D. B., and J. Arvo. 1991. Unbiased sampling techniques for image synthesis. *Computer Graphics (SIGGRAPH '91 Proceedings)*, Volume 25, 153–56.

Klassen, R. V. 1987. Modeling the effect of the atmosphere on light. *ACM Transactions on Graphics 6* (3), 215–37.

Klimaszewski, K. S., and T. W. Sederberg. 1997. Faster ray tracing using adaptive grids. *IEEE Computer Graphics and Applications 17* (1), 42–51.

Knaus, C., and M. Zwicker. 2011. Progressive photon mapping: A probabilistic approach. *ACM Transactions on Graphics 30* (3), 25:1–13.

Kniep, S., S. Häring, and M. Magnor. 2009. Efficient and accurate rendering of complex light sources. *Computer Graphics Forum (Proceedings of the 2009 Eurographics Symposium on Rendering) 28* (4), 1073–81.

Knoll, A., Y. Hijazi, C. D. Hansen, I. Wald, and H. Hagen. 2009. Fast ray tracing of arbitrary implicit surfaces with interval and affine arithmetic. *Computer Graphics Forum 28* (1), 26–40.

Knuth, D. E. 1969. *The Art of Computer Programming: Seminumerical Algorithms*. Reading, Massachusetts: Addison-Wesley.

Knuth, D. E. 1984. Literate programming. *The Computer Journal 27*, 97–111. Reprinted in D. E. Knuth, *Literate Programming*, Stanford Center for the Study of Language and Information, 1992.

Knuth, D. E. 1986. *MetaFont: The Program*. Reading, Massachusetts: Addison-Wesley.

Knuth, D. E. 1993a. *TEX: The Program*. Reading, Massachusetts: Addison-Wesley.

Knuth, D. E. 1993b. *The Stanford GraphBase*. New York: ACM Press and Addison-Wesley.

Knuth, D. E. 1999. *MMIXware: A RISC Computer for the Third Millennium*. Berlin: Springer-Verlag.

Knuth, D. E., and S. Levy. 1994. *The CWEB System of Structured Documentation: Version 3.0*. Reading, Massachusetts: Addison-Wesley.

Koerner, D., J. Novák, P. Kutz, R. Habel, and W. Jarosz. 2016. Subdivision next-event estimation for path-traced subsurface scattering. *Eurographics Symposium on Rendering— Experimental Ideas and Implementations*, 91–96.

Kolb, C., D. Mitchell, and P. Hanrahan. 1995. A realistic camera model for computer graphics. *SIGGRAPH '95 Conference Proceedings*, Annual Conference Series, 317–24.

Kollig, T., and A. Keller. 2000. Efficient bidirectional path tracing by randomized quasi-Monte Carlo integration. In *Monte Carlo and Quasi-Monte Carlo Methods 2000*, 290–305. Berlin: Springer-Verlag.

Kollig, T., and A. Keller. 2002. Efficient multidimensional sampling. *Computer Graphics Forum (Proceedings of Eurographics 2002)*, Volume 21, 557–63.

Kondapaneni, I., P. Vévoda, P. Grittmann, T. Skřivan, P. Slusallek, and J. Křivánek. 2019. Optimal multiple importance sampling. *ACM Transactions on Graphics (Proceedings of SIGGRAPH) 37* (4), 37:1–14.

Kopta, D., T. Ize, J. Spjut, E. Brunvand, A. Davis, and A. Kensler. 2012. Fast, effective BVH updates for animated scenes. In *Proceedings of the ACM SIGGRAPH Symposium on Interactive 3D Graphics and Games*, 197–204.

Křivánek, J., and E. d'Eon. 2014. A zero-variance-based sampling scheme for Monte Carlo subsurface scattering. *SIGGRAPH 2014 Talks*, 66:1.

Křivánek, J., P. Gautron, S. Pattanaik, and K. Bouatouch. 2005. Radiance caching for efficient global illumination computation. *IEEE Transactions on Visualization and Computer Graphics 11* (5), 550–61.

Kulla, C., and A. Conty Estevez. 2017. Revisiting physically based shading at Imageworks. *SIGGRAPH 2017 Course Notes 2* (3).

Kulla, C., A. Conty, C. Stein, and L. Gritz. 2018. Sony Pictures Imageworks Arnold. *ACM Transactions on Graphics 37* (3), 29:1–18.

Kulla, C., and M. Fajardo. 2012. Importance sampling techniques for path tracing in participating media. *Computer Graphics Forum (Proceedings of the 2012 Eurographics Symposium on Rendering) 31* (4), 1519–28.

Kurt, M., L. Szirmay-Kalos, and J. Křivánek. 2010. An anisotropic BRDF model for fitting and Monte Carlo rendering. *SIGGRAPH Computer Graphics 44* (1), 3:1–15.

Kutz, P., R. Habel, Y. K. Li, and J. Novák. 2017. Spectral and decomposition tracking for rendering heterogeneous volumes. *ACM Transactions on Graphics 36* (4), 111:1–16.

Kuznetsov, A., M. Hašan, Z. Xu, L.-Q. Yan, B. Walter, N. K. Kalantari, S. Marschner, and R. Ramamoorthi. 2019. Learning generative models for rendering specular microgeometry. *ACM Transactions on Graphics (Proceedings of SIGGRAPH Asia) 38* (6), 225:1–14.

Kuznetsov, A., N. K. Kalantari, and R. Ramamoorthi. 2018. Deep adaptive sampling for low sample count rendering. *Computer Graphics Forum 37* (4), 35–44.

Kuznetsov, A., K. Mullia, Z. Xu, M. Hašan, and R. Ramamoorthi. 2021. NeuMIP: Multi-resolution neural materials. *ACM Transactions on Graphics (Proceedings of SIGGRAPH) 40* (4), 175:1–13.

Lacewell, D., B. Burley, S. Boulos, and P. Shirley. 2008. Raytracing prefiltered occlusion for aggregate geometry. In *IEEE Symposium on Interactive Ray Tracing*, 19–26.

Lafortune, E., and Y. Willems. 1993. Bi-directional path tracing. *Proceedings of Compugraphics*, 145–53.

Lafortune, E., and Y. Willems. 1994. The ambient term as a variance reducing technique for Monte Carlo ray tracing. *Rendering Techniques (Proceedings of the Eurographics Workshop on Rendering)*, 163–71.

Lafortune, E., and Y. Willems. 1995. A 5D tree to reduce the variance of Monte Carlo ray tracing. In *Eurographics Workshop on Rendering Techniques 1995*, 11–20.

Lafortune, E. P., and Y. D. Willems. 1996. Rendering participating media with bidirectional path tracing. In *Eurographics Rendering Workshop 1996*, 91–100.

Lagae, A., and P. Dutré. 2005. An efficient ray-quadrilateral intersection test. *Journal of Graphics Tools 10* (4), 23–32.

Lagae, A., and P. Dutré. 2008a. Compact, fast, and robust grids for ray tracing. *Computer Graphics Forum (Proceedings of the 2008 Eurographics Symposium on Rendering) 27* (4), 1235–44.

Lagae, A., and P. Dutré. 2008b. Accelerating ray tracing using constrained tetrahedralizations. *Computer Graphics Forum (Proceedings of the 2008 Eurographics Symposium on Rendering) 27* (4), 1303–12.

Lagae, A., and P. Dutré. 2008c. A comparison of methods for generating Poisson disk distributions. *Computer Graphics Forum 27* (1), 114–29.

Lagae, A., S. Lefebvre, R. Cook, T. DeRose, G. Drettakis, D. S. Ebert, J. P. Lewis, K. Perlin, and M. Zwicker. 2010. A survey of procedural noise functions. *Computer Graphics Forum 29* (8), 2579–600.

Laine, S. 2010. Restart trail for stackless BVH traversal. In *Proceedings of High Performance Graphics 2010*, 107–11.

Laine, S., J. Hellsten, T. Karras, Y. Seol, J. Lehtinen, and T. Aila. 2020. Modular primitives for high-performance differentiable rendering. *ACM Transactions on Graphics (Proceedings of SIGGRAPH Asia) 39* (6), 194:1–14.

Laine, S., and T. Karras. 2011. Stratified sampling for stochastic transparency. In *Computer Graphics Forum 30* (4), 1197–204.

Laine, S., T. Karras, and T. Aila. 2013. Megakernels considered harmful: Wavefront path tracing on GPUs. In *Proceedings of the Fifth High-Performance Graphics Conference (HPG '13)*, 137–43.

Lambert, J. H. 1760. *Photometry, or, On the Measure and Gradations of Light, Colors, and Shade*. The Illuminating Engineering Society of North America. Translated by David L. DiLaura in 2001.

Lang, S. 1986. *An Introduction to Linear Algebra*. New York: Springer-Verlag.

Langlands, A., and L. Fascione. 2020. PhysLight: An end-to-end pipeline for scene-referred lighting. *SIGGRAPH 2020 Talks 19*, 191–2.

Lansdale, R. C. 1991. Texture mapping and resampling for computer graphics. M.S. thesis, Department of Electrical Engineering, University of Toronto.

Larson, G. W., and R. A. Shakespeare. 1998. *Rendering with Radiance: The Art and Science of Lighting Visualization*. San Francisco: Morgan Kaufmann.

Lauterbach, C., M. Garland, S. Sengupta, D. Luebke, and D. Manocha. 2009. Fast BVH construction on GPUs. *Computer Graphics Forum (Eurographics 2009 Conference Proceedings) 28* (2), 422–30.

Lauterbach, C., S.-E. Yoon, M. Tang, and D. Manocha. 2008. ReduceM: Interactive and memory efficient ray tracing of large models. *Computer Graphics Forum 27* (4), 1313–21.

Lauterbach, C., S.-E. Yoon, D. Tuft, and D. Manocha. 2006. RT-DEFORM: Interactive ray tracing of dynamic scenes using BVHs. *IEEE Symposium on Interactive Ray Tracing*, 39–46.

Lawrence, J., S. Rusinkiewicz, and R. Ramamoorthi. 2005. Adaptive numerical cumulative distribution functions for efficient importance sampling. *Rendering Techniques 2005: 16th Eurographics Workshop on Rendering*, 11–20.

L'Ecuyer, P., and R. Simard. 2007. TestU01: A C library for empirical testing of random number generators. *ACM Transactions on Mathematical Software 33* (4), 22:1–40.

Lee, J. H., A. Jarabo, D. S. Jeon, D. Gutierrez, and M. H. Kim. 2018. Practical multiple scattering for rough surfaces. *ACM Transactions on Graphics (Proceedings of SIGGRAPH Asia) 37* (6), 275:1–12.

Lee, M., B. Green, F. Xie, and E. Tabellion. 2017. Vectorized production path tracing. In *Proceedings of High Performance Graphics (HPG '17)*, 10:1–11.

Lee, M., and R. Redner. 1990. A note on the use of nonlinear filtering in computer graphics. *IEEE Computer Graphics and Applications 10* (3), 23–29.

Lee, M. E., R. A. Redner, and S. P. Uselton. 1985. Statistically optimized sampling for distributed ray tracing. In *Computer Graphics (Proceedings of SIGGRAPH '85)*, Volume 19, 61–67.

Lee, R., and C. O'Sullivan. 2007. Accelerated light propagation through participating media. *Proceedings of the Sixth Eurographics / IEEE VGTC Conference on Volume Graphics*, 17–23.

Lehtinen, J., T. Karras, S. Laine, M. Aittala, F. Durand, and T. Aila. 2013. Gradient-domain Metropolis light transport. *ACM Transactions on Graphics (Proceedings of SIGGRAPH 2013) 32* (4), 95:1–12.

Leonard, L., K. Höhlein, and R. Westermann. 2021. Learning multiple-scattering solutions for sphere-tracing of volumetric subsurface effects. *Computer Graphics Forum (Proceedings of Eurographics) 40* (2), 165–78.

Lessig, C., M. Desbrun, and E. Fiume. 2014. A constructive theory of sampling for image synthesis using reproducing kernel bases. *ACM Transactions on Graphics (Proceedings of SIGGRAPH 2014) 33* (4), 55:1–14.

Levoy, M., and P. M. Hanrahan. 1996. Light field rendering. In *Proceedings of SIGGRAPH '96*, Computer Graphics Proceedings, Annual Conference Series, 31–42.

Levoy, M., and T. Whitted. 1985. The use of points as a display primitive. *Technical Report 85-022*. Computer Science Department, University of North Carolina at Chapel Hill.

Li, T.-M., M. Aittala, F. Durand, and J. Lehtinen. 2018. Differentiable Monte Carlo ray tracing through edge sampling. *ACM Transactions on Graphics (Proceedings of SIGGRAPH Asia) 37* (6), 222:1–11.

Li, Y.-K. 2018. Mipmapping with bidirectional techniques. *https://blog.yiningkarlli.com/2018/10/bidirectional-mipmap.html*.

Lier, A., M. Martinek, M. Stamminger, and K. Selgrad. 2018a. A high-resolution compression scheme for ray tracing subdivision surfaces with displacement. *Proceedings of the ACM on Computer Graphics and Interactive Techniques 1* (2), 33:1–17.

Lier, A., M. Stamminger, and K. Selgrad. 2018b. CPU-style SIMD ray traversal on GPUs. *Proceedings of High Performance Graphics (HPG '18)*, 7:1–4.

Liktor, G., and K. Vaidyanathan. 2016. Bandwidth-efficient BVH layout for incremental hardware traversal. *Proceedings of High Performance Graphics (HPG '16)*, 51–61.

Lin, D., K. Shkurko, I. Mallett, and C. Yuksel. 2019. Dual-split trees. *Symposium on Interactive 3D Graphics and Games (I3D 2019)*, 3:1–9.

Liu, H., H. Han, and M. Jiang. 2021. Rank-1 lattices for efficient path integral estimation. *Computer Graphics Forum (Proceedings of Eurographics) 40* (2), 91–102.

Liu, J. S. 2001. *Monte Carlo Strategies in Scientific Computing*. New York: Springer-Verlag.

Liu, S., W. Chen, T. Li, and H. Li. 2019a. Soft rasterizer: Differentiable rendering for unsupervised single-view mesh reconstruction. *IEEE/CVF International Conference on Computer Vision (ICCV)*, 7708–17.

Liu, Y., K. Xu, and L.-Q. Yan. 2019b. Adaptive BRDF-oriented multiple importance sampling of many lights. *Computer Graphics Forum 38* (4), 123–33.

Logie, J. R., and J. W. Patterson. 1994. Inverse displacement mapping in the general case. *Computer Graphics Forum 14* (5), 261–73.

Lommel, E. 1889. Die Photometrie der diffusen Zurückwerfung. *Annalen der Physik 36*, 473–502.

Longbottom, Roy. 2017. Roy Longbottom's PC Benchmark Collection. *http://www.roylongbottom.org.uk/linpack%20results.htm*.

Loper, M. M., and M. J. Black. 2014. OpenDR: An approximate differentiable renderer. *European Conference on Computer Vision (Proceedings of ECCV 2014)*, 154–69.

Loubet, G., N. Holzschuch, and W. Jakob. 2019. Reparameterizing discontinuous integrands for differentiable rendering. *ACM Transactions on Graphics (Proceedings of SIGGRAPH Asia) 38* (6), 1–14.

Loubet, G., and F. Neyret. 2018. A new microflake model with microscopic self-shadowing for accurate volume downsampling. *Computer Graphics Forum 37* (2), 111–21.

Loubet, G., T. Zeltner, N. Holzschuch, and W. Jakob. 2020. Slope-space integrals for specular next event estimation. *ACM Transactions on Graphics (Proceedings of SIGGRAPH Asia) 39* (6), 239:1–13.

Löw, J., J. Kronander, A. Ynnerman, and J. Unger. 2012. BRDF models for accurate and efficient rendering of glossy surfaces. *ACM Transactions on Graphics 31* (1), 9:1–14.

Lu, H., R. Pacanowski, and X. Granier. 2013. Second-order approximation for variance reduction in multiple importance sampling. *Computer Graphics Forum 32* (7), 131–36.

Lu, H., R. Pacanowski, and X. Granier. 2015. Position-dependent importance sampling of light field luminaires. *IEEE Transactions on Visualization and Computer Graphics 21* (2), 241–51.

Lukaszewski, A. 2001. Exploiting coherence of shadow rays. In *AFRIGRAPH 2001*, 147–50. ACM SIGGRAPH.

MacDonald, J. D., and K. S. Booth. 1990. Heuristics for ray tracing using space subdivision. *The Visual Computer 6* (3), 153–66.

Machiraju, R., and R. Yagel. 1996. Reconstruction error characterization and control: A sampling theory approach. *IEEE Transactions on Visualization and Computer Graphics 2* (4), 364–78.

MacKay, D. 2003. *Information Theory, Inference, and Learning Algorithms*. Cambridge: Cambridge University Press.

Malacara, D. 2002. *Color Vision and Colorimetry: Theory and Applications*. SPIE—The International Society for Optical Engineering. Bellingham, WA.

Mallett, I., and C. Yuksel. 2019. Spectral primary decomposition for rendering with sRGB reflectance. *Eurographics Symposium on Rendering–DL-only and Industry Track*.

Mann, S., N. Litke, and T. DeRose. 1997. A coordinate free geometry ADT. *Research Report CS-97-15*, Computer Science Department, University of Waterloo.

Manson, J., and S. Schaefer. 2013. Cardinality-constrained texture filtering. *ACM Transactions on Graphics (Proceedings of SIGGRAPH 2013) 32* (4), 140:1–8.

Manson, J., and S. Schaefer. 2014. Bilinear accelerated filter approximation. *Computer Graphics Forum (Proceedings of the 2014 Eurographics Symposium on Rendering) 33* (4), 33–40.

Mansson, E., J. Munkberg, and T. Akenine-Möller. 2007. Deep coherent ray tracing. In *Proceedings of IEEE Symposium on Interactive Ray Tracing*, 79–85.

Manzi, M., M. Kettunen, M. Aittala, J. Lehtinen, F. Durand, and M. Zwicker. 2015. Gradient-domain bidirectional path tracing. *Eurographics Symposium on Rendering—Experimental Ideas & Implementations*.

Manzi, M., F. Rousselle, M. Kettunen, J. Lehtinen, and M. Zwicker. 2014. Improved sampling for gradient-domain Metropolis light transport. *ACM Transactions on Graphics (Proceedings of SIGGRAPH Asia 2014) 33* (6), 178:1–12.

Marco, J., A. Jarabo, W. Jarosz, and D. Gutierrez. 2018. Second-order occlusion-aware volumetric radiance caching. *ACM Transactions on Graphics 37* (2), 20:1–14.

Marques, R., C. Bouville, M. Ribardière, L. P. Santos, and K. Bouatouch. 2013. Spherical Fibonacci point sets for illumination integrals. *Computer Graphics Forum (Proceedings of the 2013 Eurographics Symposium on Rendering) 32* (4), 134–43.

Marschner, S. 1998. Inverse rendering for computer graphics. Ph.D. thesis, Cornell University.

Marschner, S., S. Westin, A. Arbree, and J. Moon. 2005. Measuring and modeling the appearance of finished wood. In *ACM Transactions on Graphics (Proceedings of SIGGRAPH 2005) 24* (3), 727–34.

Marschner, S. R., H. W. Jensen, M. Cammarano, S. Worley, and P. Hanrahan. 2003. Light scattering from human hair fibers. *ACM Transactions on Graphics 22* (3), 780–91.

Marschner, S. R., and R. J. Lobb. 1994. An evaluation of reconstruction filters for volume rendering. In *Proceedings of Visualization '94*, 100–107.

Martin, W., E. Cohen, R. Fish, and P. S. Shirley. 2000. Practical ray tracing of trimmed NURBS surfaces. *Journal of Graphics Tools 5* (1), 27–52.

Mas, A., I. Martín, and G. Patow. 2008. Compression and importance sampling of near-field light sources. *Computer Graphics Forum 27* (8), 2013–27.

Massó, J. P. M., and P. G. López. 2003 Automatic hybrid hierarchy creation: A cost-model based approach. *Computer Graphics Forum 22* (1), 5–13.

Matusik, W., H. Pfister, M. Brand, and L. McMillan. 2003a. Efficient isotropic BRDF measurement. In *Proceedings of the 14th Eurographics Workshop on Rendering*, 241–47.

Matusik, W., H. Pfister, M. Brand, and L. McMillan. 2003b. A data-driven reflectance model. *ACM Transactions on Graphics (Proceedings of SIGGRAPH 2003) 22* (3), 759–69.

Max, N. 2017. Improved accuracy when building an orthonormal basis. *Journal of Computer Graphics Techniques (JCGT) 6* (1), 9–16.

Max, N. L. 1986. Atmospheric illumination and shadows. In *Computer Graphics (Proceedings of SIGGRAPH '86)*, Volume 20, 117–24.

Max, N. L. 1988. Horizon mapping: Shadows for bump-mapped surfaces. *The Visual Computer 4* (2), 109–17.

Max, N. L. 1995. Optical models for direct volume rendering. *IEEE Transactions on Visualization and Computer Graphics 1* (2), 99–108.

McCluney, W. R. 1994. *Introduction to Radiometry and Photometry*. Boston: Artech House.

McCombe, J. 2013. Low power consumption ray tracing. *SIGGRAPH 2013 Course: Ray Tracing Is the Future and Ever Will Be*.

McCool, M. D. 1999. Anisotropic diffusion for Monte Carlo noise reduction. *ACM Transactions on Graphics 18* (2), 171–94.

McCool, M. D., and P. K. Harwood. 1997. Probability trees. *Proceedings of Graphics Interface '97*, 37–46.

McCormack, J., R. Perry, K. I. Farkas, and N. P. Jouppi. 1999. Feline: Fast elliptical lines for anisotropic texture mapping. In *Proceedings of SIGGRAPH '99*, Computer Graphics Proceedings, Annual Conference Series, 243–50.

McKenney, P. E. 2021. *Is Parallel Programming Hard, and, If So, What Can You Do About It? https://mirrors.edge.kernel.org/pub/linux/kernel/people/paulmck/perfbook/perfbook.html*.

McKenney, P. E., and J. D. Slingwine. 1998. Read-copy update: Using execution history to solve concurrency problems. *Parallel and Distributed Computing and Systems*, 509–18.

Mehlhorn, K., and S. Näher. 1999. *LEDA: A Platform for Combinatorial and Geometric Computing*. Cambridge: Cambridge University Press.

Meijering, E. 2002. A chronology of interpolation: From ancient astronomy to modern signal and image processing. In *Proceedings of the IEEE 90* (3), 319–42.

Meijering, E. H. W., W. J. Niessen, J. P. W. Pluim, and M. A. Viergever. 1999. Quantitative comparison of sinc-approximating kernels for medical image interpolation. *Medical Image Computing and Computer-Assisted Intervention—MICCAI 1999*, 210–17.

Meister, D., and J. Bittner. 2018a. Parallel reinsertion for bounding volume hierarchy optimization. *Computer Graphics Forum 37* (2), 463–73.

Meister, D., and J. Bittner, 2018b. Parallel locally-ordered clustering for bounding volume hierarchy construction. *IEEE Transactions on Visualization and Computer Graphics 24* (3), 1345–53.

Meister, D., J. Boksansky, M. Guthe, and J. Bittner. 2020. On ray reordering techniques for faster GPU ray tracing. *Symposium on Interactive 3D Graphics and Games (I3D '20)*, 13:1–9.

Meister, D., S. Ogaki, C. Benthin, M. J. Doyle, M. Guthe, and J. Bittner. 2021. A survey on bounding volume hierarchies for ray tracing. *Computer Graphics Forum (Eurographics State of the Art Report) 40* (2): 683–712.

Meng, J., J. Hanika, and C. Dachsbacher. 2016. Improving the Dwivedi sampling scheme. *Computer Graphics Forum 35* (4), 37–44.

Meng, J., F. Simon, J. Hanika, and C. Dachsbacher. 2015. Physically meaningful rendering using tristimulus colours. *Computer Graphics Forum (Proceedings of the 2015 Eurographics Symposium on Rendering) 34* (4), 31–40.

Metropolis, N. 1987. The beginning of the Monte Carlo method. *Los Alamos Science Special Issue 15*, 125–30.

Metropolis, N., and S. Ulam. 1949. The Monte Carlo method. *Journal of the American Statistical Association 44* (247), 335–41.

Meyer, G. W., and D. P. Greenberg. 1980. Perceptual color spaces for computer graphics. In *Computer Graphics (Proceedings of SIGGRAPH '80)*, Volume 14, 254–61.

Meyer, G. W., H. E. Rushmeier, M. F. Cohen, D. P. Greenberg, and K. E. Torrance. 1986. An experimental evaluation of computer graphics imagery. *ACM Transactions on Graphics 5* (1), 30–50.

Meyer, Q., J. Süssmuth, G. Sussner, M. Stamminger, and G. Greiner. 2010. On floating-point normal vectors. *Proceedings of the 21st Eurographics Conference on Rendering*, 1405–9.

Mikkelsen, M. 2008. Simulation of wrinkled surfaces revisited. M.S. thesis, University of Copenhagen.

Mildenhall, B., P. P. Srinivasan, M. Tancik, J. T. Barron, R. Ramamoorthi, and R. Ng. 2020. NeRF: Representing scenes as neural radiance fields for view synthesis. *European Conference on Computer Vision (ECCV)*. arXiv:2003.08934 [cs.CV].

Miller, B., I. Georgiev, and W. Jarosz. 2019. A null-scattering path integral formulation of light transport. *ACM Transactions on Graphics (Proceedings of SIGGRAPH) 38* (4), 1–13.

Miller, G. S., and C. R. Hoffman. 1984. Illumination and reflection maps: Simulated objects in simulated and real environments. *Course Notes for Advanced Computer Graphics Animation, SIGGRAPH '84.*

Mishchenko, M. I. 2013. 125 years of radiative transfer: Enduring triumphs and persisting misconceptions. *AIP Conference Proceedings 1531* (11), 11–18.

Mitchell, D. P. 1987. Generating antialiased images at low sampling densities. *Computer Graphics (SIGGRAPH '87 Proceedings)*, Volume 21, 65–72.

Mitchell, D. P. 1990. Robust ray intersection with interval arithmetic. In *Proceedings of Graphics Interface 1990*, 68–74.

Mitchell, D. P. 1991. Spectrally optimal sampling for distributed ray tracing. *Computer Graphics (SIGGRAPH '91 Proceedings)*, Volume 25, 157–64.

Mitchell, D. P. 1992. Ray tracing and irregularities of distribution. In *Third Eurographics Workshop on Rendering*, 61–69.

Mitchell, D. P. 1996. Consequences of stratified sampling in graphics. In *Proceedings of SIGGRAPH '96*, Computer Graphics Proceedings, Annual Conference Series, 277–80.

Mitchell, D. P., and P. Hanrahan. 1992. Illumination from curved reflectors. In *Computer Graphics (Proceedings of SIGGRAPH '92)*, Volume 26, 283–91.

Mitchell, D. P., and A. N. Netravali. 1988. Reconstruction filters in computer graphics. *Computer Graphics (SIGGRAPH '88 Proceedings)*, Volume 22, 221–28.

Mojzík, M., A. Fichet, and A. Wilkie. 2018. Handling fluorescence in a uni-directional spectral path tracer. *Computer Graphics Forum 37* (4), 77–94.

Møller, O. 1965. Quasi double precision in floating-point arithmetic. *BIT Numerical Mathematics 5*, 37–50.

Möller, T., and J. Hughes. 1999. Efficiently building a matrix to rotate one vector to another. *Journal of Graphics Tools 4* (4), 1–4.

Möller, T., R. Machiraju, K. Mueller, and R. Yagel. 1997. Evaluation and design of filters using a Taylor series expansion. *IEEE Transactions on Visualization and Computer Graphics 3* (2), 184–99.

Möller, T., and B. Trumbore. 1997. Fast, minimum storage ray–triangle intersection. *Journal of Graphics Tools 2* (1), 21–28.

Moon, B., Y. Byun, T.-J. Kim, P. Claudio, H.-S. Kim, Y.-J. Ban, S. W. Nam, and S.-E. Yoon. 2010. Cache-oblivious ray reordering. *ACM Transactions on Graphics 29* (3), 28:1–10.

Moon, J., and S. Marschner. 2006. Simulating multiple scattering in hair using a photon mapping approach. *ACM Transactions on Graphics (Proceedings of SIGGRAPH 2006) 25* (3), 1067–74.

Moon, J., B. Walter, and S. Marschner. 2007. Rendering discrete random media using precomputed scattering solutions. *Rendering Techniques 2007: 18th Eurographics Workshop on Rendering*, 231–42.

Moon, J., B. Walter, and S. Marschner. 2008. Efficient multiple scattering in hair using spherical harmonics. *ACM Transactions on Graphics (Proceedings of SIGGRAPH 2008) 27* (3), 31:1–7.

Moon, P., and D. E. Spencer. 1936. *The Scientific Basis of Illuminating Engineering*. New York: McGraw-Hill.

Moon, P., and D. E. Spencer. 1948. *Lighting Design*. Reading, Massachusetts: Addison-Wesley.

Moore, R. E. 1966. *Interval Analysis*. Englewood Cliffs, New Jersey: Prentice Hall.

Mora, B. 2011. Naive ray-tracing: A divide-and-conquer approach. *ACM Transactions on Graphics 30* (5), 117:1–12.

Moravec, H. 1981. 3D graphics and the wave theory. In *Computer Graphics*, Volume 15, 289–96.

Morley, R. K., S. Boulos, J. Johnson, D. Edwards, P. Shirley, M. Ashikhmin, and S. Premoze. 2006. Image synthesis using adjoint photons. In *Proceedings of Graphics Interface 2006*, 179–86.

Morovi, J. 2008. *Color Gamut Mapping*. New York: John Wiley & Sons.

Morrical, N., and S. Zellmann. 2021. Inverse transform sampling using ray tracing hardware. In Marrs, A., P. Shirley, and I. Wald (eds.), *Ray Tracing Gems II*, 625–41. Berkeley: Apress.

Morton, G. M. 1966. A computer oriented geodetic data base and a new technique in file sequencing. *IBM Technical Report*.

Motwani, R., and P. Raghavan. 1995. *Randomized Algorithms*. Cambridge, U.K.: Cambridge University Press.

Moulin, M., N. Billen, and P. Dutré. 2015. Efficient visibility heuristics for kd-trees using the RTSAH. *Eurographics Symposium on Rendering–Experimental Ideas & Implementations*, 31–39.

Muller, D. E. 1956. A method for solving algebraic equations using an automatic computer. *Mathematical Tables and Other Aids to Computation 10* (56), 208–15.

Müller, G., and D. W. Fellner. 1999. Hybrid scene structuring with application to ray tracing. *Proceedings of the International Conference on Visual Computing (ICVC '99)*, 19–26.

Müller, G., J. Meseth, M. Sattler, R. Sarlette, and R. Klein. 2005. Acquisition, synthesis and rendering of bidirectional texture functions. *Computer Graphics Forum (Eurographics State of the Art Report) 24* (1), 83–109.

Müller, K., T. Techmann, and D. Fellner. 2003. Adaptive ray tracing of subdivision surfaces. *Computer Graphics Forum 22* (3), 553–62.

Müller, T. 2019. "Practical Path Guiding" in production. *Path Guiding in Production, ACM SIGGRAPH Courses*.

Müller, T., M. Gross, and J. Novák. 2017. Practical path guiding for efficient light-transport simulation. *Computer Graphics Forum (Proceedings of EGSR 2017) 36* (4), 91–100.

Müller, T., B. McWilliams, F. Rousselle, M. Gross, and J. Novák. 2019. Neural importance sampling. *ACM Transaction on Graphics (presented at SIGGRAPH 2019) 38* (5), 145:1–19.

Müller, T., M. Papas, M. Gross, W. Jarosz, and J. Novák. 2016. Efficient rendering of heterogeneous polydisperse granular media. *ACM Transactions on Graphics (Proceedings of SIGGRAPH Asia) 35* (6), 168:1–14.

Müller, T., F. Rousselle, A. Keller, and J. Novák. 2020. Neural control variates. *ACM Transactions on Graphics (Proceedings of SIGGRAPH Asia) 39* (6), 243:1–19.

Müller, T., F. Rousselle, J. Novák, and A. Keller. 2021. Real-time neural radiance caching for path tracing. *ACM Transactions on Graphics (Proceedings of SIGGRAPH) 40* (4), 36:1–16.

Munkberg, J., and J. Hasselgren. 2020. Neural denoising with layer embeddings. *Computer Graphics Forum 39* (4), 1–12.

Munkberg, J., J. Hasselgren, P. Clarberg, M. Andersson, and T. Akenine-Möller. 2016. Texture space caching and reconstruction for ray tracing. *ACM Transactions on Graphics (Proceedings of SIGGRAPH Asia) 35* (6), 249:1–13.

Musbach, A., G. W. Meyer, F. Reitich, and S. H. Oh. 2013. Full wave modelling of light propagation and reflection. *Computer Graphics Forum 32* (6), 24–37.

Museth, K. 2013. VDB: High-resolution sparse volumes with dynamic topology. *ACM Transactions on Graphics 32* (3), 27:1–22.

Museth, K. 2021. NanoVDB: A GPU-friendly and portable VDB data structure for real-time rendering and simulation. *ACM SIGGRAPH 2021 Talks*, 1–2.

Nabata, K., K. Iwaski, Y. Dobashi, and T. Nishita. 2013. Efficient divide-and-conquer ray tracing using ray sampling. In *Proceedings of High Performance Graphics 2013*, 129–35.

Nakamaru, K., and Y. Ohno. 2002. Ray tracing for curves primitive. In *Journal of WSCG (WSCG 2002 Proceedings) 10*, 311–16.

Nalbach, O., E. Arabadzhiyska, D. Mehta, H.-P. Seidel, and T. Ritschel. 2017. Deep shading: Convolutional neural networks for screen space shading. *Computer Graphics Forum 36* (4), 65–78.

Narasimhan, S., M. Gupta, C. Donner, R. Ramamoorthi, S. Nayar, and H. W. Jensen. 2006. Acquiring scattering properties of participating media by dilution. *ACM Transactions on Graphics 25* (3), 1003–12.

Naylor, B. 1993. Constructing good partition trees. In *Proceedings of Graphics Interface 1993*, 181–91.

Ng, R., M. Levoy, M. Brédif., G. Duval, M. Horowitz, and P. Hanrahan. 2005. Light field photography with a hand-held plenoptic camera. *Stanford University Computer Science Technical Report*, CSTR 2005-02.

Nicodemus, F., J. Richmond, J. Hsia, I. Ginsburg, and T. Limperis. 1977. *Geometrical Considerations and Nomenclature for Reflectance*. NBS Monograph 160, Washington, D.C.: National Bureau of Standards, U.S. Department of Commerce.

Nicolet, B., A. Jacobson, and W. Jakob. 2021. Large steps in inverse rendering of geometry. *ACM Transactions on Graphics (Proceedings of SIGGRAPH Asia) 40* (6), 248:1–13.

Niederreiter, H. 1992. *Random Number Generation and Quasi–Monte Carlo Methods*. Philadelphia: Society for Industrial and Applied Mathematics.

Nielsen, J. B., H. W. Jensen, and R. Ramamoorthi. 2015. On optimal, minimal BRDF sampling for reflectance acquisition. *ACM Transactions on Graphics (Proceedings of SIGGRAPH Asia) 34* (6), 186:1–11.

Nimier-David, M., S. Speierer, B. Ruiz, and W. Jakob. 2020. Radiative backpropagation: An adjoint method for lightning-fast differentiable rendering. *ACM Transactions on Graphics (Proceedings of SIGGRAPH) 39* (4), 146:1–15.

Nimier-David, M., D. Vicini, T. Zeltner, W. Jakob. 2019. Mitsuba 2: A retargetable forward and inverse renderer. *ACM Transactions on Graphics (Proceedings of SIGGRAPH 2019) 38* (6), 203:1–17.

Nishita, T., Y. Miyawaki, and E. Nakamae. 1987. A shading model for atmospheric scattering considering luminous intensity distribution of light sources. In *Computer Graphics (Proceedings of SIGGRAPH '87)*, Volume 21, 303–10.

Nishita, T., and E. Nakamae. 1985. Continuous tone representation of three-dimensional objects taking account of shadows and interreflection. *SIGGRAPH Computer Graphics 19* (3), 23–30.

Nishita, T., and E. Nakamae. 1986. Continuous tone representation of three-dimensional objects illuminated by sky light. In *Computer Graphics (Proceedings of SIGGRAPH '86)*, Volume 20, 125–32.

Norton, A., A. P. Rockwood, and P. T. Skolmoski. 1982. Clamping: A method of antialiasing textured surfaces by bandwidth limiting in object space. In *Computer Graphics (Proceedings of SIGGRAPH '82)*, Volume 16, 1–8.

Novák, J., I. Georgiev, J. Hanika, and W. Jarosz. 2018. Monte Carlo methods for volumetric light transport simulation. *Computer Graphics Forum (Presented at Eurographics 2018– State of the Art Report) 37* (2), 551–76.

Novák, J., V. Havran, and C. Daschbacher. 2010. Path regeneration for interactive path tracing. *Eurographics 2010 Short Papers*, 61–64.

Novák, J., A. Selle, and W. Jarosz. 2014. Residual ratio tracking for estimating attenuation in participating media. *ACM Transactions on Graphics (Proceedings of SIGGRAPH Asia 2014) 33* (6), 179:1–11.

Nowrouzezahrai, D., E. Kalogerakis, and E. Fiume. 2009. Shadowing dynamic scenes with arbitrary BRDFs. *Computer Graphics Forum (Proceedings of Eurographics) 28* (2), 249–58.

NVIDIA, Inc. 2018. NVIDIA Turing GPU Architecture. *NVIDIA Whitepaper*.

Ogaki, S. 2020. Generalized light portals. *Proceedings of the ACM on Computer Graphics and Interactive Techniques 3* (2), 10:1–19.

Ogaki, S., and Y. Tokuyoshi. 2011. Direct ray tracing of Phong tessellation. *Computer Graphics Forum (Proceedings of the 2011 Eurographics Symposium on Rendering) 30* (4), 1337–44.

Ogaki, S., Y. Tokuyoshi, and S. Schoellhammer. 2010. An empirical fur shader. In *SIGGRAPH Asia 2010 Sketches*, 16:1–2.

Ogita, T., S. M. Rump, and S. Oishi. 2005. Accurate sum and dot product. *SIAM Journal on Scientific Computing 26* (6), 1955–88.

Oh, S. B., S. Kashyap, R. Garg, S. Chandran, and R. Raskar. 2010. Rendering wave effects with augmented light field. *Computer Graphics Forum (Eurographics 2010) 29* (2), 507–16.

Ohmer, S. 1997. Ray Tracers: Blue Sky Studios. *Animation World Network*, http://www.awn.com/animationworld/ray-tracers-blue-sky-studios.

Olano, M., and D. Baker. 2010. LEAN mapping. In *Proceedings of the 2010 ACM SIGGRAPH Symposium on Interactive 3D Graphics and Games*, 181–88.

O'Neill, M. 2014. PCG: A family of simple fast space-efficient statistically good algorithms for random number generation. Unpublished manuscript. *http://www.pcg-random.org/paper.html*.

Ooi, B. C., K. McDonell, and R. Sacks-Davis. 1987. Spatial kd-tree: A data structure for geographic databases. In *Proceedings of the IEEE COMPSAC Conference*.

OpenMP Architecture Review Board. 2013. OpenMP Application Program Interface. *http://www.openmp.org/mp-documents/OpenMP4.0.0.pdf*.

Oren, M., and S. K. Nayar. 1994. Generalization of Lambert's reflectance model. In *Proceedings of SIGGRAPH '94, Computer Graphics Proceedings, Annual Conference Series*, 239–46. New York: ACM Press.

Otsu, H., A. Kaplanyan, J. Hanika, C. Dachsbacher, and T. Hachisuka. 2017. Fusing state spaces for Markov chain Monte Carlo rendering. *ACM Transactions on Graphics (Proceedings of SIGGRAPH) 36* (4), 74:1–10.

Otsu, H., M. Yamamoto, and T. Hachisuka. 2018. Reproducing spectral reflectances from tristimulus colours. *Computer Graphics Forum 37* (6), 370–81.

Ou, J., and F. Pellacini. 2010. SafeGI: Type checking to improve correctness in rendering system implementation. *Computer Graphics Forum (Proceedings of the 2010 Eurographics Symposium on Rendering) 29* (4), 1267–77.

Ou, J., F. Xie, P. Krishnamachari, and F. Pellacini. 2012. ISHair: Importance sampling for hair scattering. *Computer Graphics Forum (Proceedings of the 2012 Eurographics Symposium on Rendering) 31* (4), 1537–45.

Ouyang, Y., S. Liu, M. Kettunen, M. Pharr, and J. Pantaleoni. 2021. ReSTIR GI: Path resampling for real-time path tracing. *Computer Graphics Forum (Proceedings of High Performance Graphics 2021), 40* (8), 17–29.

Owen, A., and Y. Zhou. 2000. Safe and effective importance sampling. *Journal of the American Statistical Association 95* (449), 135–43.

Owen, A. B. 1995. Randomly permuted (t, m, s)-nets and (t, s)-sequences. In *Monte Carlo and Quasi-Monte Carlo Methods in Scientific Computing*, 299–317.

Owen, A. B. 1998. Latin supercube sampling for very high-dimensional simulations. *Modeling and Computer Simulation 8* (1), 71–102.

Owen, A. B. 2003. Variance with alternative scramblings of digital nets. *ACM Transactions on Modeling and Computer Simulation 13* (4), 363–78.

Owen, A. B. 2019. Monte Carlo theory, methods and examples. *https://statweb.stanford.edu/~owen/mc/*.

Öztireli, A. C. 2016. Integration with stochastic point processes. *ACM Transactions on Graphics 35* (5), 160:1–16.

Öztireli, A. C. 2020. A comprehensive theory and variational framework for anti-aliasing sampling patterns. *Computer Graphics Forum 39* (4), 133–48.

Pajot, A., L. Barthe, M. Paulin, and P. Poulin. 2011. Representativity for robust and adaptive multiple importance sampling. *IEEE Transactions on Visualization and Computer Graphics 17* (8), 1108–21.

Pantaleoni, J. 2017. Charted Metropolis light transport. *ACM Transactions on Graphics (Proceedings of SIGGRAPH) 36* (4), 75:1–14.

Pantaleoni, J., L. Fascione, M. Hill, and T. Aila. 2010. PantaRay: Fast ray-traced occlusion caching of massive scenes. *ACM Transactions on Graphics (Proceedings of SIGGRAPH 2010) 29* (4), 37:1–10.

Pantaleoni, J., and D. Luebke. 2010. HLBVH: Hierarchical LBVH construction for real-time ray tracing of dynamic geometry. In *Proceedings of the Conference on High Performance Graphics 2010*, 87–95.

Papas, M., K. de Mesa, and H. W. Jensen. 2014. A physically-based BSDF for modeling the appearance of paper. *Computer Graphics Forum (Proceedings of the 2014 Eurographics Symposium on Rendering) 33* (4), 133–42.

Park, T., M. Liu, T. Wang, and J. Zhu. 2019. Semantic image synthesis with spatially-adaptive normalization. *IEEE/CVF Conference on Computer Vision and Pattern Recognition (CVPR)*, 2332–41.

Parker, S., S. Boulos, J. Bigler, and A. Robison. 2007. RTSL: A ray tracing shading language. In *Proceedings of IEEE Symposium on Interactive Ray Tracing*, 149–60.

Parker, S., W. Martin, P.-P. J. Sloan, P. S. Shirley, B. Smits, and C. Hansen. 1999. Interactive ray tracing. In *1999 ACM Symposium on Interactive 3D Graphics*, 119–26.

Parker, S. G., J. Bigler, A. Dietrich, H. Friedrich, J. Hoberock, D. Luebke, D. McAllister, M. McGuire, K. Morley, A. Robison, and M. Stich. 2010. OptiX: A general purpose ray tracing engine. *ACM Transactions on Graphics (Proceedings of SIGGRAPH 2010) 29* (4), 66:1–13.

Pattanaik, S. N., and S. P. Mudur. 1995. Adjoint equations and random walks for illumination computation. *ACM Transactions on Graphics 14* (1), 77–102.

Patterson, J. W., S. G. Hoggar, and J. R. Logie. 1991. Inverse displacement mapping. *Computer Graphics Forum 10* (2), 129–39.

Pauly, M. 1999. Robust Monte Carlo methods for photorealistic rendering of volumetric effects. Master's thesis, Universität Kaiserslautern.

Pauly, M., T. Kollig, and A. Keller. 2000. Metropolis light transport for participating media. In *Rendering Techniques 2000: 11th Eurographics Workshop on Rendering*, 11–22.

Pausinger, F., and S. Steinerberger. 2016. On the discrepancy of jittered sampling. *Journal of Complexity 33*, 199–216.

Peachey, D. R. 1985. Solid texturing of complex surfaces. *Computer Graphics (SIGGRAPH '85 Proceedings)*, Volume 19, 279–86.

Peachey, D. R. 1990. Texture on demand. *Pixar Technical Memo #217*.

Pearce, A. 1991. A recursive shadow voxel cache for ray tracing. In J. Arvo (ed.), *Graphics Gems II*, 273–74. San Diego: Academic Press.

Pediredla, A., Y. K. Chalmiani, M. G. Scopelliti, M. Chamanzar, S. Narasimhan, and I. Gkioulekas. 2020. Path tracing estimators for refractive radiative transfer. *ACM Transactions on Graphics (Proceedings of SIGGRAPH Asia) 39* (6), 241:1–15.

Peercy, M. S. 1993. Linear color representations for full spectral rendering. *Computer Graphics (SIGGRAPH '93 Proceedings)*, Volume 27, 191–98.

Peers, P., K. vom Berge, W. Matusik, R. Ramamoorthi, J. Lawrence, S. Rusinkiewicz, and P. Dutré. 2006. A compact factored representation of heterogeneous subsurface scattering. *ACM Transactions on Graphics 25* (3), 746–53.

Pegoraro, V., C. Brownlee, P. Shirley, and S. Parker. 2008a. Towards interactive global illumination effects via sequential Monte Carlo adaptation. *IEEE Symposium on Interactive Ray Tracing*, 107–14.

Pegoraro, V., and S. Parker. 2009. An analytical solution to single scattering in homogeneous participating media. *Computer Graphics Forum (Proceedings of Eurographics 2009) 28* (2), 329–35.

Pegoraro, V., M. Schott, and S. Parker. 2009. An analytical approach to single scattering for anisotropic media and light distributions. In *Proceedings of Graphics Interface 2009*, 71–77.

Pegoraro, V., M. Schott, and S. G. Parker. 2010. A closed-form solution to single scattering for general phase functions and light distributions. *Computer Graphics Forum (Proceedings of the 2010 Eurographics Symposium on Rendering) 29* (4), 1365–74.

Pegoraro, V., M. Schott, and P. Slusallek. 2011. A mathematical framework for efficient closed-form single scattering. In *Proceedings of Graphics Interface 2011*, 151–58.

Pegoraro, V., I. Wald, and S. Parker. 2008b. Sequential Monte Carlo adaptation in low-anisotropy participating media. *Computer Graphics Forum (Proceedings of the 2008 Eurographics Symposium on Rendering) 27* (4), 1097–104.

Pekelis, L., and C. Hery. 2014. A statistical framework for comparing importance sampling methods, and an application to rectangular lights. *Pixar Technical Memo 14-01*.

Pekelis, L., C. Hery, R. Villemin, and J. Ling. 2015. A data-driven light scattering model for hair. *Pixar Technical Memo 15-02*.

Pérard-Gayot, A., R. Membarth, R. Leißa, S. Hack, and P. Slusallek. 2019. Rodent: Generating renderers without writing a generator. *ACM Transactions on Graphics (Proceedings of SIGGRAPH 2019) 38* (4), 40:1–12.

Perlin, K. 1985a. An image synthesizer. In *Computer Graphics (SIGGRAPH '85 Proceedings)*, Volume 19, 287–96.

Perlin, K. 2002. Improving noise. *ACM Transactions on Graphics 21* (3), 681–82.

Perlin, K., and E. M. Hoffert. 1989. Hypertexture. In *Computer Graphics (Proceedings of SIGGRAPH '89)*, Volume 23, 253–62.

Perrier, H., D. Coeurjolly, F. Xie, M. Pharr, P. Hanrahan, and V. Ostromoukhov. 2018. Sequences with low-discrepancy blue-noise 2-D projections. *Computer Graphics Forum 37* (2), 339–53.

Peters, C. 2016. Free blue noise textures. *http://moments ingraphics.de/BlueNoise.html*.

Peters, C. 2019. Sampling projected spherical caps with multiple importance sampling. *http://momentsingraphics .de/SphericalCapMIS.html*.

Peters, C. 2021a. BRDF importance sampling for linear lights. *Computer Graphics Forum (Proceedings of High Performance Graphics) 40* (8), 31–40.

Peters, C. 2021b. BRDF importance sampling for polygonal lights. *ACM Transactions on Graphics (Proceedings of SIGGRAPH) 40* (8), 31–40.

Peters, C., and C. Dachsbacher. 2019. Sampling projected spherical caps in real time. *Proceedings of the ACM on Computer Graphics and Interactive Techniques 2* (1), 1:1–16.

Peters, C., S. Merzbach, J. Hanika, and C. Dachsbacher. 2019. Using moments to represent bounded signals for spectral rendering. *ACM Transactions on Graphics (Proceedings of SIGGRAPH) 38* (4), 136:1–14.

Petitjean, V., P. Bauszat, and E. Eisemann. 2018. Spectral gradient sampling for path tracing. *Computer Graphics Forum 37* (4), 45–53.

Pfister, H., M. Zwicker, J. van Baar, and M. Gross. 2000. Surfels: Surface elements as rendering primitives. In *Proceedings of ACM SIGGRAPH 2000*, Computer Graphics Proceedings, Annual Conference Series, 335–42.

Pharr, M. 2017. The implementation of a scalable texture cache. *https://www.pbrt.org/texcache.pdf*.

Pharr, M. 2019. Efficient generation of points that satisfy two-dimensional elementary intervals. *Journal of Computer Graphics Techniques (JCGT) 8* (1), 56–68.

Pharr, M., and P. Hanrahan. 1996. Geometry caching for ray-tracing displacement maps. In *Eurographics Rendering Workshop 1996*, 31–40.

Pharr, M., and P. M. Hanrahan. 2000. Monte Carlo evaluation of non-linear scattering equations for subsurface reflection. In *Proceedings of ACM SIGGRAPH 2000*,

Computer Graphics Proceedings, Annual Conference Series, 75–84.

Pharr, M., C. Kolb, R. Gershbein, and P. M. Hanrahan. 1997. Rendering complex scenes with memory-coherent ray tracing. In *Proceedings of SIGGRAPH '97*, Computer Graphics Proceedings, Annual Conference Series, 101–8.

Pharr, M., and W. R. Mark. 2012. ispc: A SPMD compiler for high-performance CPU programming. In *Proceedings of Innovative Parallel Computing (InPar)*, 1–13.

Pharr, Meghan. 2022. Facial approximation via manual fitting of parabolas. Personal communication.

Pharr, Sheelyn. 2022. Finding the new integration domain after a change of variables. Personal communication.

Phong, B.-T. 1975. Illumination for computer generated pictures. *Communications of the ACM 18* (6), 311–17.

Phong, B.-T., and F. C. Crow. 1975. Improved rendition of polygonal models of curved surfaces. In *Proceedings of the 2nd USA–Japan Computer Conference*.

Pilleboue, A., G. Singh, D. Coeurjolly, M. Kazhdan, and V. Ostromoukhov. 2015. Variance analysis for Monte Carlo integration. *ACM Transactions on Graphics (Proceedings of SIGGRAPH 2015) 34* (4), 124:1–14.

Piponi, D. 2012. Lossless decompression and the generation of random samples. *http://blog.sigfpe.com/2012/01/lossless-decompression-and-generation.html*.

Pixar Animation Studios. 2020. Universal Scene Description. *https://graphics.pixar.com/usd/docs/index.html*.

Popov, S., R. Dimov, I. Georgiev, and P. Slusallek. 2009. Object partitioning considered harmful: Space subdivision for BVHs. In *Proceedings of High Performance Graphics 2009*, 15–22.

Popov, S., I. Georgiev, P. Slusallek, and C. Dachsbacher. 2013. Adaptive quantization visibility caching. *Computer Graphics Forum (Proceedings of Eurographics 2013) 32* (2), 399–408.

Popov, S., J. Gunther, H. P. Seidel, and P. Slusallek. 2006. Experiences with streaming construction of SAH kd-trees. In *IEEE Symposium on Interactive Ray Tracing*, 89–94.

Potmesil, M., and I. Chakravarty. 1981. A lens and aperture camera model for synthetic image generation. In *Computer Graphics (Proceedings of SIGGRAPH '81)*, Volume 15, 297–305.

Potmesil, M., and I. Chakravarty. 1982. Synthetic image generation with a lens and aperture camera model. *ACM Transactions on Graphics 1* (2), 85–108.

Potmesil, M., and I. Chakravarty. 1983. Modeling motion blur in computer-generated images. In *Computer Graphics (Proceedings of SIGGRAPH 83)*, Volume 17, 389–99.

Poulin, P., and A. Fournier. 1990. A model for anisotropic reflection. In *Computer Graphics (Proceedings of SIGGRAPH '90)*, Volume 24, 273–82.

Poynton, C. 2002a. Frequently-asked questions about color. *www.poynton.com/ColorFAQ.html*.

Poynton, C. 2002b. Frequently-asked questions about gamma. *www.poynton.com/GammaFAQ.html*.

Praun, E., and Hoppe, H. 2003. Spherical parameterization and remeshing. *ACM Transactions on Graphics (Proceedings of SIGGRAPH 2003) 22* (3), 340–49.

Preetham, A. J., P. S. Shirley, and B. E. Smits. 1999. A practical analytic model for daylight. In *Proceedings of SIGGRAPH '99*, Computer Graphics Proceedings, Annual Conference Series, 91–100.

Preisendorfer, R. W. 1965. *Radiative Transfer on Discrete Spaces*. Oxford: Pergamon Press.

Preisendorfer, R. W. 1976. *Hydrologic Optics*. Honolulu, Hawaii: U.S. Department of Commerce, National Oceanic and Atmospheric Administration.

Prusinkiewicz, P. 1986. Graphical applications of L-systems. In *Proceedings of Graphics Interface 1986*, 247–53.

Prusinkiewicz, P., M. James, and R. Mech. 1994. Synthetic topiary. In *Proceedings of SIGGRAPH '94*, Computer Graphics Proceedings, Annual Conference Series, 351–58.

Prusinkiewicz, P., L. Mündermann, R. Karwowski, and B. Lane. 2001. The use of positional information in the modeling of plants. In *Proceedings of ACM SIGGRAPH 2001*, Computer Graphics Proceedings, Annual Conference Series, 289–300.

Purcell, T. J., I. Buck, W. R. Mark, and P. Hanrahan. 2002. Ray tracing on programmable graphics hardware. *ACM Transactions on Graphics 21* (3), 703–12.

Purcell, T. J., C. Donner, M. Cammarano, H. W. Jensen, and P. Hanrahan. 2003. Photon mapping on programmable graphics hardware. In *Graphics Hardware 2003*, 41–50.

Purgathofer, W. 1987. A statistical mothod for adaptive stochastic sampling. *Computers & Graphics 11* (2), 157–62.

Qin, H., M. Chai, Q. Hou, Z. Ren, and K. Zhou. 2014. Cone tracing for furry object rendering. *IEEE Transactions on Visualization and Computer Graphics 20* (8), 1178–88.

Quilez, I. 2010. Inverse bilinear interpolation. *https://www.iquilezles.org/www/articles/ibilinear/ibilinear.htm*.

Quilez, I. 2015. Distance estimation. *http://iquilezles.org/www/articles/distance/distance.htm*.

Quilez, I., and P. Jeremias. 2021. Shadertoy. *https://shadertoy.com*.

Raab, M., D. Seibert, and A. Keller. 2006. Unbiased global illumination with participating media. *Proc. Monte Carlo and Quasi-Monte Carlo Methods 2006*, 591–605.

Radziszewski, M., K. Boryczko, and W. Alda. 2009. An improved technique for full spectral rendering. *Journal of WSCG 17* (1-3), 9–16.

Radzivilovsky, P., Y. Galka, and S. Novgorodov. 2012. UTF-8 everywhere. *http://utf8everywhere.org*.

Rainer, G., W. Jakob, A. Ghosh, and T. Weyrich. 2019. Neural BTF compression and interpolation. *Computer Graphics Forum 38* (2), 235–44.

Rainer, R., A. Ghosh, W. Jakob, and T. Weyrich. 2020. Unified neural encoding of BTFs. *Computer Graphics Forum 39* (2), 167–78.

Ramamoorthi, R., and P. Hanrahan. 2004. A signal-processing framework for reflection. *ACM Trans. Graph. 23* (4), 1004–42.

Ramsey, S. D., K. Potter, and C. Hansen. 2004. Ray bilinear patch intersections. *Journal of Graphics Tools 9* (3), 41–47.

Ramshaw, L. 1987. Blossoming: A connect-the-dots approach to splines. *Digital Systems Research Center Technical Report*.

Ramshaw, R. 1989. Blossoms are polar forms. *Computer Aided Geometric Design 6* (4), 323–58.

Randrianandrasana, J., P. Callet, and L. Lucas. 2021. Transfer matrix based layered materials rendering. *ACM Transactions on Graphics (Proceedings of SIGGRAPH) 40* (4), 177:1–16.

Rath, A., P. Grittmann, S. Herholz, P. Vévoda, P. Slusallek, and J. Křivánek. 2020. Variance-aware path guiding. *ACM Transactions on Graphics (Proceedings of SIGGRAPH) 39* (4), 151:1–12.

Raymond, B., G. Guennebaud, and P. Barla. 2016. Multi-scale rendering of scratched materials using a structured SVBRDF model. *ACM Transactions on Graphics (Proceedings of SIGGRAPH) 35* (4), 57:1–11.

Reibold, R., J. Hanika, A. Jung, and C. Dachsbacher. 2018. Selective guided sampling with complete light transport paths. *ACM Transactions on Graphics 37* (6), 223:1–14.

Reif, J. H., J. D. Tygar, and A. Yoshida. 1994. Computability and complexity of ray tracing. *Discrete and Computational Geometry 11*, 265–88.

Reinert, B., T. Ritschel, H.-P. Seidel, and I. Georgiev. 2015. Projective blue-noise sampling. *Computer Graphics Forum 35* (1), 285–95.

Reinhard, E., T. Pouli, T. Kunkel, B. Long, A. Ballestad, and G. Damberg. 2012. Calibrated image appearance reproduction. *ACM Transactions on Graphics (Proceedings of SIGGRAPH Asia 2012) 31* (6), 201:1–11.

Reinhard, E., G. Ward, P. Debevec, S. Pattanaik, W. Heidrich, and K. Myszkowski. 2010. *High Dynamic Range Imaging: Acquisition, Display, and Image-Based Lighting*. San Francisco: Morgan Kaufmann.

Ren, P., J. Wang, M. Gong, S. Lin, X. Tong, and B. Guo. 2013. Global illumination with radiance regression functions. *ACM Transactions on Graphics (Proceedings of SIGGRAPH 2013) 32* (4), 130:1–12.

Reshetov, A. 2007. Faster ray packets–triangle intersection through vertex culling. In *Proceedings of IEEE Symposium on Interactive Ray Tracing*, 105–12.

Reshetov, A. 2019. Cool patches: A geometric approach to ray/bilinear patch intersections. In E. Haines and T. Akenine-Möller (eds.), *Ray Tracing Gems*, 95–109. Berkeley: Apress.

Reshetov, A., and D. Luebke. 2018. Phantom ray-hair intersector. *Proceedings of the ACM on Computer Graphics and Interactive Techniques 1* (2), 34:1–22.

Reshetov, A., A. Soupikov, and J. Hurley. 2005. Multi-level ray tracing algorithm. *ACM Transactions on Graphics (Proceedings of SIGGRAPH 2005) 24* (3), 1176–85.

Reshetov, R. 2017. Exploiting Budan–Fourier and Vincent's theorems for ray tracing 3D Bézier curves. *Proceedings of High Performance Graphics (HPG '17)*, 5:1–11.

Reshetov, R., A. Soupikov, and W. R. Mark. 2010. Consistent normal interpolation. *ACM Transactions on Graphics (Proceedings of SIGGRAPH Asia) 29* (6), 142:1–8.

Rhodin, H., N. Robertini, C. Richardt, H.-P. Seidel, and C. Theobalt. 2015. A versatile scene model with differentiable visibility applied to generative pose estimation. *IEEE/CVF International Conference on Computer Vision (ICCV)*. arXiv:1602.03725 [cs.CV].

Ribardière, M., B. Bringier, D. Meneveaux, and L. Simonot. 2017. STD: Student's t-distribution of slopes for microfacet based BSDFs. *Computer Graphics Forum 36* (2), 421–29.

Ribardière, M., B. Bringier, L. Simonot, and D. Meneveaux. 2019. Microfacet BSDFs generated from NDFs and explicit microgeometry. *ACM Transactions on Graphics 38* (5), 143:1–15.

Rogers, D. F., and J. A. Adams. 1990. *Mathematical Elements for Computer Graphics*. New York: McGraw-Hill.

Ronneberger, O., P. Fischer, and T. Brox. 2015. U-Net: Convolutional networks for biomedical image segmentation. *Medical Image Computing and Computer-Assisted Intervention 9351*, 234–41.

Ross, S. M. 2002. *Introduction to Probability Models* (8th ed.). San Diego: Academic Press.

Ross, V., D. Dion, and G. Potvin. 2005. Detailed analytical approach to the Gaussian surface bidirectional reflectance distribution function specular component applied to the sea surface. *Journal of the Optical Society of America 22* (11), 2442–53.

Roth, S. D. 1982. Ray casting for modeling solids. *Computer Graphics and Image Processing 18*, 109–44.

Roth, S. H., P. Diezi, and M. Gross. 2001. Ray tracing triangular Bézier patches. In *Computer Graphics Forum (Eurographics 2001 Conference Proceedings) 20* (3), 422–30.

Rougeron, G., and B. Péroche. 1997. An adaptive representation of spectral data for reflectance computations. In *Eurographics Rendering Workshop 1997*, 126–38.

Rougeron, G., and B. Péroche. 1998. Color fidelity in computer graphics: A survey. *Computer Graphics Forum 17* (1), 3–16.

Rousselle, F., P. Clarberg, L. Leblank, V. Ostromoukhov, and P. Poulin. 2008. Efficient product sampling using hierarchical thresholding. *The Visual Computer (Proceedings of CGI 2008) 24* (7–9), 465–74.

Rousselle, F., W. Jarosz, J. Novák. 2016. Image-space control variates for rendering. *ACM Transactions on Graphics (Proceedings of SIGGRAPH Asia) 35* (6), 169:1–12.

Rubin, S. M., and T. Whitted. 1980. A 3-dimensional representation for fast rendering of complex scenes. *Computer Graphics 14* (3), 110–16.

Ruckert, M. 2005. *Understanding MP3*. Wiesbaden, Germany: GWV-Vieweg.

Rupp, K. 2020. Microprocessor trend data. *https://github.com/karlrupp/microprocessor-trend-data*.

Ruppert, L., S. Herholz, and H. P. A. Lensch. 2020. Robust fitting of parallax-aware mixtures for path guiding. *ACM Transactions on Graphics (Proceedings of SIGGRAPH) 39* (4), 147:1–15.

Rushmeier, H., C. Patterson, and A. Veerasamy. 1993. Geometric simplification for indirect illumination calculations. In *Proceedings of Graphics Interface 1993*, 227–36.

Rushmeier, H. E. 1988. Realistic image synthesis for scenes with radiatively participating media. Ph.D. thesis, Cornell University.

Rushmeier, H. E., and K. E. Torrance. 1987. The zonal method for calculating light intensities in the presence of a participating medium. In *Computer Graphics (Proceedings of SIGGRAPH '87)*, Volume 21, 293–302.

Rushmeier, H. E., and G. J. Ward. 1994. Energy preserving non-linear filters. *Proceedings of SIGGRAPH 1994*, 131–38.

Rusinkiewicz, S. 1998. A new change of variables for efficient BRDF representation. In *Proceedings of the Eurographics Rendering Workshop*, 11–23.

Rusinkiewicz, S., and M. Levoy. 2000. Qsplat: A multiresolution point rendering system for large meshes. In *Proceedings of ACM SIGGRAPH 2000*, Computer Graphics Proceedings, Annual Conference Series, 343–52.

Sabbadin, M., and M. Droske. 2021. Ray tracing of blobbies. In Marrs, A., P. Shirley, and I. Wald (eds.), *Ray Tracing Gems II*, 551–68. Berkeley: Apress.

Sadeghi, I., B. Chen, and H. W. Jensen. 2009. Coherent path tracing. *Journal of Graphics, GPU & Game Tools 14* (2), 33–43.

Sadeghi, I., H. Pritchett, H. W. Jensen, and R. Tamstorf. 2010. An artist friendly hair shading system. *ACM Transactions on Graphics (Proceedings of SIGGRAPH 2010) 29* (4), 56:1–10.

Saito, T., and T. Takahashi. 1990. Comprehensible rendering of 3-D shapes. In *Computer Graphics (Proceedings of SIGGRAPH '90)*, Volume 24, 197–206.

Salesin, D., J. Stolfi, and L. Guibas. 1989. Epsilon geometry: Building robust algorithms from imprecise computations. In *Proceedings of the Fifth Annual Symposium on Computational Geometry (SCG '89)*, 208–17.

Salesin, K., and W. Jarosz. 2019. Combining point and line samples for direct illumination. *Computer Graphics Forum 38* (4), 159–69.

Sanchez-Stern, A., P. Panchekha, S. Lerner, and Z. Tatlock. 2018. Finding root causes of floating point error. *Proceedings of the 39th ACM SIGPLAN Conference on Programming Language Design and Implementation*, 256–69.

Sanzharov, V. V., V. A. Frolov, and V. A. Galaktionov. 2020. Survey of NVIDIA RTX Technology. *Programming and Computer Software 46* (4), 297–304.

Sbert, M., and V. Havran. 2017. Adaptive multiple importance sampling for general functions. *The Visual Computer 33*, 845–55.

Sbert, M., V. Havran, and L. Szirmay-Kalos. 2016. Variance analysis of multi-sample and one-sample multiple importance sampling. *Computer Graphics Forum 35* (7), 451–60.

Sbert, M., V. Havran, and L. Szirmay-Kalos. 2018. Multiple importance sampling revisited: Breaking the bounds. *EURASIP Journal on Advances in Signal Processing 15*, 1–15.

Schaufler, G., and H. W. Jensen. 2000. Ray tracing point sampled geometry. In *Rendering Techniques 2000: 11th Eurographics Workshop on Rendering*, 319–28.

Scherzer, D., L. Yang, O. Mattausch, D. Nehab, P. V. Sander, M. Wimmer, and E. Eisemann. 2011. A survey on temporal coherence methods in real-time rendering. In *EUROGRAPHICS 2011—State of the Art Reports*, 101–26.

Schied, C., C. Peters, and C. Dachsbacher. 2018. Gradient estimation for real-time adaptive temporal filtering. *Proceedings of the ACM on Computer Graphics and Interactive Techniques 1* (2), 24:1–16.

Schied, S., A. Kaplanyan, C. Wyman, A. Patney, C. R. Alla Chaitanya, J. Burgess, S. Liu, C. Dachsbacher, A. Lefohn, and M. Salvi. 2017. Spatiotemporal variance-guided filtering: Real-time reconstruction for path-traced global illumination. In *Proceedings of High Performance Graphics (HPG '17)*, 2:1–12.

Schilling, A. 1997. Toward real-time photorealistic rendering: Challenges and solutions. In *1997 SIGGRAPH/Eurographics Workshop on Graphics Hardware*, 7–16.

Schilling, A. 2001. Antialiasing of environment maps. *Computer Graphics Forum 20* (1), 5–11.

Schneider, P. J., and D. H. Eberly. 2003. *Geometric Tools for Computer Graphics*. San Francisco: Morgan Kaufmann.

Schrade, E., J. Hanika, and C. Dachsbacher. 2016. Sparse high-degree polynomials for wide-angle lenses. *Computer Graphics Forum 35* (4), 89–97.

Schuster, A. 1905. Radiation through a foggy atmosphere. *Astrophysical Journal 21* (1), 1–22.

Schuster, K., P. Trettner, and L. Kobbelt. 2020. High-performance image filters via sparse approximations. *Proceedings of the ACM on Computer Graphics and Interactive Techniques 3* (2), 14:1–19.

Schwarz, K. 2011. Darts, dice, and coins: Sampling from a discrete distribution. *http://www.keithschwarz.com/darts-dice-coins/*.

Schwarzhaupt, J., H. W. Jensen, and W. Jarosz. 2012. Practical Hessian-based error control for irradiance caching. *ACM Transactions on Graphics (Proceedings of SIGGRAPH Asia) 31* (6), 193:1–10.

Schwarzschild, K. 1906. On the equilibrium of the sun's atmosphere (Nachrichten von der Koniglichen Gesellschaft der Wissenschaften zu Gottigen). *Göttinger Nachrichten 195*, 41–53.

Segovia, B., and M. Ernst. 2010. Memory efficient ray tracing with hierarchical mesh quantization. In *Proceedings of Graphics Interface 2010*, 153–60.

Selgrad, K., A. Lier, M. Martinek, C. Buchenau, M. Guthe, F. Kranz, H. Schäfer, and M. Stamminger. 2017. A compressed representation for ray tracing parametric surfaces. *ACM Transactions on Graphics 36* (1), 5:1–13.

Sen, P., and S. Darabi. 2011. Compressive rendering: A rendering application of compressed sensing. *IEEE Transactions on Visualization and Computer Graphics 17* (4), 487–99.

Sendik, O., and D. Cohen-Or. 2017. Deep correlations for texture synthesis. *ACM Transactions on Graphics 36* (5), 161:1–15.

Shade, J., S. J. Gortler, L. W. He, and R. Szeliski. 1998. Layered depth images. In *Proceedings of SIGGRAPH 98*, Computer Graphics Proceedings, Annual Conference Series, 231–42.

Shevtsov, M., A. Soupikov, and A. Kapustin. 2007a. Ray–triangle intersection algorithm for modern CPU architectures. In *Proceedings of GraphiCon 2007*, 33–39.

Shevtsov, M., A. Soupikov, and A. Kapustin. 2007b. Highly parallel fast kd-tree construction for interactive ray tracing of dynamic scenes. In *Computer Graphics Forum (Proceedings of Eurographics 2007) 26* (3), 395–404.

Shewchuk, J. R. 1997. Adaptive precision floating-point arithmetic and fast robust geometric predicates. *Discrete & Computational Geometry 18*, 305–63.

Shinya, M. 1993. Spatial anti-aliasing for animation sequences with spatio-temporal filtering. In *Proceedings of SIGGRAPH '93*, Computer Graphics Proceedings, Annual Conference Series, 289–96.

Shinya, M., T. Takahashi, and S. Naito. 1987. Principles and applications of pencil tracing. In *Computer Graphics (Proceedings of SIGGRAPH '87)*, Volume 21, 45–54.

Shirley, P. 1990. Physically based lighting calculations for computer graphics. Ph.D. thesis, Department of Computer Science, University of Illinois, Urbana–Champaign.

Shirley, P. 1991. Discrepancy as a quality measure for sample distributions. *Eurographics '91*, 183–94.

Shirley, P. 1992. Nonuniform random point sets via warping. In D. Kirk (ed.), *Graphics Gems III*, 80–83. San Diego: Academic Press.

Shirley, P. 2011. Improved code for concentric map. *http://psgraphics.blogspot.com/2011/01/improved-code-for-concentric-map.html*.

Shirley, P. 2020. Ray Tracing in One Weekend Series. *https://raytracing.github.io/*.

Shirley, P., and K. Chiu. 1997. A low distortion map between disk and square. *Journal of Graphics Tools 2* (3), 45–52.

Shirley, P., S. Laine, D. Hart, M. Pharr, P. Clarberg, E. Haines, M. Raab, and D. Cline. 2019. Sampling transformations zoo. In E. Haines and T. Akenine-Möller (eds.), *Ray Tracing Gems*, 223–46. Berkeley: Apress.

Shirley, P., and R. K. Morley. 2003. *Realistic Ray Tracing*. Natick, Massachusetts: A. K. Peters.

Shirley, P., C. Y. Wang, and K. Zimmerman. 1996. Monte Carlo techniques for direct lighting calculations. *ACM Transactions on Graphics 15* (1), 1–36.

Shkurko, K., T. Grant, D. Kopta, I. Mallett, C. Yuksel, and E. Brunvand. 2017. Dual streaming for hardware-accelerated ray tracing. *Proceedings of High Performance Graphics (HPG '17)*, 12:1–11.

Shoemake, K., and T. Duff. 1992. Matrix animation and polar decomposition. In *Proceedings of Graphics Interface 1992*, 258–64.

Šik, M., and J. Křivánek. 2018. Survey of Markov chain Monte Carlo methods in light transport simulation. *IEEE*

Transactions on Visualization and Computer Graphics 26 (4), 1821–40.

Sillion, F., and C. Puech. 1994. *Radiosity and Global Illumination.* San Francisco: Morgan Kaufmann.

Simon, F., J. Hanika, T. Zirr, and C. Dachsbacher. 2017. Line integration for rendering heterogeneous emissive volumes. *Computer Graphics Forum 36* (4), 101–10.

Simonot, L. 2009. Photometric model of diffuse surfaces described as a distribution of interfaced Lambertian facets. *Applied Optics 48* (30), 5793–801.

Singh, G., and W. Jarosz. 2017. Convergence analysis for anisotropic Monte Carlo sampling spectra. *ACM Transactions on Graphics (Proceedings of SIGGRAPH) 36* (4), 137:1–14.

Singh, G., B. Miller, and W. Jarosz. 2017. Variance and convergence analysis of Monte Carlo line and segment sampling. *Computer Graphics Forum 36* (4), 79–89.

Singh, G., C. Öztireli, A. G. Ahmed, D. Coeurjolly, K. Subr, O. Deussen, V. Ostromoukhov, R. Ramamoorthi, and W. Jarosz. 2019a. Analysis of sample correlations for Monte Carlo rendering. *Computer Graphics Forum (Eurographics 2019—State of the Art Reports) 38* (2), 473–71.

Singh, G., K. Subr, D. Coeurjolly, V. Ostromoukhov, W. Jarosz. 2019b. Fourier analysis of correlated Monte Carlo importance sampling. *Computer Graphics Forum 38* (1), 7–19.

Slusallek, P. 1996. Vision—An architecture for physically-based rendering. Ph.D. thesis, University of Erlangen.

Slusallek, P., and H.-P. Seidel. 1995. Vision—An architecture for global illumination calculations. *IEEE Transactions on Visualization and Computer Graphics 1* (1), 77–96.

Slusallek, P., and H.-P. Seidel. 1996. Towards an open rendering kernel for image synthesis. In *Eurographics Rendering Workshop 1996*, 51–60.

Smith, A. R. 1984. Plants, fractals and formal languages. In *Computer Graphics (Proceedings of SIGGRAPH '84)*, Volume 18, 1–10.

Smith, A. R. 1995. A pixel is not a little square, a pixel is not a little square, a pixel is not a little square! (and a voxel is not a little cube). *Microsoft Technical Memo 6*.

Smith, B. 1967. Geometrical shadowing of a random rough surface. *IEEE Transactions on Antennas and Propagation 15* (5), 668–71.

Smith, J. O. 2002. Digital audio resampling home page. *http://ccrma.stanford.edu/~jos/resample/*.

Smith, W. 2007. *Modern Optical Engineering* (4th ed.). New York: McGraw-Hill Professional.

Smits, B. 1999. An RGB-to-spectrum conversion for reflectances. *Journal of Graphics Tools 4* (4), 11–22.

Smits, B., P. S. Shirley, and M. M. Stark. 2000. Direct ray tracing of displacement mapped triangles. In *Rendering Techniques 2000: 11th Eurographics Workshop on Rendering*, 307–18.

Snow, J. 2010. Terminators and Iron Men: Image-based lighting and physical shading at ILM. *SIGGRAPH 2010 Course: Physically-Based Shading Models in Film and Game Production.*

Snyder, J. M., and A. H. Barr. 1987. Ray tracing complex models containing surface tessellations. *Computer Graphics (SIGGRAPH '87 Proceedings)*, Volume 21, 119–28.

Sobol', I. 1967. On the distribution of points in a cube and the approximate evaluation of integrals. *Zh. vychisl. Mat. mat. Fiz. 7* (4), 784–802.

Sobol', I. M. 1994. *A Primer for the Monte Carlo Method.* Boca Raton: CRC Press.

Sommerfeld, A., and J. Runge. 1911. Anwendungen der vektorrechnung auf die grundlagen der geometrischen optik. *Annalen der Physik 340* (7), 277–98.

Soupikov, A., M. Shevtsov, and A. Kapustin. 2008. Improving kd-tree quality at a reasonable construction cost. In *IEEE Symposium on Interactive Ray Tracing*, 67–72.

Spanier, J., and E. M. Gelbard. 1969. *Monte Carlo Principles and Neutron Transport Problems.* Reading, Massachusetts: Addison-Wesley.

Stafford, D. 2011. Better bit mixing—improving on MurmurHash3's 64-bit finalizer. *http://zimbry.blogspot .com/2011/09/better-bit-mixing-improving-on.html.*

Stam, J. 1995. Multiple scattering as a diffusion process. In *Rendering Techniques (Proceedings of the Eurographics Rendering Workshop)*, 41–50.

Stam, J. 1999. Diffraction shaders. In *Proceedings of SIGGRAPH '99*, Computer Graphics Proceedings, Annual Conference Series, 101–10.

Stam, J. 2001. An illumination model for a skin layer bounded by rough surfaces. In *Rendering Techniques 2001: 12th Eurographics Workshop on Rendering*, 39–52.

Stam, J. 2020. Computing light transport gradients using the adjoint method. arXiv:2006.15059 [cs.GR].

Standard Performance Evaluation Corporation. 2006. CINT2006 (Integer Component of SPEC CPU2006). *https://www.spec.org/cpu2006/CINT2006/.*

Stark, M., J. Arvo, and B. Smits. 2005. Barycentric parameterizations for isotropic BRDFs. *IEEE Transactions on Visualization and Computer Graphics 11* (2), 126–38.

Steigleder, M., and M. McCool. 2003. Generalized stratified sampling using the Hilbert curve. *Journal of Graphics Tools 8* (3), 41–47.

Steinberg, S., and L.-Q. Yan. 2021. A generic framework for physical light transport. *ACM Transactions on Graphics (Proceedings of SIGGRAPH) 40* (4), 139:1–20.

Steinert, B., H. Dammertz., J. Hanika, and H. P. A. Lensch. General spectral camera lens simulation. 2011. *Computer Graphics Forum 30* (6), 1643–54.

Stephenson, I. 2007. Improving motion blur: Shutter efficiency and temporal sampling. *Journal of Graphics Tools 12* (1), 9–15.

Stich, M., H. Friedrich, and A. Dietrich. 2009. Spatial splits in bounding volume hierarchies. In *Proceedings of High Performance Graphics 2009*, 7–14.

Stokes, G. G. 1860. On the intensity of the light reflected from or transmitted through a pile of plates. In *Proceedings of the Royal Society of London 11*, 545–56.

Stolfi, J. 1991. *Oriented Projective Geometry*. San Diego: Academic Press.

Strauss, P. S. 1990. A realistic lighting model for computer animators. *IEEE Computer Graphics and Applications 10* (6), 56–64.

Ström, J., K. Åström, and T. Akenine-Möller. 2020. Immersive linear algebra. *immersivemath.com*.

Stürzlinger, W. 1998. Ray tracing triangular trimmed free-form surfaces. *IEEE Transactions on Visualization and Computer Graphics 4* (3), 202–14.

Subr, K., and J. Arvo. 2007a. Statistical hypothesis testing for assessing Monte Carlo estimators: Applications to image synthesis. In *Pacific Graphics '97*, 106–15.

Subr, K., and J. Arvo. 2007b. Steerable importance sampling. *IEEE Symposium on Interactive Ray Tracing*, 133–40.

Subr, K., and J. Kautz. 2013. Fourier analysis of stochastic sampling strategies for assessing bias and variance in integration. *ACM Transactions on Graphics (Proceedings of SIGGRAPH 2013) 32* (4), 128:1–12.

Subr, K., D. Nowrouzezahrai, W. Jarosz, J. Kautz, and K. Mitchell. 2014. Error analysis of estimators that use combinations of stochastic sampling strategies for direct illumination. *Computer Graphics Forum (Proceedings of the 2014 Eurographics Symposium on Rendering) 33* (4), 93–102.

Suffern, K. 2007. *Ray Tracing from the Ground Up*. Natick, Massachusetts: A. K. Peters.

Sun, B., R. Ramamoorthi, S. Narasimhan, and S. Nayar. 2005. A practical analytic single scattering model for real time rendering. *ACM Transactions on Graphics 24* (3), 1040–49.

Sun, W., X. Sun, N. A. Carr, D. Nowrouzezahrai, and R. Ramamoorthi. 2017. Gradient-domain vertex connection and merging. *Eurographics Symposium on Rendering—Experimental Ideas and Implementations*.

Sun, Y., F. D. Fracchia, M. S. Drew, and T. W. Calvert. 2001. A spectrally based framework for realistic image synthesis. *The Visual Computer 17* (7), 429–44.

Sung, K., J. Craighead, C. Wang, S. Bakshi, A. Pearce, and A. Woo. 1998. Design and implementation of the Maya renderer. In *Pacific Graphics '98*.

Sung, K., and P. Shirley. 1992. Ray tracing with the BSP tree. In D. Kirk (ed.), *Graphics Gems III*, 271–74. San Diego: Academic Press.

Sutherland, I. E. 1963. Sketchpad—A man–machine graphical communication system. In *Proceedings of the Spring Joint Computer Conference (AFIPS)*, 328–46.

Suykens, F., and Y. Willems. 2001. Path differentials and applications. In *Rendering Techniques 2001: 12th Eurographics Workshop on Rendering*, 257–68.

Szécsi, L., L. Szirmay-Kalos, and C. Kelemen. 2003. Variance reduction for Russian roulette. *Journal of the World Society for Computer Graphics (WSCG) 11* (1).

Szirmay-Kalos, L., I. Georgiev, M. Magdics, B. Molnár, and D. Légrády. 2017. Unbiased light transport estimators for inhomogeneous participating media. *Computer Graphics Forum 36* (2), 9–19.

Szirmay-Kalos, L., M. Magdics, and M. Sbert. 2018. Multiple scattering in inhomogeneous participating media using Rao-Blackwellization and control variates. *Computer Graphics Forum 37* (2), 63–74.

Szirmay-Kalos, L., and G. Márton. 1998. Worst-case versus average case complexity of ray-shooting. *Computing 61* (2), 103–31.

Szirmay-Kalos, L., and W. Purgathofer. 1998. Global ray-bundle tracing with hardware acceleration. *Rendering Techniques '98: 9th Eurographics Workshop on Rendering*, 247–58.

Szirmay-Kalos, L., M. Sbert, and T. Umenhoffer. 2005. Real-time multiple scattering in participating media with illumination networks. *Rendering Techniques 2005: 16th Eurographics Workshop on Rendering*, 277–82.

Szirmay-Kalos, L., B. Tóth, M. Magdics. 2011. Free path sampling in high resolution inhomogeneous participating media. *Computer Graphics Forum 30* (1), 85–97.

Tabellion, E., and A. Lamorlette. 2004. An approximate global illumination system for computer generated films. *ACM Transactions on Graphics (Proceedings of SIGGRAPH 2004) 23* (3), 469–76.

Talbot, J. 2011. Personal communication.

Talbot, J., D. Cline, and P. Egbert. 2005. Importance resampling for global illumination. *Rendering Techniques 2005: 16th Eurographics Workshop on Rendering*, 139–46.

Tan, K. S., and P. P. Boyle. 2000. Applications of randomized low discrepancy sequences to the valuation of complex securities. *Journal of Economic Dynamics and Control 24*, 1747–82.

Tannenbaum, D. C., P. Tannenbaum, and M. J. Wozny. 1994. Polarization and birefringency considerations in rendering. In *Proceedings of SIGGRAPH '94*, Computer Graphics Proceedings, Annual Conference Series, 221–22.

Tejima, T., M. Fujita, and T. Matsuoka. 2015. Direct ray tracing of full-featured subdivision surfaces with Bézier clipping. *Journal of Computer Graphics Techniques (JCGT) 4* (1), 69–83.

Tewari, A., O. Fried, J. Thies, V. Sitzmann, S. Lombardi, K. Sunkavalli, R. Martin-Brualla, T. Simon, J. Saragih, M. Nießner, R. Pandey, S. Fanello, G. Wetzstein, J.-Y. Zhu, C. Theobalt, M. Agrawala, E. Shechtman, D. B. Goldman, and M. Zollhöfer. 2020. State of the art on neural rendering. *Computer Graphics Forum (Eurographics State of the Art Report) 39* (2), 701–27.

Theußl, T., H. Hauser, and E. Gröller. 2000. Mastering windows: Improving reconstruction. In *Proceedings of the 2000 IEEE Symposium on Volume Visualization*, 101–8. New York: ACM Press.

Tódová, L., A. Wilkie, and L. Fascione. 2021. Moment-based constrained spectral uplifting. *Proceedings of the Eurographics Symposium on Rendering*, 215–24.

Toisoul, T., and A. Ghosh. 2017. Practical acquisition and rendering of diffraction effects in surface reflectance. *ACM Transactions on Graphics 36* (5), 166:1–16.

Tokuyoshi, Y., and T. Harada. 2016. Stochastic light culling. *Journal of Computer Graphics Techniques (JCGT) 5* (1), 35–60.

Tokuyoshi, Y., and A. S. Kaplanyan. 2019. Improved geometric specular antialiasing. *Proceedings of the ACM SIGGRAPH Symposium on Interactive 3D Graphics and Games (I3D '19)*, 8:1–8.

Torrance, K. E., and E. M. Sparrow. 1967. Theory for off-specular reflection from roughened surfaces. *Journal of the Optical Society of America 57* (9), 1105–14.

Tregenza, P. R. 1983. The Monte Carlo method in lighting calculations. *Lighting Research and Technology 15* (4), 163–70.

Tricard, T., S. Efremov, C. Zanni, F. Neyret, J. Martínez, and S. Lefebvre. 2019. Procedural phasor noise. *ACM Transactions on Graphics (Proceedings of SIGGRAPH) 38* (4), 57:1–15.

Trowbridge, S., and K. P. Reitz. 1975. Average irregularity representation of a rough ray reflection. *Journal of the Optical Society of America 65* (5), 531–36.

Trumbore, B., W. Lytle, and D. P. Greenberg. 1993. A testbed for image synthesis. In *Developing Large-Scale Graphics Software Toolkits*, SIGGRAPH '93 Course Notes, Volume 3, 4-7–19.

Tsai, Y. Y., C. M. Wang, C. H. Chang, and Y. M. Cheng. 2006. Tunable bounding volumes for Monte Carlo applications. *Lecture Notes in Computer Science 3980*, 171–80.

Tsakok, J. 2009. Faster incoherent rays: Multi-BVH ray stream tracing. In *Proceedings of High Performance Graphics 2009*, 151–58.

Tumblin, J., and H. E. Rushmeier. 1993. Tone reproduction for realistic images. *IEEE Computer Graphics and Applications 13* (6), 42–48.

Turk, G. 1990. Generating random points in triangles. In A. S. Glassner (ed.), *Graphics Gems I*, 24–28. San Diego: Academic Press.

Turkowski, K. 1990a. Filters for common resampling tasks. In A. S. Glassner (ed.), *Graphics Gems I*, 147–65. San Diego: Academic Press.

Turkowski, K. 1990b. Properties of surface-normal transformations. In A. S. Glassner (ed.), *Graphics Gems I*, 539–47. San Diego: Academic Press.

Turkowski, K. 1993. The differential geometry of texture-mapping and shading. *Technical Note*, Advanced Technology Group, Apple Computer.

Turquin, E., 2019. Practical multiple scattering compensation for microfacet models. *Industrial Light & Magic Technical Report*.

Twomey, S., H. Jacobowitz, and H. B. Howell. 1966. Matrix methods for multiple-scattering problems. *Journal of the Atmospheric Sciences 32*, 289–96.

Ulam, S., R. D. Richtmyer, and J. von Neumann. 1947. Statistical methods in neutron diffusion. *Los Alamos Scientific Laboratory Report LAMS-551*.

Ulichney, R. A. 1988. Dithering with blue noise. *Proceedings of the IEEE 76* (1), 56–79.

Ulichney, R. A. 1993. Void-and-cluster method for dither array generation. *Proc. SPIE 1913, Human Vision, Visual Processing, and Digital Display IV*.

Unger, J., S. Gustavson, P. Larsson, and A. Ynnerman. 2008. Free form incident light fields. *Computer Graphics Forum (Proceedings of the 2008 Eurographics Symposium on Rendering) 27* (4), 1293–1301.

Unger, J., A. Wenger, T. Hawkins, A. Gardner, and P. Debevec. 2003. Capturing and rendering with incident light fields. In *Proceedings of the Eurographics Rendering Workshop 2003*, 141–49.

Unicode Consortium. 2020. The Unicode Standard: Version 13.0. *https://www.unicode.org/versions/Unicode13.0.0/UnicodeStandard-13.0.pdf*.

Unser, M. 2000. Sampling—50 years after Shannon. In *Proceedings of the IEEE 88* (4), 569–87.

Upstill, S. 1989. *The RenderMan Companion*. Reading, Massachusetts: Addison-Wesley.

Ureña, C. 2000. Computation of irradiance from triangles by adaptive sampling. *Computer Graphics Forum* 19 (2), 165–71.

Ureña, C., M. Fajardo, and A. King. 2013. An area-preserving parametrization for spherical rectangles. *Computer Graphics Forum (Proceedings of the 2013 Eurographics Symposium on Rendering) 32* (4), 59–66.

Ureña, C., and I. Georgiev. 2018. Stratified sampling of projected spherical caps. *Computer Graphics Forum 37* (4), 13–20.

Vaidyanathan, K., T. Akenine-Möller, and M. Salvi. 2016. Watertight ray traversal with reduced precision. *High Performance Graphics (HPG '16)*, 33–40.

Vaidyanathan, K., C. Benthin, and S. Woop. 2019. Wide BVH traversal with a short stack. *High Performance Graphics (HPG '19)*, 15–19.

Valiente, G. 2002. *Algorithms on Trees and Graphs*, Berlin, Heidelberg: Springer-Verlag.

van Antwerpen, D. 2011. Improving SIMD efficiency for parallel Monte Carlo light transport on the GPU. *Proceedings of the High Performance Graphics (HPG '11)*, 41–50.

van de Hulst, H. C. 1980. *Multiple Light Scattering*. New York: Academic Press.

van de Hulst, H. C. 1981. *Light Scattering by Small Particles*. New York: Dover Publications. Originally published by John Wiley & Sons, 1957.

Van Horn, B., and G. Turk. 2008. Antialiasing procedural shaders with reduction maps. *IEEE Transactions on Visualization and Computer Graphics 14* (3), 539–50.

Van Oosterom, A., and J. Strackee. 1983. The solid angle of a plane triangle. *IEEE Transactions on Biomedical Engineering BME-30* (2), 125–26.

Vasiou, E., K. Shkurko, E. Brunvand, and C. Yuksel. 2019. Mach-RT: A many chip architecture for ray tracing. *High Performance Graphics—Short Papers*, 1–6.

Vávra, R., and J. Filip. 2016. Minimal sampling for effective acquisition of anisotropic BRDFs. *Computer Graphics Forum 35* (7), 299–309.

Veach, E. 1997. Robust Monte Carlo methods for light transport simulation. Ph.D. thesis, Stanford University.

Veach, E., and L. Guibas. 1994. Bidirectional estimators for light transport. In *Fifth Eurographics Workshop on Rendering*, 147–62.

Veach, E., and L. J. Guibas. 1995. Optimally combining sampling techniques for Monte Carlo rendering. In *Computer Graphics (SIGGRAPH '95 Proceedings)*, 419–28.

Veach, E., and L. J. Guibas. 1997. Metropolis light transport. In *Computer Graphics (SIGGRAPH '97 Proceedings)*, 65–76.

Vegdahl, N. 2021. Building a better LK hash. *https://psychopath.io/post/2021_01_30_building_a_better_lk_hash*.

Velázquez-Armendáriz, E., Z. Dong, B. Walter, and D. P. Greenberg. 2015. Complex luminaires: Illumination and appearance rendering. *ACM Transactions on Graphics (Proceedings of SIGGRAPH 2015) 34* (3), 26:1–15.

Verbeck, C. P., and D. P. Greenberg. 1984. A comprehensive light source description for computer graphics. *IEEE Computer Graphics and Applications 4* (7), 66–75.

Vévoda, P., I. Kondapaneni, and J. Křivánek. 2018. Bayesian online regression for adaptive direct illumination sampling. *ACM Transactions on Graphics (Proceedings of SIGGRAPH) 37* (4), 125:1–12.

Vicini, D., D. Adler, J. Novák, F. Rousselle, and B. Burley. 2019. Denoising deep Monte Carlo renderings. *Computer Graphics Forum 38* (1), 316–27.

Vicini, D., S. Speierer, and W. Jakob. 2021. Path replay backpropagation: Differentiating light paths using constant memory and linear time. *ACM Transactions on Graphics (Proceedings of SIGGRAPH) 40* (4), 108:1–14.

Viitanen, T., M. Koskela, P. Jääskeläinen, H. Kultala, and J. Takala. 2017. MergeTree: A fast hardware HLBVH constructor for animated ray tracing. *ACM Transactions on Graphics 36* (5), 169:1–14.

Viitanen, T., M. Koskela, P. Jääskeläinen, A. Tervo, and J. Takala. 2018. PLOCTree: A fast, high-quality hardware BVH builder. *Proceedings of the ACM on Computer Graphics and Interactive Techniques 1* (2), 35:1–19.

Villemin, R., and C. Hery. 2013. Practical illumination from flames. *Journal of Computer Graphics Techniques (JCGT) 2* (2), 142–55.

Villemin, R., M. Wrenninge, and J. Fong. 2018. Efficient unbiased rendering of thin participating media. *Journal of Computer Graphics Techniques (JCGT) 7* (3), 50–65.

Villeneuve, K., A. Gruson, I. Georgiev, and D. Nowrouze-zahrai. 2021. Practical product sampling for single scattering in media. *Proceedings of the Eurographics Symposium on Rendering*, 55–60.

Vinkler, M., J. Bittner, and V. Havran. 2017. Extended Morton codes for high-performance bounding volume hierarchy construction. *High Performance Graphics (HPG '17)*, 9:1–8.

Vinkler, M., V. Havran, J. Bittner, and J. Sochor. 2016. Parallel on-demand hierarchy construction on contemporary GPUs. *IEEE Transactions on Visualization and Computer Graphics 22* (7), 1886–98.

Vinkler, M., V. Havran, and J. Sochora. 2012. Visibility driven BVH build up algorithm for ray tracing. *Computers & Graphics 36* (4), 283–96.

Vitsas, N., K. Vardis, and G. Papaioannou. 2021. Sampling clear sky models using truncated Gaussian mixtures. *Proceedings of the Eurographics Symposium on Rendering*, 35–44.

Vitter, J. S. 1985. Random sampling with a reservoir. *ACM Transactions on Mathematical Software, 11*(1), 37–57.

Vogels, T., F. Rousselle, B. McWilliams, G. Röthlin, A. Harvill, D. Adler, M. Meyer, and J. Novák. 2018. Denoising with kernel prediction and asymmetric loss functions. *ACM Transactions on Graphics (Proceedings of SIGGRAPH) 37* (4), 124:1–15.

von Neumann, J. 1951. Various techniques used in connection with random digits. *Journal of Research of the National Bureau of Standards, Applied Mathematics Series 12*, 36–38.

Vorba, J., O. Karlík, M. Šik, T. Ritschel, and J. Křivánek. 2014. On-line learning of parametric mixture models for light transport simulation. *ACM Transactions on Graphics (Proceedings of SIGGRAPH 2014) 33* (4), 101:1–11.

Vorba, J., and J. Křivánek. 2016. Adjoint-driven Russian roulette and splitting in light transport simulation. *ACM Transactions on Graphics 35* (4), 42:1–11.

Vose, M. D. 1991. A linear algorithm for generating random numbers with a given distribution. *IEEE Transactions on Software Engineering 17* (9), 972–75.

Wächter, C. A. 2008. Quasi Monte Carlo light transport simulation by efficient ray tracing. Ph.D. thesis, University of Ulm.

Wächter, C. A., and A. Keller. 2006. Instant ray tracing: The bounding interval hierarchy. In *Rendering Techniques 2006: 17th Eurographics Workshop on Rendering*, 139–49.

Wald, I. 2007. On fast construction of SAH-based bounding volume hierarchies. In *IEEE Symposium on Interactive Ray Tracing*, 33–40.

Wald, I. 2011. Active thread compaction for GPU path tracing. *Proceedings of High Performance Graphics (HPG '11)*, 51–58.

Wald, I. 2012. Fast construction of SAH BVHs on the Intel Many Integrated Core (MIC) architecture. *IEEE Transactions on Visualization and Computer Graphics 18* (1), 47–57.

Wald, I., C. Benthin, and S. Boulos. 2008. Getting rid of packets–efficient SIMD single-ray traversal using multi-branching BVHs. In *Proceedings of the IEEE Symposium on Interactive Ray Tracing 2008*, 49–57.

Wald, I., C. Benthin, and P. Slusallek. 2003. Interactive global illumination in complex and highly occluded environments. In *Eurographics Symposium on Rendering: 14th Eurographics Workshop on Rendering*, 74–81.

Wald, I., S. Boulos, and P. Shirley. 2007a. Ray tracing deformable scenes using dynamic bounding volume hierarchies. *ACM Transactions on Graphics 26* (1), 6.

Wald, I., and V. Havran. 2006. On building fast kd-trees for ray tracing and on doing that in $O(n \log n)$. In *IEEE Symposium on Interactive Ray Tracing*, 61–69.

Wald, I., T. Kollig, C. Benthin, A. Keller, and P. Slusallek. 2002. Interactive global illumination using fast ray tracing. In *Rendering Techniques 2002: 13th Eurographics Workshop on Rendering*, 15–24.

Wald, I., W. Mark, J. Günther, S. Boulos, T. Ize, W. Hunt, S. Parker, and P. Shirley. 2007b. State of the art in ray tracing animated scenes. In *Eurographics 2007 State of the Art Reports*.

Wald, I., P. Slusallek, and C. Benthin. 2001b. Interactive distributed ray tracing of highly complex models. In *Rendering Techniques 2001: 12th Eurographics Workshop on Rendering*, 277–88.

Wald, I., P. Slusallek, C. Benthin, and M. Wagner. 2001a. Interactive rendering with coherent ray tracing. *Computer Graphics Forum 20* (3), 153–64.

Wald, I., S. Woop, C. Benthin, G. S. Johnson, and M. Ernst. 2014. Embree: A kernel framework for efficient CPU ray tracing. *ACM Transactions on Graphics (Proceedings of SIGGRAPH 2014) 33* (4), 143:1–8.

Walker, A. J. 1974. New fast method for generating discrete random numbers with arbitrary frequency distributions. *Electronics Letters 10* (8): 127–28.

Walker, A. J. 1977. An efficient method for generating discrete random variables with general distributions. *ACM Transactions on Mathematical Software 3* (3), 253–56.

Wallis, B. 1990. Forms, vectors, and transforms. In A. S. Glassner (ed.), *Graphics Gems I*, 533–38. San Diego: Academic Press.

Walt Disney Animation Studios. 2018. *Moana Island Scene*. *https://www.disneyanimation.com/resources/moana-island-scene*.

Walter, B., A. Arbree, K. Bala, and D. Greenberg. 2006. Multidimensional lightcuts. *ACM Transactions on Graphics (Proceedings of SIGGRAPH 2006) 25* (3), 1081–88.

Walter, B., K. Bala, M. Kilkarni, and K. Pingali. 2008. Fast agglomerative clustering for rendering. In *IEEE Symposium on Interactive Ray Tracing*, 81–86.

Walter, B., Z. Dong, S. Marschner, and D. Greenberg. 2015. The ellipsoid normal distribution function. *Supplemental material of* Predicting Appearance from Measured Microgeometry of Metal Surfaces, *ACM Transactions on Graphics (Proceedings of SIGGRAPH) 35* (4), 9:1–13.

Walter, B., S. Fernandez, A. Arbree, K. Bala, M. Donikian, and D. Greenberg. 2005. Lightcuts: A scalable approach to illumination. *ACM Transactions on Graphics (Proceedings of SIGGRAPH 2005) 24* (3), 1098–107.

Walter, B., P. M. Hubbard, P. Shirley, and D. F. Greenberg. 1997. Global illumination using local linear density estimation. *ACM Transactions on Graphics 16* (3), 217–59.

Walter, B., P. Khungurn, and K. Bala. 2012. Bidirectional lightcuts. *ACM Transactions on Graphics (Proceedings of SIGGRAPH 2012) 31* (4), 59:1–11.

Walter, B., S. Marschner, H. Li, and K. Torrance. 2007. Microfacet models for refraction through rough surfaces. In *Rendering Techniques 2007 (Proc. Eurographics Symposium on Rendering)*, 195–206.

Walter, B., S. Zhao, N. Holzschuch, and K. Bala. 2009. Single scattering in refractive media with triangle mesh boundaries. *ACM Transactions on Graphics (Proceedings of SIGGRAPH 2009) 28* (3), 92:1–8.

Wandell, B. 1995. *Foundations of Vision*. Sunderland, Massachusetts: Sinauer Associates.

Wang, B., M. Hašan, N. Holzschuch, and L.-Q. Yan. 2020a. Example-based microstructure rendering with constant storage. *ACM Transactions on Graphics 39* (5), 162:1–12.

Wang, B., M. Hašan, and L.-Q. Yan. 2020b. Path cuts: Efficient rendering of pure specular light transport. *ACM Transactions on Graphics (Proceedings of SIGGRAPH Asia) 39* (6), 238:1–12.

Wang, B., L. Wang, and N. Holzschuch. 2018. Fast global illumination with discrete stochastic microfacets using a filterable model. *Computer Graphics Forum 37* (7), 55–64.

Wang, C. 1992. Physically correct direct lighting for distribution ray tracing. In D. Kirk (ed.), *Graphics Gems III*, 271–74. San Diego: Academic Press.

Wang, C.-M., C.-H. Chang, N.-C. Hwang, and Y.-Y. Tsai. 2006. A novel algorithm for sampling uniformly in the directional space of a cone. *IEICE Transactions on Fundamentals of Electronics, Communications and Computer Sciences 89* (9), 2351–55.

Wang, R., and O. Åkerlund. 2009. Bidirectional importance sampling for unstructured illumination. *Computer Graphics Forum (Proceedings of Eurographics 2009) 28* (2), 269–78.

Wang, X. C., J. Maillot, E. L. Fiume, V. Ng-Thow-Hing, A. Woo, and S. Bakshi. 2000. Feature-based displacement mapping. In *Rendering Techniques 2000: 11th Eurographics Workshop on Rendering*, 257–68.

Ward, G. 1991. Adaptive shadow testing for ray tracing. In *Second Eurographics Workshop on Rendering*.

Ward, G. 1992. Real pixels. In J. Arvo (ed.), *Graphics Gems IV*, 80–83. San Diego: Academic Press.

Ward, G., and E. Eydelberg-Vileshin. 2002. Picture perfect RGB rendering using spectral prefiltering and sharp color primaries. In *Proceedings of 13th Eurographics Workshop on Rendering*, 117–24.

Ward, G. J. 1994. The Radiance lighting simulation and rendering system. In *Proceedings of SIGGRAPH '94*, 459–72.

Ward, G. J., F. M. Rubinstein, and R. D. Clear. 1988. A ray tracing solution for diffuse interreflection. *Computer Graphics (SIGGRAPH '88 Proceedings)*, Volume 22, 85–92.

Ward, K., F. Bertails, T.-Y. Kim, S. R. Marschner, M.-P. Cani, and M. Lin. 2007. A survey on hair modeling: Styling, simulation, and rendering. *IEEE Transactions on Visualization and Computer Graphics 13* (2), 213–34.

Warn, D. R. 1983. Lighting controls for synthetic images. In *Computer Graphics (Proceedings of SIGGRAPH '83)*, Volume 17, 13–21.

Warren, H. 2006. *Hacker's Delight*. Reading, Massachusetts: Addison-Wesley.

Warren, J. 2002. *Subdivision Methods for Geometric Design: A Constructive Approach*. San Francisco: Morgan Kaufmann.

Weber, P., J. Hanika, and C. Dachsbacher. 2017. Multiple vertex next event estimation for lighting in dense, forward-scattering media. *Computer Graphics Forum 36* (2), 21–30.

Weghorst, H., G. Hooper, and D. P. Greenberg. 1984. Improved computational methods for ray tracing. *ACM Transactions on Graphics 3* (1), 52–69.

Wei, L.-Y., S. Lefebvre, V. Kwatra, and G. Turk. 2009. State of the art in example-based texture synthesis. In *Eurographics 2009, State of the Art Report*.

Weidlich, A., and A. Wilkie. 2007. Arbitrarily layered micro-facet surfaces. In *Proceedings of the 5th International Conference on Computer Graphics and Interactive Techniques in Australia and Southeast Asia (GRAPHITE '07)*, 171–78.

Weier, P., and L. Belcour. 2020. Rendering layered materials with anisotropic interfaces. *Journal of Computer Graphics Techniques (JCGT) 9* (2), 37–57.

Weier, P., M. Droske, J. Hanika, A. Weidlich, and J. Vorba. 2021. Optimised path space regularisation. *Computer Graphics Forum (Proceedings of EGSR 2021) 40* (4), 139–51.

Welford, B. P. 1962. Note on a method for calculating corrected sums of squares and products. *Technometrics 4* (3), 419–20.

Werner, S., Z. Velinov, W. Jakob, and M. Hullin. 2017. Scratch iridescence: Wave-optical rendering of diffractive surface structure. *ACM Transactions on Graphics (Proceedings of SIGGRAPH Asia) 36* (6), 207:1–14.

West, W., I. Georgiev, A. Gruson, and T. Hachisuka. 2020. Continuous multiple importance sampling. *ACM Transactions on Graphics (Proceedings of SIGGRAPH) 39* (4), 136:1–12.

Westin, S., J. Arvo, and K. Torrance. 1992. Predicting reflectance functions from complex surfaces. *Computer Graphics 26* (2), 255–64.

Weyrich, T., P. Peers, W. Matusik, and S. Rusinkiewicz. 2009. Fabricating microgeometry for custom surface reflectance. *ACM Transactions on Graphics (Proceedings of SIGGRAPH 2008) 28* (3), 32:1–6.

Whitted, T. 1980. An improved illumination model for shaded display. *Communications of the ACM 23* (6), 343–49.

Whitted, T. 2020. Origins of global illumination. *IEEE Computer Graphics and Applications 40* (1), 20–27.

Wilkie, A., S. Nawaz, M. Droske, A. Weidlich, and J. Hanika. 2014. Hero wavelength spectral sampling. *Computer Graphics Forum (Proceedings of the 2014 Eurographics Symposium on Rendering) 33* (4), 123–31.

Wilkie, A., P. Vevoda, T. Bashford-Rogers, L. Hošek, T. Iser, M. Kolářová, T. Rittig, and J. Křivánek. 2021. A fitted radiance and attenuation model for realistic atmospheres. *ACM Transactions on Graphics (Proceedings of SIGGRAPH) 40* (4), 135:1–14.

Wilkie, A., and A. Weidlich. 2009. A robust illumination estimate for chromatic adaptation in rendered images. *Computer Graphics Forum (Proceedings of the 2009 Eurographics Symposium on Rendering) 28* (4), 1101–9.

Wilkie, A., and A. Weidlich. 2011. A physically plausible model for light emission from glowing solid objects. *Computer Graphics Forum (Proceedings of the 2011 Eurographics Symposium on Rendering) 30* (4), 1269–76.

Wilkie, A., and A. Weidlich. 2012. Polarised light in computer graphics. *SIGGRAPH Asia 2012 Course Notes.*

Wilkie, A., A. Weidlich, C. Larboulette, and W. Purgathofer. 2006. A reflectance model for diffuse fluorescent surfaces. In *Proceedings of GRAPHITE*, 321–31.

Wilkinson, J. H. 1994. *Rounding Errors in Algebraic Processes*. New York: Dover Publications, Inc. Originally published by Prentice-Hall Inc., 1963.

Williams, A., S. Barrus, R. K. Morley, and P. Shirley. 2005. An efficient and robust ray–box intersection algorithm. *Journal of Graphics, GPU, and Game Tools 10* (4), 49–54.

Williams, L. 1983. Pyramidal parametrics. In *Computer Graphics (SIGGRAPH '83 Proceedings)*, Volume 17, 1–11.

Wodniok, D., and M. Goesele. 2016. Recursive SAH-based bounding volume hierarchy construction. *Proceedings of Graphics Interface (GI '16)*, 101–7.

Wolff, L. B., and D. J. Kurlander. 1990. Ray tracing with polarization parameters. *IEEE Computer Graphics and Applications 10* (6), 44–55.

Woo, A., and J. Amanatides. 1990. Voxel occlusion testing: A shadow determination accelerator for ray tracing. In *Proceedings of Graphics Interface 1990*, 213–20.

Woo, A., A. Pearce, and M. Ouellette. 1996. It's really not a rendering bug, you see . . . . *IEEE Computer Graphics and Applications 16* (5), 21–25.

Woop, S., A. T. Áfra, and C. Benthin. 2017. STBVH: A spatial-temporal BVH for efficient multi-segment motion blur. *Proceedings of High Performance Graphics (HPG '17)*, 8:1–8.

Woop, S., C. Benthin, and I. Wald. 2013. Watertight ray/triangle intersection. *Journal of Computer Graphics Techniques (JCGT) 2* (1), 65–82.

Woop, S., C. Benthin, I. Wald, G. S. Johnson, and E. Tabellion. 2014. Exploiting local orientation similarity for efficient ray traversal of hair and fur. In *Proceedings of High Performance Graphics 2014*, 41–49.

Woop, S., G. Marmitt, and P. Slusallek. 2006. B-kd trees for hardware accelerated ray tracing of dynamic scenes. In *Graphics Hardware 2006: Eurographics Symposium Proceedings*, 67–76.

Woop, S., J. Schmittler, and P. Slusallek. 2005. RPU: A programmable ray processing unit for realtime ray tracing. In *ACM SIGGRAPH 2005 Papers*, 434–44.

Worley, S. P. 1996. A cellular texture basis function. In *Proceedings of SIGGRAPH '96*, Computer Graphics Proceedings, Annual Conference Series, 291–94.

Wrenninge, M. 2012. *Production Volume Rendering: Design and Implementation*. Boca Raton, Florida: A. K. Peters/CRC Press.

Wrenninge, M. 2015. Field3D. *http://magnuswrenninge .com/field3d*.

Wrenninge, M. 2016. Efficient rendering of volumetric motion blur using temporally unstructured volumes. *Journal of Computer Graphics Techniques (JCGT) 5* (1), 1–34.

Wrenninge, M., C. Kulla, and V. Lundqvist. 2013. Oz: The great and volumetric. In *ACM SIGGRAPH 2013 Talks*, 46:1.

Wrenninge, M., and R. Villemin. 2020. Product importance sampling of the volume rendering equation using virtual density segments. *Pixar Technical Memo #20-01*.

Wrenninge, M., R. Villemin, and C. Hery. 2017. Path traced subsurface scattering using anisotropic phase functions and non-exponential free flights. *Pixar Technical Memo #17-07*.

Wu, H., J. Dorsey, and H. Rushmeier. 2011. Physically-based interactive bi-scale material design. *ACM Transactions on Graphics (Proceedings of SIGGRAPH Asia 2011) 30* (6), 145:1–10.

Wu, L., L.-Q. Yan, A. Kuznetsov, and R. Ramamoorthi. 2017. Multiple axis-aligned filters for rendering of combined distribution effects. *Computer Graphics Forum 36* (4), 155–66.

Wu, L., S. Zhao, L.-Q. Yan, and R. Ramamoorthi. 2019. Accurate appearance preserving prefiltering for rendering displacement-mapped surfaces. *ACM Transactions on Graphics (Proceedings of SIGGRAPH) 38* (4), 137:1–14.

Wyman, C., and M. McGuire. 2017. Hashed alpha testing. *Proceedings of the 21st ACM SIGGRAPH Symposium on Interactive 3D Graphics and Games (I3D '17).*

Wyvill, B., and G. Wyvill. 1989. Field functions for implicit surfaces. *The Visual Computer 5* (1/2), 75–82.

Xia, M., B. Walter, C. Hery, and S. Marschner. 2020a. Gaussian product sampling for rendering layered materials. *Computer Graphics Forum 39* (1), 420–35.

Xia, M., B. Walter, E. Michielssen, D. Bindel, and S. Marschner. 2020b. A wave optics based fiber scattering model. *ACM Transactions on Graphics (Proceedings of SIGGRAPH Asia) 39* (6), 1–16.

Xie, F., and P. Hanrahan. 2018. Multiple scattering from distributions of specular v-grooves. *ACM Transactions on Graphics (Proceedings of SIGGRAPH Asia) 37* (6), 276:1–14.

Xu, B., J. Zhang, R. Wang, K. Xu, Y.-L. Yang, C. Li, and R. Tang. 2019. Adversarial Monte Carlo denoising with conditioned auxiliary feature. *ACM Transactions on Graphics (Proceedings of SIGGRAPH Asia) 38* (6), 224:1–12.

Yan, L.-Q., M. Hašan, W. Jakob, J. Lawrence, S. Marschner, and R. Ramamoorthi. 2014. Rendering glints on high-resolution normal-mapped specular surfaces. *ACM Transactions on Graphics (Proceedings of SIGGRAPH 2014) 33* (4), 116:1–9.

Yan, L.-Q., M. Hašan, S. Marschner, and R. Ramamoorthi. 2016. Position-normal distributions for efficient rendering of specular microstructure. *ACM Transactions on Graphics (Proceedings of SIGGRAPH) 35* (4), 56:1–9.

Yan, L.-Q., M. Hašan, B. Walter, S. Marschner, and R. Ramamoorthi. 2018. Rendering specular microgeometry with wave optics. *ACM Transactions on Graphics (Proceedings of SIGGRAPH) 37* (4), 75:1–10.

Yan, L.-Q., H. W. Jensen, and R. Ramamoorthi. 2017a. An efficient and practical near and far field fur reflectance model. *ACM Transactions on Graphics (Proceedings of SIGGRAPH) 36* (4), 67:1–13.

Yan, L.-Q., W. Sun, H. W. Jensen, and R. Ramamoorthi. 2017b. A BSSRDF model for efficient rendering of fur with global illumination. *ACM Transactions on Graphics (Proceedings of SIGGRAPH Asia) 36* (6), 208:1–13.

Yan, L.-Q., C.-W. Tseng, H. W. Jensen, and R. Ramamoorthi. 2015. Physically-accurate fur reflectance: Modeling, measurement, and rendering. *ACM Transactions on Graphics (Proceedings of SIGGRAPH Asia 2015) 34* (6), 185:1–13.

Yellot, J. I. 1983. Spectral consequences of photoreceptor sampling in the Rhesus retina. *Science 221*, 382–85.

Ylitie, H., T. Karras, and S. Laine. 2017. Efficient incoherent ray traversal on GPUs through compressed wide BVHs. *High Performance Graphics (HPG '17)*, 4:1–13.

Yoon, S.-E., S. Curtis, and D. Manocha. 2007. Ray tracing dynamic scenes using selective restructuring. In *Proceedings of the Eurographics Symposium on Rendering*, 73–84.

Yoon, S.-E., C. Lauterbach, and D. Manocha. 2006. R-LODs: Fast LOD-based ray tracing of massive models. *The Visual Computer 22* (9), 772–84.

Yoon, S.-E., and P. Lindstrom. 2006. Mesh layouts for block-based caches. *IEEE Transactions on Visualization and Computer Graphics 12* (5), 1213–20.

Yoon, S.-E., P. Lindstrom, V. Pascucci, and D. Manocha. 2005. Cache-oblivious mesh layouts. In *ACM Transactions on Graphics (Proceedings of SIGGRAPH 2005) 24* (3), 886–93.

Yoon, S.-E., and D. Manocha. 2006. Cache-efficient layouts of bounding volume hierarchies. In *Computer Graphics Forum: Proceedings of Eurographics 2006 25* (3), 507–16.

Yue, Y., K. Iwasaki, B.-Y. Chen, Y. Dobashi, and T. Nishita. 2010. Unbiased, adaptive stochastic sampling for rendering inhomogeneous participating media. *ACM Transactions on Graphics (Proceedings of SIGGRAPH Asia 2010) 29* (5), 177:1–7.

Yue, Y., K. Iwasaki, B.-Y. Chen, Y. Dobashi, and T. Nishita. 2011. Toward optimal space partitioning for unbiased, adaptive free path sampling of inhomogeneous participating media. *Computer Graphics Forum 30* (7), 1911–19.

Yuksel, C., and C. Yuksel. 2017. Lighting grid hierarchy for self-illuminating explosions. *ACM Transactions on Graphics (Proceedings of SIGGRAPH) 36* (4), 110:1–10.

Zachmann, G. 2002. Minimal hierarchical collision detection. In *Proceedings of the ACM Symposium on Virtual Reality Software and Technology*, 121–28.

Zellmann, S., and U. Lang. 2017. C++ compile time polymorphism for ray tracing. *Proceedings of the Conference on Vision, Modeling and Visualization (VMV '17)*, 129–36.

Zeltner, T., I. Georgiev, and W. Jakob. 2020. Specular manifold sampling for rendering high-frequency caustics and glints. *ACM Transactions on Graphics (Proceedings of SIGGRAPH) 39* (4), 149:1–15.

Zeltner, T., and W. Jakob. 2018. The layer laboratory: A calculus for additive and subtractive composition of anisotropic surface reflectance. *ACM Transactions on Graphics (Proceedings of SIGGRAPH) 37* (4), 74:1–14.

Zeltner, T., S. Speierer, I. Georgiev, and W. Jakob. 2021. Monte Carlo estimators for differential light transport. *ACM Transactions on Graphics (Proceedings of SIGGRAPH) 40* (4), 78:1–16.

Zhang, C., Z. Dong, M. Doggett, and S. Zhao. 2021a. Antithetic sampling for Monte Carlo differentiable rendering. *ACM Transactions on Graphics (Proceedings of SIGGRAPH) 40* (4), 77:1–12.

Zhang, C., B. Miller, K. Yan, I. Gkioulekas, and S. Zhao. 2020. Path-space differentiable rendering. *ACM Transactions on Graphics (Proceedings of SIGGRAPH) 39* (4), 143:1–19.

Zhang, C., L. Wu, C. Zheng, I. Gkioulekas, R. Ramamoorthi, and S. Zhao. 2019. A differential theory of radiative transfer. *ACM Transactions on Graphics (Proceedings of SIGGRAPH Asia) 38* (6), 227:1–16.

Zhang, C., Z. Yu, and S. Zhao. 2021b. Path-space differentiable rendering of participating media. *ACM Transactions on Graphics (Proceedings of SIGGRAPH) 40* (4), 76:1–15.

Zhang, C., and S. Zhao. 2020. Multi-scale appearance modeling of granular materials with continuously varying grain properties. *Computer Graphics Forum 39* (4).

Zhang, M., A. Alawneh, and T. G. Rogers. 2021. Judging a type by its pointer: Optimizing GPU virtual functions. *Proceedings of the 26th ACM International Conference on Architectural Support for Programming Languages and Operating Systems (ASPLOS 2021)*, 241–54.

Zhao, S., F. Luan, and K. Bala. 2016. Fitting procedural yarn models for realistic cloth rendering. *ACM Transactions on Graphics (Proceedings of SIGGRAPH) 35* (4), 51:1–11.

Zhao, S., L. Wu, F. Durand, and R. Ramamoorthi. 2016. Downsampling scattering parameters for rendering anisotropic media. *ACM Transactions on Graphics 35* (6), 166:1–11.

Zhao, Y., L. Belcour, and D. Nowrouzezahrai. 2019. View-dependent radiance caching. *Proceedings of Graphics Interface 2019 (GI '19)*, 22:1–9.

Zheng, Q., and M. Zwicker. 2019. Learning to importance sample in primary sample space. *Computer Graphics Forum 38* (2), 169–79.

Zhou, K., Q. Hou, R. Wang, and B. Guo. 2008. Real-time kd-tree construction on graphics hardware. *ACM Transactions on Graphics (Proceedings of SIGGRAPH Asia 2008) 27* (5), 126:1–11.

Zhu, J., Y. Bai, Z. Xu, S. Bako, E. Velázquez-Armendáriz, L. Wang, P. Sen, M. Hašan, and L.-Q. Yan. 2021. Neural complex luminaires: Representation and rendering. *ACM Transactions on Graphics (Proceedings of SIGGRAPH) 40* (4), 57:1–12.

Zhu, J., Y. Xu, and L. Wang. 2019. A stationary SVBRDF material modeling method based on discrete microsurface. *Computer Graphics Forum 38* (7), 745–54.

Zhu, S., Z. Xu, T. Sun, A. Kuznetsov, M. Meyer, H. W. Jensen, H. Su, and R. Ramamoorthi. 2021. Hierarchical neural reconstruction for path guiding using hybrid path and photon samples. *ACM Transactions on Graphics (Proceedings of SIGGRAPH) 40* (4), 35:1–16.

Zimmerman, K. 1995. Direct lighting models for ray tracing with cylindrical lamps. In *Graphics Gems V*, 285–89. San Diego: Academic Press.

Zinke, A., and A. Weber. 2007. Light scattering from filaments. *IEEE Transactions on Visualization and Computer Graphics 13* (2), 342–56.

Zinke, A., C. Yuksel, A. Weber, and J. Keyser. 2008. Dual scattering approximation for fast multiple scattering in hair. *ACM Transactions on Graphics (Proceedings of SIGGRAPH 2008) 27* (3), 32:1–10.

Zirr, T., J. Hanika, and C. Dachsbacher. 2018. Reweighting firefly samples for improved finite-sample Monte Carlo estimates. *Computer Graphics Forum 37* (6), 410–21.

Zuniga, M., and J. Uhlmann. 2006. Ray queries with wide object isolation and the S-tree. *Journal of Graphics, GPU, and Game Tools 11* (3), 27–45.

Zwicker, M., W. Jarosz, J. Lehtinen, B. Moon, R. Ramamoorthi, F. Rousselle, P. Sen, C. Soler, and S.-E. Yoon. 2015. Recent advances in adaptive sampling and reconstruction for Monte Carlo rendering. *Computer Graphics Forum (Proceedings of Eurographics 2015) 34* (2), 667–81.

Index of Fragments

Bold numbers indicate the first page of a fragment definition, *bold italic* numbers indicate an extension of the definition, and roman numbers indicate a use of the fragment.

Index of Classes
and Their Members

Bold numbers indicate the page of a class definition. Class methods and fields are indented.

Index of Miscellaneous Identifiers

Finally, this index covers functions, module-local variables, preprocessor definitions, and other miscellaneous identifiers used in the system.

Subject Index

Physically Based Rendering

FROM THEORY TO IMPLEMENTATION

This book was typeset with TeX, using the ZzTeX macro package on the Microsoft Windows 10 platform. The main body of the text is set in Minion at 9.5/12, and the margin indices are set in Bitstream Letter Gothic 12 Pitch at 5.5/7. Chapter titles are set in East Bloc ICG Open and Univers Black. Cholla Sans Bold is used for other display headings.

The manuscript for this book was written in pyweb, a literate programming markup format of the authors' own design. This input format is based heavily on the noweb system developed by Norman Ramsey. The pyweb scripts simultaneously generate the TeX files for the book and the source code of the pbrt system.

In addition, these scripts semi-automatically generate the code identifier cross-references that appear in the margin indexes, along with the fragment, class name/member, and miscellaneous back matter indexes. Wherever possible, these indexes are produced automatically by parsing the source code itself. Otherwise, usage and definition locations are explicitly tagged in the pyweb input, and these special tags are removed before the book and the code is generated. These scripts were originally written by the authors, but subsequently rewritten by Paul Anagnostopoulos in Gossip to integrate into the ZzTeX package. Small updates to the scripts were made for each edition.

Overall, the book comprises approximately 134,000 lines of pyweb input, or nearly 5.5 megabytes of text. The cover image, example renderings, and chapter images were generated by pbrt, the software that is described in this book.